D1714766

# English Origins of
# NEW ENGLAND FAMILIES

From The New England Historical
and Genealogical Register

# *English Origins* of
# *N*EW *E*NGLAND *F*AMILIES

From The New England Historical
and Genealogical Register

First Series

in Three Volumes

VOLUME II

*Selected and Introduced by*

GARY BOYD ROBERTS

*With an Index by Eleanor R. Antoniak*

*Baltimore*
GENEALOGICAL PUBLISHING CO., INC.
*1984*

# Contents

# *English Origins* of
# NEW ENGLAND FAMILIES

From The New England Historical
and Genealogical Register

# GENEALOGICAL RESEARCH IN ENGLAND

Communicated by the Committee on English Research

## HASKETT

Contributed by G. Andrews Moriarty, Jr., A.M., LL.B., of Newport, R. I.

In this article records are presented which supply new information about the English ancestry and family connections of Stephen Haskett, who settled at Salem, Mass., as early as 1668, and through two of his daughters, who married into the Derby family, was an ancestor of later generations of this well-known family. In order to make accessible in one article all the evidence thus far discovered on the English origin of this immigrant, a few records previously printed are here printed again — among them the deposition of Elizabeth, widow of Stephen Haskett, which was made in 1698 and is the starting point for investigations into his ancestry, and abstracts, with slight changes, of several English wills contributed by the late Henry FitzGilbert Waters to earlier volumes of the REGISTER. A study of the Haskett records already in print and of those here printed for the first time shows that Stephen Haskett of Salem was a son of Elias Haskett of Marnhull, co. Dorset, and Henstridge, co. Somerset, and a nephew of the Stephen Haskett of Marnhull who made his will (found by Mr. Waters) in 1648 and who was considered, eight years ago, by the contributor of this article, to have been probably the father of the Salem settler.* These records also point to an Elias or Ellis Haskett of Henstridge, who was buried 10 May 1639, as probably the grandfather of Stephen of Salem. A pedigree, in which the information derived from the records is set forth in genealogical form, will conclude the article.

## From Essex County (Mass.) Notarial Records

Elizabeth Haskitt's Oath & Certificate Entred May 30th, '98.

M$^{rs}$. Elizabeth Haskitt widow formerly the wife of Stephen Haskitt of Salem personaly appeared (before me) y$^e$ subscriber & made Oath that she hath six children liuing (viz) one sonne whose name is Elias Haskitt aged about Twenty Eight yeares & fiue Daughters Elizabeth Mary Sarah Hannah & Martha all which she had by her husband y$^e$ abouesaid m$^r$ Stephen Haskitt & Were his Children by him begotten of her body in Lawfull Wedlock being married to him by Doctor Ceauell in Exiter in y$^e$ Kingdome of England & whose sd husband serued his time with one m$^r$ Thomas Oburne a chandler and sope boyler in s$^d$ place & was y$^e$ reputed Sonne of ——— Haskit of Henstredge (so called) in Summersetshire in s$^d$ Kingdome of England & haue often heard my s$^d$ husband say that he had but one brother whose name was Elias Hasket & that he liued in said Towne of Henstredge.      Elizabeth Haskitt.

Sworne Salem May y$^e$ 30th 1698 before me John Hathorne One of y$^e$ Councill & Justice pe & Q. in y$^e$ County of Essex in his Maj$^{ties}$ province of y$^e$ Massachusets Bay in New England.†

## From the Parish Registers and Transcripts of Henstridge, co. Somerset, 1605–1699

### Baptisms

1605    Elinor Stibbs daughter of William 18 October.‡
1622    Anna Stibbs daughter of William and Edith his wife 15 December.‡
1622    Susan Hasket daughter of Elizer of Endeston§ and Christian his wife 19 March [1622/3].‡
1636    Joan bastard daughter of Aditha Hasket 27 May.‡
1636    Stephen Hasket son of Elizer Hasket, Sen.[?], clothier, and Ellinora his wife 18 December.‡
1639    William Stibbs son of William and Agnes his wife 2 February [1639/40].‡
1640    Sara Dusset daughter of George and Elizabeth 20 September.‡
1640    William Hasket son of Ellis and Sarah his wife 4 November.‡

* Cf. *Essex Institute Historical Collections*, vol. 51, p. 2.
† Printed in REGISTER, vol. 30, p. 110, from a copy made by the late Henry FitzGilbert Waters.
‡ This entry is taken from the Bishop's transcripts of the parish registers of Henstridge, these transcripts being preserved at Wells.
§ Endeston or Enston, a hamlet in Henstridge, is now called Yenston.

2

1665 Susanna daughter of Ellis Hasket, Junr., and Elizabeth 1 November.
1665 Jonathan son of William and Rebecca Hasket 23 November.
1667 Mary daughter of Ellis and Elizabeth Hasket 18 March [1667/8].
1669 Annetta daughter of William Haskett and Joan 18 November.
1670 Ellis son of Ellis and Elizabeth Haskot 8 January [1670/1].
1673 Sara daughter of Ellis and Elizabeth Haskott 2 April.
1673 Stephen son of William Hasket and Joan 21 October.
1674 Mary daughter of William Haskott and Joan 12 January [1674/5].
1675 Mary daughter of Martha Haskett, widow, 26 October.
1675 Sara daughter of William Haskott and Joan 12 January [1675/6].
1676 Samuel son of Ellis and Elizabeth Haskot 3 April.
1677 Samuel son of William Haskott and Joan 29 April.
1678 Jane daughter of William Haskott and Joan 15 September.
1681 Joan daughter of William Haskot and Joan 15 June.
1682 Thomas son of William Haskot and Joan 27 August.

## Marriages

1673 Anthony Davidge of Kington Magna, Dorset, to Mary Haskott of this parish 10 April.
1673 Robert Hellier of Stalbridge, Dorset, to Mary Haskott of this parish 10 November.
1681 William Chandoll of Marnhull, Dorset, to Joan Haskott of this parish 5 September.
1695 William Kelloway of Marnhull, Dorset, to Anna Hasket of Henstridge 25 March.
1699 Joseph Perrin and Mary Haskot 27 July.

## Burials

1605 Richard Stibbs 26 September.*
1623 Dionisia Haskett daughter of Elizer, Senior, 4 July.*
1639 Ellis Hasket, an old man, 10 May.*
1639 William Stibbs infant son of William and Agnes 16 February [1639/40].*
1640 Joane Hasket wife of William 1 March [1640/1].*
1654 William Haskott son of Wm. Haskott and Rebecca his wife 3 May.
1660 Elnor Haskett 17 June.
1666 Robert son of William Haskot 19 September.
1673 Mary daughter of Ellis Haskot of Marsh† 26 June.
1673 Elizog [?] Haskot of Enston 22 September.
1681 Johanna daughter of William Haskott 2 October.
1687 Samuel son of Wm. Haskot 23 October.
1690 Joan wife of Wm. Haskot 3 March [1690/1].
1696 Mary Haskott, widow, 21 February [1696/7].

FROM THE PARISH REGISTERS OF KINGSDON, CO. SOMERSET

1625 Willm Hescott and Joanna Hurd married 3 November.‡

FROM THE PARISH REGISTERS OF MARNHULL, CO. DORSET,
1560–1701

## Baptisms

1596 John son of John Haskett 27 June.
1597 William son of John Haskett 7 January [1597/8].
1599 Joan daughter of John Haskett 1 July.

*This entry is taken from the Bishop's transcripts of the parish registers of Henstridge, these transcripts being preserved at Wells.
†Marsh was the name of a part of Henstridge.
‡Printed in Phillimore's Somerset Parish Registers, Marriages, vol. 1, p. 96.

1601  Marie daughter of John Hasket 22 May.
1603  Thomas son of John Haskett 8 April.
1605  Robert son of John Haskett 18 September.
1608  Edeth daughter of Ellis Hasket 9 December.
1610  Ellis son of Ellis Hasket 28 October.
1615  William son of Elizeno Haskett 12 June.
1622  Elizabeth daughter of Steven Hasket 19 January [1622/3].
1624  Margaret daughter of Steven Hasket 12 January [1624/5].
1629  John son of Steven Hasket 25 June.
1648  Stephen son of Stephen Haskett the Younger and Elizabeth his wife 12 November.
1652  Elizabeth daughter of Stephen Haskett and Elizabeth his wife 7 April.
1673  Steuen son of Steuen Hasket and Marey his wife 7 May.
1675  Thomas son of Steuen Hasket and Mary his wife 15 June.
1677  John son of Steuen Hasket and Elizabeth his wife 3 October.
1678  John son of John Hasket and Joane his wife 3 September.
1680  Frances daughter of Steven Hasket and Elizabeth his wife 4 June.
1680  James son of John Hasket and Joane his wife 25 July.
1680  John and Mary twin children of Henr. Hasket and Mary his wife 9 January [1680/1].
1682  Ann daughter of Henr Hasket and Mary his wife 2 April.
1682  James son of John Hasket and Joane his wife 21 November.
1683  Jonathan son of Steven Hasket and Elizabeth his wife 28 March.
1686  Thomas son of Stephen Haskett and Anne his wife 23 June.
1687  Thomas son of John Hasket and Joane his wife 5 May.
1689  John son of John Haskett and Elizabeth his wife 23 March [1689/90].
1696  Thomas son of Thomas Hasket and Mary his wife 5 July.
1697  Stephen son of Thomas Hasket and Mary his wife 16 January [1697/8].
1699  Jonathan son of Thomas Hasket and Mary his wife 6 January [1699/1700].
1701  Ambros son of Thomas Haskett and Mary his wife 25 July.

## Marriage

1686  Richd. Fricker of Dunhead St. Mary and Elen Haskett 27 October.

## Burials

1597  Willm son of John Haskett 5 February [1597/8].
1635  Alice daughter of Stephen Haskett and Elizabeth his wife 16 November.
1635  Margarett daughter of Stephen Haskett and Elizabeth his wife 30 January [1635/6].
1648*  Steven Haskett the Elder 29 October.
1651  Steven Hasket the Elder 9 August.
1669  Robert Hasket 16 February [1669/70].
1675  Ann Hasket 28 December.
1681  James Hasket 25 November.
1682  Elizabeth Hasket of Todber 15 August.
1695  John Hasket 6 February [1695/6].
1701  Steven Hasket, Junior, 11 September.

*The entry is recorded under this year, but from the context it is evident that the year-date should have been 1649.

*Marriages**

1703  Richard Burge and Rebecca Duffet 22 February [1703/4].
1706  Charles Duffet and Martha Snook 21 July.
1709  John Calpen and Mary Dibble 16 November.

## FROM PROBATE RECORDS

The Will of WILLIAM SEAVIER of Yenston in the parish of Henstridge, co. Somerset, husbandman, dated 7 October 1604. To be buried in the parish church or churchyard of Henstridge. To that parish church 20s. and to the parish church of Kingston 10s. To Margaret Seavier £10 and to Callice Seavier £10, to remain in the executors' hands till they marry or be of age. To John Seavier, my brother Reynolde's son, £6, at one and twenty. To Reynold Seavier, my brother, a hundred weight of cheese. To my brother Presley's children a sheep apiece. To my brother Ellis Haskette's children a sheep apiece. To Gregory Royall's daughter Margery one calf of the next year's weaning. To John Collis' son William a calf of the same weaning. To Gregory Royall's son Richard and his two daughters Alice and Mary a lamb apiece. To every of my godchildren 12d. apiece. To the poor folks of Yenston four bushels of barley, to be divided amongst them. All the rest of my goods, etc., I give and bequeath to Marrian Seavier, my wife, and John Seavier, whom I make my full and whole executors. Overseers: Ellys Hasket and Gregory Royall. Proved 29 November 1604. (P. C. C., Harte, 86.) [This abstract has been adapted from the abstract of the will of William Seavier published in REGISTER, vol. 53, p. 13, and reprinted in Waters's "Genealogical Gleanings in England," vol. 2, p. 1437.]

The Will of MARIANE SEVIER of Yenstone in the parish and peculiar of Henstridge, co. Somerset, widow, dated 9 May 1607. To be buried in the churchyard of Henstridge. To the parish church of Henstridge 10s. To the poor folk of Henstridge parish 10s. To Deane Haskett, daughter of Ellis Haskitt, 40s. To Ellis Haskett's three other daughters and William Haskett, his son, £4; if any of them die before they come to the age of one and twenty years or be married, then the money is to remain to the survivors. To Margaret Sevier, daughter of Richard Sevier, a gown cloth and £10; to Alce Sevier, another daughter, a gown and £10. To Marie Royall of Henstridge, widow, one featherbed and £3. To Annis Harte 20s. To Cicely Royall, daughter of Marie Royall, £3. To Richard and Dorothie Royall, son and daughter of Marie Royall, 20s. apiece. To brother-in-law Reynold Sevier £3 and to John Sevier, his son, 40s. To Dorothie Pennie a gown. To Marrian Harris, wife to Richard Harris, five sheep. To John Moores nine sheep. To the children of John Wolfres nine sheep. To Thomas Seavier the Younger nine sheep. To the children of Gregorie Royall £4. 8s. 4d., which money is in the hands of the said Gregorie. To John and Dorothy Penny, my servants, 10s. apiece. To Rose Collis, wife of John Collis, £3. To Marie Haskett, wife of Ellis Haskett, 20s. To every of my godchildren 12d. apiece. All the rest of my goods to Gregory Royall, whom I constitute sole executor. Overseers: Ellis Haskett and Richard Chippman, and I bequeath to them 3s. 4d. apiece. Witnesses: John Bryne, William Pittman, Richard Chippman, Ellis Haskett, and John Royall. Proved 26 June 1607. (P. C. C., Huddleston, 62.) [This abstract has been adapted from the abstract of the will of Mariane Sevier published in REGISTER, vol. 40, p. 303, and reprinted in Waters's "Genealogical Gleanings in England," vol. 1, pp. 175–176.]

*Printed in Phillimore's Dorset Parish Registers, Marriages, vol. 4, pp. 42, 43.

The Will of JOHN HASKET of Todber, co. Dorset, dated 29 September, 12 James [1614]. To be buried in the parish churchyard of Stowre Estowre [sic]. To the same church and to the church of Todber. To my son William Hasket my parcel of land called Berriell, by estimation five acres, and Pitt mead, by estimation seven acres, in the parish of Sutton Mountague *alias* Montacutt, Somerset, for the term of ten years after my decease, he paying to my son John Hasket, yearly during the said term, 5s.; and after the said term of ten years I bequeath the said land wholly to my son John Haskett and the heirs male of his body, etc., with remainder to my son Thomas and then to my son Robert and the heirs male of his body for ever. To Anne, my wife, during her natural life, my parcel of land called Bushe Hayes and the arrable thereunto belonging, [she] paying her son William Haskett yearly during her life 6s. 8d., if it be lawfully demanded; and after her decease I give it to the said William, etc., with remainder to my son Michael Haskett and then to the right heir. To my son John £30, to be paid for his use when he shall be a prentice; in the meantime his mother is to have the profit, or, if he be obstinate or stubborn towards his mother in making his choice for a wife, then it shall be at the discretion of his mother and the over-seers what portion to allow him. To my son Thomas £40. To my son Robert £40. To my son Michael £40. To my two daughters, Joane Haskett and Mary Haskett, £50 apiece, to be given them at their marriage if their mother shall so long happen to live; if not, then to be paid them at their mother's decease. Also, if they should be obstinate and stubborn towards their mother in not taking their mother's good will and consent in their choice for marriage, then it shall be at their mother's discretion what portion to allow either of them. Residue to my wife Anne, whom I make my sole executrix. Overseers: my well-beloved friends Stephen Haskett, William Haskett, and George Coxe. Witnesses: Stephen Haskett, William Haskett [and others]. Proved 23 February 1614 [1614/15]. (P. C. C., Rudd, 8.) [This abstract has been adapted from the abstract of the will of John Hasket published in REGISTER, vol. 53, pp. 13–14, and reprinted in Waters's "Gen-ealogical Gleanings in England," vol. 2, pp. 1437–1438.]

The Will of JOHN HILLIER of Wincanton, co. Somerset, gentleman, dated 20 May 1619. To be buried in the churchyard of Wincanton, where I now dwell. To the parish church 5s. To the poor of Wincanton 8d. Residue to my son-in-law William Moggs and his wife Dorothye. All my lands to my said son-in-law and my daughter Dorothye, his wife, and the heirs of their bodies, and in default thereof to the said William and Dorothye Moggs in fee simple. Executors: William and Dorothye Moggs. Witnesses: John Maycock, Robert Powell, George Greenestrete, John Strode. Proved 23 October 1620. (P. C. C., Soame, 93.) [There is a very brief abstract of this will in the printed "Register Soame," p. 365.]

The Will of KATHERINE SAMPSON of the parish and peculiar jurisdiction of Hengstridge, in the Diocese of Bath and Wells, maiden, dated 30 April 1627. To be buried in the parish church of Hengstridge. To the said church, in money, 20s. To the poor of the said parish 10s. I forgive my cousin Nicholas Locke all the debts that he doth owe me. To my mother my best band of linen and my best apron. I forgive my cousin John Sampson, out of the bond of 40s. which he oweth me, 20s. thereof, and the other 20s. of the said bond I give to my cousin Susan Sampson. To my sister Joane Sampson one silver spoon. To cousin Mary Sampson, my brother William's daughter, my best gown, my best petticoat, my best hat, and £16. 10s. which is due me upon bond from Ellis Hasket and William Haskett, his son. Residue to my two sisters, Jane and Edith Sampson, and they are to be executrices. Overseers: Richard Sampson the Younger and Thomas Morris the Younger.

Brother Henry Sampson oweth me £26. Witnesses: Richard Eburne, vicar, and others. Proved 14 June 1627. (P. C. C., Skinner, 63.) [This abstract has been adapted from the abstract of the will of Katherine Sampson published in REGISTER, vol. 40, p. 303, and reprinted in Waters's "Genealogical Gleanings in England," vol. 1, p. 176.]

## GENEALOGICAL RESEARCH IN ENGLAND

Communicated by the Committee on English Research

### HASKETT (CONCLUDED)

Contributed by G. ANDREWS MORIARTY, JR., A.M., LL.B., of Newport, R. I.

The Will of WILLIAM HURD the Elder of Kingsdon, co. Somerset, gentleman, dated 14 April 1638. To be buried in the parish church or churchyard.

7

To the church and poor of Kingsdon and the poor of Ilchester and Mudford. Sundry servants and others named. My grandchild and godson Joseph Francklin. My daughter Judith Rawe. Thomas Rawe, her husband. Their children, my grandchildren. My goddaughter Judith Crane. Whereas my son-in-law William Haskett hath mortgaged unto me one messuage or tenement, with appurtenances, lying in Henstridge, for the payment of £200, my will is that he shall pay to my son William Hurd three score and ten pounds or give sufficient security to him for the payment thereof and shall likewise give unto my executors the like sufficient security for discharging of my executors of a bond of £200 which I do stand bound unto Ellioc Haskett, father of the said William Haskett, that my executors shall deliver up unto the said William Haskett the said deed of mortgage and convey and assign over all my grounds lying at Pryors Downe, with appurtenances, according to the true intent and meaning of a grant and assignment heretofore made and drawn by Mr. Richard King of Sherborne. £30 to be employed for the use and benefit of my grandchild Mary Haskett and my daughter Joane Haskett. The said Mary to marry with consent of her mother. My son George Hurd to behave himself as a dutiful and obedient son unto his mother. My daughter Hester Franklin. My son Thomas Hurd. My wife Joane Hurd. Proved 17 October 1638. (P. C. C., Lee, 129.) [This abstract has been adapted from the abstract of the will of William Hurd the Elder published in REGISTER, vol. 53, p. 14, and reprinted in Waters's "Genealogical Gleanings in England," vol. 2, p. 1438.]

The Will of STEPHEN HASKETT the Elder of Marnhull, co. Dorset, fuller, dated 24 May 1648. To be buried in the churchyard of the parish church of Marnhull. To Ellis Haskett, my son, 2s. To my son John a truckle bedstead and bed, one chest, one middling brass pan, one bell mettle pot which I bought of Nicholas Warren, and one pair of tucker's shears. To my grandchild James Young 5s. By two several indentures of lease I am now possessed of a certain messuage, tenement, and curtilage, and of divers water mills, fulling mills, and grist mills in Marnhull, Todber, and Fifehed Magdalen. The same to my wife Elizabeth for life, then to my son Stephen for life, and remainder to my daughter Elizabeth Young, as promised her in part of her marriage portion. To my son Stephen [other property, including] my racks and all other tools belonging to my fuller's trade. My wife Elizabeth to be my whole executrix. Overseers: my two friends Osmond Ploant and John Snooke. Witnesses: Elizabeth Haskett of Todber, widow, and others. Proved 27 February 1653 [?1653/4]. (P. C. C., Alchin, 320.) [This abstract has been adapted from the abstract of the will of Stephen Haskett the Elder published in REGISTER, vol. 53, pp. 14–15, and reprinted in Waters's "Genealogical Gleanings in England," vol. 2, pp. 1438–1439.]

The Will of ELIAS HASKETT of Henstridge Marsh, co. Somerset, yeoman, dated 13 February 1696 [1696/7]. To my kinswoman Mary Hoddinott £20. To the wife of Richard Shaue, late deceased, and her father-in-law Richard Shaue the Elder, now living, and the children of the said Richard Shaue, deceased, £20, to be equally divided between them. To William Heddeech, shoemaker, £20, and to his child that is now living with him £20. To Henry, Robert, Dorothy, and Anne Heddeech, brothers and sisters of the said William, £20, to be divided betwixt them. To my wife's kinsman Thomas Acstens [? Arstens] £10, and to his children £10, and £10 also to John and George Acstens, brothers of the said Thomas. To William Duffett's wife of Stalbridge Side Hill, lying in Henstridge against South Mead, and to his five children £100. To Anne Frampton and her child £5. To my wife's nephew Nicholas Buggis my now dwelling house, with appurtenances, and my two home closes called Greene Close and Marsh Close. But if he

8

die without issue, then it shall come to Elias Duffett, second son of the said William Duffett, and his heirs for ever. To John Calpen, son of William Calpen, late of Stalbridge, deceased, £10, and to William Calpen, brother of the said John, £50, at one and twenty. [Conditional bequests to Mary and Hannah, two sisters of Nicholas Buggis.] To Elias Haskett, son of Elias Haskett the baker, my close of arrable and pasture land in Henstridge called Hurleoake, and when he shall be possessed of the said close he shall pay to his brother and to his sisters Mary and Sarah £5 apiece and to his sister Susanna Hobbs, widow, £15. To William Loden's wife of Sherborne Castle Town, button-maker, £5. If Richard Calpen, my kinsman, should come to be in want, the said Elias Duffett shall pay him 20s. a year for his natural life. [Other bequests.] Executrix: my wife Mary. Proved 12 May 1698, commission being issued to Mary Crumsey, wife of Lewis Crumsey, "nepti semel remotæ prox. consanguin" [i.e., grandniece and next of kin], Mary Haskett the relict having died before taking the burden of the execution. (P. C. C., Lort, 60.) [This abstract has been adapted from the abstract of the will of Elias Haskett published in REGISTER, vol. 53, p. 15, and reprinted in Waters's "Genealogical Gleanings in England," vol. 2, p. 1439.]

FROM PROCESSES AND DECREES IN THE COURT OF DELEGATES

[Various relatives of Elias Haskett of Henstridge Marsh, co. Somerset, yeoman, the testator of 13 February 1696 [1696/7], an abstract of whose will is given above, claimed the administration *cum testamento annexo* on his estate; and their claims were brought finally before the Court of Delegates, which, after considering numerous depositions, granted the administration to Elias Haskett, son of Stephen Haskett of Salem, Mass., deceased, and nephew of the testator.

The Court of Delegates was originally a court of appeal from the Prerogative Courts of Canterbury and York and the Irish probate courts. Appeals also could be taken from the various diocesan courts to the Court of Arches and thence to the Court of Delegates. This court was called the Court of Delegates, because the judges were delegated for each particular case, the delegates being generally three puisne judges, one from each court of common law, and three or more civilians. Occasionally, however, certain specified spiritual and temporal peers were included in the Court. The Court of Delegates was abolished in 1832, when the Judicial Committee of the Privy Council was established. The processes in the Court of Delegates are preserved in the Public Record Office, London; the decrees and wills are in Somerset House, London. Some of the wills are entered also in the registers of the Prerogative Court of Canterbury or were originally proved in local courts. Cf. *The Genealogist*, New Series, vol. 11, p. 165, introduction to an article entitled "Wills and Administrations in the Court of Delegates."—EDITOR.]

Hasket *v.* Crumsey

20 April 1697. Request for administration *cum testamento annexo* on the estate of Elias Hasket, late of Henstridge [co. Somerset], deceased, by Elias and Stephen Haskett, cousins once removed ("consobrinos in gradu semel remoto") and next of kin to the deceased, Richard Gaulpin, cousin and next of kin, and Dorothy Hedich, sister of ——— Hasket, deceased, relict and executrix of the will of said Elias.

Elias and Stephen Haskett allege that Elias, the testator, died in February, leaving as executrix his widow, who died before proving the will; and they seek the administration as next of kin.

Richard Gaulpin claims to be next of kin and cousin ("consobrinum") of the deceased.

Mary Crumsey, wife of Lewis, alleges that she is grandniece ("neptem semel remotam") of the deceased, being the child of Mary Haskett *alias* Hoddinot, who was the child of William Hasket, the elder brother of the testator.

Dorothy Hedditch alleges that she was the full sister of ——— Haskett, relict and executrix of the deceased and now herself deceased. (Processes in the Court of Delegates, vol. 269, no. 630.)

24 October 1697 [after various adjournments and pleadings]. Elias and Stephen Hasket appear as above, and also Richard Gaulpin, cousin once removed ("consobrinum semel remotum"), and Mary Crumsey, Richard Sheane, and Mary Burnet, grandnieces and grandnephew ("neptes et nepotem semel remotos") of said deceased also appear. (*Ib.*)

### Depositions for Richard Gaulpin.

Egidius Hallett of Bowdon in Henstridge, where he has lived since infancy, aged 80 years, deposes that he has well known Elias Hasket for thirty years and more, but Stephen Hasket and Mary Crumsey and Dorothy Hedditch he did not know. He well knew William Stibbs, who died at Bowdon and was his neighbor. This William had five daughters, Elinor, Susanna, Ann, Margaret, and Edith Stibbs. He well knew Elias Hasket, father of Elias Hasket deceased, who was married to Ellinor Stibbs, and Elias Hasket the testator, whose estate is in issue, was the son of the said Elias Hasket and Elinor Stibbs *alias* Haskett, his wife. The testator was born in Henstridge. The sister of Elinor Stibbs, Ann Stibbs, married Thomas Gaulpin and had seven sons, the youngest of whom is Richard Gaulpin, a party to this suit. Sworn 16 September 1697.

Thomas Clarke of Yenston in Henstridge, where he has lived from infancy, husbandman, aged 77 years, deposes that he knew Elias Hasket but not Crumsey, Stephen Hasket, or Hodditch. He was a neighbor of William Stibbs, and knew his daughters Elinor and Ann. Elinor married Elias Haskett the Elder, father of Elias Hasket the testator. Ann married Thomas Gaulpin, and they were always taken for man and wife in Henstridge. They had several children, among them Richard. Sworn 16 September 1697.

William Rideout of Yenston in Henstridge, where he has lived since infancy, aged 60 years, deposes that he has known Elias Hasket and Stephen Hasket for twelve years, but does not know Crumsey or Hedditch. He was a neighbor of Elinor Hasket *alias* Stibbs and of Elias Hasket, Jr., whose estate is in litigation. Elinor was widow of Elias Hasket, Sr., the father of Elias Hasket, Jr., deceased, the testator. He deposes as the others as to the relationship of Gaulpin and Hasket. (*Ib.*)

Depositions, ordered 5 October 1697, in behalf of Mary Crumsey, to prove that she is the lawful niece once removed [i.e., grandniece], on the brother's side, of the testator, namely, that she is the daughter of William Hoddinott, deceased, by Mary Haskett, deceased, his wife, daughter of William Hasket, the elder brother of Elias Hasket the testator:

Mary Morgan, wife of Luodovic Morgan of Stalbridge [co. Dorset], where she has lived since her birth, aged 57 years, deposes that she has known Mary Crumsey from childhood, and watched with her mother, Mary Hoddinott, in her childbirth with Mary Crumsey. The said Mary Hoddinott, mother of Mary Crumsey, was daughter of William Heskott. She has known Mary Crumsey for about thirty-five years. She believes that she lives in London. Her father and mother were William and Mary Hoddinott, and she was born in Stalbridge in the house of one Taunton, in the posesssion of John Lyte. She knew her grandfather, William Hoddinot, who lived in Stalbridge. Her grandfather on the mother's side was William Hasket, but she does not know where he lived.

Ann Willowby of Stalbridge [co. Dorset], where she has lived thirty-seven years, deposes that she has known Mary Crumsey from childhood. William Haskett, her grandfather, was the elder brother of Elias Hasket the testator. Mary Crumsey lives in London, and was born in Stalbridge in the house of John Lyte. Sworn 9 November 1697.

William Webb of Henstridge [co. Somerset], where he has lived sixty years, weaver, aged 75 years, deposes in like manner, and [testifies] that Mary Crumsey now lives in London, and that Elias the testator was son of Elias and Elinor Hasket of Henstridge, where the said testator was born and always lived. Mary Crumsey's grandfather and grandmother on the mother's side were William Haskett and Mary his wife. Her great-grandfather on the mother's side was Elias Hasket the Elder.

Thomas Kensington of Henstridge [co. Somerset], where he has lived since birth, yeoman, aged 66 years, deposes that Mary Crumsey lives near the printing house in Blackfriars, London. He testifies the same as the others.

Anna Toogood of Henstridge [co. Somerset], where she has lived since birth, aged 80 years, deposes that she has known Mary Crumsey from childhood. She lives in London. She knew the father of Elias Hasket the testator, but she has forgotten her [sic, his] Christian name, but his mother's name was Elinor. They lived at Henstridge in the house of one Mr. Rogers, where Elias was born. William Hasket, the grandfather of Mary Crumsey, lived in the parish of Henstridge, where the mother of Mary Crumsey was married. She also knew his wife, her grandmother, but has forgotten her name. (Ib.)

4 June 1698. Deposition of William Hedditch of Gillingham, co. Dorset, shoemaker, aged about 30 years. He well knew Elias Hasket, deceased, who was a husbandman and kept stock. Upon his death Elias and Stephen Hasket, two of the parties to the suit, came upon the land and drove away six cows; and they attempted to take the goods from the house and did take some. [Order issued for an inventory of such goods.] (Ib.)

Inventory of the goods of Elias Hasket, husbandman, deceased, including goods in the possession of Elias Hasket the Elder and Stephen Hasket of Henstridge, made 29 May 1697, £766. 6s. 6d. (Ib.)

10 December 1697 [sic, ? 1698]. Petition of Elias Hasket, presenting his claim for administration on the estate of the testator as next of kin, being the child of Stephen Hasket, brother of Elias Hasket, Sr., deceased. Some of petitioner's witnesses are dead, and others are beyond seas and cannot be brought into Court. (Ib.)

Answers of Mary Crumsey, wife of Lewis Crumsey and great-niece and next of kin and administratrix of the goods of Elias Hasket, deceased, made to pretended articles of interrogation against her on behalf of Elias Hasket: She does not believe Elias Hasket to be of any kin to the deceased Elias Hasket, save that she hath heard that the late Elias Hasket had a brother named Stephen. Sworn 25 February 1698 [1698/9]. (Court of Delegates, Examination of Witnesses, vol. 23, 1694-1711.)

Answers of Elias Hasket to Mary Crumsey's interrogatories: He believes that Elias Hasket, this respondent's uncle, did live in Henstridge and died about 14 February 1696 [1696/7], leaving a wife Mary, who died a few days later and before the proving of the will of Elias Hasket; that some persons have pretended that he made a will and made his wife executrix, and that she died before she took execution. Suits thereupon arose and were carried on between several persons who pretend to be the next of kin to the said Elias. So proceedings were had in the Prerogative Court of Canterbury and were transmitted to this Court; but he does not believe that the pretended will was a true will or that Elias Hasket was of sound mind. The said Elias Hasket left no child nor any father or mother, brother or sister. The respondent is the son of Stephen Hasket, deceased brother of the said Elias. This Stephen was apprenticed to a soap boiler in Exeter, and, after his time was out, he did intermarry with one Elizabeth Hill of the said city and had by her a child, Elizabeth. Afterwards the said Stephen, meeting some crosses in the world, went beyond seas to a town or place called Salem, in New England; and, after he had been there some time, he sent for his wife to come over to him and bring their child. She then went over, and there said Stephen lived with his wife for several years and had several children, namely, this respondent and four sisters, Mary, Sarah, Hannah, and Martha, together with Elizabeth, the first child, who are still living; and, when the defendant grew up, he went to Barbadoes, and there married Elizabeth Rich, and there settled with her and his family, and did and does trade in shipping and merchandise, and in 1696 he came from Barbadoes in the ship *New London*, whereof he was master, to London, and on or about 28 September 1696 he arrived at Plymouth, and on 28 October at London. He unloaded, and staid in and about London until the end of the following May, and in May 1697, about the 24th of the month, he left London and went on board the *Sheerness* galley, Captain Bolles, commander, for Barbadoes, and, having touched at Ireland and Madeira, arrived in Barbadoes the latter end of August 1697. He continued there until the month of September 1698. Although in England, he did not hear of his uncle's death, and, while in England, he wrote several letters to Mr. John Ellery of Exeter, merchant, desiring of him an account of his said uncle, Elias Hasket, but could not and did not receive any answer thereto, the said Ellery being, as he has since learned, then beyond the seas; and he never gave any order to any proctor to appear for his interest until he came to England in November last, in order to prosecute this appeal. Nor did he know of any proceeding brought in the Prerogative Court about his uncle's estate until he received notice from one Mr. Dan about September 1698. Sworn 20 May 1699. (*Ib.*)

Administration with will annexed on the estate of Elias Hasket, late of Henstridge, deceased, was granted, 14 August 1699, to Elias Hasket, nephew on the brother's side and next of kin. (Decrees of the Court of Delegates, lib. 4, fo. 48.)

### From Chancery Proceedings*

10 February 1617 [1617/18]. To Sir Francis Bacon, Lord Chancellor.

WILLIAM HASKETT and wife Margaret and RALPH HUGHSON and wife Elizabeth, Margaret and Elizabeth being daughters of John Hellier, complain that said John Hellier, being seised of a capital messuage and lands in Maperton, Somerset, called the manor of Hatherley, of the yearly value of 100 marks, of goods, etc., to the value of £1800, and of leases, etc., of great value, and having only one son, above 50 and not disposed to marry, provided him with a rent of £40 a year. Plaintiffs and also William Mogge and his wife Dorothy, the third daughter, had several children. Hellier about three years ago decided to settle the above manor on his three sons-in-law and their wives, with remainder to their children, reserving to himself a life interest in the same. He promised also to lend the plaintiffs money for the purchase of land, to give £20 a year to each of Haskett's seven children, and to have his personal estate equally divided between his daughters and their children after his death. Haskett accordingly bought land to the value of £600, and, as Hellier could not fulfil his promise for help on account of disbursements made for Mogge, Haskett was obliged to sell some of his own living, worth £60 a year, for five years, to be redeemed by payment of £240. Hellier then promised help both for the above purchase and in payment of a debt of £40 which Haskett owned to one Rogers. None of these promises has been fulfilled; and the plaintiff Hughson, who married on the understanding that the third of the manor would be settled on him, has received no marriage portion with his wife. William Mogge and Dorothy, under the influence of Richard Mogge, who has been bailiff and deputy to the under sheriff of the

*Preserved in the Public Record Office, London.

county, have got possession of the deed of enfeoffment made by Hellier and of all other deeds relating to the manor, and declare that the plaintiffs have no right to the property on account of defects in the deed of enfeoffment and that Hellier has it in his power to settle it all on themselves and their children. They have also induced Hellier, who is aged and almost imbecile, to live with them, and have persuaded him to make them secret grants of the manor and to give them his money and personal estate. The plaintiffs pray that the defendants may be compelled to produce the deeds in Chancery, etc.

The King's writ, 14 February, 15 James I [1617/18], appoints commissioners to visit and examine Hellier and the other defendants, if they are not able to appear in court.

Answer of JOHN HELLYAR, WILLIAM MOGG, and his wife Dorothy, three of the defendants, to the above bill of complaint.

John Hellyar acknowledges the truth of the plaintiffs' statement as to his property, etc. His three daughters were married about nineteen or twenty years ago, and, his son, aged 50, infirm of constitution and unmarried, being provided for by some copyhold livings worth about £30 a year, he had a secret desire to settle the manor upon his grandson, the son of William Mogge and Dorothy. The marriages with Haskct and Hughson had been against his liking, and Hasket had committed some folly with the said Margaret before their marriage. Haskett, "being a man long and well experienced in Contencyouse and litigious courses," came three years ago to Hellier and urged him to settle £40 a year on his son and the manor on the three sons-in-law and their wives and children. Hellyer answered that he meant to settle the property on one only, meaning Mogge's son, but Haskett assured him that he was bound in law to divide it between the three. Finally Haskett was allowed to draw up a deed, by which the manor was settled according to his proposal, Hellier to hold for life, and the thirds of Mogge and Hughson to remain with Haskett's children. The deed was ingrossed in four parts, one being left with Hellier and the other three given to the sons-in-law. Afterwards Elizabeth Hughson, pretending to come at the request of her brother, the younger John Hellier, obtained the conveyance [several words illegible] from her father, who, being assured by Haskett that he had now only a life interest in the property, took counsel's advice thereon. Being assured that it was still in his power to dispose of the manor, etc., as he chose, he determined to make a settlement on William Mogge, his wife, and son. He granted the property last December to Richard Mogge, another of the defendants, and John Bainton, to hold to the use of himself for life and after his death to the use of William Mogge, etc. He charges the plaintiffs with disobedient and undutiful conduct towards himself, and says that Haskett before his marriage with Margaret "wrested" £100 from him, afterwards suing him at the assizes in Somerset for a further portion. The dispute was referred to the arbitration of a Mr. Swanton, who advised defendant to give Haskett £30, which he did. Haskett has also had £10 from him and the daughters £20, "besides other valuable good turnes and Curtesies." Defendant has given to his daughter Elizabeth and two of her children a copyhold tenement worth £6 a year, though she married Hughson secretly, against his will. Hughson has also had £200 from him since the marriage.

William Mogge says that until seven years ago he had no settled portion with his wife, above a sum of £50, but since that time they have been well provided for by Hellyar. The settlement of the manor on them was made by advice of learned counsel to frustrate Haskett's designs. About twelve months ago Mogge bought, at Hellyar's wish, a tenement at Wincalnton, Somerset, and Hellyar afterwards left his dwelling at Horsington to live with them there. John Hellyar is not possessed of goods and chattels to the value

13

of £1800, nor have the plaintiffs, William and Ralph, rendered him such services as they profess to have rendered, etc. (Chancery Proceedings, James I, H. 2/70.)

[Undated.] Replication of WILLIAM HASKET and wife Margaret and RALPH HUGHSON and wife Elizabeth to the answer of John Hellier the Elder, William Mogge, and his wife Dorothy.

The defendant John Hellyer, having provided for his son, promised to alter the lease of certain grounds in Marsh Court to James Hasket, the plaintiff's son, for his life, in lieu of the life and name of Mr. James Hanam, and declared his intention to settle the lands, etc., mentioned in the bill of answer among his three daughters and their heirs. When he came to deliver seisin of the deeds of conveyance drawn up to this effect, he was dissuaded by one Robert Dore, acting as the instrument of the defendant Mogges and his wife, who wished to secure the lands for themselves. The plaintiff Haskett had received only a small portion in marriage, had many children, and had left his own trade and devoted himself to the care of John Hellyer's estate. John Hellyer promised to pay £100 of a lease which Haskett bought for £300, and to provide him with cattle and household stuff. This he failed to do, and Haskett began the suit [torn] which was ended by mediation, Hellyer paying £30 besides the £100, and Haskett travelling for him in his affairs. Hellyer's wife died about three years ago, leaving much wealth, which came to the defendant [torn] and in which plaintiffs had no share. Hellyer himself had cattle, furniture, plate, etc., besides chattels, leases, etc., to the value of £700, which Mogges and his wife have gotten, besides the profits of Hellyer's lands, which amount to £140 a year. Hellyer, now old and weak and almost past sense, is completely under the influence of Mogge and his wife, who will not allow the plaintiffs to see him. They have induced him to make another deed of conveyance of the lands. Plaintiffs deny that they married their wives against Hellyer's wish and that Hellyer proposed to settle the lands upon William Mogge's son. Mogge told Hughson that he should keep him out of the land, but would give him £200. John Hellyer the Younger sent to the plaintiff, Elizabeth, his sister, to get the deed of annuity for him; but Mogge and his wife had taken it away with the intent of defrauding the said John Hellyer the Younger. As to the making of a new feoffment to the defendants, Richard Mogge and John Bainton, the plaintiffs say that John Hellyer has forfeited his estate for life reserved to him by the former conveyance, as they are entitled to enter on the lands and expel him. The £50 which Mogge had to his marriage portion was more than he deserved. Haskett's living was ten times the value of Mogge's, and he had only £130. Mogge and his wife in seven years had gotten away £2000 at least from Hellyer. (Chancery Proceedings, James I, H. 120/111.)

26 May, 3 Charles I [1627]. To Lord Coventry [Lord Keeper, 1625–1640]. The complaint of ELIZE HASKETT the Younger of Henstridge [co. Somerset], yeoman, shows that, having occasion to borrow money of a money lender, he borrowed £8, and became bound, by two bills dated on or about 24 June 1622, in a penalty of £16 to George Bingham. When the bills came due, he could not pay them; and Bingham agreed to continue the loan and thereafter agreed to take so much butter and cheese in payment as should amount to £8, and he has acknowledged the receipt thereof and promised to give the orator the several bills to cancel; but now he refuses to make delivery of the said goods in payment, and seeks to sue the orator at the common law. Wherefore the orator prays that he be compelled to deliver the said bills up for cancellation.

The answer of GEORGE BINGHAM. He denies the loan or that he is a money lender. The complainant was bound by several bills in the sum of £16, to

14

be repaid at the rate of £4 a year at the Feasts of the Annunciation of the Blessed Virgin Mary* and the Nativity of St. John the Baptist.† He denies the complainant's allegation regarding there being any request for extension and that he agreed to receive butter and cheese in payment or to deliver the bonds. (Chancery Proceedings, Charles I, C 2, H. 86/33.)

To Lord Coventry [Lord Keeper, 1625–1640].

The complaint of ELLIS HASKET of Yenston in the parish of Henstridge [co. Somerset], gentleman, shows that in or about the month of March, 7 Charles [1631/2], the orator became bound to Edward Lovel of Henstridge, yeoman, for the penal sum of £60, to secure the repayment of £30. Shortly afterwards, in March, 8 Charles [1632], the orator demised to Edward Lovell several closes of meadow and pasture, about forty acres, called West Leasures, a parcel of a tenement called Brynes in Yenston, for two years, under a yearly rent of fourscore pounds. At the same time he demised to Edward Lovell another close, called Meade Close, of six acres, at a yearly rent of £4.10s., and about March, 11 Charles [1635/6], he agreed with Lovell that he should by deed indentured make a lease to Edward Lovell and Thomas Jolliffe, gentleman, for five years next ensuing, should he, the orator, live so long, of several closes of land, meadow, and pasture, called West Grounds, belonging to Brynes tenement aforesaid in the west side of Yenston, in the occupation and tenure of the orator, and Edward Lovell was to accept the same in discharge of the bond for £60 and to deliver the same to the orator to be cancelled. The orator made the lease; but Lovell refuses to surrender the bond, and is suing the orator at common law. He prays relief.

1 July 1637. The answer of EDWARD LOVELL shows that the complainant became bound by a bond, dated 15 March, 7 Charles [1631/2], to pay £36.14s. at the defendant's house. The complainant did grant to the defendant the closes of West Leases and Meade Close. The defendant became bound for debts of the complainant, namely, to one William Ridet of Henstridge for £12, to secure the payment of £6, to Jone Hobbes, widow of ———, for £20, to secure the payment of £10, and to John Everes of Henstridge for £20, to secure the payment of £10. For the discharge of the defendant from the bonds the complainant did, about February, 11 Charles [1635/6], demise as stated to Lovell and Jolliff, to take its beginning at the Feast of the Annunciation of the Blessed Virgin Mary* next after the grant. The defendant denies, however, that he has taken the rents and profits, but believes Joliffe does, and the defendant is not discharged of his obligation in the several debts, nor was it intended so to discharge him out of the profits of the land. The complainant has not paid the £30.14s. according to the bond. Therefore the defendant has put the bond in the common law to recover his money and denies any agreement to cancel the same. (Chancery Proceedings, Charles I, H. 95/43.)

2 July 1639. The complaint of ELLIS HASKETT the Elder of Yenston, parish of Henstridge, co. Somerset, gentleman, and Ellis Haskett and William Haskett, his sons, shows that they purchased two copyhold tenements within the manor of Yenston for the term of their lives successively. So being seised, Ellis Haskett the father became indebted for money borrowed of divers persons, i.e., Thomas Willes of Sherborne, co. Dorset, mercer, £17. 10s., William Ryall of Yenston, yeoman, £30, Edmond Lovell of Yenston, husbandman, £30, John Grove of Yenston, husbandman, £10, one Lovell of Yenston, widow, £16, and Thomas Rolt of Temple Combe, co. Somerset, gentleman, £12, in all amounting to £115, for which his said sons, Ellis and William, were bound as sureties with their father. So being

---

*The Feast of the Annunciation of the Blessed Virgin Mary falls on 25 March.
†The Feast of the Nativity of St. John the Baptist falls on 24 June.

15

indebted, Ellis Haskett the father, at the suit of Thomas Rolt, steward to Sir John Jacob, Knight, owner of the manor of Yenston, about June, 14 Charles I [1638], was arrested in Marlborough, co. Wilts, and was detained in prison there two months and more, although he offered to pay said Rolt the £12 owing him; but Rolt pretended that he owed him £200 and had forfeited an obligation of £400 for nonpayment thereof, which was untrue. To pay his debts and procure his enlargement from prison, complainants sold a close of meadow called Common Close, two closes of meadow and pasture called Sawyers, and three acres of meadow in the common meadow, being in all twenty-two acres, worth about £17 a year; and the money for the same, being £250, was paid into Thomas Rolt's hands, who divided the same among the creditors and refused to pay the overplus to the complainants, the said debts not coming to more than £135. Therefore they desire that Thomas Rolt and the aforesaid creditors may have writs of subpœna directed to them to appear and answer, etc.

The answer of WILLIAM RIALL, defendant, taken at Wincalton, co. Somerset, 5 October, 15 Charles I [1639]. He says that Ellis Haskett, Senr. and Junr., owed him £80, and Ellis Haskett, Senr., owed Thomas Rolt £12, the latter of whom caused Haskett to be imprisoned, during which imprisonment defendant charged the said Haskett with his account. As to the lands sold, he denies that they were of the yearly value of £17, but of about £12. He has received from Thomas Rolt only £30, in part payment of the money due to him, and he has lately sued out process for the residue due to him.

The answer of THOMAS ROLT, gentleman, taken at Shafton, co. Dorset, 5 October 1639. He believes that the complainants purchased two copyhold tenements, as alleged, but at the time of the debt he was and yet is an officer, not steward, to Sir John Jacob, Knight. It is true that he caused the complainant, Ellis Haskett the father, to be imprisoned for debt, but he denies that he pretended that he owed him £200. He says that the lands were sold, as alleged in the bill of complaint, and that the said Haskett gave him a note of hand dated 22 July 1638, authorizing him to receive all sums of money due for the same sale. He says that he only received £157 and no more, and that he paid all the debts due and £16. 18s. for expenses incurred by said Haskett's imprisonment, as by a note delivered to him by Samuel Young, sergeant of the Corporation of Marlborough, dated 23 July 1638, ready to be produced; and that he has given the overplus of £5. 5s. 11d. to said Haskett, and has delivered up the bonds for the said debts to said Haskett or his wife. He denies that he is guilty of harsh conduct or keeping back money, etc., and he desires to be dismissed with his reasonable costs. (Chancery Proceedings, Charles I, H. 77/71.)

27 May 1647. The complaint of ELLIS HASKETT the Elder of Enson *alias* Endiston in the parish of Henstridge, co. Somerset, yeoman, shows that about fifteen years ago he purchased an estate for his own life and the lives of his two sons, William and Ellis Haskett, of and in a copyhold tenement, with the appurtenances, in Enson aforesaid, within the manor of Henstridge, called Brynes tenement or the West Living, being of the yearly value of £16, to hold to him and his said sons for the term of their lives, according to the custom of the manor; and, having been admitted, had he died, his widow would have enjoyed the same during her widowhood. About ten years ago William Haskett the Younger, aforesaid, intreated the complainant and made use of his friends to persuade him to surrender the said tenement to the use of the said William and such wife as he should marry, barring such widow as complainant should leave, and it was agreed that immediately after such surrender the said William should pay complainant an annuity of £10 a year, and, in sure confidence of this agreement being carried out,

16

complainant at the Court Baron held at Henstridge, 31 July 1638, surrendered the same to the use of the said William and such widow as he left after his death. The said William has by his marriage obtained a great portion; but, although complainant has carried out his side of the agreement and has barred his wife from her widow's estate, the said William refuses to pay the said annuity, so that complainant is much impoverished now, but is like to perish for want of payment if William dies before him, and in his old age is like to come to great want. As some witnesses to the said agreement are dead and some gone beyond the seas, complainant is deprived of their testimony, and the said William takes advantage thereof to refuse to pay or give security for doing so. Therefore complainant begs that a writ of subpœna may be directed to said William, causing him to appear, etc.

The answer of WILLIAM HASKETT to the bill of complaint of his father, Ellis Haskett, taken at Sturminster, co. Dorset, 11 October, 23 Charles I [1647].

He believes that about fifteen years ago an estate of a copyhold tenement and lands in Enson, parish of Henstridge, co. Somerset, called Brynes Tenement or the West Lyving, of the yearly value of £16, was made by copy of court roll to complainant, Ellis Haskett, and to defendant and Ellis Haskett the Younger, for their lives successively; but the money for the same was not paid by complainant but by the friends of Christian, the defendant's late mother, as part of her portion, as eighteen or twenty years before the granting of this estate an estate of the same tenement and lands was granted to complainant and Christian and Ellis Haskett the Younger, for their lives successively, and the fine for the same was paid out of the marriage portion of this defendant's mother, formerly left in her friends' hands for her benefit and disposal, and out of her love for him she, in her lifetime, surrendered up her right and interest for life in the said tenement to him, the defendant. About ten years ago the complainant was imprisoned for debt at Marlborough, and, being in want of money, persuaded the defendant and Ellis the Younger to join with him in surrendering a moiety of the said tenement, and offered to surrender his interest therein for life in the other moiety to the use of the defendant. And upon this consideration only was the surrender made. Since the surrender aforesaid the defendant has enjoyed the said moiety, and intends in time to come so to hold the same for himself and wife and family, according to the aforesaid agreement, without paying the sum of £10 a year during complainant's life. He denies making any such promise, and says that the moiety of the said tenement was sold to others and the money employed for payment of complainant's debts and enlargement from prison. As to such wife as the defendant now hath, he did not obtain her by reason of his estate in the said copyhold tenement but by God's goodness and her love and affection for him. While defendant was suitor to his wife and in service with a master and for seven years after the surrender, complainant kept the profits of defendant's moiety to his own use; and since his marriage defendant has taken the profits to his own use, as he ought to do for the maintenance of himself, his wife, and children. Complainant has £20 a year copyhold lands, and received £200 with his now wife, and therefore will not be destitute, as he pretends. Defendant desires to be dismissed with his reasonable costs. (Chancery Proceedings, Charles I, H. 29/65.) [A brief abstract of this case was published in REGISTER, vol. 53, p. 16, and reprinted in Waters's "Genealogical Gleanings in England," vol. 2, p. 1440.]

12 May [?] 1662. To Lord Clarendon.

The complaint of ELLIS HASKETT the Elder of Yenston in Henstridge [co. Somerset], yeoman, shows that about twenty years ago [i.e., about 1642] he had occasion to borrow, and repaired to William Haskett the Younger of Yenston aforesaid, yeoman, and became bound to William in a bond of £10, payable in six months from the date of the obligation, which time is now long past. When the time for payment came, the orator could not pay, and it was continued by the consent of William Haskett. Said bond was continued thus for eight or nine years, after which said William importuned the orator for his money, which the orator could not then pay. The defendant then sued the orator and recovered judgment. The orator then paid the same, with interest and costs, and defendant agreed to deliver the bond to the orator to be cancelled, and acknowledged full satisfaction; but he has failed to do so, and, "intending unjustly to extort divers sums of money from the orator doth give out speeches that he was not satisfied" of the said principal, interest, or costs; and, combining with persons unknown to the orator, he is planning to recover on it. The orator cannot make proof at the common law, as his witnesses are since dead or gone to remote parts beyond the seas; and he prays relief and a writ of subpœna, etc. [No answer attached.] (Chancery Proceedings before 1714, Collins, pt. 16, no. 585, Haskett v. Haskett.)

28 February 1682 [?1682/3]. To Lord Coventry.
The complaint of WILLIAM HASKETT of Todber, co. Dorset, yeoman, shows that his father was seised of copy or customary lands as tenant of the manor of More in the said county. He surrendered them to the lord, and received them back to himself and his son John Hasket for a lease for the life of the longest liver of them. By the custom of the manor, on the death of a tenant his wife had an estate for her life. The manor has been dissolved, and the reversion of the said copyholds has come to William Byles of Fyfehead, Nevill, co. Dorset, gentleman, and to Elizabeth Byles of Phyfin Oakford in said county, widow, and they intend to deprive complainant's wife of her estate to which she is entitled by the custom of the dissolved manor. The complainant's witnesses to the said custom are dead or old and feeble, and cannot travel to London or Weston. (Chancery Proceedings before 1714, Reynardson, 413/185.)

14 December 1694 [sic, 1697]. The complaint of DOROTHY HEDDITCH of Gillingham [co. Dorset], widow, administratrix of the estate of Mary Haskett, her late sister, widow of Elias Haskett, late of Henstridge Marsh [co. Somerset], yeoman, shows that the said Elias Haskett was seised in his demesne as of fee of lands to the value of £20 and goods and chattels in the form of ready money, household goods, mortgages, judgments, bonds, bills, securities, stock on lands, corn, grass, hay, cattle, oxen, cows, sheep, horses, wagons, carts, ploughs, tackling, chattel leases, etc., to the value of £700. Being so seised, he made his will, and disposed of the same to Mary, his then wife, and to his and her kindred and relatives, and the residue he gave to his wife. The will was dated 13 February, 9 King William [1696/7], and was as follows. [Here is set forth the will of Elias Haskett of Henstridge Marsh, co. Somerset, yeoman, dated 13 February 1696 [1696/7], an abstract of which is given above, p. 111]. Soon after the making of the will he gave, in the presence of three witnesses, all his undisposed property, in bonds, mortgages, securities, etc., which were in the house, to his wife Mary. She then stated that he had left no legacy to his baseborn child, and he told her to amend according to her desires what he had not done and declared her to be the sole legatee of his property undisposed of. He then died, on or about 19 February 1696 [1696/7]. By reason of her affection for him Mary, his wife, sickened and died five days later, in the same house, in possession of all his executory estate, intestate, before becoming executrix of his will. Thereupon the orator took out administration on her estate

18

from Samuel Mews, Clerk, Prebend of Henstridge, in the Cathedral Church of Wells, on the 3d of March following, and incurred the funeral expenses of Elias Haskett and his wife; and, as by law Mary was possessed of the residue of Elias's property, she made an inventory of the chattels of Elias, and later, in June, "bona notabilia" of Elias appearing, she made a new inventory and had it filed in the Prerogative Court of Canterbury, and took out another administration on her sister's estate, under the seal of that court, by virtue whereof she has enjoyed the executory estate of Elias. But now Elias Hasket, Stephen Hasket, Elias Hasket, Richard Gaulpin, Richard Sheene, Mary Crumsey, Luzde *alias* Lewis Crumsey, Mary the wife of Lewis *alias* Ludse Crumsey, and —— Rogers, combining with persons unknown to defeat the executory estate given to Mary, and giving out speeches that the said confederates or some of them are of the nearest kin and blood to Elias Hasket, and having gotten possession of the original will and much of the testator's estate, will oblige that administration *cum testamento annexo* on the estate of Elias Hasket be given to some of them. Complainant prays for relief and the funeral expenses. Some of the orator's witnesses are either dead or gone beyond seas; and she asks for a writ of subpœna against Elias Hasket, Stephen Hasket, Richard Gaulpin, Richard Sheene, Mary Crumsey, Lewis *alias* Ludes Crumsey and Mary his wife, —— Rogers, and Ellis Hasket. (Chancery Proceedings before 1714, Mitford, C. 8, 542/34.)

27 February 1698 [1698/9]. To Lord Somers.
The complaint of ELIAS HASKET of ——, gentleman, shows that Elias Hasket, late of Henstridge [co. Somerset], yeoman, was seised of several messuages, lands, etc., in Henstridge Marsh in Henstridge and at divers other places and parishes in the said county and elsewhere, to the yearly value of £40 and worth £800 or more, and of personalty, household stuff, plate, corn, animals, etc., to the value of £600. He died about February 1696 [1696/7], without lawful issue and intestate, leaving your orator, born beyond seas in New England, who is the only son and heir of Stephen Hasket, heretobefore of the city of Exeter, co. Devon, but late of Salem in New England, merchant, deceased, who was the only natural and lawful brother of the said Elias Hasket, deceased; and the said freehold estate ought to descend to him as heir at law, being the next and nearest relation and kin of the testator; but your orator dwelling and inhabiting some times in New England and at other times in Barbadoes beyond seas and having no intelligence till very lately of the death of his said uncle, Elias Hasket, Lewis Crumsey of the city of London and Mary, his wife, Nicholas Buggis of Henstridge, yeoman, William Dussett of Stalbridge, co. Dorset, yeoman, Elias Dusset his son, Stephen Haskett of Marnehull in Dorset, yeoman, and Dorothy Hedditch of ——, widow, combining with others unknown for the purpose of taking advantage of your orator's being beyond seas and having no intelligence till very lately of the death of his uncle, Elias Hasket, under some pretended administration, which they got by surprise, received possession of the personal and freehold estate under some pretended will, in which they pretend that they were made executors of the said Elias, and got custody of all the deeds, evidences, etc., and now they give out speeches that Elias Hasket made a will not long before his death, which they now set up, purporting to devise all the real and personal estate to them, and at other times they pretend that they are the heirs at law of the said Elias Haskett, and not your orator, when in truth the same is well known to those confederates to be the fact, and they are also well satisfied in their consciences that the said Elias Hasket, deceased, never made any such devises to them, and, if any will was obtained, it was by fraud, when the said Elias Hasket was *in extremis*, and some of the confederates were witnesses to the said

19

will and knew the truth thereof. These confederates now refuse to discover any deed or will, and refuse to deliver over the property; but they threaten to share and divide it among themselves, and have sold the greater part of the personalty or converted the same, and have made several alienations of the realty to irritate and perplex the orator's title and rights thereto, and they pretend that they have two wills, well and truly expressed, purporting to divide the estate among them, and they purpose to set them up against any suit of ejectment and so to nonsuit the orator and to refuse him evidences of discovery, and he has no relief except in equity, as the witnesses to these facts are either dead or in parts beyond the seas, remote and unknown to the orator. He prays that they be interrogated as to what property the said Elias Hasket, the orator's uncle, died seised of and its value, and where it lies; also how they are related to the said Elias Hasket, and whether the orator be not the son of Stephen Hasket, the brother of Elias Hasket, deceased, and what they know, believe, or have heard, and from whom, touching that matter, etc. (Chancery Proceedings before 1714, Mitford, B. 572/41.)

Summons to ELIAS DUSSETT, an infant about 8 years of age, to choose a guardian *ad litem*.* He chooses Thomas Gribham [?] of Yovell [Yeovil], co. Somerset, as guardian for the purposes of this suit, and a certificate thereof is produced.

The answer of WILLIAM DUSSET* shows that he believes that Elias Hasket, deceased, was seised in his demesne as of fee of three closes, called Whitefields Lane, New Close, and Long Close, and two parcels lying in South meade, in all nine acres, of the yearly value of about £8, in Henstridge, and also of a close of pastureland, called Sidehill, of three and one-half acres, of the yearly value of £5, but the defendant cannot tell the terms of the lease, as Nicholas Buggis has it. Elias Hasket, several days before he died, made his will, 13 February 1696 [1696/7], which was witnessed by Thomas Browne, William Dasset, and Alice Carly. By it he gave to the defendant's wife Sidehill close and to the defendant's sons £100, to be divided between them. He made his wife Mary the sole executrix, and she died before proving the will, some five or six days before [*sic*, after] her husband. Trouble then arose among the kindred as to who had the right to administration with the will annexed. The Court of the Arches of Canterbury gave it to Lewis Crumsey and his wife Mary, in her right, as she pretended to be the next of kin of the deceased; and thereupon the defendant, in right of his wife, entered upon Sidehill, and shortly afterwards upon the three closes and two pigtells [pightels], in the name and right of the defendant, Elias Dussett, his son, to whom they were devised; and he has held them until about twelve months since, when the complainant came into England and pretended to be the next of kin, and by threats and menaces of suits at law prevailed on the defendant to quit possession of the premises, and he refused to pay Elias Dussett or his brothers the £100. Wherefore this complainant, with other legatees, hath a suit in this Honorable Court against the complainant for recovery of the said legacies, and he believes the complainant to be no kin of the deceased, and that he obtained the administration falsely. This same Elias Hasket brought an ejectment suit against the defendant which was to be tried in the Somerset assize in May 1698, and he threatened to undo the defendant by suits at law, and prevailed on him to make an agreement with him. He also induced Alice Carley to forget her attesting of the will.

The answer of ELIAS DUSSETT by Thomas Gribham, next friend and guardian *ad litem*. This is in substance the same as the preceding answer,

* This summons and answer apparently belong to the same case with the complaint of Elias Hasket of 27 February 1698 [1698/9], given above.

and adds that Alice Carley was the testator's servant. The defendant denies that the complainant was the son of Stephen Hasket, brother of Elias Hasket the testator, who was this defendant's mother's uncle. (Chancery Proceedings before 1714, Mitford, 583/2.)

3 April 1702. The complaint of ELIAS HASKET of Henstridge Marsh [co. Somerset], Esq., cousin and heir of Ellias Hasket of Henstridge, yeoman, deceased, who left a considerable estate, shows that until very lately the complainant has traded as a merchant at Barbadoes in America, and, having some employment in the government of England, was obliged to reside there until about four years since, and then, returning into England and being at Henstridge, he found several persons in possession of the estate, who had divided it among themselves. The orator made himself known, and [showed] that he considered himself entitled to the estate, and requested them to prove their titles. They produced a will, purporting to have been made by Elias Hasket when he was in extremis and non compos, and the orator has been informed that the will was fictitious. There were several suits in the Court of Arches, this Honorable Court, and at law, whereupon several of the pretenders to the estate of Elias Hasket released their claims; but, one William Dussett of Stalbridge in Dorset, yeoman, being related to Elias Hasket, and being in possession of the premises hereafter named under the pretended will to which he pretended to be a witness, the orator brought a suit of ejectment, which was ready for trial; but then the said Dussett, who was in very mean circumstances, prevailed on the orator to give him £40 for the maintenance of himself and family, and on 22 March 1698 [1698/9] an agreement was made between the orator and Dussett that recited that, for the purpose of quashing various disputes, quarrels, and actions commenced, as well as long and tedious suits, the orator should pay the said Dussett £40, and the latter was before three calendar months to convey to the orator and his heirs all his, the said Dussett's, pretended right and title to a meadow called South Meade, containing by estimation one acre, and three fields or closes called Whitfield Lane, New Close, and Long Close, in all ten acres, together with several parcels of land in South Meade in Henstridge, late the land of inheritance of the deceased, which he pretended had been given to his, Dussett's, wife and children, and was to release all claims to the orator. The orator then gave the said Dussett a bond, with sureties, for the payment, and Dussett delivered up to him the possession of the premises, and the orator is in actual possession of them. He has asked Dussett to make the conveyance agreed on, and has tendered the £40. But now the defendant Dussett and Mary his wife and his son Elias and the children of the said Dussett, conspiring with persons unknown, pretend that they were surprised into the agreement, and that their interest was greater, and that the said William Dussett had no interest in the estate, and, if he did, it was only for his life, as guardian of his children or by their courtesy; and at other times they say that he was ready to convey, but that his wife dissuaded him and refused to join in the conveyance, and that his children are infants and cannot make an agreement; and again they say that he had settled the land on his wife and their issue. He prays discovery and a writ of subpœna.

1 August 1702. The answer of WILLIAM DUSSETT confesseth that Elias Haskett, deceased, was seised of one close called Side Hill, of three acres, worth £3 per annum, for the remainder of ninety-nine years, determinable in the deaths of persons yet living. Several days before his death Elias Hasket made a will, on 13 February 1696 [1696/7], attested by Thomas Browne of Stalbridge, scrivener, and gave the defendant and his five sons £100, and made his wife Mary sole executrix, and so died, leaving his wife

Mary, who survived her husband five or six days and died before proving the will. Trouble then arose amongst their kindred as to whom administration *cum testamento annexo* should go; but at last it was given to Lewis Crumsey and his wife Mary, by order of the Arches Court of Canterbury, as next of kin. The defendant entered the close called Sidehill in right of his wife Mary and of his son Elias on the three closes at issue, and enjoyed the same until five or six years ago the complainant came into England from beyond seas, and pretended to be nearer of kin to the testator than Mary Crumsey, and got administration with the will annexed on all the goods of the testator, and by threats and menaces of suits got the defendant timorously to desert the said demised premises, although they were given to his wife. The complainant refused the defendant the legacies and premises or to pay the £100 bequeathed to the defendant's children. The defendant denies any wrong acting, and does not believe the complainant to be of any kin or affinity with the testator, and denies that he has any deeds or evidences in his hands. The will was not obtained by fraud, and he challenges the complainant's right to the closes in question. Moreover, the complainant has admitted the validity of the will by taking administration with the will annexed. At the testator's request Thomas Browne and Alice Carly attested the will, which now remains in the Prerogative Court and it is from this that the defendant's wife and his son Elias Dusset derive their title. The deceased left two wills, the first of which was given to the complainant by Nicholas Buggis, who held the house in Henstridge late of the testator; but the defendant does not know the contents of the first will. The defendant does not believe that the complainant is the son of Stephen Haskett, brother of the testator, who was this defendant's (i. e., young Ellis Dusset's) mother's uncle. The last will was filed in the Court of Arches of Canterbury. The defendant's children are: William Dusset, aged 13 years, Elias, under 12 years, Henry, under 10 years, George, under 9 years, and James, under 6 years. The complainant has prevailed on Alice Carly to forget her attesting the will; and Thomas Browne's single evidence is not enough to prove it, according to the strict construction of the law. The only reason why he submitted to make the agreement alleged by the complainant was his inability to defend himself, and he prays that it be cancelled. (Chancery Proceedings before 1714, Reynardson, 168/44.)

FROM LAY SUBSIDIES FOR HENSTRIDGE, CO. SOMERSET*

| | |
|---|---|
| 39 Elizabeth [1596–7]. | William Sevier in goods [valuation] £3 [tax] 8d. |
| | William Stibbs in goods [valuation] £3 [tax] 8d. |
| 18 James I [1620–1]. | Elias Hasket in lands [valuation] 20s. [tax] 8d. |
| | William Stibbs in lands [valuation] 20s. [tax] 4d. |
| 3 Charles I ]1627–8]. | Elias Hasket in lands [valuation] 20s. [tax] 4d. |
| | William Haskett in lands [valuation] 40s. [tax] 8d. |
| | William Stibbs in lands [valuation] 20s. [tax] 4d. |
| 4 Charles I [1628–9]. | Elias Haskett in lands [valuation] £1 [tax] 8d. |

*Preserved in the Public Record Office, London.

|                              | William Haskett in lands [valuation] £2 [tax] 16d. |
|------------------------------|-----------------------------------------------------|
|                              | William Stibbs in lands [valuation] £1 [tax] 8d.    |
| 16 Charles I [1640–1].       | William Haskett in lands [valuation] 20s. [tax] 8d. [Assessment of first two of four payments.] |
| 16 Charles I [1640–1], Poll Tax. | Ellis Haskett [valuation] £10 [tax] 2s. |
|                              | Mr. Haskett [valuation] £20 [tax] 5s.              |
|                              | William Stibbs [valuation] £10 [tax] 2s.           |

The foregoing records contain much information about the Hasketts who in the later years of the sixteenth century and in the seventeenth century lived at Marnhull and Todbere, in the northern part of Dorsetshire, and at Henstridge, a parish in the adjoining portion of Somersetshire, among whom were the ancestors and near relatives of Stephen Haskett of Salem in New England. Ellis (or Elias) Hasket of Henstridge, who was buried there in 1639, was probably the grandfather of the emigrant to New England, and a pedigree showing two or three generations of his proved and of his probable descendants is given below. This pedigree is followed by information about the family of a John Hasket of Marnhull and Todbere, co. Dorset, who was probably closely related to Ellis Hasket of Henstridge. There are a few Hasketts mentioned in the parish registers given above whose relationship to the family of Ellis or that of John has not yet been established, as there are also several legatees and other persons named in the foregoing wills whose relationship to the testators has not yet been ascertained. New England records also have been consulted for the New England immigrant and his children.

1. ELLIS (ELIAS) HASKET, of Henstridge, co. Somerset, born probably about 1560, was buried at Henstridge, "an old man," 10 May 1639. He probably married first ———; and secondly, about 1595, MARY SEAVIER or SEVIER, sister of William Seavier of Yenston in the parish of Henstridge, husbandman, the testator of 1604. Mary (Seavier) Hasket was living 9 May 1607, when she was mentioned as a legatee in the will of her sister-in-law, Mariane Sevier, widow of William.

Ellis (Elias) Hasket appears to be the first of the name in Henstridge, as no Hasketts are to be found there in the lay subsidies of 39 and 43 Elizabeth [1596–7 and 1600–1]. He probably came to Henstridge because of his marriage with Mary Seavier, sister of William Seavier of that parish, who was taxed at Henstridge in the lay subsidy of 39 Elizabeth [1596–7], and he may have been a near relative of John Hasket of Todbere, co. Dorset, the testator of 1614, and of William Hasket, who married a daughter of John Hillier of Wincanton, co. Somerset, gentleman, the testator of 1619. He is probably the Elias Hasket who was taxed at Henstridge in the lay subsidy of 18 James I [1620–1], 3 Charles I [1627–8], and 4 Charles I [1628–9]. Children by first wife:

2. i.   ELLIS (ELIAS), probably s. of Ellis of Henstridge, b. about 1585.
3. ii.  STEPHEN, probably s. of Ellis of Henstridge, b. about 1590.

23

Children by second wife:

iii. DEANE (dau.), b. probably about 1596; bur. at Henstridge, as Dionisia Haskett, 4 July 1623; legatee in the will of Mariane Sevier, widow of William, 9 May 1607.

iv. A DAUGHTER, b. probably about 1598; living 9 May 1607 (see will of Mariane Sevier, widow, of 1607).

v. WILLIAM, of Henstridge, b. probably about 1600; m. (1) at Kingsdon, co. Somerset, 3 Nov. 1625, JOANNA HURD, bur. at Henstridge 1 Mar. 1640/1, dau. of William of Kingsdon, gentleman, the testator of 1638 (see his will, *supra*, p. 110); m. (2) REBECCA ———. Child by first wife: 1. *Mary*, living 14 Apr. 1638, when she is mentioned in the will of her grandfather, William Hurd. Children by second wife: 2. *William*, bur. at Henstridge 3 May 1654. 3. *Robert*, bur. at Henstridge 19 Sept. 1666. 4. *Jonathan*, bapt. at Henstridge 23 Nov. 1665. Perhaps others.

vi. A DAUGHTER, b. probably about 1602; living 9 May 1607 (see will of Mariane Sevier, widow, of 1607).

vii. A DAUGHTER, b. probably about 1604; living 9 May 1607 (see will of Mariane Sevier, widow, of 1607).

2. ELLIS (ELIAS) HASKET (? *Ellis*), of Marnhull, co. Dorset, and of Henstridge, co. Somerset, yeoman and gentleman, clothier, probably a son of Ellis (1), born about 1585, died before 1660. He married first, about 1608, CHRISTIAN ———, who died before 1635; and secondly, about 1635, ELEANOR STIBBS, baptized at Henstridge 18 Oct. 1605, buried there, a widow, 17 June 1660, daughter of William of Henstridge.

He appears at Marnhull, 1608–1615, and at Henstridge, where he lived in the hamlet of Enston or Yenston, from 1622 on. He was a plaintiff in Chancery suits, abstracts of which have been given above, in 1627, 1637, 1639, and 1647, the defendant in the suit of 1647 being the plaintiff's son, William Haskett.

Children by first wife:

i. EDITH, bapt. at Marnhull 9 Dec. 1608. Child (illegitimate): 1. *Joan*, bapt. at Henstridge 27 May 1636.

ii. ELLIS (ELIAS), bapt. at Marnhull 28 Oct. 1610; living 2 July 1639 (see Chancery suit); d. *s.p.* soon afterwards.

iii. WILLIAM, of Yenston in Henstridge, bapt. at Marnhull 12 June 1615; living in 1662, when he was defendant in a Chancery suit (*q.v.*); m. between 1637 and 1647 MARY ———, living 11 Oct. 1647. He was plaintiff, with his father and brother Ellis (Elias), in the Chancery suit of 1639, and was defendant in the Chancery suit brought by his father in 1647. Child: 1. *Mary*, b. probably about 1645; d. before 20 Apr. 1697; m. at Henstridge William Hoddinott, who d. before 5 Oct. 1697, s. of William of Stalbridge, co. Dorset; their dau. Mary, b. in Stalbridge about 1662, m. Lewis Crumsey, and in 1697, being then of Blackfriars, London, claimed the administration *cum testamento annexo* on the estate of Elias Haskett (2, vii), the testator of 13 Feb. 1696/7, her half great-uncle, which was granted to her in the Prerogative Court of Canterbury, 12 May 1698, but was given by the Court of Delegates, 14 Aug. 1699, to Elias Hasket (4, iii), son of the testator's own elder brother, Stephen Haskett of Salem in New England, deceased.

iv. SUSAN, bapt. at Henstridge 19 Mar. 1622/3.

Children by second wife:

4. v. STEPHEN, bapt. at Henstridge 18 December 1636.

vi. A DAUGHTER (probably), who was probably b. about 1639 and m. ———. They were probably the parents of *Mary*, b. probably about 1663, who m. about 1687 William Dussett of Stalbridge,

24

co. Dorset, yeoman, one of the defendants in the Chancery suits of 27 Feb. 1698/9 and the defendant in the suit of 1702. Both William Dussett and his wife Mary were living 1 Aug. 1702, and had then the following children: 1. William, aged 13 years. 2. Elias, under 12 years. 3. Henry, under 10 years. 4. George, under 9 years. 5. James, under 6 years. (See Chancery suit of 1702, given above.)

vii. ELIAS (ELLIS), of Henstridge Marsh, yeoman, the testator of 13 Feb. 1696/7, b. at Henstridge, probably about 1642; d. about 14 Feb. 1696/7; m. MARY ———, who d. five or six days after her husband and was bur. at Henstridge 21 Feb. 1696/7. Child: 1. *Mary*, bur. at Henstridge 26 June 1673. Elias Haskett was the father also of an illegitimate child, to whom he left no legacy in his will (see Chancery suit brought in 1697 by Dorothy Hedditch, widow, sister of Mary, wife of Elias Haskett). In his will (*vide supra*, p. 111) Elias Haskett made his wife Mary his executrix; but she died a few days after her husband, without proving the will. Various relatives and connections of the testator claimed the administration *cum testamento annexo* on his estate, and the Prerogative Court of Canterbury, in which the will was proved 12 May 1698, granted administration to Mary Crumsey, wife of Lewis Crumsey, who was grandniece of the testator, being the granddaughter of William Haskett (2, iii), deceased, an elder half brother of the testator. The contest for the administration was carried into the Court of Delegates, which on 14 Aug. 1699 granted the administration *cum testamento annexo* to the nephew of the testator, Elias Haskett, the son of Stephen Haskett of Salem in New England, deceased (4), the elder own brother of the testator. The processes in this litigation in the Court of Delegates and the Chancery suits connected with this contest (see the suits of 1697, 1698/9, and 1702) contain important information on the family connections of the testator and have been most helpful in the compiling of this pedigree. It is not possible to determine the relationship to the testator of some of the legatees in his will.

3. STEPHEN HASKETT, of Marnhull, co. Dorset, fuller, the testator of 1648, probably a son of Ellis (1), born about 1590, was buried at Marnhull 29 Oct. 1648 or 1649. He married ELIZABETH ———, who was named as executrix in his will (*q.v.*), dated 24 May 1648 and proved 27 Feb. 1653 [? 1653/4].

Children:

5. i.   ELLIS (ELIAS), b. probably about 1618.
6. ii.  STEPHEN, b. probably about 1620.
   iii. ELIZABETH, bapt. at Marnhull 19 Jan. 1622/3; living 24 May 1648; m. ——— YOUNG. Child: 1. *James*, living 24 May 1648.
   iv.  MARGARET, bapt. at Marnhull 12 Jan. 1624/5; bur. there 30 Jan. 1635/6.
   v.   ALICE, bur. at Marnhull 16 Nov. 1635.
   vi.  JOHN, bapt. at Marnhull 25 June 1629; living 24 May 1648.

4. STEPHEN HASKETT (*Ellis*, ? *Ellis*), of Exeter, co. Devon, and Salem, Mass., soap boiler, baptized at Henstridge, co. Somerset, 18 Dec. 1636, died before 30 May 1698. He married at Exeter, co. Devon, about 1666, ELIZABETH HILL of Exeter, who survived him and deposed at Salem, as his widow, 30 May 1698.

He served an apprenticeship at Exeter to one Mr. Thomas Oburne, a chandler and soap boiler there, and, after his time was out, married. Afterwards, according to the statement of his son Elias, "meeting some crosses in the world," he emigrated to Salem, in the Colony of the Massachusetts Bay, where he is found 22 Mar. 1666/7 (Salem Town Records, in *Essex Institute Historical Collections*, vol. 41, p. 122) and where he settled. After he had been there a while, he sent for his wife, who left England and joined her husband in Salem, bringing with her their daughter Elizabeth. In Nov. 1671 he deposed, aged 37 years (Records and Files of the Quarterly Courts of Essex County, vol. 4, p. 430), and his name occurs several times in the Essex County court records. He is "styled soap boiler and captain. He appears to have carried on the trade of a chandler and at the same time he was captain of a trading vessel. Capt. Stephen Hasket was employed to carry stores around Cape Cod to the army at Narragansett in 1675, and he was present at the storming of the Narragansett fort [in King Philip's War] as one of Capt. Curwin's troopers." (*Essex Institute Historical Collections*, vol. 51, p. 2.) On 30 Nov. 1677 Stephen Haskett was appointed by the Quarterly Court at Salem administrator of the estate of John Langdon, deceased, intestate, and Michaell Comes and Peter Joy, aged about 40 years, deposed on 22 Oct. 1677 that they heard John Langdon say that he gave to Elizabeth Haskitt, daughter of Mr. Stepheen Heskitt, £10, and what else there was left was to be divided among said Heskitt's children, this being said Langdon's desire when he went away with Mr. Eliezer Devenportt out of the country in Dec. 1676. John Langdon's estate was appraised at £20. 10s. (Records and Files of the Quarterly Courts of Essex County, vol. 6, p. 376. Cf. REGISTER, vol. 29, p. 318.) What, if any, relationship there was between John Langdon and the children of Stephen Haskett does not appear. The deposition of Stephen Haskett's widow, Elizabeth, of 30 May 1698, in regard to her children has been given in the early part of this article (*vide supra*, page 72); and on the same date Stephen Sewell, notary, certified that Stephen Hasket left only one son and five daughters.

Children:

i.   ELIZABETH, b. in England (probably at Exeter, co. Devon) about 1667; brought in infancy by her mother to New England; d. before 8 Apr. 1740, when administration on her estate was granted to her son-in-law, Joshua Hicks; m. (1) 6 June 1684 WILLIAM DYNN of Salem, b. at Kinsale, Ireland, about 1660, came to New England in 1678, d. in 1689–90, s. of John; m. (2) in 1691, as his second wife, ROGER DERBY, SR., of Salem, b. probably at Topsham, co. Devon, England, about 1643, came to New England in 1671, d. at Salem 26 Sept. 1698, aged 55 years. Children by first husband, b. at Salem: 1. *John*, b. 23 May 1686; living 26 July 1698, when he is mentioned in the will of his stepfather, Roger Derby; d. unm. before 18 June 1716. 2. *William*, b. 1 Aug. 1689; living 26 July 1698, when he is mentioned in the will of his stepfather, Roger Derby; d. unm. before 18 June 1716. Children by second husband, b. at Salem: 3. *Elizabeth*, b. 10 Mar. 1691/2; d. before 29 Dec. 1721, when her will was proved; m. 17 Apr. 1718 Thomas Palfray, sailmaker, b. at Salem 24 June 1689, d. before 1 Aug. 1720, when his will was proved, s. of Walter and Margaret (Manning); their only child, Elizabeth, bapt. at Salem 11 Oct. 1719, d. young. 4. *Margaret*, b. 14 Aug. 1693; d. 11 July 1765; m. 8 Feb. 1710 William Osborn, yeoman, b. 3 May 1682, d. at Danvers, Mass., 28 Sept. 1771, s. of William and Hannah (Burton) of Salem; eight children. 5.

*Ann*, b. 10 Dec. 1695; living 19 June 1752, when she was named as executrix in her husband's will; m. 2 Jan. 1717/18 Capt. Benjamin Ives, master mariner and tanner, b. at Salem about 1692, d. between 19 June 1752, when his will was dated, and 16 July 1752, when his will was proved, s. of Thomas and Elizabeth (Metcalf); nine children, b. at Salem. 6. *Martha*, b. 30 Sept. 1697; m. 22 Oct. 1719 Joshua Hicks of Salem, merchant; eight children.

ii. STEPHEN, b. at Salem in Mar. 1668/9; d. in two weeks.

iii COL. ELIAS, b. at Salem 25 Apr. 1670; m. in Barbados, about 1695 or earlier, ELIZABETH RICH. In early life he went to Barbados, where he settled and became a sea captain, merchant, and planter. He made a voyage from Barbados to England in 1696, in the ship *New London*, of which he was master, and remained in England until May 1697, when he embarked on the *Sheerness* galley, Captain Bolles, for Barbados, where he arrived in Aug. 1697. In Nov. 1698 he went again to England, and in the ensuing winter claimed in the Court of Delegates, as next of kin, administration on the estate of his uncle, Elias Haskett of Henstridge Marsh, co. Somerset, yeoman, the testator of 13 Feb. 1696/7; and he also brought a suit in Chancery, 27 Feb. 1698/9, for the possession of the estate of the deceased. On 14 Aug. 1699 administration *cum testamento annexo* on the estate of the deceased was granted to him by the Court of Delegates; but on 3 Apr. 1702, calling himself Elias Hasket of Henstridge Marsh, Esq., he brought suit in Chancery against William Dussett, husband of a niece of the deceased (cf. 2, vi), because he had not carried out an agreement which he had made with the plaintiff in connection with the latter's claim to the estate of the deceased. Meanwhile, he had been nominated by the Lords Proprietors of the Bahama Islands to be Governor of those islands, and had been vouched for by several men, presumably merchants of London, in the following letter: "To the Honble Lords Commissioners of Trade    We whose names are subscribed doe humbly certify that Capt. Elias Haskett is a person very well known unto us being personally acquainted with him for many years past, he being imployed by divers considerable Merchants of Credit and reputation as commander of severall ships and alsoe intrusted with the disposall of their Cargoes, which Trust he performed to their full satisfaction. And farther That he hath always manifested himself a Loyall and faithfull Subject to this present Government. [Signed] Hwtn.[?] Ennis Thomas Richards John Stretet Epa Charington William Deacon Jno Reynolds Rob. Heysham Mel. Holder Rowld Tryon." This letter is endorsed: " Certificate of Mr. Robert Heysham and others in behalf of Capt. Elias Hasket nominated by the Lords Proprietors of the Bahamas in the Indies to be Governour of those Islands." (State Papers, Colonial Series, vol. 13, p. 14, from Colonial Office Papers, 5, 1260, no. 42.) A bond of Elias Hasket of London, Esq., Robert Nesmith of London, Gent., and Josias Dicken of London, Gent., to John, Earl of Bath, and the other proprietors, as Governour of the Bahamas and to suppress piracy, etc., is dated 18 Apr. 1700, and is witnessed by Jo. Aleman, James Griffith, and Benj. Durgy. (*Ib.*, no. 41.) He received his commission as Governor of the Bahamas about 12 May 1701, and proceeded thither with his wife and family and took up the duties of his office. His career as Governor was brief but stormy. The people of New Providence, in an assembly held at Nassau 5 Oct. 1701, addressed to the Lords Proprietors and to the Commissioners of Trade a long statement of their grievances and of the oppressive acts of the Governor. In the statement in his own defence which he published in London in 1702, the Governor ascribes his troubles to the wicked men whom he had tried to bring to justice, who, he says, conspired with divers inhabitants of the island to stir up an insurrection against him. In Oct. 1701, the narrative continues, the conspirators seized the fort at Nassau, broke into the Governor's house, "and in a Rebellious and Hostile manner assaulted the said Governour and his Attendants, and having grevously wounded him in the Head and other Parts, to the great hazard of his Life, they carried him away Prisoner into the Fort, and kept him there confin'd in Irons; and the same Night his Wife, Sister, and Family were constrain'd for their Security, to fly into the Woods." The insurgents looted the Governor's house, and took away his own securities and money and money belonging to the King and the Lords Proprietors. They held the Governor for three days or thereabouts in the fort, and then removed him to a small house about four miles from Nassau, where he was kept a prisoner, in irons, for six weeks; and his wife and sister were kept in close confinement during a great part of this time. At length the Governor was placed on board of a small ketch, and made his escape from the Islands. Some time later, in the middle of the winter, his wife and sister were forced to board a sloop, and were cast away on a desert and uninhabited coast,* his wife succeeding in reaching Charleston in Carolina, whence she sailed for England. The Governor himself made his way to New York and New England, and on 19 Mar. 1701/2, styling himself "the Hon. Col. Elias Haskett Esquire," Governor of New Providence, in the West Indies, gave a power of attorney to Capt. Samuel Browne, merchant, of Salem, to collect his rents and sell his property, etc., in Salem. (Cf. *Essex Institute Historical Collections*, vol. 42, p. 162, and vol. 51, p. 1.) He went to England, to lay his case before the authorities, and on 3 Apr. 1702 brought the suit in Chancery against William Dussett which has been referred to above. Savage (Genealogical Dictionary, vol. 2, p. 372) states that he lived some time in Boston in the early part of the eighteenth century.

iv. MARY, b. at Salem 13 Mar. 1671/2; m. CAPT. BENJAMIN PICKMAN of Salem, b. 30 Jan. 1671/2, d. 26 Apr. 1719, s. of Benjamin and Elizabeth (Hardy). Child: 1. *John*, bapt. at Salem 12 Feb. 1698/9.

v. SARA, b. at Salem 5 Feb. 1673/4; m. 29 July 1702 SAMUEL INGERSOLL of Salem. They had issue.

vi. HANNAH, b. at Salem 2 Aug. 1675; m. 11 May 1704 RICHARD SYMMES. They had issue.

vii. MARTHA, m. 25 Feb. 1702/3 RICHARD DERBY of Salem, mariner, b. at Ipswich, Mass., 8 Oct. 1679, d. 25 July 1715, s. of Roger and his first wife, Lucretia (Kilham or Hilman), Roger Derby marrying for his second wife Elizabeth (Hasket) Dynn, eldest sister of Martha (Hasket) Derby. Children, b. at Salem: 1. *John*, b. 27 Dec. 1705. 2. *Mary*, b. 9 Jan. 1707/8; d. 9 Feb. 1736/7; m. 11 May 1727 Capt. George Mugford, mariner; two children. 3. *Richard*, of Salem, master mariner and merchant, b. 16 Sept. 1712; d. 9 Nov. 1783; m. (1) 3 Feb. 1735/6 Mary Hodges, b. 21 Dec. 1713, d. 27 Mar. 1770, dau. of Gamaliel and Sarah (Williams) of Salem; m. (2) 2 Oct. 1771 Sarah (Langley) Hersey, b. in 1712, d. 17 June 1790, widow of Dr. Ezekiel Hersey of Hingham, Mass.; six children by his first wife, of whom one was Elias Hasket Derby, the well-known Salem merchant, b. in 1739, d. in 1799. 4. *Martha*, b. 21 Sept. 1714; d. 28 Sept. 1745; m. 30 Mar. 1736 Capt. Thomas Elkins, mariner; one son.

5. ELLIS (ELIAS) HASKETT (*Stephen*, ? *Ellis*), of Enston (Yenston) in Henstridge, co. Somerset, yeoman, born probably about 1618, was buried at Henstridge 22 Sept. 1673. He married SARAH ———.

In 1662, as Ellis Haskett the Elder, he was plaintiff in a

*The documents containing the charges against Gov. Elias Haskett and his answers to these charges were collected by the contributor of this article and were printed in *Essex Institute Historical Collections*, vol. 51, pp. 1–22, 97–125, in an article entitled "The Governor of New Providence, West Indies, in 1702."

Chancery suit (q.v.) against his first cousin, William Haskett the Younger of Yenston, yeoman (2, iii).
Children:

i. WILLIAM, bapt. at Henstridge 4 Nov. 1640; probably the William Haskett who m. JOAN ——— (bur. at Henstridge 3 Mar. 1690/1). Their children, bapt. at Henstridge, were: 1. *Annetta*, bapt. 18 Nov. 1669; perhaps the Anna Hasket of Henstridge who m. there, 25 Mar. 1695, William Kelloway of Marnhull, co. Dorset. 2. *Stephen*, bapt. 21 Oct. 1673. 3. *Mary*, bapt. 12 Jan. 1674/5; perhaps the Mary Haskot who m. at Henstridge, 27 July 1699, Joseph Perrin. 4. *Sara*, bapt. 12 Jan. 1675/6. 5. *Samuel*, bapt. 29 Apr. 1677; bur. at Henstridge 23 Oct. 1687. 6. *Jane*, bapt. 15 Sept. 1678. 7. *Joan*, bapt. 15 June 1681; bur. at Henstridge 2 Oct. 1681. 8. *Thomas*, bapt. 27 Aug. 1682.

ii. ELLIS (ELIAS), of Henstridge, baker, b. probably about 1642; living in 1697, when, with his cousin Stephen Haskett (6, i), he claimed in the Court of Delegates administration *cum testamento annexo* on the estate of Elias Haskett (2, vii), the testator of 13 Feb. 1696/7; m. ELIZABETH ———. On 1 Nov. 1665 he is called "Ellis Hasket, Junr." Children, bapt. at Henstridge and all living 13 Feb. 1696/7 (see will of Elias Haskett of that date): 1. *Susanna*, bapt. 1 Nov. 1665; m. ——— Hobbs, who d. before 13 Feb. 1696/7. 2. *Mary*, bapt. 18 Mar. 1667/8. 3. *Ellis (Elias)*, bapt. 8 Jan. 1670/1. 4. *Sara*, bapt. 2 Apr. 1673. 5. *Samuel*, bapt. 3 Apr. 1676. Probably also daughters.

6. STEPHEN HASKETT (*Stephen*, ? *Ellis*), of Marnhull, co. Dorset, born probably about 1620, was buried at Marnhull 9 Aug. 1651. He married ELIZABETH ———.
Children, baptized at Marnhull:

i. STEPHEN, of Marnhull, bapt. 12 Nov. 1648; probably living 11 Sept. 1701; m. (1) MARY ———, who d. about 1675; m. (2) ELIZABETH ———, who d. about 1683; m. (3) ANNE ———. In 1697, with his cousin Elias Haskett (5, ii), he claimed in the Court of Delegates administration *cum testamento annexo* on the estate of Elias Haskett (2, vii), the testator of 13 Feb. 1696/7. Children by first wife, bapt. at Marnhull: 1. *Stephen*, bapt. 7 May 1673; bur. at Marnhull 11 Sept. 1701. 2. *Thomas*, bapt. 15 June 1675; probably the Thomas Hasket who m. Mary ——— and had children bapt. at Marnhull, viz., Thomas, bapt. 5 July 1696, Stephen, bapt. 16 Jan. 1697/8, Jonathan, bapt. 6 Jan. 1699/1700 and Ambrose, bapt. 25 July 1701. Children by second wife, bapt. at Marnhull: 3. *John*, bapt. 3 Oct. 1677. 4. *Frances* (dau.), bapt. 4 June 1680. 5. *Jonathan*, bapt. 28 Mar. 1683. Child by third wife: 6. *Thomas*, bapt. at Marnhull 23 June 1686.

ii. ELIZABETH (posthumous), bapt. 7 Apr. 1652.

JOHN HASKET, of Marnhull and Todbere, co. Dorset, the testator of 1614, perhaps a brother or a cousin of Ellis (Elias) Hasket of Henstridge, co. Somerset, with whom the pedigree given above begins, died between 29 Sept. 1614, when his will was dated, and 23 Feb. 1614/15, when his will was proved. He married ANNE ———, whom he appointed executrix of his will.

A Stephen Haskett and a William Haskett, his "well-beloved friends," were overseers and witnesses of his will. He directed that he should be buried in the churchyard of Stowre Estowre [*sic*], that is, probably, East Stower, a parish a little distance north from Todbere.

29

Children, all except the last two recorded at Marnhull, and all except the second (who died in infancy) living 29 Sept. 1614, when they are mentioned in their father's will:

i. JOHN, bapt. 27 June 1596.
ii. WILLIAM, bapt. 7 Jan. 1597/8; bur. 5 Feb. 1597/8.
iii. JOAN, bapt. 1 July 1599; living unm. 29 Sept. 1614.
iv. MARY, bapt. 22 May 1601; living unm. 29 Sept. 1614.
v. THOMAS, bapt. 8 Apr. 1603.
vi. ROBERT, bapt. 18 Sept. 1605.
vii. WILLIAM, probably b. after his father removed to Todbere.
viii. MICHAEL, probably b. after his father removed to Todbere.

## GENEALOGICAL RESEARCH IN ENGLAND

Communicated by the Committee on English Research

### SHEFFIELD

Contributed by G. ANDREWS MORIARTY, JR., A.M., LL.B., of Newport, R. I.

IN this article is given the parentage of Edmund, William, Amos, and Ichabod Sheffield, early settlers of New England, with a brief word as to the Sheffield family in England.

The Sheffield family is of Northern origin, the cradle of the race being in and about Sheffield in Yorkshire. At a very early date a gentle branch of the family was living in the neighboring county of Rutland, and in the reign of Henry III the Lincolnshire branch was already settled around Butterwick. This family became very eminent. Edmund Sheffield of Butterwick was raised to the peerage in the reign of Henry VIII as Baron Sheffield of Butterwick, and his descendant John Sheffield, Duke of Buckingham, a well-known statesman in the reign of Queen Anne, built Buckingham House, which was bought by King George III in 1761, was remodelled in the first part of the nineteenth century, and, as Buckingham Palace, is now the London residence of the English kings.

The Sheffield family of New England came from Sudbury, co. Suffolk; but the name occurs nowhere else in Suffolk, and at the time of the emigration to New England they had been there but a short time. It is probable that they were an offshoot of the Sheffields who were settled in Essex. It may be noted that the name Edmund, a favorite one in the Lincolnshire family, occurs constantly in the Sudbury family and among their descendants in New England.

### From Probate Records

Administration on the estate of EDMUND SHEIFFEILD, late of Ballingdon in the Parish of All Saints, Sudbury, deceased, was granted 4 January 1630 [1630/1] to Humphrey Sheiffeild, son of the deceased, with the consent of the widow, Thomazine. Inventory, £24. 6s. 6d. (Archdeaconry of Sudbury, Administrations [at Bury St. Edmunds], vol. 3, fo. 7.)

The Will of GEORGE SHEFFEILD of Sudbury [co. Suffolk], dated 10 July 1671. To my wife Mary all my messuages and lands in the city of Norwich or elsewhere, for life, she paying to my two children, Elizabeth and Mary Sheffield, and to my unborn child £3 each at the age of twenty-one years. After my said wife's death said estates are to be divided among my said children. Residue to my said wife, whom I make executrix. Witnesses: Marke Salter, Sam. Pannill, John Catsby. Proved 12 March 1671/2 by the executrix. (Archdeaconry of Sudbury [at Bury St. Edmunds], Register Franklin, fo. 273.)

### From the Registers of the Parish of All Saints, Sudbury, co. Suffolk

#### Baptisms

1608   Humphrey son of Edmond Sheffeld 30 November.
1610   Thomasine daughter of Edmond Sheffeild 17 July.
1612   Edmond son of Edmond Sheffeild 16 August.
1619   William son of Edmond Sheffield 15 November.
1635   Elizabeth daughter of Edmond Sheffield 12 March [1635/6].

### From the Transcripts of the Registers of the Parish of St. Peter, Sudbury, co. Suffolk*

#### Baptisms

1627   Amos son of Edmond Sheffeld — December.
1630   Ichabod son of Edmond Sheffeld 23 December.

*The entries given under this heading were found on some loose sheets at Bury St. Edmunds by Mr. J. Gardner Bartlett, who made the investigations regarding the Sheffield family.

*Burial*

1598  Thomas Sheffield, last maker, 29 June.

FROM THE RECORDS OF THE BOROUGH OF SUDBURY, CO. SUFFOLK

3 September, 8 Charles I [1632]. Thomasine Sheffield, widow, presented for not going to her parish church of All Saints.

18 January, 9 Charles I [1633/4]. Edward [*sic*] Sheffeild presented for not attending his parish church of All Saints.

From the foregoing English records and from New England sources the following pedigree has been deduced.

1. THOMAS SHEFFIELD, of Sudbury, co. Suffolk, England, last maker, born probably about 1550, was buried at St. Peter's, Sudbury, 29 June 1598. He married ———.
He was probably the father of
  2. i.  EDMUND, b. about 1580.

2. EDMUND SHEFFIELD (? *Thomas*), of the parish of All Saints, Sudbury, co. Suffolk, England, born about 1580, died before 4 Jan. 1630/1, when administration on his estate was granted to his son Humphrey. He married, about 1607, THOMAZINE ———, who was cited on 3 Sept. 1632 for not attending her parish church of All Saints.
  Children:
    i.  HUMPHREY, bapt. at All Saints', Sudbury, 30 Nov. 1608.
    ii.  THOMAZINE, bapt. at All Saints', Sudbury, 17 July 1610.
  3. iii.  EDMUND, bapt. at All Saints', Sudbury, 16 Aug. 1612.
  4. iv.  WILLIAM, bapt. at All Saints', Sudbury, 15 Nov. 1619.
    v.  AMOS, bapt. at St. Peter's, Sudbury, — Dec. 1627; apparently the Amos Sheffield who d. at Braintree, Mass., 31 Dec. 1708.
  5. vi.  ICHABOD, bapt. at St. Peter's, Sudbury, 23 Dec. 1630.

3. EDMUND SHEFFIELD (*Edmund*, ? *Thomas*), of the parish of All Saints, Sudbury, co. Suffolk, England, and of Braintree, Mass., baptized at All Saints', Sudbury, 16 Aug. 1612, died at Braintree 13 Oct. 1705, "being about 90 years." He probably married first, in England, ———, who probably died in England;* secondly, at Roxbury, Mass., 17 Apr. 1644, MARY WOODIE, who died at Braintree 30 Mar. 1662, daughter of Richard; and thirdly, at Braintree, 5 Sept. 1662, SARAH (BEALE) MARSH, who died at Braintree 9 Nov. 1710, "Aged about 84 years," daughter of John Beale of Hingham, Mass., and widow of Thomas Marsh of the same town.

He was presented at Sudbury, 18 Jan. 1633/4, for not attending his parish church of All Saints. He emigrated to New England, settled at Roxbury, Mass., and was admitted a freeman there 29 May 1644. He removed in 1645–6 to Braintree, and resided there the rest of his life. Judge Samuel Sewall, in his Diary, under date of 26 Mar. 1704, states that he heard preaching at Braintree and that "One Sheffield, a very good

*That Edmund Sheffield had a wife in England, before he came to New England, is inferred from the record of the baptism of his daughter Elizabeth at All Saints', Sudbury, 12 Mar. 1635/6.

aged Christian, of about 90 years old, was there, who, as was expected, was never like to have come abroad more."
Child by first wife:
i. ELIZABETH, bapt. at All Saints', Sudbury, 12 Mar. 1635/6; probably d. in England, since no record of her being in New England has been found.

Children by second wife, the first child born at Roxbury, the others at Braintree:
ii. JOHN, b. 6 Mar. 1644/5.
iii. EDMUND, b. 15 Dec. 1646.
iv. ANN, b. 1 Apr. 1649.
v. ISAAC, b. 15 Mar. 1650/1.
vi. MARY, b. 14 June 1653; d. at Braintree 7 Dec. 1660.
vii. MATTHEW, b. 26 May 1655.
viii. SAMUEL, b. 26 Nov. 1657.
ix. SARAH, b. 6 June 1660.

Children by third wife, born at Braintree:
x. MARY, b. 20 June 1663.
xi. NATHANIEL, b. 16 Mar. 1664/5.
xii. DEBORAH, b. 23 June 1667; d. at Braintree 18 Jan. 1690/1.

4. WILLIAM SHEFFIELD (*Edmund*, ? *Thomas*), of Sudbury, co. Suffolk, England, and of New England, baptized at All Saints', Sudbury, 15 Nov. 1619, died at Sherborn, Mass., 6 Dec. 1700. He married, about 1659, MARY ———, who died at Sherborn 31 Oct. 1714, aged 78.

It is not known at what date he came to New England; but he was residing at Dover, N. H., together with his brother Ichabod, in 1658. In 1660 he was of Braintree, Mass., in 1673 he was among the first settlers of Holliston and Sherborn, Mass., and in 1686 he paid the third highest tax in the last-mentioned town. He appears, with his brother Edmund, to have bought, prior to 1672, a tract of land of Lieut. Joshua Fisher of Dedham, Mass., at Chabboquasset, in what afterwards became Sherborn. In his will, dated 14 Oct. 1698 and proved at Cambridge 24 Mar. 1700/1, he mentions his house in Boston.
Children:
i. RACHEL, b. at Braintree 24 May 1660; d. young.
ii. HANNAH, b. 18 Apr. 1663.*
iii. DANIEL, b. 3 Mar. 1665.*
iv. WILLIAM, b. 19 Mar. 1667.*
v. MARTHA, b. 8 Jan. 1668.*
vi. JOSEPH, b. 3 Mar. 1671;* of Dover, N. H., 9 May 1733.
vii. THAMASINE, b. at Sherborn (?) 25 May 1673; m. JONATHAN ADAMS.
viii. SUSANNA, b. at Sherborn 12 Dec. 1675; m. at Sherborn, 1 Sept. 1697, ZURIEL HALL.
ix. ELIZABETH, b. at Sherborn 28 Nov. 1678.
x. NATHANIEL, b. at Sherborn 7 Mar. 1681.
xi. MARY, m. JOHN CLARK.
xii. RACHEL, m. ———.

5. ICHABOD SHEFFIELD (*Edmund*, ? *Thomas*), of Portsmouth, R. I., baptized at St. Peter's, Sudbury, co. Suffolk, England, 23 Dec. 1630, died at Newport, R. I., 4 Feb. 1712. He married at

*The birth of this child is recorded at Sherborn, but the child was probably not born there.

33

Portsmouth, in 1660, MARY PARKER, daughter of George and Frances of that town.

He first appears at Portsmouth on 10 July 1648, when he was received as a freeman there. In 1658 he was taxed at Dover, N. H., with his brother William. In 1690 he was deputy to the Rhode Island Assembly from Portsmouth. He is buried in the Clifton Burying Ground at Newport, where his gravestone states incorrectly that he was eighty-six years old.

Children, born at Portsmouth, R. I.:

i. JOSEPH,* of Portsmouth, b. 22 Aug. 1661; d. in Feb. 1705/6; m. 12 Feb. 1684/5 MARY SHERIFF, dau. of Thomas of Plymouth and Portsmouth. He was assistant, 1696 and 1698–1705, and attorney general of Rhode Island, 1704–1706, and was appointed Colonial agent to England, 2 Feb. 1702/3. Seven children.

ii. MARY, b. 30 Apr. 1664.

iii. NATHANIEL, of Newport, R. I., merchant, b. 18 Apr. 1667; d. 12 Nov. 1729; m. (1) MARY CHAMBERLAIN, dau. of William of Hull, Mass.; m. (2) CATHERINE (CLARKE) GOULD, dau. of Gov. Walter Clarke of Newport and widow of James Gould. He was assistant, 1713–14, and major for the Island, 1710, 1712, 1714–1716. He is bur. in the Clifton Burying Ground at Newport. Five children.

iv. ICHABOD,† of South Kingstown, R. I., b. 6 Mar. 1669/70; d. between 17 Sept. 1729, when his will was dated, and 4 June 1736, when it was proved; m. 27 Dec. 1694 ELIZABETH MANCHESTER, dau. of William and Mary (Cook). Six children.

v. AMOS, of Tiverton, R. I., b. 25 June 1673; d. in 1710, while serving as a captain in the expedition against Canada; m. (1) 5 Mar. 1695/6 ANNE PEARCE, dau. of John and Mary (Tallman); m. (2) 22 Dec. 1708 SARAH DAVIS, dau. of Aaron and Mary. He was selectman of Tiverton, 1705–1707, and town treasurer, 1709. His will, dated 17 Apr. 1707, was proved 7 June 1710. Four children by first wife and one son by second wife.

---

*Ancestor of the well-known Sheffield family of Rhode Island.
†Ancestor of the Sheffields of New Haven, Conn.

# GENEALOGICAL RESEARCH IN ENGLAND

### Communicated by the Committee on English Research

## BORDMAN (BOARDMAN)

#### Contributed by G. ANDREWS MORIARTY, JR., A.M., LL.B., of Newport, R. I.

MANY years ago the late Henry FitzGilbert Waters contributed to the REGISTER (vol. 49, pages 496–498, October 1895) abstracts of three wills which shewed pretty conclusively the parentage of Maj. William Bordman or Boardman of Cambridge, Mass., the fourth steward of Harvard University and the founder of a family which long occupied a prominent place among the Massachusetts Colonial gentry. Several members of the family held the office of steward of Harvard and also high offices in the Colonial government; they were large landowners in Cambridge; and they retained their important position far down into the eighteenth century, in the early part of which they were allied by marriage with the well-known Spencer Phips, for many years Lieutenant Governor of the Province of the Massachusetts Bay.

Since Mr. Waters's time considerable additional material relating to this family has been gathered in England by the contributor of this article; and the evidence now at hand proves that before Major Bordman arrived in New England with his stepfather, Stephen Day, the first printer in the Massachusetts Bay Colony, the family had attained some position in the old Cambridge beyond the Atlantic. Its members belonged to the class of well-to-do tradesmen and merchants, who were rapidly coming to the front in the days of the later Tudors; and their property, transported into New England, laid the foundation of the fortune of one of the prominent Colonial families of Massachusetts.

It should be noted that the Boardman or Boreman family of Connecticut and the Boardman family now prominent in Boston are in no way related to this family.

The records collected by Mr. Waters and by the contributor of this article concerning the English home and connections of Maj. William Bordman are given below, and are followed by a brief pedigree, in which the conclusions warranted by them in regard to this family are set forth in genealogical form.

### FROM PROBATE RECORDS

The Will of GILES BOADMAN of Cambridge in the diocese of Ely, dated 28 September 1604. To be buried in the Church of All Hallows, Cambridge. To my wife Elizabeth £100, the lease of the house I now dwell in, with all the household stuff, etc., and my tenement, messuage, burgage, or cottage, with the croft adjoining, in Ickelton, in Green Street there, in the county of Cambridge. All the rest of my goods to Robert Browne and Andrew Boadman, my brothers, whom I make executors. Proved 17 October 1604 by Robert Browne, one of the executors, with power reserved to grant a commission to Andrew Boadman, the other executor, etc. (P.C.C., Harte, 81.) [Adapted from the abstract of the will of Giles Boadman published in REGISTER, vol. 49, pp. 496–497, and reprinted in Waters's "Genealogical Gleanings in England," vol. 2, p. 1076.]

The Will of RICHARD WRIGHT of the parish of St. Edward, Cambridge, "skynner," dated 20 June, 3 James I [1605]. To my eldest son John Wright, to my son Anthony Wright, and to my son Richard Wright, to each £40 at the age of twenty-one years. To my eldest daughter Rebecca, and to my daughters Mary, Ann, and Susan, to each £20 at the age of twenty-one years or at marriage. To each godchild 5s. Residue to my wife Mary. Witnesses: Robert Sparrowe, N.P., John Symondes, and Walter Acteson. Proved 19 July 1605. (P.C.C., Hayes, 54.)

The Will of HELLINE [afterwards written Helliner] BROWNE of Cambridge, co. Cambridge, widow, dated 11 November 1616. To Robert Browne my son, besides the house which his father gave to him by will, £200, to be paid to Mr. Oliver Grenough of Nanby in Lincolnshire within three years after my decease, to the use of my said son Robert. To my son Andrew Browne £200, over and above the £100 given him by his father to be paid [as above] within two years after my decease. To my son Samuel [a similar bequest]. The said Oliver Grenough is to be "gardenier" unto my said three children. To my sons John and William Browne, to each £200, to be paid within six years after my decease. To my brother Andrewe Bordeman £5. To Thomas Jury £5. To Alice Foote, wife of ——— Foote, one of my best gowns. To the poor of Bennett parish [the parish of St. Benedict] in Cambridge 20s., at the day of my burial. To him that shall preach for me at my funeral 10s. All the rest of my goods unbequeathed I give unto Mr. John Jackesonne and Mr. Robert Birder, my sons-in-law, whom I make executors. Witnesses: Andrew Bordman and Thomas Jewry. Proved 22 January 1616 [1616/17], the executors named in the will renouncing and commission being issued to John Atkinson and Thomas Jewrie. (P.C.C., Weldon, 3.) [Adapted from the abstract of the will of Helline Browne published in REGISTER, vol. 49, p. 497, and reprinted in Waters's "Genealogical Gleanings in England," vol. 2, pp. 1076–1077.]

The Will of ANDREWE BORDMAN of Cambridge, co. Cambridge, baker, dated 10 February 1616 [1616/17]. To my eldest son Richard Bourdman and to my sons Andrewe Bordman, Thomas Bordman, and William Bordman, to each £40 at the age of one and twenty years. If any of my aforesaid four children, viz., Richard, Andrewe, Thomas, and William Bordman, depart this life before they or any of them shall attain to their several ages of one and twenty years, then he or they surviving shall be the others' heir. To my wife Rebecca Bordman my house in fee simple, which I purchased of Thomas Reade of Cambridge, carpenter, to have the same during her life; and after her decease the foresaid tenement or house is to be equally divided amongst my foresaid four sons or so many of them as shall be then living. All the rest of my goods unbequeathed I give unto my said wife. Rebecca Bordman, whom I ordain sole executrix. Proved 19 April 1617. (P.C.C., Weldon, 31.) [Adapted from the abstract of the will of Andrewe Bordman published in REGISTER, vol 49, pp. 497–498, and reprinted in Waters's "Genealogical Gleanings in England," vol. 2, p. 1077.]

The Will of ANDREW BOARDMAN of Norwich [co. Norfolk], skinner, dated 28 September 1654. To my wife Grace, whom I make executrix. Lands [mentioned] in the parish of St. George Tombland, Norwich. To my daughter Rebecca Boardman. To Lidia Farther, daughter of Thomas Farther. To my brother William Boardman. To my cousin Thomas Brooke and his wife.

Supervisors: my kinsman Mr. Thomas Lovering and Mr. William Crabb. Proved in London 9 May 1665. (P.C.C. and Archdeaconry of Norwich.) [Cf. Jay's Register of St. George Tombland, Norwich, 1891, p. 189.]

FROM THE REGISTERS OF THE PARISH OF ALL SAINTS, CAMBRIDGE

*Marriages**

1607 Mr. Oliver Gren[ough]† and Mrs. Elsebethe Bordman, widow, 3 Mar. [1607/8].
1623 Georg Bownesse and Margarit Wright 27 April.
1627 John Wright and Elzabeth Jakson 26 November.

FROM THE REGISTERS OF THE PARISH OF ST. CLEMENT, CAMBRIDGE, 1567-1636

*Baptisms*

1607 Richard Bordman son of Andrew 14 September.
1609 Andrew Bordman son of Andrew 24 November.
1610 Andrew Bordman the younger son of Andrew 13 January [1610/11].
1612 Thomas Bordman son of Andrew 29 February [1612/13].
1615 William Bordman son of Andrew 6 January [1615/16].
1619 Elizabeth Wright daughter of John 5 December.
1633 Grace Day daughter of Stephen 18 August.

*Marriages*

1589 Rychard Wakeling and Jane Day 21 November.
1593 Humfrey Averell and Alice Wright 19 November.
1604 Dennise Tyddeswell and Ann Day 13 August.
1605 Rowland Suken and Ann Wright 15 August.
1620 Anthony Wright and Jane Baker 15 January [1620/1].
1630 John Wright and Margaret Coward 22 February [1630/1].

*Burials*

1609 Andrew Buriman [sic] son of Andrew 26 November.
1616 Andrew Bordman 18 February [1616/17].
1633 Grace Day daughter of Stephen 2 February [1633/4].
1636 Ann Boureman [sic] daughter of Andrew and Grace 28 June.

FROM THE REGISTERS OF THE PARISH OF ST. EDWARD, CAMBRIDGE

*Baptisms*

158[8]‡Rebecca Wright daughter of Richard Wright 2 October.
1589 Elizabeth Wright 14 March [1589/90].
1591 John Wright 7 February [1591/2].
1593 Mary Wright 28 November.
1595 John Wright son of Richard 4 January [1595/6].
1598 Ann Wright 9 April.
1599 Anthonie Wright son of Richard 24 February [1599/1600].
1602 Susanna Wright daughter of Richard 3 May.
1604 Abell Wright son of Richard 15 April.
1605 Richard Wright son of Richard 12 May.

*Printed in Phillimore's "Cambridgeshire Parish Registers, Marriages," vol. 4.
†Although the editor of the "Cambridgeshire Parish Registers" suggests *wud* as the doubtful syllable here and the transcripts at Ely give the surname as *Greeneham*, yet it seems probable, from a passage in the will of Helline Browne, widow, the testatrix of 11 Nov. 1616 (*vide supra*), that this name should be *Grenough*.
‡The last digit in this date is missing, the margin of the page having been cut off.

37

## Marriages*

1568 Thomas Wright and Hellin Anster 2 June.
1605 Edward Woulfe and Annes Wrighte, both of this parish, 4 June.
1605 Andrew Bordman of the parish of St. Clement and Rebecca daughter of Richard Wright of this parish 24 August.
1609 Thomas Crabb and Mary Wright 25 July.
1616 Samuell Disher and Annes Wright 22 September.
1625 Henry Wright of Burwell and Julian Cooke of Swaffham Saint Mari 13 March [1625/6].

## Burials

1587 Ann Wright 9 November.
1592 John Wright 25 November.
1604 Abell son of Richard Wright 3 May.
1605 Mr. Richard Wright 30 June.
1605 Susan Wright daughter of Mr. Richard Wright 4 July.

## FROM THE REGISTERS OF THE PARISH OF ST. GEORGE TOMBLAND, NORWICH, CO. NORFOLK†

### Baptisms

1638 Ann daughter of Andrew Boandman [sic] 28 July.
1640 Rebecca daughter of Andrew Boardman 22 May.
1643 Thomas Bordman son of Andrew Bordman 13 September.

### Burial

1638 Ann daughter of Andrew Boardmā 4 August.

## FROM LAY SUBSIDIES‡

28 September, 40 Elizabeth [1598].
Cambridge Town, the Market Ward.     Giles Bordman in goods [valuation] £3 [tax] 8d.

## FROM THE RECORDS OF NORWICH, CO. NORFOLK

Andrew Boardman, locksmith, non-appr., admitted to freedom 21 September 1638. (Printed in Jay's Register of St. George Tombland, Norwich, p. 65, footnote.)

John Linsey, worsted weaver, and Anne his wife released, 1 February 1647 [1647/8], to Andrew Boardman, skinner, and Grace his wife a tenement late of Anne Harman, now occupied by the said Andrew Boardman. (Mayoralty Court Rolls, ib., p. 204.)

Francis Aylmer, woolcomber, and Grace his wife, late wife of Andrew Boardman, deceased, quitclaimed, 22 June 1661, to Richard Lynsey of Norwich, woolcomber, and Rebecca his wife, daughter of said Andrew Boardman, a messuage in Tombland where Francis and Grace Aylmer dwell, [bounded by] the churchyard on the east, a messuage now of Thomas Fairecloth and Prince's Inn on the west, King's Highway on the south, and a garden late of Edmund Brice, deceased, on the north, in default of £100 not paid as per legacy to the said Rebecca by her father's will; and Richard and Rebecca surrendered the same, 24 June 1661, to Francis and Grace. (Mayoralty Court Rolls, ib., p. 206.)

Richard Linsey of Norwich, woolcomber, and Rebecca his wife, daughter of Andrew Boardman, sold, 17 October 1661, to Francis Aylmer, woolcomber, a messuage between the churchyard on the east, a messuage

*Printed in Phillimore's "Cambridgeshire Parish Registers, Marriages," vol. 1.
†The registers of this parish, 1538-1707, edited by G. B. Jay, were published at Norwich in 1891.
‡Preserved in the Public Record Office, London.

late of Thomas Faircloth and Princes Inn on the west, King's Highway on the south, and ground of Edward [sic] Brice, deceased, on the north. (Mayoralty Court Rolls, ib., p. 206.)

The Bordman or Boardman family which forms the subject of this article apparently did not settle in the English Cambridge until the later years of the sixteenth century, for the surname is not of common occurrence in the records of that town or, indeed, in those of the county. The family was probably of Lancashire origin, the surname is frequently found in the parish registers of Bolton, near Manchester, which, unfortunately, do not begin until 1592, and in this family the Christian names of Andrew and Giles are often used. Rev. Andrew Bordman, who was born in Lancashire about 1550, was admitted a scholar of St. John's College, Cambridge, 9 Nov. 1568 and matriculated there as a pensioner three days later (12 Nov.). He received the degree of Bachelor of Arts in 1571/2, Master of Arts in 1575, Bachelor of Divinity in 1582, and Doctor of Divinity in 1594. He was admitted to a fellowship 12 Mar. 1572/3, was ordained a deacon and priest at Ely 5 July 1579, was appointed Greek lecturer of his college 5 Sept. 1580, and at the following Michaelmas was elected one of the university preachers. He was made junior bursar of his college 27 Jan. 1581/2, and in the same year was appointed minister of St. Mary's Church, in Bury St. Edmunds, co. Suffolk. In 1586 he vacated this preferment, and removed to a benefice then known as Allchurch, near Warwick (or perhaps near Norwich), and on 11 Jan. 1590/1 he was appointed by the municipality vicar of St. Mary's Church in Norwich. This united preferment he seems to have held for nearly half a century, and to have died while holding it, shortly before 16 July 1639. He was the author of various religious works. (Cf. Dictionary of National Biography and Venn's Alumni Cantabrigienses.) There can be little doubt that the brothers Giles and Andrew Bordman, the testators respectively of 1604 and 1616/17, were closely related to Rev. Andrew Bordman, D.D., and perhaps they were his nephews. The younger Andrew resided in the parish of St. Clement, Cambridge, a parish that adjoins St. John's College.

On the foregoing records and on New England authorities the following pedigree, showing the English connections and the family history of Maj. William Bordman of Cambridge, Mass., is based.

1. —— BORDMAN, probably of Lancashire, England, and perhaps a brother of the Rev. Andrew Bordman, D.D., who has been mentioned above, was the father of

    i.   GILES, of the parish of All Saints, Cambridge, the testator of 1604, d. s.p. between 28 Sept. and 17 Oct. 1604; m. ELIZABETH ——, who m. again, in the parish of All Saints, Cambridge, 3 Mar. 1607/8, Mr. Oliver Gren[ough]. Giles Boardman was taxed at Cambridge in the subsidy of 1598, and owned lands at Ickelton, co. Cambridge.

    ii.  ELEANOR, of the parish of St. Benedict, Cambridge, the testatrix of 1616, d. between 11 Nov. 1616 and 22 Jan. 1616/17; m. prior to 28 Sept. 1604 ROBERT BROWNE, whom she survived. Children (order of births uncertain), mentioned in their mother's will: 1. Robert.

39

2. *Andrew.* 3. *Samuel.* 4. *John.* 5. *William.* 6. *A daughter,*
m. Mr. John Jackesonne. 7. *A daughter,* m. Mr. Robert Birder.
2. iii. ANDREW.

2. ANDREW BORDMAN (———), of the parish of St. Clement,
Cambridge, England, baker, the testator of 10 Feb. 1616/17,
was buried in that parish 18 Feb. 1616/17. He married in the
parish of St. Edward, Cambridge, 24 Aug. 1605, REBECCA
WRIGHT, baptized in that parish 2 Oct. 158[8], daughter of
Richard of the same parish, skinner, the testator of 20 June
1605.* She married secondly, probably not long after the
death of her first husband, Stephen Day of the parish of
St. Clement, locksmith; and with him, with William Bordman,
her youngest child by her first husband, and with Stephen
and Matthew Day, two sons by her second husband, she
emigrated in 1638 to New England, where her husband, Stephen
Day, had charge of the first printing press in the Colonies,
which was set up at Cambridge, Mass., in Mar. 1638/9.† She
died at Cambridge, Mass., 17 Oct. 1658.

Children, baptized in the parish of St. Clement:

i. RICHARD, bapt. 14 Sept. 1607; living 10 Feb. 1616/17, when he was
mentioned in his father's will.

ii. ANDREW, bapt. 24 Nov. 1609; bur. in the parish of St. Clement
26 Nov. 1609.

iii. ANDREW, of Norwich, co. Norfolk, skinner, the testator of 1654,
bapt. 13 Jan. 1610/11; d. between 28 Sept. 1654, when his will
was dated, and 22 June 1661, when his wife was already married
again; m. GRACE ———, who m. (2) before 22 June 1661 Francis
Aylmer of Norwich, woolcomber, who was living 17 Oct. 1661.
Andrew Bordman resided in early life in the parish of St. Clement,
Cambridge, where a daughter named Ann was bur. 28 June 1636.
Afterwards he removed to Norwich, where another daughter named
Ann was bapt. 28 July 1638 and where he was admitted a freeman
21 Sept. 1638, being then styled a locksmith. On 1 Feb. 1647/8
Andrew Boardman, skinner, and Grace his wife bought a tenement
in Norwich, which they were already occupying at the time of the
purchase. Rev. Andrew Bordman, who was probably a great-
uncle of this younger Andrew, was settled as vicar of St. Mary's,
Norwich, from 1591 to 1639, dying in the latter year. Children:
1. *Ann,* bur. in the parish of St. Clement, Cambridge, 28 June
1636. 2. *Ann,* bapt. in the parish of St. George Tombland, Norwich,
28 July 1638; bur. there 4 Aug. 1638. 3. *Rebecca,* bapt. at St. George
Tombland 22 May 1640; m. before 22 June 1661 Richard Linsey

---

*Mr. Richard Wright was buried in the parish of St. Edward, Cambridge, 30 June 1605. For
him and his family see the abstract of his will and the records in the registers of the
various Cambridge parishes given above.

†Stephen Day, the first printer in New England, resided in 1656 at the westerly corner of Harvard
and Dunster Streets, Cambridge. He was admitted to the church 28 Feb. 1660/1, but was never
admitted a freeman. He died 22 Dec. 1668, at the age of about 75 years, since he deposed in
Apr. 1656, aged 62. His son Stephen died 1 Dec. 1639, and his son Matthew died unm. 10 May
1649. This Matthew Day was the first known steward of Harvard University, holding this office
as early as 1645 and apparently continuing in it until his death. He was admitted a freeman in
1646. In his nuncupative will, declared 10 May 1649, he gave his part "in the Garden" (a tract
of land containing about one acre and one road and situated near the College) to "the fellowes
of Harvard Colledge for ever," and, besides other bequests, left "to my mother all the estate I
have in both the houses, together with all the furniture beds & all moveables (my debts being first
paid) to her for her life, & when she dies to the little childe Moyses," who was undoubtedly Moses
Bordman, the son of the testator's half brother, William Bordman. (Cf. the will, in REGISTER,
vol. 3, pp. 181–182.) Grace, another child of Stephen and Rebecca (Wright) (Bordman) Day,
was baptized in the parish of St. Clement, Cambridge, England, 18 Aug. 1633, and was buried
there 2 Feb. 1633/4.

40

of Norwich, woolcomber; both were living 17 Oct. 1661. 4. *Thomas,*
bapt. at St. George Tombland 13 Sept. 1643.
  iv.  THOMAS, bapt. 29 Feb. 1612/13; living 10 Feb. 1616/17, when he
was mentioned in his father's will.
  3. v.  WILLIAM, bapt. 6 Jan. 1615/16.

3. MAJ. WILLIAM BORDMAN (*Andrew,* ———), of Cambridge,
Mass., tailor, baptized in the parish of St. Clement, Cambridge,
England, 6 Jan. 1615/16, died at Cambridge, Mass., 25 Mar.
1685, aged 71. He married at Cambridge, Mass., FRANCES
———, who was living 24 Aug. 1688, when she was a passenger
on a sloop in which Samuel Sewall returned from Salem to
Boston. (Cf. Sewall's Diary.)

He accompanied his mother and stepfather, Stephen Day,
to New England in 1638, sailing in the *John* of London, and
settled in Cambridge.* He was admitted a freeman in 1652,
and, with his wife Frances, joined the church in Cambridge.
About 1659 his stepfather, Stephen Day, paid to him a legacy
of £50, left to him by his father, and acknowledged that it
should have been "paid to him twenty-three years agone."
(Cf. will of Andrewe Bordman, *supra,* page 306.) "As early
as 1656, he owned and occupied the estate at the easterly
corner of Harvard Square and Dunster Street. At the death
of Day in 1668, he came into possession of the estate on the
opposite corner, to which his son Aaron added the adjoining
land, extending to Brighton Street. Both these estates
remained in the Bordman family about a hundred and fifty
years." (Paige, History of Cambridge, page 490.) He was
appointed, probably in Dec. 1663, steward of Harvard College,
but resigned this position in Dec. 1667, and was thereafter,
until his death, employed as college cook. His title of major
was probably derived from his office of steward, the steward
being looked upon as a sort of major-domo. He deposed
26 Aug. 1672, aged 57.

Children:

    i.  MOSES, b. probably about 1640; d. 16 Mar. 1661/2. He was probably
of age when he died, since he owned real estate. He is undoubtedly
the "little childe Moyses" who is mentioned in the nuncupative
will of Matthew Day, his father's half brother, 10 May 1649.
(*Vide supra,* p. 310, second footnote.)
    ii.  REBECCA, b. 1 Nov. 1643 and bapt. in the First Church, Cambridge;
m. at Cambridge, 4 Aug. 1664, JOHN PALFREY.
    iii.  ANDREW, of Cambridge, tailor, b. about 1645 and bapt. in the First
Church, Cambridge; d. 15 July 1687, aged 42; m. at Cambridge,
15 Oct. 1669, RUTH BULL, who d. 17 Dec. 1690, in her 40th year.
He was freeman, 1674, inherited his father's homestead, was
appointed steward of Harvard College in 1682, and succeeded his
father as cook of the College. On 23 July 1686 the Corporation
of the College voted that he "henceforward manage the office of
Steward in the manner as of late," and he held these two college
offices until his death. He also kept a shop or variety store. Five
children.†

*Pope (Pioneers of Massachusetts, p. 57) is evidently in error in identifying a William Boreman
who appears in Lechford's Note-Book as an apprentice, in 1639, to Richard Gridley of Boston,
brickmaker, and to others in quick succession, with William Bordman (3) of Cambridge.

†Cf. Paige's "History of Cambridge," p. 490, and the Bordman family record in REGISTER,
vol. 76, pp. 312-313.

iv.  LIEUT. AARON, of Cambridge, locksmith, b. about 1649 and bapt. in the First Church, Cambridge; d. 15 Jan. 1702/3, in his 54th year; m. MARY ———, who was living in 1717. "He inherited his father's estate on the westerly side of Dunster Street [Cambridge], to which he made large additions, and became an extensive land-holder in the town." (Paige, History of Cambridge, p. 491.) He was "appointed to take charge of the College clock, and also to serve as College Smith, 1675; and succeeded his brother as College Cook and Steward." (*Ib.*, p. 490.) He remained in office as steward until his death, and was succeeded by his nephew Andrew Bordman, son of Andrew, who was steward for more than forty-four years, until his death, and was in turn succeeded in this office by his only son, Andrew.* Seven children.

v.  FRANCES, b. about 1650 and bapt. in the First Church, Cambridge; d. unm. 16 Sept. 1718, in her 69th year.

vi.  MARTHA, b. about 1653 and bapt. in the First Church, Cambridge; d. 9 Feb. 1692; m. 17 Apr. 1672 DANIEL EPES of Salem.

vii.  MARY, b. 9 Mar. 1655/6; d. before 17 July 1688; m. about 1682, as his first wife, ROBERT KITCHEN of Salem, Mass., merchant, bapt. at the First Church, Salem, 15 Apr. 1655, d. at Salem 28 Oct. 1712, s. of John and Elizabeth (Grafton) (Sanders). Three children. (Cf. *Essex Institute Historical Collections*, vol. 51, pp. 128–129.)

viii.  WILLIAM, b. 6 Dec. 1657; perhaps the William Bordman of Malden, Mass., 1684, carpenter, who m. SARAH ——— and d. at Rumney Marsh, Mass., 14 Mar. 1695/6. He was freeman in 1690. One daughter.

ix.  ELIZABETH, b. 17 Aug. 1660 and bapt. in the First Church, Cambridge, 26 Aug. 1660; d. 15 Nov. 1714; m. at Cambridge, 28 Apr. 1686, JOHN COOPER.

*Cf. *Proceedings of the Massachusetts Historical Society*, 1860–1862, pp. 154–158.

# GENEALOGICAL GLEANINGS IN ENGLAND

## I

Contributed by G. ANDREWS MORIARTY, JR., A.M., LL.B., of Newport, R. I.,
and communicated by the Committee on English Research

[To the present issue of the REGISTER the Committee on English Research communicates the first of a series of articles contributed by G. Andrews Moriarty, Jr., Esq., Chairman of the Committee, and consisting for the most part of abstracts of records relating to the English ancestry and connections of various early settlers of New England which are not sufficient to serve as foundations for such extended articles as have appeared in recent years in the REGISTER under the title "Genealogical Research in England." These records, however, are of considerable interest and importance in supplying additional information about families whose histories have already been published in the REGISTER or elsewhere or in furnishing clues which may be helpful in further research. Most of them were collected personally by Mr. Moriarty during his stay in England in the winter of 1920–21 and again in the late winter and spring of 1923, and others have been found and copied by searchers working under his immediate direction and at his expense. A few items have been secured from other investigators by gift or purchase. This collection of records has been generously placed at the disposal of the Committee by Mr. Moriarty, whose longer articles on the English ancestry of New England families which have been printed in the REGISTER from time to time during the last six years have been highly appreciated by those interested in English genealogical research. Comparatively few wills are included in these records, for the bulk of the material has been taken from documents in the Public Record Office, London, where the greater part of Mr. Moriarty's research work was done. — EDITOR.]

### HASKETT
**

IN the REGISTER, vol. 77, pages 71–77, 110–133, there were published records and a pedigree relating to the English ancestry and family connections of Stephen Haskett of Salem, Mass., including numerous documents pertaining to the lawsuits in which various members of the Haskett family in England were involved and especially to the cases arising from the contest for the estate of Elias Haskett of Henstridge Marsh, co. Somerset (who died in Feb. 1696/7), of which the nephew of the deceased, Elias Haskett, son of Stephen of Salem, Mass., was finally appointed administrator *cum testamento annexo*. The following records throw additional light on the history of this family. Among them may be found the marriage record of Stephen Haskett, the emigrant to New England, and numerous interesting depositions in cases to which Elias Haskett, son of Stephen, was a party and in some earlier cases. These records supply also further details about the movements of Stephen Haskett before he went to New England, and confirm the conjecture of the previous article that William Dussett or Duffett* married a niece of Elias Haskett of Henstridge Marsh. The deposition of Elias Haskett the Elder, of Henstridge, baker, "aged about 60," proves that the

---

* This name is given in some records as Dussett and in others as Duffett.

**Pages 1–30, this volume.

approximate date for his birth (namely, 1642) given in the pedigree (REGISTER, vol. 77, page 132) is correct. **

## FROM THE REGISTERS OF THE PARISH OF ST. SIDWELL, EXETER, CO. DEVON

1659 Stephen Heskett and Elizabeth Hill married 2 August.

[This record places the marriage of Stephen Haskett some seven years earlier than the approximate date ("about 1666") assigned for it in REGISTER, vol. 77, p. 128.]

## FROM PROBATE RECORDS

The Will of WILLIAM ALBERT of Winterbourne Strickland, co. Dorset, dated 10 August 1639. To my wife Anne, to my sons Richard and William, [and] to my unmarried daughters, Elizabeth, Anne, and Joane [sundry bequests]. "I give and bequeath unto my eldest daughter Sarah which is married to Ellis Haskett the some of tenn pounds upon condition that it come not to her husbands handes but to remaine in my executors or one of theire handes to her use and to be disposed of after her owne discretion." To each of my grandchildren 20s., to be employed for their benefit, "soe as it come not to theire father's hands," to be paid them at their marriages or at the age of twenty-one years. Executors: my wife Anne and my son Richard. Overseers: Edward Heighmore, clerk, and William Mace. Witnesses: John Blanchard, James Prevet, Julyan Hunt. Proved 24 October 1639 by the executors named in the will. (P. C. C., Harvey, 156.)

[From this will it appears that the wife of Ellis or Elias Haskett (Cf. REGISTER, vol. 77, p. 131, No. 5 of the pedigree) was Sarah, eldest daughter of William Albert of Winterbourne Strickland, co. Dorset.] **

## FROM THE RECORDS OF THE COURT OF REQUESTS*

1639. THOMAS HASKETT of Todbere, co. Dorset, husbandman, complains that, whereas one Richard Combe of West Orchett [West Orchard], husbandman, about November, 12 Charles [November 1636], was seised of a messuage or tenement and garden and orchard, with appurtenances, in West Orchett, either for the life of the said Richard Combe or for many years then yet to come, determinable at the death of the said Richard and worth £40 per annum, the said Richard, wishing to marry his daughter Elizabeth Combe with the said Haskett, well knowing that Haskett had a good estate of inheritance of lands and tenements, of good value, in the county of Somerset, induced the said Haskett to become a suitor for the said Elizabeth, and the said Richard then and there did promise that, upon the marriage, the said Thomas and Elizabeth should have the use of the said Richard's dwelling house in West Orchett and of a meadow called Greene Cliste, Broad Lands, and Ryebrook, from the Feast of the Blessed Virgin Mary† next following, to wit, in 1639. About Lady Day in 1637 the complainant intermarried with Elizabeth Combe, his now wife, and sold to Richard Combe a horse, which the defendant promised to pay for. The complainant has continued to live upon the premises, but now the said Richard Combe, conspiring with one Andrew Combe, his son, Robert Lanninge, and William Card, both of Orchett, to do your poor subject out of his agreement and also of his moneys, goods, boxes, deeds, etc., about Easter last past came to your subject's house when he was from home, and, waiting until your subject's wife was out of doors upon her necessary affairs, the said Andrew did shout out the said Elizabeth and your subject and refused them and still refuses them entrance

---

* Preserved in the Public Record Office, London.
† The Feast of the Annunciation of the Blessed Virgin Mary, commonly called Lady Day, falls on 25 March.
**For pp. 131 & 132 see pp. 28 & 29 this volume.

or to let them take their goods. The said Andrew falsely and wickedly has worked upon the weakness, submissiveness, and feebleness of Richard Combe by reason of his old age. Your subject had by agreement brought thither his goods, which the said defendants are keeping. (Court of Requests, uncalendared, 58, Part I (660), Charles I, 1639.)

[Thomas Haskett, the complainant in this case, was probably the Thomas Haskett who was baptized at Marnhull, co. Dorset, 8 Apr. 1603, son of John of Marnhull and afterwards of Todbere, co. Dorset. Cf. REGISTER, vol. 77, pp. 74,** 133. This record reveals the name of the wife of Thomas.]

## FROM PLEA ROLLS*

1655. Dorset. WILLIAM HASKETT, late of Henstridge, co. Somerset, gentleman, was summoned to answer Robert Jones, gentleman, and Bridgett his wife, late called Bridgett Burbidge, in a plea that he owed them £80, which he unjustly detains. They say, by their attorney, John Cole, that on 30 April 1650, at Blandford, William Haskett by his obligatory bill, bound himself and his heirs in the sum of £80, to pay the said Bridget, whilst she was unmarried, at the dwelling house of Robert Burbidge, gentleman, in Sturminster Newton, £41. 12s., on 1 November following. This he refused to do. William Haskett, by Robert Burbidge, his attorney, came and said nothing in bar of the plea. It is considered that Robert Jones and Bridgett shall recover their debt and damages, and William is in mercy, etc. (Plea Roll 2658, m. 1282, Trinity Term, 1655.)

1655. Somerset. WILLIAM HASKETT, late of Taunton, co. Somerset, gentleman, otherwise called William Haskett of Yenston in the parish of Henstridge, co. Somerset, gentleman, was summoned to answer Jonathan Cooth in a plea that he should pay him £56 which he owes him, as appears by the bond which William Haskett made at Taunton on 28 February 1653. William Haskett, by William Talbot, his attorney, came and demanded that the condition of the bond should be read. The condition is that William Haskett mortgaged to Jonathan Cooth for two years, if the said William or Rebecca his wife should live so long, his copyhold tenement formerly called Brynes and now called the Leases and Longgoare, together with a Fursie close adjacent to Hooke lane, called Hurne, all which premises lie in Yenston and are in the possession of William Haskett and contain about forty acres. [Certain conditions as to the sowing of the land.] If William and Rebecca shall die before the end of two years, then Henry Smith shall pay any money still owing to the said Jonathan. William Haskett says that he ought not to be charged with the debt, because the writing is not his deed. They put themselves upon the country. Adjourned till Trinity Term. (Plea Roll 2659, m. 1606d, Trinity Term, 1655.)

[The William Haskett of this and the preceding record is the William who m. (1) Joanna Hurd and (2) Rebecca ———. Cf. the Haskett pedigree, 1, v (REGISTER, vol. 77, p. 127).] **

## FROM CHANCERY DEPOSITIONS

[Haskett v. Duffett et al., *circa* 1700]

Interrogatories to be administered to witnesses on behalf of Elias Haskett, gentleman, in a cause depending between the said Elias Haskett, plaintiff, and William Duffett, Elias Duffett, Stephen Haskett, Dorothy Hedditch, and Lewis Crumsey and Mary his wife, defendants.

1. Do you know the parties?
2. Did you know Stephen Haskett, formerly of Exeter, co. Devon, but

*Preserved in the Public Record Office, London.
**For pp. 74 & 127 see pp. 4 and 24, this volume.

afterwards of Salem in New England, soapboiler, lately deceased. When and where did he die? When did he go to New England, and was he a soapboiler till his death? What family did he bring with him, and did they live at Salem? Is the plaintiff his eldest son, and where was he born? Is his mother now living at Salem?

3. Did you know Elias Haskett, late of Henstridge Marsh, co. Somerset? When and where did he die?

4. Was he sensible till his death? What did he say of his brother and his children beyond the sea? Did he say that he had made his last will?

5. Did you see Elias Haskett sign his will, dated 13 February 1696/7, by which he made bequests to his kinswoman Mary Hoddinott; to the widow and children of Richard Shane and to Richard Shane the Elder, his father; to William Heddeech, shoemaker, and his child; to Henry, Robert, Dorothy, and Anne Heddeech, brothers and sisters of the said William; to his wife's kinsman Thomas Acstons and his children; to John and George Acstons, his brothers; to the wife of William Duffett of Stalbridge Side hill in Henstridge, against South mead, and to his five children, £100; to Anne Frampton and her child; to his wife's nephew, Nicholas Buggis, his dwelling house and two closes, but if the said Nicholas shall die without issue, remainder thereof to Elias, second son of the said William Duffett, and his heirs; to John and William Calpen, sons of William Calpen, late of Stalbridge, deceased, when they are twenty-one; to Mary and Hannah, sisters of Nicholas Buggis; to the said Elias Duffett three closes, on condition that he pays £40 towards the payment of legacies; to Elias Haskett, son of Elias Haskett the baker, a close called Hurle Oake in Henstridge, on condition that he pays to his brother and his sisters Mary and Sarah £5 each and to his sister Susannah Hobbs, widow, £15.; to the wife of William Loden of Sherborne Castle Town, button maker; to his servant Alice Carley; to Richard Downe of Stalbridge, clerk; to the poor of Henstridge; to his kinsman John Calpen, if he shall come to be in want; and to his wife Mary, whom he appointed his executrix. He appointed John Smith the Elder, Henry Snook, and the said William Duffett to be trustees and overseers of his will. The witnesses were William Duffett, Alice Carley, and Thomas Browne. Were you a witness?

6. Was Elias Haskett of a sound mind when he made this will? How long after did he live? Was the reading of the will in the testator's presence opposed by anyone? Is William Duffett the witness the same as William Duffett the defendant? Was he told that he could not be a witness to the will, and what did he answer?

Depositions of witnesses taken at Henstridge on Monday, 23 September 1700, on behalf of the plaintiff.

Amy Hopkins of Henstridge, widow, aged 53, says that she knew Elias Haskett, deceased, well. He was about 60 when he died at his house in Henstridge, about three years ago.

4. She attended him during his last sickness, which was a fever. He was often light-headed, but never spoke of making his will.

Thomas Browne, a witness for the defendants and now examined for the plaintiff, says:

4. He made the will quoted, and believes that the testator was of sound mind when it was made, and afterwards, as he was told by a woman who nursed him, named Jane Shearing, afterwards married to one Parsons. The testator lived about four days after the will was made. When it was made, he said that he would give to his brother and children beyond sea some legacies, as he had done by a former will, but that he believed that they were all dead.

Alice, wife of Joseph Eyres, late Alice Carley, aged about 30, says:

46

3. She knew Elias Haskett for a year before his death, as she lived with him as his covenant servant. He died 14 February 1696 [1696/7] in his house at Henstridge Marsh.

4. He was never sensible, but always light-headed. She never heard him wish to make his will.

6. She was asked by William Duffett, the defendant, on 13 February 1696 [1696/7], to sign a paper that he shewed her, one Thomas Browne being also present there. He afterwards told her that it was a will, but did not say whose will. No one else signed it when she put her mark, which she did in her master's bedroom; but he did not see her do it, as he was very ill and the curtains of his bed were close drawn.

Susannah Hobbs of Henstridge, widow, aged about 30, says:

3. She has always known Elias Haskett. He died 14 February 1696 [1696/7], aged about 55, as she believes.

4. She saw him during his sickness, and the day before his death, when he was very light-headed.

6. He was quite incapable of making a will. She has been told that William Duffett's wife and children had several legacies given them by the will made 13 February 1696/7.

Elias Haskett the Elder of Henstridge, baker, aged about 60, says:

4. He was with Elias Haskett for about three hours on the Sunday before his death. He had a fever and was light-headed at intervals. He never mentioned making a will, but said that he had business to go abroad.

Charles Mackarty of Henstridge, servant to the plaintiff, aged 32, says:

7. That a few days ago he was sent by his master to fetch Thomas Browne of Stalbridge, co. Dorset, weaver, to speak with him. When he came, this deponent talked with him. about Elias Haskett's will, which was written by the said Thomas Browne, and asked him if the testator was sensible when it was made, to which Thomas Browne replied that he was not.

Elizabeth Warde of the parish of St. Thomas, co. Devon, widow, aged about 59, says:

1. She knows the plaintiff, but not the defendants.

2. She knew Stephen Haskett, formerly of Exeter, co. Devon, for fifty years. He came out of the eastern parts of Somersetshire, but from what parish she does not know. He was bound an apprentice to one Thomas Oborne, a soapboiler of Exeter, and served seven years apprenticeship with him. He afterwards married Elizabeth Hill, spinster, and lived for some time with his said wife in Exeter, and had one daughter called Elizabeth. Afterwards he went to Ireland, as he told this deponent on his return. He then stayed in Exeter about half a year, and then went to New England. About two or three years after he sent for his wife and child, then in Exeter, to come to him there, which they did. She knows that they arrived safely, because she received a letter from Stephen Haskett's wife, dated in New England.

John Bingham of Exeter, soapboiler, aged about 60, says:

2. He well knew Stephen Haskett, who was the only brother of Elias Haskett, late of Henstbridge [sic], deceased. Deponent was a schoolfellow of Elias Haskett at Henstridge. Deposes the same as last witness. He has been told by several of his acquaintance who came from New England that Stephen Haskett was settled in Salem in New England, and did first on his arrival there trade on fishing, and afterwards used the trade of soapboiling. It is about forty years since Stephen Haskett lived in Exeter. He died in New England.

Josias Burgesse of Topisham, co. Devon, soapboiler, aged about 63, says:

2. He knew Stephen Haskett when he was an apprentice in Exeter, about forty years ago. He told the deponent that he was born in Henstridge and

had a brother Elias. He was present at the marriage of the said Stephen to Elizabeth Hill, which took place in the Church of St. Sidwell in Exeter. He gave away the bride, and afterwards gave them a wedding dinner at an inn there. Stephen Haskett stayed in Ireland about six months, and then went again into Ireland, and from thence to New England. The master of a vessel from New England came to this deponent with a request to him from Stephen Haskett that he would buy necessary clothing for his wife and child and ship them direct to him in New England. They were not to be delivered to his wife, because he was doubtful whether she would come over to New England to join him. The deponent thinks that the wife and child sailed in the same ship as the clothing. He has several times received greetings from the wife of Stephen Haskett, sent by friends who have come from New England, in one of which communications she told him that her husband was dead. Stephen Haskett had several children born at Salem. He believes the plaintiff to be one of his children or very nearly related to him. Stephen Haskett's wife is still living in Salem.

John Ellery of the parish of St. Thomas the Apostle, co. Devon, serge-maker, aged about 48, says:

1. He has known the plaintiff for seven years, but does not know the defendants.

2. He did not know Stephen Haskett, but was very well acquainted with Elizabeth, his widow. He visited her several times in Salem, about seven years ago, when she told him she was an Exeter woman. She also told him that her husband was dead and had left one son and five daughters, and that the plaintiff, Elias Haskett, then present, was the only son she had then living by her said deceased husband. He became well acquainted with both mother and son. About three years later this deponent was in Bridgetowne in Barbadoes, where he met the plaintiff, Elias Haskett, then living some distance from the said town, and renewed acquaintance with him. He has been meeting him lately in Exeter, and they have discussed their former acquaintance in New England and Barbadoes. The plaintiff is the same person as he met there. He first met Elizabeth, widow of Stephen Haskett, in New England about ten or eleven years ago, when she told him that she had an only son, then at sea, which son this deponent saw the next time he went to New England, which was about seven years ago.

Interrogatories to be administered to witnesses examined on behalf of William Duffett and his wife and others, defendants.

1. Do you know the parties? Did you know Elias Haskett of Henstridge, deceased?

2. Of what lands in Henstridge was Elias Haskett seised in fee simple, and what goods, etc., did he possess?

3. Did he send for you to take his instructions concerning the making of his will? Did you read it to him, and did he understand it? Who were present, and who witnessed it? Declare what you know.

4. Did the relict and executrix of Elias Haskett survive him? Did he deliver to her all his personal estate, and did she die in possession thereof? Did the plaintiff try to wrest from her her claim thereto?

5. After Elias Haskett's death into whose custody did his estate come? What has the plaintiff taken of the same?

6. How did the plaintiff get from the defendants possession of any part of the real estate of Elias Haskett, and what part did he get?

Witnesses for the defendants.

Thomas Browne of Stalbridge, co. Dorset, weaver, aged about 53, says:

1. He has known the plaintiff for about a year and the defendants about twenty years and Elias Haskett for about three years before his death.

2. 3. Elias Haskett sent for him to make his will, and shewed him a former

will. He gave him an account of several parcels of land in Henstridge which he wished to devise. He believes that Elias died possessed of goods to the value of £500. He made the will, and read it to the testator, who was then sensible, and who signed it in the presence of this deponent, William Duffett, Alice Carley (who held the testator up in bed whilst he signed), and of his wife, who all (except his wife) were witnesses to it. He remembers several small legacies in it, and considerable ones to Wm. Duffett's wife and children. He bequeathed messuages and lands to Elias, one of the sons of Wm. Duffett, and to ——— Buggis, who now lives in the house in which Elias Haskett died. Of this will he made his wife Mary sole executrix. By his former will Elias Haskett bequeathed £100 to his brother beyond the seas, if he should return. To this will Wm. Douch of Stalbridge, Edward Young of Henstridge, and Susanna Duffett of Stalbridge Weston, spinster, were witnesses. He does not remember the date of this former will.

Edward Young of Henstridge, yeoman, aged about 50, says:
1. He has known the plaintiff ever since he came into this country, about a year and a half ago, and the defendants, Wm. Duffett and Mary his wife, about ten years, and Elias Haskett about twenty years before his death.
2. Elias died possessed of lands in Henstridge — one parcel worth £10 yearly and another parcel held by lease worth 50s. yearly. His goods were worth £630.
3. He has heard that he was sensible when his said will was made.
4. When he came to the funeral of Elias Haskett, he found that the relict and administratrix of the deceased had died that morning.
5. After their deaths one part of his real estate was possessed by Nicholas Buggis and Elias Haskett, both of Henstridge, and the other part by Wm. Duffett, one of the defendants. All the bills, bonds, and specialities were locked up in a trunk and deposited with Anthony Rogers of Henstridge, the keys of which were intrusted to this deponent, till, on an order from the Prerogative Court of Canterbury, he delivered them up to Nicholas Shirley of Bagber in Sturminster Newton, attorney at law.
6. The plaintiff has some part of the testator's real estate in his possession, and Nicholas Buggis rents one other part, and Elias Haskett of Henstridge rents or occupies another part. At the assizes held at Taunton, twelve months before, there was a trial at common law brought between the plaintiff and the defendant, Wm. Duffett, when the latter, feeling that he was not so well provided as he should be, referred the matters on his part to Mr. Bingham of Exeter and to this deponent. They at the assizes gave their opinion verbally, which was that the plaintiff should pay Wm. Duffett £40, for which Wm. Duffett was to deliver up to him that part of the estate which was bequeathed to Wm. Duffett, for which the said William gave him a bond for the quiet enjoyment thereof.

Jane, wife of John Parsons of Henstridge, yeoman, aged about 40, says:
3. She visited Elias Haskett on the Saturday before his death, when he told her that he had made his will on the previous day. The next day, being Sunday, his servant Alice Carley came to her house and told her that her master had made his will on the previous Friday, to which she had been a witness, and that in it she had been left a legacy. This deponent visited him again on the following Tuesday and found him quite sensible. She did not see him again until half an hour before his death, which took place on the following Friday.
5. Mary, the relict, died on the Tuesday after her husband's death. She believes that, after he made his last will, he delivered into his wife's possession all his bonds, etc.

Jane, wife of Richard Parsons of Keynton Magna, co. Dorset, white baker, aged about 22, says:
3. On Friday in the sickness of Elias Haskett Alice Carley sent for her to

help nurse him during the night. She met Thomas Browne of Stalbridge and Wm. Duffett, the defendant, her then master, coming from the house. When she reached the house, Elias told her that he was very well, and asked for roasted apples, bread, and butter, of which he ate plentifully. The next morning he sent them to move his cattle from one close to another. Alice Carley told her that her master had made his will on the previous day, and had left, among other legacies, the ground below and above his dwelling house, called Greene Close, Marsh Close, Long Close, and two others, called Broade Close and Whitefeild Lane, to Elias, son of Wm. Duffett, and the close called Side Hill to Mary, wife of the defendant Duffett.

Frances Strong of Stalbridge, widow, aged 36, says:
3. She visited Elias Haskett on Shrove Tuesday, being the Tuesday after he had made his will and before the Friday on which he died. She reproved him for discussing his worldly affairs, such as his sheep and cattle, with his servant Alice, on which he was silent for a considerable time, and then fetched a great sigh and in an audible voice prayed very devoutly and sensibly for about half a quarter of an hour. She had lived in his house for about one and three-fourth years, during which time he usually prayed in his own family. She stayed till next day with him, and found him quite sensible. When she left, he asked her to go to Wm. Duffett and his wife and tell them that he wished to speak to them, "for they must be the persons that must look after their Aunt (meaning his wife) when he was dead."

John Smith of Henstridge, yeoman, aged about 63, says:
2. Much the same as Edward Young deposed.
3. He saw Elias Haskett on the Saturday before he died, when he told him that he had made his will on the previous day. He saw him again on Sunday and Monday. On Sunday he went for him to Dr. Wattson, who was attending him, and fetched some physic. He was quite sensible all those three days.
5. Nothing new.

Robert Dann of Exeter says:
To the last interrogatory, that at Christmas, a year ago, he was at the house of Mr. Wm. Berkenhead of Henstridge, with Mr. Elias Haskett, the plaintiff, and Elias Haskett the Elder of Henstridge, baker, when the latter told the plaintiff that Alice Carley was a witness to Elias Haskett's will. He asked where she was now, and was told that she was newly married in Dorsetshire. The next morning, when going to Stalbridge, this deponent met Elias Haskett the Elder and Alice Carley, with her husband, as he supposed. The same day he went to the house of Elias Haskett the Elder, and found in a room together the plaintiff, Elias the baker and his wife, and Alice Carley. The plaintiff asked her if she knew anything about his uncle's will. She said that she was sent by him to fetch Wm. Duffett of Stalbridge, because he wished to make his will. She brought him and one Browne to write the will. The plaintiff asked her to do him a kindness concerning the will, and said that, if she would, she should never want as long as she lived. He asked her to go with him next day to make affidavit that he was not in his right senses when the will was made, and that she did not see it signed. He asked Elias Haskett the Elder to give her a piece of gold for him, which he at first refused to do, but afterwards did. This deponent told him that it would be dangerous if it was discovered. He replied that he would say it was given her as a legacy, under the will. The plaintiff asked this deponent to go with Alice the next morning to the alehouse, to spend a shilling for her there, to keep her in the same humour. She promised to make affidavit, "as she hoped to get more by the plaintiff than by the other rogues, for they had almost starved her," which she accordingly did before a master in Chancery. The plaintiff also gave Amy Hopkins, another witness, a new

50

gown, and said that he would tamper with Thomas Browne. (Chancery Depositions before 1714, 622/36.)

[Duffett et al. *v.* Haskett, *circa* 1700]

Interrogatories to be administered to witnesses to be examined on behalf of William Duffett and others, plaintiffs, against Elias Haskett, defendant.

1. Do you know the parties? Did you know Elias Haskett, late of Henstridge, yeoman, deceased?

2. What lands, goods, and chattels did the said Elias Haskett, deceased, possess?

3. Did the said Elias Haskett make his will before his death? What do you know about it?

4. Did his widow survive him, and did he deliver to her his personal estate?

5. After his death, into whose hands did his estate come? What part of them [*sic*] has the defendant got into his custody?

6. How did the defendant get such possession from the plaintiffs?

7. What else do you know?

Depositions of witnesses taken at the house or inn of John Munnings, called The Bell, in Sherborne, co. Dorset, 5 October 1700.

Thomas Browne of Stalbridge, co. Dorset, yeoman, aged about 53, deposes much as in the former suit [i.e., Haskett *v.* Duffett et al., 622/36].

Nicholas Shirley of Bagber in the parish of Sturminster Newton, gentleman, aged about 38, says:

5. After several disputes between persons who claimed nearness of kin to Elias Haskett, the testator, and to his wife, one Mary, wife of Lewis Crumsey, came to this deponent for advice about the right of administration to the said testator's personal estate. On examining the matter he considered that she was the nearest of kin. This was examined in the Prerogative Court, when counsel was retained by all the parties claiming, and Mary Crumsey proved her pedigree and was granted an administration out of the same court. She possessed herself of about £500 or £600. Some time after the defendant, coming into England, declared that he was the son of Stephen Haskett of Salem in New England, who was brother to Elias Haskett, the testator. He said that he had the greatest right to the administratory estate of the testator, he being his uncle. A commission was sued forth and witnesses examined, and, on the whole matter being heard before the Court of Delegates, the administration of Mary Crumsey was made void and given to the defendant. She delivered up to the defendant all that remained of the said personal estate, after legacies and law expenses were paid, which amounted to about £400.

Frances Stronge of Stalbridge, widow, aged about 36, says the same as before [622/36].

Jane, wife of Richard Parsons of Keynton Magna, co. Dorset, baker, aged about 21, deposes as before [622/36].

Edward Younge of Henstridge, gentleman, aged about 50, says:

2. 4. The same as before [622/36]. He believes that all the real estate of which the testator died possessed is now in the hands of the defendant.

6. [Answers as in 622/36.]

7. It being reported that Amy Hopkins of Henstridge had sworn that Elias Haskett was not sensible in any of his last sickness, she was asked the reason for saying so. She utterly denied that she had so said, for she was not with him, and knew nothing of it till after his will was made.

Jane, wife of John Parsons of Henstridge, aged about 39, deposes as before [622/36].

John Smith of Henstridge, gentleman, aged about 63, says much the same as before [622/36]. He adds that Elias Haskett, deceased, told him that he had made him a trustee of his will, and William Duffett, one of the plaintiffs, and Henry Snooke were to be his partners. The testator was then of sound and perfect mind.

Nicholas Buggis of Henstridge, tailor, aged about 34, says:

2. Elias Haskett in his lifetime was seised in fee of a tenement and lands in Henstridge, worth yearly £16 or £18, and was possessed of a leasehold estate called Sidehills, worth yearly about 50s. His personal estate was worth about £746. He knows this because he made an inventory of the goods.

3. He believes that the testator bequeathed £100, to be divided equally between the five children of William Duffett, the plaintiff.

4. Mary, the wife of the testator, died in actual possession of his goods, bonds, securities, etc., which he gave her, before his death, in a box or cabinet.

5. The defendant, Elias Haskett, is now possessed of all the testator's real estate, except one small close called Hurle Oake, worth about 40s. yearly, which he gave up to Elias Haskett the Younger of Henstridge, baker, as it was bequeathed to him by the said will. He believes that the defendant has possessed himself of part of the personal estate of the testator.

William Hedditch of Gillingham, co. Dorset, cordwinder, aged about 35, says:

Some of the goods of Elias Haskett came into the possession of Dorothy Hedditch of Gillingham, widow, his mother, to the value of £22. 15s. 6d.

Interrogatories to be administered to witnesses produced on behalf of Elias Haskett, defendant.

[These interrogatories are practically the same as those in the case of Haskett v. Duffett et al., 622/36. The will of Elias Haskett, deceased, is described again at great length, as in Interrogatory 5. Interrogatory 2, concerning Stephen Haskett and his family, is omitted in this list. No answers have been found to these interrogatories on behalf of Elias Haskett, the defendant in this suit, but a reference (S Oc 170) which cannot be identified, is probably to the missing answers.] (Chancery Depositions before 1714, 1023/8.)

## Metcalf

For many years the statement has repeatedly appeared in print that Michael Metcalf, the dornick* weaver, of Norwich, co. Norfolk, England, and later of Dedham, Mass., was the son of Rev. Leonard Metcalf, parson of Tatterford, co. Norfolk, and that he was baptized at Tatterford 3 Sept. 1586. An examination of the parish registers of Tatterford proves this statement to be an error, for on 3 Sept. 1586 Leonard Metcalf, son of Leonard, was baptized there. This error was probably made by some zealous American who could not read the sixteenth-century writing but was determined to find the parentage of the redoubtable Michael. All that can be said at present is that the parentage of Michael Metcalf is unknown. He was, however, probably born about 1592, since in his examination on embarking for New England, in Apr. 1637, his age was given as 45. (Cf. Pope, "Pioneers of Massachusetts," page 312, and Savage, "Genealogical Dictionary," vol. 3, page 203.)

*Dornick or dornock, a coarse sort of damask, originally made at Tournai (in Flemish, Doornick), Belgium.

Below are given the Metcalf entries in the early parish registers of Tatterford and the entries relating to the children of Michael Metcalf found in the registers of the parishes of St. Benedict and St. Edmund, Norwich.

### From the Parish Registers of Tatterford, co. Norfolk

#### Baptisms

1583 John Metcalf son of Leonard and his wife 15 August.
1586 Leonard Metcalf son of Leonard and his wife 3 September.
1587 Nicholas Metcalf son of Leonard and his wife 8 July.
1594 Matthew Metcalf son of Leonard and his wife 18 December.
1596 Nynian Metcalf 10 June.
1601 Marie Metcalf daughter of Leonard Metcalf and his wife 28 August.
1613 Leonard Metcalf son of Richard and Mary 15 August.
1614 Richard Metcalf son of Richard and Mary 15 January [1614/15].
1618 John Metcalf son of Richard 15 November.
1639 Mary Metcalf daughter of Richard and Alice 23 August.
1652 Richard Metcalf son of Leonard and Margaret 9 November.

#### Burials

1601 Maria Metcalf 7 December.
1602 Amy Metcalf 22 December.
1604 John Metcalf 17 March [1604/5].
1616 Leonard Metcalf, clerk, 22 September.
1618 John Metcalf son of Richard (clerk) 31 January [1618/19].
1643 Mary Metcalf wife of Richard (clerk) 24 March [1643/4].
1656 Richard Metcalf, clerk, 11 March [1656/7].
1694 Elizabeth Metcalf 3 March [1694/5].
1695 Leonard Metcalf, rector of Sherford,* 23 November.

### From the Registers of the Parish of St. Benedict, Norwich, co. Norfolk

#### Baptisms

1617 Michael Medcalfe son of Michael 30 November.
1624† Saray [Saray *written over* Mary *and also in the margin*] Medcalfe 10 March [1624/5].
1626 Elizabeth Medcalfe daughter of Michael 20 September.
1628 Martha Medcalfe daughter of Michael 27 March.

#### Burial

1617 Michael Medcalfe son of Michaell 20 January [1617/18].

### From the Registers of the Parish of St. Edmund, Norwich, co. Norfolk‡

#### Baptisms

1629 Thomas Medcalf son of Michael and Sara 11 January [1629/30].
1631 Anne Metcalfe daughter of Michael and Sara 4 March [1631/2].
1633§ Jane Metcalfe daughter of Michael and Sara 29 March.
1635 Rebecky [Katherine *erased*] Metcalfe daughter of Michael 12 April.

*Probably Shereford, co. Norfolk, and not Sherford, co. Devon.
†The pages containing the entries for 1619 and 1620 are missing.
‡The register of the parish of St. Edmund, Norwich, contains many corrections and additions. It suffered severely in the great flood at Norwich some years ago, but the copy of the entries here given was made before that disaster occurred.
§1632 has been added at the side.

*Burials*

1632   Jane Metcalfe daughter of Michaell and Susanna* 29 March. [*All this entry is crossed out with a pen in a contemporary handwriting.*]
1632   Mary† Metcalf daughter of Michael and Suzanna* 13 May.

---

## GENEALOGICAL GLEANINGS IN ENGLAND
### II

Contributed by G. ANDREWS MORIARTY, JR., A.M., LL.B., of Newport, R. I., and communicated by the Committee on English Research

### BOWDITCH

IN the REGISTER, vol. 72, pages 223–240,** an article was published establishing the parentage, English ancestry, and family connections of William Bowditch, who died at Salem, Mass., in 1681, the progenitor of the well-known Bowditch family of Salem and Boston, which includes among its illustrious members Nathaniel Bowditch, the famous mathematician and astronomer. Below are given additional Bowditch records, which supplement the previous article on this family. It is through the courtesy of Mrs. Rose-Troup of Ottery St. Mary, Devonshire, that the contributor of this article is enabled to include in it the Chancery suit of 1699.

#### FROM PROBATE RECORDS

The Will of WILLIAM BOWDITCH of Winsham [co. Somerset], husbandman, dated 19 November 1573. To be buried in Winsham churchyard. To my godchildren. To the Cathedral Church of Wells. To Edye Long. To Agnes Howper. To John Alvord. Residue to my wife Joane. Proved 23 February 1574 [? 1573/4]. (P.C.C., Martyn, 9.)

#### FROM THE PARISH REGISTERS OF WINSHAM, CO. SOMERSET

*Marriages*

1567   Robert Bowdiche and Margaret Sparke 12 January [1567/8].
1567   William Hall and Agnes Bowditch 3 February [1567/8].
1572   Heracles Bogwell and Mary Bowdiche 28 January [1572/3].
1576   William Palfrey and Joan Bowditch 4 October.
1587   Jeanne [?] Welche and Agnes Bowditch 14 January [1587/8].
1601   William Cowkeny and Catherine Bowdiche 4 October.

*Burials*

1567   Joan Bowditch 18 February [1567/8].
1573   Margery widow of John Bowditch and daughter of William Bowditch of Chardstock 30 November.
1582   Joanna Bowdiche, widow, 24 June.

*An error for Sarah.
†Apparently an error for Ann.
**See Vol. I of this work, pp. 528-545.

FROM CHANCERY PROCEEDINGS*

[Bowditch v. Guppy, circa 1624/5]

[Replication only.] The replication of GEORGE BOWDITCH, complainant, to the answer of Ezekiel Guppy, defendant, shows that the defendant promised that he would procure the arrest of one Daniell[?] and would discharge the complainant of his obligation, as is alleged in the bill. This defendant is a hard man and is accustomed to take advantages. Sworn Hilary term, 22 James I [January 1624/5]. (Chancery Proceedings, James I, C. 2, B. 31/47.)

[Whether George Bowditch, the complainant in this suit, belongs to the Bowditch family of Devon and Dorset has not been ascertained.]

[Bowditch et al. v. Bowditch, 1699]

21 November 1699. The complaint of SARAH BOWDITCH, widow, relict of William Bowditch the Younger, late of Thornecombe, co. Devon, deceased, and their son William Bowditch, John Crow of Thorncombe and Sarah his wife, and Matthew Staple of Thornecombe, yeoman, and Joan his wife (Sarah and Joan being daughters of William and Sarah Bowditch abovenamed) shows that William Bowditch the Elder, father of said William the Younger, deceased, by indenture bearing date 1 September 1663, assigned to his son William on his marriage with said Sarah, then Sarah Beer, as a dower for her and her children in case of William the Younger's death, a tenement and lands called Stonelake in Thornecombe, she giving him her portion of £100, in trust for his said son and his wife after the death of him, William the Elder, and his wife Joan. The said marriage was solemnized; and they had issue William Bowditch, Sarah married to John Crow, and Joan married to Matthew Staple. But now William Bowditch the Elder, confederating with others, gives out that he made no such settlement, and that, if he did, it was voluntary and he never received £100, the marriage portion of said Sarah, and that before that time he had mortgaged the premises; and he refuses to produce the indenture or deeds, but says that they will see them when he is dead. Complainants desire that the said William Bowditch the Elder may be caused to appear to answer the premises.

The answer of WILLIAM BOWDITCH the Elder, taken at Chard, co. Somerset, 5 February 1699 [1699/1700]. He says that, by indenture bearing date 1 September 1663, made between himself of the first part, John and Robert Beare of the second part, and his son William Bowditch, since deceased, and the complainant Sarah Bowditch, widow, then Sarah Beare, of the third part, he assigned to John and Robert Beare the messuage called Stonelake, wherein he dwelt, in Thorncombe, with five closes and a messuage thereunto adjoining, and another messuage and lands at Laymore, in the parish of Crewkerne, as follows: the said messuage called Stonelake to the use of himself and his [wife] Joan, since deceased, for their lives, with contingent remainders to his son William, the said Sarah, and the children of William and Sarah; in default to defendant's second son, John Bowditch, and his issue, to defendant's third son, Michael, and his issue, and to his fourth son, Daniel, and his issue; the other tenement in Thornecombe in like manner; and the tenement called Laymore to said William and Sarah. The defendant has the said indenture in his keeping, but [has] no other deeds, and believes that his son William had all the earlier deeds concerning said premises. The little messuage in Thornecombe his said son William sold to Jonas Clarke, and [it] is now in the possession of Mary Corner, widow; and the premises in Crewkerne, whereof his said son William had possession, was [sic] entered upon by the lord thereof for some forfeiture. He denies that he ever at-

*Preserved in the Public Record Office, London.

55

tempted to defraud the complainants, but says that he paid great sums of money at various times for his said son, which are still due from his executors or administrators, and that he had educated the complainant William for about eight years and the complainant Joan Staple for fourteen years "since the going away of his said son William," and that he has received nothing for so doing. He says that Sarah and Joan are the children of his son William, born under wedlock, and that the complainant Sarah Bowditch, widow, divers years after her said husband had gone to New England, . . . went to her husband in New England, and had a son William, "and then died there."* William Bowditch his mark. (Chancery Proceedings before 1714, Hamilton Division, 604/2.)

FROM LAY SUBSIDIES FOR THORNCOMBE, CO. DEVON†

15–16 Henry VIII [1523–1525].   Robert Boudyche, Sen., in goods [valuation] £5 [tax] 2s. 6d.
Robert Boudyche, Jur., in goods [valuation] £4 [tax] 2s.
Robert Boudyche in goods [valuation] 40s. [tax] 7d.

[The extracts from the lay subsidies of 15–16 Henry VIII, given above, make it almost certain that the father of John Bowditch of Thorncombe, who died in 1563 (No. 1 of the Bowditch pedigree printed in REGISTER, vol. 72, p. 236), was named Robert, and perhaps his grandfather also had the same Christian name. **
It is to be noted that John Bowditch had a son named Robert (No. 2 of the pedigree), and that this last-mentioned Robert also had a son Robert. The Margery Bowditch whose burial at Winsham is given above was probably the widow of this John Bowditch of Thorncombe. It is clear that this Thorncombe family originated in the neighboring parish of Chardstock, co. Dorset, where the Bowditches or Bowdiches had been settled from very early times as a family of small gentry.
The abstract of the Chancery suit brought in 1699 by Sarah Bowditch, widow of William Bowditch of Salem, Mass., against her father-in-law proves that William Bowditch the Elder (No. 5 of the pedigree) was not the William Bowridge who was buried at Thorncombe 16 Jan. 1680/1, but was evidently the William Bowditch who was buried there 27 Mar. 1701 (cf. REGISTER, vol. 72, pp. 238, ** 234). This suit also shows that Sarah Bowditch, daughter of the Salem settler, married John Crow of Thorncombe, that Joan (or Johanna) Bowditch, her sister, married Matthew Staple of Thorncombe, yeoman, and that these two sisters and their husbands were living 21 Nov. 1699. The husband of Joan Staple appears as Mathew Staple of Thorncombe, comber, in the bond given by William Bowditch, his brother-in-law, in 1705, in which he was a surety (ib., vol. 72, p. 227). The ** John and Robert Beare who are mentioned in the answer of William Bowditch the Elder to the complaint of his daughter-in-law are evidently near kinsmen of Sarah (Bear) Bowditch, probably her father and brother. It also appears from this answer that William Bowditch the Elder, father of the immigrant to New England, had a son John, who is called his second son. This suit gives the names of the closes in Thorncombe owned by the family and proves that they had lands also in Crewkerne, co. Somerset.]

*The reading of the text here seems uncertain. The person who died in New England was undoubtedly William Bowditch the Younger, husband of the complainant Sarah Bowditch. The statement of this complainant that her children were William Bowditch, Sarah, and Joan makes it unlikely that the son William mentioned in the last sentence of the answer of the defendant was a second William in the family of William and Sarah (Bear) Bowditch. Cf. REGISTER, vol. 72, ** pp. 238–240. A few words of the answer of the defendant, referring to the complainant Sarah Bowditch, have been omitted in the printed record. — EDITOR.

†Preserved in the Public Record Office, London. Thorncombe, formerly a parish in co. Devon, is now in co. Dorset.

**See the last footnote at the bottom of p. 54, this volume.

# COCKE

In April 1922 the Committee on English Research communicated to the REGISTER (vol. 76, pages 115–129) an article contributed by* Mrs. Elizabeth (French) Bartlett, which made known the English ancestry of James Weeden, the founder of a well-known Rhode Island family, who came to New England in 1638. This James Weeden, as was stated in the article in question, married first, at Chesham, co. Bucks, England, 11 Sept. 1615, Phillip Cock (or Cocke), who was baptized at Chesham 14 Jan. 1587/8 and was living as late as 1632, daughter of William and Joan Cocke of Belenden in the parish of Chesham. She was the mother of James Weeden's six children, all of whom were born in England. (Cf. REGISTER, vol. 76, page 129.)

Below are given abstracts of sundry probate records relating to the Cockes of Chesham and also all records of baptisms, marriages, and burials of members of the various branches of the Cocke family that are found in the parish registers of Chesham down to the early part of the seventeenth century. It is not possible to establish the relationship of all the persons mentioned in these records to Phillip, wife of James Weeden; but the printing of these entries in this article may be helpful to those undertaking further research in the history of this family, which was one of the most prolific in the parish. Chesham was a very large parish, and contained several different hamlets or settlements. The particular branch of the Cocke family to which Phillip (Cocke) Weeden belonged lived in the section known as Belenden.

The records are followed by a pedigree, in which the ancestry and family connections of Phillip Cocke, in so far as they have been traced, are set forth in genealogical form.

## FROM PROBATE RECORDS

The Will of WILLIAM COKKE of Chesham [co. Bucks], 1485, appoints as executrix and executor the testator's wife Joan and son John. (Archdeaconry of Bucks [Somerset House], Case 1, fo. 201d.)

The Will of WILLIAM COCK of Chesham [co. Bucks], dated 13 October 1558. To be buried in Chesham churchyard. To Chesham church 3s. 4d. To my son William Cock a cow, three carts, five horses, and a plough. To my wife Joan all the goods she brought with her, four sheep, hemp, wheat, etc. To my daughter Agnes a cow, six sheep, pewter plates, a christening sheet, and a mattress. To my daughter Jane a cow, six sheep, pewter plates, a tablecloth, and a candlestick. To my daughter Joan, the younger, six sheep, four pewter plates, sheets, and a tablecloth. To Leonard Twychille's children, Joan, Alice, Mary, and Henry, to each a ewe. To William, son of Richard Cock, a ewe. To William Awby, my godson, a sheep. To John Wedon, my godson, a sheep. To my son-in-law ——— Gold 100 [sic] of timber. To my daughter Isabel Gold wheat. Residuary legatee and executor: my son Thomas. Overseer: my brother Ro. Cock. Witnesses: Leonard T[wichell], William Gold, Henry Prat, and Henry Barnard. Proved 4 July 1559. (Archdeaconry of Bucks [Somerset House], Case 1558-9, fo. 4.)

*See Vol. I of this work, pp. 700-714.

57

The Will of THOMAS COCKE of Bellenden, parish of Great Chesham, co. Bucks, husbandman, dated 2 November 1585. To my wife Ann £6. 13s. 4d. and a chamber in my house. To my son William Cocke a cupboard, a coffer, a bed, etc. To my son Henry £6. 13s. 4d., and a like bequest to my son Thomas, to my daughters Joan and Alice Cocke, to my son Robert Cocke, and to my daughter Ann Cocke at nineteen. Residuary legatee and executor: my son William. Overseers: Henry Putnam, Thomas Puttnam. Witnesses: Rychard Grover, Henry Warde, Thomas Puttnam. Proved 11 April 1586 by the executor. (Archdeaconry of Bucks [Somerset House], 1586, original will.)

FROM THE PARISH REGISTERS OF CHESHAM, CO. BUCKS*

*Baptisms, 1538–1610*

1538  Jone daughter of Will[ia]m Cocke 14 March [1538/9].
1539  Nicholas son of John Cocke 25 October.
1540  Jone daughter of Thomas Cocke 8 October.
1540  Rychard son of Henry Cocke 26 October.
1541  Raufe son of Will[ia]m Cocke 11 December.
1542  Nicholas son of Henry Cock 3 January [1542/3].
1544  Nicholas son of Rychard Cocke 5 December.
1544  Nicholas son of Will[ia]m Cocke 22 January [1544/5].
1547  Symon son of Will[ia]m Cocke 21 September.
1547  Nicholas son of John Cocke 22 January [1547/8].
1548  Agnes the daughter of Rychard Cocke 29 November.
1549  Joan the daughter of Henry Cock 4 April.
1549  Will[ia]m son of John Cocke 28 November.
1550  Jone daughter of Thomas Cocke 31 January [1550/1].
1550  Will[ia]m son of Richard Cock 9 February [1550/1].
1551  Jaane daughter of Henry Cocke 14 April.
1560  Henry son of Thomas Cocke of Ashly Greene 8 September.
1561  Richard son of Henry Cock 18 May.
1562  Henry son of Thomas Cocke of Belend[en] 13 July.
1562  Hugh son of Nicho[las] Cock of Whelpleyhill 20 August.
1563  W[illia]m son of John Cocke of Ly Greene 11 July.
1563  Thomas son of Henry Cock 1 August.
1564  Richard son of Will[ia]m Cock of Ly Grene 23 April.
1564  Margarite daughter of Ric[hard] Cock of Botl[ey] 10 December.
1564  Thomas son of Thomas Cocke 7 January [1564/5].
1565  Thomas son of John Cock of Ly Grene 30 September.
1567  John son of Henry Cocke 25 March.
1567  Helenor daughter of Thomas Cocke 22 June.
1567  Rychard son of John Cocke 11 January [1567/8].
1567  Agnes daughter of Henry Cocke 22 February [1567/8].
1568  Joan daughter of Tho[mas] Cock of Belend[en] 13 February [1568/9].
1569  Anne daughter of Rychard Cock of Botley 24 December.
1570  Will[ia]m son of Henry Cocke 27 August.
1570  Henry son of John Cock of Ly Greene 26 November.
1571  Alice daughter of Thomas Cocke of Belend[en] 23 December.
1573  John son of John & Elyzabeth Cocke of Lyegreene 1 November.
1574  Rychard son of Thomas & Anne Cock of Belend[en] 16 May.
1574  Agnes daughter of Thomas & Alice Cocke of Lygreene 28 November.
1575  Mary & Elyzab[eth] daughters of Elyz[abeth] Cock, widow, & of Henry Cocke, her husband, deceased, 4 April.

*The parish registers of Chesham begin in October 1538, and the first volume, extending *to* 25 Mar. 1636/7, copied and edited by J. W. Garrett-Pegge, has been printed (London, 1904). There are no entries for the year 1546 nor for the first part of the year 1547 (prior to September), nor for the greater part of the years 1553–1559.

58

1576  Abraham son of Jo[hn] & Elyzab[eth] Cocke of Ly Greene 1 April.
1576  Rob[er]t son of Thomas & Anne Cock of Belend[en] 2 December.
1577  Susan daughter of Nic[holas] & Isbell Cocke, Jr., of Ly Grene 21
      July.
1577  Agnes daughter of Ric[hard] & Agnes Cock, wheeler, 15 September.
1578  Jaane daughter of Nicholas & Emme Cock, laborer, 21 September.
1578  Georg[e] son of Bennet & Elyzabeth Cocke 2 November.
1580  Will[ia]m son of Nic[holas] & Isbell Cock of Lygreene 5 June.
1580  Agnes daughter of Thom[as] & Anne Cock of Belend[en] 24 July.
1580  Nathanael son of Ric[hard] & Agnes Cock, wheeler, 14 August.
1580  Priscilla daughter of Nicholas & Emme Cock, laborer, 15 January
      [1580/1].
1580  Timothie son of John & Elyzab[eth] Cocke of Lyegreene 29 January
      [1580/1].
1581  Josias son of George & Margarite Cock, the seconde of that name,
      3 December.
1581  Timothie son of Nic[holas] & Elyzab[eth] Cock, Ju[nio]r, of Lygreene
      6 January [1581/2].
1581  Ric[hard] son of Ric[hard] & Agnes Cock, wheler, 11 February [1581/2].
1583  Lidia daughter of Nicholas & Emme Cocke, laborer, 24 November.
1584  Nathanael son of Nic[holas] & Elyzab[eth] Cock, Jr., of Lygreene
      8 June.
1584  Daniel son of George & Margarite Cocke 9 June.
1584  Richard son of Nicho[las] & Isbell Cocke of Lygreene 23 August.
1585  Daniel son of Ric[hard] & Agnes Cocke, wheler, 24 October.
1586  Daniel son of Nic[holas] & Elyzab[eth] Cock, Jr., of Ly Greene 18
      April.
1586  Elyzab[eth] daughter of old W[illia]m & Ellenor Cock of Lygrene
      19 June.
1586  Rebecca daughter of Georg[e] & Margarite Cocke 19 March [1586/7].
1587  Thomas son of John & Isbell Cock, Jr., laborer, 3 December.
1587  Phillip daughter of W[illia]m & Joan Cock of Belend[en] 14 January
      [1587/8].
1589  Ric[hard] son of Nic[holas] & Elyzab[eth] Cock, Ju[nio]r, of Ly Grene
      15 June.
1590  Elyzabeth daughter of Will[ia]m and Joan Cock of Belend[en] 15
      April.
1590  Thomas son of Nicholas & Emme Cock, laborer, 25 November.
1590  Susanna daughter of John & Isbell Cock, Jr., laborer, 6 January
      [1590/1].
1590  Samuel son of Georg[e] & Margarite Cock 25 January [1590/1].
1592  Elyzabeth daughter of Nicholas & Elyzab[eth] Cock, Jr., of Lygrene
      11 June.
1592  Rob[er]t son of Will[ia]m & Joan Cock of Lygrene 13 August.
1592  Mary daughter of Will[ia]m & Joan Cock of Belend[en] 26 December.
1593  Sara daughter of John & Isbell Cock, Jr., laborer, 29 April.
1593  Dorcas daughter of Georg[e] & Margarite Cocke 1 November.
1595  Samuell son of Will[ia]m & Joan Cock of Lygreene 13 July.
1595  Hester daughter of Ryc[hard] & Agnes Cocke of Ly Greene 20 July.
1595  Samuel son of John & Isbell Cock, Jr., laborer, — December.
1596  Martha daughter of Will[ia]m and Joan Cock of Belend[en] 9 May.
1597  Martha daughter of Ryc[hard] & Agnes Cock of Ly Grene 10 April.
1597  Thomas son of Thomas & Elyzabeth Cocke of Bois 8 February [1597/8].
1597  Agnes daughter of Georg[e] & Margarite Cocke 5 March [1597/8].
1598  Agnes daughter of Will[ia]m & Joan Cocke of Ly Greene 3 May.
1598  Will[ia]m son of Will[ia]m and Joan Cocke of Belend[en] 14 January
      [1598/9].

1599  Elyzabeth daughter of Rychard & Agnes Cock of Ly Greene 25 March.
1600  Martha daughter of Will[ia]m & Alice Cocke 14 May.
1600  John son of Thomas & Elyzab[eth] Cocke of Bois 28 September.
1600  Jeremy son of Georg[e] & Margarite Cocke 7 December.
1600  Thomas son of Will[ia]m & Joan Cocke of Lyegreene 21 January [1600/1].
1601  Nicholas son of Willia[m] & Joan Cocke of Belend[en] 12 November.
1603  Anne daughter of Will[ia]m & Joan Cock of Belend[en] 4 May.
1603  Tho[mas] son of Tho[mas] & Agnes Cock, laborer, 18 October.
1604  Henry son of Will[ia]m & Joan Cock of Lye Greene 23 May.
1606  James son of Thomas & Elizabeth Cock of Boys 5 October.
1607  Martha daughter of George & Margaret Cock 26 May.
1607  Sarah daughter of William & Joane Cock [of] Lygreen 14 March [1607/8].
1607  William son of Richard & Agnes Cock [of] Lygreene 20 March [1607/8].
1608  Henry son of Timothie & Rebecca Cock 18 September.
1609  Richard son of Richard & Martha Cock of Leyhill 11 June.
1609  William son of Timothie & Rebecca Cock 21 January [1609/10].
1610  Anne daughter of William & Dorothie Cocke [of] Lygr[eene] 2 September.
1610  John son of John & Martha Cocke 7 October.
1610  Martha daughter of William & Joane Cocke 30 January [1610/11].
1610  William son of Richard & Martha Cocke of the Mose 10 February [1610/11].

*Marriages, 1538–1600*

1539  Thomas son of Nic[holas] Cock & Alice Carter 28 September.
1540  Henry Hudnoll & Alice daughter of Henry Cocke 24 October.
1541  Jeames son of John Harding of Northchurch and Alice daughter of John Cocke 26 November.
1542  Will[ia]m son of Nicholas Cock & Agnes daughter of John Gate 7 May.
1542  Richard son of John Cock & Joan daughter of Roger Weedon 8 October.
1543  Rob[er]t son of W[illia]m Gate & Joan daughter of John Cocke 7 October.
1543  Rychard son of Nicholas Cock & Margery Berry 15 October.
1544  Rychard son of John Longe & Joan daughter of John Cocke 7 September.
1545  John the son of Nicholas Cocke 5 October.
1548  Rychard Allen & Christian Cocke — June.*
1551  John Grante & Agnes Cocke 10 October.
1561  Edward Shyre & Joan Cocke 19 May.
1561  Henry Tookefeild & Joan Cock, widow, 13 November.
1564  John Sutton & Margarite Cock of Amersam 27 April.
1564  Edmond Putna[m] & Joan Cocke 6 November.
1569  Will[ia]m Blackborne of Hegeley & Elyzabeth Cocke 23 October.
1571  Bennet Cocke & Elyzabeth Dell 20 September.
1572  Richard Cock & Agnes Allen 21 January [1571/2].
1572  Will[ia]m Cock of Ly Grene & Elenor Weedon 15 June.
1572  Nicholas Roberde & Elyzabeth Cocke 21 July.
1576  Will[ia]m Gryffin & Elyzab[eth] widow of Henry Cocke 13 May.
1576  Nicholas son of Will[ia]m Cock of Lye Greene & Isbell Hobbes daughter of the wife of Nicholas Heerne 9 July.
1576  Gilbert Wardall and Agnes daughter of Rychard Cocke of Botley 30 July.

*The last marriage recorded in June 1548. This marriage and two other marriages preceding it follow a marriage recorded on 17 June.

1577 Nicholas son of John Cocke, laborer, & servant to Mr. Tho[mas] Ash-
feild & Emme Sam servant to Ric[hard] Byrch of the parsonage
28 November.
1580 Nicholas son of Thomas Cock of Lygreene and Elyzabeth Shaake-
maple of Bovington, widow, 16 January [1580/1].
1580 Georg[e] Cocke & Margarite East s[ervan]t to John West 24 January
[1580/1].
1580 John Russell & Isbell Cock servant to Ric[hard] Tookef[eild] [?] of
Cherietrees 6 February [1580/1].
1581 Rychard Crane & Elyzab[eth] daughter of W[illia]m Cock of Lygreene
28 September.
1583 Rychard Hawes servant to Ric[hard] Grace of Lye Greene and Elyza-
b[eth] widow of John Cocke of the same 2 July.
1586 John son of John Cock, laborer, & Isbell Blackwell servant to Hugh
Smyth, smyth, 31 December.
1593 Thomas son of John Cocke of Lye Grene, deceased, and Elyzabeth
daughter of Henry Tookefeild of Chartridge 29 October.
1593 Rychard Norwood & Agnes the widow of Richard Cock, wheeler,
11 March [1593/4].
1594 Rychard brother of Nicholas Cock, Sr., of Ly Greene & Agnes daughter
of Ric[hard] Putna[m], deceased, & daughter by law of Gabriel
Yong of Wiginton 27 June.
1595 Rychard son of John Cocke of Lye Grene, deceased, & Sara daughter
of Mr. John Smyth, deceased, some tyme vicar of Chesham, 9
October.
1596 Rychard Kytson, myller, s[ervan]t to Thomas Monke & Anne daughter
of the widow of Richard Cocke 18 October.
1598 Thomas son of Thomas Cock of Belend[en], deceased, & Agnes the
daughter of John Gregory of Wilstorne Grene in the parish of
Greate Trynge, both s[ervan]ts of John Turner, married at Hawrich
8 May.

*Burials, 1538–1606*

1538 John son of John Cock the Yo[u]ng[e]r 19 November.
1538 Christian daughter of Henry Cock 5 March [1538/9].
1540 Henry Cock 28 October.
1541 Rychard Cock 2 February [1541/2].
1547 Joan daughter of Richard Cocke of London 3 January [1547/8].
1549 Thomas son of John Cocke 2 June.
1550 The wife of Will[ia]m Cock of Belenden 2 February [1550/1].
1552 Joan the wife of Nicholas Cocke 28 October.
1552 Mother Cocke 6 March [1552/3].
1557 Nicholas Cocke 15 February [1557/8].
1560 Rychard Cocke of Ly Greene 8 April.
1567 John son of Henry Cocke 28 March.
1567 Elenor daughter of Thomas Cock 14 March [1567/8].
1568 John Cock 11 August.
1569 Agnes Cock of Ly Greene, widow, 8 December.
1569 Elyzabeth wife of Bennet Cock of Ly Greene 30 December.
1571 Agnes wife of Will[ia]m Cocke of Ly Greene 22 May.
1571 Will[ia]m son of Richard Cocke 28 May.
1571 Isbell wife of Bennet Cocke 23 November.
1571 Joan daughter of Will[ia]m Cock 10 March [1571/2].
1574 Henry Cock 17 January [1574/5].
1575 Elyzabeth daughter of Elyzab[eth] Cocke, widow, 13 April.
1579 Richard Cock of Botley 23 July.
1579 Margarite of the said Richard Cocke 26 July.

1580   Thomas Cocke of Ly Greene 31 October.
1580   Nathanael son of Richard & Agnes Cock, wheeler, 24 January [1580/1].
1582   John Cockc of Ly Greene 12 January [1582/3].
1585   Thomas Cocke of Belenden 6 November.
1590   Old Will[ia]m Cock of Lygreene 6 January [1590/1].
1592   Susanna daughter of John Cock, Jr., laborer, & Isbell 16 July.
1593   Elyzabeth daughter of Nicholas & Elyzabeth Cock, Jr., of Lygrene
       1 August.
1593   Thomas son of John Cock, Jr., laborer, 20 August.
1593   Rychard Cocke, wheeler, 25 September.
1593   Agnes daughter of old W[illia]m Cock of Ly Grene, deceased, & of
       Ellen his wife 19 October.
1594   Sara daughter of John & Isbell Cock, Jr., laborer, 12 August.
1594   Sara daughter of Thomas & Elyzabeth Cock of Bois 16 January
       [1594/5].
1595   Hester daughter of Ric[hard] & Agnes Cock of Ly Greene 13 No-
       vember.
1598   Alice widow of Thomas Cocke of Lygreene 4 June.
1598   Mary daughter of Thomas Cock of Belend[en] 19 June.
1598   Mary daughter of Ric[hard] Cock of Botley, deceased, 21 November.
1598   Anne wife of old John Cock of the towne 25 November.
1601   Rychard son of Rychard Cocke, wheeler, 24 October.
1601   Nicholas son of Willia[m] & Joan Cocke of Belend[en] 13 November.
1602   Elyzabeth wife of Nicholas Cock, Jr., of Lye Greene 11 April.
1602   Ellen the widow of Will[ia]m Cock of Lyegreene 25 June.
1602   Mathew son of Rychard & Agnes Cocke of Lye Greene 19 July.
1602   Sara wife of Rychard Cock, tayler, 4 November.
1603   Old John Cock of the towne, laborer, 17 July.
1603   Susan daughter of Nicholas & S Isbell Cock, Jr., of Ly Greene 26
       July.
1606   Agnes Geery, widow, & mother of William Cock [of] Belend[en],
       2 February [1606/7].
1606   Richard Cock, tailor, 24 February [1606/7].

From the records given above genealogical information about several Cocke families of the parish of Chesham, co. Bucks, might undoubtedly be derived; but the following pedigree relates only to the
immediate ancestors of Phillip Cocke, wife of James Weeden, and
the children of these ancestors, as they are disclosed by those records.

1. WILLIAM COCKE of Belenden in the parish of Chesham, the
testator of 13 Oct. 1558, born probably about 1500, died between 13
October 1558 and 4 July 1559.  Perhaps he was a grandson of William
Cokke of Chesham, the testator of 1485.  He probably married first
———, who was buried at Chesham 2 Feb. 1550/1; and secondly
JOAN ———, who was named in his will and who was perhaps the
Joan Cock, widow, who married at Chesham, 13 Nov. 1561, Henry
Tookefeild.  His brother, Robert Cock, was appointed overseer in
his will.
       Children by first wife, named in their father's will:
   i.   WILLIAM, b. probably about 1528.
   ii.  ISABEL, b. probably about 1530; m. before 13 Oct. 1558 ———
        (probably WILLIAM) GOLD.
   iii. AGNES, b. probably about 1532.
 2. iv. THOMAS, b. probably about 1534.

v. JANE, b. probably about 1536.
vi. JOAN, "the younger," b. probably 1538 and perhaps the Jone, dau. of William Cocke, who was bapt. at Chesham 14 Mar. 1538/9. Perhaps another daughter, among the older children, who m. LEONARD TWYCHILLE (or TWICHELL), whose children, *Joan, Alice, Mary,* and *Henry,* are mentioned in William Cocke's will.

2. THOMAS COCKE *(William),* of Belenden in the parish of Chesham, husbandman, the testator of 2 Nov. 1585, born probably about 1534, was buried at Chesham 6 Nov. 1585. He married ANN (or AGNES) ——, who married secondly —— Geery and was buried at Chesham 2 Feb. 1606/7.
  Children:
3. i. WILLIAM, b. probably about 1560.
  ii. HENRY, bapt. at Chesham 13 July 1562.
  iii. THOMAS, bapt. at Chesham 7 Jan. 1564/5; m. at Hawridge, co. Bucks, 8 May 1598, AGNES GREGORY, dau. of John of Wilstorne Green in the parish of Great Tring, co. Hertford. In the marriage record he and his wife are described as servants of John Turner.
    Child:
    1. *Mary,* bur. at Chesham 19 June 1598.
  iv. ELENOR (probably dau. of this Thomas Cocke), bapt. at Chesham 22 June 1567; bur. there 14 Mar. 1567/8.
  v. JOAN, bapt. at Chesham 13 Feb. 1568/9.
  vi. ALICE, bapt. at Chesham 23 Dec. 1571.
  vii. RICHARD, bapt. at Chesham 16 May 1574.
  viii. ROBERT, bapt. at Chesham 2 Dec. 1576.
  ix. AGNES (or ANN), bapt. at Chesham 24 July 1580.

3. WILLIAM COCKE *(Thomas, William),* of Belenden in the parish of Chesham, was born probably about 1560. He married JOAN ——, who was perhaps the Joan Cock, widow, who was buried at Chesham 7 May 1623 (cf. the printed Register of Chesham, page 317).
  Children, baptized at Chesham:
  i. PHILLIP, bapt. 14 Jan. 1587/8; living in 1632; m. at Chesham, 11 Sept. 1615, JAMES WEEDEN, bapt. at Chesham 30 July 1585, d. probably before 17 Dec. 1673, s. of Richard and Joan (or Jane) of Botley in the parish of Chesham. James Weeden emigrated to New England in 1638, and lived at Newport and later at Portsmouth, R. I. He m. (2) in New England, about 1650, Rose (——) (Grinnell) Paine, widow successively of Matthew Grinnell and Anthony Paine. She survived her third husband. Six children, b. in England, the baptisms of five of them being recorded at Chesham. (Cf. REGISTER, vol. 76, p. 129.)
  ii. ELIZABETH, bapt. 15 Apr. 1590.
  iii. MARY, bapt. 26 Dec. 1592.
  iv. MARTHA, bapt. 9 May 1596; perhaps d. young.
  v. WILLIAM, bapt. 14 Jan. 1598/9.
  vi. NICHOLAS, bapt. 12 Nov. 1601; bur. at Chesham 13 Nov. 1601.
  vii. ANNE, bapt. 4 May 1603.
  viii. MARTHA (perhaps dau. of this William), bapt. 30 Jan. 1610/11; perhaps the Martha, dau. of Jone Cock, widow, deceased, who was bur. at Chesham 13 May 1623 (cf. the printed Register of Chesham, p. 317).

# GENEALOGICAL GLEANINGS IN ENGLAND
## III

Contributed by G. Andrews Moriarty, Jr., A.M., LL.B., of Newport, R. I.,
and communicated by the Committee on English Research

### Stokes–Pemberton–Williams–Zinzan

THE records published in this section refer to English relatives and connections of Roger Williams, the founder of Providence Plantations, and supplement the wills and notes communicated by the late Henry FitzGilbert Waters, A.M., to the REGISTER in 1889 (vol. 43, pages 290 *et seq.*) and in 1893 (vol. 47, pages 498 *et seq.*)* and other material that has been printed at various times on the Williams and Pemberton families and families allied with them.

#### FROM PROBATE RECORDS

The Will of JOHANE STOKES of Redburne [co. Herts], dated 30 June 1560. To the church of St. Albans. To Joone Wetheredde. To Robert Stowke. To Roger Stokes. To Walter Beech one acre. To John Beche's wife. To Katherine Thorne. To John Cranwell. To Alice Beche. To Elizabeth Beche. To Henry Beche one acre. Overseer: John Beche. Executor: my brother, Roger Stokes. Proved 12 October 1560. (Archdeaconry of St. Albans [Somerset House], Finkelcaster, 230.)

The Will of ROGER STOKES of St. Albans [co. Herts], mercer [made before 29 March 1578]. To the poor of St. Albans. To the parson of St. Albans to preach a sermon on my death. To the reparation of the free school in St. Albans. To my son Robert, on the decease of my wife Ellen, my lands in Pottersworth, both free and copy, provided he pay to Roger, my youngest son, £60 in four years. To my wife Ellen my house in St. Peter's Street in St. Albans, now in the tenure of Henry Webb, gentleman, and also a tenement in Fish Pole Street in St. Albans, in the tenure of John Durye. My two sons are to be brought up at Oxford or Cambridge University until they are twenty-six years old. To my son Roger my lands in St. Peter's Street, upon my wife's death. To my cousin Roger Pemberton. Executrix: my wife Ellen. Supervisors: Thomas Howldinge, gentleman, and my brother-in-law Robert Pemberton. Proved 29 March 1578. (Archdeaconry of St. Albans [Somerset House], Finkelcaster, 66.)

[Johane Stokes and Roger Stokes, abstracts of whose wills are given above, were sister and brother, respectively, of Catherine Stokes, who became the wife of Robert Pemberton, father of Alice (Pemberton) Williams and grandfather of Roger Williams.]

----

#### FROM LAY SUBSIDIES FOR ST. ALBANS, CO. HERTS†

34–36 Henry VIII [1542–1545] (121/158).

| | |
|---|---|
| Myddlewarde. | Robert Wolley in goods [tax] 3s. 4d. |
| St. Peter's warde. | William Pate in goods [tax] 2d. |
| St. Stephen's ward. | Mother Stoke, widow, in lands [tax] 2d. |
| | Henry Stoke in goods [tax] 2s. |

8 Elizabeth [1565–66].

| | |
|---|---|
| Myddlewarde. | Robert Pemb[er]ton in goods [valuation] £3 [tax] 3s. |

----

*Reprinted in Waters's Genealogical Gleanings in England, vol. 1, pp. 327 *et seq.* and 771 *et seq.*
†Preserved in the Public Record Office, London.

18 Elizabeth [1575–76] (121/228).

Myddlewarde.

John Arnolde in goods [valuation] £3 [tax] 5d.
Ralph Moore in goods [valuation] £3 [tax] 5d.
Robert Pemberton in goods [valuation] £3 [tax] 5d.
Robert Woolley in goods [valuation] £26 [tax] £4. 3s. 4d.
Thomas Wolley in goods [valuation] £3 [tax] 5d.

St. Peter's Ward.

John Williams in goods [valuation] £3 [tax] 5d.

FROM THE RECORDS OF THE COURT OF REQUESTS*

[After 30 September 1594.] The bill of ROGER PEMBERTON of St. Albans in the county of Hertford, gentleman, and ROBERT GROOME of the parish of Redbourne in the said county, yeoman, recites that one Thomas Sibley, late of Redbourne, deceased, was in his life seised in his demesne as of fee of one messuage or toft and one acre of land in Redbourne, and held the same of Your Majesty, before you came to the crown, as of your manor of Redbourne, [as] by copy of the court roll doth appear. The said Thomas Sibley about the fourth or fifth year of your sister, Queen Mary, being on his deathbed, surrendered his lands, according to the custom of the manor, into your hands, by some of the customary tenants, to the use of Joan Sibley, then the wife of the said Thomas, and after her decease to the use of Edward Sibley, son of the said Thomas, and his heirs, and the said Thomas died; and at the next court at Redburn it was presented by the homages that Thomas Sibley was dead, and that in life he had surrendered the said lands to the use of Joan, his wife, for life, and then to the said Edward Sibley and his heirs. The said Joan appeared and prayed to be admitted, and she was admitted and paid her fine therefor. Thereafter, on 30 June, 1 Elizabeth [1559], Edward Sibley came and desired to be admitted to the reversion after the death of the said Jone or her surrender or forfeiture. By the Queen Majesty's steward seisin was granted to him and his heirs in reversion, and Edward Sibley paid his fine and did fealty and was admitted to the reversion on the decease, forfeiture, or surrender of Joane, his mother. At a Court holden 30 June, 1 Elizabeth [1559], the homages found that Edward Sibley surrendered all his interest to the use of Vincent Roade, son of Sir Richard Roade, Knight, and his heirs, and the said Vincent Road, being then present, was given seisin and paid his fine and was admitted to the reversion.

Afterwards, to wit, in 5 Elizabeth [1562–63], Johane Sibley died, and Roade entered, as was lawful, and in 18 Elizabeth [1575–76] he surrendered the said messuage and one acre, amongst other things, by the name of one cottage with a garden near Redburne Heath and one acre late Edward Sibley's to the use of Francis Sylls, and at a court held 28 November, 19 Elizabeth [1576], the said Francis was admitted.

On 18 September, 35 Elizabeth [1593], the said Sylls surrendered the lands in question to the use of Roger Pemberton. That same day Roger Pemberton was admitted. On 30 September, 36 Elizabeth [1594], Roger Pemberton let the said messuage to Robert Grome for three years. But now John Beeche the Elder of Jerames in the parish of Redburn, yeoman, and one Robert Sybley of Redburn, yeoman, and one John Sybley of Hartingfordbury, yeoman, combining to trouble your orators, have obtained unlawfully all copies of the said court roll, and they have suborned some of

*Preserved in the Public Record Office, London.

the stewards or clerks to get the court rolls, and they claim that the said lands must descend unto Robert Sibley, the eldest son of the said Thomas. The witnesses and homages are all dead, and Beeche is setting on the said Robert Sibley, and he it is who will pay the expenses. And to give semblance to his title, the said Robert has colorably leased the premises to John Sybley. Your orators pray for a writ of subpœna, etc.

The answer of ROBERT SIBLEY. He denies the surrender of the reversion to Edward Sibley, and says that he himself was absent at the time and therefore could not enter at his father's death; and he further states that he made his leases of the premises by advice of learned counsel. (Court of Requests, B. 36, no. 53.)

INSCRIPTION ON THE MEMORIAL BRASS OF ROGER PEMBERTON, ESQ., IN ST. PETER'S CHURCH, ST. ALBANS, CO. HERTS

Here lieth Roger Pemberton Esqre sometime high sheriff of this County, who by his last will ordained six almshouses to be built near this church for six poor widows; and hath given out of his manor of Shelton, in the County of Bedford, thirtye pounds per annum for their maintenance: to whose pious memory, Elizabeth his loving wife and Ralph Pemberton their dutyful son, mayor of this town, executors of his last will, have dedicated this remembrance. He lived well and departed this life the 13th of November 1627, in the 72d year of his age. Here now his body rests, in expectation of a joyfull ressurection.

Filii dicti Rogeri et Elizabethæ      Filiæ dicti Rogeri et Elizabethæ
Ralph, Robert, et Johannes      Elizabeth, Elizabeth, Tecla.

[The names of the taxpayers in the entries in the Lay Subsidies given above are those of relatives or connections of Roger Williams, the Robert Pemberton mentioned there being undoubtedly his grandfather. The Roger Pemberton of the case in the Court of Requests and of the memorial brass was the uncle and godfather of Roger Williams; for Alice Pemberton, sister of Roger, married James Williams, citizen and merchant tailor of London, and they were the parents of Roger Williams. For Roger Pemberton's will see REGISTER, vol. 43, pp. 294–295, and "Genealogical Gleanings in England," vol. 1, p. 331. He was high sheriff of Herts in 1618, and was the heir of his cousins, Robert and Roger Stokes, abstracts of whose wills are published in the REGISTER, vol. 43, p. 294, and in "Genealogical Gleanings in England," vol. 1, pp. 330–331. They were sons of Roger Stokes, the testator whose will is given in abstract above. Roger Pemberton's son Ralph, who was mayor of St. Albans in 1627 and 1638, was, by his wife Frances, daughter of Francis Kempe, the father of Sir Francis Pemberton (1625–1697), Lord Chief Justice of the King's Bench and afterwards of the Common Pleas (1681–1683).]

FROM THE REGISTERS OF ST. ALBANS ABBEY, CO. HERTS

1607    Roger son of Mr. Lewis Williams baptized 3 August.

FROM THE PARISH REGISTERS OF PUTNEY, CO. SURREY

1637    The wife of Sidrach Williams, gentleman, buried 10 July.

FROM THE RECORDS OF THE COURT OF REQUESTS*

[*Circa* 1636.] The complaint of SIDRACH WILLIAMS of Putney in the county of Surry, gentleman, shews that for many years since passed he has used to trade and traffic in the way of merchandise, as was well known to William Langhorne and Thomas Harbie, who about 1625 were partners and both resident at Legorne in Italy, as factors for divers merchants. They solicited the complainant to send them from England a ship laden

*Preserved in the Public Record Office, London.

with red herrings, and the complainant was to credit them with one-fourth of the said herrings. Accordingly, in 1625, your complainant went from London to Great Yarmouth, and hired the ship *Mayflower* of Yarmouth, of 240 tons, Walter Wallward master. The complainant then bought 1475 barrels of red herrings to send to Langhorne and Harbin, and he shipped one-fourth for the use of the said Langhorne and Harbin, which amounted to £430. 6s. 9d. In December 1625 the *Mayflower* sailed from Yarmouth, and arrived in convenient time at Legorne in Italie; and the barrels of herrings were discharged and delivered to them. And now your complainant hoped that they would pay him the money due him for the cost and charge of one-fourth of the said herrings; but they have utterly refused so to pay, and the said Harby is now since deceased, and the said money is due for about eleven years. The complainant prays that Langhorne may answer whether about 1625 he was a partner of Harby, and whether they were resident in Legorne as factors to several merchants in the said country, and if, either alone or with Harby, he did not write letters to the complainant to send a shipload of red herrings, they to have one-fourth on their own account, and if he did not so send the *Mayflower* of Yarmouth with 1475 barrels of red herrings, and whether they did not receive them, and why they have not paid him for one-fourth thereof.

The answer of WILLIAM LANGHORNE. The defendant denies that either Harby or himself did solicit the said Williams to send the ship laden with red herrings, but says that at the time mentioned he had his abode at Legorne and the complainant dwelt in London. The complainant was willing to adventure to those parts, and asked the defendants to advise him concerning prices at Legorne, which he did. The defendant confesses that Thomas Harby was in the adventure of herrings, but denies that either Harby or himself ever asked the complainant to give them credit for a one-fourth part thereof, nor did they need the complainant's credit, for Thomas Harby then paid to the complainant in London £420 on account, namely, twelve shillings more than a one-fourth part of the herrings came unto, as is witnessed under the complainant's hand and is ready to be produced in court, and there a one-fourth part was set forth in the bill to the use of the said Harby; and the defendant denies that it amounted to £430. 9s. 9d. He confesses that the ship did arrive safely at Legorne and the said barrels were delivered to the defendants upon the agreement.

The account was made up about December 1625, and it there appears that the one-fourth part came up to less than the £420 paid to the complainant, namely, he was overpaid, as well as 12s. 12d. [*sic*] and £42. 8s. 4d. that was owing by the complainant to the defendant and Harby for their half part of the net proceeds of 20 barrels of argol, and this credit later was allowed by the complainant. Moreover, two years after, in 1627, the defendant came to London from Leghorn, and had other tradings with the complainant for 290 pigs of lead, and the complainant in the account allowed them for other sums of money owing them. Thomas Harby is now dead, and he died in Florence, in parts beyond the seas, about five or six years agone, and he had been a short time before in London, where he was for six months, and this complainant never made any demand and never claimed any such thing as is now contained in this pretended bill of complaint. (Court of Requests, uncalendared, Charles I, B. 44, part 2.)

[Sidrach Williams was a brother of Roger Williams; and in the REGISTER, * vol. 75, pp. 234–235, records in Chancery cases were published which described some of his activities as a merchant of London and proved that he was the brother whom Roger Williams called "a Turkey merchant in London." The records printed in this article reveal him as trading with the Italian port of Leghorn and as residing at Putney, near London, in 1636 and 1637.]

*See Vol. I of this work, pp. 646-647.

FROM PROBATE RECORDS

The Will of ALEXANDER ZINZIN of St. Stephens next St. Albans [co. Herts], dated 21 September 1557. To my son a damask gown, etc., that my lord of Warwycke gave me. To my son Alexander Zinzin. To my daughter Dorythe. To my daughter Aime. Executrix: my wife Ann. Overseer: Mr. Harryball Zinzin. Proved 13 December 1559. (Archdeaconry of St. Albans [Somerset House], Finkilcaster, 205.)

The nuncupative will of SIR ROBERT ZINZAN *alias* ALEXANDER, Knight, of Walton upon Thames [co. Surrey], declared on St. Matthew's Day [21 September], 1607. To Dame Margaret Zinzan his lands for life. To his two sons, Sir Sigismund Zinzan *alias* Alexander and Henry Zinzan *alias* Alexander, his patents granted to him by the late Queen Elizabeth. Proved 27 June 1608. (P. C. C., Windebanck, 1.)

The Will of ANDREW ZINZAN *alias* ALEXANDER of Reading [co. Berks], Esq., dated 14 March 1622 [1622/3]. To the church of St. Mary, Reading. To my nephew Henry Zinzan *alias* Alexander. To my servant Roger Baily. To my nephew Sir Sigismund Zinzan *alias* Alexander, Knight. Executors: my nephews, Henry and Sir Sigismund Zinzan.
Codicil. To Dr. Bird for pains taken in this my sickness. To my servant Thomas Hapenny. To my nephew Robert Zinzan. To Richard Zinzan, son of Henry the Elder. To Robert and Sigismund Zinzan, sons of Sir Sigismund Zinzan. To John Canna the Elder of Reading. To my servant Thomas Hemphrey. To Alexander Zinzan. Proved 22 February 1625/6. (P. C. C., Hele, 26.)

[The Zinzan wills are interesting, for Andrew Zinzan was one of the witnesses to the nuncupative will of Rev. Roger Williams of St. Albans, declared 26 June 1619. Cf. note by the late Henry FitzGilbert Waters, A.M., in REGISTER, vol. 43, p. 295, and in "Genealogical Gleanings in England," vol. 1, p. 332. In the Visitation of Berkshire, 1665–66 (*Publications of the Harleian Society*, vol. 56, p. 320), there is a pedigree of Zinzan *alias* Alexander of Tilehurst, from which it appears that Sir Robert Zinzan of St. Albans, co. Herts, married a daughter of —— Wescot of Hansaker Hall, co. Stafford. They were the parents of Henry Zinzan, the eldest son, of Walton upon Thames, co. Surrey, who married Elizabeth, daughter of —— Alder of Reading; of Robert Zinzan, second son, who died *s.p.;* of Sir Sigismund Zinzan, third son, of Molesey, co. Surrey, who married Margaret, daughter of Sir Philip Sterley of Sterley, co. Notts, Knight, died in 1663, and had children, who are entered in the pedigree; of Mary, who married —— Digby; and of Dulcibella, who married —— Williams of St. Albans. The wife of Rev. Roger Williams of St. Albans, to whom in his nuncupative will of 26 June 1619 he left all his estate, was named Affradosa, and, as Mrs. Aphrodoza Moore, widow, had been married to Mr. Roger Williams at St. Albans, 7 June 1613, a little more than two months after the burial of his former wife, Alice (Asheton), whom he had married nearly thirty years earlier. Mrs. Aphrodoza Williams was daughter of Alexander Zinzan of St. Michael in St. Albans, gentleman, and widow of William Moore of St. Albans, gentleman. Cf. REGISTER, vol. 43, pp. 296, 297. Who was the Williams of St. Albans who married Dulcibella, daughter of Sir Robert Zinzan?]

# GENEALOGICAL GLEANINGS IN ENGLAND
## IV

Contributed by G. ANDREWS MORIARTY, JR., A.M., LL.B., of Newport, R. I.,
and communicated by the Committee on English Research

## ALMY

IN the REGISTER, vol. 71, pages 310–324, may be found an article
by George Walter Chamberlain, M.S., entitled "The English Ancestry of William Almy of Portsmouth, R. I.," which is based in
part on an earlier article contributed by the present Chairman of
the Committee on English Research to the *Essex Institute Historical
Collections*, vol. 49, pages 172–176. The records printed below supply
additional information about this Almy family in its English home.
It should be noted, however, that the statement· made by Mr.
Chamberlain in his article in the REGISTER (vol. 71, page 319),
that Thomas Almey of Dunton-Bassett, co. Leicester (No. 2 of Pedigree I), was born about 1550, is obviously an error, for William
Almey, son of this Thomas, was born about 1556, as is stated in
the article in question and as is proved by the deposition of William,
made in 1625, when he was aged 68 years (*ib.*, page 318). Therefore
Thomas Almey, father of William, was born probably about 1530,
and Thomas's father, John Almey, with whom Mr. Chamberlain's
pedigree begins, was born probably about 1500–1505.

### FROM LAY SUBSIDIES FOR CO. LEICESTER*

15 Henry VIII [1523–24].
Dunton-Bassett. Christopher Almey in goods [valuation]
£3 [tax] 18d.
William Almey in goods [valuation]
£10 [tax] 5d.
John Reynold in goods [valuation] £10
[tax] 12d.
Robert Rynold in goods [valuation] £30
[tax] 30s.

13 Elizabeth [1570–71].
Bitteswell. John Wale in goods [valuation] £3
[tax] 5d.
Dunton-Bassett. Thomas Almye in goods [valuation]
£4 [tax] 6s. 8d.
Robert Reynolds in lands [valuation]
£26. 8s. [tax] 3s. 6d.
North Kilworth. Robert Wale in goods [valuation] £10
[tax] 8s. 4d.

39 Elizabeth [1596–97], first payment.
Dunton-Bassett. Thomas Almye in goods [valuation]
£3 [tax] 8d.
Lutterworth. John Almy in goods [valuation] £3 [tax]
8d.
Henry Clarke in goods [valuation] £3
[tax] 8d.

*Preserved in the Public Record Office, London.

69

39 Elizabeth [1596–97], second payment.

Dunton-Bassett. Thomas Almey in goods [valuation] £3 [tax] 8d.

Lutterworth. John Almey in goods [valuation] £3 [tax] 8d.

39 Elizabeth [1596–97], third payment.

Bitteswell. William Almy in lands [valuation] 20s. [tax] 4d.
John Wale in lands [valuation] 20s. [tax] 4d.

Dunton-Bassett. Thomas Almy in goods [valuation] £3 [tax] 8d.

7 James I [1609–10].

Bitteswell. William Almeye in goods [valuation] £3 [tax] 5d.
William Clarke in goods [valuation] £3 [tax] 5d.
Thomas Wale in lands [valuation] 20s. [tax] 2s. 8d.

Dunton-Bassett. Thomas Almye in goods [valuation] £3 [tax] 5d.

North Kilworth. Margaret Wale in lands [valuation] 20s. [tax] 2s. 8d.

2 Charles I [1626–27].

Bitteswell. William Allmye in goods [valuation] £3 [tax] 8d.

South Kilworth. William Aulmye in goods [valuation] £3 [tax] 8d.

[The entries in the lay subsidies given above show that John Almey of Dunton-Bassett, co. Leicester (No. 1 of Pedigree I in Mr. Chamberlain's article), was undoubtedly the son either of William Almey or of Christopher Almey of the subsidy of 15 Henry VIII [1523–24]. These two men may have been brothers, and in that case they were born undoubtedly in the last quarter of the fifteenth century; or they may have been father and son. The other two men, John Reynold and Robert Rynold, of the subsidy of 1523–24 at Dunton-Bassett, and also Robert Reynolds, of the subsidy of 13 Elizabeth [1570–71], were probably relatives of the wife of John Almey (No. 1 of Pedigree I), who was a Reignolds. The wife of Thomas Almey (No. 2 of Pedigree I) was Joan Wale, and the surname Wale is found in several of the entries given above. The first wife of Christopher Almey (No. 6 of Pedigree I) was ——— Clarke, daughter of ——— Clarke of Lutterworth, co. Leicester, and the Henry Clarke of the subsidy of 39 Elizabeth [1596–97] was probably her father.]

FROM THE RECORDS OF THE COURT OF REQUESTS*

February, 22 James I [February, 1624/5]. EDMUND CLEMENT of Lutterworth [co. Leicester], clerk, recites that on Easter last past he exhibited his bill of complaint against one Christopher Almey of South Kilworth [co. Leicester], yeoman. Twenty-seven years ago the complainant by suretyships undertook for his friends and by other losses and misfortunes became indebted to divers persons, some in London and others in the counties of Leicester, Northampton, and elsewhere, in the sum of £1200 in all, and desiring to pay this great debt out of what should yearly accrue out of your subject's parsonage and incumbency at Lutterworth and wishing his creditors to receive from time to time out of the yearly profits equally and indifferently such sums of money as in twelve years would make full satisfaction of the principal due, being all his poor estate could bear, your subject about 38

*Preserved in the Public Record Office, London.

Elizabeth [1595-96] exhibited his bill, in the nature of a humble petition to the said late Queen of famous memory, in Your Highness's High Court of Whitehall at Westminster, and thereby set forth that your subject was indebted to William Miller of Whitebrook, co. Warwick, gentleman, William Tilley, citizen and merchant tailor of London, Richard Halford of Gilmorton in Leicester, gentleman, John Robinson, merchant of the Staple, Thomas Hoddiler, citizen and salter of London, William Hericke, citizen and goldsmith of London, Thomas Garwaie, merchant of the Staple of England, Thomas Ashley of Kirby, co. Northampton, husbandman, John Mobbey of Leicester town, yeoman, Christopher Almey, then of Lutterworth, yeoman, and divers others, to the number of thirty or more, in divers sums, amounting to £1200, and, having no way to pay his debts but the profits of his living and being desirous to give contentment out of his living by yearly payments to prevent many suits then growing and more likely to grow, he prayed for a commission out of the Court or under the privy seal to be directed, amongst others, to the Right Worshipful Sir Edward Hastings and Henrie Turvile, Esq., justices of the peace of the county of Leicester, commanding them or any one of them to call your subject and all his creditors and to mediate and end discords touching the said debts, as the estate would afford and as might give contentment to the creditors. A commission was accordingly awarded to Sir Edward Hastings and William [sic] Turvile in 38 Elizabeth [1595-96], and they called the creditors and examined your subject's estate, which they found to be very weak for so great a debt. In a treaty in what manner they would be contented to receive their due, amongst others the said Christopher Almey, then of Lutterworth, yeoman, was present, and acquainted the said Commissioners with his debt of £27, and stated that he would be content with yearly payments at such times and in such manner as contented the other creditors. The commissioners, then perceiving a charitable inclination of the said Christopher Almey and the other creditors to take small payments, with the consent of all the creditors determined that, if the creditors would abate by one half their debt, which divers did, then your subject should provide some able men to whom your said subject should make a list of his tithes and parsonage, and should be bound to pay the rest of the said sum so abated in two or three years, at the most, in yearly payments, but such as would not abate any of their claims should receive payments in ten years by yearly payments; and the commissioners directed your subject that tithes and other profits of the parsonage of Lutterworth (except a matter of £20, which your subject received for his livelihood) were to be paid to Robert Garfield of London, dyer, and Robert Smith of Lutterworth, barber, to have and to hold for twelve years next ensuing, for the yearly rent of a peppercorn, and on such lease they should enter into a bond with the creditors for the payment of their yearly sums. All this was done, and a schedule of debt was made, and Christopher Almey was to be paid £2. 5s. on 2 February 1598, £2. 5s. on 2 February 1599, and £2. 5s. on 2 February 1600 [and similar yearly payments down through 2 February 1608, amounting to £27]. These sums were to be paid to Christopher Almey by the said Smith and Garfield, and said Almey did from time to time deliver up to the said lessees their several bonds, to the number of ten specialties, and all the other persons also were paid, to the amount of £1200, and the creditors did deliver up their bonds and your subject's old bonds originally given to the said creditors, and Robert Smith demanded of the said Almey his said old bond, as well as of the said other creditors. But Almey refused, as he feared the lessees would not perform their agreements, and for the purpose of vexing and troubling your subject did retain the old bond, and, as the said lessees were only entrusted by your subject to take up the other bonds and as they forgot to continue to demand the same, the said Almey kept his bond after the last payment made in 1608 for ten years and never molested your subject, and then, well knowing that the commissioners and most of the others concerned were dead, the said Almey, about the year 1616, threatened your poor subject that, if he would not make a new bond for £100 for the payment of £50 (that being the full forfeiture on the old bond) at a day shortly to come and now long past, he would immediately arrest and imprison your said subject on the old bond; and your poor subject, to avoid open discredit and fearing to be deprived of the public exercise of his ministry, it being the only comfort of his life, was driven to enter into the £100 bond for payment of the £50, and said Almey, well knowing that your subject could not pay then, promised not to use any extreme course thereupon against your subject or compel him to pay any more than his means would afford, but, contrarily, he entered upon a suit in the Common Pleas on the bond, and threatened your subject with prison, and would have undone him in his estate, if he had not been relieved by Your Most Excellent Majesty; and your subject then prayed for a writ of privy seal against the said Christopher Allmey, to answer in the premises, and an injunction to stay proceedings at the law. And at a full hearing by counsel on both sides it appeared that the said defendant had confessed that about twenty-seven years last past he had accounted for the several payments but that the money paid was for interest only. Now, upon consideration, the Commission [sic] ordered that an injunction should be awarded against this defendant, his attorney, counsel, and solicitors, for a stay of proceedings. Since when the said Christopher Almey made his last will and testament and lately died, since which death his son William Almey and his executors proved the said will* and prosecuted suits at law with great violence against your poor subject, and they threaten him on his bond to arrest him, and your subject is forced to keep to his house and to neglect his ministry since before Christmas last past. He prays for a writ of privy seal against William Almey, and that he be enjoined as his father, Christopher Almey, was.

The answer of WILLIAM ALMEY, executor of the will of Christopher Almey, deceased, defendant to the above-set-forth bill, asserts the insufficiency of the said bill, which is carelessly exhibited to trouble him and put him at unnecessary expenses and charges in the law rather than upon any good cause. The complainant did heretofore put in his bill against Christopher Almey, who answered the same, and this answer is true. The complainant did owe the deceased Christopher Almey the sum of £50, in a bond of £100. The testator never did in 1616 threaten the complainant, in order to make him give a penalty bond of £100. That bond was made upon a just reckoning and on this complainant's request for a longer time to pay the £50 due on the old bond, and the complainant did entreat Mr. Henry Flamell, the testator's attorney, not long before the testator's death, to get the testator to forbear the £50 a longer time, offering to pay the interest long past due, and not by fear of discredit was he drawn into giving the bond or by the testator's promise not to go to extremes on the said bond. True it is that about five months last past Christopher Almey made his will, and made the defendant executor of the same; and about Christmas last past the said complainant did in the presence of divers persons acknowledge and confess the debt of the £50 as still due, and that it was a just and true debt still unpaid, and the complainant has been instigated by others to commence this suit, and the complainant has offered the defendant a very good security to pay £25 on the Feast of St. Luke the Evangelist† next coming and £27 on that day come twelve months. This complainant also wrote divers letters

*His will, dated 2 Oct. 1624, was proved 29 Oct. 1624. Christopher Almey was buried at South Kilworth, co. Leicester, 4 Oct. 1624. (REGISTER, vol. 71, pp. 314, 317, 320.)
†The Feast of St. Luke the Evangelist falls on 18 October.

to the testator to intreat him for forbearance, and, moreover, the testator on his deathbed and in the time of his sickness declared that the said money was due on the bond of £100 and that it was a just debt. Defendant prays that the debt be adjudged due and that it be caused to be paid, as the testator's personal estate is not able to pay all the debts owing, and this defendant, the executor, has become indebted and payeth interest upon £200, and not with £50 can he satisfy the just debts due from the estate. This complainant's estate hath been sequestered for great debts, and, he being unable to make satisfaction, the testator had prosecuted his claim against this complainant, who is better able to pay than the defendant to loose the £50, having enjoyed a very good parsonage of the value of eight score pounds per annum and having no charges of wife or child to maintain. True it is that the complainant [sic] intended to put the bond in suit at the common law, and the more so as the testator was much damnified by the complainant's long delay in making payment. (Court of Requests, uncalendared, James I, B. 38, part 2.)

[In the article by Mr. Chamberlain to which reference has been made above an abstract was given (REGISTER, vol. 71, p. 318) of a document in the records of the Court of Requests which, it was stated, showed that in 1625 Edward Clement, clerk, sued William Almey, yeoman, son and executor of Christopher Almey, deceased, about the parsonage of Lutterworth [co. Leicester] and a bond connected therewith, the suit having been brought first against Christopher Almey and, after his death, against his son and executor William Almey. The documents of which abstracts are given above supply full particulars about this case, in which the defendant was William Almey (No. 7 of Pedigree I in Mr. Chamberlain's article), who emigrated to New England and finally settled at Portsmouth, R. I. This case is of considerable interest from the point of view of the legal antiquary as illustrating the process employed in bankruptcy proceedings in England in the early part of the seventeenth century. The commissioners correspond to the modern referee in bankruptcy, the two men appointed by them to receive the debtor's moneys and apply them correspond to our trustees in bankruptcy, and the action appears to have been begun by a petition to the Court at Westminster.]

## SLOCUM

To the REGISTER of July 1916 (vol. 70, pages 283–284) the present Chairman of the Committee on English Research contributed a note entitled "Parentage of Giles Slocum of Portsmouth, R. I.," in which abstracts of English wills were given that made it appear probable that Giles Slocombe, son of Charity (Bickham) Slocombe of Old Cleeve, co. Somerset, was identical with Giles Slocum, an early settler of Portsmouth, R. I. The will of Charity Slocombe of Old Cleeve, widow, dated 21 Nov. 1642, was proved 26 Jan. 1642/3, her son Giles being sole executor; and in the note in the REGISTER it was pointed out that Giles Slocum of Portsmouth, R. I., probably did not arrive in New England until 1647 or 1648, in spite of the assumption of some genealogists that he was at Portsmouth as early as or soon after 1638. The records printed below undoubtedly give the marriage of the parents of Giles Slocum, the Portsmouth settler, and his own baptism. He probably emigrated to New England shortly after the death of his mother, lived for a few years at Taunton, Mass., where Anthony Slocum, who afterwards migrated to Carolina, was then residing, and settled at Portsmouth in or shortly before 1648. The entries taken from the lay subsidies show that

*See p. 75, this volume.

73

there were many Slocums in Old Cleeve and in neighboring parishes in the last years of the sixteenth and the first half of the seventeenth century.

From the Transcripts of the Parish Registers of Old Cleeve, co. Somerset*

1621  Philip Slocum and Charity Bickham married 20 November.
1623  Giles Slocum son of Philip baptized 28 September.

From Lay Subsidies for co. Somerset†

39 Elizabeth [1596–97].
  Huish-Champflower.               Richard Slocum in lands [valuation] £20.
  Nettlecombe.                     George Slocum in goods [valuation] 4s. [tax] 8d.
  Old Cleeve.                       Aldred Bickham in goods [valuation] £3 [tax] 10s.
  Over Stowey.                    Robert Slocum in lands [valuation] 20s. [tax] 4d.
  Watchet.                         Thomas Slocombe in lands [valuation] 20s. [tax] 4d.
22 James I [1624–25].
  Old Cleeve.                       Aldred Bickham in lands [valuation] 20s. [tax] 4d.
4 Charles I [1628–29].
  Nettlecombe.                     Richard Slocombe in goods [valuation] £4 [tax] 10s. 8d.
16 Charles I [1640–41].
  Nettlecombe.                     Thomas Slocombe in lands [valuation] 4s. [tax] 4d.

From the Somerset Protestation Roll, 1642‡

27 February 1642.
  Old Cleeve.                       Gilles Slocum.

*Preserved in the Diocesan Registry at Wells, co. Somerset.
†Preserved in the Public Record Office, London.
‡In the custody of the Librarian of the House of Lords.

Parentage of Giles Slocum of Portsmouth, R. I. — In the Slocums of America, compiled by Dr. Charles Elihu Slocum, there is an extended notice of the English Slocums; and Giles Slocum of Portsmouth, R. I., is given as a son of Anthony Slocum of Taunton, Mass., in spite of the fact that in the will of Anthony Slocum of Albemarle County in the Province of Carolina, dated 26 Nov. 1688 and proved 7 Jan. 1689/90, neither Giles nor his children are mentioned. There is no doubt of the identity of the Anthony Slocum of Albemarle County in Carolina with the Anthony Slocum who was formerly of Taunton, Mass., and the omission in the will of any reference to Giles Slocum or his children shows conclusively that Giles was not Anthony's son.

In Dr. Slocum's account of the English Slocums is given an abstract of the will of Charity Slocombe, widow, of the parish of Old Cleeve, co. Somerset, dated 21 Nov. 1642 and proved 26 Jan. 1642/3. The testatrix mentions brother Aldred Bickham, sister Joane Studdier, kinswomen Isoll Oatford and Mary Wills, widow, the latter of Envier, and son Giles Slocombe, who is made sole executor of the will. The English genealogist employed by Dr. Slocum to carry on the search in England concluded that this Giles could not be Giles of Rhode Island, because he assumed that the latter was at Portsmouth, R. I., as early as or soon after 1638. This assumption is not warranted by the records. The first mention of Giles Slocum on record in New England is on 4 Sept. 1648, when he was granted land in Portsmouth. He does not appear in Rhode Island previous to that date, and he was not in Plymouth Colony in Aug. 1643, when Anthony Slocum of Taunton was on the list of men able to bear arms. It would therefore appear that he did not arrive in New England until 1647 or 1648, and in this case it is very probable that he was the Giles, son of Charity Slocombe, who was her executor in 1643.

Abstracts of the wills of the father and mother of Charity (Bickham) Slocombe and of her brothers William and Aldred follow.

The will of Aldred Byccombe of Old Cleve, co. Somerset, clothier, dated 21 July 1610 and proved 2 Feb. 1610/11 by Hellen Byccombe the relict, contains bequests to daughter Charitie (£50, being a debt due to him from his brother William Byccombe), to daughter Mary at 21, to daughter Joane, to son William Byccombe, and to Isott Lanham, daughter of daughter Ann Lanham, deceased. Son Aldred to succeed in the house. Residue to wife Helen, executrix. Overseers: brother William Byccombe, friend Andrew Speede, and brother-in-law Thomas Cridland. (Somersetshire Wills, Series 2, p. 67.)

The will of Ellen Bickham of Old Cleve, co. Somerset, widow, dated 24 June 1642 and proved 20 June 1646 by Aldred Bickham, contains bequests to sister Anne Ashe, to daughter Charitie Slocombe, to daughter Joan, the wife of John Studdier, to son Aldred Bickham's daughter Ellen, to cousins Nicholas and Roger Colles, to uncle John Colles's widow, mentions chattels left to the testatrix by her son William Bickham, and bequeaths the residue of the estate to son Aldred Bickham. There are bequests to the poor of Spaxton, Bishop's Lyddiard, and Old Cleeve. (Ib., Series 2, p. 68.)

The will of William Bickham of Old Cleeve, co. Somerset, bachelor, dated 2 Mar. 1626 [1626/7] and proved 12 June 1627, contains bequests to sister's eldest daughter, to Aldred Bickham, Jr., to brother Aldred, to brother-in-law John Studdier, and to testator's mother, Ellen Bickham. (Ib., Series 2, p. 67.)

The will of Aldred Bickham of Old Cleeve, co. Somerset, clothier, dated 7 Feb. 1651 [1651/2] and proved 24 May 1652, contains bequests to eldest son Richard Bickham ("a silver salt guilded with gold & six silver spoons, according to my grandfather's will to remain for ever to the eldest son of his line & blood"), to wife Thomasine, to daughter Ellen Escott, wife of Richard Escott, to sons Aldred Bickham, William, and Hugh, to daughters Johan, Mary, and Anne, to daughter Isott Bickham, to Mary and Joan, daughters of daughter Ellen Escott, and to brother-in-law Hugh Slocombe. Residue to son Aldred, executor. Overseer: Richard Escott. (Ib., Series 3, p. 87.)

Abstracts of wills of other members of the Bickham family are printed in Somersetshire Wills, and subsequent records in Somersetshire show that by the beginning of the eighteenth century the family had risen to the ranks of the gentry and that they resided in Taunton, co. Somerset, and also in Exeter, co. Devon.

In view of these facts a further search should be made in the records of Somerset and Devon, and the parish registers or Bishop's transcripts for Old Cleeve and the neighboring parishes ought to be examined, as there can be little doubt that Giles Slocombe, son of Charity of Old Cleeve, and Giles of Portsmouth, R. I., are identical. Giles was probably a near relative of Anthony of Taunton, Mass., and the latter probably came to New England in the company of Mistress Elizabeth Poole, who founded Taunton and who, being a native of the West Country, brought the earliest settlers of Taunton from the counties of Devon, Somerset, and Dorset.

*Newport, R. I.*                                    G. Andrews Moriarty, Jr.

---

Giles Slocum of Portsmouth, R. I. — In The Register (vol. 70, pp. 28–3 * 84; vol. 78, pp. 395–96) the writer contributed two notes regarding the parentage of Giles Slocum, the early settler of Portsmouth, and suggested that he was probably identical with the Giles, son of Philip and Charity (Bickham) Slocum, who was baptized at Old Cleeve, co. Somerset, 28 Sept. 1623. The following will amplify this suggestion.

The statement has frequently been made that Giles was in Portsmouth as early as 1638, but the writer has found no evidence of this. His first appearance in Portsmouth was 4 Sept. 1648, when he was granted thirty acres there by the town (Records of the Town of Portsmouth, p. 38). He lived next to Thomas Cook, who first appears in Portsmouth in 1643 (ibid., p. 23), and Thomas Cook in his will, dated 6 Feb. 1673-4, calls him "my brother Giles Slocum" (Austin's Gen. Dic. of R.I., p. 282). Giles may have married a sister of Thomas Cook or vise versa and there are, of course, other possible combinations. The births of the children of Giles and his wife, Joan, are recorded in the records of the Portsmouth Quaker Meeting, and their eldest child Joanna was born 16 May 1642 (Austin, op. cit., p. 181), hence Giles must have married in 1641, when Giles, son of Philip, was only 18 or 19 years of age. This is rather young, but quite possible,

*See pp. 73-76, this volume.

and it must be noted that his mother Charity Slocum, in her will, dated 21 Nov. 1642, proved 26 Jan. 1642-3, made him her sole executor, when he was but 20 years old (Somersetshire Wills; THE REGISTER, vol. 78, p. 395).*

Prior to his arrival in Portsmouth, Giles had been in Taunton, Plymouth Colony. The early town records of Taunton were, for the most part, destroyed by fire many years ago, but in what remain there are two references to Giles. He is named in a list of Taunton proprietors made prior to 5 July 1664 and in a like list, made about 1675, Nicholas White, Sr., held "the right which was Giles Slocum's" (Bailies New Plymouth, vol. II, p. 280). Anthony Slocum was among the first settlers of Taunton in 1637; he came with Mistress Elizabeth Poole, the daughter of the famous West Country antiquary, Sir William Poole, from Somerset and Dorset, and settled Taunton. In or about 1670 Anthony removed to Albemarle County, N. C., where he was a prominent citizen. In 1680 "Anthony Slocum Esq., one of ye Lds Proprs Deputies" deposed "aged 90 years or thereabouts". His will, dated 26 Nov. 1688, was proved 7 Jan. 1689-90 (Crapo's "Certain Comeverers", vol. I, p. 336). It seems probable that Giles was a nephew or other near relative of Anthony, and that this was the reason for his emigration to Taunton.

The following is a statement of the suggested early life of Giles Slocum:

20 Nov. 1621.  Philip Slocombe married Charity Bickham at Old Cleeve, co. Somerset.

28 Sept. 1623.  Giles Slocombe, their son was baptized there.

About 1641.  Giles married Joan, perhaps the sister of Thomas Cook, of Portsmouth (1642).

16 May 1642.  Joanna, eldest child of Giles and Joan was born.

21 Nov. 1642.  Giles was named as sole executor in the will of his mother Charity Slocombe of Old Cleeve.

27 Feb. 1642-3.  Giles signed the Somerset Protestion Roll (Library, House of Lords).

Prior to 1648 he removed to Taunton, Plymouth Colony, where Anthony Slocum lived.

4 Sept. 1648.  He was granted land in Portsmouth, R.I., and resided next to Thomas Cook.

31 Aug. 1679.  Joan, wife of Giles Slocum died.

1683.  Giles Slocum died (Austin, *op. cit.*, p. 18½).

It is submitted that Giles of Portsmouth is probably identical with the Giles baptized at Old Cleeve on 28 Sept. 1623.

*Wells, Maine.*                    G. ANDREWS MORIARTY, F.S.A., F.S.G.

---

*Page 73, this volume.

# GENEALOGICAL GLEANINGS IN ENGLAND
## V

Contributed by G. ANDREWS MORIARTY, JR., A.M., LL.B., of Newport, R. I.,
and communicated by the Committee on English Research

## PAYNE

IN the REGISTER for July 1915 (vol. 69, pp. 248–252)[*] there were
published entries found in the parish registers of Lavenham, co.
Suffolk, relating to the Payne family and to the Aires (or Eyre) and
Page families, which were allied with the Paynes. A brief Aires
pedigree accompanied these records. In that article it was proved
that William and Agnes (Neves) Payne of Lavenham were the
parents of William Payne, who was baptized at Lavenham 20 Feb.
1596/7 and was later of Ipswich and Boston, Mass., and of three
daughters who migrated to New England, viz., Elizabeth Payne,
baptized at Lavenham 11 Sept. 1586 and married there 9 June 1605
to William Hamond (or Hammond), Phebe Payne, baptized at
Lavenham 1 Apr. 1594 and married there 5 June 1621 to John Page,
and Dorothy Payne, born about 1598 and married, probably about
1616, to Simon Aires (or Eyre). The following records supply further
information regarding the Payne family, and offer a clue to the
parentage of William Payne of Lavenham, husband of Agnes Neves.

### FROM PROBATE RECORDS AT BURY ST. EDMUNDS, CO. SUFFOLK

The Will of THOMAS PAYNE of Boxsted [co. Suffolk], yeoman, dated 2
February 1544/5. To be buried in Boxsted churchyard. To my wife Alice
and my son Richard Payne my lease that I hold of Sir John Cresson, knight,
during my wife's life, and afterwards to my said son. To my son John £4.
To my son William £8. To my daughter Alice £3. To my son Robert £4.
To my goddaughter Margery Fyrmyn 40s. at full age. To Richard Wright,
Christian Warde, and Ann Slypper, to each 6s. 8d. To my wife Alice £6.
13s. 4d. and household goods. Residuary legatees and executors: my wife
and my son Richard. Witnesses: Sir Henry Gascogne, priest, John Paynne,
and John Gooddynge. Proved 25 February 1544/5. (Archdeaconry of
Sudbury, book 13, fo. 484.)

The Will of RICHARD PAYNE of Boxsted [co. Suffolk], clothier, dated 13
January 1574/5. To be buried in Boxsted churchyard. To my wife Margaret
my tenement in Somerton's Boxsted for life, and then to my son Richard
Payne and his heirs, except the Ray meadow, which I give to my son Thomas
Payne, with £40. To my son Richard Payne £20. To my son John Payne
£40 for life, and then to his children. To my servant Thomas Cocky a horse.
To Marion and Joane Firmyne 6s. 8d. each. To my brother William Payne's
children 4 nobles. To John Firmin 5s. To John Payne, sometime my
servant, 3s. 4d. To Marion Hale 13s. 4d. To Susan Hale £6. 13s. 4d. To
William Halle not demanding the £10 I owe him. To Sir John Hallidaye
£10. To Cle Ellett 4 nobles. Executors: my wife Margaret and my sons
John, Richard, and Thomas. Proved 9 November 1575 by the sons, the wife
Margaret being dead. (Archdeaconry of Sudbury, book 33, fo. 102.)

The Will of ROGER PAYNE of Long Melford [co. Suffolk], husbandman,
dated 1 February 1583/4. To be buried in Melford churchyard. To my
mother 6s. 8d. To my sister Ann 6s. 8d. To my sisters Rose, Jane, and

*See Vol. I of this work, pp. 383-387.

Agnes, to each 6s. 8d. To Elizabeth, daughter of William Payne, 6s. 8d. To his son John 3s. 4d. To his son Edward 3s. 4d. To my brother Giles 2s. 8d. All to be paid by my godfather William Payne out of what he owes me. To my brother William my apparel. To my unborn child 46s. 8d. at the age of twenty-one. Residuary legatee and executrix: my wife Margaret. Proved 14 April 1584. (Archdeaconry of Sudbury, book 35, fo. 156.)

Administration on the estate of GILES PAYNE of Bury St. Edmunds [co. Suffolk] was granted 31 May 1585 to his relict Joan, William Payne of Lavenham [co. Suffolk] being surety. (Bury St. Edmunds Act Book, vol. 1, fo. 65.)

The Will of JOHN PAYNE of Bury [Bury St. Edmunds, co. Suffolk], butcher, dated 3 September 1587. To my wife Alice for life my tenement where I dwell, and then to my son John and his heirs. To my son Edward my tenement and barn. To my son George my close and £10. To my daughter Ann £10 at the age of twenty-one. If all die without issue, my brother Bartholomew Payne is to have my tenement. To my brother Edward Payne 40s. To my sister Ann Payne 40s. Residuary legatee and executrix: my wife Alice. Proved 5 September 1587. (Archdeaconry of Sudbury, book 36, fo. 149.)

The Will of JOHN PAYNE of Boxsted [co. Suffolk], clothier, dated 27 November, 42 Elizabeth [1599]. To be buried in Boxsted churchyard. To my wife Margery. To my son Walter my house in Boxsted and certain fields there, he paying to my sons John and Ambrose £70 bequeathed to them by their grandfather Richard Paine, at the age of twenty-three years. To my son Thomas £30. My son Walter is to pay to my daughters Martha and Dorothy £60 each at the age of twenty-six. To my son William a silver goblet. Executor: my son Walter. Overseer: my son Richard Paine. Proved 29 April 1600. (Archdeaconry of Sudbury, book 41, fo. 24.)

The Will of ANN PAYNE of Lavenham, co. Suffolk, widow, dated 8 December 1635. To be buried in Lavenham churchyard. To my son Richard Payne 10s. To my daughter Susan Payne my capital messuage in the market place in Lavenham, in the tenure of one Thomas Dister and myself. Executrix and residuary legatee: my daughter Susan Payne. Proved 25 April 1646. (Archdeaconry of Sudbury, book 55, fo. 291.)

[The testatrix, Ann (or Agnes) (Neves) Payne, was the widow of William Payne of Lavenham and the mother of William Payne and his married sisters who emigrated to New England. She was buried at Lavenham 8 Oct. 1645.]

FROM THE ARCHDEACON'S TRANSCRIPTS OF THE PARISH REGISTERS OF LAVENHAM, CO. SUFFOLK

1563 Richard son of Richard Payne baptized 13 August.

FROM THE SUBSIDY OF 1568 FOR CO. SUFFOLK*

| | |
|---|---|
| Bury St. Edmunds. | Robert Payne in goods [? valuation] £3. |
| Lavenham. | William Payne in goods [? valuation] £3. |

ASSESSMENTS FOR SHIP MONEY

| | |
|---|---|
| Boxsted. | Widow Elizabeth Hammond 8s. |
| | Walter Paine 7s. 8d. |
| Lavenham. | Richard Payne 8s. 4d. |
| | Thomas Payne 1s. 5d. |

*Published in Suffolk Green Books.

[An examination of the Payne entries in the Lavenham registers published in the REGISTER, vol. 69, pp. 251–252, shows that a Thomas Payne married Agnes Wyat 16 Nov. 1561, and had Agnes, baptized 19 July 1562, and John, baptized 6 July 1564. A William Payne had Thomas, baptized 25 Jan. 1559 (the year in the Lavenham registers, previous to 1570, beginning on 1 Jan.), and William was buried 17 Nov. 1587. A Joane Payne, widow, was buried 8 Oct. 1594. An Agnes Payne was married to George Sergeantson 5 Oct. 1565. Finally, William Payne, the father of the emigrants to New England, married Agnes Neves 28 Dec. 1584, their children were baptized at Lavenham, and William was buried there 9 June 1621. The name *Payne* is very widely spread in Suffolk, especially in the southwestern corner of the county; but it seems in the highest degree probable, when the contiguity of Boxsted and Lavenham is considered, that William Payne, son of Thomas Payne of Boxsted (the testator of 2 Feb. 1544/5), had issue William, Thomas, and Agnes (wife of George Sergeantson), who appear in the early Payne entries in the Lavenham registers, that these children are the ones mentioned in the will of Richard Payne of Boxsted (the testator of 13 Jan. 1574/5) as "my brother William Payne's children," and that the William Payne who married Agnes Neves was a great-grandson of Thomas Payne of Boxsted (the testator of 2 Feb. 1544/5), being the son of William, who in turn was the son of William (the brother of Richard) and the grandson of Thomas of Boxsted.

It may be noted that the records published in the REGISTER in July 1915 proved that this Payne family was not descended from the gentle family living at Hengrave Hall in Suffolk, as was asserted in the "Paine Genealogy," by Albert W. Paine, Bangor, Me., 1881.]

## COGGESHALL

To the REGISTER for January 1919 (vol. 73, pp. 19–32) the Com-[**]mittee on English Research communicated an article contributed by Hon. Frederick Samuel Fish, A.B., of South Bend, Ind., and containing records relating to the English ancestry of John Coggeshall, one of the early settlers of Rhode Island and first president of that Colony. Among those records was an abstract of a complaint in Chancery brought in 1620 by Anne Coggeshall, widow, in the name of her son, John Coggeshall the Younger (the later settler in Rhode Island), then a minor, against William Sydaie (or Sidey), his son John Sydaie (or Sidey), and Walter Bright, with the answers of the defendants. Below is given an abstract of a deposition belonging to the same case.

### FROM CHANCERY PROCEEDINGS[*]

Coggeshall *v.* Sydey. Richard Micklefield of Earl's Colne, co. Essex, cook, aged 64 years or thereabouts, deposes that he knew John Coggeshall, gentleman, named in the complaint, and also John Sidey, and that he knew well John Coggeshall, gentleman, deceased, late father of the complainant, and John Sidey, late of Pebmarsh in Essex. It is true that, at the burial of John Sidey, the complainant's late father came to William Sydey, father of John Sidey, about an agreement concerning the return of lands and woods called Miller's Cloose, Swift's Crofte, and Swift's Greene in Halsted [co. Essex], formerly mortgaged by the said John Coggeshall, this complainant's late father, to John Sidey, deceased. This deponent heard John Sydey say that John Coggeshall did borrow of him £100. (Chancery Proceedings, Town Depositions, Bundle 478, Hilary Term, 18 James I [1620/1]. Copy for Sydaie, 14 June 1623.)

*Preserved in the Public Record Office, London.

**See Vol. I of this work, pp. 556–569.

# GENEALOGICAL GLEANINGS IN ENGLAND
## VI

Contributed by G. ANDREWS MORIARTY, JR., A.M., LL.B., of Newport, R. I.,
and communicated by the Committee on English Research

### HUTCHINSON–FREESTONE–RAITHBECK–THEW

IN an article entitled "Freestone–Raithbeck–Thew," which the
Committee on English Research communicated a few years ago to
the REGISTER in two instalments (vol. 72, pp. 51–63, and vol. 74,
pp. 140–146), the present writer submitted records and pedigrees *
which confirmed and supplemented what he had previously published
(*Essex Institute Historical Collections*, vol. 48, pp. 265–268) about
the English ancestry and connections of Frances, Ann, and Elizabeth Freestone, who were daughters of Richard Freestone of Horncastle, co. Lincoln, and kinswomen (first cousins once removed) of
William Hutchinson of Boston and of Portsmouth, R. I., the husband of the famous Anne (Marbury) Hutchinson, their father's
mother, Mary (Hutchinson) Freestone, being a sister of Edward
Hutchinson of Alford, co. Lincoln, who was the father of William
Hutchinson of New England. These three Freestone sisters came
to New England, where Frances became the wife of Valentine Hill,
a Boston merchant, and Elizabeth married Robert Turner of Boston,
the ancestor of a well-known Salem family. The records given below furnish further information about various members of this
group of connected Lincolnshire families which formed the subject
of the writer's previous article in the REGISTER, and supply also
certain items relating to the Hutchinsons; and the conclusions that
may be drawn from them are set forth at the end of the article in a
note by the contributor.

### FROM PROBATE RECORDS

The Will of CHRISTOPHER HUTCHINSON, clarke, parson of the south part
of Leasingham [co. Lincoln], dated 18 November 1554. To be buried in the

*See Vol. I of this work, pp. 510-522 and pp. 588-594.

chancel of Leasingham. To the poor of Leasingham and Scremby. To my brother William Hutchinson and his wife and children. To my brother John Hutchinson my best gown and my am[b]ling nag, and to his children and to my sister Margaret, his wife. To my sister Alice Remyngton. To Nicholas Hornell and his sisters Helene and Elizabeth. To Sir Robert Halydaye. To various servants. To "Sir Alexander yf he tary in seruyce at Lessingham [sic] either with me or with my brother parson of Leasingham a brown blewe gown and a new testament in Lattyn and Inglyshe." To Robert Martyn. To Sir William Saundersonn, parson of Willoughbye, my "latynn byble." To Sir Robert Bartonn, parson of Quaryngton [a book (?)]. To Sir John Pechell, chaplain to Mres Wymbyshe [books (?)]. To Margaret Brown. To Agnes Neylsonn. To John Haye. To Richard Crowder. To Margarete Huchynsonn, daughter of [my] brother Thomas. Executor and residuary legatee: my brother John Huchynsonn. Supervisor: George Chippingdale. Proved 8 July 1556. (Consistory Court of Lincoln, 1557, book 4, fo. 73.)

The Will of RICHARD FREESTON of Horncastle [co. Lincoln], woolen draper, dated 28 December 1627. To my three sons, at the age of twenty-one, namely, to Robert, the eldest, £200, to Samuel £120, and to George £80. To my daughters Susan and Frances, both under twenty-one years of age, £100 each. To my daughters Marie, Ann, Elizabeth, and Faith £80 each, at the age of twenty-one. Executors: my father-in-law, Robert Freiston of Thimolby [sic, ? Thimbleby], and my uncle, Mr. Edward Hutchinson of Alford. Supervisors: my brother-in-law John Broxholme and my cousin Robert Hutchinson of Horncastle. Proved 17 January 1627 [1627/8]. (Consistory Court of Lincoln, 1627, fo. 571d.)

The Will of ROBERT FREISTON of Thimelbye [sic, ? Thimbleby, co. Lincoln], doctor of physick, dated 24 September 1638. To be buried in Horncastle church. To my eldest son, Robert Freeston, at the age of twenty-one, my manor house. To my wife Mary. Lands in Thimelby [sic], Horncastle, and elsewhere in Lincoln are to be sold to pay my debts and for payment of other portions that I have in my hands of my brother Frestone's children and to pay the portions of William Hill and for portions for the rest of my children, Thomas, Matthew, and Frances. Executrix: my wife Mary. Proved 12 November 1638. (Consistory Court of Lincoln, 1638, fo. 358.)

FROM THE PARISH REGISTERS OF ALFORD, CO. LINCOLN*

1541   John son of George Freeston buried 31 January [1541/2].
1543   Margaret daughter of George Freeston buried 30 March.
1543   Robert son of George Freeston buried 17 December.
1563   Elena daughter of Richard Dickson baptized 24 March [1563/4].
1567   Dorcas daughter of Richard Dickson baptized 17 January [1567/8].
1570   Anna daughter of Richard Dickson baptized 8 April.

FROM LAY SUBSIDIES FOR CO. LINCOLN†

14-15 Henry VIII [1522-1524] (136/310).

Ashby Puerorum.       John Becke in wages 20s. [tax] 4d.
                       Richard Freestone in wages 20s. [tax] 4d.
                       Robert Freestone in goods [valuation] £10 [tax] 12d.

*Printed in *The Publications of the Lincoln Record Society, Parish Register Section*, vol. 5.
†Preserved in the Public Record Office, London.

| Salmonby. | John Freestone in goods [valuation] £4 [tax] 2d.<br>John Freestone in wages 20s. [tax] 4d.<br>William Freestone in wages 20s. [tax] 4d. |

34 Henry VIII [1542–43] (137/380).

| Horncastle. | Thomas Rathbecke in goods [valuation] £20 [tax] 13s. 4d. |

34–35 Henry VIII [1542–1544] (137/397).

| Horncastle. | Thomas Rathbecke in goods [valuation] £24 [tax] 6s. |

35 Henry VIII [1543–1544] (137/373).

| Ashby Puerorum. | Robert Becke in goods [valuation] £6 [tax] 2s. 2d.<br>Agnes Thewe in goods [valuation] £20 [tax] 13s. 4d.<br>Edmund Thewe in goods [valuation] £4 [tax] 8d.<br>William Thewe in goods [valuation] £20 [tax] 13s. 4d. |
| Brinkhill. | Richard Freestone in goods [valuation] £4 [tax] 6d.<br>William Freestone in goods [valuation] £6 [tax] 10d. |
| Salmonby. | Robert Freestone in goods [valuation] £10 [tax] 4d.<br>William Thewe in goods [valuation] £24 [tax] 16s.<br>William Thewe, Jr., in goods [valuation] £12 [tax] 8s. 8d. |

35 Henry VIII [1543–44] (137/400).

| Ashby Puerorum. | Robert Becke in goods [valuation] £7 [tax] 1s. 1d.<br>Edmund Thewe in goods [valuation] £4 [tax] 4d.<br>John Weyght in goods [valuation] £5 [tax] 10d.<br>Robert Weyght in goods [valuation] 20s. [tax] 1d. |
| Brinkhill. | Richard Freestone in goods [valuation] £4 [tax] 4d.<br>William Freestone in goods [valuation] £6 [tax] 12d. |
| Salmonby. | Robert Freestone in goods [valuation] £10 [tax] 2s. |

## From Chancery Proceedings*

[Circa 1600.] To Sir Thomas Edgerton, Lord Chancellor.

The complaint of WILLIAM HUTCHINSON of Louth [co. Lincoln], yeoman, son and heir of Christopher Hutchinson, late of Mablethorpe [co. Lincoln], yeoman, against Ann Madyson, sometime the wife of Christopher Hutchinson, who by "some indirect way hath gotten into her hands" the lands which his father had held in Mablethorpe. Sworn in June 1600.

The answer of ANN MADISON, late wife of Christopher Hutchinson, states that the said Christopher was seised in his life by an indenture deed dated

*Preserved in the Public Record Office, London.

83

4 September, 25 Elizabeth [1583], and that, being so seised, he enfeoffed John Neale and Richard Wilson of said Mablethorpe of the lands in question, then or later in the occupation of Thomas Hutchinson, to the use of Christopher Hutchinson and the defendant and the heirs of the body of the said Christopher and, in default of such, to the right heirs of said Christopher. The defendant hath in her possession a deed of feoffment dated 20 May, 23 Elizabeth [1581], whereby the said Christopher purchased the said lands of Thomas Hutchinson, his brother. (Chancery Proceedings, Elizabeth.)

## FROM THE RECORDS OF THE COURT OF REQUESTS*

[*Circa* 1602.] ROBERT HUTCHINSON complains of Edward Hutchinson and Thomas Hutchinson regarding the lands of Christopher Hutchinson situated in Lincoln City, Mablethorpe, and Theddlethorpe [co. Lincoln]. Complainant states that the said Christopher made his will 31 August 1592, and left the lands to his wife Ann and to two daughters and to his eldest son, when of age. The daughters, Mary and Frances, were under age. In this will he bequeathed to his sons Robert and Christopher Hutchinson, and made his brother, Thomas Hutchinson of Louth, and Edward Hutchinson of Alford, mercer, his executors. The supervisors were Mr. Thomas Copledike, Esq., and John Neale of Horncastle, tanner.

The answer of THOMAS HUTCHINSON mentions Robert Freston.

Richard Rose of Lincoln, glover, testifies, 2 September, 44 Elizabeth [1602], that he was a tenant of Christopher Hutchinson, deceased, on his lands in St. Botolph's Parish, Lincoln. At this time William Hutchinson of Remington, aged 35 years, deposed, as did also Arthur Hutchinson of Beesby, aged 50 years. (Court of Requests, Elizabeth, B. 33/7.)

## FROM THE RECORDS OF THE COURT OF STAR CHAMBER*

[*Circa* 1612.] ROBERT FREESTON of Thymblebye [*sic*, ? Thimbleby, co. Lincoln], gentleman, complains that he is seised in his demesne as of fee of lands and meadows in the manor of Thymblebye [*sic*], in the town of Thymbleby [*sic*], which is a champaign town having small store of pastures. Your subject has a private family, and, wanting sufficient pasture for his milch kine and dairy and for his horses and draught cattle, about two years since he inclosed his own freehold, six acres of meadow only, for feeding his milch kine, geldings, and draught horses, and had the same ditched and hedged and set with thorses [?], quickset, and willows, and other wood. But now, may it please your good Lordship, divers inhabitants of Horncastle, of seditious, factious, and turbulent spirit, apt to raise tumult and rebellion and to disturb the quiet and settled state and peace of the majority of the whole kingdom and to revive the like late-quieted uproars, and desirous to blow the coals of the new kindlings of the like or a greater fire, pretend that Horncastle town, which is a neighboring one having a small piece of field, mostly inclosed, and next the field of Thymbleby [*sic*] — having combined and drawn together the common and poor people not only of Horncastle but of divers other towns, have appointed divers conventicles and mutinous meetings secretly in the nighttime to raise companies and to cast down your subject's close, and your subject fears this is but the color and pretence for greater and more dangerous mischief. Now Edward Harrin, George Shotten [?], Gilbert Midel, William Taylor, John Hammerton, Robert Hammerton, Robert Taylor, Frances [*sic*] Taylor, Thomas Taylor, Henry Kinge, and George Taylor, all of Horncastle, and persons to your orator unknown, by the advice of one Richard Enderby, gentleman, an attorney at the common law and high steward of Horncastle, riotously and unlawfully, on 12 April, 10 James I [1612], in the nighttime, met and as-

*Preserved in the Public Record Office, London.

sembled, armed with spades, shovels, pickaxes, and other like tools, and in such warlike manner marched from Horncastle to the close in Thimbleby, and riotously and wickedly, under the advice of the said Richard Enderby, "raised down" the hedges and ditches of your said subject, and, not yet herewith satisfied, they riotously and wickedly, being in warlike manner weaponed and armed and arrayed with swords, rapiers, daggers, long pikes, staves, pistols, and other weapons, as well offensive as defensive, did gather together the whole herdship of Horncastle's cattle, in the number of five hundred, and did with great noise, shouts, and cries drive the said cattle to the said close of your subject, and did beat and wound one Edward Lawson and Thomas Cruste, your subject's servants, being in God's peace and without any weapon, and threatened to kill them and to put the said cattle and herdship in the said close, saying that they were there to do it and would do it, and kept them there to eat up the grass of your poor subject. And now, on 13 April, your poor subject, having notice thereof, came down to drive the said cattle out of there to the pound for trial of the title, but then the said Harrin, Shotten [?], Kinge, and others, being riotously guarding the cattle there, assaulted your subject and threatened to beat and kill him and his men, and threatened him how he should not live a year after making the said inclosure, and, further, the said persons, by the advice of the said Richard Enderby, have combined to continue it and have raised money for his [sic] maintenance. Prays for a writ of commitment against them and that they appear and answer in the premises. Sworn 24 June, 10 James I [1612]. (Court of Star Chamber, James I, B. 445/20.)

[Christopher Hutchinson, the testator of 18 Nov. 1554, was a brother of John Hutchinson, mayor of Lincoln, Eng., who was the common ancestor of the Boston (Mass.) Hutchinsons and of the Earls of Donoughmore. William Hutchinson of Boston and Portsmouth, R. I., was a grandson of John Hutchinson, mayor of Lincoln. Christopher Hutchinson took his degree of Bachelor of Arts at the University of Cambridge in 1509/10, and was probably rector of Scremby, co. Lincoln, in 1526 and rector of Leasingham, in the same county, in 1535. His will has often been referred to but has never hitherto been printed. (Cf. Venn, Alumni Cantabrigienses, part 1, vol. 2, p. 439, and REGISTER, vol. 20, p. 356.)

William Hutchinson of Louth, co. Lincoln, the complainant in the Chancery case given above, was the eldest son of Christopher Hutchinson of Mablethorpe, co. Lincoln, and a grandson of William Hutchinson, who was a brother of Rev. Christopher and of John, the mayor of Lincoln, and was himself elected mayor of Lincoln in Sept. 1552. (Cf. REGISTER, vol. 20, p. 356.) This William Hutchinson of Louth is mentioned in the will of his father (REGISTER, vol. 51, p. 120, and Waters's Genealogical Gleanings in England, vol. 2, pp. 1261–1262). The will of his grandfather, William, mayor of Lincoln, has also been printed (REGISTER, vol. 51, pp. 118–119, and Waters's Gleanings, vol. 2, p. 1260). Strangely enough, William Hutchinson of Louth is entirely omitted in the Hutchinson pedigree given in "Lincolnshire Pedigrees" (Publications of the Harleian Society, vol. 51, p. 536). For this Hutchinson family of Lincolnshire, to which William Hutchinson of Boston and Portsmouth, R. I., belonged, the genealogy compiled by the late Col. Joseph Lemuel Chester and published in the REGISTER, vol. 20, pp. 355 et seq., still stands unshaken; but unfortunately the same statement cannot be made of Colonel Chester's pedigree of the Hutchinsons of Salem, Mass., which breaks down at Richard Hutchinson, the immigrant.

Robert Hutchinson, the complainant in the case before the Court of Requests, was a brother of William Hutchinson of Louth; and Edward Hutchinson of Alford, mercer, was the father of William of New England. Arthur Hutchinson of Beesby was apparently a son of John, the mayor of Lincoln (cf. REGISTER, vol. 20, p. 358, and Lincolnshire Pedigrees, ut supra, p. 535).

Passing now to the Freestone family, the subsidy entries given above tend to confirm the supposition made in the REGISTER, vol. 74, p. 141, that Richard * Frestonne of Brinkhill (No. 2 of the pedigree) was a son of Richard Freston of

*See Vol. I of this work, p. 589.

85

Ashby Puerorum (No. 1 of the pedigree). The subsidy of 1522–1524 shows both a Richard Freestone and a Robert Freestone at Ashby Puerorum. The will of Richard Freston of Ashby Puerorum, dated 16 Feb. 1533/4 (REGISTER, vol. 72, pp. 51–52), is evidently that of a young man, as his children are all * under the age of fourteen. The Richard Freestone of the subsidy of 1522–1524 is also a young man, as he is taxed on his wages, while the Robert Freestone of the same subsidy is clearly an older man. The first Richard Freston (No. 1) of the pedigree was, therefore, undoubtedly the father of Richard of Brinkhill (No. 2 of the pedigree), and the Robert Freestone of Ashby Puerorum who appears in the subsidy of 1522–1524 was undoubtedly the father of Richard of Ashby and the grandfather of Richard of Brinkhill. Richard of Ashby had at least three sons, namely, Richard of Brinkhill, Thomas, and Robert of Brink- * hill, the testator of 11 Feb. 1566/7 (REGISTER, vol. 72, p. 53). Robert of Ashby, * the grandfather of the three men last-mentioned, probably had, besides Richard, their father, a son George, who settled in Alford, whose children appear among the early entries in the Alford parish registers, and also a son John, of Brink- * hill, the testator of 14 Feb. 1548/9 (REGISTER, vol. 72, p. 52). It should be * noted that Richard of Brinkhill (No. 2 of the pedigree) appears to have named his son George for his (Richard's) uncle, George of Alford. It is, therefore, probable that Richard of Brinkhill (No. 2) was born about 1521, and that his daughter Anne, who married about 1563 Richard Dixon or Dickson of Alford, was born about 1545 (cf. the Dickson entries in the parish registers of Alford, given above). Richard of Ashby Puerorum (No. 1 of the pedigree) was probably born about 1497, and his father, Robert of Ashby Puerorum, was probably born about 1465. Thus it is possible to trace this family, with a fair degree of certainty, back almost to the middle of the fifteenth century.

Richard Freeston of Horncastle, woolen draper, the testator of 28 Dec. 1627, was the father of the three sisters, Frances, Ann, and Elizabeth Freestone, who emigrated to New England; and Robert Freiston of Thimbleby, the testator of 24 Sept. 1638 and the complainant in the Star Chamber case given above, was the uncle of these three young women, but it should be noted that he was not a brother of their father, Richard Freeston, but of their mother, Margery Freeston, their father having married his first cousin. This Robert Freiston or Freeston was admitted a fellow commoner at Emmanuel College, Cambridge, in 1608, was B.A., 1609/10, M.A., 1613 (?), and M.D., 1628, and evidently acquired the manor of Thimbleby (cf. Venn, Alumni Cantabrigienses, part 1, vol. 2, p. 180, and REGISTER, vol. 74, p. 142, where he is No. 4, i, of the pedigree).] *

*For pp. 51, 52, 53 & 142 see Vol. I of this work, pp. 510, 511. 512 & 590.

# GENEALOGICAL GLEANINGS IN ENGLAND
## VII

Contributed by G. Andrews Moriarty, Jr., A.M., LL.B., of Newport, R. I., and communicated by the Committee on English Research

### HATHORNE

To the REGISTER, vol. 67, pp. 248–260 (July 1913), the Committee* on English Research communicated records and a pedigree that disclosed four generations of the ancestry of Maj. William Hathorne of Salem, Mass., and his brother John Hathorne (who also settled in Massachusetts), whose parentage had been proved by the late Henry FitzGilbert Waters in the REGISTER, vol. 38, pp. 201–204 (April 1884). The records given below furnish additional information about various members of this English family and other families allied with it. From Maj. William Hathorne of Salem, some of whose ancestors appear in these records, Nathaniel Hawthorne, the novelist, was descended.

### FROM PROBATE RECORDS

THOMAS HATHORNE was named as an overseer in the will of Thomas Martyn, 1548, and was a witness to the will of John Bishop of East Oakley in the parish of Bray, co. Berks, 20 May 1551. (Archdeaconry of Berks [Somerset House]).

[This Thomas Hathorne was the great-great-grandfather of Maj. William Hathorne of Salem, Mass., and is given as No. 1 in the pedigree in the REGISTER, vol. 67, p. 255.]

The Will of JAMES BISHOP of Bray [co. Berks], carpenter, dated 14 March, 13 Elizabeth [1570/1]. To my brothers Robert Bishop and Robert Bishop the Younger. To my brother-in-law Humphrey Smith. To my elder brother's children. To my mother, Elizabeth Hathorne, who is to be executrix. Overseer: Robert Winch of Bray. Proved 29 October 1572. (Archdeaconry of Berks [Somerset House], Register F, fo. 334.)

[Elizabeth Hathorne, the mother of this testator, was probably the widow of Robert Hathorne (1, iii, of the pedigree in the REGISTER), an abstract of whose will is given in the REGISTER, vol. 67, pp. 248–249. Before her marriage to Robert Hathorne she must have married ——— Bishop.]

The Will of JOSEPH MERIE of East Oakley in the parish of Bray [co. Berks], dated 15 September, 23 Elizabeth [1581]. To my son Christopher Merie one-third of my goods and chattels, excepting a lease held of Mr. Gurmonde and his wife, which I give to my wife for life, and on her death it is to revert to the said Christopher. To the son of William Hathorne. To Robert and Margaret Merie. To Thomas, the son of John Hathorne. To Jane Ollyn, my servant. To William, Thomas, and Jane Hathorne, children of William Hathorne. Overseers: John and William Hathorne. Witnesses: John Hathorne the Elder and William Hathorne the Elder. Proved 5 January 1581/2. (Archdeaconry of Berks [Somerset House], Register G, fo. 304.

The Will of JOHN TAYLOR of Wargrave [co. Berks], gentleman, dated 17 November 1643. To the churches of Binfield and Wargrave. To my brother Austin Taylor, my godson John Taylor, my son Hugh Taylor, and

*See Vol. I of this work, pp. 267-279.

the children of my brother Austin Taylor. My son-in-law Stephen Squibb and his wife. To my godson Stephen Squibb and my son Captain Squibb. To my cousin Mr. Humphrey Broughton and his children. To my daughter Mrs. Mary Davison. To Arthur Squibb's children. To my brother-in-law Francis Webb. To my sister Rebecca and her son Francis and her daughters Jane, Susan, and Rebecca. My late uncle Thomas Taylor and his sons and daughters. To Elizabeth, the daughter of my brother Henry, deceased. To the two daughters of my late sister Ford. To my cousin Lane, widow, to my cousins Mr. Henry Jennens and Mrs. Anne Browne. To my kinsmen William Holloway and Nathaniel Hathorne, gentleman, and to my brother-in-law Francis Webb. To the poor of Binfield, Warfield, Easthampstead, Wokingham, Finchampstead, Barkham, Arborfield, Hurst, Wargrave, Ruscombe, and Lawrence Waltham. [No record of probate.] (P. C. C., Twisse, 155.)

[Nathaniel Hathorne, gentleman, kinsman of this testator, was Nathaniel Hathorne of Cookham, co. Berks (3, iii, of the pedigree in the REGISTER), an abstract of whose will is given in the REGISTER, vol. 67, pp. 251–252. He was ** the complainant in the Chancery suit of 1630 and in the suit before the Court of Requests in 1638 and one of the defendants in the Star Chamber case in 1619 (vide infra).]

The Will of RICHARD HATHORNE of Lawrence Waltham [co. Berks], yeoman, dated 24 October 1644. To my eldest son, Richard Hathorne, at the age of thirty years, my lands in Bray. To my two grandsons, Thomas and Robert, and my three daughters, Jone, Marie, and Elizabeth. Testator mentions lands in Bray, bought of William Hathorne. Overseers: Thomas Foote, alderman of London, Thomas Wilkinson, minister, and Mark Theabridge of Lawrence Waltham. Proved 15 January 1644/5. (P. C. C., Rivers, 23.)

### FROM LAY SUBSIDIES FOR CO. BERKS*

15 Henry VIII [1523–24].
Binfield.                     Robert Hothorne in goods [tax] 4s.

### FROM CHANCERY PROCEEDINGS*

[Prior to the divorce of Catherine of Aragon, first wife of King Henry VIII, in 1533.] ROBERT BROOKE, Esq., complains that he is seised of fee of a messuage, mills, 100 [? 102] acres of land, 40 acres of meadow, 46 acres of wood, and £3 rent in Binfield, co. Berks, held of Katherine, Queen of England, as of her manor of Cookham, co. Berks. One John Horthorne of Horthorne, co. Berks, intending by craft to disinherit complainant, has of late sued a writ of right close out of the Chancery, directed to the Queen's bailiff of Cookham Manor, against the complainant. One Richard Ward of Berks, Esq., John Norres, and one Stafferton are the maintainers, bearers, and procurers of the matter against the complainant, and give money to John Horthorne to maintain the suit, so that, if Horthorne happen to recover the premises, they may have them for little money. Stafferton, the special maintainer of the matter, has married one of the daughters of Sir Richard Weston, Knight, the Queen's steward of Cookham Manor. By such unlawful maintenance and because the complainant has no acquaintance nor allies in those parts where the lands lie, being a stranger not wont to reside there, the complainant is like to be disinherited. Prays for a writ of subpœna against Horthorne and an injunction for him to cease pursuing his action against the complainant. (Early Chancery Proceedings, 607/48.)

[John Horthorne or Hathorne, the defendant in this Chancery case, was evidently of Hawthorn Hill, on the border of the parishes of Warfield and Bray,

*Preserved in the Public Record Office, London.

**See Vol. I of this work, pp. 270–271.

co. Berks, and it is very likely that he was the progenitor of the Hathornes of both of those parishes. Possibly he was the father of Thomas and Robert Hathorne of Bray, who appear in the subsidy of 1523–24 (REGISTER, vol. 67, p. 254), for this Thomas (No. 1 of the pedigree in the REGISTER) held lands at Crychefeld, in the southern part of Bray, in 1535, a place that was contiguous to Hawthorn Hill in Warfield (*ib.*, p. 255).]

23 October 1605.  To Lord Chancellor Ellesmere.

THOMAS HATHORNE of Bray [co. Berks], yeoman, and JOHN FERMORE of Warfield [co. Berks], yeoman, complain that the said Thomas Hathorne, being possessed in or about 40 Elizabeth [1597–98] of four score ewes and twenty lambs, committed the same to the said John Fermore, for the good opinion he had of him, to sell them for the said Hathorne.  As the said John was driving them to London, he lay at Bedfount [Bedfont] in Middlesex, and, meeting one William Pitts of Bedfount, yeoman, there, he sold him the sheep for £25, and it was agreed that the said Pitts should pay Thomas Hathorne.  The said Pitts hath refused to pay either of them, although often in a friendly manner requested to do so.  The complainant is lacking evidences of writing and witnesses of the sale, and prays for a writ of subpœna against Pitts.  (Chancery Proceedings, James I, Series 2, 274/94.)

[The Thomas Hathorne of this case is apparently the Thomas who appears as 2, iii, of the pedigree in the REGISTER (vol. 67, p. 256), a son of Thomas and Jone Hathorne.]

14 April 1630.  To the Lord Chancellor Coventry.

NATHANIEL HATHORNE of Cookham, co. Berks, gentleman, complains that John Fitz James of South Broham [South Brewham] in Somerset, Esq., about the day of this instant and previously by himself and his agents, sold to the orator the manor of South Broham, and induced the orator to purchase by himself and by Sir Robert Grey, Knight, James Fitz James, gentleman, and Robert Woodford, gentleman, who represented that the said John Fitz James was seised of the said manor, and your orator agreed to pay the sum of £2500 on conveyance and £1500, the residue of the price, on a day fixed, and your orator paid £50 at once, to bind the bargain; but the premises were encumbered with leases and mortgages, judgments, and other encumbrances put thereon by the said John Fitz James or his father John Fitz James or his aunt or others, and they now deny any evidence of the same.  Moreover, one William Symes hath a lease of a great part thereof, and it is made back to John Fitz James, and they together have conveyed away the evidences thereof.

The answer of SIR ROBERT GREY, Knight, 3 May 1630, denies the agreement to sell the manor of South Broham in the parish of Charlton Musgrove to the orator.  (Chancery Proceedings, Charles I, Series 2, 404/117.)

FROM THE RECORDS OF THE COURT OF REQUESTS*

[1638.]  NATHANIEL HAUTHORNE of Cookham, co. Berks, gentleman, complains that, whereas your subject was seised in his demesne as of fee in the manor of South Brewham, co. Somerset, with its members and appurtenances, and, moreover, there be divers tenements of freehold within the said manor, and one Saunders was seised of a tenement to him and his heirs in the said manor, of the value of £16, and he died without heirs of the body or otherwise, and the said tenement by right came back to the lord of the manor, and no heir has claimed the said tenement, although there have been many courts since that time, the last court being held 28 December 1637, now, in or about July 1637, John Fitz James, Esq., the lord of the manor of South Brewham, and his agent had many communications

*Preserved in the Public Record Office, London.
**For pp. 254 & 256 see Vol. I of this work, pp. 273 & 275.

and treaties for encouraging your subject to the buying of the said manor, and, for the better inducing him thereto, the said John Fitz James and his agent alleged that the said tenement had escheated and fallen to the said Fitz James, and did thereupon draw your said subject to a higher and greater value than otherwise he would have given, and, an agreement being made between them, on or about Michaelmas last, to buy and sell and to convey the said manor to the complainant and his heirs, the complainant had thereupon livery of seisin made unto him, as is his right. But now one Robert Matthews of ———, within the Isle of Wight, in the county of Southampton, gentleman, and Edward Curle of ———, gentleman, have since Saunders' death entered into the said tenement and kept your subject out of possession, sometimes pretending that they or one of them is heir of the said Saunders at the common law, and at others they pretend some conveyance or assurance from the said Saunders; but they are not his heirs and they have no such assurance from him, and, if any such there be, the same is contrived, as your subject hopeth to prove, to defeat him of his inheritance, as they have never come to any of the courts held for the same manor or to lay claim to the same, nor have they produced the conveyances; and they, with persons unknown, have contrived among themselves divers fraudulent and secret estates, so that your subject does not know against whom to bring his action at the common law; and, about March last past, one Saunders entered the tenement and pretended himself heir of the deceased Saunders, which he is not, nor is he of the kindred or blood of the said Saunders; and these three, to wit, Matthews, Curle and Saunders, have contrived a secret feoffment, and they have gotten into their hands some of your subject's charters and evidences, with the proofs of the tenure and that it is held of the manor of South Brewham, so that he is disabled to take his course at the common law. Prays that the defendants answer on their oaths their claims and demands, and that they disclose what conveyances and assurances they have contrived and made, and prays for a writ of Privy Seal directed to them.

The defendants in reply demur that the bill is insufficient, and that complainant was not lord of the manor until about December last. Demurrer dated 13 July, 14 Charles I [1638]. (Court of Requests, uncalendared, Charles I, B. 630, part 2.)

### From the Records of the Court of Star Chamber*

8 June, 17 James I [1619]. RICHARD WINCH of Reading [co. Berks], clothier, guardian of William, Richard, John, George, Joane, and Judith Winch, children of Joane Winch, late of Bray [co. Berks], widow, complains that the said Joan was possessed of corn, grain, wheat, rye, barley, pease, vetches, beans, and oats, part growing on the land in occupation of the said Joan and part in barns, houses, and rooks of the said Joan, to the value of £500 at least, and of horses, kine, oxen, sheep, swine, and other beasts and cattle, worth £300, and plate, rings, jewels, brass, pewter, bed linen, and other household stuff, worth £200, and ploughs, carts, harrows, harness, and other husbandry tools, worth £100, and £500 ready money, and obligations, bills, etc., to the value of £500, being in all £2100. The said Joan, about June last past, fell sick, and sent for William Hawthorne of Binfield in Berks, yeoman, and Nathaniel Hathorne of Cookham, yeoman, to confer about her will. She desired William Winch, her eldest son, to be her sole executor. They begged her to bestow upon William and Nathaniel Hathorne £10 apiece, which she refused, and declared that her personal estate should go to her children, saving only some small legacies to the children of Robert Winch, her late husband, then deceased, and some small trifles to the poor.

*Preserved in the Public Record Office, London.

90

But, the said Joan being extremely sick and past all hope of recovery and very weak in her understanding, they combined to obtain the great part of her chattles and defraud the said children. Accordingly they got her to name them as her executors, and William Hathorne wrote the will and gave some legacies to the children, amounting to not half of the personal estate or very little more, and the residue of £1000 she, on 27 February 1618 (i. e., 16 James), bequeathed to William and Nathaniel Hawthorne, and they corruptly inserted this into her will without her direction: "all the rest and residue unbequeathed I give unto William and Nathaniel Hawthorne my brothers." And the said Joan died that day or the next, and they have proved the fraudulent will and claim £1000 worth of the goods of Joan. This complainant already hath a suit in the spiritual court, [and] before the officials of the county proved that the said clause was inserted without her knowledge or consent and that her intent was for the children to have all. These children are poor orphans, without father or mother. Prays for a writ of subpœna against the defendants.

The answers of NATHANIEL and WILLIAM HATHORNE. They answer severally.

NATHANIEL HAWTHORNE says that Joan Winch was possessed of goods amounting to £1093. 1s. 4d., as per an inventory made up by three indifferent appraisers. The said Joan fell grieviously ill in January last past and sent for them to confer about her will. She spake about her eldest son William Winch, and was told that, if he should be executor, being under age, he would have to prove by a guardian. She then entreated these defendants to be her executors and to write her will. The said Joan, after legacies of £10 apiece to each of her six children, gave other legacies to the amount of £923, and on 28 February 1618 William Hathorne wrote the will. The residue she gave to Nathaniel and William Hathorne, and made them her executors. The will was proved by witnesses. These said witnesses were sent for to her house in Bray. They found her very sick and lying in her bed in the upper chamber, and openly and distinctly they read her the will; and, on being asked by William Hathorne if her will was as it was written, she said that it was; and, being asked if she would set her hand and seal, she sat up in bed and set her mark, which was laid upon a trencher, and she took of the seal which was set in the will and delivered it to William Hathorne and Nathaniel Hathorne. She was in perfect mind, for she spake sensibly and well and knew those that were then there. And she, being requested by one of these witnesses to remember one Elizabeth Slye, her servant, she presently answered that she, the said Joane Winch, was to pay for her £20, for a legacy given her by her grandfather, which Robert Winch, her husband (if he had lived) should have paid to the said Elizabeth, and she told her executors to pay the same. This was after she signed the will, and the next day, at night, the said Joan died. Afterwards William Hathorne (by reason of the troubles that he saw and thought would ensue) renounced the will in court before the official of the diocese of Sarum, and then Nathaniel did try to prove the will, and he believes this will to be her true one.

WILLIAM HATHORNE acknowledges that by reason of his love and good will to his sister's children, but not by reason of any speeches used by the said Joan, he had no meaning to make any gain out of his sister's goods; and the defendants say there was a suit against them in the spiritual court of Berks, but Nathaniel for just reasons hath appealed into the Court of the Arches. They deny that the estate amounted to £2000, and that all the legacies were given to the children, [and] also that she refused to give these defendants £10 apiece. They acknowledge the gift to the children of Robert Winch and to the poor of Bray, but deny that Joan was weak in her understanding; and they did not combine or practise to obtain her property. They deny that the suit in the spiritual court of this complainant has sufficiently proved that this clause was inserted without any directions from Joan or that she did not intend them to have the residue. But true it is that this complainant hath obtained a sentence to that effect against Nathaniel Hathorne in the spiritual court. (Court of Star Chamber, James I, 293/16.)

[The William Hathorne of this case is the father of Maj. William Hathorne of Salem, Mass.; and Nathaniel Hathorne is Nathaniel of Cookham, co. Berks, later styled "gentleman," the uncle of the New England settlers. Nathaniel was afterwards lord of the manor of South Brewham, co. Somerset (*vide supra*), and appears to have been at the time of the emigration the great man of the family, whose name was handed down among his American kinsmen. This case proves that Joane (Hathorne) Winch (3, i, of the pedigree in the REGISTER), sister of William and Nathaniel Hathorne, died on 27 or 28 February 1618/19, that she had a son William (her eldest son), besides the five children named in the pedigree in the REGISTER, that her husband, then deceased, had been married before his marriage to Joane Hathorne, and that children by her husband's former wife were living in February 1618/19. Cf. pedigree in the REGISTER, vol. 67, pp. 256–260.] *

## RYDER

THE following certificate, the original of which is preserved among uncalendared deeds in the public library at Northampton, England, shows that Samuel Ryder, Sr., and his son, Samuel Ryder, Jr., had lived together in the towns of Plymouth and Yarmouth, in the Plymouth Colony, for some thirty years prior to 3 Dec. 1662, and that Samuel Ryder, Sr., had previously lived at Northampton, England. Cf. Savage, "Genealogical Dictionary," vol. 3, p. 540, vol. 4, p. 697, and Pope, "Pioneers of Massachusetts," p. 385.

These may Certify all whom it may Concerne That Samuell Ryder Junio[r] the bearer heerof, is the Reputed sonne of Samuell Ryder seno[r]; which said Samuell Ryder seni[r] sometimes lived in the Towne of Northampton in the Countey of Northampton in the Parish of Alhallowes in old England, and the said Samuell Ryder Juni[r]: hath lived with his said father in the Township of Yarmouth in the Jurisdiction of Plymouth in new England in America and in the Towne of Plymouth in the aforesaid Jurisdiction the space of thirty yeares or thereaboutes in witnes to the truth of this Certifycate and Testimony wee have affixed the seale of our Gou[r]ment of Plymouth aforsaid third day of December Ann[o] Dom' one Thousand six hundred sixty and two: 1662

| [Seal, at the left | [Signed] W[m] Collier Deputie |
| of the lower part | Tho: Southworth Assistant |
| of the certificate.] | By us in the Absence |
| | of the Gouernor |

*See Vol. I of this work, pp. 275-279.

# GENEALOGICAL RESEARCH IN ENGLAND

Contributed by G. ANDREWS MORIARTY, JR., A.M., LL.B., of Newport, R. I.,
and communicated by the Committee on English Research

## DERBY

It has long been known that Roger Derby, the immigrant ancestor
of the Derby family of Salem, Mass., resided in the parish of Topsham, co. Devon, England, before his migration to New England
(cf. Savage's Genealogical Dictionary, vol. 2, p. 40), for his marriage
in Topsham, 23 Aug. 1668, to Lucretia ————, his arrival in Boston
18 July 1671, and the births of his oldest child in Topsham and of
his other children in Ipswich and Salem, Mass., were entered in the
records of the Essex County (Mass.) Quarterly Court and may now
be found in the printed "Vital Records of Salem," vols. 1 and 3.
In 1886 Dr. Richard H. Derby communicated to the *Essex Institute
Historical Collections*, vol. 23, pp. 229–230, a statement about Roger
Derby, of which the first paragraph reads as follows:

"Roger Derby was born at Topsham in Devonshire, England, in 1643.
He married Lucretia Hilman at Topsham August 23rd 1668; they arrived
at Boston July 18th 1671 with their child Charles and settled first at Ipswich;
they afterwards removed to Salem where she died May 25th 1689. The
above dates are taken from old papers in the possession of the writer of
these brief memoranda."

The statement that the maiden name of Roger Derby's wife was
Hilman seems to be supported by entries in the parish registers of
Topsham which are given below (p. 415). That Roger Derby himself was born at Topsham has not been proved by any English
records thus far discovered. That he was born in 1643 seems to be
an inference from his age (55 years) at death, in 1698.

Dr. Derby went on, in the article cited, to tell of his discovery in
Devonshire, in 1885, of the records of the grant to Roger Darby, in
1671, of letters of administration on the estates of his brother and
sister (*vide infra*, p. 414); and he gave also the baptismal records of
Lucretia Hilman and of Charles Derby, son of Roger and Lucretia,
as he found them in the parish registers of Topsham (*vide infra*,
p. 415). He was not able, however, to throw any light on the ancestry
of Roger Derby.

About ten years ago, therefore, some of the descendants of Roger
Derby engaged Mr. F. J. Pope of London, a fellow of the Royal
Historical Society, to search for the English ancestry and connec-
tions of their immigrant ancestor. His work was supervised by the
late Mrs. Lucy (Derby) Fuller, who had been interested for many
years in her family history, and it resulted in the discovery of records
that disclosed three generations of the paternal ancestors of Roger
Derby and brought to light much interesting information about the
Derby family and the families with which it was allied by marriage.
Through the courtesy of another Derby descendant a copy of Mr.
Pope's reports has been placed, at the request of the Committee on

English Research, in the Library of the New England Historic Genealogical Society, and permission has been given to the Committee to communicate it to the REGISTER. In the present article, therefore, the abstracts of English records made by Mr. Pope have been classified, a few other records have been inserted by the Committee, and the history of this Derby family, from the middle of the sixteenth to the later years of the seventeenth century, as revealed by the evidences cited, has been arranged in the usual genealogical form.

## FROM PROBATE RECORDS

The Will of NICHOLAS HARDIE of Askerswell [co. Dorset], dated 20 January 1552, shows that Sir Robert Darbye, parson, was a debtor to the testator and a witness to the will. Proved in 1573. (P. C. C., Peter, 31.)

The Will of CLEMENT KYCHE of Beaminster, co. Dorset, dated in 1567, mentions a debt of £8. 5s. "for ware" due from Sir Robert Darby, parson of Askerswell [co. Dorset], and appoints Bartilmew Darby of Beaminster an overseer of the will. Proved in 1570. (Court of the Dean of Sarum, book 2, fo. 78.)

The Will of JOHN GREGORIE *alias* WHETCOMBE of Marsh in the parish of Burton [Burton-Bradstock, co. Dorset], dated 2 December 1576, mentions a debt of £11. 14s. 8d. due to the testator from Nicholas Derbie of Sturtle [Sterthill in Burton-Bradstock]. Proved in 1576. (P. C. C., Carew, 39.)

The Will of JOHN WADHAM of Catherston, co. Dorset, gentleman, dated in 1583, refers to a lifehold estate in Bryanspuddle sold by the testator to Nicholas Darby. Proved in 1584. (P. C. C., Watson, 2.)

Administration on the estate of NICHOLAS DERBY of Sturthill, co. Dorset, w as granted 28 April 1600 to his relict Catherine. (P. C. C.)

The Will of CHRISTOPHER DARBYE of Askerswell, co. Dorset, yeoman, dated 14 March 1603. Towards repairs of the church 10s. For the poor of Askerswell £10. To the children of Arthur Fowkes the Elder of Symesburye [Symondsbury] a bond for £116. To the children of John Peason of Lelington [Lillington], co. Dorset, yeoman, £100. Residuary legatees: "my two daughters," Jone Fowkes and Jone Peason. Proved in 1604. (P. C. C., Harte, 52.)

Administration on the estate of NICHOLAS DERBYE of Sturthill, co. Dorset, w as granted 11 February 1606 to his son Christopher. (P. C. C.)

Administration on the estate of HENRY DARBY of Affpuddle, co. Dorset, w as granted 24 September 1607 to his relict Joane. (P. C. C.)

The Will of MORGAN HOLMAN of Barwicke in the parish of Swyre, co. Dorset, gentleman, dated 19 June 1614, bequeathed to the testator's son John, etc., the lease of the tithes of certain parcels of land, etc., belonging to the free chapel of St. Luke's and lately purchased by the testator of Nicholas Darbye, Lawrence Darbye, and Roger Darbye. Proved 19 April 1623. (P. C. C., Swann, 33.) [For lengthy extracts from this will see the REGISTER, vol. 72, pp. 186–188.]

The Will of ROGER LEACHLAND of Chard [co. Somerset], merchant, at ed 6 February 1620 [1620/1]. To the poor of Chard 10s. To the church 5s. All my goods are to be equally divided among my wife Margaret, my sons

94

William and Thomas, and my daughters Margaret, Jane, and Alice. Executrix: my wife. Overseer: my brother William Leachland. [Signed] Roger Leachland. Witnesses: William Leachland, Thos. Pitts, scr. Proved 31 October 1621 by the executrix named in the will. (P. C. C., Dale, 83.)

The Will of LAURENCE DERBY of Nether Sturthill [co. Dorset], gentleman, undated. Wife Ann. Son Mathew [to whom nothing is left]. To son Laurence the sum of £100, at the age of twenty years. To daughters [all unmarried], Anne, Catherine, and Elizabeth, £100 each. Brother Nicholas Derby. Brother-in-law William Jacob. Proved in 1624 by the relict, Ann. (P. C. C., Byrde, 82.)

The Will of WILLIAM SYMONS of Exeter, co. Devon, gentleman, dated 20 February, 9 Charles 1 [1633/4]. To be buried near my wife in Exeter Cathedral. To my sister's daughter, Mary Stevens, £5. To my sister's daughter, Alice Gill, £5. To the wife of Henry Thomas of Widworthy £5. To John Hore of Axminster, his son, £6. 13s. 4d. "To Rebecca my daughter for terme of her life the parcell of land called Newlands within the parish of Whittchurch Co. Dorset, purchased from George Wadham, Esq. I also give unto her the house and land in Axminster as it is purchased by copie of Court Rolls, unto her and unto her sister Agnes Derbye for terme of their lives. Item I give and bequeath unto Anthonie Salter my son-in-law, one cuppe covered with silver wayinge twentie ounces and upwards given unto me by my brother Richard Symons. Item I give and bequeath unto Christopher Derbye my son-in-law one salt wayinge twentie ounces and upwards and also two gobletts parcell gilt wayinge eight or nine ounces either of them. One other small goblet the fellowe of that which I gave unto William Derbyes Wife. Also I give unto him fifteen silver spoons with one cruse cupp covered with silver. Item my will is that these parcells of plate following shall remayne in the custodie of Marcella my daughter and executrice and hereafter named, as long as she liveth, that is to say one bason and yeore of silver parcell gilt weighing three score and three ounces or thereabouts, and also two silver potts gylted for beere wayinge twenty ounces each of them or thereabouts, these parcells of plate before mentioned my will is that they shall remayne to the use of Southcott Hewish (after my executrix) and to his assigns forever." To Southcott Hewish, my nephew, a bond of my son Anthony for £312. To my wife's kinswoman, Elizabeth Rockey, £3. To Christopher Sandford, servant to my executrix, 40s. To my godson, William Seaward, 22s. Executrix: my daughter Marsella Herbert. [Signed] William Symondes. Witnesses: John Mayne, James Calthropp, Henry Rowcliffe. Proved 20 February 1634 [1634/5] by the executrix named in the will. (P. C. C., Sadler, 16.)

The Will of HENRY THOMAS of Wydworthie [Widworthy], co. Devon, yeoman, dated 10 December 1644. Son-in-law Thomas Derbie [an overseer of the will]. Grandchildren Ann Derbie and Rebecca Derbie. Proved in 1650. (P. C. C., Pembroke, 101.)

The Will of ANNE DERBY of Sturthill, co. Dorset, widow, dated 6 October 1645.

"In the name of God Amen I anne Derby of Sturthill in the County of Dorset vid: beinge sicke in body but whole and sound in memory thanks be unto Almightie God Doe ordaine and make this my last Will and Testamt in manner and forme followeing vizt. imprimis I give and bequeath my soule into the hands of the Lord God my Creator, hopeinge by the death and passion of Jesus Christ his only sonne my Saviour to obtaine the full remission and pardon of all my sinns and my body to Christian buriall. Item I give and bequeath unto my sonne William Derby Twelve pence. Item I give unto my sonne John Twelve pence. Item I give to the poore of the

95

parish of Shipton five shillings to be distributed by mine Executor. All the rest of my goods Cattles and Chattles corne graine howshould stuffe plough and plough geere and whatsoever els I die possessed of I give and bequeath unto Richard Derby my sonne whom I ordaine and make sole Executor. of this my last Will and Testamt. And I doe hereby intreate my trustie and wel-beloved friends of John Parker of Allington gent and John Tucker of Loader Clarke and Thomas Hallett of Askerswell husbandman to be the Overseers of this my last Will and Testament. In witness whereof I have set my hand and seale Geeven the sixt day of October Anno Dni one thousand sixe hundred forty five. The marke of Ann Derby"

Proved 22 February 1649 by Richard Derby, son of the deceased and the executor named in the will. (P. C. C., Pembroke, 21.)

Administration on the estate of THOMAS DARBY of Axminster, co. Devon, was granted in January 1648 to John Clarke and Ann his wife, late widow of the said Thomas Darby. (P. C. C.)

Administration on the estate of JOHN DARBY of Sturthill, co. Dorset, was granted 7 August 1651 to his sister, Anne Darby, spinster. (P. C. C.)

The Will of MARGARET LEACHLAND of Chard, co. Somerset, widow, dated 31 August 1654. To be buried in the parish church of Chard. To the poor of that town 20s. To my daughter Joan Thorne a petticoat and apron, a chest, a table board and a bed, and a Bible. To my grandchildren Margaret and Joan Thorne all my linen. To Florence Cade a box and looking-glass. To my daughter Margaret Turner a petticoat. To my daughter Alice Darby a gown. To my grandchild Alice Leachland a feather bed. Residuary legatee and executor: my son Thomas Leachland. Overseer: Mr. William Coggan of Chard. The mark of Margaret Leachland. Witnesses: Christopher Webb, John Daye. Proved 22 July 1655 by the executor named in the will. (P. C. C., Aylett, 65.)

The Will of MATHEW DERBY of Dorchester, co. Dorset, gentleman, dated 13 December 1655. To the poor of Dorchester, to every almsman and almswoman in the three almshouses in Dorchester, and to the poor of Bockhampton, "where I was born," [small sums]. To the poor of Mayne Martell 20s. yearly for ever, and to the poor of Burton near Bridport 20s. yearly for ever. The sum of £3 yearly for ever is to be paid for and towards the placing of poor children apprentices to handy craftsmen out of the several places and parishes before named. To the poor prisoners in the county prison 20s. yearly for ever. A rent of £3 had been charged on the testator's dwelling house in Dorchester for the schoolmasters, and for this purpose the will adds 40s. yearly. All these yearly payments are charged on the testator's lands in Broadmayne, otherwise Mayne Martell. Bequests of lands in Broskenhurst and Bolder, co. Southampton, the tithes of a farm at Cherlton, co. Dorset, and a tenement in Haselbury-Bryan, co. Dorset. To my mother a house in Dorchester. My wife Martha. My sisters, Anne (wife of John Williams, gentleman), Cicily (wife of William Polden, woollendraper), Elizabeth Whittell, deceased, and Katharine Bryer. My kinsman Mathew, son of Mr. Michaell Derby, and Mr. Robert Derby, who had issue. Proved in 1657. (P. C. C., Ruthen, 180.)

The Will of MARCELLA DUKE of Salcombe, co. Devon, widow, dated 17 December 1656. My sister Rebecka Salter. My cousin John Hooper of Salcombe, "who married my Kinswoman Ann Darby." Proved 10 December 1657. (P. C. C., Ruthen, 368.)

The Will of REBECCA SALTER of the parish of St. Stephen in Exeter [co. Devon], widow, dated 13 November, 14 Charles II [1662]. To be buried in the Cathedral Church of Exeter, near my father's and mother's graves. To my cousin Anne Darby, daughter of "my Nephew Mr. William Darby of Dorset," £40. To my cousin Samuell Darby, "sonne of my nephew Mr. Richard Darby," £40. My cousin Anne Hooper, wife of John Hooper. My cousin Anne Darby, that lives with the said John Hooper. To my cousin Roger Darby, "now living in Topsham," 10s. To my cousin Anne Darby, "daughter of my nephew Mr. Richard Darby," all my household goods and implements, except my linen and what I have formerly herein thereof given. Residue to my executrix, for the benefit of "my two cousens Samuell Darby & Anne Darby the sonne and daughter of my nephew Mr. Richard Darby." [The testatrix lived in the house of Nathaniel Salter, who was perhaps her stepson. Other stepchildren (called "son-in-law" and "daughter-in-law") were Dr. Anthony Salter, and Mrs. Jane Penny, wife of Mr. Allan Penny of Exeter, merchant.] Proved 24 November 1662. (Archdeaconry of Exeter [Exeter].)

Administration on the estate of SAMUEL DARBY of Exeter [co. Devon] was granted 14 April 1671 to his brother, Roger Darby of Topsham [co. Devon], chandler. (Archdeaconry of Exeter.)

Administration on the estate of ANN DARBY of Exeter [co. Devon] was granted 28 April 1671 to her brother, Roger Darby of Topsham [co. Devon], chandler. (Archdeaconry of Exeter.)

The Will of WILLIAM DERBY of Honiton, co. Devon, apothecary, dated 8 May 1682. Testator owned tithes at Neither Stirthill, formerly belonging to St. Luke's in Dorsetshire, which were left to him by his father, who died 6 March 1676, and whose will was proved at Bridport, co. Dorset. My wife Susanna. To my son William Derby (under twenty-one) £150. To my daughters (under twenty-one) Susannah Derby and Margaret Derby, to each £100. "Sons-in-law" and "daughter-in-law," surnamed Deeme. Overseer: Joseph Deeme the Elder of Honiton. Proved in 1682. (P. C. C., Cottle, 117.)

### FROM PARISH REGISTERS IN CO. DORSET*

#### Allington

1589 Henry ———— and Elizabeth Darby married 9 May.
1654 Robert Darby and Joane Pummery *alias* Wrixen married 25 September.

#### Askerswell

1571 Christopher Darby son of Nicholas Darby baptized.
1572 Christopher Darby and Agnes ———— married 10 April.
1576 Roger Derby son of Nicholas Derby baptized.
1603 Christopher Derby buried.
1609 George Primrose and Edith Darby, widow, married 4 November.

#### Burton-Bradstock

1623 Christopher Derby buried.
1627 Simon Pinson and Dorothy Darby married 2 October.

#### Marshwood

1618 William Holman and Elizabeth Darbie married 3 November.

#### Symondsbury

1594 Arthur Fowke, gentleman, and Joane Darbye married 5 August.
1612 Mar. Gorge Broune and Mrs. Joane Fowkes married 12 December.
1615 Wylliam Balson and Joan Darby married 5 March [1615/16].

*The marriages at Allington, Askerswell, Burton-Bradstock, Marshwood, and Symondsbury have been printed in Phillimore's Dorset Parish Registers, Marriages.

1628  Alice wife of Mr. Wm. Symons buried 28 July.
1634  Mr. Wm. Symons, gentleman, buried 8 January [1634/5].

## FROM THE PARISH REGISTERS OF TOPSHAM, CO. DEVON*

### Baptisms

1632  Mary Helman daughter of Vincent and Mary 16 September.
1634  Vinsent Hilman son of Vincent and Marie 14 December.
1637  Parnell Hellman son [sic] of Vincent 8 April.
1639  Parnell Hellman daughter of Vincent 10 November.
1641  Margrett Hellman daughter of John 24 July.
1641  Vincent Hellman son of Vincent 13 February [1641/2].
1641  Roger Lechland son of Thomas and Sara 15 March [1641/2].
1643  Sara Leachland [Lesland *in the Bishop's transcripts*] daughter of
      Thomas and Sara 25 July.
1643  Lucretia Helman daughter of John and Honour 6 August.
1647  Josias Helman son of John and Honner 20 May.
1648  Charles Helman son of John and Honnor 8 February [1648/9].
1669  Charles Derbey son of Roger and Lucretia 30 July.

### Burials

1639  Parnell Hellman daughter of Vincent 20 June.
1639  Vincent Hellman son of Vincent 17 August.
1641  Parnell Hellman daughter of Vincent 15 June.
1642  Roger Leachland son of Thomas and Sara 22 April.
1643  Vensent [Vincent *in the Bishop's transcripts*] Helman 20 January
      [1643/4].
1651  Charles Hillman son of John 18 May.
1654  Lucretia Hillman, wid[ow], 13 April.
1658  Sarah Leachland wife of Thomas 22 March [1658/9].
1669  Joane Darbey wife of Tristrum 29 March.
1669  Thomas Leachland 3 September.

## FROM LAY SUBSIDIES FOR CO. DORSET.†

14 and 15 Henry VIII [1522–1524] (103/125).
    Burton-Bradstock.        John Derby in goods [valuation] 100s.
16 Henry VIII [1524–25] (103/122).
    Askerswell.        John Derby in goods [valuation] £10.
34 Henry VIII [1542–43] (104/155).
    Askerswell.        Oswald Darby in goods [valuation] £4.
    Burton-Bradstock.        John Darby in goods [valuation] 40s.
3 and 4 Edward VI [1549–1551] (104/199).
    Askerswell.        Oswald Derby in goods [valuation] £10.
                        Robert Derby in goods [valuation] £17.
1 Elizabeth [1558–59] (104/216).
    Askerswell.        Robert Darbye in goods [valuation] £8.
39 Elizabeth [1596–97] (105/266 and 252).
    Askerswell.        Christopher Darby in goods [valuation]
                        £14.
    Stirthill.        Nicholas Darbye in goods [valuation]
                        £16.

*Published by the Devon & Cornwall Record Society.
†Preserved in the Public Record Office, London.

22 James I [1624–25] (105/309).
    Shepton [Shipton-George].    Nicholas Derby in annuity 20s.
    Sturthill.    Ann Derby, widow, in annuity 20s.
                Christopher Darby, gentleman, in lands
                [valuation] £4.

### FROM MUSTER ROLLS, CO. DORSET*

34 Henry VIII [1542–43].
    Askerswell.    A. B. John Darby haithe a bill.†
                John Darby Junur haithe a bowe vi
                arowes.
                Oswald Darbye haithe a bowe vi
                arowes.
                (Miscellaneous Books of the Ex-
                    chequer, Treasury of the Receipt,
                    vol. 17.)
    Burton-Bradstock.    John Darby a byll a Salett.† (*Ib.*, vol.
                51.)

11 Elizabeth [1568–69].
    Askerswell.    Nicholas Darby byllman. (State
                Papers, Domestic Series, Elizabeth,
                vol. 56.)

### FROM INQUISITIONS POST MORTEM‡

14 Henry VIII [1522–23]. Henry Derby was one of the jurors who held inquisition on the estate of SIR JOHN GREY, Knight, who died seised of the manor of Askerswell [co. Dorset] and the advowson of the rectory there and of other lands. (Chancery Inquisitions Post Mortem, vol. 39, no. 122.)

[The only Henry Derby in Dorset at this time, so far as is known, was Henry Derby of Wyke-Regis. A juror was always a freeholder.]

19 May, 42 Elizabeth [1600]. The jurors find that NICHOLAS DARBY, gentleman, was at his death seised in fee of a moiety of the manor of Brians-puddle, co. Dorset, and six messuages, six gardens, six orchards, fifty acres of arable land, ten acres of meadow, forty acres of pasture, and twenty acres of wood, and all that capital messuage called the Free Chapel of St. Luke's and Sterthill, late dissolved, and all tithes belonging to the said chapel. And so seised the said Nicholas, by indenture made between himself of the one part and his sons Christopher Darby, Roger Darby, Laurence Darby, and Nicholas Darby [of the other part], conveyed the said lands and tithes in Sterthill to the said Roger, Laurence, and Nicholas for their lives, and afterwards to the said Christopher and his male heirs, or in default of such heirs to the said Roger, Laurence, and Nicholas and their heirs in succession. Nicholas, the father, died 30 October, 41 Elizabeth [1599], and the said Christopher is his son and next heir and was aged 25 years and more at his father's death. (Chancery Inquisitions Post Mortem, Series 2, vol. 260, no. 122.)

### FROM FEET OF FINES‡

Final Concord between Henry Darbye, John Crome, and Henry Smyth, querents, and George Wadham, Esq., deforciant, of the manor of Bryans-puddle and eight messuages, a mill, four hundred and ten acres, and a rent

---

*The musters in the reign of Henry VIII included the names of all males between the ages of 16 and 60. The muster of 1569 included only able-bodied men.
†A.B. stands for Able Billman. A salett (sallet) was a light kind of helmet.
‡Preserved in the Public Record Office, London.

of 16s. 8d. in Bryanspuddle and Affpuddle, co. Dorset. (Feet of Fines, Dorset, Easter Term, 32 Elizabeth [1590].)

Final Concord between Thomas Darby and Richard Hardey, querents, and Cristofer Morgan, Esq., and Anne, his wife, deforciants, of a messuage and two hundred and fifty acres in Burton, Shepton, Swyer, and Sturtell, co. Dorset. (Feet of Fines, Dorset, Michaelmas Term, 32–33 Elizabeth [1590].)

Final Concord between Cristofer Darby, gentleman, querent, and Henry Darby, deforciant, of a moiety of the manor of Brianspuddle and twelve messuages, eight cottages, etc., a water mill, and one thousand five hundred and eighty acres (including one thousand and thirty acres of furze, heath, and moor) in Brianspuddle, Arthpuddle *alias* Athpuddle, Tolpuddle, and Throope, co. Dorset. (Feet of Fines, Dorset, Michaelmas Term, 42–43 Elizabeth [1600].)

Final Concord between Thomas Derby, querent, and Christopher Derby, gentleman, and William Derby, gentleman, deforciants, of a messuage and fifty-eight acres in Sterthill and tithes of sheaves, hay, wool, and lambs in Barwick, Bredye Fearme, Graveston, Brode Sterthill, Nether Sterthill, Swyre, and Byrtonne, co. Dorset. (Feet of Fines, Dorset, Michaelmas Term, 15 Charles I [1639].)

### From Recoveries*

[January 1635/6.] Gilbert Loder, gentleman, and Robert Holman, gentleman, *v.* Andrew Loope, gentleman, for a moiety of the manor of Brianspuddle and four messuages, a mill, and three hundred and forty acres in Brianspuddle, Arthpuddle, Tolepuddle, and Throope [co. Dorset]. Vouchee: William Derby, who calls Christopher Derby. (Recoveries, Hilary Term, 11 Charles I [1635/6], m. 11.)

[January 1640/1.] Henry Martyn, gentleman, *v.* William Chilcott, gentleman, for a messuage and fifty-eight acres in Sterthill and tithes in Barwicke, Bredy farm, Graveston, Broadstirthill, Nether Stirthill, Swyre, and Birton [co. Dorset]. Vouchee: William Derby, gentleman. (Recoveries, Hilary Term, 16 Charles I [1640/1], m. 24.)

### From the Records of the Court of Queen's Bench*

[1555/6.] Walter Grey, Esq., sues Robert Derby, clerk, for slander uttered by said Robert at Brydport [Bridport], co. Dorset, 1 and 2 Philip and Mary [1554–55], the words complained of being: "Master Grey is a false perjured man." Plaintiff claims £100 as damages. Defendant pleads not guilty. (Coram Rege Rolls, Hilary Term, 2 and 3 Philip and Mary [1555/6], 1177, m. 65.)

[Walter Grey was lord of the manor of Askerswell, co. Dorset, and patron of the rectory there.]

[1569/70.] Henry Medewaye sues Robert Derby, clerk, for slander uttered by said Robert at Dorchester [co. Dorset], 20 June, 10 Elizabeth [1568], the words complained of being: "Thou art an arrant theif and I will prove itt for thou hast stolen a lambe of myne." Defendant states that his lamb has been found among Medewaye's sheep. (Coram Rege Rolls, Hilary Term, 12 Elizabeth [1569/70], 1232, m. 281.)

[1570/1.] John Samwayes, gentleman, sues Christopher Darbye for trespass and damage committed by said Christopher 1 January, 11 Elizabeth [1568/9], on lands of said John at Toller-Fratram, co. Dorset. (Coram Rege Rolls, Hilary Term, 13 Elizabeth [1570/1], 1236, m. 227.)

*Preserved in the Public Record Office, London.

[1568.] Cristofer Derby of Stynsford, co. Dorset, husbandman, executor of the last will of Robert Derby of Askerswell, co. Dorset, yeoman, was summoned to answer John Wade, son of John Wade of Burton, co. Dorset, deceased, concerning a plea that he should render to him £300, due on a certain bond executed by said Robert at Dorchester [co. Dorset] on 11 May, 1 Elizabeth [1559].

And the said Cristofer came by his attorney and defended, putting forward a bond executed by Thomas Grey, son of Walter Grey, late of Barwyck in the parish of Swyre, co. Dorset, Esq. (Plea Rolls, Easter Term, 10 Elizabeth [1568], 1269, m. 1406.)

[This record shows that Christopher Derby of Askerswell was temporarily living at Stinsford (a mile east from Dorchester) in 1568. Brockhampton in Stinsford was the residence of the Jacob family, one of whom later became the wife of Laurence Derby. The above-mentioned Robert Derby is named on subsidy rolls at Askerswell in and after 1550, and died, as is here indicated, before 1568. It seems likely that he was father of Christopher, Henry, and Nicholas Derby.]

[1570.] Nicholas Longe of Wotton Abbott, co. Dorset, yeoman, was summoned to answer Henry Darby of Asshekerswell [Askerswell], co. Dorset, husbandman, concerning a bond, dated at Dorchester 25 January, 11 Elizabeth [1568/9], for a debt of £12, to be paid at the house of Walter Mone in the town of Burporte [Bridport], co. Dorset. (Plea Rolls, Michaelmas Term, 12 and 13 Elizabeth [1570], 1286, m. 108.)

[1571.] Robert Darbye of Askerswell [co. Dorset], clerk, is attached to answer John Hardy on a charge of slander. Said Robert at Symondsbury [co. Dorset], on 1 November, 12 Elizabeth [1570], spoke these words to said John: "Thou arte a theif and I wyll prove yt and Justyfy yt."

Said Darbye defends, justifying his words. (Plea Rolls, Michaelmas Term, 13 and 14 Elizabeth [1571], 1297, m. 1405.)

[1571.] John Hardye of Askerswell, co. Dorset, husbandman, is attached to answer Robert Darbye, clerk, concerning the seizure of certain horses of Alice Hardye at Askerswell. (Plea Rolls, Michaelmas Term, 13 and 14 Elizabeth [1571], 1299, m. 312.)

[A similar entry in the Plea Rolls, Michaelmas Term, 14 and 15 Elizabeth [1572], 1306, m. 111, shows that Robert Darby was living as late as 1572.]

[1578/9.] Richard Sydenham of Wynforde Egle [Winford-Eagle], co. Dorset, gentleman, is attached to answer Cristofer Darby of Askerswell [co. Dorset], yeoman, concerning a bond for £20, executed by said Richard at Birtporte [Bridport], co. Dorset, 24 June, 14 Elizabeth [1572]. (Plea Rolls, Hilary Term, 21 Elizabeth [1578/9], 1364, m. 1310.)

16 January, 16 Charles I [1640/1]. Deed between Nicholas Derby of Shepton [Shipton], co. Dorset, gentleman, William Derby of Sterthill, co. Dorset, gentleman, and Richard Derby and Thomas Derby, brothers of the said William, of the one part, and William Chilcott of Briddey [Bredy], co. Dorset, gentleman [of the other part]. The said Nicholas and William Derby, at the request of the said Richard and Thomas, in consideration of £700, convey to the said Chilcott the late dissolved free chapel called Sterthill alias St. Luke's, co. Dorset, with the houses and lands pertaining thereto in Sterthill and Nether Sterthill (part in the possession of Matthewe Derby, gentleman), and two acres in Barwicke Meadowe and all tithes belonging to

*Preserved in the Public Record Office, London.

the chapel (now in the possession of the said Matthewe Derby and the said William Derby and Agnes, his mother, and others), which Nicholas Derby, gentleman, now deceased (late father of the said Nicholas Derby and grandfather of the said William, Richard, and Thomas Derby), purchased from William Gould of Gussage St. Andrews, co. Dorset, gentleman. The tithes were from lands in Sterthill, Nether Sterthill, Greencombe, and a farm called Graveston. (Deed enrolled in Common Pleas, Hilary Term, 16 Charles I [1640/1].)

[1667/8.] George Derby, an attorney of Common Pleas, obtains judgment against William Derby of Sturthill, co. Dorset, gentleman, for the sum of £300. (Plea Rolls, Hilary Term, 19 and 20 Charles II [1667/8], 2839, m. 1894.)

### From the Records of the Court of Chancery*

5 February 1596. The plaintiff, Raphe Hurding of Longebreedye [Long Bredy, co. Dorset], gentleman, states that in 36 Elizabeth [1593–94] he borrowed £50 from Christopher Darby of Askerswell [co. Dorset] and other sums later, and, having made default in payment of the debt, said Darby has caused plaintiff's cattle to be taken in execution. Christopher Darby in his answer mentions his son-in-law Arthur Fowks, Esq. (Chancery Proceedings, Elizabeth, H. 20/40.)

22 May 1601. John Everye of Wycroft, co. Devon, gentleman, and William Everye, his son and heir, sue Christopher Darbye, the object of the suit being to test the title of the defendant to "the manor house & farme of Stertell otherwise Upper Sterthill and Nether Stertell, Dorset," late in tenure of Nicholas Darbye and now of his son Christopher Darbye.

Christopher Darby answers that Hugh Cheverell, Esq., by deed of 24 July, 18 Elizabeth [1576], between the said Hugh Cheverell of the one part and the said Nicholas Darbye of the other part, in consideration of £700, demised to said Nicholas the farm or farms of Upper Sturthill and Nether Sturthill and all his grounds there in the parish of Barton [Burton-Bradstock, co. Dorset], to hold from the Feast of St. Michael the Archangel, 1578, for ninety-nine years, if the said Nicholas and his sons Christopher and Richard should so long live, at a rent of £10.13s. 4d. yearly. By another deed of the same date, Hugh Cheverell was bound to Nicholas Darbye in a sum of £1000 for the due performances of the articles and grants in the firstnamed deed. And about three years since Nicholas Darbye assigned all his estate in the said farm or farms to his son Christopher, and died about one and a half years since. (Chancery Proceedings, Series 2, 268/3.)

9 June, 44 Elizabeth [1602]. John Every, plaintiff, v. Christopher Darby, defendant.

Thomas Jones of Burton [Burton-Bradstock], co. Dorset, husbandman, aged 44 years, deposed that he was for thirteen years servant to Nicholas Darby, "in wᶜʰ tyme he sayth he did by his Mʳˢ appoyntment carrye and paid unto Mʳ Hughe Cheverell money for rent for the Farmes of Upper Sterthill & Nether Sterthill and he sayth that sometymes the said rent was paid quarterly and then he comonly carryed and paid fiftie shillings and ten groates for the Quarter but sometymes the said Hughe Cheverell when he had occasion to use money did send for a quarter's rent sometymes half a yeeres aforehand." The deponent further refers to his conversations with William Ferret, bailiff to Cheverell, respecting Nicholas Darby's estate in the farms.

*Preserved in the Public Record Office, London.

Alexander Buckler of Evershoute [Evershot], co. Dorset, yeoman, aged 34 years, deposed that he had been servant to Hugh Cheverell and "served him as clerke and did wayt on him when he rode abrode as much or more than any other man he had and did very well know Nichas Darby decessed the defend<sup>ts</sup> father." Said Darby, speaking of his estate in the farms, had said to deponent: "What care I for a further estate I will not scorse the estate I have alreade therein for thy master's estate," and then showed deponent his lease of the farms, dated 24 July, 18 Elizabeth [1576]. Thereupon deponent replied to said Nicholas: "Unkle (for so he commonly called him) I think yo<sup>r</sup> estate for the fourscore and nineteen yeares in remainder mentconed cannot be good in lawe." And Nicholas answered: "Hould thy peace for I have a fyne from thy master and mistris and the fyne is all and looke thou heere," and showed deponent a fine acknowledged by said Cheverell and Anne his wife to Nicholas Darby. (Town Depositions, Chancery, Trinity Term, 44 Elizabeth [1602].)

[The will of Alexander Buckler of Woolcombe Matravers in Melbury Bubb (adjoining Evershot), co. Dorset, yeoman, dated 24 February 1567 [1567/8] and proved 30 March 1568 (P. C. C., Babington, 6), and the will of his widow, Elizabeth Buckler of the same place, dated 15 November 1579 and proved 5 February 1579 [1579/80] (P. C. C., Arundel, 8), mention among the daughters of the testators a Katherine; and, since the above-mentioned deponent, Alexander Buckler of Evershot, calls Nicholas Derby his uncle, it is probable that the Katherine named in these two wills is identical with Nicholas Derby's wife Catherine. *Vide infra*, p. 431.]

November 1630. Christopher Derby of Sturthill, co. Dorset, gentleman, sues Sir John Strove of Chauntmerle, co. Dorset, Knight, and others, and complains concerning a bond for a sum of money, dated Oct. 1612, to which he was a party, having been a surety with William Hardy (now deceased) for a debt of Henry Harding of Long Bredy, co. Dorset, Esq. (now deceased). Harding had been imprisoned for debt and remained a long time in prison. The suit concerned the plaintiff's liability for the debt, the defendants being the executors of the creditor. (Chancery Proceedings, Charles I, D. 26/38.)

Phelps *v.* Gardiner, June, 8 Charles I [1632]. Among deponents are Matthew Derby of Dorchester, gentleman, aged 24, and William Derby of Dorchester, mercer, aged 25. They depose in regard to conversations with one Matthew Coker concerning Coker's share in a ship called *The Content* of Weymouth and a prize taken at sea by *The Content.* (Chancery Depositions before 1714, 693/20.)

3 February 1636. John Guppie of Crewkerne, co. Somerset, mercer, William Guppie, and William Browne sue Christopher Darby of Sturthill in the parish of Shepton [*sic*], co. Dorset, gentleman, and his sons William Darby and Richard Darby. The plaintiffs state that the said John Guppie, having had dealings in "wares and comodities" with Christopher Darby, became indebted to him. The defendants, William Darby and Richard Darby, had "used" the trade of mercery or linen drapery, together with their father, and had sold a large stock of their wares to John Guppie. The suit concerned the value of the goods and the condition of a bond which, by way of payment, Guppie had given to Christopher Darby.

The answer, signed by the three defendants, deals at great length with the matter in question, and states that Richard Darby had lived with his brother William as an apprentice to the mercer's trade. (Chancery Proceedings, Charles I, G. 56/53.)

Hide *v.* Coker, 26 September 1638. A suit relating to the manor and advowson of Walton Fitzpaine, co. Dorset, with which the Jacob family of Brockhampton, co. Dorset, was concerned. William Jacob was father of

"Mistress Derby," who was mother of a deponent in the suit, viz., Mathew Derby of Dorchester, gentleman, aged 30 years. (Chancery Depositions before 1714, 366/3, 367/33.)

8 May 1647. Roger Preston of Uppotterie, co. Devon, Esq., sues Richard Derby, gentleman, stating that he [Preston] had been a surety for John Clegg of Axminster, co. Devon, yeoman, who had borrowed money from Richard Derby, the defendant, who was then resident at Chard, co. Somerset.

Richard Derby dates his answer at Bridport, co. Dorset, and signs the same, Arthur Fowke being a witness to his signature. (Chancery Proceedings before 1714, Bridges, 416/117.)

21 May 1650. William Derby of Upper Stirthill [co. Dorset], gentleman, sues Richard Derby. Plaintiff complains that his father, Christopher Derby of Upper Stirthill, now deceased, about the time of the latter's marriage with the plaintiff's mother, Ann Derby, also now deceased, had settled on her a jointure of about £70 a year out of the farm of Upper Stirthill. And in 1632 it was agreed between the said Christopher and his son, the said William, that William should enjoy some part of the farm during the remainder of the term of ninety-nine years for which Christopher held the same. By mutual consent the lease was deposited in a chest "wth.in the Church in the borough of Bridport," but the agreement and a certain bond, given by William, had come into the hands of his brother, Richard Derby. After the death of Christopher Derby (the plaintiff's father) the plaintiff's mother, Ann, had entered on part of the farm, and she and her son Richard Derby and Richard's wife and family had enjoyed this part of the farm till her death one year since. Richard had committed waste on the farm and taken possession of some of his mother's goods. (Chancery Proceedings before 1714, Hamilton, 100/22.)

30 November 1650. John Clarke of Axminster, co. Devon, vintner, sues Tristram Hooper and Julyan his wife, John Clegg, and others. Plaintiff complains that Henry Thomas, being possessed of a personal estate of £500, about five years since made his will, appointing Anne Darby and Rebecca Derby, then infants of tender age, executrices, and died shortly afterwards. The latter executrix is also dead, and John Clarke was granted administration of the estate, with the will annexed, during the minority of Anne Derby, who is now ten years of age. Most of the estate had come into the hands of Tristram Hooper and Julyan his wife (a daughter of the said Henry Thomas), John Clegg (who married a daughter of Henry Thomas), and others. (Chancery Proceedings before 1714, Mitford, 119/37.)

25 November 1651. Anne Derby of Ottery St. Mary, co. Devon, spinster, sues John Clarke of Axminster, co. Devon, and Anne his wife and William Derby. Plaintiff complains that her grandfather, Christopher Derby of Sterthill, co. Dorset, gentleman, left by will £40 to her brother, John Derby (son of Christopher's son John Derby). Christopher's youngest son, Thomas Derby, was executor of the will. The testator died shortly afterwards, and Anne's brother, John Derby, died two or three years since, when administration of his goods was granted to his said sister Anne. Anne [the defendant] had possessed herself of his estate, valued at £1000 and upwards, and had since married John Clarke of Axminster. One William Derby, now a defendant, had been bound in a sum of money to pay the legacy to John. (Chancery Proceedings, Charles II, D. 47/15.)

27 June 1653. Thomas Leachland of Chard, co. Somerset, merchant, sues Richard Darby, mercer, and Alice his wife. Plaintiff complains that about twelve years since he had been surety for his mother, Margaret Leachland of Chard, widow, for a debt of £20 borrowed from his sister Alice Leach-

land, then unmarried. A house in the town of Chard, now occupied by the said Margaret, together with bonds, formed security for the debt. For two or three years after lending the money Alice lived with her mother, Margaret, and then married Richard Darby of Combe St. Nicholas, co. Somerset, mercer. After the marriage Derby and Alice, his wife, sojourned for two years in the house at Chard with Margaret Leachland, and Derby there carried on his trade as mercer. One year since Derby and his wife caused Thomas Leachland to be arrested for the debt. (Chancery Proceedings before 1714, Mitford, 116/108.)

12 February 1654 [1654/5]. Richard Derby of Beare, co. Devon, mercer, and Alice his wife, and Joane Thorne, widow, sue Thomas Leachland. The plaintiffs state that the said Alice and Joane were daughters of Margarett Leachland of Chard, co. Somerset, widow, who, by will dated 20 October 1654, left legacies to the said Alice and Joane and to two children of Joane. Margaret Leachland died 24 October following. Thomas Leachland, now defendant, though appointed executor of the will, has not proved it and has not paid the legacies.

Thomas Leachland, in answering, mentions that the will was dated 31 August 1654. (Chancery Proceedings before 1714, Mitford, 98/32.)

2 February 1656. William Derby of Stirthill, co. Dorset, gentleman, sues George Derby, the eldest son of the plaintiff. Plaintiff states that Hugh Cheverell, Esq., by indenture dated 18 or 19 Elizabeth [1575–76 or 1576–77] demised to the plaintiff's grandfather, Nicholas Derby, the farm of Upper Stirthill and Nether Stirthill, co. Dorset, for a term of ninety-nine years, if Christopher Derby (the plaintiff's father) and Richard Derby, both sons of the said Nicholas and both now deceased, should so long live, at a yearly rent of £10. 13s. 4d. Nicholas Derby settled the farm on his son Christopher Derby, who, by indenture dated September, 7 Charles I [1631], granted it in trust to George Harrington, an alderman of Bristol, William Baldwyn, citizen and woollendraper of London, and Symon Baldwyn (brother of the last-named), for the benefit successively of the said Christopher Derby and his wife (the plaintiff's father and mother) and of the plaintiff's wife Johan, with remainder to the plaintiff and his heirs. And William Derby (the plaintiff) had issue by his said wife Johan the following children, viz., George, Christopher, William, Johan, Ann, Hannah, Elizabeth, and Mary. And about July last, in order to make provision for his younger children, several deeds were executed by the plaintiff and his sons and the said trustees. But the plaintiff's eldest son, the said George Derby, having obtained possession of these deeds, retains them and refuses to return them to plaintiff. (Chancery Proceedings, Series 2, 440/80.)

[After 1656.] William Derby of Sturthill, co. Dorset, gentleman, sues George Derby, living at Clonmell in co. Tipperary in the Kingdom of Ireland. Plaintiff states that, having been possessed for many years past of the farms of Upper and Nether Sturthill in the parish of Burton-Bradstock, co. Dorset, for the remainder of a term of years, he had intended to settle the farms for the benefit of his children, who were many. But his eldest son, George Derby, "an unditiful son," had obtained possession of the deeds and evidences of the estate, so that the settlement could not then be effected. Whereupon William had filed a bill in Chancery against George. By the mediation of friends, however, an agreement was reached, to the effect that George should receive from his father lands of the value of £200 and an annuity of £20 during the lives of George and Temperance, his wife, and that the deeds and evidences should be surrendered to William. And William, by an indenture dated 1656, granted to George land in Whitchurch, co. Dorset, "of which George has since made above £300." And on 26 July

1656 George surrendered all claim to the farms of Upper and Nether Stirthill, and gave a bond for the delivery of the writings, but has not fulfilled the agreement. (Chancery Proceedings before 1714, Collins, 572/69.)

1 December 1663. William Derby of Sturthill, co. Dorset, gentleman, sues John Warren.

Plaintiff was administrator of the goods of Nicholas Derby of Shepton Gorges [Shipton-George], co. Dorset, gentleman, deceased, and executor of the will of Mabell Derby, widow of the said Nicholas. William Derby states that the said Nicholas Derby possessed a lease of Whites Tenement in Shepton Gorges for a term of ninety-nine years from 20 December, 15 Charles I [1639], if the said Nicholas and Robert Derby (son of Roger Derby, deceased) should so long live, and a lease of Spencers Tenement in Shepton Gorges for a term of ninety-nine years from 10 December, 20 James I [1622], if the said Nicholas and Mabell his wife and Laurence Derby (son of Laurence Derby, deceased), and Michaell Derby (son of Roger Derby) should so long live, and a lease of a close called Farborough in Shepton Gorges for ninety-nine years, if the said Nicholas and Laurence Derby (son of Laurence Derby, deceased) and the said Michaell Derby should so long live, and a barn called Gulliford Barne in Shepton Gorges, with two acres, and a house called Napper House, held for the lives of the said Nicholas and Mary Davy, daughter of William Davy of Lyme-Regis, co. Dorset. And, by indenture of 20 April, 21 Charles I [1645], between the said Nicholas Derby of one part and the said William Derby (now plaintiff), Henry Hardy of Sturthill, yeoman, Matthew Derby of Dorchester, gentleman, and William Warren of Shepton Gorges, yeoman, of the other part, Nicholas Derby granted to the other parties to the deed all the aforesaid lands, etc., in trust for the use of the said Nicholas and Mabell his wife for their lives, with remainder to John Williams. Mabell Derby had by will bequeathed to the plaintiff, William Derby, all her goods. The said Hardy, Matthew Derby, and William Warren are all dead, but Laurence Derby and Michaell Derby are both living. John Warren, the defendant, has claimed the lands.

The defendant, son of the said William Warren, answers that Nicholas Derby, by indenture of 3 May, 20 Charles I [1644], assigned to Richard Darby of Higher Sturthill, mercer, and Henry Hardy of Broad Sturthill in the parish of Burton, yeoman, all his goods, cattle, etc., in trust for the benefit of the said Mabell Derby. And Mabell, "out of the love she bore" to Joane Warren of Shepton Gorges, widow (defendant's mother), by deed of 11 April 1659 granted to the said Joane and to the defendant all her right and interest in Spencers Tenement (eighteen acres) and in a tenement called Gulliford Hay (one and one-half acres) and all her bills, bonds, etc. With the purpose of trying the defendant's title to the premises, William Derby, son of the plaintiff William Derby, brought an action for ejectment against the now defendant, John Warren, putting forth a lease made by plaintiff to his son William Derby, dated 20 April, 15 Charles II [1663], the lands being then described as two messuages, two gardens, and forty-six acres in Shepton Gorges. The cause was tried at the assizes for co. Dorset, when documents were produced and witnesses examined, Derby being nonsuited. (Chancery Proceedings before 1714, Hamilton, 474.)

Drake et al. *v.* the Mayor and Burgesses of the City of Exeter, etc., 1663. John Drake and Ursula, widow and administratrix of Vincent Hillman, etc., sue the Mayor and Burgesses of Exeter concerning fishing rights in the manor of Exe Island and land there called "The Bunhay," both in co. Devon. It is stated that Vincent Hillman of Topsham, co. Devon, shipwright, died about twelve years since. Among deponents is Thomas Leachland of Topsham, co. Devon, merchant, aged 45, who deposed for the plaintiffs. (Chancery Depositions before 1714, 779/49.)

[*Circa* 1667.] George Derby of Clonmell in the Kingdom of Ireland, attorney-at-law, sues John Symes of Frampton-Cotterell, co. Gloucester, Esq., and his son, Henry Symes, and William Derby. Plaintiff states that about 1651 he was employed by the said John and Henry Symes to "lett and sett certain ymproppriate gleabe lands comonly called by ye name of St. Lukes in ye County of Dorsett." Derby was then living in England at Bradford-Abbas, co. Dorset, and was so employed till 1657. This suit concerned accounts and fees and salary claimed by the plaintiff. The plaintiff's father, William Derby, is called on to show cause why he should not deliver up certain bonds. [The answer is dated 6 October 1667.] (Chancery Proceedings before 1714, Hamilton, 492/83.)

Penny *v.* Starr, 17 June 1674. Among deponents is George Derby of Chard, co. Somerset, gentleman, aged 41 years. (Chancery Depositions before 1714, 414/50.)

15 May 1675. Henry Walroud of Ilebrewers [Isle-Brewers], co. Somerset, Esq., sues William Derby of Honiton, co. Devon, apothecary, and his brother George Derby of Chard, co. Somerset, gentleman. The suit relates to the payment for "medicaments pills and potions" supplied by the defendant William Derby during the sickness of Walroud's wife. (Chancery Proceedings before 1714, Collins, bundle 66.)

Davey *v.* Drew, 1676. Among deponents is William Derby of Honiton, co. Devon, apothecary, aged 35 years, who had supplied "drugs & apothecary wares" for Andrew Davey in 1669, his bill amounting to £4. 4s. 10d. (Chancery Depositions before 1714, 898/24.)

28 November 1678. Henry Bishop of Chilcombe, co. Dorset, Esq., and another plaintiff sue William Baldwyne, William Derby, George Derby, William Levermore and Ann his wife, Elizabeth Derby, and William Boler and Mary his wife, the defendants, William Derby, George, Ann, Elizabeth, and Mary, being children of William Derby, deceased. Plaintiffs state that, by indenture dated July, 18 Elizabeth [1576], Hugh Cheverell of Chantmarle in Cattistock, co. Dorset, Esq., granted to Nicholas Derby of Stirthill, co. Dorset, gentleman, the farm or farms of Upper Stirthill and Nether Stirthill in the parish of Burton-Bradstock [co. Dorset] for a term of ninety-nine years and for the lives of the said Nicholas and his sons Christopher and Richard. After the death of Nicholas his eldest son Christopher held the lands . . . [*manuscript illegible*]. And, by indenture dated [*illegible*] Charles I, between the said Christopher Derby and Agnes his wife of one part and George Harrington (then an alderman of Bristol), William Baldwyne of London [?], Symon Baldwyne (his brother), William Derby (eldest son of the said Christopher), and Joane (daughter of William Baldwyne), the lands in question were settled on the marriage of the said William Derby to Joane Baldwyne. Christopher Derby died 20 January 1639, and his wife Agnes is now also dead. Joane, wife of William Derby, died 6 November 1673, and her husband and her children above-mentioned survived her. [The manuscript is here illegible; but the plaintiffs apparently claim that Humphrey Bishop, Esq. (father of the plaintiff Henry), purchased the farms from William Derby and his eldest son, George Derby.] (Chancery Proceedings before 1714, Collins, 514/106.)

1693. Jennings Derby of Chard, co. Somerset, gentleman, sues Michael Pope of Bristol, grocer. Plaintiff states that his father, George Derby, was son of Joane Derby, who was daughter of William Baldwin; and he sues concerning the estate of the said Baldwin and Baldwin's lands in co. Gloucester and Bristol. (Chancery Proceedings before 1714, Mitford, 439/79.)

107

Commission dated 23 February, 41 Elizabeth [1598/9].

The plaintiff, Robert Mason, states that he was and yet is seised of the site and demesnes of the manor of Burton, co. Dorset, for a term of years, and that he and Richard Arnold, Esq., had for the last two years possessed 600 sheep depasturing on the lands. And about 21 September last John Greene of Dorchester [co. Dorset], ironmonger, Thomas Moundyn of Burton [Burton-Bradstock, co. Dorset], husbandman, Henry Allen of Charmester [Charminster, co. Dorset], —— Newe, and Nicholas Derby assembled at Dorchester and "Sett downe a corse Rioltouslye Unlawfullye secretlye and Injuriouslye to enter on the said scite and demeanes," and to convey away the said sheep by night in secret. And all these persons "about 10 or 12 of the clokke in the night seazon assembled at Burton and there did armme and arraye themselves wᵗʰ long staves Picks Swordes Daggers and other Weapons and Municōn" and entered the sheepfold and carried away the 600 sheep and "did before the daye appeared the next mornige drive [them] soe farre and by such strainge wayes towards the sea coste as your said subject could not knowe howe to finde them," and drove the sheep into a secret ground of the said Nicholas Darbye "in an obscure corner of the countrye neere the sea environed wᵗʰ hills." The sheep, however, were seized by the under sheriff. Subsequently Thomas Chapman, Thomas Woods, —— Darbye, and others unknown, to the number of fifteen, armed with weapons, rescued the sheep from the said sheriff and his ministers and assaulted the sheriff. Then "the said Nicholas Darby cominge himself to the place where the said sheep weare he wᵗʰ beatinge his hands and settinge one of Doggs caused the said sheep to Runne from the said Sheriff . . . and the said Shrief findinge faulte wᵗʰ the said disorde affirmed to the said Nicholas Darbye that he was like to be slaine unto wᶜʰ speach the said Nicholas Darby answered that if he had bin slaine he had had his omens in his hands usinge other proud and arrogant wordes that he was worth twenty thousand poundes and in defence of his cause would laye upp fortye shilling a weeke to be spente therein to the greate hinderance of youʳ said subject contempt of authoritye and breach of youʳ mᵗⁱᵉˢ peace."

Nicholas Darbye answers 14 April, 41 Elizabeth [1599], stating that about the time mentioned in the bill he bought from the said Moundyn about 100 sheep, which he placed in his own ground. But the plaintiff came into this defendant's pasture with the sheriff and others [and] drove away the said sheep, together with 200 other of defendant's sheep. This defendant's servant, Thomas Wood, informed defendant, whereon he "willed" Wood to go to the sheriff and request him to "stay the said sheep" until the defendant arrived. On arrival Darbye told the sheriff how he had bought the sheep, and, the sheriff seeming to be contented, Darbye "did fanne with his hande to torne the said sheepe," and the sheriff and his servants departed. Darbye denies that he was guilty of any riot, unlawful assembly, or misdemeanor, and prays to be discharged out of the Court. [Darbye was sworn in the presence of Henry Harlyn and Matthew Chubb, and the answer was signed by Robert Jacob, apparently the attorney or counsellor who drafted the document.] (Court of Star Chamber, Elizabeth, M. 45/33.)

## MISCELLANEOUS RECORDS

In the Return of Church Goods for Dorset in 1552 Sir William Derby appears as parson of the parish of Askerswell, and among the custodians of the goods are Robert Derby, Senior, and Christopher Darby.

[Apparently the parson's name should have been given as Robert (not William) Derby, for "Robert Darby, presbyter," was instituted at Askerswell in 1534.

*Preserved in the Public Record Office, London.

"Sir" was an honorary title of respect given to certain of the clergy in the sixteenth century.]

Among the Contributors to the Defence of the Realm at the time of the Spanish Armada — the "loan" was raised in 1589 — was Christopher Darby of Askerswell, co. Dorset, £25.

[Letter from the Privy Council to the Marquis of Winchester]

24 June 1597. "Whereas wee have bin informed by John Browne collonell of one of the divisions within the countie of Dorcett that one Christopher Darby sonne of Nicholas Darby of Sturtle in the sayd countie hath of late very lewdlie behaved himself in contempt of her Majesty's service and to the disgrace of the sayd Mr. Browne in the place he beareth in that the sayd Darby (as it is alleged) being amongst others chosen and appointed for a soldier to be employed in this present intended service and accordingly warned by the constables of the lymittes where he dwelleth to make his appearance at the muster he thereuppon presentlie after such warninge to him given procured himself to be retayned unto our very good Lord the Lord Vicount Bindon with purpose to protect himself from such employment and being so admitted as a retaynour to the said Lord Vicount came to the muster with his Lordships livery on his back, whose prectize heerein being discovered to the Captaine havinge charg of the soldiers leavied in that countie by the constable that warned Darby the sayd Captaine delivered to him his imprest money and the rather for that he was both for his hability and personage fitt for the service which imprest the said Darby receaving in very disdainefull and scornefull manner made his repaire the next day to the howse of Mr. Browne and there in most contemptous sort threw the same to the ground using very unreverent and unfitt speaches and utterly refused to serve in regard he was retayned to the Lord Viscount as aforesaid whose misdemeanours being afterwards at larg made known to Sir Oliver Lambert Knight at his cominge into the country to take vew of the soldiers he complayned thereof to the Deputie Leiutenants as a matter of great abuse and meete to be punished for example sake to others.

"We therefore uppon due consideration of the premises have thought good to referr the ordering and reformacion of this misdemeanor and offence to your Lordship her Majesty's Leiutenant of that countie praying and requiring your Lordship to give present direction to your Deputy Leiutenants or some of them to call the said Cristofer Darby before them and particularly to examyn the matter of complaint made against him and fynding the same to be such as is informed to cause him to be punished according to his desert or otherwise to certifie us of their proceedings and opyions [sic] in the matter and in whome the fault shalbe found. And for your better proceeding heerein you shall do well to acquaint the Lord Vicount Bondon with the order and direction that we have given you by this our letter."

[Plea of Christopher Derby about his Composition for Knighthood]

10 April 1632. At Sherborne. Christopher Derbie of Sturthill, co. Dorset, gentleman, appearing before the King's Majesty's Commissioners at Sherbourne in the said county, maketh answer that he hath already entered his plea of record to His Majesty's writ in His Highness's Court of Exchequer that he, the said Christopher, had not freehold lands, etc., of the yearly value of £10 per annum or above at the time of the King's Majesty's coronation and in three years before, which his said plea he saith he is ready to verify, and saith that all his freehold lands, etc., are not of the clear yearly value of 20 marks; for the farms of Upper Sturthill and Nether Sturthill, whereof the said Christofer is possessed, is [sic] not nor ever was the freehold of him, the said Christofer, but he holdeth it only by virtue of a lease for

years now shewed forth, bearing date the 28th day of July, 18 Elizabeth [1576], shewed forth to the said Commissioners, all which the said Christofer is ready to verify on his oath or by any other ways as the said Commissioners shall appoint. Christopher Derby. (Special Commission of the Exchequer, no. 5254.)

January 1632 [1632/3]. William Darbye, mercer, is admitted into the liberties of the City for [to] be married to Joan, daughter of Mr. William Baldwyn. (Bristol Burgess Book.)

The Dorset Protestation Rolls* show that in February and March 1641/2 the oath was taken by Nicholas Derby, Thomas Derby, and William Derby (a churchwarden), from Shepton Gorges [Shipton-George] and Stirthill, and by William Darby and Christopher Derby, from Burton [Burton-Bradstock]. [All who took the oath were over eighteen years of age.]

[Deposition of Ann Hoskins at Plymouth in New England, taken 2 March 1641/2†]

"Ann Hinde, the wife of Willam Hoskins, aged 25 yeares or therabouts, being examined and deposed before M<sup>r</sup> Edward Winslow in a case between John Darbey and John Chipman, afeirmeth vpon oath as followeth: —

"That the said Ann liued in the house of M<sup>r</sup> Darbeyes father with the said John Chipman att such time as the said John Chipman came from thence to New England to serue M<sup>r</sup> Richard Darbey, his [John Darbey's] brother; and that the said Ann came afterwards likewise ouer to serue the said Richard Darbey, when old M<sup>r</sup> Darbey requested this deponant to comend him to his cozen Chipman, and tell him if hee were a good boy hee would send him ouer the money that was due to him when hee saw good; and further, wheras this deponant heard the said John Darbey affeirme that his money was payed to John Chipmans mother, shee further deposeth that his said mother was dead a quarter of a yeare or therabouts before her old master sent this message to his cozen Chipman; all which this deponant sweareth, and further knoweth not.

"Before mee,          Edward Winslow.
"Taken the 2<sup>cond</sup> of March, 1641."

[William Derby is adjudged not guilty of delinquency]

23 January 1649 [1649/50]. "Whereas a charge of delinquency hath been exhibited beefore us against William Derby of Sturthill in this Countie [Dorset] gent., and the witnesses in the same cause examined viva voce and whereas vpon the same examinacõns it was laboured to bee proved that the said Mr. Derby was in armes with the Clubb men against the govrnor of Lyme and his souldiers neare Bridport, wee find vpon the testimony of honest men that the said Mr. Derby was not then and there in armes (as was suggested).

"And whereas it was likewise indeavered to be proved against him by one Metyard that hee was at Sherbourne (when Prince Maurice, the Marquis of Hartford and the Sheriff of the Countie were there) and tooke the Kinge's oath (which the said Metyard averred to bee done in his sight), but vpon further examinacõn of the matter the said Metyard confessed that hee could not tell in what manner hee tooke it, though beefore he averred that it was done in his sight: now vpon a full debate of the whole matter in charge, and the said Mr. Derby's answeare thereunto, wee doe adjudge and declare that hee the said Mr. Derby is not sequestrable within any ordinance of

*In the custody of the Librarian of the House of Lords.
†This deposition is printed in Plymouth Colony Records, Court Orders, vol. 4, p. 98, the General Court of the Plymouth Colony having ordered that it be recorded 7 June 1665.

110

Parliment, notwithstanding anything in the said charge alleaged against him, and therefore doe order that the said Mr. Derby and his assignes shall and may quietly hold and injoy all his Estate both reall and p'sonall; and all Sequestrators Sollicitors and other officers under this Committee, whom it may concerne, are required to take notice heereof, and to yeeld obedience heereunto." (Minute Books of the Dorset Standing Committee, 23 January 1649.)

Lent Assizes, 1656. George Derby of Yeovil, co. Somerset, gentleman, is bailed by John Clarke of Chard, co. Somerset, innkeeper, and Richard Derby of Beere, co. Devon, mercer. (Assize Records of the Western Circuit, Bail Book No. 1.)

[Statement of John Chipman of Barnstable in the Plymouth Colony, dated at Barnstable 8 February 1657/8*]

"A Brief Declaration . . . in y$^e$ behalf of John Chipman, now of Barnstable . . . in New England . . . y$^e$ only Son & Heir of M$^r$ Thomas Chipman Late Deceased at Brinspittlle [Bryanspuddle] about five miles from Dorchester in Dorsetshire . . . concerning some Certain Tenement or Tenements with a Mill & other Edifice thereunto belonging Lying & being in Whitechurch of Marshwood vale near Burfort Alias Breadport in Dorsetshire afores$^d$ hertofore worth 40 or 50 Pounds p' Annum which were y$^e$ Lands of y$^e$ s$^d$ Thomas Chipman being Entailed to him & his Heirs for Ever but hath for Sundry years [been] Detained from y$^e$ s$^d$ John Chipman the right & only Proper Heir Thereunto, By reason of Some kinde of Sale made of Inconsiderable value by the s$^d$ Thomas (In the time of his Single Estate not then minding marriage) unto his kinsman M$^r$ Christopher Derbe Living Sometime in Sturtle near Burfort afors$^d$ being as the said John hath been Informed but for 40$^{ll}$ And to be maintained Like a man with Diet Apparel &c by the s$^d$ Christopher as Long as the s$^d$ Thomas Should Live whereat y$^e$ Lawyer w$^c$ made the Evidences being troubled at his Weakness in taking Such An Inconsiderable Price tendered him to Lend him money or to give to him . . . Seven hundred Pounds for y$^e$ s$^d$ Lands But . . . The Vote of the Country who had knowledge of it was that the s$^d$ Thomas had much wrong in it Especially After it pleased God to Change his Condition, and to give him Children, being turned off by the s$^d$ Christopher only with a poor Cottage and Garden Spott instead of his fors$^d$ Maintenance to the great wrong of his Children Especially of his Son John Afors$^d$ to whom y$^e$ s$^d$ Lands by right of Entailment did belong. Insomuch that m$^r$ William Derbe who had the s$^d$ Lands in his Possession then from his father Christopher Derbe told the s$^d$ John but if y$^e$ s$^d$ Lands prospered with him that he would then Consider the s$^d$ John to do for him in way of recompence for the same when he should be of Capacity in years to make use thereof The s$^d$ John further Declareth that one m$^r$ Derbe A Lawyer of Dorchester (he Supposes y$^e$ father of that m$^r$ Derbe now Living In Dorchester) being

*Although this statement has been in print for many years, its genealogical importance is such that the essential parts of it are reproduced here. It was published in the REGISTER in Jan. 1850 (vol. 4, pp. 23–24), from a copy communicated by Rev. Richard Manning Chipman, A.M.; but, on account of sundry typographical errors in the statement as printed in 1850, a new copy, made by the late D. P. Corey of Malden from the manuscript of the statement, then in the possession of William Churchill Chipman of Sandwich, Mass., was printed in the REGISTER in Apr. 1881 (vol. 35, pp. 127–128), and this second printed copy has been followed in the extracts here given, except for the date of the statement, which in the two texts published in the REGISTER was unfortunately printed as "8th of Feb. (51)," but in Swift's edition of Otis's Barnstable Families (vol. 1, p. 154) is given as "8th of Feb. (57.)." That Swift read the date correctly is proved by the inscription on the gravestone of Elder John Chipman at Sandwich, which states that he died 7 Apr. 1708, aged 88 years. He was, therefore, born about 1620, a date which is in accord with his statement of 8 Feb. 1657/8 that he supposed "his Age to be About thirty seven years." The manuscript from which Mr. Corey made his copy was not in the handwriting of John Chipman himself, but was probably a contemporary transcript of a document sent to England.

a friend to the mother of the s^d John; Told her being Acquaind with y^e Business and sorry for the Injury to her Heir, that if it pleased God he Liv'd to be of Age he would himself upon his own Charge make A Tryal for the recovery of it and in Case he recovered it Shee Should give him 10^ll Else he would have nothing for his trouble and Charge. Furthermore John Derbe Late Deceased of Yarmouth in New Plimouth Goverment Afors^d hath Acknowledged here to the s^d John Chipman that his father Christopher had done him much wrong in the fors^d Lands but y^e s^d John Chipman . . . being now Stirred up by Some friends . . . hath Therfore Desired . . . Some Searh may be made . . . into the Records the Conveyance of the Said Lands being made as he Judgeth about Threescore years Since as Also that Enquiry be made of his Sisters which he Supposeth lived about those parts. . . . John Chipman Desires his Love be presented to his Sisters Hanner and Tamson and to hear particularly from them if Living and . . . that Enquiry be made of m^r Oliver Lawrence of Arpittle who was an Intimate friend of his fathers. Barnstable . . . this 8^th of Feb. (57) . . . The s^d John Chipman Supposeth his Age to be About thirty seven years; it being next may Twenty & one year since he Come out of England."

The Return of the Hearth Tax for Dorset, due Michaelmas, 1664, shows that Mr. William Derby of Stirthill paid for nine hearths in his house there. (Rawlinson MSS. [Bodleian Library, Oxford], B, 292–6.)

The foregoing records show that in the sixteenth and seventeenth centuries the surname *Darby* or *Derby* was common in the western part of Dorset, especially in the parish of Askerswell, about five miles east from Bridport and about ten and one-half miles west from Dorchester, and in the eastern part of the neighboring county of Devon. Among the bearers of this name may be mentioned a Henry Derby, probably of Wyke-Regis, co. Dorset, who in 14 Henry VIII [1522–23] was one of the jurors in the inquisition post mortem of Sir John Grey, Knight, who died seised of the manor of Askerswell and the advowson of the rectory there. A Robert Derby, clerk, was instituted as rector of Askerswell in 1534,* was a witness to the will of Nicholas Hardie in 1552, was charged with slander in the Coram Rege Rolls in 1555/6 and 1569/70 and in the Plea Rolls in 1571, and was living as late as 1572. Another Robert Derby (probably the Robert Derby, Sr., who was a custodian of the church goods at Askerswell in 1552) was taxed at Askerswell in 3 and 4 Edward VI [1549–1551] and in 1 Elizabeth [1558–59], and was apparently the Robert Derby of Askerswell, yeoman, who executed a bond at Dorchester 11 May, 1 Elizabeth [1559], and died not later than Easter Term, 10 Elizabeth [1568], when Christopher Derby of Stinsford, co. Dorset, husbandman, as executor of Robert's will, was defendant in a suit in the Court of Common Pleas.

This Christopher Derby, who was probably a son of the last-mentioned Robert, was, it seems likely, the man who was sued for trespass in the Court of Queen's Bench in 1570/1 and, as Christopher Derby of Askerswell, was plaintiff in a suit in Common Pleas in Jan. 1578/9, was sued in Chancery in 1596, and in 1589 contributed £25 for the defence of the realm against the Spaniards. In 39 Elizabeth

*Hutchins, History of Dorset, vol. 4, p. 431.

[1596–97] he or another man of the same name was taxed at Askerswell on goods valued at £14. He is evidently the Christopher
Derby who married at Askerswell, 10 Apr. 1572, Agnes ———, and
was buried there in 1603, his will, of 14 Mar. 1603, proved in 1604,
naming as residuary legatees his two daughters, Jone Fowkes and
Jone Peason, and containing bequests to the children of Arthur
Fowkes the Elder of Symondsbury, co. Dorset, and to the children
of John Peason of Lillington, co. Dorset, yeoman. These children
were grandchildren of the testator, the parish registers of Symonds-
bury recording the marriage, 5 Aug. 1594, of Arthur Fowke, gentleman (called "Antho. Foulke" in the "Addenda to the Visitation of
Dorsetshire, 1623," published in 1888), and Joane Darby, and "The
Visitation of Dorsetshire, 1623," p. 76 (*Publications of the Harleian
Society*, vol. 20, anno 1885), showing that "Joh: Peasinge" of Lilling-
ton, co. Dorset, who was living in 1623, married Joane, daughter of
"Christʳ Darby of Askeruille," co. Dorset, and had issue by her.
After the death of her first husband Joane (Darby) Fowkes married
secondly, at Symondsbury, 12 Dec. 1612, "Maʳ. Gorge Broune"
(Symondsbury registers), who is described in the "Addenda to the
Visitation of Dorsetshire, 1623," p. 8, as George Browne of Taunton,
Esq., a barrister of the Middle Temple, *s.p.*, æt. 45 in 1627, whose
will was proved 27 May 1631 (P. C. C., St. John, 59). These records
about Christopher Derby, the testator of 1603, and his daughters
have been given, because he was probably a brother of Nicholas
Derby, the earliest ancestor of the Derby name from whom the
descent of Roger Derby of Salem, Mass., has been traced, although
positive proof of the relationship between Christopher and Nicholas
Derby has not yet been discovered.

Another man who seems to have been closely related to Christopher
Derby, the testator of 1603, and to Nicholas Derby, was Henry
Darby of Askerswell, husbandman, who was probably their brother.
In 1570 he sued Nicholas Longe concerning a bond for a debt of
£12. He is presumably the Henry Darby who held a moiety of the
manor of Bryanspuddle, in the parish of Affpuddle, co. Dorset, and
other holdings, which he sold in 1600 to Christopher Darby, gentleman, a son of Nicholas, and he was probably the Henry Darby of
Affpuddle on whose estate administration was granted, 24 Sept. 1607,
to his relict, Joane.

It is likely, therefore, but not yet proved, that Robert Derby of
Askerswell, yeoman, was the father of Christopher Derby, yeoman,
of Henry Darby, husbandman, and of the Nicholas Derby, gentleman, who was the great-grandfather of Roger Derby of Salem, Mass.
Robert Derby was a man of considerable property for one of his
station in life, and, if the other three men were his sons, they probably owed their own evident prosperity in part to the portions which
they received from their father's estate.

In the following genealogy, based on the records given in the preceding pages, on some additional entries in parish registers consulted by Mr. Pope, on certain New England records, and on a few
authoritative compilations, an account is presented of Nicholas Derby

of Sterthill* in the parish of Burton-Bradstock, co. Dorset, gentleman, and his descendants of the name to the later years of the seventeenth century, and the relationship of John and Richard Derby of the Plymouth Colony in New England and of Roger Derby of Salem to one another and to Nicholas Derby of Sterthill is made clear.

1. NICHOLAS DERBY, of Askerswell, co. Dorset, and later of Sterthill in the parish of Burton-Bradstock, in the same county, gentleman, probably, as stated above, a son of Robert Derby of Askerswell, yeoman, and a brother of Christopher Derby of Askerswell, yeoman, and Henry Darby of Askerswell, husbandman, was the great-grandfather of Roger Derby of Salem, Mass., and died 30 Oct. 1599. He married CATHERINE ———,† who was living 28 Apr. 1600 but apparently was dead by 11 Feb. 1606.

He resided at Askerswell in 11 Elizabeth [1568–69], when he was entered in the Dorset Muster Rolls as a billman; but on 24 July 1576 he purchased of Hugh Cheverell of Chantmarle in Cattistock, co. Dorset, Esq., for £700, the lease of the farms of Upper Sterthill and Nether Sterthill and all said Cheverell's grounds there, in the parish of Burton-Bradstock, for a term of ninety-nine years from the Feast of St. Michael the Archangel [29 Sept.], 1578, if the said Nicholas and his sons Christopher and Richard should so long live, at a yearly rent of £10. 13s. 4d. John Gregorie *alias* Whetcombe of Marsh in the parish of Burton-Bradstock, in his will dated 2 Dec. 1576, states that Nicholas Derby of Sterthill owed him, the testator, the sum of £11. 14s. 8d. As early as 1583 Nicholas Derby had bought of John Wadham of Catherston, co. Dorset, gentleman, as the will of the latter shows, a lifehold estate in Bryanspuddle, in the parish of Affpuddle,‡ co. Dorset, and he also purchased from William Gould of Gussage St. Andrews, co. Dorset, gentleman, at an unknown date, the late dissolved free chapel called Sterthill *alias* St. Luke's, co. Dorset, with the houses and lands pertaining thereto in Sterthill and Nether Sterthill, and two acres in Barwicke Meadow, and all tithes belonging to the chapel, these tithes being from lands in Sterthill, Nether Sterthill, Greencombe, and a farm called Graveston. In 39 Elizabeth [1596–97] he was taxed at Sterthill on goods valued at £16. About 1598 he assigned all his estate in the farms of Upper Sterthill and Nether Sterthill to his son Christopher. That he owned a large number of sheep is evident from a case before the Court of Star Chamber in 41 Elizabeth [1598–99], in which he and others were accused of driving off sheep belonging to Robert Mason and Richard Arnold, his defense being that the sheep in question belonged to him.

The inquisition post mortem of Nicholas Derby, gentleman, dated 19 May, 42 Elizabeth [1600], shows that at his death he was seised in fee of a moiety of the manor of Bryanspuddle, co. Dorset,

---

*In the records this name appears in various forms, such as Sterthill, Stirthill, and Sturthill; and on these pages no attempt has been made at uniformity in the spelling of the name. Sterthill is a tithing in the parish of Burton-Bradstock.

†Probably Catherine Buckler. *Vide supra*, p. 420, note to Chancery deposition of 9 June 1602.

‡The parish of Affpuddle or Affpiddle is situated on the River Piddle, nine miles east from Dorchester, co. Dorset. Bryanspuddle or Bryanspiddle is a tithing of this parish.

of lands at Sterthill, and of the capital messuage called the Free Chapel of St. Luke's at Sterthill, with the tithes pertaining thereto, and that he had conveyed to his sons Roger, Laurence, and Nicholas Darby the said lands and tithes in Sterthill for their lives, and afterwards to his son Christopher Darby and his male heirs, or, in default of such heirs, to the said Roger, Laurence, and Nicholas and their heirs in succession. The jurors found that Christopher Darby was the son and next heir of Nicholas Darby and was aged 25 years and more at his father's death.

Administration on the estate of Nicholas Derby of Sturthill was granted in the Prerogative Court of Canterbury, 28 Apr. 1600, to his widow, Catherine, and on 11 Feb. 1606 to his son Christopher, the widow having probably died in the interval.

Children:

2.  i. CHRISTOPHER, bapt. at Askerswell in 1571.
   ii. RICHARD, living 24 July 1576, when he was evidently a very young child (*vide supra*, Chancery cases of 22 May 1601, 2 Feb. 1656, and 28 Nov. 1678); probably d. *s.p.* in the lifetime of his father.
  iii. ROGER, bapt. at Askerswell in 1576; d. before 20 Dec. 1639 (*vide supra*, Chancery case of 1 Dec. 1663); m. ———.
       Children:
       1. *Michael*, living 1 Dec. 1663. He had a son Matthew, living 13 Dec. 1655.
       2. *Robert*, living 13 Dec. 1655. He had issue.
   iv. LAURENCE, of Nether Sterthill, gentleman, d. in or before 1624, when his will was proved; m. ANN JACOB, who was living 13 Dec. 1655, daughter of William Jacob of Brockhampton, co. Dorset. As Ann Derby, widow, she was taxed on an annuity 20s. at Sterthill in 22 James I [1624–25]. In his will Laurence Derby directed that he should be buried in the church of Burton-Bradstock, co. Dorset.
       Children:
       1. *Matthew*, of Dorchester, co. Dorset, gentleman, solicitor, the testator of 13 Dec. 1655, b. at Brockhampton about 1608; d. *s.p.* in or before 1657, when his will was proved; m. at the Church of the Holy Trinity, Dorchester, 21 Sept. 1634, Martha Jollyffe, who m. (2) Henry Maber of Dorchester, merchant, and d. about 1672.
       2. *Laurence*, under 20 when his father made his will; living 1 Dec. 1663.
       3. *Anne*, living 13 Dec. 1655; m. before that date John Williams, gentleman, living 13 Dec. 1655.
       4. *Catherine*, living 13 Dec. 1655; m. before that date ——— Bryer.
       5. *Elizabeth*, d. before 13 Dec. 1655; m. ——— Whittell.
       6. *Cicely*, living 13 Dec. 1655; m. before that date William Polden of Dorchester, woolen draper, living 13 Dec. 1655.
    v. NICHOLAS, of Shipton-George, co. Dorset, gentleman, living 20 Apr. 1645; d. *s.p.*, probably before 11 Apr. 1659; m. MABEL ———, who survived her husband but d. not later than 1662, when her will was proved in the Archdeaconry Court. William Derby of Sterthill, co. Dorset, gentleman (3), nephew of this Nicholas Derby, was administrator of his estate and executor of the will of his widow, Mabel Derby. The various leases held by Nicholas Derby in Shipton-George and the disposition made of them by Nicholas and afterwards by Mabel Derby are set forth in a Chancery case of 1 Dec. 1663 (*vide supra*, p. 423), which contains much important genealogical information about the Derby family. Nicholas Derby was taxed on an annuity 20s. at Shipton-George in 22 James I [1624–25]. As "Nicholas Darbie of Shepton" he is included in "A Note of all such as have usurpt the

115

name and Titles of Gentlemen without Authoritie and were disclaimed at Bridport com. Dorcest. 1623 Sept. 10. Ignobiles omnes."\* But he is called gentleman in the Chancery case of 1 Dec. 1663, already mentioned, and also in his lifetime, in a deed of 16 Jan. 1640/1, in which he and his nephew, William Derby of Sterthill, gentleman, at the request of Richard and Thomas Derby, William's brothers, and in consideration of £700, convey to William Chilcott of Bredy, co. Dorset, gentleman, the late dissolved free chapel called Sterthill *alias* St. Luke's, with the houses and lands pertaining thereto in Sterthill and Nether Sterthill and all the tithes belonging to the chapel, which Nicholas Derby, gentleman, deceased, father of the said Nicholas and grandfather of the said William, Richard, and Thomas Derby, purchased from William Gould of Gussage St. Andrews, co. Dorset, gentleman.† The Dorset Protestation Rolls show that Nicholas Derby took the oath in 1641/2.

2. CHRISTOPHER DERBY (*Nicholas*), of Sterthill in the parish of Burton-Bradstock, co. Dorset, gentleman, baptized at Askerswell, co. Dorset, in 1571, died 20 Jan. 1639/40, and was buried at Shipton-George, co. Dorset. He married ANN (or AGNES) SYMONDS, the testatrix of 6 Oct. 1645, who died probably about May 1649, her will being proved 22 Feb. 1649/50 by her son and executor, Richard Derby (4), and who was a daughter of William Symonds of Exeter, co. Devon, gentleman, the testator of 20 Feb. 1633/4, and his wife Alice (Moone), and a sister of Marcella (Symonds) (Herbert) Duke, the testatrix of 17 Dec. 1656, and Rebecca (Symonds) Salter, the testatrix of 13 Nov. 1662.‡

While his father was still living, Christopher Derby was accused by the Privy Council, in a letter dated 24 June 1597 and addressed to the Marquis of Winchester, of trying to evade military service by becoming a retainer of Viscount Bindon; but whether this accusation was justified does not appear. (*Vide supra*, p. 426.) About 1598 his father assigned to him all his (the father's) estate in the farms of Upper Sterthill and Nether Sterthill, and on 22 May 1601 Christopher Derby was the defendant in a suit in Chancery (*vide supra*, p. 419), the purpose of which was to test his title to the manor house and farm of Sterthill, otherwise Upper Sterthill and Nether Sterthill, late in the tenure of Nicholas Derby and then in the tenure of the latter's son Christopher Derby. Records of several law suits in which Christopher Derby was a party are given above, and are of great help in tracing the genealogy of the family.

\*Visitation of Dorsetshire, 1623, p. 4 (*Publications of the Harleian Society*, vol. 20, anno 1885).
†Not long before 19 June 1614 Nicholas Derby (1, v) and his brothers Laurence and Roger sold to Morgan Holman of Barwicke in the parish of Swyre, co. Dorset, gentleman, the lease of some, at least, of the tithes belonging to the free chapel of St. Luke's. (Cf. the will of Morgan Holman, *supra*, p. 411.)
‡From the Symonds pedigree printed in The Visitation of the County of Devon in the Year 1620, p. 280 (*Publications of the Harleian Society*, vol. 6, anno 1872), it appears that William Simonds of Exeter, 1620 (son of Thomas Simondes of Taunton, co. Somerset), married Alice, daughter of —— Moone of Bampton, co. Dorset, and had three daughters, viz., Marcella, wife of Richard Harbert (or Herbert) of Exeter, Ann, wife of Christopher Darby of Sturtle, co. Dorset, and Rebecka, wife of Anthony Salter of Exeter. According to Tuckett's Devonshire Pedigrees, p. 40, and Hutchins's History of Dorset, vol. 3, p. 238, the father of Alice (Moone) Symonds was Robert Moone.

As has already been stated, Nicholas Derby, father of Christopher, bought of John Wadham of Catherston, co. Dorset, gentleman, as early as 1583, a lifehold estate in Bryanspuddle, in the parish of Affpuddle, co. Dorset, and at his death was seised in fee of a moiety of the manor of Bryanspuddle. In 1590 Henry Darby (probably a brother of Nicholas Derby) and others purchased from George Wadham, Esq., the manor of Bryanspuddle and certain lands, etc., in Bryanspuddle; and in 1600 Christopher Derby bought of Henry Darby a moiety of the manor of Bryanspuddle and much land in Bryanspuddle and other places nearby. (*Vide supra*, records from Feet of Fines.) Christopher Derby, therefore, seems to have come into possession of the whole of the manor of Bryanspuddle.

Perhaps some transaction connected with the acquisition of the Bryanspuddle estate and its dependencies may have given rise to a statement made 8 Feb. 1657/8, eighteen years after Christopher Derby's death, by John Chipman of Barnstable in the Plymouth Colony in New England, to the effect that his (John Chipman's) father, Mr. Thomas Chipman, late deceased at "Brinspittlle" [Bryanspuddle], "about five miles from Dorchester," co. Dorset, had sold, some threescore years since [that is, about 1598] to " his kinsman M$^r$ Christopher Derbe Living Sometime in Sturtle " [Sturthill] a " Tenement or Tenements with a Mill & other Edifice thereunto belonging . . . in Whitechurch of Marshwood vale near Burfort Alias Breadport [Bridport] in Dorsetshire " worth £40 or £50 per annum, " which were y$^e$ Lands of y$^e$ s$^d$ Thomas Chipman being Entailed to him & his Heirs for Ever." According to the statement Thomas Chipman, then unmarried, had conveyed this property to Christopher Derby for the inconsiderable sum of £40 and an agreement that he should be " maintained Like a man with Diet Apparel &c by the s$^d$ Christopher as Long as the s$^d$ Thomas Should Live; " but later, after Thomas Chipman had married and had children, he had been " turned off by the s$^d$ Christopher only with a poor Cottage and Garden Spott . . . to the great wrong of his Children Especially of his Son John Afors$^d$ to whom y$^e$ s$^d$ Lands by right of Entailment did belong." The lawyer who " made the Evidences," the " Vote of the Country who had knowledge of it," Christopher Derby's son " m$^r$ William Derbe who had the s$^d$ Lands in his Possession then from his father," Christopher's son " John Derbe Late Deceased of Yarmouth in New Plimouth Goverment," and " one m$^r$ Derbe A Lawyer of Dorchester " had all, according to this declaration, recognized that Thomas Chipman had been wronged in this transaction, and therefore his son John wished to have English records searched for further light on the matter.

John Chipman in this statement calls himself "y$^e$ only Son & Heir of M$^r$ Thomas Chipman Late Deceased at Brinspittlle," and mentions his sisters "Hanner" [Hannah] and "Tamson"

[Thomasine]. Since he adds to his declaration that he "Supposeth his Age to be About thirty seven years: it being next may [May 1658] Twenty & one year since he Come out of England," it is evident that he was born about 1620 and came to New England in May 1637. In Mar. 1641/2, probably soon after he had attained his majority, he seems to have tried to recover from John Derby (4) of the Plymouth Colony, a son of Christopher, money due to him from the elder Derby, for Ann Hinde, the wife of William Hoskins, aged 25 years or thereabouts, deposed on 2 Mar. of that year, before Mr. Edward Winslow, in a case between John Darbey and John Chipman, that she lived in the house of Mr. [John] Derby's father at the time when John Chipman, who also lived there, went out to New England as a servant of Mr. Richard Derby, John Derby's brother, that is, in the spring of 1637, and that when she, the said Ann, afterwards likewise went out to serve Richard Derby, "old Mʳ Darbey" requested her "to comend him to his cozen Chipman, and tell him if hee were a good boy hee would send him ouer the money that was due to him when hee saw good." Ann Hoskins deposed further, in reference to a statement of John Derby that the money was paid to John Chipman's mother, that the said mother was dead a quarter of a year or thereabouts before the deponent's "old master" sent the message to "his cozen Chipman." Whether John Chipman ever recovered anything from Christopher Derby or his son John does not appear, nor is it possible to determine the merits of his claim; but his declaration and the deposition of Ann Hoskins are of great importance in the history of the Derby family as well as the Chipmans.*

In 22 James I [1624-25] Christopher Derby, gentleman, was taxed at Sturthill on lands valued at £4. On 10 Apr. 1632 he appeared before the King's commissioners at Sherborne, co. Dorset, and excused himself for not compounding for knighthood on the occasion of the King's coronation by stating that he did not have at that time freehold lands of the yearly value of £10 and that all his freehold lands were not of the clear yearly value of 20 marks, for the farms of Upper Sturthill and Nether Sturthill, of which he was possessed, he held not as freehold lands but only by virtue of a lease, dated

*See the full text of the deposition of Ann Hoskins and lengthy extracts from the statement of John Chipman, supra, pp. 427 and 428. In what way Mr. Thomas Chipman, father of John Chipman, was a kinsman of Mr. Christopher Derby has not been discovered. Catherine, wife of Nicholas Derby (1), may have been a sister of Thomas Chipman's father or mother, or Thomas Chipman's mother may have been a sister of Nicholas Derby. In any one of these contingencies Thomas Chipman and Christopher Derby (2) would have been first cousins. As a youth John Chipman lived in the household of Christopher Derby, and he came to New England in May 1637, when about sixteen years old, as a servant of Christopher's son Richard, probably crossing the Atlantic in the same ship with his master, the first record of whom in New England is found in a Plymouth deed dated 12 July 1637. He became a prominent resident of Barnstable, and in 1670 was chosen and ordained one of the ruling elders of the church there. Later he removed to Sandwich, and died 7 Apr. 1708, aged (according to his gravestone) 88 years. His first wife, the mother of all his children, was Hope Howland, a daughter of John and Elizabeth (Tilley) Howland, both of whom were passengers in the Mayflower in 1620. His numerous living descendants are now widely scattered in the United States and in the Dominion of Canada.

28 July, 18 Elizabeth [1576], for a term of years. A Chancery case of 3 Feb. 1636 [1636/7], in which Christopher Derby and his sons William and Richard were defendants, shows that he had been engaged with his two sons in "the trade of mercery of linen drapery."

About the time of his marriage Christopher Derby settled on his wife a jointure of about £70 a year out of the farm of Upper Sterthill, and in Sept. 1631 he granted the farms of Upper and Nether Sterthill to certain trustees for the benefit of himself and wife and the wife of his son William, with remainder to William and his heirs. In 1632 it was agreed between Christopher and William that William should enjoy part of the farm of Upper Sterthill during the remainder of the lease of ninety-nine years. (Cf. Chancery cases of 21 May 1650, 2 Feb. 1656, and 28 Nov. 1678.)

Christopher Derby's will, which is no longer extant, was proved by his youngest son, Thomas Derby. After Christopher's death his widow, Ann, entered on part of the Upper Sterthill farm, and she and her son Richard Derby and the latter's wife and family enjoyed this part of the farm until the death of Ann, in 1649. (Cf. Chancery case of 21 May 1650.)

Children:

i.    CHRISTOPHER, bapt. in the parish of All Hallows, Exeter, co. Devon, in 1607; bur. at Burton-Bradstock, co. Dorset, in 1623.

3. ii.   WILLIAM, b. about 1608 (*vide infra*, p. 437, first footnote).

4. iii.  JOHN, b. probably about 1610.

5. iv.  RICHARD, bapt. in the Cathedral Church of St. Peter, Exeter, co. Devon, 16 Nov. 1613 (*vide infra*, p. 443, first footnote).

v.    THOMAS, of Axminster, co. Devon, youngest son, bapt. at Burton-Bradstock, co. Dorset, in 1616; living 10 Dec. 1644; d. before Jan. 1648/9, when administration on his estate was granted to John Clarke and Ann, his wife, late widow of Thomas Derby; m. ANN THOMAS, daughter of Henry Thomas of Widworthy, co. Devon, yeoman, the testator of 10 Dec. 1644. She m. (2) as early as Jan. 1648/9 John Clarke of Axminster, vintner. Thomas Derby is mentioned as a brother of William and Richard Derby and a grandson of the first Nicholas Derby (1) in the deed of 16 Jan. 1640/1, described in the account of the second Nicholas Derby (1, v), by which the free chapel of St. Luke's, etc., was conveyed to William Chilcott; and he is called youngest son of Christopher Derby and executor of his will in the Chancery case of 25 Nov. 1651.

Children:

1.  *Ann*, b. about 1640; named in the will of her grandfather, Henry Thomas, dated 10 Dec. 1644 — according to the record of the Chancery case of 30 Nov. 1650 she and her sister Rebecca, who were infants of tender age on 10 Dec. 1644, were named as executrices of this will; living unm. with John Hooper and his wife (her first cousin, Anne, daughter of her father's brother, John Derby) at Salcombe, co. Devon, 13 Nov. 1662 (see will of Rebecca Salter, *supra*).

2.  *Rebecca*, named in the will of her grandfather, Henry Thomas, 10 Dec. 1644; d. before 30 Nov. 1650. (See account of her sister Ann, *supra*.)

**3.** WILLIAM DERBY (*Christopher, Nicholas*), of Sterthill in the parish of Burton-Bradstock, co. Dorset, gentleman, mercer, born about 1608,* died 6 Mar. 1676. He married, not earlier than Jan. 1632 (when he was admitted to the liberties of the city of Bristol in order to be married), JOAN BALDWYN, who died 6 Nov. 1673 and was buried at Burton-Bradstock, daughter of Mr. William Baldwyn of Bristol and London.

In a Chancery case in June 1632 he appears as a deponent and is called William Derby of Dorchester, mercer, aged 25, and the Chancery case of 3 Feb. 1636 shows that he was associated with his father and brother Richard in the mercer's trade and that his brother Richard had been apprenticed to him in this trade.† His interest in the Sterthill farms has been mentioned above, in the account of his father; he joined his uncle, Nicholas Derby (1, v), in the sale, 16 Jan. 1640/1, of the late dissolved free chapel of St. Luke's, with the houses and lands pertaining thereto in Sterthill and Nether Sterthill, etc.; and he was a party in numerous law suits, charging his brother Richard, 21 May 1650, with committing waste on the farm of Upper Stirthill and with taking possession of some of their mother's goods after her death, and being involved in his later years in litigation with his eldest son George. On 23 Jan. 1649/50 he was adjudged by the Dorset Standing Committee not guilty of delinquency. In 1664 he paid a hearth tax for nine hearths in his house at Stirthill. His will, which is no longer extant, was proved at Bridport, co. Dorset.

Children:

i. GEORGE, in his later years of Chard, co. Somerset, gentleman, solicitor, b. about 1633; d. between 28 Nov. 1678 and 1693; m. TEMPERANCE ——— [? JENNINGS of Yeovil, co. Somerset]. He lived in his earlier years at Bradford Abbas, co. Dorset, at Yeovil, co. Somerset, and at Clonmell, co. Tipperary, Ireland. The Chancery records show that he was involved in litigation with his father and with others.

    Child:

    1. *Jennings,* of Chard, co. Somerset, gentleman, solicitor, living in 1733. He brought suit in Chancery in 1693 concerning the estate of his great-grandfather, William Baldwin. He had issue, viz., George Derby, vicar of Collompton, co. Devon, and other children.

ii. CHRISTOPHER, living 2 Feb. 1656.

*Although his age is given as 25 years in June 1632, he seems to have been born about 1608, since Christopher Derby, his brother, who was apparently older than William, was baptized in 1607.

†On 8 Nov. 1638 Ralfe Sprague of Charlestown in New England, planter, and Joane his wife, one of the daughters of Richard Warren, late of Fordington, co. Dorset, yeoman, deceased, gave a power of attorney to William Derby of Dorchester, co. Dorset, gentleman, to receive their portions from the estate of the said Richard Warren (Lechford's Note-Book, pp. 36–37). This was accompanied by a letter from Ralfe Sprague addressed to "my very worthy and good ffreind M$^r$. William Derby at his home in Dorchester or at his lodging in Terme tyme at the Sugerloafe in Sheerelane, London" (*ib.*, p. 37); and Ralfe Sprague also sent a letter to his sister, Alice Eames, "at Pomberry milles neare Dorchester" (*ib.*, p. 38). These letters show that this Mr. William Derby was a lawyer, and it is hardly likely that he was identical with the William Derby of Sterthill, gentleman, mercer, of this pedigree, although the latter may possibly have entered the legal profession after 1632. It is more probable that the man to whom Ralfe Sprague and his wife gave the power of attorney was the "Will'm Darby" who was deputy recorder of the town and borough of Dorchester on 9 Aug. 1623. (Cf. Visitation of Dorsetshire, 1623, p. 3, in *Publications of the Harleian Society*, vol. 20.)

iii. WILLIAM, of Honiton, co. Devon, apothecary, the testator of 8 May 1682, b. about 1641; d. in 1682; bur. at Burton-Bradstock, co. Dorset; m. SUSANNA (———) DEEME, widow of ——— Deeme. The "sons-in-law" and "daughter-in-law" surnamed Deeme who were mentioned in his will were his stepchildren. He owned tithes at Nether Sterthill, co. Dorset, formerly belonging to St. Luke's, which were left to him by his father. He was a defendant in a Chancery case 15 May 1675 and deposed in 1676, aged 35 years.

    Children:
1. *William*, d. in infancy in 1683.
2. *Susannah*, } under 21 8 May 1682.
3. *Margaret*, }

iv. JOHN, bapt. at Burton-Bradstock, co. Dorset, in 1639; apparently d. before 2 Feb. 1656.

v. JOHAN, living 2 Feb. 1656; apparently d. before 28 Nov. 1678.

vi. ANN, living 28 Nov. 1678, when she was the wife of WILLIAM LEVER-MORE. A legacy of £40 was left to her in the will of Mrs. Rebecca Salter, dated 13 Nov. 1662, the testatrix calling her "my cousin Anne Darby, daughter of my nephew Mr. William Darby of Dorset."

vii. HANNAH, living 2 Feb. 1656; apparently d. before 28 Nov. 1678.

viii. ELIZABETH, living unm. 28 Nov. 1678.

ix. MARY, living 28 Nov. 1678, when she was the wife of WILLIAM BOLER.

4. JOHN DERBY (*Christopher, Nicholas*), of Plymouth and Yarmouth in the Plymouth Colony in New England, born, probably in the parish of Burton-Bradstock, co. Dorset, about 1610, died in New England (probably at Yarmouth) between 4 Oct. 1655, when he made a complaint against Masshantampaine, an Indian, and 22 Feb. 1655/6, when the inventory of his estate was taken. John Chipman, in his statement dated 8 Feb. 1657/8, mentions him as "John Derbe Late Deceased of Yarmouth in New Plimouth Goverment," and shows that he was a son of Christopher Derby. He married ALICE ———,* who survived him and married secondly, at Barnstable in the Plymouth Colony, 4 Jan. 1658 [1658/9], as his third wife, Abraham Blush of Barnstable (Plymouth Colony Records, Miscellaneous Records, p. 41), who died 7 Sept. 1683, his wife Alice surviving him.†

    John Derby is found at Plymouth in New England in 1637, being granted threescore acres of land at Mounts Hill by the Court of Assistants on 6 Aug. of that year (Plymouth Colony

---

*She may have been his second wife, and perhaps he married her in New England, for two of his children, John and Anne (*vide infra*), lived in England and apparently never came to New England. He may have migrated to New England after the death of his first wife, leaving these two children with relatives in England. But it is, of course, possible that he had only one wife, the mother of all his children, and that she went with him or followed him to New England.

†Abraham Blush or Blish of Barnstable had accounts with John Cole in 1637, was proposed for freeman 1 June 1641, and was on the list of those able to bear arms in 1643. He was a town officer. By his first wife, Ann ———, who was buried 16 May 1651, he had two children, Sarah, born 2 Dec. 1641 and baptized 5 Dec. 1641, and Joseph, born 5 Apr. 1648 and baptized 9 Apr. 1648 (who married and had children in Barnstable). By his second wife, Hannah (Williams) Barker, daughter of John Williams of Scituate and widow of John Barker of Duxbury and Marshfield, who was buried about 16 Mar. 1658 [1657/8], he had Abraham, born about 16 Oct. 1654. His will, dated 17 Apr. 1682 and proved 5 Mar. 1683/4, mentions his wife Alice, his sons Joseph and Abraham, and his daughter Sarah Orchyard and her five children. (Plymouth Colony Records, Miscellaneous Records, p. 41; Savage's Genealogical Dictionary, vol. 1, p. 200; Pope's Pioneers of Massachusetts, p. 55.)

Records, Court Orders, vol. 1, p. 64). He had probably accompanied his brother Richard (5) to Plymouth or had crossed the Atlantic about the same time as his brother. On 4 Dec. 1637 "M^r John Darbys former graunt at Mounts Hill" was confirmed by the Court of Assistants (*ib.*, vol. 1, p. 69). In the records of the Court of Assistants of 5 Feb. 1637/8 "Derbys Pond, on the south side of Monts Hill chase," is mentioned (*ib.*, vol. 1, p. 76), and at a meeting of the General Court of the Colony, 6 Mar. 1637/8, "John Derby [and others] desired to be admitted freemen this Court" (*ib.*, vol. 1, p. 79). The deposition of Ann Hoskins of 2 Mar. 1641/2, taken before Mr. Edward Winslow, in the case between John Darbey and John Chipman, has already been mentioned in the account of Christopher Derby (2), and furnishes additional proof of John Derby's parentage. The inventory of the goods of William Swyft of Sandwich, deceased, exhibited 29 Jan. 1642 [1642/3], shows that the deceased owed John Derby 14s. (*The Mayflower Descendant*, vol. 4, p. 170), while according to the inventory of Mr. John Atwood, deceased, taken 27 Feb. 1643 [1643/4], John Derby owed the deceased 3s. (*ib.*, vol. 5, p. 158). His mother, Anne Derby, in her will of 6 Oct. 1645, bequeathed to him 12d.

About 1643 John Derby removed to Yarmouth, and his name appears in that year on the Yarmouth list of men able to bear arms (Plymouth Colony Records, Miscellaneous Records, p. 194). He was a supervisor of the highways at Yarmouth 1 June 1647 (Plymouth Colony Records, Court Orders, vol. 2, p. 115); and on 14 May 1648, at Yarmouth, where Captain Standish had been authorized by the Court held at Plymouth 7 Mar. 1647/8 to hold a hearing and to put an end to all differences remaining in the town of Yarmouth, it was granted "to John Darby to haue six acares of meadow in the Easteren Swan Pond Meadowe, in lewe of 4 acars dew to William Chase, for a debt the town owed him" (*ib.*, vol. 2, p. 129). On 20 Sept. 1655 Willam Pearse of Yarmouth and Elizabeth his wife conveyed unto John Darbey of Yarmouth "all our Right and Interest in our Dwelling house with sertaine appurtenances thereunto belonging heerunder specifyed and alsoe thirty and eight acres of upland more or lesse with the ffencing about p̄te of it and nine acres of meddow more or lesse; the said house and land and meddow lying and being on the basspond River; To have and to hold unto the said John Darbey," etc., "from after the first Day of May Next ensuing the Day of the Date heerof." Sundry articles of furniture included in the sale were enumerated, in the "outward Rome" and in the "Inward Rome," and the deed was witnessed by Willam Nicarson and Nicolas Nicarson. (*The Mayflower Descendant*, vol. 11, pp. 17–18, from Plymouth Colony Deeds.) At the General Court held at Plymouth 4 Oct. 1655 various complaints were made against Masshantampaine [an Indian], and John Darbey of Yarmouth stated that "his [Masshantampaine's] doges did him wrong amongst his cattell, and did much hurt one of them," whereupon the Court ordered and requested Mr. Prence and Thomas Boardman "to heare and determine the said diference as M$^r$ Prence goeth home." (Plymouth Colony Records, Court Orders, vol. 3, p. 91.)

The inventory of the estate of John Darby of Yarmouth was taken 22 Feb. 1655/6 by Edmund Hawes and Robert Dennis, and was proved before Mr. Thomas Prence 6 June 1656. Among the items were five acres of rye on the ground, children's bedding, ten acres of meadow "which hee bought of goodman Seares which is to pay for," and "one house and 38 Acars of upland and 9 Acars of meddow which hee bought of Willam Pearse," £15. The estate was indebted to Mr. Hedge, William Falland, "David the Irishman," "Peeter the Scotsman," Goodman Wells, James Lewis, Goodman Sturgis, Goodman Nicarson, Thomas Phelps, William Chase, Goodman Seares for land, £6, and "goodman Pearse for house & land," £15. (*The Mayflower Descendant*, vol. 14, p. 112, from Plymouth Colony Wills and Inventories.) At a General Court held at Plymouth 5 Mar. 1655/6 Mr. Prence was ordered and requested "to adminnester an oath vnto the widdow Darbey, somtimes the wife of John Darbey, of Yarmouth, deceased, for the truth of the inuentory of his estate." (Plymouth Colony Records, Court Orders, vol. 3, p. 96.)

All his sons appear to have died without issue, but his daughters married and had children.

Children (the first two perhaps by an earlier wife than the wife who survived him):

i.   JOHN, of Sterthill, in the parish of Burton-Bradstock, co. Dorset, probably b. in England; d. *s.p.* about 1649, administration on his estate being granted 7 Aug. 1651 to his sister, Anne Darby, spinster (*vide supra*, p. 413). That this John was a son of John the son of Christopher Derby is proved by the Chancery case of 25 Nov. 1651, given above (p. 421). Apparently he was left in England when his father went to New England.

ii.  ANNE, probably b. in England; living 13 Nov. 1662, when she was mentioned in the will of her great-aunt, Rebecca (Symonds) Salter (*vide supra*, p. 413), as "my cousin Anne Hooper, wife of John Hooper;" m. after 25 Nov. 1651 (when, as Anne Derby of Ottery St. Mary, co. Devon, spinster, she brought a suit in Chancery in regard to the estate of her brother John, of which she had been appointed administratrix on 7 Aug. preceding) JOHN HOOPER of Salcombe, co. Devon. Apparently she, too, was left in England when her father went to New England.

iii. ABRAHAM, probably b. in New England about 1640; m. HANNAH ———, b. about 1642. "Hannah Darbey, aged thirty two or therabouts," deposed on 19 Nov. 1674, and said "that my husband, Abraham Darbey, gaue vnto my brother in law, Jabez Lumbert, liueing in Barnstable, in the jurisdiction of New Plymouth, order to sell all the lands left him by his father, John Darbey, deceased, within the bounds of Yarmouth, in the aforsaid jurisdiction, with all the priulidges and appurtenances thervnto belonging, and for the which I receiued p̄te of the payment in my husbands absence, by my brother Lumbert, which when my husband came home I aquainted my husband therwith, and hee was satisfyed with my brother Lumbert, for soe much as I had

123

receiued, and in what hee had doñ in the sale of the aforsaid lands." (Plymouth Colony Records, Court Orders, vol. 5, p. 158.) Another deposition about Abraham Darbey's lands was made 4, 1 mo. 1674/5 by "John Gorum, Senir, aged 53 yeares, or therabouts," who testified "that some time since, hee being desired to write a memorandum of an agreement between Jabez Lumbert and Zachariah Ryder, concerning lands of Abraham Darbey, which is in the bounds of Yarmouth, and they coñitted the writing, after it was written, to my keeping, some space of time after, Abraham Darbey, coming from Verginnia, put in on the othersyde of the Cape, and come to my house, and I told him that his brother, Jabez Lumbert, had sold all rights of lands in the bounds of the towne of Yarmouth, and Abraham Darbey said what hee had done in that respeċt hee had giuen him order soe to doe, and it should be made good, or to that very purpose." (Ib., vol. 5, p. 157, and The Mayflower Descendant, vol. 5, p. 28.) It would appear, from John Gorham's deposition, that Abraham Derby was a mariner. No record of children has been found.

iv. SARAH, probably b. in New England about 1642; m. at Barnstable, 1 Dec. 1660, JABEZ LUMBART [i.e., LOMBARD] of Barnstable, b. at Barnstable about 1 July 1642, son of Bernard Lumbart (Barnstable records, in The Mayflower Descendant, vol. 11, p. 96).

Children (surname Lumbart), b. at Barnstable (ib., vol. 11, pp. 96–97*):

1. *A son*, b. 18 Feb. 1661/2; d. the same day.
2. *Elizabeth*, b. in June 1663; m. 10 Mar. 1684 Ben Gage.
3. *Mary*, b. in Apr. 1666; m. in May 1686 James Lovell.
4. *Bernard*, b. in Apr. 1668; m. and had children b. at Barnstable.
5. *John*, b. in Apr. 1670.
6. *Matthew*, b. 20 Aug. 1672.
7. *Mehitable*, b. in Sept. 1674; m. 24 Sept. 1693 William Lovell.
8. *Abigail*, b. in Apr. 1677.
9. *Nathaniel*, b. 1 Aug. 1679; m. and had children b. at Barnstable.
10. *Hepthsibah*, b. in Dec. 1681.

v. MARY, probably b. in New England about 1644; d. 16 Mar. 1705/6; living unm. 12, 8 mo. 1662, when Jone Swift of Sandwich, in her will of that date, bequeathed "unto Mary Darbey my wearing clothes" (The Mayflower Descendant, vol. 16, p. 21, from Plymouth Colony Wills and Inventories), a bequest which seems to indicate that Mary Darbey was a relative of the testatrix or perhaps a servant in her household; m. about 1663, as his second wife, NICHOLAS NICKERSON of Yarmouth, b. in England probably about 1630, d. before 26 Mar. 1681/2, when the inventory of his estate was taken, son (apparently the eldest) of William and Anne (Busby) Nickerson. The estate of Nicholas Nickerson, amounting to £125. 9s. 3d., was settled 31 Oct. 1682 (Plymouth Colony Records, Court Orders, vol. 6, p. 99). Some time after his death, and later, of course, than 7 Sept. 1683, the date of the death of Abraham Blush, the Court ordered that the land on Monk's Hill in Plymouth should be divided between Widow Blush [formerly the wife of John Derby] and Widow Nicarson, who had received nothing of her father, John Darby, deceased, before (Pope, Pioneers of Massachusetts, p. 130). Administration on the estate of Mary (Derby) Nickerson was granted 16 Apr. 1706 to her son John, and the estate was settled 14 May 1706 by an agreement signed by William, John, Elizabeth, and Patience Nickerson,

---

* See also for this family Otis's The Lumbert or Lombard Family, in Library of Cape Cod History and Genealogy, no. 54, Savage's Genealogical Dictionary, vol. 3, p. 106 (who gives Sarah, wife of Jabez Lumbart, as daughter of Martha Derby), and REGISTER, vol. 3, p. 272, and vol. 12, p. 249. The marriages of these children are given on the authority of Otis.

children, and Jonathan White of Yarmouth, Simon Crosby of Harwich, and John Burg [Burgess] of Yarmouth, sons-in-law.*

Children (surname *Nickerson*), b. at Yarmouth:

1. *John*, of Yarmouth, b. 10 Sept. 1664; m. Elizabeth Baker of Yarmouth.
2. *A child*, d. in Oct. 1667, a jury of inquest finding on 14 Oct. 1667 that the child, lately deceased, of Nicholas Nicarson was choked by a piece of pumpkin shell which was found in its windpipe (Plymouth Colony Records, Court Orders, vol. 4, p. 170).
3. *Mary*, b. in the last week of July, 1668; m. at Eastham, 27 Aug. 1691, Simon Crosby (*The Mayflower Descendant*, vol. 5, p. 195). Residence, Harwich.
4. *Sarah*, b. 1 May 1674; m. John Burgess of Yarmouth.
5. *Patience*, b. 3 Apr. 1682; living unm. 14 May 1706.

vi. ELIZABETH (probably a daughter of John Derby), probably b. at Yarmouth about 1646; m. at Barnstable, 23 Dec. 1665, THOMAS LUMBARD [i.e., LOMBARD] of Barnstable (Barnstable records, in *The Mayflower Descendant*, vol. 11, p. 97). The relationship of this Thomas Lumbard to the Jabez Lumbart who m. Sarah Derby seems not to have been determined.†

Children (surname *Lumbart*), b. at Barnstable (*ib.*, vol. 11, p. 97‡):

1. *Sarah*, b. in Dec. 1666; d. 5 May 1753; m. 30 May 1689 John Phinney.
2. *Thomas*, b. in Mar. 1667; d. 30 May 1761; m. and had children b. at Barnstable.
3. *Elizabeth*, b. in Sept. 1668.
4. *Mary*, b. in Apr. 1669; m. 11 Dec. 1689 Daniel Parker.
5. *Hannah*, b. in Dec. 1671.
6. *Jabez*, b. in Feb. 1673; d. aged about 8 days.
7. *Rebecca*, b. in May 1676; m. 8 Dec. 1698 Benjamin Parker.
8. *Jabez*, b. in June 1678.
9. *Bethiah*, b. in July 1680; m. 7 Dec. 1704 Joseph Robinson.
10. *Bathshua*, b. in Aug. 1682.
11. *Patience*, b. in Sept. 1684; m. 6 Apr. 1704 Judah Rogers.
12. *Martha*, bapt. in 1686.§

vii. A SON, b. at Yarmouth "the last of" Feb. 1647/8 (Plymouth Colony Records, Miscellaneous Records, p. 3); probably d. young, as no further record of him has been found.

viii. MATHEW, of Barnstable, b. at Yarmouth 8 Feb. 1649/50 (Plymouth Colony Records, Miscellaneous Records, p. 9); d., probably *s.p.*, between 6 July 1671 and 1 Mar. 1674/5, for on 6 July 1671, in the settlement of the estate of John Turner, the Court declared that Mathew Darbey was entitled to all of said Turner's estate except a mare (*The Mayflower Descendant*, vol. 19, p. 61), and on 1 Mar. 1674/5, it appearing "to the Court [held at Plymouth], that Jabez Lumbert was left by Mathew Darbey, deceased, with order to looke after his estate in his absence, which hee hath in

*For Nicholas Nickerson and his children see, in addition to the references given in the text, Hawes's William Nickerson and Children of William (1) Nickerson, in Library of Cape Cod History and Genealogy, nos. 102 and 91. Abundant references to authorities are given in these two pamphlets. Since Mary Derby was unmarried on 12 Oct. 1662, a fact which had not been published when Mr. Hawes prepared his account of the Nickerson family, it is clear that she was not the mother of the three oldest children of Nicholas Nickerson, viz., Hester, b. in the last week of Oct., 1656 (who m. 2 Feb. 1682/3 Jonathan White of Marshfield, son of Peregrine White), William, b. 12 Jan. 1658/9 (who m. at Eastham, 22 Jan. 1690/1, Mary Snow, daughter of Mark and Jane (Prence) Snow of Eastham, and lived first at Eastham and then at Harwich), and Elizabeth, b. in Dec. 1662 (who was living unm. 14 May 1706). Among those who signed the agreement of 14 May 1706 for the settlement of the estate of Mary (Derby) Nickerson were therefore the stepchildren as well as the children of the deceased. Cf. *The Mayflower Descendant*, vol. 2, p. 208, and vol. 4, p. 33.

†Savage says that this Thomas was perhaps brother, perhaps son of Bernard, and Otis gives him as a son of Bernard and therefore a brother of the Jabez Lumbart who m. Sarah Derby.

‡*Vide supra*, p. 441, footnote. The marriages and deaths of these children, except the death of the first Jabez, are given on the authority of Otis.

§This child is given on the authority of Otis, *op. cit.*

this collonie, this Court therfore doth order, that the said Jabez Lumbert doe looke after and gather in all such dues and debts as are owing and belonging to the said Darbeyes estate, and keepe a faire accompt of the same, soe as hee may be reddy to giue in the said accompt, when any heire shall appeer, or when the Court shall see cause to require it." A note in the margin against this record shows that the Court granted to the said Lumbert administration on this estate. (Plymouth Colony Records, Court Orders, vol. 5, p. 160.) Jabez Lumbert was the husband of Mathew Derby's sister Sarah (4, iv).

5. RICHARD DERBY (*Christopher, Nicholas*), of Sterthill in the parish of Burton-Bradstock, co. Dorset, gentleman, mercer, later of Plymouth in New England, and later again of England, baptized in the Cathedral Church of St. Peter, Exeter, co. Devon, 16 Nov. 1613,* was living 13 Nov. 1662, when he was mentioned in the will of his aunt, Rebecca (Symonds) Salter, but died probably before 14 Apr. 1671, when administration on the estate of his son Samuel was granted to his (Richard's) son Roger (6). He married, about 1642, ALICE LEACHLAND, born before 6 Feb. 1620/1, when she was mentioned in her father's will, living 12 Feb. 1654/5, daughter of Roger Leachland of Chard, co. Somerset, merchant, and his wife, Margaret (Jones) Leachland.†

He lived with his brother William (3) as an apprentice in the mercer's trade, and on 3 Feb. 1636 [1636/7] was a defendant, with his father and his brother William, in a case in Chancery that related to their transactions in the trade of mercery of linen drapery. Soon afterwards, apparently in May 1637, he went to New England, taking with him as a servant his kinsman John Chipman (see deposition of Ann Hoskins and statement of John Chipman, *supra*, pp. 427, 428). Very likely his brother, John Derby (4), accompanied him on his voyage to New England. He was in Plymouth on 12 July 1637, as appears by a deed of that date of which the essential portions are here given.

Edward Dotey, in consideration of the sum of £150, conveyed to Richard Derby "All those his Messuages houses and tennements at the heigh Cliffe or Skeart hill together w^th the foure lotts of lands and three other acres purchased of Josuah Pratt Phineas Pratt & John Shaw." . . . Richard Derby agreed to pay the sum of £150 "in manner following That is to say Twenty pounds by Bill of Exchaunge in old England (if the said Edward Dotey can p'cure the same here) or els in lue thereof one heiffer which the said Edward shall make choyce of to be valued by two indifferent men to be chosen by eich p'te w^ch said sume to be in p't of payment of the said hundred and fifty pounds & the residue of the said hundred & fifty pounds to be payd at the returne of the said Richard Derby forth of old England w^ch wilbe w^thin two yeares now next ensuing (if God p'mitt.)." Richard Derby "shall haue p'sent possession of all the said cheif Messuage

---

*See the Register of Exeter Cathedral, published by the Devon & Cornwall Record Society, p. 5. The baptism is given as that of Richard Darbye, son of Mr. Darbye, and undoubtedly refers to the Richard Derby (5) of this pedigree.

†See the wills of Alice Leachland's parents, *supra*, pp. 411, 413, and also the Lechland pedigree in The Visitation of the County of Somerset in the Year 1623, p. 67 (*Publications of the Harleian Society*, vol. 11, anno 1876).

(except one inner chamber wherein the said Edward Dotey layeth his Corne) and of one lott & three acres of the said lands, and as much more as he cann conveyniently take in & make vse of to plant vpon. . . . Edward Dotey shalbe in possession of thother house & thother three lotts of land vntill he shalbe . . . payd the said hundred & fifty pounds and . . . it shalbe lawfull for him to reape this crop & another crop the next yeare and then if the said Richard Derby shall not be returned forth of old England or haue not payd . . . the 150li by that tyme yt shall be lawfull for the said Edward Dotey to sowe the second Crop and reape it and so a third vntill the said Richard Derby shall haue payd . . . the said 150li. . . . Richard Derby shall p'cure one able man servant to be brought ouer to serue the said Edward Dotey for the terme of fiue six or seauen yeares for whose passage the said Edward Dotey shall pay fiue pounds to the said Richard Derby & p'forme such other couenants to the said servant as the said Edward shall agree vpon wth twelue bushells of Indian graine at thend of his terme.". . . Edward Dotey shall "make vse of the two oute houses for the houseing of his Corne and Cattle vntill he be payd the said 150li wch said houses the said Edward shall keepe and leaue in as good repaire (as now they are) when he leaues them as also the dwelling house (he is to use as aforesd) & the fence vpon the lands as sufficient as now they are. . . . Wm Hodgkinson shall hold his tyme in such p'te of the said lands as hee now occupyeth for his terme, wch is two crops more besids this p'sent crop now vpon the ground." [This agreement was signed by Richard Derby, and Edward Dotey made his mark thereunto.] (Plymouth Colony Records, Deeds, vol. 1, pp. 20–21.)

Mr. Richard Derby seems to have gone back to England soon after the date of this agreement with Edward Dotey, and to have returned to Plymouth a few months later — he probably went in the autumn of 1637 and returned in the spring of 1638, for on 31 Aug. 1638 the following memorandum was entered in the records of the Court of Assistants at Plymouth:

"Whereas Willm Snow was lately brought ouer out of Old England by Mr Richard Derby, and is his couenant servant for fiue yeares, as appeares by his indenture, beareing date the xxth of Februar., 1637 [1637/8], — now the said Richard Derby hath assigned ouer the said Willm Snow vnto Edward Dotey, to serue him the residue of the said terme of fiue yeares, and two yeares longer, that is to say, for the terme of seuen yeares from the xxth day of October next ensuing. . . ." (Plymouth Colony Records, Court Orders, vol. 1, p. 94.)

In bringing over from England William Snow and in assigning him to Edward Dotey as a servant Richard Derby fulfilled one clause of his agreement with Edward Dotey of 12 July 1637. Ann Hinde, afterwards Ann Hoskins, who was living in the house of Mr. Christopher Derby when John Chipman "came from thence to New England to serue Mr Richard Darbey" [i.e., in May 1637] and who "came afterwards likewise ouer to serue the said Richard Darbey," bringing a message from "old Mr Darbey" to "his cozen Chipman," may have made the voyage with Richard Derby on his return to Plymouth in 1638 (see her deposition, *supra*);* and on 24 Oct. 1638 "Richard Clark, servant to Mʳ Richard Derby, is turned ou' to Mʳ Atwood" (Plymouth Colony Records, Court Orders, vol. 1, p. 100). Richard Derby's father advanced the passage money for at least one immigrant to New England, as the following deposition of 8 Nov. 1638 shows:

Thomas Harvey of Cohannett, yeoman, aged 21 years or thereabouts, deposed and said that he, the deponent, "haueing a bond or writing vnder the hand and seale of Walter Knight carpenter whereby the said Walter Knight stood endebted in the sume of five pounds sterl' vnto Mʳ Christopher Derby wᶜʰ was payd for his passage ouer the wᶜʰ five pounds is to be payd vnto Mʳ Richard Derby here [at Plymouth]: as this deponent was reading the same (at the sᵈ Knights request) in the ship as they came ouer The said Walter Knight snatched the said bond or writing out of this deponᵗˢ hands and iñediately tore the same in peeces." (Plymouth Colony Records, Deeds, vol. 1, pp. 38–39.)

At a Court of Assistants held at Plymouth 3 Sept. 1638 "Mʳ Rich: Derbye requesteth lands towards the six miles brooke" (Plymouth Colony Records, Court Orders, vol. 1, p. 95), and at a General Court held the next day (4 Sept.) "Richard Derbye" served on a jury which found three men guilty of murdering and robbing an Indian (*ib.*, vol. 1, pp. 96–97). On the same day also Richard Derby, gentleman, was surety, in the sum of £20, for the appearance of Richard Clough before the next General Court (*ib.*, vol. 1, p. 97). The agreement of 12 July 1637 in regard to the sale of Edward Dotey's property at High Cliff to Richard Derby was not carried out, as appears by the following entry in the records of the Court of Assistants of 1 Oct. 1638:

"Whereas sixtie acres of lands were graunted to Edward Dotey . . . vpon report that he had sould his house and land at Heigh Cliffe to Mʳ Richard Derby, wᶜʰ bargaine is now relinquished, the said Edward Dotey doth also relinquish the said grant" (*ib.*, vol. 1, p. 99).

On 25 Oct. 1638 "Richard Derby complaines agˢᵗ Edward Dotey, in an action vpon the case, to the dañ of xiiijˡⁱ" (Plymouth Colony Records, Judicial Acts, p. 10). On 16 Apr. 1639 Richard Derby, gentleman, was bound in the sum of £40 to appear at the next General Court to answer charges "concʳning the ympoysoning of the body of John Dunford, (whereby he is disabled to worke,)," and John Barnes of Plymouth, yeoman, and Gyles Rickett of the same became sureties for him in the sum of £20 each. (Plymouth Colony Records, Court Orders, vol. 1, pp. 120–121.) At the next General Court, on 4 June 1639, Richard Derby of Plymouth, gentleman, is again bound in the sum of £40, John Combes of Plymouth, gentleman, and Edward Dotey of Plymouth, yeoman, being sureties, each in the sum of £20, to answer charges "concʳneing the giueing of an empoysoned potion of drinke to John Dunford & diuers others at his comeing out

*She was married 21 Dec. 1638, as his second wife, to Mr. William Hoskins of Plymouth, planter. (Cf. Pope's Pioneers of Massachusetts, p. 234.)

of England, whereby they were endangered of their liues"
(*ib.*, vol. 1, p. 128); and John Danford on the same date
brought a complaint against Richard Derby, gentleman, "in
an action vpon the case, to the dam̃ of xxˡⁱ," the jury finding
for the plaintiff and assessing the damages at £20, in addition to the charges of the Court. (Plymouth Colony Records,
Judicial Acts, p. 12.) John Dunford, however, seems to have
been an undesirable inhabitant of the Colony, for at the same
General Court, on 4 June 1639, he was sued for slander by
William Hoskine and Ann his wife, who asked for £60 as
damages. The jury found for the plaintiffs, and assessed the
damages at 20s. and the charges of the Court (*ib.*); and "John
Dunford, for his slaunders, clamors, lude & euell carriage,
p'ued as well by his owne confession as otherwise, is cen-
sured to depᵗ the gou'ment wᵗʰin the space of three months
next ensuing, and in the meane tyme well to behaue himself, and if after his depᵗure he shalbe found wᵗʰin the
gou'ment againe, to be whipt & sent from constable to constable out of the gou'ment" (Plymouth Colony Records,
Court Orders, vol. 1, p. 128).

Richard Derby was a party to another real-estate transaction during his brief residence in Plymouth. On 24 Sept.
1639 Edward Dotey of Plymouth, planter, in consideration of
the sum of £22, "to him in hand payd by Mʳ Richard Derby,"
sold to the said Richard Derby "one lott of Land contayne-
ing twenty acrees lying at the heigh Cliff the Lands of John
Winslow lying on the North side thereof and the lands of the
said Edward Dotey on the South side;" and on the same
day Richard Derby, in consideration of the sums of 20s., "to
him in hand payd," and £20, "to be payd in England by the
appoyntment of Samuell King of Plym̃," sold to the said
Samuell King "the abouesaid xx acres of lands at the heigh
Cliffe & fence about the same," etc. (Plymouth Colony
Records, Deeds, vol. 1, pp. 46–47.)

At a General Court held on 1 Sept. 1640 John Shawe complained against "Mʳ Richard Derby, in an action of trespas
vpon the case, to the dam̃ of vjˡⁱ." The jury found for the
plaintiff and assessed 50s. damages and the charges of the
Court. (Plymouth Colony Records, Judicial Acts, p. 18.)
Whether Richard Derby was still at Plymouth when this action was brought may be doubted. At any rate, he was back
in England by 16 Jan. 1640/1 (*vide infra*), and at the Court
of Assistants held at Plymouth on 3 Jan. 1642/3 execution
was granted to John Shawe against John Barnes, "for Richard Derby." In the records of the same court is found the
following entry:

"Whereas Richard Willis is endebted vnto Richard Derby the sum
of fourty shillings for a bedd, the which bed not being seene by the
said Willis, but taken vpon the said Derbys word, and it now appeare-
ing, by the oath of Willm Nelson, that the said bed was not answerable
to that goodness the said Derby affirmed it to be of, nor of such

129

waight by sixteene pounds as he affirmed also it was, and that the tick of the said bed was full of patches, for w<sup>ch</sup> the said Willis was to haue payd three pounds fiue shillings, whereof xxv<sup>s</sup> is payd, — now, the Court doth order that twenty shillings more shalbe payd in full satisfaccõn for it, & no more." (Plymouth Colony Records, Court Orders, vol. 2, p. 50.)

The entry given above is the last statement about Richard Derby that has been found in New England records. His father, Christopher Derby, gentleman, died in England on 20 Jan. 1639/40, and Richard seems to have returned to England soon after receiving the tidings of his father's death, for on 16 Jan. 1640/1 he joined his uncle, Nicholas Derby (1, v), and his brothers, William Derby (3) and Thomas Derby (2, v), in conveying to William Chilcott the late dissolved free chapel called Sterthill *alias* St. Luke's, etc. (*vide supra*, p. 418). For a while he resided at Combe St. Nicholas, co. Somerset, apparently carrying on his trade as mercer there, and after his marriage with Alice Leachland, about 1642, he and his wife lived for two years with his wife's mother, Margaret Leachland, widow, at Chard, co. Somerset, where also he carried on his trade as mercer (see Chancery case of 27 June 1653, *supra*, p. 421). Then he and his wife and family lived with his mother on part of the farm of Upper Stirthill, co. Dorset; and after his mother's death, which occurred about 1649, he was sued by his brother William for committing waste on the farm and for taking possession of some of his mother's goods (see Chancery case of 21 May 1650, *supra*, p. 421). His mother, in her will dated 6 Oct. 1645, bequeathed 12d. to her son William, 12d. to her son John, and 5s. to the poor of Shipton, and made her son Richard her residuary legatee and executor of her will. On 27 June 1653 his brother-in-law, Thomas Leachland of Chard, co. Somerset, merchant, sued Richard Darby, mercer, and Alice his wife, this litigation arising from matters connected with a loan of £20 made about twelve years before by Alice Leachland, then unmarried, to her mother (see Chancery case of this date). On 12 Feb. 1654/5 Richard Derby, then of Beare [in Seaton], co. Devon, mercer, with Alice his wife and Joane Thorne, widow, his sister-in-law, sued Thomas Leachland, the executor of the will of Margaret Leachland, Thomas's mother, for legacies bequeathed in this will to the said Alice and Joane and to two children of Joane, the mother Margaret having died on 24 Oct. 1654 (see Chancery case, *supra*, p. 422). On 13 Nov. 1662, as already stated, "Mr. Richard Darby" was mentioned in the will of his aunt, Rebecca (Symonds) Salter, and he probably died between that date and 14 Apr. 1671.

Children:

6. i. ROGER, b., probably at Chard, co. Somerset, about 1643.
   ii. SAMUEL, of Exeter, co. Devon, d. before 14 Apr. 1671, when administration on his estate was granted to his brother, Roger Darby of Topsham, co. Devon, chandler (*vide supra*, p. 414). He was named as a legatee in the will of his great-aunt, Rebecca (Symonds) Salter, dated 13 Nov. 1662.

iii. ANN, of Exeter, co. Devon, d. unm. before 28 Apr. 1671, when administration on her estate was granted to her brother, Roger Darby of Topsham, co. Devon, chandler (*vide supra*, p. 414). She was named as a legatee in the will of her great-aunt, Rebecca (Symonds) Salter, dated 13 Nov. 1662.

6. ROGER DERBY (*Richard, Christopher, Nicholas*), of Topsham, co. Devon, chandler, and afterwards of Ipswich and Salem, Mass., born, probably at Chard, co. Somerset, about 1643, died at Salem 26 Sept. 1698, aged 55 years. He married first, at Topsham, co. Devon, 23 Aug. 1668, LUCRETIA HILMAN, baptized at Topsham 6 Aug. 1643, died at Salem, Mass., 25 May 1689, daughter of John and Honor Hilman (or Holman) of Woodbury and Topsham, co. Devon;* and secondly, in 1691, ELIZABETH (HASKETT) DYNN, born in England (probably at Exeter, co. Devon) about 1667, died before 8 Apr. 1740 (when administration on her estate was granted to her son-in-law, Joshua Hicks), daughter of Stephen and Elizabeth (Hill) Haskett of Exeter, co. Devon, and Salem, Mass., and widow of William Dynn of Salem (born at Kinsale, Ireland, about 1660, came to New England in 1678, died in 1689–90), to whom she had been married 6 June 1684 and by whom she had two sons, John and William, who were mentioned in the will of their stepfather, Roger Derby, dated 26 July 1698.†

Roger Derby, the founder of a distinguished Salem family, was living in Topsham, co. Devon, 13 Nov. 1662, when he was named as a legatee in the will of his great-aunt, Rebecca (Symonds) Salter; and, as Roger Darby of Topsham, co. Devon, chandler, he was appointed administrator of the estate of his brother Samuel Darby of Exeter, 14 Apr. 1671, and of his sister Ann Darby of Exeter, 28 Apr. 1671. Very soon after this last-mentioned date he must have embarked for

*For the baptism of Lucretia Hilman and for other Hilman data see extracts from the parish registers of Topsham, *supra*, p. 415. The marriage of Roger Derby and Lucretia ——— is printed in the Vital Records of Salem, vol. 3, p. 293, from the records of the Essex County Quarterly Court.

From a note furnished by the late Mrs. Lucy (Derby) Fuller, wife of Rev. Samuel Richard Fuller and daughter of the late Elias Hasket Derby, A.M. (whose descent from Roger Derby of Salem is given in REGISTER, vol. 35, p. 198), it appears that John Hilman, father of Lucretia (Hilman) Derby, was the son of Vincent Hilman (or Holman) of Woodbury and Topsham, co. Devon, and that, when Vincent and John Hilman died, their estates were administered as belonging to Topsham, but John was buried at Woodbury. This John Hilman, according to Mrs. Fuller's note, apparently had a house at Woodbury called "Pilehays," where he carried on his farming, but followed his occupation of shipbuilder at Topsham. In the Devon poll tax of 1660 (Subsidy Rolls, Topsham, 245/14) he paid the tax for himself, his wife, two daughters (Margaret and Lucretia), and three servants. His wife Honor was buried at Woodbury in 1672, and his son John was administrator of his estate in 1674. The children of John and Honor Hilman were: 1. John. 2. Margaret, bapt. at Topsham 24 July 1641; living in 1660. 3. Lucretia, bapt. at Topsham 6 Aug. 1643; m. Roger Derby. 4. Josias, bapt. at Topsham 20 May 1647; d. in 1697; a sailor on H. M. ship *Medway*. 5. Charles, bapt. at Topsham 8 Feb. 1648/9; buried there 18 May 1651; his name was borne by the first child of Roger and Lucretia Derby. A Vincent Helman, probably the father of John, was buried at Topsham 20 Jan. 1643/4, and a Lucretia Hillman, widow, probably John's mother, was buried there 13 Apr. 1654. In a Chancery deposition of 1663, given above (p. 423), Vincent Hillman of Topsham, co. Devon, shipwright, is said to have died about twelve years since [i.e., about 1651], and his widow, Ursula, appears as administratrix of his estate. This Vincent was presumably a brother of John, the father of Roger Derby's wife, and the baptisms of five of his children are recorded in the Topsham registers, from 16 Sept. 1632 to 13 Feb. 1641/2. He seems to have had two wives, Mary and Ursula.

†*Vide* REGISTER, vol. 77, pp. 128–129. (Pages 25–26, this volume.)

New England, for he arrived in Boston 18 July 1671,* accompanied by his wife Lucretia and his son Charles, then a few days less than two years old. He settled first at Ipswich, Mass., but in 1681 he removed to Salem, his home for the remainder of his life, where he was a shopkeeper.† During their stay at Ipswich Mr. Roger Derby and his wife Lucretia were repeatedly presented and fined for absence from the public meeting on the Lord's days.‡

Children by first wife:§

i.  CHARLES, b. at Topsham, co. Devon, 27 July 1669, and bapt. there 30 July 1669; d. in the expedition against Quebec, 8 Oct. 1690. He deposed 7 Apr. 1682, aged about 13 years (Essex Court Records, vol. 8, p. 341).

ii. EXPERIENCE, b. at Ipswich 18 Dec. 1671; m. at Salem, 22 June 1698, JOSEPH FLINT.

iii. SAMUEL, b. at Ipswich 24, 9 mo. 1673.

iv. ROGER, b. at Ipswich 1 Jan. 1675.

v.  JOHN, b. at Ipswich 25 Feb. 1677.

vi. RICHARD, of Salem, mariner, b. at Ipswich 8 Oct. 1679; d. at Salem 25 July 1715; m. at Salem, 25 Feb. 1702 [1702/3], MARTHA HASKETT, who d. at Salem 2 May 1746, youngest daughter of Stephen and Elizabeth (Hill) Haskett of Exeter, co. Devon, and Salem, Mass., and sister of Elizabeth (Haskett) Dynn, who became, in 1691, the second wife of Richard Derby's father, Roger Derby. Four children, of whom the third, *Richard*, of Salem, master mariner and merchant, 1712–1783, was the father of Elias Hasket Derby, the well-known Salem merchant, 1739–1799.

vii. LUCRETIA, b. at Salem 17 Aug. 1681.

viii. EBENEZER, b. at Salem 9, 9 mo. 1683; d. 20 Jan. 1688.

Children by second wife, born at Salem:‖

ix. ELIZABETH, b. 10 Mar. 1691/2; d. before 29 Dec. 1721, when her will was proved; m. at Salem, 17 Apr. 1718, THOMAS PALFREY, sailmaker, b. at Salem 24 June 1689, d. before 1 Aug. 1720, when his will was proved, son of Walter and Margaret (Manning) Palfrey. One daughter, who d. young.

x.  MARGARET, b. 14 Aug. 1693; d. 11 July 1765; m. at Salem, 8 Feb. 1710/11, WILLIAM OSBORNE, yeoman, b. 3 May 1682, d. at Danvers, Mass., 28 Sept. 1771, son of William and Hannah (Burton) Osborne of Salem. Eight children.

xi. ANN, b. 10 Dec. 1695; living 19 June 1752, when she was named as executrix in her husband's will; m. at Salem, 2 Jan. 1717/18, CAPT. BENJAMIN IVES, master mariner and tanner, b. at Salem about 1692, d. between 19 June 1752, when his will was dated, and 16 July 1752, when his will was proved, son of Thomas and Elizabeth (Metcalf) Ives. Nine children, b. at Salem.

xii. MARTHA, b. 30 Sept. 1697; m. at Salem, 22 Oct. 1719, JOSHUA HICKS of Salem, merchant. Eight children.

*Vital Records of Salem, *loc. cit.*
†Savage, Genealogical Dictionary, vol. 2, p. 40.
‡Records and Files of the Quarterly Courts of Essex County, Mass., *passim*.
§Cf. Vital Records of Salem, *passim*; Savage, *loc. cit.*; REGISTER, vol. 77, p. 131 (for Richard).**
‖Cf. Vital Records of Salem, *passim*; Savage, *loc. cit.*; REGISTER, vol. 77, pp. 129–130.**

**For pp. 131 & 129-130 see pp. 28 & 26-27, this volume.

## GENEALOGICAL RESEARCH IN ENGLAND

Contributed by G. ANDREWS MORIARTY, JR., A.M., LL.B., of Newport, R. I.,
and communicated by the Committee on English Research

### DUNSTER

IN 1854 the Massachusetts Historical Society published in its *Collections* (Series 4, vol. 2, pp. 190–198) several papers which had belonged to Henry Dunster, the first president of Harvard College, and had descended from him to a great-great-granddaughter, Hannah Dunster of Pembroke, Mass., by whom they had been presented in 1852 to Edward Swift Dunster, a member of the Harvard Class of 1856, who had found them in Miss Dunster's house. Edward Swift Dunster afterwards became well known in the medical profession, served as an assistant surgeon in the Union Army in the Civil War, and was professor of obstetrics in various medical schools and universities from 1868 until his death in 1888.[*]

The first of these papers was a letter, dated 20 Mar. 1640/1 and written by Henry Dunster of Balehoult (or Baleholt), an estate in the parish of Bury, co. Lancaster, England, to his son, Rev. Henry Dunster, who in the preceding summer had entered upon his fourteen years' service as the first president of Harvard. This letter disclosed the name of President Dunster's father and his English home, gave considerable information about his immediate relatives, and told also of the advance of the Scots into England, on the eve of the Civil War.[†]

Efforts, however, to identify in the parish registers of Bury the record of the baptism of President Dunster were for many years unsuccessful, the parish clerk of Bury persisting in his statement

[*] Cf. Henry Dunster and His Descendants, by Samuel Dunster (father of Edward Swift Dunster), 1876, pp. 316–322.

[†] This letter has been printed also in Chaplin's Life of Henry Dunster, 1872, and in Dunster's Henry Dunster and His Descendants, 1876.

that the Henry Dunster who was baptized there in Nov. 1609 was recorded as the son of "Thos. Dunster" and not as the son of Henry Dunster. But in 1898 the Lancashire Parish Register Society published the first volume of the parish registers of Bury, containing the baptisms, marriages, and burials from 1590 to the end of 1616; and in this volume the baptism of 26 Nov. 1609 is given as that of "Henry s. of Henrye Dunster," this entry having evidently been misread by the parish clerk in previous years. Two other volumes, published by the same society in 1901 and in 1905, brought the printed registers of Bury down to the year 1698; and from the Dunster entries in these registers and from sundry American records Mr. J. Gardner Bartlett, the well-known genealogist, was enabled to compile a brief genealogy of the early generations of the family, which he communicated to the REGISTER in Apr. 1907 (vol. 61, pp. 186–189).*

After the appearance of Mr. Bartlett's communication no further interest, apparently, was manifested in the family and antecedents of the first president of Harvard until the present writer undertook to make a careful search of the Lancashire records, including the Lancashire wills and administrations preserved in the Consistory Court of Chester, the Court Rolls of the Manor of Tottington, in the parish of Bury, which are preserved at Clitheroe Castle, the Feet of Fines, etc. Abstracts of such recently discovered records as throw light on the Dunster family are given below, and reveal the paternal ancestry of President Dunster back to his great-grandfather (Mr. Bartlett's genealogy had not established the line with certainty back of the President's grandfather) and his probable descent from a still more remote ancestor. These abstracts are followed by a pedigree of the early generations of the family, in which the substance of Mr. Bartlett's pedigree is repeated, with such corrections and additions as the records presented in this article show to be necessary. The so-called Balehoult letter and the Dunster entries in the early parish registers of Bury, being easily accessible in print, are not reproduced here; but the information derived from the parish registers is given in the pedigree.

### FROM PROBATE RECORDS

The Will of ROBERT DUNSTURE of Tottington, co. Lancaster, husbandman, dated 3 August 1599. My goods are to be divided into three parts, one to Jony, my wife, another to Henry Dunsture, my son, and the third for myself. To Robert Dunsture, son of Henry, 10s. To Henry, Alice, and Elizabeth, children of Henry Dunsture, my brother, 12d. apiece. To the three children of Robert Battersbie 12d. To James, son of Ellis Lomax, and the three children of Rauffe Wosencrofte 12d. To my brother Henry Dunsture my best hose and doublet. All my arks, chests, carts, husbandry gear, etc., to my said son Henry, my wife to have the use thereof until he attains the age of twenty-one years. The residue of my estate equally to my wife and son. Executors: Jony, my wife, and Thomas Warberton of Elton, he to have the tuition of my son. Overseers: Peter Shawe, clerk, parson of Bury, Henry Dunsture, my brother, John Barlow of Heape Bridge, and George Scholes, my brother-in-law.

Debts owing to the testator: Ryc. Fletcher of Redyvalles, 50s.; Thomas Key of Elton, 20s.; Thomas Battersbie, my brother-in-law, for hire of a cow, 12s.; in lent money, Henry, my brother, 30s., and, for various items,

*See Vol. I of this work, pp. 8-11.

58s. 4d.; Rychard Booth by bond £11, etc. Debts I owe: To Robert, James, and Thomas, children of Richard Fletcher of Redivalles, to every of them 13s. 4d., when of age. Witnesses: Peter Shawe and Thomas Dearden, clerk, the writer of this will.

The Inventory of the goods of Robert Dunster, deceased the last day of August, 41 Elizabeth, 1599, "prysed" by John Bouthe, Ryc. Holte, Peter Lomax, and Thomas Nuttall, includes: a yoke of oxen, £8. 6s. 8d.; two horses, £8. 6s. 8d.; four kine, £10. 6s. 8d.; five young beasts, £7. 6s. 8d.; corn and hay, £14; saddle, bridle, boots, sword, dagger, bows and arrows, 20s.; total value, £106. 5s. 4d.

Proved 16 November 1599 by the executors named, before the rector of Bury, by commission. (Consistory Court of Chester.)

The Will of Elizabeth Dunster, late wife of Henry Dunstier of Tottington, co. Lancaster, deceased, dated 30 May 1602, being weak in body. To Isabel Holt 40s. To James Lomaxe, son of Ellis, 13s. 4d. To my brother George Undsworthe 6s. 8d. To the wife of Ralph Wolsoncrofte 40s. To my son Henry Dunstier the long chest under the ladder. To the wife of Thomas Battersbye my best brass pot, my two best gowns, two petticoats, cloak, and linen clothes. To my servant or servants at my death 3s. 4d. apiece. Executors: Henry Dunstier, my son, and Thomas Battersbye, my son-in-law. Supervisors: Thomas Whithead the Elder and Henry Whithead, his brother, and I give to either of them 13s. 4d. Residue: one part to the children of my son Henry Dunstier and Elizabeth his wife, the other part to the children of Thomas Battersbye and his wife Katherine, when [said children are] married or when they shall attain the age of twenty-one years. Witnesses: Thomas Nuttall, Richard Smethurst *alias* Nichols, and Ralph Asinall [?Aspinwall]. Inventory taken 2 May 1605 by John Bouthe, Thomas Nuttall, George Undsworth, and Tho: Warberton, £94. 13s. The will of Elizabeth Dunster of Tottington, widow, was proved 16 June 1605 by the executors named. (Consistory Court of Chester.)

Administration on the estate of Henry Dunster of Elton, co. Lancaster, deceased, was granted 23 January 1610 [1610/11] to Elizabeth, his relict, before Hugh Watmoughe, clerk, rector of Bury, by commission.

Inventory taken and "priced" 19 January 1610/11 by Thomas Kaye of Elton, John Kaye of Widdell, Richard Greenhalgh of Tottington, Laurence Lorte, Ralph Brocke, Richard Grinhalgh of Bury, and James Barlowe, butcher, £86. 7s. 10d.

"Certayn debts owing to the deceased Henry Dunster on the daie of his departure, viz., Mr. John Grynehaulgh, Esq., £11; Robert Rydinge, £10; Wm. Potts, gent., £3; Henry Dunstier, £20: 3: 4; James Dunstier, £3: 10: 0; Water Swawev, gent., 15/; Thomas Baterson, 40/; Summa, £50/8/4."

Total of debts and goods, £136. 16s. 2d. Exhibited 12 February 1610 [1610/11]. The widow and relict sworn. (Consistory Court of Chester.)

Administration on the goods of Henry Dunster of Bury, co. Lancaster, was granted 29 April 1614 to Elizabeth Dunster, his widow and relict, before Hugh Watmough, clerk, rector of Bury, by virtue of a commission dated 28 March 1614.

A true and perfect account of Elizabeth Dunster, widow, relict and administratrix of the goods of Henry Dunster, late of the parish of Bury, deceased, taken and examined before Mr. Hugh Watmough, clerk, parson of Bury, by virtue of a commission out of the Consistory Court of Chester, dated 28 March 1614.

"Goods, etc., in her hands, 138/9/6. Whereof she hath paid as followeth: Unto Elizabeth Fenton of the parish of Bury the residue of a bill of £5: 10: 0, [viz.] £3:15:0. Expenses, £3:8:0. Letters of administration, £1:2:0. Unto Thomas Allen, tanner, by Bill, 40/. James Barlow of Bury, by Bond, £11. John Grennaugh of Ainsworth, half a Bill for £8/6/8, 4/3/4. Elizabeth Entwisell, extrix of the will of Richard Entwisell of Broadhead, decd., half remainder of a bill of £7, 1/16/8. Frances Hamer of Chessune, by Bond, £4. Roger Kaye of Tottington, by Bond, £5:10:0. Ralph Brook of Tottington, by Bill, 6:12:0. Ann Meadowcroft of Haslame, By Bond, £5:10:0. Thomas Holt, gent., by Bond, £4, by Bill, £8. Thurstane Raustome of Dovelach, by Bill, 30/. James Sarocold of Leach, by Bond, £7. Richard Spakeman of Newton, by Bill, £3:6:0. John Lomas, upon Bill made unto his wife while she was sole, 58/8. For a Commission for taking this Accomptant's oath upon these accounts, etc., 33/4. Total receipts, £138:9:6. Total payments, £152:7:8. Excess payments, £4: 8:2." (Consistory Court of Chester.)

The Will of HENRY DUNSTER of Baleholt in the parish of Bury, co. Lancaster, yeoman, dated 6 December 1645, being weak in body. Whereas I have assured £50 unto Joan, my wife, at the making hereof, all the rest and remainder [of my estate I give] to my three children, Richard, Alice, and Elizabeth Dunster, equally. Executors: my said three children. Witnesses: William Alte, Tho: Whitehead, George Woods. Proved 14 December 1646 by Richard Dunster, with power reserved for the remaining executors.

The Inventory of the goods of Henry Dunster of Baleholt, co. Lancaster, yeoman, late deceased, "prysed" 28 September 1646 by Rich. Kaye, Senior, Thomas Kaye, William Greenhalghe, yeoman, Rich: Lomaxe, cowper, and John Booth, joiner, includes: six kine, £22. 10s.; three oxe stirkes and a why stirke, £10. 10s.; five calves, £6. 6s. 8d.; one graye stoned horse, £7; one ould gray paceing gelding, £4. 10s.; one young gray fillye, 3 years old, £6; one other gray fillye, £5; oats unthreshen, £16; pewter, £2. 14s.; potte metle, £4. 4s.; the High Chamber over the parlour above; the other high chamber; the Parlour above; the Parlour below; the high chamber below; the Brewhouse; the great arke in Roberts [sic], 12s.; bookes of all sorts, 13s. 4d. In the House: one greate Table, a stoole at the end, a forme at the side, and a table under the wyndowe, £1. 6s. 8d.; one harvest cart, wheels, and cart rope, £1; linnen, £2. 18s.; apparell, £5. 10s.; total, £165. 12s. 11d.

Debts owing by the testator, Henry Dunster: to Richard, Alice, and Elizabeth Dunster 20 markes apeece, by two bonds, £40; to the wife of Robert Dunster £1. 8s.; to Robert Smythe, his servant, £1. 2s.; to Dorothy Houlte, his servant, 2s.; to William Querall, Smyth, for work, 3s.; to John Kaye of Borras, for grass, £1. 13s. 4d.; to George Wood, for oil, £1. 6s.; to Mr. Fleetwood, in arrears of rent, £18; owing for his tithe of corn £1.12s.; in borrowed moneys to Alice and Elizabeth Dunster £6; to Richard Dunster £3; total, £75. 13s.

Funeral expenses of the said Henry Dunster: for meat bought in Boulton, £3. 3s. 3d.; ale, 6s.; wine, 6s.; for a coffin and a cloth to lay over the corpse, 7s.; to the clerk, 4s.; to the poor, £1. 10s.; to the cook, 7s.; spent in town, 2s.; for wheat bread, 3s. 4d.; in wheat, malt, meal, and butter, £1. 15s.; total, £8. 4s. 1d.

A like account of the funeral expenses of Joane, late wife of the said Henry Dunster: for spices of all sorts, 10s.; wheat bread and ale, 10s. 6d.; meat bought in Boulton, £1. 5s. 6d.; to Roger Kaye for going to Eccles, 1s.; to the poor, £1. 3s. 4d.; to the cook, 6s. 6d.; to the clerk, 4s.; for a coffin and cloth, 7s.; spent in town, 1s. 6d.; to John Fletcher, for meal, £1. 10s.; to Mris Croston, for two pigs, 5s.; to Richard Greenehalghe, for other two pigs, 4s.; for helping to serve, 5s.; wheat, malt, meal, and butter, £1. 14s.;

to the church wardens, for church dues for them both, 6s. 6d.; total, £8. 4s. 10d.

4 June 1647. Inventory exhibited on behalf of the relict and administratrix, administration having been previously granted in 1646. [There is no Act Book for this year.] (Consistory Court of Chester.)

The Inventory of the goods of ROBERT DUNSTER of Tottington, co. Lancaster, exhibited 24 August 1646 [a fragment only of the inventory remains, the top, with the endorsement of the administration grant, being gone], includes: corne, £7; hay, £4; brass of all sorts, £1. 17s.; pewter, 7s.; wool and yarn, £1. 9s.; apparell, £4; total, £48. 10s. 4d. [No Act Book for 1646.] (Consistory Court of Chester.)

FROM CHESTER MARRIAGE LICENCES*

1608    Arthur Kay and Joan Dunster, Parish of Bury, Lanc. Bondsman, Richard Lever. At Bury. 23 February [1608/9]. (Vol. 1, p. 53.)

1610    William Fletcher and Alice Dunster, Parish of Bury, Lanc. Bondsman, Francis Key of Burrowes. At Bury. 29 December. (*Ib.*, p. 91.)

1621    Robert Dunster and Mary Gerrard, Spinster, Parish of Bury, Lanc. Bondsman, Robert Whittaker. Licence to Mr. Hugh Watmough. 19 September. (Vol. 2, p. 144.)

1625    Daniel Dunster and Elizabeth Fletcher, Spinster. Bondsman, William Pilkington. At Leyland, Lanc., or Rufforth, Lanc. 16 June. (Vol. 3, p. 32.)

FROM THE COURT ROLLS OF THE MANOR OF TOTTINGTON,<br>HONOR OF CLITHEROE, CO. LANCASTER†

Halmote held at Holcome on Saturday after the Feast of Corpus Christi, 2 Henry VIII [1 June 1510]. . . . Inquisition taken from the Fee of Todyngton upon the oaths of Geoffrey Nuttau, George Kyrkman, Henry Dunster, Richard Ryder, Edmund Bukley, and Nicholas Whytheide. . . . (Vol. 3, p. 275.)

Halmote held at Totyngton on 20 March, 2 Henry VIII [1510/11]. . . . Inquisition taken from the Fee upon the oath of Lawrence Kay and Ralph Kay, constables of the Fee of Midilton; John Dunster and Thomas Bradley, constables of the Fee of Alcryngton; . . . (*Ib.*, p. 276.)

Halmote of the Manor of Tottyngton, held at Holcom on Saturday after St. Michael the Archangel, 20 Henry VIII [3 October 1528]. . . . From Tottyngton Fee the jurors present that Ellis Flecher (20d.) made a fray upon Robert Doustere, and the said Robert (20d.) upon the said Ellis. . . . (*Ib.*, p. 303.)

Halmote of the Manor of Tottyngton, held at Holcom on Saturday next before Pentecost, 22 Henry VIII [4 June 1530]. . . . Charles Nuttoo sues John Dunster and Thomas Werberton, his pledge, for 26s. 8d. debt, for the salary of the chapel of Holcom. The jury award the whole debt to the plaintiff. . . . (*Ib.*, p. 306.)

Halmote of the Manor of Tottyngton, held at Holcome on Saturday next before the Feast of Saints Simon and Jude, Apostles, 36 Henry VIII [25

---

*The marriage licences here given have been adapted from the printed volumes entitled Marriage Licences granted within the Archdeaconry of Chester in the Diocese of Chester, which have been published by the Lancashire & Cheshire Record Society. The reference in parentheses at the end of each entry indicates the volume and page of the printed Marriage Licences where the entry may be found.

†These entries down to the year 1567 have been printed in volume 3 of The Court Rolls of the Honor of Clitheroe, in the County of Lancaster, edited by William Farrer and published from 1897 to 1913, and the references to the pages of this volume are given in parentheses after each of the early entries.

October 1544]. . . . The jury say that . . . Thomas Grenealgh (6d.) of Tottyngton and the relict of Robert Dunster (6d.) diverted a stream at Schoe Gapp. . . . (*Ib.*, p. 340.)

Halmote of Tottington, held at Holcome 25 October, 30 Elizabeth [1588]. The Fee. The jurors present Robert Dunstyre and Richard Grenehaulghe for making an affray against the Queen's peace. Each is fined 20d.

Halmote of the Manor of Tottington, held at Holcome on Friday, 8 June, 41 Elizabeth [1599], before Sir Richard Mollineux, Knight, chief steward there. The Fee. Henry Dunstyre and Thomas Spackman are fined 12d. each for unlawfully obstructing Thomas Bothe from making and grinding his corn crop at Tottington Mill on 25 January last [1598/9] to the grave damage of the said Thomas Bothe.

At a Halmote of the Manor of Tottington, held at Holcome on Saturday, 7 May, 12 James I [1614], came Richard Assheton of Middleton, Knight, Robert Holte and William Holte, Esquires, and Robert Heywood, Gentleman, and gave notice that, at the special demand of John Greenhalgh, junr., of Brandlesome, Gentleman, John Greenhalgh and Henry Cowpe, customary tenants of the said manor, surrendered a messuage, sixteen acres of land, meadow, and pasture in Tottington, with land in Alden, late in the tenure of Henry Dunster, to the use of the said Henry Dunster and his assigns for a term of twenty-one years. The said Henry Dunster was admitted and gave 5s. 8d. as fine.

1 June 1622. The commissioners for dividing the commons of Tottington amongst the copyholders and freeholders set forth to Henry Dunster three acres, twenty-eight falls of land on the common called Affetsyde in Tottington, in right of his freehold land in the said manor, bounded on the west by Watling Street, on the north by Mr. Bradshay's land, on the south by John Warberton's, and on the east by John Greenhalgh's.

## From Feet of Fines, Palatinate of Lancaster*

Final Concord between Margaret Meadowcroft, widow, querent, and Henry Dunster and Isabel, his wife, deforciants, of a messuage, garden, three acres of land, one acre of meadow, and three acres of pasture and common of pasture in Tottington [co. Lancaster], with warranty against the heirs of Henry. Consideration, £66. 13s. 4d. (Palatinate of Lancaster, Fines, 17/114, m. 70, dated Monday in the fifth week of Lent, 4 Charles I [1628].)

Final Concord between John Lomax, querent, and Henry Dunster and Isabel, his wife, deforciants, of a messuage, two gardens, four acres of land, one acre of meadow, six acres of pasture, one acre of wood, ten acres of gorse and heath, four acres of moor, and four acres of turf and common of pasture in Tottington [co. Lancaster], with quitclaim from the heirs of Henry. Consideration, £66. 13s. 4d. Covenant signed at Breighmett, 12 August, 12 Charles I [1636]. (Palatinate of Lancaster, Fines, 17/129, m. 40, dated Monday, 22 August, 12 Charles I [1636].)

The Dunsters, a family of small yeomen, had long been settled in or near the parish of Bury, co. Lancaster. A John Dunster who was of Tottington, in the parish of Bury, in 1510/11, was perhaps the father of the John Dunster who was of Tottington in 1530. A Henry Dunster, of Tottington in 1510, was born probably about 1480, and was perhaps the father of Robert Dunster, of Tottington in 1528, who was born probably about 1505 and was dead in 1544. (*Vide supra*, Court Rolls of the Manor of Tottington.) This Robert Dunster was probably the father of

*Preserved in the Public Record Office, London.

1. HENRY· DUNSTER, of Tottington, in the parish of Bury, co. Lancaster, who was born probably about 1530, and was buried at Bury 11 Apr. 1592.  He married ELIZABETH ——— [? UNDSWORTH], the testatrix of 30 May 1602, who was buried at Bury 1 May 1605, her will being proved 16 June 1605.
Children:

2. i. ROBERT, b. about 1555.
   ii. KATHERINE, m. THOMAS BATTERSBY, and had children under age and unmarried 30 May 1602.
3. iii. HENRY, b. about 1560.

2. ROBERT DUNSTER (*Henry*), of Baleholt, an estate in Bury, co. Lancaster, the testator of 3 Aug. 1599, born about 1555, was buried at Bury the last of Aug. 1599.  He married JONY ——— [? SCHOLES], who was buried at Bury 21 Nov. 1624.
Children:

4. i. HENRY, b. about 1580.
   ii. JONY, m. at Bury, 27 Feb 1608/9, ARTHUR KAYE.
   iii. ELIZABETH, m. at Bury, 14 Feb. 1608/9, JAMES KAYE.

3. HENRY DUNSTER (*Henry*), of Elton, a hamlet in Bury, co. Lancaster, born about 1560, was buried at Bury 16 Jan. 1610/11. He married ELIZABETH ———, who was buried at Bury 8 Apr. 1617.
   Administration on his estate was granted to his widow on 23 Jan. 1610/11 and again on 29 Apr. 1614.
   Children, the baptisms of all except the first one being recorded at Bury:

   i. ALICE, b. about 1590; m. at Bury, 4 Jan. 1610/11, WILLIAM FLETCHER of Gosforth in Bury, who was bur. at Bury 19 Aug. 1626.
      Children (surname *Fletcher*), bapt. at Bury:
      1. *Jane*, bapt. 22 Sept. 1611; bur. at Bury 5 Sept. 1612.
      2. *Isabel*, bapt. 4 July 1613; bur. at Bury 19 Mar. 1616/17.
      3. *Alice*, bapt. 24 June 1615; probably the Alice Dunster of Tottington in Bury who d. 29 Sept. 1688 and was bur. at Bury 1 Oct. 1688; m. at Bury, 27 Sept. 1636, as his second wife, her second cousin, Robert Dunster (6), *q.v.*
   ii. JOHN, bapt. 16 Apr. 1591; bur. at Bury 22 May 1591.
5. iii. HENRY, bapt. 30 Apr. 1592.
   iv. ROBERT, bapt. 1 June 1595; m. at Bury, 22 Sept. 1621, MARY GERRET.
      Child:
      1. *Daniel*, bapt. at Bury 10 Mar. 1621/2.
   v. ELIZABETH, bapt. 12 Mar. 1597/8.
   vi. DANIEL, bapt. 24 Aug. 1600; m. at Bury, 16 June 1625, ELIZABETH FLETCHER.
   vii. JAMES, bapt. 13 Mar. 1602/3; m. at Bury 19 May 1635 SUSAN FITTON.

4. HENRY DUNSTER (*Robert, Henry*), of Baleholt in the parish of Bury, co. Lancaster, yeoman, the testator of 6 Dec. 1645, born about 1580, was buried at Bury 16 Sept. 1646.  He married first, about 1602, ———,* who was buried at Bury 7 Feb.

*Possibly she was the Isabel, wife of Henry Dunster, who joined with her husband in 1628 and 1636 in sales of land at Tottington.

1643/4; and secondly, at Bury, 4 Dec. 1644, JOAN ORPE, who was buried there 19 Sept. 1646.

It was a letter of 20 Mar. 1640/1, written by him and addressed to his son Henry in New England, that revealed the English home and parentage of the first president of Harvard College. (*Vide supra*, p. 86.)

Children by first wife, baptized at Bury:*

    i.  ISABEL, bapt. 1 May 1603; bur. at Bury 10 June 1611.
6.  ii.  ROBERT, bapt. 18 Aug. 1605.
    iii.  JOHN, bapt. 24 Aug. 1606; probably d. young.
    iv.  MARGARET, bapt. 17 Jan. 1607/8; bur. at Bury 20 Aug. 1625.
7.  v.  HENRY, bapt. 26 Nov. 1609.
    vi.  THOMAS, bapt. 8 Dec. 1611/12; living, a widower, at Bury 20 Mar. 1640/1, the letter from his father of that date stating that Thomas "is now a widower for both wife and children are dead since Michaelmas."
    vii.  ALICE, bapt. 19 Dec. 1613; living unm. in 1646.
    viii.  RICHARD. He came to New England with his brother Henry in 1640, but apparently returned after a few years to Bury in Lancashire. (Cf. the Balehoult letter.)
    ix.  ELIZABETH, bapt. 26 Apr. 1619; came to New England between 1647 and 1651; m. in 1651, as his second wife, MAJ. SIMON WILLARD† of Concord, Mass.; d. *s.p.* about six months after her marriage. Maj. Simon Willard m. (3) in the latter part of 1652 Mary Dunster, who had come to New England in the summer of 1652 and was either the Mary Dunster (6, ii) who was bapt. at Bury 5 Dec. 1630, daughter of Robert Dunster and niece of Simon Willard's second wife, or the Mary Dunster (5, vii) who was bapt. at Bury 25 Oct. 1629, daughter of Henry Dunster (5) and second cousin of Simon Willard's second wife. President Dunster in his will refers to Mary (Dunster) Willard as "sister Willard," because her husband, Maj. Simon Willard, was his brother-in-law, having been the husband of the President's sister, Elizabeth Dunster. By his third wife, Mary Dunster, Maj. Simon Willard had eight children, and after his death she m. (2) 14 July 1680 Dea. Joseph Noyes of Sudbury, Mass., and d. in Dec. 1715.

5.  HENRY DUNSTER (*Henry, Henry*), of Elton, a hamlet in Bury, co. Lancaster, was baptized at Bury 30 Apr. 1592. He married at Bury, 10 Oct. 1615, ISABEL KAYE, who was buried there 10 Dec. 1638.

Children, baptized at Bury:

    i.  RICHARD, bapt. 23 Mar. 1616/17.
    ii.  MARY, bapt. 14 June 1618; bur. at Bury 19 May 1620.
    iii.  HENRY, bapt. 29 Nov. 1620.
    iv.  JOHN, of Elton, bapt. 4 May 1623; had issue.
    v.  DANIEL, bapt. 8 Aug. 1625.
    vi.  ALICE, bapt. 16 Dec. 1627.
    vii.  MARY, bapt. 25 Oct. 1629; perhaps the Mary Dunster who came to New England in 1652 and m. (1) in 1652, as his third wife, MAJ. SIMON WILLARD, and (2) 14 July 1680 DEA. JOSEPH NOYES. (*Vide supra*, under 4, ix.)
    viii.  ELIZABETH, bapt. 15 July 1632; perhaps the Elizabeth Dunster who came to New England and m. at Cambridge, Mass., 9 Dec. 1653, BENANUEL BOWERS of Cambridge. They were Baptists and

---

*The record of the baptism of Richard has not been found, but it is probable that he was baptized at Bury.

†Maj. Simon Willard married (1) in England, about 1631, Mary Sharpe, by whom he had nine children.

Quakers, and suffered persecution for twenty years. She is mentioned in President Dunster's will as "cousin Bowers."* Nine children.

ix.  JAMES, bapt. 26 Apr. 1635.

6.  ROBERT DUNSTER (*Henry, Robert, Henry*), of Tottington and Baleholt, in the parish of Bury, co. Lancaster, baptized at Bury 18 Aug. 1605, was buried there 24 Sept. 1644. He married first ———, who was buried at Bury 31 Dec. 1634; and secondly, at Bury, 27 Sept. 1636, his second cousin, ALICE FLETCHER (3, i, 3), who was baptized at Bury 24 June 1615 and was probably the Alice Dunster of Tottington in Bury who died 29 Sept. 1688 and was buried at Bury 1 Oct. 1688, daughter of William and Alice (Dunster) Fletcher of Bury.

Children by first wife, baptized at Bury:

i.  MARGARET, bapt. 30 Mar. 1628/9.
ii.  MARY, bapt. 5 Dec. 1630; perhaps the Mary Dunster who came to New England in 1652 and m. (1) in 1652, as his third wife, MAJ. SIMON WILLARD, and (2) 14 July 1680 DEA. JOSEPH NOYES. (*Vide supra*, under 4, ix.)
iii.  HENRY, bapt. 18 Mar. 1631/2; bur. at Bury 12 Oct. 1632.
iv.  HENRY, bapt. in Nov. 1634; bur. at Bury 1 Oct. 1641.

Children by second wife, baptized at Bury:*

v.  BETHIA, bapt. 9 Dec. 1638; bur. at Bury 29 Jan. 1647/8.
vi.  FAITH, bapt. 7 Mar. 1640/1; came to New England; m. 12 May 1664 JOHN PAGE of Watertown and Groton, Mass. She is mentioned in President Dunster's will as "cousin Faith Dunster," the word "cousin" being used in the sense of "niece." The Pages of Groton and Salem, Mass., are descendants of John and Faith (Dunster) Page.
vii.  ALICE, bapt. 15 Jan. 1642/3; bur. at Bury 1 Oct. 1644.

7.  REV. HENRY DUNSTER (*Henry, Robert, Henry*), the first president of Harvard College, baptized at Bury, co. Lancaster, 26 Nov. 1609, died at Scituate in the Plymouth Colony in New England 27 Feb. 1658/9. He married first, at Cambridge, Mass., 22 June 1641, ELIZABETH (HARRIS) GLOVER, who died 23 Aug. 1643, having had no children by President Dunster, sister of Richard Harris and widow of Rev. Josse Glover, who had died on the voyage to New England in 1638; and secondly, in 1644, ELIZABETH ———, born about 1627, died at Cambridge 12 Sept. 1690, perhaps daughter of that Hugh Atkinson of Kendall, co. Westmoreland, England, whose daughter Helen Atkinson came to New England and married, in Jan. 1655/6, as his third wife, Capt. Joseph Hills of Malden, Mass.

Henry Dunster was matriculated at Magdalene College, Cambridge, England, in 1627, and was admitted to the degree of Bachelor of Arts in 1630/1 and to that of Master of

*See REGISTER, vol. 64, pp. 186–187, for evidence tending to show that the Elizabeth Dunster ** who married Benanuel Bowers was a niece of President Dunster. In that case she was probably a daughter of the President's brother, Robert Dunster (6), and his second wife, Alice (Fletcher) Dunster, and was probably born between 27 Sept. 1636, the date of their marriage, and 9 Dec. 1638, the date of the baptism of their daughter Bethia. President Dunster mentioned in his will "my cousin Bowers," but he may have used the word "cousin" in the sense of "niece," as he certainly used it when he mentioned "my cousin Faith Dunster." *Vide infra*, p. 95. — EDITOR.

**See Vol. I of this work, pp. 9–10.

Arts in 1634.   He taught school at Bury for several years, and was curate of Bury in 1634.*   Among the contributions from the clergy in the Diocese of Chester, 1634–1636, was one of 3s. 4d. from Henry Dunster, curate of Bury, in the Deanery of Manchester.   In the will of Henry Bury of Bury, clerk, dated 22 Oct. 1634, a legacy of 20s. is left to "Mr. Dunster that studious and painfull minister."   In the summer of 1640 he migrated to New England, and was immediately made the first president of Harvard College, holding this office from 27 Aug. 1640 to 24 Oct. 1654, when, having announced his opposition to infant baptism, he was forced to resign the presidency of the College.   Soon afterwards he settled at Scituate in the Plymouth Colony, where he was minister until his death.   In accordance with the directions of his will he was buried at Cambridge, Mass.   In his will he mentioned, among others, "my cousin Bowers," "my cousin Faith Dunster," "my sister Willard of Concord," and "my sister Mrs. Hills of Malden."

Children by second wife:

i.    DAVID, b. at Cambridge, Mass., 16 May 1645;  supposed to have gone to England.
ii.   DOROTHY, b. at Cambridge, Mass., 29 Feb. 1647/8;  d. young.
iii.  HENRY, b. at Cambridge, Mass., in 1650;  d. young.
iv.   JONATHAN, of Cambridge, farmer, b. at Cambridge, Mass., 28 Sept. or 27 Oct. 1653;  m. thrice.  Through him the American Dunsters who are descendants of President Dunster trace their descent.†
v.    ELIZABETH, b. (probably at Scituate, but her birth is recorded at Cambridge, Mass.) 29 Dec. 1656;  d. in 1729;  m. (1) about 1686 MAJ. JONATHAN WADE of Medford, Mass., who d. 24 Nov. 1689; m. (2) about 1714 COL. NATHANIEL THOMAS of Marshfield, Mass. Two daughters by first husband, both of whom d. unm.

*Venn, Alumni Cantabrigienses, part 1, vol. 2, p. 76.
†Cf. Henry Dunster and His Descendants, by Samuel Dunster, 1876, p. 23 *et seq.*

# GENEALOGICAL RESEARCH IN ENGLAND

Communicated by the Committee on English Research

## METCALF

Contributed by CHARLES EDWARD BANKS, M.D., Colonel, U. S. A., Retired, of Chicago, Ill.

THE presumed English ancestry of Michael Metcalf of Dedham, Mass., which represents him as a son of the Rev. Leonard Metcalf of Tatterford, co. Norfolk, while reasonably entertained as possible, has been held in abeyance through a misapprehension of the evidence relating to it. An examination of the parish registers of Tatterford disclosed a Nicholas [sic], baptized in 1586, son of the Rev. Leonard Metcalf, who was rector of Tatterford, and Amy, his wife. This had been assumed as an error for Michael; but this assumption, of course, was rejected as an unsound inference and the relationship of the Rev. Leonard Metcalf to Michael, the emigrant, rejected as a consequence. The error in this conclusion lies in the fact that the registers of Tatterford are a piece of patchwork, constructed prior to 1616 by the wardens of the parish from the then existing Bishops' transcripts. On the first written page of the registers is found this statement:

"True Coppies of certeyne Bills Indented of the Marriages Christninges and Burialls . . . extracted owte of the office of Registershipp of the Archdeconry of Norff: as followeth."

The actual registered entries begin in 1616, but the continuity from 1569 is broken. Bills for the years 1570, 1579, 1580, 1585, and 1590 are marked as "not to be found." Four later years are also recorded as "not found," but 1590 is the significant loss in connection with Michael Metcalf, as will be explained. This fact has not been taken into account by previous investigators.

The Rev. Leonard Metcalf became rector of this parish in 1574, and was the only head of a family of his name there; but, while it is known that he had a large family, only the baptisms of five sons are of record, namely, John, in 1583, Leonard and Nicholas, in 1586, Mathew, in 1592, and Nynian, in 1596. The writer, however, has found in the Diocesan Registry at Norwich (in the Consistorial Deposition Books) a deposition of Michael Metcalf, in which he describes himself as of Norwich, dornick weaver, aged 45 years, and born in Tatterford.* This carries his birth year back to 1590, and, as the records for that year are missing in the synthetically prepared registers, it explains why it is impossible to produce positive evidence of his parentage; but the negative evidence is quite as strong, for, in addition to his own statement of age and birthplace, there is nothing to show that any other Metcalf family lived there, and the Rev. Leonard Metcalf was by all reasonable circumstantial

---

*Although Colonel Banks does not give the date of this deposition, it was evidently made in 1635. — EDITOR.

evidence his father. His place in the family is in the gap between Nicholas and Mathew shown above.

Confirmatory collateral evidence is found in the fact that Michael Metcalf was warden of St. Benedict's, Norwich, 1619–1634, a natural position for the son of a clergyman to occupy, and his fine signatures on the deposition and the Wardens' Account Book, written with a sure hand ending in a graceful flourish, further indicate his early training and association in an educated family.

The statement in the Metcalf genealogy published in the REGISTER (vol. 6, p. 171), that his wife Sarah was born at "Waynham," should be corrected, for an entry in the records of the First Church of Dedham, Mass., states that she was born at Heigham, near Norwich [co. Norfolk], 17 June 1593. She was a daughter of Thomas and Elizabeth (Benslye) Elwyn of that parish (see Mr. Moriarty's article on "The Elwyns of Norfolk," in *Miscellanea Genealogica et Heraldica* for March 1926), the Elwyns being a distinguished family in that county.

In another deposition in the same court made in 1614, the Rev. Leonard Metcalf, clerk, rector of the parish of Tatterford, states that he was 73 years of age, that he had been the incumbent there for forty years, and that he was born at Apperside in the North Riding of Yorkshire.

These facts lay the foundation for further research into the earlier generations of the Metcalf family, which seems to be peculiar to Yorkshire. Amy, wife of the Rev. Leonard Metcalf, died in 1602, and his estate was administered in 1616 as of West Barsham, Norfolk, of which he was vicar, holding this living as well as the rectory of Tatterford.

[Colonel Banks is to be congratulated on having discovered at last something definite regarding the ancestry of Michael Metcalf. With regard to my article in the REGISTER of January 1924, referred to by him, I should like to point out * that at the time that was written there was no definite proof that Michael was born at Tatterford, such as is furnished in the deposition discovered by Colonel Banks. Moreover, the record of his age then known was that of the shipping list, which made him born in 1586, the year in which Leonard, son of Rev. Leonard Metcalf, was baptized, a baptism which has been called a baptism of Michael, which was clearly wrong. I agree with Colonel Banks that Michael must be a son of Rev. Leonard Metcalf, born in a year of which no baptismal records remain, about 1590, because there was no other Metcalf in the parish at this time. Colonel Banks has made a slight error when he says that Rev. Leonard Metcalf had sons Nicholas and Leonard baptized in 1586. Leonard was baptized 3 Sept. 1586, but Nicholas was baptized 8 July 1587. Matthew was baptized on 18 Dec. 1594, and not in 1592, as stated above. There are no records in the registers for 1592. In addition to the above children, Rev. Leonard Metcalf had a daughter Marie, baptized 28 Aug. 1601. Rev. Leonard Metcalf was undoubtedly the father of Richard Metcalf of Tatterford and of Michael Metcalf. Thanks to Colonel Banks's discovery, we now have a good starting point for further investigation regarding Michael Metcalf's ancestry. Apperside is a hamlet in the vale of Wensleydale, North Riding of Yorkshire. — G. ANDREWS MORIARTY, JR.]

## MOODY

### Contributed by Miss LILIAN J. REDSTONE of London, England

ACCORDING to Rev. John Eliot's record of the members of the church at Roxbury, Mass., John Moody "came to the Land in the
*Pages 52-54, this volume.

Yeare 1633." He had a wife, Sarah, but no children. He had, however, two "vngodly" men servants, who were drowned on the "oister bank." (See Rev. John Eliot's account in the REGISTER, vol. 35, p. 242, and also Winthrop's History of New England, vol. 1, p. 126, edition of 1853. Winthrop gives 6 Aug. 1633 as the date of the drowning.) "Mr." John Moody was admitted a freeman 5 Nov. 1633 and was a deputy in 1635. He soon removed to Hartford, Conn., and died not earlier than 25 July 1655. He had a son Samuel, born in New England, who finally settled at Hadley, Mass., where his mother, the Widow Sarah Moody, died in 1671. Samuel Moody was the progenitor of numerous descendants. (Cf. Savage's Genealogical Dictionary, vol. 3, pp. 225–226, Pope's Pioneers of Massachusetts, p. 316, and Records of the Governor and Company of the Massachusetts Bay, vol. 1.)

In 1850 the late H. G. Somerby communicated to the REGISTER (vol. 4, pp. 178–180) several pedigrees extracted from the Candler Manuscript in the British Museum, among them a brief Moody pedigree which gave John Moody who "went into New England" as a son of George Moody of Moulton [co. Suffolk].* In 1885 the late Henry FitzGilbert Waters communicated to the REGISTER (vol. 39, pp. 68–69) abstracts of the wills of George Moody and Samuel Moody of Moulton, brothers of the New England immigrant, and also what is apparently a more accurate copy of the pedigree contributed by Mr. Somerby in 1850. In the present article records are given that throw additional light on the Moody family in England and its connections, and not only confirm the statements previously made that John Moody the immigrant was a son of George Moody of Moulton but also carry the ancestral line back to Richard Moody, the immigrant's grandfather. A pedigree setting forth in genealogical form the history of the family follows the records.

### FROM PROBATE RECORDS

The Will of RICHARDE MODYE of Moulton, co. Suffolk, dated 14 January 1572 [1572/3]. To be buried in Moulton church. To my wife Anne the house that I now inhabit called Fryettes and all those lands which I of late bought of the executors of Roger Fryett, viz., George Tayler and Thomas Harvye, for life, in recompense of her dower, all my winter corn growing on the said land and forty combs seed barley to sow the said land, four bullocks, four horses in Mason's stable, a plough, a cart, ten combs malt, and one-half of my household stuff, my wife to release her thirds in all my other lands, yielding them up in the parish church of Moulton or elsewhere at the executor's discretion, and, if she refuses, all legacies to her are to be void. To George, my eldest son, all lands and tenements, free and copyhold, in Moulton [and Kentford added in will of 2 February 1572/3], at the age of twenty-one years, to him and the heirs of his body for ever, with contingent remainder first to John, my [third in later will] son, and the heirs of his body, at twenty-one, and secondly to Edmond, my youngest† son, at twenty-one. To my son Edmond, at twenty-one, houses and lands in Gaseley, in tail, a lease of ten acres of land in Moulton, bought of Mr. Byrde, all my corn grow-

*Harleian MS. 6071, fo. 254 b. Candler wrote in the middle of the seventeenth century, and was acquainted with the Puritan families of western and southern Suffolk. The words attached to John Moody's name in the manuscript are probably "went over to New England." ✱✱
†The word youngest is omitted in the will of 2 February 1572/3.

✱✱See Vol. III of this work, pp. 575-577.

ing in Gaseley, and fourteen score wether sheep now going with Mr. James Tayler of Gaseley. To my son John, at twenty-one, my lease at Cavenham bought of Thomas Rampling [Richard Rampley *in later will*], with all my sheep there going. To Robert, my son, at twenty-one, all leases and stocks of cattle or money in Okingbury, Wessen, Illington, or elsewhere, in co. Huntingdon, a bond of William Goodinche and what William owes, and, to make up all these sums, £80. To Grace, Margaret, and Mary, my daughters, one-half of my household stuff, nine bullocks, one hundred and twenty combs rye, and £20, to be equally divided between them when they are severally eighteen. To Thomasin, my eldest daughter, at eighteen, four hundred sheep now going at Isleham. To Anne, my daughter, at eighteen, £40. To George, my eldest son, at twenty-one, the rest of my sheep at Moulton, six horses, a plough and plough gear, a cart and cart gear, so much rye as now grows on the ground, and so much rye as is now left on the loft at Moulton end.

Forasmuch as my great care and desire is that my children may be well and virtuously brought up in the fear of God and good learning and education, the executors shall take all the mean profits bequeathed to the children until their several ages, trusting that they will have great care for their good education.

I will that Thomas Smithe, son and heir apparent of Thomas Smith, one of my executors, shall have the education and bringing up of John, my son, with all the goods and stock, etc., bequeathed to John, till twenty-one. Richard Grene of Newmarket is similarly to bring up my son Robert. The residue of my goods is to be divided among my children at the discretion of my executors.

Executors: Thomas Smythe of Asheley and John Smythe of Newmarket. Overseer: Thomas Sutevile of Dalham, co. Suffolk, Esq., to whom I give my silver salt and a bay colt. To Robert and Elizabeth Gynner ten combs rye and ten combs malt. To every poor house in Moulton one bl. rye. To every godchild 10s. To every servant 10s. Witnesses: Richard Grene, John Midlediche, John Kynge, Davye Ayre, John Phillipp.

Memorandum, that on Sunday, 25 April 1574, instead of giving to my daughter Thomasin four hundred sheep at Isleham [*sic*], I give to her £100, payable at her marriage. To the child my wife now goeth with £40. Witnesses: Richard Grene, Christopher Funston, John Trace, John Leche, Richard Johnson, Robert Browne.

Proved 30 April 1574 by George Haryson, notary public, procurator for the executors. (P. C. C., Martyn, 16.)

[This will was declared null and void 10 June 1574. *Vide infra.*]

The Will of RICHARD MODYE of Moulton, co. Suffolk, yeoman, dated 2 February 1572 [1572/3], disannulling all former wills.* To the reparations of Moulton church 6s. 8d. To the poor of Gaseley 6s. 8d. To the poor of Dalham 6s. 8d. To the poor of Kentford 6s. 8d. To the poor of Newmarket 10s. To my wife Anne the house called Fryettes [as in the former will], for life, with remainder to my son George Modye and his heirs for ever. To my son John the contingent remainder of the Gaseley lands, failing heirs of my son Edmond. The lease of ten acres in Moulton was held of Mrs. Higham, widow. To my wife Anne all my household stuff, on condition that she give to my son George £20 at the age of twenty-one, and also one-half of my bullocks, one-half of my horses, one-half of my carts and ploughs, all the corn growing on the land late Fryettes and the tilth thereof, the lands to be sown with barley, forty combs barley to sow them, twenty combs malt, and twenty combs rye. To my son George the other half of the horses, bullocks, carts,

*Only the new provisions or the chief differences from the provisions of the former will, dated 14 January 1572/3, are here given.

and ploughs, and the residue of the corn growing in Moulton, with the tilth and seed barley. To my wife Anne and son George all wethers in Moulton. To my son George the lease of a sheep ground in Moulton held of the demise of John Trace, Gentleman. My "gossoppe" Christopher Founstone is to have the use and profit of the leases and sheep in Cavenham till my son John is twenty-one, on condition that he bring John up in good learning. To my daughter Thomazine £100 at marriage. To my son John sheep at Kennet with John Cheverrye. To my daughter Grace £20 at marriage. To my daughter Anne £40 at marriage. To my daughter Margaret £20 at marriage. To my daughter Mary £20 at marriage. My friend Mr. Taylor is to take the revenues of the lands and tenements given to my son George till he is twenty-one, on condition that "he shall keepe & bringge upp hym godleye and vertuousleye" and shall maintain the lands and tenements, and account to my son George at twenty-one, deducting reasonable expenses. To Richard Lamberte one comb rye. To Robert Wilsonne, my servant, my worst coat, hose, and doublet. To Thomas Archer one comb wheat. To John Modye of Cambridge two stone wool, one black, one white. My friend Thomas Smythe of Assheleye is to take the profits of the lands given to my son Edmond, finding him and keeping him in good learning. The residue of my goods is to be evenly divided between my four daughters, viz., Grace, Anne, Margarett, and Mary, at their marriage. To the child my wife is now withall £40. Executors: my trusty friends Thomas Smithe of Assheleye and Roger Tompson of Clare, to whom I give £5 each. Supervisor: my trusty and very friend Mr. Stuttevile of Dalham, to whom I give my silver salt and bay colt. Witnesses: Richard Lamberte, Richard Grene, and Christopher Funstone. My wife Anne is to have the use of my daughters' legacies till their marriage. (P. C. C., Martyn, 25.)

On 10 June 1574 sentence was promulgated in the house of the commissary of the Prerogative Court of Canterbury, in Sermon Lane, in favor of the above will, exhibited by the widow, Anne, against Thomas and John Smythe, executors of the will previously proved and now annulled.

On 16 June 1574 a commission was issued to the widow, Anne Modye, to administer the goods according to the above will, upon the renunciation of the executors.

The Will of GEORGE MOODYE of Moulton [co. Suffolk], yeoman, dated 5 August, 5 James [1607]. To be buried in the parish church of Moulton, in such sort as shall be thought best by my executor. To George Moodye, my eldest son, and his heirs my mansion house wherein I dwell in Moulton, called Fryettes, sixscore acres of arable land, and the "sheepstour" pertaining, occupied by itself. To my executor [Thomas Kilborne, son-in-law of the testator] the tenement in Moulton Inne in Moulton sometime held by Thomas Cooke as my farmer, the round meadow and osier pightel held by lease of Mr. Tracey, a messuage and croft in Moulton and twelve acres of arable land in possession of John Seeley, my servant, and a messuage and croft and fourteen acres of land in Moulton occupied by John Mathewe *alias* Philip, all for eleven years, with remainder to my son George. From the profits of the above premises during the eleven years my executor is to pay the following legacies: to my son Samuel Moodye £200 at the age of twenty-four; "Unto John Moodye my youngest sonne" £200 at the age of twenty-four; to Elizabeth Moody, my eldest daughter, £100 within two years of my death; to my daughter Sara Moodye 100 marks at the age of twenty-two; to my daughters Margaret Moodie, Anne Moodye, and Mary Moodye 100 marks at the age of twenty-one. To my wife, Christian Moodye, the bedstead, feather bed, bolster, three pillows, blankets, and coverlet which I lie on, standing in my hall chamber. To my wife all her own apparel, two chests which she use[s] to lay her apparel in, one-half dozen table-napkins

147

"wrought with a stitch," three pairs of sheets (one of the best, two of the middle sort), a little brass pot which she brought with her, a little green chair, and two green stools. To Elizabeth Moodye and Frauncys Kilborne four of my best silver spoons, equally. To Anne Kilborne, my grandchild, one pot tipped with silver, one silver spoon, and six of my best table-napkins. To Eleazer Moodie, an apprentice in Bury, £5 at the age of twenty-four. To the poor of Gaseley, Kentford, Dalham, and Barrow 13s. 4d. each. To the poor of Denham 20s. To the poor of Moulton 20s. To my son-in-law, Thomas Kilborne, my residuary legatee and executor, 20 marks, leviable out of the rents of the lands demised to him for eleven years. [Signed] George Moodye senior. Witnesses: John Newman, Christopher Raghett [sic, ? Haggett, a Christopher Haggett becoming later the husband of Margaret Moody], W. Harte, George Moodye. Proved 20 November 1607 by Thomas Kilborne, the executor named in the will. (P. C. C., Hudleston, 87.)

The Will of Christopher Cox [of Bury St. Edmunds, co. Suffolk], dated 7 April 1624. "I X. Cox . . . being . . . in health of bodie and minde and willing . . . to be prepared to leave this sinfull world when the Lord seeth best to call me and beinge full of yeares 70 yeares ould att Barnabas daie next 1624 [11 June 1624] And havinge receiued extraordinary blessings from the Lord aboue any of my fathers Children I here doe desire to make knowne with earnest humble thanksgiuing to my mercifull father in Jesus Christ retorninge to the holy speritt for that measure of illuminacion vouchsafed unto me and all those which the Lord hath given unto me And having by the Lordes great and exceedinge loue granted vnto me Two yokefellowes of speciall vnderstanding for the good of their soules & for their bodies The first beinge an heire to 3 M' And seeing the Lord in mercie in soe manie kindes have granted soe much that I may take serious Accoumpte of them & never to forgett the Lordes benefitts upon my sonnes and daughters," etc., I ordain my wife Marie my sole and whole executrix. Proved 11 February 1624/5 by Mary Cox, widow of the deceased. (P. C. C., Clarke, 25.)

The Will of George Moody of Moulton, co. Suffolk, yeoman, dated 20 February 1651 [1651/2]. Administration, with the will annexed, on the estate of this testator was granted 3 May 1654 to Samuel Moody, brother of the deceased, the executors having renounced the trust. [An abstract of this will was published in the Register, vol. 39, p. 68, and was reprinted in Waters's "Genealogical Gleanings in England," vol. 1, p. 96.]

The Will of Samuel Moody of Mowlton, co. Suffolk, Esq., dated 18 February 1657 [1657/8], was proved by the executor, John Moody, son of the testator, 28 June 1658. [An abstract of this will was published in the Register, vol. 39, pp. 68–69, and was reprinted in Waters's "Genealogical Gleanings in England," vol. 1, pp. 96–97.]

From the Registers of the Parish of St. James, Bury St. Edmunds, co. Suffolk*

*Baptisms*

1588    Elizabeth Coxe daughter of Christopher 1 January [1588/9].
1590    John Coxe son of Christopher 11 November.
1593    Henry Coxe son of Samuell "owt of the jaole" 16 April.
1593    Thomasen Coxe daughter of Christopher 18 July.
1596    Mary Coxe daughter of Christopher 28 April.
1598    Sarah Coxe daughter of Christopher 17 May.
1603    Samuell Cox son of Christopher 4 December.

*Printed in the Suffolk Green Books, no. 17 (3 vols.).

1604    Mary Coxe daughter of Christopher 23 January [1604/5].
1606    William Cox son of Christopher 11 May.
1610    Margaret Cox daughter of Richard 15 July.
1616    George Moody son of Samuel 4 July.
1617    John Moody son of John 3 December.
1618    John Moody son of John 1 January [1618/19].
1619    Mary Moody daughter of Samuel 11 April.
1619    William Cox son of Richard 21 April.
1620    Samuell Moodie son of Samuell 9 June.
1621    John Moodie son of John 3 March [1621/2].
1623    Sarah Moody daughter of Samuell 13 March [1623/4].
1624    Hanna Mody daughter of John 11 November.
1625    Ann Modie daughter of Samvell 3 July.
1626    Samuell Cox son of William 29 November.
1627    Thomas Mody son of Samuell 27 September.
1627    Mary Coxe daughter of William 21 March [1627/8].
1629    Sarah Cox daughter of William 9 January [1629/30].
1630    Elizabeth Mody daughter of Samuell 2 May.
1631    Samuell Mody son of John 16 July.
1632    Henry Mody son of Samuell 7 August.
1649    Sam Moody son of Gorge — June, "Borne ye 21."
1650    George Moody son of George 28 February [1650/1].
1652    George Moody son of George 10 January [1652/3].
1654    Ambroes Moodey son of George 9 June.
1655    John Moodey son of George 18 August.
1658    Anne Moodey daughter of George 6 October [Oct. 19 *added*].

## Marriages

1606    Raphe Cantrell, Gent., and Anne Cox, widow, — September.
1610    John Pratt and Elizabeth Moody 2 April.
1612    Thomas Clover and Elizabeth Cox per license 29 April.
1615    Roberte Greene and Mary Cox 3 May.
1617    John Mody and Sarah Cox by license 8 September.
1622    John Salmon and Mary Moody 24 October.
1627    Milles Borowes, widower, and Mary Cox, widow, by licenses 21 March [1627/8].
1649    William Cooke and Sara Modye — December.
      [From the autumn of 1653 to the autumn of 1658 marriages take place before justices of the peace, among them, in the first months of this period, being Samuell Moody, Gent.]
1673    John Cooke and Frances Moody 8 May.
1674    Thomas Moody and Sarah Walter 10 September.

## Burials

1599    The wife of Christopher Coxe 12 January [1599/1600].
1610    A child of Christopher Cox, unbaptized, 15 March [1610/11].
1612    Raphe Cox 16 August.
1618    John Moody son of John 5 January [1618/19].
1621    John Moodie son of John 5 March [1621/2].
1624    Hanna Mody daughter of John 11 November.
1624    Christover Coxe, "masur," 29 January [1624/5].
1631    Samuell Mody son of John 19 July.
1634    William Cox son of William 14 July.
1645    Thomas Moody son of Mr. Samuell Moody 30 December.
1656    John Moody son of George 13 February [1656/7].
1663    Ann wife of George Moody "drnd" [? drowned] 2 July.
1684    George the third son of Mr. George Moody 5 July.

1692  Mr. Samuell Modey 28 April.
1694  Mrs. Ann Mody daughter of Mr. Samuell 3 July.
1695  Mr. George Mody, sen., 29 July.

## FROM THE PARISH REGISTERS OF MOULTON, CO. SUFFOLK

### Baptisms

1568  Margaret daughter of Richard Mody 1 November.
1570  Edmund son of Richard Mody 24 June.
1572  Mary daughter of Richard Mody 22 September.
1574  Judith daughter of Richard Mody 31 July.
1582  Elizabeth daughter of George Mody 2 October.
1584  Francys daughter of George Mody 11 October.
1586  George son of George Mody 19 February [1586/7].
1589  Sarah daughter of George Mody 8 May.
1592  Samuel son of George Modye 31 March.
1593  John son of George Modye 8 April.
1595  Margaret daughter of George Modye 19 July.
1599  Anne daughter of George Modye 5 September.
1602  Mary daughter of George Modye 25 January [1602/3].
1632  John Moodie son of John Moodie — October.

### Marriages

1574  Edward Coult, Gent., and Anne Moody, widow, 6 September.
1575  Henery Smith and Thomasin Mody 23 January [1575/6].
1579  Edward Coulte, Gent., and Mary Maris[?] 20 August.
1585  Albert Ramont and Anne Mody 18 October.
1589  Christopher Hagget and Margaret Moody 9 May.
1593  Mr. Browne, minister, and Mary Moody 1 [or 2] October.
1602  Edmund Fowler and Judith Moodye 5 April.
1604  George Moody and Christian Cramp 5 September.
1604  Thomas Kilbourne and Frances Mody 5 September.

### Burials

1574  Richard Moody 28 April.
1576  Anne Coult wife of Edward Coult, Gent., 14 March [1576/7].
1602  Margaret wife of George Moodye 25 January [1602/3].
1607  George Moodye 23 August.
1651  Mr. George Moodye 23 February [1651/2].
1660  Mrs. Moodye wife of Mr. George Moodye 23 June.

## FROM THE TRANSCRIPTS OF PARISH REGISTERS IN THE ARCHDEACONRY OF SUDBURY*

### Marriages, 1561–1640

1595  Edmund Moodye and Agnes Clarke, at Wood Ditton [co. Cambridge], 26 May.
1600  George Moody and Margy. Bacon, at All Saints', Sudbury, 19 January [1600/1].
1603  William Moodye and Agnes Collyn, at All Saints', Sudbury, 2 July.
1608  George Moodie of Moulton, Gent., and Lidia Hovell, daughter of Robt. Hovell, at Ashfield Magna, Wednesday, 25 May.
1615  Thos. Warren and Margt. Moody, at Bradley Magna [co. Suffolk], 24 May.
1615  Saml. Moody and Mary Boldero, at Fornham Martin [Fornham St. Martin, co. Suffolk], 10 August.
1629  John Brewington and Sarah Moody, at Gaseley [co. Suffolk], 22 October.

*Preserved at Bury St. Edmunds, co. Suffolk.

150

1630     Clement Brewington and Mary Moody, at Gaseley [co. Suffolk], 8 April.

1632     Thos. Moody and Alice Wrench, at Gaseley [co. Suffolk], 1 May.

1634     Giles Coppinge of Kentford, widower, and Susan Moody of Gaseley, 18 January 1634 [1634/5].

1635     Robt. Moodie and Alice Bird, at Denham [co. Suffolk], 26 October.

*Baptism at Ashley Magna, co. Suffolk*

1567     Agnes Clarke daughter of William and Agnes 25 April.

*Baptisms at Gazeley, co. Suffolk, 1561–1660*

1599     Anne Moody daughter of Edmund and Agnes 23 September.

1601     Rich. Moodie son of Edmund and Anne 6 April.

1615     Margaret Moody daughter of Edmund and Anne 18 October.

1633     Mary Moody daughter of Thos. and Alice 26 May.

1633     Sarah Brewington daughter of John and Sarah 23 February [1633/4].

1636     Thos. Moody son of Thos. and Alice 1 January [1636/7].

1638     William Brewington son of John and Sarah 13 January [1638/9].

MARRIAGE LICENCE

1609     John Pratte, single man, of Woodditton [co. Cambridge], and Elizabeth Moodye, single woman, of St. James, Bury St. Edmunds. Sureties: Thos. Kilbourne of Woodditton, yeoman, and Walter Pratt of Woodditton, Gent. 5 March [1609/10]. (Acta Books, Archdeaconry of Sudbury [at Bury St. Edmunds], book 5, p. 78.)

FROM INQUISITIONS POST MORTEM*

Inquisition taken at Bury St. Edmunds [co. Suffolk], 22 July, 16 Elizabeth [1574], before commissioners, including Francis Boldero. The jurors say that RICHARD MOODYE, yeoman, was seised in demesne as of fee 20 acres of arable land in Moulton, in Millwayefelde, acquired of [*blank*] Burgent, Gent., and held of the Queen as of the Honor of Clare by knight's service, and worth 10s. yearly.

He died 28 April last past [1574]. His son and heir, George Moodye, was aged 14 years, 7 months, at his father's death.†   (Chancery Inquisitions Post Mortem, Elizabeth, vol. 167, no. 105.)

Inquisition taken at Bury St. Edmunds [co. Suffolk], 4 November, 5 James I [1607]. The jurors say that GEORGE MOODY, yeoman, held in demesne as of fee 20 acres of arable land in Millwayefeld, acquired of the executors of Thomas Burgent, Gent., and held of the King as of the Honor of Clare, and worth 20s. yearly, and 2 messuages, 5 cottages, 200 acres of land, 2 acres of pasture, and 1 acre of meadow in Moulton, held of John Tracy, Gent., as of the Manor of Frenshall, co. Suffolk, in free and common socage, by rent of 6s. 7d.

He died 24 August, 5 James I [1607]. George Moody, his son and heir, was aged 20 years, 6 months, 28 days, at his father's death.‡  (*Ib.*, James I, vol. 298, no. 25.)

FROM CHANCERY PROCEEDINGS§

[Undated, but between 1558 and 1574, the year of the death of the complainant.]

The complaint of RICHARD MODYE of Moulton, co. Suffolk, yeoman, shows that, whereas he is seised in fee of a messuage in Moulton called

---

*Preserved in the Public Record Office, London.

†He was born, therefore, about Sept. 1559.

‡He was born, therefore, 27 Jan. 1586/7.

§Preserved in the Public Record Office, London.

Lanwades and 120 acres of land and 10 acres of pasture, with the liberty of a fold-course belonging to the said messuage, a great part of the deeds written in the handwriting of Thomas Burgeant have late come into the hands of Sir Clement Higham, Knight, Richard Hyldersham, Gent., and Thomas Burgeant, who refuse to give them up.

The answer of THOMAS BURGEANT, Gent., states that he copied the deeds concerning the premises and delivered them to the complainant. He has no other deeds relating thereto. (Chancery Proceedings, Series 2, 121/54.)

FROM COPINGER'S CALENDAR OF FEET OF FINES, HENRY VIII–ELIZABETH

Easter Term, 2 Mary I [15 April–8 May 1555]. Thos. Moody v. Christopher Funston, tenement in Multon [Moulton, co. Suffolk]. (197.)
Michaelmas Term, 1 Elizabeth [2-25 November 1558]. Mathew Rand v. Richard Mody, tenement in Multon [Moulton, co. Suffolk]. (57.)
Easter Term, 4 Elizabeth [15 April–8 May 1562]. Richard Modye v. John Shorte, tenements in Moulton [co. Suffolk]. (354.)
Easter Term, 14 Elizabeth [15 April–8 May 1572]. Richard Moodye and others v. Beatrice Byrde, [lands] in Moulton, Gazeley [co. Suffolk], etc. (1660.)
Trinity Term, 29 Elizabeth [22 May–12 June 1587]. John Moody v. Lionel Costen, etc., [lands] in Multon [Moulton, co. Suffolk]. (4172.)
Trinity Term, 29 Elizabeth [22 May–12 June 1587]. Edm. Moody v. Rich. Emyn, etc., [lands] in Bury St. Edmunds [co. Suffolk]. (4855.)

FROM ADDITIONAL CHARTERS, IN THE BRITISH MUSEUM

10 April, 1 and 2 Philip and Mary [1555]. Praecipe to Christopher Funsdon and Petronella, his wife, to keep a covenant with Thomas Mody, clerk, touching a messuage, 6 acres of land, and 4 acres of pasture in Multon [Moulton, co. Suffolk]. (25283.)

FROM LAY SUBSIDIES FOR CO. SUFFOLK*

1327 Exning.     John Mody [tax] 2s. (Suffolk Green Books, no. 9, p. 102.)
1524 Barrow.     John Mody [among "laborers" taxed] 8s. 8d. (Ib., no. 10, p. 340.)
     Lindsey.     John Mody [valuation] £5. [tax] 2s. 6d. (Ib., no. 10, p. 160.)
     Lydgate.     John Mody [Amount illegible]. (Ib., no. 10, p. 298.)
1568 Moulton.    Richard Modye in goods [valuation] £40. [tax] £1. 13s. 4d. (Ib., no. 12, p. 214.)

From the foregoing records and from other records duly cited below the following account of the Moody family of Moulton, co. Suffolk, to which Mr. John Moody, the emigrant to New England, belonged, has been derived.

The surname *Mody* is found occasionally in the early lay subsidies in western Suffolk (*vide supra*), but the earliest known connection of the Moody family with Moulton, a parish in the western part of Suffolk, on the border of Cambridgeshire, was about 1555, when Thomas Moody, clerk, acquired a house and land there. (Cf. Copinger's Calendar of Feet of Fines, *supra*, and the praecipe following it.) He was probably the Thomas Moody who had been

---

*Preserved in the Public Record Office, London. The Suffolk subsidies for 1327, 1524, and 1568 have been printed in the "Suffolk Green Books."

rector of Lackford, also in western Suffolk, from 1542 to about 1551. This living was in the patronage of the King, who presented Thomas Moody on 16 Dec. 1542, his induction taking place on 21 Jan. following. He resigned the rectorship, probably in 1551, as his successor, Robert Peacock, was presented on 24 Apr. of that year. A deed of sale, in the Moulton register, dated 8 Elizabeth [1565-66], is signed by Thomas Moody, Rector and Patron. (See Inductions, Archdeaconry of Sudbury, 1537-1641, and also Davy's Suffolk Pedigrees, in British Museum, Additional MSS., 19142.) His will has not been found in either of the Suffolk courts or in the Prerogative Court of Canterbury. He was probably related (but in what way has not been ascertained) to the Richard Moody with whom the following pedigree begins.

1. RICHARD MOODY, of Moulton, co. Suffolk, yeoman, the testator of 14 Jan. and 2 Feb. 1572/3, is the earliest Moody from whom the descent of the New England settler has been proved. He died 28 Apr. 1574, and was buried at Moulton on the same day. He married ANNE ———, who survived him and married secondly, at Moulton, 6 Sept. 1574, Edward Coult, Gentleman. She was buried at Moulton 14 Mar. 1576/7, and Edward Coult married again at Moulton, 20 Aug. 1579, Mary Maris [?].

Richard Moody was dealing with a tenement in Moulton in the autumn of 1558, and purchased lands there in 1562 and lands in Moulton and Gazeley, a parish two miles east from Moulton, in 1572. (Cf. Copinger's Calendar of Feet of Fines, *supra*.) In or after 1558 he brought a suit in Chancery against Thomas Burgeant, to recover the title deeds relating to a leasehold house and lands in Moulton, called Lanwades. (*Vide supra*.) He evidently acquired a considerable landed estate in western Suffolk, chiefly by purchase. He lived in a house called Fryettes, in Moulton, which he had bought from the executors of a certain Roger Fryett. Besides his lands in Moulton and Gazeley he had leasehold and other land in Cavenham and Kentford, co. Suffolk, a flock of four hundred sheep at Isleham, co. Cambridge, and land at Okingbury, Wessen, and Illington, co. Huntingdon. The only lands held by him in chief of the Crown seem to have been twenty acres in Millwayefelde, in Moulton (*vide supra*, Inquisitions Post Mortem), which were apparently the lands mentioned in the Chancery suit, for they were acquired from ——— Burgeant, Gentleman.

Richard Moody made two wills, one on 14 Jan. and the other on 2 Feb. 1572/3. In his anxiety to provide for the virtuous upbringing of his children in the fear of God and good learning and education, he distributed the care of his younger sons, with their lands, among various friends. Under both wills the house called Fryettes was to go to Anne, his wife, but under the second will she was to have it for life only, with remainder to the eldest son, George. This son was also to have other lands in Moulton and certain stock, farm produce, etc. On Sunday, 25 Apr. 1574, only three days before his death, Richard Moody added — to the *earlier* will, strangely enough — a codicil; and on 30 Apr. 1574, two days after the death of the testator, the executors named in the first will, by their procurator, proved it, together with the codicil. In June 1574, however, Anne Moody, the widow, brought forward the second will, in which Thomas Smythe of Ashley (one of the executors of the first will) and Roger Tompson of Clare were appointed executors, and the Court gave judgment, 10 June, in favor of this will. The executors refusing to act, administration on the estate was granted to the widow, 16 June 1574.

Children (order of births somewhat uncertain):*

    i.  THOMASINE, eldest daughter, under 18 on 14 Jan. 1572/3; m. at Moulton, 23 Jan. 1575/6, HENRY SMITH.

2. ii.  GEORGE, eldest son, b. about Sept. 1559 (*vide supra*, Inquisitions Post Mortem).

    iii.  GRACE, living 14 Jan. 1572/3.

    iv.  ANNE, m. at Moulton, 18 Oct. 1585, ALBERT RAMONT.

    v.  ROBERT, bapt. at Moulton 20 Mar. 1563.† He was to have, by his father's will, lands in co. Huntingdon.

    vi.  JOHN, third son. His father left to him lands in Cavenham. He was dealing with lands in Moulton in 1587 (Feet of Fines).

    vii.  MARGARET, bapt. at Moulton 1 Nov. 1568; m. at Moulton, 9 May 1589, CHRISTOPHER HAGGET.

    viii.  EDMUND, youngest son, bapt. at Moulton 24 June 1570; m. at Wood Ditton, co. Cambridge, 26 May 1595, AGNES CLARKE. His father left to him houses and lands in Gazeley.

        Children, bapt. at Gazeley:

        1.  *Anne* (daughter of Edmund and Agnes), bapt. 23 Sept. 1599.

        2.  *Richard*, bapt. 6 Apr. 1601.

        3.  *Margaret*, bapt. 18 Oct. 1615.

        Probably others.

    ix.  MARY, bapt. at Moulton 22 Sept. 1572; m. there, 1 Oct. 1593, Mr. [JOHN] BROWNE, minister. The living of Moulton was sequestered, 17 .Mar. 1644 [1644/5], from John Brown because he would not pray for a blessing on Parliament (Walker's Sufferings of the Clergy). Davy, in his "Suffolk Collections" (British Museum, Additional MSS., 19103), copies from Tom Martin's "Church Notes" two letters from George Moody (2, iii) and Jonas Alston (1651), sequestrators of the living, to Mr. Mason, who had occupied the living but whom they rejected as a "scandalous" minister.

    x.  JUDITH (posthumous), bapt. at Moulton 31 July 1574; m. there, 5 Apr. 1602, EDMUND FOWLER.

2. GEORGE MOODY (*Richard*), of Moulton, co. Suffolk, yeoman, the testator of 5 Aug. 1607, called "eldest sonne" in his father's wills, was born about Sept. 1559 (*vide supra*, Inquisitions Post Mortem), and was buried at Moulton 23 Aug. 1607. He married first MARGARET ———, who was buried at Moulton 25 Jan. 1602/3, on the day of the baptism of their daughter Mary; and secondly, at Moulton, 5 Sept. 1604, CHRISTIAN CRAMP, who was living 5 Aug. 1607.‡

According to the second will of his father, George Moody

---

*Davy, in his Suffolk Pedigrees, in British Museum, Additional MSS., 19142, fo. 189, gives Richard Moody as the father of six of the children named below, including George.

†This baptism is given in Davy's Suffolk Pedigrees.

‡A George Moody and Marg[er]y Bacon were married at All Saints', Sudbury, co. Suffolk, 19 Jan. 1600/1. If this George Moody is identical with George Moody (No. 2) of the pedigree, then all of the latter's children except Mary, the ninth and youngest child, were children by an earlier wife, whose name is unknown, who died between the birth of the eighth child, Anne (baptized 5 Sept. 1599), and 19 Jan. 1600/1. In that case the Margaret (or Margery), wife of George Moodye, who was buried at Moulton 25 Jan. 1602/3, was his second wife and mother of the ninth child only, and Christian Cramp, whom he married 5 Sept. 1604, was his third wife. — EDITOR.

154

was to be brought up by the father's friend, Mr. Taylor, who was possibly the George Tayler who was one of the two executors of Roger Fryett from whom Richard Moody had bought his house at Moulton. This Mr. Taylor may have been a godfather to George Moody. The youth must have been brought up either in the Taylor family or by his stepfather, Edward Coult, and he took livery of his father's lands at Moulton, including Fryettes, in 24 Elizabeth [1581–82]. (Davy's Suffolk Pedigrees.) According to what the contributor of this article believes to be the correct reading of Candler's pedigree, George Moody was "famous for his housekeeping & honest & plain dealing."

There is no indication that George Moody's lands extended beyond Moulton. His father's outlying estates had been distributed among a large family; and George Moody, in his will of 5 Aug. 1607, left Fryettes to his eldest son, George, and various other tenements in Moulton were to be held by the executor, the testator's son-in-law Thomas Kilborne, for eleven years, with remainder to the son George. The executor would thus be enabled to pay certain lump sums to the other children when they reached the ages specified in the will (from twenty-one to twenty-four years).

Children by first wife, baptized at Moulton:

i.    ELIZABETH, bapt. 2 Oct. 1582; m. in the parish of St. James, Bury St. Edmunds, 2 Apr. 1610, JOHN PRATT of Wood Ditton, co. Cambridge, bachelor, the marriage licence being dated 5 Mar. 1609 [1609/10]. By her father's will Elizabeth Moody was to receive £100 within two years of his death.

ii.    FRANCES, bapt. 11 Oct. 1584; m. at Moulton, 5 Sept. 1604, THOMAS KILBOURNE (or KILBORNE) of Wood Ditton, co. Cambridge, yeoman, who was executor of her father's will, which he proved 20 Nov. 1607. They had a daughter, *Anne*, who was mentioned in her grandfather's will.

iii.    GEORGE, of Moulton, yeoman, bapt. 19 Feb. 1586/7; d. *s.p.*; bur. at Moulton, as "Mr. George Moodye," 23 Feb. 1651/2; m. at Ashfield Magna, co. Suffolk, 25 May 1608, as "George Moodie of Moulton, gent.," LYDIA HOVELL, daughter of Robert Hovell *alias* Smith, who, as "Mrs. Moodye, wife of Mr. George Moodye," was buried at Moulton 23 June 1660. This George Moody received under the will of his father the mansion house called Fryettes, in Moulton, with much land. In the Civil War he was a Parliamentarian, and was one of the sequestrators of the living of Moulton when the minister, John Browne, apparently his aunt's husband, was suspended for not praying for a blessing on Parliament (*vide supra*, p. 323). The family of Hovell *alias* Smith, to which his wife belonged, was a well-known Suffolk family, of which the elder members were usually styled "gentlemen," while the younger sons became clothiers, physicians, apothecaries, and clergymen.* In his will, dated 20 Feb. 1651 [1651/2], he left Fryettes to his wife Lydia and made bequests to his sister, Margaret Warren, and her children and to other relatives and connections, including his brother Samuel Moody. An abstract of the will, which contains much genealogical information, is given in the REGISTER, vol. 39, p. 68.

iv.    SARAH, bapt. 8 May 1589. By her father's will she was to receive 100 marks at the age of twenty-two.

*For an account of this family see Muskett's Suffolk Manorial Families, vol. 2, pp. 1 *et seq.*

v.  SAMUEL, of Bury St. Edmunds and Moulton, co. Suffolk, Esq.,
M.P., bapt. 31 Mar. 1592; d. between 18 Feb. 1657/8, when his
will was dated, and 28 June 1658, when it was proved; m. at Fornham St. Martin, co. Suffolk, 10 Aug. 1615, MARY BOLDERO,
daughter of John Boldero of Bury St. Edmunds, Gentleman. By
his father's will he was to receive £200 at the age of twenty-four.
He became a woollen draper at Bury St. Edmunds, was an alderman there, a justice of the peace, and a member of Parliament
for Bury in 1654 and 1656. He was the most notable member of
the family at that period. As justice of the peace he performed
marriages from the autumn of 1653 on for several months. In the
later years of his life he resided at Moulton, having succeeded to
his father's estate there after the death of his brother George. His
eldest son, George, occupied the mansion at Bury after the father
left it. An abstract of the will of Samuel Moody, Esq., may be
found in the REGISTER, vol. 39, pp. 68–69.

Children, bapt. in the parish of St. James, Bury St. Edmunds:
1.  *George,* of Bury St. Edmunds, woollen draper, bapt. 4 July
1616; bur. at Bury St. Edmunds 29 July 1695; m. Anne
Biggs, who was drowned [?] 2 July 1663, daughter of Ambrose Biggs of Glemsford, co. Suffolk, Gentleman. (Cf.
Candler's pedigree.) Children, recorded in the parish of
St. James, Bury St. Edmunds: (1) Samuel, b. 21 June
1649, bur. 28 Apr. 1692; (2) George, bapt. 28 Feb. 1650/1,
probably d. young; (3) George, bapt. 10 Jan. 1652/3, bur.
5 July 1684; (4) Ambrose, bapt. 9 June 1654; (5) John,
bapt. 18 Aug. 1655, bur. 13 Feb. 1656/7; (6) Anne, bapt.
19 Oct. 1658.
2.  *Mary,* bapt. 11 Apr. 1619; m. in 1658 John Browne, Alderman of Bury St. Edmunds. (Cf. Candler's pedigree.)
3.  *Samuel,* bapt. 9 June 1620; probably d. *s.p.* before his father,
as he was not mentioned in his father's will. He was a
captain. (Cf. Candler's pedigree.)
4.  *John,* of Ipswich, co. Suffolk, Gentleman, living in 1664,
when he registered his pedigree in the Visitation of Suffolk;[*]
m. Anne Bull, one of the daughters and coheirs of Thomas
Bull of Flowton, co. Suffolk. As executor he proved his
father's will, 28 June 1658, his father leaving to him all his
lands in Ireland. He was a captain of Foot and afterwards
a sergeant major of Horse in the service of Parliament.
Still later he was a merchant in Ipswich. (Cf. Candler's
pedigree.) Children, according to the Visitation of Suffolk:
(1) John, son and heir, aged 14 in 1664; (2) Thomas; (3)
Mary.
5.  *Sarah,* bapt. 13 Mar. 1623/4; m. in the parish of St. James,
Bury St. Edmunds, in Dec. 1649, William Cooke of Bury,
linen draper.
6.  *Ann,* bapt. 3 July 1625.
7.  *Thomas,* bapt. 27 Sept. 1627; bur. at Bury St. Edmunds 30
Dec. 1645.
8.  *Elizabeth,* bapt. 2 May 1630.
9.  *Henry,* bapt. 7 Aug. 1632; living 18 Feb. 1657/8, when his
father in his will left to him lands in Gaywood near Lynn,
co. Norfolk; d. *s.p.*
10.  *Margaret,* d. in 1704 (Davy); m. before 18 Feb. 1657/8
(marriage settlement dated 4 May 1652, according to
Davy) Major Westhropp of Hundon, co. Suffolk.

*\*Publications of the Harleian Society,* vol. 61, p. 9. There is a saying — little more than a
legend — that the arms claimed by Moody of Ipswich in the Visitation of Suffolk in 1664 were the
arms granted, 6 Oct., 32 Henry VIII [1540], to Edmund Moody, who afterwards lived at Bury St.
Edmunds, in recognition of his having saved the life of King Henry VIII by leaping into a ditch
into which the King had fallen and lifting up his head. (Cf. Davy's Suffolk Pedigrees, in British
Museum, Additional MSS., 19142, fo. 194.) This deed has also been ascribed to Edward Moody
of Aldersfield, co. Worcester.

3. vi. JOHN, the emigrant to New England, bapt. 8 Apr. 1593.
   vii. MARGARET, bapt. 19 July 1595; living 20 Feb. 1651/2, when she and her children are named as beneficiaries in the will of her brother, George Moody; m. at Bradley Magna, co. Suffolk, 24 May 1615, THOMAS WARREN, who was living 20 Feb. 1651/2. By her father's will she was to receive 100 marks at the age of twenty-one.
   viii. ANNE, bapt. 5 Sept. 1599. By her father's will she was to receive 100 marks at the age of twenty-one.
   ix. MARY,* bapt. 25 Jan. 1602/3; m. in the parish of St. James, Bury St. Edmunds, 24 Oct. 1622, JOHN SALMON, who was living 20 Feb. 1651/2, when he is named in the will of his brother-in-law, George Moody. By her father's will Mary Moody was to receive 100 marks at the age of twenty-one. Children of John and Mary (Moody) Salmon are mentioned in the will of their uncle, George Moody.

3. JOHN MOODY (*George, Richard*), of Moulton and Bury St. Edmunds, co. Suffolk, of Roxbury, Mass., and of Hartford, Conn., was baptized at Moulton 8 Apr. 1593, and died in New England on or after 25 July 1655, the date of his will. He married in the parish of St. James, Bury St. Edmunds, 8 Sept. 1617, SARAH Cox, who was baptized in that parish 17 May 1598 and died at Hadley, Mass., in 1671, daughter of Christopher Cox, macer.†

He was about ten years old when his mother died and over fourteen at his father's death, and he was probably brought up either by his stepmother, Christian (Cramp) Moody, or by his brother-in-law, Thomas Kilborne, the executor of his father's will, according to which he was to receive £200 at the age of twenty-four. This legacy was probably paid to him before his marriage.

As has been stated in the first paragraph of this article, John Moody emigrated to New England in 1633. He and his wife Sarah settled in Roxbury, Mass., and he was styled "Mr.," was admitted a freeman, and was a deputy to the General Court of the Colony. He had two men servants, who were drowned 6 Aug. 1633. His wife had borne to him children in England, but probably all these children died before the parents left their native land. He soon moved from Roxbury to Hartford, Conn.

Children:

*Perhaps a half sister of the older children. *Vide supra*, p. 323, third footnote. — EDITOR.

†Christopher Cox, of Bury St. Edmunds, co. Suffolk, macer [i.e., grocer or spicer], the testator of 7 Apr. 1624, was born 11 June 1554 (see his will, *supra*) and was buried in the parish of St. James, Bury St. Edmunds, 29 Jan. 1624/5. He married first ———, who was buried in the parish of St. James 12 Jan. 1599/1600; and secondly Mary ———, who proved his will 11 Feb. 1624/5 and married secondly, in the parish of St. James, 21 Mar. 1627/8, Milles Borowes, widower. The first wife of Christopher Cox was, according to his will, a woman of considerable fortune, being heir to "3 M'" [? £3000], and both his wives were "of speciall vnderstanding for the good of their soules and for their bodies." He himself came from a West-Country family. Children by first wife, recorded in the parish of St. James: 1. Elizabeth, bapt. 1 Jan. 1588/9; m. 29 Apr. 1612 Thomas Clover. 2. John, bapt. 11 Nov. 1590. 3. Thomasen, bapt. 18 July 1593. 4. Mary, bapt. 28 Apr. 1596; m. 3 May 1615 Robert Greene. 5. Sarah, bapt. 17 May 1598; m. 8 Sept. 1617 John Moody, as stated above. Children by second wife, recorded in the parish of St. James: 6. Samuel, bapt. 4 Dec. 1603. 7. Mary, bapt. 23 Jan. 1604/5. 8. William, bapt. 11 May 1606. 9. A child, bur. unbapt. 15 Mar. 1610/11.

i.   JOHN, bapt. in the parish of St. James, Bury St. Edmunds, 3 Dec.
     1617; probably d. young.*
ii.  JOHN, bapt. in the same parish 1 Jan. 1618/19; bur. there 5 Jan.
     1618/19.
iii. JOHN, bapt. in the same parish 3 Mar. 1621/2; bur. there 5 Mar.
     1621/2.
iv.  HANNA, bapt. in the same parish 11 Nov. 1624; bur. there the same
     day.
v.   SAMUEL, bapt. in the same parish 16 July 1631; bur. there 19 July
     1631.
vi.  JOHN (probably a son of John Moody, the New England settler),
     bapt. at Moulton in Oct. 1632; probably d. within a few months.
vii. SAMUEL,† of Hartford, Conn., and Hadley, Mass., b. in New Eng-
     land; d. 22 Sept. 1689; m. SARAH DEMING[?], who d. in 1714,
     probably daughter of the first John Deming of Wethersfield,
     Conn. He removed to Hadley about 1660.
     Children:
     1.  Sarah, b. about 1660; d. 19 Sept. 1689; m. 23 Dec. 1680
         Joseph Kellogg.
     2.  John, of Hartford, b. 24 July 1661; d. at Hartford 5 Nov.
         1732. Nine children.
     3.  Hannah, b. 5 Mar. 1662/3; d. unm. 6 Jan. 1712/13.
     4.  Mary.
     5.  Samuel, b. 28 Nov. 1670; d. at Hadley 10 Nov. 1744; m.
         5 Sept. 1700 Sarah Lane, who was living in Jan. 1758,
         daughter of Samuel Lane of Suffield, Conn. Seven children.
     6.  Ebenezer, b. 23 Oct. 1675; d. at South Hadley, Mass., 11 Nov.
         1757; m. Editha ——, who d. 19 Aug. 1757, in her 75th
         year. Nine children.

---

## GENEALOGICAL RESEARCH IN ENGLAND

Contributed by G. ANDREWS MORIARTY, JR., A.M., LL.B., of Newport, R. I.,
and communicated by the Committee on English Research

### SYMONDS–FEMELL

To the REGISTER for October 1925 (vol. 79, pp. 410–449)* the
Committee on English Research communicated an article con-
tributed by its Chairman, G. Andrews Moriarty, Jr., Esq., in which
the English ancestry and connections of Roger Derby, the immigrant
ancestor of the well-known Derby family of Salem, Mass., were set
forth and the descent of Roger Derby from Nicholas Derby of
Askerswell, co. Dorset, and later of Sterthill in the parish of Burton-
Bradstock, in the same county, gentleman, was proved. This
Nicholas Derby was the great-grandfather of Roger Derby; and
Christopher Derby of Sterthill, gentleman, who was baptized at
Askerswell in 1571 and died 20 Jan. 1639/40, the son of Nicholas
and the grandfather of Roger of Salem, was shown to have married
Ann (or Agnes) Symonds, who died probably about May 1649,
daughter of William Symonds of Exeter, co. Devon, gentleman, and
his wife Alice (Moone). (REGISTER, vol. 79, p. 433.) In the
present article it is the purpose of the Chairman of the Committee
to lay before the readers of the REGISTER records relating to this
*Pages 93-132, this volume.

Symonds family and also to the Femell family, to which the mother of William Symonds belonged; and these records will be followed by two pedigrees, in which the most important facts disclosed by them are arranged in genealogical form. Articles on other English families that were connected by marriage with the Derby family will appear in future numbers of the REGISTER.

Before presenting the Symonds and Femell records, however, it is necessary to mention and to refute an erroneous statement about the origin of the Symonds family which was believed and recorded in the second quarter of the seventeenth century by Sir Simonds D'Ewes, Bart. (1602–1650), a famous Suffolk antiquary, who was himself a grandson of Richard Symonds, one of the brothers of William Symonds, the father-in-law of Christopher Derby.

In Harleian Manuscript 381, in the British Museum, are to be found various papers of Sir Simonds D'Ewes and copies of records made by him, and among them are pedigrees, partly in his own handwriting, in which, as well as in his autobiography, published in 1845, he identifies his great-grandfather, Thomas Symonds of Taunton, co. Somerset, merchant, with a Thomas Simonds whose father, Thomas Simonds, was an illegitimate son of Sir Giles Strange-ways of Melbury-Sampford, co. Dorset, Knight. This identification was made on the strength of information given to Sir Simonds by Sir John Strangeways, a descendant of Sir Giles, and by Sir Simonds's great-uncle, William Symonds of Exeter, the latter asserting, in response to questions from Sir Simonds D'Ewes, that he did not remember the name of his [William's] grandfather, but that this grandfather "lived in Melberry in Dorset, at length came to tanton & there died."*

Now it is perfectly clear that Sir Giles Strangeways of Melbury-Sampford had an illegitimate son named Thomas Simonds or Symonds, who bore his mother's surname, for in his will, dated 20 Sept. 1546 and proved 29 Dec. 1546 (P. C. C., Alen, 24), Sir Giles bequeathed to his "bastard son, Thomas Symondes, the occupation and profit of my parsonage of Abbottsbury, with reversion to the said Giles" [i.e., Giles Strangeways, the testator's grandson, son of his son Henry], and the parsonage of Sydling, with reversion to Henry Strangeways, younger son of the testator's son Henry. Sir Giles also bequeathed to his bastard son, Thomas Symonds, "my whole term and interest in my farm of Wrakelford, parcel of the prebend of Stratton, with the stock and store thereof for ever," and "the issues and profits of the 'Wayhouse' in Castell towne in Shurborne and the profits of castell towne market during the life of one Hugh Whitewood." This Thomas Symonds, the illegitimate son of Sir Giles Strangeways, was of Woodsford and West Stafford, co. Dorset, and in his will, dated 2 Jan. 1562/3 and proved 17 May 1566, he named, among others, his sons Giles and Thomas, and mentioned his sheep upon his farm of Wrakelford and Woodesford. (See his will, *infra*, p. 351.) It is this last-mentioned Thomas, son of the bastard Thomas, whom Sir Simonds D'Ewes identified with

*Vide infra, p. 350.

159

his [Sir Simonds's] great-grandfather, Thomas Symonds of Taunton, pewterer and merchant.

Now this identification is clearly wrong. Thomas Symonds of Taunton, the great-grandfather of Sir Simonds D'Ewes, made his will 13 Oct. 1572 and was buried in the parish of St. Mary Magdalene, Taunton, 22 Oct. 1572 (see will and parish register entry, *infra*), while administration on the estate of Thomas Symonds of Woodefforde Castle was granted 22 Dec. 1612 to his relict Ann (P: C. C.), and a further administration was granted 20 July 1613 to Thomas, son of the deceased, the widow, Ann, not having fully administered the estate. (Cf. *Notes & Queries for Somerset and Dorset*, vol. 3, p. 13.) Moreover, a deposition taken at Dorchester, co. Dorset, 29 Aug., 12 James I [1614], in the case of Symonds *v.* Fulhurst (Chancery Depositions, Elizabeth, James I, Charles I, S, 44/5) states that Thomas Symonds, father of the plaintiff (Thomas Symonds, gentleman), had died possessed of a lease of a capital messuage and demesne lands called Woddesford Castle, etc., which the said Thomas (the father) had bought of his elder brother, Giles Symonds, the deponent, etc. Thus Sir Simonds D'Ewes's identification of Thomas Symonds of Taunton, his own great-grandfather, with Thomas Symonds, son of Thomas of Woodesford and brother of Giles, is effectually disproved. Furthermore, the two families used distinct coats of arms, which Burke and other writers have confused, owing to the mistake of Sir Simonds. William Symonds of Lyme-Regis, co. Dorset, in 1587, and later of Exeter and Axminster, co. Devon, son of Thomas of Taunton and great-uncle of Sir Simonds D'Ewes, was granted in 1587, by Robert Cooke, Clarenceux King-of-Arms, the following coat: *Party per fesse sable and argent a pale counterchanged, three trefoils of the second*, with the crest: *On a mount vert an ermine proper holding in his mouth a pannce [pansy] or;*[*] but Giles Symonds and his descendants used an entirely different coat, viz., *Argent, a bend engrailed between two fire balls proper*, and in 1596 Dethick, Garter King-of-Arms, granted to Giles Symonds as a crest: *A Moor's arm tied with a scarf, in the hand a fire ball.* In this grant Giles is described as son of Thomas Symonds of West Stafford, co. Dorset.

The statement of Sir Simonds D'Ewes that his great-grandfather, Thomas Symonds of Taunton, was a son of Thomas Symonds of Woodsford, an illegitimate son of Sir Giles Strangeways, having been effectually disproved, the following Symonds and Femell records are presented.

---

[*]From the records of the College of Arms. Cf. the arms on the monument to Richard Symonds in the Chardstock church, co. Dorset, as described *infra*, p. 347, footnote. In The Visitation of the County of Devon in the Year 1620, p. 280 (*Publications of the Harleian Society*, vol. 6), in the brief Symonds pedigree filed by Richard Herbert for his father-in-law, William Symonds, the Symonds arms are given as *Per fess sable and argent, a pale counterchanged, three trefoils slipped of the second*, with the crest: *On a mount vert an ermine holding in the mouth a pansy, all proper.* This Devonshire pedigree is described in the REGISTER, vol. 79, p. 433, third footnote. ✳✳

✳✳Page 116, this volume.

"I was born . . . at Coxden, in the parish of Chardstock, in the county of Dorset, upon Saturday, the 18th day of December, about five of the clock in the morning, in the year of our Lord, 1602. . . . I was baptized upon the 29th day of the same month, . . . in the open gallery of Coxden aforesaid, (in respect of the extreme coldness of the season,) by Mr. Richard White, the vicar of Chardstock. My godfathers were my uncle William Simonds, being son and heir of my great-grandfather Thomas Simonds, and his second brother Richard Simonds, of Coxden, aforesaid, Esq., being the second son of the said Thomas, and father to Cecilia, my most endeared mother. . . . The house, being for the most part fairly built of freestone, with the demesnes thereof, commonly called the manor of Coxden, I still enjoy as the inheritance of my mother, descended unto her from the said Richard Simonds, her father, whose sole daughter and heir she was." (Vol. 1, pp. 1–2.)

"Paul D'Ewes, of Milding, in the county of Suffolk, . . . Esq., my father, was ordinarily resident in the vacation time at Welshall, in the said parish of Milding, (for during the terms he attended his law-studies in the Middle Temple, and after the year 1607, his office being one of the six clerks of the Chanery,)." (Vol. 1, pp. 3–4.)

"I could never yet add anything . . . to that [information about my paternal ancestors] which I received from my father, . . . as followeth: That his father was named Geerardt D'Ewes, being a citizen of London; that his mother was named Grace Hynde, and descended of the family of the Hyndes of Cambridgeshire, and a widow big with child when my grandfather married her. But . . . he never enquired, nor could ever inform me, what was his grandfather's Christian name by his mother's side, nor who was her first husband." (Vol. 1, p. 7.)

"The child my grandmother was first delivered of after she married my grandfather, though it had been begotten by her former husband, yet bare my grandfather's surname. . . . It was named John D'Ewes, and died in its infancy, and was buried the 3d of September A.D. 1563. My grandfather had afterwards a son named Paul, born in 1563, which died before the said John a day or two, and was buried September 1, 1563. My father was the second son, and . . . was called Paul also, . . . [having been] born upon the 25th day of January, . . . 1567." (Vol. 1, p. 8.)

"My grandfather had only one daughter, named Alice, married to William Lathum of Upminster, in the county of Essex, Esquire. This Geerardt [my grandfather] was . . . son and heir to Adrian D'Ewes, who first came from the dition [i.e., government, lordship] of Kessel in the Duchy of Guelderland into England in Henry the Eighth's time, and settled here and married Alice Ravenscroft, being a gentlewoman of a good family, and had issue by her, Geerardt his son and heir aforesaid, Peter, James, and Andrew, all named in the last will, as is also Alice, his wife, who overlived him." (Vol. 1, pp. 8–9.)

"She [Alice], by her unfortunate second marriage with one William Ramsey, (after the said Adrian's decease in July, A.D. 1551,) was the cause that her son and heir Geerardt aforesaid (who overlived his said father near upon

*Cf. The Autobiography and Correspondence of Sir Simonds D'Ewes, Bart., edited by James Orchard Halliwell, 2 vols., London, 1845. The original manuscript of the autobiography is in the British Museum, in Harleian MS. 646. The spelling of the manuscript has apparently been corrected or modernized by the editor in preparing the copy for publication. A Simonds pedigree and other pedigrees and papers, wholly or partly in the handwriting of Sir Simonds D'Ewes, may be found in Harleian MS. 381. The extracts from the Autobiography and the summaries of certain passages in it given in this article are chiefly of a genealogical nature and have, for the most part, not been used in the excellent life of Sir Simonds D'Ewes in the Dictionary of National Biography, to which the reader is referred for a comprehensive account of his career.

forty years, dying April 2d, 1591,) was enforced to betake himself to a city life; for the said Ramsey wasted and spent most of that estate her first husband left her, who unadvisedly made her his sole executrix." (Vol. 1, p. 10.)

"I did search long . . . to have found the endenization of my great-grandfather Adrian, but never could discover it; so, as I believe, he lived and died here an alien." (Vol. 1, p. 11.)

[Sir Simonds D'Ewes adds much more about his father's ancestral line.]

"Of my mother's family I can say little; she brought to my father, or to me his son and heir, (whom Richard Simonds, Esq. made his sole executor,)] in lands, leases, goods, and ready money, about ten thousand pounds. She was the sole daughter and heir of the said Richard, and of Johanna his wife, the daughter of William Stephens of Kent, and of Ellen his wife, the daughter and heir of a Lovelace, (as hath been received by tradition,) and that she was heir to the said Ellen her mother, being her father's second wife; and hence my said grandfather did, about forty-five years since, reckoning from this present year (1636), cause to be depicted over the chimney of his dining-room at Coxden in Dorsetshire, his own coat-armour empaled with Lovelace and Ensham quarterly, as accounting the said two coat-armours to belong by right of inheritance to the said Johanna his wife; which depiction remaining still upon the said chimney-piece, being of wainscot, may yet be seen. These coats quarterly were thus empaled in my grandfather Simonds's funeral escutcheons, and in my mother's, both enquartered with Simonds, and so empaled with my father's paternal coat.* I know nothing to the contrary, but that I might enquarter these coat-armours; and yet, so sincere hath my proceedings been in the searching out of these truths, as I have yet forborne ordinarily to insert the said coat-armours of Lovelace and Ensham into my shield, because I first desired to have some proof of them. What proofs my grandfather aforesaid had to assert his assuming of them, I know not; but they are all now perished, if he had any: for my father, shortly after his decease, brought up all his writings from his said house at Coxden, together with the evidences and leases of my estate there, which were all burnt together with many other writings of moment, in the Six Clerks' Office in 1621 [20 December], when . . . there happened a lamentable fire.

"My said grandfather Simonds, who ordinarily wrote his surname with a *y*, had an elder brother called William, before remembered, and three younger brothers, viz. Thomas, Laurence, and Robert. Their father was Thomas Simonds, who died in the year 1570 [*sic*, 1572], and lieth buried in St. Mary Magdalen's church in Taunton, whither he removed divers years before his death from Melbury, in Dorsetshire, where Thomas Simonds his father inhabited, as my great-uncle William Simonds sent me word,† who lived till he was near ninety years old, and died in the city of

*According to a contributor to *Notes & Queries for Somerset and Dorset*, vol. 13, pp. 127–128 (for the year 1912–13), a Simonds monument was standing in the church of Chardstock as late as 1874 or 1875, for Pulman, in The Book of the Axe, 1875, p. 567, in his description of Chardstock church, writes: "The most interesting monument in the church is a mural one to the memory of some members of the Simonds family. It contains effigies of a gentleman and lady kneeling before a desk, with other figures, including mutilated ones of three children." Pulman then gives the inscription. The contributor to *Notes & Queries*, writing probably about 1912, states that the "only remaining portions of this monument are now on the north wall of the tower and consist of the slab with the inscription and by its side a stone shield of arms. . . . The effigies are now gone." The arms on the shield, according to this contributor, are *Per fesse sable and argent, a pale counter-charged [sic], on each of the first a trefoil slipped of the second*, for Symonds, impaling quarterly, 1 and 4, presumably Lovelace, and 2 and 3, presumably Ensham, These quarterings are described by the contributor. The Symonds crest is broken, but, as given by Burke, was *On a mount vert an ermine ppr, holding in the mouth a cinquefoil or.*

†What William Symonds wrote to his grandnephew, Sir Simonds D'Ewes, was that his [William's] "grandfather [*not his father*] lived in Melberry in Dorset, at length came to tanton & there died." *Vide infra*, p. 350. (Page 165, this volume.)

162

Exeter in 1635 [sic, he was buried 8 January 1634/5]. But I could never yet* learn from him what his grandfather's Christian name was, nor anything else touching the original of this surname. . . . The wife of this Thomas Simonds, and mother of my grandfather and his four brethren, was Agnes, the daughter of Richard Femel, a wealthy Dutchman, who came out of Normandy into England." (Vol. 1, pp. 20–22.)

The writer of the autobiography records the death of his Grandmother Simonds, at Coxden, 16 February 1610/11, and her burial in the Chardstock church, 23 February 1610/11, and also the death of his Grandfather Simonds, at Coxden, 27 June 1611, and adds that his uncle, William Simonds, "my grandfather's elder brother, being come from Exeter during the time of his sickness, to visit him, and being at Coxden when he died," sent word of his death to the writer's father and mother, who were in London, and they sent for their son Simonds [then only in his ninth year] to come from Lavenham, co. Suffolk [where he was at school], and join them. "Being come to London, I went straightway into Chancery Lane, to my father's office [His father was one of the six clerks of Chancery]; there I found my uncle Thomas Simonds, my grandfather's younger brother," and about 5 July [1611] the writer's father, with his mother, himself, and his two elder sisters, left London for Coxden, "for my two younger sisters, Mary and Cecilia, remained still near Welshall [the father's manor in Suffolk], with their nurses." His grandfather "was aged, at the time of his death, about sixty and one years, . . . [and] did by his last will and testament, constitute and appoint me his sole executor, which bare date the 14th day of January, 1608 [1608/9], . . . leaving me thereby a great personal estate, in ready money, debts upon specialities, leases, household stuff, and other goods and chattels; but appointing my father to be administrator during my minority. . . . My grandfather was interred upon Thursday, the 11th day of the same July [1611], fourteen days after his death, in the same upper end of the middle aisle [in Chardstock church], by my grandmother, his wife, . . . and care was taken not only to bring my grandfather with honour to his grave; but a fair monument, according to his own appointment in his will, was erected and set up on the north side of his grave, in Chardestock church, to the memory of himself and my grandmother."† (Vol. 1, pp. 37–43.)

Simonds D'Ewes was brought up by his Grandfather and Grandmother Simonds at Coxden until October 1610, when he was nearly eight years old; then he lived with his parents at Welshall, their home in Suffolk, and from there was sent to school in Lavenham, Suffolk; and after the death of his Grandfather Simonds he remained in the "West Country" until 1614, being at school at Wambroke, co. Dorset, some three miles from Coxden, for three full years from about the end of September 1611. (Vol. 1, pp. 30, 36, 45, 46.) "In the year 1614, I went to the city of Exeter to keep my Easter with my uncle William Simonds, who had been also one of my witnesses at my baptizing. I was most affectionately entertained by him and his wife my aunt. . . . This was the first time that I conversed and spake with my aged uncle, departing finally out of the West Country this year [in November]." (Vol. 1, p. 61.)

*A footnote in the printed autobiography (vol. 1, p. 21) states that the following note was here added by D'Ewes in the margin: "This I wrote in the year 1636; since which time, I was informed by Sir John Strangwaies of Melburie Sampford, in the County of Dorset, Knight, that the said Thomas Simonds was the natural son of Sir Giles Strangwaies, Knight, which is proved by record also, viz. Escaet. de a°. 1°. E. 6. N°. 34°. Dorset, by which my mother enquartered divers great and noble coat-armours." The pedigrees in Harleian MS. 381 give the Strangeway line and the supposed illegitimate descent of Thomas Simonds from that family, which has been disproved in one of the introductory paragraphs of this article (supra, p. 345). ✳

† Vide supra, p. 347, footnote. ✳

*For pp. 345 & 347 see pp. 160 & 162, this volume.

Soon after the death of his Grandfather Simonds the writer's father, Paul D'Ewes, lost the manors of Welshall, co. Suffolk, which were recovered from him by Mrs. Ann Sherland, widow of Thomas Sherland, from whom Paul D'Ewes had bought them, the wife of Sherland not having relinquished her rights therein, as she had promised to do. (Vol. 1, p. 43.) In 1611 Paul D'Ewes purchased Lavenham Hall, Suffolk, with the manor and town of Lavenham, and there he settled with his family, in 1613, Coxden being leased to others. (Vol. 1, pp. 54–55.) In 1614 he bought the manor of Stowlangtoft, co. Suffolk, some five miles from Bury St. Edmunds, the capital messuage and site of the manor being called Stow Hall, and thither he moved soon afterwards, with his family, from Lavenham Hall, and resided there in vacation time until his death. (Vol. 1, p. 65.)

The education of Simond D'Ewes had been continued under a teacher in London, where his father resided in term time, and afterwards under the upper master of the school at Bury, and on 21 May 1618 he was admitted to St. John's College, Cambridge, as a fellow commoner. (Vol. 1, p. 107.)

The mother of Sir Simonds D'Ewes died at Stow Hall 31 July 1618, and was buried in Stowlangtoft church 6 August 1618. (Vol. 1, pp. 110–111.) "She was the sole daughter and heir of Richard Simonds of Coxden, . . . yet was not born in the western parts whence her paternal family did originally spring; but at the town of Feversham, in the county of Kent, the 29th day of November, being Sunday, about two of the clock in the afternoon . . . , A. D. 1579. Her birth happened to be in the place by reason it had been formerly resided in by Johan, her mother, being at the time her father married her, the widow of John Nethersole, Esq., and being the daughter also of a Stephens, which is a surname very ancient in that shire, but of small eminence in these days; yet she was nearly allied unto (if not descended from an inheritance of) the family of Lovelace. She brought a great personal estate to the said Richard Simond's, her last husband, and a daughter also, having ever before remained barren. After he had a few years inhabited with her in her own country, she removed with him into the western parts, and first inhabited Wycraft Castle, in Devonshire, not far from Axminster; where they increasing with wealth, and their daughter in delicacy and beauty, educated also by her mother very carefully and virtuously, she was sought in marriage by divers of the western gentry. But her father having gained the acquaintance of Paul D'Ewes, after of Milding, in the county of Suffolk, and lastly of Stow Hall, in the same county, Esq., at London; his father Geerardt D'Ewes being deceased some three years before, and knowing him to be a great husband [i.e., a careful person], and to be well moneyed, he accepted of him for his son-in-law; and married him to his daughter at Axminster, aforesaid, (Wycraft Castle standing in that parish,) upon Tuesday the tenth day of December, . . . A. D. 1594; his said daughter being then but fourteen years old and about a fortnight over. . . . She having lived with her husband awhile after her marriage at Wycraft Castle, in her father's house, removed thence to Broad Street, in London, and afterwards settled awhile at Malden, in the county of Essex. . . . At last, my father buying the manor of Wellshall in Milding, in the county of Suffolk, of one Shorland, and removing thither in or about the year 1579 [sic, ? 1599] to reside, it pleased God in mercy to grant unto her what she begged of Him in so many zealous prayers, and to give her not only one but many children, as well sons as daughters." (Vol. 1, pp. 112–115.)

In September 1620 Simonds D'Ewes left Cambridge University, and in October of the same year he went to London, where since 1607 his father had been one of the six clerks in Chancery, and entered the Middle Temple. (Vol. 1, pp. 147, 149.) On 5 March 1622/3 his father married secondly, in St. Faith's Church, under St. Paul's, London, Dame Elizabeth Denton, widow of Sir Anthony Denton, Knight, late of Tunbridge, co. Kent, and eldest daughter of Thomas Isham, Esq., of Langport in Northamptonshire, deceased. She was then about forty-five years old. (Vol. 1, pp. 227–229.) On 24 October 1626 Simonds himself married, in Blackfriars Church, London, Anne Clopton, born in February 1612 [1612/13],* sole surviving daughter and heir of Sir William Clopton, Knight (who died 11 March 1618/19), by his first wife, Dame Anne Clopton, who was a younger daughter of Sir Thomas Barnardiston, Knight, and Dame Anne Barnardiston, Sir Thomas's last wife. (Vol. 1, pp. 133, 322, 332.) On 6 December 1626 Simonds D'Ewes was knighted by King Charles at Whitehall. (Vol. 1, p. 325.) [He was made a baronet on 15 July 1641.] In 1629/30 Sir Simonds's father delivered to him "three fair silver goblets, which were given by Thomas Simonds, my great-grandfather, to Richard Simonds, Esq., of Coxden, . . . my mother's father, being the second son of the same Thomas." (Vol. 1, p. 429.) On 4 August 1630 Sir Simonds and his wife "went to Edmonton, to my cousin Thomas Simonds' house, (being my mother's cousin-german, and the son and heir of her uncle, Thomas Simonds,) where we lay." (Vol. 1, p. 435.)

"Tuesday, February the 22nd [1630/1], my father fell sick of a fever, joined with a pleurisy, of which disease he lingered three weeks before he deceased, during which time I had many sad and heavy journeys to him. [Sir Simonds and his wife were living in Islington, and his father lived at the Six Clerks' Office, in Chancery Lane.] . . . [He] departed out of this life about a quarter of an hour after five of the clock in the afternoon, . . . Monday, March the 14th [1630/1]," and was buried in the church at Stow-langtoft, co. Suffolk, 25 April 1631. (Vol. 2, pp. 5–11, 30–31.)

[Sir Simonds writes about his father's will, which was dated 8 January 1629/30, and about the family dissensions which arose out of its provisions (vol. 2, pp. 22–26), and gives an account of his father's children and their marriages (vol. 2, pp. 11–21), of which the most important genealogical data are given in the pedigree near the end of this article. The autobiography ends with a narration of events of 14 May 1636.]

Information furnished to Sir Simonds D'Ewes by William Simonds of Exeter, co. Devon.†

[Endorsement.] "The answeares which my uncle William Simonds of the cittie of Exeter then aged aboue 80 yeares sent mee in the yeare 1635‡ to certaine questions I desired one Robert Cogan to ask him touching some of his ancestors; Hee was eldest brother to Richard Simonds Esquire my grandfather by my mothers side."

"I pray carrie this bre͠ w^th you & under these next questions write my uncles answeeres & soe cutt off this peice of paper & send it mee."

"1. What was the Christian name of his owne grandfather, whether Thomas or William, his fathers name was Thomas Simonds.
*his grandfathers name he remembers not*
"2 Whether his father weere a yonger brother or his grandfather & whether his grandfather dwelt in Tanton as Thomas Simonds his father did: & whether his ancestors weere anciently townes men in Tanton or liued elseweere in Somersetshire & at what place.
*Whether his grandfather or father wer a yonger brother he knowes not, his grandfather lived in Melberry in Dorset, at length came to tanton & there died.*

*She was born 14 Feb. 1612/13, at Clare Priory, co. Suffolk, the home of her grandfather, Sir Thomas Barnardiston. (Autobiography, vol. 1, pp. 52–53.)
†From Harleian MS. 381, fo. 147. The writing is all in the hand of Sir Simonds D'Ewes, except the answers, which are printed in italics.
‡William Simonds was buried 8 Jan. 1634/5, and, according to the autobiography of Sir Simonds D'Ewes (vide supra), "lived till he was near ninety years old."

"3. If Agnes his mother was not his fathers second wife & if shee were not the daughter of one Richard Femel a Dutchman & whose daughter his grandmother was & what her name.

"*Agnes his mother was his fathers second wife daughter to one Richard Femell a Norman as he thinkes*"

### FROM PROBATE RECORDS

The Will of THOMAS SYMONDES of Woodesford, co. Dorset, gent., dated 2 January 1562 [1562/3]. To William, Nicholas, Elizabeth, and Anne, my children, £100 each, at their ages of twenty-one, to be paid out of the increase of my sheep upon my farm of Wrakelford and Woodesford. To my sons Thomas and George the years I have in reversion of Hugh Pesin in Est Ayleworth farm in the parish of Abbotisbury, co. Dorset, and £100. Residuary legatees and executors: my wife Alice and my son Giles. Overseers: George and Hugh Watkins and Thomas Golloppe. [Signed] Thomas Symondes. Witnesses: Heughe Watkins, John Chubbe, Thomas Golupp, Robert Wolton. Proved 17 May 1566 by Thomas Willett, notary public, proctor to the executors. (P. C. C., Crymes, 12.)

[The will given above is that of the Thomas Symonds who was an illegitimate son of Sir Giles Strangeways of Melbury–Sampford, co. Dorset, Knight; and the testator's son Thomas, named in the will, is the man who was erroneously identified by Sir Simonds D'Ewes with his (Sir Simonds's) great-grandfather, Thomas Symonds of Taunton, co. Somerset. *Vide supra*, p. 344.]

The nuncupative Will of JOHN SYMMONS of Taunton, co. Somerset, declared 14 January 1570 [1570/1]. He gave to his wife, Emma Symmons, all his goods wheresoever, on this side or beyond the seas. Witnesses: Mr. Nicholas Goodland, M.A., Walter Bryan, clerk.

A commission was issued 27 January 1570 [1570/1] to Emma Symons, relict of the deceased, to administer his goods, etc., in the person of Mr. John Lewes, notary public, her proctor. (P. C. C., Holney, 1.)

The Will of THOMAS SYMONS of Taunton, co. Somerset, merchant, dated 13 October 1572. To be buried in the church of St. Mary Magdalene. To the said church 10s. To the poor of the parish 40s. To my son Richard, after the decease of my wife Agnes, all my lands in Grascrofte, to him and his heirs for ever. To my son Henry, at his age of twenty-four, £40 and half my "mowles" and tools. Residuary legatee and executrix: My wife Agnes. Overseers: my brother Henry Femall and my son-in-law William Leonard. The mark of Thomas Symons. Witnesses: Henry Femall, Willyam Leonard, Willyam Symonds, Thomas Carlell, Wallter Bryand. Proved 10 January 1572 [1572/3] by Walter Smith, proctor to the executrix. (P. C. C., Peter, 1.)

The Will of JOHANNE FEMELL of St. Mary Magdalene in Taunton, co. Somerset, dated 29 June 1576, being "sicke of bodie." To be buried in the church of Mary Magdalene, Taunton. To the church of St. Andrew's, Wells, 4d. To St. Mary Magdalene, Taunton, 6s. 8d. To the poor at burial 40s. To my daughter Agnes Calvarte "one flatt pece called the p'es pece" and £20 in money. To Thomas Symons, Laurence Symonds, Robert Symons, and Jane Symondes a riall of gold apiece. To my daughter Anstice Lawrence my interest in the house where she now dwelleth, with the implements and household stuff therein, a goblet, six spoons with rolled knobs, my second-best featherbed [and other household stuff]. To Henry Lawrence, son of William Lawrence, at the age of twenty-four or at marriage, £10. To Anstice Lawrence, daughter of William Lawrence, at the age of twenty-four or at marriage, £10. To Mary and Margaret Femell, daughters of my son Laurence Femell, £20 each at the age of twenty-four or at marriage.

To Richard Femell, son unto my son John Femell, deceased, a gilt goblet and six silver spoons. To Thomas Femell, son to the said John, at the age of twenty-four, £20, a gilt goblet, six silver spoons, and a parcel-gilt salt. My executor is to find said Thomas meat, drink, and apparel, and to find him to school for two years after my decease, or he is to have £10 towards his finding and schooling elsewhere. Unto John Femell, son of the said John Femell, one obligation of £13. 6s. 8d., "due to be paid by John Symons his maister that he nowe dwelleth with at thende and tearme of his prentishippe." Residuary legatee and executor: my son Henry Femell. Overseers: Nicholas Calvarte, Symon Saunders. Witnesses: Nicholas Calvarte, Thomas Jones, clerk. Proved 4 February 1577/8 by Edward Orwell, notary public, proctor for the executor. (P. C. C., Langley, 8.)

The Will of RICHARD SYMONDES of Coxden, co. Dorset, Esq., dated 14 January 1608 [1608/9]. I desire a monument to be made of me and my late wife, cut in some semblance of us and put in the walk at the end of my seat. To Cecilia Riche and my man, William Case, £10 each. To my brothers, William and Thomas Symondes, plate engraved with my name to the value of £10 each. To the poor of Chardstock £5 and to the poor of Tanton £5. To my grandchild Joan Dewes, at age of eighteen or marriage, £50, and she is to give her brother Symonde Dewes the piece of plate given her at her christening by my wife, that he may have the goblets that were my father's. To Grace and Mary Dewes and Cecilia £50 each, at like age. To my servant Thomas Tibbes £15. To all my other servants 20s. each. I desire Paul Dewes to care for Thomas Tibbes. To Richard Stevens and Mary Leonard a gold ring each. To my friends, Mr. Edward Aldworthe, Anthony Luther, John Bruester, commonly in mess with me in the Temple, a double sovereign each, to buy a pair of gloves. To Mr. Thomas Parmyter 10s. To William Gibbes, Esq., and Mary, his wife, rings. To my daughter [not named] £50. Residuary legatee and executor: my grandchild, Symond Dewes, and his father, Paul Dewes, during Symond's minority. If he die before the age of eighteen, then his mother, my daughter Cecilia, is to be executrix, and then his sisters, Joan, Grace, and Mary are to be residuary legatees. [Signed] Richard Symonds. Witnesses: John Mogredge, Thomas Parris, Thomas Payne of Symondsberry [his mark].

Administration was granted 26 October 1611 to Paul Dewes, Esq., during the minority of Symond Dewes. Proved 1 October 1633 by Sir Symond Dewes, Knight, the executor named in the will, the administration granted to Paul Dewes now ceasing. (P. C. C., Wood, 79.)

The Will of WILLIAM SYMONS of Exeter, co. Devon, gentleman, dated 20 February, 9 Charles I [1633/4]. The testator bequeaths to his sister's daughter, Mary Stevens, to his sister's daughter, Alice Gill, to the wife of Henry Thomas of Widworthy, to the son of John Hore of Axminster, to his daughter Rebecca [Salter] and her sister Agnes Derbye, to his son-in-law Anthonie Salter, to his son-in-law Christopher Derbye, to his daughter Marcella Herbert, whom he appoints executrix, to his nephew [i.e., grandson] Southcott Hewish, to his wife's kinswoman, Elizabeth Rockey, to Christopher Sandford, servant to his executrix, and to his godson William Seaward. He mentions land called Newlands, within the parish of Whittchurch, co. Dorset, purchased from George Wadham, Esq., a house and land in Axminster, various articles of plate, his brother Richard Symons [deceased], and William Derbye's wife. He signs the will as "William Symondes." Witnesses: John Mayne, James Calthropp, Henry Rowcliffe. Proved 20 February 1634 [1634/5] by the executrix. (P. C. C., Sadler, 16.) [A longer abstract of this will, with the portion disposing of lands and plate quoted *verbatim*, was published in the REGISTER, vol. 79, p. 412.] *

*Page 95, this volume.

FROM THE PARISH REGISTERS OF CHARDSTOCK, CO. DORSET

1602 Symondes Dewes son of Paul Dewes, Esquire, baptized 29 December.
1610 Joan wife of Richard Symondes, Esquire, one of his Majesties Justices of the Peace, buried 23 February [1610/11].
1611 Richard Symondes, Esq., J. P., buried 11 July.

FROM THE REGISTERS OF THE CATHEDRAL, EXETER, CO. DEVON*

1628 Alice wife of Mr. William Symons buried 26 July.
1634 Mr. William Symons, gent., buried 8 January [1634/5].

FROM THE REGISTERS OF THE PARISH OF ST. MARY MAGDALENE, TAUNTON, CO. SOMERSET

*Baptisms*

1559 Ellinor Symons 20 September.
1559 Marie Femell 7 December.
1559 John Femell 18 December.
1560 Margarett Symons 16 April.
1560 Lawrence Symons 16 March [1560/1].
1561 Annes Femell 13 April.
1564 Elinor Femell 1 April.
1564 Johane Femell 15 March [1564/5].
1565 Robert Simons 12 December.
1567 Lawrence son of John Femell 11 April.
1567 Robert Simons 8 February [1567/8].
1580 Nicholas Simons 8 January [1580/1].
1581 Robert Simons 18 February [1581/2].
1593 Ambrose son of Roger Symmons 8 October.
1596 Agenstice daughter of Roger Symons 19 January [1596/7].
1605 Henry son of Lawrence Femall *alias* Morse 17 November.
1606 Ratcher daughter of Lawrence Femell *alias* Morse 18 February [1606/7].
1613 Eme daughter of Henry Simons 15 March [1613/14].
1614 Robert son of William Symons 24 November.
1631 Katherine daughter of Henry Simmons 22 January [1631/2].

*Marriages†*

1566 Henrie Sherborne and Johane Simons 9 May.
1568 John Simons and Em Pope 13 September.
1571 William Simons and Alice Moone 14 September.
1573 William Hill and Annies Femell 14 December.
1573 Nicholas Colvord and Agnes Simons 11 March [1573/4].
1575 John Rich and Elnor Simons 21 November.
1578 Roger Simons and Alice Spreate 31 January [1578/9].
1596 Nicholas Yeat and Agnes Simons 29 July.
1606 Henrye Symons and Luce Browne 23 June.
1611 William Simons and Dorethy Carter 8 February [1611/12].
1613 Henry Simons and Margarett Pitts 12 April.
1614 William Hill and Judith Femall 30 June.
1620 John Broaley and Dorothy Symmons 5 August.
1629 Henry Symons and Elizabeth Longe 4 May.

*The registers of the Cathedral of Exeter were published by The Devon & Cornwall Record Society, 1910.

†The marriages recorded in the registers of the parish of St. Mary Magdalene, Taunton, have been printed in Phillimore's Somerset Parish Registers, Marriages, vols. 9 and 10.

## Burials

1559 Annes Simons 12 July.
1565 Robert Symons 4 January [1565/6].
1565 Annes Femell 28 March [1565/6].
1566 William Symons 21 April.
1569 Lawrence Femell 10 April.
1570 John Simons 16 January [1570/1].
1572 Lawrence Femell 28 May.
1572 Thomas Simons 22 October.
1574 Henrie Simons 27 August.
1577 Joane Femell 9 October.
1590 Joane Simons, widow, 7 August.
1596 Elizabeth Symons 17 July.
1597 Joane Simons 18 April.
1598 Mr. Henry Femell 23 January [1598/9].
1612 Eme wife of Henry Simons 3 August.
1612 Rachell daughter of Lawrence Femall 4 October.
1615 Joane wife of Henry Femall 9 November.
1616 Roger Symons 16 January [1616/17].
1616 William Symons 16 February [1616/17].
1617 Alice wife of Roger Symons 15 June.
1617 Eme Symons 23 September.

### From the Portreeves' Accounts, Taunton, co. Somerset

1569 Thomas Symonds, constable of Taunton.
1573 ⎫
1579 ⎬ Henry Femell, constable of Taunton.
1589 ⎭
1594 Thomas Femell, constable of Taunton.

### From Inquisitions Post Mortem*

Inquisition on Richard Simons, Esq., of [Cox]sden, co. Dorset, taken at Bridport, co. Dorset, 24 September, 9 James I [1611], in pursuance of a writ of *diem clausit extremum* dated 16 July, 9 James I [1611].

The jurors say that long before the death of the said Richard a certain Thomas Symonds and Lawrence Symonds were seised in demesne as of fee of the manor, capital messuage, or barton of Coxsden, co. Dorset, of 1 mill, 1 garden, 40 acres of arable land, 30 acres of meadow, 30 acres of pasture, 12 acres of wood, and 2s. rent in Coxsden and Tiderleigh, co. Dorset, and by indenture dated 8[?] November, 36 Elizabeth [8 November 1594], granted the said premises to Thomas Tomlynson and John Searle to the use of the said Richard Symonds for life, with remainder to Paul Dewes, gent., and Cecily, daughter of the said Richard Symonds, and the heirs of their bodies, with remainder to the heirs of the body of the said Cecily, with remainder to the right heirs of the said Richard Symonds.

The said Richard Symonds held the said premises for life, and died at Coxsden 27 June last [1611].

The manor was held of the Bishop of Salisbury, as of his Manor of Chardstoke, in free socage, by rent of 2s. yearly, and is worth 40s. yearly.

Cecily, now the wife of Paul Dewes, daughter and heir of said Richard Symonds, was aged 30 when the inquisition was taken. (Chancery Inquisitions Post Mortem, Series 2, vol. 323, no. 3.)

*Preserved in the Public Record Office, London.

169

Final Concord made on the Octave of St. Michael, 2 and 3 Philip and Mary [6 October 1555], between Henry Femell, querent, and William Browne and Joan, his wife, deforciants, concerning two burgages and one garden in Taunton [co. Somerset]. William and Joan have acknowledged the aforesaid premises to be the right of Henry, and they have remised them from William and Joan and the heirs of Joan to Henry and the heirs of Henry for ever. Consideration, £40.† (Feet of Fines, Somersetshire, Michaelmas Term, 2 and 3 Philip and Mary.)

## FROM LAY SUBSIDIES FOR CO. SOMERSET*

9 Edward IV [1469–70] (169/117).

In an inquisition at Bridgewater, 23 September, 9 Edward IV [1469], concerning aliens in co. Somerset, the name *Femell* does not occur.

14 and 15 Henry VIII [1522–1524], second payment of the subsidy of these years (169/154).

Taunton Borough, Forestrete.             Frenchemen.

* * *

Ric. Femyll in goods [valuation] £20 [tax] 20s.

32 Henry VIII [1540–41], second payment of the subsidy of that year (170/193).

Taunton Boro[ugh].            "De Ricō Femell alyn' in bonis" [valuation] £40 [tax] 40s.

## FROM A LIST OF SUBSCRIBERS TOWARDS THE DEFENCE OF THE COUNTRY AT THE TIME OF THE SPANISH ARMADA, 1588‡

William Symondes, of Lyme-Regis [co. Dorset], Merchant, £25.

## FROM CHANCERY PROCEEDINGS*

The bill of JOHN FEMALL of Taunton [co. Somerset], goldsmith, filed 23 January 1566 [1566/7], shows that, whereas John Combe of Taunton, about the Feast of St. Michael, 5 Elizabeth [i.e., about 29 September 1563], desired the complainant, being a goldsmith, to dress and garnish a couple of stone cruises or cups with silver and double-gilt, promising to pay for the stuff and workmanship at the rate of 9s. per oz., whereupon the complainant bestowed thereon 20 oz. of silver, double-gilt, and delivered them to Combe on the Feast of St. Luke [18 October] next following, and Combe promised to pay £9 and also purchased of him [the complainant] six silver spoons weighing 6 oz., promising to pay 36s. for them, now the said Combe refuses to pay. [The answer of the defendant is missing.]

The replication of JOHN FEMELL denies that he owed the defendant £9. 14d. for wares bought, or that the "said Mary" had satisfied him for the silver spoons. (Chancery Proceedings, Series 2, Elizabeth, 63/47.)

The bill of WILLIAM SYMONDS of Lyme-Regis, co. Dorset, gent., dated 6 November 1592, shows that, whereas about 19 Henry VIII [1527–28] one Richard Moone, then of Howchurche, co. Dorset, gent., took of the Abbey of Newneham, co. Devon [*sic*], then lord of the manor of Axminster [co. Devon], by copy of court roll, to himself and to Robert Moone and

---

*Preserved in the Public Record Office, London.
†Translated from the Latin and abridged.
‡From *Notes & Queries for Somerset and Dorset*, vol. 1, p. 39.

Walter Moone, his sons, an estate for their three lives successively of a messuage, tenement, and gardens, parcel of Axminster manor in Axminster parish, to take effect from the death of one "Florence Wood *alias* Tailor," then tenant in possession, and whereas about 26 Henry VIII [1534–35], Florence Taylor then being living, the said Richard Moone procured from the said Abbey as lord of the said manor, by indenture, an estate for diverse years yet to come in the premises, after which the said Richard died, about the last year of Henry VIII [1546], the said Florence being still living, and [whereas] after Richard's death the said Robert Moone compounded with the said Florence and had for a good time during her life the occupation of the premises, and the said Florence died about the last year of Queen Mary [1558], the said Robert being still in possession, and [whereas] about 2 Elizabeth [1559–60] the said Robert compounded with his brother Walter Moone, that Walter should surrender the estate procured by copy of court roll to the use of Robert, and should quitclaim all right therein, this the said Walter did about 2 Elizabeth [1559–60], when Robert and Walter at a court holden for Axminster surrendered to the lord, and Robert became sole tenant, by force of the Abbot's lease for years, and also Walter made a deed of release.

Thereby the said Robert held in peace during the life of Walter, "which was for the space of 20 years or thereabouts," and during Walter's life, viz., about 22 Elizabeth [1579–80], conveyed the premises by good and lawful assurance to the complainant, in consideration of a marriage between the complainant and Alice Moone, daughter of the said Robert, to be had and solemnized, and in consideration of £50 paid by the complainant to Robert.

Now the said Robert, having become, a little before his death, by the visitation of God, very weak and of no memory, died at Baunton, co. Dorset [*sic*], about 23 Elizabeth [1580–81], and made Margaret Moone, his then wife, his sole executor, who ought to have all the writings.

And the said Margaret, being partly moved in regard of the necessity and want of one Morgaine Moone, now of Burpot [Bridport], co. Dorset, one of the sons of the said Walter Moone, then deceased, and partly by her need for help in her business and affairs abroad, took the said Morgaine to be her helper, who thus saw her evidences and the release from Walter; and the said Morgaine, thus seeing the release to be an absolute bar to him and other children of Walter, his father, and intending to drive the complainant to expenses in law or to some composition with him or some other children of Walter, did, before or after the death of the said Robert, convey away and embezzle the release made by his father Walter and also sundry letters written in his own hand by Walter to Robert, which would testify to the release. This the said Morgaine did without Margaret's knowledge and contrary to her trust in him.

Now the said Morgaine gives out openly that the complainant has no right to the premises and that, after the surrender, they ought to have belonged to the said Walter, and he boasts that he will recover them at common law. And the complainant prays for Her Majesty's writ of subpœna, etc.

A writ of subpœna to Morgan Moone was issued 21 November, 35 Elizabeth [21 November 1592].

The answer of MORGAN MONE, gent., states that Richard Mone, the father of Robert and Walter, by his will devised the term of years in the premises to Walter Mone, the defendant's father, and the said Richard made Johane, his wife, executrix. At Richard's death the said Robert kept this will secret, so that its substance did not come to Walter's knowledge. Robert, "being a worldly man," suppressed the lease for years, and, having compounded with Florence Taylor, persuaded his brother Walter that there was no other estate but that by copy, which estate by copy the defendant does not know whether the said Walter agreed that the said Robert should enjoy. The defendant has only heard that Robert tendered Walter a release in general words, and this was not executed. The said Johane made Walter her executor, and after her death Walter made Edith, his wife, the defendant's mother, his executrix, and one Richard Tyggins married Edith. Edith died intestate, and Tyggins and the defendant took the administration of the goods of the said Walter after her death, and, the defendant having notice of Walter's right through the lease for the term of years, Tyggins released all right therein to him [the defendant]. The defendant denies that the said Robert made any agreement with Walter touching the term of years. (Chancery Proceedings, Series 2, 250/2.)

### From Chancery Depositions*

Depositions taken at Axminster [co. Devon], 31 March, 10 James I [31 March 1612], in the case of Thomas Long *v.* Alexander Chick, concerning Axminster Church Houses.

William Simons of Exeter [co. Devon], gent., aged threescore years or thereabouts, deposes that he has known the parties twenty years and "hath ben dwelling in the parish of Axminster for the space of 10 yeres past or thereabout." He deposes that John Launder, deceased, was father of the defendant's wife and some times dwelt in a house which he hired of the deponent. Launder died in the house. The deponent commenced an action of trespass against the defendant for taking away boards out of the house, but deponent ceased his suit after he had had speech with William Longe about the controversy, the matter being referred to the award of Walter Harris and William Bellamy. Longe was solicitor for the deponent. (Chancery Depositions, Elizabeth, L, 29/1.)

### From the Records of the Court of Star Chamber†
### [Combe et al. *v.* Chaplyn et al.]

Commission to hear depositions dated 14 November, 8 Elizabeth [1566]. Depositions taken at Taunton [co. Somerset], 18 December, 9 Elizabeth [1566], on behalf of the complainants in the case between John Combe and his wife Mary and their daughter Elizabeth, complainants, and John Chaplyn, Thomas Lecheland, John Femell, and John Nycholles, defendants.

Laurence Carvanell of Taunton, merchant, aged 67, saith:
About a year or more past, before 11 October, 7 Elizabeth [1565], there was variance between Mary Combe and Margret Peirs of Taunton, and afterwards the variance was appeased. On said 11 October (being the day of the imprisonment of Mary and Elizabeth Combe in Taunton) Mary Combe was a little scratched in the face, and told deponent that it was Margret Peirs that did hurt her. The hurt was "no otherwyse then skratchinge might be betwene two children." On that day, 11 October, 7 Elizabeth, Mary Combe came to deponent's house in Taunton, accompanied with Elizabeth, her daughter, to show deponent that Margret Peirs and she had fought together. Deponent was not deputy to the constable, Hannyvorde, but Hannyvorde had prayed him, if he had need, that he would be "his speale." Nevertheless, deponent did not act as deputy, because Hannyvorde had appointed Skoryer to be his deputy, as Skoryer told deponent. As deponent came from his house with Mary Combe and her daughter Elizabeth, John Chaplyn, Thomas Lecheland, and John Nicholls, defendants, assembled together in the streets and met with deponent at Magdalen Lane

---

*Preserved in the Public Record Office, London.
†Preserved in the Public Record Office, London, the following depositions being found in Star Chamber Proceedings, Elizabeth, C, 5/34.

end. They were so assembled to apprehend Mary Combe, for that she had broken the peace about half an hour and more before. John Chaplyn, as bailiff, Thomas Lecheland, as deputy bailiff to Robert Hendley, and John Nycholls, as one of the aldermen of Forestreet in Taunton, made the assembly to imprison Mary and Elizabeth by the commandments of William Cleve-hanger and William Skoryer, deputy constables of the town, as they said. Deponent did not see Femell until he was returning from the prison and until he came against John Chaplyn's house, being distant from the prison by the space of a butlength. Deponent does not know that any companies were assembled in the streets by the procurement of John Chaplyn and all the other defendants; but Hugh Joy, an alderman of Taunton, came in their company. When deponent came from his house with Mary Combe, passing towards her house, John Chaplyn, then meeting with them, "gave a huppe and the sayed John Nycholls gave a huppe agane to him," Nycholls being distant from him about 40 feet. When Chaplyn hupped, Nycholls came, but how many came with him deponent does not know. No violence was offered to Mary, "she being taken by the Arme by John Chaplyn and was caryed ymatly to the Pryson." Deponent went to the door of the prison with her, and requested Chaplyn and the others to suffer her to depart quietly, offering himself to stand bound for her forthcoming the next morrow and to answer anything that should be laid to her charge. His bond was refused; he does not know that any other was offered. Elizabeth was imprisoned in the prison called the Cowhouse; and Mary was imprisoned in the prison called the Cowhouse [sic]. Upon the first apprehension of Mary there were about six persons; when she was imprisoned there were about twenty persons, men, women, and children, and none of them "weap-oned" other than John Chaplyn and Thomas Lecheland having two staves accustomed to be used in the execution of their office. Deponent denies that he said to Mary: "Be of good comforte Mary Combe for I thinke we shall bothe [be] slayne." Mary, as she was going into the prison, held deponent by the girdle, and then the bailiffs putting her into the prison against her will, she broke the girdle of deponent; he did not hold her girdle. She was imprisoned, but not pulled over the stocks, nor drawn upon the ground violently by the hair, head, or garments. There was a witch im-prisoned in the prison called the Cowhouse a little before. Deponent does not know anything as to whether the devil had appeared to the witch every night while she was in prison, nor whether the prison were filthy. John Chaplyn, at the time of the imprisonment, was bailiff and had been sworn; a bailiff elected to office may execute his office without being sworn. Mary was presented at a Lawday at Taunton to be a disquieter of her neighbors. Deponent, two constables, and William Skoryere were of the jury which presented her. Mary neither railed on those who apprehended her nor made a great noise.

Asked what manner of person John Femell was, and of what disposition, deponent answers that Femell is of the mystery of a goldsmith and of honest disposition.

Richard Wylson of Taunton, merchant, aged 22, saith:

Mary Combe was scratched on both sides of her face, with three scratches on one side. She was in Carvanell's house on 11 October, 7 Elizabeth, as well to sup as to declare her hurt and grief. Margret Peirs and Mary Combe had fought together on 11 October, at night. Chaplyn, Lecheland, Nycholls, and Femell were assembled together at the stocks by the prison door, bring-ing Mary towards the prison, some having her by one arm, some by the other, some thrusting behind, with such cruelty as "he hath not seen and yet he hath seen diuers imprysoned." About twelve persons put her into prison; deponent heard say there were more assembled in the town. Asked whether drink and candlelight were denied Mary, deponent answers that, when one of the town had given her a candle into the prison, John Chaplyn, one of the bailiffs, came after and took it from her, at which time she requested him to get her some sack and she would pay for it. Deponent does not know whether she had it. Chaplyn commanded that no person should give her candlelight upon pain of imprisonment.

John Femell is a goldsmith and "of honest conuersacion."

John Gressham of Taunton, skinner, aged 40, saith:

He judges there were forty persons assembled with Chaplyn and the rest in the night season to imprison Mary; this he judges by the noise made in the street. Among them were Henry Wylmett and his wife, Richard Nutt, John Jenkyns, and many others. Chaplyn and the others took Mary with great force and cruelty, she holding Carvanell by the girdle till she burst his girdle. The bailiffs told Carvanell they had no commission to take his bond for Mary's appearance in the morning. Robert Wylson and one Julyan, servant to Elizabeth Wylson, on behalf of Elizabeth offered bond likewise; he does not know whether the bailiffs heard. The Cowhouse is the vilest prison in Taunton. Mary was forced to go over the stocks in the prison; the prison is "very stinckinge." A witch had been imprisoned there a little before; he can say nothing as to the devil's appearances to her. When Mary cried for help and said her daughter was like to perish, asking for drink and candlelight, Chaplyn said she should have some small drink anon. He and Femell gave open commandment to all there not to bring Mary or Elizabeth any meat, drink, or candlelight on pain of imprisonment for three days and three nights. Deponent "did mynde" to bring Mary candlelight, and Femell watched at his door until 12 of the clock in the night, so that he could not.

"John Femell ys a buseye man and will doo more than ys his dewtye."

John Thomson of Taunton, bowyer, saith:

Chaplyn, Lecheland, Nycholls, and four or five aldermen of Taunton were assembled on the said 11 October in the streets of Taunton in two several companies, distant from one another a pair of butlengths and more, and, when Carvanell and Mary Combe were about Magdalene Lane, one of each company gave the other a "huppe" to give warning of Mary's coming. Thereupon they came together and apprehended her and Elizabeth. Carvanell asked for what cause; the bailiffs answered for breaking the Queen's peace. When they came to the prison door, they were in all about fourteen persons; deponent supposes diverse of them came by reason of the noise.

Femell is to his knowledge an honest man.

Thomas Pawlyn of Taunton, barber, aged 26, saith:

He came into the street by reason of the noise. About forty persons were assembled at the Cornhill, going towards the Cowhouse. Deponent returned to his house to see to the safety of a young child from the fire there, and immediately repaired to the Cowhouse, where he understood Mary and Elizabeth were imprisoned, and saw Chaplyn and Nycholles and also one West and one Dawlie. At least threescore persons were standing abroad at their doors and diverse places in the streets, having come there by reason of the great noise.

Deponent knoweth not but that John Femell is an honest man.

Richard Warre of Heastercombe, Esq., aged 45, saith:

Next morning after the affray Mary Combe sent her son and one Gresham of Taunton to declare that she and her daughter Elizabeth were imprisoned in the Cowhouse by John Chaplyn and others for affray that had happened between her and Margrett Peirs. Deponent sent his precept to the constables of Taunton, commanding them to bring before him Mary and Margrett. They came to his house, Margrett having a "blacke face" and Mary her face scratched. He bound them to keep the peace and appear at the next sessions, at which sessions a bill of indictment was found against diverse of the town of Taunton for a riot or wrong imprisonment of Mary Combe and her daughter; deponent was then sitting on the Bench. About a sevennight after Carvanell declared to deponent that Mary came to his house about 6 or 7 o'clock in the afternoon, saying: "I am come unto you to declare what hath happened betwine Margarett Peyers and me as it doth appere in my face which you may see." Thereupon Carvanell said: "Yt shalbe well Inough Come goe with me and I will bringe you saffe whome to yoᵣ owne howse." On meeting the defendants, Chaplyn and others said to Carvanell: "Geve vs the Quenes Prysoner." Who answered: "I will yeld her unto you to morrowe in the morninge bodie for bodie." But Chaplyn, with others, said: "Nay we will not, we will have her nowe." They went forwards towards the prison, Mary's hand being fastened in the girdle of Carvanell. When they reached the prison, Chaplyn rigorously pulled her away from Carvanell, with which pulling Carvanell's girdle broke and his purse fell to the ground. And Mary said: "take hede to yoᵣ Purse yt ys fallen downe;" and forthwith [he] whirled her into the prison and locked the door. Carvanell told deponent that Hannyvord and Davydge were constables and Hannyvord had desired him to be his deputy till he returned from Wells.

Henry Hurforde of Taunton, groom, aged 20, saith:-
John Chaplyn, Thomas Lecheland, and John Nycholles were assembled to take Mary to prison; Femell came to take them before they came to the prison. Whuppes were made by the persons assembled, whereby twenty persons came together. Near the prison Elizabeth fell down and cried out because she would not go to the prison. It is a vile prison; cannot tell whether it is the worst or not. Mary was thrust over the stocks standing at the prison door. Besides Chaplyn and Nycholles there were present Richard Robyns, Anthony the baker, "Adrye the toker," Dawlye, Mannynge, and others.
Deponent heard Carvanell say: "Be of good comfort Mary I thincke we shalbe both slayne." He heard the witch, who was before imprisoned in the Cowhouse, say that the devil came to her diverse times and tempted to hang herself with her girdle. Mary cried out that her daughter was nearly dead, and called for a candle and wine. Chaplyn answered she should have some small beer. Mary said: "No I will have some wyne for I am able to pay for yt," and said she thought her daughter would die. Elizabeth has had a more sickly colour since the imprisonment than before; deponent does not know whether this is by reason of the imprisonment. Chaplyn threatened imprisonment for three days and nights to any who should bring Mary candlelight, after he took away the candle which was put in the window of the prison by one byrdes wife. These words he spoke at the prison door.
"He can say nothing But that John Femell is an honest man as he supposeth."

John Nomys of Taunton, shoemaker, aged 40, saith:
He repaired to the Cowhouse by reason of the noise. Mary and Elizabeth were then newly imprisoned, but the door not yet locked. All sorts of people, about one hundred altogether, were assembled. About twelve months before Mother Nyneacres, a witch, was imprisoned there.
John Femell is an honest man, as he supposeth.

[Depositions on behalf of the defendants.]

Henry Femell of Taunton, merchant, brother to John Femell, one of the defendants, of the age of 40 or thereabouts, saith:
The constables sent for Mary Combe to come before them by one John

Femell, then one of the bailiffs of the town, before Margrett Pyers was hurt. Mary refused to go to the constables, saying they were not her friends, and, if they had anything to do with her, they should come to her, for she would not come unto them. Then the said bailiff "presting to goo to her," she held up a knife and said: "come no here unto me, but yf thow do at thy perill," reviling the said bailiff and calling him knave and harelip, with other railing words, whereof the said bailiff called deponent, Mr. More, and one John Pyers to be witness.

About Easter last, at the meeting at Taunton, of Sir Hugh Pawlett, Knight, Humphrey Colles, Henry Portman, Richard Warre, John Francis, and Robt. Hyll, Esquires, chosen to be arbitrators by both parties, deponent was present in the house of Wm. Clevehanger of Taunton, when both parties sealed bonds to stand by the arbitrators' award. The award was then read; it was very well liked of both parties. Deponent read it. Deponent was present when the Bishop of Bath offered John Combe a release according to the effect of the reward, which Combe refused to seal.

Thomas Symons of Taunton, pewterer, brother-in-law to John Femell, one of the defendants, aged 42 or thereabouts, knows both parties. He heard a glazier and Johanne Garrett and Alford's boy of Taunton say that Elizabeth Combe, when she saw Margret Pyers coming in the streets of Taunton, said: "Now she comyth, now she comyth." And Margret passing by the said Mary Combe between the stall and her, Mary said to Margret: "What thow whore dust thow take my stalle of me," and thereupon leaped unto Margret and smote her in the face with her fists, and [they] "fell togeathers by the eares" and so continued till the glazier and Garrett's wife parted them, as the glazier, etc., declared to the constables in deponent's hearing, Mary saying then that what she did was in self-defence.

Deponent being one of the constables of the town about ten days before Michaelmas next before the affray, he and his fellow constable sent John Femell, one of the bailiffs, to require Mary to come before them. He returned and said she had replied she had as good a house to receive them, [and] if they would anything to her, should come to her; and [he] reported that she had a knife in her hand.

At the Lawday held at Taunton in October, 7 Elizabeth, Oliver Hester gave evidence to the jury for the Queen that Mary Combe had said [that] rather than the said Oliver should dwell so near her she would set fire to his house; but there was no such matter found according to his evidence. At the same Lawday a bill was found that Mary Combe was a common scold and perturber of her neighbors. Deponent was present in Clevehanger's house when obligations were sealed to abide by the award. Deponent read the award. Oliver Hester and Anthony Longe confess that they had sealed to John and Mary Combe a release of all actions and Mary made a similar release to Oliver and Anthony in her own name. John and Mary have refused to seal a release in accordance with the award offered them at two several times before the constables and others.

William Clevehanger of Taunton, clothier, late constable of Taunton, age 60, saith:

He heard Elizabeth Combe say to her mother, "when Margrett Peyers came out of her dores towardes Lechelandes" to supper, "she cometh she cometh." Margret came about 7 o'clock in the evening at Mary Combe's door. And there Margrett and Mary met. Johanne Garrett showed deponent that Mary made the affray upon Margrett. Johanne said Margrett would have been worse handled, had not she been there. Immediately after the affray Margaret Pyers, accompanied with Thomas Lecheland and Johanne Garrett, repaired to deponent and William Skoryeire, then deputies to the constables. By the space of fifty years, to deponent's knowledge, the constables and bailiffs have used to make deputies. Seeing the hurt on Margrett and having examined the witness Johanne, deponent and William Skoreyer commanded John Chaplyn, bailiff, and Thomas Lecheland, substitute to the other bailiff, to apprehend Mary and Elizabeth and put them in ward for breaking the Queen's peace.

Thomas Pope of Taunton, merchant, sometime constable of Taunton, saith:

When he was last constable, he sent John Femell, the bailiff, for Mary Combe, to come to be examined for railing words that she had used against "one Symondes wyefe" and others.

Thomas Shoell of Combeflory, glazier, aged 52, saith:

He was going home from work towards his host's house in the street at Taunton about 7 o'clock in the night, and saw Mistress Combe standing in the street from her stall before her door, and her daughter at her door, and Margaret Pyers and another woman coming from Peyers his house towards her, and [she] was passing between Mistress Combe and her stall towards Lechelands house, whereupon they fell immediately by the ears. Deponent does not know who gave the first stripe; [but] he saw the woman with Mistress Peyers pluck away Mistress Combes daughter from Mistress Combes, and Mistress Peyers and Mistress Combes then lying fighting together; he parted them.

John Hannyford of Taunton, merchant, constable at the time of the imprisonment, aged 40, saith:

He was at Wells fair when the affray was made. On his return he and his fellow constable, Thomas Davage, examined Mary and Margret as to the cause of the affray. Mary would not confess who gave the first blow; she said she was standing at her door, thinking to go to Lawrence Carvanell's to supper. Margrett said she was going to Thomas Lechelands to supper, and, as she passed, she found Mary standing her length from her town stall and went between her and the stall.

Departing from Taunton towards Mr. Colles house at Barton, [and] meeting Carvanell in the street at Taunton, deponent said: "I pray you execute my office of constableship until I return from Mr Colles agayne," meaning to return that date. Afterwards, going on to Wells, deponent appointed Skoryer his deputy, telling him to "disappoint" Carvanell.

Johanne Garrett of Taunton, widow, aged 50, saith:

She and Margrett were going to supper at Lecheland's house about 6 at night, after the purification of Margaret Vowell. As they came against John Combes house, saw Mary going over the street and her daughter standing in her door. Mary, seeing Margrett coming, stayed, and, Margrett passing betwixt Mary and her own stall, Mary was therewith offended and said: "Thow queane duste thou take my stalle from me beinge my owne grounde." And with that she plucked Margaret out by the bosom, whereupon they went together by the ears, and Elizabeth lay on Margrett's back till deponent plucked her off. Mary gave the first blow.

[William Lancaster of Mylverton, co. Somerset, gentleman, aged 50, also deposed.]

Depositions taken at Taunton [co. Somerset], 13 and 14 January, 9 Elizabeth [1566/7].

Johanne Harrys of Taunton, widow, aged 74, saith:

A little after Michaelmas was twelve months, when Margery Vowell made her purification, deponent, being midwife in the town of Taunton and present at Vowell's house with other women of the town according to their old usage in the town, offered to one Margaret Swayne a cup of wine, wherewith Mary Combe, being offended for that she had not first offered her the cup, thrust deponent in the side with her fist, saying: "Dost thou not know thy betters to whom thou shuldes offred the cuppe fyrst." In the church afterwards she heard a noise; does not know who made it; but after, as the said Vowell's wife and the rest of the women were going homewards from the church, Margaret Peyers and the wife of Skoreyer, seeing "olde Mother Goldsmyth" coming after them, required her to go forth with them. And therewith Mary Combes, being offended, said: "Shall this French Dogge" or "French knaves wyefe goo before me," and would have plucked her back again, but Margaret Peyers and Johanne Scoryer would not suffer her. And therewith Mary Combes, being much offended, went forth and back, sometimes before the wives that went before her, and sometimes before the constables' wives, and sometimes behind them.

Anestice Lawrence, wife of William Lawrence of Taunton, merchant, aged 33, saith:

After Margaret Vowell had made her purification in the church, a little after Michaelmas was twelve months since, on the way homewards Johane Skoreyer and Margaret Peyers, "knowing Johane Femell to be an auncient woman of the towne," took her to go forth with them. Then Mary Combe came out of her pew, and took Johane Femell by the arm, and plucked her back. Margaret Peyers said: "Mistress Combe you came hither before in quiet, and so I pray you goo home agayne." Whereat Mary Combe said: "Sett her before thyselfe, For thou shalt sett no Frenche knaves wyefe and Frenche curres wyefe before me." Then Johane Femell said: "good wyfe Combe yf I shall not goe before you I pray lett me goo with you." Then said Mary Combe: "Thow shalt not goo with me for I am thy better by two hundred pounds." As the wives were going forth of the church, Mary Combes said to Johane Scoreyer, who stayed: "Will you goo forth," and Johane Scoreyer said: "Goo you forth for I like this company very well." With that Mary went out before Johane Scoreyer, and ceased not till she came to the constable's wife, and then returned [and said]: "I defye you all For the best and prowdest of you all have bin beholding unto me." And she said to Margt. Peyers: "A vengeance upon the thow arte mayntayned by my goods. For I am the worse by £200 for thy father. And the same vengeance upon them both," meaning the father-in-law and husband of Margaret.

Peter Cable of Taunton, pewterer, servant to Mr. Symonds, aged 27, saith:

About 9 of the clock of the night Mary Combes was imprisoned, deponent came to the Cowhouse door, and saw John Chaplyn fetch out the candle of the Cowhouse. Therefore she called Chaplyn knave, saying that "If she were at here owne house she wold have Light Inough." Then Chaplyn came to the door again, and Mary required drink of him, and, he bidding his man fetch her a cup of beer, she said: "No knave I will drinke none of thy bere I will have clarret wyne and suger for I am as well hable to pay for yt as the proudest knave of you all." "Yt is no matter," quoth the said John Chaplyn, "what you saye I will geve you no yvell words." And thereupon Chaplyn commanded all the people assembled to depart home or else he would put them all in the Cowhouse, as many as it would hold.

George Fisher, of Wylton, co. Somerset, aged 30, yeoman, saith:

. . . Just before Oliver Hester last passed into Flanders, he released all actions to John Combes, upon Mary's promise to be good neighbor to his wife and to give him a like release; but the release was in her name only and not her husband's. When Hester protested at this, she said: "Dust thou not know that I rule all."

Richard Matthew of Taunton, draper, aged 52, knows Mary to be a common "Skoldester."

[Depositions were also made by Mark Porter of Taunton, apothecary, aged 30, Richard Bult of Taunton, yeoman, aged 30, William Collerd of Taunton, tailor, aged 31, William Dawley of Taunton, capper, aged 34, William Skoreyer of Taunton, merchant, aged 54, Johane Scoryere, wife of William Scoryere, aged 30, and Alexander Coxe of Taunton, groom, aged 14 or 15.]

From the foregoing records, from papers and pedigrees formerly belonging to Sir Simonds D'Ewes and now in Harleian MS. 381 in the British Museum, and from other records and authorities cited below, the following Symonds pedigree has been compiled.

1. —— SYMONDS, certainly *not* the Thomas Symonds who was an illegitimate son of Sir Giles Strangeways of Melbury-Sampford, co. Dorset (*vide supra*, p. 345), but probably the William Symons who was buried at St. Mary Magdalene's, Taunton, co. Somerset, 21 Apr. 1566, lived at Melbury, at length came to Taunton, and there died. He was the father of

   2. i.  THOMAS, b. about 1524.
     ii.  JOHN, of Taunton, second son, the testator of 14 Jan. 1570/1, d. *s.p.* at Taunton; bur. at St. Mary Magdalene's, Taunton, 16 Jan. 1570/1; m. there, 13 Sept. 1568, EMMA POPE, to whom he left all his goods and to whom administration on his goods was granted 27 Jan. 1570/1.

2. THOMAS SYMONDS, of Taunton, co. Somerset, gentleman, pewterer and merchant, the testator of 1572, born about 1524, was buried at St. Mary Magdalene's, Taunton, 22 Oct. 1572. He married first ——; and secondly AGNES FEMELL, daughter of Richard Femell of Taunton, goldsmith, and his wife, Johan (Crow), who was the testatrix of 1576 and was buried at St. Mary Magdalene's, Taunton, 9 Oct. 1577.* Agnes (Femell) Symonds, who was residuary legatee and executrix of the will of her first husband, married secondly, at St. Mary Magdalene's, Taunton, 11 Mar. 1573/4, Nicholas Colvord or Calvarte (see will of her mother, Johan Femell, dated 29 June 1576), and lastly Jeffery Moore, Esq. She died about 1584, and was buried beside her first husband in the Church of St. Mary Magdalene, Taunton.

   Thomas Symonds was constable of Taunton in 1565 and 1569.

   Children by second wife (order of births somewhat uncertain):

   3. i.  WILLIAM, b. about 1547.
   4. ii.  RICHARD, b. about 1550.
     iii.  HENRY, under twenty-four in 1572, when he is mentioned in his father's will; bur. in the parish of St. Mary Magdalene, Taunton, 27 Aug. 1574.
     iv.  THOMAS, of London, a wealthy merchant, b. about 1555; d. 1 Sept. 1620, aged about 65 years, "and was there [in London] buryed with greate solemnitye;" m. (1) ELIZABETH MUNS, daughter of John Mun[s] of London; m. (2) MARIE WADE, third daughter of William Wade of Bildeston, co. Suffolk. He was fined sheriff

*See the Femell pedigree, *infra*, p. 368.   (Page 183, this volume.)

of London, and is mentioned in the Autobiography of Sir Simonds D'Ewes, his grandnephew.

Children by first wife:
1. *Thomas*, son and heir, living at Edmonton on 4 Aug. 1630, when Sir Simonds D'Ewes and his wife visited him.
2. *A child.**
3. *A child.**
4. *A child.**

Children by second wife:
5. *William*, d. in infancy.
6. *Susan*, eldest daughter by second wife, m. Thomas Kiriage of London.†
7. *Hester*, second daughter by second wife, m. Charles Hales of co. Warwick, Esq.

v. MARY, eldest daughter, m. before 13 Oct. 1572 WILLIAM LEONARD of Taunton, gentleman, who was living at that date, when he was mentioned in the will of his father-in-law, Thomas Symonds. One son and two daughters.

vi. ELEANOR, second daughter, bapt. at St. Mary Magdalene's, Taunton, 20 Sept. 1559; m. there, 21 Nov. 1575, JOHN RICH of Lydeard St. Lawrence, co. Somerset, gentleman. They had issue.

vii. LAWRENCE, bapt. at St. Mary Magdalene's, Taunton, 16 Mar. 1560/1; d. *s.p.* at Leghorn, Italy; m. SUSAN BOYS, daughter of William Boys of Barnstable, co. Devon. She survived him and m. (2) Elias Wood, grocer, a citizen of London.

viii. JANE, third and youngest daughter, m. WALTER EDNIE, Esq. They had issue.

ix. ROBERT, bapt. at St. Mary Magdalene's, Taunton, 12 Dec. 1565; bur. there 4 Jan. 1565/6.

x. ROBERT, youngest son, bapt. at St. Mary Magdalene's, Taunton, 8 Feb. 1567/8; d. at sea, unm.

3. WILLIAM SYMONDS (*Thomas*), of Lyme-Regis, co. Dorset, and Axminster and Exeter, co. Devon, gentleman, heir to his father, the testator of 20 Feb. 1633/4, was born about 1547 (since he is said to have been "aged about 80 yeares" in 1627), and was buried at Exeter 8 Jan. 1634/5 (registers of Exeter Cathedral). He married at St. Mary Magdalene's, Taunton, co. Somerset, 14 Sept. 1571, ALICE MOONE, who was buried in Exeter Cathedral 26 July 1628, daughter of Robert Mohun *alias* Moone of Bampton and of Fleete near Burport [Bridport], co. Dorset, gentleman, and his wife, Margaret (Hyde).‡

In 1587, being then of Lyme-Regis, William Symonds was granted arms by Robert Cooke, Clarenceux King-of-Arms (*vide supra*, p. 345). In 1588, being then also of Lyme-Regis, merchant, he subscribed £25 towards the defence of the country against the Spaniards, and in 1592, being still of Lyme-Regis, he was the complainant in a case in Chancery

---

*More information about this child is said to be given in Harleian MS. 381.

†He appears in the Visitation of Suffolk, 1664–1668, p. 151 (*Publications of the Harleian Society*, vol. 61), as Thomas Kerridge of Shelley [Hall], co. Suffolk, Esq., high sheriff of that county, and his marriage to Susan, daughter of Thomas Symons of London, merchant, is there given. Their son, Samuell Kerridge of Shelley, gent., had this brief pedigree entered in the Visitation in 1664. No arms are tricked in this pedigree. Thomas Kiriage or Kerridge was high sheriff of Suffolk in 1647 and a director of the East India Company. He was a descendant of William Kerrich, who belonged to the Kerrich family about which information was published in the REGISTER, vol. 75, pp. 290–301. See p. 298 of that volume, No. 3, iii, 2, of the Kerrich pedigree.

‡Proof of the marriage of Robert Moone and Margaret Hyde will be given in an article on the Moone family that will be published in a future number of the REGISTER.

against Morgan Moone, gentleman, his wife's cousin. On 31 Mar. 1612, as William Simons of Exeter, gentleman, aged "threescore years or thereabouts," he deposed that he "hath ben dwelling in the parish of Axminster for the space of 10 yeres past or thereabout." In 1614 the young Simonds D'Ewes, his grandnephew, visited him at Exeter, and many years later, shortly before his death, William Symonds answered certain questions which this grandnephew had sent to him in regard to the Symonds family.
Children:

i. MARCELLA, eldest daughter and coheir, d. between 17 Dec. 1656, when her will was dated, being then of Salcombe, co. Devon, and 10 Dec. 1657, when it was proved (see the will of Marcella Duke, widow, in the REGISTER, vol. 79, p. 413); m. (1) HENRY HEWISH (or HUISH), gentleman; m. (2) not later than 1620 RICHARD HERBERT of Exeter; m. (3) after 20 Feb. 1634/5 ———— DUKE, whom she survived. She was named as executrix in her father's will, which she proved 20 Feb. 1634/5.
Child by first husband (surname *Hewish*):
1. *Southcott*, living 20 Feb. 1633/4, when he is called "my nephew" [i.e., grandson] in the will of William Symonds, his grandfather. He was unmarried in 1627.

ii. WILLIAM, only son, d. unm. before 20 Feb. 1633/4, the date of his father's will.

iii. ANNE (or AGNES), second daughter and coheir, d. probably about May 1649, her will, dated 6 Oct. 1645, being proved 22 Feb. 1649/50 (see the will of Anne Derby of Sturthill, co. Dorset, widow, in the REGISTER, vol. 79, pp. 412–413); m. not later than 1607 CHRISTOPHER DERBY of Sterthill in the parish of Burton-Bradstock, co. Dorset, gentleman, bapt. at Askerswell, co. Dorset, in 1571, d. 20 Jan. 1639/40, bur. at Shipton-George, co. Dorset, son of Nicholas Derby of Askerswell and later of Sterthill, gentleman, and his wife Catherine. Christopher and Anne (Symonds) Derby were the ancestors of the Derby family of Salem, Mass. For their descendants see the REGISTER, vol. 79, pp. 433– * 449.

iv. REBECCA, third daughter and coheir, d. *s.p.* between 13 Nov. 1662, when her will was dated, being then of the parish of St. Stephen in Exeter, and 24 Nov. 1662, when it was proved (see the will of Rebecca Salter, widow, in the REGISTER, vol. 79, pp. 413–414); m. not later than 1620 ANTHONY SALTER of Exeter, widower, living 20 Feb. 1633/4, whom she survived.

4. RICHARD SYMONDS (*Thomas*), of Coxden, in the parish of Chardstock, co. Dorset, Esq., J. P., barrister of the Middle Temple, the testator of 14 Jan. 1608/9, born about 1550, died at Coxden 27 June 1611, aged about 61, and was buried in the church at Chardstock 11 July 1611. He married JOAN (STEPHENS) NETHERSOLE, who died at Coxden 16 Feb. 1610/11 and was buried in the church at Chardstock 23 Feb. 1610/11, daughter of William Stephens of Kent and his second wife, Ellen (Lovelace [?]), and widow of John Nethersole, Esq.
Child:

i. CECILIA, sole daughter and heir to her father, b. at Faversham, co. Kent, 29 Nov. 1579; d. at Stow Hall, in the parish of Stowlangtoft, co. Suffolk, 31 July 1618; bur. in the church of Stowlangtoft 6 Aug. 1618; m. at Axminster, co. Devon, 10 Dec. 1594, PAUL D'EWES of Wellshall, in the parish of Milden, co. Suffolk,

*Pages 116-132, this volume.

later of Lavenham, co. Suffolk, and still later of Stowlangtoft, Esq., member of the Middle Temple, one of the six clerks in Chancery from 1607 until his death, b. 25 Jan. 1567, d. in London 14 Mar. 1630/1, bur. in the church at Stowlangtoft 25 Apr. 1631, son of Geerardt D'Ewes, printer, citizen of London, and his wife Grace (Hynde) ———, who was a widow when Geerardt D'Ewes married her.* Paul D'Ewes m. (2) in St. Faith's Church, under St. Paul's, London, 5 Mar. 1622/3, Elizabeth (Isham) Denton, who was born about 1578 and survived her husband, eldest daughter of Thomas Isham of Langport in Northamptonshire, Esq., deceased, and widow of Sir Anthony Denton, of Tunbridge, co. Kent, Knight. Paul D'Ewes had no issue by his second wife. By the burning of the offices of the six clerks in Chancery, on 20 Dec. 1621, he lost much money and many valuable heirlooms, records, business papers, deeds, etc., a loss which was keenly felt by his son, Simonds, in his researches into the history of his family and in the management of his property.

Children (surname *D'Ewes*):

1. *Johan*, b. at Wellshall 1 Feb. 1600/1 and bapt. in the neighboring church of Brunt Illeigh 18 Feb. 1600/1; living in 1637; m. in St. Faith's Church, under St. Paul's, London, 7 Feb. 1620/1, as his third wife, Sir William Elliot of Busbridge in the parish of Godalming, co. Surrey, Knight, son of Lawrence Elliot of Busbridge, Esq., and his wife, Mary (Barker). Sir William Elliot was "a discreet honest man, (hard to find in this corrupt age,)." They had issue.

2. *Sir Simonds*, Bart., of Stow Hall, antiquary, member of the Middle Temple, knighted 6 Dec. 1626, sheriff of Suffolk, 1639, M.P. for the borough of Sudbury, in the Long Parliament, 1640–1648, created a baronet 15 July 1641, b. at Coxden 18 Dec. 1602 and bapt. there 29 Dec. 1602; d. at Stow Hall 8 Apr. 1650; m. (1) in Blackfriars Church, London, 24 Oct. 1626, Anne Clopton, b. at Clare Priory, co. Suffolk, 14 Feb. 1612/13, d. at Stow Hall in July 1641, sole surviving daughter and heir of Sir William Clopton of Lutons Hall (Kentwell), Melford, co. Suffolk, Knight, deceased, by his first wife, Anne (Barnardiston); m. (2) Elizabeth Willoughby, daughter and coheir of Sir Henry Willoughby, Bart., of Risley, co. Derby. She m. (2) Sir John Wray, Bart. Seven children by first wife and one son by second wife.†

3. *Grace*, b. at Wellshall 14 May 1604 and bapt. in the parish church of Milden 30 May 1604; living in 1636; m. in the

*The D'Ewes family was of Dutch origin. See Autobiography of Sir Simonds D'Ewes (*supra*) and brief biography of Geerardt D'Ewes in Dictionary of National Biography.

†For a longer account of the career of Sir Simonds D'Ewes see the Dictionary of National Biography and his Autobiography. Cf. also *Notes & Queries for Somerset and Dorset*, vol. 13, pp. 129–130. There are some errors in dates in the statements in *Notes & Queries*, and the failure to use double dating there for the periods from 1 Jan. to 24 Mar., inclusive, is confusing. The list of children of Sir Simonds D'Ewes, as given in *Notes & Queries* and corrected, when possible, by the Autobiography, is as follows: Children by first wife: 1. *Anne*, b. at Islington 30 Apr. 1630 and bapt. there 13 May 1630; living in 1638. 2. *Clopton*, b. at Lavenham 24 June 1631 and bapt. there 5 July 1631; d. at Lavenham 9 July 1631; bur. there 10 July 1631. 3. *Adrian* (twin), b. at Bury St. Edmunds 10 Mar. 1632/3 and bapt. there 11 Mar. 1632/3; d. at Bury St. Edmunds 13 Mar. 1632/3; bur. at Lavenham 14 Mar. 1632/3. 4. *Geerardt* (twin), b. at Bury St. Edmunds 10 Mar. 1632/3 and bapt. there on the same day; d. there on the same day; bur. at Lavenham 12 Mar. 1632/3. 5. *Clopton*, b. at Ixworth Abbey, near Bury St. Edmunds, 18 July 1634 and bapt. in Ixworth church 1 Aug. 1634; d. at Stowlangtoft 9 May 1636; bur. there 10 May 1636. 6. *Cecilia*, b. at Stow Hall 25 Nov. 1635 and bapt. there on the same day; living in 1638. 7. *Adrian*, an infant in the cradle in 1639; d. young. Child by second wife: 8. *Sir Willoughby*, heir to his father, b. about 1650; d. 13 June 1685; succeeded his father as second baronet, and was succeeded by his son, Sir Simonds D'Ewes, as third baronet, who in turn was succeeded by his son, Sir Jermyn D'Ewes, the fourth and last baronet, who d. in 1731.

church of Stowlangtoft, 22 Sept. 1625, Wiseman Bokenham, Esq., son and heir of Sir Henry Bokenham of Great Thornham Hall, co. Suffolk, Knight. They had issue.

4. *Paul,* b. at Wellshall 3 Jan. 1605/6 and bapt. at Milden 16 Jan. 1605/6; d. 10 July 1607; bur. in Milden church.

5. *Mary,* b. at Wellshall 27 June 1608 and bapt. 29 June 1608; living in 1636; m. in St. Faith's Church, under St. Paul's, London, 4 Dec. 1626, Sir Thomas Bowes of Much Bromley, co. Essex, Knight, son of Thomas and Bridget (Starling) Bowes. They had issue.

6. *Cecilia,* b. at Wellshall 7 May 1610 and bapt. at Milden 16 May 1610; d. in London 17 Nov. 1620; bur. in St. Stephen's Church, Walbrook, London, 19 Nov. 1620.

7. *Richard,* b. at Stow Hall 14 Oct. 1615 and bapt. at Stowlangtoft 29 Oct. 1615; living unm. in 1636. He was admitted to the Middle Temple 19 Apr. 1632.

8. *Elizabeth,* b. at Stow Hall 23 Jan. 1617/18 and bapt. at Stowlangtoft 4 Feb. 1617/18; m. in the church of Stowlangtoft, 15 Mar. 1635/6, Sir William Poley of Boxted, co. Suffolk, Knight, second son and heir of Sir William Poley of Boxted, Knight. They had issue.

From the records given in this article, supplemented by certain statements in the papers of Sir Simonds D'Ewes (Harleian MS. 381), the following facts about Richard Femell and his family have been derived.

RICHARD FEMELL, of Taunton, co. Somerset, goldsmith, was probably already dead in Oct. 1565 and was certainly dead by 29 June 1576, when his wife's will was dated. He married JOHAN CROW, who was buried at St. Mary Magdalene's, Taunton, 9 Oct. 1577, daughter of ——— Crow of Taunton, gentleman.

Richard Femell was "a wealthy Dutchman, who came out of Normandy into England," according to the Autobiography of Sir Simonds D'Ewes, who also, in his papers, calls him a Frenchman.* In the second payment of the subsidy of 14 and 15 Henry VIII [1522–1524], levied in the "Forestrete," Taunton Borough, he was listed as a Frenchman and was taxed 20s. on goods valued at £20. In the second payment of the subsidy of 32 Henry VIII [1540–41], in Taunton Borough, he was taxed 40s. on goods valued at £40, and was described as a foreigner [*alyn'* = *aliengino*]. A Johan Femell, who was undoubtedly his wife or widow, appears in a deposition in the Star Chamber case given above, which refers to events occurring in 1565, as "an auncient woman of the towne" [Taunton], and was reviled by Mary Combe as a "Frenche knaves wyefe and Frenche curres wyefe." She is probably identical with the "olde Mother Goldsmyth" of another deposition in this case, of whom Mary Combe spoke as "this French Dogge" or "French knaves wyefe." In her will she bequeathed "a riall of gold apiece" to Thomas, Laurence, Robert, and Jane Symonds [her grandchildren]; and from this will and from the depositions in the Star Chamber case much information about her children and her other grandchildren has been obtained.

*In Rietstap's Armorial Général, tome 1, pp. 660, 661 (deuxième édition), the arms of Fermanel of Normandy are given as *D'azur à trois fers de lance d'or, rangés en fasce,* and the arms of Fernel of Maine as *D'azur à trois bâtons écotés d'or.*

Children (order of births somewhat uncertain):*

i.    HENRY, of Taunton, merchant, b. about 1526 (being aged 40 or
      thereabouts on 18 Dec. 1566); bur. at St. Mary Magdalene's,
      Taunton, 23 Jan. 1598/9; m. JOANE ———, who was bur. at St.
      Mary Magdalene's 9 Nov. 1615. He deposed in the Star Chamber
      case in Dec. 1566, was constable of Taunton in 1573, 1579, and
      1589, and was residuary legatee and executor of his mother's will,
      which was proved 4 Feb. 1577/8.

ii.   AGNES, d. about 1584; m. (1), as his second wife, THOMAS SYMONDS;
      m. (2) NICHOLAS COLVORD (or CALVARTE); m. (3) JEFFERY
      MOORE. For her and her children see Symonds pedigree, under
      No. 2 (supra, p. 364).

iii.  ANSTISS, b. about 1533 (being aged 33 in Jan. 1566/7); living 29
      June 1576; m. before Jan. 1566/7 WILLIAM LAWRENCE of Taun-
      ton, merchant.
         Children (surname Lawrence):
         1.  Henry,  } both under 24 and unm. 29 June 1576.
         2.  Anstiss,

iv.   LAWRENCE, perhaps the Lawrence Femell who was bur. at St. Mary
      Magdalene's 10 Apr. 1569 or the one who was bur. there 28 May
      1572, but it is more likely that he was living 29 June 1576;   m.
      ———.
         Children:
         1.  Mary, bapt. at St. Mary Magdalene's 7 Dec. 1559; living
             unm. 29 June 1576.
         2.  Margaret, living unm. and under 24 on 29 June 1576.

v.    JOHN, of Taunton, goldsmith, d. between 23 Jan. 1566/7 and 29
      June 1576; m. ———. He was bailiff in 1565 and one of the
      defendants in the Star Chamber case of 1566, in which several
      witnesses deposed that he was an honest man. He filed a bill in
      Chancery against John Combe of Taunton 23 Jan. 1566/7, and
      the "said Mary" mentioned in John Femell's replication in this
      suit was probably the Mary Combe who was a prominent party in
      the Star Chamber case.
         Children:
         1.  Richard, living 29 June 1576.
         2.  Thomas, living 29 June 1576, when he was under 24.
         3.  John, bapt. at St. Mary Magdalene's 18 Dec. 1559; living
             29 June 1576, when he was an apprentice of John Symon[d]s.
         4.  Lawrence, bapt. at St. Mary Magdalene's 11 Apr. 1567; not
             mentioned in his grandmother's will of 29 June 1576;
             probably bur. at St. Mary Magdalene's 10 Apr. 1569 or
             28 May 1572.
         Perhaps others.

*The names of several unidentified Femells appear in the registers of St. Mary Magdalene,
Taunton. Vide supra, pp. 353-354. (Pages 168-169, this volume.)

SYMONDS-FEMELL: ADDITION: — In THE REGISTER, vol. 80, p. 364,[*] the account of Thomas Symonds of London (born *ca.* 1555, died 1 Sept. 1620), son of Thomas Symonds of Taunton, and his family there given, is based upon the notes of his great-nephew, Sir Symonds D'Ewes. At the time it was published the writer was not aware that Mr. Waters had published his will in THE REGISTER (vol. 51, p. 279). The will of Thomas Symonds of London, skinner, dated 30 Nov. 1619, proved 6 Sept. 1620, enables one to add to the account of his children in the above article.

He names his wife Mary Symonds, his sons Thomas and Richard, and his daughters Elizabeth Hawes, Mary Peate, Joan Symonds, Anne Shepard, Susan Symonds, and Hester Symonds. He also names his eldest brother, William Symonds, his wife, and his three sons-in-law. Also mentioned are his brother Abraham Cartwrite, his brother Thomas Mun and his wife, Edward Abbot's wife, sister Wood, cousin William Riche and cousin Sisilia Rich and her husband. He left also to his three grandchildren Mary Peat, Joan Peat, and Mary Sheppard. Also named are his cousin John Vassal and his wife, brother William Wade, his wife and their son William, as well as cousin Coels [?], his daughter Mary Mason, and cousin Gyll and his wife. He made a bequest of plate to the Skinner's Company and to the poor of Taunton, "where I was born". There was also a legacy to Richard Stens and his wife and to her sister and her husband living in Taunton.

[For a more extended account of this will, see Mr. Waters' abstract above noted.]

*Wells, Maine.*                                    G. ANDREWS MORIARTY.

*Page 179, this volume.

185

# GENEALOGICAL RESEARCH IN ENGLAND

Contributed by G. ANDREWS MORIARTY, JR., A.M., LL.B., of Newport, R. I.,
and communicated by the Committee on English Research

## MOHUN (OR MOONE)–HYDE

IN the article which was published in the REGISTER for October
1926 (vol. 80, pp. 343–369), under the subheading "Symonds– *
Femell," one of the series of articles communicated by the Committee
on English Research and entitled "Genealogical Research in England," the English connections of William Symonds of Exeter, co.
Devon, gentleman, an ancestor of Roger Derby of Salem, Mass.,
were set forth, and it was announced that in future numbers of the
REGISTER articles on other English families connected with the
Derby family would appear. In accordance with this announcement
records and pedigrees relating to the Mohun (or Moone) and Hyde
families of Dorset are presented in this article, Alice Moone, the
wife of William Symonds, being a daughter of Robert Mohun *alias*
Moone and his wife, Margaret (Hyde) Moone.

### FROM PROBATE RECORDS

The Will of JOHN HYDE of the King's Exchequer, dated 14 August 1543.
[Bequests to London pensions.] To the children of Roger Belamy 20s. each.
To my daughter Agnes the profits of the lease of the Cranes, the Aley in St.
Augustine's, Watling Street, London, late possession of the Priory called
Elsing Spital, Cripplegate, London. To my daughter Elizabeth Cartmyll
my·lease of the manor of Albury, co. Herts. I remit to the King the £10
which I lately loaned him. To my wife Margaret £20 and a third of my
plate, the residue of my plate to my daughters. To my wife the use of my
stuff at my house at Hyde, co. Dorset. To my son Thomas my best gown.
To Sir William Barker, priest, a gown. Gowns to Mr. Tregoys, priest, and
"to brother Hugh." To my servant Henry Darell 13s. 4d. To my brother
Steven all I owe him for rent. My son is to have what is owing me by the
purchase I have begun with Mr. Babyngton. Executors: my son Thomas
and John Butler, gent. [Signed] John Hyde. [No witnesses.] Proved
1 October 1545 by Thomas Hyde, power being reserved to the other executor
when he shall apply for the same. (P. C. C., Pynnyng, 36.)

The Will of WALTER MOONE of Birport [Bridport], co. Dorset, dated 23
May 1571. To be buried in Birport church, near my father. [Bequests to
the poor of the almshouses of Birport and other poor there.] To my daughter
Joan £20 at her marriage and my house in Poole. To my daughter Martha
£20 at her marriage. To my daughter Alice £20 at her marriage. To my
wife Edith my leases. To my son Morgan my leases of my tithing corn of
Uploders, Upton, and Matravers, to him and his issue, and, in default of such,
to my son John, and, in default, to my other sons. To my sons Anthony,
George, Richard, and John my leases of the tithing of Brodpole and my barn
in Birport. To my son Richard, after his mother's death, my house in Birport wherein I dwell. Residuary legatee and executrix: my wife. Overseers: Robert Moone, Richard Davidge the Elder, Gilbert Holman, Richard
Davidge the Younger, John Belmy. Witnesses: Robert Moone, Thomas
Coker, John Sampson, John Hayward, Robert Roper. Proved 2 December
1572 by George Heiball, proctor to the executrix.

*Pages 158-185, this volume.

A commission was issued 14 November 1581 to Morgan Moone, son of the deceased, and Richard Tyggyn of Birport, merchant, to administer the goods of deceased left unadministered by the executrix, in the person of Edward Barker, Dr. of Laws. (P. C. C., Daper, 43.)

The Will of ROBERT MOONE of Weymouth–Melcombe-Regis, co. Dorset, dated 1 September 1578. To be buried in the south aisle of Burport church, near my father and mother. To the vicar of Loders, for my tithes, 5s. To the hospital of Mary Magdalene, Athlington, 10s. To the almshouses at Burport 10s. To the poor of Bothenhampton 5s., of Fleet 20s., of Weymouth and Melcombe-Regis 20s., and of Loder and Uploder 20s. To my cousins Morgan Moone and Alice, his wife, £5 each, and to the rest of my brothers' and sisters' children 20s. each. To Gilbert Holman, William Holman, Sir Martin Smith, parson of Burport, and Edith Holman [small legacies in money]. To my daughters Mary, Joan, and Margaret £600 amongst them, at their ages of twenty-one. To my sons Robert, Maximilian, and John the parsonage of Bothenhampton. To my daughters Joan and Mary a tenement in Walton, in the manor of Symonds Borough. To my daughter Alice Symonds £100. To my wife Margaret my lands in Bothenhampton and Burton, co. Dorset, with remainder, after her death, to my son Robert and his issue, with contingent remainders, in default of his issue, to my sons Maximilian and John and their issue, to my issue, and to my right heirs. To my wife my manor of Loder Matravers, co. Dorset, and a burgage in Burport, with remainders as above; also my manors of East and West Fleet, the rectory and parsonage of East and West Fleet, the parsonage of Chaldon, and a burgage in Burport, with remainders to my son Maximilian and my other sons, etc. [as before]; also my manor of Maugertonne, co. Dorset, and another burgage in Burport, with remainders to my son John and other sons, etc. [as before]. To my daughter Margaret a house in Burport, in East Street. Overseers: my cousin Edmond Anderson, Esq., sergeant at law,* my son-in-law Richard Sydwaye, head customer, my cousin Christoper Symes, John Belmy, and Gilbert Holman. Executrix: my wife. [Signed] Robert Moone. Witnesses: William Pytt, Henry Mychell, Richard Boolle, clerk, Thomas Martyn, Henry Pitt. Proved 9 November 1581 by Edward Orwell, notary public, proctor to the executrix. (P. C. C., Darcy, 38.)

Sentence was pronounced 22 May 1585 in a suit between John Davidge *alias* Moone of the one part and Margaret Moone, widow, executrix of the will of Robert Moone, late of Bothenhampton, diocese of Bristol, declaring in favor of the will produced by said Margaret and confirming the probate thereof. (P. C. C., Brudenell, 26.)

Administration on the estate of RICHARD MOONE of Birtport, co. Dorset, was granted 4 February 1586 [1586/7] to Morgan Moone, next of kin [of the deceased]. (*Notes & Queries for Somerset and Dorset,* vol. 2, p. 132, from P. C. C., Act Books.)

Administration on the estate of ANTHONY MOONE of Lyme-Regis, co. Dorset, was granted 1 March 1609 [1609/10] to Morgan Moone, brother [of the deceased]. (*Ib.,* vol. 2, p. 298, from P. C. C., Act Books.)

Administration on the estate of ANTHONY MOONE of Lyme-Regis, co. Dorset, was granted 13 September 1611 to Martha Davidge *alias* Moone, wife of Christopher Davidge, sister [of the deceased], Morgan Moone, brother [of the deceased], not having fully administered the estate. (*Ib.,* vol. 3, p. 13, from P. C. C., Act Books.)

*Sir Edmund Anderson, afterwards chief justice of the Court of Common Pleas, who was at this time a sergeant at law.

Administration on the estate of MORGAN MOONE of Burport, co. Dorset, was granted 26 December 1611 to Dionisie, relict [of the deceased]. (*Ib.*, vol. 3, p. 13, from P. C. C., Act Books.)

Administration on the estate of DIONISIUS [*sic*, ? DIONISIA] MOONE of Bridport, co. Dorset, was granted 1 March 1620 [1620/1] to Walter [Moone], son [of the deceased]. (*Ib.*, vol. 3, p. 93, from P. C. C., Act Books.)

## FROM INQUISITIONS POST MORTEM*

Inquisition on Robert Moone of Bothenhampton, co. Dorset, gent., taken at Dorchester, co. Dorset, on Monday, 4 September, 23 Elizabeth [1581], among the jurors being Gilbert Moone, gent.

The jurors say that Robert Moone was seised of the manor of Loder Matravers, held of the Queen and worth £18 yearly, the manor of Maugerton *alias* Maggerton, held of Edmund Hardye, Esq., as of Wotton Fitzpayne, and worth £10. 13s. 8d. yearly, the manor of Fleet and the advowson of Fleet church, held of the Queen, as of East Greenwich, and worth respectively £7 and £4 yearly, the rectory of East Chaldon, held of the Queen, as of Stokenham, co. Devon, and worth 13s. 4d. yearly, 1 tenement in Bothenhampton, late of Lyon Monastery, co. Middlesex, held of the Queen, as of East Greenwich, and worth 7 marks yearly, 4 other tenements in Bothenhampton, held of the Queen, as of East Greenwich, and worth 50s. yearly, 5 closes [named] in Bothenhampton, held of the Queen, as of East Greenwich, and worth 50s. yearly, 11 acres of arable land in the common fields of Bothenhampton, held of the Queen, as of East Greenwich, and worth 50s. yearly, 14 acres of arable land in the parish of Burt[on], called Portmanfeild, held of the Queen, as of Realton, co. Cornwall, and worth 13s. 4d. yearly, a messuage in Loder, late of Cannington Priory, co. Somerset, held of the Queen, as of East Greenwich, and worth 11s. yearly, a messuage with 7 acres of arable land in Westfleete, formerly in the tenure of Thomas Wilshere, held of the Queen, as of East Greenwich, and worth 6s. 8d. yearly, and 4 burgages in the borough of Bridport, held of the Queen, as of East Greenwich, and worth 40s. yearly.

The will of the said Robert Moone is recited. He died 14 November last [1580], and Robert Moone, his son and heir, was then aged 21 and more. (Chancery Inquisitions Post Mortem, Series 2, vol. 193, no. 45.)

Inquisition on Robert Moone of Bothenhampton, co. Dorset, gent., taken at Shafton 14 October, 40 Elizabeth [1598], in pursuance of a writ of *diem clausit extremum* dated 3 October, 40 Elizabeth [1598].

The jurors say that Robert Moone was seised in fee tail of the manor of Loder Matravers, held of the Queen and worth £18 yearly, to him and the heirs of his body, with contingent successive remainders to Maximilian Moone, his brother, in tail, John Moone, his brother, in tail, and the right heirs of Robert Moone, father of the said Robert.

He was seised similarly of 4 messuages, a dovecote, 4 gardens, 34 acres of arable land, 30 acres of meadow, 140 acres of pasture, and common pasture for 12 cows in Bothenhampton and Loders, held of the Queen and worth 1 rose yearly. By fine levied on the Octave of St. Michael, 31 Elizabeth [6 October 1589], the said Robert and Maximilian granted these messuages, etc., to Gilbert Holeman and John Pytt, Junior, for ninety-nine years after the death of Robert, if Meliora Moone, wife of the same Robert, should so long live, [they] rendering to Robert and Maximilian a rose yearly, at the Nativity of St. John the Baptist [24 June].

The said Robert Moone died at Bothenhampton 17 August, 40 Elizabeth [1598]. His wife Meliora survives.

*Preserved in the Public Record Office, London.

On the day of his death the said Robert Moone had three daughters, viz., Meliora Moone, Margaret Moone, and Anne Moone, who are his heirs, and at the date of the inquisition are aged respectively 11¾ years, 10¼ years and 14 days, and 4 years, 10 weeks. (Chancery Inquisitions Post Mortem, Series 2, vol. 252, no. 35.)

Inquisition on Robert Moone, gent., taken at Shafton 7 April 42 Elizabeth [1600], in pursuance of a writ dated 22 February, 42 Elizabeth [1599/1600], to inquire touching the tenure of the manor of Loder Matravers, returned as held by the said Robert by inquisition of 14 October, 40 Elizabeth [1598].

The jurors say that the manor was held of the Queen by a one-fourth knight's fee. (Chancery Inquisitions Post Mortem, Séries 2, vol. 259, no. 93.)

Inquisition on Maximilian Moone, Esq., taken at Blandford Market, co. Dorset, 19 January, 10 James I [1612/13], in pursuance of a writ dated 4 November, 10 James I [1612].

The jurors say that Robert Moone, deceased, late father of the said Maximilian, was seised in demesne as of fee of the manors of East Fleet and West Fleet in East Fleet, of 1 messuage and 16 acres of arable land in West Fleet, formerly in the tenure of Thomas Wilshire, of 1 burgage in the East Street of Bridport, formerly in the tenure of Edward Prymrose, of the rectory or parsonage and tithes of Fleet *alias* East Fleet, of the advowson of the vicarages of East Fleet and West Fleet, and of the rectory, parsonage, and tithes of East Chaldon.

The will of the said Robert Moone, dated 20 March [*sic*] 1578, is recited, whereby the said Robert bequeathed the premises (1) to Margaret, his wife, until the said Maximilian, his son, should be twenty-four years of age, and (2) to the said Maximilian and the heirs of his body, with contingent remainder (3) to Robert Moone, Junior, son and heir apparent of the said Robert the testator, and the heirs of the body of Robert, Junior, (4) to John Moone, another son of the said Robert the father, and the heirs of his body, and (5) to Gilbert Holman and his heirs for ever.

Robert Moone the father died 14 November, 22 Elizabeth [1580]. Margaret survived. Maximilian was twenty-four years of age on 1 February, 30 Elizabeth [1587/8], and then entered upon the premises.

The said Maximilian was seised at his death of the manor of Maugerton *alias* Maggerton, a messuage, land, and pasture in East Chaldon, another burgage in Bridport, formerly in the tenure of Henry Browne, and the rectory or parsonage of Brapple [or Brappole].

By a fine levied on the Octave of St. Hilary, 36 Elizabeth [20 January 1593/4], between Richard Swaine, Esq., John Churchill, and William Churchill, querents, and the said Robert Moone, son of the said Robert Moone the father, the said Maximilian Moone, and John Moone, deforciants, concerning the said manors of East Fleet and West Fleet, by the name of the manor of Fleet, and concerning the rectory of Fleet, the deforciants granted the premises to the querents for eighty years, should Anne Moone, wife of the said Maximilian, live so long. The fine and an indenture dated 16 August, 25 Elizabeth [1583], were to provide a jointure for the said Anne.

The will of the said Maximilian [P. C. C., Capell, 12] is recited, by which the testator bequeathed Brappole rectory to his wife Anne for the good of his children, until his eldest son, Maximilian, should be twenty-one years of age.

The said Maximilian [the father] died at West Fleet 23 October last past [1612]. Anne, his widow, survives at West Fleet. (Chancery Inquisitions Post Mortem, Series 2, vol. 330, no. 94.)

# GENEALOGICAL RESEARCH IN ENGLAND

Contributed by G. ANDREWS MORIARTY, JR., A.M., LL.B., of Newport, R. I.,
and communicated by the Committee on English Research

## MOHUN (OR MOONE)–HYDE (CONTINUED)

### FROM FEET OF FINES†

Final Concord made on the Morrow of the Purification of the Blessed
Virgin Mary, 2 Elizabeth [3 February 1559/60] between Robert Mone,
gentleman, querent, and Henry Earl of Arundel and John Lumley, knight,
Lord Lumley, and Jane, his wife, deforciants, concerning the manor of Loder
Matryvers, 40 messuages, 10 cottages, 50 gardens, 50 orchards, 2000 acres
of land, 1000 acres of meadow, 2000 acres of pasture, and 40s. rent in Loder
Matryvers, Askerwell, Lytton, and Pourestok [co. Dorset]. The deforciants
have acknowledged the aforesaid premises to be the right of Robert, and
they have remised them from John and Jane and the heirs of John to Robert
and his heirs for ever. Warranty against the heirs of the Earl. Consideration, £360. (Feet of Fines, Dorset, Hilary Term, 2 Elizabeth.)

Final Concord made on the Quindene of Easter, 5 Elizabeth [1562–63],
between Christopher Hardy, Thomas Hardy, and John Hardy, querents,
and Robert Moone, gentleman, deforciant, concerning 10 acres of land,
10 acres of meadow, 300 acres of pasture, 6 acres of wood, and 80 acres of

†Preserved in the Public Record Office, London.

broom and heath in North Yarden[?] and Lytton. The deforciant has acknowledged the aforesaid premises to be the right of Christopher, Thomas, and John, and has remised them to Christopher, Thomas, and John and the heirs of Christopher for ever. Consideration, from Christopher, Thomas, and John, 100 marks. (Feet of Fines, Dorset, Easter Term, 5 Elizabeth.)

## FROM PATENT ROLLS*

10 February, 13 Elizabeth [10 February 1570/1]. Whereas Robert Moone the Younger, son of Robert Moone the Elder, will do his best to frustrate at law, at his own charges, letters patent of Queen Mary, dated 17 July, 2 Mary [17 July 1554], granting to John Grene and William Jennings, in fee simple, a messuage and lands thereto belonging in the occupation of Robert Moone† in Bothenhampton and late belonging to Syon Abbey, in consideration of a yearly rent of £7. 6s. 8d., reserved upon the lands below, which till now have paid to the Crown £4 a year only, the Queen lets to farm to the said Robert Moone the Younger (1) certain closes called Courte Close, Bertlease, Bonehampton Meade, Bonehampton Wood, Shipton Furseys, etc., etc., in Bothenhampton, parcel of Loders manor and now or late in the tenure of Robert Mone the Elder and late parcel of the possessions of Katherine, Queen of England, and before of Syon Abbey, and (2) the customary works of Bothenhampton, for life, with remainder (a) to Maximilian Moone, brother of Robert Moone the Younger, for life, and (b) to John Moone, brother of said Robert Moone the Younger, for life. (Patent Rolls, 13 Elizabeth, part 4, 1074, m. 20.)

## FROM CHANCERY PROCEEDINGS*

The bill of WATER MOONE, gent., filed 27 October 1562, complains that, whereas the Duchess of Somerset that now is had assigned to her by Edward VI the manor of Symondsbury, during the minority of the Earl of Hertford that now is, of which manor the complainant was bailiff during the time the Duchess held it and collected rents, on 6 May, 2 Philip and Mary [6 May 1556], the complainant desired Giles Aclough of Salisbury to pay £10 to the Duchess for him. In accordance with a request from Giles he sent the £10 by his brother, Robert Mone, gent., to the house of Giles in Salisbury, and Robert, because Giles was not at home, delivered it to Anne, then wife of Giles and now of Thomas Hussey of Eustam, co. Dorset, gent. Anne delivered it to her husband, but he never paid it to the Duchess; and about six years past he died, leaving to Anne, his executrix, about £500 in goods and chattels. The complainant has no written obligation from Giles for the payment of the £10 to the Duchess.

The answer of THOMAS HUSEE and ANNE states that they have paid out greater sums on behalf of Giles than his estate amounted to. They deny that Robert ever delivered the £10 at Giles's house; if he did, he delivered it to one Olyver, who was servant to Giles and kept his book of receipts, and Olyver repaid it to one Coteryngton, a clothier. [This the complainant denies.] (Chancery Proceedings, Series 2, 128/31.)

The bill of ROGER CLAVELL of Corffe Castle, co. Dorset, gent., 25 January 1574 [? 1574/5], shows that the complainant's grandfather, Roger Clavell, gent., deceased, had by grant from the late Abbey of Byndon, co. Dorset, the farm of Chaldon parsonage, co. Dorset (then in the tenure of Richard Clyffe for life), for ninety-nine years after Clyffe's death. Being seised of the lease in reversion, Roger, the grandfather, by deed of 6 April, 5 Edward

---

*Preserved in the Public Record Office, London.
†This is evidently a recital of the earlier patent, without specifying which Robert Moone is intended.

VI [6 April 1551], for the zeal which he bare to the name of the Clavells, conveyed the lease to Walter Clavell, gent., deceased, the complainant's father, and his issue male. Walter had issue male, viz., the complainant and his brother, Henry Clavell, and died. Afterwards Clyffe died, and Henry Clavell surrendered his interest to the complainant. But Robert Moone, having by casual means gotten the lease into his hands, has contrived to make secret estates to persons unknown, who have entered upon the parsonage.

The answer of ROBERT MOONE states that the lease was made by the Abbey "a very short space & long time within the year next before the suppression of the house" and is therefore void and of no force. Accordingly, when Clyffe died, the defendant entered, "being lawfully entitled." Thereon Marmaduke Lovell, who had married the late wife of Walter Clavell, pretending a title in his wife's right, reëntered. Thereupon, about sixteen years past, the defendant brought an action at common law against Lovell, and, when it was ready to be tried, Lovell surrendered his claim and paid a certain sum to Moone not to prosecute, and took a lease from the defendant at a greater rent than before. (Chancery Proceedings, Series 2, 45/30.)

### FROM CHANCERY DEPOSITIONS*

#### [Symonds v. Moone]

Interrogatories on behalf of the complainant in the case of William Symonds, gent., v. Morgan Moone, gent.†

Did you know Walter Moone that was father to the defendant and Robert Moone that was father-in-law to the complainant? Was not Walter Moone a clerk unto Mathew Colthurst that was officer to Henry VIII? And could not Walter very well both write and read the secretary and court hand? How long ago did they die?

Depositions taken at Bridport [co. Dorset] 19 April, 35 Elizabeth [19 April 1593].

Henry Waye of Bradpoole [co. Dorset], yeoman, aged 50, saith that he knew Robert and Walter Moone. Walter could well write and read the secretary hand and could write a "Basterde court hand." Walter died about twenty-two years past. Robert died about twelve years past. Deponent knew Walter in familiar acquaintance some ten years before his death. During that time Walter was accounted "a man learned & verie well experienced in the world aswell in drawing of conveyances as in making of other writings & instruments." Walter "after he departed from his office of Searcher in the Port of Poole and his return from beyond the Seas did for the space of some eight or ten years make his most abode in Bridport where he dwelt." Deponent knew by report that Walter and Robert Moone had an estate for the term of their lives of a tenement called Mills [*elsewhere* Miles] Warrens Tenement in Loders near Bridport, and that Walter sold their interest to Mylles Warren, the then tenant. He thinks this was done with Robert's consent, "for that the saide Robert was sythens one of the Farmers of the said Mannor where the said Tenement laie." He has seen a joint lease of Bradpool parsonage to Walter and Robert. Robert survived Walter and enjoyed the same till he died.

Deponent has heard that Walter Moone was present when his father Richard made his will. He has heard that Walter wrote the will, and that

*Preserved in the Public Record Office, London.

†For an abstract of the bill of William Symonds of Lyme-Regis, co. Dorset, gent., dated 6 November 1592, and of the answer of Morgan Mone, gent., see REGISTER, vol. 80, pp. 355–357. The ** interrogatories and depositions here given in this case are found in Chancery Depositions, Elizabeth, S, 56/12.

**For pp. 355-357 see pp. 170-172, this volume.

Robert and Walter had a copyhold in certain houses and lands in Axminster [co. Devon] successively, and Robert and his assigns have enjoyed the same for thirty years or thereabouts until this day.

He deposes to the handwriting of Walter Moone in the letter following:

"Lyke as y<sup>e</sup> take me to bee in all my doengs inconstant the w<sup>ch</sup> you nor no man hath so proved in me Even so I doubt very moche you woll not performe suche promasses as ye made unto me when I by my owne hand writynge passyd awaye my title in Axmyster.

"The fyest is you promysyd mee the deputacion in Waymoth for £4 by the yere and this yere to give yt me free and everye owre ye are royllinge at me thowe shults owte owte ye knowe I have not offendyd And yf I haue let me aunswere it quietly w<sup>t</sup> Suerties from the first owre I toke it in £200 band reson wolde I shulde have some assurance therein.

"The 2<sup>de</sup> is ye promysyd me the next reuercion that shulde fall in your manor of Loder Matravers in Recompense off Axmyster ye knowe I have none assurance but yo<sup>r</sup> worde.

"The 3<sup>de</sup> y<sup>e</sup> promysyd me a lesse in Sadlers House for 30 yeres before Thomas Mason, reson wolde ye shulde fullfylle yo<sup>r</sup> promas as I trust ye woll do, but I wolbe right to see it don.

"The 4<sup>th</sup> ys ye knowe I solde my right and title in Myles Warens Bargayne by yo<sup>r</sup> owne assent or ells I cowde not have don it and I had the some of £60 and yo had no peny thereof I am contentyd ye allowe yo<sup>r</sup>selfe oute of Axmyster one £100 and let me have but the 4th parte of the rest of the mony ye do Sell yt for. This is but reson I thinke

"These are the causes I wolde be aunsweryd w<sup>t</sup> quietnes at yo<sup>r</sup> hande prainge yo to be no more offendyd w<sup>t</sup> me in Dowting the worst seinge every man is mortall and not to be so hasty to Surrender my tytle so quicly upon yo<sup>r</sup> promasses but that first in recompense of so good a thinge at yo<sup>r</sup> hande to have some assuraunce as reson wolde I am sewre I have never ment but when ye wolde I am redye to come to the court and to Surrender accordingly nother in no worde that ever I said unto you that I wolde not do it but that ye were in a grete chafynge as who shulde saye I were yo<sup>r</sup> bondman or slave and that I shuld not darre to saye or reson w<sup>t</sup> yo for any matter

"Notw<sup>t</sup>standynge ye have hard my greffe before in the 4 articles the whiche I refer upon yo<sup>r</sup> concyence and honestye and forasmoche as fors partely causeth me consyderinge yo<sup>r</sup> honesty peradventure resteth upon my cominge to the Court of Axminster nowe at the next laweday court there to be holden and there to Surrender my tytle &c. I am contentyd to come at any tyme upon one dayes warninge and if ye performe yo<sup>r</sup> promasses before so it is, yf not the more ye ar to blame But, whether ye do or do not I woll come to Axmyster at all tymes and there to performe my promasse accordinge as before is saide

"In the worshipp of yo<sup>r</sup> fayre I have sent yo<sup>r</sup> wyffe 6 Raylles I praye let M<sup>r</sup> W<sup>m</sup> Raffe the vice Comptroller etc some parte of them w<sup>th</sup> you. From Burport this presente Saterdaye St. Mathies daye 1560.
                    "Yo<sup>r</sup> poore Brother     Walter Moone
"The Raylles were kylled Thurysdaie last"

Henry Waye further deposes that he thinks the defendant "is a man like to take away & secretlie kepe . . . any writing . . . that might hinder" his title to the houses in Axminster.

There is a chest at Bridport which contains several writings "of such as be dead." There were in it only two leases concerning Walter and Robert Moone and their children, viz., one lease of the tithe garb of Bradpoole, the other of a burgage in Bridport lying in the South Street called the Porch Howse. Deponent and the defendant did not break up the chest; but [Richard] Tyggens did break up a box sealed with five seals, wherein the leases were, which box lay in the Town Chest aforesaid. And the said Richard Tyggens was for his breach thereof put from his place of trust and office in the said Corporation; but he cannot depose that the defendant was put from office for the same reason [as the interrogation suggests].

Richard Davidge of Bridport [co. Dorset], merchant, aged 80, saith that he knew that Walter Moone was a clerk to Mathew Colthurst that was officer unto Henry VIII, and did write very well. He knew Walter Moone from his infancy until he died. Walter enjoyed the tithe garb of Bradpoole after his mother's death, during all his life. Walter was present when Richard Moone, his father, made his will, and Walter wrote the will in the presence of deponent and of Robert Moone and Christopher Betscombe.

Deponent thinks that the defendant will make no question for his profit to detain any writing or release that might better his pretended title.

John Clare of Bridport [co. Dorset], saddler, aged 52, saith that he was tenant to both Robert and Walter Moone in their lifetimes. Robert Moone admitted to deponent that the tithe of Bradpoole belonged to Robert, and that Walter enjoyed it for divers years until Robert's death. He heard Robert declare, after the death of Walter, in the Guildhall of Bridport (whither deponent was called by Robert and by [Edith] the late wife of Walter Moone, his sister-in-law, upon some speech of a marriage then likely to take effect between one Tiggens and Edith), in the presence of the masters of the town, that he (Robert) had passed away his right in the tithe of Bradpoole for such right as Walter had in the houses and lands in Axminster, exhorting his sister-in-law to give after her death the residue of the term of the lease unto four of the sons of the said Walter Moone, to the end that no man that should marry her should take any benefit of the said lease, whereunto his said sister-in-law yielded and accordingly conveyed the same.

Walter Moon in his lifetime was greatly beholden to his brother Robert, who gave him diverse sums of money for the better preferment of Walter's children, as Robert declared to deponent.

It is only of late that question has been made by Walter or his executrix or the defendent as to the title to Axminster houses. The defendant is likely to detain any writing that might hinder his claim.

Richard Russell of Bridport [co. Dorset], gent., aged 37, deposes that Morgan Moone admitted to him and to one Robert Moone, gent., that the letter (copied above) was in the writing of Walter Moone (his father).

Richard Davidge of Lyme-Regis [co. Dorset], merchant, aged 48, deposes that the letter is in Walter's hand and is verbally as Henry Waie has deposed.

Maximilian Moone of Fleet [co. Dorset], gent., aged 28, called by the defendant, deposes that he has seen the will of Richard Moone, deceased, his (deponent's) grandfather, which remains in deponent's custody.

Richard Davidge of Bridport [co. Dorset], merchant, aged 80, deposes that he has heard Richard Moone's will read and that thereby he gave all his land and leases for a term of years to Walter Moone, his son, the defendant's father, reserving the profits thereof to his then wife for her life. This he knows, because he was present at the writing of the will.

Richard Tyggen of Bridport [co. Dorset], merchant, aged 70, saith that he knew Richard Moone, Walter Moone, and Robert Moone, sons of the said Richard, deceased. He has heard by the report of Edith Moone, relict of Walter, whom this deponent married, that Robert Moone concealed the will of Richard Moone, deceased, and that she never came by sight of it; but about two years past the defendant, upon request of Maximilian Moone, perusing his writings in a chest of Margaret Moone, mother to the said Maximilian, saw and read some part of the will. He heard this by report from Maximilian and the defendant. Deponent gave money unto one friend of his to make search and inquire to find the same extant in Record for twenty years past, and since he has searched himself; but he hath not found it in record. He heard Walter Moone declare, shortly after his return from beyond the seas, that he had right to the lands in Axminster in question, and that Robert did him wrong to detain them from him. Walter's widow desired deponent many times to sue for the lands; but deponent would not, because in all her life he could never come by sight of the will of Richard. On her deathbed she charged her son, the defendent, to sue for the same; whereupon the defendant procured administration of the goods and chattels of Richard Moone, his grandfather, supposing him to have died intestate because he could not find his will in record.

After the death of Edith, Walter Moone's executrix, she dying intestate, deponent took administration of the goods of Walter Moone not then administered, and the lease of the lands in question was returned upon the inventory. By his deed deponent has released to the defendant all title therein.

Depositions taken at Lyme-Regis [co. Dorset] 9 August, 35 Elizabeth [9 August 1593].

Margaret Moone of West Fleet [co. Dorset], widow, aged 70, saith that she has known the defendant from his youth and the plaintiff for sixteen years last past. Robert Moone was her husband and father-in-law to the plaintiff. Walter Moone died about twenty years past, and Robert Moone about seven years past. She knew Walter more than twenty years before he died. He dwelt at Bridport at the time of his death. Walter was deputy searcher in the port of Poole under Robert Moone, deponent's late husband. Robert had an estate for life in a bargain called Myles Warrens Bargain, in a place called Loder, near Bridport. The same was sold by Walter, by Robert's consent, for £60, which Walter had to his own use. Walter had the tithe in Bradpooll which she thinks was Robert's. Walter wrote his father's will.

Robert and Walter had a copyhold estate successively of the houses and land in question. She has heard her husband say that Walter surrendered their copyhold estates in the court of Axminster and thereafter Robert claimed to hold the same land by lease, "was within a year next after the surrender," and, when the said Robert Moone enjoyed the land in question by copy, he was pained or compelled to dwell upon the same. Since the surrender of the copyhold estate, made by Robert and Walter, Robert and his assigns have quietly enjoyed the same by lease until about this suit now attempted. She thinks that Walter knew that Robert enjoyed the same by lease. She was present when Walter made his will and in her hearing bequeathed the land in question and appointed his wife Edith executrix.

Walter was beholden to Robert, who paid some debts for him amounting to about £200. The defendant was employed by deponent in diverse of her business after her husband's death and in looking over his writings. She thinks that the defendant is set on to the suit by others, viz., John Bellamie.

John Bellamie of Lyme-Regis [co. Dorset], merchant, aged 50, saith that he knows the plaintiff and knew Robert and Walter Moone. Walter died about twenty-two years past, Robert about twelve years past. Walter could write a plain secretary hand and was accounted well-learned and experienced in the world.

The defendant was discontinued and put out of the Corporation of Bridport.

Robert Moone of Baunton [co. Dorset], gent., aged 34, deposes that the letter is in Walter Moone's secretary hand. He thinks that if any writing concerning the land in question came to the defendant's hands in perusing the evidences of Robert Moone, deceased, the defendant would convey the same away. The defendant, presuming upon deponent's courtesy, wrote a letter in deponent's name to one of deponent's tenants to receive certain money, which he received, but at the day when the tenant should have paid the same money to deponent, deponent was truly paid thereof again.

William Bellamie of Axminster [co. Devon], yeoman, aged 54, saith that Robert Moone, deceased, sometime held by copy of court roll the houses and land in question and claimed to hold the same by lease. When he held the same by copy, he was compelled to dwell thereon.

Gilbert Moone of Bridport [co. Dorset], merchant, aged 54, deposes that the [above] letter "directed to Robert Moone" was in the hand of Walter. Deeds as well of townsmen as of the country were wont to be put in the town chest at Bridport for safety. Deeds relating to Robert and Walter Moone and their children were taken therefrom, as it was suspected, by the defendant. Deponent does not know who took them; but the defendant and Richard Tiggens were, upon suspicion of the taking away of the writings, put out of the company or corporation of Bridport. Tiggens confessed that he took away the writings.

John Bellamie of Lyme-Regis [co. Dorset], merchant, aged 50, called for the defendant, saith that he has heard that the said Richard Moone first took an estate of the lands and tenements in question by copy of court roll to himself and his sons Robert and Walter successively, to begin after the death, surrender, or forfeiture of Richard Wood and Florence, his wife. Richard Moone also took a lease for ninety-one years, to begin as above. After Richard's death, viz., about twenty-four years past, deponent wrote a copy of the lease. Robert Moone, after the estates of Richard and Florence Wood were determined, enjoyed the lands and dwelled upon them. Whether he was compelled to dwell thereon, deponent knows not.

Deponent was servant to Robert Moone when he enjoyed the premises. Deponent was sent by Robert with a copy of the lease, and written over it: "This is the true copie of my lease and I will stand to yt," to Mr. Dannett, then lord of Axminster manor.

William Bellamie of Axminster [co. Devon], yeoman, aged 54, deposes that Mr Dannett refused to receive Robert Moone's rent for many years. He heard Walter Moone say that, if the land was held by lease, it belonged to him. Walter wrote to deponent's father that, "if it be claimed by lease, you shall have it."

Deponent heard it reported by Hugh Bragge and John Bettey, deceased, that Robert Moone showed two leases touching the lands in question, "or els the Stewarde of the mannor did read the same leases falselie out." Deponent cannot depose that it was to keep his brother Walter from the lands in question.

Deponent produces a letter to himself from John Dannett, dated 14 January, 15 Elizabeth [14 January 1572/3], touching [in detail] arrears of Mr. Moone's rent.

Richard Davidge of Lyme-Regis [co. Dorset], merchant, aged 50, saith that he has had search made for the probate of Richard Moone's will both in the Prerogative Court of Canterbury and in the country, and he by no means can find the same, which giveth him occasion to think that it has been suppressed.

Margaret Moone of West Fleet [co. Dorset], widow, aged 70, saith that Walter Moone gave her husband a writing touching the Axminster lands, which writing was drawn up by Castle of Exeter. She also deposes that her husband granted by writing to the complainant, in consideration of marriage, his estate in the land in question, about the time of the complainant's marriage with deponent's daughter. Robert was of perfect memory at the time of the grant. Deponent is bound to the complainant for the enjoying of the lands in question.

## [Moone v. Wade and Moone]

Depositions taken at Bridport [co. Dorset] 3 October, 42 Elizabeth [3 October 1600].*

Walter Hallet, bailiff of the borough of Bridport [co. Dorset], brought out of the town chest a writing purporting to be a lease of Bradpoll parsonage, dated 10 July, 24 Henry VIII [10 July 1532]. He said that he had not seen it before; in diverse parts it is "eaten and consumed," and the seal is covered with linen cloth.

Richard Tiggins of Exmouth [co. Devon], yeoman, aged 40, servant to the defendant Henry Wade, saith that he heard his father, Richard Tiggins (who married the widow of Walter Moone), in his lifetime say that his wife should tell his said father [sic] that the supposed lease was put into the town chest of Bridport for some fault therein. He further deposes that his father told him that his wife made him swear not to buy the lease for any of his own children (which he would otherwise have done to avoid troubles). He deposes that Henry Waye (sometime town clerk of Bridport) told him that he should see troubles about the lease because the seal was wrapped up.

Richard Gibbes of Bridport [co. Dorset], gent., aged 45, who has from childhood seen many writings made by Walter Moone, saith that the writing on the lease is like Walter's, but differs somewhat from his usual hand. He has heard Richard Tiggins, deceased, say that the lease was somewhat suspicious. He has heard that counterfeit keys had been made to the town chest to take writings touching this matter.

Richard Rossell of Bridport [co. Dorset], gent., aged 44, saith that some letters and words in the lease resemble Walter Moone's writing.

Lionel Browne of Bradpoll [co. Dorset], aged 42, saith that he heard the defendant, Morgan Moone, say, in the presence of deponent and of Henry Wade, the other defendant, that he could make the supposed lease of Bradpoll parsonage either good or bad, if it pleased him.† Before that deponent and some of his neighbours "had a price of the said parsonage" from Robert Moone.

Walter Hallett, the bailiff, deposes that he has heard say that the defendant Wade bought from Robert Moone (brother to the complainant Maximilian Moone) twelve years in Bradpoll rectory for £240.

Richard Gibbes, above [who has previously deposed], saith that, when he was a scholar at Bridport, about twenty [sic] years past, he heard that Walter Moone had an interest in the parsonage. At that time Walter had tithing corn brought from Bradpoll to his barn in Bridport.

Richard Rossell, above [who has previously deposed], deposes that he has heard that the rectory was granted long since to Richard Moone, grandfather of the now complainant, and to Walter Moone and Robert Moone, his two sons, for seventy years. He deposes that the rectory has been enjoyed "by the same Moones" for thirty years. He has heard that the lease was put in the common chest of Bridport when Richard Tiggins married the wife of Walter Moone, so that Tiggins should not defraud the children of Walter of their interest therein given them in Walter's will.

*The depositions here given in this suit brought by Maximilian Moone, gent., against Henry Wade, gent., and Morgan Moone, gent., are found in Chancery Depositions, Michaelmas Term, 42–43 Elizabeth, no. 15 (Dorset).

†Others also deposed that Morgan Moone said this.

Deanes Moone, wife of Morgan Moone, one of the defendants, aged 50, saith that she has heard that the lease was put in the town chest about the time when Richard Tiggins, her "father," married Edith Moone, relict of Walter Moone, which was about thirty years past. And they could not agree to be married until the lease was put into the chest. She heard that it was put there because the interest was supposed of right to belong to the issue and children of Robert Moone, deceased, one of the lessees, and was withholden from them by the children of the said Walter Moone, and for that cause, for the better concealment of the same, was put into the town chest. About twelve years since, there being one John Bellamye marrying one of the daughters of Walter Moone, and from the rest of the said Walter's children holding the same parsonage, Morgan Moone, deponent's husband, demanding from Bellamye his part and portion of the parsonage and Bellamye then refusing, contention and debate grew between Bellamye and Morgan Moone, and Morgan then told Bellamy that, if he might not have his part, he would make him lose his whole parsonage, meaning, as it seemed, to impart the same to Robert Moone, the complainant's brother, unto whom of right the interest did appertain. Thereupon Bellamy entreated deponent to be a means to accord her husband and Bellamy, promising that he would give Morgan Moone out of the parsonage £10 or £5 (she does not remember which) and that she should never want if her husband happened to die. But this promise did not take any effect. And thereupon, as she taketh it, the said Robert Moone came to the knowledge of his interest in the same.

------

# GENEALOGICAL RESEARCH IN ENGLAND

Contributed by G. Andrews Moriarty, Jr., A.M., LL.B., of Newport, R. I., and communicated by the Committee on English Research

## Mohun (or Moone)–Hyde (concluded)

### From the Corporation Records of Bridport, co. Dorset

#### Calendar of Leases, 1461–1612

12 September 1529. Robert Hasard and Richard Furlock, cofferers, grant to Richard Mone a parcel of hempland called Morterhay, on the east side of South Street, for eighty-one years, at 2s. a year. (D, 339.) [Another draft of this record adds: "on which Thomas Moleyns has made an orchard." (D, 330.)]

26 August 1536 to 19 July 1537. Richard Mone, as bailiff, is a party to town leases, with Richard Davage, bailiff.

12 September 1544 to 26 May 1545. Richard Mone, as bailiff, is a party to town leases, with John Cooper.

10 June 1553. Robert Mone of Baunton, "marchante," grants to Richard Alforde, "bourcher," Margaret, his wife, and John, their son, for their lives, a messuage and garden on the north side of East Street, at 6s. 8d. a year. (D, 1860.)

25 September 1577. Ric. Tiggin, cofferer. (D, 26.)

20 September 1578. Ric. Tiggins, bailiff.

15 November 1585. Bailiffs and cofferers [including Richard Tiggins, cofferer] grant to Richard Tiggins, Sr., merchant, for forty-one years, a messuage called Bridge House, with a barn and lands, in Waldiche and Shipton. Fine, £40. Rent, £6 a year. (D, 1865.)

The Mohun family was one of the most ancient Norman houses of the West Country, and derived its name from Moyon in Normandy. The founder of the family in England, William de Mohun, appears in Domesday as an important tenant in chief in the counties of Somerset and Dorset. The *caput* of their barony was at Dunster Castle, in Somerset, and their history has been fully set forth by Sir Henry Churchill Maxwell-Lyte in his history of "Dunster and its Lords."

The Moones of Fleet, co. Dorset (for the name *Mohun* became corrupted into *Moone*), were a cadet branch, who claimed to descend from Sir Robert Mohun of Porlock, co. Somerset, the fifth son of Sir John de Mohun of Dunster, who died in 1330. But the descent is obscure, and the ancestry of this branch has not been proved farther back than Richard Mohun *alias* Moone with whom the following pedigree begins. This pedigree sets forth briefly the genealogy of Richard Mohun *alias* Moone and his descendants for a few generations. For details in regard to the lands held by members of the family and the litigation in which they were involved see the preceding records.

1. Richard Mohun *alias* Moone, of Bridport, co. Dorset, Gentleman, died, an old man, about 1570, and was buried in Bridport

199

church. The name of his wife, who also was buried in Bridport church, is unknown.

He was of Hawkchurch, co. Dorset, in the early part of the reign of Henry VIII, and held land also in Axminster, co. Devon, in 1529. He removed to Bridport at that time, and was granted land there 12 Sept. 1529. He was bailiff of Bridport in 27 and 28 Henry VIII [1535–1537] (Hutchins's History of Dorset) and also in 1544–45.

Children:

2. i. ROBERT.
3. ii. WALTER.
   Other sons and daughters, whose names are unknown.

2. ROBERT MOHUN *alias* MOONE (*Richard*), of Bridport and Bothenhampton, co. Dorset, Esq., died 14 Nov. 1580. He married MARGARET HYDE, born probably about 1523, died 1 Dec. 1603, daughter and coheiress of Stephen Hyde of Hyde, co. Dorset, Esq. (See Hyde pedigree, *infra*.)

On the north wall of the chancel of the Church of the Holy Trinity, the parish church of Fleet, co. Dorset, there is (according to Hutchins, *op. cit*, vol. 1, p. 546) a brass plate, with the figures of a man and a woman kneeling at a desk, and behind the man are represented nine sons and behind the woman eight daughters. Above are the arms of Mohun impaling Hyde. Below is the following inscription:

> "HIC IACET MARGARITA, QUONDAM CASTISSIMA VIRI DIGNISSIMI ROBERTI MOHUN, ALIAS MOUN DE BOTHENHAMPTON, IN COMITATU DORCESTRENSI ARMIGERI, QUÆ QUIDEM MARGARITA FUIT FILIA ET COHERES STEPHANI HYDE DE HYDE, IN EODEM ETIAM COMITATU ARMIGERI. HÆC XVII LIBERORUM FÆLICISSIMA FUIT PARENS, VIXIT ANNOS CIRCITER XC, AC IN DOMINO REQUIESCIT. OBIIT PRIMO DIE DECEMBRIS, ANNO REGNI SERENISSIMI JACOBI ANGLORUM REGIS I. AC SCOTIÆ XXXVI. SALUTIS, MDCIII."

Margaret (Hyde) Mohun, mother of nine sons and eight daughters, was probably born about 1523, instead of about 1513, as the inscription on the brass indicates; for in the Chancery case of Symonds *v.* Moone she deposed on 9 Aug. 1593, aged 70 years. Another reason for believing that she was born later than 1513 is the fact that on 1 Sept. 1578, when her husband made his will, three of their daughters, Mary, Joan, and Margaret, were under twenty-one.

Robert Mohun (or Moone) acquired large wealth, bought the manors of Loders Matravers and Fleet, lands in Baunton (Bothenhampton), and the manor of Maugerton, co. Dorset, and held lands in Axminster, co. Devon, that had been his father's and four burgages in Bridport. He was searcher of the Port of Poole and a burgess in Parliament for Bridport in 1558. (See Hutchins, *op. cit.*) His will, dated 1 Sept. 1578, was proved 9 Nov. 1581 (*supra*, p. 92), and his inquisition post mortem was taken 4 Sept. 1581 (*supra*, p. 93). ✱

✱For pp. 92 & 93 see pp. 187-188, this volume.

Children:*

i. ROBERT, of Bothenhampton, co. Dorset, Gentleman, son and heir, b. about 1559; d. 17 Aug. 1598; m. MELIORA PITT of Blanford, co. Dorset, who survived him. His inquisition post mortem was taken 14 Oct. 1598 (*supra*, pp. 93–94).
   Children:
   1. *Meliora*, b. in 1586; m. —— Dakcomb (or Jackson).
   2. *Margaret*, b. in 1588; m. at Stoke Damerel, co. Devon, 5 Dec. 1609, Thomas Heale, son and heir of John Heale of Plymouth, co. Devon, Esq.
   3. *Anne*, b. in 1594; m. —— Heale of co. Devon.

ii. MAXIMILIAN, of Fleet, co. Dorset, Esq., b. 1 Feb. 1563/4; d. at West Fleet 23 Oct. 1612;† m 4 Oct. 1593 ANN CHURCHILL, who survived him, daughter and coheiress of John Churchill of Corton, co. Dorset, Gentleman. His inquisition post mortem was taken 19 Jan. 1612/13 (*supra*, p. 94). His brass, in Fleet church, as described by Hutchins, *op. cit.*, vol. 1, p. 546, shows a man and woman, with five sons behind the man and eight daughters behind the woman. Above are the arms of Mohun quartering Hyde and impaling a lion rampant debruised with a bendlet (Churchill), with a crescent for difference. Below is the following inscription: "Hic jacet *Maximilianus Mohun*, armiger, filius Roberti Mohun alias Moun, de Bothenhampton, in comitatu Dorcestrensi armigeri, qui quidem Maximilianus Mohun, una cum uxore, castissima filia et coherede Johannis Churchill de Corton, generosi, tredecim liberorum felicissimus fuit parens. Vixit annos 48, ac vita bene beata peracta in Domino requiescit. Obiit XIV. die Octobris, anno regni, serenissimi Jacobi Anglorum regis 10, ac Scotiae 45to, anno Salutis 1612."
   Children:‡
   1. *Mary*, b. in 1595; m. in 1610 John (or Cornelius) Weston of Hethell, co. Devon, Gentleman.
   2. *Maximilian*, of Fleet, Esq., bapt. in 1596; d. in 1673; m. Elizabeth Chawcott (or Chaldecot), daughter of Francis Chawcott (or Chaldecot) of Whitwaye (Whiteway), co. Dorset, Esq. He was an active adherent of King Charles, and in 1650 the sequestration of his estate was proposed, but he was later excused (Hutchins, *op. cit.*, vol. 1, p. 545). The pedigree of Mohun of Fleet given in the Visitation of Dorset, 1623, begins with Robert (2), father of Maximilian (2, ii), gives fragmentary information about the elder Maximilian's brothers and sisters, and gives also the five sons of the latter and five of his eight daughters. It was entered in the Visitation of 1623 by "Ed: Shawe for Mr Max Moone" (2, ii, 2).
      The arms of the family, according to the pedigree in the Visitation were: "Quarterly: 1 and 4, Gules, a maunch ermine, the hand, proper, holding a fleur-de-lis or, all within a bordure argent; 2, Or, a chevron between three lozenges azure, on a chief gules an eagle displayed of the first [HYDE]; 3, Sable, a lion rampant argent, debruised by a bendlet gules [CHURCHILL]. Over all four quarterings a crescent for difference. Crest: A maunch ermine, the hand, proper, holding a fleur-de-lis [or], a crescent for

*For descendants of Robert Mohun *alias* Moone cf. also the Visitation of Dorsetshire, 1623, p. 72 (*Publications of the Harleian Society*, vol. 20), and the pedigree in Hutchins's History of Dorset, vol. 1, p. 545. As is customary in pedigrees in English visitations, county histories, and similar works, the sons are given first in the order of their births, and the daughters follow the sons.

†Inquisition post mortem. His brass in Fleet church, the inscription on which is given in the text, states that he died on 14 Oct. 1612.

‡The dates given for some of these children in the pedigree in Hutchins's History of Dorset make it possible to arrange their names approximately in the order of their births.

difference. Mohun of Fleet thus Quartered under the hand of William Camden, Clarentiulx, with this Crest."

According to the pedigree in the Visitation this Maximilian (2, ii, 2) had two children living in 1623, viz., Maximilian, son and heir, aged 3 years, and a daughter, aged 1 year. According to the pedigree given in Hutchins, *loc. cit.*, the boy Maximilian d. young, and the line was continued through his father's second son, Francis Mohun of Fleet, Esq., b. in 1625, d. in 1710 (25 Feb. 1711/12, according to his monument in Fleet church, described by Hutchins, vol. 1, p. 546), who m. Elenor Sheldon, a niece of Archbishop Sheldon. This Francis had two brothers, besides the elder brother who d. young, and two sisters. On the death *s.p.* in 1758 of Robert Mohun of Fleet, Esq., grandson of the Francis above-mentioned, the estate at Fleet passed to Robert's two sisters, each of whom was twice married.

3. *Churchill, d. s.p.*
4. *Robert.*
5. *Elizabeth*, m. in 1615 or 1625 John Gollop, Gentleman.
6. *Anne*, b. in 1692 [*sic*, ? 1602].
7. *John*, b. in 1605.
8. *Margaret*, b. in 1606.
9. *George*, b. in 1607.
10. *Eleanor.*
11. *Thomasine*, b. in 1610.
12. *Catharine*, b. in 1612.
13. *A daughter.*

iii. JOHN, of Maugerton, co. Dorset, Gentleman.
iv. ALICE, bur. in Exeter Cathedral 26 July 1628; m. at St. Mary Magdalene's, Taunton, co. Somerset, 14 Sept. 1571, WILLIAM SYMONDS of Lyme-Regis, co. Dorset, and Exeter, co. Devon, Gentleman. and had issue. (See REGISTER, vol. 80, pp. 353, 365–366.) *

v. MARY,  
vi. JOAN, } under twenty-one in 1578.  
vii. MARGARET,  

Six other sons and four other daughters, according to the monumental brass of their mother in Fleet church.

3. WALTER MOONE (*Richard*), of Bridport, co. Dorset, died in 1572, his will being dated 23 May 1571 and proved 2 Dec. 1572. He married EDITH ———, who married secondly, soon after the death of her first husband, Richard Tiggins, merchant, burgess of Bridport, born about 1523, died between 19 Apr. 1593 and 3 Oct. 1600. She died before 14 Nov. 1581, when administration on the goods of Walter Moone, deceased, which were left unadministered by the executrix Edith, was granted to Morgan Moone, his son, and Richard Tyggyn.

Walter Moone was clerk of Matthew Colthurst, officer of King Henry VIII. He was appointed searcher of the Port of Poole 22 Nov., 36 Henry VIII [22 Nov. 1544] (Letters and Papers Foreign and Domestic, vol. 19, no. 690), and was bailiff of Bridport in 2 Elizabeth [1559–60] (Hutchins's History of Dorset).

Children:

i. MORGAN, d. before 13 Sept. 1611; m. (1) ALICE ———; m. (2) DIONISIA TIGGINS, b. about 1550, living 26 Dec. 1611, d. before

*See pp. 168 & 180-181, this volume.

1 Mar. 1620/1, daughter of Richard Tiggins, burgess of Bridport. Morgan Moone inherited land in Loders, Upton, and Matravers. He had issue.

ii. ANTHONY, of Lyme-Regis, co. Dorset, d. before 1 Mar. 1609/10, when administration on his estate was granted to Morgan Moone, his brother.

iii. GEORGE.

iv. RICHARD, of Bridport, co. Dorset, d. before 4 Feb. 1586/7, when administration on his estate was granted to Morgan Moone, next of kin.

v. JOHN.

vi. JOAN, unm. 23 May 1571.*

vii. MARTHA, living 13 Sept. 1611; m. after 23 May 1571 CHRISTOPHER DAVIDGE, who was living 13 Sept. 1611.

viii. ALICE, unm. 23 May 1571.*

The established genealogy of the Hyde family, to which Margaret Hyde, wife of Robert Mohun *alias* Moone, belonged, begins with her grandfather, John Hyde, and the chief facts that are known about the early generations of this family are assembled in the following pedigree. According to Hutchins (History of Dorset, vol. 1, p. 359) the family takes its name from Hyde, a hamlet in the parish of Bothenhampton, co. Dorset; but from the grant of arms described below, under No. 1, it appears that there was an estate or locality called Hyde in the parish of Lodres (Loders), co. Dorset.

1. JOHN HYDE, of Hyde in the parish of Lodres, co. Dorset, "gentilhome," the name of whose wife is unknown, received from Sir Thomas Wryothesley, Garter King of Arms, and from Thomas Benolte, Clarencieux King of Arms, the following grant of arms, dated 22 Dec. 1525:

"D'or, a vng chiveron entre trois lozenges dasura a vng chief de gueules, sur le chief vne saltier engrelée entre deux aiegles closées du champ ar son tymbie sa teste d'ung fesant rasée d'asure crestée becquée de purpre tenant en son dit becquee la fleur d'ung pansee en sa propre colore lestoc et le fuilles de vert aiant sur son dit col une lozenge d'or entre quatre besants affis sur un corsse d'argent et de sable, mantelle de gueules doublé d'argent sicome la picture en le marge cy devant le demonstre." (*Notes & Queries for Somerset and Dorset*, vol. 18, pp. 154–155, with illustration between pp. 144 and 145 of the same volume.)

Children:

2. i. STEPHEN.

3. ii. JOHN.

iii. RICHARD, of Bothenhampton, living 24 Oct. 1545, when he was named in the inquisition post mortem of his brother John as one of John's tenants in co. Dorset.

2. STEPHEN HYDE (*John*), of Hyde, co. Dorset, was living 24 Oct. 1545, when he was named in the inquisition post mortem of his brother John as one of John's tenants in co. Dorset. The name of his wife is unknown.

In a rental and survey of the lands of his brother John, made about 1544, there is mention of "my [John's] howse and grownde called Hyde which my brother Stephen holdyth at wyll." (*Vide infra*, No. 3.)

*Either Joan or Alice married about 1588 John Bellamye. One John Bellamie of Lyme-Regis, co. Dorset, merchant, aged 50, deposed 9 Aug. 1593 in the Chancery case of Symonds *v.* Moone.

Children:

  i.   MARGARET, coheiress of her father, b. probably about 1523; d. 1
       Dec. 1603; m. ROBERT MOHUN *alias* MOONE (*supra*, Mohun
       pedigree, No. 2). From them descended the Mohuns of Fleet,
       co. Dorset.
 ii.   A DAUGHTER, coheiress of her father.

3. JOHN HYDE (*John*), of London, lawyer, died 20 Sept. 1545. He
married MARGARET BUTLER, sister of William Butler of
Aldbury, co. Herts.

In 1529 he appears in the Exchequer as a clerk of the Pipe
(an engrosser of the great Pipe Roll), and states that he has
held the office for the past eight years. He petitions that he
may be allowed to appear as attorney or counsel in the King's
Exchequer. (Letters and Papers Foreign and Domestic, vol.
5, part 3, app. 250.) In the decade from 1530 to 1540 he
acquired a large estate in the confiscated lands of the monasteries (*ib.*). A rental and survey of his lands made about
1544 (*The Herts Genealogist and Antiquary*, vol. 3, pp. 257–
258) and statements taken from the Feet of Fines (*ib.*) show
that he had a considerable estate in Hertfordshire, where he
bought part of the manor of Aldbury, and in Dorset, and
among his Dorset holdings are mentioned "my howse and
grownde called Hyde which my brother Stephen holdyth at
wyll." Hutchins (History of Dorset, vol. 1, p. 359) states
that Hyde, in the parish of Bothenhampton, had been a
parcel of the manor and priory of Loders, that the premises
were granted in 34 Henry VIII [1542–43] to Richard Andrews,
who had licence to alienate them to John Hyde, and that the
latter, at his death in 37 Henry VIII [1545–46], held the
premises of Queen Catharine, as of her manor of Loders,
by knight's service. The premises consisted of a capital
messuage and sixty acres of land, in Hyde and Waldish, and
were valued at 33s. 8d.

The will of John Hyde of the King's Exchequer, dated 14
Aug. 1543 and proved 1 Oct. 1545, mentions, among others,
the testator's wife Margaret, his son Thomas, his daughter
Agnes, his daughter Elizabeth Cartmyll, and his brother
Steven. (See abstract of the will, *supra*, p. 91.) His inquisition post mortem for Dorset was taken at Bridport 24 Oct.
1545, names Stephen Hyde and Richard Hyde as tenants of
tenements in Hyde, Waldyche, and Loders, and states that
he died 20 Sept. 1545 and that Thomas Hyde, his son and
heir, was aged 26 years and more at his father's death (*The
Herts Genealogist and Antiquary*, vol. 3, p. 258).

Children:

4. i.   THOMAS, b. about 1518.
 ii.   AGNES, to whom her father, in his will, left the profits of certain
       holdings in London.
iii.   ELIZABETH, m. before 14 Aug. 1543 JOHN CARTMYLL of Aldbury,
       co. Herts. Her father, in his will, left to her his lease of the
       manor of Aldbury.

4. Thomas Hyde (*John, John*), of Hyde, co. Dorset, and of Ald-
,bury, co. Herts, born about 1518 (since he was aged 26 years
and more at his father's death), died in 1570. He married
Frances ———.
  He succeeded his father in the estate at Hyde, the premises
being valued in the same year in which his father died at £9.
18s. (Hutchins's History of Dorset, *loc. cit.*)
  Children:

    i.   George, of Aldbury, b. about 1547; d. about 29 Elizabeth [1586–87],
        when his brother Robert was his heir. He succeeded his father
        in the estate at Hyde.

   ii.   Robert, of Aldbury, Esq., d. before 7 Apr. 1608, when his inquisition
        post mortem was taken at St. Albans, co. Herts. (*The Herts
        Genealogist and Antiquary*, vol. 3, p. 261.) He succeeded his
        brother George in the estate at Hyde, which he held in 1586–87.*
        In 1586 he received from Cooke a grant of the following arms,
        which are impaled on the brass of Margaret Hyde, widow of
        Robert Moone: "Or, a chevron between three lozenges azure, on
        a chief gules an eagle displayed of the first." (British Museum,
        Additional MS. 4966, fo. 84*b*.)

5. iii.   Nicholas, b. about 1567.

5. Sir Nicholas Hyde (*Thomas, John, John*), of Aldbury, co.
Herts, Bart., born about 1567 (since he was aged 40 years
and more when the inquisition post mortem of his brother
Robert was taken in 1608), died at Aldbury 21 Mar. 1624/5
(see his inquisition post mortem, in *The Herts Genealogist
and Antiquary*, vol. 3, p. 262). He married Bridget Sandes,
daughter of Michael Sandes of Latimer, co. Bucks, Esq.
  He was sheriff of Herts, 1619–20, and was created a baronet
in 1621.
  Child:

    i.   Sir Thomas, of Aldbury, Bart., b. about 1597 (since he was aged
        28 years and more on 5 Aug. 1625, when the inquisition post
        mortem of his father was taken); d. 18 May 1665; m. Mary
        Whitechurch, daughter of John Whitechurch of Walton, co.
        Bucks, Esq.
        Child:
      1.  *Bridget*, heiress of her father, m. Peregrine Osborne, second
          Duke of Leeds. From them descend the later Dukes of
          Leeds.

### LEACHLAND

  Richard Derby, father of Roger Derby of Salem, Mass., married,
about 1642, Alice Leachland, daughter of Roger Leachland of Chard,
co. Somerset, merchant, and his wife, Margaret (Jones) Leachland **
(cf. Register, vol. 79, p. 443). The following records and pedigree
relate to this Leachland family.

### FROM PROBATE RECORDS

  The Will of Thomas Leachland, late of London, now of Taunton, co.
Somerset, merchant, dated 2 February 1595 [1595/6]. To the poor of
Taunton 40s. To my mother, Alice Leachland, £40, when the money due

---

*Hyde was finally sold to ——— Hardy, in the time of Charles II (Hutchins, *op. et loc. cit.*).

**Page 126, this volume.

by bond dated 6 May, 36 Elizabeth [6 May 1594], of Edmond Coggan of Oxford becomes due. To my brother, Roger Leachland, £20 at like time. To Frances, wife of my brother William Leachland, two cypress chests in the keeping of Thomas Calton of London, my brother-in-law, and £10. Residuary legatee and executor: my brother William Leachlande. Overseers: Thomas Gregorie, merchant, and John Gibbons. Witnesses: John Hutchins, Thomas Gregorie. Proved 7 May 1596 by the executor named in the will. (P.C.C., Drake, 33.)

The Will of WILLIAM LECHLAND of Westmounton, co. Somerset, yeoman, being "sicke in bodie," dated 12 January 1615 [1615/16]. To my two daughters, Anne Harte and Eleanor Palfrey, £20 each on the 24th of June after my decease. To my daughter Anne Harte's children, which are, at this time, five, and to my daughter Eleanor Palfrey's children, which are, at this time, four, £6 each at their ages of twenty-one or marriage. To my wife two "petticoats clothes" which are at Collaton, one "gownes clothe," with one chest which was her own, and all the linen which she had or hath, [and] also all my household stuff at the price it is appraised. Richard Elwell of Colliton and Roger Whicker of Southley are to be released of debts. All my shop debts specified in books in my chest at Collaton are to be remitted. Remainder to my wife, except two feather beds, which shall remain after her decease to my said daughters, Anne and Eleanor. Executors: Hugh Hardinge, John Sampson the Younger, Gregory Sampson the Younger of Coliton, to each of whom I give 10s. [Signed] Willm Lechland. Witnesses: Peter Bagwell, Simon Repington, Richard Osborne. Proved 21 February 1615 [1615/16] by the executors named in the will. (P.C.C., Cope, 18.)

The Will of ROGER LEACHLAND of Chard [co. Somerset], merchant, dated 6 February 1620 [1620/1]. To the poor of Chard 10s. To the church 5s. All my goods are to be equally divided among my wife Margaret, my sons William and Thomas, and my daughters Margaret, Jane, and Alice. Executrix: my wife. Overseers: my brother William Leachland. [Signed] Roger Leachland. Witnesses: William Leachland, Thos. Pitts, scr. Proved 31 October 1621 by the executrix named in the will. (P.C.C., Dale, 83.) [A similar abstract of this will was published in the REGISTER, vol. 79, pp. 411–412.] *

The Will of MARGARET LECHLAND of Fitzhead [co. Somerset], widow, dated 30 January 1621 [1621/2]. To be buried in the church or churchyard of Fitzhead. To William Pearce, my son, 5s. To Elinor Pecke, my daughter, 5s. To William Dier, my nephew, 10s. To Phillippe Dier, my nephew, 10s. To Mary Dyer, my niece, 10s. To Ancilla Pearce, my niece, 10s. To Lawrence Pecke, my nephew, 12d. To Ancilla Pearce, aforesaid, one wainscott chest standing in the hall chamber. To Edward Lechland, my nephew, one truckle bedstead in the little chamber over the buttrye. To Anne Dier, my daughter, one standing bedstead standing in the hall chamber over the fire [?]. To Mary Dier, aforesaid, one sideboard standing in the hall chamber. To John Dier, my son-in-law, one chest standing in the hall chamber, commonly called the cushion chest. To Emme Pounde my daughter's four children, Thomas, John, William, and Edward, 6d. apiece. The rest of all my goods and chattels to my daughter Joane Lechland, executrix. Overseers: John Dier, my son-in-law, and Thomas Cheeke of Wineliscombe, each of whom is to have 6d. My will is that my executrix shall have one year's liberty after my death for the payment of the several legacies aforesaid. Witnesses: Richard Cade, William Cornish. Proved 22 August 1622, and administration granted to the executrix. [No inventory.] (Wells Probate Registry.)

*Pages 94-95, this volume.

The Will of WILLIAM LECHLAND of Taunton, co. Somerset, gent., dated 4 January 1637 [1637/8]. I desire to be buried in the north aisle of the parish church of St. Mary Magdalene, Taunton. To my kinswoman Florence Newporte, daughter of Emanuel Newport, late of Enmore, deceased (in consideration I have for thirty-two years and more had £100 and household stuff of her father's, which was given her by his will in 44 Elizabeth [1601–02]), all my lands for life, and after her death to Frances Newport and her issue, and in default [of such issue] to my next heirs. To my sister Ann Calton of London £5 a year for life. To my servant Ann Lane, who has been with me twenty-six years, the house where Henry Symons dwells at Poulewall, for her life. Executrix: the said Florence Newport. Overseers: Mr. Robert Browne of Taunton Castle, my cousins, Mr. John Davedge of Cheddon and Mr. John Jeane of Taunton, and Mr. Thomas Brooke of Glaston. 25 May 1638. [Signed] William Leachland. Witnesses: Hugh Pitcher, William Chaplin, Barnard Pitcher. Confirmed 29 January 1638 [1638/9]. Witnesses: Roger Prowse, Phillip Lissant, Senr. and Junr. Again confirmed 4 April 1639. Witnesses: Antho: Pardoe, William Chaplin, Barnard Pitcher. Proved 20 May 1639 by the executrix named in the will. (P.C.C., Harvey, 94.)

The Will of MARGARET LEACHLAND of Chard, co. Somerset, widow, dated 31 August 1654. To be buried in the parish church of Chard. To the poor of that town 20s. To my daughter Jane Thorne a petticoat and apron, a chest, a table board and a bed, and a Bible. To my grandchildren Margaret and Joan Thorne all my linen. To Florence Cade a box and a looking-glass. To my daughter Margaret Turner a petticoat. To my daughter Alice Darby a gown. To my grandchild Alice Leachland a feather bed. Residuary legatee and executor: my son Thomas Leachland. Overseer: Mr. William Coggan of Chard. The mark of Margaret Leachland. Witnesses: Christopher Webb, John Daye. Proved 22 July 1655 by the executor named in the will. (P.C.C., Aylett, 65.) [A similar abstract of this will was published in the REGISTER, vol. 79, p. 413; but in that abstract the first-named daughter of the testatrix is called Joan (not Jane) Thorne.]

FROM THE PARISH REGISTERS OF COLYTON, CO. DEVON

*Baptisms*

1551 William Lechland son of John 27 August.
1553 Joan Lechland daughter of John 21 October.
1555 Ambrose Lechland son of John 7 September.
1559 Alice Lechland daughter of John 4 November.
1561 Agnes Lechland daughter of John 24 February [1561/2].

FROM THE REGISTERS OF THE PARISH OF ST. MARY MAGDALENE, TAUNTON, CO. SOMERSET

*Baptisms*

1560 Luce Lechland 28 July.
1561 Ellinor Lechland 4 January [1561/2].
1564 Johan Lechland 20 May.
1565 Annes Lechland 2 December.
1566 Robert Lechland 25 January [1566/7].
1568 Annes Lechland 24 July.
1568 Thomas Lechland 13 October.
1570 Joan Lechland 10 December.
1570 Roger Lechland 25 December.
1571 Lawrence Lechland 9 November.

## Marriage

1567   Lawrence Leachland and Margaret Perse 30 September.

## Burials

1564   Annes Leshland 13 August.
1574   Lawrence Leshland 29 [*sic*] February [1574/5].
1593   Mr. Thomas Lechland 30 November.
1595   Thomas Lechland 8 February [1595/6].
1596   Alice Leachland, widow, 12 February [1596/7].

# GENEALOGICAL RESEARCH IN ENGLAND

Contributed by G. Andrews Moriarty, Jr., A.M., LL.B., of Newport, R. I.,
and communicated by the Committee on English Research

## Leachland (continued)

### Mural Memorial in the Church of St. Mary Magdalene, Taunton, co. Somerset†

"Here under lyethe the bodye of Fraunces the wyffe of William Lechland
of Tanton gentleman  the saide Fraunces was the daughter of Henrye
Cornishe of Greenwitch Esquyre by Margarete his wyffe sister too
Sir John Younge of Bristoll Knighte the saide Henrye Cornishe beinge
godsonn to King Henrye the eight: was placed by him Captain of the
Castle of Jersey and their they boyth lived elven yeares, after which
beinge called home they lived & dyed here  The saide Fraunces after
a longe sackness wherin she was a patterne of patience as she was of
vertues in her liffe deceased the 18 day of marche anno do. 1631 to
whom her said husban after fortye & nyne yeares and sixe monethe
livinne with her in maryage hath given this laste righte a grave and
this stone  Her age was 76."

### From Lay Subsidies for co. Devon‡

14 Henry VIII [1522–23].

Parish of Colyton.  Among names of persons having lands or goods
above the value of £40 appears the name of
John Lestland, in goods, £60 (97/186). This
entry occurs again in 99/307, where he is
assessed on the same date £3 on the above-
mentioned £60.

14 and 15 Henry VIII [1522–1524], subsidy paid before 24 April 1523.

Parish of Colyton.  Nicholas Lecheland, [valuation] £10, [tax] 20s.
(97/193).

8 May, 16 Henry VIII [8 May 1524].

Parish of Colyton.  John Lechelond, in goods and chattels, [valua-
tion] £60, [tax] 60s.§
Nicholaus Lechelond, in goods and chattels,
[valuation] £10, [tax] 5s. (96/183).

10 December, 16 Henry VIII [10 December 1524].

Parish of Colyton.  Certificate of second payment on same subsidy
shows John Lechlond, "pro bonis," £60, [tax]
60s., and Nicholas Lechelond, "pro bonis,"
£10, [tax] 5s. (96/151).

### From Ministers' Accounts

Possessions of the Earl of Devon, 17–18 Henry VII [1501–1503].

Colyton, New Rents.  An entry relating to John Lechelond, as in Ministers' Accounts, Henry VIII, 523 (see below).  Roger Trelaweny accounts
as bailiff of Colyton Hundred.  (Ministers' Accounts, Henry VII, 1096.)

---

†This tablet is on the east wall of the north transept of the church, and on it is inscribed a coat
of arms.
‡Preserved in the Public Record Office, London.
§Very few others pay as much. Alan Haydon pays 66s. 8d., John Byrde 60s., and John Morys
60s.

Account of the lands of Katherine, Countess of Devon, "Daughter [Sister] & Aunt of Kings," from Michaelmas, 17 Henry VIII, to Michaelmas, 18 Henry VIII [29 September 1525 to 29 September 1526].

### Account of John Byrche, Reeve of Colyton Manor

"New Rents." He answers for 20d. new rent of John Lechelond, for one parcel of land called le More, lying next Parkemede, late in the tenure of Robert Nueton, as let to the said John this year among other things by court roll there from 12 Henry VII [1496–97] for life, according to the custom of the manor, but more than the ancient rent formerly charged by the year, as is contained in the roll of the court of the manor that same year.

"Quittances & Default of Rents." He accounts in default of rent of two closes there, called Milham and Hakenham, charged above at 12s. per annum, whereof [there are] no issues this year except 6s. therefrom raised from John Lechelond, and thus [he is] in default 6s.

### Account of John Lechelond, Bailiff of Colyton Hundred for the time aforesaid

He is charged with arrears from the last account.* He accounts for perquisites of the hundred court. He is allowed a fee for a bailiff. He renders his account to the lady's receiver. (Ministers' Accounts, Henry VIII, 523.)

### From Court Rolls of the Hundred and Manor of Colyton, co. Devon†

18 January, 1 Mary [18 January 1553/4). In the court of the manor and "law" of the hundred of Colyton John Lecheland and Agnes, his wife, and Nicholas Lecheland were presented for default of suit. (Miscellaneous Books, Augmentation Office, 86.)

12 October, 1 and 2 Philip and Mary [12 October 1554]. "Law" court of the hundred and manor of Colyton. The jurors include John Lechelond. The jurors present that Thomas Lechelond acquired from John Lechelond of Colyton, co. Devon, merchant, all that messuage and tenement lying in Colyton and divers closes of land, meadow, and pasture lying within the manor of Colyton, to have and to hold to the said Thomas and the heirs of his body for ever, whereof relief happens, viz., 13s., as appears by deed thereof dated 24 January, 6 Edward VI [24 January 1552/3.]. Said Thomas is to do fealty. Walter Lechelond (John Spiller, pledge) and eighteen others, including John Spiller, are presented as common players at tables and other games against the form of the statute. (Ib., 85, fols. 10 and 12.)

19 April, 1 and 2 Philip and Mary [19 April 1555]. "Law" court of the hundred and manor of Colyton. The jurors include John Lecheland. The jurors present Richard Dassell, Nicholas Lechelond (present in court), Henry Hore, and Elizabeth Roggers, widow, for keeping a brothel. John Abbott brings a plea of debt against Walter Lechelond. (Ib., 85, fols. 29b and 30.)

### From Chancery Proceedings†

Sir Thomas Audley, Lord Chancellor [1533–1538].

Johane Lechelond of Colyton, co. Devon, widow and executrix of John Lechelond, late of Colyton, v. Robert Waddon and Johane, his wife.

The plaintiff shows that one William Holcombe, late of Lyme Regis, co. Dorset, merchant, deceased, in his lifetime was indebted to her late husband in the sum of £6. He died without having made payment, and appointed his wife Johane executrix of his will. She afterwards married Robert Waddon, and, although often asked to pay the debt, both she and her said husband refuse to do so. (Early Chancery Proceedings, F, 844/26.)

[The Leachland pedigree will be published in the Register of January 1928. — Editor.]

*Apparently he had accounted in the previous year also, for otherwise the previous accountant is usually named.

†Preserved in the Public Record Office, London.

The following records relate to the Jones family of Bridgwater, co. Somerset, to which Margaret Jones, wife of Roger Leachland of Chard, co. Somerset, and grandmother of Roger Derby of Salem, Mass., belonged.

## FROM PROBATE RECORDS

The Will of WILLIAM JONES of Bridgwater [co. Somerset], merchant, being sick of body, dated 20 March 1592 [1592/3]. To St. Andrew's Church, Wells, 5s. To the Bridgwater church 20s. To the Chilton church 12d. To the poor there 20s. To the Mayor, Aldermen, and Burgesses of Bridgwater £50, to the use of the poor, the profit to be used yearly, "being (I hope) £5 at the least," to be bestowed at Christmas and Easter. To the poor of Brodway 20s. To my wife Jane the use and occupation of my house in Bridgwater wherein I now dwell, during her widowhood only, with remainder immediately after her death to my right heirs, and £300. To my daughter Margarett £200 within four years of my death, my overseers immediately after the receipt of the same to employ it to her use until she shall be sixteen. To my daughter Margaret a tenement in Chilton, late John Pymmes, for life, if my term of years so long endure, with remainder to my daughter Alice. To my daughter Alice £300 within four years after my death, my overseers employing the same immediately after its receipt to her use till sixteen. To my daughter Alice the term of years in a tenement near Crophill, late of Robert Stevens, for her life, with remainder to my daughter Jane for life and contingent remainder to my daughter Margaret for life. To my daughter Jane £200 within six years after my death, my overseers to employ the same immediately after its receipt till she shall be sixteen. To my daughter Jane the term of years in 9 acres of ground called Pickle Meare, in Bridgewater, late in the tenure of Robert Chute, for life, with remainder to my other two daughters, one after the other successively, first to Margaret, then to Alice, for life. If all or any of my daughters die under the age of sixteen, their portion is to remain to my son Robert, if he be then living, otherwise to be divided equally among my daughters surviving. To "every my Brothers and sisters Children" 40s. apiece. To Ralphe Masters, my servant, Martha Sheppard, my servant, and Eleanor Vernon 40s. each. Residuary legatee and executor: my son Robert. If he die under the age of twenty, his portion is to go to my daughters then living equally. If any of my daughters marry without my overseers' consent, she shall forfeit her portion. "My Brethren Alexander Jones, Henry Jones & John Michell to be the overseers" and to have the custody of my children's portions until my daughters be sixteen and my said son twenty, and to have the keeping, rule, and government of my children, taking care that they be well and virtuously brought up. To my brother Alexander my great horse. To my brother Henry my scarlet gown. To the said John Michell £5. My said wife, upon reasonable assurance, is to have meet and convenient household stuff and furniture to be used by her in the house aforesaid during her widowhood and then redelivered to my overseers for my executor. I have caused this will to be indented and have subscribed the same and sealed the same with my seal. [Signed] William Jones. Witnesses: Alexander Jones, Tho: Leyson, Nicholas Strete, Tho: Harte, John Chick, Robert Barrell, John Michell, Henry Jones.

A commission was issued 28 July 1593 to Alexander and Henry Jones, brothers of the testator and overseers named in the will, during the minority of the executor.

Proved 1 May 1607 by Robert Jones, the son and executor, the former commission having expired upon the majority of the said Robert. (P. C. C., Nevill, 56.)

The Will of ALEXANDER JONES of Bridgewater, co. Somerset, merchant, being sick of body, dated 6 April 1608. To [name omitted*] a "messuage tenement seller a Roome underneath the same with divers things belonging" within the city of Bristol, occupied by George Holland. To "my nephew Alexander Jones one other of the sonnes of the sayd Henry Jones" the term of years in a house, curtilage, and garden in Bridgewater, called the "Crown," and the household stuff and implements there, in the occupation of one Richard Newman, from the end of two years after my death. To Abel Harris and Anne, his wife, the term of years in another house and stable in Bridgewater. To John Beard and Alice, his wife, a house and garden in Frieren Street, Bridgwater, in the occupation (leasehold) of Robert Bowring. To John White, the tanner, and his wife the term of years in a house and court in Eastover Street, Bridgewater, next the house of Robert Barrett. To Thomas Harte's children, which are named in the lease thereof, a stable and garden in Eastover. To my wife Margaret 10 acres of ground in Bridgewater, late in the tenure of William Thomas, deceased, parcel of the inheritance of the Mayor and Commonalty of the City of Bristol for the remainder of a term of years, for her life, with remainder to my said nephew Alexander Jones. "Unto William Kirtons fower Children which he hath begotten on the body of Mary my kinswoman" £10 each at the age of twelve years. The said William Kirton is to be released from a debt of £40. To Margaret Marchant, daughter of one William Marchant, deceased, £40 within four years. To three of Raphe Deamont's children, viz., Alice, Robert, and Eleanor, £10 each within three years. To all of Thomas Harte's children unmarried (his daughter Elizabeth only excepted) £10 each at the age of sixteen. To my mother, Alice Jones, 40s. a year for life, payable quarterly. To John Davie 20s. To John Long, the glover, 20s. To the Widow Rooke 20s. To Alice Copner 20s. To Tristram Hunt 20s. To Thomas Chilcott 20s. To John Fudge, the shoemaker, 20s. To Robert Chicke 40s. To William Dowdney 20s. To Richard Yeo, the pavier, 20s. To Richard Blake, the shoemaker, 20s. To Richard Swaish *alias* Hewes 20s. To Walter Pilcorne 20s. within a year. Dominick Fisher is to be forgiven a bond for 40s. John Pierce is to be forgiven a bond for 40s. To Robert Evans and his wife £10 within a year, if the wife so long live. To Abel Harris and Anne, his wife, £40. Whereas my nephew Robert Jones, son of William Jones, my brother, deceased, is to pay me £100 within a certain time after my decease, in respect of certain lands in Hunspill which I have assured unto him for divers years yet to come, I give the £100 to the Mayor, Aldermen, and Burgesses of Bridgewater, to use for reasonable gain and the gain to be distributed by their discretion among such poor people as shall be placed in three almshouses which I have builded without the Southgate of the said borough, under one roof. The said almshouses are to be repaired with part of the profit of the £100, and the almshouse is to be under the direction of the Mayor, Aldermen, and Burgesses for the habitation of such poor as they shall place therein. To my wife Margaret 600 bushels of salt now lying in the cellar of William Parsons in Bridgewater, all my beasts, goods, plate, household stuff, and debts, and also the adventure of £600 odd which I have before this time sent into the Straights, in a ship called the eagle of Northam, master John Shereman, in which John Wipple and Henry Jones are factors. The rest of my goods are to be disposed of as expressed in a schedule [not registered]. Executrix: my wife Margaret. Overseers: John Michell, Mayor, Henry Jones, my brother,

*The name of this legatee was omitted by the clerk in registering the will. The legatee was obviously one of the sons of Henry Jones and a nephew of the testator.

and Nicholas Streete, eldest son of Nicholas Streete, Town Clerk of Bridge-water; and to each I give £5. [Signed] Alexander Jones. Witnesses: Nicholas Streete, junior, George Gray, [the mark of] John Otway, Abell Harris. Proved 20 June 1609 by Margaret Jones, the executrix named in the will. (P. C. C., Dorset, 67.)

The Will of HENRY JONES of Bridgewater, co. Somerset, gentleman, dated 1 March 1609 [1609/10]. To be buried in Bridgewater churchyard, adjoin-ing my wife. To my daughter Tacye Jones £100, her mother's apparel, a chest with linen, a bed, and so forth. To my daughter Margaret £100, my barn at North Gate, Bridgewater, and a bed. To my daughter Deanes £100 and a bed. To my youngest daughter, Alice Jones, £100 and a bed. All [these bequests] are to be paid at their [the daughters'] ages of sixteen. To my son Henry a house adjoining mine, for life, with remainder to my son William. To my son Alexander £20. To my son William the rent due from my two houses in which Mr. Clowler and Robert Dudding dwell, the house the latter dwells in, and £10. To my son Robert my houses and land without the west gate, Bridgewater, being four houses, and £40. To my mother, Alice Jones, 10s. To William Spencer, senr., 40s. To my god-daughter Eleanor Spencer 10s. To Widow Colridge 20s. To the poor of Bridgewater £5. Overseers: Thomas Warre, Esq., and George Bond of Bridgewater, gentleman. Residuary legatee and executor: my eldest son, Mark Jones. [Signed] Henry Jones. Witnesses: George Graye, William Spencer the Elder.
Codicil, dated 13 March 1609 [1609/10], directs that John Stradling and Toby Venner, gentlemen, be "joined Overseers." Witnesses: William Spencer, senr., Richard Barrell, Alexr. Neale.
Codicil, dated 17 March 1609 [1609/10]: I have in my hands £200 of Jane Jones, daughter of my brother William Jones, deceased, and the same is to be paid her. [Signed] Henry Jones. Witnesses: John Stradling, George Bond, Thobye Venner, Thomas Bragg, Richard Barrell.
Codicil, dated 19 March 1609 [1609/10], provides further legacies to sons already named. To my kinswoman Alice Bearde my garden lying in North Lane, Bridgewater. [Signed] Henry Jones. Witnesses: Robert Oliver, William Spencer, George Graye, William Pyne, Edmond Dawes [his mark].
A commission was issued 3 December 1610 to Henry Jones, son of the deceased, one of the executors named in the will of Mark Jones, deceased, the executor named in the will of the said testator, who died without taking the executorship upon him, to administer the goods, etc., of the said Henry, with power reserved to Rowland Jones, the other executor named in Mark's will. (P. C. C., Wingfield, 100.)

The Will of MARGARETT JONES of Bridgwater, widow, being sick of body, dated 19 January 1615 [1615/16]. To St. Andrew's Church, Wells, 2s. 6d. To the Bridgewater church 20s. To John White the Elder, merchant, for his relief for life, £8 a year, and after his death to the four children of John White the Younger, my kinsman, of Bridgewater, tanner, for their relief and bringing up until they be twenty-one, and, if they all die under twenty-one, to John White aforesaid and Margaret, his wife, their father and mother. The sum of £100 is to be put into the hands of the Mayor, Alder-men, and Burgesses of Bridgewater to pay the above legacy. To Judith White, one of the daughters of the said John White the Younger, £25 at twenty-one, if John White the Elder be not then living; otherwise, within a month of his decease. To Edward White, son of John White the Younger, £25 at twenty-one, on similar conditions. To Margaret White, second daughter of John White the Younger, £25 at twenty-one, on similar condi-tions, and the same sum, on similar conditions, to Elizabeth White, youngest daughter of John White the Younger. To the Mayor and Aldermen and Bailiffs of Bridgwater 40s., out of the use of the £100 in their hands, for their pains in respect to this will, viz., 10s. to the Mayor, 10s. each to the two Aldermen, and 5s. each to the two Bailiffs. To the Mayor, Aldermen, and Common Council of Bridgwater my great silver salt, appraised at £9. 11s. 9d. in the inventory, to be used by the Mayor during his year of office. George Turner and Joan, his wife, are to be put in the next almshouse vacant outside Southgate and are to have £10 and the bed they now lie on. To Alice Cottner, £5. The bond of Mr. William Kyrton of £10 [I give] to Margaret Marchant, his daughter-in-law, and also £10. To William Harte £10. To Thomas White, my man, a flock bed and 40s. To Thomas Chilcott, Michael Glasse, tucker, John Longe, glover, Richard Blake, shoemaker, Richard Gilbert, the widow of Robert Chick, deceased, James Herringe, Robert Ball, William James, Robert Bell, Isaac Gennyngs, Matthew Burd, Katherine Satterford, Robert Mancell, Elizabeth Dowdney, widow, the Widow Peverell, Joan Pilcorne, Eleanor Pike *alias* Olyver, Florence Shute, and Ann Currie 20s. each. To John Pearce, William Fenner, Symon Chilcott, and Alice Portingall 40s. each. To Dominick Fisher and Richard Batten 20s. each. To John White the Elder, merchant, the bed he lieth upon, two pairs of sheets, one pair of blankets, a coverlet, a rug, etc., and £5. To the said John White the Younger, my kinsman, £10. To Nicholas Wastell, my kinsman, £10. To Margaret Evans, daughter of Robt. Evans, 40s. To my godson Raffe Demont the Younger £5. To my goddaughter Margaret Lesland the Younger 40s. To John Michell £5 and a gold ring with the "Turkey" stone. To his son George Michell £5. To Dorothy, wife of John Michell, apparel and a spectacle case. To William Sealy £5 and a gold ring with the lizard's head, and to Joan, his wife, a gold "Gynny" ring. To George Gray £5, two leather cushions painted, one embroidered cushion, and one red velvet cushion. To the preacher of this town for the time being and the vicar, 13s. 4d. to him that preacheth at my funeral, and 6s. 8d. to the other. To the three clerks of the Bridgwater church 20s. To the Westgate almspeople 20s. To the Southgate almspeople 20s. To the poor of Bridgwater £5. To Joyce Chilcott 40s. To Sara Gray, wife of the said George, my saddle and the furniture of my horse. To Margaret White my working day's apparel, an old still, and a Lymbick. To Anne Demont, wife of Raffe Demont, my gown and "skamell" petticoat that I made last and my gold ring which I wear upon my finger. To Alice Cottner a featherbed, etc. To John White the Younger a featherbed, etc. Residuary legatee and executor: my loving friend Nicholas Box. Overseers: John Michell, George Gray, and William Sealy of Bridgwater. Witnesses: Thomas Bragge, notary public, Jacob Androes, Dominick Fisher, Thomas Sheppard. Proved 20 April 1616 by Nicholas Box, the executor named in the will. (P. C. C., Cope, 36.)

The Will of ROBERT JONES of Bridgewater, co. Somerset, gentleman, dated 3 May 1639. To the church of Bridgewater 10s. To the poor there £5. To Margaret, my wife, £20, besides her jointure, and three kine and one mare. To my eldest daughter, Elizabeth Jones, £500. To my daughter Margaret, £400. To my daughter Christabel £300. To my second son, Robert, ground called Poplands, in South Brent, for ninety-nine years, he paying to the lords of the same the yearly rent of 3s. 4d., and to him £200. To my son William all other my lands in South Brent. To my son Nathaniel all my estate called Malkeinge Orchard, in Bridgewater, and £100, he to surrender to his brother William the copyhold messuage called Deyhouse or Deyhouse Close, in Chirston, of the grant of Sir Arthur Cabell, Knight. To my son Hugh all the lands I bought of the Chamber of Bristol and lands called Thomas his grounds, leased of the said Chamber, and a copyhold messuage in Puriton. Residuary legatee and executor: my son William. Overseers: Edmund Wyndham of London, Esq., John Pyne of Curry Mallett, Esq., and George Pitts of Norton under Hamdon, gentleman. [Signed] Robte Jones. Witnesses: William Champion, Edward Carey, John Townsend. Proved 15 November 1639 by the executor named in the will.

A commission was issued 22 September 1660 to Nathaniel Jones, son of the deceased, to administer the goods, etc., left unadministered by William Jones, son and executor of the deceased, now also dead. (P. C. C., Harvey, 180.)

# GENEALOGICAL RESEARCH IN ENGLAND

Contributed by G. ANDREWS MORIARTY, JR., A.M., LL.B., of Newport, R. I.,
and communicated by the Committee on English Research

## JONES (CONCLUDED)

### FROM THE PARISH REGISTERS OF BRIDGWATER, CO. SOMERSET†

*Baptisms*

1558 Thomas Jones 17 November.
1559 Christopher Jones *als*. Bedoe 19 January [1559/60].
1560 Robert Bishoppe 7 June.
1563 John Derbye 26 October.
1567 Mathew Symo 7 December.
1568 John Neale 1 August.
1568 Agnes Darby 7 November.
1569 Henry Jones 1 September.
1569 Thomas Symons 7 October.
1570 Joan Neale 10 November.
1571 Agnes Jones 25 February [1571/2].
1573 William Neale 4 December.
1574 Anne Jones 4 June.
1576 Agnes Jones 1 March [1576/7].
1577 Robert Symons 31 March.
1580 Elizabeth Symons 13 September.
1582 Frauncis Symons 6 March [1582/3].
1585 John Jones 15 July.
1585 Robert Jones 1 August.
1585 Robert Jones 20 February [1585/6].
1586 Samuell Jones 16 October.
1586 Margery Jones 13 January [1586/7].
1586 William Godbeare 30 January [1586/7].
1588 Richard Bedowe 2 October.
1589 Alice Jones 9 August.
1589 Markes Jones 23 November.
1590 Margaret Jones 12 November.
1591 Jane Jones 20 February [1591/2].
1591 Elizabeth Beadowe 24 February [1591/2].
1592 William Godbeare and Hercules Godbeare 17 October.
1592 Alexander Jones 21 January [1592/3].
1593 John Jones *als*. Beadow 3 December.
1594 William Jones 15 July.
1595 Tacy Jones 7 July.
1596 Samuell Jones *als*. Bedowe 20 April.
1596 Robert Jones 11 July.
1597 William Jones 9 October.
1598 Alexander Jones *als*. Beadowe 26 March.
1598 William Symons 20 November.
1599 Margaret Jones 12 June.

†These registers begin in 1558. The records of baptisms have been examined to 6 Mar. 1630/1, those of marriages to 1631/2, and those of burials to 10 Mar. 1630/1. Entries relating to persons of other surnames who may have been connected with the Derby family and allied families are also given.

1599   Mary Jones *als*. Bedowe 4 September.
1600   Deanes Jones 12 October.
1601   Agnes Symons 28 March.
1601   Joan Jones *als*. Beadoe 3 April.
1601   Alice Jones 21 February [1601/2].
1601   Amy Jones 19 March [1601/2].
1602   Tacy Jones *als*. Beedowe 21 November.
1603   John Symondes 6 July.
1604   Elizabeth daughter of John Jones *als*. Beddoe 6 January [1604/5].
1605   Erasmus son of Humfrey Simmons and Joane his wife 15 March [1605/6].
1606   John son of John Beddow and Christian his wife 1 March [1606/7].
1607   Thomas son of Morgan Jones and Agnes 28 February [1607/8].
1609   Anstice daughter of Morgan Jones and Agnes 22 February [1609/10].
1609   Jane daughter of Rouland Jones and Judith his wife 21 March [1609/10].
1611   Edward son of Henry Jones and Elizabeth 2 October.
1612   Simon Courte eldest son of Edward Courte, gent., and Katherine his wife 23 April.
1612   Rouland son of Rouland and Judith Jones 2 August.
1613   John son of John Courte, gent., and Joan 9 October.
1613   Amia Jones daughter of Henry and Elizabeth 24 October.
1615   Joan daughter of Morgan and Katherine Jones 17 September.
1615   Joan Jones daughter of Henry and Elizabeth 8 March [1615/16].
1617   William Jones son of Morgan and Kat. his wife 11 September.
1617   Hugo Jones son of Robert and Margaret 21 January [1617/18].
1618   Henry Jones son of Henry and Elizabeth 1 December.
1620   Thomas Jones son of Morgan and Kat. 23 July.
1621   Tace Jones son of Henry and Elizabeth 4 June.
1621   Elenora daughter of Morgan Jones and Katherine 5 July.
1621   Walter Jones son of Walter and Matilda 18 August.
1624   Margery daughter of Walter and Matilda Jones 18 May.
1624   Christabella Jones daughter of Robert and Margaret 14 November.
1625   Rich[ar]d son of William Godbeare and Mary 10 June.*
1625   William Jones son of Richard and Agneta 4 September.
1625   Mary daughter of Rich[ar]d Jones and Elenore his wife 12 February [1625/6].
1627   Thomas Jones son of Richard and Elenora 20 May.
1627   Thomas Jones son of Richard and Anna 30 December.
1627   Taceu [*sic*,? Tacy] Jones "fil." Henry and Elizabeth — March.
1628   Martha Jones daughter of Walter and Matilda 8 April.
1629   Francisca daughter of Rich[ar]d Jones and Elenora 8 April.
1630   Richard Jones son of Richard and Agnes 6 March [1630/1].

### *Marriages*

1560   John Yrishe and Elizabeth Strong 11 October.
1560   David Jones and Joan Cowrt 31 January [1560/1].
1562   John Galynton and Joan Jones 2 August.
1564   Thomas Neale and Helen More 9 September.
1565   Thomas Galynton and Jacob [*sic*] Hivgered 23 October.
1567   Henry Jones and Agnes Mychell 26 May.
1567   Alexander Jones and Margaret Baker 28 February [1567/8].
1568   Lewes Jones and Elsabeth Yerishe 18 January [1568/9].
1570   John Symons and Margaret Loges 5 February [1570/1].
1575   David Jones and Agnes Davies 25 October.

*The baptisms of other children of William and Mary Godbeare are also recorded in these registers.

1577 Jeffrye Jones and Sibly Cocks 21 October.
1577 Thomas Mote and Sibly Cocks 21 October.
1584 Henry Jones and Joan Neale 15 September.
1585 William Jones and Jane Bishopp 1 June.
1585 Jelber [sic] Symons and Agnes Jones 11 January [1585/6].
1586 Gabriell Jones and Eleanor Dirron 30 [sic] February [1586/7].
1592 John Darby and Joan Donne 12 August.
1597 John Jones alias Bedowe and Christian Richardes 4 July.
1597 Humphry Symons and Joan Hucker 24 October.
1600 Henry Jones and Julyan Cordent 23 September.
1601 Morgan Jones and Agnes Stronge 8 June.
1604 Roger Leathland and Margaret Jones 11 February [1604/5].
1605 John Hodges and Susan Jones 7 August.
1609 Thomas Smyth and Julian Jones 16 October.
1610 Henry Jones and Elizabeth Baber 21 July.
1613 Henry Traylman and Margaret Jones 14 November.
1620 William Adams and Elizabeth Jones 30 April.
1621 William Godbeare and Maria Jones als. Bedowe 9 April.
1623 Philip Jones and Martha Williams 26 October.
1624 William Gilbert and Johanna Jones 8 June.
1624 Richard Jones and Anna Batten 27 November.
1624 Richard Jones and Elenora Stonnard 17 January [1624/5].
1626 Richard Oteway and Joanna Jones als. Beddowe 31 May.

*Burials*

1561 Agnes Yerishe 7 August.
1561 Richard Jones 19 February [1561/2].
1561 Marget Jones 20 February [1561/2].
1565 Helen Jone 23 October.
1565 Alice Yerishe 6 November.
1565 John Yerishe 10 November.
1568 John Darbye 18 July.
1569 Alexander Jones 15 February [1569/70].
1571 John Neale 29 March.
1571 Elizabeth Symons 30 September.
1572 Catherine Derby 18 May.
1573 Joan Baker 6 December.
1574 Thomas ffemale* 11 October.
1575 Barnabe ffannell* 24 August.
1576 Agnes Jones 2 May.
1577 Robert Symons 22 April.
1578 Thomas Bishopp 1 January [1578/9].
1579 Margaret Bishop 29 April.
1579 John Iriske 9 June.
1579 Xper Jones drowned 21 February [1579/80].
1582 Florence ffemall* 17 July.
1582 Margaret Jones 5 December.
1582 Fraunces Symons 7 March [1582/3].
1583 Elizabeth Symons 15 April.
1584 Thomas Neale 29 May.
1584 Julian Bishopp 6 June.
1584 Alice Jones 26 August.
1585 David Jones 10 April.
1585 Robert Jones 5 August.
1585 Elizabeth Bishopp 30 August.

*This surname is perhaps a form of *Femell*. Cf. records and pedigrees relating to "Symonds-Femell," in REGISTER, vol. 80, pp. 343-369 (October 1926). **

**Pages 158-185, this volume.

1587   Gabriel Jones 31 March.
1588   John Jones 30 June.
1588   Richard Bedoe 6 October.
1588   Joan Bishoppe 5 November.
1588   Samuell Jones 22 November.
1590   Joan Jones ba: 23 August.
1590   Catheryne Symons 23 December.
1591   Joan Jones 23 October.
1593   John Darby 5 April.
1593   William Jones 30 July.
1596   Mary Beadowe *als.* Jones 7 December.
1597   George Neale 4 June.
1597   Philip Jones 19 June.
1599   Alexander Jones *als.* Bedoe 10 October.
1601   Robert Baker of Bridgwater 15 August.
1601   Robert Baker of Hargrove 30 August.
1602   Agnes Symondes 2 May.
1603   Jeremy Baker 7 March.
1605   Benjamin Baker 25 April.
1605   John Jones *als.* Beddow 18 October.
1607   Joan Jones 20 June.
1608   Henry Jones 8 November.
1608   Geffery Jones *als.* [*illegible**] 9 November.
1608   John Jones *als.* [*illegible**] 19 February [1608/9].
1609   Alexander Jones, Mayor, 11 April.
1609   William Neale of Mary-Stoke 24 October.
1609   Joan Symons 4 March [1609/10].
1610   Henry Jones 3 April.
1612   Joannes Jones 24 May.
1613   Humphry Simons 25 August.
1615   Margaret Jones 6 February [1615/16].
1616   Agnes Michell 28 January [1616/17].
1616   John Michell 24 March [1616/17].
1617   Joan Jones 10 October.
1617   William Simmons 26 October.
1619   Edward Coort, gent., 7 August.
1620   Christiana Jones *als.* Beddow, wid., 28 December.
1623   Alexander Jones 4 June.
1623   Simon Court 1 August.
1624   Rich[ar]d Symons 22 March [1624/5].
1625   Maria Jones 8 March [1625/6].
1627   Walter Jones 20 March.
1627   Thomas Jones 6 February [1627/8].

*Churchwardens*

1601   John Jones *als.* Beddow.
1628   William Godbeare.

FROM RECORDS OF THE BOROUGH OF BRIDGWATER, CO. SOMERSET†

1597   Alexander Jones Member of Parliament for Bridgwater.

1588 ⎤
1592 ⎬ Alexander Jones Mayor of Bridgwater.‡
1608 ⎦

*The edge of the page has been cut off.
†Printed.
‡He died in office, and was buried 11 Apr. 1609. *Vide supra.*

1592 William Jones Mayor of Bridgwater.
1594 }
1602 } Henry Jones Mayor of Bridgwater.
1607 John Mitchell Mayor of Bridgwater.

FROM DEEDS OF THE CORPORATION OF BRIDGWATER, CO. SOMERSET

16 December, 15 Henry VIII [1523]. Thomas Jones a witness to a livery of seisin. (Nos. 288, 858.)

5 July, 22 Henry VIII [1530]. Bond of Jn Davy, tailor, and Ralph Benett, merchant, to the mayor for £10, as bail for Robert Jones, that he will keep the peace. (No. 1049.)

22 October, 25 Henry VIII [1533]. Acquittance from Charles Bulkeley to Rd. Gapper and Thomas Jonys, bailiffs of Bridgwater, for the sum of £10 due at Michaelmas, 24 Henry VIII [1532]. (No. 2034.)

32 Henry VIII [1540–41]. Thomas Jonys and Jamys Baysse mentioned as bailiffs in a book containing accounts of John Parc, water bailiff. (No. 1441.)

30 July 1545. Maurice Jones a witness to a livery of seisin. (No. 919.)

9 April, 37 Henry VIII [1546]. John Bentley, shoemaker, grants to Thomas Jones, John Page, Thomas Holcombe, John Long, Thomas Hale, and Will Bryan his tenement in Bridgwater. (No. 645.)

1548. In the churchwardens' accounts Thomas Jonis is mentioned as bailiff, and an entry reads: To Thomas Jonis for mending the great bell clypper, 2s. (No. 1447.)

1548. In the water bailiff's accounts Thomas Jones and Jeffre Shercum are mentioned as bailiffs. (No. 1447.)

1549. In the water bailiff's accounts Thomas Jonys and Jeffery [also Geoffrey] Shyrcum are mentioned as bailiffs. (No. 1446.)

1 September, 2 Edward VI [1548]. Thomas Jonys appears as a witness. (No. 612.)

25 September 1551. Richard Jones is mentioned as attorney. (No. 500.)

5 Edward VI [1550/1–1551/2]. In a book containing water bailiffs' accounts is found "the account of Rycherde Jonse, water bailiff of Bridgwater made 5 Edw. 6." (No. 1456.)

1 February 1552 [1552/3]. The will of John Colford bequeaths all the testator's other land and tenements to Margaret, his wife, for life, and after her death to James Boyes, Thomas Holcombe, Xper Hoskins, and Rychard Jones, to sell for the profit of the town. (No. 1201.)

Michaelmas, 1 Mary [1553]. Copy of a final concord in the Court of Common Pleas at Westminster, whereby Robert Mullyns and Rd. Gybbes recover against John Legge, Joan, his wife, James Boyes, Thos. Holcombe, Xper Hoskyns, and Rd. Jones messuages, cottages, burgages, etc., in Bridgwater, Wemdon, North Petherton, and Chilton, co. Somerset, and said Robert and Rd. grant to said John and Joan an annuity of 26s. 8d. out of the premises, and also grant the premises to said James, Thos., Xper, and Rd., with settlement on the heirs of said James. (No. 1483.)

12 July, 2 Mary [1554]. Richd. Jones appears as a trustee in the conveyance of John Colvord's land to the mayor and bailiffs. (No. 691.)

20 July, 2 Mary [1554]. A grant by Hugh Hamonde, son and heir of John Hamonde, merchant, deceased, to James Boyesse, John Page, John Chappell, Geoffrey Shyrcombe, Richd. Gybbes, Wm. Goolde, Rd. Castleman, Robert Byshoppe, John Hamonde, Rd. Hyott, Francis Fromond, and Richard Jones of a messuage or burgage in the town of Bridgwater, on the north side of High Street, formerly granted by Giles Dobyll, gent., 20 August, 29 Henry VIII [1537], to John Hamonde,

father of the grantor, and John Walshe *als.* Oder. [*Endorsed*] A feoffment of the Church house. (No. 1360.)

1557. An account of money, weapons, and harness taxed on the inhabitants of Bridgwater. Under the heading "names of brothers of councel" is found: Richard Jones, 3s. 4d., ¼ harness, bow, sheaf of arrows. (No. 124.)

1560. A thin book is entitled: "1560, The accompte book of Richerde Jones, recever of all the lands perteyninge to the Town, etc." (No. 1536.)

1560. A book is entitled: "the accompte book of Rycherd Jones, recever for myllstones and grynynge stones 1560." (No. 1537.)

1560. Account of Barnard Radbart, Rychard Jones, and Edmond Clowther, receivers, 1560. (No. 1902.)

1587. Water bailiff's accounts audited and signed by Alexander Jones, mayor. (No. 1579.)

1591. The water bailiff's accounts include accounts of Robert Buckin, W. Jones, Alexr. Jones, Henry Jones, and John Stradling. (No. 1478.)

20 November 1592. Receivers' accounts audited and signed by Wyllyam Jones, mayor. (No. 1580.)

26 March, 35 Elizabeth [1593]. An indenture of apprenticeship of John Jones of Bridgwater, æt. 12, to Thomas Bond, goldsmith, and Agnes, his wife, for a term of eight years. (No. 854.)

6 December 1594. Receivers' accounts, audited and signed by Henry Jones, mayor. (No. 1582.)

1597–98. Mr. Alexander Jones, mayor. (No. 1482.)

December, 41 Elizabeth [1598]. Grant of two houses and a garden, sometime parcel of the inheritance of John Colford, by Richd. Aishe to John Michell, Hen. Jones, and others, merchants, and conveyance of the property by these feoffees to the mayor and aldermen. (Nos. 418–420.)

1598–99. Account of Alex Jones, Richd. Godbeard, and others, overseers, and of Geo. Grey and Thos. Rowland, collectors for the poor. (No. 2285.)

15 April, 41 Elizabeth [1599]. Accounts of the town of Bridgwater entitled: "Payments towards relefe of the poore to begin at Christmas 1598," audited and signed by Alex. Jones, mayor. (No. 2083.)

1599. Acquittances by Alexander Jones, mayor of Bridgwater, for £40 his fee for the mayoralty to 5d. received. (No. 2122.)

42 Elizabeth [1599–1600]. Will. Culverwell, æt. 5, apprenticed to Agnes Symons of Bridgwater, wid., "in domestic science." (No. 1036.)

23 June, 42 Elizabeth [1600.] Alexander Jones, alderman and justice of the peace. (No. 1032.)

6 August, 42 Elizabeth [1600]. Robert Chute of Bridgwater, gent., and Henni Jones of Bridgwater, merchant, lease of barn and land for ninety-nine years or for the lives of Robert Tacye and others. (No. 1302.)

2 September 1600. Alexander Jones, alderman and justice of the peace. (No. 73.)

12 October, 43 Elizabeth [1601]. Signatures of Alex. and Henry Jones, "marchants." (No. 489.)

2 August 1602. Alex. Jones, justice of the peace and alderman. (No. 1033.)

1602. Water bailiff's account, audited and signed by Henry Jones, mayor. (No. 1485.)

23 July, 2 James I [1604]. Indented deed of surrender by Alexander Jones of Bridgwater, merchant, to the mayor, aldermen, and bailiffs of the borough of Bridgwater, of all the rectory and parsonage of Bridgwater,

with tithes, etc., and his term of years unexpired therein, for the remainder of the term. (No. 2189.)

1605. Water bailiff's accounts, audited and signed by Alexander Jones. (No. 1489.)

29 September 1607. Deed of surrender and resignation by Alexander Jones of the borough of Bridgwater, merchant, of the office of alderman and the aldermanship within the borough. (No. 1937.)

Michaelmas, 6 James I [1608]. Conveyance by fine and counterpart from Robert Chute, gent., and Anne, his wife, to Alex Jones, Humphry Blake, and Nich. Strete, Jr., of twenty-three messuages, twenty-three gardens, etc., in Bridgwater. (Nos. 2253, 2254.)

26 September, 8 James I [1610]. Lease from the mayor, etc., to John Leakye, draper, for ninety-nine years, of a one-half burgage of land without West Gate, in North Street, sometime in the occupation of William Jones, deceased, and now in the tenure of the mayor, etc. Rent, 12d. Warranty against Robert Jones, son of William Jones, deceased. [*Memorandum, pinned to the lease*:] "late in tenure of Robert son of William Jones deceased." (No. 1313.)

1616. Account of £100 given by Mr. Alex. Jones, deceased, to the corporation for maintaining the poor, repairs of almshouses at South-gate, etc. (No. 1724.)

6 June, 2 Charles I [1626]. Acquittance from Edw. White, son of John White of Bridgwater, tanner, to the mayor, aldermen, and bailiffs of the Borough of Bridgwater, for £25 bequeathed to him by the late Margaret Jones of Bridgwater, widow. (No. 1729.)

[*Undated.*] Lease by the mayor and bailiffs to Thos. Yeudall, Agnes, his wife, and Abraham, his son, for a fine of 20s., of a garden in Fryeren Street, between land of the Queen on the north of [*sic*, ? and] lands of John Popham, Esq., Solicitor General to Her Majesty our Sovereign, which was in the tenure of Jefferye Joanes *als.* Beddowe. (No. 1254.)

## From the Somerset Muster Roll, 1569

Bridgwater.   Alexander Jones, one paire of almain rivets, one harquebut. William Jones, one harquebut.

## From Lay Subsidies for co. Somerset*

34 and 35 Henry VIII [1542–1544], first payment of subsidy.
Borough of Bridgwater.  Thomas Jones in goods, [valuation] £20, [tax] 13s. 4d.

Maurice Jones in goods, [valuation] 20s., [tax] 2d.

William Jones in goods, [valuation] 20s., [tax] 2d.

William Jones in goods, [valuation] 20s., [tax] 2d.

William Jones in goods, [valuation] 40s., [tax] 4d.

William Jones in goods, [valuation] 20s., [tax] 2d.

[*Endorsed*] The commissioners delivered up this certificate 28 November, 35 Henry VIII [1543]. (170/203.)

8 March, 36 Henry VIII [1544/45], Names of People paying Benevolence.
Borough of Bridgwater. Thomas Jones, 30s. (170/213.)

38 Henry VIII [1546],† Names of People paying Benevolence.
Borough of Bridgwater. Thomas Jones, 12s. 6d. (170/230.)

*Preserved in the Public Record Office, London.
†This date, 38 Henry VIII, is given in the calendar of Lay Subsidies.

222

From the foregoing records — chiefly from the probate records and the parish registers — the following Jones pedigree has been compiled. Many other persons of this surname appear in the Bridgwater records, but their relationship to the family of this pedigree has not been discovered.

William Jones, Henry Jones, and Alexander Jones, all of Bridgwater, co. Somerset, were living in the last half of the sixteenth century, and were *perhaps* brothers. William Jones (No. 1 of this pedigree) and some of his descendants are given below. Henry Jones married at Bridgwater, 26 May 1567, Agnes Mychell, and was buried at Bridgwater 8 Nov. 1608. Alexander Jones married at Bridgwater, 28 Feb. 1567/8, Margaret Baker, and was buried at Bridgwater 15 Feb. 1569/70. The Henry Jones who was baptized at Bridgwater 1 Sept. 1569 was probably their son.

1. WILLIAM JONES, of Bridgwater, co. Somerset, is perhaps the William Jones of the muster roll of 1569. He married ALICE ———, who was living 1 Mar. 1609/10, when her son Henry made his will.
Children:

    2. i.  HENRY.
       ii.  ALEXANDER, of Bridgwater, merchant, the testator of 6 Apr. 1608, d. *s.p.*; bur. at Bridgwater 11 Apr. 1609; m. MARGARET ———, the testatrix of 19 Jan. 1615/16, who was bur. at Bridgwater 6 Feb. 1615/16. Her will deserves careful study. Alexander Jones was a member of Parliament for Bridgwater in 1597 and mayor of Bridgwater in 1588, 1592, and 1608. He died while holding the office of mayor.
    3. iii.  WILLIAM.
       iv.  DOROTHY (perhaps daughter of William), m. JOHN MICHELL, mayor of Bridgwater.

2. HENRY JONES (William), of Bridgwater, co. Somerset, gentleman, the testator of 1 Mar. 1609/10, was buried at Bridgwater 3 Apr. 1610. He married at Bridgwater, 15 Sept. 1584, JOAN NEALE, who died before her husband, probably the Joan Neale who was baptized at Bridgwater 10 November 1570 and probably the Joan Jones who was buried at Bridgwater 20 June 1607.

He was mayor of Bridgwater in 1594 and 1602.
Children (recorded at Bridgwater):

    i.  ROBERT, bapt. 1 Aug. 1585; bur. 5 Aug. 1585.
    ii.  MARK, bapt. 23 Nov. 1589; d. in 1610, before 3 Dec.
    iii.  HENRY, m. at Bridgwater, 21 July 1610, ELIZABETH BABER.
         Children (recorded at Bridgwater):
          1.  *Edward*, bapt. 2 Oct. 1611.
          2.  *Amia*, bapt. 24 Oct. 1613.
          3.  *Joan*, bapt. 8 Mar. 1615/16.
          4.  *Henry*, bapt. 1 Dec. 1618.
          5.  *Tacy*, bapt. 4 June 1621; probably d. young.
          6.  *Tacy*, bapt. in Mar. 1627.
    iv.  ALEXANDER, bapt. 21 Jan. 1592/3; bur. 4 June 1623.
    v.  WILLIAM, bapt. 15 July 1594; probably d. young.
    vi.  TACY (daughter), bapt. 7 July 1595; living unm. 1 Mar. 1609/10.
    vii.  ROBERT, of Bridgwater, gentleman, the testator of 3 May 1639, bapt. 11 July 1596; d. between 3 May 1639 and 15 Nov. 1639; m. MARGARET ———, who was living 3 May 1639.

Children (all named in their father's will, but order of births somewhat uncertain):

1. *William*, living 3 May 1639; d. before 22 Sept. 1660. He was executor of his father's will.
2. *Robert*, second son, living 3 May 1639.
3. *Nathaniel*, living 22 Sept. 1660.
4. *Hugh*, bapt. at Bridgwater 21 Jan. 1617/18; living 3 May 1639.
5. *Elizabeth*, eldest daughter, living unm. 3 May 1639.
6. *Margaret*, living 3 May 1639.
7. *Christabel*, bapt. at Bridgwater 14 Nov. 1624; living 3 May 1639.

viii. WILLIAM, bapt. 9 Oct. 1597; living 19 Mar. 1609/10.
ix. MARGARET, bapt. 12 June 1599; living 1 Mar. 1609/10.
x. DEANES (daughter), bapt. 12 Oct. 1600; living 1 Mar. 1609/10.
xi. ALICE, bapt. 21 Feb. 1601/2; living 1 Mar. 1609/10.

3. WILLIAM JONES (*William*), of Bridgwater, co. Somerset, merchant, the testator of 20 Mar. 1592/3, was buried at Bridgwater 30 July 1593. He married at Bridgwater, 1 June 1585, JANE BISHOPP, who was living 20 Mar. 1592/3.

He was mayor of Bridgwater in 1592.

Children (baptized at Bridgwater):

i. ROBERT, bapt. 20 Feb. 1585/6; living 6 Apr. 1608, when his uncle, Alexander Jones, made his will.
ii. ALICE, bapt. 9 Aug. 1589; living 20 Mar. 1592/3.
iii. MARGARET, bapt. 12 Nov. 1590; d. 24 Oct. 1654 (REGISTER, vol. 79, p. 422); m. at Bridgwater, 11 Feb. 1604/5, ROGER LEACHLAND of Chard, co. Somerset, merchant, for whom see pedigree of Leachland, *infra*, p. 65.
iv. JANE, bapt. 20 Feb. 1591/2; living unm. 17 Mar. 1609/10.

LEACHLAND (CONCLUDED)

From the Leachland records given in the REGISTER, vol. 81, pp.** 320–323, 486–487, from the Lechland pedigree in "The Visitation of the County of Somerset in the Year 1623" (*Publications of the Harleian Society*, vol. 11, p. 67), and from other records mentioned below, the following pedigree of the earliest known generations of the Leachland or Lechland family of Colyton, co. Devon, and Taunton, co. Somerset, has been compiled.

1. JOHN LECHLAND* held land in Colyton Manor, co. Devon, in 1496–97 and in 1525, when he was bailiff of Colyton Hundred. He was taxed on £60 in the subsidy of 1524. He married, according to the Visitation of 1623, ISABEL -——, but the Chancery case given in REGISTER, vol. 81, p. 487, shows that his widow was named JOHANE.

Children:

2. i. JOHN.
ii. NICHOLAS (perhaps a son of No. 1), taxed on £10 in 1524.
iii. JOAN (perhaps a daughter of No. 1), bur. 28 Apr. 1582; m. JOHN WESTON of Colyton, who was bur. 10 June 1555.†

*According to the Visitation of Somersetshire, 1623, he was the son of -—— Lechland and his wife, who was a daughter of -—— St. Lowe of co. Devon.
†Cf. Vivian's Visitation of Devon, p. 780.

**For references to Vol. 81, pp. 320-323 & 486-487 see pp. 205-211, this volume.

Children (surname *Weston*):
1. *Walter.*
2. *Robert.*

2. JOHN LECHLAND (*John*) was of Colyton, co. Devon, in 1550. He married AGNES STARRE of Beare, co. Devon.
   Children:
   i. EDWARD, of London, lawyer.
   3. ii. THOMAS.
   iii. LAWRENCE, of Taunton, co. Somerset, m. at Taunton, 30 Sept. 1567, MARGARET (———) PERSE, widow, the testatrix of 30 Jan. 1621/2, who in her will calls herself of Fitzhead [co. Somerset] and who d. between 30 Jan. 1621/2 and 22 Aug. 1622. Lawrence Leachland was constable of Taunton in 1583 (Taunton Portreeves' Accounts).
       Children, bapt. at Taunton:
       1. *Annes*, bapt. 24 July 1568; m. John Dier; both were living 30 Jan. 1621/2.
       2. *Joan*, bapt. 10 Dec. 1570; living unm. 30 Jan. 1621/2.
       3. *Lawrence* (perhaps son of No. 2, iii), bapt. 9 Nov. 1571; bur. at Taunton 29 [*sic*] Feb. 1574/5.
   iv. ROBERT, who went to Spain and m. a Spanish woman.
   v. WILLIAM, of Westmounton, co. Somerset, yeoman, the testator of 12 Jan. 1615/16; bapt. at Colyton 27 Aug. 1551; d. between 12 Jan. 1615/16 and 21 Feb. 1615/16; m. ———, who was living 12 Jan. 1615/16.
       Children:
       1. *Anne*, m. ——— Harte. Five children living and under twenty-one 12 Jan. 1615/16.
       2. *Eleanor*, m. ——— Palfrey. Four children living and under twenty-one 12 Jan. 1615/16.
   vi. JOAN, bapt. at Colyton 21 Oct. 1553.
   vii. AMBROSE, bapt. at Colyton 7 Sept. 1555.
   viii. ALICE, bapt. at Colyton 4 Nov. 1559.
   ix. AGNES, bapt. at Colyton 24 Feb. 1561/2.

3. THOMAS LECHLAND (*John, John*), of Colyton, co. Devon, and Taunton, co. Somerset, was buried at Taunton, as "Mr." Thomas Lechland, 30 Nov. 1593. He married ALICE VINEY, who, as Alice Leachland, widow, was buried at Taunton 12 Feb. 1596/7, daughter of William Viney of Taunton (constable of Taunton in 1542, 1549, 1551, and 1554*).
   Thomas Lechland was deputy bailiff of Taunton in 1566 and constable of Taunton in 1572 and 1580.*
   Children:
   i. WILLIAM, of Taunton, gentleman, the testator of 4 Jan. 1637/8, d. *s.p.* between 4 Apr. 1639 and 20 May 1639; m. in 1582 FRANCES CORNISH, who d. 18 Mar. 1631, aged 76, daughter of Henry Cornish of Greenwich, Esq., captain of Jersey Castle and godson of King Henry VIII.† William Lechland was constable of Taunton in 1603, 1610, 1619, and 1627 (Taunton Portreeves' Accounts), and he was also mayor of Taunton. He entered the Lechland pedigree in the Visitation of Somersetshire in 1623, but no arms were recorded with it.
   ii. LUCY, bapt. at Taunton 28 July 1560,
   iii. ELEANOR, bapt. at Taunton 4 Jan. 1561/2,
   iv. ANNES, bur. at Taunton 13 Aug. 1564,
   v. JOHAN, bapt. at Taunton 20 May 1564,
   } perhaps children of No. 3.

---

*Taunton Portreeves' Accounts, in possession of H. Byard Sheppard of Taunton.
†See her mural tablet, REGISTER, vol. 81, p. 486.

vi. ANNES, bapt. at Taunton 2 Dec. 1565; m. before 2 Feb. 1595/6 THOMAS CALTON of London.

vii. ROBERT, bapt. at Taunton 25 Jan. 1566/7; d. *s.p.*

viii. THOMAS, of London and Taunton, merchant, the testator of 2 Feb. 1595/6, bapt. at Taunton 13 Oct. 1568; d. *s.p.*; bur. at Taunton 8 Feb. 1595/6.

4. ix. ROGER, bapt. at Taunton 25 Dec. 1570.

4. ROGER LEACHLAND (*Thomas, John, John*), of Chard, co. Somerset, merchant, the testator of 6 Feb. 1620/1, baptized at Taunton, co. Somerset, 25 Dec. 1570, died between 6 Feb. 1620/1 and 31 Oct. 1621. He married at Bridgwater, co. Somerset, 11 Feb. 1604/5, MARGARET JONES, who was baptized at Bridgwater 12 Nov. 1590 and died 24 Oct. 1654 (REGISTER, vol. 79, p. 422), daughter of William and Jane (Bishopp) Jones of Bridgwater (see pedigree of Jones *supra*, p. 63). As Margaret Leachland of Chard, co. Somerset, widow, she made her will (*q.v.*) 31 Aug. 1654.

Children:

i. WILLIAM, b. about 1608, since according to the Visitation pedigree he was aged 15 in 1623; probably d. before 31 Aug. 1654, since he is not mentioned in his mother's will.

ii. MARGARET, living 31 Aug. 1654; m. before that date ———— TURNER.

iii. JANE (or JOANE), living, a widow, 12 Feb. 1654/5 (REGISTER, vol. 79, p. 422); m. ———— THORNE.
    Children (surname *Thorne*), living 31 Aug. 1654:
    1. *Margaret.*
    2. *Joan.*

iv. THOMAS, of Chard, co. Somerset, merchant, b. about 1616, since according to the Visitation pedigree he was aged 7 in 1623; bur. at Topsham, co. Devon, 3 Sept. 1669; m. SARAH ————, who was bur. at Topsham 22 Mar. 1658/9. As executor, he proved his mother's will, 22 July 1655; and he was involved in litigation with his brother-in-law, Richard Derby, mercer, and his sister, Alice, wife of the latter, in 1653 and subsequent years. (*Cf.* REGISTER, vol. 79, pp. 415, 421–422, 447.) Thomas Leachland's son *Roger* was bapt. at Topsham 15 Mar. 1641/2 and was bur. there 22 Apr. 1642, and his daughter *Sara* was bapt. there 25 July 1643 (*ib.*, vol. 79, p. 415).

v. ALICE, b. before 6 Feb. 1620/1, when she was mentioned in her father's will; living 12 Feb. 1654/5 (REGISTER, vol. 79, p. 422); m. about 1642 RICHARD DERBY, gentleman, mercer, for whom see REGISTER, vol. 79, pp. 443–448. They were the parents of *Roger Derby*, the immigrant ancestor of the Derby family of Salem, Mass., and of two other children (*ib.*, vol. 79, pp. 448–449).

## DERBY (ADDITIONAL RECORDS)

THE Chairman of the Committee on English Research is indebted to his friend, Rev. R. Grosvenor Bartelot, F.S.A., of Fordington St. George, co. Dorset, the well-known antiquary, for the following additional records relating to the Derby family of Dorset, to which Roger Derby, the immigrant ancestor of the Derby family of Salem, Mass., belonged. These records supplement the records and pedigree given in the REGISTER, vol. 79, pp. 410–449, in an article con-* tributed by the Chairman of the Committee, in which the English ancestry and connections of the Salem settler were set forth.

*For references to Vol. 79, pp. 410-449 see pp. 93-132, this volume.

### Baptisms

1615   Mary Derby daughter of Laurence 10 August.*
1616   Thomas Derby son of Christopher of Sturtell 18 August.†
1617   Edith Derby daughter of Laurence 27 November.*
1635   Margaret Derby daughter of William 10 February [1635/6].‡
1637   Mary Derby daughter of William and Lucy 9 January [1637/8].‡
1639   John Derby son of William and Lucy 1 March [1639/40].‡

### Marriages

1620   Robert Beere and Johan Derby 3 November.
1627   Simon Pinson and Dorothy Derby 2 October.§

### Burials

1620   Jone daughter of Nicholas Derby 20 February [1620/1].||
1621   Laurence Derby 26 November.¶
1623   Christopher Derby son of Christopher 27 July.**
1633   Joan Derby 16 July.
1634   Mary Derby daughter of Christopher [?] ———.
1639   Christopher Derby, gentleman, of Sturthill 3 February [1639/40].††
1665   Luce Derby wife of William 10 March [1665/6].

From notes assembled by Rev. R. Grosvenor Bartelot it appears that William Derby of Dorchester, co. Dorset, gentleman, was aged 37 years on 20 March, 2 Charles I [1626/7]. He married at Beaminster, co. Dorset, 19 April 1615, Mary, daughter of Joseph Bradstock, and had issue: Joseph, aged 43 on 12 December 1663, Matthew of Dorchester, and Paul of Dorchester. Cf. Register, vol. 79, p. 437, second footnote.

## Mohun (Additions and Corrections)****

Sundry additions and corrections for the pedigree of Mohun (or Moone), which was published in the Register, vol. 81, pp. 314–318, are here presented, and are followed by some additional records pertaining to this family.

Richard Mohun *alias* Moone (No. 1 of the pedigree) was born about 1485 and died about 1547 (*not* about 1570, as stated in the pedigree). He married Joan (———) Howman, a widow (cf. Court Rolls of the Manor of Axminster, 21 July 1528, *infra*).
A large parchment pedigree of the Mohuns of Fleet, co. Dorset, was compiled in 1606 by the Garter Dethick for Maximilian Mohun (No. 2, ii,

---

*For Laurence Derby, father of this child, see Register, vol. 79, p. 432, where he appears as No. 1, iv, of the Derby pedigree. This child should be added to the list of his children there given.
†This entry gives the exact date of the baptism of Thomas Derby (No. 2, v, of the Derby pedigree), who is listed in Register, vol. 79, p. 436.
‡If this William Derby is identical with the William Derby who appears as No. 3 of the Derby pedigree (Register, vol. 79, p. 437), he must have had a wife named Lucy before he married Joan Baldwyn. But see *infra*, last entry under *Burials*, 10 Mar. 1665/6.
§This entry was given in Register, vol. 79, p. 414.
||This Nicholas Derby appears as No. 1, v, in the Derby pedigree (Register, vol. 79, pp. 432–433).
¶No. 1, iv, of the Derby pedigree (Register, vol. 79, p. 432).
**This entry gives the exact date of the burial of Christopher Derby (No. 2, i, of the Derby pedigree), who is said in Register, vol. 79, p. 414 and p. 436, to have been buried at Burton-Bradstock in 1623.
††No. 2 of the Derby pedigree, who is said in Register, vol. 79, p. 433, to have died 20 Jan. 1639/40 and to have been buried at Shipton-George, co. Dorset. Shipton-George, a parochial chapelry, is near Burton-Bradstock, both being about three miles southeasterly from Bridport. The registers of Shipton-George are included in the registers of Burton-Bradstock.
***See the footnote on p. 226, this volume.
****For references to Vol. 81, pp. 314-318 see pp. 186-190, this volume.

of the pedigree published in the REGISTER), son of Robert Mohun *alias* Moone (No. 2 of the pedigree) and grandson of Richard Mohun *alias* Moone (No. 1 of the pedigree). In this parchment pedigree Richard Mohun (No. 1) is given as the son of John Mohun of Ottery St. Mary, co. Devon; and, since Maximilian Mohun, for whom the parchment pedigree was drawn up, was a grandson of this Richard, it is probable that this statement is correct, especially as in the court rolls of Ottery St. Mary, now among the muniments of Lord Coleridge, it appears that on 14 Apr. 1516 John Mohun of Ottery St. Mary was surety for William Salter, an out-tenant. This John Mohun was evidently the son of Richard Moyne of Ottery St. Mary, who died between 21 Nov. 1515 and 24 Jan. 1515/16, seised of half a ferling of land at "Four Elms," of the tenure of "antique berton" and leaving a wife, Elizabeth. (Court Rolls of Ottery St. Mary, m. 106*d*.)

Maximilian Mohun (No. 2, ii, 2), of Fleet, Esq., was born in 1596 and was matriculated at Oxford in Apr. 1613. In 1631 he paid £10 for exemption from knighthood. He was an active adherent of King Charles, his estate was sequestered for seven years by the Parliament, and he compounded for £1540. 18s. 4d. He was imprisoned for some time at Weymouth, co. Dorset.

Francis Mohun, of Fleet, Esq., son of Maximilian Mohun (No. 2, ii, 2), married Eleanor, daughter of Ralph Sheldon of Stanton, co. Stafford, and niece of Gilbert Sheldon, Archbishop of Canterbury. Francis Mohun was one of the Dorsetshire gentlemen who in 1688 refused to support the repeal of the Penal Laws. (Cf. History of Dunster, by Sir Henry Churchill Maxwell-Lyte, K.C.B., vol. 2, app. A, p. 472 *et seq*.)

Churchill Mohun (No. 2, ii, 3) was matriculated at Oxford in Apr. 1613.

Robert Mohun (No. 2, ii, 4), of Birckham near Beaminster, co. Dorset, married in 1634 Elizabeth, daughter of John Hillary of Meerclay. He was a major in King Charles's Army, was taken prisoner near Bridgwater, co. Somerset, by the forces of the Parliament, and later compounded for his estates.

John Mohun (No. 2, iii) was matriculated at St. Albans Hall, Oxford, in 1581, aged 16 years, and was therefore born about 1565. On 4 Oct. 1593 he was a student at the Middle Temple.

The heir general of Mohun of Fleet is Sir Henry Churchill Maxwell-Lyte, K.C.B., of Lyte's Cary, co. Somerset, a distinguished scholar, who, until recently, was head of the Public Record Office, London. He is an honorary member of the New England Historic Genealogical Society, having been elected 1 Apr. 1924.

FROM THE PARISH REGISTERS OF PORTESHAM, CO. DORSET*

*Baptisms*

1605  John Mohun son of Maximilian and Ann 19 May.
1606  Margaret Mohun daughter of Maximilian and Ann 28 September.
1608  George Mohun son of Maximilian and Ann 10 December.
1610  Tamsie Mohun daughter of Maximilian and Ann 15 July.

FROM THE COURT ROLLS OF THE MANOR OF AXMINSTER, CO. DEVON†

10 February, 19 Henry VIII [1527/8]. To the court of the manor came Richard Mowne of Hawkechurch and took of the lord, John Cabell, Abbot, and the monastery of Newham the reversion of a parcel of land called Stoneyats, lying next Beber [*or* Bever], which Elizabeth Yorke, widow, now holds,

*These entries are from the manuscript collections of Rev. R. Grosvenor Bartelot, F.S.A., of Dorchester, co. Dorset, and relate to the family of Maximilian Mohun (No. 2, ii, of the pedigree).
†Preserved in the Public Library of Exeter, co. Devon. Cf. bill in Chancery of William Symonds, dated 6 Nov. 1592, in REGISTER, vol. 80, pp. 355-357. (Pages 170-172, this volume.)

to hold the said parcel of land to the said Richard Mowne and Robert and Walter, his sons, immediately after the death, surrender, or forfeiture of the said Elizabeth, for their lives and the lives of the longest liver, paying yearly at the usual terms 10s. and other dues, rents, and services formerly due and of right accustomed. And he gave to the lord as fine for having this estate 10s., paid in hand, and is admitted to the reversion, and fealties are respited.

To this court came Richard Mowne and took of the lord, John Cabell, Abbot, and the monastery of Newham the reversion of a tenement, with appurtenances, in Axminster, which Richard Wod *alias* Tayllor now holds, and the reversion of one parcel of land of the lord's demesne, called Stodehays, and of one acre of land, called Beare acre, and of one parcell of pasture or moor of the lord's demesne, lying under Southfyld, containing 4 acres, and also of one parcel of pasture "de solo domini," lying above [*or* upon, *supra*] Furseley downe, at Boroughhute [*elsewhere* Boroughshete], all of which the said Richard Wod *alias* Tayllour now holds, to hold the said tenement, with appurtenances, and all the land, pasture, and premises to the said Richard Mowne and Robert and Walter, his sons, immediately after the death, surrender, or forfeiture of the said Richard Wod *alias* Tayllour, for their lives and the life of the longest liver, successively, according to the custom of the manor, paying therefor yearly, viz., for the tenement 6s. 10d. and for the said parcell of land called Stoneyats 10s., and for Beare acre 8d., for the pasture under Southfyld 4s., and for the parcel upon Fursely downe 3s. 4d., and all other dues and services, etc. And, by an agreement made, the said Richard, Robert, and Walter are to repair hedges and fences between the lord's and their own land upon Furseley downe during the said term, at their own cost. And said Richard gave to the lord as fine for the estate £14 and a horse worth 40s., paid in hand. And they are admitted to the reversion, and their fealties respited.

21 July, 20 Henry VIII [1528]. To this court came Richard Mowne and took of the lord, John Cabelle, Abbot of Newham, and the convent the reversion of a tenement and two gardens, which Elizabeth Yorke, widow, now holds, to hold the said tenement and two gardens, together with two closes of the demesne, called Stoneyats, to said Richard Mowne, Joan, his wife, and John Howman, son of said Joan, immediately after the death, surrender, or forfeiture of said Elizabeth Yorke, for their lives and the life of the longest liver, successively, according to the custom of the manor for rent and services due and of right accustomed. And he gave to the lord as fine for such estate 46s. 8d., in hand paid, and was admitted to reversion, and fealty respited.

12 December, 22 Henry VIII [1530]. To this court came Elizabeth Yorke, who held of the lord one cottage, with appurtenances, and certain land of the barton of the lord, called Stoneyattys, and the said cottage, with premises and appurtenances, surrendered into the hands of the lord, to the use of Richard Mone, and nothing falls as heriot, because there is no heriot, upon which came the said Richard and took of the lord, Richard Gyll, Abbot of Newham, said cottage and said parcel of land called Stoneyatts, to have and to hold, etc.

26 July, 23 Henry VIII [1531]. Messor comes *ex officio* and presents that Richard Taylor *als*. Wode allows his ditch lying over against Fursse Downe called the Gore to be ruinous and in decay, to the great damage of the lord: in mercy 3d.

Pain laid on Richard Mone (6s. 8d.) to remove from the said house [*sic*] a certain John Halsshe and Joan, his wife. [Repeated 8 August, 23 Henry VIII [1531]. "recess" is written over the name of John Halsshe.]

9 October, 23 Henry VIII [1531]. Legal court, with view of frankpledge. It is presented that John Nuton and Richard Monne absent themselves from their tenements which they hold of the lord according to the custom of the

manor, and the bailiff is ordered to seize the land and tenements into the hands of the lord. Richard Mone (3d.) and William Symond (3d.) for suit.

6 November, 23 Henry VIII [1531]. The bailiff is in mercy because he did not distrain Richard Monne (3d.) [among other] to answer to the lord for divers trespasses. [Repeated 18 December, 23 January, 20 February, and 16 April.]

14 May, 24 Henry VIII [1532]. Legal court. Richard Monne (3d.) for suit.

14 November, 24 Henry VIII [1532]. Richard Mone (3d.) for suit.*

## GARDE
### PARENTAGE OF ROGER GARDE, THE FIRST NEW ENGLAND MAYOR

ONE of the most interesting characters of early New England and one about whom we know very little was Roger Garde of York, Me. He was recorder of York and mayor of Agamenticus or Gorgeana under Sir Ferdinando Gorges, and hence he was, beyond all doubt, the first mayor in New England.

Roger Garde had a relative, John Garde, an English merchant at Fayal in the Azores (cf. Aspinwall's Notarial Record, p. 109), who later came to Boston; for on 15 Mar. 1661/2 John Davesse and wife discharged to "John Gard, merchant, now living at Boston," a mortgage that they held on Roger Garde's land south of the Agamenticus River in York (cf. York Deeds, vol. 1, part 1, fo. 119). John Garde lived the latter part of his life in Newport, R. I., on the south side of Thames Street, where Southwick's sporting-goods store recently stood. His wife, Harte Garde, was buried back of the store, having died on 16 Sept. 1660, aged 55 years. On 7 Aug. 1665 "John Garde merchant" died, aged 61 years, and was buried beside his wife. The stones, two large, flat, sandstone slabs, were removed many years ago to the Island Cemetery at Newport, where they are the two oldest stones in that burying ground.

Last summer, while examining copies of certain Devonshire parish registers in the possession of the Devon & Cornwall Record Society, the writer came upon the following entries:

### FROM THE PARISH REGISTERS OF ALVINGTON, CO. DEVON

#### Baptisms

1589    William son of John Garde 29 March.
1590    Elizabeth daughter of John Garde 13 May.

#### Marriage

1588    John Garde and Mary Suthcott 12 November.

### FROM THE PARISH REGISTERS OF BIDEFORD, CO. DEVON

#### Baptisms

1608    Philip son of George Mountjoye 27 October.
1613    Elizabeth daughter of Roger Garde 16 February [1613/14].
1616    Rebecca daughter of Roger Garde 9 May.
1618    John son of Roger Garde 8 November.
1620    Thomas son of Roger Garde 21 January [1620/1].

*This series of court rolls begins in 1514 and ends in 1536, but no reference to Richard Mone is found after that of 14 Nov. 1532. Richard Taylor *als.* Wod was still alive in 26 Henry VIII [1534–35].

1623  Patience daughter of Roger Garde 13 July.
1626  Mary daughter of Roger Garde 1 February [1626/7].
1631  Abraham son of John Garde 24 April.
1632  Vlalia daughter of John Garde 5 February [1632/3].
1644  Mary daughter of William Champlen 29 September.
1646  Christian daughter of John Gord 28 August.
1650  Isacke son of John Goorde 13 March [1650/1].

## Marriages

1610  Roger Garde and Philip Gist 4 July.
1625  Richard Sheere and Joan Garde 18 July.
1629  John Garde and Rebecca Copp 27 September.
1641  William Champlen and Rebecca Garde 25 November.
1644  Richard Greade and Mary Dany 9 October.

## Burials

1614  Joane Montjoye 2 February [1614/15].
1634  Philip wife of Roger Garde 1 February [1634/5].
1646  Elizabeth Garde 10 June.

In Rhode Island, on 9 Apr. 1675, John Champlin, late of Fayal, now of Newport, merchant, sold land of John Garde in that town to Peleg Sanford of Newport, merchant (Rhode Island Land Evidence). On 30 Mar. 16 — John Champlin, "heire to John Garde deceased," gave freedom to the latter's negro, Salmerdore (entered between documents dated 17 Mar. 1672/3 and 8 June 1673, in Rhode Island Land Evidence, vol. 1, 1648–1676; cf. also *Magazine of New England History*, vol. 3, pp. 232 *et seq.*). This John Champlin occupied land in Newport adjoining that of Jeffrey Champlin, an early settler of Newport in 1638 and the founder of the Rhode Island family of Champlin. John Champlin apparently remained only a few years in Newport, and then vanished utterly from the Rhode Island records.

It is probable that Roger Garde, the mayor of Agamenticus or Gorgeana, was an unrecorded child of Roger Garde of Bideford, co. Devon, and that John Garde of Fayal, Boston, and Newport was his uncle and the great-uncle of John Champlin of Fayal and Newport. Furthermore, this John Champlin was evidently a near kinsman of Jeffrey Champlin, the founder of the Rhode Island family of Champlin, who must seek their origin in and around Bideford in co. Devon. The Garde family apparently moved, early in the seventeenth century, from Alvington to Bideford.

The George Mountjoy who appears in the Bideford parish registers is evidently a kinsman of George Mountjoy, the early settler of Falmouth (Portland), Me., and later of Boston.

As a student of early Newport history, it is gratifying to the writer to be able to clear up, to some extent, the history of that hitherto mysterious person, John Garde, and at the same time to point out the probable origin of the Rhode Island Champlins and of that sturdy opponent of the Massachusetts Puritans, Roger Garde of the Maine coast, the first mayor that New England ever had.

# GENEALOGICAL RESEARCH IN ENGLAND

Contributed by G. ANDREWS MORIARTY, JR., A.M., LL.B., of Newport, R. I., and communicated by the Committee on English and Foreign Research

## GARDE (CORRECTION)

THE attention of the Chairman of the Committee on English and Foreign Research has been called by Col. Charles Edward Banks, M.D., to the fact that Roger Garde, although he was mayor of Gorgeana (York) in 1644–45, was not "the first mayor in New England," as was stated on page 69 of the present volume of the * REGISTER. In this matter Colonel Banks is quite correct. The article published in the REGISTER was written in the country, without books of reference at hand; hence the misstatement. Roger Garde was, however, recorder of York and one of the first aldermen of Gorgeana, Thomas Gorges, nephew of Sir Ferdinando Gorges, being the first mayor. (Cf. Moody's History of the Town of York, p. 22.)

It may be stated also that Charles Thornton Libby, Esq., of Yarmouth, Me., the leading authority on early Maine genealogy, thinks that Roger Garde of Bideford in Devon was identical with the York recorder; and this opinion, from such an eminent antiquary as Mr. Libby, is entitled to great weight.

## GORTON

ALTHOUGH the birthplace of the redoubtable Samuel Gorton of Warwick, R. I., has always been known (for in his letter to Nathaniel Morton, printed in Force's Tracts, vol. 4, he states that he was born at Gorton, a chapelry within the parish of Manchester [co. Lancaster, England], where the "fathers of my body have dwelt for many generations"), no effort has been made hitherto to establish his ancestry. The present article is an effort in that direction, but the result is not very satisfactory, owing to the late date for the beginning of the Manchester registers, the fact that the Gortons had, apparently, been long settled in that vicinity, and the paucity of wills — circumstances that combine to make the tracing of the pedigree a difficult matter.

In a letter to John Winthrop, Jr., dated 11 Aug. 1674, Samuel Gorton gives his age as "four score and two years," and there can, therefore, be little doubt that he was the Samuel Gorton, son of Thomas, who was baptized at Manchester 12 Feb. 1592/3, and that the record of the burial there, 2 Nov. 1616, of Samuel, son of Thomas Gorton of Gorton, does not refer to him, but to a child of Thomas and Agnes (Grimshaw) Gorton (who were married at Manchester, 14 Sept. 1612), whose baptism is not recorded. The Thomas Gorton who married Agnes Grimshaw was apparently a brother of Samuel Gorton of Rhode Island, and was baptized at Manchester 17 Nov. 1588. He seems to have accompanied his younger brother to New

*Page 230, this volume.

232

England, as he appears with him in Plymouth in 1637 and later in Portsmouth, R. I., where, apparently, he died between 16 July and 21 Nov. 1649.

Samuel Gorton boasts that his family "was not unknown in the heraldry of England," and at a later time the Gortons of Gorton appear to have used as arms *Gules, ten billets or, a chief indented of the last*, and as a crest *A goat's head erased argent, ducally gorged or.** Samuel Gorton also, on the title page of his book, describes himself as "Samuel Gorton gent." The facts appear to be that an ancient family, with some pretensions to gentility, was settled in and about Gorton and the neighboring parish of Atherton as early as 1332, but that by the latter half of the sixteenth century the race had multiplied and the members of the family settled at Gorton had sunk to the position of small tenant farmers. Samuel Gorton went early to London, became a clothier, married Mary Maplett, the daughter of a well-to-do merchant (cf. REGISTER, vol. 70, pp. 115–118), and appears to have raised himself considerably in the social scale. In the eighteenth century some members of the family in Gorton rose through trade at Manchester, acquired considerable wealth, and once more styled themselves Gorton of Gorton; but financial disaster overtook them early in the nineteenth century, and they disappeared from that vicinity.†

### FROM PROBATE RECORDS

The Will of JOHN HOLMES of London, founder of Blackrod School, Lancashire, dated 18 September 1568, mentions Thomas Gorton of Adlington and his son Robert, the issue of Thomas Gorton of Aspull, the issue of James Gorton of Hawghton, his cousin James Gorton of Westhawghton, his cousin Alice Gorton of the same place, Richard Gorton of Winwick parish, the daughter and widow of Robert Gorton, Agnes Gorton, etc. (This abstract is published in Mr. Higson's article in *Miscellanea Genealogica et Heraldica*, New Series, vol. 1, p. 321.)

The Will of WILLIAM GORTON of Gorton in the parish of Manchester, co. Lancaster, being somewhat infirm and weak in body, dated 20 May 1588. To be buried in Manchester churchyard. By consent of the Right Worshipful Sr. John Byrd, knight, my good Mr., my brother Frannces Gorton shall occupy and enjoy this messuage and tenement wherein my father, Ric. Gorton, is now possessed immediately after the death of my said father, provided that Joan, my wife, shall enjoy and quietly possess the half of the foresaid housing and tenement, according to the ancient use and custom of this town, keeping herself in my name and in honest report and fame. My goods [are] to be divided into two parts, one for myself, to pay debts, etc., with reversion to my wife, and the other for my wife, Joan Gorton. To Katherin, my sister, 53s. 4d. To my brother Frannces Gorton his children, being six in number, £7 equally among them. To Alexander Bexwicke 6s., Roger Rydar 12d., and Thomas Gorton 12d. To every godchild 12d. To George Wharmbye, minister, for writing my will, 2s. Reversion of my part to Frannces, my brother. Executors: Frannces, my brother, and my wife. Supervisors: Thomas Gorton and Thomas Birch. Witnesses: Robert Baguley, John Bexwicke, George Wharmbie.

---

*Vide supra*, pp. 156 and 167.

†Cf. Mr. John Higson's account of the family in *Miscellanea Genealogica et Heraldica*, New Series, vol. 1, pp. 321–325, 1874.

Debts owing to [sic] me: To [sic] the widow of Robert Birtenshall £6., to [sic] Mr. Chaderton of Nuthurste or his administrators 23s., to [sic] Thomas Pycrofte £6. 13s. 4d.

6 June 1588. Inventory by John Bexwicke, Thomas Gorton, Edward Bexwicke, William Whitakars, and George Wharmby, minister: In Yarn, £18. 5s.; Current money and coin, £23. 11s.; Brass, 53s. 4d.; Pewter, 13s. 4d.; Iron ware, 7s.; His apparel, 13s. 4d. Total, £50. 6s. 8d.

Proved 11 June 1588 by Francis Gorton, one of the executors named in the will, power being reserved for the other executor. (Consistory Court of Chester [District Probate Registry, Chester].*)

The Will of HENRIE GORTON of Brinhill, co. Lancaster, yeoman, "Ffelinge my self diseased comynge by the visitatione of Almightie God," dated 24 September 1605. To be buried in the parish church of Brinhill, near the place where my father and mother lieth. To every godchild 12d. To Margaret Gorton, my son John's daughter, 6s. 8d. My worst pair of "shodd wheles" to my son-in-law Thomas Anderton. To my son John one plow, with irons, etc. To my wife Margaret 20s. To Isabell, my son John's wife, 3s. 4d. To Elizabeth, daughter of my son John, 3s. 4d. To two children of James Aspedeyne, to either 12d. The rest and residue [of my estate] to Thomas Gorton, my younger son. Executors: he and said wife Margaret. I delivered to my son-in-law Thomas Anderton three pounds, to buy his wife clothes withall. Witnesses: John Blackeledge, James Farclough.

Debts owing unto me: My son-in-law Thomas Anderton £6.; Evan Gerrarde, 5s. 6d.

Debts which I owe: To three children of Xtofer Leeds, given them by Ric. wife Eastam, their aunt [sic], 20s.; to my son John 7s.

Inventory by Lawrence Haydocke, John Blackledge, Willm. Shorrocke, and Thomas Anderton, 25 April 1606, shows the usual items, amounting to about £50. Debts owing to Elyn Trige, dec'd, 46s. 8d.; to Rauffe Anderton 4s.

Proved 8 August 1606 by the executors named in the will, before Mr. Makinson, Dean of Leyland.

The Will of WILLIAM GORTOUN of Sephtoun, co. Lancaster, husbandman, "sicke in body," dated 19 February 1608 [1608/9]. To be buried within the "bellfree" of the church of Sephtoun. To Alice Carter £13. 6s. 8d. To Elizabeth Carter, alias Gorton, my base daughter, £10. To Alice Carter, alias Gorton, my base daughter, £10. To Henry Foackes, alias Gorton, my base son, £6. To Elizabeth Winstanley, my niece, £5. To Elizabeth Guddicker 20s. To James Norrice 12d. To Henry Norrice 6d. To Robert Molineux 6d. To Margery, wife of Robert Molineux, 6d. To Alice Boulton 6d. To Jane Anderton 12d. To Bridget Abbey 12d. To William Livesey 12d. To Anthony Hesketh 12d. To John Higanson 3s. 4d. To Robert Harrison 6d. To Robert Walton 5s. To Richard Snape 3s. 4d. The rest and residue [of my estate] to my abovesaid three base children and to Alice Carter, the mother of two of them. Executors: Robert Woorrall and William Smyth of Darbye, co. Lancaster, husbandmen. Witnesses: Lawrence Starkie, Humfrey Dale, Robert Harrisoun × (his mark). [Various debts.]

Inventory by Robert Molineux, Robert Boultoun, Anthony Burgess, and Humphrey Shepparde, 26 February 1608 [1608/9], shows a total, including debts, of £81. 11s. 2d.

Proved 24 March 1608 [1608/9] by the executors named in the Will.

*The following wills also, nine in number, were proved in the Consistory Court of Chester and may be found in the District Probate Registry at Chester.

234

The Will of THOMAS GORTON of Gorton in the parish of Manchester, co. Lancaster, husbandman, "being greeved with sickness in body," dated 31 December 1610. To be buried in the parish church of Manchester. The moiety of the lease on my dwelling house to Anne, my wife, with reversion of the same to my eldest son Nicholas, to whom [I give] the other moiety. My said son Nicholas is to give to my children Thomas and Samuel 20s. each and to Edward and Mary 30s. each. Reversion of the tenement to my said sons, in tail. My goods are to be divided into three parts, one for myself, the second for Anne, my wife, and the third equally among my seven children, Nicholas, Thomas, Samuel, Edward, Elizabeth, Catherine, and Mary. Out of my part [I give] to Anne, my wife, my cloak; to Edward, my son, my best breeches; to Thomas Gorton, son of William Gorton, 12d.; to Jane Hibbert 12d.; to Raphe Shelmerdyne, to whom I am grandfather, 12d.; to Raphe Shelmerdyne, my son-in-law, my jerkin; to James Ellor my leather breeches; to Mary, my daughter, my best hat. The rest and residue [of my estate is to be divided] equally among my six younger children. Executors: Anne, my wife, and Nicholas, my son. Overseers: Hugh Kenyon and William Howorth, my neighbors.

Debts which I owe: To Thomas Watson 7s. 4d.; to William Howorth 12d.; to Thomas Prestwch ———; to Edward Walker 12s.

My children under age [are] to be under the tuition of my wife until twenty-one. Witnesses: Hugh Kenyon, Thomas Watson, John Ellor, Robert Mason, William Howorth, George Somerset, Thomas Beswyck, Roger Beswyck.

Inventory by Hugh Kenyon, Thomas Graver, William Howorth, Thomas Watson, Thomas Beswyck, and William Gorton, 24 January 1610 [1610/11], £25. 5s. 8d.

Proved 26 January 1610 [1610/11] by the executors named in the will.

The Will of THOMAS GORTON of Failsworthe, co. Lancaster, carpenter, "beinge of greate and manye years of Age," dated 17 September, 15 James (51 of Scotland), 1617. Debts and funeral expenses paid, the rest of my goods shall be divided into three equal parts, one part for Issabell, my loving wife, and one other part for my son Adame and my daughter Issabell, and the third part as followeth: To my sister Johane Smethurste 20s. To Margaret Gorton, my brother's daughter, 2s. 6d. To the poor of the parish where it shall please God I shall be buried 40s. To Thomas Tayleor of Failsworth 12d. The rest and residue [of my estate I give] to the said Issabell, my wife. Executor: my loving son-in-law Thomas Whittyker of Chatterton. Overseers: my dear and loving friend Adame Hollande the Elder of Newton and Nycholas Kempe of Failsworth. Witnesses: Robarte Kershawe, Leonard Tetlowe, Hughe Pollett.

Inventory of the goods of Thomas Gorton in the County of Lancaster, carpenter, deceased 27 March, by Robarte Kershawe, Hughe Cleaton, Robarte Ogden, and Nycholas Kempe, 17 April 1618:

"In bylls and bounds as followeth viz."

Robarte Marler, Adame Hollande, and Raffe Marler, by "bounde" to pay 1 February 1618 [1618/19] £ 44.

Hughe Cleaton by "bylle" . . . £22.

Raffe Marler and John Ramesdayne by "bounde" to pay . . . £11.

Total, £109. 7s. 6d.

Proved 5 November 1618 by the executor named in the will, the testator being described as late of Chatherton, deceased.

The Will of ADAM GORTON of Dreilsden within the parish of Manchester, co. Lancaster, yeoman, "Sick in bodie," dated 17 December 1628, 4 Charles. To be buried in the churchyard of Manchester. After my debts, if any, are deducted, my goods shall be divided into two equal parts, one to myself and the other equally between my two daughters, Ales Hudson and Marie Knott. My funeral charges [shall be paid] out of my part, and all the rest [I give] unto Thomas Gorton, my son. "And as touchinge such harnishe wherewith I am charged in servite unto my soveraigne lord the kinge it is my will that it shallbee and remaine at my house as an heireloome, for the use and behoofe of my aforesaid sonne Thomas Gorton." To my grand-child Adam Gorton [sundry goods], to remain his. Whole and sole executor: Thomas, my son. Overseers: Adam Baguley the Elder of Fealesworth and John Gromishaw of Drilseden, my neighbors. Witnesses: James Halle, Raphe Grimshaw, Adam Holland.

Inventory by Edward [illegible, ? Wro], James Gromishaw, George Kenion, and Adam Holland, 12 January 1628 [1628/9], mentions the "Clocke" chamber, the "kitchinge" chamber, the chamber over the "worke house," in the "parlour" above, the "sellar" — total, £57. 12s. 3d.

Proved 9 April 1629 by the sole executor named in the will.

The Will of ALICE GORTON of Culcheth, co. Lancaster, widow, dated 20 March 1629 [1629/30]. To be buried at my parish church of Winwick. Richard Gorton, my son, shall have all the money owing by Thomas Shaw. The residue [of my estate], after payment of debts, etc., [is] to be divided into three parts, whereof two shall remain to Richard, my son, and the third I give to Raphe Lowton, alias Oldam. Executors: William Smyth and Richard Gorton, my son. Overseers: William Bate and Thomas Smith. [Signed] Alice Gorton, her X mark. Witnesses: George Boydell, his X mark, Cicely Fichet, alias Renykers, her X mark, Geo: Benchall.

Inventory by Nicholas Hey, George Flitcroft, John Yate, and Robert Leegh, 8 May 1631, amounting to £60.

Proved 30 May 1631 by the executors named in the will.

The Will of ROBERT GORTON of Adlington, co. Lancaster, "lynnenman" ["carrier" in inventory], "sicke in bodie," dated 10 September 1637. To be buried within my parish church at Standishe. After debts and funeral expenses are paid, the residue and remainder [of my estate] shall be and remain to my wife and daughter. Sole executrix: my wife Dorothie.

[Schedule of debts, to various persons.]

Debts owing unto me: James Gorton of Broadhead, £8. 8s. 4d.; James Gorton (more), £1. 1s.; Mr. Hatton, £6.; Thomas Foster, als. French, and his wife Margaret, £1.; Edward Haskine, for his wife, Mres. Margarett Adlington, in lent money, 20s., in "camebricke," 10s., in all, £1. 10s.; Mr. Ryley of Preston, for carriage of our trun[illegible] of Tobacco, £1.

Inventory by Rauffe Bayley, Robte Rothwell, Roger Rigby, and John Worthington of Adlington, 25 September 1637, about £50.

Proved 7 July 1638 by the executrix named in the will.

The Will of RAPHE SHELMERDYNE the Elder of Gorton, co. Lancaster, yeoman, dated 29 May 1639. My body to be buried in Christian manner in the parish church or churchyard of Manchester, near to the place where my late loving wife, Anne Shelmerdyne, lieth interred, or elsewhere where the Lord shall appoint. My debts and funeral expenses shall be paid out of my whole goods. I devise all my messuage, land, and tenement called the Greene Head, with the appurtenances, situate in Gorton aforesaid, to my eldest son, Raphe Shelmerdyne, his heirs and assigns for ever. And for default of such issue to Thomas Shelmerdyne, my second son, and his heirs and assigns for ever. And for default of such issue to my six daughters, Jane Shelmerdyne, Elizabeth, Anne, Margaret, Alice, and Marie Shelmer-dyne, their heirs and assigns for ever. My said son Raphe Shelmerdyne shall, in consideration that I do give him my said lands and tenements at the Greene Heade, pay to his sister Jane Shelmerdyne the yearly rent of 40s. during the term of sixty years, if she shall so long live, with power to distrain for the same upon the closes called the Intake and Pingotte. Thomas Shelmerdyne shall, in consideration that I have given him all my lands, messuage, and tenement at Banke Topp in Gorton, pay to his sister Jane Shelmerdyne the yearly rent of 20s. during the term of sixty years, if she so long live, with power to distrain for the same on the close called the Barley Croft, being parcel of my messuage and tenement at Banke Topp aforesaid. To my daughter Ann Shelmerdyne £30. To my son-in-law James Thorpe £10, to be paid within one month after the decease of Widow Thorpe of Newton. To three of the youngest children of my son-in-law James Thorpe 33s. 4d. apiece, when twenty-one years of age. My said son Thomas Shelmerdyne shall have the use and benefit of the said three children's legacies, to be employed for their best commodity and profit, and he shall pay the same, with the advantage thereof, when they attain the said age; and, if my son Thomas shall depart this life before the said sums of money be paid to my said grandchildren, the said lands at the Banketopp shall be charged with the payment thereof. Also, my said son Thomas Shelmerdyne shall pay to my three daughters, Margaret, Alice, and Marie, £20 apiece out of my land at Banketopp. It is my will that my son-in-law James Thorpe and Elizabeth, his wife, my daughter, shall hold them[selves] satisfied in regard I have given them sufficient portions formerly. To my said son Thomas Shelmerdyne these parcels of goods hereafter named remaining in my said house at Bank Topp, viz., the greatest coffer, two tables in the house, a cubboard and dishboard, a great swine trough and cheese press, in consideration whereof he shall give to his three sisters, Margaret, Alice, and Marie, £3 equally amongst them. All the residue of my goods, etc., I give to my said three daughters, Margaret, Alice, and Marie, equally amongst them. I make my said son Thomas Shelmerdyne sole executor of this my last will. Also, I desire my loving neighbors, Thomas Jackson, clerk, and Raphe Wood the Younger, to be overseers. [Signed] Raphe Shelmyerdyne, his ✕ marke. Witnesses: Tho. Jackson, John Cocke, his marke, John Jacksonn.

Inventory, taken by Thomas Grauer the Elder of Gorton, Raph Wood the Younger, William Berkinshaw, and John Cocke, 1 November 1639, mentions farming stock, household goods, etc., contains the expressions "in the little house," "in the loom house," "in the parlor at the west end of the house," "in the north side of the house," "in the west end of the house," "in the west chamber," and "in the kitchen chamber," and appraises one musket at 13s. 4d., bills, bonds, and debts at £8. 6s., and "more in bonds" at £40, no total valuation being given.

Proved at Chester, 4 November 1639, by the sole executor named in the will.

The Will of ADAM GORTON of Droylsden, parish of Manchester, co. Lancaster, yeoman, "sick in bodie," dated 28 December 1650. To be buried in the parish church of Manchester. After funeral expenses and debts [are] discharged, one third part to my loving wife, Catterin Gorton, and the other two equal parts to my three children, viz., Thomas Gorton, John Gorton, and Mary Gorton, and wife is to have their tuition. To Thomas Gorton, my son, my messuage, house, barns, stables, etc., with all closes, in Droilsden, now in my possession or otherwise in my mother's possession, to him and his heirs for ever. In default of such heirs to John, my second son, and his heirs male and female; and in default of such to Mary Gorton, my daughter, and her heirs male or female; and in default of such to

John Gorton, my brother, and his heirs for ever, with remainder to my own right heirs. My wife is to enjoy a one-third part of all my lands. My son Thomas is to give his brother and sister £100 betwixt them. Executors: my uncle, Rodger Bate of Cheadell, co. Chester, yeoman, and John Gorton, my brother. Overseers: my friends and brothers-in-law John Tilesley and James Tilesley of Worseley. [Signed] Adam Gorton. Witnesses: Adam Holland, John Knott, George Worseley, his mark I.

Inventory by Robert Glossop, Willm Parr, Richard Heape, and James Hall, 6 February 1650 [1650/1], mentions the "House," the "Clocke chamber," the "sellor," and the "milkhouse," the total valuation (not given) being about £75.

Proved 20 April 1661 [sic, ? 1651] by the executors named in the will.

FROM THE REGISTERS OF THE CATHEDRAL CHURCH OF MANCHESTER, CO. LANCASTER, 1573-1653 *

*Baptisms*

1573 Elizabeth daughter of Alice Gorton, "base gott," 24 January [1573/4].
1574 Elline daughter of Georg Gorton 20 July.
1574 Elizabethe daughter of Nicholas Gorton 6 December.
1575 Nicholas son of Thomas Gorton 5 May.
1575 Nicholas son of Thomas Gorton 4 June.
1575 Will[ia]m son of Frannces Gorton 31 July.
1576 Thomas son of Thomas Gorton 3 November.
1576 James son of James Gorton 9 February [1576/7].
1577 Elizabeth daughter of Franncys Gorton 8 March [1577/8].
1579 Thomas son of Will[ia]m Gorton, "basegott," 6 August.
1580 Franncis son of Franncis Gortonn 3 April.
1582 Thomas son of Thomas Gorton 16 February [1582/3].
1582 Issabell daughter of Frannces Gorton 20 March [1582/3].
1584 Katherine daughter of Thomas Gorton 4 October.
1584 Otywell son [sic] of Adame Gortonne 29 November.
1585 George son of Franncis Gortonn 21 November.
1586 Mary daughter of Franncis Gorton 4 April.
1587 Will[ia]m son of Thomas Gortonne 30 April.
1588 Thomas son of Thomas Gorton 17 November.
1590 Martha daughter of Adam Gorton 31 January [1590/1].
1591 Franncis son of Thomas Gorton 18 December.
1592 Samuell son of Thomas Gortonne 12 February [1592/3].
1593 Adam son of Adame Gortonne 9 September.
1593 Thomas bastard of Ric: Gorton and Anne Bridge 16 September.
1597 Mary daughter of Adam Gorton and Jone Gorton, "base," 12 March [1597/8].
1598 Thomas son of Williame Gortonne 14 January [1598/9].
1599 Thomas son of Will[ia]m Gortonn 2 March [1599/1600].
1600 Adam son of Adam Gorton 15 June.
1601 Samuel son of Adam Gorton 2 October.†
1604 Margaret daughter of William Gortonn 5 March [1604/5].
1607 Elizabeth daughter of William Gorton of Gorton 29 March.
1610 George son of Will[ia]m Gorton of Gorton 20 January [1610/11].
1613 Thomas son of Nicholas Gorton of Gorton 25 July.

*The entries of baptisms, marriages, and burials here given are based on the *verbatim* copy published by the Lancashire Parish Register Society in two volumes, 1908, 1918–19.
†This baptism does not appear in the copy of the registers printed by the Lancashire Parish Register Society, but it is given by Mr. Higson in his article in the *Miscellanea Genealogica et Heraldica*, vol. 1, p. 321.

1614 Samuell son of Will[ia]m Gorton of Gorton 1 May.
1616 Anne daughter of William Gorton of Gorton 20 May.
1616 Samuell son of Nicholas Gorton of Gorton 23 June.
1616 Adam son of Thomas Gorton of Droilesden 17 November.
1618 Samuell son of Thomas Gorton of M: [?Moston] 10 January [1618/19].
1618 Marye daughter of Thomas Gorton of Droilsden 7 March [1618/19].
1619 Ellin daughter of Alice Parcivall and Edward Gorton, both of Gorton
     within the parish of M[anchester], 13 February [1619/20].
1620 Martha daughter of Nicholas Gorton of Gorton 20 August.
1620 Marye daughter of Thomas Gorton of M: 25 February [1620/1].
1621 James son of James Gorton of Droilsden 30 March.
1622 William son of Marye Gorton of Droylseden and Mr. William Boothe
     of Ashton 4 August.
1622 Martha daughter of Frannces Gorton of Gorton 18 August.
1622 Anne daughter of Thomas Gorton of M: 9 February [1622/3].
1623 Margaret daughter of Alice Parcivall and Edmund Gortō, both of
     Gorton, 30 March.
1625 Roharte son of Anne Fletch[e]r and Edmunde Gorton of Gorton 20
     November.
1626 George son of Thomas Gorton of M: 2 April.
1629 John son of Thomas Gorton of Droylsden 14 March [1629/30].
1631 Marye daughter of Thomas Gorton of Droylsden 28 January [1631/2].
1634 Anna daughter of Thomas Gorton of Droilsden 18 May.
1644 Ellin daughter of Samuell Gorton of M: 15 September.
1646 Marie daughter of Samuell Gorton of M: 25 October.
1649 Ann daughter of Robert Gorton of M: 1 April.
1650 James son of Sámuel Gorton of M: 18 August.

*Marriages*

1574 Franncis Gorton and Elizabeth Buerdsell *istius* 4 May.
1574 Nicholas Gorton and Anne Greene *istius* 22 September.
1593 Thomas Hawle and Elline Gorton *istius* 19 November.
1602 Edmund Cowell and Issabell Gorton 9 May.
1605 Raphe Shelmerdeyne and Katherin Gorton 22 April.
1608 John Gorton and Katheryn Leighe 1 May.
1609 John Towneley and Elizabeth Gorton 22 April.
1611 William Betson and Elizabeth Gorton 27 April.
1612 Thomas Gorton and Agnes Grimshaw 14 September.
1612 James Gorton and Margaret Chorlton 16 September.
1613 John Hulme and Grace Gorton *huius* 7 April.
1613 Richard Hudson and Alice Gorton, by licence, 7 September.
1614 Raphe Briddocke and Elizabeth Gorton 1 August.
1617 Thomas Gorton and Elizabeth P[er]civall 10 January [1617/18].
1619 Frannces Gorton and Marye Nicholson 28 June.
1625 Allexander Birche and Marye Gorton 2 January [1625/6].
1625 Peeter Bowker and Isabell Gorton, L[icence], 2 February [1625/6].
1626 Edwarde Gorton and Alice Parcivall 12 May.
1626 Franncis Gorton and Isabell Smythe 28 December.
1630 James Dawson and Margrett Gorton 4 April.
1634 Thomas Boardman and Elizabeth Gorton 20 November.
1641 Samuell Gorton and Anne Hulme 28 December.
1642 Adam Gorton and Katherin Tyldisley p[ar]ish of Eccles 3 January
     [1642/3].
1651 James Holland and Mary Gorton 3 April.
1651 John Gorton and Elizabeth Smith 20 March [1651/2].

239

*Burials*

1576 Thomas son of Thomas Gortonn 4 February [1576/7].
1578 Elizabeth wife of Thomas Gorton 29 August.
1586 An infant son of Tho: Gorton 10 April.
1586 Elizabeth widow of Tho: Gortonne 11 April.
1587 Cicely wife of Richard Gorton 23 September.
1588 Will[ia]m Gorton of Gorton, hou[seholder], 26 May.
1588 Richard Gorton of Gorton, hous[e]holder, 23 January [1588/9].
1589 Francys son of Franncys Gorton 30 March.
1591 Martha daughter of Adam Gorton 15 April.
1592 Franncys son of Thomas Gorton 16 April.
1597 Frannces Gorton of Gorton 29 March.
1597 Rauffe Gorton of Drylsdeyne, ho[useholder], 26 February [1597/8].
1599 Thomas son of Will[ia]m Gorton 2 April.
1600 Adam son of Adam Gorton 6 October.
1604 Issabell daughter of Francys Gorton 6 May.
1608 Anne widow of Nicholas Gorton of Gorton 24 June.
1609 Jane wife of Rauffe Gorton of Drilsden 19 March.*
1609 Elizabeth widow of Franncis Gorton of Gorton 11 January [1609/10].
1610 Thomas Gorton of Gorton, househould[e]r, 3 January [1610/11].
1615 Samuell son of Wm. Gorton of Gorton 9 April.
1615 Joane widow of William Gorton of Gorton 20 September.
1615 Thomas son of William Gorton of Gorton 29 November.
1616 Samuell son of Thomas Gorton of Gorton 2 November.
1617 William Gorton of Gorton 29 December.
1619 Katherin wid[ow] of Thomas Gorton of Moston 3 March [1619/20].
1619 Ellin daughter of Edward Gorton of Gorton 9 March [1619/20].
1619 Katherin Gorton of M: linenwebster, 13 March [1619/20].
1621 Jane Gorton of Cheetam, spinster, 21 January [1621/2].
1623 William son of William Boothe deceased at Adam Gorton's of Droilsden 9 May.
1623 Anne wid[ow] of Thomas Gorton of Gorton 1 November.
1625 William Irlame deceased at Nicholas Gorton's in M: 27 June.
1625 Jane w[ife] of Adam Gorton of Gorton 22 August.
1625 Margaret w[ife] of James Gorton of M: 21 October.
1625 Margerye Gorton of M: 18 November.
1627 Marye daughter of Thomas Gorton of M: 11 April.
1627 George son of Thomas Gorton of M: 14 May.
1628 Adam Gorton of Droylsden, yeoman, 5 January [1628/9].
1629 Elizabeth wife of James Gorton 6 September.
1629 Marye daughter of Thomas Gorton of Droylsden 24 December.
1633 George son of William Gorton of Gorton 23 September.
1640 John Gorton of M:, "Alehowsekeeper," 4 December.
1642 An infant of Samuell Gorton of M: 17 October.
1645 Ann daughter of Thomas Gorton of M: 17 July.
1645 The wife of Thomas Gorton of M: 30 July.
1645 Thomas Gorton of M: 31 July.
1645 Katharine wife of John Gorton of M: 6 September.
1645 Thomas Gorton of Droylsden, yeoman, 17 February [1645/6].
1647 Robert son of Robert Gorton of M: 2 December.
1650 Isabell wife of Francis Gorton of M: 2 April.

[The rest of the Gorton records, with a pedigree of the family, will be published in the REGISTER of July 1928. — EDITOR.]

*The year 1609 in this parish register begins on 1 January. This date is equivalent to 19 March 1608/9.

# GENEALOGICAL RESEARCH IN ENGLAND

Contributed by G. Andrews Moriarty, Jr., A.M., LL.B., of Newport, R. I.,
and communicated by the Committee on English and Foreign Research

## Gorton (concluded)[*]

### From Lay Subsidies for co. Lancaster[†]

1332. Atherton. Thomas de Gorton, [tax] 2s.
1524. Parish of Manchester. Thomas Gorton in goods, [valuation] 40s.,
[tax] 12d. (Exchequer Lay Subsidies, 130/79.)
1543. Aspull. Robert Gorton in goods, [valuation] 20s., [tax] 2d.
Gorton. Thomas Gorton in goods, [valuation] £4, [tax] 8d.

### From Duchy of Lancaster Inquisitions Post Mortem[†]

Inquisition taken at Bolton, co. Lancaster, 22 April, 18 James I [1620],
before the King's escheator there. The jurors [named] say that William
Gorton, late of Gorton, deceased, was seised the day he died of a messuage,
a garden, an orchard, and 9 acres of land, meadow, and pasture in Gorton,
held *in capite*, by knight's tenure, of the King, as of his Duchy of Lancaster,
and worth 10s. per annum.
Said William died at Gorton 24 December, 16 James I [1618], and Francis
Gorton is his son and next heir, and aged 17 years, 6 months, 5 days. (Vol.
22, no. 11.)

Inquisition taken at Wigan [co. Lancaster] 9 September, 1 Charles I
[1625]. The jurors [named] say that Robert Gorton was seised of a messuage,
a garden, an orchard, 10 acres of land, 4 acres of meadow, and 6 acres of
pasture in Aspull, bought of Thomas Lathume, late of Wolfall.
Said Robert died 10 December last past [1624], and James Gorton is his
son and next heir, and is now aged 40 years and more. (Vol. 26, no. 48.)

Inquisition taken at Leigh, co. Lancaster, 17 April, 4 Charles I [1628].
The jurors [named] say that James Gorton, yeoman, was seised of a messuage, a garden, an orchard, 10 acres of land, 4 acres of meadow, and 6
acres of pasture in Aspull, late bought of Thomas Lathorne of Woofall.
Said James died 10 November, 2 Charles I [1626], and Robert Gorton is
his son and next heir, and is aged 15 years. (Vol. 26, no. 11.)

†Preserved in the Public Record Office, London.
*For references to pp. 185-193 see pp. 232-240, this volume.

FROM CHANCERY PROCEEDINGS*

Michaelmas Term, 6 Edward VI [1552]. Complaint by Robert Gorton of West Haghton, co. Lancaster, that James Browne of West Haghton, gent., James Lathemyt, and others, to the number of twenty, assembled on 3 May, 6 Edward VI at West Haghton, and with force entered complainant's house there, plucked two of his children out of their beds, tossing up the bedding and bedstraw, and telling complainant's wife that they intended to kill him. He desires that they may be called to answer for the same. (Chancery Proceedings, Duchy of Lancaster, vol. 29, no. G. 9.)

35 Elizabeth [1592–93]. [No Bill of Complaint.] Answer of Roger Fidler, in regard to property left by John Bold, states that John Bold married Grace Gorton, widow, and that after Bold's death said Fidler married her. (Chancery Proceedings, Duchy of Lancaster, vol. 160, no. B. 13.)

19 April 1594. Complaint by Henry Bolde of Northmeiles, co. Lancaster, gent., that a house in Preston, late the property of John Bold, deceased, has come into the hands of Richard Gorton of Preston, who wrongfully detains it. Richard Gorton says that by deed dated 12 October, 27 Elizabeth [1585], John Bold conveyed the same to Henry Gorton, Grace, his then wife, late mother of said Richard, and to their son, the said Richard, for one hundred years. Henry Gorton died, and Grace entered into the same, and on her death he, the said Richard, still a minor, entered into the same, as by right he was entitled to do. (Chancery Proceedings, Duchy of Lancaster, vol. 162, no. B. 18.)

Bill of Complaint (filed 18 August 1615) of Richard Clough of Gorton, co. Lancaster, yeoman, and Thomas Picroste [later written Picrofte] of the same, yeoman, states that, whereas, about five years since, complainants, together with William Whittaker, Nicolas Gorton, William Gorton, Miles Birtinshaw, John Leigh, Ambrose Birch, James Somestʳ, and Raph Clough, all of the said town, yeomen, and others, purchased to themselves and their heirs severally, from Sir John Biron, Knight, divers lands in Gorton, and not long afterwards Rowland Moseley of Manchester, Esq., being lord of the said town of Manchester, laid claim to a rent of £30. 11s. issuing out of the said lands, and exhibited an information in the Court of Wards at Westminster against complainants and William Howarth, another purchaser, thereupon, about April, 11 James I [1613], complainants agreed with Whittaker and the rest that Whittaker and the rest should contribute towards the costs of the suit. But now Whittaker and the rest refuse to pay towards the cost of a suit brought at Westminster by Biron. (Chancery Bills in Palatinate of Lancaster, unnumbered, 6/3.)

[No answer between August 1615 and August 1616. Depositions, 10/11, contain only Moseley v. Picroft. No Gorton occurs.]

Gorton v. Foster and Lambe.

Bill of Complaint (filed 10 February 1634 [1634/5]) of Samuel Gorton of London, clothier.

Whereas complainant about January 1633 [1633/4] sold to William Lambe of London 15 score pair of "mixt" stockings at 4s. 3d. per pair, the total amounting to £63. 15s., which Lambe was to pay in ready money, and about 22 February following complainant (upon Lambe's affirming that he was possessed of certain Scotch yarn) bought from Lambe 958 small weight of Scotch yarn, viz., 618 pound weight at 17d. the lb. and 340 pound weight at 16½ d. per lb., the sum total being £67. 3s. 4d. Lambe gave com-

*Preserved in the Public Record Office, London.

242

plainant a bill of parcels, writ by himself, of the said yarn, making it bought
of him only. The yarn was weighed at His Majesty's beam at Cornhill
and entered as bought of Lambe, and of truth it was Lambe's when he sold it
to complainant. Being so mutually indebted, complainant often required
Lambe either to pay the £63. 15s. or to deduct it out of the £67. 3s. 4d.
and complainant would pay the remainder, viz., £3. 8s. 4d. Lambe refused
to take the £3. 8s. 4d. when it was tendered, or to pay the £63. 15s. Complainant, in order, therefore, to recover the £63. 15s., about May last entered
a plaint into His Majesty's Court before the Mayor and Aldermen of
London, in a plea of debt of £70, and (according to the custom of the City)
attached the £63. 15s. in his own hands as the money of Lambe, and tendered the residue (£3. 8s. 4d.). But now (after judgment and execution
upon the said attachment) Lambe, in confederacy with one Thomas Foster,
a draper, has agreed to cause complainant to pay the £67. 3s. 4d., and
Foster has commenced suit against complainant for 618 lb. of Scottish
yarn at 17d. per lb. and 340 lb. at 16½d. (total £67. 3s. 4d.), and intends
to prosecute the suit and thereby defeat the judgment in the Mayor's Court.
Foster intends to produce Lambe as a witness that, when complainant
bought the yarn, it was Foster's, not Lambe's, whereas in truth it was then
Lambe's. Foster has often acknowledged that Lambe gave him an accompt
of the yarn, which he had of the said Foster, at another rate than that
which complainant agreed for for the yarn he bought of Lambe. Lambe
also often required the money from complainant, saying to complainant
"pay mee my money," and said withall that he would spend £100 but he
would have his money, and offered complainant to refer it to arbitrement.
Complainant did not know that anyone else claimed the yarn until Lambe
entered an action at the suit of Foster and sent a note that complainant
should either put in bail or serjeants should attend him, which was at least
nine months after complainant bought the yarn from Lambe. Lambe has
often acknowledged that he does not know whether he bought the yarn
which he sold to complainant from Foster or from some other man. Complainant hopes to prove that Lambe had it of some other. Lambe has
often confessed that Foster often called upon him for money for the yarn
and never named complainant as the debtor; but Foster acknowledges that
he often threatened to take some course against Lambe to recover the
money; and to avoid this Lambe has now combined with him to sue complainant. Complainant prays for a writ of subpœna against Lambe and
Foster.

Joint Answer of Foster and Lambe, sworn 17 February 1634 [1634/5].
Lambe for five years has been a factor in London for buying, selling, and
bartering several commodities for citizens or countrymen who employ him
and satisfy him for his pains. He was heretofore employed by William
Mercer to buy a parcel of stockings, and, having notice of complainant's
parcel, repaired to him about the time stated in the bill and bargained for
the stockings for Mercer at the rate stated in the bill; but six months was
limited for the time of payment for the stockings. Afterwards, long before
the money was due and before Lambe had taken any of the stockings, viz.,
fourteen days after the bargain, Lambe, having acquainted Mercer of the
agreement, who disliked thereof, repaired to complainant and desired him
to release him of the bargain, because it had been made for a friend who disliked the price. Thereupon complainant (in consideration of a promise
then made by Lambe to spend 5s. in a breakfast upon complainant, which
Lambe is and ever since has been ready to perform) discharged Lambe of
the bargain for the stockings and told him he would dispose of them otherwise. Thereupon Lambe left the stockings with complainant and never
intermeddled further with them. Complainant bought the yarn of Lambe,

243

at the time and rates stated in the bill, and all of it was owned by Foster, who employed Lambe as his factor in this and agreed to allow him 40s. in every 100 pound's worth of yarn sold. Lambe informed Foster of the sale, but admits that he used his own name in the bill and in weighing of the yarn; and this is usual among factors in London, but in their particular books they keep an account of the parcels sold for different persons. At the time of the sale of the yarn complainant further discharged Lambe of the bargain touching the stockings. After complainant had got possession of the yarn, he did most "uncontionablie" and dishonestly demand abatement of the pretended sum of £63. 15s. for the stockings; so Lambe refused to take the £3. 8s. 4d. which complainant proffered. Neither before nor after the said judgment in the Mayor's Court has Lambe acknowledged that £3. 8s. 4d. only were due for the yarn. Lambe denies that he acted otherwise than as Foster's lawful factor. Foster denies that he has threatened to sue Lambe. (Chancery Proceedings, Charles I, C. 2, G. 27/34.)

5 February 1635 [1635/6]. Complaint by Samuel Gorton of Stratfourd Langton, co. Essex, merchant, that divers bargains had been made between him and William Lambe of London, merchant, in regard to wools and merchandise, and complainant had faithfully performed his contracts. In January 1633 [1633/4] he sold Lambe 15 score pairs of stockings, at 4s. 3d. a pair, totalling £63. 15s. 0d., which he promised to pay for at certain dates, but has not done so. Complainant is now afraid that Lambe may withdraw himself to Scotland, where he was born. He attached him in April 1634 in the Lord Mayor's Court at London for the money due. But in September 1634 Lambe conspired with Thomas Forster, of London, draper, and commenced a suit against complainant in the Lord Mayor's Court for money due for yarn, and he was forced to pay it to Forster, but Lambe still refuses to pay for the stockings. Complainant begs that Lambe may be caused to appear to answer the premises. [No answer.]

Demurrer of complainant (who appeared in person), confirming his bill. (Chancery Proceedings, Charles I, C. 2, G. 4/57.)

### Gorton v. Walker.

27 January 1647 [1647/8]. Bill of Samuell Gorton of New England. "Whereas your orator on or about the yeere" 1634 "had familier acquaintance with one John Duckingfeild of London Gent. and [said Duckingfeild] being a Batchellor had noe residinge place but recourse to such freinds and acquaintance as at the present gaue him hopes to be enterteyned most freely with the least charge and to draw on such familiarity and to be provided for with necessarys did use to pretend true love to the parties and would at the tyme of his death be a great advantage to such freinds or their children with whom hee sojourned . . . and would continually deposite great somes of money and divers . . . bonds . . . and writings touching his estate into the custody of such freinds . . . and being beyond measure troublesome and the burthen where he lay soe great noe freind in expectacion of his favour did admitt any long tryall of him and soe from others he came vnto your Orators then dwelling howse scituate in the parish of St Bottolphe Algate and your Orator being before acquainted with his person but knew not his Condicion vpon leaving others of his acquaintance he desired entertainemt of your Orator," pretending great love for complainant and promising him what reward should be just. Continuing some time in complainant's house, he brought in several moneys and carried from complainant (with whom he had deposited writings, such as bonds, bills and accounts) other moneys, upon pretence of bartering and letting out moneys to use and receiving money from use, in all of which complainant perceived nothing but that he was a very fair dealing man. Complainant, having occasion to

244

use money, desired Duckingfeild to lend him £100 upon bond. He consented, lent the £100, and complainant gave him a bond for payment of the same in twelve months without interest. Duckingfield, being possessed of the bond, and having obliged complainant to bear with all offences and to supply him free of charge with meat, drink, and lodging, [did] break forth openly to abuse diverse other persons, men of quality, with whom he had resided and had been freely entertained. Before the time of payment was due, Duckingfield found some new entertainment, left complainant's house, and took from him all his bonds, bills, and writings, carrying them into Cambridgeshire, and reserved his friends in London for his entertainment when he came about his business. Complainant being indebted to him, he used to take up his holding in complainant's house, and complainant, "being desired by some mutuall freinds to leave this Countrie and to live in New England acquainted the said Duckingfeild with his intention and did crave his advise therein." So soon as Duckingfeild heard this, he called in the £100, and would not continue the loan upon any conditions. Having some experience of his abusing carriage, complainant was unwilling to leave him any occasion to revile your orator in others' hearing, as he had done others. Complainant therefore paid him the money; but Duckingfield, having embursed it, pretended that the bond was with a friend in Cambridgeshire, and promised to return it cancelled, and meantime to give a release of all actions upon it. Complainant, having the release, expected the return of the bond; but Duckingfield, going down into Cambridgeshire at "some festival or Comencement," being entertained by friends, by some excess therein had a surfeit and died soon after. Complainant knew not of whom to demand the bond, and was advised by counsel that his release would be a good bar to it when produced. "And your Orators mind altering he stayed in old England a long tyme after the money was paid and after the death of the said Duckingfeild," and heard no demand made. "But in the tyme that your Orator stayed in old England there was some difference in opinion betweene your Orator and George Walter [sic] minister of Wattling streete parish Church London who preposed a Charitable contribucion to be made on or about the yeere" 1638 or 1639, "which collection was pretended to be conveyed to poore ministers in Lancasheire and the fraud being discouered by your Orator hee with drew his hand and by his example diverse others who had in that charitable pretence bin very free." This action bred great discontent in the said Walker, who, as complainant has since understood, was Duckingfield's coexecutor, with others, to dispose of his estate for charitable uses and the educating of one or more scholars at the University. Finding this bond among Duckingfield's writings and having knowledge (as complainant believes) that the money was paid, Walker did not publish the bond, and, having true knowledge that complainant was going beyond the seas to New England and being upon the said voyage, sent privately, in the same ship wherein complainant and his family passed over, to some of his brethren in New England that, so soon as complainant was seated there, they should prosecute the bond in New England, where it was hoped that complainant would get no bail, or, if he did, that the release should be left here or lost. Walker's plot was thus effectually put into action. So soon as complainant was well placed and in repute for his civil course of life and for his doctrine he there taught, Walker's agents attached his goods for £60, which was due to Walker in old England, alleging there that to avoid payment complainant came to that place; but, having obtained some good justice in that country, the defence was preferred as more honest than the accusation, and, when complainant had put in bail to answer the suit, Walker's agents declared upon the bond of £100 due to Duckingfield. Complainant pleaded the release there in New England, and was forced, at the hearing of the cause in the winter time, not only to great expense but also to the hazard of his life to travel through the wilderness sixty miles to the court of justice, where he produced his release before Sir H. Vane as Governor. The release was allowed, and the action dismissed, and complainant thought that Walker, "having his publique notice," was satisfied. Complainant, employed about some affairs for the state of New England, about 1645 coming into old England, into the Cities of London and Westminster, where Walker lived, he, having knowledge of where complainant lived for two years together, complainant being continually employed about the town, did not demand the money; but, having intelligence that complainant and his company had finished the business they had come about and were ready to depart to New England again, and that the ship and all things were ready for their passage and stayed only for opportunity of weather, Walker (endeavoring the ruin of complainant and his family) entered an action against complainant in the Counter of Woodstreet, London, for £200, by which he hopes (complainant being a stranger in the land for his habitation) that complainant should endure imprisonment or be compelled to pay. Walker caused complainant's arrest; but, contrary to expectation, some friends bailed complainant, and Walker (finding complainant had left the release behind him) prosecuted the suit with violence, endeavoring to have judgment before complainant could obtain relief. Complainant was obliged to remove the action into the King's Bench, and, not knowing the course of the court, his attorney did not inform him of any rules to make answer in the term time, nor did his attorney call for any answer, as the attorney alleges. Thereby complainant neglected to move the Court for an imparlance till complainant could send for the release, and upon this omission the attorney for the plaintiff in this vacation presseth for an answer, and complainant was forced to plead and hath given order to plead conditions performed, and Walker upon the plea purposeth to go to trial, although complainant has procured him a testimonial under Vane's hand of the trial in New England. Walker pretends not to be satisfied, and will not treat with complainant or his friends. Thereby complainant is not only kept from the company of his wife and children, who are in danger not only to lose their estates but to have their lives taken from them, and from divers others who expect his coming daily to give an account of the trust reposed in him, or else complainant must pay the whole £100 with interest and charges. Complainant prays for a writ of subpoena against Walker. [No answer here.] (Chancery Proceedings, Charles I, C. 2, G. 20/44.)

## MISCELLANEOUS RECORDS

Friday after the Festival of the Assumption,* 9 Henry V [22 August, 1421]. Thomas de Gorton *et al.*, querents, and John, son of Peter Gerard, Knight, and Ellen, his wife, deforciants, concerning the manors of Aspull and Ince by Wygan. (Lancashire Feet of Fines, 27, *m.* 12.)

13 Henry VIII [1521–22]. Ellen Gorton, widow of Roger Gorton, *v.* John Haryson and Katherine, his wife, *et al.*, concerning lands in Cockersand and Westhaughton, held by her late husband, Roger Gorton, for nineteen years, of the Abbot of Cockersand, according to the custom of the manor. Among the witnesses was Ellys Gorton of Horwich, aged 34 years. Ellys Penhulbury deposed that John and Elys Gorton were tenants, and that John Haryson and forty men in "hernez" came and took Nicholas Gorton to the bailiff's house and threatened to take him to Lancaster, etc. (Duchy of Lancaster Depositions, vol. 12, col. 6.)

10 July 1581. Richard Gorton, Nicholas Gorton, Thomas Gorton, and Elizabeth Gorton, four tenant farmers, surrendered their leases to the

*The Festival of the Assumption of the Blessed Virgin Mary occurred on 15 August.

Byrons of Clayton. (*Miscellanea Genealogica et Heraldica*, New Series, vol. 1, p. 321.)

1607. Adam Gorton [was] one of the two constables of Droylsden, near Manchester. (*Ib.*)

10 March 1608 [?1607/8]. William Gorton and Elizabeth Gorton, two tenant farmers, surrendered their leases to Sir John Byron, etc. (*Ib.*)

1614. William Gorton and Nicholas Gorton [are] two of the late purchasers of estates in Gorton who refused to pay the chief rent reserved by the Byrons. (*Ib.*, p. 322.)

14 October 1616. Precept to the constable of Gorton to apprehend Francis Gorton of Gorton, linenwebster, to show cause why he left the service of John Cocker of Gorton, he being his apprentice. (Manchester Sessions.)

1 April 1618. Robert Andrewe of Gorton *et al.* are bound to keep the peace towards Nicholas Gorton. (*Ib.*)

14 April 1618. Thomas Gorton of Manchester, lynner [?], is bound to keep the peace to Elizei [Ellis] Kenion. (*Ib.*)

1 July 1620. Ann Gorton of Gorton, widow, *v.* Paul Nicholson of Redich and Mary, his wife. (*Ib.*)

1628. Peeter Travis and Samuel Gorton [were] paid 6d. for warding at Milne End Gate, per the town's desire. (*Vide* Manchester Court Leet Records.) (*Miscellanea Genealogica et Heraldica*, New Series, vol. 1, p. 322.)

1636. Edward Gorton resided in Levenshulme, near Gorton. (*Vide* History of Birch, p. 43.) (*Ib.*)

The Gorton family was a very ancient family in Lancashire. Thomas de Gorton was assessed 2s. in the parish of Atherton in the subsidy of 1332; and in 1421 another Thomas de Gorton held the manor of Aspull, near Gorton. The arms borne by the Gortons have been described in the introduction to this article (*supra*, p. 186). On some of the foregoing and on other English records and on sundry New England records the following outline of the English ancestry and immediate family connections of Samuel Gorton of Rhode Island is based.

1. THOMAS GORTON, of Gorton, in the parish of Manchester, co. Lancaster, a descendant of the early Gortons of Gorton and of Aspull, was assessed 12d. on goods valued at 40s. in the subsidy of 1524. The name of his wife is unknown.

He was *probably* the father of

  2. i.  THOMAS.
  3. ii.  RICHARD.

2. THOMAS GORTON (probably a son of No. 1), of Gorton, in the parish of Manchester, co. Lancaster, was assessed 8d. on goods valued at £4 in the subsidy of 1543. The name of his wife is unknown.

He was *probably* the father of

    i.    NICHOLAS, of Gorton, living 10 July 1581, when, a tenant farmer, he surrendered his lease to the Byrons of Clayton; m. 22 Sept. 1574* ANNE GREENE, who was bur. 24 June 1608.
        Child:
        1.  *Elizabeth*, bapt. 6 Dec. 1574.
4. ii.   THOMAS.
   iii.  RICHARD. By Anne Bridge he had an illegitimate son, *Thomas*, bapt. 16 Sept. 1593.
   iv.  JAMES, m. ———.
        Child:
        1.  *James*, bapt. 9 Feb. 1576/7; m. 16 Sept. 1612 Margaret Chorlton.
    v.  ALICE. She had an illegitimate daughter, *Elizabeth*, bapt. 24 Jan. 1573/4.

3. RICHARD GORTON (probably a son of No. 1), of Gorton, in the parish of Manchester, co. Lancaster, a tenant farmer, surrendered his lease to the Byrons of Clayton 10 July 1581, and was buried 23 Jan. 1588/9. He married CICELY ———, who was buried 23 Sept. 1587.

    Children (the first two *probably* and the others *certainly* children of this Richard):
    i.    GEORGE, m. ———.
        Child:
        1.  *Ellen*, bapt. 20 July 1574; m. 19 Nov. 1593 Thomas Hawle.
    ii.   THOMAS, d. before 11 Apr. 1586; m. ELIZABETH ———, who, as his widow, was bur. 11 Apr. 1586.
        Children:
        1.  *Nicholas*, bapt. 4 June 1575.
        2.  *Thomas*, bapt. 3 Nov. 1576; bur. 4 Feb. 1576/7.
   iii.  WILLIAM, of Gorton, the testator of 20 May 1588, bur. 26 May 1588; m. JOAN ———, who survived him and was bur. 20 Sept. 1615. He had an illegitimate son, *Thomas*, bapt. 6 Aug. 1579.
   iv.  KATHERINE, living 20 May 1588, when she was mentioned as a legatee in her brother William's will.
5. v.   FRANCIS.

4. THOMAS GORTON (probably a son of No. 2), of Gorton, in the parish of Manchester, co. Lancaster, husbandman, the testator of 31 Dec. 1610, was buried 3 Jan. 1610/11. He married first ELIZABETH ———, who was buried 29 Aug. 1578; and secondly, about 1581, ANNE ———, who survived him and was buried 1 Nov. 1623.

    Children by first wife:
    i.    NICHOLAS, bapt. 5 May 1575; m. ———.
        Children:
        1.  *Thomas*, bapt. 25 July 1613.
        2.  *Samuel*, bapt. 23 June 1616.
        3.  *Martha*, bapt. 20 Aug. 1620.
    ii.   ELIZABETH (perhaps a child by the second wife), m. 27 Apr. 1611 WILLIAM BETSON.

    Children by second wife:
   iii.  THOMAS, bapt. 16 Feb. 1582/3; d. young.
   iv.  KATHERINE, bapt. 4 Oct. 1584; living 31 Dec. 1610, when she is mentioned in her father's will; m. 22 Apr. 1605 RALPH SHELMER-

*Dates of baptisms, marriages, and burials are taken from the registers of the Cathedral Church of Manchester, co. Lancaster (*vide supra*, pp. 191–193), unless otherwise stated or unless the context shows that they occurred elsewhere.

DYNE of Gorton, yeoman, the testator of 29 May 1639, who d. between 29 May 1639 and 1 Nov. 1639, when the inventory of his estate was taken. He m. (2) Anne ———, who d. before 29 May 1639. He had issue by his first wife. (See wills of Ralph Shelmerdyne and his father-in-law, Thomas Gorton.)

v. A SON, d. in infancy; bur. 10 Apr. 1586.
vi. WILLIAM, bapt. 30 Apr. 1587; d. young.
vii. THOMAS, bapt. 17 Nov. 1588; probably d. in New England between 16 July and 21 Nov. 1649; m. at Manchester, Eng., 14 Sept. 1612, AGNES GRIMSHAW, who may or may not have been the wife whom he had in Rhode Island about 1646 (see below).

As previously stated (*supra*, pp. 185–186), he seems to have accompanied his younger brother Samuel to New England, as he appears with him at Plymouth in New England in 1637 and later at Portsmouth, R. I. Among the volunteers for the Pequot War from Plymouth were "Mr. Goarton" (i.e., Samuel Gorton) and "Thomas Goarton" (Orr's Pequot War, p. xiv); in the Rhode Island Colonial Records (Chapin's Documentary History, vol. 2) it appears that Thomas Gorton was on a petit jury at the Quarter Sessions, 1 Dec. 1641 (p. 132), that he attended the General Court 16 Mar. 1641/2, being freeman and sergeant (pp. 119, 168), that at the General Court, 13, 1 mo. 1644, he was chosen ensign for Portsmouth (p. 128), and that in the suit of Richard Morris of Portsmouth against Thomas Gorton of the same place (an undated case, 1641–1648, but after 6 Oct. 1646) the plaintiff was awarded £20 as damages "for extravagancie of his [Gorton's] wive's tongue in abusing said Richard," but, the woman having acknowledged her fault, the fine was remitted (p. 161); and the printed town records of Portsmouth, R. I., show that Thomas Gorton was chosen ferryman 7 Sept. 1640, that he had land by the ferry 1 Nov. 1642, that he was present at a town meeting 29 Aug. 1644, that the town was to agree with him about the ferry (entry of 1 June 1647), that to Thomas Brooks and to Thomas Gorton 30 acres apiece were to be laid out at Wading River (entry of 25 June 1648), that on 16 July 1649 Thomas Gorton was chosen town sergeant and water "baily," and that on 21 Nov. 1649 John Albro was chosen sergeant in place of Thomas Gorton. As the entry of 21 Nov. 1649 contains the last reference to Thomas Gorton in the Portsmouth records, it is reasonable to suppose that he died shortly before this date.

Child:
1. *Samuel* (probably child of Thomas and Agnes), bur. at Manchester, Eng., 2 Nov. 1616.

viii. FRANCIS, bapt. 18 Dec. 1591; bur. 16 Apr. 1592.
ix. SAMUEL, of London and of New England, clothier, bapt. at Manchester, Eng., 12 Feb. 1592/3; living 11 Aug. 1674; m. before 11 Jan. 1629/30 MARY MAPLETT, bapt. in the parish of St. Lawrence Jewry, London, 12 Mar. 1608/9, a legatee in the will of her brother, John Maplett of Bath, co. Somerset, Eng., "Doctor of Physick," dated 13 Apr. 1670, daughter of John Maplett of London, haberdasher, and his second wife, Mary (———).*

Samuel Gorton, well-known in the annals of early New England, was of Plymouth in 1637, and migrated thence to Rhode Island, where he was of Portsmouth in 1639 and of Warwick in 1642. He was aged 82 in 1674.

Children:
1. *Samuel*, b. about 1630; m. 11 Dec. 1684 Susanna Burton, and had issue.
2. *John*, d. 3 Feb. 1714/15; m. 28 June 1668 Margaret Wheaton, and had issue.
3. *Benjamin*, m. 5 Dec. 1672 Sarah Carder, and had issue.

*For the ancestry and family connections of Mary Maplett, wife of Samuel Gorton, see REGISTER, vol. 70, pp. 115–118.

4. *Mahershalalhashbaz*, m. Daniel Cole.
5. *Mary*, d. before 1688; m. (1) Peter Greene of Warwick, R. I.; m. (2) John Sanford of Portsmouth, R. I. She had issue.
6. *Sarah*, m. William Mace.
7. *Ann*, m. 4 Aug. 1670 John Warner.
8. *Elizabeth*, m. 18 June 1673 John Crandall.
9. *Susanna*, m. 18 June 1672 Benjamin Barton.
x. MARY, m. 2 Jan. 1625/6 ALEXANDER BIRCHE.
xi. EDWARD, living at Levenshulme near Gorton in 1636; m. 12 May 1626 ALICE PARCIVALL. Before their marriage they had two daughters, *Ellen*, bapt. 13 Feb. 1619/20, bur. 9 Mar. 1619/20, and *Margaret*, bapt. 30 Mar. 1623.

5. FRANCIS GORTON (son of Richard, No. 3), of Gorton, in the parish of Manchester, co. Lancaster, was buried 29 Mar. 1597. He married, 4 May 1574, ELIZABETH BUERDSELL, who survived him and was buried 11 Jan. 1609/10.

Children:

i. WILLIAM, of Gorton, bapt. 31 July 1575; m. ———.
   Children:
   1. *Thomas*, bapt. 14 Jan. 1598/9; bur. 2 Apr. 1599.
   2. *Thomas*, bapt. 2 Mar. 1599/1600; bur. 29 Nov. 1615.
   3. *Margaret*, bapt. 5 Mar. 1604/5; m. 4 Apr. 1630 James Dawson.
   4. *Elizabeth*, bapt. 29 Mar. 1607; m. 20 Nov. 1634 Thomas Boardman.
   5. *George*, bapt. 20 Jan. 1610/11.
   6. *Samuel*, bapt. 1 May 1614; bur. 9 Apr. 1615.
   7. *Anne*, bapt. 20 May 1616.
ii. ELIZABETH, bapt. 8 Mar. 1577/8; m. 22 Apr. 1609 JOHN TOWNELEY.
iii. FRANCIS, bapt. 3 Apr. 1580; bur. 30 Mar. 1589.
iv. ISABEL, bapt. 20 Mar. 1582/3; bur. 6 May 1604.
v. GEORGE, bapt. 21 Nov. 1585 [*sic*].
vi. MARY, bapt. 4 Apr. 1586 [*sic*].

# GENEALOGICAL RESEARCH IN ENGLAND

Contributed by G. ANDREWS MORIARTY, JR., A.M., LL.B., of Newport, R. I.,
and communicated by the Committee on English and Foreign Research

## GOODSPEED <sup>*</sup>

IN this article records and a pedigree are presented which show the English ancestry and family connections of Roger Goodspeed, who was at Barnstable in the Plymouth Colony in New England as early as December 1641 and was the founder of a well-known New England family.

### FROM PROBATE RECORDS

The Will of THOMAS GOODSPEEDE of Wingrave, co. Bucks, husbandman, dated 5 January 1604 [1604/5]. To my wife Jane the little portion of land I bought, with the close and profits thereunto belonging, for twelve years after my death, for the bringing up of my children. Then it is to be sold, and out of the same I bequeath to my wife 20 marks, to my son Edward 20 marks, and the residue of the money from the said sale to my other children. The household stuff is to be divided, one half to my wife and one half to my daughters. Executrix: my wife Jane. [Signed] Thomas Goodspeede, his mark. Witnesses: Thomas Theed, his mark, William Goodspeede, John Putnam, Richard Haunce, Bennet Quarryndon, Wm. Heddge. Debts owing to my brother, William Goodspeed, Robert Lukas, Mr. Nicson. Proved 14 April 1606 by the executrix. (Archdeaconry of Bucks, No. 125 [filed will].)

The Will of NICHOLAS GODSPED of Wingrave, co. Bucks, husbandman, dated 20 January 1605/6. To be buried in Wingrave churchyard. To Thomas Collens of Hollingdon, parish of Soulbery, 20 marks, and to his children 12d. each. To the children of John Keene 12d. each. To the children of Robert Seabrocke 12d. each. To my wife Margaret £30 and my messuage in Wingrave, now in the tenure of Edward Jones, for her life. To the poor of Wingrave 10s. To my son-in-law Robert Seabrocke the said messuage after my wife's death, being a lease of one thousand years, purchased of Roger Henshawe of Wingrave. To Joseph Keene £10. Residuary legatees: My wife and the said Robt. Seabrocke. Executor: Robert Seabrocke. Overseers: George Etheridge of Tyscott and George Brocks of Wingrave. Witnesses: George Etheridge, George Brokes, William Heddy, writer. Debts owing by John Keene, Richard Newell of Hadnole, Roger Wygginton of Wigginton, Thomas Hill of Wigginton, Adkins of Berkhamstead, late of Tring, John Newman of Little Gadsden. Proved 17 February 1605/6. (Archdeaconry of Bucks, 1604–5, fo. 91.)

The Will of THOMAS GOODSPEED of Cranborrowe, co. Bucks, yeoman, dated 8 September 1622. To my son Hugh all my lands and tenements. To my son Robert £10. To my son William £10, when he comes from beyond the seas. To my son Bartholomew £10. To my daughter Jane Goodspeed £10. To my son Thomas £10. To my daughter Margaret 12d. Executor: my son Hugh. [Signed] Thomas Goodspeed, his mark. Witnesses: Samuel Clutterbucke, clerk, William Burton, P ———, the writer hereof. Proved 5 March 1626/7 by Hugh Goodspeed, son and executor of the deceased. (P. C. C., Skynner, 28.)

*For pp. 443-453 see pp. 251-261, this volume.

The Will of WILLIAM GOODSPEED of Rowsham, co. Bucks, yeoman, dated 7 October 1626. To the poor of Wingrave 10s. To my godson John Gurney £5. To my goddaughter Sara Brookes, daughter of Elizabeth Brookes, £5. To William and Hugh Peaseley, sons of my daughter Mary Peaseley, £10 each. To Susan Gaffield, daughter of William Gaffield, £5. To my god-daughter Joan Lucas, £5. To my daughter Anne Goodspeed and her heirs for ever my quarter of a yardland of meadow in the fields of Wingrave and Rowsham and £60, and she is to keep her mother, my wife, until her thirds be paid. To Thomas Gurney my malt mill. Residuary legatee and executrix: my daughter Anne. Overseers: William Gaffield and Nicholas Lucas, my friends. [Signed] William Goodspeed. Witnesses: John Seabright, Fra: Stevens.

Codicil [not dated]. To my daughter Mary Peeasley £20. To Ann and Joan Brookes, daughters of Elizabeth Brookes, my daughter, £10. To Alice and William Gaffield, children of Joan, my daughter, £4. To Sarah Lucas 40s., being daughter of Alice, my daughter. To the three daughters of my daughter Katherine £6. [Signed] William Goodspeed, his mark. Witnesses: William Gaffield, Nicholas Lucas, George Etheridge.

Proved 12 June 1628 by Anne Goodspeed, executrix. (Archdeaconry of Bucks, No. 86 [filed will].)

The Will of BENNETT GOODSPEEDE of Weston Turvile, co. Bucks, carpenter, dated 9 July 1638. To be buried in Weston churchyard. To my wife, for life, the occupation of my house and little close wherein I now dwell; on her marriage or death the same is to go to my son Bennett Goodspeede. To my wife 20s. a year for life. To Thomas, my second son, £10, at his age of twenty-one. To my three daughters [not named] £5 each. Executrix: my wife. Supervisor: Mr. John Latimer, rector of Halton, co. Bucks. [Signed] Bennett Goodspeede. Witnesses: John Latymer, Elizabeth Gerrarde, her mark. Proved 22 October 1638 by the executrix [name not given]. (Archdeaconry of Bucks, 1638, fo. 116.)

The Will of ROBERT GOODSPEEDE of Wingrave, co. Bucks, yeoman, dated 15 September 1658. To my wife Alice all my household stuff in my house at Wingrave, my grain, two cows, and twelve sheep. To my son Henry Good-speed £20. To my son Nicholas Goodspeed £5. To my sons Roger, Bennett, and Thomas Goodspeed £6. 13s. 4d. each, if they or any of them return from beyond the seas within ten years after my decease; if they do not return, then his or their share not returning is to go to my children Henry, Nicholas, Margaret Bate, Mary Seabrooke, Jane Lucas, and Mathew Moores. To my grandchild Robert Goodspeed, son of Robert Goodspeed, deceased, 40s., at their ages [sic] of twenty-one. To my grandchildren William Bate, Rebecca Bate, and Robert and Richard Bate, children of my daughter Margaret Bate, 20s. each, at their ages of twenty-one. To John Bate, son of the said [sic] William Bate, 20s., at his age of twenty-one. To my daughter Margaret Bate £5. To John, son of my son Nicholas Goodspeed, £5, at his age of twenty-one. To John Goodspeed, son of my son Henry, 40s., at said age. To my grandchild Jane Seabrooke 40s., at said age. To my grandchild Mary Moores 40s., at said age. To my said daughters, Margaret Bate, Mary Seabrooke, Jane Lucas, and Mathew Moores, 40s. each. To Jane and Mary Lucas, daughters of said Jane Lucas, 20s. each. Residuary legatee and executor: my son John Goodspeede. [Signed] Robert Good-speede, his mark. Witnesses: John Robins, Tho. Howson, scr. Proved 13 February 1660 [1660/1] by the executor named in the will. (Archdeaconry of Bucks, 1660.)

*Baptisms*

1553 Alice Goodspeed 27 March.
1553 Thomas Goodspeed 3 April.
1553 Elizabeth Goodspeed 30 April.
1553 Elizabeth Goodspeed 6 August.
1555 Nicholas son of Robert Goodspeed 13 December.
1556 John Goodspeed 9 August.
1556 Margaret daughter of Jo. and Elizabeth Goodspeed, Nicholas Goodspeed godfather, Margaret Theed and Margaret Milner godmothers,
16 August.
[1556 Nicholas Goodspeed is godfather to Jo: Biggs 18 August.]
1557 Jo: Goodspeed son of Jo: Goodspeed 27 August.
1558 Wm. Goodspeed 9 October.
1560 Bennett son of John Goodspeed 25 December.
1561 Agnes daughter of Robert and Isabel Goodspeed 15 April.
1561 Matthew son of Thomas and Joan Goodspeed 21 September.
1564 William son of John and Elizabeth Goodspeed 25 April.
1564 William son of Thomas and Joan Goodspeed 18 October.
1564 Thomas son of Robert and Isabel Goodspeed 27 December.
1565 John son of Thomas and Joan Goodspeed 22 January [1565/6].
1567 Ann daughter of Robert and Isabel Goodspeed 17 August.
1568 Margaret daughter of Nicholas and Margt. Goodspeed 14 November.
1570 Roger son of Robert and Isabel Goodspeed 22 October.
1573 Joan daughter of Nicholas Goodspeed 21 September.
1576 Alice daughter of Nicholas Goodspeed 19 August.†
1577 Margaret daughter of Robert Goodspeed 11 August.
1578 Robert son of Robert Goodspeed 3 August.
1583 Bennett son of Robert Goodspeed 22 September.
1586 Joan daughter of Nicholas Goodspeed 8 April.
1587 Robert son of Nicholas Goodspeed 18 October.
1589 Jo: daughter of Nicholas Goodspeed 16 October.
1589 Katherine daughter of William Goodspeed 3 December.
1590 Edward son of Thomas Goodspeed 13 September.
1591 Elizabeth daughter of William Goodspeed 26 December.
1592 Mary daughter of Thomas Goodspeed 25 December.
1593 Henry son of Nicholas Goodspeed 11 November.
1594 Dorothy daughter of Thomas Goodspeed 1 January [1594/5].
1595 Mary daughter of William Goodspeed 19 December.
1598 Joan daughter of William Goodspeed 23 July.
1598 Alice daughter of Thomas Goodspeed 17 December.
1599 Alice daughter of William Goodspeed 28 December.
1601 Susan daughter of Thomas Goodspeed 24 June.
1603 Eliz. daughter of Thomas Goodspeed 10 June.
1603 Thos. and Eliz. children of Roger Goodspeed 31 July.
1603 William son of William Goodspeed 29 September.
1604 Robert son of Roger Goodspeed 5 January [1604/5].
1606 Jo: son of William Goodspeed 4 July.
1606 Richard son of Roger Goodspeed 13 July.

*The entries from 1550 to the end of 1611 in the first volume of these registers are in one hand-
writing, except for a few entries at the end of the volume, and are evidently copies of the original
records. There are comparatively few burial entries, and apparently the burials were not so
carefully copied as the baptisms. After December 1611 there are no entries in this volume,
except a few written at the end, most of which belong to the years 1649–1652, although the book
is supposed to extend to 1656. The second volume of the registers has only scattered entries
prior to 1679, when a continuous series of entries begins.
†*Vide infra,* p. 446, first footnote.

1607   Ann daughter of William Goodspeed 6 March [1607/8].
1611   Robert son of Robert Goodspeed 20 November.
1650   Jane daughter of Hugh and Jane Goodspeed 22 June.*
1651   John son of Hugh Goodspeed 8 February [?1651/2].*
1652   Ann daughter of Hugh Goodspeed 25 August.*

### Marriages

1550   Robert Hebbes of Tilsworth and Margaret Goodspeed 25 February [1550/1].
1552   Robert Goodspeed and Isabel Allyn 30 October.
1584   Nicholas Goodspeed and Mary Benett of Adstocke 5 July.
1586   Richard Jeffes and Agnes Goodspeed 17 November.
1588   Benett Goodspeed and Agnes Strange 28 July.
1588   Thomas Goodspeed and Jane Chersley 28 September.
1588   Jo: Kyne and Margaret Goodspeed 10 November.
1596   Robert Seabrooke and Alice Goodspeed 12 September.
1598   Roger Woodbridge and Mary Goodspeed 30 October.
1602   William Goodspeed and Eliz. Lucas 11 October.
1602   Roger Goodspeed and Alice Grace 4 November.
1606   Roger Goodspeed and Alice Spindler 16 January [1606/7].
1611   Edw. Briginshaw and Jane Goodspeed, widow, 8 November.

### Burials

1558   Margaret daughter of Thomas Goodspeed 28 April.
1558   Jo. son of Thomas Goodspeed 3 October.
1558   Ann Goodspeed 4 October.
1563   Edw. son of Jo. Goodspeed 27 December.†
1583   Isabel wife of Robert Goodspeed 9 March [1583/4].
1593   Nicholas Goodspeed 21 April.
1600   Robert Goodspeed 8 November.
1602   Alice wife of William Goodspeed 17 June.
1602   Jo: Goodspeed 20 January [1602/3].
1605   Thomas Goodspeed 7 January [1605/6].
1606   Alice wife of Roger Goodspeed 17 July.
1606   Jo: son of William Goodspeed 8 August.
1608   Margaret Goodspeed, widow, 4 February [1608/9].

### From Lay Subsidies for co. Bucks‡

16 Henry VIII [1524–25].  Assessment of subsidy, Cottesloe Hundred.
  Wingrave with Rowsham.    Alicia Goodspeede in goods [valuation] £3, [tax] 18d.
                                  Nicholas Goodspeede in goods, [valuation] 16s., [tax] 4d.
                                  William Goodspeede in goods, [valuation] 20s., [tax] 4d.  (78/105.)
14 November, 33 Henry VIII [1541].  Assessment of subsidy.
  Wingrave.               Nicholas Goodspeade for goods, 10s. [sic]. (78/122.)
37 Henry VIII [1545–46].  Assessment of subsidy.
  Wyngrave with Rowlesham.   Nicholas Goodspede, 16d.
                            [Illegible]na Goodspede, 1d.  (78/134.)

---

*Entered at the end of the first volume of the parish registers.  This entry is not in the same handwriting as that of the main portion of the volume, and it is evidently an original record and not a copy.  Vide supra, p. 445, first footnote.

†Entered at the end of the first volume of the parish registers.

‡Preserved in the Public Record Office, London.

18 February, 37 Henry VIII [1545/6].  Assessment of subsidy.
Wyngrave with Rowlesham.  Nicholas Goodspead in goods, [valuation] £8, [tax] 5s. 4d.  (78/148.)
23 March, 1 Edward VI [1546/7].  Assessment of subsidy.
Wyngrave with Rowlesham.  Nicholas Goodspeade for goods, 5s. 4d. (78/149.)
26 July, 1 Elizabeth [1559].  Assessment of subsidy.
Wyngrave.  Robert Goodspede in goods, [valuation] £6, [tax] 10s.  (79/186.)
17 October, 36 Elizabeth [1594].  Assessment of subsidy.
Wingrave with Rolsham.  William Goodspeed in goods, [valuation] £3, [tax] 8s.  (79/217.)
4 October, 40 Elizabeth [1598].  Assessment of subsidy.
Wyngrave with Rowlsham.  Nicholas Goodspeede in goods, [valuation] £4, [tax] 10s. 8d.
William Goodspeed in goods, [valuation] £3, [tax] 8s.  (79/229.)
1 October, 41 Elizabeth [1599].  } Assessment of subsidy, as on 4 October,
10 October, 42 Elizabeth [1600].  }  40 Elizabeth [1598].  (79/242, 79/240.)
16 August 1622.  Contribution towards the recovery of the Palatinate, a schedule of names of such men of ability as have contributed.
Wingrave.  William Goodspeede, 8s.  (79/270a.)
15 March, 22 James I [1624/5].  Assessment of subsidy.
·Wingrave with Rowsham.  William Goodspeed in goods, [valuation] £3, [tax] 8s.  (79/278.)
1 April, 17 Charles I [1641].  Assessment of subsidy.
Wingrave with Rowlsham.  Robert Goodspeed in lands, [valuation] £1, [tax] 8s.  (80/299.)
22 March, 16 Charles II [1664/5].  Assessment of subsidy.
Wingrave.  John Goodspeede in lands, [valuation] £1, [tax] 8s.  (80/337.)
4 January 1670 [1670/1].  Return by the churchwardens of Wingrave, of whom John Goodspeed is one, of persons in Wingrave whose houses are under 20s. in value.  [No Goodspeed among them.]  (Bundle 324.)
Charles II.  Cotteslow Hundred.  Hearth tax.
Wingrave.*  Hugh Goodspeede, 1.
John Goodspeede, 2.  (80/352.)

FROM COURT ROLLS

Monday in the Feast of St. Dunstan, 26 Henry VI [1447–48].  Court held at Albury.† Rental of Tiscote with Wingrave.  Rent of bondmen [sic, ? bondsmen] of William Duncome for land late in the tenure of Richard Gudspede in Aldrewyke, 20s. 4d.  (Court Roll, 176/120)
27 September, 30 Henry VIII [1538].  Court Baron of John de Gostwyke, Esq., and Joan, his wife, held at Wyngrave.  Nicholas Godspede, juror.  To this court came Nicholas Godspede, and took from the lord one pightell or close in Eastwelwyk between the messuage of [illegible] on the west and a virgate of land and meadow in Rowsam and Wyngrave, late in the tenure of Richard Bysshop, paying yearly 16s. and suit of court, and gave as fine ———— [blank] and a heriot when due of 6s. 8d., and did fealty.
20 October, 32 Henry VIII [1540].  Court Baron of the said John Gostwyke held at Wingrave.  Nicholas Godspeede, juror.

*This list is much torn, and about three names are torn and illegible for this parish.
†Apparently a court for the Honor of Berkhampstead with Albury and Wingrave.

22 November, 33 Henry VIII [1541].   Court held.   Nicholas Godspede, juror.

16 January, 34 Henry VIII [1542/3].   View of frankpledge with court of Sir John Gostwyk, Knight, held at Wingrave.   Nicholas Goodspede, juror.

8 November, 35 Henry VIII [1543].   Court held.   Nicholas Goodspede, juror.   (Court Roll, 155/34.)

5 April, 2 Edward VI [1548].   Court Baron held at Wyngrave.   Nicholas Goodspede, juror.

8 December, 3 Edward VI [1549].   Court Baron held at Wyngrave. Nicholas Goodspede, juror.

11 July, 6 Edward VI [1552].   Court Baron held at Wyngrave.   Nicholas Goodspede, juror.   To this court came Nicholas Goodspede and showed here in court his copy, by which it appears he took a close lying in Eastwell-wyk, formerly Richard Bysshop's, and one virgate of land and meadow in Rollosham and Wyngrave, to him and his heirs, rendering yearly 16s. rent and other services.   (Court Roll, 155/35.)

7 September, 3 and 4 Philip and Mary [1556].   Court held at Wyngrave. Nicholas Goodspede, juror.

21 July, 4 and 5 Philip and Mary [1557].   Court held at Wyngrave. Nicholas Goodspede, juror.

24 September, 5 and 6 Philip and Mary [1558].   Court held at Wyngrave. It is presented that Nicholas Goodspede, who held by copy a close in Castell-wyk [*sic*, ? Eastwellwyk], late Richard Bishop's, and a virgate of meadow in Rollosham and Wyngrave, by rent of 16s., has died, and there falls due a heriot of 6s. 8d. [*illegible*].   Copy to Robert Goodspede for life.   (Court Roll, 155/36.)

Robert Goodspede was a juror at courts held at Wyngrave on Wednesday in Easter week, 2 Elizabeth [1560], 16 April, 5 Elizabeth [1563], 25 April, 7 Elizabeth [1565], 19 April, 8 Elizabeth [1566], 7 April, 9 Elizabeth [1567], 19 January, 10 Elizabeth [1567/8], 7 October, 10 Elizabeth [1568], and 3 March, 11 Elizabeth [1568/9].   (Court Roll, 155/37.)

Robert Goodspede was a juror at courts held on 25 October, 18 Elizabeth [1576], 23 Elizabeth [1580–81], 20 September, 24 Elizabeth [1582], and 31 October, 24 Elizabeth [1582].   (Court Roll, 155/39.)

17 April, 5 Elizabeth [1563].   Court Baron held at Tiscote [apparently for Tiscote with Wingrave].   John Godspede, juror.

20 September, 12 Elizabeth [1570].   Court Baron held at Tiscote [apparently for Tiscote with Wingrave].   John Goodspeede, juror.   (Court Roll, 178/67.)

MISCELLANEOUS

1637.   Roger Goodspeed of Wingrave appears in a list of delinquents for nonpayment of the ship money subsidy for Buckinghamshire.   (Public Record Office, 273/5.)

From the foregoing records and from a few other records and authorities hereafter cited the following pedigree has been compiled.

1. —— GOODSPEED, of Wingrave, co. Bucks, married ALICE ——, who was taxed 18d. on goods valued at £3 in the subsidy of 1524–25.

Children:

2.  i.  WILLIAM.
3.  ii.  NICHOLAS.

2. WILLIAM GOODSPEED, of Wingrave, co. Bucks, died about 1535. He married ANNA ———, who was buried at Wingrave 4 Oct. 1558.

He was taxed 4d. on goods valued at 20s. in the subsidy of 1524–25, and his widow was taxed 1d. in the subsidy of 1545–46.

Children:

4. i. JOHN.
5. ii. THOMAS.
iii. MARGARET, m. at Wingrave 25 Feb. 1550/1 ROBERT HEBBES of Tilsworth.

3. NICHOLAS GOODSPEED, of Wingrave, co. Bucks, died between 21 July 1557 and 24 Sept. 1558. The name of his wife is unknown.

He was taxed 4d. on goods valued at 16s. in the subsidy of 1524–25, 10s. [sic] on 14 Nov. 1541, 16d. in 1545–46, 5s. 4d. on goods valued at £8 on 18 Feb. 1545/6, and 5s. 4d. on goods on 23 Mar. 1546/7. He appears on the court rolls as a juror at various times from 27 Sept. 1538 to 21 July 1557, and the land which he held is mentioned in the court rolls of 27 Sept. 1538, 11 July 1552, and (after his death) 24 Sept. 1558, when it descended to Robert Goodspeed [his son].

Children:

6. i. ROBERT.
ii. NICHOLAS, of Wingrave, husbandman, the testator of 20 Jan. 1605/6, d. between 20 Jan. and 17 Feb. 1605/6; m. MARGARET ———, who was bur. at Wingrave 4 Feb. 1608/9. He was taxed 10s. 8d. on goods valued at £4 on 4 Oct. 1598.
Children, bapt. at Wingrave:
1. *Margaret*, bapt. 14 Nov. 1568; probably d. before her father, as she is not mentioned in his will; m. at Wingrave, 10 Nov. 1588, John Kyne (or Keene), whose children were legatees in her father's will.
2. *Joan*, bapt. 21 Sept. 1573; probably d. before her father, as she is not mentioned in his will; probably m. Thomas Collens of Hollingdon, parish of Soulbury [co. Bucks], to whom and to whose children her father left bequests.
3. *Alice*, bapt. 19 Aug. 1576; probably d. before her father, as she is not mentioned in his will; m. at Wingrave, 12 Sept. 1596, Robert Seabrooke, a legatee, with his children, in the will of her father.

4. JOHN GOODSPEED (*William*), of Wingrave, co. Bucks, was buried there 20 Jan. 1602/3. He married ELIZABETH ———.

Children:

i. ELIZABETH, bapt. at Wingrave 6 Aug. 1553.
ii. EDWARD, bur. at Wingrave 27 Dec. 1563.
iii. MARGARET, bapt. at Wingrave 16 Aug. 1556.
iv. JOHN, bapt. at Wingrave 27 Aug. 1557.
v. BENNETT, bapt. at Wingrave 25 Dec. 1560; m. there, 28 July 1588, AGNES STRANGE.
vi. WILLIAM, of Rowsham, co. Bucks, yeoman, the testator of 7 Oct. 1626, bapt. at Wingrave 25 Apr. 1564; d. between 7 Oct. 1626 and 12 June 1628; m. (1) at Drayton-Parslow, co. Bucks, 19 May 1588, ALICE BOUDE (Phillimore's Buckinghamshire Parish Registers, Marriages, vol. 3), who was bur. at Wingrave 17 June

1602; m. (2) at Wingrave, 11 Oct. 1602, ELIZABETH LUCAS, living
7 Oct. 1626. He was probably the William Goodspeed who was
taxed 8s. on goods valued at £3 in the subsidies of 17 Oct. 1594,
4 Oct. 1598, 1 Oct. 1599, and 10 Oct. 1600, who contributed 8s.
on 16 Aug. 1622 towards the recovery of the Palatinate, and who
was taxed 8s. on goods valued at £3 on 15 Mar. 1624/5.
Children by first wife, bapt. at Wingrave:
1.  *Katherine*, bapt. 3 Dec. 1589; m. ———; three daughters,
    mentioned in her father's will.
2.  *Elizabeth*, bapt. 26 Dec. 1591; m. ——— Brookes; three
    daughters, Sara, Ann, and Joan Brookes, named in her
    father's will.
3.  *Mary*, bapt. 19 Dec. 1595; living 7 Oct. 1626; m. ———
    Peaseley; two sons, William and Hugh Peaseley, named
    in her father's will.
4.  *Joan*, bapt. 23 July 1598; m. William Gaffield, who was
    living 7 Oct. 1626; three children, Susan, Alice, and
    William Gaffield, named in her father's will.
5.  *Alice*, bapt. 28 Dec. 1599; m. ——— [perhaps Nicholas]
    Lucas; probably two daughters, Joan and Sarah Lucas,
    named in her father's will.
Children by second wife, bapt. at Wingrave:
6.  *William*, bapt. 29 Sept. 1603; probably d. young, since he
    is not mentioned in his father's will.
7.  *John*, bapt. 4 July 1606; bur. at Wingrave 8 Aug. 1606.
8.  *Anne*, bapt. 6 Mar. 1607/8; living 12 June 1628, when, as
    executrix, she proved her father's will.*

5.  THOMAS GOODSPEED (*William*), of Wingrave, co. Bucks, married
    JOAN ———.
    Children:
    i.   THOMAS, of Wingrave, husbandman, the testator of 5 Jan. 1604/5,
         bapt. at Wingrave 3 Apr. 1553; bur. there 7 Jan. 1605/6; m.
         there, 28 Sept. 1588, JANE CHERSLEY, who survived him and
         m. (2) at Wingrave, 8 Nov. 1611, Edward Briginshaw.
         Children, bapt. at Wingrave:
         1.  *Edward*, bapt. 13 Sept. 1590; living 5 Jan. 1604/5.
         2.  *Mary*, bapt. 25 Dec. 1592.
         3.  *Dorothy*, bapt. 1 Jan. 1594/5.
         4.  *Alice*, bapt. 17 Dec. 1598.
         5.  *Susan*, bapt. 24 June 1601.
         6.  *Elizabeth*, bapt. 10 June 1603.
    ii.  JOHN, bapt. at Wingrave 9 Aug. 1556; bur. there 3 Oct. 1558.
    iii. MARGARET, bur. at Wingrave 28 Apr. 1558.
    iv.  WILLIAM, bapt. at Wingrave 9 Oct. 1558; probably d. young.
    v.   MATTHEW, bapt. at Wingrave 21 Sept. 1561.
    vi.  WILLIAM, bapt. at Wingrave 18 Oct. 1564.
    vii. JOHN, bapt. at Wingrave 22 Jan. 1565/6.
    viii. MARY (probably daughter of Thomas, No. 5), m. at Wingrave,
         30 Oct. 1598, ROGER WOODBRIDGE.

6.  ROBERT GOODSPEED (*Nicholas*), of Wingrave, co. Bucks, was
    buried at Wingrave 8 Nov. 1600. He married at Wingrave,
    30 Oct. 1552, ISABEL ALLYN, who was buried there 9 Mar.
    1583/4.
    He succeeded, 24 Sept. 1558, to the lands formerly held by
    his father, Nicholas Goodspeed, deceased, and was taxed 10s.

*Perhaps William Goodspeed had another child (probably by his first wife), who married ———
Gurney; for the first individual legacy in his will is one of £5 to his godson John Gurney, and he
leaves his malt mill to Thomas Gurney (perhaps his son-in-law).

on goods valued at £6, in the subsidy of 26 July 1559. He appears as a juror at numerous courts from 1560 to 1582, inclusive.

Children, baptized at Wingrave:

i. ALICE, bapt. 27 Mar. 1553.
ii. NICHOLAS, bapt. 13 Dec. 1555; bur. at Wingrave 21 Apr. 1593; m. there, 5 July 1584, MARY BENETT of Adstocke.
   Children, bapt. at Wingrave:
   1. *Joan,* bapt. 8 Apr. 1586; probably d. young.
   2. *Robert,* bapt. 18 Oct. 1587.
   3. *Joan,** bapt. 16 Oct. 1589.
   4. *Henry,* bapt. 11 Nov. 1593.
iii. AGNES, bapt. 15 Apr. 1561; probably d. young.
iv. THOMAS, bapt. 27 Dec. 1564. Possibly he was the Thomas Goodspeed of Cranborrowe, co. Bucks, yeoman, an abstract of whose will, dated 8 Sept. 1622, is given above (p. 443).
v. ANN (AGNES), bapt. 17 Aug. 1567; m. at Wingrave, 17 Nov. 1586, RICHARD JEFFES.
vi. ROGER, of Wingrave, bapt. 22 Oct. 1570; living in 1637; m. (1) at Wingrave, 4 Nov. 1602, ALICE GRACE, who was bur. there 17 July 1606; m. (2) at Wingrave, 16 Jan. 1606/7, ALICE SPINDLER. In 1637 he appears in a list of delinquents for nonpayment of the ship money subsidy for Buckinghamshire.
   Children by first wife, bapt. at Wingrave:
   1. *Thomas*  }  (twins), bapt. 31 July 1603.
   2. *Elizabeth* }
   3. *Robert,* bapt. 5 Jan. 1604/5.
   4. *Richard,* bapt. 13 July 1606.
vii. MARGARET, bapt. 11 Aug. 1577.
7. viii. ROBERT, bapt. 3 Aug. 1578.
ix. BENNETT, of Weston-Turville, co. Bucks, carpenter, the testator of 9 July 1638, bapt. 22 Sept. 1583; d. between 9 July and 22 Oct. 1638; m. ——, who survived him and proved his will 22 Oct. 1638.
   Children:
   1. *Bennett,* living 9 July 1638.
   2. *Thomas,* under twenty-one 9 July 1638.
   3. *A daughter,* ⎫
   4. *A daughter,* ⎬ living 9 July 1638.
   5. *A daughter,* ⎭

7. ROBERT GOODSPEED (*Robert, Nicholas*), of Wingrave, co. Bucks, yeoman, the testator of 15 Sept. 1658, baptized at Wingrave 3 Aug. 1578, died between 15 Sept. 1658 and 13 Feb. 1660/1. He married at Soulbury, co. Bucks, 6 Nov. 1609, ALICE HARRIS (Phillimore's Buckinghamshire Parish Registers, Marriages, vol. 1), who was living 15 Sept. 1658.

He was taxed 8s. on lands valued at £1 on 1 Apr. 1641.

Children:

i. ROBERT, bapt. at Wingrave 20 Nov. 1611; d. before 15 Sept. 1658; m. ——.
   Child:
   1. *Robert,* under twenty-one 15 Sept. 1658.
ii. JOHN, living 13 Feb. 1660/1, when, as executor, he proved his father's will. He was probably the John Goodspeed who was taxed at Wingrave 8s. on lands valued at £1 on 22 Mar. 1664/5, who was a churchwarden there 4 Jan. 1670/1, and who was taxed there for two hearths in the reign of Charles II.

*Entered in the parish register as "Jo: daughter of Nicholas Goodspeed."

iii. HENRY, living 15 Sept. 1658; m. ———.
   Child:
      1. *John*, under twenty-one 15 Sept. 1658.
iv. NICHOLAS, living 15 Sept. 1658; m. ———.
   Child:
      1. *John*, under twenty-one 15 Sept. 1658.
8. v. ROGER, ⎫ to each of whom their father, in his will, dated 15 Sept.
vi. BENNETT, ⎬ 1658, bequeathed £6. 13s. 4d., "if they or any of them
vii. THOMAS, ⎭ return from beyond the seas within ten years after
                  my decease."
viii. MARGARET, living 15 Sept. 1658; m. before that date WILLIAM BATE.
   Children (surname *Bate*):
      1. *William*, ⎫
      2. *Rebecca*, ⎪
      3. *Robert*, ⎬ under twenty-one 15 Sept. 1658.
      4. *Richard*, ⎪
      5. *John*, ⎭
ix. MARY, living 15 Sept. 1658; m. before that date ——— SEABROOKE.
   Child (surname *Seabrooke*):
      1. *Jane*, under twenty-one 15 Sept. 1658.
x. JANE, living 15 Sept. 1658; m. before that date ——— LUCAS.
   Children (surname *Lucas*):
      1. *Jane*, ⎱ living 15 Sept. 1658.
      2. *Mary*, ⎰
xi. MATHEW (daughter), living 15 Sept. 1658; m. before that date
   ——— MOORES.
   Child (surname *Moores*):
      1. *Mary*, under twenty-one 15 Sept. 1658.

8. ROGER GOODSPEED (*Robert, Robert, Nicholas*), of Barnstable in
   the Plymouth Colony, farmer, the immigrant ancestor of the
   American Goodspeeds, was born probably at Wingrave, co.
   Bucks, and died intestate in 1685. He married at Barnstable,
   1 Dec. 1641, ALICE LAYTON, who died between 10 Jan. 1688/9,
   when her will was dated, and 4 Sept. 1689, when it was proved.
      As stated above, his father, in his will dated 15 Sept. 1658,
   bequeathed to him and to his brothers Bennett and Thomas
   £6. 13s. 4d. each, "if they or any of them return from beyond
   the seas within ten years after my decease." He came to
   Barnstable in 1639, and in 1643 was on the list of those able
   to bear arms. His wife was admitted to the church 31 Dec.
   1643, and he was admitted to the church 28 July 1644.*
      Children, born at Barnstable:*

i. NATHANIEL, of Barnstable, b. 6 Oct. 1642; bapt. at Barnstable 14
   Jan. 1643/4; d. in 1670; m. in Nov. 1666 ELIZABETH BURSLEY,
   daughter of Mr. John Bursley. She m. (2) in Oct. 1675 Increase
   Clap. Two children.
ii. JOHN, of Barnstable, b. 15 June 1645; d. in 1719; m. 9 Jan. 1668/9
   EXPERIENCE HOLWAY (or HOLLEY). Seven children.
iii. MARY, b. in July 1647; m. 14 Dec. 1664 SAMUEL HINCKLEY.
iv. BENJAMIN, of Barnstable, b. 6 May 1649; bapt. at Barnstable
   19 May 1649; m. MARY DAVIS, daughter of John Davis. She
   m. (2) 24 Nov. 1697 Ensign John Hinckley. One daughter.
v. RUTH, b. 10 Apr. 1652; bapt. at Barnstable 15 May 1652; m. 2 Feb.
   1674/5 JOHN DAVIS, JR.

*Cf. Savage's Genealogical Dictionary, Pope's Pioneers of Massachusetts, and Swift's Genea-
logical Notes of Barnstable Families, vol. 1, 1888. Swift gives details about Roger Goodspeed's
lands in Barnstable.

vi. EBENEZER, of Barnstable, b. in Dec. 1655; living 30 Dec. 1746; m. 15 Feb. 1677/8 LYDIA CROWELL of Yarmouth. Thirteen children.

vii. ELIZABETH, b. 1 May 1658; living unm. in 1688.

———

GOODSPEED. — On page 2 of the "Collections of the New-York Historical Society for the Year 1892," a volume containing abstracts of wills on file in the surrogate's office in New York City, 1665–1707, the following abstract, taken from liber 1–2, page 5, of the records, is printed:

Roger Goodspeede, of Barnstable, Massachusetts, had wife Alice, who was sister and "next heire" of John Layton, "late of Middleborrough, *alias* New Towne, upon Long Island." Upon application of their son Nathaniel Goodspeede, Letters of Administration were granted to his parents January 2, 1665.

This abstract gives additional information about the wife and family of Roger Goodspeed, as printed in the REGISTER, vol. 82, page 452. *

*Bristol, R. I.* G. ANDREWS MORIARTY, F.S.A.

— — —

*
GOODSPEED (THE REGISTER, volume 82, pages 443–453): ADDITION AND COR-RECTION: — Page 449. *To* Margaret, daughter of John Goodspeed, bapt. 16 Aug. 1556 *add* Married at Wingrave, 30 Jan. 1577/8, Nicholas Putnam of Wingrave. Parents of John Putnam, the early settler of Salem Village, Mass. (When this article was written there was some uncertainty as to this marriage, which has since been removed by a recent examination of the Wingrave Parish Register.)

Page 452. Roger Goodspeed of Barnstable *delete* "died intestate" *and add* his will is printed in volume I of the "History of the Goodspeed Family", by Weston A. Goodspeed.

*Wells, Maine.* G. ANDREWS MORIARTY.

*For pp. 443–453 see pp. 251–261, this volume.

# GENEALOGICAL RESEARCH IN ENGLAND

Contributed by G. Andrews Moriarty, Jr., A.M., LL.B., of Newport, R.I.,
and communicated by the Committee on English and Foreign Research

## Morse

On 15 Apr. 1635 there embarked on the *Increase,* from London, England, for New England, Samuel Morse, husbandman, aged 50 years, Elizabeth Morse, aged 48 years, Joseph Morse, aged 20 years, and Elizabeth Daniel, aged 2 years, Joseph Morse being without doubt a son and Elizabeth Daniel probably a granddaughter of Samuel and Elizabeth Morse. Samuel Morse settled first in Watertown, Mass., but moved to Dedham, Mass., at its first settlement in 1636 and died in 1654, leaving a will. Of his children who are found in New England the eldest son was John Morse, the second Daniel Morse, the third Joseph Morse, and the youngest child, apparently, was Mary, who married, 10 Aug. 1641, Samuel Bullen of Watertown and Medfield, Mass., whither also the Morses went. From the date of Mary's marriage it may be inferred that she was born about 1620. A Thomas Morse who appears in the Dedham church records on 5, 2 mo. 1640 and 28, 4 mo. 1640 was probably another son of Samuel Morse, and, as nothing more is heard about him, he probably died childless soon afterwards.

Samuel Morse's son Daniel came to New England before his father, and settled at Watertown, for on 6 May 1635 Daniel and Joseph Morse of Watertown were admitted as freemen. This Joseph Morse was not Joseph the son of Samuel, as the latter Joseph came in the ship with his father, but he was apparently the Joseph Morse, aged 24, who embarked at Ipswich, England, 1 Apr. 1634, on the *Elizabeth.* He appears to have been a son of Joseph and Dorothy Morse of Dedham, England; and his father migrated to Ipswich, Mass., and in his will in 1646 mentions a son Joseph. That Joseph Morse of Ipswich, Mass., was a relative of Samuel Morse of Dedham, Mass., will appear from the records given in the following pages.

For many years the question of the ancestry of Samuel Morse of Dedham, whose descendants are numerous, has puzzled New England genealogists. It is with pleasure, therefore, that the Committee on English and Foreign Research presents English records and a pedigree based on them which show very conclusively the ancestry of Samuel Morse and the parentage of his wife Elizabeth.

Acknowledgment is due to Mrs. Sidney Morse of London for information contained in her valuable notes, from which the clue leading to the parish of Redgrave, Suffolk, was first obtained.

### FROM PROBATE RECORDS

The Will of ROBERT MORSE of Stoke Nayland [co. Suffolk], husbandman, dated 5 October 1551. To my son John the Elder the house where I live, he paying to my eldest son Thomas £3 in three years. To Robert and Thomas, sons of my son Thomas, who now dwells with me, 20s. towards their keeping. To my son Richard the house and lands called Canons, at his age of twenty-one. To my son John the Younger half of my tenement called Paulling, at his age of twenty-one. To my daughters Alice, Jone, Margaret, and Katherine. To my wife Agnes my dun mare. Executrix: my wife Agnes. Proved 15 September 1552. (Archdeaconry of Sudbury [Bury St. Edmunds], book 27, fo. 90.)

The Will of JOHN MOSSE THE ELDER of Stoke by Nayland [co. Suffolk], yeoman, dated 23 September 1577. To Agnes Pood a cow. To the three daughters of John Awford three calves. To my sister Wellam a calf. To Agnes Langley three calves. To Elizabeth Bacon a cow. To William Pudney a lamb. To Alice Clark a lamb. To the wife of my nephew Robert Mosse the tenement called Gilberts and the house and lands called Dales, which are to be sold to my son-in-law John Bacon. To my nephew Robert Mosse my lands called Pondyard, Burgise, and Cookucks. To the poor of Stoke £8 a year. To my nephew Thomas Mosse the Elder one croft bought of Benight Langley's widow. Other lands to my wife and nephew Robert Mosse, for life, and then to Robert, son of my brother Richard Mosse. Supervisor: Robert Genner. Executors: my wife Katherine and my nephew Robert Mosse. Proved at Bury St. Edmunds 12 December 1577. (Archdeaconry of Sudbury [Bury St. Edmunds].)

The nuncupative Will of AGNES MOSSE of Stoke by Nayland [co. Suffolk], declared 13 January 1578/9. To my son John 5s., for the poor. To Alice Elsing. To Margaret Mosse. To Lancelot Mosse, John Mosse the Younger, Richard Mosse, and Robert, son of Richard Mosse the Elder. Residue to my son John, who is to be executor. Proved at Bury St. Edmunds 1 February 1578/9. (Archdeaconry of Sudbury [Bury St. Edmunds].)

The Will of WILLIAM MORSE of Suffolk, clothier [not dated]. Land in tenure of Anthony Morse. To my five children, Robert, Edward, John, Alice, and Samuel. To my three cousins Hubbard gold rings. To Brother Reme and wife, Brother Bugge and wife, Brother Aldrich and wife, and Sister Bloyse. Executors: Robert Causdell and Anthony Morse. Proved 12 September 1582. (P. C. C., Tirwhite, 36.)

The Will of THOMAS MORSE, "minister of God his worde in the County of Essex," dated 10 November 1596. To my "nyne children noew living nyne score pounds," namely, to John, Samuel, Daniell, Joseph, Jeremye, James, Nathaniel, and Philip, my sons, and to Sara, my daughter, at the age of twenty-three, Sara to receive her twenty pounds at twenty-one. To my brother Richard Mosse 50s. To my sister Margaret Morse 20s. To my eight youngest children eight "Bybles." To my eldest son all my books in my "studdye." To the poor of Foxearth 10s. Residue of goods, money, plate, bonds, mortgages, cattle, household stuff, etc., to my wife Margaret, and she is to bring up my children in learning. If my wife Margaret die unmarried, she is to give to the four children by my first wife £20. Proved 28 April 1597. (P. C. C., Cobham, 26.)

The Will of ROBERT MOSSE of Stoke by Nayland [co. Suffolk], single man, dated 21 August 1600. Testator bequeathes his house and other property in Stoke to Gillian Bacon, his executrix. Proved at the Bishop's Court, Norwich, in 1602.

The Will of ANTHONY MORSE* of Hinderclay [co. Suffolk], dated 4 August 1603. To my wife Elizabeth lands in Stoke by Nayland for life, and then to my nephew Azaell, son of my brother Edward Morse. To my wife lands in Boxted, co. Essex, for life, and then to said Azell, if he pay to the children of my brother Nathaniel Morse £20. To the children of my brother William, i.e., Edward, John, and Samuel, to each £40. To Robert Snow of Stratford £20. To John Pigott £20 per annum for life. To poor students of Cambridge £4. To the poor of Stratford £40. To the poor of Hinderclay £40. To Cousin Bond and wife a ring. To Sister Mary Morse of Stratford a ring and the furniture in my house at Stratford. To Mr. Dow, a preacher of God's word at Stratford. To Mr. Smyth of Rickinghall a book. Like bequests to Mr. Ravens, Mr. Wallys, Mr. Hall, and Mr. Chamberlain of Hunson. To Nathaniel Hollingston of Cambridge. Executrix: my wife Elizabeth. Supervisor: Henry Farr. Proved 20 September 1604. (P. C. C., Harte, 77.)

The Will of WILLIAM GLOVER of Dedham, co. Essex, clothier, dated 26 January, 6 James [1608/9], bequeaths to Joseph Morse of Dedham 40s. and to the Widow Morse, in the Valley, 20s. Proved 5 May 1609. (P.C.C., Dorsett, 39.) [An abstract of this will may be found in the REGISTER, vol. 46, pp. 312–313, and in Waters's "Genealogical Gleanings in England," vol. 1, pp. 582–583.]

The Will of LANCLETT JASPER of Redgrave [co. Suffolk], husbandman, being "sick of body," dated 17 February 1616 [1616/17]. To William, my son, and Francis [sic] his wife, for their lives, the tenement wherein I dwell, which I purchased of Gregorye Fysher, with the hemp land and croft thereto belonging, on condition that they pay to Rose, my wife, for her life, 40s. a year, quarterly; otherwise my son Henrie is to enter thereon. If William and Frances pay the annuity, then the tenement shall, after their decease, be equally divided among the children of my said son William and Frances, his wife, viz., Nathaniell, Jonathan, Joseph, Jerymie, Elizabeth, Bridgett, and Marye. To my son Nathaniell Jasper and his heirs £5. 6s. 8d., payable by my son William within one year of the death of my wife Rose. To my son William and his heirs 1 acre of land which I purchased of Elizabeth Sheppard, he to plough and sow it with hempseed during the life of my wife Rose, and the hemp to be equally divided between himself and my wife Rose. My son William is to pay to Annes Morse, my daughter, £3 within two years of the decease of my wife Rose, and to Elizabeth Morse, my daughter, £3 within three years of the decease of my wife Rose. To my son Jeremye and his heirs, if it please God he overlive me, a piece of land (2 acres) which I purchased of Edmond Fowle, he paying to Rose, my wife,

*This Anthony Morse, a prominent Presbyterian minister, was the son of Edward and Julyan (Forth) Morse of the Stratford St. Mary branch of the family.

13s. 4d. a year for her life. My son Jeremye shall pay to my son Daniell Jasper £5 within one whole year of the decease of Rose, my wife, and to my son John Jasper £5 within two years of the decease of said Rose. If Jeremye die before his mother, "wch God defende," and "before he hath taken yt upp," then my son Henrie Jasper shall have the two acres, paying to his mother her annuity and to his two brethren, Daniell and John, the portions last-named; and in default of payment Daniell and John are to enter on the land. My wife Rose shall have those rooms and fruit trees which I have reserved and which are now in my tenure out of the before-bequeathed premises, with ingress and egress and to the fire, for life. To my wife Rose one bed complete, as it standeth in my chamber, with one cupboard, a cupboard table, two coffers, a chest, a kettle, a little brass pot, a warming pan, two ale firkins, one mortar with the pestle, and a candlestick. Executor: my son William. Witnesses: Roberte Debenham, Edmond Fowle, Robert Fysher. Proved at Bury St. Edmunds, 3 March 1616 [1616/17], by the executor. (Archdeaconry of Sudbury [Bury St. Edmunds], book 46, fo. 185.)

The Will of Robert Morse of Stoke by Nayland [co. Suffolk], yeoman, dated 6 May 1619. To my wife Ann 3s. per annum for life and her dwelling in the house where I now dwell and her board, etc., at the charge of her son Richard. To my son Richard all my freehold land in Stoke. To my son Robert £20, at twenty-one years of age, and the lands given to him by his grandfather Richard Morse, deceased, after the death of his brother Joseph. To my daughter Lydia, at twenty-two years of age. To my son John, at twenty-six years of age. To my son Francis, at eighteen years of age. [Testator's son Joseph was not yet eighteen years of age.] Executor: my son Richard. Proved in the Bishop's Court, Norwich, 19 September 1622.

The Will of John Anger of Dedham, co. Essex, clothier, dated 19 January 1623 [1623/4], contains a bequest of 20s. to Joseph Morse the Elder. Proved 18 February 1623 [1623/4]. (P. C. C., Byrde, 19.) [A lengthy abstract of this will may be found in the Register, vol. 50, pp. 400–402, and in Waters's "Genealogical Gleanings in England," vol. 2, pp. 1187–1189.]

The Will of John Pye of Dedham, co. Essex, clothier, dated 8 November 1624, contains a bequest of Joseph Morse, Sr., of Dedham, and mentions Jeremie Morse. Proved 24 February 1624 [1624/5]. (P. C. C., Clarke, 13.) [A lengthy abstract of this will may be found in the Register, vol. 50, pp. 386–387, and in Waters's "Genealogical Gleanings in England," vol. 2, pp. 1173–1174.]

The Will of Ann Anger, dated 2 September 1625, mentions Joseph Morse. Jerimiah Morse is a witness. Proved at Colchester 16 December 1625. (Commisary Court of London for Essex and Herts [Somerset House, London], 1625–26, no. 177.) [A lengthy abstract of this will may be found in the Register, vol. 50, pp. 402–403, and in Waters's "Genealogical Gleanings in England," vol. 2, pp. 1189–1190.]

The Will of Anne Copping of Burgate [co. Suffolk], dated 7 July 1626, is witnessed by Elizabeth Morse, wife of Samuel Morse. (Archdeaconry of Sudbury [Bury St. Edmunds], book 49, fo. 550.)

The nuncupative Will of Mary Mosse of Dedham, co. Essex, single, declared 9 May 1631. To my three unmarried sisters apparel at the discretion of Francis Gibbes. Witnesses: Jeremy Mosse, Margt. Mosse. Proved 25 January 1631/2 by Fras. Gibbes. (P. C. C., Audley, 6.)

The Will of RICHARD MORSE of the parish of Duddinghurst, co. Essex, yeoman, being "weak in body," dated 16 August 1632. To my brother Edward Morse all moveables, he paying £70 to my loving wife Margaret. To my wife Margaret £5 yearly, towards the bringing up of her child until it be fourteen years of age. My executor is to pay the whole fine for my land, so that my wife may enjoy her third part without fine; otherwise he shall pay her £10. To my elder daughter Margereth £100, viz., £50 at her age of eighteen and £50 at her age of twenty-one; if she marry and have issue before her age of twenty-one, her issue is to have the mother's portion [it is not expressly stated that this portion is to go to the issue on the mother's death]; if she die without issue in the meantime, the latter part of the portion shall go to her younger sister; if she die under eighteen years of age, the whole portion shall go to the younger sister. My executor is to bring up my elder daughter or to put her forth to some sufficient man, with her portion. To my younger daughter [not named] £100, payable at the same ages; but, if she die, [her portion] is to remain in my executor's hands. To my wife the bed [manuscript torn]. To the poor of Duddinghurst 20s. The mark of Recherd Morse. Witnesses: Samuel Petchey, the mark of Samuel Merden, the mark of Nicholas Ouerall.

Administration with the will annexed was granted 1 November 1632 to Edward Morse, brother of the deceased, no executor having been named in the will. (Archdeaconry of Essex [Somerset House, London], filed copy.)

The nuncupative Will of ROBT. MORSE of Hinderclay [co. Suffolk], husbandman, declared 6 January 1633/4, makes the testator's wife, Judith, the sole legatee, and she is to bring up his children. Witnesses: Mary Locke, Kath. Scarphe. Proved 13 January 1633/4 by the relict, Judith. (Consistory Court of Norwich, 1633, fo. 398.)

The Will of JEAMES MORSE of Bargham, co. Suffolk, being "weak of body but of p'fect memorie," dated 2 September 1638. To my brother Joseph Morse and his heirs all my lands and tenements, both free and copyhold; and my said brother Joseph shall make sale of so many of the said lands and tenements as shall raise these sums of money following, and dispose of the said money in the legacies hereafter mentioned: To my brother Nathaniell Morse £20. To my brother Phillip £5. To the child of my brother Daniell Morse £5. To my brother Mr. John Morse of Rumforde £5. To my brother Samuell Morse £10. To my cousin Joseph Morse 40s. To Mr. Catlin and Mr. Candler and Mr. Swayne, to each of them 40s. and a pair of gloves, and the like pair to Mr. Fowle. To Edward Ines, Andrew Wills, Edwarde Sacker, and Elisabeth Sacker, to each of them 20s. To Richard Aldridge 20s. To Richard Balewe and Margery Colstone, to each 10s. To Willm. Studde, Danell Dale, and Steven Blomfeild, to each of them 5s. To every serv[an]t in this house, besides these before named, to each of them 2s. 6d. "And my will is yt my Executor doe give to every-one of my fellowes servts [a] payer of gloves and Ribond." To Mrs. Wardd, Goodman Mapes, Goodman Harvye, and Goodman Tayler, to each of them 20s. To my good Mrs. Bacon 40s. for a pair of gloves, and to Mrs. Nathaniell Bacon and Mrs. Francis Bacon, to each of them 20s. for a pair of gloves, and the like legacy to Mrs. Phillip Bacon. To Mr. Lyonell Bacon 40s. To Robert Baker, Mr. Arthur, Mr. Burgh, Mr. Fowle, and Goodman Fouldger of Disse, to each of them 40s. To Katherin Westbrowne £5. To Mr. Nathaniell Bacon and Mr. Francis Bacon, to each of them 5s. To Goodman Aldridge, Goodman Turner, and Goodman Warde, to each of them 20s. To the poor of Codenhall 40s., and to the poor of Bargham [sic] 40s. Sole executor: my brother Joseph Morse. Immediately after my death my said brother Joseph shall make proffer of the sale of all my lands in Stowmakett to Mr. Yonge, of whom I bought them, at the same price that I had them of him; and, if he shall refuse to purchase them upon the offer, after the rate aforesaid, then my will is that they be immediately sold to any other body, at the best value, by my said executor. I give to my said executor all the overplus of my whole estate, my deb[ts] and legacies being discharged. Witnesses: Fr. Bacon [evidently the writer of the will], John Swaine, Thomas Fowle. [Signed] James Morse. Proved at Ipswich 8 September 1638 by the executor named in the will. (Ipswich, uncalendared wills, 1638, 101a.)

Administration on the goods of ALICE MORSE of Beccles [co. Suffolk was granted in 1644 to her husband, John. (Ipswich, Act Books, 21, fo. 9.)

The Will of JOHN MORSE, Mnr. [i.e., minister], of Romford [co. Essex], dated 14 July 1645. To Dorothe, my younger daughter, £100, to be paid by my executrix within two years after my decease or at the day of her marriage. To Elizabeth, my elder daughter, £5, to be paid within one year after my decease. To my brothers or brothers' children £30, to be paid within two years after my decease at my dwelling house in Romford and to be divided among them at the discretion of my executrix. To my beloved wife Dorothe all my lands and tenements, for life, and she is to be sole executrix and to dispose what else she see meet [sic] to the poor. [Signed] John Morse [with seal]. Witnesses: Daniel Cramphorne, the mark of Mary Cramphorne. Proved at Brentwood 25 May 1648 by Dorothy Morse, widow and executrix. Valuation, £133. 15s. (Archdeaconry of Essex [Somerset House, London], original will. Cf. Archdeaconry of Essex, Act Books, 19, fo. 31b).

The Will of JUDITH MORRIS of Dedham, co. Essex, widow, dated 25 January 1645 [1645/6], contains a bequest of 20s. to "Joseph Morse in New England," "if he be living;" and, "if he be dead," to "William Stone in New England." Proved 17 March 1645 [1645/6]. (P. C. C., Twisse, 33.) [A lengthy abstract of this will may be found in the REGISTER, vol. 48, pp. 118–119, and in Waters's "Genealogical Gleanings in England," vol. 1, pp. 818–819.]

The Will of SAMUELL MOSE of Littell Walden in the parish of Great Walden, co. Essex, labourer, being "week in body," dated 14 November 1647. To Robart Mosy, my second son, a hutch, a kneeding trough, and one-half of my working tools. To my daughter Margett, now wife of Henry Bechshop, my little tenement, paying ———. To Edward Mosy, my eldest son, 12s. To James Mosy, my youngest son, a table and form in the parlour. Residuary legatee and executrix: my wife Alce. The mark of Samuell Mose. Witnesses: Thos. Wenham, Francis Belleham. Proved at Dunmowe Magna 1 January 1647 [1647/8] by William Wood for the executrix. (Commissary Court of London for Essex and Herts [Somerset House, London], filed copy, January 1647, Clarke, 71.)

Administration of the goods of JOSEPH MORSE of Palgrave [co. Suffolk] was granted in 1648 to Elizabeth, relict of the deceased. (Bury St. Edmunds, Act Books, 3, fo. 122.)

The Will of JEREMY MOSSE of Dedham, co. Essex, clothworker, dated 14 May 1663. To be decently buried, with a sermon. To my wife Abigall and to her heirs for ever the house where I dwell in Dedham, with residue of household stuff and shop stuff. Executrix: my wife Abigael. Supervisors: Thos. Luffkin, gent., and Joseph Gleason, grocer, both of Dedham. Witnesses: Jeremiah How and Jeremiah Songer. Proved at Colchester 20 May 1664 by the oath of the executrix. (Commissary Court of London for Essex and Herts [Somerset House, London], Alderton, 329.)

The Will of ABIGAIL MOSSE of Dedham, co. Essex, widow, being sick, dated 8 January, 17 Charles II [1665/6]. To Cousin Henry Robinson and his heirs my messuage and tenement in Dedham, upon Prensall Green, and all moveables, "to this intent and purpose her Daughter mentioned." [*sic* in register.] To Maryan Greene £5; if she then be dead, to Henry, Saml., and John Robinson, her grandchildren; payable to Maryan Greene or her grandchildren six months after my decease. To Sister Rebecca Hall £5, my red undercoat with red golden lace and a suit of "linning," and a white apron. To Sister Dorcase, wife of Henry Cracknell, £5. To Cousin Thomas Greene 40s.; to his son Thomas Greene 20s. To Sister Rebecca Olester 40s. To William Hall 40s. apiece [*sic*]. To Rebecca Olester and Abigail Hall, daughters of my sister Rebecca Hall, a suit of "linning" and a white apron each. To Sister Dorcase Cracknell the like. To Nathaniel Flouerd 5s. for gloves. To Mr. Richard Culferwell and his wife Mary gloves. My loving kinsman Henry Robinson, executor, is to sell my house and goods and to discharge debts and legacies. The mark of Abigail Mosse. Witnesses: William Barker, Jonas Lawrell, Elizabeth Picks. Proved by the executor 23 February 1665 [1665/6]. (Commissary Court of London for Essex and Herts [Somerset House, London], Waller, 276.)

Administration of the goods of ANTHONY LIST of Sproughton [co. Suffolk] was granted 3 June 1677 to his wife Elizabeth, Daniel Mosse, Sr., and Daniel Mosse, Jr., of Ipswich, being sureties. (Ipswich, Act Books, 29, fo. 62.)

The Will of SAMUEL MORS [calendared as of "foreign parts"], dated 14 June 1677. My mother, Rebecca Butcher, and my brothers Joseph Mors, Daniel Mors, Nathaniel Mors, Robert Mors, and Thomas Mors. My friends Justice William Wood and Mrs. Jane Wood, his wife. My brother John Mors. All my wages that shall become due "from shipp new London" and all my clothes sold after my decease by my commander, Capt. George Erwin, and my trunk of clothes at Justice Wood's in Wapping [? to whom]. Executor: my brother John Mors. Witnesses: Robert Chester, Benjamin Franklin, Charles Price. Proved 15 August 1678 by the executor. (P. C. C., Reeve, 86.)

Administration of the goods of SUSAN M[ORSE] of Ipswich was granted 8 July 1682 to Mary, wife of Robert Morse, and Sarah Morse, wife of Benjamin Hornigold, niece *ex fratre* of the deceased. (Ipswich, Act Books, 34, fo. 56.)

The Will of DANIELL MORS of London, gent., dated 20 October 1688. Sole legatee and executor: my brother Robert Mors, citizen and barber-surgeon of London. Witnesses: Jane Pownsett, John Mors, Wm. Pownsett. Proved 8 June 1695 by Robert Mors. (P. C. C., Irby, 99.) [The probate act book describes him as Daniel Mors, late deceased in parts beyond the seas; and the calendar describes him as "of Ireland."]

The Will of NATHANIEL MORSE of Ipswich, co. Suffolk, mariner, bound out to sea, dated 7 May 1689. To my loving cousin Benjamin M[orse] 1s., in full of what he may claim. To my brother-in-law Benjamin Hornigold of Ipswich, mariner, 20s. for a ring. Residuary legatees: my sisters Sarah, wife of said Benjamin Hornigold, and Susan Morse of St. Paul's, Shadwell, co. Middlesex, widow; and their children are to benefit should they be dead. Executor: my brother-in-law Benjn. Hornigold. Witnesses: Geo. Curting, Robt. Reed, Jr., John Cosin, Scr. Proved 6 May 1690 by the executor. (P. C. C., Dyke, 75.)

Administration of the goods of SPACHETT MORSE of Uggeshall [co. Suffolk] was granted 12 December 1691 to his sister Martha. (Ipswich, Act Books, 36, fo. 15.)

Administration of the goods of WILLIAM MORSE of Southolt [co. Suffolk] was granted [? in 1691 or later] to his brother Robert Morse. (Ipswich, Act Books, 36, fo. 39.)

The Will of JOSEPH MOSSE of Danbury, co. Essex, yeoman, dated 11 December 1693. To be buried in Danbury churchyard. To my eldest son, Joseph Mosse, stock on Wickhams Farm, he paying £60 to my executors for my wife Mary, in discharge of my bond to her before marriage. To my wife Mary the Darby mare, for her own riding. To my daughter Mary a broad piece of gold, the mare always called hers, and £10. To my youngest son, Gervase Mosse, £5. The residue [is to be divided] equally among my five children, "Charles, Mary, Robt., Francis, and Gervase Mosse." Executors: my sons Charles and Francis. Witnesses: Thos. Spurgion, R. Coker, John Honden. Proved 6 July 1694 by Chas. Mosse, the other executor renouncing. (Commissary Court of London for Essex and Herts [Somerset House, London], Lowing, 287.)

Administration of the goods of BARBARA MORSE, widow, was granted 4 April 1698 to her son John. (Ipswich, Act Books, 36, fo. 84.)

The Will of SAMUEL MOSSE of London, merchant, dated 28 December 1698. To my honoured father, Mr. Robert Mosse, the interest on £500, and after his death to my honoured mother, and after her death the principal, £500, to my brother, Mr. Robert Mosse. To Susanne, wife of Robt. Abell of Norwich, weaver, £5 per annum, and to her sister, Sarah Knap, £5 per annum, and on their deaths the principal, £400, as follows: to my brother Wm. Mosse £200, and to my brother Chas. Mosse £200. To Mr. Saml. Edwards, cashier at His Majesty's Exchequer, and his sister now living with him '£100. £60 for mourning for the family of Sir William Gore. Mourning for Christopher Barry and Mr. Hawly and his wife. Residuary legatee: my brother Robt. Executors: my brother Robert M[osse] and said Saml. Edwards. Witnesses: Saml. Stone, Fran: Batch, John Kettle, Chris: Barry. Proved 18 January 1698/9 by Robt. Mosse, with power reserved for the other executor. (P. C. C., Pett, 10.)

### FROM THE PARISH REGISTERS OF BARHAM, CO. SUFFOLK*

1638   James Morse, a servant in Shribland [sic] Hall, buried in the "Ile belonging thereunto" 5 September.

### FROM THE PARISH REGISTERS OF BOXTED, CO. ESSEX

*Baptisms, 1559–1616*

1574   John Mors son of Thomas Mors, minister, 20 February [1574/5].
1576   Samuell Mors son of Thomas Mors, minister, 12 June.
1576   Joseph Mors son of Richard 4 November.
1578   Sarae Mors daughter of Thomas Mors, minister, 11 June.
1579   Joane Kinge daughter of Thos. Kynge ————.
1579   Nathaniell Mors son of Richard Mors 10 May.
1580   Daniell Mors son of Thomas Mors, minister, 29 June, "being St. Peters Day."
1582   Daniell Mors son of Richard Mors 6 December.

*The registers of this parish begin regularly in 1563, but there are a few scattered items in earlier years. The records of baptisms, 1577–1619, are missing. The record of the burial of James Morse is the only Morse entry prior to 1640.

1582    Thomas Kynge son of Thomas Kynge 14 February [1582/3].
1583    Daniell Mors son of Thomas Mors, minister, 2 May.
1585    John Kynge son of Thomas Kynge 1 November.
1587    Ann Boggas daughter of John Boggas 7 March [1587/8].
1589    Elizabeth Kynge daughter of Thomas Kynge 27 July.
1590    Margret Bogas daughter of John Bogas 7 April.
1591    Robert Bogas son of John Bogas 14 March [1591/2].
1594    Wm. Bogas son of John Bogas 17 October.
1614    Suzan Kinge daughter of Thomas 27 November.
1616    Alice Kinge daughter of Thomas 12 December.
[Gap in baptisms from 1616 to 1644.]

### Marriages, 1573–1616

1573    Thomas Mors and Margarett King 26 May.
1578    Thomas King and Joane Cullpeck 26 December.
1582    Sydracke Barnes and Elizabeth King ———.
1585    Mr. Thomas Mors, "Mynister of Hynderclaye," and Margerye Boggas 24 November.

### Burials, 1559–1616

1565    Edward Boggas 27 April.
1577    The wife of Thomas Kinge 16 January [1577/8].
1602    Thomas Kynge the elder 12 May.
1605    Rebecka Kyng, widow, 1 January [1605/6].
[Gap from 1616 to 1662.]

### Miscellaneous Records

Thomas Gleason signs as vicar, evidently signing the copy of the entries from 1559 on. The baptism of Alice Kinge, 12 December 1616, is among the last entries in Gleason's handwriting.

1643    Covenant signed by Nath. Kirkland, vicar, and by the parishioners, including Daniell King and Thomas Kinge, but no Morse.

## From the Parish Registers of Burgate, co. Suffolk, 1560–1676

### Baptisms

1616    Sara Morse daughter of Samuel Morse 25 August.*
1620    Mary Morse daughter of Samuel Morse 13 August.*
1663    Susan daughter of John and Martha Moss 20 April.

### Burials

1626    Samuel Morse, Junior, 11 May.*
1665    Ann daughter of John and Martha Moss 16 July.
1667    Henry son of John and Martha Moss 18 March [1667/8].
1676    Martha wife of John Moss 2 September.

## From the Registers of the Parish of St. Nicholas, Colchester, co. Essex

1621    Richard Mosse and Ann Porter married 25 March.

## From the Parish Registers of Dedham, co. Essex

### Baptisms

1583    Michaell Morse son of Nathaniel 13 August.
1585    John Morse son of Nathaniel 11 May.
1586    William Morse son of Nathaniel 11 October.
1587    Samuel Morse son of Richard 25 July.

* Translated and abridged from the original entry, which is written in Latin.

1590 Sara Morse daughter of Richard and Margery 10 November.
1591 Mary Morse daughter of Nathaniel 17 August.
1594 Hanna Morse daughter of Richard 14 June.
1612 Elizabeth Morse daughter of Nathaniel 8 June [sic].
1612 Elizabeth Morse daughter of Nathaniel 3 July [sic].
1620 Thomas Morse son of Jeremie 2 February [1620/1].

### Marriages

1573 Nathaniel Mors and Joane Upcher 10 December.
1586 Richard Morse and Margery Symsone 15 February [1586/7].

### Burials

1603 Richard Morse 30 June.
        [Gap from April 1605 to April 1610.]
1612 Elizabeth daughter of Nathaniel Morse 9 August.
        [Gap from 17 April 1613 to May 1641.]
1651 Wm. Mouse 23 May.
1663 Goodman Jeremy Moss 14 July.
1664 Ann Moss 2 November.
1666 Widow Moss and Grisle Mouse 12 January [1666/7].

### FROM THE PARISH REGISTERS OF FOXEARTH, CO. ESSEX

#### Baptisms, 1594–1617*

1595 Philip Mors son of Thomas, rector of this parish, 14 March [1595/6].†

### FROM THE PARISH REGISTERS OF HIGHAM, CO. SUFFOLK

#### Baptisms

1544 Anne daughter of Wm. Mors 3 January [1544/5].
1549 Margaret daughter of Wm. Morse "last of" March.
1551 John son of Wm. Morse 5 January [1551/2].
1554 Jane daughter of Wm. Mors 27 September.
1580 Joan daughter of Brian and Anne Morse 27 November.
1583 Mary daughter of Brian and Anne Morse 15 March [1583/4].
1586 Sylva daughter of Brian and Anne Morse 16 October.
1590 Thomas son of John and Anne Morse 6 September.

#### Burials

1580 Nath'l son of Nath'l Morse 27 May.
1587 Anne wife of Wm. Mose 8 June.
1594 Ales [sic] wife of John Morse 8 August.

### FROM THE PARISH REGISTERS OF HINDERCLAY, CO. SUFFOLK

#### Baptisms, 1568–1650

1588 Jeremiah Morse son of Thomas Morse, Clericus, 11 August.
1590 James Morse son of Thomas Morse, Clericus, 10 November.
1592 Nathaniel Morse son of Thomas Morse, Clericus, 13 March [1592/3].
1611 Judith daughter of Robert Morse 17 April.
1613 Richard Mosse son of Robte. Mosse 1 November.
1615 Robert Mosse son of Robte. Mosse 7 February [1615/16].
1618 Thomas Mosse son of Robte Mosse 19 August.
1620 James Mosse son of Robte. Mosse 24 March [1620/1].
1623 William Mosse son of Robt. Mosse 10 January [1623/4].

*Baptisms begin in 1551, but many pages of the book are missing. No marriage entries and no burial entries exist for this period. There is a gap from 1617 to 1705.
†Translated from the Latin of the original entry.

| | |
|---|---|
| 1626 | Margaret Mosse daughter of Robte. Mosse 27 March. |
| 1630 | Anne Mosse daughter of John Mosse 19 September. |
| 1633 | John Mosse son of John Mosse 5 May. |
| 1635 | Margaret Mosse daughter of John Mosse 5 April. |
| 1637 | Robte Mosse son of John Mosse and Anne his wife 17 September. |
| 1639 [or 1640] | Susan Mosse daughter of Richard and Susan Mosse ———. |
| 1641 | John Mosse son of Richard Mosse and Susā his wife 6 January [1641/2]. |
| 1643 | Margaret Mosse daughter of Richard Mosse and Susā his wife 21 February [1643/4]. |
| 1644 | Mary Mosse daughter of John Mosse and Anne his wife 23 August. |
| 1645 | Robert Mosse son of Robert Mosse 25 July. |
| 1646 | Richard Mosse son of Richard Mosse and Susan his wife 21 June. |
| 1646 | John Mosse son of Robert Mosse 24 November. |
| 1650 | Mary Mosse daughter of Robert Mosse and Mary his wife 25 March. |
| 1650 | Jeames Mosse son of James and Margaret his wife 30 September. |
| 1650 | William Mosse son of Richard Mosse and Susan his wife 25 November. |

*Marriages*

| | |
|---|---|
| 1639 [or 1640] | Richard Mosse and Susan Tillett ——— [just previous to the baptism of their daughter Susan]. |
| 1647 | James Mosse and Margaret Tillett 22 October. |

*Burials*

| | |
|---|---|
| 1585 | Margaret Morse wife of Thomas Morse, Clk., 28 July. |
| 1633 | Robert Mosse 7 January [1633/4]. |
| 1637 | Judith Mosse, widow, 14 January [1637/8]. |
| 1657 | John Mosse 28 September. |

### FROM THE PARISH REGISTERS OF NAYLAND, CO. SUFFOLK

*Baptisms*

| | |
|---|---|
| 1602 | Marie daughter of Robert Morse 10 December. |
| 1621 | Susan daughter of Charles Morsse 25 December. |

### FROM THE PARISH REGISTERS OF PALGRAVE, CO. SUFFOLK

*Baptisms*

| | |
|---|---|
| 1619 | John Mors son of Josephe Mors 3 October.* |
| 1620 | John Mors son of Josephe Mors 8 December.* |
| 1626 | Benjamin Mosse son of Josephe Mosse 20 November [?].* |
| 1628 | Mary Mosse daughter of Josephe Mosse 17 August.* |

*Burials*

| | |
|---|---|
| 1619 | John Mors son of Josephe Mors 3 February [1619/20].* |
| 1638 | Mary Morse daughter of Josephe Morse 10 September.* |
| 1643 | Joseph Morse son of Josephe Morse 13 November.* |

### FROM THE PARISH REGISTERS OF REDGRAVE, CO. SUFFOLK, 1570–1674

*Baptisms*

| | |
|---|---|
| 1574 | William Jasper son of Lancelet Jasper 6 February [1574/5].* |
| 1577 | Anna Jasper daughter of Lancelet Jasper 28 September.* |
| 1578 | Elizabeth Jasper daughter of Lancelet Jasper 8 October.* |
| 1579 | Elizabeth Jasper daughter of Lancelet Jasper 30 January [1579/80].* |

*Translated and abridged from the original entry, which is written in Latin.

1581   Henrie Jasper son of Lancelet Jasper 26 May.*
1583   Rachel Jasper daughter of Lancelet Jasper 6 August.*
1585   Samuel Jasper son of Lancelet Jasper 2 February [1585/6].*
1588   Jeremiah Jasper son of Lancelet 2 November.*
1590   Nathaniel Jasper son of Lancelet Jasper 24 May.*
1592   Daniell Jasper son of Lancelet Jasper 23 April.*
1593   John Jasper son of Lancelet Jasper 2 February [1593/4].*†
1593   John Jasper son of Lancelet Jasper 11 February [1593/4].*†
1605   Elizabeth Morse daughter of Samuell Morse 6 March [1605/6].*
1607   Joseph Jasper son of William Jasper 26 July.
1607   John Morse son of Samuell Morse 28 February [1607/8].
1608   Johne Jasper son of Samuell Jasper 5 July.
1609   Jeremy Jasper son of Willi[am] Jasper 6 August.*
1612   Henry Jasper son of Henry Jasper 7 April.
1613   Joseph Morse son of Samuel Morse 2 May.*
1613   Mary Jasper daughter of William Jasper 30 October.*
1616   Bridget daughter of William Jasper 25 August.*
1618   Ruth Jasper daughter of Henry Jasper 11 November.*
1619   Liddia Jasper daughter of William Jasper 31 March.*
1634   William Jasp[er] daughter [sic] of Joseph Jasp[er] 4 May.*
1654   John wife [sic] of Tho[mas] Mosse born 3 February [1654/5].
1660   Susan Lance alias Jasper daughter of Jeremiah Lance alias Jasper 31 October.
1671   Mary Mosse daughter of John Mosse and Ruth his wife 16 December.
1674   John Mosse son of John Mosse of Botesdale and Ruth his wife 12 April.

### Marriages

1602   Samuel Morse and Elizabeth Jasper 29 June.*
1605   Joseph Morse and Ann Jasper 29 October.
1607   Samuell Jasper and Anne Edwards 21 September.
1630   John Kynge and Mary Peper 29 September.
1638   John Westinge and Maria Jasp[er] 25 July.
1639   Edward Skarffe and Jane Jasper 23 July.
1639   Samuel Skarffe and Jane Jasper 25 July.
1656   Robert Fedl, single man, and Margarett Morss, single woman [day and month not given].

### Burials

1608   Joseph Jasper son of Samyel Jasper 15 July.
1616   Launcelett Jasper 2 February [1616/17].*
1625   Rose Jasper, widow, 3 September.*
1631   ——— wife of William Jasper 3 November.*
1637   Joseph Jasper son of William Jasper 28 April.*
1640   Jonathan Jasper son of William Jasper 19 October.*
1640   Henry Jasper 27 January [1640/1].*
1657   John Moss son of John Moss 28 September.
1659   Amye Mosse wife of John Moss 19 October.
1661   Mary Lance alias Jasper daughter of Jeremiah Lance alias Jasper 6 April.
1671   Elizabeth Mosse wife of Richard Mosse 1 January [1671/2].

*Translated and abridged from the original entry, which is written in Latin.
†According to the parish register these two entries are in the same year, 1593. Whether the second entry was intended as a correction of the preceding entry or whether it should have been placed under burials is not clear.

## From the Parish Registers of Romford, co. Essex *

### Baptisms

1616 John son of John Morse, "Minister of the Word," 2 March [1616/17].
1619 Lydia daughter of John Morse 19 June.
1620 Thomas son of John Morse, "Minister of Romford," 10 September.
1621 Ann daughter of John Morse, "Minister of Romford," 3 March [1621/2].
1624 Thomas son of John Morse 6 June.

### Burials

1627 Ann daughter of John Morse, "Minister of Romford," 30 May.
1627 Thomas son of John Morse 3 November.
1629 John son of John Morse, "Minister of the Word," 16 July.

## From the Parish Registers of Stoke-by-Nayland, co. Suffolk†

### Baptisms

1559 John son of John Morsse, junior, 2 January [1559/60].
1560 Margarite daughter of John Morsse, junior, labourer, 18 October.
1562 Robert son of John Morsse, junior, 10 May.
1564 Anne daughter of John Morsse, junior, husbandman, 2 July.
1565 Robt. son of Richard Morsse, husbandman, 17 March [1565/6].
1566 William son of John Morsse, junior, 2 June.
1567 Thomas son of Agnes Morsse, widow, 14 September.
1568 Briget daughter of John Morsse, junior, 9 May.
1571 Jeremie son of John Morsse, junior, 14 June.
1571 Margerie daughter of Richard Morsse 9 December.
1573 Richard son of John Morsse, junior, 13 March [1573/4].
1574 Elizabeth daughter of Richard Morsse 12 April.
1576 Richard son of Richard Morsse 12 August.
1593 Elizh. daughter of George Morsse 7 March [1593/4].
1596 —— —— of George Morsse 25 April.
1600 Francis [sic] daughter of George Morsse 20 April.
1602 John son of George Mosse 17 November.
[Entries from September 1605 to April 1606, inclusive, are wanting.]
1606 Joseph son of Robt. Mosse 21 June.
1606 George son of George Mosse 21 June.
1608 John son of Robard Mose 26 June.
1609 William and Grace children of George Mosse 7 November.
1612 Richard son of George Mosse 5 April.
1612 Francis son of Robert Morse 11 October.
1621 Anne daughter of Richard Morsse 10 February [1621/2].
1623 Elizh. [altered from Mary] daughter of Richard Mosse 8 July.
1628 Ann daughter of John Morsse 7 December.
1629 Elizh. daughter of Richard Morsse 4 June.
1630 Marie daughter of John Mosse —— [1630/1].
1632 Elizh. daughter of John Mosse 4 August.

### Marriages

1562 Richard Morsse and Margerie Wood 18 October.
1570 Robert Elsinge, widower, and Katherine Morsse 12 September.
1593 William Morsse and Anne Kirkham 11 November.
1594 Thomas Gentrie and Margerie Morsse 15 September.

*Taken from G. E. C.'s Essex Extracts.
†The registers of Stoke-by-Nayland begin in 1558, and have been searched from 1558 to 1635, inclusive, for baptisms and marriages, and from 1558 to 1690 for burials.

1595  Robert Morsse and Anne Hedge 12 October.
1597  Thomas Bull and Anne Morsse 9 October.
1604  John Crosse and Elizabeth Mosse 9 September.
1608  Philip Morise and Jane Houlten of Nayland 15 May.
1619  Thos. Stanlye and Francis [sic] Mosse 22 July.
1619  Andrewe Allen and Anne Mosse 28 October.
1620  Richard Mose and Ann Porter 15 March [1620/1].
1621  William Lewes and Leedye Morsse 25 October.
[The page containing the entries from February 1629/30 to April 1631, inclusive, has been cut out of the register.]

### Burials

1566  Thomas Morsse, labourer, 17 February [1566/7].
1574  Agnes Morsse, widow, 5 April.
1576  Richard son of Richard Morsse 30 September.
1577  John Morsse, senr., æt. 57, 25 September.
1578  "Mother Morsse vid: Ætat. 80 annorum" 17 January [1578/9].
1594  Katherine Morsse, widow, æt. 63, 26 August.
1602  Robertt Mosse, single man, 26 June.
1609  Katherin wife of John Mosse 13 November.
1609  Grace daughter of Geo. Mosse 22 November.
1609  William son of Geo. Mosse 29 November.
1609  Margery wife of Richard Mosse 26 February [1609/10].
1611  M[ist]ris Morriff, widow, 11 April.
1614  The son of William Morse 17 April.
1614  Richard Morse, widower, 8 August.
1619  Robert Mosse 11 May.
1621  John Morsse, aged 88, 11 May.
1626  Anne wife of Rich. Mosse 14 January [1626/7].
1637  Anne wife of John Morse 4 December.
[Gap, 1645–1652.]
1654  Mary Morse 20 June.
[Gap, 1656/7–1663.]
1665  Anne Mosse, single woman, 26 February [1665/6].
1667  John Mosse, widower, 2 July.
1672  Elizabeth Mosse 20 January [1672/3].

### Churchwardens

1615  Robert Morse signs as churchwarden.
1655 }
1656 }  John Morse signs as churchwarden.

## FROM THE PARISH REGISTERS OF STRATFORD ST. MARY, CO. SUFFOLK

### Baptisms

1570  Robt. son of Wm. and Anne Morsse 29 July.
1572  Edw. son of Wm. and Anne Morsse 28 July.
1573  Alice daughter of Wm. and Anne Morsse 8 January [1573/4].
1575  Nath'l son of Nath'l Morsse 14 August.
1576  John son of Wm. and Rachell Morss 7 April.
1582  Sara daughter of Edw. and Marye Morss, gent. [sic], 10 October.
1608  Mary daughter of Asabell [sic, ? Asahell] Morse 9 October.

### Burial

1589  Wm. Morse 16 April.

275

FROM THE PARISH REGISTERS OF WRENTHAM, CO. SUFFOLK

### Baptisms*

1605   Mary daughter of Thos. and Margaret Morse.†
1608   Anne daughter of Thos. and Margaret Morse.
1613   Bridget daughter of Thos. and Margaret Morse.

### Marriages

1622   John Allen and Margaret Morse.
1630   Brian Fox and Sara Morse.

### Burials

1638   Margaret Morse.
1653   Thomas Morse, aged 88.

## GENEALOGICAL RESEARCH IN ENGLAND

Contributed by G. ANDREWS MORIARTY, A.M., LL.B., F.S.A., of Newport, R. I.,
and communicated by the Committee on English and Foreign Research

### MORSE (CONCLUDED)

#### FROM LAY SUBSIDIES FOR CO. SUFFOLK**

##### Parish of Stoke-by-Nayland ***

| | |
|---|---|
| 16 Henry VIII [1524–25]. | Robert Morse, [valuation] £3, [tax] 1s. 6d. |
| | William Morse, [valuation] £3, [tax] 1s. 6d. |
| 35 Henry VIII [1543–44]. | Robert Morse in goods, [valuation] £6, [tax] 2s. |
| | Thomas Morse in goods, [valuation] 20s., [tax] 2d. (181/225.) |
| 37 Henry VIII [1545–46]. | Robert Morse in goods, [valuation] £6, [tax] 12d. (181/247, returned 15 November, 37 Henry VIII [1545].) |
| 12 February, 37 Henry VIII [1545/6]. | Robert Morsse in goods, [valuation] £6, [tax] 4s. (181/275.) |

#### FROM THE SUFFOLK MUSTER ROLL, 1638

| | |
|---|---|
| Covehithe.   Thomas Morse. | Shadingfield.   Henry and John Morse. |
| Frostenden.   Nicholas Morse. | South Cove.   Edward Morse, Constable. |
| Monk-Soham.   John Morse. | Stuston.   John Morse. |
| Palgrave.   Joseph Morse, Jr. | Wrentham.   Thomas Morse. |

#### FROM ESSEX SHIP MONEY, 1635 AND 1636

Dedham.   Jeremy Morse.        Romford.   Mr. Mosse, Clerk.

#### FROM SUFFOLK SHIP MONEY, 1639/40

| | |
|---|---|
| Hinderclay.   John Morse, 5s. | Redgrave.   William Jasper, 4½d. |
|      Richard Morse, 9s. | Stuston.   John Mosse, 8s. 7d. |
| Palgrave.   Joseph Morse, Constable. |      Robert Morse, Gent., £2. 7s. 6d. |

Among the "Outsitters."   John Morse, 6d.

---

*Children of a Francis Morse are also recorded, beginning in 1637.
†This Mary Morse married Robt. Darby.
** Preserved in the Public Record Office, London.

***For references to pp. 70-84 and 278-294 see pp. 262-292, this volume.

19 September, 22 Elizabeth [1580], Monday. Court at Dedham Hall. Anthony Morse does fealty as customary tenant for a tenement, 2 acres of land called Little Reades, and one-half a tenement called Legges, next Dedham Bridge, which he took to himself and his heirs while he was within age, to wit, at the court on Wednesday, 21 August, 2 Elizabeth [1560], after the death of Edward Morse, his father. He also fines to be excused from suit of court at 2d. per annum. Henry Moyse is mentioned as a customary tenant.

12 April 1581, Wednesday. Court at Dedham Hall. On m. 10*d* the surrender of a tenement by Edward Morsse to Ralph Starling, at a court holden on the Sunday after the Feast of the Ascension, 7 Edward VI [1553], is cited. (Court Rolls, Bundle 60, No. 740.)

17 April, 29 Elizabeth [1587], Monday. Court at Dedham Hall. Homage present that Anthony Morse, a customary tenant, without the court, surrendered into the hands of Nicholas Gillam, in the presence of Edwd. Thedam and Roger Vaughan, customary tenants, the tenement called Reades, which the lord regranted to said Anthony and Elizabeth, his wife, their heirs and assigns.

10 April, 30 Elizabeth [1588], Wednesday. First court of Chas. Sekford for Overhall and Netherhall, Dedham. Henry Mose attorned tenant. Anthony Morse fined 4d. a year to have respite of suit of court. (Court Rolls, Bundle 60, No. 741.)

1 October, 38 Elizabeth [1596]. Court at Dedham Hall. Presentment that Stephen Upcher surrendered a tenement in the presence of Anthony Morse and John Whitlocke, customary tenants.

Same court. Presentment that Thomas Glover, who died before this court and had surrendered his tenements to the use of his will, made his will 17 November 1596 [*sic*], bequeathing, *inter alia*, to his son Edward and his heirs, after the decease of the testator's wife Margret, all the messuage or tenement wherein one Richard Morse now dwelleth in Dedham, adjoining the capital messuage where the testator dwells, which also is bequeathed to the testator's wife Margret. Testator bequeaths "to Richard Morse my Weaver 20s." Livery of the same tenements to the widow, Margaret. (Court Rolls, Bundle 60, No. 742.)

## From Rentals and Surveys, Duchy of Lancaster

### Dedham, co. Essex

| | |
|---|---|
| Anthony Morse for a messuage and lands called Helland | 8s. 6¾ |
| "1 1601" The same for a close called Calendon | 9½ |
| The same for a tenement late Bawdes | 8¾ |
| *with the meadow and suit fines the half year 6s. 4d.*† | |

Sum 9s. 1d.‡

### From Rental of Dedham Hall, Lady Day, 1594§

Anthonie Morse, a cottage, garden, and croft called little reades. the moity of a tenement called Legges next Dedham Bridge.

---

*Preserved in the Public Record Office, London.

†The words in italics are an interlineation.

‡The foregoing items about Anthony Morse are taken from Rentals and Surveys, etc., 2/22, from what is an undated rental, evidently of the manors of Overhall and Netherhall in Dedham, probably for Lady Day [25 March], 1594. The outer wrapper is inscribed "Rental Ladyday 1594 and Mich. 1625." "1 1601" may mean "living 1601."

Below the items about Anthony Morse are given the lands of Henry Moyse, viz., 1 acre of Garroldes tenement (5), 8 acres of the same tenement (2s. 8¼), and a croft called Seabrights (8d.).

§Another book in the same cover.

In the search, under the auspices of the Committee on English and Foreign Research, for the ancestry of Samuel Morse of Dedham, Mass., records pertaining to several Morse families in the counties of Essex and Suffolk, England, have been collected, and abstracts of these records have been presented in the preceding pages of this article. Some of them relate to families whose connection, if there was one, with the family to which the New England immigrant belonged has not yet been established; but these are helpful, nevertheless, in showing who were *not* his ancestors. Many other records, however, point unmistakably to a family that included two clergymen of the Church of England, namely, Rev. Thomas Morse, vicar of Boxted, co. Essex, and rector of Hinderclay, co. Suffolk, and Foxearth, co. Essex, in the reign of Queen Elizabeth, and his son, Rev. John Morse, M.A., curate of Romford, co. Essex, in addition to other charges, for many years in the reigns of James I and Charles I; and in the following pedigree, based on some of the foregoing English records, on a few English authorities cited below, and on various New England records and authorities, it will be shown that Samuel Morse of Dedham, Mass., was a son of Rev. Thomas Morse, who, in turn, was probably a grandson of a Robert Morse, husbandman, who lived at Stoke-by-Nayland, co. Suffolk, in the first half of the sixteenth century. It will also be shown that Joseph Morse, planter, who was at Ipswich, Mass., as early as 1637 and died in 1646, leaving descendants, belonged to the same family and was a first cousin of Samuel Morse; and several erroneous statements that have been made in the existing Morse genealogies in regard to the children of Samuel Morse will be corrected.

The late Rev. Abner Morse, compiler of the "Memorial of the Morses," which was published in 1850, expressed the opinion, in a note attached to the copy of the will of Rev. Thomas Morse of Foxearth which was printed in the REGISTER in July 1865 (vol. 19, p. 264), that the testator "was no doubt the father of Samuel of Dedham;" but he had not found the entries in the various parish registers of Essex and Suffolk nor the other wills that prove the truth of his conjecture, and J. Howard Morse and the late Miss Emily W. Leavitt, who, under the auspices of the Morse Society, compiled a revision of the "Memorial of the Morses," under the title of "Morse Genealogy," which was published in two parts in 1903 and 1905, identified Samuel Morse of Dedham, Mass., with the Samuel, son of Richard and Margery (Symsone) Morse, who was baptized at Dedham in England 25 July 1587 and was a half brother of Joseph Morse of Ipswich, Mass. (Cf. the following pedigree, Nos. 5, i; 5, iv; 6; and 7.) The "Morse Genealogy," it may be added, throws no light on the relationship between Samuel Morse of Dedham and Joseph Morse of Ipswich, Mass.

1. ROBERT MORSE, of Stoke-by-Nayland, co. Suffolk, husbandman, the testator of 1551, died between 5 Oct. 1551, when his will was dated, and 15 Sept. 1552, when it was proved. He married AGNES ———, who declared her nuncupative will (*q.v.*) 13 Jan. 1578/9

and was buried at Stoke-by-Nayland 17 Jan. 1578/9, "Ætat. 80 annorum."

He was taxed at Stoke-by-Nayland 1s. 6d., on property valued at £3, in the subsidy of 1524–25, 2s., on goods valued at £6, in the subsidy of 1543–44, 12d., on goods valued at £6, in a subsidy returned 15 Nov. 1545, and 4s., on goods valued at £6, in a subsidy of 12 Feb. 1545/6.

His father, whose Christian name is unknown, was probably living at Stoke-by-Nayland about 1490; and William Morse, who was taxed at Stoke-by-Nayland 1s. 6d., on property valued at £3, in the subsidy of 1524–25, was perhaps his (Robert Morse's) brother.

Children, named in their father's will, 5 Oct. 1551:

2. i. THOMAS, b. before 1520.
   ii. JOHN, the Elder, of Stoke-by-Nayland, yeoman, the testator of 23 Sept. 1577, b. about 1520; d. *s.p.*; bur. at Stoke-by-Nayland 25 Sept. 1577, æt. 57; m. KATHERINE ———, who, as Katherine Morsse, widow, was bur. at Stoke-by-Nayland 26 Aug. 1594, æt. 63.
3. iii. RICHARD.
   iv. JOHN, the Younger, of Stoke-by-Nayland, husbandman, under 21 in 1551; bur. at Stoke-by-Nayland 11 May 1621, aged 88; m. ———.

    Children, bapt. at Stoke-by-Nayland:
    1. *John*, bapt. 2 Jan. 1559/60; m. Katherine ———, who was bur. at Stoke-by-Nayland 13 Nov. 1609.
    2. *Margaret*, bapt. 18 Oct. 1560.
    3. *Robert*, of Stoke-by-Nayland, the testator of 21 Aug. 1600, bapt. 10 May 1562; d. unm. at Stoke-by-Nayland 26 June 1602.
    4. *Anne*, bapt. 2 July 1564; m. at Stoke-by-Nayland, 9 Oct. 1597, Thomas Bull.
    5. *William*, bapt. 2 June 1566; m. at Stoke-by-Nayland, 11 Nov. 1593, Anne Kirkham. A son was bur. at Stoke-by-Nayland 17 Apr. 1614.
    6. *Bridget*, bapt. 9 May 1568.
    7. *Jeremie*, bapt. 14 June 1571.
    8. *Richard*, bapt. 13 Mar. 1573/4.
   v. ALICE, living 13 Jan. 1578/9; m. at Stoke-by-Nayland, 12 Sept. 1570, ROBERT ELSINGE, widower.*
   vi. JOAN, living 5 Oct. 1551.
   vii. MARGARET, living 13 Jan. 1578/9.
   viii. KATHERINE, living 5 Oct. 1551.*

2. THOMAS MORSE (*Robert*), of Stoke-by-Nayland, co. Suffolk, labourer, called "eldest son" in his father's will, 5 Oct. 1551, and at that time dwelling with his father, was born before 1520, and was buried at Stoke-by-Nayland 17 Feb. 1566/7. He married AGNES ———, who survived him and, as a widow, was buried at Stoke-by-Nayland 5 Apr. 1574.

Perhaps he was the Thomas Morse who was taxed at Stoke-by-Nayland 2d., on goods valued at 20s., in the subsidy of 1543–44.

*The parish registers of Stoke-by-Nayland record the marriage, on 12 Sept. 1570, of Robert Elsinge, widower, and Katherine Morsse; but Agnes Mosse, mother of Alice and Katherine, in her nuncupative will of 13 Jan. 1578/9, bequeaths to Alice Elsing and does not mention Katherine, who was probably then deceased.

Children:
- i. ROBERT, named, as living, in the will of his grandfather, Robert Morse, 5 Oct. 1551, and in the will of his uncle, John Mosse the Elder, 23 Sept. 1577.
- 4. ii. THOMAS, named, as living, in the will of his grandfather, Robert Morse, 5 Oct. 1551, and, as Thomas Mosse the Elder, in the will of his uncle, John Mosse the Elder, 23 Sept. 1577, and probably identical with the Rev. Thomas Morse who is given as No. 4 of this pedigree (vide infra).
- 5. iii. RICHARD, b. about 1540, probably the Richard Mosse who was named in the will of his brother, Rev. Thomas Morse, 10 Nov. 1596.
- iv. LANCELOT, living 13 Jan. 1578/9, when he was named in the nuncupative will of his grandmother, Agnes Mosse.
- v. MARGARET, probably the Margaret Morse who was living unm. 10 Nov. 1596, when she was named in the will of her brother, Rev. Thomas Morse.
- vi. THOMAS (posthumous), bapt. at Stoke-by-Nayland 14 Sept. 1567.

3. RICHARD MORSE (*Robert*), of Stoke-by-Nayland, co. Suffolk, husbandman, born after 5 Oct. 1530, since he was under 21 on 5 Oct. 1551, when his father made his will, was buried at Stoke-by-Nayland 8 Aug. 1614. He married at Stoke-by-Nayland, 18 Oct. 1562, MARGERIE WOOD, who was buried there 26 Feb. 1609/10.

Children, baptized at Stoke-by-Nayland:
- i. ROBERT, of Stoke-by-Nayland, yeoman, the testator of 6 May 1619, bapt. 17 Mar. 1565/6; bur. at Stoke-by-Nayland 11 May 1619; m. there, 12 Oct. 1595, ANNE HEDGE, who was living 6 May 1619. He was named in the nuncupative will of his grandmother, Agnes Mosse (Morse), declared 13 Jan. 1578/9, as "Robert, son of Richard Mosse the Elder."

   Children:
   1. *Richard*, m. at Stoke-by-Nayland, 15 Mar. 1620/1, Ann Porter,* who was bur. at Stoke-by-Nayland 14 Jan. 1626/7. They had (1) Anne, bapt. at Stoke-by-Nayland 10 Feb. 1621/2, perhaps the Anne Mosse, single woman, who was bur. at Stoke-by-Nayland 26 Feb. 1665/6, and (2) Elizabeth, bapt. at Stoke-by-Nayland 8 July 1623, who probably d. young, since another Elizabeth, daughter of Richard Morsse [by another wife], was bapt. at Stoke-by-Nayland 4 June 1629 and was perhaps the Elizabeth Mosse who was bur. at Stoke-by-Nayland 20 Jan. 1672/3.
   2. *Robert*, under 21 on 6 May 1619, to whom his father bequeathed £20 and the lands given to him by his grandfather, Richard Morse, deceased, after the death of his [Robert's] brother Joseph.
   3. *Mary*, bapt. at Nayland, co. Suffolk, 10 Dec. 1602; probably d. young, as she was not mentioned in her father's will.
   4. *Lydia*, under 22 on 6 May 1619; m. at Stoke-by-Nayland, 25 Oct. 1621, William Lewes.
   5. *Joseph*, bapt. at Stoke-by-Nayland 21 June 1606; living 6 May 1619.
   6. *John*, bapt. at Stoke-by-Nayland 26 June 1608; living 6 May 1619.
   7. *Francis*, bapt. at Stoke-by-Nayland 11 Oct. 1612; living 6 May 1619.

*In the registers of the parish of St. Nicholas, Colchester, co. Essex, is recorded, under date of 25 March 1621, the marriage of Richard Mosse and Ann Porter. (*Vide supra*, p. 78.)

ii.   MARGERIE, bapt. 9 Dec. 1571;  m. at Stoke-by-Nayland, 15 Sept. 1594, THOMAS GENTRIE.

iii.  ELIZABETH, bapt. 12 Apr. 1574;  m. at Stoke-by-Nayland, 9 Sept. 1604, JOHN CROSSE.

iv.   RICHARD, bapt. 12 Aug. 1576;  bur. at Stoke-by-Nayland 30 Sept. 1576.

4. REV. THOMAS MORSE (? *Thomas, Robert*), clerk, named in the will of his grandfather, Robert Morse, 5 Oct. 1551,* made his own will on 10 Nov. 1596 and died between that date and 10 Mar. 1596/7, when John Fermin, his successor as rector of Foxearth, co. Essex, was presented by the patron of that living, Anne Butts, widow (Whitgift, vol. 2, p. 280, and Newcourt, Repertorium, vol. 2, p. 80). He married first, at Boxted, co. Essex, 26 May 1573, MARGARET KING, who was buried at Hinderclay, co. Suffolk, 28 July 1585; and secondly, at Boxted, 24 Nov. 1585, MARGERY BOGGAS, who was living 10 Nov. 1596, when her husband made his will.

Rev. Thomas Morse was presented to the vicarage of Boxted, co. Essex, of which the Bishop of London was patron, in 1573, and held this living until 1578, when he resigned, his successor, Rev. Philip Silgate, being presented on 18 Mar. 1578 [1578/9] (Newcourt's Repertorium, 1710, vol. 2, p. 80). Apparently he continued to live at Boxted until 1583, for the baptisms of his five children by his first wife, down to and including the Daniel who was baptized 2 May 1583, were recorded there.  On 14 July 1583 he was inducted as rector of Hinderclay, in northern Suffolk (Induction Books, Archdeaconry of Sudbury, at Bury St. Edmunds), and from about 1594 until his death he was rector of Foxearth, co. Essex, his son Nathaniel being baptized at Hinderclay 13 Mar. 1592/3 and his next and youngest child, Philip, being baptized at Foxearth 14 Mar. 1595/6.  On 28 Aug., 37 Elizabeth [1595], Thomas Morse, clerk, compounded' for the first fruits of the rectory of Foxearth (First Fruits Composition, book 12, fo. 36).†

In his will, dated 10 Nov. 1596 and proved 28 Apr. 1597, Rev. Thomas Morse bequeathed to his "nyne children noew living nyne score pounds," that is, twenty pounds to every child, the eight sons, who were named, to receive their legacies at the age of twenty-three, and the daughter, Sara, to receive her twenty pounds at the age of twenty-one.  He bequeathed also to his brother, Richard Mosse, 50s., and to his sister, Margaret Morse, 20s.  To his eldest son he gave all the

---

*Although it is not *certain* that Rev. Thomas Morse was identical with the Thomas who, with his brother Robert, was named in the will of Robert Morse of Stoke-by-Nayland (No. 1) as son of the testator's son Thomas, yet a careful study of the wills of Robert Morse (No. 1), his widow, Agnes, and their son, John Mosse the Elder, together with the mention by Rev. Thomas Morse, in his own will, of his brother Richard and sister Margaret, makes this identification seem most likely.  Thomas Morse (No. 2), son of Robert, was father not only of the Robert and Thomas who were named in their grandfather's will but also of a posthumous son Thomas; and it should be noted that John Mosse the Elder, brother of Thomas (No. 2), mentions in his will his nephew, Thomas Mosse the Elder.  (For these wills *vide supra*, p. 71.)

†See foot of p. 294, Addendum.

books in his study and to his wife Margaret the residue of his estate, and she was to bring up his children in learning.* Children by first wife, baptized at Boxted:

i. REV. JOHN, M.A., clerk, the testator of 14 July 1645, bapt. 20 Feb. 1574/5; bur. at Romford, co. Essex, 31 Jan. 1647/8; m. (by licence granted by the Bishop of London, 16 Apr. 1610) DOROTHY BURNAP, who survived him and proved his will 25 May 1648, daughter of Thomas Burnap of Stanstead-Abbots, co. Herts. He was admitted pensioner at Emmanuel College, Cambridge, 12 Aug. 1591, was matriculated about 1591, was admitted Bachelor of Arts in 1594–5 [?] and Master of Arts in 1598, was ordained deacon in London 28 June and priest 29 June 1601, aged 26, and was rector of Little Ilford, co. Essex, 1607–1615, rector of Digwell, co. Herts, 1612–1615, and perpetual curate of Romford, co. Essex, 1615–1647/8. As Mr. Mosse, Clerk, he was entered, from Romford, on the Essex Ship Money Roll in 1635 and 1636. In his will he bequeathed £5 to his elder daughter, Elizabeth, £100 to his younger daughter, Dorothy, then unm., £30 to his brothers or brothers' children, and to his wife Dorothy all his lands and tenements, for life. His estate was appraised at £133. 15s.
    Children:
    1. *Elizabeth*, living 14 July 1645.
    2. *Dorothy*, living unm. 14 July 1645.
    3. *John*, bapt. at Romford 2 Mar. 1616/17; bur. there 16 July 1629.
    4. *Lydia*, bapt. at Romford 19 June 1619; probably d. young.
    5. *Thomas*, bapt. at Romford 10 Sept. 1620; probably d. young.
    6. *Ann*, bapt. at Romford 3 Mar. 1621/2; bur. there 30 May 1627.
    7. *Thomas*, bapt. at Romford 6 June 1624; bur. there 3 Nov. 1627.

6. ii. SAMUEL, bapt. 12 June 1576. For reasons for believing that he was the Samuel Morse who emigrated to New England in 1635 see below, under No. 6.
   iii. SARA, bapt. 11 June 1578; living 10 Nov. 1596.
   iv. DANIEL, bapt. 29 June 1580; probably d. young.
   v. DANIEL, bapt. 2 May 1583. [He was later of Ipswich, co. Suffolk.] He had a child living 2 Sept. 1638, when his half brother, James Morse, bequeathed to it £5.

Children by second wife:

vi. JOSEPH, of Palgrave, co. Suffolk, b. about 1586; living in 1639/40, when, as Joseph Morse, Constable, he was entered, from Palgrave, on the Suffolk Ship Money roll; d. not later than 1648, when administration on his goods was granted to his relict, Elizabeth; m. (1) at Redgrave, co. Suffolk, 29 Oct. 1605, ANN JASPER, bapt. at Redgrave 28 Sept. 1577, living 17 Feb. 1616/17, when, as "Annes Morse, my daughter," she was given a legacy of £3 in her father's will, daughter of Lancelot Jasper of Redgrave, husbandman, and sister of Elizabeth (Jasper) Morse, wife of Samuel Morse, her husband's brother; m. (2) ELIZABETH ———, who survived him and was appointed administratrix of his goods in 1648. On 8 Sept. 1638, as executor, he proved the will of his brother James.
    Children (by which wife is uncertain):
    1. *Joseph*, bur. at Palgrave 13 Nov. 1643. He was enrolled on the Suffolk Muster Roll, in 1638, from Palgrave, as Joseph Morse, Jr.
    2. *John*, bapt. at Palgrave 3 Oct. 1619; bur. there 3 Feb. 1619/20.

*The complete text of the will of Rev. Thomas Morse, of which a brief abstract has been given in the preceding instalment of this article (*supra*, pp. 71–72), may be found in the REGISTER, vol. 19, pp. 264–265, from a copy by the late Horatio G. Somerby.

3. *John,* bapt. at Palgrave 8 Dec. 1620.
4. *Benjamin,* bapt. at Palgrave 20 Nov. [?] 1626.
5. *Mary,* bapt. at Palgrave 17 Aug. 1628; bur. there 10 Sept. 1638.

vii. JEREMIAH, of Dedham, co. Essex, clothworker, the testator of 14 May 1663, bapt. at Hinderclay, co. Suffolk, 11 Aug. 1588; d. without living issue; bur. at Dedham, as "Goodman Jeremy Moss," 14 July 1663; m. ABIGAIL ———, the testatrix of 8 Jan. 1665/6, who proved her husband's will 20 May 1664 and d. between 8 Jan. 1665/6 and 23 Feb. 1665/6, when her will was proved. As Jeremy Morse he was entered, from Dedham, on the Essex Ship Money Roll in 1635 and 1636.
Child:
1. *Thomas,* bapt. at Dedham 2 Feb. 1620/1; d. before his father.

viii. JAMES, of Bargham [Barham], co. Suffolk, the testator of 2 Sept. 1638, bapt. at Hinderclay, co. Suffolk, 10 Nov. 1590; d. *s.p.*; bur. at Barham 5 Sept. 1638, his burial being entered in the parish registers as that of James Morse, a servant in Shribland [*sic*] Hall, buried in the "Ile belonging thereunto." His will was proved at Ipswich, co. Suffolk, 8 Sept. 1638, by his brother Joseph Morse, whom he had made sole executor, to whom he left all his lands and tenements, with the residue of his estate, subject to the payment of numerous legacies, including £20 to his (the testator's) brother Nathaniel Morse, £5 to his brother Philip, £5 to the child of his brother Daniel Morse, £5 to his brother, Mr. John Morse of Rumforde, £10 to his brother Samuel Morse, and 40s. to his cousin Joseph Morse. The testator was a man of considerable means, and seems to have held a high position in the "Hall." He made bequests to "every serv[an]t in this house," and directed his executor to "give to everyone of my fellowes servts [a] payer of gloves and Ribond."

ix. NATHANIEL, bapt. at Hinderclay, co. Suffolk, 13 Mar. 1592/3; living 2 Sept. 1638.

x. PHILIP, bapt. at Foxearth, co. Essex, 14 Mar. 1595/6; living 2 Sept. 1638.

5. RICHARD MORSE (*Thomas, Robert*), of Boxted and Dedham, co. Essex, weaver, born about 1540, was buried at Dedham 30 June 1603. He married first ———; and secondly, at Dedham, 15 Feb. 1586/7, MARGERY SYMSONE.

He was named, with his brother Lancelot, in the nuncupative will of his grandmother, Agnes Mosse, declared 13 Jan. 1578/9; and by the will of his brother, Rev. Thomas Morse, dated 10 Nov. 1596, he was to receive a legacy of 50s. He was occupying a messuage in Dedham in 1596 (court record), when Thomas Glover bequeathed to him 20s.

Children by first wife, baptized at Boxted:

7. i. JOSEPH, bapt. 4 Nov. 1576.
ii. NATHANIEL, bapt. 10 May 1579; perhaps the Nathaniel Morse whose daughter *Elizabeth* was bapt. at Dedham 8 June or 3 July 1612 and was bur. there 9 Aug. 1612.
iii. DANIEL, bapt. 6 Dec. 1582.

Children by second wife, baptized at Dedham:

iv. SAMUEL, bapt. 25 July 1587.
v. SARA, bapt. 10 Nov. 1590.
vi. HANNA, bapt. 14 June 1594.

6. SAMUEL MORSE (*Rev. Thomas, ? Thomas, Robert*), of Redgrave and Burgate, co. Suffolk, and of Watertown, Dedham, and

Medfield, Mass., husbandman, baptized at Boxted, co. Essex, 12 June 1576, when his father was rector of that parish, died at Medfield, Mass., 5 Dec. 1654 (Medfield Vital Records). He married at Redgrave, co. Suffolk, 29 June 1602, as will be shown below, ELIZABETH JASPER, baptized at Redgrave 30 Jan. 1579/80, died at Medfield, Mass., 20 June 1655, daughter of Lancelot Jasper of Redgrave, husbandman, and younger sister of the Ann Jasper who married at Redgrave, 29 Oct. 1605, Joseph Morse, brother of Samuel Morse.*

Children of Samuel Morse are recorded at Redgrave from 1605/6 to 1613 and at Burgate from 1616 to 1626, and he may have lived at times elsewhere in England, as the records of the baptisms of some of his children have not been found. On 7 July 1626 his wife, Elizabeth Morse, witnessed the will of Anne Copping of Burgate. On 2 Sept. 1638 his half brother, James Morse of Barham, co. Suffolk, bequeathed to him £10, without indicating, however, where he (Samuel) was then living.

On 15 Apr. 1635, as has been stated in the first paragraph of this article (*supra*, p. 70), a Samuel Morse, husbandman, aged 50 years, with Elizabeth Morse, his wife, aged 48 years, Joseph Morse [without doubt their son], aged 20 years, and Elizabeth Daniell [probably their granddaughter], aged 2 years, embarked on the ship *Increase*, bound from London for New England.† The chief reasons for believing that this passenger, Samuel Morse, was the Samuel who was a son of Rev. Thomas Morse (4) are as follows.

The records published in the first instalment of this article disclose three Samuel Morses who should be considered in any attempt to identify the Samuel Morse who emigrated to New England in 1635. The first of the three is Samuel, son of William Morse of Suffolk, clothier, who in his will, not dated, but proved 12 September 1582, names his five children, Robert, Edward, John, Alice, and Samuel (*vide supra*, p. 71). This testator is evidently the William Morse of Stratford St. Mary, co. Suffolk, the baptisms of four of whose children are recorded in that parish, viz., Robert, 29 July 1570, Edward, 28 July 1572, Alice, 8 Jan. 1573/4 (these three by a wife named Anne), and John, 7 Apr. 1576 (by a wife named Rachel). The son Samuel, whose baptism does not appear to be on record at Stratford St. Mary, was probably the youngest child, as he was named last in the list of children in his father's will, and was born, therefore, between 1576 and 1582. He would, accordingly, have been from 53 to 58 years of age when the *Increase* sailed for New England in 1635, and might well have been entered in the shipping list as aged 50, for it must be remembered that the ages given in the shipping lists are often notoriously inaccurate, the original lists having been carelessly made and only copies having come down to the present day,

*For the Jasper family *vide infra*, p. 293, Addendum.
†See Drake's Founders of New England, p. 26, and Hotten's Original Lists, pp. 64–65.

so that, when an age given in a shipping list corresponds with that revealed by a baptismal record, it is corroborative evidence, but, when it is not confirmed by a baptismal or other record, it is by no means certain that it is the correct age. Since, however, none of the names found in the family of William Morse of Stratford St. Mary, except John, are repeated in the family of Samuel Morse of New England, his son Samuel is not likely to be the New England immigrant of 1635.*

The second Samuel Morse to be considered as possibly the New England immigrant of 1635 is the Samuel (5, iv, of this pedigree) who was baptized at Dedham, co. Essex, 25 July 1587, the son of Richard and Margery (Symsone) Morse. He would have been nearly 48 years of age when the *Increase* sailed in 1635, only about two years below the age assigned to Samuel Morse in the shipping list; and in the "Morse Genealogy" he is assumed to be the New England settler, although Rev. Abner Morse, in 1865, was of the opinion that the Samuel Morse of the *Increase* was a son of Rev. Thomas Morse (4). Both Richard Morse of Dedham (5) and Samuel Morse of New England (6) had sons named Joseph and Daniel; but the names of the parents of the Samuel who was baptized at Dedham in 1587 are not found among the names of the children of Samuel of New England, and this fact makes it almost certain that Samuel Morse of Dedham, co. Essex, was not the Samuel Morse who migrated to New England in 1635.

The third Samuel Morse who may have been the passenger in the *Increase* is Samuel, second son and second child of Rev. Thomas Morse (4) by his first wife, Margaret (King) Morse. This Samuel was baptized at Boxted, co. Essex, 12 June 1576, and would have been, therefore, almost 59 years old when the *Increase* sailed, an age which would exclude him from consideration were it not for the frequent errors in the ages given in the shipping lists, as already mentioned, and for the following facts that make it likely that he was the emigrant to New England. Samuel, son of Rev. Thomas Morse, had two own brothers named John and

*From the records published in the previous instalment of this article it appears that William Morse, clothier, whose will was proved in 1582, had at least three brothers, namely, Edward, who had a wife Mary and children Azaell (or Asahel) and Sara, Nathaniel, whose son Nathaniel was baptized at Stratford St. Mary 14 Aug. 1575, and Anthony, one of the executors of his brother William's will, whose own will, dated 4 Aug. 1603 and proved 20 Sept. 1604, shows that he had a wife Elizabeth but evidently no children living. He mentions his brothers and their children; and, since he leaves to his wife, for life, lands in Stoke-by-Nayland and Boxted, he and his brothers may have been related to the family to which Robert Morse of Stoke-by-Nayland (1) belonged. The searcher of English records employed by the Committee on English and Foreign Research stated that this Anthony Morse was the son of Edward and Julyan (Forth) Morse of the Stratford St. Mary branch of the family, and that he was a prominent Presbyterian. (*Vide supra*, p. 72, footnote.) His will describes him as of Hinderclay, the Suffolk parish of which Rev. Thomas Morse was rector from 1583 to about 1594. Information about him may be found in Usher's Presbyterian Movement in the Reign of Elizabeth, a work in which it is sometimes difficult to distinguish Rev. Thomas Morse from Anthony Morse, when each is described merely as Mr. Morse. (Cf. also Alumni Cantabrigienses, part 1, vol. 3, p. 216, and Court Rolls and Rentals and Surveys, *supra*, p. 279.)

Daniel (an earlier brother Daniel having died young, it is supposed), an own sister named Sara, and five half brothers, Joseph, Jeremiah, James, Nathaniel, and Philip. His seven brothers and his sister were named, with Samuel himself, in the will of their father, dated 10 Nov. 1596. Of these names, John, Daniel, Joseph, and Sara were given to children of Samuel and Elizabeth Morse of New England, and they had one grandson named Jeremiah and two grandsons named Nathaniel. Two others of their eight known children were named respectively Thomas (if the Thomas Morse who was in Dedham, Mass., in 1640 was a son of Samuel) and Elizabeth, Thomas bearing the name, presumably, of his father's father and Elizabeth the name of her mother. The remaining children were Mary and Samuel. Moreover, Samuel, son of Rev. Thomas Morse, was living (or was believed to be living) on 2 Sept. 1638, when his half brother, James Morse of Barham, co. Suffolk, named him in his will, together with his (the testator's) own brothers, Joseph, Nathaniel, and Philip, the child of his half brother Daniel Morse, probably then deceased, and his half brother, Mr. John Morse of "Rumforde." The testator's own brother Jeremiah is the only one of the brothers who was not mentioned in the will — for what reason is not known, as he was then living. James Morse also left a legacy to his "cousin," that is, his nephew, Joseph Morse, undoubtedly the son of Samuel. The testator does not, however, state where his brother Samuel and his "cousin" Joseph were then living. Furthermore, the Samuel Morse who embarked in the *Increase* in 1635 had a wife Elizabeth, whose age was given as 48 years. Now the parish registers of Redgrave, co. Suffolk, record the marriage of Samuel Morse and Elizabeth Jasper on 29 June 1602 and that of Joseph Morse and Ann Jasper on 29 Oct. 1605; and they show also that these two brides were daughters of Lancelot Jasper and that Elizabeth was baptized at Redgrave 30 Jan. 1579/80. Lancelot Jasper, in his will, dated 17 Feb. 1616/17, mentions his daughters Elizabeth Morse and Annes Morse. That the Samuel Morse and Joseph Morse who married these two sisters at Redgrave were the sons of Rev. Thomas Morse appears extremely likely, when the geographical situation of some of the Suffolk and Essex parishes mentioned in this article is studied. Stoke-by-Nayland, the home of the probable father and grandfather of Rev. Thomas Morse, is in southern Suffolk, only two miles north from Nayland, which is on the River Stour, that separates Suffolk from Essex. Boxted, where Rev. Thomas Morse was vicar from 1573 to 1578 and where he apparently continued to live for some five years more, his fifth child having been baptized there in 1583, was only a mile or two southeast from Nayland, on the Essex side of the Stour, and Dedham, also in Essex, was a few miles farther down the river. In 1583 Rev. Thomas Morse became rector of Hinderclay, a parish in northern Suffolk, about thirteen miles northeast from Bury St. Edmunds and very near Redgrave, on the Norfolk border. A short distance easterly from Redgrave was Palgrave, where Joseph Morse, a son of Rev. Thomas Morse, settled. Samuel Morse, therefore, must have been taken by his father to Hinderclay when he was only seven years old, and probably remained there at least until he was seventeen or eighteen years of age, for his father did not leave Hinderclay and become rector of Foxearth in Essex until about 1594. Presumably Samuel became acquainted with the neighboring parish of Redgrave while his father was rector of Hinderclay, and in 1602 married a Redgrave young woman, his brother Joseph marrying a sister of Samuel's wife some three years later. Certainly this Samuel Morse, the son of Rev. Thomas Morse, is much more likely to be the man who married Elizabeth Jasper of Redgrave than either of the other two Samuels who have been considered, the first belonging to Stratford St. Mary, on the extreme southern border of Suffolk, and the second having been baptized at Dedham in Essex, in 1587 and being therefore too young to have married in 1602. Elizabeth (Jasper) Morse, to be sure, would have been 55 years of age when the *Increase* sailed, instead of 48, as recorded in the shipping list; but this discrepancy may be disregarded, as already explained, in the face of the other evidence. It may be added that Samuel Morse's son Joseph, whose age is given in the shipping list of the *Increase* as 20 years, was baptized at Redgrave 2 May 1613 and was therefore about 22 years old in the spring of 1635, an age that corresponds better with the age in the shipping list than do the ages of his father and mother.

On his arrival in New England Samuel Morse went first to Watertown, Mass., where he was admitted to the church and where his son Daniel, who had crossed the Atlantic before his father, had already settled. Daniel Morse and his second cousin, Joseph Morse (7, i), had been admitted as freemen at Watertown on 6 May 1635. Samuel Morse remained only a short time in Watertown. In 1636 he was a proprietor of Dedham, where he was prominent in the early settlement of the town, a member of the First Church there at its organization, a freeman 8 Oct. 1640, and a town officer. His last days were spent at Medfield, Mass., which had been set off from Dedham in 1651 and was the home of his daughter Mary, the wife of Dea. Samuel Bullen. The son of a minister of the Church of England, Samuel Morse was a man of fair education and of considerable importance in the Massachusetts communities in which he lived. Among his numerous descendants were several ministers, graduates of Harvard.

In his will, dated 2 Dec. 1654, Samuel Morse bequeathed all his estate, whether moveable or immoveable, to his wife, Elizabeth Morse, for life, and directed that after her decease it should be divided amongst his children, John Morse, Daniel

Morse, Mary Bullin, and Ann Morse, the widow of his son Joseph, "who with my said children shall have an equall portion upon a just division with them for the childrens sake of my beloved Joseph. Therefore my will is that the above named Ann . . . shall make an equall distribution of all that portion upon division unto every child of my sonne Joseph when they & every one of them shall grow up to the age of one & twenty years." He made his wife Elizabeth the executrix of the will. (Cf. abstract of this will in REGISTER, vol. 5, p. 299, and the full text in the Morse Genealogy, by J. Howard Morse and Emily W. Leavitt, part 1, 1903.) The inventory of the estate of Samuel Morse of Medfield, taken 5 Dec. 1654, was accepted at a County Court held in Boston, 30 Jan. 1654/5, and showed a valuation of £124. 7s. (REGISTER, vol. 9, p. 141.)

Children:

i. THOMAS (probably son of Samuel), of Dedham, Mass. He was proposed for membership in the church at Dedham at its formation in 1638, was admitted to the church 28 June 1640, and probably d. *s.p.* soon afterwards, as no further record of him has been found.

ii. ELIZABETH, bapt. at Redgrave, co. Suffolk, 6 Mar. 1605/6; probably m. ——— DANIEL, and d., leaving a daughter, *Elizabeth*, b. about 1633, who was probably the Elizabeth Daniel, aged 2 years, who was taken to New England in 1635 by Samuel Morse and his wife.

iii. JOHN, of Dedham and Boston, Mass., tailor, bapt. at Redgrave, co. Suffolk, 28 Feb. 1607/8; d., probably in Boston, 26 May 1657; m. about 1636 ANNAS CHICKERING, who survived him and d. in 1691. Whether he came to New England before or after his father is uncertain; but he was admitted freeman 13 May 1640. He moved from Dedham to Boston in 1654, and on 18 Dec. 1655, "now undertakeing a voyage for England," made his will, in which he named his wife Annas and his eight living children and made his wife and her brother, Francis Chickering, executors. Francis Chickering, however, renounced the executorship 18 June 1657. The inventory of the estate of John Morse, tailor, of Boston, deceased, dated 9 June 1657, amounted to £385. 9s. 5d. (Cf. abstract of the will in REGISTER, vol. 8, p. 278, and text in the Morse Genealogy, part 1, 1903.)

Children:

1. *Ruth*, b. 3 June 1637; living 18 Dec. 1655.
2. *John*, b. 8 June 1639; living 18 Dec. 1655.
3. *Samuel* (twin), } bapt. 15 Mar. 1639/40; d. young.
4. *Rachel* (twin),
5. *Joseph*, b. 3 Feb. 1640/1 and bapt. 6 July 1641; living 18 Dec. 1655.
6. *Ezra*, bapt. 4 Feb. (but recorded as b. 5 Feb.) 1643/4; living 18 Dec. 1655.
7. *Abigail*, b. 2 Mar. and bapt. 8 Mar. 1646/7; living 18 Dec. 1655.
8. *Ephraim*, b. 19 July and bapt. 30 July 1648; living 18 Dec. 1655.
9. *Bethia*, b. 28 Mar. and bapt. 6 Apr. 1651; living 18 Dec. 1655.
10. *Nathaniel*, b. 2 May 1653; living 18 Dec. 1655.

iv. DANIEL, of Watertown, Dedham, Medfield, and Sherborn, Mass., d. at Sherborn 5 June 1688; m. LYDIA FISHER, who d. at Sherborn 29 Jan. 1690/1, aged 70, daughter of Anthony Fisher of Dedham. Daniel Morse came to New England before his father and settled at Watertown, being admitted a freeman 6 May 1635. He soon moved to Dedham, and was later of Medfield and finally of Sherborn, where he was selectman. In his will, made 9 Mar. 1687/8, he provided for his wife, gave his homestead to his youngest child Samuel, and named his sons Obediah, Daniel, Jonathan, and Nathaniel and his daughters Bathiah Perry, Mary West, Bathsheba Fiske, and Lydia Wight (Memorial of the Morses, Appendix).

Children, all living in 1687/8, when they were named in their father's will:

1. *Obadiah,* b. at Dedham 8 Aug. 1639.
2. *Daniel,* b. at Dedham 31 Jan. and bapt. 7 Feb. 1640/1.
3. *Jonathan,* b. at Dedham 8 Mar. and bapt. 12 Mar. 1642/3.
4. *Lydia,* bapt. at Dedham 13 Apr. 1645.
5. *Bethia,* b. at Dedham 24 Mar. 1647/8 and bapt. 2 Apr. 1648.
6. *Mary,* bapt. at Dedham 29 Sept. 1650.
7. *Bathshua (Bathsheba),* b. at Medfield 20 July 1653.
8. *Nathaniel,* b. at Medfield 20 Jan. 1657/8.
9. *Samuel,* b. at Medfield 12 May 1661.

v. JOSEPH, of Watertown, Dedham, Medfield, and Dorchester, Mass., bapt. at Redgrave, co. Suffolk, 2 May 1613; d. in the lifetime of his father, on or before 20 June 1654, when the inventory of his estate at Medfield was taken; m. 1 Sept. 1638 HANNAH PHILLIPS of Watertown, perhaps a sister of Rev. George Phillips. She m. (2) 3 Nov. 1658 Thomas Boyden of Watertown. Joseph Morse came to New England with his father and mother in the *Increase* in 1635, aged, according to the shipping lists, 20 years.* His uncle, James Morse of Barham, co. Suffolk, in his will dated 2 Sept. 1638, bequeathed to him 40s., describing him as "my cousin Joseph Morse." In New England he lived first at Watertown, and then was, with his brother Daniel, among the first to whom land was allotted in Dedham, in 1636. He moved to Dedham in 1637. In 1649 he was one of the proprietors of that part of Dedham which was set off in 1651 as the town of Medfield, and he settled there, with his father. At his death, however, he was of Dorchester, being so described in the "Inventory of yt pte of the Estate wch he had at Meadfield," which was taken 20 June 1654 and amounted to £183. (Cf. REGISTER, vol. 8, p. 277.) His father, in his will dated 2 Dec. 1654, refers to him as deceased. On 18 Oct. 1661 Thomas Boyden, "late of Boston, now of meadfeild, co. Suffolk, in New England, yeoman," gave a bond of £300, "together with the house, upland & meadow now in my possession, lately the Inheritance of Joseph Morse, late of Meadfeild," to ensure the suitable maintenance and bringing up of the "severall children of ye late Joseph Morse & Hannah his [Boyden's] now wife during the time of theire Nonage or Unmarried Condicon, or till they choose theire Guardians," and the payment to them "at theire severall marriages or days of Age" of "the severall portions to them Assigned by the County Court at Boston In January last." (REGISTER, vol. 30, p. 433.)

Children:

1. *Samuel,* b. 10 Jan. 1639/40.
2. *Hannah,* b. 8 Aug. 1641.
3. *Sarah,* b. 16 Sept. 1643.
4. *Dorcas,* b. 24 Aug. 1645.
5. *Elizabeth,* b. 1 Sept. 1647.
6. *Joseph,* b. 26 Sept. 1649.
7. *Jeremiah,* b. 10 June 1651.
8. *A child,* b. shortly before the father's death.

vi. SARA, bapt. at Burgate, co. Suffolk, 25 Aug. 1616; probably d. young.

vii. MARY, bapt. at Burgate, co. Suffolk, 13 Aug. 1620; d. at Medfield, Mass., 14 Feb. 1691/2; m. 10 Aug. 1641 SAMUEL BULLEN of

*Vide supra, p. 286.

289

Dedham and later of Medfield, Mass., who d. at Medfield 16 Jan. 1691/2. When and how she came to New England is unknown. Her husband had been admitted freeman 2 June 1641, and is called deacon in the record of his death (Medfield Vital Records).

Children (surname *Bullen*):

1. *Mary*, b. at Dedham 20 July 1642.
2. *Samuel*, b. at Dedham 19 Dec. 1644.
3. *Elizabeth*, b. at Dedham 3 Feb. 1646/7.
4. *Joseph*, b. at Medfield 6 Sept. 1651.
5. *Ephraim*, b. at Medfield 18 July 1653.
6. *Meletiah*, b. at Medfield 15 Sept. 1655.
7. *Elisha*, b. at Medfield 26 Dec. 1657.
8. *John*.
9. *Eliezer*, b. at Medfield 26 Apr. 1662; d. there 3 May 1662.
10. *Bethia*, b. at Medfield 1 Aug. 1664.

viii. SAMUEL, bur. at Burgate, co. Suffolk, 11 May 1626.*

7. JOSEPH MORSE (*Richard*, ? *Thomas*, *Robert*), of Dedham, co. Essex, and Ipswich, Mass., planter, baptized at Boxted, co. Essex, 4 Nov. 1576, died in New England (probably at Ipswich) between 24 Apr. 1646, the date of his will, and 28 Sept. 1646, the date of the inventory of his estate. He married in England DOROTHY ――――, who was living 24 Apr. 1646, when she was named as a legatee and as executrix in her husband's will.

William Glover of Dedham, co. Essex, clothier, in his will, dated 26 Jan. 1608/9, bequeathed 40s. to Joseph Morse of Dedham and 20s. to the Widow Morse, in the Valley. John Anger of Dedham, clothier, in his will, dated 19 Jan. 1623/4, bequeathed 20s. to Joseph Morse the Elder. John Pye of Dedham, clothier, in his will, dated 8 Nov. 1624, made a gift to Joseph Morse, Sr., of Dedham. Ann Anger, in her will, dated 2 Sept. 1625 and proved at Colchester, co. Essex, 16 Dec. 1625, mentioned Joseph Morse. Judith Morris of Dedham, widow, in her will, dated 25 Jan. 1645/6, bequeathed 20s. to "Joseph Morse in New England," "if he be living;" and, "if he be dead," to "William Stone in New England."

The exact time of Joseph Morse's emigration to New England is unknown; but he was a proprietor of Ipswich in 1637. His son Joseph and perhaps also his son John had gone to New England before him. In his will, dated 24 Apr. and

---

*In his list of children of Samuel Morse (6), published in the Memorial of the Morses, in 1850, Rev. Abner Morse did not include Thomas, Elizabeth, and Sara — these two daughters, of course, did not appear in New England records; but he assigned to the immigrant a daughter Abigail and a son Jeremiah, who were not his children, although he had grandchildren bearing those names. He also gave to the immigrant a son Samuel, who, he said, married Mary Bullen and died "at the Eastward," 24 Sept. 1688. In his note attached to the will of Rev. Thomas Morse (REGISTER, vol. 19, p. 265) Rev. Abner Morse stated that this son Samuel "returned to England and served as Colonel under Cromwell," and in the Morse Genealogy (part 1, 1903) he is said to have served under Cromwell, to have fled at the Restoration, and to have died at the Eastward. Now no son Samuel was named in the will of Samuel Morse (6), nor is there any evidence that he had a son of that name except the Samuel who was buried at Burgate, co. Suffolk, 11 May 1626. Among the descendants, however, of Samuel Morse (6) were three grandsons named Samuel Morse (cf. 6, iii, 3, iv, 9, and v, 1); and one of these grandsons, the eldest child of Joseph Morse (6, v), married 10 Feb. 1664/5 Elizabeth Moore and had Samuel, born 8 Feb. 1665/6, and eight other children (cf. Savage's Dictionary and Vital Records of Medfield, Mass.). This last-named Samuel, son of Samuel and Elizabeth (Moore) Morse and great-grandson of Samuel Morse the immigrant (6), died "att ye eastward" 24 Feb. (*not* 24 Sept.) 1688 [1688/9], according to the Vital Records of Medfield. He, at any rate, could not have served in Cromwell's army. — EDITORS.

proved 29 Sept. 1646, he bequeathed to his wife Dorothy, his sons Joseph and John, and his daughter Hannah, and made his wife executrix. The inventory of his estate, taken 28 Sept. 1646, amounted to £83. 1s. 10d. (The Probate Records of Essex County, vol. 1, pp. 53–55, Salem, Mass., 1916.)

Children:

i.  JOSEPH, of Watertown, Mass., b. in England, probably about 1610; d. at Watertown, Mass., 4 Mar. 1690/1; m. at Watertown, about 1636, ESTHER PIERCE, daughter of John Pierce of Watertown. He came to New England in 1634 in the *Elizabeth*, from Ipswich, co. Suffolk, aged 24 years, according to the shipping lists, and may have been sent over by his father. He settled in Watertown, was admitted freeman 6 May 1635, together with his second cousin, Daniel Morse, and was a proprietor of Watertown in 1636. Administration on his estate was granted to his son John.

Children:

| | | | |
|---|---|---|---|
| 1. | *Joseph*, b. 30 Apr. 1637. | 5. | *Esther*, b. 7 Mar. 1645/6. |
| 2. | *John*, b. 28 Feb. 1638/9. | 6. | *Sarah*. |
| 3. | *Jonathan*, bur. 12 May 1643. | 7. | *Jeremiah*. |
| 4. | *Jonathan*, b. 7 Nov. 1643. | 8. | *Isaac*. |

ii.  JOHN, of Ipswich, Watertown, and Groton, Mass., husbandman, b. in England; d. in 1697; m. DINAH ⸺, who survived him.* He may have come to New England before his father. On 4 Jan. 1663 [1663/4] he sold his house and lot at Ipswich and soon afterwards went to Watertown and thence to Groton, where he was town clerk, 1670–1676 and 1680–81. While holding this office he was carried into captivity by the Indians, 12 May 1676, but was released on the payment of a ransom of £5. He returned to Groton, where he again served as town clerk. (Cf. the Morse Genealogy, part 1.)

Children:

1. *Elizabeth*, b. at Ipswich 29 Mar. 1657; d. there 7 June 1659.
2. *Mary*, b. at Ipswich 15 Jan. 1660/1.
3. *John*.

iii.  HANNAH, m. at Ipswich, Mass., 8 June 1665, THOMAS NEWMAN.

## ADDENDUM

### THE JASPER FAMILY OF REDGRAVE, CO. SUFFOLK

FROM entries in the parish registers of Redgrave, co. Suffolk, and from the will of Lancelot Jasper, printed in the previous instalment of this article, the following facts in regard to Lancelot Jasper, the father-in-law of Samuel Morse of New England, and his family have been derived.

LANCELOT JASPER, of Redgrave, co. Suffolk, husbandman, born probably about 1550, was buried at Redgrave 2 [*sic*, ? 22] Feb. 1616/17. He married ROSE ⸺, who survived him, and, as Rose Jasper, widow, was buried at Redgrave 3 Sept. 1625.

In his will, dated 17 Feb. 1616/17 and proved at Bury St. Edmunds, co. Suffolk, 3 Mar. 1616/17, he names his wife Rose, his son William, with William's wife Francis [*sic*] and their children

---

*Savage (Genealogical Dictionary) assigns to him a wife Dinah and gives the year of his death as 1697. In the Morse Genealogy (part 1, 1903) his wife's name is given as Elizabeth, and his son John is said to have married at Woburn, Mass., 5 Mar. 1686 [1686/7], Dinah Knight, daughter of John and Hannah Knight.

Nathaniel, Jonathan, Joseph, Jeremy, Elizabeth, Bridget, and Mary, his [the testator's] son Nathaniel, his [the testator's] daughters Annes Morse (who is to receive £3 within two years of the decease of the testator's wife Rose) and Elizabeth Morse (who is to receive £3 within three years of the decease of the said Rose), and his sons Jeremy, Daniel, John, and Henry. His son William was appointed executor, and proved the will.

Children, recorded at Redgrave:

i. WILLIAM, bapt. 6 Feb. 1574/5; living 3 Nov. 1631, when the burial of his wife is recorded; m. FRANCES ———, who, with her husband William, was named in the will of her father-in-law, 17 Feb. 1616/17.

    Children, recorded at Redgrave:
1. *Nathaniel*, living 17 Feb. 1616/17.
2. *Jonathan*, bur. 19 Oct. 1640.
3. *Elizabeth*, living 17 Feb. 1616/17.
4. *Joseph*, bapt. 26 July 1607; bur. 28 Apr. 1637; m. ———, and had William, bapt. 4 May 1634.
5. *Jeremy*, bapt. 6 Aug. 1609; living 17 Feb. 1616/17. Susan Lance *alias* Jasper was bapt. at Redgrave 31 Oct. 1660, and Mary Lance *alias* Jasper was bur. at Redgrave 6 Apr. 1661, both being daughters of Jeremiah Lance *alias* Jasper.
6. *Mary*, bapt. 30 Oct. 1613; living 17 Feb. 1616/17; perhaps the Maria Jasper who m. at Redgrave, 25 July 1638, John Westinge.
7. *Bridget*, bapt. 25 Aug. 1616; living 17 Feb. 1616/17.
8. *Lydia*, bapt. 31 Mar. 1619.

ii. ANN, bapt. 28 Sept. 1577; living 17 Feb. 1616/17; m. at Redgrave, 29 Oct. 1605, JOSEPH MORSE. (*Vide supra*, Morse Pedigree, 4, vi.)

iii. ELIZABETH, bapt. 8 Oct. 1578; probably d. young.

iv. ELIZABETH, bapt. 30 Jan. 1579/80; d. at Medfield, Mass., 20 June 1655; m. at Redgrave, 29 June 1602, SAMUEL MORSE, with whom she migrated to New England in 1635. She was named in her father's will, 17 Feb. 1616/17. (*Vide supra*, Morse Pedigree, 6.)

v. HENRY, bapt. 26 May 1581; living 17 Feb. 1616/17; perhaps the Henry Jasper who was bur. at Redgrave 27 Jan. 1640/1; m. ———.

    Children, bapt. at Redgrave:
1. *Henry*, bapt. 7 Apr. 1612.
2. *Ruth*, bapt. 11 Nov. 1618.

vi. RACHEL, bapt. 5 Aug. 1583; not named in her father's will of 17 Feb. 1616/17.

vii. SAMUEL, bapt. 2 Feb. 1685/6; not named in his father's will of 17 Feb. 1616/17; m. at Redgrave, 21 Sept. 1607, ANNE EDWARDS.

    Children (perhaps twins), recorded at Redgrave:
1. *John*, bapt. 5 July 1608.
2. *Joseph*, bur. 15 July 1608.

viii. JEREMIAH (JEREMY), bapt. 2 Nov. 1588; ⎫
ix. NATHANIEL, bapt. 24 May 1590; ⎪ living 17 Feb. 1616/17.
x. DANIEL, bapt. 23 Apr. 1592; ⎬
xi. JOHN, bapt. 2 or 11 Feb. 1593/4; ⎭

ADDENDUM to page 283 (No. 4): Rev. Thomas Morse (4) was one of the signers of a letter from Dedham, co. Essex, dated 19 Apr. 1583, to Mr. Thomas Cartwrighte, pastor of the Church of the English Merchants at Middelburg, in the Low Countries, urging him forward in his work of criticizing the Jesuits' translation of the New Testament. He was probably the Mr. Morse who took part in the meetings of the Dedham Classis at Boxted, 4 Mar. 1582/3, and at "Barfold" [i.e., East Bergholt], 8 Apr. 1583. (Cf. Usher's Presbyterian Movement in the Reign of Elizabeth.)

# GENEALOGICAL RESEARCH IN ENGLAND

Communicated by the Committee on English and Foreign Research

## THE BORDENS OF HEADCORN, CO. KENT

Contributed by G. Andrews Moriarty, A.M., LL.B., F.S.A.,
of Bristol, R. I.

The records of which abstracts are given in this article relate to the Bordens of the parish of Headcorn, co. Kent, the family to which Richard Borden, one of the early settlers of Portsmouth, R. I., belonged.

In 1901 there was printed in Philadelphia, Pa., for private distribution, a book compiled by Thomas Allen Glenn of that city and entitled "Pedigree of Richard Borden, who removed from the County of Kent, Old England, 1637–1638, and settled at Portsmouth, Rhode Island." In this book Mr. Glenn represents Richard Borden, the Portsmouth settler, as eighth in descent from a certain Henry Borden of Headcorn, who was born about 1370–1380, through Thomas, John, William, Edmund, William, Thomas, and Matthew Borden, the father of the immigrant to Rhode Island.

The weak link in this pedigree is the statement that Edmund Borden, great-great-grandfather of Richard Borden of Rhode Island, was a son of the William Borden whose will (*vide infra*) was dated 11 Feb. 1530/1 and was proved 25 Sept. 1531. Edmund Borden was not named in the will of this William Borden, but Mr. Glenn claims that he was the son of William, because certain lands and tenements on the High Street of Headcorn and elsewhere which had formerly been the property of this William Borden and his ancestors were, "by operation of the custom of Gavelkind," held by the heirs of Edmund, and because Stephen Borden, a son of Edmund's son William, "by operation of custom of Gavelkind became seized of certain lands at Bydynden which had once belonged to John Borden (died 1469) and to his ancestors." Mr. Glenn also declares "that a glance at the pedigree of the Bordens of Hedcorn shows, aside from positive proof offered, that Edmund Borden could not have been the son of any other Borden of Hedcorn, but William."

Unfortunately, Mr. Glenn does not present in his book this evidence so essential in establishing the parentage of Edmund Borden; and investigations made personally at Canterbury some years ago by the contributor of this article showed that there was another William Borden at Headcorn, a contemporary of the William Borden who died in 1531, and that the Bordens were so numerous in Headcorn at that time as to make it impossible, without further evidence, to identify the father of the Edmund Borden from whom Richard Borden of Rhode Island was fourth in descent.

Mr. Glenn was in error also in identifying Bennett, wife of John Borden (grandson of the Henry Borden with whom his pedigree begins), with Bennett Borden, widow, the testatrix of 15 Oct. 1518, daughter of Thomas Turnor, for the Turner wills given below show that Bennett, daughter of Thomas Turnor, was wife of the other William Borden mentioned above, a contemporary of the William Borden who died in 1531.

The records given in the present article comprise abstracts of wills of the Bordens of Headcorn and a few of the neighboring parishes (several of which appear—for the most part in briefer form—in Mr. Glenn's book), of two Borden administrations, and of two Turner wills (not given by Mr. Glenn), Borden entries from the Bishop's transcripts of the parish registers of Biddenden, Frittenden, and Headcorn, co. Kent, which have been supplemented by a few entries from the original registers of Headcorn, many abstracts of records of the purchase and sale of lands, preserved in the so-called Feet of Fines, a few items from the Lay Subsidies, and an abstract of an early Chancery suit that supplies much information about the family of Thomas Borden, son of the Henry Borden with whom Mr. Glenn's pedigree begins. The pedigree that ends this article begins with Edmund Borden, the testator of 13 Apr. 1539, beyond whom the ancestral line of Richard Borden of Portsmouth, R. I., has not yet been proved.

## From Probate Records

The Will of JOHN BORDEN of Headcorne [co. Kent], dated 26 April 1469. To be buried in the churchyard of St. Peter and St. Paul there. [Bequests for lights in the church.] To Thomelyn, my servant, 40s. To Isabel Seede, my servant, 20s. To each executor 6d. Residue to Thomas Hovynden, Richard Borden, and John Holstrete, my executors, to dispose of for my soul.

My will regarding my lands. To my feoffees, Thomas Phylip, Richard Borden, William Ive, John Holstrete, and Robert Hovynden, all my lands and tenements in Headcorn, and they are to permit Benedicta, my wife, to have during her widowhood [a place] in hall and kitchen for fire and flet, with a chamber and a portion of the garden and a cow to be kept on the land. After the term of her widowhood she is to have a messuage and lands and her clothing and apparel and a one-fourth part of all things in her room, but the other three parts are to go to my children and executors. My executors are to have until the Michaelmas next after my death to carry out my will, and are then to let out the lands at the best price until my son William reaches the age of twenty years, and are to pay £20 to my daughters at the age of twenty years, and, if one daughter die under twenty, then her share is to go to the other daughter. When William Borden is twenty years old, he is to have the lands and tenements, except such as are sold, in fee simple; but, if he die within age, then all the lands I had from my father or obtained myself are to go to my daughters, in fee simple, except such as the feoffees must sell to perform the will. If both William and my daughters die within age, then I give to the son of the above-mentioned Richard Borden, if he have one, all the lands that were my father's, and the remainder are to be disposed of for an honest priest to sing in Headcorn church for my soul and the souls of Thomas, my father, and Isabel, my mother, and of Henry Borden and Roberga, his wife, and of Thomas Sander, for two years, and to buy a silver cross for Headcorn church. [No date of probate.] (Archdeaconry of Canterbury, vol. 2, fo. 1.)

The nuncupative Will of Richard Burden of Rolvinden, co. Kent, spoken 15 June, 13 Edward IV [1473], to William Patynden, John Watts, Sr., of Beninden, Richard Duke, and John Burden of Rolvinden, my feoffees of all my lands and tenements in Beninden and elsewhere in Kent. They are to grant to my mother, Joan, 4s. yearly rent from my messuage, with garden and a piece of arable land and wood, etc., in Beninden, at Skullisgate, which belonged to William Burden, my father, for her life, which is then to be sold, and from the proceeds 10 silver marks are to be given to my sister Agnes, on her marriage, if she be ruled by Joan, her mother, and my executors; if not, then they are to be given, with the residue of the proceeds, to charity. William Patynden and John Watt, the feoffees of my grandfather, John Burden, are to deliver to my executors, Richard Duke and John Sextayn, in fee simple, a piece of land called Park, lying near the aforesaid messuage and garden and piece of land, which the said John Burden by his will gave to me. My executors are to sell the same and expend the proceeds on a priest, to sing for my soul in Rolvinden church for one year, and for other charitable purposes. To be buried in Rolvinden churchyard. The residue of my goods is to be disposed of by my executors for the good of my soul. Overseer: my uncle, John Burden. Proved 17 June 1477. (Archdeaconry of Canterbury, vol. 3, fo. 112.)

The Will of Thomas Turnor of Hedcorn [co. Kent], dated 15 January 1476/7. To be buried in the churchyard of St. Peter and St. Paul at Hedcorn. [Bequests for lights in Headcorn church.] Residue to my wife, Margery, and she and Thomas Hauersham are to be executors.

My will regarding my lands. Thomas Hauersham and others are to be my feoffees. To Margery, my wife, for life, my messuage, garden, and two pieces of land (3 acres in all) in Headcorn, with reversion to my daughter Benedict; and, if she die before my wife, then to my wife and her heirs. Proved 20 May 1477. (Archdeaconry of Canterbury, vol. 3, fo. 95.)

The Will of Robert Borden, Jr., of Hedcorn [co. Kent], dated 27 January 1479/80. To be buried in Headcorn churchyard. To Roger Marketman, my godson, a cow. To Alice at Well, my goddaughter, a cow. My moveable goods to John Wedynbrok, Thomas at Well, William Man, and Thomas at Crouch, Sr., my feoffees. My messuage and lands at Eastowne are to be sold, and the money is to be paid to my executors to pay my debts and for a chaplain to sing for my soul for half a year. To each of the children of my brothers and sisters now living 6s. 8d., if they marry with the consent of their fathers. To the repair of the road at Steven bridge 6s. 8d. To Maogle Boycott 6s. 8d. To Eme Dor, my mother, 6s. 8d. To Richard Marketman 6s. 8d. To each feoffee 8d. Residue to my mother, Eme Dor, and Richard Marketman, my executors, for my soul. Proved 6 June 1480. (Archdeaconry of Canterbury, vol. 3, fo. 304.)

The Will of James Burden of Hedcorn [co. Kent], dated 27 February 1479/80. To be buried in Hedcorn churchyard. To James Walter 4d. To Godlove, my wife, 20d., and to Henry Man 20d., and they are to be my executors.

My will regarding my lands. Two parcels of land called Petrsde[?] and Gretecroft are to be sold, and the proceeds to go to pay my debts and to my wife Godleve and my son. My wife is to have my messuage and all my other lands, for life; and, if my son die under the age of twenty, without issue, then, on the death of Godleve, they are to be sold and the money is to be used for a priest to sing for our souls in Hedcorn church for a year and to pay to each of my brothers and sisters then living 40s. To my mother, Emma, 6s. 8d. Proved 26 September 1480. (Archdeaconry of Canterbury, vol. 3, fo. 326.)

The Will of RICHARD BORDEN of Hedcorn [co. Kent], dated 6 May 1490. To be buried in Hedcorn churchyard. To my son John (under twenty-four years of age) and my daughter Isabel, equally, bedding, napery, and six silver cups. Residue to my executors, for my children. Executors: my daughter Isabel and Roger Litell of Hedcorn. Witnesses: William Borden [and others].

My will regarding my lands. Feoffees: John Southland, Roger Litill, Thomas atte Crouche, Jr., of Headcorn, and many others [named]. Lands in Hedcorn, Bidinden, Frittenden, Ashford, and Westwell or elsewhere in Kent [mentioned]. All my lands are to be let until my son John is twenty-two years old; and Isabella, my daughter, is to have 40 marks within eight years of my death. If John die without issue, then to Isabella; and, if she die without issue, then William, son of Henry Borden, is to have my messuage at Crotynden and all my lands in the dens of Blechynden and Staplehurst, in fee simple, he paying to my feoffees 20 marks, of which 10 marks are to go to the wife of Thomas Mapillisden of Marden and 10 marks to Hedcorn church. Robert Borden, brother of the said William, is to have the lands on the dens of Thornherst, Borden, and Maxinden, in fee simple, paying to my executors 20 marks for pious purposes. William, son of John Borden, is to have two pieces of land called Stouredes. To John Nettar of Great Chart, son of John Nettar of Ashford, my messuages, lands, etc., in Ashford and Westwell and Brodmede meadow. All my other messuages, etc., in Hedcorn, Bidinden, Frittenden, or elsewhere are to be sold, and the money is to go to Hedcorn church. Proved 21 October 1490. (Archdeaconry of Canterbury, vol. 5, fo. 234.)

The Will of LETICIA BORDEN of Frittenden, co. Kent, widow, dated 1 May 1492. To be buried in Frittenden churchyard. My feoffees and executors are to sell 18 acres in Chart next Sutton Valance, and the money is to go to my daughter at her marriage; and, if she die unmarried, then to Richard Bovinden and Thomas Huth, my sons. [Bequests to the churches of Frittenden, Stokebury, Chart *juxta* Sutton Valance, Staplehurst, Hedcorn, and Massefield in Sussex, and to William Wele, Thomas Turner, and Thomas Hooth, my son, at the age of twenty years.] Residue to James Taylor and Richard Bovynden. Proved 14 January 1492/3. (Archdeaconry of Canterbury, vol. 5. fo. 341.)

The Will of MARGERY TURNER of Headcorn [co. Kent], dated 10 July 1500. To be buried in the churchyard of St. Peter and St. Paul in Headcorn. [Bequest for lights.] Residue to be distributed at the discretion of Thomas Atwell and Thomas Wentspawehawke, my executors. Witnesses: William Borden, Stephen Bowman, William Borden, laborer, and others.

My will regarding my lands. My executors are to be my feoffees, and are to sell my messuage and garden at Estonn, and the proceeds are to be dispensed for a priest to sing in Headcorn church for my and my husband's soul and all Christian souls, 33s. 4d. To Elizabeth, daughter of William Borden, laborer, household goods and 20s., at the age of eighteen or marriage. To Robergie, daughter of the said William, 6s. 8d. and a posnet. To Agnes Borden 6s. 8d. and a pottle pan. To Bennett Borden 6s. 8d. To Joan, daughter of William Burden, 6s. 8d. To Roger and William, sons of said William Borden, 6s. 8d. To my servant, Joan Caveney, 20s., corn, and household goods. For repairing the way from my gate to Estonne cross 6s. 8d. To Joan Atwood, my goddaughter, 4s. To Margaret and Joan Fox 20s. each. To Alice Pisham 20d. and a taper to burn before the rood, value 20d. To my executors 6s. 8d. each. Residue to my household goods to Benet, wife of William Borden, laborer, at the discretion of William Borden, yeoman, whom I make my overseer. Residue of my money for pious works. Proved 23 September 1500. (Archdeaconry of Canterbury, vol. 8, fo. 1.)

The Will of HENRY BORDEN of Frittenden [co. Kent], dated 2 April 1502. To be buried in Frittenden churchyard. Debt owed to Robert Borden [mentioned]. To my daughters Elizabeth and Joan. To my wife Alice. To my son Robert Borden.

My will regarding my lands. My house and all my lands [I give] to my wife, for life, with remainder to Robert Borden, my son, who is to pay to my son John Borden 26s. 8d. after my wife's death. Proved 14 June 1502. (Archdeaconry of Canterbury, vol. 8, fo. 203.)

Administration on the goods of ROGER BORDEN of Hedcorn [co. Kent] was granted 12 July 1508 to Dionisia, his widow. (Archdeaconry of Canterbury, Act Book 3, fo. 32.)

The Will of BENNETT BORDEN of Hedcorn [co. Kent], widow, dated 15 October 1518. To be buried in Hedcorn churchyard. To William, my son. To Joan, my daughter. To Isabel, my daughter, and her child. To Roberge, my daughter. To John Borden a calf. To Ann Borden. To the friars of Winchelsea, Lossyngham, and Aylesford, and to the Grey Friars of Canterbury. To Roger, my son, my house and garden and two pieces of land that I inherited from my father, Thomas Turnor. Residue to my son Roger, who is to be my executor. Proved 16 November 1518. (Archdeaconry of Canterbury, vol. 13, fo. 225.)

The Will of WILLIAM BORDEN of Hedcorn [co. Kent], dated 10 February 1530/1. To be buried in the Church of Our Lady, between my two wives, Joan and Thamasine [Bequests for charitable and pious purposes.] My four crofts, two of them called Byrchetts and the other two lying beside the Moore of Blachynden, which I purchased of Richard Whitsphawk and Henry Webbe, my old servants, are to be given to them. To my daughter Elizabeth a standing cup with silver and gilt and its cover. To Ann, my daughter, £20, at her marriage, with reversion to Thomas, my son. Executors: Walter Hendeley, Gent., and William Lynch; and Nicholas Batnor is to be their solicitor. Overseer: Sir Edward Wotten, Knight, and he is to have my gold ring with mother of pearl for his pains. To my daughter Katherine my messuage, two gardens, a forstall, three pieces of land sometime old Southland's, two pieces of land purchased of John Southland's heirs, and two pieces called Ryngsell purchased of Sir William Hetlesden, sometime vicar of Hedcorn, with reversion to my son Thomas.

My will regarding my lands. Feoffees: Edward Wotten, Knight, George Goldysford, Esq., and six others [named]. Lands in Hedcorn, Frittenden, and Smarden [mentioned]. My feoffees are to let to farm my two meadows, with "were banks and wilget," that I purchased of Stephen Baker, citizen and stationer of London, lying unto the Church Bridge upon the den of Crothenden, to be sought out of a pair of indentures between Edward Borden and me; and the profits are to be used for an obit for me and my friends in Our Lady's Church. My son Edward Borden is to be content with the lands and tenements which he had of my gift, i.e., my tenement in Borden and 100 acres of land and meadow and my tenement at Wilse, with such lands as be holdeth of me by indenture under a false pretense of marriage with Joan, daughter of John Alyn, one of the barons of the King's Exchequer. My wife Rose is to occupy during her widowhood my principal messuage of Horcheyard Podsole, with the lands purchased of Richard Thomas and John Thomas, and my tenement where Marmaduke Peper dwelleth, in a piece of land called Brofyld; and she is to keep my son Thomas and my daughter Ann until they be able to be set to learning. My feoffees are to let to farm two pieces of land called Thets and Somerlese and all my other lands on the north side of the street that leads from Hedcorn to Lenham, in the occupation of Thomas Whit and others, and nine pieces of land, with a barn and a lodge, in the occupation of John Lytle, and my tenement of Balden and seven pieces of land, containing 55 acres, in Hedcorn and Frittenden, on the dens of Holland and Hasylden, until my son Thomas is twenty-four years old. My feoffees are to buy also certain lands for the use of my son Thomas. To my son Thomas my three shops and a stall, and he is to pay to the lord of the town 8d. a year and to receive of Thomas Whitte 2d. yearly for a shop which he bought of me, with reversion to my daughters Elizabeth, Katherine, and Anna. The furnishings in the hall, little parlor, great parlor, and chambers of my principal messuage I give to my son Thomas. To my son Thomas 10 acres of land called Pikesfeld, lying to the hall door of his brother Edmund. Proved 25 September 1531. (Archdeaconry of Canterbury, vol. 19, fo. 224.)

The Will of EDMUND BORDEN of Hedcorne [co. Kent], dated 13 April 1539. To be buried in Hedcorn churchyard. To two priests at my burial and to the poor 20s. To my daughter Joan £5, to be paid to Rauff Champ to her use. To Maryon, my daughter, £5, to be paid to John Lytle to her use, at the age of twenty years, if they be not married before, or at their marriage. To Margaret, Alice, and Julyan, my daughters, £5 each, at their ages of twenty years or at their marriages. If any of my daughters die under twenty, unmarried, their legacies are to go to my sons then living. To Margaret, my wife. Residue of my goods to Edward, John, and William, my sons, equally. If my wife is pregnant with a woman child, I give to that child £5. Executors: Thomas Madocke and John Phylyke. Proved 18 June 1539. (Archdeaconry of Canterbury, vol. 21, fo. 209.)

The Will of JOHN BURDEN of Biddenden, co. Kent, dated 8 April 1541. To be buried in Biddenden churchyard. To William Boone. To Stephen Burdon, my brother. Executors: Stephen and William Burden.
My will regarding my lands. To my brother Stephen Burden my tenement and lands in Crunynden. To Margarie Boone the house John Petygrewe dwells in and 6 acres at Apuldore. To my sisters Alice and Elynor the house and lands I dwell in. To Christopher Burdon the lands bought of William Gybbon. To Robert Burdon the lands that Thomas Bewlde bought of Allen aand Stare, if he overcome the trouble he is now in, or else to my next heirs. To William Boone my annuity at Newstreets. The lands I bought of John and Thomas Halsenode and of Thomas Collyer are to be sold to the performance of my will, and also the annuity at John Best's. Proved 27 April 1541. (Archdeaconry of Canterbury, vol. 21, fo. 231.)

Administration on the estate of ROBERT BURDEN of Biddenden [co. Kent] was granted 27 July 1541 to his brother Christopher of Sandwich [co. Kent]. (Archdeaconry of Canterbury, Act Book 8, fo. 76.)

The Will of ALICE BURDON of Headcorn [co. Kent], widow, dated 22 March 1547/8. To be buried in Headcorn churchyard. All my goods I give to my son Robert Burdon, whom I make my executor, to dispose of them for my soul and all Christian souls. Witnesses: Thomas Burden and others. Proved 26 April 1548. (Archdeaconry of Canterbury, vol. 26, fo. 133.)

The Will of STEPHEN BURDEN of Biddenden, co. Kent, yeoman, dated 15 December 1553. To be buried in Biddenden churchyard. To my daughter Lettys, at her marriage. My wife is to pay to my son Thomas 43s. 4d. that is owing him. Residue to my wife Ursula. Executors: the said Ursula and John Jordayn.
My will regarding my lands. To my wife Ursula my messuage, garden, and three pieces of land thereunto belonging, for the nonage of James and John, my sons, until they are twenty-two years of age. She is to keep them until they can get their own living, and she is to pay to my daughter Lettys, at her marriage, £3. 6s. 8d., and, when my sons are twenty-two, they are to divide the said land equally. To my said sons, after my wife's decease, four pieces of land called Gauntes, and each son is to be the other's heir in the said messuage and lands, with reversion to my daughters Jane and Lettys Burden. To my sons Thomas and George Burden one piece of land called Gaunts als. Lakefelde, containing 4 acres, in Biddenden, on the den of Horrynden, to the King's high street against the lands of John Mayne, Gent., to the east, south on my lands, and north on Thomas Hendleighe, after my decease; and they are to allow my sons James and John a right of way and to pay Jane, if she be living, £3. 6s. 8d. If my wife die during the minority of my children, John Jordayn is to be their governor. Proved 16 March 1556 [1556/7]. (Archdeaconry of Canterbury, vol. 33, fo. 7.)

The Will of WILLIAM BURDON of Headcorn, co. Kent, undated. To Joan, my wife, £20 and a feather bed, etc. To Thomas Burdon, my son, £10. To Edward, my son, £10. To John, my son, £6. To Stephen, my son, £10. To Elizabeth, my daughter, £3. 6s. 8d. To my daughters Thomesy and Ann and to Edmonde, my son, a cow each. Executors: Joan, my wife, and Edward, my son. Residue to Joan, my wife, and to my sons Edward, Thomas, and Stephen, equally. Edward is to occupy John's and Stephen's parts until they are twenty years old. Overseer: John Kippinge. Witnesses: Nicholas Boodes, Nicholas Haurmersham, and others [not named]. Proved 8 June 1557. (Archdeaconry of Canterbury, vol. 30, fo. 134.)

The Will of EDWARD BORDEN of Headcorn, co. Kent, dated 28 January 1559/60. To be buried in Headcorn churchyard. My wife Margaret is to be my executor, and she is to pay to my brother Stephen Borden £17. 6s., which was given him of my father. To my mother, to Thomas Borden, my brother, to Edmunde Borden, my brother, to John Borden, and to my brother Steven Borden, to each 20s. To my sister Thamasin, to my sister Agnes, and to my sister Elizabeth, to each 10s. To John, Thomas, and Christopher Batnor 26s. 8d. each, at sixteen years of age. To Alice Warner £5, at twenty years of age. To the poor, at my burial, 10s. To my mother £5, which I owe her. Witnesses: John Kyppyr, Nycholas Boods, Nicholas Homersham, and others [not named]. Proved 26 March 1560. (Archdeaconry of Canterbury, vol. 34, fo. 199.)

The Will of AGNES BORDEN of Headcorn [co. Kent], widow, dated 13 February 1560/1. To be buried in Headcorn churchyard. To my brother Bodd's wife. To Parnell Semarke, my sister. To my daughter-in-law

Joan Borden. To Philpott's widow. To Isabel, my "keper." To Barnard's widow. To Henry Baker's widow. To John Dowde's widow. To Moise's widow. To the wife of Nicholas Todd and to the wife of James Reignes. To each godchild 1s. To Heles Wood 6d. To Joan Little 4d. To Polkyn's widow 4d. To my goddaughter Agnes Buddes. To my goddaughter Agnes Semarke. To Richard Hadd's wife. To Lawrence Draper what he has brought into my house. To John and Thomas Colingham, my sons, the residue of my goods. The children of my brother Nicholas Budds and Petronyll Semarke, my sister. Executor: my brother Nicholas Budds. Overseer: Thomas Tange. Proved 17 May 1561. (Archdeaconry of Canterbury, vol. 35, fo. 170.)

The Will of THOMAS BORDEN of Headcorn [co. Kent], yeoman, dated 13 April 1587. To be buried in the parish church of Headcorn. To the poor, at my burial, 20s. To my daughter Agnes, wife of Jonas Gorham, £10, one bedstead standing next to the parlor door, with a flock bed, a pair of blankets, a pair of sheets, one coverlet, a bolster, a pillow, a pillowbere, the greatest brass pot save one, three platters, three pewter dishes, a cow, a yard kercher, two neckerchers, two cross-clothes, a linen apron, and four bushels of wheat. To my brother Stephen Borden £4. To my sister Elizabeth Borden £4. To Edward Mills, my servant, 10s. To my maid, Tabitha Dame, 10s. Executor: my son Matthew Borden, and he is to be residuary legatee of my goods and chattles real. Witnesses: John Fotherbie, Edmund Meles, and Thomas Fravant. Proved 26 April 1592. (Archdeaconry of Canterbury, vol. 48, fo. 279.)

The Will of MATTHEW BORDEN of Headcorn [co. Kent], yeoman, dated 26 September 1620. To the poor of Headcorn, at my burial, 20s. To my wife Joan two beds and a bedstead, with all things belonging, in the inner chamber over the hall, and the bed and bedstead, with furniture belonging, in the next chamber, wherein I now lie, and a fourth part of all the rest of my household goods, except my bedding, which is to be equally divided, and £8 a year out of my farm called Sim Harnden's, in Smarden, Kent, in the tenure of Edward Watts, broadweaver, until my son John reaches the age of twenty-one years, and after that £4 a year for life to my said wife, the rent of my houses in Headcorn, wherein Zacharias Elye dwells, during her life, the rent of my farm called Grinnett, in Headcorn, in the occupation of Robert Marrance, for her life, and the rent of the tenement where Robert Jones dwells, until my son Edward is twenty-one years old. To my daughter Amye Borden £60 out of my Smarden lands, in the occupation of James Rich, butcher, at twenty years of age or marriage, to be paid by my son William, one of my executors. To my daughter Amye a feather bed, with a bedstead and furniture belonging thereto. To my daughter Mary Borden, wife of John Rowe, £16 promised at her marriage. To my son Edward £40, at twenty-one years of age, and two houses and land, etc., one in Headcorn, in the occupation of Zacharias Elye aforesaid, the other in the den of Blechenden, in the tenure of Robert Jones, sawyer. To my son Edward a feather bed and a bedstead, with furniture thereto belonging, three pewter platters, three pewter dishes, a brass pot, and a brass kettle. To my son John Borden my house and lands called Sym Harnden's, in Smarden. To my son John a like gift of personalty and £10, at twenty-one years of age. To my daughter Amye a dozen of pewter, a brass pot, a brass kettle, and a spit. To Tomson Cuery, my servant, 10s. To my son Richard my two houses and land in Hedcorn, in the tenure of George Brett and Robert Marrannte. To my son William £40, towards the performance of my daughter Amye's marriage money, to be paid out of my goods before a division is made. To my son William Borden my house and land in Smarden, in the tenure of James Riche, and William is to pay to my wife, his mother, £5 per year for life. Executors and residuary legatees: my sons Richard and William. Supervisor: Thomas Samson of Cranbrook, yeoman. Witnesses: Obedia Vyne and Richard Pabworth. Written by Jonas Bottinge. Proved by Richard Borden 27 October 1620 and by William Borden 30 November 1620. (Archdeaconry of Canterbury, vol. 63, fo. 134.)

## FROM PARISH REGISTERS

### BIDDENDEN, CO. KENT*

1588    Thomas son of Matthew Borden baptized 1 September.

### FRITTENDEN, CO. KENT*

#### Baptisms

——    Judeth Burdon 23 March.
——    Mathew Borden 30 September.
1563    Rose Burdon daughter of Richard 12 March [1563/4].
1564    Ann Burdon daughter of Thomas 26 December.
1569    Gilbert Burdon son of William 25 April.
1573    Richard Burdon son of John 11 May.
1574    Grace Burdon daughter of Richard 24 October.

#### Marriages

1571    John Bertune and Joan Burdune 24 August.
1573    Richard Borden and Margaret Benson, widow, 28 April.
1589    Peter Payne and Alice Borden 15 September.
1621    Alexander Burden and Ann Swadford 23 October.

#### Burials

1570    Thomas Burtun 30 November.
1571    Christian[?] Burdon daughter of Richard 24 December.
1573    Eleanor Borden 17 October.
1575    Richard Barden the sexton 21 April.

### HEADCORN, CO. KENT, 1560–1630†

#### Baptisms

1562    Agnes daughter of Edward Borden 25 January [1562/3] (R).
1568    Anne daughter of Edward Booreman 5 September.
1571    Kateryne daughter of Edward Boreman 19 August.
1572    William son of Edward Boreman 28 December.
1577    Xtopher son of Edward Boreman 26 April.
1578    Stephen son of Edward Boreman 8 May.
1579    Marye Booreman 21 June.
1582    Elizabeth daughter of Edward Booreman 25 March.

*The entries from the Biddenden and Frittenden registers have been taken not from the original registers but from the Bishop's transcripts of the registers, which are preserved at Canterbury.
†The entries from the Headcorn registers have been taken from a copy of the Bishop's transcripts of the registers which is in the College of Arms, London; and some entries found in the original registers but not appearing in the transcripts have been inserted in their proper chronological places and have been indicated by the letter R in brackets [R]. Names and dates in the original registers which differ from the corresponding names and dates in the copy of the Bishop's transcripts have been indicated in the same way. In the original registers of Headcorn, which have been searched from 1560 to 1640, no records of burials are extant from 2 May 1610 to 13 May 1631. In September 1626 William Borden signed the transcripts as a "sideman."

1585    Stephen son of Edward Booreman 12 August.
1588    Stephen son of Edward Booreman 21 January [1588/9].
1593    ———— Borden [Joan daughter of Matthew Borden, R] 29 April.
1594    John [son of Matthew, R] Borden 28 April.
1595    Richard son of Matthewe Borden 22 February [1595/6].
1600    William son of Matthew Borden 1 June [R].
1603    Anne [sic, ? Amye] daughter of Matthewe Borden 26 April.
1605    Edward son of Mathew Borden 14 April [R].
1606    John son of Mathew Borden 22 February [1606/7] [R].
1622    Margaret daughter of Richard Balden 26 January [1622/3] [R].
1626    Richard son of Richard Borden 9 July.
1626    Thomas son of Richard Borden 3 October [sic] [R].

## Marriages

1560    Edward Borden and Agnes Tassell 10 February [1560/1].
1561    John Marden and Agnes Booreman 22 September.
1566    Edward Booreman and Katerin Henecar 7 October.
1573    Stephen Denet [Steven Donet, R] and Elizabeth Boorden [Borden, R] 24 August.
1582    Robert Howtenge [Howtinge, R] and Agnes Boorden [Borden, R] 4 February [1582/3, sic, ? 1583/4].
1584    Thomas Borden and Margaret Reader, widow,* 2 May [1583, R].
1584    Robert Wyldegate [Wildegate, R] and Margaret Burden [Borden, R], widow,* 9 November.
1584    Francis Cooper and Alice Balden 11 January [1584/5] [R].
1585    Richard Standen and Anne Boreman 19 April.
1585    Jonas Gorram [Gorham, R] and Agnes Borden 2 August.
1620    John Roe and Mary Borden 4 May [R].
1625    Richard Borden and Joane Fowle 28 September.
1629    John Borman and Elizabeth Clagget 21 April.

## Burials

1560    Agnes Borden, widow, 9 March [1560/1].
1561    Katherin daughter of Edward Borden 17 May.
1564    Edmund son of Edward Borden 16 December [1563, R].
1571    Jone [Johanc, R] daughter of Thomas Borden 5 April.
1571    Katteren daughter of Edward Borman 28 August.
1572    William son of Edward Borman 23 March [1572/3].
1576    Edward Boorden [Borden, R], householder, 7 January [1576/7].
1577    Xtopher son of Edward Boorman 27 April.
1578    Stephen son of Edward Boreman 10 May.
————    Thomas son of Thomas Borden 30 May [30 April 1580, R].
————    The wife of Thomas Borden 20 May [1581, R].
1581    ———— [John, R] Borden, servant,* 15 November.
1582    Mary daughter of Edward Boreman 27 July.
1584    Edward [? Borden's] widow [Widow Borden, R] 25 March.
1589    Margaret wife of Thomas Borden 25 September [R].
1590    Joane Borden 5 February [1590/1].
1592    Thomas Borden [paterfamilias, R] 21 April.
1593    ———— [Joan daughter of Mathew, R] Borden 11 June.
1593·    Elizabeth Barden [Borden, R] 9 December.
1607    Margaret Balden, widow, 13 May [R].
1611    Tho[mas] son of Mathew Borden 6 November.
1615    William Borman 16 January [1615/16].
1620    Mathew Borden 4 October.

*This word is omitted in the original registers.

# From Feet of Fines*

Final Concord made in the King's Court at Westminster, on the Morrow of St. John the Baptist, 5 Henry VIII [25 June 1513], before the King's justices there, between William Borden, querent, and Richard Worme and Margery, his wife, and Thomas Ford and Agnes, his wife, deforciants, concerning two parts of one messuage, one garden, five acres of land, and two acres of meadow in Hedcron [*sic,* Headcorn], in five parts divided. Plea of covenant. Richard and Margery and Thomas and Agnes have acknowledged the same to be the right of William, as of their gift, and for themselves and the heirs of Margery and Agnes have quitclaimed and remised the same to William and his heirs for ever, and have warranted him and his heirs in the same against all men for ever. For this grant, etc., William has given them £5 sterling. (Feet of Fines, Kent, Henry VIII, Bundle 19, File 106, No. 9.)

Final Concord made in the King's Court at Westminster, on the Morrow of All Souls, 5 Henry VIII [3 November 1513], before the King's justices there, between Edward Borden and John Ady, querents, and William Mower and Margaret, his wife, deforciants, concerning two messuages and seventeen acres of land in Smarden. Plea of covenant. William and Margaret have acknowledged the same to be the right of Edward, as of their gift, and for themselves and the heirs of Margaret have remised and quitclaimed the same to Edward and John and the heirs of Edward for ever, and have warranted them and the heirs of Edward therein against all men for ever. For this acknowledgment, etc., Edward has granted the same to the said John [*sic*] and his heirs, to hold of the chief lords of the fee for ever. (Feet of Fines, Kent, Henry VIII, Bundle 19, File 106, No. 25.)

Final Concord made in the King's Court at Westminster, on the Morrow of Ascension Day, 7 Henry VIII [1515], before the King's justices there, between William Borden, querent, and Thomas Lacchynden and Margery, his wife, deforciants, concerning the eighth part of a messuage, a garden, and eleven acres of land in Hedcron [*sic,* Headcorn]. Plea of covenant. Thomas and Margery have acknowledged the same to be the right of William, as of their gift, and for themselves and the heirs of Margery have remised and quitclaimed the same to him and his heirs, and have warranted him and his heirs therein against all men for ever. For this acknowledgment, etc., William has given them £10 sterling. (Feet of Fines, Kent, Henry VIII, Bundle 19, File 106, No. 3.)

Final Concord made in the King's Court at Westminster, on the Morrow of the Purification of the Blessed Virgin Mary, 10 Henry VIII [3 February 1518/19], before the King's justices there, between William Borden, querent, and John Larke and Agnes, his wife, deforciants, concerning the moiety of one messuage, one garden, and eleven acres of land in Hedcron [*sic,* Headcorn]. Plea of covenant. John and Agnes have acknowledged the same to be the right of William, as of their gift, and for themselves and the heirs of Agnes have remised and quitclaimed the same to William and his heirs for ever, and have warranted him and his heirs therein against all men for ever. For this acknowledgment, etc., William has given them 40 marks of silver. (Feet of Fines, Kent, Henry VIII, Bundle 19, File 111, No. 34.)

*Preserved in the Public Record Office, London. The text of the Feet of Fines given in this article has been translated from the original Latin and abridged.

Final Concord made in the King's Court at Westminster, from Easter Day in three weeks, 20 Henry VIII [1528–29], before the King's justices there, between Edward Borden, querent, and William Newenden and Joan, his wife, deforciants, concerning one messuage, two gardens, and five acres of land in Hedcron [*sic*, Headcorn], and concerning the third part of one garden, called Oldetowne, containing two acres, in Smarden. Plea of covenant. William and Joan have acknowledged the same to be the right of Edward, as of their gift, and for themselves and the heirs of Joan have remised and quitclaimed the same to Edward and his heirs for ever, and have warranted Edward and his heirs therein against all men for ever. For this acknowledgment, etc., Edward has given William and Joan £40 sterling. (Feet of Fines, Kent, Henry VIII, Bundle 21, File 121, No. 4.)

Final Concord made in the King's Court at Westminster, on the Morrow of All Souls, 32 Henry VIII [3 November 1540], before the King's justices there, between John Wysperhawke and Elizabeth, his wife, querents, and William Borden and Joan, his wife, deforciants, concerning a messuage, a barn, a garden, and two acres of land in Hedcorne [*sic*, Headcorn]. Plea of covenant. William and Joan have acknowledged the same to be the right of Elizabeth, as of their gift, and for themselves and their heirs have remised and quitclaimed the same to John and Elizabeth and the heirs of Elizabeth for ever, and for themselves and the heirs of Joan have warranted John and Elizabeth and the heirs of Elizabeth therein against all men for ever. For this acknowledgment, etc., John and Elizabeth have given William and Joan £30 sterling. (Feet of Fines, Kent, Henry VIII, Bundle 22, File 138, No. 21.)

Final Concord made in the Queen's Court at Westminster, in the Octaves of Hilary, 14 Elizabeth [14–20 January 1571/2], before the Queen's justices there, between George Mephum, querent, and John Burden, deforciant, concerning one messuage, one orchard, one toft, one garden, ten acres of land, and twenty acres of pasture in Byddenden. Plea of covenant. John has acknowledged the same to be the right of George, as of his gift, and has remised and quitclaimed the same to him and his heirs, and for himself and his heirs has warranted George and his heirs therein against all men for ever. And the said George for the said acknowledgment, etc., has given John £40 sterling. (Feet of Fines, Kent, Hilary Term, 14 Elizabeth.)

Final Concord made in the Queen's Court at Westminster, in the Octaves of Michaelmas, 21 Elizabeth [30 September–6 October 1579], before the Queen's justices there, between John Walter, querent, and Richard Burden and Petronilla, his wife, deforciants, concerning ten acres of land and ten acres of pasture in Marden. Plea of covenant. Richard and Petronilla have acknowledged the same to be the right of John, as of their gift, and have remised and quitclaimed the same to him and his heirs for ever, and for themselves and the heirs of Richard have warranted John and his heirs therein against Richard and Petronilla and the heirs of Richard for ever. For this acknowledgment, etc., John has given Richard and Petronilla £40 sterling. (Feet of Fines, Kent, Michaelmas Term, 21–22 Elizabeth, Part 1.)

Final Concord made in the Queen's Court at Westminster, in the Octaves of Michaelmas, 21 Elizabeth [30 September–6 October 1579], before the Queen's justices there, between Peter Lymytory, clerk, querent, and Richard Burdon and Petronilla, his wife, deforciants, concerning one messuage, one barn, three acres of land, two acres of meadow, and three acres of pasture in Marden. Plea of covenant. Richard and Petronilla have acknowledged the same to be the right of Peter, as of their gift, and have remised and quitclaimed the same to Peter and his heirs for ever, and for themselves and the heirs of Richard have warranted Peter and his heirs in the same against all claiming by the said Richard for ever. For this grant, etc., Peter has given them £80 sterling. (Feet of Fines, Kent, Michaelmas Term, 21–22 Elizabeth, Part 1.)

Final Concord made in the Queen's Court at Westminster, in the Octaves of Hilary, 26 Elizabeth [14–20 January 1583/4], before the Queen's justices there, between William Burdon, querent, and Edward Young and Agnes, his wife, deforciants, concerning one messuage, one garden, eight acres of land, six acres of meadow, and six acres of pasture in Boughton Mounchelsey. Plea of covenant. Edward and Agnes have acknowledged the same to be the right of William, as of their gift, and for themselves and their heirs have remised and quitclaimed the same to William and his heirs for ever, and for themselves and the heirs of Edward have warranted William and his heirs therein against the said Edward and Agnes and the heirs of Edward for ever. For this acknowledgment, etc., William has given them £80 sterling. (Feet of Fines, Kent, Hilary Term, 26 Elizabeth.)

Final Concord made in the Queen's Court at Westminster, in the Octaves of Michaelmas, 26 Elizabeth [30 September–6 October 1584], before the Queen's justices there, between James Usborne, querent, and Richard Burden and Petronilla, his wife, deforciants, concerning two messuages and two gardens and concerning the fourth part of five acres of land and two acres of meadow in Marden. Plea of covenant. Richard and Petronilla have acknowledged the same to be the right of James, as of their gift, and for themselves and their heirs have remised and quitclaimed the same to James and his heirs for ever, and for themselves and the heirs of Richard have warranted James and his heirs therein against themselves and the heirs of Richard for ever. For this acknowledgment, etc., James has given them 100 marks of silver. (Feet of Fines, Kent, Michaelmas Term, 26–27 Elizabeth, Part 1.)

Final Concord made in the Queen's Court at Westminster, in the Octaves of St. Michael, 28 Elizabeth [30 September–6 October 1586], before the Queen's justices there, between Thomas Fowle, querent, and Alexander Tayler and Joan, his wife, deforciants, concerning one messuage, one garden, two orchards, ten acres of land, ten acres of meadow, ten acres of pasture, and two acres of wood in Biddenden. Plea of covenant. Alexander and Joan have acknowledged the same to be the right of Thomas, as of their gift, and for themselves and their heirs have remised and quitclaimed the same to Thomas and his heirs for ever, and for themselves and the heirs of Alexander have warranted Thomas and his heirs therein against all men for ever. For this acknowledgment, etc., Thomas has given them £120 sterling. (Feet of Fines, Kent, Michaelmas Term, 28–29 Elizabeth, Part 1.)

[The above-named Thomas Fowle was of Frittenden, co. Kent. He was the father of Richard Fowle of Frittenden and Headcorn, whose daughter Joan married Richard Borden of Headcorn and went with him to New England. For records and a pedigree showing the ancestry of Joan (Fowle) Borden see REGISTER, vol. 75, pp. 226–233.] *

*See Vol. I of this work, pp. 638–645.

305

Final Concord made in the Queen's Court at Westminster, in the Octaves of Michaelmas, 36 Elizabeth [30 September–6 October 1594], before the Queen's justices there, between Mathew Borden, querent, and William Lorkin and Mary, his wife, and John Batherst and Elizabeth, his wife, deforciants, concerning one messuage, one barn, one garden, and two acres of land in Hedcrone [sic, Headcorn]. Plea of covenant. William and Mary and John and Elizabeth have acknowledged the same to be the right of Mathew, as of their gift, and for themselves and their heirs have remised and quitclaimed the same to Mathew and his heirs for ever, and the said William and Mary, for themselves and the heirs of William, have warranted Mathew and his heirs therein against themselves and the heirs of William for ever, and John and Elizabeth, for themselves and the heirs of John, have warranted him and his heirs therein against all men for ever. For this grant, etc., Mathew has given them £40 sterling. (Feet of Fines, Kent, Michaelmas Term, 36–37 Elizabeth, Part 2.)

Final Concord made in the Queen's Court at Westminster, on the Morrow of the Purification of the Blessed Virgin Mary, 38 Elizabeth [3 February 1595/6], before the Queen's justices there, between Mathew Borden, querent, and Thomas Nokes and Joan, his wife, deforciants, concerning one messuage, one barn, one garden, ten acres of land, and ten acres of pasture in Smarden. Plea of covenant. Thomas and Joan have acknowledged the same to be the right of Mathew, as of their gift, and for themselves and their heirs have remised and quitclaimed the same to Mathew and his heirs for ever, and for themselves and the heirs of Joan have warranted Mathew and his heirs therein against themselves and the heirs of Joan for ever. For this acknowledgment, etc., Mathew has given them £80 sterling. (Feet of Fines, Kent, Hilary Term, 38 Elizabeth.)

Kent. [Final Concord] between John Powell, querent, and Francis Fowle and Mary, his wife, deforciants, concerning one messuage, one barn, one garden, one orchard, six acres of land, six acres of pasture, and four acres of wood in Marden. Plea of covenant. Francis and Mary have acknowledged the same to be the right of John, as of their gift, and have remised and quitclaimed the same to him and his heirs for ever, and for themselves and the heirs of Francis have warranted him and his heirs therein against themselves and the heirs of Francis for ever. For this acknowledgment, etc., he has given them £41 sterling. The Morrow of Trinity, 6 James I [1608]. (C. P. 26/2 [Notes of Fines], Trinity Term, 6 James I.*)

[This Francis Fowle was of Cranbrook, co. Kent, and was a clothier. He was brother of Richard Fowle of Frittenden and Headcorn and uncle of Joan, wife of Richard Borden of Rhode Island.]

Final Concord made in the King's Court at Westminster, in the Octaves of Michaelmas, 15 James I [30 September–6 October 1617], before the King's justices there, between Richard Fowle, querent, and John Fullager alias Dounne and Anne, his wife, deforciants, concerning a messuage, a barn, a garden, two orchards, and two acres of meadow in Hedcorne [sic, Headcorn]. Plea of covenant. John and Anne have acknowledged the same to be the right of Richard, as of their gift, and for themselves and the heirs of John have remised and quitclaimed the same to Richard and his heirs for ever, and have warranted him and his heirs therein for ever against themselves and the heirs of John. For this acknowledgment, etc.,

*No Feet of Fines are extant for this term.

Richard has given John and Anne £41 sterling. (C. P. 25 [Feet of Fines], Kent, Michaelmas Term, 15 James I, File 1.)

[Richard Fowle was the father of Joan, wife of Richard Borden of Portsmouth, R. I.]

Final Concord made in the King's Court at Westminster, from Easter Day in fifteen days, 18 James I [1620], before the King's justices there, between Richard Fowle, querent, and William Wathers and Isabel, his wife, deforciants, concerning one messuage, three barns, a garden, twenty acres of land, seven acres of meadow, and seventeen acres of pasture in Frittenden. Plea of covenant. William and Isabel have acknowledged the same to be the right of Richard, as of their gift, and have remised and quitclaimed the same to him and his heirs for ever, and for themselves and the heirs of William have warranted him and his heirs therein against themselves and the heirs of William for ever. For this acknowledgment, etc., Richard has given William and Isabel £60 sterling. (C. P. 25 [Feet of Fines], Kent, Easter Term, 18 James I, File 1.)

[This Richard Fowle is apparently the Richard Fowle who was the father of Joan, wife of Richard Borden.]

Final Concord made in the King's Court at Westminster, in the Octaves of St. Martin, 4 Charles I [12–18 November 1628], before the King's justices there, between Richard Fowle, querent, and William Borden and Alice, his wife, deforciants, concerning one messuage, one barn, one garden, one orchard, seventeen acres of land, and five acres of pasture in Smarden. Plea of Covenant. William and Alice have acknowledged the same to be the right of Richard, as of their gift, and have remised and quitclaimed the same to him and his heirs for ever, and for themselves and the heirs of William have warranted him and his heirs therein against all men for ever. For this acknowledgment, etc., Richard has given them £60 sterling. (C. P. 25 [Feet of Fines], Kent, Michaelmas Term, 4 Charles I, File 1.)

[This Richard Fowle was perhaps the Richard Fowle of Frittenden and Headcorn whose daughter Joan married Richard Borden; and William Borden was probably the William Borden, son of Matthew, who was baptized at Headcorn 1 June 1600 and was brother of Richard Borden of Portsmouth, R. I.]

# GENEALOGICAL RESEARCH IN ENGLAND

Communicated by the Committee on English and Foreign Research

## THE BORDENS OF HEADCORN, CO. KENT

Contributed by G. Andrews Moriarty, A.M., LL.B., F.S.A.,
of Bristol, R. I.

## From Lay Subsidies for co. Kent*

15 Henry VIII [1523–24].
   Lathe of Aylesford, Hundred of Ayhorne.
      Halyngherste in Hedcorne.   William Borden in goods, [valuation]
                                  20s., [tax] 4d.
                                  William Borden in goods, [valuation]
                                  £10, [tax] 5s.
      Hedcorne.                   William Borden in goods, [valuation]
                                  £40, [tax] 40s.
      Hallyngherst in Smarden.    Symond Borden in goods, [valuation]
                                  £3, [tax] 18d. (Lay Subsidies,
                                  124/192.)

35 Henry VIII [1543–44].
   Hundred of Ayhorne.            Thomas Borden in goods, [tax] 2d.
                                  (Ib., 125/280.)
   Hedcorne.                      Edward Bourdon in lands, [tax] 4d.
                                  William Bourdon in goods, [tax] 2s.
                                  Thomas Maddocke for Edmond Bor-
                                  den "heyres goods," [tax] 8d. (Ib.,
                                  125/268.)

10 November, 36 Henry VIII [1544], Indenture.
   Hundred of Cranbrooke.         Robert Burden in goods, [valuation]
                                  £5, [tax] 10d.
   Hundred of Marden.             Thomas Borden in goods, [valuation]
                                  £3, [tax] 3d. (Ib., 125/273.)

Henry VIII [undated].
   Hundred of Cranbrooke.         John Burden, Jr., on wages [amount]
                                  20s., [tax] 4d.
                                  Thomas Burden on wages, [amount]
                                  20s., [tax] 4d. (Ib., 125/324.)

40 Elizabeth [1597–98].
   Hundred of Eythorne,
      Parish of Headcorne.        Mathew Borden in goods, [valuation]
                                  £4, [tax] 6s, 8d. (Ib., 127/535.)

## From Early Chancery Proceedings†

To the right gracious Lord Chancellor of England.

Henry Burden, one of the sons and heirs of Thomas Burden, late of
Headcorn, co. Kent, complainant, v. Nicholas Cutbussh of Beaynden, defendant.

*Preserved in the Public Record Office, London.
†Preserved in the Public Record Office, London.   The Early Chancery Proceedings are of
the fourteenth and fifteenth centuries.

The complainant shews that his said father was seised of a messuage, lands, rents, and services in Headcorn, Fretynden, and Stapilherst, co. Kent, and enfeoffed thereof William Burden, Richard Burden, Thomas Burden the Younger, and one Nicholas Cutbussh, upon condition that they should enfeoff Roberge, wife of the said Thos. Burden, in a messuage and twenty-five acres of land in Headcorn, "upon the dene of Burdn," for the term of her life, with remainder to Herry, John, and Thomas, sons of the said Thomas Burden, for ever, and that the said William, Richard, Thomas, and Nicholas should suffer the said Roberge to have and receive all issues and profits of all other lands which they had of the gift of the said Thomas Burden, for the term of two years next after his death, without any more declaration and mention made thereof in his last will; so that by right, after the said two years, it should remain to the complainant as son and next heir of Thomas Burden, because his brothers, John and Thomas, died without heirs of their bodies, and the said William, Richard, and Thomas have made him estate according to the last will of his father. But Nicholas Cutbussh, one of the feoffees, has at all times refused, and still doth. He desires that a writ of subpœna may be directed to the said Nicholas.

Pledges for { William Godyng of co. Surrey, gentleman.
prosecuting. { William Swyenden[?] of co. Kent, gentleman.

[Endorsed] Writ returnable in the Octave of the Purification. [No answer.] (Early Chancery Proceedings, Bundle 70, No. 60.)

The following pedigree shows all that has been *proved* in regard to the paternal ancestry of Richard Borden of Portsmouth, R. I.

1. EDMUND BORDEN, of Headcorn, co. Kent, the testator of 13 Apr. 1539, born about 1480, died between 13 Apr. and 18 June 1539, when his will was proved. His estate was taxed 8d. in 1543–44. He married MARGARET ———.

Children:

    i.    EDWARD, of Headcorn, b. about 1505.
    ii.   JOHN, b. about 1508.
2. iii.   WILLIAM, b. about 1510.
    iv.   JOAN, b. about 1515; m. shortly before 13 Apr. 1539 RALPH CHAMP.
    v.    MARION, b. about 1520; betrothed on or before 13 Apr. 1539 to JOHN LITTLE.
    vi.   MARGARET, b. about 1522.
    vii.  ALICE, b. about 1525.
    viii.  JULIAN (a daughter), b. about 1527.

2. WILLIAM BORDEN (*Edmund*), of Headcorn, born about 1510, died before 8 June 1557, when his will, undated, was proved. Perhaps he was the William Borden who was taxed 2s. at Headcorn in the subsidy of 1543–44. He married JOAN ———, who was living 28 Jan. 1559/60.

Children:

3. i.    THOMAS, b. about 1533.
    ii.   EDWARD, the testator of 28 Jan. 1559/60, b. about 1535; d. *s.p.* between 28 Jan. 1559/60 and 26 Mar. 1560, when his will was proved; m. MARGARET ———, who was living 28 Jan. 1559/60.
    iii.  JOHN, b. about 1539; d. 15 Nov. 1581.
    iv.  STEPHEN, b. about 1541; living 13 Apr. 1587.

v. ELIZABETH. b. about 1543; living unm. 13 Apr. 1587. Probably she was the Elizabeth Borden who was bur. at Headcorn 9 Dec. 1593.
vi. THAMASINE, b. about 1545.
vii. ANN (or AGNES), b. about 1547; living 28 Jan. 1559/60; probably the Agnes Booreman who m. at Headcorn, 22 Sept. 1561, JOHN MARDEN.
viii. EDMUND, b. about 1548; living 28 Jan. 1559/60.

3. THOMAS BORDEN (*William, Edmund*), of Headcorn, yeoman, the testator of 13 Apr. 1587, born about 1533, was buried at Headcorn 21 Apr. 1592. He married first ———, who was buried at Headcorn 20 May 1581; and secondly, at Headcorn, 2 May 1584, MARGARET READER, widow, who was buried at Headcorn 25 Sept. 1589.

Children by first wife:

i. THOMAS, b. about 1560; bur. at Headcorn 30 Apr. 1580.
4. ii. MATTHEW, bapt. at Frittenden, co. Kent, 30 Sept. —— [about 1563].
iii. JOAN, b. about 1565; bur. at Headcorn 5 Apr. 1571.
iv. AGNES, b. about 1567; living 13 Apr. 1587; m. at Headcorn, 2 Aug. 1585, JONAS GORHAM.

4. MATTHEW BORDEN (*Thomas, William, Edmund*), of Headcorn, yeoman, the testator of 26 Sept. 1620, baptized at Frittenden, co. Kent, 30 Sept. —— [about 1563], was buried at Headcorn 4 Oct. 1620. He married first, at Biddenden, co. Kent, 21 Feb. 1584, ELEANOR TAYLOR (Canterbury Marriage Licences); and secondly JOAN ———, who was living 26 Sept. 1620 and was the mother of his surviving children.

He owned lands in Headcorn, Smarden, and Bletchenden, co. Kent, was taxed 6s. 8d. at Headcorn on goods valued at £4 in the subsidy of 1597–98, and was churchwarden at Headcorn in 1598.

Child, probably by first wife:

i. THOMAS, bapt. at Biddenden 1 Sept. 1588; bur. at Headcorn 6 Nov. 1611.

Children by second wife:

ii. JOAN, bapt. at Headcorn 29 Apr. 1593; bur. there 11 June 1593.
iii. JOHN, bapt. at Headcorn 28 Apr. 1594; d. young.
5. iv. RICHARD, bapt. at Headcorn 22 Feb. 1595/6, the emigrant to New England.
v. MARY, b. about 1598; m. at Headcorn, 4 May 1620, JOHN ROE.
vi. WILLIAM, bapt. at Headcorn 1 June 1600.
vii. AMY (called ANNE in the Bishop's transcripts), bapt. at Headcorn 26 Apr. 1603.
viii. EDWARD, bapt. at Headcorn 14 Apr. 1605.
ix. JOHN, bapt. at Headcorn 22 Feb. 1606/7. He inherited his father's land in Smarden, co. Kent. Probably he was the John Borden who m. at Headcorn, 21 Apr. 1629, ELIZABETH CLAGGET, who must have d. soon afterwards, as he appears in 1635 on the shipping list of the *Elizabeth & Ann*, bound for New England, aged 28 years, with a wife JOAN, aged 23 years, a son Matthew, aged 8 years, and a daughter Elizabeth, aged 3 years. Nothing is known of him in New England.

5. RICHARD BORDEN (*Matthew, Thomas, William, Edmund*), of Headcorn and Cranbrook, co. Kent, and of Portsmouth, R. I., baptized at Headcorn 22 Feb. 1595/6, died at Portsmouth 25 May 1671. He married at Headcorn, 28 Sept. 1625, JOANE FOWLE, who died at Portsmouth 15 July 1688, daughter of Richard Fowle of Frittenden and Headcorn, co. Kent, yeoman.*

Richard Borden inherited from his father lands in Headcorn, but in 1628 he moved to Cranbrook, where his wife had relatives. She, by the will of her uncle, Francis Fowle of Cranbrook, clothier, dated 8 Oct. 1632 and proved 3 Apr. 1633, was to receive his messuages in Cranbrook, after the death of his widow, Elizabeth Fowle.† In 1637/8 Richard Borden emigrated from Cranbrook to New England, and settled at Portsmouth, R. I., where he held various public offices. He was freeman there 16 Mar. 1640/1, a member of a committee to treat with the Dutch, 18 May 1653, assistant at Portsmouth, 1653, 1654, treasurer, 1654, 1655, commissioner, 1654, 1656, 1657, and deputy from Portsmouth to the Rhode Island General Assembly, 1667, 1670. He was a surveyor, and acquired large tracts of land in Rhode Island and in East Jersey (Monmouth County). He was buried in the burial ground of the Society of Friends at Portsmouth. His nuncupative will, of which an abstract is given in Austin's "Genealogical Dictionary of Rhode Island," was admitted to probate by the town council of Portsmouth 31 May 1671. It mentions his wife Joan and all his children except Richard and Elizabeth, who probably died young. Five of his children were born in England, and the remaining seven at Portsmouth, R. I.‡

Children:

i.   RICHARD, bapt. at Headcorn 9 July 1626; probably d. young.
ii.  THOMAS, of Portsmouth and Providence, R. I., bapt. at Headcorn 3 Oct. 1627; d. 25 Nov. 1676; m. 20 Jan. 1663/4 MARY HARRIS, who d. 22 Mar. 1717/18, daughter of William and Susanna Harris of Providence. Eight children.
iii. FRANCIS, of Portsmouth, R. I., and Shrewsbury, Monmouth Co., East Jersey, bapt. at Cranbrook 23 Dec. 1628; d. in Monmouth Co., East Jersey, 19, 1 mo. 1705/6; m. 12, 4 mo. 1677 JANE VICKARS. He moved to Shrewsbury about 1677. In his will, dated 4 May 1703, he bequeathed to his son Francis his land in the parish of Goudhurst, co. Kent, "as the same is conveyed to me by virtue of Francis Fowle of Cranbrook in said county of Kent" by his will dated 8 Oct. 1632.§ He was the ancestor of the Pennsylvania Bordens. Four children.
iv.  MARY, bapt. at Cranbrook 13 Jan. 1632/3; d. before 1691; m. JOHN COOKE of Portsmouth, R. I., who d. in 1691, son of Thomas Cook. Eleven children.

*For records and a pedigree showing the ancestry of Joane Fowle see REGISTER, vol. 75, pp. 226-233. **
†See abstract of this will in REGISTER, vol. 75, p. 229.
‡In order to make this article complete in itself, this account of Richard Borden, the immigrant, and the following list of his children have been repeated, with a few changes and additions, from REGISTER, vol. 75, p. 233.
§See abstract of the will of Francis Fowle in REGISTER, vol. 75, p. 229. It mentions messuages in Cranbrook, *not* in Goudhurst.
**For pp. 226-233 see Vol. I of this work, pp. 638-645.

v. ELIZABETH, bapt. at Cranbrook 25 May 1634; probably d. young.
vi. MATTHEW, of Portsmouth, R. I., b. at Portsmouth in May 1638, and said in the Friends' records to be "the first English child born on Rhode Island;" d. 5 July 1708; m. 4 Mar. 1673/4 SARAH CLAYTON, b. in 1654, d. 19 Apr. 1735. His will was dated 28 Mar. 1705. Ten children.
vii. JOHN, of Portsmouth, R. I., b. at Portsmouth in Sept. 1640; d. 4 June 1716; m. 25 Dec. 1670 MARY EARLE, b. about 1655, d. in June 1734, daughter of William and Mary (Walker) Earle. His will was dated 24 Feb. 1715/16 and was proved 9 July 1716. Nine children.
viii. JOSEPH, of Portsmouth, R. I., and Barbados, B. W. I., b. at Portsmouth 3 July 1643; m. HOPE ———. Three children recorded in Rhode Island before 1674.
ix. SARAH, b. at Portsmouth in May 1644; d. after 1705; m. JONATHAN HOLMES of Newport, R. I., who d. in 1713, son of Obadiah and Catharine Holmes. Nine children.
x. SAMUEL, of Portsmouth, R. I., and Westchester, N. Y., b. at Portsmouth in July 1645; m. 1 June 1679, being then of Westchester, ELIZABETH CROSSE. Probably he left issue.
xi. BENJAMIN, of Portsmouth, R. I., and of Monmouth and Burlington Counties, N. J., b. at Portsmouth in May 1649; d. after 1718; m. 22 Sept. 1670 ABIGAIL GROVER, daughter of James Grover. He was in Burlington Co., N. J., by 1670. Ten children.
xii. AMEY, b. at Portsmouth in Feb. 1653/4; d. on shipboard at New York 5 Feb. 1683/4; bur. at Gravesend; m. 27 Mar. 1678 WILLIAM RICHARDSON of Newport, R. I., and Flushing, N. Y. Three children.

[Vincent Boys of Goodnestone, co. Kent, in his will, proved in 1558, mentioned his wife Mary, his sons Thomas and William, his daughters Mildred, Judith, Bennet, Margaret, and ———, and his brother Thomas Honeywood and daughter Joan. The testator left his lands in Headcorn that were late of his uncle, Edward Borden, to his son, Thomas, with remainder to his right heirs, and his lands in Headcorn, Frittenden, and Smarden that were late of his uncle, Thomas Borden, to his son William, with remainder to his son John and his heirs. (Archdeaconry of Canterbury, vol. 27, fo. 252.) This Vincent Boys appears to have been a grandson of William Borden of Headcorn, the testator of 10 Feb. 1530/1, a correction in the printed abstract of whose will is given below.]

CORRECTION

Vol. 84, page 75, line 22 (in the will of William Borden of Headcorn, dated 10 Feb. 1530/1. *For* Edmund *read* Edward. *

## HASKETT: ADDITIONAL RECORDS

Contributed by G. ANDREWS MORIARTY, A.M., LL.B., F.S.A., of Bristol, R. I.

IN the REGISTER, vol. 77, pages 71–77 and 110–133, there were ** published records and a pedigree relating to the English ancestry and family connections of Stephen Haskett, who settled at Salem, Mass., as early as 22 Mar. 1666/7. These records included numerous documents pertaining to the lawsuits in which various members of the Haskett family in England were involved; and they were followed in vol. 78, pages 54–63, of the REGISTER by other records, chiefly relating to litigation in England, which supplied more information about this family. In the present issue of the REGISTER the publication of additional Haskett records, which have been brought to light since 1924,
*Page 307, this volume.
**For pp. 71-77 & 110-133 see pp. 1-30, this volume; for pp. 54-63 see pp. 43-52, this volume.

is begun, and will be continued in one or more future issues of the magazine.

## FROM FEET OF FINES*

Final Concord made on the Quindene of St. Martin, 20 Henry VII [25 November 1504], between Thomas Frowyk, Knight, Richard Empson, Knight, Anthony FitzHerbert, Richard Hasket, Robert Ap Rees, and John Litilbury, querents, and Richard Andrews and Elizabeth, his wife, deforciants, concerning the manors of Athlyngton and Pymor and forty acres of land, etc., in Othe. Richard and Elizabeth and the heirs of Elizabeth have quitclaimed the same to the querents and to the heirs of John Litilbury, and the querents have given to the deforciants £500. (Feet of Fines, Dorset, Henry VII, Bundle 51, File 63, No. 17.)

Final Concord made at Westminster, on the Quindene of Michaelmas, 10 James I [13 October 1612], between Elizeus Haskett, querent, and Maurice Carrent, Esq., and Elizabeth, his wife, deforciants, concerning three acres of meadow in Hengestridge. Plea of covenant. Maurice and Elizabeth have granted to Elizeus the meadow, to hold from the Feast of the Annunciation [25 March] for ninety-nine years, if William Haskett, son of Elizeus, Alice Haskett, daughter of Elizeus, and Elizeus Haskett, son of Elizeus, so long live, rendering yearly to Maurice and Elizabeth and the heirs of Maurice 3s. at the Annunciation [25 March] and at Michaelmas [29 September], by equal portions, if William, Alice, and Elizeus Haskett, son of Elizeus Haskett, the Younger, so long live. And Maurice and Elizabeth and the heirs of Maurice shall warrant to Elizeus the aforesaid meadow against Maurice and Elizabeth and the heirs of Maurice for the whole term, if William, Alice, and Elizeus Haskett, son of Elizeus Haskett, the Younger, so long live. And Elizeus Haskett, the Elder, has given to Maurice and Elizabeth £41 sterling. (Feet of Fines, Somerset, Michaelmas Term, 10 James I.)

Final Concord made at Westminster, on the Octave of St. Michael, 11 James I [6 October 1613], between John Haskett, the Elder, querent, and Maurice Carent, Esq., and Elizabeth, his wife, deforciants, concerning six acres of land, four acres of pasture, and common of pasture for all manner of beasts in Todber *alias* Todebere *alias* Todbeare. Plea of covenant. Maurice and Elizabeth have acknowledged the tenements and common of pasture to be the right of John, as those which John has of the gift of Maurice and Elizabeth, and they have remised and quitclaimed the same from Maurice and Elizabeth and their heirs to John and his heirs for ever. And moreover Maurice and Elizabeth have granted for themselves and the heirs of Maurice that they will warrant to John and his heirs the aforesaid tenements and common of pasture against Maurice and Elizabeth and the heirs of Maurice and against the heirs of William Carent, Knight, deceased, great-grandfather of Maurice, and against the heirs of Leonard Carent, Esq., deceased, grandfather of Maurice, and against the heirs of William Carent, Esq., deceased, father of Maurice. And for this John has given Maurice and Elizabeth £41 sterling. (Feet of Fines, Dorset, Michaelmas Term, 11 James I.)

Final Concord made at Westminster, on the Octave of Michaelmas, 14 James I [6 October 1616], between William Haskett, querent, and John Rogers, deforciant, concerning three acres of meadow and thirty acres of pasture in Sutton-Montague *alias* Montacute. Plea of covenant. John

*Preserved in the Public Record Office, London. The text of the Feet of Fines given in this article has been translated from the original Latin and abridged.

313

has acknowledged the tenements to be the right of William, as those which William has of the gift of John, and he has remised and quitclaimed the same from himself and his heirs to William and his heirs for ever. And John has granted for himself and his heirs that he will warrant to William and his heirs the tenements against John and his heirs for ever. And for this William has given John £41. (Feet of Fines, Somerset, Michaelmas Term, 14 James I.)

# GENEALOGICAL RESEARCH IN ENGLAND

Communicated by the Committee on English and Foreign Research

## HASKETT: ADDITIONAL RECORDS

Contributed by G. Andrews Moriarty, A.M., LL.B., F.S.A.,
of Bristol, R. I.

## From Feet of Fines (concluded)*

Final Concord made at Westminster, in three weeks of Michaelmas, 19 James I [20 October 1621], between William Mogg and Dorothy, his wife, querents, and William Haskett and Margaret, his wife, and Ralph Hudson and Elizabeth, his wife, deforciants, concerning the manor of Hatherley and twenty acres of land, twenty acres of meadow, eighty acres of pasture, and twelve acres of wood in Hatherley, Maperton, and Wincanton. Plea of covenant. William Haskett and Margaret and Ralph and Elizabeth have acknowledged the manor and tenements to be the right of William Mogg, as those which William and Dorothy have of the gift of William Haskett and Margaret and Ralph and Elizabeth, and they have remised and quitclaimed the same from themselves and their heirs to William and Dorothy and the heirs of William for ever. And William Haskett and Margaret have granted for themselves and the heirs of Margaret that they will warrant to William Mogg and Dorothy and the heirs of William the aforesaid manor and tenements against William Haskett and Margaret and the heirs of Margaret for ever. And further Ralph and Elizabeth have granted for themselves and the heirs of Elizabeth that they will warrant to William Mogg and Dorothy and the heirs of William the manor and tenements against Ralph and Elizabeth and the heirs of Elizabeth for ever. And for this William Mogg and Dorothy have given William Haskett and Margaret and Ralph and Elizabeth £160. (Feet of Fines, Somerset, Michaelmas Term, 19 James I.)

Final Concord made at Westminster, in three weeks of Easter, 21 James I [4 May 1623], between William Haskett, the Elder, querent, and Mervin, Lord Awdely, Earl of Castlehaven, and Elizabeth, his wife, deforciants, concerning ten acres of meadow and sixty acres of pasture in Stalbridg. Plea of covenant. The Earl and Elizabeth have granted to William the aforesaid tenements, to hold to William from the Annunciation [25 March] last past for the term of ninety-nine years, if the said William, Margery Lillye, and William Haskett, the Younger, or any of them, so long live, rendering yearly to the Earl and his heirs 60s. yearly at [four terms named]. And the Earl and his heirs will warrant to William Haskett, the Elder, the aforesaid tenement against the Earl and Elizabeth and the heirs of the Earl for the whole term aforesaid, if William, Margery, and William, or any of them, so long live. And for this William Haskett, the Elder, has given the Earl and Elizabeth £100 sterling. (Feet of Fines, Dorset, Easter Term, 21 James I.)

Final Concord made at Westminster, in one month of Easter, 4 Charles I [11 May 1628], between Richard Adames, querent, and William Haskett and Margaret, his wife, and Thomas Hole and Elizabeth, his wife, de-

*Preserved in the Public Record Office, London. The text of the Feet of Fines given in this article has been translated from the original Latin and abridged.

forciants, concerning eleven acres of pasture in Sutton-Mountague. Plea of covenant. William and Margaret and Thomas and Elizabeth have granted to Richard the aforesaid tenements, and have rendered them to him in the same court, to hold to Richard from 16 April last past for the term of ninety-nine years, if Anne Adames, Margaret Adames, and Grace Adames, daughters of Richard, so long live, rendering yearly to William and his heirs 13s. 4d. at Michaelmas [29 September] and the Annunciation [25 March] by equal portions, if Anne, Margaret, and Grace so long live. And William and Margaret and Thomas and Elizabeth and the heirs of William will warrant to Richard the aforesaid tenements against William and Margaret and Thomas and Elizabeth and the heirs of William for the whole term aforesaid, if Anne, Margaret, and Grace so long live. And for this Richard has given William and Margaret and Thomas and Elizabeth £41. (Feet of Fines, Somerset, Easter Term, 4 Charles I.)

Final Concord made at Westminster, on the Octave of St. Hilary, 6 Charles I [20 January 1630/1], between James Haskett, querent, and John Hodges, Gentleman, and Margery, his wife, deforciants, concerning one messuage, one garden, one orchard, seventeen acres of land, five acres of meadow, and seven acres of pasture in Wedmore and Weschombe. Plea of covenant. John and Margery have granted to James the aforesaid tenements, and have rendered them to him in the same court, to hold to James from 1 November last past for the term of ninety-nine years, if the aforesaid James, Elizabeth Hodges, daughter of Edward Hodges, Gentleman, and John Hodges, son of James Hodges, Gentleman, so long live, rendering yearly to John and Margery and the heirs of John 10s. at the Annunciation [25 March] and Michaelmas [29 September], by equal portions, payable for the whole term aforesaid, if James, Elizabeth, and John Hodges, the son, so long live. And John and Margery and the heirs of John will warrant to James the aforesaid tenements against John and Margery and their heirs for the whole term aforesaid, if James, Elizabeth, and John Hodges, the son, so long live. And for this James has given John and Margery £60. (Feet of Fines, Somerset, Hilary Term, 6 Charles I.)

Final Concord made at Westminster on the Morrow of the Holy Trinity, 10 Charles I [2 June 1634], between Walter Bricke, querent, and William Haskett, Gentleman, John Haskett, James Baker and Joan, his wife, Thomas Hole and Elizabeth, his wife, and Margaret Haskett, widow, deforciants, concerning three acres of meadow and thirty acres of pasture in Sutton-Montacute alias Montague. Plea of covenant. William, John, James and Joan, Thomas and Elizabeth, and Margaret have acknowledged the aforesaid tenements to be the right of Walter, as those which Walter has of the gift of William, John, James and Joan, Thomas and Elizabeth, and Margaret, and have remised and quitclaimed them from William, John, James and Joan, Thomas and Elizabeth, and Margaret and their heirs to Walter and his heirs for ever. And William has granted for himself and his heirs that they will warrant to Walter and his heirs the aforesaid tenements against William and his heirs for ever. And John has granted for himself and his heirs that they will warrant to Walter and his heirs the aforesaid tenements against John and his heirs for ever. And John and Joan have granted for themselves and the heirs of Joan that they will warrant to Walter and his heirs the aforesaid tenements against James and Joan and the heirs of Joan for ever. And Thomas and Elizabeth have granted for themselves and the heirs of Elizabeth that they will warrant to Walter and his heirs the aforesaid tenements against Thomas and Elizabeth and the heirs of Elizabeth for ever. And Margaret has granted for herself and her heirs that she will warrant to Walter and his heirs the aforesaid tenements against Margaret and her heirs for ever. And for this Walter has given William, John, James and Joan, Thomas and Elizabeth, and Margaret £100. (Feet of Fines, Somerset, Trinity Term, 10 Charles I.)

Final Concord made at Westminster on the Quindene of Easter, 11 Charles I [12 April 1635], between Andrew Loder and James Loder, querents, and William Haskett and Joan, his wife, deforciants, concerning ten acres of meadow and sixty acres of pasture in Stalbridge. Plea of covenant. William and Joan have granted to Andrew and James the aforesaid tenements, and have rendered them to them in the same court, to hold to Andrew and James for the term of eighty years next after the death of the aforesaid William, if Margery Lyllie and William Haskett, the Younger, or either of them, so long live, rendering therefor yearly to the heirs of William one grain of pepper at Michaelmas [29 September]. And William and Joan and the heirs of William will warrant to Andrew and James the aforesaid tenements against William and Joan and the heirs of William for the whole term aforesaid, if Margery and William Haskett, the Younger, or either of them, so long live. And for this Andrew and James have given to William and Joan £100 sterling. (Feet of Fines, Dorset, Easter Term, 11 Charles I.)

Final Concord made at Westminster in three weeks of Michaelmas, 1649 [20 October 1649], between Stephen Haskett, querent, and John Windsor and Mary, his wife, deforciants, concerning two messuages, sixteen acres of land, twelve acres of meadow, and sixteen acres of pasture in Coxeley, Wyke, and Wells. Plea of covenant. John and Mary have acknowledged the aforesaid tenements to be the right of Stephen, as those which Stephen has of the gift of John and Mary, and they have remised and quitclaimed the same from John and Mary and the heirs of John to Stephen and his heirs for ever. And John and Mary have granted for themselves and the heirs of John that they will warrant to Stephen and his heirs the aforesaid tenements for ever. And for this Stephen has given John and Mary £60. (Feet of Fines, Somerset, Michaelmas Term, 1649.)

Final Concord made at Westminster on the Morrow of St. Martin [12 November], 1659, between Katherine Harte, widow, querent, and Robert Haskett. the Elder, and Judith, his wife, Robert Haskett, the Younger, John Bartlett and Edith, his wife, and William Bryne and Mary, his wife, deforciants, concerning fourteen acres of meadow in Sutton-Montacute *alias* Mountague. Plea of covenant. Robert and Judith, Robert, John and Edith, and William and Mary have acknowledged the tenements to be the right of Katherine, as those which Katherine has of the gift of Robert and Judith, Robert, John and Edith, and William and Mary, and they have remised and quitclaimed the same from Robert and Judith, Robert, John and Edith, William and Mary, and their heirs to Katherine and her heirs for ever. And Robert Haskett, the Elder, and Judith have granted for themselves and the heirs of Robert that they will warrant to Katherine and her heirs the aforesaid tenements against Robert and Judith and the heirs of Robert for ever. And Robert Haskett, the Younger, has granted for himself and his heirs that they will warrant to Katherine and her heirs the aforesaid tenements against Robert and his heirs for ever. And John and Edith have granted for themselves and the heirs of John that they will warrant to Katherine and her heirs the aforesaid tenements against John and Edith and the heirs of John for ever. And

317

William and Mary have granted for themselves and the heirs of William that they will warrant to Katherine and her heirs the aforesaid tenements against William and Mary and the heirs of William for ever. And for this Katherine has given Robert and Judith, Robert, John and Edith, and William and Mary £60. (Feet of Fines, Somerset, Michaelmas Term, 1659.)

Final Concord made at Westminster on the Quindene of St. Martin, 12 Charles II [25 November 1660], between William Doun [or Donn] [querent] and John Jacob, Knight, William Haskett and Rebecca, his wife, John Derby, Clerk, and John Snooke, deforciants, concerning one messuage, one cottage, two gardens, two orchards, eight acres of land, eight acres of meadow, eleven acres of pasture, and common of pasture in Yenston and Henstridge. Plea of covenant. John, William Haskett and Rebecca, John, and John have acknowledged the aforesaid tenements and common of pasture to be the right of William Doun, as those which William has of the gift of John, William Haskett and Rebecca, John, and John, and they have remised and quitclaimed the same from John, William Haskett and Rebecca, John, John, and their heirs to William Doun and his heirs. And John Jacob has granted for himself and his heirs that they will warrant to William Doun and his heirs the aforesaid tenements and common of pasture against John and his heirs for ever. And William Haskett and Rebecca have granted for themselves and the heirs of William that they will warrant to William Doun and his heirs the aforesaid tenements and common of pasture against William Haskett and Rebecca and the heirs of William for ever. And John Derby has granted for himself and his heirs that they will warrant to William Doun and his heirs the aforesaid tenements and common of pasture against John and his heirs for ever. And John Snooke has granted for himself and his heirs that they will warrant to William Doun and his heirs the aforesaid tenements and common of pasture against John and his heirs for ever. And for this William Doun has given John, William Haskett and Rebecca, John, and John £100. (Feet of Fines, Somerset, Michaelmas Term, 12 Charles II.)

## FROM THE RECORDS OF THE COURT OF STAR CHAMBER*

### [Haskett v. Dibben et al.]

Commission to take answers of Robert Wake the Elder, Edith Child, Joan Dibbin, and Alice Panter, at Bruton [co. Somerset], 23 November, 37 Elizabeth [1594].

Bill [undated] of John Haskott and William Haskott of Hengestridge [Henstridge, co. Somerset], woollen drapers.

Complainants came to the fair at West Lydford [co. Somerset] to trade. William came first with his pack of cloth, intending to provide a standing. Meeting William Ditty of Wincaunton, co. Somerset, woollen draper, he asked courteously to whom the ladders, etc., lying on the green for hire, appertained. Ditty answered: "They belong to the man of the house," pointing to the house of William Bridge, near by. Haskott replied gently: "Then I will have this ladder and of him will hire poles and forks to build my standing." Contracted with Bridges for many poles and forks. William Haskett took up one burden of these, and Bridges' son another burden, and carried them on their backs to the place where

*Preserved in the Public Record Office, London, the commission and the bill being found in Star Chamber Proceedings, Elizabeth, H, 77/18, and the interrogations and depositions in Star Chamber Proceedings, Elizabeth, H. 45/10.

he meant to set up his standing. John Haskott came after to the fair, with his horses laden with packs of woollen cloth, and began also to set up the standing. Finding one fork too long, William Haskett began to cut it, as he lawfully might, the place then growing full of company of buyers and sellers. Robert Wake the Elder, a man of exceeding choleric disposition, well known to be contentious, spying William Haskett sharpening and fitting the pole, and envious that any should gain by letting forks besides himself, having two of his sons, Robert and Thomas, lying in readiness, came towards complainants, swearing and saying to Wm. Haskett: "Thou shalt cut noe forkes of myne." Wm. Haskett answered modestly: "If I cutt anie I cutt non of yours," whereupon Wake in a great rage swore they were his, and gathered together his sons and Abraham Morris, Barnard Coles, and other riotous persons. Wake laid hold of the forks. Wm. Haskett said they had hired them of his neighbour, Bridges. The sons, Robt. and Thos. Wake, struck complainants with poles, and complainants, having but one pole between them, were forced to hold it up for their defence, their cloths and goods lying about openly upon the ground. Some of the elder Wake's companions struck Wm. Haskett a blow on the hand, rending the flesh from the bone, so that he was not able for long after to help himself. The broil abated, but the elder Wake's rage increased. Ditty, meeting him and being friendly to him, since he used ever to "host" in Wake's house for that fair, reproached him that, being an old man, he should maintain quarrels. Wake, incensed, ran upon Ditty with a long pole, saying: "Godes Woundes. Wilt thou have to doe with itt and lye too," and would have struck him, had not a neighbour named Edmund Harte resisted him. On the same day Wake and his sons, with long poles, beat complainants and their friends and carried away William Bridge's forks and poles and departed. Complainants continued quietly to set up their standing, and one of Wake's sons came back and stirred them to ire with opprobrious speeches, challenging them to fight, which they refused, and threatening Wm. Haskett with violence; but he thrust him away with his hand. Thereupon Robt. Wake the Elder and the rest of defendants assembled, declaring that ere they returned from the fair they would "stick out" complainants' brains. Fifteen or sixteen of them marched thro' the fair, to the great terror of those present. Complainants were rescued by bystanders, and Wm. Haskett, being greatly amazed, took him to his dagger, having no other weapon, and John Haskett to his meteyard. Bystanders interposed. Nicholas Panter, one of the rioters, a man of very ill name, with Richard Dibben and Thomas Chiles, who had married the daughter of Robt. Wake the Elder (Dibben having before lived a disordered life, so that his neighbours have lost much cattle by his shifts and filching, being a butcher, and thereby grown to great wealth and by his malicious killing of their cattle with engines) also interposed, Panter pretending to be a constable and Dibben and Chiles tithingmen. These required Wm. Haskett in the Queen's name to put up his dagger. This he did. Then they laid hands on him and pulled him from the standing, threatening to carry him to a justice of the peace or prison, and detained him a long time, while Robt. Wake the Elder and the rest were assisting, and Robt. Wake the Elder came round to John Haskett, taking from him his yard. John Haskett suffered this patiently and followed Robt. the Younger thro' the fair, gently entreating him to deliver the yard. Robt. called out: "I am an officer, keep him from me." Robt. the Younger, saying nothing, with a great pole of elm seven foot long, held in both hands, struck John Haskett on the head, so that he fell for dead, the sound of the blow being heard eightscore yards. John lay on the ground, terribly wounded, for one-fourth hour, the bystanders despairing of his life and no man giving him any assistance. He languished for six days, not being able to speak, sleep, or drink.

Defendants answer that they are not guilty of any riot, etc.

Examinations of Robt. Wake of West Lydford, husbandman, aged 60, Alice, wife of Nicholas Panter, and Edith, wife of Thomas Chiles.

Interrogations to be administered to Richard Dibben, Nicholas Panter, Robert Wake the Younger, Thomas Wake, and Thomas Chiles, defendants, on behalf of John Haskett and William Hasket, complainants.

1. Did you see complainants setting up a standing, in which they meant to set forth such woollen cloth as they had to sell, on 1 August (Lammas Day), at a fair at West Lydford, co. Somerset?

2. Were there lying on the ground by the complainants "lugges or polles" for setting up their standing, which they had got together? Of whom were they hired? Were they the property of Robert Wake the Elder?

3. Did complainants set about cutting or sharpening these and cutting them shorter for their occasions, whereupon Robert Wake the Elder, in swearing and furious manner, claimed them and forbade complainants to cut them?

4. Did the said Robt. Wake the Elder, with his sons Robt. the Younger and Thomas Wake, soon after beat, wound, hurt, or evil entreat complainants, violently carrying away the polls which complainants had hired from William Bridge?

5. Did Thomas Wake then return to the place where complainants were quietly building their standing, using these words at several times: "The prowdest of you both come now forth and fight with me"?

6. After this "proud challenge" did Robert Wake the Elder, Robt. Wake the Younger, Thomas Wake, Richard Dibben and Johan, his wife, Nicholas Panter and Alice, his wife, Thomas Chiles and Edith, his wife, come running into the fair with lugges, polls, staves, etc., in their hands to assault complainants?

7. Did you (Dibben, Panter, and Chiles only), after Robert Wake the Elder and his associates came into the fair so eagerly running, come to the side of the standing where William Haskett stood holding his dagger drawn in his hand to use for his safety, and did you, Painter, take upon you the office of constable, and require him in the Queen's name to put up his dagger and to keep the peace?

8. After his dagger was put up, did Panter, falsely pretending to be a constable, seize William Haskett, taking him by the "handwrestes," aided by Dibben and Chiles, and violently haul him clean from his standing, saying they would carry him to Sir Harry Beckley, and violently detained him till John Haskett, being on the other side, was stricken down by your company and lay as dead?

9. Did not Dibben, Panter, and Chiles counsel Robert Wake the Younger, who had so stricken down John Haskett, to get under the hedge there and fly away?

11.* For this purpose did Dibben, Panter, and Chiles deliver Robt. Wake the Younger money to put in his purse, and did Robert lie hidden in or near the house of Dibben?

12. Have you (Dibben) been indicted at sundry times for stealing cattle and sheep in Somerset and Dorset, and have you uncharitably and maliciously destroyed your neighbour's cattle?

13. And have you (Dibben) been accused of so doing?

14. Did you (Panter) meet Leonard Leicester in the same fair, and

*No interrogation numbered 10 appears in this abstract.

320

say, touching the riot, "Anything that is donne I repent not but am sorie I have not donne more"?

Examinations taken 26 November, 37 Elizabeth [1594], on behalf of John Hesket.

Richard Dibben of Shepston-Mountague [co. Somerset], yeoman, aged 40, says:
Did not see complainants building the standing at the fair, nor the polls lying on the ground. Was not party to any violent assault. Denies 6, 7, 8, 9, 10, 11. Numbers 12 and 13 he says not to concern the bill.

Thomas Chiles of West Lydford [co. Somerset], husbandman, aged 34, says:
Was at the fair, but did not see complainants building their standing, nor see the lugs and poles on the ground. Knows nothing of any assault on complainants; but, as he passed by complainant at the fair time, he saw his face bloody but drying. He does not know, of his own knowledge, how he came by that hurt. Denies 8, so far as the violence against William Haskett is concerned, or that any of defendants struck or wounded either complainant. Was not in any place where John Haskett was struck, but heard that Robert Wake struck him. Denies 10 and 12.

Thomas Wake of West Lydford [co. Somerset], husbandman, aged 19, says:
Was at the fair and saw complainants standing about the place where they intended erecting a standing, but not setting it up. Had never seen them before. Saw many polls and lugs lying on the ground, some of which belonged to Robert Wake the Elder, defendant's father. Heard that complainants cut his father's poles, which his father disliked. Denies 4. As he was passing on some business along the place where complainants, with John Bridge and Thomas Bridge, were assembled together, Thomas Bridge, picking a quarrel with defendant, said: "Thou Calf dost thou challenge our polle?" Defendant answered: "I challenge none." Then one of the complainants, he thinks John Haskett, said "Goe thy waies thou art bredd of a whelpe," and, as defendant was going, struck him upon the side of his head with a great yard or "ells rodd" and broke his head. Denies the rest. One of the complainants assaulted defendant, and with his fist did beat and break his face without any cause.

Robert Wake of Westlidford [co. Somerset], husbandman, aged 21, says:
Was at the fair. Did not see complainants erecting a standing, but saw them, or one of them, cutting a pole or short lug. Had never seen them before. Many poles were lying there, some being defendant's father's, brought thither to hire to those who had occasion to use them. Does not know that complainants procured any others. John Haskett cut one of the poles, which was Robt. Wake the Elder's, whereupon Robt. Wake claimed it. Robt. Wake the Elder, understanding that complainants had broken the head of his son Thomas, came to inquire by what occasion it had been done. When he had been talking for some while with complainants, defendant heard him call for help, hastened to the place, and saw complainants offering violence and using threatening words to his father. Thinking it his bounden duty to rescue his father, he took up a pole lying on the ground and struck one of the complainants (which he cannot tell) to the ground. Did not carry away the poles which complainants had procured from Wm. Bridges. Knows nothing of 5. Denies 6.

Examinations taken 28 January, 37 Elizabeth [28 January 1594/5].

Nicholas Painter of West Lidford, yeoman, aged 45, says:
Was at the fair but did not see or know the complainants. Heard that complainants went about to cut a pole which was Robt. Wake's the Elder. Shortly afterwards defendant, coming to the place where William Haskett was, heard there had been some contention between complainants and the Wakes about the cutting of the pole, and that, on very hard usage, which one of them offered in drawing a dagger at Robt. Wake the Elder and striking Robert the Younger and Thomas, Robert the Younger did strike John Haskett with one of the poles. Denies 6. Saw Wm. Haskett standing, but not with dagger drawn, and did not take upon himself the office of constable "to his remembrance;" but, being told that Wm. Haskett was the man who had so beaten and abused Robert the Elder and Thomas, asked complainant upon what counsel he offered violence to "this defendant's father and brothers," taking him by one of the handwrists; but did not offer violence nor haul him from the standing. Has heard that John Haskett was stricken down by Robt. the Younger with a pole. Did not advise Robt. the Younger to run away; of his own mind he went to one of his friend's houses for three or four days. Thinks he had no cause to run away. Met Leicester in the fair and said: "What they have don (meaning Robt. Wake the Younger and Thos. Wake) let them aunswere. But what I have don I wold doe if yt were to be don againe for I have don nothinge at all."

[For more about this case see the next following record, the first record from De Banco Rolls.]

## From De Banco Rolls*

### [Haskett v. Wake, 1597]

Somerset. Robert Wake the Elder, late of Westlydford, co. Somerset, husbandman, Robert Wake the Younger, of the same, husbandman, and Thomas Wake, late of the same, husbandman, were attached to answer John Haskett in a plea that they assaulted the said John at West Lydford by force and arms, and beat, wounded, and illtreated him, so that his life was despaired of, to the damage of the said John and against the Queen's peace. And whereof the said John, by William Bower, his attorney, complains that on 1 August, 36 Elizabeth [1594], by force and arms, viz., with sticks, swords, and knives, they assaulted and wounded him at Westlydford. He claims damages to the value of £40.

Robert, Robert, and Thomas, by William Colborn, their attorney, say that, as to the force and arms, they are in nowise guilty, and put themselves on their country. And John likewise. And as to the rest of the supposed trespass, Robt., Robt., and Thos. say that John ought not to have his action against them, because on that day and year, at Westlydford, John assaulted them, and beat, wounded, and illtreated them, whereby the said Robt., Robt., and Thos. defended themselves against him. And they say that the damage or injury (if any happened) to the said John was from his own assault. And they seek judgment whether John ought to have his action against them.

And John says that he ought not to be stayed from his action by any said allegation, because they assaulted him without any cause (as alleged). And on this he seeks that inquisition be made by his country. And Robert, Robt., and Thos. likewise.

Mandate is issued to the sheriff to cause twelve to come here on St. Martin in fifteen days [25 November 1597]. The parties come then, but

*Preserved in the Public Record Office, London.

322

not the jurors. Then precept is issued to the sheriff to have them on the Octave of St. Hilary [20 January 1597/8]. Then the cause is adjourned till Easter in fifteen days, unless first the justices of assize come to Chard [co. Somerset]; and on Wednesday, 1 March [1597/8], at Chard, before the justices of assize, the parties came, but only two of the jurors (John Midland and John Elys). Therefore, at the request of John Haskett and by command of the justices, other jurors are impanelled (viz., John Hunt, Jasper Gredy, John White, John Phelpes, George Slade, Thomas Lacy, Oliver Lottesham, Thomas Hearne, John Lambert, and John Sellack), who say that Robt., Robt., and Thos., by force and arms, on the day and year aforesaid, assaulted John of their own wrong and without cause, and wounded him; and they assess his damages at 10s. and the costs of the suit at 20s. Therefore he is to recover 30s. under the jurors' assessment; and the court (at his request) adjudges him in addition as costs 90s. Which damage in the whole amounts to £6. And no fine is levied from Robt., Robt., and Thos. because they are pardoned. (De Banco Roll 1596, m. 332, Michaelmas Term, 39 and 40 Elizabeth [1597].)

Dorset, Michaelmas Term, 39 and 40 Elizabeth [1597]. John Haskett offered himself against Robert Kember of Stalbridge, Thomas Combe of Marnhull, and Anthony Stone of Purscandell, husbandmen, in a plea of debt. Adjourned. (De Banco Roll, 1597, m. 1169, Michaelmas Term, 39 and 40 Elizabeth [1597].)

Somerset, Michaelmas Term, 39 and 40 Elizabeth [1597]. Stephen Haskett v. Robt. Welmothe of Milborne Porte, James Cluett of Templecombe, and others, in a plea of debt. (De Banco Roll 1600, m. 2591, Michaelmas Term, 39 and 40 Elizabeth [1597].)

Trinity Term, 1600. William Horton offered himself against William Haskett, late of North Cadbury, co. Somerset, in a plea of debt. (De Banco Roll 1646, m. 2310d, Trinity Term, 1600.)

## From Chancery Depositions*

### [Nurse v. Carent]

Land in Milborne-Port [co. Somerset]. Depositions taken at Castle Come[?], co. Dorset, 22 April, 4 Charles I [1628].

Ellis Haskett of Henstridge, co. Somerset, yeoman, aged about three score and six, and William Haskett, aged about 32 years, son of Ellis, deposed. (Chancery Depositions, Elizabeth to Charles I, N, 4/13.)

### [Daccomb v. Ridout]

7 June, 10 Charles I [1634]. William Haskett of Henstridge, co. Somerset, clothier, aged about 37 years, deposed. (Chancery Depositions, Elizabeth to Charles I, D, 4/15.)

### [Heskett v. Heskett]

23 November, 24 Charles I [1648]. Commission to Peter Hoskins and others to take depositions on behalf of Ellis Heskett, complainant, and William Heskett, defendant.†

Interrogations on behalf of William Heskett include:

*Preserved in the Public Record Office, London.
†For the bill of complaint of Ellis Haskett the Elder, 27 May 1647, and the answer of William Haskett, 11 October 1647, from Chancery Proceedings, see Register, vol. 77, pp. 119-120.**
**Pages 16-17, this volume.

323

2. Was there a grant by copy of court roll of a tenement in Ensome, in the parish of Hestridge [sic], co. Somerset, called Brynes tenement or the West [Living], to the complainant and the defendant and to Ellis Hasket the Younger, the complainant's son? Was not the money for the fine paid by some of the friends of Christian, complainant's late wife, the defendant's late mother, as part of her portion?

3. Was there, about eighteen years since, an estate made, by copy of court roll, on surrender of the said estate by the lord of Henstridge Manor to the complainant, the defendant and his wife, and Ellis Hasket the Younger, for their lives successively, and did not the defendant and complainant afterwards deliver up the copyhold to the benefit of the defendant and his said brother, [Ellis] Haskett?

4. Was not complainant imprisoned in Marlborough for debt ten years ago?

Depositions taken at Sturmi[n]ster-Newton Castle 15 [December( ?)], 24 Charles I, 1648, on behalf of William Haskett, the defendant:

John Woodridge of Henstridge, yeoman, aged 71 or thereabouts, has known complainant for about forty years and defendant for about twenty-two years. Has heard that complainant, Ellis Haskett, being imprisoned in the town of Marleburrough, co. Wilts, for debts, did for the payment of the said debts and the obtaining of his freedom desire defendant to join with him and with Ellis Haskett, brother to the defendant, in surrendering about half of the tenement and lands in question. About eight or nine years past one moiety was sold for complainant's debts, and deponent was present when the same was surrendered by the said William Haskett.

John Nayle of Henstridge, yeoman, aged about 41, has known complainant about ten years and defendant about eleven years. Defendant was taken tenant unto a copyhold tenement and lands in Ensome, in the parish of Henstridge, called Sayers, being [parcel of the tenement called] Brines. Ellis Haskett the Younger hath enjoyed that moiety of the tenement which is in question, which is now occupied by the defendant. Deponent has rented several leas from Ellis Haskett the Younger for four or five years past. Complainant has estate in one copyhold for life, over and above the tenement in controversy and over and above that which his son Ellis hath estate in, and worth £14 per annum; and his wife is to have a life estate therein, if she survive him. Defendant's brother, Ellis Haskett the Younger, has taken other beasts to feed upon that moiety of the tenement which is in the defendant's occupation.

Richard Chant of Ensome in Henstridge, yeoman, aged 60 and upwards, has known complainant for about forty years and defendant from his childhood. Has heard that the defendant and Ellis Haskett the Younger, sons of the complainant, have an estate successively by copy of court roll, but does not know whose money paid the fine for the estate in the first interrogation. Believes that Christian, the late wife of the said complainant [paid the fine in the second interrogation], because complainant had no estate Complainant is estated in a copyhold tenement worth about £17 per annum, and his widow hath a possibility of her widow's estate therein. Ellis Haskett the Younger, brother to defendant, is bound to defendant in several sums of money and has been sued at law for the same by the defendant, since which this deponent has been employed as a friend to mediate between them. About four[illegible] pounds was made by the sale of the closes called the Common Close, parcel of the premises. (Chancery Depositions before 1714, 260/45.)

[Young *v.* Hilsden]

18 April 1670. Elizabeth Haskett of Todber [co. Dorset], spinster, aged about 30 years, deposed. (Chancery Depositions before 1714, 483/22.)

[Strangeways *v.* Bisse]

29 January, 5 William and Mary [29 January 1693/4]. Stephen Haskett of Marnhull [co. Dorset], fuller, aged 45 years or thereabouts, deposed. (Chancery Depositions before 1714, 178/22, and 179/16.)

## From Chancery Proceedings*

### [Doune *v.* Haskett, 1676]

Bill [filed 28 November 1676] of William Doune of Odcombe, co. Somerset, yeoman, complaining that, whereas William Haskett of Yenston, in the parish of Hengstridge, co. Somerset, gentleman, John Derby of Abbotts [*sic*, ? Abbas] Combe, co. Somerset, clerk, and John Snoake of Temple Combe, co. Somerset, linen weaver [a rough duplicate reads: skinner], being seised of a messuage and copyhold tenement in Yenston, then in the occupation of Ellis Haskett, father of the said William Haskett, by deed about 20 June, 12 Charles II [1660], enfeoffed complainant of the premises, of which he had livery of seisin and attornment of the said Ellis Haskett, deceased, and it was the custom of the manor of Yenston that the copyholder's widow should enjoy his tenement, during widowhood, as her free bank, since complainant purchased the tenement Ellis Haskett is dead, and on his death, his widow, Martha Haskett of Hengestridge, entered upon the tenement, keeping it in repair, as she ought; but now she takes advantage of the dismemberment of the tenement, whereby it is taken from the said member, so that complainant cannot keep any court baron upon the same and force her to keep the tenement in repair nor to perform the customary services, for she has never attorned tenant. She not only refuses to pay complainant rent for the tenement, but suffers it to fall into decay, and threatens to convert the ancient pasture and meadow to tillage, and to commit much waste. Complainant has not the court rolls of the manor, nor any copy thereof, and cannot force Martha to attorn nor find out what are the accustomed rents from the tenement.

The answer of Martha Haskett of Yeanson [*sic*], in the parish of Henstridge, co. Somerset, widow. She is ready to attorn for the premises, if the Court think fit, but is advised that such attornment would be nugatory, since the reversion of the premises passed by the livery in the bill mentioned without attornment. The rent payable is 8s. 2d. yearly and she has always been ready to pay it. She has not converted pasture into arable [land]. The premises are in as good repair as when she came into them. She is a poor widow, and complainant is trying to fright her into a composition. (Chancery Proceedings, C. 8, 300/34.)

### [Hedditch *v.* Gaulpin, Sheene, Haskett, et al.]

The complaint of Dorothy Hedditch of Gillingham [co. Dorset], widow, dated 14 December 1697. [For this bill see Register, vol. 77, pp. 121-122.]

The answer of Richard Gaulpin to the bill of complaint of Dorothy Hedditch.

*Preserved in the Public Record Office, London.

Ellis Haskett was seised of lands and tenements to the value of £20, and had at his death goods, etc. [Reference is made to the will of Ellis (or Elias) Haskett, for an abstract of which see REGISTER, vol. 77, p. 111.] Mary, the relict of Ellis, died some days after her husband, and left the complainant in the dwelling house where both had dwelt; and the complainant seized the moneys, etc., in the house. He does not know if Ellis in his lifetime gave his wife a box with bonds, mortgages, specialties, etc., in it or had any discourse concerning the deceased's baseborn child. The complainant took care of the burial of Ellis and Mary Haskett, and spent a considerable sum therefor, which should be allowed her; but she has no right to anything else in the residuary estate, as she is no heir of the testator. The complainant after the burial sued out letters of administration on the estate of Mary, with the will of Ellis annexed; but defendant does not know if it was granted to her in the Prerogative Court of Canterbury. Administration was, however, granted to Mary Crumsey, one of the defendants in this bill, as nearest kin to the testator. Defendant denies that he had any of the deceased's goods, but as one of the nearest of kin he claims a share in the residuary estate. (Chancery Proceedings before 1714, Mitford, 571/75.)

The answer of Richard Sheene to the bill of complaint of Dorothy Hedditch, dated 17 January 1697 [1697/8].

Defendant knows that Ellis Haskett had property, but whether he intended to dispose of it to Mary, his then wife, and his or her kindred, or whether he intended that his wife should have the residue, he does not know. Nor does he know if Ellis Haskett made such a will or gave his wife a box of writings, or if there was any discourse as per the bill. Defendant has heard and believes that the relict, Mary, died intestate four or five days after her husband, without proving the will; and he denies that he has tried to burn or destroy the will or the pretended will, nor has he ever had it in his custody. But he intends to prove that Ellis Haskett was his, the defendant's, great-uncle by the father's side, he, this defendant, being the only son living of Richard Sheene, deceased, this defendant's father, who was the only son and issue living of Richard Sheene and Agnes, his wife, this defendant's grandfather and grandmother, which said Agnes was sister of the half blood, by the father's side, of the said Ellis Haskett; and this defendant is next of kin or at least as nearly related to Ellis Haskett as any other person whatsoever. In case it be found that the said Elias Hasket died intestate, defendant prays that he may be found entitled to a share of the personal estate; and, if the will is good, then [defendant prays] that he may be found entitled to a one-third share of a legacy of £20, to be given to the wife of Richard Sheene and his children, to be equally divided. This defendant is a stranger to all matters and allegations in the bill; but he believes that the relict, Mary, continued in the same house where Ellis Haskett died up to the time of her death, and that administration has been lately granted to Mary, wife of Lewis, *alias* Luzes Crumsey, which said Mary is next of kin to the said Ellis Haskett in equal degree with this defendant; but this defendant by reason of his poverty took no steps to obtain the same. (*Ib.*)

The answer of Elias Haskett to the bill of complaint of Dorothy Hedditch, dated 26 January 1697 [1697/8].

Defendant says that Elias Haskett of Henstridge Marsh was seised and possessed of a real and personal estate, and made his will, and gave the legacies mentioned in the will, and made his wife Mary his executrix; but defendant does not know whether he gave her all his residuary estate or the box of mortgages, etc. Mary dying soon afterwards without proving the will, this defendant was advised that administration of the estate of Ellis Haskett ought to be granted to his next of kin, *cum testamento annexo*; and this defendant conceives that he is entitled to a share of the personal estate, being a near relative of the testator; and he did possess himself of goods to the value of £30, but a true inventory thereof and the will were exhibited in the Prerogative Court of Canterbury, and administration is not yet granted or the will proved, the matter not yet being determined in the said spiritual court. This defendant is ready to deliver the property that he has of the testator or to pay the full value thereof. (*Ib.*)

[Nicholas Buggis and Thomas Austen *alias* Acsten brought a bill of complaint in Chancery against Richard Sheene et al.; and the answer of Richard Sheene, dated 5 July 1698, is chiefly a repetition of much of the answer of Richard Sheene to the bill of complaint of Dorothy Hedditch.]

## From the Records of the Court of Requests*

### [Fell v. Coombe]

Land in Stalbridge [co. Dorset]. William Haskett of Henstridge [co. Somerset], gentleman, deposed 12 April, 12 Charles I [1636], aged about 40 years. (Court of Requests, Charles I, Bundle 84.)

### [Haskett v. Jolliffe and Lovell†]

14 Charles I [1638–39]. Ellis Haskett of Yenston [in the parish of Henstridge, co. Somerset], gentleman, complains that about three years since he held for life a messuage in Yenston, a parcel of Henstridge Manor, and, being indebted to divers creditors, to wit, Thomas Eastmond of Dunhead in co. Wilts, gentleman, Edmund Lovell of Yenston, yeoman, Thomas Wills of Sherborne, co. Dorset, mercer, Samuel Duffett of Durrisen[?], co. Dorset, husbandman, and John Parsons of Sherborne, haberdasher, in April, about two years since, he made over to Thomas Jolliffe of Haselber [*sic*, Haselbury], co. Dorset, gentleman, and to the said Edmund Lovell a messuage worth 40 marks per annum, and they undertook to satisfy his creditors out of it, which they have not done. Jolliffe had formerly married one of the complainant's daughters, and Lovell was his near neighbour and intimate friend. They have failed to satisfy his creditors, as agreed.

In his answer Edmund Lovell acknowledges the agreement as regards Jolliffe, but denies it as to himself. Jolliffe was to account for the surplus. The complainant and his sons, William and Ellis Haskett, are bound to the defendant Lovell for a debt of £36; and this defendant has a judgment against the complainant and intends to arrest him, as is his right. (Court of Requests, Charles I, B. 3, Part 2.)

### [Haskett v. Coombe]

Thomas Haskett of Todbere, co. Dorset, deposed 17 June, 16 Charles I [1640], aged about 41 years.‡ (Court of Requests, Charles I, Bundle 92.)

## From Plea Rolls*

1655. Somerset. William Haskett, late of Charlton-Horethorne, co.

*Preserved in the Public Record Office, London.
†For records from Chancery Proceedings pertaining to this litigation see Register, vol. 77, p. 118.
‡For the complaint of Thomas Haskett against Richard Combe, made in 1639 in the Court of Requests, see Register, vol. 78, p. 55. (Page 44, this volume.)

Somerset, husbandman, was attached to answer Francis Davenish, gentleman, in a plea wherefore with force and arms he entered the tenement called Brynes and twelve acres of land, ten acres of meadow, and thirty acres of pasture in Yenston, in the parish of Henstridge [co. Somerset], which Nicholas Bingham the Younger demised to the said Francis for a term not yet past, and ejected him from his said farm. Nicholas Bingham demised the tenement to Francis 1 May 1655, to occupy from 28 April last for three years. On the same 1 May Francis says that William ejected him from his said farm. He claims £50 damages. William, by Robert Burbidge, his attorney, pleads that he is not guilty of the ejectment. Both parties put themselves upon the country. The sheriff is to have twelve [jurors] here on Trinity in three weeks. (Plea Roll 2659, m. 1606, Trinity Term, 1655.)*

[The rest of these additional Haskett records, with a brief statement of their bearing on the history of the family, will be published in the REGISTER of October 1930.—EDITORS.]

## BORDEN: ADDITIONAL INFORMATION

ON page 227 of the present volume of the REGISTER (April 1930) ** it is said that John Borden (No. 4, ix, of the Borden pedigree), brother of the Richard Borden who emigrated to New England in 1637/8 and settled at Portsmouth, R. I., was probably the John Borden who, with his wife and two children, embarked for New England in the *Elizabeth & Ann* in 1635, but that nothing was known of him in New England. This last statement, however, should be modified, for it is likely that the John Borden who came to New England in the *Elizabeth & Ann* was identical with the John Bourden or Borden of the Colony of Connecticut, the administrators of whose estate, at a court held at Hartford 14 May 1685, applied for authority (which was granted to them) to confirm certain transfers of land. (Cf. The Public Records of the Colony of Connecticut, May, 1678–June, 1689, p. 171.)

*For two other cases from the Plea Rolls in 1655 in which this William Haskett was the defendant see REGISTER, vol. 78, p. 56. This case evidently belongs between the two cases there given. (Page 45, this volume.)

**Page 310, this volume.

# GENEALOGICAL RESEARCH IN ENGLAND

Communicated by the Committee on English and Foreign Research

## HASKETT: ADDITIONAL RECORDS

Contributed by G. ANDREWS MORIARTY, A.M., LL.B., F.S.A.,
of Bristol, R. I.

## MISCELLANEOUS RECORDS

26 October 1625. Licence to solemnize marriage between William Haskett of Henstridge [co. Somerset], clothier, and Joan Hurd of Kingesdon [co. Somerset], spinster, at Kingesdon. Bondsmen: Stephen Haskett of Wells [co. Somerset], mercer, and Lawrence Bull of Wells, gentleman. (Licence Book at Wells.)

29 April 1641. The Will of ROBERT MACKEREL of Corfe-Mullen [co. Dorset], yeoman, contains bequests to sons William, John, Thomas, George, and Robert Mackerel (Robert being then under twenty-one years of age), to daughters Joane Elliot and Agnes Haskett, and to son-in-law William Haskett. (P. C. C.)

16 Charles I [1640–41]. On a Lay Subsidy Roll for Henstridge [co. Somerset] Ellis Haskett, William Stibbs, and William Stibbs are taxed 2s. each on property valued at £10 for each one, and Mr. Haskett is taxed 5s. on property valued at £20. (Lay Subsidies, Somerset, 16 Charles I, 172/408.)

1641 [?]. "Mr. Jeat* (if wth conveniency) I shall desier you wille plese send me what money you can spare it is all 8l 8s 5d as I make it wch I hope is Right otherwise it shalbe amended, I am sorry to trouble you againe herein But I p[ro]test I am in such a strain for want of

*Mr. Jett, the registrar.

money that I cannot tell wch way to turn by reason of the deadnes of the times that I cannot get in debte thus desiringe you not to take it amisse [I] rest Yor lovinge frd to use [Signed] Stephen Haskett." (From an undated letter, probably written in 1641, since it is with other letters of 1640–1642 in the Diocesan Registry at Wells, co. Somerset.)

4 March 1669 [? 1669/70]. Administration on the estate of ROBERT HASKETT of Marnhull, co. Dorset, was granted to John Haskett of Marnhull, husbandman, the natural son of the deceased. Surety: William Bryne of Stalbridge, co. Dorset, yeoman. (Archdeaconry of Dorset.)

3 October 1695. The Will of EDITH COX of Fifehead-Magdalen, co. Dorset, dated 3 October 1695 and proved 9 June 1696, contains bequests to Robert Davidge, son of John Davidge of Fifehead-Magdalen, at the age of twenty-one, and to his sister Mary; to kinswomen Ann Haskett and Joan Hassem; to kinsman Roger Clarke; to Thomas Willetts of Stower [co. Dorset]; to kinswoman Margaret Haskett, sons-in-law William Cox and Robert Cox, and Robert's three children; to kinsmen Thomas, John, William, and Roger Haskett and Roger's two children; to kinswomen Elizabeth Short and Joane Eaton; to kinsman Jonathan Snooke; to kinsmen Martin Metyard and Robert Metyard and their sister Elizabeth Metyard; to kinsman Robert Blackmoore; to John, the son, and to the two daughters of kinsman Stephen Skener; to kinsman John Freeke and kinswomen Thomasin Snooke and Mary Bennett; and to servant Catherine Gullifer. Executors: the two kinsmen of the testatrix, Roger Clarke of Todber [co. Dorset] and Ellis Haskett of Shafton, co. Dorset. (P. C. C., Bond.)

The additional records relating to the Haskett family in England which have been printed in this number of the REGISTER and in the two numbers immediately preceding make necessary a few additions and corrections in the pedigree of the family given in the REGISTER, *vol. 77, pp. 126–133. In the following paragraphs the numerals in parentheses serve to identify the persons in the pedigree to whom the newly discovered facts refer.

The original Ellis Haskett (1), who was buried at Henstridge, co. Somerset, 10 May 1639, was born in 1563; and his son William (1, v), who married Joan Hurd in 1625, was born in or about 1597. Stephen Haskett of Wells, co. Somerset, mercer, who was a bondsman on the marriage licence of William Haskett and Joan Hurd, was evidently a near kinsman of William, perhaps a son of a brother of William's father, Ellis, Sr. (1). John and William Haskett, who were of Henstridge in 1594, were probably elder brothers of Ellis, Sr., and John may be the John of Todbere, the testator of 1614, whose son John was born in 1594, while William may be the William who was of Stalbridge, co. Dorset. William Haskett of Stalbridge had a son named William, while William, son of John of Todbere, seems to be identical with the William Haskett who married Margaret, daughter of John Hellier of Wincanton, co. Somerset.

The Elizeus Haskett who was querent in the final concord of 1612 **(vide supra, p. 230) was apparently Ellis Haskett, Sr. (1), and the concord shows that he had sons William and Elizeus (Ellis) and a daughter Alice; but it seems strange that Ellis, who was clearly the elder son, should be named after William. If, however, Ellis Has-

*See the last footnote on p. 312, this volume.
**Page 313, this volume.

330

kett, Jr. (2), was the querent in the final concord of 1612, then this querent had a son William, who was alive in 1612 but died soon afterwards, and another son William, who was baptized at Marnhull 12 June 1615. Ellis Haskett, Jr. (2), had a daughter, Edith, who was baptized at Marnhull 9 Dec. 1608 and was married to Thomas Joliffe of Haselbury, co. Dorset, by 1627; and therefore Ellis, Jr., was probably born a little earlier than appears in the pedigree in the REGISTER, very likely at some time between 1580 and 1585.

Furthermore, it is now known that the William Haskett who married Rebecca ———— was not William, son of Ellis, Sr., who had married Joan Hurd in 1625, but William, son of Ellis, Jr., and that the first wife of this William was named Mary. This William Haskett appears to have lost all his children by his second wife, Rebecca; and the only child who survived him was Mary, his daughter by his first wife. He seems to have resided also in Taunton and Charlton Magna, co. Somerset, and to have been styled both gentleman and husbandman. The Chancery suit of 1662 (*vide supra*, vol. 77, p. 120) was a suit between Ellis, Jr. (2), and this son William, and not a suit between William and a cousin.

Ellis Haskett, Jr. (2), lived to a good old age, being alive in 1660, when his second wife, Eleanor (Stibbs), was buried; and he appears to have married a third wife, Martha, who survived him and was living in 1676. He had, as was not uncommon in those days, two sons named Ellis (or Elias), whose lives overlapped. The elder of the two, who was baptized at Marnhull 28 Oct. 1610, a son by the first wife, was living as late as 1647/8, and probably died without issue. The younger of the two, a child by the second wife, was born probably about 1642 and was the testator of 13 Feb. 1696/7, whose estate was the subject of protracted litigation.

The answer of Richard Sheene to the bill of complaint of Dorothy Hedditch, dated 17 Jan. 1697/8 (*vide supra*, p. 284), shows that the said Richard Sheene was the only son then living of Richard Sheene, deceased, and that this Richard Sheene, the father, was the only surviving child of Richard and Agnes (Haskett) Sheene, the said Agnes (Haskett) Sheene being a daughter of Ellis Haskett, Jr. (2), by Christian, his first wife, and therefore a half sister of Ellis Haskett (2, vii), the testator of 13 Feb. 1696/7.

## ADDENDUM

### RECORDS RELATING TO THE STIBBS FAMILY

#### [Hayne v. Pope]

Easter, 36 Elizabeth [1594]. William Hayne of Belchuwell[?], co. Dorset, yeoman. sues Robert Pope of Milborne-Port, co. Somerset, yeoman, Thomas Hussey, Esq., and Robert Brooke, yeoman, complaining that Thomas Hussey was seised in his demesne as of fee of the manor of Bowden and did grant to the complainant a parcel of the said manor late in the tenure of Hercules Stibbs. One Stibbs pretended an estate in the said tenement for his life, and it was understood that the said Stibbs was suddenly dead. Three witnesses testified as to the custom of the manor, but they gave false testimony. They were Richard Stibbs, William Ryall, and William Mears. Richard Stibbs falsely testified that one Robert Stibbs did surrender his own copy estate in the manor in a certain way, but he had not so surrendered it.

In his answer, dated 16 September, 38 Elizabeth [1596], William Ryall denied that he had deposed that one Robert Stibbs did surrender his copy into the hands of the lord of the manor, in the manner stated. (Star Chamber Proceedings, Elizabeth, H, 27/22.)

39 Elizabeth [1596–97]. On a Lay Subsidy Roll for Rympton [Rimpton], co. Somerset, Richard Stibbs is taxed 8d. on goods valued at £3. (Lay Subsidies, Somerset, 39 Elizabeth, 171/316.)

18 April 1655. The Will of William Foster of Sherborne [co. Dorset], yeoman, dated 18 April 1655, contains bequests to grandchild William Stibbs, son-in-law [i. e., stepson] of Richard Swetman, and to daughter Agnes, wife of Richard Swetman of North Wotten [North Wootton, co. Dorset.].

[Popley v. Lambert et al.]

19 October 1663. Thomas Galpin and his wife Ann [and] Christopher French deposed that William Stibbs of Bowden, co. Somerset, yeoman, died about ten years since, and that he was the father of Robert Stibbs and of a daughter, Edith, who married the defendant French and died about four years since. The suit relates to a settlement on the marriage of said Edith and to lands in Milborne-Port, co. Somerset. Said Edith had held a close in Milborne-Port for the life of the defendant Lambert and his wife Mary, now deceased, and John Lambert, their son, and a close called Milborne Hill, in Milborne-Port, for her own life. (Chancery Depositions before 1714, B, 142/12.)

[The Stibbs records given above throw light on the family connections of * Ellen or Eleanor Stibbs, the second wife of Ellis Haskett of Henstridge, co. Somerset (No. 2 of the Haskett pedigree, in REGISTER, vol. 77, p. 127), and the mother of Stephen Haskett of Salem, Mass. William Stibbs, Sr., of Bowden in Henstridge, father of Eleanor (Stibbs) Haskett, married Edith —— ——, and had William Stibbs, Jr., of Bowden in Henstridge, who held lands in Milborne-Port, co. Somerset, married Agnes Foster, daughter of William Foster of Sherborne, co. Dorset, yeoman, the testator of 18 Apr. 1655, and died about 1653, his widow, Agnes, being on 18 Apr. 1655 the wife of Richard Swetman of North Wootton, co. Dorset. William Stibbs, Jr., had, perhaps by an earlier wife, a son, Robert, and a daughter, Edith, who married Christopher French and died about 1659. By his wife Agnes (Foster) William Stibbs, Jr., had William, baptized at Henstridge 2 Feb. 1639/40, buried there 16 Feb. 1639/40 (REGISTER, vol. 77, pp. 72, 73), and a second William, who was a legatee in the will of his grandfather, William Foster, dated 18 Apr. 1655, and died before 1663. William Stibbs, Sr., had also five[?] daughters, namely, Eleanor, baptized at Henstridge 18 Oct. 1605 (ib., p. 72), who married Ellis Haskett, Anna, baptized at Henstridge 15 Dec. 1622 (ib., p. 72), and three[?] other daughters. In the reign of Elizabeth one Hercules Stibbs held a parcel of the manor of Bowden, but died before Easter, 36 Elizabeth [1594]. The Richard Stibbs and Robert Stibbs who are mentioned in the Star Chamber case of Hayne v. Pope, in 1594 and 1596 (vide supra), may have been sons or brothers of Hercules Stibbs. Richard Stibbs was taxed 8d., on goods valued at £3, at Rimpton, co. Somerset, in 1596–97, and was probably the Richard Stibbs who was buried at Henstridge 26 Sept. 1605 (REGISTER, vol. 77, p. 73). Either he or Robert Stibbs was probably the father of William Stibbs, Sr., whose daughter Eleanor married Ellis Haskett.—G. A. M.]

*See the last footnote on p. 312, this volume.

# LOTHROP

Contributed by G. Andrews Moriarty, A.M., LL.B., F.S.A.,
of Bristol, R. I.

The English ancestry of Rev. John Lothrop, the well-known minister at Scituate and Barnstable in the Plymouth Colony in New England, was traced correctly many years ago by the late Horatio Gates Somerby, and may be found in the Lothrop genealogy compiled by the late Rev. E. B. Huntington, A.M., and published in 1884, several years after the death of the compiler, by Mrs. Julia M. Huntington, under the title "A Genealogical Memoir of the Lo-Lathrop Family." To the records there printed in regard to Rev. John Lothrop and his ancestors and other relatives the following gleanings from English sources may be added.

## From Lay Subsidies for co. York*

15 Henry VIII [1523–24], Assessment for the first payment.
Wapentake of Herthill.

| | |
|---|---|
| Cherry Burton. | John Lowthr[o]p in goods, [valuation] £13. 11s. 8d., [tax] 6s. 8d. (Lay Subsidies, 203/183.) |

32 Henry VIII [1540–41], Assessment of £20 and upward.

| | |
|---|---|
| North Burton. | John Lowthrop in goods, [valuation] £20, [tax] 20s. (*Ib.*, 203/191.) |

35 and 36 Henry VIII [1543–1545].

| | |
|---|---|
| Burton. | Robert Lowthorppe at Isabella Lowthorpe's, *in manibus* John Milsoin, in goods, [valuation] £4, [tax] 4d. |

39 Elizabeth [1596–97].

| | |
|---|---|
| Etton. | William Akyett in goods, [valuation] £5, [tax] 13s. 4d. |
| | Thomas Lowthorpe in goods, [valuation] £6, [tax] 16s. |
| North Burton. | Robert Lowthorpe in goods, [valuation] £3, [tax] 8s. |
| | Lawrence Lowthorpe in goods, [valuation] £4, [tax] 16s. |
| | Robert Patterson in goods, [valuation] £4, [tax] 8s. (*Ib.*, 204/348.) |

## From the Records of the Court of Star Chamber*

Petition [undated] of James Carter and his wife Agnes and Thomas Layton and his wife Isabell states that they are seised of one acre of customary land in the manor of South Dalton, co. York, with appurtenances in Chery Burton, co. York, called Coke Merys, as of fee in right of Agnes and Isabel, whereon in 24 Henry VIII [1532–33] they sowed good wheat, which prospered till it was ready to be reaped, and that they then reaped a great part of the wheat, bound it in sheaves, and made thirty stooks, each containing twelve sheaves, according to the custom of that country, and intended to reap the rest. But now John Lawthrop, William Bynkys, Robert Lawthrop, William Patton, and John Burne, of their malicious and riotous minds, with clubs, staves, swords, daggers, pikes, etc., by force

*Preserved in the Public Record Office, London.

of arms, about Monday sennight next after the Feast of the Assumption of the Blessed Virgin,* 25 Henry VIII [1533–34], entered the land, took away the wheat which had been reaped, and reaped and carried off the rest, making assault upon James Carter, beating and wounding him, and putting him in jeopardy of his life. Petitioners pray for a writ of subpœna for Lawthrop and the rest to appear before the King's Court at Westminster. (Star Chamber Proceedings, Henry VIII, vol. 9, no. 61.)

Answer [undated] of John Lowthorp to the petition of James Carter and the others sets forth that the matter of the petitioners is determinable within the Court of the Provost of Beverley, within his lordship of South Dalton, as the land specified is a parcel of the manor of South Dalton. Said Lowthorp denies that he is guilty of any riot or any other misdemeanor. Further, if he had committed any such riot or misdemeanor, the King, by authority of Parliament, has pardoned to all his subjects all riots and misdemeanors committed before 3 November last, before which time the riot is said to have taken place. He prays that the petition be dismissed with costs. (*Ib.*, Henry VIII, vol. 9, no. 62.)

Richard Lowthropp of Etton [co. York], yeoman, William Archer of Etton, yeoman, William Blackstone of Etton, gentleman, and Thomas Johnson of Beverley [co. York], gentleman, complain against Thomas Aulaby, Esq., and his wife Sarah, Thomas Pottinger, William Downing, bailiff, Gervaise and Edward Harmon, gentlemen, Ralph Eastabye, Marmaduke Hooper, John Carlin, and others for excessive fines in Etton and Coatgartle court-leets, and for building a house on the waste land of the lordship, perjury, pulling it down, and assault. (Star Chamber Proceedings, James I, B, 199/1.)

3 May 1632. At a conventicle at the house of one Barnett, a brewer's clerk dwelling in Blackfriars, the minister was one John Latropp, and among those present were Pennina Howse and Sarah Barbon. During the examination of Latropp [i. e., Rev. John Lothrop] by the Bishop of St. David's he was asked: "Were you not Dr. King's, the Bishop of London's, sizar at Oxford? I take it you were."† (Star Chamber Proceedings, Ecclesiastical Division of the Court of High Commission. Cf. REGISTER, vol. 69, p. 284.)

### FROM PROBATE RECORDS

The Will of THOMAS LOTHROP of Dengie, co. Essex, clerk, dated 20 October 1628. To daughters Ann, Jane, Elizabeth, and Mary—all under twenty-one years of age. Wife Elizabeth. Brother-in-law William Akett of Leckenfield [Leconfield], co. York. My sister Mary, wife of John Gallant. Brothers William Lathrop and John Lathrop. Proved 6 May 1629. (Consistory Court of London [Somerset House], Bellamy, 324. Cf. Lothrop genealogy, p. 18.)

[It is apparent that Robert Lathrop of Cherry Burton, co. York, with whom the pedigree compiled by Somerby begins, was undoubtedly the son of the John Lowthrop who was taxed at Cherry Burton in 1523–24 and was one of the defendants in the Star Chamber case in the reign of Henry VIII.

The will of Thomas Lothrop, clerk, of which a brief abstract is given above, taken with the other records published in the Lothrop genealogy, establishes the parentage of Rev. John Lothrop, the minister at Scituate and Barnstable

*The Feast of the Assumption of the Blessed Virgin Mary falls on 15 August.

†Rev. John King, D.D., was made Dean of Christ Church College, Oxford, 5 Aug. 1605, and was Vice Chancellor of the University of Oxford, 1607–1610, and Bishop of London, 1611–1621.

in the Plymouth Colony in New England. The father of Rev. John Lothrop, Thomas Lathop of Etton, co. York, did not mention in his will either his son John or his son. Thomas, the testator of 1628, probably because they had received their portions of their father's estate in the cost of their education. But Thomas Lathrop of Etton did mention in his will his son-in-law William Akett, his son--in-law John Gallant, and his son William.

Rev. John Lothrop evidently entered first Christ Church College, Oxford, for according to Foster's "Alumni Oxonienses" John Lowthroppe of Yorkshire, aged sixteen years, was admitted a pleb of Christ Church, Oxford, 15 Oct. 1602. Thence he went to Cambridge, where, according to Venn's "Alumni Cantabrigienses" John Loothrop, Lathrop, or Lothropp, who was baptized at Etton, Yorkshire, 20 Dec. 1584, son of Thomas of Etton, was admitted to the degree of Bachelor of Arts from Queen's College in 1606 and to that of Master of Arts in 1609. A brief biographical notice of him is given by Venn. His brother, Rev. Thomas Lothrop, was admitted sizar at Queen's College, Cambridge, 30 June 1601, took his bachelor's degree in 1604/5 and his master's degree in 1608, was rector of Dengie in Essex, 1613–1629, and died in 1629. (Venn, *op. cit.*)—G. A. M.]

---

                                                                         \*

LOTHROP-LATHROP-LOWTHORP.—In THE REGISTER, October 1930, pp.437-9, Mr. G. Andrews Moriarty contributed further information on the ancestry of Rev. John Lothrop, early settler of Barnstable, New England.

The following extracts, from "Yorkshire Fines", may be of added interest to Lowthorp descendants:

"Easter, 1596—William Dixon, Thomas Pattenson, Lawrence Lowthropp, John Constable, and Thomas Lowthropp, *versus* Brian Pattenson and Alice, his wife, re property in Etton".

"Hilary, 1557/8—Robert Lowthorpe *versus* Marmaduke Whytyng and Alice, his wife, re lands in Wolkyngton".

Many data concerning the early Lowthrops may be obtained from the "Bridlington Chartulary" and from "Transactions, East Riding Antiquarian Society", vol. 21. These pertain to the period prior to 1400.

*Arlington, Va.*                                                    JOHN G. HUNT.

\*Pages 333-335, this volume.

# GENEALOGICAL RESEARCH IN GERMANY AND ENGLAND

Communicated by the Committee on English and Foreign Research

## THE TALLMAN FAMILY

Contributed by G. Andrews Moriarty, A.M., LL.B., F.S.A.,
of Bristol, R. I.

To the Register, vol. 69, page 90 (January 1915), the writer of this article contributed a deposition, found in the town records of Portsmouth, R. I., and made by Joseph Sheffield on 17 Mar. 1702/3, concerning a declaration made to him by Peter Tallman of Portsmouth on 13 Mar. 1702/3. In this declaration Peter Tallman stated that he was then 80 years of age, that in the year 1647 he came from Hambrough [Hamburg] to the Island of Barbados, that within two years after his arrival he was married, in Christ Church Parish in said Island, to Ann Hill, daughter of Philip Hill and Ann, his wife, that seven or eight months after his marriage he moved from Barbados to Rhode Island, bringing with him his wife and his wife's brother, Robert Hill, and also his wife's mother, who after said Philip Hill's death married Mr. John Elten, and that Mrs. Elten remained in Rhode Island about one year with her son Robert and afterwards moved to Flushing on Long Island, thence to Staten Island, and then, with her son Robert Hill, to Virginia, where she had "a child or more by Capt Hudson, who, as is reported, she married," and where her son, Robert Hill, settled. The said Peter Tallman further declared that the Peter Tallman whose habitation was then [17 Mar. 1702/3] at Guildford [Guilford], New Haven Co., Conn., was the "eldest lawfull son of said Peter Tallman." This declaration of Peter Tallman was evidently made when Peter Tallman, Jr., was going to Virginia, to dispose of the property of Robert Hill, as heir at law.

The registers of Christ Church Parish, Barbados, contain a record of the marriage on 2 Jan. 1649 [? 1648/9] of "Peter Tolman and Ann Hill" (REGISTER, *loc. cit.*) ; and in the "Aspinwall Notarial Records," page 259 (No. 32 of the series of Boston records published by the Registry Department of the City of Boston), the following agreement for the transportation of Peter Tallman and his goods from Barbados to New England is entered:

13 (9) 1649 Agreed on this 2ᵈ of June 1648. in & betweene Nath. Maverick* of the one pty & Peter Talmo of the other pty as followeth. Imprs the afores^d Nathaniel Maverick doth covenant to transport the afores^d Peter Talmon his goods for New Engl. in the shipp golden Dolphin he paying for the fores^d goods 3ˡⁱ. sterl p tonne for all cask, & for Cotton 5 farthings p pound & for Tobacco one penny p pound in consideration whereof the fore said Talmo doth covenant to shipp uppon the fores^d ship to the value of ten tonns at or before the fifteenth day of this instant June, & in case any more of the afores^d Talmon his goods shall be ready by this time specifyed I doe ingage my selfe to take them aboard it is further agreed that the afores^d Talmon shall have the passage of one Englishman & three negros he putting in pvisions for them. Witnes oʳ hands

testi       Peter Talmon
John Ewin     Nathaniel Mavericke.
Walter Hanbery.

Acting upon the clues given above, the Chairman of the Committee on English and Foreign Research commissioned Dr. Henry Presch, Jr., of Hamburg, Germany, to make researches in the Hamburg records for the parentage and ancestry of Peter Tallman of Rhode Island; and the records relating to the Tallman family brought to light by Dr. Presch are herewith submitted.

FROM THE BAPTISMAL REGISTER OF THE CHURCH OF ST. NICHOLAS, HAMBURG

### Baptisms

1608 Anna, daughter of Peter Talemann, 18 May. Godparents: Susanna, widow of Jacob Melchior Jacobsen, Anna Talemanns, Wilbert de Voss.

1616 Anna Maria, daughter of Henry Talemann, 20 September. Godparents: Margaret, wife of Vincent Moellers, Elisabeth, wife of John Wetcken, Hermann Wetcken, cannoneer.

1619 Elisabeth, daughter of Henry Talemann, 24 March. Godparents: Gesche von Eitzen, Catherine Wetckens, Erich Wortenhoff.

### FROM THE HAMBURG BURGHER BOOK

1636 Peter Talemann made free 21 October. { Both were admitted as
1646 Peter Talemann made free 14 August. { sons of burghers.†

*Nathaniel Maverick of Barbados was the eldest son of Samuel Maverick of Noddle's Island in Boston Harbor, now East Boston. Cf. REGISTER, vol. 67, pp. 365-367 (October 1913).
†Sons of burghers were usually admitted at the age of twenty-one years.

From the Inheritance Book of the Parish of St. Nicholas, Hamburg

5 October 1610. Dr. Stephen Schoenefeldt, body physician to John Adolphus, Duke of Schleswig-Holstein, gave an inheritance in Dreckwall to Peter Talemann; and it was conveyed to Marilius de Corput, as trustee, since Talemann was not a burgher of Hamburg. (Vol. 3, fo. 53.)

3 May 1644. Peter Talemann conveyed a part of the above-mentioned premises on the Alster to Diego Charles. (Vol. 4, fo. 60.)

3 July 1663. Peter Talemann conveyed the remainder of the said premises to Henry Schwarte, as trustee for Ahrend, Sr. (Vol. 4, fo. 180.)

From the Rent Book of the Parish of St. Nicholas, Hamburg

21 November 1656. On this day Peter Talemann recovered a judgment, and on 23 January 1657 [1656/7] he entered an annuity of 124 bank marks for his daughter Susanna. On 9 October 1663 Susanna Talemann, by her curator [guardian], Hans Erlekamp, cancelled this annuity entry. (Vol. 9, fo. 219.)

The Tallman entries found in the Hamburg records by Dr. Presch, combined with the declaration of Peter Tallman of 13 Mar. 1702/3 and other New England records, make it possible to construct, with considerable certainty, the following brief pedigree, according to which Peter Tallman of Barbados and Rhode Island was probably a son of Henry Tallman of Hamburg, who appears to have come to Hamburg from the Duchy of Schleswig-Holstein.

1. ——— Talemann, apparently of the Duchy of Schleswig-Holstein, was born about 1558. He married ———, and had, beyond doubt, the following

    Children:

  **2. i.**  Peter, b., probably in Schleswig-Holstein, about 1582.
    ii.  Susanna, b. about 1584; m. prior to 18 May 1608, when she was a widow, Jacob Melchior Jacobsen. She was a godmother at the baptism of Anna, daughter of her brother Peter Tallman, in the Church of St. Nicholas, Hamburg, on 18 May 1608.
  **3. iii.**  Henry, b., probably in Schleswig-Holstein, about 1586.
    iv.  Anna (perhaps a sister of Peter, No. 2), b. probably about 1588. She was a godmother at the baptism of Peter's daughter Anna on 18 May 1608; but it is, however, possible that this Anna was a sister-in-law of Peter, i. e., his brother's wife.

2. Peter Tallman, of Hamburg, born, probably in Schleswig-Holstein, about 1582, presumably settled in Hamburg in the opening years of the seventeenth century, for he was living in the Parish of St. Nicholas in 1608, when his daughter Anna was baptized. The name of his wife is unknown.

On 5 Oct. 1610 he received from Dr. Stephen Schoenefeldt, body physician to John Adolphus, Duke of Schleswig-Holstein, an inheritance in Dreckwall [a part of Hamburg], which was conveyed to Marilius de Corput as trustee, since Peter Tallman was not at that time a burgher of Hamburg. Later, however, he evidently became a burgher of Hamburg, for two Peter

338

Tallmans, one probably a son and the other probably a nephew of this Peter, were admitted as burghers in 1636 and in 1646, respectively, both being admitted as sons of burghers.

Children:

    i.    ANNA, bapt. in the Church of St. Nicholas, Hamburg, 18 May 1608.

4. ii.    PETER, b. about 1615.

    Probably other children.

3.    HENRY TALLMAN, of Hamburg, born, probably in Schleswig-Holstein, about 1586, was living in the Parish of St. Nicholas, Hamburg, as late as 24 Mar. 1619, and probably lived for several years after that date. He probably married ANNA ———, who may have been the Anna Talemanns who was a godmother at the baptism of Anna, daughter of Peter Tallman, on 18 May 1608.

He was residing in the Parish of St. Nicholas, Hamburg, on 20 September 1616, when his daughter Anna Maria was baptized there. He evidently became a burgher of Hamburg, if the Peter Talemann who was admitted a burgher in 1646 was his son.

Children:

    i.    ANNA MARIA, bapt. in the Church of St. Nicholas, Hamburg, 20 Sept. 1616.

    ii.    ELISABETH, bapt. in the Church of St. Nicholas, Hamburg, 24 Mar. 1619.

5. iii.    PETER (probably son of Henry), b. about 1623, the emigrant to Barbados and New England.

4.    PETER TALLMAN (*Peter*), of Hamburg, born about 1615, died probably between 3 July 1663 and 9 Oct. 1663. The name of his wife is unknown.

He was admitted a burgher of Hamburg, as the son of a burgher, on 21 Oct. 1636. On 3 May 1644 he sold part of the land that had belonged to his father, and on 3 July 1663 he sold the remainder of it. On 21 Nov. 1656 he recovered a judgment, and on 23 Jan. 1656/7 he obtained an annuity of 124 bank marks for his daughter Susanna.

Children:

    i.    SUSANNA, b. about 1645. The annuity which her father had obtained for her on 23 Jan. 1656/7 she sold, by her guardian, on 9 Oct. 1663.

    ii.    JOHN ADOLPHUS (perhaps a son of Peter, No. 4), admitted as a burgher of Hamburg in 1660.

5.    PETER TALLMAN (*Henry*), of Hamburg, Barbados, and New England, born probably in Hamburg, about 1623, died in 1708. He married first, in the Parish of Christ Church, Barbados, 2 Jan. 1649 [? 1648/9], ANN HILL, whom he divorced in New England in 1665, daughter of Philip and Ann Hill of the Parish of Christ Church, Barbados; secondly (marriage settlement dated 24 July 1665) JOAN BRIGGS of Taunton, then in the Plymouth Colony; and thirdly, about 1686, ESTHER ———.

He was admitted a burgher of Hamburg, as the son of a

burger, on 14 Aug. 1646, and disappears thereafter from the Hamburg records. In 1647 he emigrated from Hamburg to the Island of Barbados, and seven or eight months after his marriage at Barbados he migrated from Barbados to Rhode Island, accompanied by his wife, her brother, Robert Hill, and her mother, having agreed with Nathaniel Maverick on 2 June 1648 for transportation from Barbados to New England. On 18 Nov. 1650, as "Peter Talman of Newport on Roade Iland Apothecary," he gave a power of attorney to "my welbeloved frend M$^r$ John Elton" to collect what was due to him from "M$^r$ Samuel Maverick of Noddles Iland in the Massachusetts gent." and "to take upp & to seaze upon a Negro man of mine w$^{ch}$ I am informed is w$^{th}$in the Jurisdiction of the Massachusetts. The Negro is named Mingoe & but a yong man & hath the marke of I : P : on his left shoulder : & did unlawfully dept from my house in Newport about six months since." (Aspinwal Notarial Records, pp. 370-371, entered under date of 5 (12) 1650 [5 Feb. 1650/1].) He had, therefore, arrived in Newport at least as early as May 1650. Soon, however, he moved to Portsmouth, R. I., where he was a landowner and merchant and was a freeman in 1655. He was one of the early purchasers of land on Martha's Vineyard, and was very active in the settlement of that island. (Cf. Banks's History of Martha's Vineyard.) He appears also in the Connecticut records on 20 May 1652, when he is called "Dutchman." (Colonial Records of Connecticut, vol. 1, p. 231.) He bought lands from the Indians within the bounds of the Plymouth Colony (Plymouth Colony Records, vol. 5, p. 151), and was apparently for some time at Flushing, on Long Island. From 1655 to 1658 his name is frequently found in the court records of New Amsterdam, where he sometimes acted as interpreter between the English and the Dutch. (Records of New Amsterdam, 1653–1674, vols. 1 and 2.) He purchased much land in Dartmouth, Mass., and the neighboring towns, but his principal place of residence was Portsmouth, R. I. His estate was settled on 8 May 1709.

Children by first wife :*

i.  MARY, b. about 1651; d. in 1720; m. about 1668 JOHN PEARCE of Portsmouth and Bristol. Eight children.

ii.  ELIZABETH, b. about 1654; d. 20 May 1701; m. in 1674, as his second wife, ISAAC LAWTON of Portsmouth. Eleven children.

iii.  PETER, of Guilford, Conn., cordwainer and physician, b. about 1655; d. 6 July 1726; m. 7 Nov. 1683 ANN WALSTONE. On 5 Nov. 1703 he sold the land in Farnham Parish, near Dragon Swamp, Essex Co., Va., which had belonged to his maternal uncle, Robert Hill of Rappahannock County (afterwards Essex County), Va. (Essex County, Va., Deeds, book 11, p. 115.) Three children.

iv.  ANN, b. about 1658; m. 8 Mar. 1678/9 STEPHEN BRAYTON of Portsmouth. Five children.

*The names Elizabeth, Ann (Anna), and Susanna, which were given to daughters of Peter Tallman of Portsmouth, R. I., are found also in the Tallman family of Hamburg; and Mary, the name of Peter Tallman's eldest child, may be compared with Anna Maria, the name of a daughter of Henry Tallman of Hamburg.

v. JOSEPH, b. about 1660; living 3 May 1709.
vi. SUSANNA, b. about 1662; m. ———— BECKITT.
vii. A DAUGHTER, b. about 1664; d. before 1732; m. about 1684 WIL-
LIAM WILBOR of Portsmouth, R. I., and Little Compton, then in
the Plymouth Colony. Twelve children.

Children by second wife:

viii. JONATHAN, of Dartmouth, Mass., b. about 1666; d. in 1762; m.
about 1689 SARAH ————. Eight children.
ix. JAMES, of Portsmouth, physician, b. about 1668; d. in 1724; m.
(1) 18 Mar. 1689/90 MARY ————; m. (2) 14 Sept. 1701 HAN-
NAH SWAIN. Three children by first wife and nine children by
second wife.
x. A DAUGHTER, b. about 1670; m. WILLIAM POTTER. Three children.
xi. JOHN, of Flushing, Long Island, b. about 1672; d. about 1707–
1709; m. about 1693 MARY ————. Nine children.
xii. A DAUGHTER, b. about 1674; m. about 1689 ISRAEL SHAW of Little Compton, then in the Plymouth Colony. Thirteen children.
xiii. BENJAMIN, of Warwick, R. I., b. 28 Jan. 1684/5; d. 20 May 1759;
m. (1) 23 Sept. 1708 PATIENCE DURFEE; m. (2) 7 June 1724
DEBORAH COOK. Eight children.

Child by third wife:

xiv. SAMUEL, b. 14 Jan. 1687/8.

## THE SEALY BROTHERS OF THE ISLES OF SHOALS

Contributed by WALTER GOODWIN DAVIS, B.A., LL.B.,
of Portland, Me.

THE broad estuary of the River Teign, in the county of Devon, is
bounded on the west by a range of rounded hills, which descend
sharply to the water. About a mile from the mouth of the river a
steep lane ascends a wooded valley, which winds through the hills,
and from its highest point one looks down on the ancient gray church
tower and clustered thatched roofs of the little village of Stoke-in-
Teignhead, backed by another line of Devon combes. In this peace-
ful country spot, with no visible hint of the sea, but only a short walk
from the Channel cliffs and the still harbor of Teignmouth, lived in
the seventeenth century a hardy seafaring population, which sent
many sons on the New World adventure, among them the four Sealy
brothers of the Isles of Shoals.

The parish registers of Stoke-in-Teignhead begin in 1538. Before
1574 there is no mention of the Sealy family, which possibly came
from the country to the eastward, between the Rivers Teign and Exe,
where, in the parish of Kenton, a Thomas Sely was vicar in 1452 and
the name is commonly met with for two succeeding centuries. The
following records, however, make it possible to trace the English
ancestry of the Sealy brothers of the Isles of Shoals back to their
grandfather, Richard Sealy of Stoke-in-Teignhead, and supply much
information about his family.

### FROM PROBATE RECORDS

1. The Will of RICHARD SEALIE of the parish of Stokentinhead, co.
Devon, dated 10 April 1620. To the church stoore a sheepe. To the
poor people of the parish 5s. To John Sealy, the son-in-law of John
Wills, a sheepe. To George Sealie's children a sheepe apiece and all the

rest of my goods after the death of my wife, Gillian Sealie. My sonne Andrew is to be executor. Proved by the executor 5 May 1620. Inventory, £21. 18s. 4d. (Archdeaconry Court of Exeter.)

2. Administration on the goods of GEORGE SEELY, late of Stokeinteignhead, co. Devon, sayler, was granted, 27 October 1637, to his widow, Dorothea Seely, and Thomas Andrew, marriner, both of Stokeinteignhead. Inventory, £31. 16s. 2d., taken by Thomas Andrew, Andrew Sely, and Richard Andrew 3 October 1637. (Archdeaconry Court of Exeter.)

3. The Will of GREGORY SEALEY of the parish of Stokeinteignhead, co. Devon, dated 14 February 1639 [1639/40]. To the poor of the parish 5s. To George and John Sealey, sonnes of my brother George Sealey, 40s. each. The rest to my mother, Winifred Wills, who is to be sole executrix. Witnesses: Richard Isacke, Richard White. Proved 14 January 1640/1. Inventory, taken by Will^m knolls and Richard White 11 December 1640, including an item "dew unto the said Gregory for his newfoundland voyage." (Archdeaconry Court of Exeter.)

4. Administration on the goods of JOHN SEALY, late of Stokeinteignhead, co. Devon, was granted, 30 November 1644, to his widow, Agnes Sealy. Inventory, amounting to £17. 17s., taken by Elles Blakkaller and Michell Endell 10 July 1643. (Archdeaconry Court of Exeter.)

5. The Will of ANDREWE SEALY of Kingstainton, co. Devon, yeoman, dated 14 April 1664. To the poor of Kingstainton 3s. 4d. To my son John Sealy 20s., the greatest brasse pott, one iron barr, and the glasse of the windowes. To my son George Sealy 20s. and my greatest brasse panne. To my son William Sealy £8 within one yeare. To my son Thomas Sealy £4 within one yeare, my second best brasse pott, two little brasse pannes, and two pewter dishes. To my grandchildren, sons and daughters of my son John Sealy, 10s. each. To my grandchild Robert Sealy of Plymouth one colte or 40s. To the daughters of my son Andrew Sealy 50s. each, when twenty-one. Residue to my son Andrew, who is to be executor. Witnesses: John Selman, John Wilking. Proved 15 April 1665. Inventory, £55. 17s. 6d. (Archdeaconry Court of Totnes.)

FROM THE PARISH REGISTERS OF STOKE-IN-TEIGNHEAD, CO. DEVON

*Baptisms*

1574  Alise, daughter of Richard Sealie, 23 May.
1576  Elizabeth, daughter of Richard Sealie, 9 December.
1591  John, son of Richard Sealie, 29 November.
1597  Andrew, son of Richard Sealie, 8 April.
1597  Elizabeth, daughter of George Sealie, 18 October.
1599  George, son of George Sealie, 26 January [1599/1600].
1602  Johan, daughter of George Sealie, 8 June.
1604  John, son of George Sealie, 13 August.
1607  Gregory, son of Gregory Sealey, 4 October.
1610  Christopher, son of George Sealey, 16 September.
1620  Richard, son of Andrew Sealie, 4 February [1620/1].
1622  George, son of Andrew Sealie, 19 December.
1626  Andrew, son of Andrew Sealye, 25 February [1626/7].
1629  George, son of George Sealey, 3 April.
1629  Robert, son of Andrew Sealey, 7 June.
1631  John, son of George Sealye, 13 November.
1632  William, son of Andrew Sealye, 30 July.

1634 Thomas, son of Andrew Sealye, 30 January [1634/5].
1636 Doritie, daughter of John Sealie, 18 October.
1638 Thomas, son of Andrew Sealy, 28 July.
1638 John, son of John Sealy, 13 October.

## Marriages

1579 Robert Selie and Elizabeth Peter 23 November.
1590 Richard Sealie and Julian Selman 26 January [1590/1].
1596 George Sealie and Winifred Selman 25 November.
1612 John Wills and Winifred Sealie 18 February [1612/13].
1628 George Sealye and Doritie Andrew 21 January [1628/9].
1645 John Hooper and Agnes Sealye 8 January [1645/6].
1664 John Cealie and Agnes Tapley 8 December.

## Burials

1580 Elizabeth, wife of Robert Sealie, 15 September.
1590 Elizabeth, daughter of Richard Sealie, 29 July.
1590 Annis, daughter of Richard Sealie, 30 July.
1590 Johan, wife of Richard Sealie, 13 August.
1603 Johan, daughter of George Sealie, 16 August.
1625 Joane, daughter of Andrew Sealie, 22 December.
1643 John Seely 28 June.

From the foregoing English records, supplemented by sundry New England records, the following pedigree of the Sealy family of Stoke-in-Teignhead, co. Devon, and of the Isles of Shoals has been prepared.

1. RICHARD SEALY, of Stoke-in-Teignhead, co. Devon, the testator of 10 Apr. 1620, was born probably in some neighboring Devon parish, and died between 10 Apr. and 5 May 1620, when his will was proved. He married first JOAN ———, who was buried at Stoke-in-Teignhead 13 Aug. 1590; and secondly, in that parish, 26 Jan. 1590/1, JULIAN SELMAN, undoubtedly the widow of Thomas Selman of Stoke-in-Teignhead, whose will, dated 16 June and proved 20 Oct. 1590, left the principal portion of his estate to his wife Julian (Archdeaconry Court of Exeter). As to her maiden name there are two possibilities, as Thomas Selman mentions in his will two fathers-in-law, Humphrey Alyghe and William Medycote, one of whom was doubtless his stepfather.

In his own will, after legacies to the church and the poor, Richard Sealy leaves a sheep to John Sealy, son-in-law [stepson] of John Wills, a sheep apiece and the residue of his property to the children of George Sealy, after the death of the testator's wife Julian, and makes his son Andrew his executor.

Children by first wife:

  i.  GEORGE, d. before 18 Feb. 1612/13, when his widow, Winifred, m. John Wills; m. at Stoke-in-Teignhead, 25 Nov. 1596, WINIFRED SELMAN.
    Children, bapt. at Stoke-in-Teignhead:
    1. *Elizabeth,* bapt. 18 Oct. 1597.
    2. *George,* sailor, bapt. 26 Jan. 1599/1600; d. before 27 Oct. 1637, when administration on his goods was granted to his widow, Dorothy Sealy, and to Thomas Andrew; m. 21 Jan. 1628/29 Dorothy Andrew. His sons George (bapt. 3

343

Apr. 1629) and John (bapt. 13 Nov. 1631) were legatees of their uncle, Gregory Sealey, in 1639/40.

3. *Johan,* bapt. 8 June 1602; bur. at Stoke-in-Teignhead 16 Aug. 1603.

4. *John,* bapt. 13 Aug. 1604; d. before 30 Nov. 1644, when administration on his goods was granted to his widow, Agnes; m. Agnes ———, who m. (2) 8 Jan. 1645/6 John Hooper. Children: Dorothy (bapt. 18 Oct. 1636) and John (bapt. 13 Oct. 1638), who probably m. 8 Dec. 1664 Agnes Tapley.

5. *Gregory,* the testator of 14 Feb. 1639/40, bapt. 4 Oct. 1607; d. unm. between 14 Feb. 1639/40 and 14 Jan 1640/1. He had been on a voyage to Newfoundland shortly before his death. In his will he leaves 40s. each to George and John Sealy, sons of his brother George, and the residue of his estate to his mother, Winifred Wills.

6. *Christopher,* bapt. 16 Sept. 1610.

ii. ALICE, bapt. at Stoke-in-Teignhead 23 May 1574; probably d. unm. before 10 Apr. 1620, as she is not mentioned in her father's will.

iii. ELIZABETH, bapt. at Stoke-in-Teignhead 9 Dec. 1576; bur. there 29 July 1590.

iv. ANNIS, bur. at Stoke-in-Teignhead 30 July 1590.

Children by second wife:

v. JOHN, bapt. at Stoke-in-Teignhead 29 Nov. 1591; d. probably before 10 Apr. 1620, as he is not mentioned in his father's will.

2. vi. ANDREW, bapt. at Stoke-in-Teignhead 8 Apr. 1597.

2. ANDREW SEALY (*Richard*), of Stoke-in-Teignhead and King's Teignton,* co. Devon, yeoman, the testator of 14 Apr. 1664, was baptized at Stoke-in-Teignhead 8 Apr. 1597, and died between 14 Apr. 1664 and 15 Apr. 1665, when his will was proved. He married, about 1618, ———, who died probably before 14 Apr. 1664.

In his will he leaves small legacies to his sons John, George, William, and Thomas, to the sons and daughters of his son John, to the daughters of his son Andrew, and to his grandchild Robert Sealy of Plymouth, and gives the residue of his estate to his son and executor, Andrew Sealy.

Children:

i. CAPT. JOHN, of the Isles of Shoals, New England, b. in England about 1618; d. before 30 June 1670, when his brother William petitioned for the administration of his estate; m. ———, and had sons and daughters before the making of his father's will in 1664, but they probably remained in England. He was a sea captain, making his New England headquarters at the Isles of Shoals, where a warrant from Boston was directed to him and Antipas Maverick in 1647. Probably he was the Mr. Sealy who was taxed in Dover, N. H., in 1648. He called himself "of Kingstanton, Devon," in 1651, when he acknowledged himself indebted to his brothers Richard and George Sealy and to George Moncke "of Stockingtynhee."† He sold property on Star Island in 1651, signed a petition asking that the Isles of Shoals be made a township in 1653, was captain of the ship

*The parish registers of King's Teignton, co. Devon, begin in 1670, too late for the purposes of this article.

†In 1624 Richard Selman of Stoke-in-Teignhead made his will, leaving property to his daughter Isabel Monk and to Richard and George Monk, presumably her sons. (Archdeaconry Court of Exeter.) George Monk was with the Sealy brothers on the Isles of Shoals, where he was appointed constable by the Dover Court in 1649.

*Dolphin* in 1659, and bought property on Great Island in 1660. William Sealy and Elias Stileman were appointed administrators of Capt. John Sealy's estate in 1670, the papers mentioning his wife and children. In 1676 Mr. William Henderson, bearing a power of attorney from William and Joanna Tapping in England, claimed the estate of Captain Sealy which was in possession of Mr. Stileman, "to Look after ye same till a right claim should be made by ye said Jno Sealys heirs and administrators out of England;" and the Court, after examining Mr. Henderson's credentials, ordered that "Housen and land wch are on Doctors Island" be delivered to him for the use of William and Joanna Tapping.

ii.   RICHARD, of the Isles of Shoals and possibly also of Saco, Me., bapt. at Stoke-in-Teignhead 4 Feb. 1620/1; living in 1678; m. ————. He was fishing master at the Isles of Shoals in 1651, when Henry Shrimpton drew a bill of exchange for £300 on London, payable to Mr. Richard Seely, in payment for merchantable dry codfish. He signed the petition of the inhabitants to be constituted a township, and was named commissioner to end small causes in 1653. He was not mentioned in his father's will in 1664. He moved to Saco, where the name of Goodwife Sily appears in the meeting-house seating-list in 1666.* In 1670 he gave a bond to Henry Kemble, to deliver 10,000 feet of merchantable timber, and a mortgage on his house and land at Winter Harbor (Saco) to secure it; and in the same year he gave a bond to Robert Brimsdon, to pay £30. 15s., and a mortgage on all his estate to secure it. He was a refugee in Salem, Mass., during King Philip's War; and he took the oath of allegiance to the Massachusetts Bay Colony in Boston in 1678. Probably at least two daughters and one son survived him.†

iii.  GEORGE, of the Isles of Shoals, New England, bapt. at Stoke-in-Teignhead 19 Dec. 1622; living 14 Apr. 1664, when he was named as a legatee in his father's will. He engaged in the fishing trade at the Isles of Shoals, was a creditor of his brother, John Sealy, in 1651, as set forth above, and signed the petition of the inhabitants of the Isles of Shoals to be made a township in 1653. No further record of him has been found in New England.

iv.   JOANE, bur. at Stoke-in-Teignhead 22 Dec. 1625.

v.    ANDREW, bapt. at Stoke-in-Teignhead 25 Feb. 1626/7; living 14 Apr. 1664, when he was named as executor and residuary legatee in his father's will and had daughters under twenty-one; m. ————.

vi.   ROBERT, bapt. at Stoke-in-Teignhead 7 June 1629. He was not mentioned in his father's will in 1664; but the "grandchild Robert Sealy of Plymouth" may have been his son.

vii.  WILLIAM, of the Isles of Shoals, New England, bapt. at Stoke-in-Teignhead 30 July 1632, d. before 13 Dec. 1671, when the inventory of his estate, amounting to £621, was taken; m. ELIZABETH LINN, daughter of Henry and Sarah Linn of Boston and of York, Me., and stepdaughter of Hugh Gunnison of Kittery, Me. She survived him, and m. (2) before 3 Jan. 1678 (when she and her second husband conveyed Sealy property in Kittery) Thomas Cowell of Kittery. William Sealy was at the Isles of Shoals in 1653, when he signed the petition for incorporation as a township and bought a house, fishing stage, shallop, cables, anchor, and skiff from Emanuell Hillyer. He was en-

*Mr. Charles Thornton Libby points out the possibility that Richard Sealy of the Isles of Shoals and Richard Sealy of Saco may have been two distinct persons.
†The second generation of this family of Sealy in New England presents problems of identification which are not as yet satisfactorily solved. Cf. Hoyt's Old Families of Salisbury and Amesbury, Mass., pp. 569, 892-893, 1058, and *Maine Genealogist and Biographer*, vol. 2, pp. 76-79, 123-124.

sign of the military company, constable in 1655, and a member of the grand jury in 1656 and 1660. He took the oath of allegiance in 1658, leased land at Spruce Creek, Kittery, from his wife's stepfather, Hugh Gunnison, in 1658/9, purchased a messuage on Smuttynose Island from William Colley in 1664, and sold it to William Harris in 1666. He was named as a legatee in the will of his father in 1664, had grants of land in Kittery in 1667, sold the property bought from Hillyer to Francis Wainwright in 1669, and deposed 25 June 1670, giving his age as about 39 years. Administration on his estate was granted to his widow, Elizabeth Sealy, 2 Apr. 1672. No children have been identified.

viii. THOMAS, bapt. at Stoke-in-Teignhead 30 Jan. 1634/5; d. in infancy.

ix. THOMAS, bapt. at Stoke-in-Teignhead 28 July 1638; living 14 Apr. 1664, when he was named as a legatee in his father's will. A Thomas Sellie was living on the west side of the Kennebec River, in Maine, in 1665, and was a refugee in Braintree, Mass., where the oath of allegiance of Thomas Scilley was recorded in Jan. 1678/9.

## ANCESTRY OF GEORGE ABBOTT OF ANDOVER, MASS.

Contributed by G. ANDREWS MORIARTY, A.M., LL.B., F.S.A.,
of Bristol, R. I.

[Several years ago the late J. Gardner Bartlett, a member of the New England Historic Genealogical Society, while carrying on genealogical researches in England, found records that established the paternal ancestry of George Abbott, a settler at Andover, Mass., towards the middle of the seventeenth century, and compiled the pedigree here given, which is based on the English records brought to light by Mr. Bartlett and on sundry New England records. This pedigree was purchased by me from Mr. Bartlett, and is now made accessible to readers of the REGISTER. A short article entitled "Abbotts of Bishop's Stortford, co. Herts, England, Probable Ancestors of George Abbott of Andover, Mass." was published in the issue of *The New York Genealogical and Biographical Record* for July 1930 (vol. 61, pp. 224-225); but, as it is based chiefly on the parish registers of Bishops-Stortford and does not include the items found by Mr. Bartlett in the lay subsidies and court rolls, and as, moreover, it traces the ancestral line of George Abbott only as far back as his great-grandfather, it seems desirable to print here the longer pedigree and more abundant material contained in Mr. Bartlett's compilation.—G. ANDREWS MORIARTY.]

THE earliest known ancestor of George Abbott, who came to New England in 1637, and, after living for a few years at Roxbury, Mass., settled at Andover, Mass., where he was the founder of a well-known family,* was William Abbott of Bishops-Stortford, co. Herts, England, who was born about 1470 and is given as No. 1 in this pedigree.

The surname *Abbott* is, of course, derived from the title of abbot, which was borne by the head of a monastery; and there have been numerous different families of the name in various parts of England, of totally distinct origins, as is usual in the case of family names derived from offices, occupations, or patronymics. Such surnames came into use in England about the time of King Edward I (1272–1307).

*There was an older immigrant named George Abbott, who came early to Rowley, Mass., where he died in 1647. He left sons, namely, Thomas, Sr., born about 1628, George, born about 1630, Nehemiah, born about 1632, and Thomas, Jr., born about 1634. Of these sons George and Thomas, Jr., settled in Andover, Mass., about 1655 and 1660, respectively.

The most distinguished Abbott family of England originated in Guildford, co. Surrey, a town about thirty miles southwest from London. Maurice or Morris Abbott, said to have been born in Farnham, co. Surrey, about 1520, but of unknown ancestry, became a successful clothier at Guildford, where he died in 1606. Of his six sons three became especially eminent. The third son, Robert Abbot, D.D., born about 1560, rose in the church to the high position of Bishop of Salisbury in 1615. The fourth son, George Abbot, D.D., born in 1562, became Bishop of Lichfield in 1609, Bishop of London in 1610, and in 1611 attained the highest preferment in the church when he was appointed Archbishop of Canterbury. The fifth son, Sir Morris Abbot, Knight, born about 1564, became an eminent London merchant, a member of Parliament, governor of the East India Company, and Lord Mayor of London in 1638. The coat of arms of this distinguished Abbott family was *Gules, a chevron between three pears pendent stalked, or*. Although there is no known or even likely connection between this Abbott family and the Abbotts of Herts, it is a curious fact that on the original will of John Abbott, yeoman, of Sawbridgeworth, co. Herts (a parish five miles south from Bishops-Stortford), dated 20 Mar. 1637/8, is a seal having a chevron between three small objects which are difficult to distinguish, but which may be meant for pears. (Commissary Court of London for Essex and Herts, original will, 1638, no. 107.)

Bishops-Stortford, the home of at least five generations of the paternal ancestors of George Abbott of Roxbury and Andover, Mass., is a thriving market town and parish about thirty miles northeast from London, on the extreme eastern border of Hertfordshire, adjoining the county of Essex. The parish is bounded on the north by Farnham, on the east by Birchanger and Great Hallingbury, all in Essex, on the south by Thorley, and on the west by Little Hadham, both in Herts. The place has been known for centuries as Bishops-Stortford, because the manor of Stortford has belonged to the Bishops of London from a period prior to the Norman Conquest. For centuries the parish has had a population of a few thousand, and its present inhabitants number about eight thousand. Grain dealing and malt manufacture have long been the largest industries of the town.

The parish church, dedicated to St. Michael, is situated on a hill, and is a fine, large, stone structure, dating from early in the fourteenth century. A peal of ten bells hangs in the massive tower. The registers begin in 1561, although they are imperfect for the earlier years; and there are unusually valuable church wardens' accounts, dating from as early as 1431.

The descent of George Abbott of Roxbury and Andover, Mass., progenitor of a numerous New England family, from William Abbott of Bishops-Stortford, co. Herts, who lived about 1470–1532, is set forth in the following pedigree.

1. WILLIAM ABBOTT, of Bishops-Stortford, co. Herts, born probably about 1470, was living as late as 21 Nov. 1532. The name of his wife is unknown.

He is first found in the records in 1509, when he was a church warden, an office which he held also in 1517 and 1518, as is shown by the ancient churchwardens' accounts. In 1523 his name appears at Stortford in a subsidy of 14 Henry VIII, the amount of his assessment being illegible on the badly damaged roll. (Lay Subsidies, Herts, 120/117, in the Public Record Office, London.) At a general court of the manor of Bishops-Stortford, held on the Thursday before St. Catherine's Day,* 24 Henry VIII [21 Nov. 1532], Will. Abbot was one of twenty-four jurors on an inquisition. (Court Roll 171/37, in the Public Record Office, London.) These five records furnish all the information that has been found concerning William Abbott.

While no positive proof has been discovered that he had a family, it is probable that he was father of at least one

Child :

2. i.    JOHN, b. about 1495.

2.    JOHN ABBOTT (*William*), of Bishops-Stortford, co. Herts, born about 1495, was living as late as 1545. The name of his wife is unknown.

He was a resident of Bishops-Stortford as early as 1523, when he was assessed in a subsidy of 14 Henry VIII, for goods worth 40s., the amount of his tax being illegible. (Lay Subsidies, Herts, 120/117.) He also appears in the following later subsidies : in 34 Henry VIII [1542–43], tax 3s. 4d.; in 35 Henry VIII [1543–44], tax 3s. 4d. on goods worth £10; and in 37 Henry VIII [1545–46], tax also 3s. 4d. (*Ib.* 120/160, 121/157, 121/171.) In a rental roll of the Bishop of London for his manor of Stortford in 37 Henry VIII [1545–46] it appears that "John Abot paies for a tenement that he dwelleth in on the est syed of northstrete by yere xx d." (Court Roll 299, in the Public Record Office, London.) As John Abbott left no will, the names of his children cannot be stated with certainty; but he was probably father of at least two

Children :

i.    JOHN, of Bishops-Stortford, b. about 1520; bur. at Bishops-Stortford 8 Apr. 1570; m. about 1543 JOANE CARROWE, daughter of Thomas and Joane Carrowe. The will of his father-in-law, of which an abstract is here given, supplies some information about his family :
The Will of Thomas Carrowe of Stortford, co. Herts, dated 25 June 1548. To my wife Joane, my son Thomas (under twenty-one), and my daughters Mary, Dorothy, and Grace (under twenty-one). To my daughter Kyng and my son-in-law Robert Kyng. I give my daughter Joane no money, as it would not serve her husband two months; therefore I give her for life my house in Northgate where Whayt now dwells and my house where the Coryor dwells. Remainders at her decease to her sons John Abbot and Awbery Abbot. To John Abbot, my daughter's son, £10 at twenty-one, to her son Awbery £6. 8s. 4d., and to her daughter Joane £5 at eighteen. Executors : William Archer and Robt. Kyng. Proved 3 May 1551. (P. C. C., Bucke, 14.)
Children :

*The Feast of St. Catherine fell on 25 November.

348

1. *John,* of Bishops-Stortford, b. about 1543; bur. at Bishops-Stortford 26 Oct. 1579; m. 18 Sept. 1569 Susanna Sherewood. In 1575 Francis Saunton *als.* Mathewe was querent *v.* John Abbotte and his wife Susanna, deforciants, for a messuage in Stortford. (Feet of Fines, Herts, Easter Term, 17 Elizabeth, in the Public Record Office, London.) Children: Mary, bapt. 5 May 1570; m. 3 Apr. 1592 Thomas Durdefall. Thomas, bapt. 1 July 1572.

2. *Awbery,* b. about 1545.

3. *Joane,* b. about 1547; m. 27 Apr. 1578 John Momford.

3. ii. WILLIAM, b. about 1525 and probably named for his grandfather.

3. WILLIAM ABBOTT (*John, William*), of Bishops-Stortford, co. Herts, born at Bishops-Stortford about 1525, died in Mar. 1569. He married, about 1550, MARGARET ———.

He was a man of good estate, and appears in the churchwardens' accounts as paying poor-rate assessments of 12d. in 1558 and of 4s. 4d. in 1566. In the autumn of 1564 Henry Parseley was querent *v.* William Abbott and his wife Margaret, deforciants, for a messuage and land in Stortford. (Feet of Fines, Herts, Michaelmas Term, 6 and 7 Elizabeth.) William Abbott is also of record in two subsidies at Stortford, paying in 5 Elizabeth [1563] 10s 8d. on lands worth £4 and in 8 Elizabeth [1566] 5s. 4d. on lands worth £4. (Lay Subsidies, Herts, 121/202, 121/208.) An abstract of his will is here given.

The Will of WILLIAM ABBOTT of Stortford, co. Herts, dated 12 Mar. 1568/9. To my wife Margarett my messuage where I dwell, with the tenement adjoining, where Thomas Smith dwells, together with the appertaining crofts, lands, etc., until my son George be twenty-one years old, and then it is to remain to him. To my said wife Margaret my other lands in Stortford and a piece of land which I late bought of my cousin Elliott in Farnham, with remainder to my sons, John, Robert, and Thomas Abbott (all under twenty-one). All the residue to my wife Margaret, to bring up my children, and she is to be sole executrix. Supervisor: my cousin Rowland Elliot. Witnesses: Robert Gooday, William Barnarde. Proved 29 Mar. 1569. (Commissary Court of London for Essex and Herts, Meade, 111.)

Children:

4. i. GEORGE, b. at Bishops-Stortford about 1550.

ii. JOHN.

iii. ROBERT.

iv. THOMAS.

4. GEORGE ABBOTT (*William, John, William*), of Bishops-Stortford, co. Herts, yeoman, born at Bishops-Stortford about 1550, was buried 11 Jan. 1619/20. He married, about 1576, BRIDGET ———, who was buried 13 Aug. 1625.

George Abbott succeeded to the homestead of his father according to the latter's will. His name appears several times on the court rolls of the manor of Bishops-Stortford. On 13 Apr. 1577 he was amerced 3d. for default of suit of court; on 6 Apr. 1583, 30 Mar. 1585, and 27 Sept. 1585, he was one of the chief pledges; and on 1 Oct. 1604 he was ordered to make two easy stiles in his croft out of Napton Field into London Lane before Hallowtyde [All Saints' Day, 1 November] next, and so to keep them, upon pain of forfeiting 10s. (Court Rolls 205/21, 206/2, 206/3, and 189/30.) In 1596 he sold some property in Bishops-Stortford by the following fine: John Gace and Thomas Myller, querents, *v.* George Abbott and his wife Bridget and Edward Hake, gentleman, and his wife Margaret, deforciants, for two messuages, with lands, in Stortford. (Feet of Fines, Herts, Easter Term, 38 Elizabeth.) On 20 Sept. 1602 he was a witness to the will of John Gace of Stortford (P.C.C., Montague, 61), and in 1608 he was churchwarden. An abstract of his will follows.

The Will of GEORGE ABBOTT THE ELDER of Stortford, co. Herts, yeoman, dated 12 Oct. 1619. To my eldest son, George Abbott, my table and frame, stools, benchboard, and cupboard in the hall of the messuage in Stortford where I dwell, and also the bedstead in the chamber over said room. To my wife Bridgitt all my other household stuff, maintenance for life in my said messuage, meet for an aged woman, and an annuity of 40s. out of my said messuage, with lands of eighteen acres, to be paid at the four quarterly feasts, and these bequests are to be in lieu of dower; but, if she prefer to remove from said messuage and to live elsewhere, then she is to have an annuity of £6 out of my said messuage, in lieu of dower. To my said son George Abbott and his heirs my said messuage and lands at my decease, he paying to my wife as aforesaid and also paying to my son Edward Abbott, within one year of my decease, £30, so as ———— Marshe of Chrissing, co. Essex, yeoman (father-in-law to my said son Edward) shall deliver, within six months of my decease, to my said son George an obligation wherein said Marshe shall be bound in £60 to my said son George to pay within one year to my son Edward Abbott £40 of the £50 which he promised on the marriage of his daughter to my son Edward; and, if said Marshe fail to pay, then my gift to my son Edward is to be void. If my son George fail to pay the £30 to my son Edward, the latter is to have my croft of three acres, in two parcels, next the commons, called Chalnerscroft or Chalkcroft. To my daughter Joane (if she happen to be a widow before her two children be of age) £10. To the two daughters of my daughter Anne (now wife of Mathewe Reeve) 20s. each at twenty-one or marriage. All the residue to my son George Abbott, who is to be sole executor. Witnesses: Thomas Miller, Thomas Barnarde, Sr., scr. [Signed] Georg Abbott. Proved 8 Feb. 1619/20 by the executor. (Commissary Court of London for Essex and Herts, original will, 1619, no. 133.)

Children, recorded at Bishops-Stortford:

i. GEORGE, bapt. 17 July 1577; bur. 10 Aug. 1577.
ii. JOHN, b. probably in 1579; bur. 2 Apr. 1589.
iii. ANNE, bapt. 3 Dec. 1581; living 12 Oct. 1619; m. before 12 Oct. 1619 MATTHEW REEVE. Two daughters, under twenty-one and unm. 12 Oct. 1619.
iv. JOHANNE, bapt. 17 June 1584; d. young.
v. GRACE, bapt. 10 Oct. 1585; bur. 6 Jan. 1585/6.
5. vi. GEORGE, bapt. 28 May 1587.
vii. JOHANE, bapt. 5 Apr. 1590; living, a married woman, 12 Oct. 1619;

perhaps m. at Farnham, 23 Nov. 1617, DANIEL FORDHAM. Two
children under age 12 Oct. 1619.

viii. EDWARD, bapt. 19 Dec. 1591; living 12 Oct. 1619; m. before 12
Oct. 1619 ———— MARSH of Chrissing [Chrishall], co. Essex.

5. GEORGE ABBOTT (*George, William, John, William*), of Bishops-
Stortford, co. Herts, baptized at Bishops-Stortford 28 May
1587, was living there as late as 1628, when his child Christopher was born, but his further history has not been discovered,
and no will or administration of his estate has been found. He
married, about 1615, ELIZABETH ————.

He succeeded to the homestead farm formerly of his grandfather and father, according to the latter's will, of which he
was the sole executor.

Children, recorded at Bishops-Stortford:

6. i. GEORGE, "George Abbot sonne of George & Elizabeth baptized
May xxij^th 1617."

ii. EDWARD, bapt. 25 Mar. 1623.

iii. JOHN, bapt. 16 Oct. 1625.

iv. CHRISTOPHER, bapt. 2 Nov. 1628.

6. GEORGE ABBOTT (*George, George, William, John, William*), of
Bishops-Stortford, co. Herts, and of Roxbury and Andover,
Mass., baptized at Bishops-Stortford 22 May 1617, died at
Andover, Mass., 24 Dec. 1681. He married at Roxbury, Mass.,
12 Dec. 1646, HANNAH CHANDLER, baptized at Bishops-Stortford 22 May 1630, died 2 June 1711, in her 82d year, daughter
of William and Annis (Bayford) Chandler, who brought her
to New England in 1637. She married secondly, in 1690, as
his third wife, her stepbrother, Rev. Francis Dane of Andover,
Mass., who was baptized at Bishops-Stortford 20 Nov. 1615
and died at Andover 17 Feb. 1696/7, whom she survived.

About the time George Abbott came of age, he emigrated to
New England, coming, according to a tradition among his descendants which was published nearly a century ago, in the
same ship which brought the family of Hannah Chandler,
whom he married a few years later. As it is now proved that
he came from the same place in England as the Chandlers, the
tradition that he accompanied them may be considered to be
correct; and therefore his emigration took place in 1637, as the
church records of Roxbury state that the Chandlers came in
that year. Doubtless the influence and preaching of Rev. John
Eliot were responsible for the emigration to New England of
George Abbott, as they were for the emigration of many of the
other early settlers of Roxbury.

George Abbott lived for a few years at Roxbury, but, when a
new plantation was planned at Andover, in 1643, he became
one of the first proprietors and settlers of that town. He lived
at first in the northern section of the town, but about 1660 he
established a farm in the South Parish, part of which still continues in the family. His house, which was fortified for a garrison against Indian attacks, was owned and occupied by his
descendants for seven generations, until it was demolished

about 1860. During King Philip's War a force of Indians made an attack on Andover, on 8 Apr. 1676. The villagers fled to the garrisons for protection; but two of George Abbott's sons, Joseph and Timothy, were intercepted in the fields. After a desperate fight the former was killed, and the latter was taken prisoner; but he afterwards escaped and returned to his home. The rest of the family reached their garrison, and succeeded in repulsing the attacks of the savages.

George Abbott was not active in public affairs, holding only minor town offices, such as surveyor of highways in 1673 and brander of cattle in 1676; but that he was one of the most substantial citizens of the town is shown by the tax rate made on 3 Sept. 1679, when, among ninety taxpayers, he was assessed 10s. 5d., only six persons having a larger assessment. In a list of one hundred and sixteen male inhabitants of Andover above the age of sixteen years who took the oath of allegiance to the King on 11 Feb. 1678/9 appear George Abbott, Sr., and [his sons] John, George, Jr., William, and Benjamin Abbott. (Ipswich Deeds, at Salem, vol. 4, fo. 237.) On 18 Nov. 1656 George Abbott, aged about forty years, deposed about John Perley coming to Andover. (Essex County Court Files, for 9 Apr. 1657.) An abstract of the will of George Abbott follows.

The Will of "GEORGE ABBUT" of Andover, co. Essex, aged and "crasey" in body, dated 12 Dec. 1681. Considering the great love and affection I have unto my loving wife Hannah Abbut and the tender love she hath had to me and her care and diligence in helping me to get and save what God has blessed us with and also her prudence in management of the same, I leave her my whole estate for life, she to dispose of the same among my children, with the advice of my overseers, my eldest son, John Abbot, to have a double portion. My wife is to be sole executrix, and my brothers Thomas and William Chandler and my friend John Barker are to be overseers. [Signed] Georg Abbott. Witnesses: Thomas Chandler, Timothy Abbott. Proved 28 Mar. 1682.

The inventory of his estate, taken by the overseers and presented by the widow and executrix on 28 Mar. 1682, showed real estate appraised at £350, live stock, £91, and household goods and husbandry utensils, £46. 12s. 5d., a total of £487. 12s. 5d. (Essex Probate Records, file no. 43.)

Children, born at Andover:

i.  DEA. JOHN, b. 2 Mar. 1647/8; d. 19 Mar. 1720/1; m. 17 Nov. 1673 SARAH BARKER, daughter of Richard Barker. Nine children.
ii.  JOSEPH, b. 11 Mar. 1648/9; d. 24 June 1650.
iii.  HANNAH, b. 9 June 1650; m. 20 Dec. 1676 CAPT. JOHN CHANDLER.
iv.  JOSEPH, b. 30 Mar. 1652; killed on his father's farm by Indians 8 Apr. 1676.
v.  GEORGE, b. 7 June 1655; m. 17 Apr. 1668 DORCAS GRAVES, daughter of Mark Graves. Nine children.
vi.  WILLIAM, b. 18 Nov. 1657; d. 24 Oct. 1713; m. 19 June 1682 ELIZABETH GEARY, daughter of Nathaniel Geary of Roxbury. Twelve children.
vii.  SARAH, b. 14 Nov. 1659; m. 11 Oct. 1680 EPHRAIM STEVENS.

viii. BENJAMIN, b. 20 Dec. 1661; d. 30 Mar. 1703; m. 22 Apr. 1685 SARAH FARNUM, daughter of Ralph Farnum. Four sons.

ix. TIMOTHY, b. 17 Nov. 1663; d. 9 Sept. 1730; m. 27 Dec. 1689 HANNAH GRAVES, daughter of Mark Graves. Three children.

x. THOMAS, b. 6 May 1666; d. 28 Apr. 1728; m. 7 Dec. 1697 HANNAH GRAY. Nine children.

xi. EDWARD, d. young.

xii. NATHANIEL, b. 4 July 1671; d. 1 Dec. 1749; m. 22 Oct. 1695 DORCAS HIBBERT. Eleven children.

xiii. ELIZABETH, b. 9 Feb. 1672/3; m. 24 Nov. 1692 NATHAN STEVENS.

---

ABBOTT-ELIOT CONNECTION: — In THE REGISTER (vol. 85, pp. 79–86) will be * found the English ancestry of George Abbott, the early settler of Andover, Mass., and at page 82 will be found the will of his great-grandfather, William Abbott, of Bishop's Stortford, co. Herts., dated 12 March 1568/9, proved 28 March 1569, in which he mentions land "bought of my cousin Eliot in Farnham" [the adjoining parish] and makes "my cousin Rowland Eliot" supervisor. Here will be considered a possible solution to the relationship between William Abbot and the Eliots.

Rowland Eliot belonged to the gentle family of Eliot of Hertfordshire and the adjoining county of Essex, whose pedigree is recorded in the Visitations. Their pedigree will be found in THE REGISTER (vol. 28, p. 144), which may be corrected and added to by reference to the Eliot wills and the valuable note published in THE REGISTER (vol. 48, pp. 385–403) by the late Henry FitzGilbert Waters, Esq.

The family descended from Thomas Eliot of Cottered and Hunsdon, co. Herts., who flourished about 1500, and his wife Elizabeth, daughter of Thomas Wilson, of Cottered, who, upon his death married Thomas Greene of Stanford Rivers, yeoman (will dated 23 March 1534, proved 12 Jan. 1537, cf. THE REGISTER, vol. 48, pp. 385–86, 399–400). Thomas and Elizabeth had issue five sons, John, the elder, of Bishop's Stortford, ancestor of the Visitation family, George of Bishop's Stortford, John, the younger, of Widford, Robert of Hunsden, and Thomas of Widford (cf. ibid., vol. 48, op. cit.).

John, the elder, whose will was dated 22 Oct. 1557, had, among other children, Rowland, who is called "cousin" by William Abbott (ibid., p. 390). George, brother of this John, whose will, dated 12 Jan. 1548/9, proved 29 Jan. 1554 (ibid., p. 386), mentions his lands in Farnham, among other places, which he devised to his son Magnus.

The children of Thomas Eliot of Cottered were evidently born about 1500–1520 and William Abbott was born about 1525 (cf. THE REGISTER, vol. 85, p. 82). Rowland Eliot, son of John the elder, was born about 1525–1535. The term "cousin" was a loose one, which generally denoted a nephew but which was also used in the present sense, and often more loosely, to connote a more remote relationship. In the present instance, there are, of course, a number of combinations which could apply to the relationship between William Abbott and Rowland Eliot. But the most likely appear to be that William Abbott's wife, Margaret, was a sister of John, the elder, and a daughter of Thomas Eliot of Cottered, in which case William Abbott would be uncle by marriage to Rowland Eliot and also to Magnus of Farnham, or else William's father John Abbott, who occurs 1523–1545 (ibid., vol. 85, p. 81), married a daughter of Thomas Eliot of Cottered, in which case William Abbott would be a first cousin of Rowland and Magnus. From the chronology, this would appear the more likely. It should be noted that the Visitation pedigree of Eliot gives the wife of Thomas of Cottered as Margaret, and although the evidence is clear that his widow was Elizabeth (Wilson), it may well be that he had an earlier wife, Margaret, who was the mother of John Abbott's wife. William Abbott named his eldest son George, apparently for George Abbott, Esq., of Bishop's Stortford, son of Thomas of Cottered, and this strongly suggests that the relationship came through the Eliots rather than in some other way.

These Eliots bore as arms: Silver a fesse gules between 4 cotises wavy azure.

*Wells, Maine.*                                        G. ANDREWS MORIARTY.

*For pp. 79-86 see pp. 346-353, this volume.

## GENEALOGICAL RESEARCH IN ENGLAND

Communicated by the Committee on English and Foreign Research

### ANCESTRY OF WILLIAM CHANDLER OF ROXBURY, MASS.

Contributed by G. ANDREWS MORIARTY, A.M., LL.B., F.S.A.,
of Bristol, R. I.

[In the article here published the paternal ancestry of William Chandler of Roxbury, Mass., whose daughter Hannah became the wife of George Abbott of Roxbury and later of Andover, Mass., is traced through four generations in England to his great-great-grandfather, Thomas Chandler of Bishops-Stortford, co. Herts, who was born probably about 1475 and died probably about 1550. Like the article on the ancestry of George Abbott of Andover, which may be found in the REGISTER for January 1931 (*supra*, pp. 79-86), this article was compiled several years ago by the late J. Gardner Bartlett from English records brought to light by him and from sundry New England records, and was purchased by me from Mr. Bartlett. It is here offered to readers of the REGISTER as a companion article to the one giving the ancestry of George Abbott.—G. ANDREWS MORIARTY.] **

THE earliest known ancestor of William Chandler, who came to New England in 1637 and settled at Roxbury, Mass., whose daughter Hannah married George Abbott, then of Roxbury but later of Andover, Mass. (*vide supra*, p. 84), was Thomas Chandler of Bishops-Stortford, co. Herts, England,* who was born about 1475 and is given as No. 1 in this pedigree.

The surname *Chandler* originally meant a maker or seller of candles, an occupation in which many men in all parts of England were formerly engaged. Like many other names of occupations, it became an hereditary surname early in the fourteenth century, when family names derived from offices, occupations, or patronymics came into general use. There were, accordingly, numerous distinct families of the name, descended from different progenitors and, as a rule, not related to one another.

*For a brief description of Bishops-Stortford *vide supra*, p. 80.

** For pp. 79-86 see pp. 346-353, this volume.

1.  THOMAS CHANDLER, of Bishops-Stortford, co. Herts, probably a chandler by occupation as well as by name (*vide infra*), born probably about 1475, was living 19 Mar., 2 Edward VI [1547/8], but died in or before Hilary Term, 3 and 4 Edward VI [11 to 31 Jan. 1550/1], since in a fine in that term his son Thomas (whose wife Agnes also appears in the fine) is called "Thomas Chaundeler, Senior." (*Vide infra, 2.*) He married, about 1500, ———, who was buried in 1514, according to an entry in the accounts of the churchwardens of Bishops-Stortford for that year, given below.

As the court rolls of the manor of Stortford from 1399 to 1423 and the accounts of the churchwardens of St. Michael's Church from 1431 on have been preserved, and as no Chandlers appear therein until this Thomas Chandler is mentioned in 1514, it may be inferred that he was the first of the family to settle at Bishops-Stortford. No will or administration on his estate has been found; and all that is known about him has been revealed by a few entries in the accounts of the churchwardens of St. Michael's Church, Bishops-Stortford, and in the lay subsidies. The items in the churchwardens' accounts are as follows:

1514. Item, of Thomas Chaundeler for waste of Torchis at the buryyng of his wife, xvj d.

1518. Item, delyverd to Andrew Clyfton and Thomas Chaundeler for to fynde w\(^t\)alle a lyght before Seynt Myghell for a hole yere v s.

1521, 1522, 1536. Thomas Chaundeler a churchwarden.

1537, Palm Sunday. Inventory of church goods. M\(^d\), delyv'd to old Chaundeler ij canstiks [candlesticks].

19 Mar., 2 Edward VI [1547/8]. Inventory of church goods. Item, iiij canstikes delyvered to old Chaundeler and Thomas Snowe. Item, wex weyng cv li sold by old Chaundeler.

This Thomas Chandler was taxed, as "Thomas Chaundeler," at Bishops-Stortford in the subsidy of 14 Henry VIII [1522–23], the amount of the tax being illegible, as "Thomas Chaundeler," in the subsidy of 34 Henry VIII [1542–43], the amount of the tax being 14s. 8d., and, as "Thomas Chaundler," in the subsidy of 37 Henry VIII [1545–46], on goods valued at £20, the amount of the tax being illegible. (Lay Subsidies, Herts, 120/117, 121/160, 121/177, in the Public Record Office, London.) In the two later of these subsidies his son, "Thomas Chandeler junior," also appears.

Child:

2. i.   THOMAS, b. about 1500.

2.  THOMAS CHANDLER (*Thomas*), of Bishops-Stortford, co. Herts, born about 1500, died in the spring of 1554. He married, about 1525, AGNES ———, who survived him.

Since he is the only person of the family name in his generation who appears in Bishops-Stortford, it may be assumed that he was the only surviving son of his father. He seems to have been successful and prosperous, as there are evidences that he acquired considerable property and left a good estate. The earliest mention found of him is in 1532, in one of four land transactions by fine in which he participated, in three as

355

a purchaser and in one as a vendor, which may be summarized as follows:

1532. Richard Glascok, Thomas Chaundeler, John Jacobbe, Thomas Smyth, and William Sybthorpe, querents v. George Thompson and his wife Margaret, deforciants, for two messuages and lands in Stortford. (Feet of Fines, Herts, Easter Term, 24 Henry VIII.)

1532. Richard Glascok and Thomas Chaundeler, querents, v. John Nobill and his wife Joane and Thomas Clyfton and his wife Joan, for a messuage and lands in Stortford. (Ib., Michaelmas Term, 24 Henry VIII.)

1541/2. Thomas Chaundeler, querent, v. George Tomson, gentleman, and his wife Margaret, deforciants, for a barn and land in Stortford. (Ib., Hilary Term, 33 Henry VIII.)

1550/1. Nicholas Marden, querent, v. Thomas Chaundeler, Sr., and his wife Agnes, deforciants, for a messuage in Stortford. (Ib., Hilary Term, 4 Edward VI.)

Some of the properties held by Thomas Chandler are shown in a rental roll of the Bishop of London for his manor of Bishops-Stortford in 37 Henry VIII [1545–46], as follows:

Thomas Chanler for a tenement that he dwelth in on the sowth syed of the heyght, by yere ij s. vj d. The same Thomas for certene lands late parcell of Hawers, ij s. iiij d. Itm, the same Thomas for a tenement in Sowth stret on the West syed called Sampson, by yere xix d. Itm, the same Thomas for a tenement in the wyder end of sowth strete on the est syed, by yere xxiij d. Itm, the same Thomas for a garden in basburne lane, by yere vj d. Itm, the same Thomas for the dovehowse and garden at Hacryelbryge, by yere ij d. (Court Roll 299, in the Public Record Office, London.)

As Thomas Chandler, Jr., he was assessed at Stortford 10d. on lands in the subsidy of 33 Henry VIII [1541–42], 10s. in 34 Henry VIII [1542–43], 2d. on goods valued at 40s. in 35 and 36 Henry VIII [1543–1545], and 3s. 4d. on lands valued at 40s. in 37 Henry VIII [1545–46]; and as Thomas Chaundler, Sr., he was assessed at Stortford 18s. on goods in the subsidy of 4 Edward VI [1549/50–1550/1]. (Lay Subsidies, Herts, 121/151, 121/160, 121/157, 121/177, 121/185, in the Public Record Office, London.) In 1546, 1548, and 1553 Thomas Chandler was one of the churchwardens of Bishops-Stortford, as appears from the accounts of that board, preserved in the church. An abstract of his will follows:

The Will of THOMAS CHAUNDELER of Stortford, dated 30 Mar. 1554. To my son John Chaundler and his heirs and assigns for ever the messuage I now dwell in, together with one garden in Basborn Lane to the said messuage [belonging (?)], and one croft enclosed at Waldinge, of four acres, with one meadow by the waterside, and one croft in Thorley that I late bought of Richard Pilleston, the said John paying yearly to Agneis, my wife, the rent of said premises during her life. To my son Thomas Chaundler and his heirs and assigns for ever a grove I late bought of Henry Perker, gentleman, of Berden, deceased, and my messuage in Northstreet I late bought of Edward Willay, the said Thomas paying yearly the rent thereof to the said Agneis, my wife, for life. To my said son Thomas for life my meadow of two acres I late bought of Mr. Tomson in Stortford, on the backside of Cawton the tanner, with remainder to my son Robert Chaundler and his heirs, and, if the said Robert die without issue, then remainder to my son John Chaundeler and his heirs. To my son Robert Chaundler and his heirs and assigns for ever my dove house, yard, and barn, my tenement in Stortford I late bought of Wardall, and my croft and pasture I late bought of John Turnor. I will have it remembered that I have surrendered my copyhold lands and tenements by the hands of Raf Smyth and Richard Bedwell, tenants of the lord's customary, for the use of Robert Chaundler, my son, and his heirs and assigns, he paying yearly to my wife Agneis the rent thereof for life. To Robert Chaundler £20. I will that my son Robert Chaundler pay to Anne Chaundler, the daughter of John Chaundler, 5 marks at the day of his [sic] marriage, and to Barbara Chaundler, daughter of Thomas Chaundler, 5 marks at the day of her marriage, and to Margaret Bedwell, my daughter's daughter, 5 marks at the day of her marriage. To my wife Agneis a lease of a meadow and tenement I late bought of Stonard. To six poor men of Stortford a pair of hose each. To six poor children of the same town a coat each. All the residue of my goods to my wife Agneis, who is to be executrix; and John Chaundler and Robert Chaundler are to be executors with her. Supervisor: my son-in-law Richard Bedwell. Witnesses: Raif Smythe, George Hawkyns, and Willm Bardnerd. Proved on the oaths of Agnes and Robert Chaundler, executors, 23 May 1554, with power reserved for John Chandler, the other executor, when he shall demand it. (Commissary Court of London for Essex and Herts, Garland, 7.)

Children, born probably at Bishops-Stortford:

3. i. JOHN, b. about 1525.
4. ii. THOMAS, ancestor of the Chandler family in America, b. about 1528.
   iii. AGNES, b. about 1530; m. about 1550 RICHARD BEDWELL of Bishops-Stortford.
   iv. ROBERT, b. about 1532; bur. at Stortford 2 Aug. 1611; m. before 1560 JOANE ———.
       He was an executor of his father's will in 1554, paid an assessment of 10d. on the churchwardens' accounts in 1558, and was taxed at Bishops-Stortford 2s. 8d. on lands valued at 20s. in the subsidy of 5 Elizabeth [1562–63], 16d. on lands valued at 20s. in the subsidy of 8 Elizabeth [1565–66], and 10s. 8d. on goods valued at £4 in the subsidy of 39 Elizabeth [1596–97]. (Lay Subsidies, Herts, 121/202, 121/208, 121/271.) In 1570 John Miller was querent v. Robert Chaundeler and his wife Joan, deforciants, for a messuage in Stortford (Feet of Fines, Herts, Easter Term, 12 Elizabeth). On 6 Apr. 1583, 24 Sept. 1583, and 27 Sept. 1585, Robert Chaundler appears as one of the chief pledges at courts and views of frankpledge held for the manor of Stortford (Court Rolls of Ecclesiastical Commissioners, 206/2, 206/3, in the Public Record Office, London). He left no will; and, as the parish registers do not give the names of the parents of infants baptized prior to 1580, the list of his children that follows, while probably correct, should not be considered as positively proved.
       Children, recorded at Bishops-Stortford:
       1. *Frances*, bapt. 6 Dec. 1562; d. young.
       2. *Mary*, b. perhaps about 1565; bur. 4 Nov. 1582.

357

3.  *Frances,* bapt. 6 Jan. 1567/8; bur. 11 Jan. 1574/5.
4.  *Thomas,* bapt. 5 Feb. 1569/70; bur. 30 May 1571.
5.  *Richard,* bapt. 16 Feb. 1572/3; living at Bishops-Stortford in 1614; m. ———, and had children as follows: (1) Robert, bapt. 24 June 1601. (2) Elizabeth, bapt. 17 Oct. 1602; probably m. 1 Nov. 1624 John Gryce. (3) Johane, bapt. 19 Aug. 1604. (4) Richard, bapt. 10 Apr. 1614.
6.  *Thomas,* bapt. 6 Nov. 1575; bur. 9 Sept. 1597.

3.  JOHN CHANDLER (*Thomas, Thomas*), of Bishops-Stortford, co. Herts, born, probably at Bishops-Stortford, about 1525, was living 17 Mar. 1581/2. He married, about 1550, JOANE ———.

He was a considerable legatee in his father's will of 1554, and was also named in it as an executor. But little mention of him, however, has been found. In 1563 John Denyzon was querent *v.* John Chaundeler and his wife Joane, deforciants, for a messuage and lands in Stortford (Feet of Fines, Herts, Easter Term, 5 Elizabeth, in the Public Record Office, London). At a court and view of frankpledge of the manor of Stortford, held 17 Mar. 1581/2, John Chandler appears as one of the chief pledges (Court Rolls of Ecclesiastical Commissioners, 206/2, in the Public Record Office, London). As he left no will, and as the parish registers of Bishops-Stortford do not give the names of the parents of children baptized before 1580, the names of his children are not known with certainty, but are probably here given.

Children, recorded at Bishops-Stortford:

i.  TOBIAS, of Bishops-Stortford, tanner, b. about 1551; bur. at Bishops-Stortford, as "Tobias Chandler old man," 24 Oct. 1629; m. 21 Sept. 1574 JOHANE MOMFORD, who was bur. at Bishops-Stortford 29 June 1618.

He was churchwarden at Bishops-Stortford in 1598. He was taxed at Stortford on goods in the subsidy of 39 Elizabeth [1596–97], the amount of the tax being illegible, and he was taxed there 8s. on goods valued at £3 in the subsidy of 43 Elizabeth [1600–01]. (Lay Subsidies, Herts, 121/271, 121/280.) At a court of the manor of Pigotts in Stortford, held there 1 Oct., 4 James I [1606], Tobias Chaundeler, Sr., appeared as essoin for Thomas Chaundeler, probably his uncle (*Herts Genealogist and Antiquary,* vol. 2, pp. 377–378). On 9 Dec. 1618 he was a witness to the will of his cousin, Henry Chandler (5).

The will of Tobias Chandler, Sr., of Stortford, co. Herts, tanner, was dated 20 Aug. 1627. In it he bequeathed to his three daughters, Margaret, Jhone, and Grace, beds, blankets, sheets, etc.; to his son John a doublet, etc., and his least Bible; to his son Robert his best horse and greatest Bible; to his son George his horseman's "coote," etc.; to Henry Moncke a shirt; and to Mr. Dillingham 6s. 8d., to preach at his burial. Witnesses: William Dillingham, Tho: Jennynges. The will was proved 24 Nov. 1629. (Commissary Court of London for Essex and Herts, original will, 1629.)

Children, recorded at Bishops-Stortford:

1.  *Tobias,* probably a son of Tobias and Johane (Momford) Chandler, although he was not named in the will of his supposed father, bapt. at Bishops-Stortford 21 Sept. 1575 as Tobias Chandler [parents' names not given]; m. 22 Apr. 1604 Katherine Johnson, who in her will, dated 16

Apr. 1662 and proved 4 Oct. 1662, names her son-in-law, William Gyatt, her sons Henry and Thomas, her grand-child Alice Birch, her grand-children Luce and Mary Shuckford, and her son-in-law Thomas Shuckford, whom she makes executor. Witnesses: Thomas Rennals, George Osbuern, and Mathew Gurney. (Commissary Court of London for Essex and Herts, original will.) Children: (1) Tobias, bapt. 13 Jan. 1604/5; d. 16 Nov. 1613. (2) Henry, bapt. 19 Jan. 1605/6; living in 1662. (3) Thomas, bapt. 23 Feb. 1606/7; living in 1662. (4) John, bapt. 3 July 1608. (5) Jone, bapt. 3 Dec. 1609. (6) Alice, bapt. 21 Apr. 1611. (7) Mary, bapt. 11 Oct. 1612; m. 28 Oct. 1635 Thomas Shugford.

2. *Margaret,* bapt. 13 Oct. 1577; d. at Roxbury, Mass., 3 Feb. 1645/6; m. (1) Henry Munck (or Monck), who was bur. 10 Dec. 1602; m. (2) at Bishops-Stortford, 7 Nov. 1603, William Denison of Bishops-Stortford, bapt. there 3 Feb. 1571/2, d. at Roxbury 25 Jan. 1653/4. William Denison and his wife Margaret, with three of their six sons,* emigrated to New England in 1631 and settled at Rox-bury, where they appear in Rev. John Eliot's church records. He was admitted freeman 3 July 1632 and was a representative in the General Court in 1635; but in 1637, being an adherent of Rev. John Wheelwright, he was dis-armed. His descendants were numerous and influential. (Cf. Savage's Genealogical Dictionary, Pope's Pioneers of Massachusetts, and REGISTER, vol. 46, pp. 352-354, 127-133.)

3. *John,* bapt. 4 Oct. 1579; living at Bishops-Stortford in 1629; m. 18 Sept. 1615 Jane Miller. Children: (1) John, bapt. 12 July 1616; living in 1667. (2) A daughter, b. and bur. 1 Mar. 1617/18. (3) Robert, bapt. 10 July 1619. (4) William, b. in 1623; d. *s. p.* in 1665, leaving a will. (5) George, bapt. 3 May 1623; d. in 1667, leaving by will† his estate to a widow, Dorcas, and two children. (6) Thomas, bapt. 11 Feb. 1626/7. (7) Edward, bapt. 7 Apr. 1629; bur. 9 Apr. 1630.

4. *George,* of Bishops-Stortford, bapt. 1 Nov. 1581; d. at Bishops-Stortford 23 May 1628. Children: (1) Elizabeth, bapt. 23 Aug. 1601; probably m. 27 May 1621 Thomas West. (2) Jeremy, bapt. 24 Oct. 1602. (3) Anna, bapt. 16 Dec. 1604. (4) Grace, bapt. 26 Jan. 1605/6. (5) John, bapt. 11 Jan. 1606/7. (6) Alice, bapt. 17 Jan. 1607/8. (7) Sarah, bapt. 14 May 1609; probably m. 30 Nov. 1629 Henry Abram. (8) William, bapt. 21 Oct. 1610; bur. 14 Feb. 1612/13. (9) Margaret, bapt. 21 June 1612.

5. *Thomas,* bapt. 17 Dec. 1583; bur. 11 Mar. 1606/7.
6. *Joane,* bapt. 10 Apr. 1586; d. young.
7. *Joane,* bapt. 23 Mar. 1587/8; d. young.
8. *Frances,* bapt. 12 Apr. 1590; d. young.
9. *Joane,* bapt. 11 June 1592.
10. *Robert,* tallow chandler, bapt. 31 Mar. 1594; bur. at Bishops-Stortford 10 June 1638; m. in 1617 Sarah ———. By his nuncupative will, declared 8 June 1638 and proved 23 July 1638, he left all his estate to his wife Sarah, for the bringing up of his children (Commissary Court of London for Essex and Herts, original will). Children: (1) Robert, bapt. 18 Apr. 1618. (2) Jane, bapt. 29 Apr. 1620. (3) Grace, bapt. 26 Oct. 1622. (4) Thomas, bapt. 7 Aug. 1625. (5) Henry, bapt. 27 Apr. 1628; bur. 6 July 1631.

*They had also a daughter, Sarah, bapt. and bur. at Bishop-Stortford in 1615.
†This will has a seal on which is inscribed a fleur-de-lis.

(6) William, bapt. 2 May 1630. (7) Mary, bapt. 4 Nov. 1632. (8) Joane, bapt. 19 July 1635. (9) Martha, bapt. 22 Apr. 1638.

      11. *Grace,* bapt. 10 Sept. 1598.

  ii.   ANNE, b. about 1553; mentioned in the will of her grandfather, Thomas Chandler (2), in 1554.

  iii.  SUSANNA, b. about 1556; m. 4 Oct. 1579 JOSEPH TAYLOR.

  iv.  GRACE, b. about 1560; m. 3 Oct. 1585 WILLIAM ROGERS.

4. THOMAS CHANDLER (*Thomas, Thomas*), of Bishops-Stortford, co. Herts, ancestor of the Chandler family of America, was born, probably at Bishops-Stortford, about 1528, and was buried there 4 June 1611, aged over 83 years. He married, about 1552, JOANE ———, who was buried at Bishops-Stortford 11 Mar. 1606/7.

The earliest mention found of him is in the subsidy of 4 Edward VI [1549/50–1550/1], when as "Thomas Chaundler jun." he was assessed at Stortford 10s. on goods. He is taxed at Stortford in subsequent subsidies as follows: in 5 Elizabeth [1562–63], as "Thomas Chaundeler," 13s. 4d. on goods valued at £8; in 8 Elizabeth [1565–66] and in 13 Elizabeth [1570–71], as "Thomas Chandler," 8s. on goods valued at £8; in 39 Elizabeth [1596–97], as "Thomas Chandler," on goods, the amount of the tax being illegible; in 43 Elizabeth [1600–01], as "Thomas Chandeler," 8s. on lands worth 40s.; and in 3 James I [1605–6] as "Thomas Chandler," on lands worth 20s., the amount of the tax being illegible. (Lay Subsidies, Herts, 121/185, 121/202, 121/208, 121/225, 121/271, 121/280, 121/302, in the Public Record Office, London.)

In 1556 Henry Hoye was querent *v.* Thomas Chaundeler and his wife Joane, deforciants, for a messuage and lands in Stortford (Feet of Fines, Herts, Trinity Term, 2 and 3 Philip and Mary).

Thomas Chandler also appears for many years in the churchwardens' accounts. In 1558 he paid an assessment of 12d.; in 1562 he paid 5s. for wood in Thorleywyk; in 1573 he was collector for the market house and in 1582 he paid 12s. rent. The churchwardens' rental accounts show that in 1592 Philologus Bush and Robert Smith held a double tenement in South Street, formerly Bowyers, where they resided, each paying 6d. per year. In the next year (1593) the said double tenement was held by Philologus Bush and Thomas Chandler, the latter evidently having secured Smith's moiety. Philologus Bush and Thomas Chandler continue to reside there, and appear there yearly until 1600, when Thomas Chandler is succeeded by Henry Chandler. Then Philologus Bush and Henry Chandler appear there yearly until 1619, when the latter is succeeded by his widow. These records are important, since they show that Henry Chandler was undoubtedly a son of Thomas Chandler and about 1600 received from him this half tenement. After the death of Thomas Chandler in 1611, it is recorded that Edward Chandeler held Lowemeade, late Thomas

Chandler's and formerly Mr. Tompson's; this shows that Edward also was a son of Thomas.

At a court of the manor of Pigotts, in Bishops-Stortford, held 1 Oct., 4 James I [1606], Tobias Chaundeler, Sr., appears as essoin for Thomas Chaundeler (*Herts Genealogist and Antiquary*, vol. 2, pp. 377–378). Thomas Chandler also appears on several of the court rolls for views of frankpledge of the manor of Bishops-Stortford. At the courts held 13 Apr. 1577 and 27 Sept. 1577 he was one of the jurors; and at the courts of 5 Apr. 1578, 12 Apr. 1580, 4 Apr. 1581, 24 Sept. 1583, and 30 Mar. 1585 he was one of the chief pledges. At the courts of 5 Apr. and 27 Sept. 1578 Richard Comfrey was ordered to open up a right of way for Thomas Chaundler to go and come to and from Southmill field. (Court Rolls of Ecclesiastical Commissioners, 205/21, 206/1, 206/2, 206/3, in the Public Record Office, London.)

Thomas Chandler was churchwarden at Bishops-Stortford in 1562, 1563, and 1574. He left no will and, as the parish registers do not give the names of the parents of infants baptized prior to 1580, the names of all his children cannot be given with certainty; but there is proof that he had at least three children, Barbara, Henry, and Edward.

Children:

i. BARBARA, b. about 1553; living in 1554, when she was mentioned in the will of her grandfather, Thomas Chandler (2).
ii. AGNES, bur. at Bishops-Stortford 20 Feb. 1599/1600.
5. iii. HENRY, ancestor of the Chandler family in America, b. at Bishops-Stortford about 1560.
iv. SARAH, bapt. at Bishops-Stortford 5 July 1562; m. there, 20 Sept. 1580, JOHN INGHAM.
v. RICHARD, b. about 1565; bur. at Bishops-Stortford 2 Feb. 1592/3.
vi. EDWARD, of Stortford, silk weaver, b. about 1568; bur. at Stortford, as "Old Edward Chandler," 9 Nov. 1653; m. about 1600 ANN ———, who survived him.
   In the subsidy of 3 James I [1605–06] Edward Chandler was taxed at Stortford on goods valued at 60s., the amount of the tax being illegible (Lay Subsidies, Herts, 121/302). He succeeded to "Lowemeade late Thomas Chandlers" in 1611, and for many years paid rent therefor (*vide supra*). In 1614 he served as churchwarden (Churchwardens' Rentals and Accounts). An abstract of his will follows.
   The Will of EDWARD CHAUNDLER of Stentford [*sic*], co. Herts, silk weaver, being aged, dated 1 Jan. 1652/3. To my wife Ann, with whom I have lived a long season, all my household goods. To my son-in-law Justinian Aylmer, after the death of my wife, a tenement in Stortford where my son-in-law Symon Rutland now dwells, he paying to my daughter Susan, wife of Francis Onge, £30, and to my grandson Samuel Coe £5 at twenty-one. To my son Francis Chandler a silver beaker. All the residue of my estate to my wife Ann, whom I make executrix. Witnesses: John Rowe, John Howe, Theophilus Aylmer. Proved 17 Jan. 1653/4. (P. C. C., Alchin, 188.)
   Children, recorded at Bishops-Stortford:
   1. *Edward*, of the neighboring parish of Ware, draper, bapt. 1 Feb. 1600/1; d. in 1650; m. about 1623 Elizabeth ———. In his will, dated 8 May 1650 and proved 24 Apr. 1651,

Edward Chandler named his wife Elizabeth, his sons Edward and Daniel Chandler, his daughters Mary Holley and Sarah Chandler, his daughter Susan Chandler (under twenty), and his children Martha, Job, Noah, and Rebecca Chandler (all under eighteen). (P. C. C., Grey, 63.) His eldest child was baptized at Stortford, and six other children were baptized at Ware. Children: (1) Elizabeth, bapt. 2 Oct. 1624; d. young. (2) Edward, b. about 1626. (3) Mary, b. about 1628; m. ——— Holly. (4) Susan, b. in 1630. (5) Martha, b. in 1632. (6) John, bapt. 31 Aug. 1634; d. young. (7) Sarah, bapt. 25 Oct. 1635. (8) Daniel, bapt. 6 Nov. 1636. (9) Job, bapt. 2 June 1639. (10) John, bapt. 26 July 1640; d. young. (11) Noah, bapt. 22 Aug. 1641. (12) Rebecca, b. about 1644.

2. *Daniel,* bapt. 23 Sept. 1604.
3. *Margaret,* bapt. 11 Jan. 1606/7.
4. *Susan,* bapt. 29 Jan. 1608/9.
5. *Ann,* bapt. 15 Apr. 1610.
6. *John,* bapt. 28 July 1612.
7. *Winifred,* bapt. 16 Mar. 1613/14.
8. *Francis,* bapt. 6 Jan. 1618/19.

vii. WILLIAM, bapt. at Bishops-Stortford 31 Aug. 1570; bur. there 8 July 1590.

viii. JOHN, bapt. at Bishops-Stortford 10 Aug. 1573; bur. there 9 May 1592.

ix. THOMAS, d. 23 May 1592.

5. HENRY CHANDLER (*Thomas, Thomas, Thomas*), of Bishops-Stortford, co. Herts, glover, ancestor of the Chandler family of America, was born at Bishops-Stortford about 1560, and was buried there 17 Dec. 1618. He married, about 1590, ANNE ———, who survived him and married secondly, 8 July 1622, as his second wife, John Miller, Sr., of Bishops-Stortford.

Although Henry Chandler's baptism is not recorded and his father left no will, it is nevertheless clear that he was a son of Thomas Chandler, as he succeeded to the moiety of the double house occupied by the latter (*vide supra,* p. 139).* Appended are the entries in the churchwardens' rental roll for this property in 1600:

Of Phillologus Bush for part of a tenement in Southstreet where he resides formerly of John Bowyer the elder, 6d.

Of Henry Chaundeler for the other part of said tenement where he resides, 6d.

Bush and Chandler thereafter appear on the yearly rolls as residing on this property until 1619, when the latter is succeeded by his widow.

Except for mentions of his name in the parish registers, no other information about Henry Chandler has been found, apart from his will, an abstract of which is here given:

The Will of HENRY CHANDELER of Stortford, co. Herts, glover, dated 9 Dec. 1618. To my wife Anne, for life, the tenement in Stortford where I now dwell (my daughter Elizabeth to have the chamber therein in which she lodges); with remainder to Samuell Chandeler, my youngest son, he paying to my daughter Sara, within

*Page 360, this volume.

four years after the death of my wife, £5 in money, and to my daughter Elizabeth, for life, an annuity of 20s., payable at the usual quarterly feasts. "Itm. I give & bequeath vnto Willm myne eldest sonne ffower pownds of lawfull mony to be payd to him wi<sup>th</sup>in fower yeres next after my decesse, that is to say yerely in e[v'r]y of the said yeres Twenty shillings, if my said sonne live so long, To be pd to my Wife, her executors, or ass." To my daughters Elizabeth and Sarah, beds, etc., and to said daughter Sarah a linen wheel that was her grandmother's. All the residue of my estate to my wife Anne, whom I make sole executrix. Wit[nesses]: Tobias Channler, Willm Denyson, Tho: Jeninges, Thomas Barnarde, Sen., Sc. The mark of Henrici Chandeler. [Seal, a fleur-de-lis.] Proved by the executrix 15 Mar. 1618/19. (Commissary Court of London for Essex and Herts, original will.)

Children, recorded at Bishops-Stortford:

|   | i.   | RICHARD, bapt. 21 Nov. 1591; d. young. |
|---|------|----------------------------------------|
| 6. | ii.  | WILLIAM, emigrant to New England in 1637, bapt. 12 Oct. 1595. |
|   | iii. | SARAH, bapt. 11 Mar. 1597/8; living unm. in 1618. |
|   | iv.  | ELIZABETH, b. probably about 1601; perhaps m. 2 May 1619 JOHN BREWER. |
|   | v.   | SAMUEL, bapt. 13 Oct. 1605; bur. 11 May 1606. |
|   | vi.  | SAMUEL, bapt. 19 July 1607; m. 29 June 1629 MARGARET GRAY. |

Children:
1. *Mary*, bapt. 11 Apr. 1630.
2. *Henry*, bapt. 25 Dec. 1631.

6. WILLIAM CHANDLER (*Henry, Thomas, Thomas, Thomas*), of Bishops-Stortford, co. Herts, and of Roxbury, Mass., pointer, immigrant ancestor of the Chandler family in America, was baptized at Bishops-Stortford 12 Oct. 1595, and died at Roxbury 26 Jan. 1641/2, the Roxbury church records containing the following entry: "1641. Month 11<sup>to</sup> day 26. Willia' Chandler, a Christian & godly broth<sup>r</sup> dyed of a Consumption." (Roxbury Land and Church Records, printed, p. 170.) He married first, at Bishops-Stortford, 29 Jan. 1621/2, ALICE THOROGOOD of Farnham, co. Essex, the parish north of Bishops-Stortford, who was buried at Bishops-Stortford, as "Alice Chandeler, wife of William Chandler, poynter," 15 June 1625; and secondly, at Farnham, 6 Nov. 1625, ANNIS (or AGNES or ANN) BAYFORD, baptized there 12 June 1603, daughter of Francis and Johan Bayford.* Annis (Bayford) Chandler migrated to New England with her husband and four children in 1637, and, surviving William Chandler, married secondly, at Roxbury, 2 July 1643, as his second wife, John Dane of Ipswich and Roxbury, Mass., who was buried at Roxbury 14 Sept. 1658. She married thirdly, at Roxbury, 9 Aug. 1660, as

*Francis Bayford was baptized at Farnham, co. Essex, 13 Apr. 1567, the second son of Richard and Joan (Searl) Bayford who were married 10 Apr. 1564. An abstract of the will of Francis Bayford follows:

The Will of Francis Bayford of Farnham, co. Essex, husbandman, dated 9 June 1614. My copyhold lands to my wife Johan, for life, with remainder to my eldest son Richard and my younger son John, the former to pay to my daughter Agnes £14 and the latter to pay to her £6 within three years of the death of my wife. The residue of my goods to my wife Johan, executrix, to bring up my young children. Witnesses: Edmond Byshop, Richard Allis, Thomas Allis. Proved 3 Dec. 1622. (Commissary Court of London for Essex and Herts, original will, 1622, No. 141.)

his second wife, Dea. John Parmenter of Sudbury, Mass., later of Roxbury, who died at Roxbury 1 May 1671, aged 83 years. She survived her third husband, and died 15 Mar. 1682/3, the Roxbury church records giving her burial as follows: "1683. M.I., d. 17, Old Mother Parmiter, a blessed Saint." (Roxbury Land and Church Records, printed, p. 184.)

William Chandler learned the trade of point making, the making of the lace tags for fastening clothing which were in vogue before buttons came into use. By his father's will, in 1618, he received only £4, and it is, therefore, probable that he had already received from his father a portion of his patrimony.

Except for the references to him in the parish registers and in his father's will, no records of him have been found at Bishops-Stortford, where he resided until he emigrated with his family to New England in 1637. His emigration was due, without doubt, to the preaching of Rev. John Eliot, the Puritan minister known as the "Apostle to the Indians," who was born in the neighboring parish of Widford in 1604, went to New England in 1631, and became pastor of the church at Roxbury, Mass., being accompanied or followed thither by many adherents who had lived in the parishes on the borders of Herts and Essex.

William Chandler appears among the early proprietors and householders of Roxbury, and was admitted a freeman of Massachusetts on 13 May 1640. (Records of the Colony of the Massachusetts Bay, printed, vol. 1, p. 377.) He owned an estate of twenty-two acres, described as follows:

"John Dane his house and lott with a swamp before the house, butting upon the way leading to the house of John Watson east, in all five accres and a halfe more or lesse, upon John Watson's swamp south, upon the heires of Thomas Ruggles west, and upon the heires of George Alcocke north. And in the nookes next Dorchester being the second lott lying betweene Phillip Tory and the assignes of Joseph Patching ten accres and a halfe. And in the thousand accres neare Deddam.* All the lands with the house above mentioned were latly belonging to the heires of William Chandler." (Roxbury Land and Church Records, printed, pp. 5, 39.)

This homestead of William Chandler was situated at the southerly corner of the present Bartlett and Washington streets, in Roxbury (see Drake's Town of Roxbury, p. 368); and it later became the property of John Dane, who married the widow of William Chandler, by grant of the Massachusetts General Court, as appears from the following documents:

"1649. At a Gen'all Co'te, at Boston, the 17ᵗʰ of the 8ᵗʰ Mᵒ. Upon the petition of John Dayne, the house & land wᶜʰ was Wᵐ Chamb'ˢ [*sic*] is settled upon yᵉ said Dayne, he haveing paid more debts of Chamb'ˢ [*sic*] then yᵉ house & land was worth, & also

*Number of acres not given.

364

brought up y$^e$ children of Chandler. w$^{ch}$ have bene chargable to him."

"19 Oct. 1649. In ans$^r$ to the peticon of John Dajne ffor the settling the howse and lands of W$^m$ Chandler (whose wyddow he marryed, & children brought up) on him, the said John Dajne, his request was graunted, & y$^e$ said howse and lands confirmed on him by this Courte." (Records of the Colony of the Massachusetts Bay, printed, vol. 2, p. 283, vol. 3, p. 177.)

The following account of William Chandler, given in the list of members of the Roxbury church by his pastor, Rev. John Eliot, well describes his circumstances and character:

"William Chandler he came to N. E. aboute the yeare 1637: he brought 4 small childr, Thomas, Hana, John, Willia': his 5$^t$ child Sarah was borne here; he lived a very religious & Godly life among us, & fell into a consumption, to w$^h$ he had bene long inclined; he lay neare a yeare sick, in all w$^h$ time, his faith, patiens, & Godlynesse & contentation so shined, y$^t$ Christ was much gloryfied in him; he was a man of weake pts, but excellent fath & holyness, he was very thankful man, & much magnified Gods goodnesse, he was pore, but God so opened the hearts of his nabs to him y$^t$ he never wanted y$^t$ w$^h$ was (at least in his esteeme) very plentifull & comfortable to him; he dyed about the [*blank*] in yeare 1641, & left a sweet memory & savor behind him." (Roxbury Land and Church Records, printed, p. 83.)

Children by first wife, recorded at Bishops-Stortford:

i.    ELIZABETH, bapt. 10 Jan. 1622/3; bur. 30 Sept. 1636.
ii.   SARAH, bapt. 19 Dec. 1624; bur. 19 Jan. 1626/7.

Children by second wife, recorded (except the youngest) at Bishops-Stortford:

iii.  WILLIAM, bapt. 26 Mar. 1627; bur. 27 Nov. 1633.
iv.  CAPT. THOMAS, of Andover, Mass., blacksmith and iron worker, bapt. 9 Aug. 1628; d. early in 1702/3; m. HANNAH BREWER, who survived him and d. at Andover 25 Oct. 1717, perhaps aged 87, and perhaps daughter of Daniel Brewer.
    He was brought to New England by his parents in 1637, was of Andover in 1645, and was a representative from Andover in the General Court in 1678 and 1679. His will, dated 13 Sept. 1700, was proved 8 Feb. 1702/3. Eight children.
v.   HANNAH, bapt. 22 May 1630; brought to New England by her parents in 1637; d. 2 June 1711, in her 82d year; m. (1) at Roxbury, 12 Dec. 1646, GEORGE ABBOTT of Roxbury and later of Andover, Mass., for whom see pp. 84–86 of the present volume of the REGISTER; m. (2) in 1690, as his third wife, her stepbrother, REV. FRANCIS DANE of Andover, bapt. at Bishops-Stortford 20 Nov. 1615, d. at Andover 17 Feb. 1696/7, son of John and Frances Dane. Thirteen children by first husband (*vide supra*, pp. 85–86).
vi.  HENRY, bapt. 13 Aug. 1632; d. young.
vii.  DEA. JOHN, of Roxbury, Mass., and Woodstock, then belonging to Massachusetts but since 1752 a part of Connecticut, husbandman, bapt. at Bishops-Stortford 27 July 1634; d. at Woodstock 15 Apr. 1703, aged about 68 years (gravestone); m. at Roxbury, 16 Feb. 1658/9, ELIZABETH DOUGLAS, b. in Boston, Mass., 26 Aug. 1641, d. at New London, Conn., 23 Sept. 1705, daughter of William and Anna (Matlat or Motley) Douglas of Ipswich and Boston, Mass., and New London, Conn.
    He was brought to New England by his parents in 1637,

and lived in Roxbury until 1686, when he became one of the pioneer settlers of Woodstock, where he was selectman, moderator of the town meeting and deacon in the church. His will was dated 1 June 1702. Eight children, b. at Roxbury.

viii. WILLIAM, of Andover, Mass., yeoman, brickmaker, innkeeper, bapt. at Bishops-Stortford 20 Mar. 1635/6; d. at Andover in 1698; m. (1) at Ipswich, Mass. (recorded at Andover), 18 or 24 Aug. 1658, MARY DANE, b. at Ipswich about 1639, d. at Andover 10 May 1679, daughter of Dr. John and Eleanor (Clark) Dane; m. (2) at Chelmsford, Mass., 8 Oct. 1679, MRS. BRIDGET (HENCHMAN) RICHARDSON, b. about 1640, said to have d. 6 Mar. 1731, daughter of Maj. Thomas and Elizabeth Henchman and widow of Lieut. James Richardson, all of Chelmsford.

He was brought to New England by his parents in 1637, and was admitted freeman in 1669. His will, dated 15 Sept. 1697, was proved 12 Dec. 1698. Eleven children by first wife and three children by second wife.

ix. SARAH, b. at Roxbury; m. (1) 4 Nov. 1659 WILLIAM CLEVES of Roxbury, who was killed by the Indians at Sudbury, Mass., in King Philip's War, 29 Apr. 1676; m. (2) —— WILSON; m. (3) 11 Oct. 1688 EPHRAIM STEVENS; m. (4) —— ALLEN. She had issue.✻✻

# GENEALOGICAL RESEARCH IN ENGLAND

Communicated by the Committee on English and Foreign Research

## BELKNAP: ADDITIONAL RECORDS

Contributed by HENRY WYCKOFF BELKNAP of Salem, Mass.

IN the REGISTER, vol. 68, pages 83–92 and 190–198 (January and April, 1914), there was published an article by the present writer entitled "The English Ancestry of the American Belknaps," in which records from English sources were presented that showed that Abraham[1] Belknap, who was a landowner at Lynn, Mass., in 1635 or thereabouts, was baptized at Sawbridgeworth, co. Herts, England, 10 Mar. 1589/90, and that he was a son of Bennet Beltoft *alias* Belknap and a grandson of Richard Beltoft *alias* Belknap, both of the same parish. Richard Beltoft *alias* Belknap, grandfather of the Lynn settler, was considered in the article to have been probably a son of a Henry Beltoft of Sawbridgeworth, who, in turn, was regarded as perhaps a brother of a John Beltoft of Sawbridgeworth who died about 1546 and an Edmond Beltoft who was living in the same year. The Christian name of the father of these brothers was then unknown.✻

Since 1914 more records that throw light on the Beltofts or Belknaps of Sawbridgeworth have been discovered among the proceedings of the Court of Chancery, in the Public Record Office in London, by Mr. Charles A. Bernau of London, who carried on the researches that led to the preparation of the article published in 1914. These additional records show that the Christian name of the Beltoft with whom the pedigree published in 1914 begins was Richard, that he

*The article on the English ancestry of Abraham Belknap which was published in the REGISTER in January and April 1914 was reprinted for the present writer; but almost the entire edition of the little book was consumed in the great fire in Salem, having been received by the writer from the binder only a few days before that catastrophe. Those who wish to consult the article will find it, of course, in the REGISTER (vol. 68).

✻✻ Further information about the children of William Chandler, the immigrant (6), may be found in Dr. George Chandler's The Chandler Family, second edition, Worcester, Mass., 1883.

lived in Sawbridgeworth and died probably in the first decade of the sixteenth century (1501–1510) or perhaps even earlier, that he had a wife named Christian, who survived him and was probably, although not certainly, the mother of his children, and that in his will he mentioned six children, John (given in the pedigree in 1914), Laurence (not given in 1914), Edmund (given in 1914), Thomas (not given in 1914), and two daughters (also not given in 1914). Henry, given in the pedigree of 1914 as perhaps a brother of John and Edmund, was not their brother. The newly discovered records show also that Richard Beltoft, the grandfather of the Lynn settler, was probably a son, or, in the opinion of Mr. Bernau, a grandson, of Laurence Beltoft, a son of the first Richard.

These records are here presented, and are followed by a more detailed statement as to the conclusions to be drawn from them, when combined with the records published in 1914, and the changes in the pedigree of 1914 that they make necessary.

### From Chancery Proceedings

#### I

[Westwood *v.* Gyrton, a suit for the possession of a messuage, etc., in Sawbridgeworth called Nidelles, 1550–51.]

[The Bill of Complaint of Thomas Westwood against William Gyrton, 1550.]

To the right honourable s<sup>r</sup> Rychard Ryche knyght lord Ryche & lord Chauncello<sup>r</sup> of Englond.

In most humble Wyse sheweth and complayneth unto yo<sup>r</sup> good lordship youre dayly orato<sup>r</sup> Thomas Westwood that where oon John Beltofte late of Sabrygeworth in the Contye of Hertf was seysed of & in oon mesuage xxx Acres of lond medoe & past<sup>r</sup> with thapp<sup>r</sup>tennces callyd Nydellys sett liyng and beyng in the psshe of Sabrygeworthe aforeseyd in his demeane as of fee And so beyng therof seysed by his dede indentyd sufficyent in the lawe beryng date aboute Apryle in the xxxvj<sup>th</sup> yere of the Reign of oure late sov'aign lord Kyng Henry the viij<sup>th</sup> [1544–45]* dyd gyve & gr<sup>a</sup>unte unte the same to oon Henry Chacy theld<sup>r</sup> & Robt. Godday thelder & other to yo<sup>r</sup> orato<sup>r</sup> unknowen To hold to them & to theyr heyres to thuse & behoyff of the seyd John Beltofte for t'me of his lyfe and aft<sup>r</sup> the death of the seyd John Beltoft to thuse & behoyff of Margaret then hys wyfe & of her Assignez unto the full Ende & t'me of xv yeres then next & immedyatly following the death of the seyd John Beltoft and aft<sup>r</sup> that t'me of xv yeres ended to thuse & behoyff of Edmond Beltoft brother of the seyd John Beltoft & of hys heyres & assignez for ev' by force of which gyft & of the late statute of usez the seyd John Beltoft was therof seysed accordyngly the Remaynder ov' to the psons aforeseyd & which John thissues & pffitts therof quyetly dyd take & pceyve to his owne only use duryng his lyfe as lawfull was for hym to do and the seyd John Beltoft aboute v yeres last past dyed & the seyd Margaret hym ou'lyved aft<sup>r</sup> whose death the seyd Margaret entred into the p'mysses & was therof possessed accordyngly & thissuez & pfitts therof dyd quyetly pceyve & take to her owne use And the seyd Margaret so beyng of the p'mysses possessed toke to husbond yor seyd orator by vertu wherof yo<sup>r</sup> seyd orato<sup>r</sup>

*The exact date, as it appears below, was 4 April 1545.

& the seyd Margaret were possessed of the p'mysses & occupied the p'mysses accordyngly And the seyd Margaret by lycence of yo$^r$ seyd orato$^r$ made her wyll & by the same dyd gyve & graunte the seyd t'me of yeres in the p'mysses unto yo$^r$ seyd orato$^r$ w$^t$ all the Residue of her goods & Cattalls & dyed levyng issue by yo$^r$ seyd orato$^r$ yet lyvyng After whose death yo$^r$ seyd orato$^r$ had & ought to have the p'mysses duryng the rest of the seyd t'me as in his owne right aswell by reason of the seyd mariage as by the seyd Wyll & had the Admynystracon of all the goods & Cattalls of the seyd Margaret to hym comytted by theordynary of the Dyoces wherby yo$^r$ seyd orato$^r$ entred into the p'mysses & was therof possessed accordyngly & so he contynued long tyme untyll aboute the last daye of Marche last past [about 31 March 1550] that oon Wyllm Gyrton by colo$^r$ that the seyd dede made & executed of the p'mysses to thusez aforeseyd & other evydences touchyng the pfittyng of the state & t'me of yo$^r$ orato$^r$ of & in the p'mysses & to yo$^r$ orato$^r$ belongyng duryng the rest of the seyd yere as com to the hands of the seyd Willm. he the seyd Willm. w$^t$ out just ground or tytle hath entred into the p'mysses & therof hath expulsed yo$^r$ seyd orato$^r$ & suche goods & Cattalls as yo$^r$ seyd orato$^r$ had in the p'mysses the seyd Wyllm Gyrton then & there hath cast out of the p'mysses to thutt$^r$ undoyng of yo$^r$ seyd orato$^r$ for ev' onles spedy remedy be had herin And because youre orato$^r$ doith not knowe the date of the seyd dede ne the names of all the seyd feoffeez ne the certen contents of the same dede ne the certen nombre of the seyd other evydences & writyngs ne wherin they be conteyned ne the certen contents ne t'mes of the same yo$^r$ seyd orato$^r$ can thefore have no remedy ne recov the p'mysses by thorder of the coen lawe ne maynteyne and Accon at the same for the p'mysses And so shall lose the same except that the seyd dede & Evydence by order of yo$^r$ good lordship may be brought into this honorable Co$^r$te & delyv'yd to yo$^r$ orato$^r$ for his tyme & t' me orells be inrolled or otherwyse [*a few words illegible*] yo$^r$ seyd orato$^r$ maye have the same or thinrollment therof for the mayntenance & p's$^r$vacon of his estate duryng the [*a few words illegible*] yeres may it therfore please yo$^r$ good lordship the p'mysses considered to graunte the Kyngs wrytt of suppen to be dyrected to the seyd Willm. Gyrton comandyng hym by the same psonally to Apcre before yo$^r$ good lordship in the kyngs high Courte of Ch$^a$unc$^r$y at a certen daye & under A payne by yo$^r$ good lordship to be apoynted there to Answer to the p'mysses & to be further ordred therin according to right & Equtie And yo$^r$ seyd orato$^r$ wyll dayly p$^a$ye to god for the p's$^r$vacon of yo$^r$ good lordships Estate p'sp'ously long in hono$^r$ to endure   [Signed] R. Broke Antony Broun

The Answer of Willm. Gyrton to ye bill of Compleynt of Thomas Westwood [1550].

The said Willm. Gyrton for answer sayethe that longe tyme before ye said John Beltofte in ye said bill of copleynt resited ony thinge had in ye said [*a few words illegible*] medowe and pasture in the said bill of Compleynt mencioned that one Richard Beltofte father to the said John Beltofte was lawfully seasid by his dead sufficient in the lawe then enfeffed oon Thomas Lentroope and other to have and to hold the same to them & to ther heyrs to ye use of the said Richard Beltoft & his heyrs by reson wherof the said Thomas Lentroope and other his cofeoffees wer seased of ye p'misses in ther demeane as of fee to thuse aforesaid And after ye said Richard Beltoft ordeynid made and declared his last will and testamet and by ye same he willyd yt his feoffees shuld stond and be seasid of ye p'misses to thuse of on Cristian then his wyf onto ye full age of John his sone And after to thuse of the said John Beltofte and of theyrs of his body lawfully begotten w$^t$ div's other remaynders ov' as in ye said will more playnly apperithe and died after whose deathe the said Thomas Lentroope and other his cofeoffees wer seasid of ye p'misses in ther demeane as of fee* unto ye use of ye said John Beltoft and of theires of his body lawfully begotten and for defaut of such yssue to such use as in the said will is expressed and declared And after ye said John dyd cum to his full age that is to wete to the age of xxj yeres And then the said feoffees wer seasid of and in ye p'misses to thuse of the said John Beltoft and theirs of his body lawfully begotten by force wherof ye said feoffees entrid in to ye p'misses and thissues and pfits therof cumyng peaceable toke unto ye forthe day of February in the xxvij$^{th}$ yere of ye reigne of ye late prince of famous Memorye Kynge Henry theyght [4 February 1535/6] At w$^{ch}$ day ye said John Beltofte was therof sole seasid in his demeane as of fee tayle by force of ye statute therto made for extinguisement of usis and willes And he so beynge of ye p'misses seasid toke to wife one Isabell and had by her issue one Johan And ye said Johan toke to husebond one Willm. Waller and had issue betwene them on Mergret now wife to ye said defend$^t$ And then ye said Johan died and after ye said John Beltofte died after whose deathe ye p'misses descendid and cam and of right owght to discend and cume unto ye said Mergret wif of ye said defendant [a few words illegible] next heire of ye said John Beltofte that is to say dowghter & heire of ye body of ye said Johan Waller dowghter & heire of ye said John Beltofte by force wherof ye said defendant as in ye right of his wif entered into ye p'misses and therof was seasid in his demeane as of fee taile as in ye right of ye said Mergret untill the Compleynants and other wrongfully and w$^t$ force expulsed & put out for w$^{ch}$ wrong dissession and expulsion w$^t$ force at a Sessions holden at Pookeridge in the said Countie of Hertford the xxix day of Marche last past in this p'sent fourt yere of ye reigne of our sovereigne lord Kinge Edward ye sixt [29 March 1550] before Sir Raffe Sadler knight s$^r$ Henry Parker knight and other the Kynges Justics of peace of ye same shere ther beynge accordynge to ye lawes and statutes of this realme ye said Thomas Westwood on John Toller Richard Underwood and Raffe Roke wer iustly Indited for entringe in to ye p'misses in forceble man' uppon ye possession of ye said Will$^a$m and Margaret his wiffe now defendants of ye estatute mad in ye eyght yere of Kynge Henry the sixt late Kynge of England [1429–30] and kepinge of them owt w$^t$ force upon wyche enditmet ye said Justics accordyng to ye said estatute awarded a writ of restotutio to one John Gats knight shrife of ye same shere to put ye said Will$^a$m and Margaret in possession of ye p'misses and suche goods and cattelles as the copleynant then had in the p'misses ye said Will$^a$m Girton cast owt of ye p'misses as lawful was and is for him to doe w$^t$ owt yt ye said John Beltofte was ev' seasid of ye p'misses in his demeane as of fee or yt he by his dead indentid sufficient in ye law did gyve or gr$^a$unt ye same to one Henry Chacy the elder and others in ye bill of compleint resited to have to them and to ther heires to the use of ye said John Beltoft for terme of his liffe and after to ye use of Mergeret then his wife for xv yeres next after his death and after to thuse of Emond [sic] Beltofte in man' and forme as in ye said bill is resited And w$^t$ owt yt ye said Mergeret was ev' possessid lawfully of ye p'misses or peasably toke ye pfits therof or by reson of ye esspowsells had betwene ye said Mergeret by license of ye copleyn$^a$nt made any will or did

*Several lines here are a repetition of the lines immediately preceding and have therefore been omitted.—EDITORS.

geve or might lawfully geve the p'misses to the copleyn^a nt or that after her deathe the copleyn^a nt owght to have ye p'misses in man' and forme as in ye said bill is surmised And w^t owt yt that ye said defendant hathe any dedes Charters munemetts and writinges doo of right belonge unto him but ye defendant sayeth that ye Compleynant hathe in his handes custody and possession all ye deades charters and wrytynges yt do cos^r ne ye p'misses and do belonge to ye defendant ye w^ch he shewed at Pukeredge aforesaid ye friday in Ester weke last past unto S^r Raffe Sadler knight in ye p'sens of div's and many men of woorshipe and other wherfore this defendant prayeth that by the order of this honerable Corte ye compleyn^a nt might bring into this honerable Cort ye said dedes charters and writings yt they might be deliverid to ye right honor [i. e., owner] of them And w^t owt yt yt ye complen^a nt dothe not knowe ye date of ye said dede nether ye names of ye said fefees or yt he is wt owt remedy by ye comen law if he have any right And w^t owt that yt any other thing comprised in ye said faynid bill w^ch is matereall to be answerid unto and in this answer not confessid avoyded traversid or denied is trew All w^ch matters ye said defendant is redy to aver and prove as this honerable cort shall award and prayeth to be dismissed w^t his resonable costs and charge susteind in this behalfe.

The Replycacon of Thomas Westwood to the Onswere of Wyllm. Gyrton.*

The said Thomas Westwood seyth and av'yth all and ev'y thyng and matter comprysed in hys seid byll of compl. to be good c'ten suffycyent and trewe in man' and form as in the same ys det'mynable in this hon^r ble court & nott set forth for ony syche intent or p^r pose as in the seid onswere ys alledged wyhtoute that the seid Rychard Beltofte named in the seid onswere father to the seid John Beltoft beyng seased of the seid mesuage and xxx acres of lond medowe and pasture menconed in the seid byll of compl. in hys demene as of fe by hys dede suffycent in the lawe therof infeffed one Thomas Lentroope and other to have and to hold the same to them and to theyr heyres to thuse of the seid Rychard and of hys heyres as in the seid onswere ys alledged and wythowte that the seid Rychard Beltofte ordeined made and declared hys last wyll and testament and by the same wylled that hys feoffees shold stond and be seased of the p'mysses to thuse of one Chrystyan than hys wyff unto the full age of John hys sun and after the seid John Beltofte and of theyres of hys body lawfully begotten wyth dyv'z remaynders as in the seid onswereys also untrewly s'mysed And wythoute that that the seid Thomas Lentroppe and hys Cofeffees after the deth of the seid Rychard were seased of the p'mysses in theyr demene as of fee unto thuse of the seid Christian untyll the full age of the seid John & after to thuse of the seid John Beltofte and of theyres of hys bodye lawfully begotten and for default of syche yssue to the syche uses as in the seid wyll ys s'mysed in man' and form as ys also in the seid onswer s'mysed And wythowte that that after the seid John Beltofte cam to thage of xxj yeres the seid feoffees werre seased of & in the p'mysses to thuse of the seid John Beltoft and of theyres of hys body lawfully begotten or by force therof the said John by the sufferaunce of the seid feoffees ent'ed into the p'mysses and dyd take thissues & pffytts therof untyll the iiij^th day of February in the xxxvij^th yere of the reygn of the late Kyng Henri theyght [4 February 1545/6] as ys further in the seid onswere untrewly s'mysed And wythowte

*On the left of this line are the names "A. Broune" and "Powle," probably Westwood's lawyers.

370

that that the seid John Beltofte was at that day sole seased of the p'mysses in hys demene as of fee Tayle by force of the statute made for the extinguyshement of uses as ys also in the seid onswere most ontrewly s'mysed And yf ony syche feffement to ony syche use was had or made by the seid Rychard Beltoft as ther was nott and also yf the seid Rychard Beltoft made & declared ony syche wyll of the p'mysses as ys aforeseid as he dyd nott or therby declared & devysed the p'mysses in tayle as ys above-seid as he dyd nott yett the seid compl. seyth that yt ys nott mat'yll for the seid compl. do sey that the seid John Beltoft after the deth of the seid Rychard that ys to sey abought therd [*sic,* ? thend, i. e., the end] of the reygn of ower late sov'eyn lord Kyng Henri the viij[th] dyd infeffe Henri Chauncey & others to thuse of the seid John Beltoft for t'me of xv yeres next after the decese of the seid John Beltofte for t'me of his lyef & after the decese of the seid John Beltoft to thuse of Margarett then hys wyef for the t'me of xv yeres next after the decese of the seid John Beltofte and after that t'me endyed to thuse of Edmond Beltoft Brother of the seid John Beltoft and of hys heyres for ev' by v'tue wherof the seid John Beltoft ent'd into the p'mysses and was seased of the p'mysses for t'me of hys lyef and thyssues & pfytts thernf dyd take quyetly Accordingly and dyed and the seid Margarett hym ov'lyved and after toke to hushond the seid Thomas Westwood nowe compl. wherby the seid Westwood and Margarett as in the right of the seid Margarett toke thissues & pfytte to thuse of the seid compl. and after the seid Margarett wylled as in the seid byll of compl. is alledged & dyed after whose deth the seid complayn'nt had the admynstracon of all the goods & chattells of the seid Mar-garett to hym lawfully comytted wherby youer seid oratour contynewed possessyon of the p'mysses and hath lying in the howses ther of whete barley otes & pese abought xxx[ti] quarters sum throssed and sume un-throssed & abought iiij loods of hay & xij heves of bees in the gar-den there & also hath ther abought ij loods of fuell and also the seid deft hath tylled . . . abought xviij acres & hath sewen the same wyth corne of hys owen & hath abought xij acres in falowe wyche youer seid compl. to hys grete costs charges labours ... hath hetherto ymployed & conv'ted to comen utylyte intendyng the same to be to hys comfort & the comfort of hys pore chyldren and yett the seid defendtin Marche last past cont'ri to right & good conshyens hath ent'ed into the p'mysses & the seid whete barley otes pese be heves hay fuell corne on the grond & fallowe do take use & conv't to hys owen use & pfytt to the otter on-doyng of youer seid oratour & hys Chyldern for ev' & to the greate com-fort of all syche yll doers that wrongfully shall intend hereafter to attempt the lyke yll & to the greate sklander of Justyce & equyte wythoute that that ther ys ony other thyng or matter mat'yall or effectuall to be replyed onto contheyned or especyfyed in the seid onswere not in the replycacon suf-fyceently confessed & avoyded trav'sed or denyed ys trewe all whyche matt's the seid compl. ys able to av' & pve as this hon'able court wyll award & prayeth as he in hys seid byll of compl. hath prayed.

The Reieynder of Willm. Girton to the Replication of Thomas Westwood.*
The said Answer hathe said that Richarde Beltoft father of the said John Beltoft was lawfully seasid of the said Mesuage and xxx acres of lond and other the p'mysses in the sayd bill and answer resitid in his demeane as of fee and he so beinge therof seasid infeoffid the said

*On the left of this line are the names "Hadley Hanchett" and "Garth," probably Gyrton's lawyers.

371

Tomas leventhorpe and other in the Answer resitid to have to them and to ther heirs by force wherof they werr seasid of the p'misses in ther demeane as of fee to thissue afore said And after the said Richard Beltoft ordeyned and made his last will and testamet and willid that his feoffees shuld stand & be seasid of the p'misses to the use of one Christiane then his wiffe untill the full age of John his sone and after to the use of the said John beltofte and of the heirs of his body lawfully begotten w^t divers remaynders over as in the said [*some words obviously omitted*]cofeffees wer seasid to the use of the said Christian w^t divers Remaynders over in man' and forme as in the said answer trewly is alleadgid And that by vertew of the statute made in the xxvij yere of kynge Henry theight [1535–36] for extinguizmet of uses and willes the said John beltofte was sole seasid in his demeane as of fee tayle in man' and forme as in the said Answer trewly is alleadgid And further the said defendant averrithe all & every other thinge and things in his said Answer conteynid to be good and trew w^t owt that that the said John Beltofte after the death of the said Richard dyd infeffe Henry Chauncy and other to any suche use or intent as in the said Replication untrewly is surmised And the defendant sayethe that the compleyn^ant hathe lienge in the said howse divers quarteres of Corne and grayne that is to saye xiij quarters of malt vj quarteres ots and hathe also x hives of bees & other ij lodes of heye ther about the w^ch the defendant hathe bine allweies hetherto redy to deliv' and yet is if the Compleyn^ant wold fetche it a way And the defendant sayethe moreover that ther is in the said howse whett peson and otes and sume barley but how miche he knowethe not with out that the Compleyn^ant hathe ther any more or other Corne thresshid then before is declarid or hathe tillys of the p'mysses about xviij acres or hathe sowine the same yf he have yet it is not matereall to this defendant for the Cawsis before rehersid And withe owt that that the defendant hathe conv'tid any of the Corne before rehersid to his owine use or that he hathe done any thinge to the slaunder of Justice or any other thinge to the Comforte of any evill doeres in man' and forme as in the said Replication slaunderously ys alleadgid And withe owt that that any other thinge comprisid in the said Replication w^ch is materiall or effectuall to be Reioynid unto and in this reioynder not sufficiently confessid avoydid traversid or denied is trew All whiche matteres the said defendant is redy to averre & prove as this honerable Co^rt shall award And prayethe as he is in his said Answer hathe prayed. (Early Chancery Proceedings, Bundle 1276.)

Int'rogatories uppon the part & behalfe of Thomas Westwood Agenst Willm. Gyrton.

Imp'mis whed^r oon John Beltofte late of Sabrygeworth alias Sabbesford in the Coutye of Hertf. was saysed of an estate of enherytance of and in oon mesuage xxx Acres of land medowe & pasture or thereabouts with thapp'tennces called Nydells sett lying & beyng in the pysshe of Sabrygeworth aforeseid alias Sabbesford or not.

Itm. wheder the seid John Beltofte by hys dede indented beyryng date aboute Aprill in the xxxvj^th yere of the reygn of Kyng Henry the viij^th [1544–45]* dyd gyve and graunte the seid mease & lands With thapp'tennces to oon Henry Chacy thelder & Robert Godday thelder & other theyr Cofeoffeez To hold to them & to theyr heyres to the use & behoif of the said John Beltofte for t'me of his lyfe And After the death of the same John Beltofte to the use & behof of Margarett

*The exact date, as it appears below, was 4 April 1545.

372

then his Wyfe and of her Assignez to the full ende & t'me of xv yeres then next Immediatly folowyng aft<sup>r</sup> the death of the seid John Beltofte And aft<sup>r</sup> thende of the seid xv yeres then to thuse of Edmond Beltofte his brother & his heyres for ev' or not.

Itm. wheder the seid Edmond Beltofte be yet in lyfe or not.

Itm. whed<sup>r</sup> the seid Margarett the late Wyfe of the seid John Beltofte by force of the seid gyfte & conveyance aft<sup>r</sup> the deceas of the seid John Beltofte her husband was possessed of the p'mysses & peacybly toke the pfitts therof to her own use by the space of v yeres or not or by what space.

Itm. whed<sup>r</sup> the seid Margarett aft<sup>r</sup> the deceas of the seid John Beltofte her husband dyd marrye the seid Thomas Westwod or not And whether the syd Thoms. Westwod & Margarett aft<sup>r</sup> marriage had betwen them were peacybly possessed of the seid tente and lands & by how long tyme

Itm wheder the seyd Thomas Westwood aft<sup>r</sup> the deceas of the seid Margarett were peacybly pssessed of the p'mysses by the space of A yere & an half or thereabouts or not,

Itm. wheder the seid Wyllm. Gyrton entrid into the p'mysses and therof expulsed the seid Thomas Westwod And yet kepeth hym from the possession of the same or not

Itm. what ye esteme the seid mease and land to be clerely Worth by Yere.

Ex pte Thomas Westwood cont. Willm. Gyrton p. Antoniu. Skynner testes examinati.

Henry Chauncy of Sabrycheworth in the Countie of Hertf. Esquyr of the Age of fourty yeres swoorne and examynyd the xxix<sup>th</sup> daye of Octobr in the fourth yere of the reign of King Edward the sixt [29 October 1550] sayeth as he supposeth in his conscyence that one John Beltoft late of Sabryggeworth otherwyse Sabbesford aforesd. was seased on An estate of inherytaunce of and in one Messuage xxx<sup>ti</sup> Acres of land Medowe and pasture or therabouts w<sup>t</sup> ther App'tenances called Nydellys sett lying and being in the pysshe of Sabryggeworth aforesd otherwyse Sabbesford Insomoche that the said John Beltoft by his dede indentyd beryng date the fourth daye of Aprell in the xxxvj<sup>th</sup> yere of the reign of Kyng Henry the viij<sup>th</sup> [4 April 1545] dyd geve and grant the said messe. and lands w<sup>t</sup> thapp'tenenances to this deponent and Robt. Gooddaye thelder to hold to them and to there heyres to thuse and behoff of the sd. John Beltoft for t'me of his lyff And after his decesse to thuse and behoff of Margarett then his wiff and of her Assignes to the full end and t'me of xv yeres then next and ymmediatly folowyng after the deth of the sd. John Beltoft And after the end of the sd xv yeres then the p'mysses to remayn to thuse of Edmond Beltoft his brother and to his heyres and assignes for ev' wheruppon the sd John Beltoft dyd execute An estate by v'tue of the seid dede of p'mysses to the use exp'ssed in the said dede that is to say he in ppre pson after the dede being opynly redde dyd delyv' the said dede and the Ryng of the doore of the said Messuage into the hands of this deponent and of the said Goodaye Ther being p'sent John Pery the elder and George Turner and dyv'se other being nowe decessed And sayeth he is p'vey that the sd Edmond Beltoft ys yet lyvyng And ferther is p'vey that the said Margarett late the wyff of the said John Beltoft beforce of the said gyft and conveyance after the dethe of the said John Beltoft her husbond was possessyd of the p'mysses and peaseably toke the pffitts therof to her owne use by the space of iij yeres or thereabouts And ferther sayeth that the said Margarett after the decesse of the said John

Beltoft her late husband dyd marry the said Thomas Westwood which the said Thomas Westwood after maryage had betwene them were peaseably possessed of the seyd tent. and lands by the space of iiij yeres at the lest Also he is p'vey that the said Thomas Westwood after the decesse of the said Margarett was peaceably possessyd of the p'mysses by the space of one yere at the lest And doth knowe that the said Willm. Gyrton ent'yd into the p'mysses and therof expulsyd the said Thom. Westwood And this deponent doth exteime the said Mess. and lands to be of the clere yerely valewe of xl⁸ And other wyse he cannott depose. [Signed] p me Henric. Chauncy.

Robarte Goodaye thelder of Sabrygworthe in the Countie of Hertf. Clothier of the Age of lxviij yeres sworne and examynd the daye and yere above wrytten [29 October 1550] sayethe as he suposethe in his conscience that one John Beltoft late of Sabrigworthe otherwyse Sabbesford was seasid of an estate of inherytaunce of and in one messuage xxx<sup>tt</sup> acres of land medowe and pasture or thereaboutes wythe thappurtenaunces caullyd Nydellys sett liinge and beinge in the pysshe of Sabrygworthe aforsaid otherwyse Sabbesford whiche he knowethe is true by reason that the said John Beltoft by his dede indentyd berynge date the iiij<sup>th</sup> daye of Aprell in the xxxvj yere of the reigne of Kynge Henry the viij<sup>th</sup> [4 April 1545] dyd geve and graunte the said mease and londes wythe thappurtenaunces to this deponent and to Henry Chauncey Esquyer to hold to them and to theire heyres to the use and behoff of the said John Beltoft for terme of hys lyff And after his decesse to the use and behoff of Margarett then hys wyff and of theire assignes to the full yend and terme of xv yeres then next and ymmedyatly foloynge after the [decease of the] said John Beltoft and after the yend of the said xv yeres then the p'mysses to remayne to the use of Edmond Beltoft his brother and to his heyres and assignes for ever wheruppon the said John Beltoft dyd execute an estate by vertue of the said dede of the p'mysses to the use expressyd in the said dede that is to saye he in pprie pson after the dede being openly redd dyd delyver the same dede and the Rynge of the doore of the said messuage into thands of this deponent and of the said Chauncey then beinge p'sent John Pery thelder and George Turner and dyverse other beinge now deceasyd And sayethe he is prevye that the said Edmond Beltoft is yet lyvnge And is also p'vye that the said Margarett late the wyff of the said John Beltoft byforce of the said gyfte and conveyaunce after the dethe of the said John Beltoft her husband was possessyd of the premysses and peaseably tooke the proffets therof to her owne use by the space of iiij yeres or therabouts And further sayeth that the said Margarett after the decesse of the said John Beltoft her late husband did mary the said Thomas Westwood which said Thomas Westwood and Margarett after maryage hadd betwene them were peaseably possessyd of the said tenement and landes by the space of iiij yeres at the lest Also he is p'rvye that the said Thomas Westwood after the decesse of the said Margarett was peaceably possessyd of the premysses by the space of one yere at the lest And dothe knowe that that [sic] the said Willm. Gyrton enteryd into the premysses and therof expulsyd the said Thoms. Westwood who yet kepyth the same from the possession of the said Thoms. Westwood And this deponent dothe exteime the Meese and londes to be of the clere yerely valewe of xl⁸ And other wyse he cannott depose.

George Turner of Sappisford in the Countie of Hertf. husbandman of the Age of fyfty yeres sworne and examynyd the xviij<sup>th</sup> daye of Aprell in the fyft yere of the said Kyng's reign [18 April 1551] sayeth he is p'vey that one John Beltoft late of Sabrygeworth als. Sabbesford aforesaid was seased takyng the pffetts of An estate of inherytance of and in one messuage xxx$^{ti}$ Acres of lond medowe and pasture or therabouts w$^t$ there App'tenances callyd Nydellys sett lying and being in Sabrygeworth als. Sabbysford aforesaid And further he sayeth that the said John Beltoft being so seased of the said p'mysses by his dede indented beryng date in Aprell in the xxxvj$^{th}$ yere of the reign of the late Kyng of famous memory Kyng Henry the viij$^{th}$ [1544–45]* dyd geve and grant the said Messe and londs w$^t$ ther App'tenancs to one Henry Chacy the elder and Robt. Goodaye the elder To have to them and to there heyres to thuse and behof of the said John Beltoft for t'me of his lyff And after his decesse to thuse of Margarett then his wyff and of her Assignes unto the end and t'me of xv yeres then next Immediatly folowyng after the deth of the said John Beltoft And after the end of the said xv yeres then to thuse of Edmund Beltoft his brother and of his heyres for ev' Wheruppon the said John Beltoft executyd An estate of the p'mysses and delyv'yd possession of the same to the said Chacy and Goodaye by delyv'e of the Ryng of the doore of the said Messuage to them Ther being p'sent one Payn one John Pery John Galuwaye Richard Garland Denys Adam and this deponent And sayeth that the said Margarett the late wyff of the said John Beltoft by reason of the said gyft and conveyance after the decesse of the said John Beltoft her husbond was possessyd of the p'mysses and peaseably toke the p'ffetts therof to her owne use by the space of v yeres or therabouts to his remembrance Also this deponent is p'vey that the sd Margarett after the deth of the said John Beltoft her late husbond dyd mary the said Thoms. Westwood which Westwood and Margarett after the maryage betwene them were peaseably possessed of the said tent and lands by the space of towe yeres or therabouts to his remembrance And he doth p'fetly remembre that the said Thoms. Westwood after the decesse of the said Margarett was peaseably possessyd of the p'mysses by the space of a yere and A half w$^{th}$in lyttle And sayeth that Willm. Gyrton ent'yd into the p'ymsses and therof expulsyd the said Thoms. Westwood who yet kepyth the said Westwood from the possession of the same wych Messe. and lands be Clerely worth xl$^s$ by the yere as he supposeth And otherwise he cannott depose. (Chancery Proceedings, Town Depositions, Bundle 30.)

Interogatores for Witnesses to be examinid on the pte of Willm. Gyrton agaynst Thomas Westwood.

Imprimis whether on Richard Beltoft was seasid in his demeane as of fee of and in one Mesuage xxx Acres of lond in Sabbridgeworthe called Nidelles yf he wer whether he enfeffid therof on Thomas Leventhorppe and other or who wer his feoffes yf he ded & to whose use.

Itm whether the said Richard Beltoft ordeinyd and made any Will or Testament yf he ded whether he willid that his feofees shud stand and be seasid of the p'mysses to the use of Chrystian then his wiffe uto the full age of Jhon his sonne the Remaynder therof To the sayde John Beltoft and to the heyres of his body lawfully begotten And who were the sayd Richardes executores.

Itm whether the sayd John Beltoft by the sufferaunce of the said feoffees entrid into the p'misses and yf he did by how longe tyme.

Itm what corne and graine of the Compleyn'nts do Remayne thresshed and unthreshed in the sayd howse and to what valewe.

*The exact date, as it appears above, was 4 April 1545.

375

Itm whether the Complen'nt migh have had all that his corne and grayne that Remaynid in the sayd howse.

Itm whether yt any of these deponents ev' had or hathe the last Will and Testament of the sayd Richard or did ev' see it or hard it or Red it and yf they did here it Red who did Red it & where and how longe synce.

Itm whether the [said] John did ev' enfeoffe on Henry Chauncy and other of the londs in contencyon ye or no and yf he so did to what use the same was and howe longe before his deathe and whether he wer then of pfect memory or not And whether he sealid the deade of foeffement or not.

Itm whether the sayd John Beltoft declared and sayd at the Deathe or at any tym before y' he could not geve the landes and tenets in contention from the sayd Gyrtonis Wiffe for then he should do her Wronge and breake his fatheres Will.

Ex parte Willi. Gyrton v'sus Thomam Westwood testes examynati p Willm. Bromley.

Richard Beltofte of Sabridgeworthe in the Countie of Hertf. & of the age of xxx yeres or more sworne and examyned the xiiij[th] daye of Octobre in the fourthe yere of the reigne of o' sov'aigne lord Edward the sixt, &c. [14 October 1550], saieth and disposethe by v'tue of his othe that he doth not ko [i. e., know] whether one Richard Beltofte was seasyd in his demeane as of fee of and in one mesuage xxx acres of land in Sabridgeworth called Nidelles or not k[nowe]th whether he enfeoffed any psone or psones therof or not nev'thelesse he saieth that he did dwell with one John Beltofte the son of the said Richard Beltofte by the space of xx yeres together or therabouts in the said house called Nydelles in whiche tyme he saieth the same John Beltofte fell sicke and was likely then to have died and at the same tyme he saieth he hard the same John Beltofte in the said house call for his fathers last will which being brought to hym was delyv'yd unto one Thomas Helam Curate there then being p'sent to reade it who at the same tyme reade it ou[t] before the same John Beltofte this depo' and dyvers other whom he nowe remembreth not wherin he saiethe he remembreth well that the same Thomas Helam amongst other things reade at the same tyme that the said Richard gave or willid the p'misses to remayne to John his sonn and the heyres of his body lawfully begotten and for lacke of soche issue to remayne to his son laurence and the heyres of his body lawfully begotten and for lacke of soche issue to remayne to Edmond his son and the heyres of his body lawfully begotten and for lacke of soche issue to remayne to his son Thomas and the heyres of his body lawfully begotten and if all his sones should die without issue of their bodyes lawfully begotten then he willed the same to be sold and the money therof comyng to be devyded bytwene his two doughters but what be their names he remembreth not nor can any more or otherwise depose in this matter.

Michaell Waller of Sabridgworth in the said Countie of Hertf. & of the age of xxxj yeres sworne and examyned the daie and yere abovesaid [14 October 1550] saieth and disposeth by v'tue of his othe that as by report of dyvers aunciant old men of Sabridgeworth as namely John Pery the elder and Robert Nodds he k[nowe]th that one Richard Beltofte was seasyd in his demeane as of fee of and in one mesuage and xxx acres of land in Sabrridgeworthe called Nidelles and as by the said report he saieth that the sayd Richard Beltofte enfeoffed therof one leventhorpe and other but to what use they were enfeoffed he k[nowe]th not nev'thelesse he saieth that aboute vij yeres past or more [i. e., about 1543] one John

Beltofte late of Sabridgeworth being sick in the said house called Nidelles and like to have died sent for one Thomas Elam Clerke Curate there to make his Will and mynistre the sacrement unto hym and also sent for this depo$^t$ and dyvers other of his neighbors to heare his will red and then being p'sent Richard Beltofte and William lyon the said John Beltofte called for his fathers will wherupon ther was a will brought to hym made in the name of Richard Beltofte his father whiche was there reade openly by the said Thomas Elam in the hearing of this depo$^t$ and the psones abovesaid wherin amongest other things he saieth the said Thomas Elam read that the said Richard Beltofte gave the p'misses to the said John Beltofte his son and to the heyres of his body lawfully begotten and if the same John should die without issue of his body lawfully begotten then he willed that laurence his son should have it to hym and the heyres of his body lawfully begotten and if laurence should die without issue lawfully begotten of his body then that Edmond his son should have it to hym and the heyres of his body lawfully begotten and if Edmond should die without issue of his body lawfully begotten then he willed that Thomas his son should have it to hym and the heyres of his body lawfully begottyn and if all his sons should die without issue of their bodyes lawfully begotten then he willed it to be sold and ptyd betwyne his two doughters but what be their names he nowe remembrethe not but this depo$^t$ saieth that by all the tyme of the remembraunce of this depo$^t$ the said John Beltofte did occupie the p'misses And saieth he k[nowe]th not that the said John Beltofte did at any tyme enfeoffe one Henry Chancy or any other of the lands in contencion or any pcell therof Albeit he saieth that he hath hard the said John Beltofte being in helthe declare and saie that he could not geve the lands and tents. in contention from the said Gyrton his wif for then he should do her wrong and breake his fathers will but more or otherwise he saieth he cannot depose. [Signed] Mychaell Waller.

John Hellam of Sabridgeworth in the said Countie of Hertf. & of the age of xlj yeres or more sworne and examynd the thyrd daie of November in the yere abovesaid [3 November 1550] saith and esposeth by v'tue of his othe that as by report he k[nowe]th one Richard Beltofte was seasyd in his demeane as of fee of and in one mesuage and xxx acres of land in Sabridgeworth called Nidelles and enfeoffed therof one Thomas leventhorppe and one whose name he nowe remembreth not to the use of Christian then his wyff unto the full age of John his son The remaynder therof to the said John Beltofte and to the heyres of his body lawfully begotten and ordeyned and made his last will and testm$^t$ therby willing that his feoffes should stand and be seasyd of the p'misses to the use aforesaid but he k[nowe]th not whome he made his Executors and as by the report he saieth that the said John Beltofte was put in possession of the p'misses by the said Thomas leventhorp at the tyme of his full age and the said Christian put oute of the same but howe longe the same John Beltofte was in possession therof this depo$^t$ k[nowe]th not but he saieth he k[nowe]th hym in possession at Michaelmas was xiij yeres [i. e., on 29 September 1537] and he contynued in possession therof till his deathe and he died about seynt Barthilimew tyde was fyve yeres [i. e., about 24 August 1545] and saieth he dothe not nowe remembre what or howe moche corne and grayne of the Complaynants did remayne threshed or un-threshed in the said house not with standing that he made a taile therof but he saieth that all the same corne and grayne except a little howse [*the two last words are indistinct and may not be correct*] of pease conteynyng by estimacon aboute foure or fyve busshells was redelyved agayne unto the said Complaynant by the said Richard [sic] Gyrton in the p'sence of this depo^t being Constable Thomas Sedcole William Browne and dyvers other whose names he nowe remembreth not and at the same tyme he saieth that the said Complaynant might have had the said pease likewyse or a recompense therfore whether he wold but this depo^t hath not nor nev' had the said last will and testam. of the said Richard nor yet at any tyme see or heare it red but he saieth he hath hard one John Kyrkham report that he hath red the said will And this depo^t sayeth that aboute two yeres next before the deathe of the said John Beltofte this depo^t demaunded of the same John Beltofte who should have his land after his deathe and he made answer agayne that Megge his doughters doughter nowe wiffe of the said Richard [sic] Gyrton should have it or ells he should do her wronge but as by report afterwards he conceyvyd displeasure towards her for that she bestwoed herself upon the said William Gyrton being then but a pore yonge man and unlykely to thrive and therfore wold have sought wayes if he could to have put her from it but otherwise he saieth he cannot depose.  [The mark of the deponent.]

John Kyrkham of Shynglehall in the parishe of Shabridgeworth servyng man and servant unto Edward Leventhorppe Esquyer of the age of xliij yeres or thereabouts sworn and axamyned the daie and yere last above writtyn [3 November 1550] saieth and deposeth by v'tue of his othe that he doth not ko [i. e., know] whether Richard Beltofte was seasyd in his demeane as of fee or otherwyse of and in one mesuage and xxx acres of land in Sabridgeworth or any pcell therof or not nev' the lesse he saieth that about fyve yeres past [i. e., about 1545] at whiche tyme one John Beltofte late of Sabridgeworth aforsaid lay on his death bed in the custody of the same John Beltofte he did see a will in pchement made in the name of the said Richard Beltofte wherby amongst other things therin conteynd he saieth it apperyd that the said Richard Beltofte gave the p'misses unto John Beltofte and the heyres of his body lawfully begotten and for lacke of soche issue to remayne to one or other of the Beltofts (whose name he remembreth not) and to the heyres of his body lawfully begotten and for lacke of soche issue of the said John Beltofte and the other p'sones recytyd in the said will he willyd the p'misses to remayne to two sisters (whose names he now remembreth not) and the heyres of their two bodyes lawfully begotten and the said John Beltofte confessed the same to be his fathers will and said he must do as he was directyd by the same will and then det'myned to send it to Mr Cocke late solicit^r to the late noble Kat'yn Quene of England decessed to have his advise therin and it was then delyv'yd to one Dennys Adam and William Garland who went therwith oute of said house called Nidelles and said that they wold go to the said Mr Cocke but whether they so did or not he k[nowe]th not nor remembreth the conclusion of the rest of the same remaynders nor can any more otherwise depose in this matter.  [Signed] By me John Kyrkhm   (Chancery Proceedings, Town Depositions, Bundle 18.)

### Decree int. Westwood et Gyrton.

Where matter of varyaunce hath dependyd in thys court betwene Thomas Westwood playntyf and Willm. Gyrton def. for and touchyng a messe and xxx acres of land and pasture w^t thapp^atten^ances in Sabrychesford in the county of Hartf, the sayd compleyn^ante claymyng the same for terme of xv yeres by a feoffamanent made by one John Beltoft a wyll declared upon the same to Margaret hys Wyfe for the terme of xv yeres after hys deceas Which Margaret after the deceas of the sayd John

Beltofte dyd mary the sayd compleynaunt And the sayd def. p'tendyng to avoyd the sayd inte'st for terme of yeares by reason of a former conveyance ôf entayle made of the p'mysses Wherunder Margaret the Wyf of the said Gyrton is heyre apon the delybat hearing of Which sayd matter beyng at pfytt Issue and apon the hearyng of the deposycons of Wytnesses of both pties and upon pusyng of their sev'all evydencs the sayd pties by mediacon of the sayd Court dyd submyt them selfs to thordre of the same Court and that the same ordre shuld be decreed by the same court for a fynall end of the same matter Wherupon it is this last day of Novembr in this p'sent fyveth yere of the Raigne of our sov'aigne lord kyng Edward the syxt [30 November 1551] by the grace of God of England Fraunce and ireland kynge defendor of the fayth and in yerth the supreme hedd of the churche of England and Ireland by the mutuall assents and full consents of both the sayd parties orderid and decreed by the right honorable Syr Rychard Ryche knyght lord Ryche and lord Chauncelour of England and by the Court of Chancery that the sayd Wyllyam Gyrton and hys sayd Wyfe hys executors and assignes shall peasubly have hold occupye and enioye the sayd tent. and p'mysses with thapp°ten°unces and the Issues and p'fytts of the same from the feast of saynt Mychell tharchangell last past [29 September 1551] duryng fourc yeres from thensfurth next ensuyng Without lett trouble or int'upcyon of the sayd Westwood or of any other by hys int'est the sayd Gyrton and hys Wyfe hys and their heyres executors or assignes [paying] a yerely rent of xlvj s., viij d. at the feasts of thanuncyacyon of our ladye and seynt Mychell tharchangell by evyn porcyons And that after the ende of the sayd foure yeres the sayd Gyrton and hys sayd Wyfe their heyres executors and assignes shall pmytt and suffre the sayd Westwood hys executors or assignes peasably to entre into the p'mysses and to have hold and inioye the same Without lett int'upcyon or impedyment of the sayd Gyrton and hys Wyfe their heyres executors and assignes duryng fyve other yeres next ensuyng after thende of the sayd foure yeres Without anythyng payeng for the same and after thend of the sayd fyve yeres that the sayd Westwood his executors and assignes shall relynguysshe & leave the possessyon of the p'mysses. (Chancery Proceedings, Decrees, Roll 6, No. 76.)

## II

[Beltoft v. Westwood, a suit for the possession of a tenement, etc., in Sawbridgeworth called Currants, 1549–1551.]

[For the Bill of Complaint of Richard Beltoft against Thomas Westwood see REGISTER, vol. 68, pp. 84–85.]

[For the Answer of Thomas Westwood to the Bill of Complaint of Richard Beltoft see ib., pp. 85–86.]

[For the Interrogatories for Witnesses to be examined in behalf of Richard Beltoft against Thomas Westwood and the Depositions of Michael Waller, John Hongston, John Tredegold, and Robert Chauncy see ib., pp. 86–90.]

[The Interrogatories for Witnesses to be examined in behalf of Thomas Westwood against Richard Beltoft and the Depositions of four witnesses, which had not been discovered when the previous article on the English ancestry of the American Belknaps was published in 1914, are here presented.]

Interrogator ad exaiand testes ex pte Thome Westwood contra Ricu Beltofte.

Imp'mis whyther John Beltofte were verey owner and seased of the lands and Tents. nowe in varyaunce betwene the said parties called Currans lienge and beinge in Sabbysford in the Countye of Hertf.

Itm. whyther he so beinge therof seased dyd therof Infeoff John Payne thelder & George Mathewe to have to them & there heires in fee to thuse of the said John Beltofte for the terme of his lyfe and after his decesse to thuse of Marg'ett his wyfe and of her heires ye or no.

Itm. whyther the said Thoms Westwood and Marg'ett his wyfe late wyff of the said John Beltofte after the decesse of the said John Beltofte were seased of the p'mysses and toke the pffytts thereof.

Itm. whyther the said Thomas Westwood had any Childe by the said Marg'tt his wyff and what was the name or names of the said Children.

Ex pte Thome Westwood con. Ricu Beltoft p Antoniu. Skynner tests examinati.

Rauff Rooke of Sappesford in the Countye of Herf. husbandman of the Age of fyfty and towe yeres sworne and examynd the viij th daye of Novembr. in the third yere of the reign of Kyng Edward the sixt [8 November 1549] sayeth that he knewe John Beltoft by the space of xvj yeres next before his decesse seasyd as very owner to hym and to his heres for ev' of the lands and tents. nowe being in varyaunce betwene the seyd ptyes called Currans lying and being in Sabbysford in the sd Countye of Hertf. insomoche the deponent doth remember that the sd. John Beltoft bought the sd. lands and tents, of one Mr Chancy. And he sayeth that the sd. John Beltoft being seased as before he hath declared of the sd. p'mysses that he dyd infeffe by dede A lyttle befor Bartilmewe tyde last past was fyve yeres [before 24 August 1544] John Payne the elder and George Mathewe to have to them and to there heyres to thuse of the sd. John Beltoft for the t'me of his lyff and after his decesse to thuse of Margarett his wyff and of her heyres insomoche that one John Galuwaye being namyd in A lre of Attorny in the said dede dyd delyv' possession of the p'mysses to the sd. Payne to thuse exp'ssyd in the said dede by delyv'ie of the Ryng of the doore in a tent. uppon the strete syde in Sappysford aforesd. Then being p'sent this deponent Henry Chancy Gent. and Willm. Tredgold And sayeth that Thomas Westwood and Margaret his wyff late the wyff of the sd. John Beltoft after the same John Beltoftes decesse were seased of the p'mysses and toke the pffetts therof Also he sayeth that the sd. Thomas Westwood had ij Children by the sd. Margarett his wyff the elder being namyd Thomas Westwood and the other being namyd Nicholus Westwood And otherwyse he cannot depose.

Willm. Tredgold of Sappysford in the Countye of Hertf. husbondman of the Age of xxxiij te yeres sworne and examynd the daye and yere above wryttn [8 November 1549] sayeth that he knewe John Beltoft seased as v'y owner takyng the pffetts of the lands and tents. nowe being in debate betwene the sd. ptyes callyd Currans lying and being in Sappysford aforesd. long before his decesse And the said John Beltoft being so seasyd of the p'mysses A lyttle before Bartilimewe tyd last past was fyve yeres [before 24 August 1544] to his remembraunce dyd infeffe therof by dede one John Payn the elder and George Mathew to have to them and to there heyres in fee to thuse of the sd. John Beltoft for t'me of his lyff and after his decesse to thuse of Margarett his wyff and of her heyres

And possession was delyv'yed by one John Galawaye to thuse of the sd. Payne to thuse exp'ssyd in the sd. dede then being p'sent Rauff Rooke & Henry Chawcy Gent. And he sayeth assone as ev' that the estate was executed this deponent came to the tent. in Sappesford where the said estate was exacutyd And then the said Payne sayed to this deponent in this wyse in effect folowyng Godman Tredgold we sent for you to the intent you shuld have been on the estate execuyng for yo<sup>r</sup> Sister And we have doon before you dyd come notw<sup>th</sup>standyng I do declare unto you that wee have takyn possession to thuse of her and of her heyres And therunto I wold that you bere wytnes Them heryng the sd. coicacon [i. e., communication] the sd. Chawcy and the said Rooke And sayeth that the said Thoms. Westwood and Margarett his wyff late the wyff of the said John Beltoft after the death of the said John Beltoft were seased of the p'mysses and toke the pfetts of them And sayeth that the said Thoms. Westwood had ij Children by the said Margaret that ys to say Thoms. Westwood and Nicholus Westwood And otherwyse he cannot depose as he sayeth.

George Mathewe of Sabbsford in the countye of Hertf. clothier of the Age of xxx<sup>te</sup> yeres sworne and examynd the xiiij<sup>th</sup> daye of Novembr in the yere above writtyn [14 November 1549] sayeth that John Beltoft was v'y owner by his owne report and was seased of the lands and tents. nowe being in varyaunce betwene the said ptyes called Currans lying and being in Sabbysford aforesd. at the tyme of his decesse and long tyme before And sayeth that the said John Beltoft being so seased of the p'mysses this deponent ys p'vy that he dyd infeffe therof by dede one John Payn thelder and George Mathewe to have to them and to there heyres in fee to thuse of the said John Beltoft for t'me of his lyff And after his decesse to thuse of Margarett his wiff and of her heyres forev' wheruppon the said John Beltoft by one Galuwaye being namyd in a lre. of Attorney in the said dede did delyv' possession of the p'mysses to the said Payn and Mathewe to thuse exp'ssyd in the said dede And as soone as that the estate was executyd this deponent being sent for dyd come to them And then the said Payn dyd [*word illegible*] this deponent what they had doon then and there being p'sent one Rauff Roke Mr Chacy Gent. this deponent the said Galuwaye and Tredgold and other And he sayeth he is p'vy that the said Thomas Westwood and Margarett his wiff late the wyff of the said John Beltoft were seased of the p'mysses and toke the pffetts of them And further this deponent ys c'teyn that the said Thomas Westwood had towe Childern by the said Margarett his wyff the one of them being namyd Thomas Westwood and the other Nicholus Westwood And otherwise he cannott depose.

Henry Chauncey of Sabbrycheworth in the Countye of Hertf. Gent. of the Age of xl<sup>te</sup> yeres sworne and examynyd the daye and yere abov wrytten [14 November 1549] sayeth he ys p'vey that John Beltoft late decessyd was v'y owner and seased to hym and to his heyres forev' of the lands and tents. nowe being in varyaunce betwene the sayd ptyes called Currauns lying and being in Sabrycheworth aforesaid And this deponent ys p'vey that the said John Beltoft being so seasyd of the p'mysses dyd therof infeffe by dede one John Payn and George Mathewe to have to them and to there heyres in fee to thuse of the said John Beltoft for t'me of hys lyff And after his decesse to thuse of Margarett his wyff and of her heyres forev' which he knows ys true for he devysed and caused to be engrossed the said dede And sayeth that the said John Beltoft made lyv'e and seased of the said tents. and lands accordyng by one John Galuwaye his Attorney namyd in the said dede by delyv'ie of the ringe of doore of the said tent. into the hands of the said Payn There being p'sent this deponent which redd the said dede the said Payn Rauff Rooke Willm. Tredgold and other whose names he remembryth not And as this deponent doth [*two or three words missing, the paper being torn*] said Thomas Westwood and Margarett his wyff late wyff of the said John Beltoft after the decesse of the said John Beltoft were peaseably seased of the p'mysses and toke the yssues and pffetts of them And further as this deponent hath herd it comynly reportyd the said Thomas Westwood had c'ten childcrn by the said Margarett his late wyff but what the name or names of the said Chyldern be this deponent cannot depose And otherwyse he cannott saye. (Chancery Proceedings, Town Depositions, Bundle 30.)

[For the Decree of the Court of Chancery in this suit of Beltoft *v.* Westwood, dated 24 April 1551, see REGISTER, vol. 68, p. 90.]

The records given above, combined with those published in 1914, make necessary the following revision of the early generations of the pedigree of that date. Mr. Charles A. Bernau's summary of the two Chancery cases and his conclusions about the parentage of Richard Beltoft, the grandfather of the settler at Lynn, Mass., have been accepted, with a few changes.

1. RICHARD BELTOFT, of Sawbridgeworth, co. Herts, died probably in the first decade of the sixteenth century (1501–1510) or perhaps even earlier, since his son John, who was under twenty-one years of age when Richard died, had a granddaughter who was married as early as 1545, and therefore John could hardly have been born later than 1490. He married CHRISTIAN ———, who survived him. No proof has been found that she was the mother of his children, although this is probable.

From the records in the Chancery suit of Westwood *v.* Gyrton, 1550–51 (*vide supra,* pp. 266–278) it appears that Richard Beltoft * owned a messuage, with thirty acres of land, meadow, and pasture, situated in Sawbridgeworth and called Nidelles, the annual value of which was estimated in 1550 at 40s. This messuage, etc., he settled upon his wife, with the proviso that he should retain the use of it as long as he lived and that after his death the possession of it should be in accordance with the terms of his will; and he appointed Thomas Leventhrop and others as trustees, to hold the property in trust for these purposes. Unfortunately this will is now lost; but the substance of its provisions in reference to this property is known from the depositions of some of the witnesses in the above-mentioned Chancery suit.

The testator, according to these depositions, directed in his will that his wife Christian should enjoy the property until his son John should attain his majority, when it should pass to the said son John and the heirs of his body, and in default of such issue to the testator's son Laurence and the heirs of his body, and in default of such issue to the testator's son Edmund and the heirs of his body, and in default of such issue to the testator's son Thomas and the heirs of his body, and in default of such issue the property, according to one account of the

*Pages 367-369, this volume.

will, was to be sold and the proceeds were to be divided between the testator's two daughters (whose names are not given in the depositions), while, according to another account of the will, the property itself was to go to the testator's two daughters and the heirs of their bodies. From the description of the will it is, therefore, clear that Richard Beltoft, when he made his will, had only four sons living, and that, if he had had other sons, they had died without issue. Therefore Henry Beltoft (No. 2 of the pedigree printed in 1914) could not have been a son of this Richard and a brother of John and Edmund, as was suggested in the earlier article on this family.

On the death of Richard Beltoft his widow Christian, in accordance with her husband's will, came into possession of the property; and, when the son John came of age, she was obliged to surrender it to him. It is stated that John was in possession of Nidelles at least fourteen years before 1550, that is, not later than 1536. However, he must have come into possession many years before 1536, for, as stated above, he could hardly have been born later than 1490, and would therefore have attained his majority not later than 1511. Since John had "heirs of his body," the other remainders mentioned in his father's will never came into force.

Children:

2. i. JOHN, b. probably not later than 1490.
3. ii. LAURENCE, named in his father's will.
  iii. EDMUND, living 29 Oct. 1550; d. probably before 1558, when the parish registers of Sawbridgeworth begin.
  iv. THOMAS, named in his father's will.
  v. A DAUGHTER, mentioned in her father's will.*
  vi. A DAUGHTER, mentioned in her father's will.*

2. JOHN BELTOFT (*Richard*) of Sawbridgeworth, co. Herts, born probably not later than 1490, died 4 Feb. 1545/6. He married first ISABEL ———; and secondly MARGARET TREDGOLD, who was probably many years younger than her husband, for her brother was only thirty-three years old in 1549. She survived John Beltoft, married secondly, probably in 1546, Thomas Westwood (who in 1551 was of Laver-Magdalen, co. Essex), and died about 25 July 1548, possibly in childbirth, when her son, Nicholas Westwood, was born. By her second husband, who survived her, she had two sons, Thomas Westwood, who was three years old in 1549, and Nicholas Westwood, who died in or before 1549.

On attaining his majority John Beltoft, in accordance with the terms of his father's will, succeeded his father's widow in the possession of the messuage, etc., in Sawbridgeworth called Nidelles, which he held until his death. He owned also one tenement, with a garden and two acres of arable land or thereabouts thereunto belonging, situated in Sawbridgeworth and called Currants, which he bought from a Mr. Chauncey in or before 1530. The Chancery suit of Westwood *v.* Gyrton, in 1550–51,

*The place to be assigned to each daughter in the list of children is not known, for the four sons are evidently named first, in the order of their births.

was for the possession of Nidelles; the Chancery suit of Beltoft v. Westwood, in 1549–1551, was for the possession of Currants.

By his first wife John Beltoft had a daughter named Joan, who married William Waller and died not later than 1543, leaving a daughter, Margaret Waller, known also as Meg, who married about 1545 William Gyrton, thereby incurring the displeasure of her grandfather, because William Gyrton was "but a pore yonge man and unlykely to thrive." On the death of her grandfather, her mother being already dead, Margaret (Waller) Gyrton was undoubtedly heir to the property called Nidelles, because according to the will of her great-grand-father, Richard Beltoft, this property was to descend to John Beltoft and the heirs of his body. That John Beltoft was well aware of the terms of his father's will and that he acknowl-edged his granddaughter as the one who was to succeed to Nidelles after his death is proved by the following two well-authenticated incidents:

(1) In or before 1543 John Beltoft lay sick in the house called Nidelles, and it was thought then that he was dying. He sent for the curate, Rev. Thomas Elam (or Helam), to draw up his will for him and to administer the last sacrament. He sent also for his neighbors, Michael Waller and William Lyon, and John Kyrkham also was present, although later, in his depo-sition, Kyrkham makes a mistake of about two years in fixing the date of this incident. Another who was present was Rich-ard Beltoft (No. 4 of this pedigree and No. 3 of the pedigree of 1914), whose relationship to John Beltoft is not stated, but he was probably a nephew* of John, for in 1550 his age was given as thirty years or more and he deposed that he had lived with John Beltoft, in the house called Nidelles, for about twenty years before John's death. On the occasion referred to John Beltoft called for his father's will, which was in his possession, and it was handed to Rev. Thomas Elam to read aloud. When it had been read, John Beltoft said that he must act in accordance with it, and he decided to send it to Mr. Cocke, solicitor to Queen Katherine, for his advice. The will was then handed to Dennis Adam and William Garland, who took it with them when they left the house, saying that they would go to Mr. Cocke, but whether they actually did see Mr. Cocke is unknown.

(2) About this same time John Beltoft's neighbor, John Helam, asked him who would have his land after his death, and he replied that Meg, his daughter's daughter, should have it, for otherwise he would be doing her a wrong and acting con-trary to his father's will.

John Beltoft, however, recovered from this illness, and lived some two years longer. During this time his granddaughter

*Mr. Charles A. Bernau thinks it more likely that Richard Beltoft was a grandnephew of John Beltoft. See below, p. 287, footnote.

incurred his displeasure by marrying William Gyrton, and John Beltoft tried to prevent the property from descending to her. Therefore, on 4 Apr. 1545, he made Henry Chauncey, Sr., and Robert Goodday, Sr., trustees, to hold in trust the property called Nidelles on the following terms, namely, that he should retain the use of it so long as he lived, that after his death his wife Margaret and her assigns should hold it for fifteen years, and that it should then go to his brother Edmund Beltoft and his heirs or assigns; and to these trustees he formally delivered possession of the said premises in the presence of several witnesses.

The attempt of John Beltoft to prevent his granddaughter from succeeding to Nidelles led to litigation after his death. Margaret, his widow, was in possession of Nidelles for a few years after John's death, and by her will left the unexpired portion of her term of years in the property, with all the rest of her goods, to her second husband, Thomas Westwood. She died about 25 July 1548, and about a year or a year and a half after her death William Gyrton, husband of John Beltoft's granddaughter, got possession of the property, but was turned out of it by force by Thomas Westwood, with the help of John Toller, Richard Underwood, and Ralph Roke. For this proceeding these four men were indicted, 29 Mar. 1550, at a court held before Sir Ralph Saddler, Knight, and other judges, at Puckeridge, co. Herts, and Gyrton obtained a writ of restitution, by virtue of which he regained possession of the premises two days later, and cast out Westwood's goods, which consisted of wheat, barley, oats, pease, hay, hives of bees, and fuel, the quantity of each article being later in dispute. Thereupon Westwood filed a bill of complaint in Chancery against Gyrton; Gyrton made his answer to the same; Westwood made his replication to Gyrton's answer; Gyrton made his rejoinder to Westwood's replication; witnesses were heard both for Westwood and for Gyrton; and the Court, on 30 Nov. 1551, decreed that Gyrton and his wife should enjoy the premises for four years, as from Michaelmas 1551 (i. e., to 29 Sept. 1555), paying Westwood 46s. 8d. rent per annum, that for the next five years (i. e., to 29 Sept. 1560) Westwood should have possession free of any rent, and that at the expiration of these five years he should relinquish possession to Gyrton. (Cf. the records of this suit given above. They show, *inter alia*, that Edmund Beltoft, brother of John Beltoft, was still living on 29 Oct. 1550.)

The other property owned by John Beltoft in Sawbridgeworth, the tenement, with a garden and two acres of arable land or thereabouts thereunto belonging, called Currants, which, as already stated, he had bought from a Mr. Chauncey not later than 1530, and which, in the estimation of some of the witnesses in the case of Beltoft v. Westwood, had in 1549 an annual value of from 13s. 4d. to 17s., that is, considerably less than one-half the annual value of Nidelles, was also in litigation in 1549–1551, a few years after John's death. A little while before the Feast of St. Bartholomew (24 Aug.), 1544, Beltoft appointed John Payne, Sr., and George Mathewe as trustees, to hold the property in trust, providing that he should retain the use of it as long as he lived and that his wife Margaret and her heirs should have it after his death; and formal delivery of the property was thereupon made to the trustees. Soon, however, deciding to make a new settlement of this property, in order to provide for Richard Beltoft, probably John's nephew, who was born about 1520 and had lived with him at Nidelles from early boyhood, since about 1525 or 1526, John Beltoft, about Candlemas Day (2 Feb.), 1544/5, appointed Henry Chauncey and others as trustees, to hold the property in trust, providing that after his death his wife Margaret should possess it for twenty years, if she should live so long, and that then it should go to Richard Beltoft and his heirs, and, in default of such, to Edmund Beltoft (John's brother) and his heirs; and formal delivery of possession was made to Margaret and to Richard, Margaret, having had no children by John Beltoft, apparently making no objection to this new settlement. After the death of John Beltoft his widow, Margaret, took possession of the property, as she was entitled to do under both the first and the second settlement made by her husband. After her death (about 25 July 1548), however, her second husband, Thomas Westwood, remained in possession of the premises, claiming a right to do so under the so-called "courtesy of England" (i. e., the right of a widower to hold for life the property of his late wife) and also in behalf of her heir, Thomas Westwood, Jr. Richard Beltoft, accordingly, who claimed that, under the settlement of Candlemas Day or thereabouts, 1544/5, possession of the premises should have come to him, filed a bill of complaint in Chancery against Thomas Westwood (printed in the REGISTER, vol. 68, pp. 84–85); Westwood made his answer to this bill (ib., pp. 85–86); and Richard Beltoft made his replication, which is lost but is mentioned in the decree of the Court in this suit. Witnesses for the complainant were examined in Oct. 1549 and in Jan. 1549/50 (ib., pp. 86–90), and for the defendant in Nov. 1549 (vide supra, pp. 279–281); and on 24 Apr. 1551 the Court decreed (REGISTER, vol. 68, p. 90) that Westwood and his heirs by his late wife, Margaret, should have the premises for ever more, but that they should pay to Richard Beltoft £6 in two instalments, namely, £3. 6s. 8d. "at the consignment of this decree" and 53s. 4d. in the parish church of Sawbridgeworth on the following Christmas (1551). As this decree was made with the consent of both parties to the suit, it appears that Richard Beltoft compromised his claim for the sum of £6.

386

Child by first wife:

i. JOAN, d. probably not later than 1543; m. WILLIAM WALLER.
Child (surname *Waller*):
1. *Margaret* (*Meg*), living 30 Nov. 1551; m. about 1545 William Gyrton, also living 30 Nov. 1551, the defendant in the Chancery case of Westwood *v.* Gyrton, which has been described above.

3. LAURENCE BELTOFT (*Richard*), named in the will of his father as next in succession, after his elder brother John and the heirs of John's body, to the property called Nidelles, in Sawbridgeworth, co. Herts, died probably before 2 Feb. 1544/5 (Candlemas Day), for he was not mentioned by his brother John in the settlement which John made about that time of the property called Currants in Sawbridgworth, which, after John's widow, Margaret, had held it for twenty years, if she should live so long, was to go to Richard Beltoft and his heirs, and, in default of such, to Edmund Beltoft (younger brother of John and also of Laurence) and his heirs; nor was Laurence mentioned in the settlement which John made on 4 Apr. 1545 of the property called Nidelles, although the younger brother, Edmund Beltoft, and his heirs or assigns, were placed next to John's widow, Margaret, in the succession to this property. If, as is suggested below, Richard Beltoft was a son of Laurence and was for that reason placed before Edmund Beltoft in the succession to Currants, it is probable that Laurence had died when Richard was very young, since Richard had lived with John Beltoft at Nidelles since early boyhood, that is, since 1525 or thereabouts. The only positive information about Laurence Beltoft thus far found is the statement that in his father's will he and the heirs of his body were placed next to his elder brother John and the heirs of John's body in the succession to Nidelles. Probably Laurence Beltoft had the following
Children (order of births unknown):

4. i. RICHARD, b. about 1520.*
ii. ALICE (perhaps a sister of Richard Beltoft), m. at Sawbridgeworth. 14 Apr. 1562, WILLIAM STUBBS.
iii. A DAUGHTER (known to be a sister of Richard Beltoft), m. ———— SUTTON.
Children (surname *Sutton*):
1. *Clement*, ) living at Docksall. co. Essex, 20 Aug. 1594, when
2. *William*, } they were named in the will of their uncle, Rich-
3. *Richard*, ) ard Beltoft, a legacy of 3s. 4d. being left to each.

4. RICHARD BELTOFT (? *Laurence, Richard*), of Sawbridgeworth, co. Herts, husbandman, the testator of 20 Aug. 1594 (see REGISTER, vol. 68. pp. 90–91), who appears as No. 3 in the pedigree published in 1914 and was the grandfather of Abraham Belknap, the settler at Lynn, Mass., was born about 1520, since he deposed 14 Oct. 1550, aged 30 years or more, and was bur-

*For the reasons for the statement that Richard Beltoft was probably a son of Laurence Beltoft see below, under No. 4.

ied at Sawbridgeworth 2 Dec. 1599. He married ———,* who was buried at Sawbridgeworth 17 Jan. 1588/9.

Positive proof of the parentage of this Richard Beltoft has not been found. He was evidently closely related to John Beltoft (2) of Nidelles and Currants, in Sawbridgeworth, for he deposed on 14 Oct. 1550 that he dwelt with John Beltoft, in the house called Nidelles, for about twenty years (that is, from about 1525 or 1526, when he was only five or six years old, to the death of John Beltoft, 4 Feb. 1545/6). He was not John's son or grandson, for in that case he would have succeeded to Nidelles in preference to John's daughter Joan and her daughter Margaret. He was born too late (about 1520) to have been a younger brother of John, and moreover, had he been a son of the first Richard Beltoft, his father in his will would probably have included him among the possible successors to Nidelles. He was not a cousin of John's, for then John would hardly have placed him before his (John's) brother Edmund in the succession to Currants. For the same reason it is very unlikely that this Richard Beltoft was Edmund's son, for one would scarcely name a young man in a settlement and then, in default of his issue, leave the remainder to the young man's father. John had only three brothers, Laurence, Edmund, and Thomas, who, with the heirs of their bodies, were named in that order by their father as successors to Nidelles, in default of John and the heirs of John's body. Richard Beltoft, therefore, was probably a son either of Laurence or of Thomas; and, as Laurence was Edmund's elder brother and the settlement of the succession to Currants made by John about 2 Feb. 1544/5 placed Richard and his heirs before Edmund, it is reasonable to conclude that Richard was probably a son of Laurence.†

Richard Beltoft was the complainant in 1549–1551 in a Chancery suit against Thomas Westwood for the possession of Currants, and he deposed in 1550 in the Chancery suit of Westwood v. Gyrton for the possession of Nidelles. An account of these suits has been given above, under John Beltoft (No. 2). The will of Richard Beltoft, in which he leaves a legacy to his young grandson, Abraham Beltoft (*alias* Belknap), afterwards the settler at Lynn, Mass., shows that he was a well-to-do husbandman. For his children and grandchildren and some of his more remote descendants see the records and pedigree published in the REGISTER in 1914 (vol. 68).

HENRY BELTOFTE, who was buried at Sawbridgeworth, co. Herts, 5 July 1561, could not have been a brother of John Beltoft of Nidelles

*The Christian name of Richard Beltoft's wife is stated in the pedigree of 1914 to have been Elizabeth, but no authority for this name seems to be given.—EDITORS.
†Mr. Charles A. Bernau thinks it more likely that Richard Beltoft was a grandson, rather then a son, of Laurence; but, as Richard was born about 1520, that would hardly be possible, unless the births of Laurence and his elder brother, John, occurred several years earlier than 1490. See above, under No. 1 of this pedigree.

and Currants and of Edmund Beltoft, as was suggested in the REG-ISTER, vol. 68, p. 193. This is proved by the accounts given in the present article of the will of Richard Beltoft (No. 1). His relationship to the other Beltofts of the pedigree remains unknown. The Elizabeth Beltofte who was buried at Sawbridgeworth 14 Jan. 1560/1 may have been his wife.

ABRAHAM BELKNAPP, of Northweald Bassett, co. Essex, yeoman, aged 38 years or thereabouts, deposed 31 Jan., 2 Charles I [31 Jan. 1626/7], in the Chancery suit of Bird v. Westwood and Campe. (Chancery Proceedings. Town Depositions, Bundle 527). He was probably the Abraham Belknap who emigrated to New England and settled at Lynn, Mass., whose son (probably) was buried at Nettes-well, co. Essex, 6 Dec. 1620. (See the REGISTER, vol. 68, pp. 193, 194–195.)

---

## GENEALOGICAL RESEARCH IN ENGLAND

Communicated by the Committee on English and Foreign Research

### COWES OF IPSWICH, MASS.

Contributed by WALTER GOODWIN DAVIS, B.A., LL.B.,
of Portland, Me.

A STUDY of wills and administrations in the probate registries of Devonshire under the name of Cowes and its many variants shows that the name was largely confined to the seacoast country between Exeter and Plymouth, with a marked concentration in the parish of Stoke-in-Teignhead. When the registers of this parish were begun in 1538 the family was already numerous, and it continued so for the succeeding century and a half, a condition which makes publication of the Cowes entries, as a basis for the following article on the ancestry of Giles and Christopher Cowes of Ipswich, Mass., impractical because of their great number. The same statement applies to the probate records, there being twenty-four available documents of the Stoke-in-Teignhead family, all of which have been examined in the search for material for this article. From entries in the parish registers of Stoke-in-Teignhead, from probate records preserved at Exeter, and from sundry New England records the following pedigree has been compiled.

1. WILLIAM COWES, of Stoke-in-Teignhead, co. Devon, possibly that son of William Cowes who was baptized at Stoke-in-Teignhead 4 May 1561, was buried 28 Apr. 1621. He married first, 18 Oct. 1588, ELIZABETH TAPLEY, who was buried 6 Dec. 1593; and secondly, 6 June 1594, HONOR LANGE, who survived him.

In his will, dated 26 Mar. and proved 29 May 1621, he directed that he be buried in the churchyard of Stoke-in-Teignhead, left small legacies to his sons Giles, John, William, and Thomas, to his daughters Charity and Dorothy Cowes and Joan Halley, and to Gideon and Richard Zevy, and named his wife Honor Cowes residuary legatee and executrix. The will was witnessed by Richard Lang and John Simon, and an inventory in the sum of £53 was returned by John

Ford, Gregory Aleygh, and Richard Lang. (Principal Registry, Exeter, co. Devon.)

Children by first wife, recorded at Stoke-in-Teignhead:

i.   ELLINOR, bapt. 4 Oct. 1589.
ii.  JULIAN, bapt. 18 Oct. 1590; m. 8 Dec. 1612 JOHN ZEVIE. She was doubtless the mother of the Gideon and Richard Zevy mentioned in her father's will.

Children by second wife, recorded at Stoke-in-Teignhead:

iii. JOHAN, bapt. 20 Nov. 1595; d. in infancy.
iv.  JOAN, bapt. 14 June 1599; m. before 26 Mar. 1621, when she was a legatee in the will of her father, ——— HALLEY.
v.   CHRISTOPHER, bapt. 8 Nov. 1600; bur. 9 Feb. 1600 [1600/1].
vi.  GILLES, bapt. 21 Feb. 1601 [1601/2]; m. 15 Jan. 1626 [1626/7] MARY CADE, who in her will, dated 2 Feb. 1660 [1660/1] and proved 26 June 1669, left property to John Halley, Hannah Martyn, her godson Giles Cowes, Mary Holley, and Mary Tasker, and devised her land at Knighton in the parish of Hennock, at Higher Rixtell in the parish of Bishop's Teignton, and at Highweek at Tingbridgcend to her son and executor, Gilbert Cowes. (Archdeaconry Court of Exeter.)
     Children, recorded at Stoke-in-Teignhead.
     1.  *John*, bapt. 11 Nov. 1627; bur. 11 Jan. 1629 [1629/30].
     2.  *Gilbert*, bapt. 28 Feb. 1629 [1629/30]; m. 23 Jan. 1662 [1662/3] Marian Clyffe.
vii. CHARITIE, bapt. 9 Aug. 1604; m. 13 Nov. 1623 RICHARD LADIMORE.
viii. JOHN, bapt. 23 Nov. 1606.
ix.  WILLIAM, bapt. 12 July 1609.
2. x. THOMAS, bapt. 9 Nov. 1611.
xi.  DOROTIE, bapt. 19 Oct. 1617.

2.  THOMAS COWES (*William*), of Stoke-in-Teignhead, co. Devon, baptized 9 Nov. 1611, died between 24 Feb. 1680 [1680/1] and 23 Jan. 1681 [1681/2], the dates of the making and proving of his will. He married, 12 Apr. 1640, MARY LUX, who survived him and died between 19 Aug. 1690 and 27 June 1691, the dates of the making and the proving of her will.

In his will he left small gifts to his sons Giles, Thomas, William, and Richard and to his daughters Mary Cowes and Julian Loring, his land called Pegens to his daughter Susanna Cowes, after the death of his wife, and his homestead to his daughter Julian Loring, with the same limitation, and named his wife Mary residuary legatee and executrix. (Archdeaconry Court of Exeter.)

Mary Cowes, his widow, in her will, mentions her sons Giles and Richard, her daughter Mary Coysh [Couch], her grandchildren Robert Lang and Susan and Elizabeth Cowes (children of her deceased son Thomas), her brother John Lux (to whom she gives a parcel of land called Peagens, given to her by her father), and her godchildren Mary Rendall, William Buffett, Elias Payne, and Dorothy Colaton, and leaves the residue of her estate to her daughter Julian Lang, executrix. (Archdeaconry Court of Exeter.)

Children, recorded at Stoke-in-Teignhead:

i.   JULIAN, bapt. 25 Jan. 1640/1; m. (1) ——— LORING; m. (2) between 1680 and 1690 ———— LANG. She was a legatee in the wills of her father and mother.

3. ii. GILES, bapt. 22 Oct. 1642.

iii. THOMAS, a legatee in the will of his father in 1680; d. before 1690, leaving two daughters, *Susan* and *Elizabeth,* who were mentioned in the will of their grandmother.

iv. CHRISTOPHER, bapt. 22 Nov. 1648; d. before 1 Apr. 1677, when administration of his estate was granted to his father and sister Susanna. (Archdeaconry Court of Exeter.)

He emigrated to America, and was a sailor in the ketch *Dove* of Ipswich, Mass., in 1673, his name appearing in an account dated 14 Feb. 1673/4, for a voyage from Ipswich to Barbados. (Records and Files of the Quarterly Courts of Essex County, vol. 5, p. 340.) Although, as stated above, administration on his estate was granted in Devonshire, the amount of the administrator's bond was left blank, and no inventory was filed; and on 11 Aug. 1677 the Essex County Court granted administration to his brother Giles Cowes of Ipswich, it apparently having been decided that this court had proper jurisdiction. (The Probate Records of Essex County, vol. 3, p. 155.)

v. WILLIAM, a legatee in the will of his father, but not mentioned in the will of his mother in 1690.

vi. MARY, m. ———— COYSH [COUCH] before 1690, when she was a legatee in the will of her mother.

vii. ISET, bapt. 3 Dec. 1651; d. in infancy.

viii. RICHARD, b. 20 Nov. 1655; a legatee in the wills of his father and mother.

ix. SUSAN, b. 11 Aug. 1657; a legatee in the will of her father in 1680; not living in 1690.

3. GILES COWES (*Thomas, William*), of Stoke-in-Teignhead, co. Devon, and Ipswich, Mass., baptized at Stoke-in-Teignhead 22 Oct. 1642, died at Ipswich 14 Aug. 1696. He married first, at Ipswich, 29 July 1668, MARY DUTCH, who died 22 Oct. 1672, daughter of Robert and Mary (Kimball) Dutch; and secondly, at Ipswich, 27 Feb. 1672/3, AGNES BERRY, who died, "an antient widow," 15 Sept. 1731, daughter of Thomas Berry.

From a desposition made 21 Mar. 1671/2, in which he stated that he was about twenty-seven years old, it appears that he was fishing at the Isles of Shoals in 1666. (Records and Files of the Quarterly Courts of Essex County, vol. 5, p. 8.) When he settled in Ipswich he was a shipmaster, engaged in a coasting trade, although he may have undertaken voyages to England as well. He was administrator of the estate of his brother Christopher in 1677, and was remembered with small legacies by his father and mother in England in 1680 and 1690. In 1690 he was master of the bark *Speedwell,* which was captured by the French and recaptured by Capt. John Alden at Port Royal. In 1693 he administered the estate of his father-in-law, Thomas Berry, a dyer who came to Ipswich from Barbados, and "Mrs. Cowes personally appeared and prayed further time in bringing in an Inventory in behalf of her Husband." (Essex County Probate Records, vol. 303, p. 116.)

Giles Cowes does not seem to have owned land in Ipswich until 1695, when he bought 8 acres from John Pengry and 3 acres from Bonus Norton. He died intestate, and his widow was appointed administratrix of his estate 19 May 1697. In the account of the division of his property a list of his children appears, as follows: William Cowes, eldest son, Mary Cowes, Hannah Oliver, Agnes Cowes, Elizabeth Cowes, and Giles Cowes. (Essex County Probate Records, vol. 305, p. 295, vol. 306, p. 61.)

The widow of Giles Cowes was assigned a prominent seat in the Ipswich meeting house in 1719/20. In her will, dated 27 July 1722, she left 3s. to her son Giles, "if he come to demand it, he having had a sufficient part of his father's estate," and the residue of her estate to her daughter Elizabeth, wife of John Harris, and her (Elizabeth's) children. Harris and his wife, with whom the testatrix lived, were named executors, and proved the will 23 Oct. 1731. (Essex County Probate Records, vol. 319, pp. 474-475.)

Children by first wife, recorded at Ipswich:

i.   MARY, b. 30 Aug. 1670; living in 1702, when she was the wife of EDWARD DOLIVER and signed a receipt for her share of her father's estate.
ii.  HANNAH, b. 16 Oct. 1672; living in 1701, when she was the wife of JOHN OLIVER of Kittery, Me., who in that year gave a receipt for her share in her father's estate.

Children by second wife, recorded at Ipswich:

iii. THOMAS, b. 15 Nov. 1673; d. in infancy.
iv.  A SON, b. 27 Nov. 1675; d. 6 Dec. 1675.
v.   AGNES, b. 6 Apr. 1681; d. unm. 20 Feb. 1721/2.
vi.  WILLIAM, b. 12 Aug. 1683; living in 1698; not mentioned in his mother's will in 1722.*
vii. ELIZABETH, b. 6 Mar. 1691 [1691/2]; m. (intention recorded at Ipswich, 26 Oct. 1717) JOHN HARRIS, son of John and Grace (Searle) Harris of Ipswich.
viii. GILES, b. 28 Jan. 1692 [1692/3]; d., presumably *s.p.*, in Nov. 1752. He was a tailor in Ipswich in 1717, when he sold all his rights in his father's land to Philip Fowler, his mother buying them back from Fowler in 1718 (Essex County Deeds, vol. 34, p. 252, vol. 35, p. 80). In 1733 he sold to Mary Calef, widow, his rights in the common lands granted to his father's heirs (*ib.*, vol. 69, p. 158).

## SCRUGGS OF SALEM, MASS.

Contributed by WALTER GOODWIN DAVIS, B.A., LL.B.,
of Portland, Me.

THE name Scroggs or Scruggs, fortunately for the cause of euphony, is very uncommon. It is probably of Scotch origin, the names of Robert and Simon de Scrogges and Adam and William del Scrogges appearing in thirteenth century records of that country while in the fifteenth century David del Scrogges was a provost of the town of Aberdeen.

With the exception of an isolated family in Preston-in-Holderness,

*A William Coas, seaman, married in Gloucester, Mass., 5 Feb. 1722/3, Mary Gardner, and his estate was distributed in 1765 to his widow, his son William, and his daughters Mary and Joanna; but possibly he was another Devon sailor.

co. York, most of the name in England can be traced with more or less certainty to Thomas Skeyff *alias* Scrogs, who by his marriage with Agnes Harleston, an heiress, became possessed of the manor of Patmore Hall, Albury, co. Herts, and other extensive property, about the year 1519.* In the inquisition post mortem, taken after his death in 1538, his son Francis Scroggs, aged eighteen and more, was found to be his heir, and two sons by a second marriage, Alexander and Richard Scroggs of Renhold, co. Bedford, have been identified. It is possible, though unproved, that other sons survived, and that one of them founded the family of London merchants, members of the Butchers' Company, with which this article deals and to which Mr. Thomas Scruggs, emigrant to Salem and follower of Anne Hutchinson, belonged.

## FROM PROBATE RECORDS

1. Administration on the goods of JOHN SCROGGES, late of Christ Church [London], intestate, was granted 4 April 1597 to his widow, Mary Scrogges. Inventory of personal property, £23. (Commissary Court of London, Act Book, 1596–97, fo. 36.)

2. The Will of WILLIAM SCROGGES of "St. Pulcars" [St. Sepulchre's], co. Middlesex, butcher, dated February, 3 James 1 [February, 1605/6]. To my wife Margaret the leases which were hers before I married her and £40. To my son William the lease of the house wherein I dwell, subject to the payment of rent and to the payment of £5 apiece each year during the life of the lease to my son Adam and to my daughter Rachel. To my son Thomas £40. To my daughter Margaret £5. To my maidservant Jane £5. My children are to receive their legacies at the age of twenty-one or at my executor's discretion, and the legacies are to be abated or increased proportionately according to the size of my estate. Executor: Mr. Barnaby Newman of Turnbold Street, Clerkenwell. Overseers: John Batemanson, butcher, dwelling near Cow Cross, and Mr. Zachary, dwelling near St. Jones [*sic*] Street. Proved 13 July 1609; and, upon the renunciation of Mr. Newman, administration *cum testamento annexo* was granted to William Scrogges, son of the testator. (Commissary Court of London.)

3. Administration on the goods of JOHN SCROGGES, late of St. Sepulchre's, London, intestate, was granted to his widow, Jane Scrogges. Inventory of personal property, £16. (Commissary Court of London, Act Book, 1612–13, fo. 185.)

4. The Will of MARGARET SCRUGGES of St. Sepulchre's without Newgate, widow, "well stricken in years and at this present verie sicke and weake," dated 19 April 1633. To be buried in St. Sepulchre's Church, as near to my late husband, William Scrugges, as may be. To my grandson William Scrugges, son of my son-in-law [i. e., stepson] William Scrugges, my small wine cup. To my cousin Martha Walker of Westminster my best kettle. To my goddaughter Margaret Harford. To my loving friend Anne Percivall and her daughter Margaret Percivall. To the Livery Company of Butchers a supper, if they shall accompany my body to the earth on the day of my funeral. To my neighbors, being butchers'

*Pedigree of the Scroggs Family, by J. Renton Dunlop, F.S.A., in *Miscellanea Genealogica et Heraldica*, Fifth Series, vol. 3, 1918–19, pp. 65-82.

wives near Smithfield barrs, attending my funeral, a supper. Residue to my daughter Jane Scrugges, spinster, who is to be sole executrix. Overseers: my son [stepson] William Scrugges and my friend Thomas Jonson, butcher. Proved 28 September 1633. (P. C. C., Russell, 78.)

5. The Will of WILLIAM SCRUGGES, the Elder, of Rainham, co. Essex, gentleman, dated 9 September 1647. To my grandchildren Anne and Elizabeth Scrugges, daughters of my son William, £100 equally, at their majority or at marriage, but, if both die, it is to go to any other children that William may have. To my daughter-in-law Anne Scrugges, wife of my son William, my old grey mare, entreating her not to sell it or do away with it. To my sister Margaret Raymond, widow, 20s. for a ring. To my other sister, Jane Games, £5. I forgive Thomas Rands, butcher at Smithfield Bars, London, £10 in his hands in satisfaction of £5 he paid for ending a suit occasioned by my business. To my granddaughters, daughter-in-law, and executors decent mourning apparel. If my wife, being formerly a widow, claims her household goods, my son William is to have the equivalent. Residue to my wife Elizabeth and my son William, who are to be executors. Proved 5 January 1647/8 (P. C. C., Essex, 11.)

6. The Will of ELIZABETH SCROGGS, widow, of London, dated 13 August 1651. To my son William Scroggs £5. To my daughter-in-law Anne Scrogg my wearing apparel. Residue (including the lease of a farm in Holloway, Islington Parish, occupied by John Munns, and a lease from the Girdlers' Company of tenements at Cowe Cross, St. Sepulchre's, London) to my two grandchildren, Ann and Elizabeth Scroggs, who are also to be executrices. Witnesses: Anthony Gosling, Rich. Goldston, Robert Chamberlaine. Proved 8 November 1651; and a commission was issued to William Scroggs, gentleman, father of the executrices, to act during their minority. (P. C. C., Grey, 226.)

7. The Will of JANE GAYMES of St. Sepulchre's Parish, co. Middlesex, widow, dated 3 January 1660/1. To my daughter Jane Gaymes my wedding ring of gold. To my daughters Jane, Hannah, and Elizabeth Gaymes £25, equally divided between them. To my daughter Elizabeth Gaymes my term of years in a messuage in the occupation of Thomas Taylor, butcher, at or near West Smithfield Bars, in the parish of St. Sepulchre's, which I hold by lease for several years yet to come. Residue to be equally divided between my daughters Hannah and Jane Gaymes. Executor: my friend Mr. Richard Lowe. Proved 9 December 1664. (Commissary Court of London, filed copy.)

FROM PARISH REGISTERS

CHRIST CHURCH, NEWGATE STREET, LONDON

*Baptisms*

1573 Fraunces, son of John Scroggs, 20 December.
1576 Elyzabethe, daughter of John Skroggs, 3 December.
1579 John, son of John Skroggs, 28 October.

*Marriages*

1572 William Wyllye and Mary Scrogges 9 July.
1572 John Scrogges and Mary Stocklye 31 October.
1579 William Scrogh, butcher, and Rachel Prentice 3 August.

*Burials*

1576 John, son [of] John Skrougs, 19 February [1576/7].

1579    Margaret Sanders, servant to Mr. Skroggs, butcher, 14 September.
1583    Mary Scroggs, a child, of the plague, 25 July.

St. Helen's, Bishopsgate, London

*Marriages*

1580    David Thomas and Agnes Scrogs 3 April.
1621    William Scroggs of St. Sepulchre's, London, butcher, and Elizabeth Mansfield of the same, widow, by licence, 21 May.

St. Nicholas, Great Yarmouth, co. Norfolk

*Baptisms*

1619    Rachel Scruggs, of Tho. and Ma$^r$gy, 2 February [1619/20].
1623    Thomas Scruggs, of Tho. and M$^r$g$^r$y, 7 December.
1627    Rachell Srugges, of Tho. and Rachell [*sic*], 23 May.

*Burials*

1625    Rachell Scruggs, *puell*[*a*], 14 October.
1625    Eliz. Scruggs, *puella*, 2 November.
1625    Thomas Scruggs, *pu*[*er*], 12 November.

From the foregoing records and from other records whose source is obvious from the context the following genealogical arrangement has been drawn up:

1. ———— Scroggs. Purely for convenience in tabulation a common origin is ascribed to four persons of the name who were married in London between 1562 and 1580:

     i.    Mary, m. at Christ Church, Newgate Street, London, 9 July 1572, William Wyllye.
2. ii.    John, b. about 1546.
3. iii.    William, b. about 1557.
     iv.    Agnes, m. at St. Helen's Bishopsgate, London, 3 Apr. 1580, David Thomas. Her son *Francis* was bapt. in the same parish 19 June 1580.

2.    John Scroggs, of the parish of Christ Church, Newgate Street, London, born about 1546, died before 4 Apr. 1597, when administration on his estate was granted to his widow, Mary Scrogges. He married at Christ Church, 31 Oct. 1572, Mary Stocklye, who survived him and was administratrix of his estate. Her brother, Fulke Stocklye, citizen and blacksmith of London, left by will in 1598 £8 apiece to "John, Raphe and Samuel Scrogges, sons of my late brother-in-law John Scrogges, citizen and butcher, of London, and to their sister Marie Scrogges." (P.C.C., Kidd, 23.)

     He was presented as an apprentice by Richard Bramleye of the Butchers' Company in 1558 or 1559, and was admitted to the Company by service in 1566 or 1567.

     Children:

     i.    Francis, bapt. at Christ Church 20 Dec. 1573.
     ii.    Mary. Mary Scroggs, a child, d. of the plague, and was bur. at Christ Church 25 July 1583.
     iii.    John, living in 1598; probably the John Scrogges, late of St. Sepulchre's Parish, London, on whose estate administration was granted in 1612 or 1613 to the widow, Jane Scrogges. As son

of John Scroggs, late citizen and butcher of London, deceased, he was presented as an apprentice by John Awsten of the Butchers' Company for a term of seven years from St. Mark's Day [25 Apr.], 1598.

iv. RALPH. As son of John Scroggs, late citizen and butcher of London, deceased, he was presented as an apprentice by George Hawton of the Butchers' Company for a term of eight years from St. Bartholomew's Day [24 Aug.], 1599.

v. SAMUEL. As son of John Scrogges, butcher, late of London, deceased, he was presented as an apprentice by Francis Green of the Butchers' Company for a term of eight years from 1 July 1600.

vi. MARY, living in 1598, when she was a legatee in the will of her uncle, Fulke Stocklye.

3. WILLIAM SCROGGS, of St. Sepulchre's Parish,* London, butcher, the testator of Feb. 1605/6, born about 1557, died between Feb. 1605/6 and 13 July 1609, the dates of the making of his will and the proving thereof. He married first, at Christ Church, Newgate Street, London, 3 Aug. 1579, RACHEL PRENTICE; and secondly MARGARET ———, probably a widow, who survived him and died between 19 Apr. and 28 Sept. 1633, the dates of the making and the proving of her will.

He was apprenticed to Andrew Woodcock, a member of the Butchers' Company of London, in 1569 or 1570, and received his freedom by service in 1577 or 1578. He began paying "quarterage" and "barge-money" as a yeoman of the Company at once, and continued to do so until 1605, when he was advanced in rank to liveryman. Among the apprentices whom he presented were Henry Budworth (1593–94), Thomas, son of Alexander Weston of Northampton (1595–96), William Holland (1598–99), Peter, son of Peter Baldam of Tichfield, co. Hants (1602–03), Thomas, son of Richard Knight of Belbroughton, co. Worcester (1603–04), and Humphrey, son of Richard Thomas of Bishops-Castle, co. Salop (1608–09). He paid numerous fines for absence and lateness at the Company's meetings, and on two occasions he was fined for selling mutton for lamb and for giving false weight.

In his will he left his property to his wife Margaret and his children William, Thomas, Adam, Rachel, and Margaret Scroggs, and named Mr. Barnaby Newman executor. Mr. Newman refused the trust, and William Scroggs, the testator's son, was appointed administrator *cum testamento annexo*.

The widow, Margaret Scroggs, in her will, gave interesting directions for her funeral, and, after making several small gifts, including a wine cup to William Scroggs, son of her stepson William Scroggs, left her estate to her daughter Jane Scroggs, who had not been mentioned in her father's will, probably because of the prospective legacy from her mother, whose only child she appears to have been.

Children by first wife:

4. i. WILLIAM, b. about 1582.

*The early registers of St. Sepulchre's Parish were destroyed in the Great Fire of London.

5. ii. THOMAS, b. about 1590.
   iii. ADAM. He was made free of the Butchers' Company by patrimony 8 July 1630, and was of Smithfield Bars, St. Sepulchre's Parish, in 1641, as reported by the master of the Butchers' Company in the lay subsidy of that year. (Lay Subsidies, 251/22, in the Public Record Office, London.)
   iv. MARGARET, m. before 1647 ———— RAYMOND, if William Scroggs of Rainham, co. Essex, the testator of 1647, was her brother.
   v. RACHEL.

Child by second wife:

   vi. JANE, m. before 1647 ———— GAYMES, if William Scroggs of Rainham, co. Essex, the testator of 1647, was her brother. Jane Gaymes of St. Sepulchre's Parish, co. Middlesex, widow, the testatrix of 1660/1, left her property to her three daughters, Jane, Hannah, and Elizabeth Gaymes, and made her friend Mr. Richard Lowe executor.

4. WILLIAM SCROGGS (*William*), of St. Sepulchre's Parish, London, butcher, born about 1582, died (if he was identical with William Scroggs of Rainham, co. Essex, gentleman, the testator of 1647) between 9 Sept. 1647, when he made his will, and 5 Jan. 1647/8, when his will was proved. He married first ————; and secondly, at St. Helen's, Bishopsgate, London, 21 May 1621, ELIZABETH MANSFIELD of St. Sepulchre's Parish, widow.

He received the freedom of the Butchers' Company by patrimony in 1603 or 1604, on payment of 3s. 6d. and a gilt spoon. He passed through the various ranks of the Company from yeoman to assistant, and was at one time its master, his name appearing on a list of former masters dated 29 June 1641. On 30 June 1625 "Thomas Randes apprentice of William Dente was made free by William Scrugges," on payment of 3s. 6d. and a silver spoon. His last payment of dues to the Company was made in 1643.

That William Scroggs, the successful London merchant, retired with a sufficient fortune, and died as William Scroggs of Rainham, co. Essex, gentleman, the testator of 1647, and the father of Sir William Scroggs, who was Lord Chief Justice of England, 1678–1681, is indicated by strong circumstantial evidence, as follows: (a) The London butcher had sisters Margaret and Jane; the Rainham gentleman mentioned in his will his sisters Margaret and Jane. (b) The London butcher freed an apprentice named Thomas Randes in 1625; the Rainham gentleman left a legacy to "Thomas Rands, butcher at Smithfield Bars, London, . . . for ending a suit occasioned by my business." (c) The London butcher's second wife was a widow, named Elizabeth, and they lived in St. Sepulchre's Parish; the Rainham gentleman's wife was named Elizabeth, "being formerly a widow," and by her will it appears that she held leases at West Smithfield Bars, in St. Sepulchre's Parish. On the other hand, J. Renton Dunlop, F.S.A., in his "Pedigree of the Scroggs Family," states that William Scroggs of Rainham was a son of William Scroggs of Wood Street, London, mercer and innholder, who was a younger son of Francis Scroggs, Esq., of Patmore Hall. Mr. Dunlop gives no evidence in support of this conclusion except the Lord Chief Justice's hazy conjecture that he was a great-grandson of Francis Scroggs through that gentleman's son Thomas, who, as a matter of fact, died *s.p.**  But there is contemporary evidence showing that the Lord Chief Justice, who did not know his grandfather's name, was in fact the son of a butcher.  Sir William Dugdale, who was in the College of Arms when Sir William Scroggs was knighted, stated that he was "the son of an one-ey'd butcher near Smithfield Bars," and the "Dictionary of National Biography" says that "the squibs with which he was assailed in after-life constantly alluded to his father's business as that of a butcher."

William Scroggs of Rainham, gentleman, the testator of 1647, left his property to his grandchildren Anne and Elizabeth, daughters of his son William, his daughter-in-law Anne Scroggs, his sisters Margaret Raymond and Jane Games, his son William, and his wife Elizabeth.

The widow returned to London, and died between 13 Aug. and 8 Nov. 1651, the dates of the making and the proving of her will.  Her only legatees were her daughter-in-law Anne Scroggs and her two grandchildren, Anne and Elizabeth Scroggs.

Child by first wife:

i. SIMON, probably d. *s.p.* before 1647. As son of William Scruggs, citizen and butcher of London, he was apprenticed to Ric. Lewis for a term of eight years from 7 Feb. 1621/2.

Child by second wife:

ii. SIR WILLIAM, B.A., M.A., Lord Chief Justice of England, 1678–1681, b. about 1622, as he was free of the Butchers' Company in 1643; d. in London 25 Oct. 1683; m. ANNE FETTYPLACE, daughter of Edmund Fettyplace of Denchworth, Berkshire. One son and three daughters.  For an account of his life see the "Dictionary of National Biography."

5. THOMAS SCRUGGS (*William*), of Great Yarmouth, co. Norfolk, and Salem, Mass., born, probably in St. Sepulchre's Parish, London, about 1590, died at Salem not later than 29 June 1654. He married, before 1619, MARGERY ———, who survived him and died at Salem 26 Jan. 1662/3.

No record of his apprenticeship appears in the books of the Butchers' Company in London, but some time before 1619/20, when the record of the baptisms of his children begins in the parish registers, he settled at Great Yarmouth, co. Norfolk, and carried on the family trade.  His name appears in a subsidy of 1629 as the owner of land in the Second North Ward of the town (Lay Subsidies, 153/607, in the Public Record Office, London).  The corporation records contain no mention

*This article was submitted to Mr. Dunlop before publication, but the condition of his health made it impossible for him to give it consideration.

of him until 1631, when Thomas Scrugges and five others were presented for keeping "certain houses within this town for slaying beasts called slaughter houses to the grave annoyance of their neighbors;" and on the same day he and seventeen others were presented, "being inhabitants of the said town of Great Yarmouth aforesaid and occupying [i.e., trading] as burgesses of the said town whereas in truth they are not burgesses." Similar records are found until the Monday after the Feast of St. Barnabas,* 9 Charles I [June 1633]. In Feb. 1634/5 Scruggs and his wife were cited to appear before the Archdeaconry Court of Norwich, probably for failure to attend church. They did not appear, and at the following session Mrs. Scruggs was fined 7s. 8d. and costs. In the margin of the record are the words: "att New England." (Act Book, Archdeaconry of Norwich.)

There was undoubtedly a religious reason for the emigration of Thomas Scruggs and his wife. On his arrival at Salem, in the Bay Colony, he immediately became prominent in the church-state. He was sworn a freeman on 2 Sept. 1635, was a deputy to the General Courts of 3 Mar. 1635/6, 8 Sept. 1636, and 7 Dec. 1636, a commissioner of the Salem Court in 1636 and 1637, and a selectman of the town in the same years. In 1637, however, he became deeply involved in religious controversy as a partisan of Mrs. Hutchinson, and upon her banishment he and six other Salem men were disarmed as a danger to the community. Except for services as a trial juror in 1645 and a grand juror in 1647 his public career was ended.

Scruggs's first land grant of 300 acres was returned by him to the town in 1636, and Salem tradition states that it was the projected site of the college which was later established at Cambridge. In its stead he received a farm of 200 acres in what later became Beverly, originally granted to Capt. William Trask, one of the "old planters."

Thomas Scruggs died in 1654, and his widow Margery was appointed administratrix of his estate on 29 June of that year. The inventory, amounting to £244. 10s. 2d., included "a silver boule." Mrs. Scruggs conveyed the estate to her son-in-law, John Raymond, in consideration of £5 to be paid at once, £5 to be at her disposal on her death, the use of the household goods, and an annual income of £20 to be paid quarterly during her lifetime.

Children, baptized at Great Yarmouth:

i. RACHEL, bapt. 2 Feb. 1619/20; bur. 14 Oct. 1625.
ii. THOMAS, bapt. 7 Dec. 1623; bur. 12 Nov. 1625.
iii. ELIZABETH, bur. 2 Nov. 1625.
iv. RACHEL, bapt. 23 May 1627; brought by her parents to New England; m. before 1654 JOHN RAYMOND.

*The Feast of St. Barnabas falls on 11 June.

# STEVENS OF NEWBURY AND ANDOVER, MASS.

Contributed by G. ANDREWS MORIARTY, A.M., LL.B., F.S.A.,
of Bristol, R. I.

THE parentage of John Stevens, who came to New England in the *Confidence* in 1638, with his wife, his mother, his brother William, and two servants, and, after living for a few years at Newbury, moved to Andover, Mass., where he resided until his death, 11 Apr. 1662, was discovered many years ago by the late Horatio Gates Somerby, who found a number of Stevens entries in the parish registers of Caversham, co. Oxford. These entries, however, have not hitherto been published; and the contributor of this article now places them before the readers of the REGISTER, together with items from the Lay Subsidies that show that the Stevens family was settled at Caversham as far back as 1524–25, although, owing to the absence of wills relating to the family, the ancestry of the American immigrants, John and William, cannot be traced with certainty beyond their father.

## FROM LAY SUBSIDIES FOR CO. OXFORD*

### CAVERSHAM

16 Henry VIII [1524–25].
>    Richard Stevins in goods, [valuation] 11s., [tax] 12d.
>    Thomas Stevins on wages, [valuation] 20s., [tax] 4d.
>    William Stevins in goods, [valuation] £16, [tax] 8d.
>                                    (Lay Subsidies, 161/195.)
>    Amy Steuyns in goods, [valuation] £11, [tax] 5s. 6d.
>    Peter Steuyns on wages, [valuation] 26s., [tax] 4d.
>    Richard Steuyns on wages, [valuation] 20s., [tax] 4d.
>    Thomas Steuyns on wages, [valuation] 20s., [tax] 4d.
>                                    (*Ib.*, 161/201.)

37 Henry VIII [1545–46].
>    Peter Stevens in goods, [valuation] 20s., [tax] 1d.
>    Wylliam Stevens in goods, [valuation] £7, [tax] 4d.
>                                    (*Ib.*, 162/236.)
>    Rychard Stevens in goods, [valuation] £20, [tax] 13s. 4d.
>                                    (*Ib.*, 162/239.)
>    Richard Stephens in goods, [valuation] £20, [tax] 26s. 8d.
>                                    (*Ib.*, 162/247.)

1 Elizabeth [1558–59].
>    Richard Stevyns in goods, [valuation] £30.
>                                    (*Ib.*, 162/317.)

10 Elizabeth [1567–68].
>    Richard Stevens in goods, [valuation] £16, [tax] 13s. 4d.
>                                    (*Ib.*, 162/331.)

19 Elizabeth [1576–77].
>    John Stevens in goods, [valuation] £3, [tax] 3s.
>    William Stevens in goods, [valuation] £3, [tax] 3s.
>                                    (*Ib.*, 162/341.)

23 Elizabeth [1580–81].
>    John Stevens in goods, [valuation] £3, [tax] 5s.

*Preserved in the Public Record Office, London.

Richard Stevens in lands, [valuation] 20s., [tax] 2s. 6d.
William Stevens in goods, [valuation] £3, [tax] 5s.
(Ib., 162/346.)

36 Elizabeth [1593–94].
> John Stevens in goods, [valuation] £5, [tax] 13s. 4d.
> Rychard Stevens in lands, [valuation] 20s., [tax] 4s.
> William Stevens in goods, [valuation] £3, [tax] 8d.
(Ib., 163/381.)

41 Elizabeth [1598–99].
> John Stevens in goods, [valuation] £5, [tax] 13s. 4d.
> William Stevens in goods, [valuation] £3, [tax] 8d.
(Ib., 163/394.)

## FROM PARISH REGISTERS

### CAVERSHAM, CO. OXFORD*

#### *Baptisms*

1601   Elizabeth, daughter of Ralph Stevens, 20 August.
1602   Jane, daughter of John Stevens, 2 January [1602/3].
1605   John, son of John Stevens, 7 July.
1607   Humphrey, son of John Stevens *alias* Atwell, 19 June.
1608   William, son of Ralph Stevens, born 29 January and baptized 5 February [1608/9].
1611   Barbara, daughter of John Stevens, 11 September.
1616   William, son of John and Alice Stevens, 1 September.
1623   John, son of Ralph Stevens, 13 January [1623/4].
1624   Henry, son of Henry Stevens, 20 January [1624/5].
1628   Tomasin, daughter of Henry Stevens, 13 April.
1636   Richard, son of Richard Stevens, 16 October.

#### *Marriages*

1597   John Stevens and Alice Atkins 27 February [1597/8].
1600   Ralph Stevens and Christian Nash 15 November.
1619   Ralph Stevens and Margaret Billingsby 18 October.
1623   Thomas Stevens and Joan Jeffrey 21 September.
1629   Richard Stevens and Eleanor Mathie 23 April.

#### *Burials*

1601   Cecily, wife of William Stevens, 20 February [1601/2].
1602   Edith, wife of Richard Stevens, 12 October.
1615   Christian, wife of Ralph Stevens, 24 August.
1617   Susan, daughter of John Stevens, 28 July.
1617   John Stevens 11 January [1617/18].
1623   Richard Stevens 15 April.
1627   John Stevens 21 September.
1630   Henry Stevens 3 January [1630/1].
1631   Mary Stevens 27 March.
1636   Widow Stevens 25 July.

## FROM THE LIST OF PASSENGERS IN THE "CONFIDENCE," 1638†

The List of the Names of the Passeng<sup>rs</sup> Intended for New England in the good shipp the Confidence of London of C C. tonnes, John Jobson,

*From the Somerby Papers.

†This list of passengers in the *Confidence* in 1638 was found in the British State Papers, America and the West Indies, vol. 5, p. 375, and was printed in the REGISTER, vol. 2, pp. 108-110. The late Samuel G. Drake included it, in corrected form, in his article entitled The Founders of New England, which was published in the REGISTER, vol. 14, pp. 297-359

M$^r$   And thus by vertue of the Lord Treas$^{rs}$ warr$^t$ of the xj$^{th}$ of Aprill, 1638.

Southampton, 24° Aprill, 1638.

Ages.

\* \* \*

John Stephens    } of Gonsham\* in           31
William Stephens } Oxon$^r$ *husbandmen*  21
Eliza: Stephens *his wife*†
Alice Stephens *his Mother*
John Lowgie     }                                16
Grace Lowgie    } *seruants*

\* \* \*

[*Endorsement*.]—So$^u$thton, 1638.  The Cert. and List of the Passeng$^{rs}$ names gone for New-England in the Confidence of London in Aprill 1638.

Although the records given above show that the Stevens family was settled at Caversham, co. Oxford, as early as 1524–25, that is, in the first quarter of the sixteenth century, several persons of the name being taxed there in the subsidy of that year and in later subsidies down almost to the end of the century, and the parish registers, which go back to 1597, containing many entries of baptisms, marriages, and burials in this family, it is not possible, from the data thus far assembled, to establish with certainty the relationship of the early Stevenses to one another or to the father of the two brothers, John and William Stevens, who emigrated to New England in the *Confidence* in 1638.  The following pedigree, therefore, based on some of the records given above and on various New England records, begins with the parents of the two brothers.

1. JOHN STEVENS, of Caversham, co. Oxford (probably a son either of the John Stevens of Caversham who was taxed there in the subsidies of 1576–77, 1580–81, 1593–94, and 1598–99 and was presumably the John Stevens who was buried there 11 Jan. 1617/18, or of the William Stevens of the same parish who was taxed in the same four subsidies, whose wife, Cecily, was buried there 20 Feb. 1601/2), was born perhaps about 1575, and was probably the John Stevens who was buried at Caversham 21 Sept. 1627.  He married at Caversham,

(Oct. 1860), and was reprinted in book form, Boston, 1860.  The list as here given appears in the REGISTER, vol. 14, p. 335, and in the reprint, The Founders of New England, p. 59. The number of passengers in this list, "greate and little," amounts, in the words of the record itself, to "Cx soules."

\*This place name appears in the REGISTER, vol. 2, p. 109, as Gowsham, which is also given on the same page as the English home of Thomas Jones and John Binson.  In the REGISTER, vol. 14, p. 335, it appears as Gonsham, as given above; but, since no parish of that name could be found in England, Mr. Drake suggested Godestow, in the parish of Woolvercott, Oxfordshire, as a possible reading, although the Gowsham of the list in vol. 2 had been corrected to Caversham in the REGISTER, vol. 4, p. 387.  Savage, in his Genealogical Dictionary, vol. 4, p. 186, gives the correct name of the parish, Caversham; but Pope, in his Pioneers of Massachusetts, pp. 433, 434, repeats the old error, Gonsham.  The entries in the parish registers of Caversham, given above, show that that parish was the home of the family, and that the forms Gowsham and Gonsham were misreadings for Caversham.

†John and William Stephens (or Stevens) were undoubtedly brothers, Elizabeth Stephens must be the wife of John, and Alice Stephens the mother both of John and William.  Pope (p. 434) makes the Elizabeth who came in the *Confidence* with John and William the wife of William; but William married later, at Newbury, Mass., 19 May 1645, Elizabeth ———.

403

27 Feb. 1597/8, ALICE ATKINS, who survived her husband, accompanied her sons John and William when they emigrated to New England in the *Confidence* in Apr. 1638, and was perhaps identical with the Anne Stevens, widow, who was buried at Newbury, Mass., where her son William had settled, 17 July 1650.

Children, recorded at Caversham:*

    i.    JANE, bapt. 2 Jan. 1602/3.
2.  ii.   JOHN, bapt. 7 July 1605.
    iii.  BARBARA, bapt. 11 Sept. 1611.
3.  iv.   WILLIAM, bapt. 1 Sept. 1616.
    v.    SUSAN, bur. 28 July 1617.

2.  JOHN STEVENS (*John*), of Caversham, co. Oxford, and of Newbury and Andover, Mass., husbandman, baptized at Caversham 7 July 1605, died at Andover 11 Apr. 1662, in his 57th year. He married in England, before sailing for New England in Apr. 1638, ELIZABETH ——— (probably PARKER), who was born about 1613, survived her husband, and died at Andover 1 May 1694, aged about 81.

John Stevens (or Stephens), aged 31, with William Stevens (or Stephens), aged 21, undoubtedly his brother, his (John's) wife Elizabeth, his mother Alice Stephens, and two servants, John Lowgie, aged 16, and Grace Lowgie, sailed from Southampton, England, for New England, in Apr. 1638, in the ship *Confidence* of London, of 200 tons, of which John Jobson was master, the total number of passengers on this voyage being 110. He settled first at Newbury, where he was a proprietor, and he was admitted freeman 18 May 1642. Soon afterwards he moved to Andover, where he made his home for the rest of his life.

His wife Elizabeth deposed 16 June 1673, aged 60 years, concerning Samuel, son of her brother Joseph Parker of Andover (Pope's Pioneers of Massachusetts, p. 433, from Middlesex Court Files).†

Administration on the estate of John Stevens was granted 24 June 1662 to Elizabeth, his widow, who in her will, dated 21 Oct. 1687 (with a codicil added 7 Sept. 1691) and proved 25 Sept. 1694, bequeathed to her sons John, Timothy, Nathan, Ephraim, Joseph, and Benjamin Stevens, her daughters Elizabeth Woodman and Mary Barker, and their children.

Children:

    i.    LIEUT. JOHN, b. at Newbury 20 June 1639; d. at Casco 4 or 5 Mar.
          1688/9; m. (1) at Andover, 13 June 1662, HANNAH BARNARD,
          who d. there 13 Mar. 1674/5; m. (2) at Andover, 10 Aug. 1676,
          ESTHER BARKER, who d. 25 June 1713, aged 62 years, 1 month.
          Six children by first wife and seven children by second wife,
          all recorded at Andover.

*Humphrey, son of John Stevens *alias* Atwell, was baptized at Caversham 19 June 1607; but his father was probably not identical with the John Stevens whose five children are here given.

†Joseph Parker of Newbury, co. Berks, tanner, aged 24, was one of the passengers in the *Confidence* in Apr. 1638, on the voyage on which John Stevens and his wife and brother and mother came to New England. (REGISTER, vol. 14, p. 335). He settled first at Newbury, Mass., and was afterwards of Andover. He had a wife Mary and a large family.

ii. CAPT. TIMOTHY, of Roxbury, Mass., b. at Newbury 22 Sept. 1641; d. at Roxbury 31 Jan. 1707/8, aged about 68; m. at Roxbury, 12 Mar. 1664/5, SARAH DAVIS. who d. at Roxbury 5 Apr. 1695, aged about 48. Ten children.

iii. CORNET NATHAN, said to have been the first white child born at Andover, b. about 1644; d. there 19 Feb. 1717/18, in his 75th year.

iv. ENSIGN EPHRAIM, b. about 1649; d. 15 June 1718, in his 70th year; m. at Andover, 11 Oct. 1680, SARAH ABBOTT, b. at Andover 14 Nov. 1659, d. there 29 June 1711, aged 51, daughter of George[1] and Hannah (Chandler) Abbott. Seven children.

v. ELIZABETH, m. at Andover, 22 Jan. 1665/6, JOSHUA WOODMAN. Seven children recorded at Andover.

vi. MARY, b. about 1651; d. at Andover 1 May 1703, aged 52; m. at Andover, 6 July 1670, JOHN BARKER, sergeant and captain. Seven children recorded at Andover.

vii. DEA. JOSEPH, b. at Andover 15 May 1654; d. there 25 Feb. 1742/3, in his 89th year; m. (1) at Andover, 28 May 1679, MARY INGALLS, who d. at Andover 21 Sept. 1699; m. (2) at Salem, Mass., 13 Nov. 1700, ELIZABETH BROWN of Salem, who survived· her husband and d. at Andover 16 Sept. 1745. Five children by first wife and two children by second wife, all recorded at Andover.

viii. CAPT. BENJAMIN, b. at Andover 24 June 1656; d. there, probably s.p., 8 Jan. 1729/30, aged 74; m. (intention recorded at Andover, 3 Sept. 1715) Mrs. SUSANNA CHICKERIN[G] of Bradford, Mass., who survived him and d. at Andover 30 or 31 July 1753, in her 83d year.

3. WILLIAM STEVENS (*John*), of Caversham, co. Oxford, and of Newbury, Mass., husbandman, baptized at Caversham 1 Sept. 1616, died at Newbury 19 May 1653. He married at Newbury, 19 May 1645, ELIZABETH ——— (probably BITFIELD), who married secondly, at Newbury, 3 Mar. 1653/4, William Titcomb.

He came to New England in 1638 in the *Confidence* from Southampton, being described on the passenger list as a husbandman, aged 21, his brother John, John's wife Elizabeth, and their mother Alice Stephens being fellow passengers in the same ship. (See above, under 2.) He settled at Newbury, where he was a proprietor, and he was admitted freeman 18 May 1642, on the same day with his brother.

In his will, dated 19 May 1653 and proved 30 June 1653, he names only his wife Elizabeth, whom he appoints as executrix, and his sons John and Samuel.

Children, born at Newbury:

i. BITFIELD, b. 16 Mar. 1648/9; d. at Newbury 23 July 1649.

ii. JOHN, of Newbury and Haverhill, Mass., b. 19 Nov. 1650; m. at Newbury, 9 Mar. 1669/70, MARY CHASE, b. at Newbury 3 Feb. 1650/1, daughter of Aquila[1] and Ann (Wheeler) Chase.

Children:
1. *Mary,* b. at Newbury 10 Feb. 1670/1.
2. *A son,* b. at Newbury 22 Mar. 1673/4.
3. *Thomas,* b. at Newbury 3 July 1676.
4. *A daughter,* b. at Newbury 7 Sept. 1680.
5. *Aaron,* b. at Haverhill 7 Apr. 1685.
6. *Joseph,* b. at Haverhill 19 Nov. 1689.
7. *Benjamin,* b. at Haverhill 25 Jan. 1692/3.

iii. SAMUEL, b. 18 Nov. 1652; probably (according to Savage) the sergeant who was killed by the Indians at Bloody Brook, with

some of his fellow townsmen, 18 Sept. 1675; m. at Salem, Mass.,
17 Dec. 1672, REBECCA REA, b. at Salem 4 Sept. 1656, daughter of
Joshua and Sara (Waters) Rea or Ray. She survived him and
m. (2) at Salem, 28 Feb. 1675/6, Symond Horne. She was administratrix of the estate of her first husband, Samuel Stevens.
   Children, b. at Salem:
1.  *Samuel*, b. in Sept. 1673; d. in Oct. 1673.
2.  *Sarah*, b. 8 Nov. 1674; survived her father.

---

# GENEALOGICAL RESEARCH IN ENGLAND

Communicated by the Committee on English and Foreign Research

## BURT–MARCH

Contributed by GEORGE SKELTON TERRY, B.SC., of Buffalo, N. Y.

IT is the purpose of the contributor of this article to present records
that throw light on the English connections of Henry Burt, who was
at Roxbury, Mass., in 1639, and settled in the following year at
Springfield, and his wife, Ulalia March, whom he married 28 Dec.
1619 in England, where several of their children were born. The
conclusions drawn from the records will be given in genealogical
form in the latter part of the article. The researches in England were
carried on for the contributor by Miss Lilian J. Redstone of London.

### FROM PROBATE RECORDS

Administration on the estate of HENRY BURD, late of Harberton [co.
Devon], deceased, intestate, was granted 2 May 1603 to Joan, his relict,
provided she give to Walter and Jane, his children, etc. [as stated below].
Bond given by Johanna Burd of Harberton, widow, and Walter Burd of
the same, weaver, 2 May 1603. Johanna is to distribute to Walter and
Jane, her children, such portion of the goods of the deceased as by the
Archdeacon shall be thought fit.
   Inventory, taken 28 April 1603 by Gyles Hooper and Thomas [*torn*]:
a pair of "lumbres," 6s.; . . . his "woodinge" vessel . . . ; 6 silver
spoons . . . ; 1 piece of melley cloth . . . ; total [*torn*]. (Archdeaconry of
Totnes.)

   The Will of WILLIAM MARCHE the Elder of Shereford [co. Devon],
yeoman, dated 29 April 1612. To be buried in the church of the parish

406

of Shereford. To George March, my son, 40s. To my eldest daughter, Joane Hinde[?], 40s. To each of the rest of my daughters, namely, Grace Neale, Jane Bickforde, Prudence Jackson[?], and Sarah Pounde, 6s. 8d. To each of the seven children of my son Richard Marche, deceased, 6s. 8d. To the poor of Sherford 5s. Residue to Joane Marche, my daughter-in-law, executor. She is to receive no benefit of my goods (except for necessaries about my funeral and necessary use about the children) until she has discharged my debts. [No signature or witnesses.] Proved 8 September 1615.

Inventory, taken 11 February 1613 by Arthur Wakeham, Will Randall, and Thomas Marche of Sherford: 53 sheep, £15; 10 hogs, £3. 10s.; 3 young bullocks, £2. 13s. 4d.; 3 kine, £9; 3 mares, £5; geese and poultry, 8s. (Archdeaconry of Totnes.)

The Will of JOHANE MARCHE of Sherford, co. Devon, widow, dated and sealed 21 May 1616.* To be buried in the church of the parish of Sherford. To the poor of Sherford 10s., to be distributed by my overseers at my burial. To my eldest daughter, Alice March, £5, to be paid within a half year after my death. To my second daughter, Elizabeth March, £5, within one year after my death. To each of the rest of my daughters, namely, Ulalia March, Amias March, Jane March, and Johane March, 50s., to be paid within a year after my death. Residue (with all my rents and reservations) to William March, my son, executor. I do request William Randall, John Bickford, and Gregory Bickford to be overseers. The sign of Johan Marche. Witnesses: George March, Nicholas Jackston[?]. Proved 21 June 1616.

Inventory, taken 10 June 1616 by Arthur Wakeham, William Randall, and Thomas March and exhibited 21 June 1616, includes farm stock and apparel, £5; no household goods; 20 ewes, £7. 13s. 4d.; 19 lambs, £4; 3 kine, £10. 10s.; swine, £3; lease in reversion of twenty-one years in a tenement called Sand Wills, £60, total, £140. 7s. (Archdeaconry of Totnes.)

The Will of HENRY BURTT of Harberton [co. Devon], clothier, dated 10 July 1617. To the poor of the parish of Harberton 30s. To my son Henry and his heirs and assigns [sic] my close of land situate in Harberton Ford, called by the name of the Racheparke, together with the house that John Tummells now dwelleth in and the house that George Causie and Johan Pearse now dwell in and the house that Andrew Pearse and Edward Adams now dwell in, as also the orchard, nursery, herb gardens, backsides, and other appurtenances belonging. To the said Henry, my son, the mansion house of that land commonly called Crobers Land which Thomas Wood now dwelleth in, together with the sheep pen, orchard, herb garden, and bakehouse, during the term of his life. To my said son Henry £100, to be paid within a year after my death. To Isett, my wife, for life, one chamber over the shop, called the forechamber, with the bedstead and bed performed that I use to lie in. My wife shall have yearly, during her life, £6. 13s. 4d., issuing out of that land or tenement called Crobers Land; and my executor shall find her and one to attend her, during her life, sufficient meat, drink, and firewood for her own use; and, if my said wife do dislike her diet & do leave it, then my will is that she shall have £3. 6s. 8d., in lieu of her diet, out of the lands aforesaid, for her life. To my said wife and son Henry the half of my household stuff, equally to be divided between them; and the other half is to remain to my executor. To Raddegan, my daughter, £60, to be paid within three months

*The seal is covered with paper and was probably only a drop of wax.

after she shall be of the age of twenty-one. To Allies, my daughter, £40, to be paid at the age of twenty. To Agnes, my daughter, £40, at the age of twenty. To Elizabeth, my daughter, £40, at the age of twenty. Whereas I promised my son-in-law, Chrispine Saunder, £40 at his marriage, and because he is not as yet paid, my executor shall pay it. Also I promised him other £20 when my daughter Johan, his wife, for the term of her life or for fifty years determinable upon her life, should be assured of that tenement that Thomasine Saunders now dwelleth in or of some other as good, then my executor shall pay him £20 towards the same. To Joseph Saunders and Samuel Saunders, my grandchildren, £5 each. To my brothers' and sisters' children 2s. each. To every of my godchildren 12d. To Nycholas Hyans, my apprentice, 30s., to be paid at the end of his apprentice[ship]. Residue to my son John Burte. Witnesses: Will Huxham and Thos. Colton. Proved 19 September 1617.

Inventory, taken 10 September 1617 by Thomas Colton and Paule Symons and exhibited 19 September 1617, includes apparel, £8; cloth and yarn, £102; money, £70; 93 sheep, £31; 32 lambs, £6; other farm stock; an estate in certain grounds, £61; an estate in house, meadow, and garden, £20; two pairs of "lumbes," warping pins, raggles, quilt torns, and one spinning-turn with sleyes, £2. 10s.; brass pans, cauldrons, and pots £10. 13s. 4d.; for household cloth already made, £3; 13 silver spoons, £3; desperate debts, £140; total, £602. 7s. 9d. (Archdeaconry of Totnes.)

The Will of ELIZABETH MARCH of Ratterie, co. Devon, spinster, undated. To the poor of Ratterie 10s. To the poor of Sherford 10s. To my aunt, Alce March, 20s. I give 10s. to be bestowed in a ring unto him that shall preach my funeral sermon. To Marie Marche, the daughter of Thomas March of Sherford, 6s. To Silvester Risdon, Robert Rogers, and Symon Thorne, three of my uncle's, Mr. Henrie Martyne's, servants, 12d. apiece. To my brother William March a yeowe[? ewe]. To my godchild, Peter Cooke, 12d. To my sister Amyas all my apparel and a yeowe [? ewe]. The residue of my goods (except as hereunder excepted) to my five sisters, equally to be divided amongst them. But, always excepted, if Alce, my eldest sister, shall marry to my Uncle Martine's good liking and [that] of her friends, my will is that she shall have 40s. more than the rest. Lastly, I do entreat my uncle, Mr. Henry Martyn, to be my executor, and for his pains I bequeath unto him a gold ring which my mother gave unto me. Witnesses: William Hele, Luce Martyn, Christian Hele. Proved 14 May 1619.

Inventory, taken 12 May 1619 and exhibited by Henry Marten, clerk and executor, 14 May 1619: Due unto her in money the sixth part of £140, £23. 6s. 8d. Due unto her for the use of the same money for two years, £4. 13s. 4d. Give[n] her by her mother's will, to be paid within one year after her death, £5. For the use of said £5 for two years, ————. Due to her the sixth part of one-third part of a bargain in Sherford, which amounted by the year to £15, besides all charges, and to her part to 50s., besides reparations, £2. 10s. Her clothes, £2. 10s. One gold ring given unto her by her mother, £1. Two yeowes[? ewes], 14s. Total, £39. 14s. (Archdeaconry of Totnes.)

The Will of HENRY MARTYN, clerk, vicar of Rattery [co. Devon], "Written with myne owne hand" 13 November 1619. To the poor of Rotterye 13s. 4d. My chattel of Yeoland to Richard Martyn, my son, and Chrystijan, my daughter, jointly, and the whole years unto the survivor of them. To my son Heale all my books and my table board in my hall. To my son Heale the advowson of the vicarage of Ratterye. To Thomas

Martyn, Peter Martyn, and John Martyn, my brothers, to each of them a gold ring, the price of one noble, for a remembrance. To Mrs. Philip Saverye the gold ring which my cousin Saverye gave me. To my cousin Johan Saverye and my cousin Jane Saverye my virginals which are in Willinge house. To my wife Luce Martyn and Richard Martyn, my son, the lease of years in the sanctuary grounds, which is the Ball, the Marrell Parke, and Frogwell. To my daughter Chrystyan, if her husband procure her her life in some bargain, as he promised, then I give unto her 20 nobles, to be paid yearly as long as the lease doth last. To Ames Marche, who dwelleth with me, one yeowe [ewe] sheep. To Thomas Beare, the son of Thomas Beare, one yeow [ewe] sheep. To Henry Beare, the son of Thomas Beare, one yeow [ewe] sheep. To each of my servants 12d. Residue to Luce Martyn, my wife, and Richard Martyn, my son, executors. I do appoint my cousin Thomas Beare in trust, to deal for my son Richard Martyn in his absence, and for his pains I give him a gold ring. Overseers: my cousin Robert Saverye, Esq., and William Heale, my son-in-law. To my cousin Savery for his pains the gold ring which my father gave me, and to my son Heale a gold ring of 10s. Witnesses: Robert Savery and Wm. Heale. Proved 25 April 1620, and administration committed to Lucee Martyn, the relict.

Inventory taken on the last day of January 1619 [1619/20] by John Byckford and Thos. Head: farm stock and household goods; in books, £20; 20 yards or thereabout of new cloth, £3. 10s.; total £534. 5s. 11d. (Archdeaconry of Totnes.)

The Will of JOHN BICKFORDE of Ratterye [co. Devon], yeoman, weak and sickly in body, dated 23 May 1625 (1 Charles I). To be buried in the church or churchyard of Rattery. To the poor of Ratterye £20, to be employed by the four men, rulers or overseers of said parish, towards keeping the poor at work, as other money is now employed in said parish. To my son Thomas Bickeford, my executor, a term of fifteen years in a tenement and two mills in Rattery called Croutes Bargine. To my son John Bickeforde the residue of the term which shall be to come in all said ten[ement] and mills, which term is during the lives of my said son John Bickeforde and my son William Bickeforde, and also one meadow called Marleye Meadow in Rattery. If my son John pays to my son Thomas £100 towards payment of my debts, Thomas is to have no estate for fifteen years in the ten[ement] and mills called Crotes Bargine. My son John is to pay to my daughter Anne Bickford £20 on the surrender of her estate in Marlaye Meadow aforesaid; but, if she will not give the surrender, he shall pay her nothing. I give more[over] to my son Thomas an estate for eight years in the ground that is held between me and my brother Gregorye Bickeforde in Rattery, towards payment of debts and legacies. To William Bickeforde, my son, £10, in two years after my death. To Symon Bickeforde, my son, £10, in two years after my death. To my son Richard Bickeforde £10, in two years, and an estate for one year in the ground before mentioned which is held between me and my brother Gregory, to begin next after the end of the said one years [sic]. Residue of the term which is to come in said ground, which is during the lives of Jane Bickeforde, wife of said Gregory Bickeforde, and my said son John Bickeford, I give to my sons Symon Bickeforde and Richd. Bickeforde, to be held jointly bet[ween] them. To Anne Bickeford, my daughter, £30, one year after my death. To Jaune Bickeford, my daughter, £30, 3 years after my death. To Marye Bickeford, my daughter, £30, 3 years after my death. Residue to my son Thomas, whom I appoint executor. Overseers: my brother Gregorye Bickeford and my brother-in-law Thomas Headd. In witness that I affirm this my last will I have hereunto set my hand and seal the 6 Oct[ober] in the year first above written. Witnesses: Xper Windeat and Alexander Halse. Proved 16 December 1625.

Inventory of the goods of John Bickford of Ratterie the Elder, lately deceased, taken 14 December 1625 by Gregorie Bickford of Rattery, yeoman, and Thomas Head of Dean Prior, yeoman, and exhibited by Thomas Bickford, executor, 16 December 1625: 3 oxen, 5 kine, 2 yearlings, 3 calves, 3 horses, 15 wethers, and 15 ewes, pigs, and poultry; wearing apparel, £5; 14 silver spoons, £5; other household goods; chattel lease of Ratterie Hills, £60; total £188. 8s. (Archdeaconry of Totnes.)

The Will of CHRISPIN SAUNDERS of Harberton [co. Devon], sick in body, dated 16 October 1626. To my three eldest sons my three pairs of lumes. To Daniell, my son, one chest. To Rebecca, my daughter, one chest. My executor shall pay to my son Joseph the sum of £5 which was given him by his grandfather, and she shall pay to Samuell, my son, £5 likewise given him by his grandfather. Residue to Johan, my wife, executor. Overseers: John Huxham, my uncle, John Huxham, his son, and Thomas Voysey. Witnesses: William Walplate, John Burtt, John Huxham, Thos. Voysey. Proved 8 December 1626.

Inventory, taken 1 December 1626 by John Huxham, John Burt, and Thos. Voysey, and exhibited 8 December 1626 by Johan Saunders, relict and executor: wearing apparel, £5; one mill to make clean seed wheat, 13s. 4d.; sword, musket, & birding piece, 13s. 4d.; his wool and yarn, 8s.; his books, 13s. 4d.; one skaskett and one thread turn, 1s.; all his "sleas," 3s.; one cupboard, one glass case, his chairs, his presses to bind books withal, £1; three pairs of looms, £3; his quilturns, one spinning-turn, warping pins, and ragle, 3s. 4d.; corn in the barns, £14; 2 kine, his sheep, and a labor beast, £8; all his pigs, £2. 10s.; total, £53. 16s. 10d. (Archdeaconry of Totnes.)

The Nuncupative Will of ISOTT BURTE of Harberton [co. Devon], being of perfect mind and memory, declared 14 March, or thereabout, 1629 [1629/30], in the presence of John Burte and Joane Saunders, with others, in manner and form following: she gave all her goods unto Agnes Burte and Elizabeth Burte, her daughters, whom she made her executors. Proved 9 July 1630 by Elizabeth Burte, one of the executors named in said will, with power reserved to grant administration to Agnes Burte, the other executor.

Inventory, taken 8 July 1630 by Henry Burt and Symon Trumelles and exhibited 9 July 1630 by Elizabeth Burte: her wearing apparel £5; household goods only; total, £9. 13s. 4d. [Signed] Henry Burtt. The mark of Symon Trummells. (Archdeaconry of Totnes.)

The Will of GREGORY BICKFORD of Rattery [co. Devon], yeoman, weak in body, dated 3 July 1630. To the poor of Rattery 40s., to be employed as of late the like gifts have been. To the poor of Modbury 10s., to be employed as at the present time such legacies are employed in Rattery. To the minister that shall give me Christian burial 20s. To Allan Belfeild and Joane Belfeild, children of Allan Belfeild the Elder, £100, for procuring to them a state [i. e., an estate] for their lives in this my living of Knoll or some other like unto it, which sum I appoint to be paid out of my living at Modbury and Rattery Hills. Out of my said living at Modbury and my grounds at Rattery Hills there shall be paid immediately, after this £100 is satisfied, £100 more, to be divided equally between Margarett

410

Benfeild and Joane Benfeild, the daughters of Allan Benfeild [sic]. If Allan Benfeild the Elder do make his son Allan Benfeild sole heir of all his land, then, after the payment of the said £200 and after the death of my executrix, the said Allan Benfeild the Younger shall have and enjoy the whole living and means in Modbury. The said Allan Benfeild the Younger is to have half of all the household [goods] in my house at Knowle, after the death of my executrix. To each of those that shall be my household servants at the day of my death 5s., but to my servant Mary Marche I give 10s. Executrix: my beloved wife, Jane Bickford. Overseers: Allan Benfeild, my son-in-law, and my cousin Richard Marten, to each of whom I give 40s. Witnesses: John Knight, John Rowland, Late [?] Martyn. Proved 17 December 1630.

Inventory, taken 22 September, 6 Charles I [1630], by Thomas Hedd, gentleman, Richd. Martyn, merchant, and Thomas Bickford and Geffery Wyndeate, yeoman, and exhibited 17 December 1630 by Jane Bickford, relict and administratrix: ready money and plate, £30; wearing apparel, £20; 5 fat oxen, £22; 8 fat bullocks, £21; 8 plough oxen, £32; 9 milch kine, £27; 17 young bullocks, £30. 10s.; 304 sheep, £101. 6s. 8d.; 4 score lambs, £16, and other stock; 312 fleeces of wool, £30; a chattel lease in one-half of certain grounds near Rattery Church called the Heele, for years to come determinable on two lives, £80; a chattel lease of a tenement in Rattery called Crabbacrosse, determinable on one life, £20; a chattel lease in a tenement in Rattery, parcel of a tenement called Holwill, for about six years to come, £60; a chattel lease for a tenement in Rattery, late Johane Halse's, for about two years, £6. 13s. 4d.; two other chattel leases in two several tenements in Modbury, co. Devon, determinable on three lives, £400 apiece; total £1236. 9s. 2d. [Signatures of Thos. Head, Richard Martin, and Jeffery Windeatt.] (Archdeaconry of Totnes.)

Administration on the goods of HENRY BURT of Abbots-Kerswell, co. Devon, was granted in 1634. (Principal Registry, Exeter.)

Administration on the estate of LUCY MARTIN of Rattery [co. Devon], widow, deceased, intestate, was granted 20 September 1639 to Richard Martin, son of the deceased.

Inventory, taken 15 August, 15 Charles I [1639], by Thomas Head the Elder of Deane Prior and Geffery Windeate of the same, yeomen, and exhibited 20 September 1639 by Richd. Martyn, son and administrator: wearing apparel, £10; 1 silver boll [bowl], 1 gilt boll, 1 double-gilt salt, 1 little silver cup, 6 silver spoons, £8. 10s.; beds, bedding, etc., of high value; wheat, barley, oats and peas in the ground, £28; 66 sheep, 20 lambs, cows, etc.; a good debt owing for wool, £2. 5s.; total, £162. 18s. 10d. Bond by Richd. Martyn of Totnes, merchant, for £300, 20 September 1639. [Signed] Richd. Martin thelder. [A seal covered with paper.] (Archdeaconry of Totnes.)

FROM PARISH REGISTERS, CO. DEVON

ABBOTS-KERSWELL

1630    Luke Burt, son of Henry Burt, baptized.*

CREDITON†

*Baptisms*

1634    Anna, daughter of Samuell Saunders and Ulalaiah, 1 June.

*This entry was found in the transcripts of the parish registers, at Exeter, co. Devon.
†The Crediton entries are taken from the transcripts of the parish registers, at the Exeter Library.

1636 Samuel, son of Samuell Saunders and Ulalie, 18 June.
1638 John, son of Samuell Saunders and Ulalie, 24 March [1638/9].
1645 Susannah, daughter of Samuell Saunders and Ulalie, 8 June.

## DARTMOUTH (ST. SAVIOUR'S CHURCH)

1604 Joan, daughter of Henry Byrt, baptized 19 April.
1607 Anna, daughter of Henry Byrt, baptized 11 December.

## DEAN-PRIOR

### Baptism
1571 Allen, son of John Berd, 2 September.

### Marriages
1619 Henrie Burt and Ulalia March 28 December.
1646 George March and Sibell Taylor 14 April.

### Burial
1582 John, son of Henry Berd, 6 March [1582/3].

## HARBERTON

### Baptisms
1620 Sarah, daughter of Henry and Eulalia Burt, 14 January [1620/1].*
1624 Samuel, son of John Burt, — April.
1624 Jonathan, son of Henry Burt and [blank] his wife, 23 January [1624/5].
1628 John, son of John Burt and Wilmote, his wife, — February [1628/9].
1629 David, son of Henry Burt and Ulalia, his wife, 18 October.
1632 Mary, daughter of Henry Burt and Ulalia, his wife, 2[?] April.
1632 Nathaniel, son of John Burt and Wilmote, his wife, 15 April.
1635 Mary, daughter of Henry Burt and Ulalia, his wife, 13 April.
1637 Nathaniel, son of Henry Burt and Eulaliah, his wife, [on or after 23] March [1637/8].
1638 Elizabeth, daughter of Henry Burt and Ulaiah, his wife, 4 December.
1650 John, son of Nicholas Marche and Elizabeth, his wife, 21 January [1650/1].

### Marriage
1649 Nicholas March and Elizabeth Voysey 26 December.

### Burials
1612 Christian, daughter of Henry Burt, 11 November.*
1625 Samuell, son of Henry Burt, 21 November.
1629 Isack Burt 13 March [1629/30].
1634 Mary, daughter of Henry Burt, 18 July.

## ILSINGTON

1615 Thomas Paunsford and Isott March married 23 October.

## PAIGNTON

### Baptisms
1642 Will., son of William Burte, 25 November.

*This entry was found in the transcripts of the parish registers, at Exeter.

1661 ——— [ ? Wm.], son of Wm. Burt, 30 November.

*Marriages*

1650 David Narracot and Joane Beard 18 June.
1660 William Burt and Florence Horne 26 February [1660/1].

*Burial*

1659 Ann, wife of William Burt, 17 January [1659/60].

# GENEALOGICAL RESEARCH IN ENGLAND

Communicated by the Committee on English and Foreign Research

## BURT–MARCH

Contributed by GEORGE SKELTON TERRY, B.Sc., of Buffalo, N. Y.

### FROM LAY SUBSIDIES FOR CO. DEVON, 1624*

| Parishes | Persons taxed |
|---|---|
| Chivelstone | John Marche |
| | William Marche |
| East Portlemouth | Grace Marche |
| Harberton | Henry Burt, in land |
| | John Burt |
| | Crispyn Saunders |
| Modbury | Nichola Marche |
| Plymstock | Richard Burte, in land |
| Rattery | Luce Martyn |
| Sherford | William Marche |
| Wembury | John Burte, in goods |

### FROM THE COURT ROLLS OF THE MANOR OF STOKENHAM,† CO. DEVON

Court held 30 September, 12 Elizabeth [1570]. John Marche is to answer to the lord for a trespass, because he unjustly diverted the water at Allymore from its right course so that the water could not run to the lord's mill. (The same entry is found in the records of the court held in September, 11 Elizabeth [1569]).

Court held 3 January, 23 Elizabeth [1580/1]. Will Marche, son of John Marche, is mentioned.

Court held 9 October, 29 Elizabeth [1587]. John Hooper demised part of his tenement to Peter, son of John Marche, a stranger, against the custom of the manor.

Court Roll, 42–43 Elizabeth [1599–1601]. Peter March, a stranger, is mentioned.

Court held 29 March, 44 Elizabeth [1602]. Robert Marche and Richard Marche of Alvington are distrained to answer to the lord, because they are hunters [*venatores*] in the manor.

In an undated list of tenants of the manor [probably of 1608] the name of Thos. Marche, of Mattyscombe, is found.

Court held 9 October 1610. Chillingtu[n]. William March, sen., has stopped the church path leading through a close called le Lower Holbrooke from the village of Chillingtu[n] to the parish church of Stockingham. Thos. Marche paid a fine to the lord, *magn' preposit'*, for this year.

Court held 15 January, 8 James I [1610/11]. William Marche, be-

*From a transcript of this subsidy preserved at Exeter, co. Devon.
†This name also appears in these rolls as Stakenham, Stockenham, Stockingham, and Stokingham.

cause he doth deny the water to be turned out of a certain "drange," which usually hath been turned out of the same without licence, for the better making of the hedge there, [the matter is] referred to Mr. John Peter and the steward of the manor, to be viewed and determined by them before "Midsomer" next. [A similar entry is found in the records of the next court.]

24 June 1647. Lease by Sir Edw. Cary to William March of Sherford of land at Bessand in Stokenham for ninety-nine years, if said William and his sons, Geo. and Will. Marche, so long live.

From the foregoing records the following conclusions may be drawn in regard to the English home and family connections of Henry[1] Burt of Roxbury and Springfield, Mass., and his wife, Ulalia March.

## I. THE BURT FAMILY

The Burt family is found at Harberton, co. Devon, in the early decades of the seventeenth century. A HENRY BURD of Harberton died intestate not later than 28 Apr. 1603, when the inventory of his estate was taken; and administration on his estate was granted, 2 May 1603, to Joan Burd, his widow, who was to distribute to Walter and Jane, her children, such portion of the goods of the deceased as the Archdeacon [of Totnes] should think fit. The Walter Burd of Harberton, weaver, who was surety on the bond of the administratrix, was undoubtedly the son of the deceased. (*Vide supra*, p. 77.) *No relationship has been proved, however, between this Henry Burd and the Henry Burtt who was possibly the father of the New England settler and appears in the following paragraph as No. 1. In fact, the surname *Burd* may be a form of *Beard*, which occurs in that neighborhood, rather than a form of *Burt*.

1. HENRY BURTT, of Harberton, co. Devon, clothier, the testator of 10 July 1617, died between 10 July 1617, when his will was dated, and 10 Sept. 1617, when the inventory of his estate was taken. He married ISETT (or ISOTT) ————, who survived her husband and died between 14 Mar. 1629/30, when she declared her nuncupative will, and 8 July 1630, when the inventory of her estate was taken.

He was a prosperous clothier and landholder, who had his own flock of sheep and owned at his death a considerable stock of cloth and yarn. The value of his estate, according to the inventory, was £602. 7s. 9d. In his will he gave 30s. to the poor of the parish of Harberton, and bequeathed to his wife Isett, his sons Henry and John, his daughters Raddegan (under twenty-one), Allies [Alice], Agnes, and Elizabeth (these three under twenty), another daughter, Johan, who was the wife of Christine [Crispin] Saunder[s], his grandchildren, Joseph and Samuel Saunders, his brothers' and sisters' children, and others. His son John was apparently his executor. (See his will, *supra*, pp. 78–79.)

His widow, Isott Burte, in her nuncupative will of 14 Mar. 1629/30, or thereabouts, gave all her goods to her daughters Agnes Burte and Elizabeth Burte, whom she made her executors. Her estate

*Page 406, this volume.

(personal property only), was appraised at £9. 13s. 4d. (*Vide supra,* p. 81.)

Children:

    i.   JOHN, residuary legatee and executor of his father's will, 1617, and therefore possibly the elder son, was probably the John Burt of Harberton whose wife's Christian name was WILMOTE. He was taxed at Harberton in the subsidy of 1624. and had sons bapt. there from 1624 to 1632. He was present at the declaration of the nuncupative will of his mother. 14 Mar. 1629/30, or thereabouts.

       Children of John and Wilmote Burt, bapt. at Harberton:
1. *Samuel,* bapt. in April 1624.
2. *John,* bapt. in February 1628/9.
3. *Nathaniel,* bapt. 15 Apr. 1632.

2. ii.  HENRY, living 10 July 1617, probably the immigrant to Massachusetts.

    iii.  JOHAN, living 14 Mar., or thereabouts, 1629/30, when she was present at the declaration of the nuncupative will of her mother; m. before 10 July 1617 (when her father made his will) CHRISPIN [CRISPIN] SAUNDERS of Harberton, the testator of 16 Oct. 1626, who d. between that date and 1 Dec. 1626, when the inventory of his estate, amounting to £53. 16s. 10d., was taken. Among the items in the inventory were one mill to make clean seed wheat, 13s. 4d., his books, 13s. 4d., his presses to bind books withal, and three pairs of looms, £3. The will was proved 8 Dec. 1626, his wife, Johan, being his residuary legatee and executor. (*Vide supra,* p. 81.) He was taxed at Harberton in the subsidy of 1624.

       Children (surname *Saunders*), mentioned in their father's will:
1. *Joseph,* b. before 10 July 1617, when his grandfather, Henry Burtt, bequeathed to him £5; living 16 Oct. 1626.
2. *Samuel,* of Crediton, co. Devon, b. before 10 July 1617, when his grandfather, Henry Burtt, bequeathed to him £5; probably living 8 June 1645, when his daughter Susannah was bapt. at Crediton; m. before 1 June 1634 Ulalaiah [Ulalie] ———, who was probably living 8 June 1645. The baptisms of four children of Samuel and Ulalaiah [Ulalie] Saunders are recorded at Crediton, namely, Anna, 1 June 1634; Samuel, 18 June 1636; John, 24 Mar. 1638/9; Susannah, 8 June 1645. The name of Samuel Saunders's wife, Ulalie, is noticeable.
3. *Daniel,*    ⎫
4. *A son,*\*   ⎬ probably b. after 10 July 1617; living 16 Oct.
5. *Rebecca,*   ⎭ 1626.

    iv.  RADDEGAN, living 10 July 1617, when she was under twenty-one.
    v.   ALLIES [ALICE], living 10 July 1617, when she was under twenty.
    vi.  AGNES,    ⎫ both under twenty on 10 July 1617, and both living,
    vii.  ELIZABETH, ⎭ unm., 9 July 1630.

2.  HENRY BURT (probably son of Henry Burtt (No. 1) of Harberton, co. Devon, clothier, the testator of 1617), of Harberton, co. Devon, and of Roxbury and Springfield, Mass., born probably about 1595, died at Springfield 30 Apr. 1662. He married at Dean Prior, co. Devon, 28 Dec. 1619, ULALIA (or EULALIA) MARCH, who died in New England 29 Aug. 1690, daughter of

---

\*Crispin Saunders in his will mentions "my three eldest sons;" and, as it is known that Joseph and Samuel, who are named in the will, were his two eldest sons. and as he *names* only one other son, Daniel, he must have had a third son older than Daniel.

Richard and Joan    Martyn[?]) March (*vide infra,* March pedigree).

Henry Burt was taxed *on land* at Harberton in the subsidy of 1624 — cf. the bequest of lands and houses made by Henry Burt (No. 1), the testator of 10 July 1617, to *his* son Henry (*supra,* p. 78).** He emigrated to New England, probably in the winter of 1638/9 or in the spring or summer of 1639, and probably also with his wife and his seven surviving children, two children having died in England. In New England he is found first at Roxbury, Mass., where his house was burned; and the General Court made a grant of £8 to the town in November 1639 because of this loss. In the following year (1640) he moved to Springfield, where he was clerk of the writs, although he did not record the births of his own children (at least four more) who were born in Massachusetts.

Children :*

i.    SARAH, bapt. at Harberton 14 Jan. 1620/1; living in New England 11 July 1689; m. (1) in New England, 20 June 1643, JUDAH GREGORY of Springfield; m. (2) HENRY WAKLEY of Hartford and Stratford, Conn., who in his will, dated 11 July 1689, named his wife Sarah, three sons, and three daughters.

ii.   SAMUEL, bur. at Harberton 21 Nov. 1625.

iii.  ABIGAIL, b. in England about 1623; m. (1) at Springfield, in 1644, FRANCIS BALL of Springfield, who was drowned in the Connecticut River in October 1648; m. (2) in 1649 BENJAMIN MUNN of Springfield, who d. in November 1675; m. (3) 14 Dec. 1676, as his second wife, LIEUT. THOMAS STEBBINS of Springfield, who d. 15 (or 25) Sept. 1683. Two sons by first husband and five children by second husband.

iv.   DEA. JONATHAN, of Springfield, bapt. at Harberton 23 Jan. 1624/5; d. 19 Oct. 1715; m. (1) in Boston, 20 Oct. 1651, ELIZABETH LOBDELL, who d. 11 Nov. 1684; m. (2) 14 Dec. 1686 DELIVERANCE HANCHET, widow of Thomas Hanchet. Six children by first wife.

v.    DAVID, of Northampton, Mass., bapt. at Harberton 18 Oct. 1629; d. in 1690; m. 18 Nov. 1655 MARY HOLTON, who m. (2) Joseph Root and d. in 1718. Thirteen children.

vi.   MARY, bapt. at Harberton 2[?] Apr. 1632; bur. there 18 July 1634.

vii.  MARY, bapt. at Harberton 13 Apr. 1635; d. in 1689; m. in 1654 WILLIAM BROOKS of Springfield and of Deerfield, Mass., who d. in 1688. Eight sons and eight daughters.

viii. NATHANIEL, of that part of Springfield which was incorporated later as the town of Longmeadow, bapt. at Harberton on or after 23 Mar. 1637/8; d. 29 Sept. 1720; m. 15 Jan. 1662/3 REBECCA SIKES, who d. 28 Jan. 1711/12. Eight children.

ix.   ELIZABETH, bapt. at Harberton 4 Dec. 1638; m. (1) 24 Nov. 1653 SAMUEL WRIGHT, JR., of Springfield and Northampton, Mass., a soldier in King Philip's War, who was killed by the Indians at Northfield, Mass., 2 Sept. 1675; m. (2) 16 Sept. 1684, as his second wife, NATHANIEL DICKINSON of Hatfield, Mass., who had a third wife and d. 11 Oct. 1710. Eight children by first husband.

x.    PATIENCE, b. in New England; m. at Springfield, 7 Oct. 1667, JOHN BLISS of Northampton and Springfield, Mass., who d. 10 Sept. 1702. Seven children, b. 1669—1683.

xi.   MERCY, b. in New England; m. 7 Jan. 1666/7 JUDAH WRIGHT of Northampton, Mass., who m. (2) 11 July 1706 Sarah Burk, widow of Richard Burk, and d. 26 Nov. 1725. Nine children.

*Cf. the parish registers of Harberton (*supra*) and Savage's Genealogical Dictionary.

**Page 407, this volume.

xii. HANNAH, b. in New England; m. in 1659 JOHN BAGG of Spring-field. Ten children.

xiii. DORCAS, b. in New England; m. 28 Oct. 1658 JOHN STILES of Windsor, Conn., who d. 8 Dec. 1683. Five children.

Communicated by the Committee on English and Foreign Research

BURT–MARCH

Contributed by GEORGE SKELTON TERRY, B.Sc., of Buffalo, N. Y.

II. THE MARCH FAMILY

The March family seems to have been in the neighborhood of Sherford, co. Devon, as early as September 1569, when a John Marche was charged in the court of the manor of Stokenham, co. Devon, with diverting the water at Allymore from its right course, so that it could not run to the mill of the lord of the manor. The same charge against John Marche is found in the records of the court of the manor of 30 Sept. 1570. On 3 Jan. 1580/1 William Marche, son of John Marche, is mentioned in the court rolls of the manor, and on 9 Oct. 1587 Peter Marche, a stranger, son of John Marche, appears in the rolls, as does Peter March, a stranger, probably the same man, in 1599–1601. Moreover, on 29 Mar. 1602, Robert Marche and Richard Marche of Alvington, co. Devon, were distrained to answer to the lord for hunting in Stokenham manor. Since the parish registers of Sherford begin late (in 1713), probably because Sherford was formerly a chapelry of Stokenham, where the registers begin in 1578, the exact relationship of these early Marches to the family to which Ulalia (March) Burt belonged has not been determined; but it seems likely that the John Marche of 1569 and 1570, who had sons William (1580/1) and Peter (1587, 1599–1601), was the great-grandfather of Ulalia March, the wife of Henry Burt, John's son William being probably identical with William Marche, the Elder, the testator of 1612, with whom the following pedigree begins.

1. WILLIAM MARCHE, the Elder, of Sherford, co. Devon, yeoman, the testator of 29 Apr. 1612, probably a son of the John Marche whose name appears in the records of the court of the manor of Stokenham, co. Devon, in 1569 and 1570, died between 29 Apr. 1612 and 11 Feb. 1613/14, when the inventory of his personal estate was taken. The name of his wife, who was not mentioned in his will and was probably deceased when it was drawn up, is unknown.

The "Will Marche," son of John Marche, who is mentioned in the court rolls of the manor of Stokenham 3 Jan. 1580/1, is probably identical with this testator of 1612. In a court of the manor held 9 Oct. 1610 he, called "William Marche, sen.," was said to have stopped the church path leading from the village of Chillingtun to the parish church of Stokenham; and on 15 Jan. 1610/11 the case of William Marche, who "doth deny the water to be turned out of a certain 'drange,'" was referred to Mr. John Peter and the steward of the manor.

419

In his will William Marche, the Elder, bequeathed 40s. to his surviving son, George March, 40s. to his eldest daughter, Joane Hinde[?], 6s. 8d. to each of his other daughters, namely, Grace Neale, Jane Bickforde, Prudence Jackson[?], and Sarah Pounde, and 6s. 8d. to each of the seven children of his deceased son, Richard Marche. He directed that he be buried in the parish church of Sherford, and he bequeathed 5s. to the poor of Sherford. The residue of his estate he left to his daughter-in-law, Joane Marche, widow of his son Richard, whom he appointed executor.

Although William Marche must have died not later than 11 Feb. 1613/14, when the inventory of his personal estate was taken, yet his will was not proved until 8 Sept. 1615. This delay may have been due to a clause in the will forbidding the executrix to receive any benefit from the testator's goods (except for necessaries about his funeral "and necessary use about the children" [i. e., Richard's children]) until she had paid his debts. Only farm animals—horses, cattle, sheep, hogs, geese, and poultry—were listed in the inventory.

Children, named in the will of their father:

2. i. RICHARD, d. before 29 Apr. 1612.
   ii. GEORGE, living 21 May 1616, when he witnessed the will of his sister-in-law, Johane Marche, widow of his brother Richard Marche; perhaps m. ALCE (or ALICE) ——, for his niece, Elizabeth March, in her will proved 14 May 1619, bequeathed 20s. to "my aunt, Alce March," who, however, may have been a great-aunt of the testatrix, a sister of her grandfather, William Marche, the Elder. Perhaps the William March of Sherford who on 24 June 1647 took a lease of land in Stokenham and had sons George and William (*supra*, p. 217) was a son of this George.
   iii. JOANE (eldest daughter), m. before 29 Apr. 1612 —— HINDE[?].
   iv. GRACE, m. before 29 Apr. 1612 —— NEALE.
   v. JANE, living 17 Dec. 1630, when she exhibited the inventory of the estate of her late husband; m. before 29 Apr. 1612 GREGORY BICKFORDE of Rattery, co. Devon, yeoman, the testator of 3 July 1630, who d. between 3 July 1630 and 22 Sept. 1630, when the inventory of his estate was taken. He and his brother, John Bickforde of Rattery, yeoman, the testator of 23 May 1625 (who d. between 6 Oct. 1625, when he set his hand and seal to his will, and 14 Dec. 1625, when the inventory of his estate was taken), held land in common in Rattery; and Gregory Bickforde was named as an overseer in his brother's will and, with Thomas Headd of Dean Prior, co. Devon, yeoman, brother-in-law of the testator, took the inventory of his brother's estate. (See the will of John Bickforde, *supra*, pp. 80-81, which contains much information about * the testator's family.) In his own will Gregory Bickford bequeathed 40s. to the poor of Rattery, 10s. to the poor of Modbury, co. Devon, and 20s. to "the minister that shall give me Christian burial." He mentioned his livings at Knoll (he had a house at Knoll or Knowle), Modbury, and Rattery Hills, and provided liberally for his grandchildren, Allan, Joane, and Margaret Benfeild (or Belfeild), the children of his son-in-law, Allan Benfeild, the Elder, whom he made one of the overseers of his will. To each of those that should be his household servants at the day of his death he left 5s., but to his servant Mary Marche (undoubtedly a relative of his wife) he gave 10s. He appointed his wife, Jane Bickford,

*Pages 409-410, this volume.

420

executrix. The inventory of his estate showed property appraised at £1236. 9s. 2d., including ready money and plate, wearing apparel, livestock (304 sheep, 80 lambs, and many other animals), wool, and several leases of lands and tenements.

Child (surname *Bickforde*):

1. *A daughter*, d. probably before 3 July 1630; m. Allan Benfeild (or Belfeild), who was living 3 July 1630. Their three children, Allan, Joane, and Margaret, were living (the daughters unm.) 3 July 1630. (See will of Gregory Bickford, *supra*, pp. 81-82.)

vi. PRUDENCE, m. before 29 Apr. 1612 ——— JACKSON[?]. Perhaps he was the Nicholas Jackston[?] who witnessed the will of Johane Marche, widow of Prudence's brother Richard Marche, 21 May 1616.

vii. SARAH, m. before 29 Apr. 1612 ——— POUNDE.

2. RICHARD MARCHE (*William*), of Sherford, co. Devon. died before 29 Apr. 1612. He married JOANE ——— [? MARTYN], the testatrix of 21 May 1616, who died between that date and 10 June 1616, when the inventory of her estate was taken. She was probably a sister of Rev. Henry Martyn, vicar of Rattery, co. Devon, the testator of 13 Nov. 1619, or of his wife, Lucy Martyn, administration on whose estate was granted 20 Sept. 1639, for, since Elizabeth March of Rattery, spinster, daughter of Richard and Joane Marche, in her will proved 14 May 1619, called Mr. Henry Martyn her uncle, there can be little doubt that Elizabeth's mother was Henry Martyn's sister or sister-in-law.*

William Marche, father of Richard Marche, in his will dated 29 Apr. 1612, had bequeathed to each of his seven children of his (the testator's) son Richard, deceased, 6s. 8d., and had made his daughter-in-law, Joane Marche, his residuary legatee and executor. In her own will, dated 21 May 1616 and proved 21 June 1616, Joane Marche of Sherford, co. Devon, widow, disposed of an estate appraised (according to the inventory of 10 June 1616) at £140. 7s., including apparel, live stock, and a lease in reversion of twenty-one years in a tenement called Sand Wills. She directed that she be buried in the parish church of Sherford, and bequeathed 10s. to the poor of Sherford. She left £5 to her eldest daughter, Alice March, to be paid within a half year after her death, £5 to her second daughter, Elizabeth March, to be paid within one year after her death, and 50s. to each of the rest of her daughters, namely, Ulalia March, Amias March, Jane March, and Johane March, to be paid within a year after her death. She made William March, her son, her executor and residuary legatee. John Bickford and Gregory Bickford were two of the overseers of her will, and George March, undoubtedly her brother-in-law, was a witness.

Children, named in their mother's will, dated 21 May 1616:

i. WILLIAM, a legatee in the will of his grandfather, William Marche, the Elder, executor of his mother's will, and her resi-

*For Henry Martyn and his family and relatives *vide infra*, Addendum.

duary legatee, apparently d. *s. p.* about a year after his mother, i. e., about May or June 1617, for although he was a legatee in his sister Elizabeth's will, which was undated but was proved 14 May 1619, the inventory of her estate, taken 12 May 1619, showed that there was due to her the sixth part of £140, viz, £23. 6s. 8d., with interest (£4. 13s. 4d.) for two years, as well as the legacy of £5 given to her by her mother's will, with interest for two years, and the sixth part of a one-third part of a "bargain" [a small farm] in Sherford, etc. In other words, Elizabeth and her five sisters had inherited the estate of their deceased brother, with interest for two yeaars.

ii.   ALICE (eldest daughter), a legatee in the will of her grandfather, William Marche, the Elder, and in her mother's will, living unm. when her sister Elizabeth made her will, probably about 1616 or 1617.

iii.  ELIZABETH (second daughter), a legatee in the will of her grandfather, William Marche, the Elder, and in her mother's will, d. unm. not later than 12 May 1619, when the inventory of her estate was taken. In her will, undated but probably made soon after her mother's death, i. e., about 1616 or 1617, and proved 14 May 1619, she styled herself Elizabeth March of Ratterie, co. Devon, spinster, bequeathed 10s. to the poor of Rattery and the same amount to the poor of Sherford, and gave 10s. for a ring for "him that shall preach my funeral sermon." She left 6s. to Marie Marche, daughter of Thomas Marche of Sherford, probably a near relative and perhaps identical with "my servant Mary Marche," to whom Gregory Bickford of Rattery, in his will dated 3 July 1630, gave 10s. She also bequeathed 12d. apiece to "three of my uncle's, Mr. Henrie Martyne's, [men]servants," whose names she gave, a ewe to her brother, William March, 12d. to her godchild, Peter Cooke, and all her apparel and a ewe to her sister Amyas. The residue of her goods was to be equally divided among her five sisters, except that, if Alce (Alice), her eldest sister, should marry "to my Uncle Martine's good liking and [that] of her friends," she was to have 40s. more than the others. "Lastly, I do entreat my uncle, Mr. Henry Martyn, to be my executor, and for his pains I bequeath unto him a gold ring which my mother gave unto me." The witnesses to the will were Luce Martyn [wife of Mr. Henry Martyn] and William and Christian Hele (or Heale) [son-in-law and daughter of Henry Martyn]. The inventory of her estate, taken 12 May 1619 and exhibited by Henry Marten, clerk and executor, 14 May 1619, showed, as explained above, in the account of her brother William, that she had inherited a sixth part of her brother's estate. Her estate was appraised at £39. 14s. Elizabeth probably, and her sister Amyas certainly (see will of Henry Martyn, *supra*. pp. 79-80), lived with her uncle, Henry Martyn, at Rattery.*

iv.   ULALIA (probably third daughter), a legatee in the will of her grandfather, William Marche, the Elder, and in her mother's will, heir to one-sixth of her brother William's estate, and entitled to one-fifth of the residue of the estate of her sister Elizabeth, m. at Dean Prior, co. Devon, 28 Dec. 1619, HENRY BURT of Harberton, co. Devon. She emigrated to New England in 1638 or 1639, probably in company with her husband and surviving children, and d. in New England 29 Aug. 1690. Her property, including the bequests in her grandfather's and mother's will and her share in the estates of her brother and her sister Elizabeth, probably amounted to £36 or more at the time of her marriage. For further information about her

*Pages 408-409, this volume.

husband and for her thirteen children see the Burt pedigree, *supra*, pp. 218-220.

v.  AMIAS (or AMYAS) (probably fourth daughter), a legatee in the will of her grandfather, William Marche, the Elder, and in her mother's will, heir to one-sixth of the estate of her brother William, a legatee in the will of her sister Elizabeth, and entitled to one-fifth of the residue of Elizabeth's estate, was living unm. 13 Nov. 1619, when her uncle, Rev. Henry Martyn, mentioned her in his will as "Ames Marche, who dwelleth with me," and bequeathed to her a ewe.

vi.  JANE (probably fifth daughter), living when her sister Elizabeth made her will, about 1616 or 1617. She was a legatee in the will of her grandfather, William Marche, the Elder, and in her mother's will, heir to one-sixth of the estate of her brother William, and entitled to one-fifth of the residue of the estate of her sister Elizabeth.

vii.  JOHANE (probably sixth daughter), living when her sister Elizabeth made her will, about 1616 or 1617. She was a legatee in the same wills as her sister Jane (*supra*), and shared in the same proportion in the same estates.

THOMAS MARCHE of Sherford, co. Devon, was one of three men who took the inventory of the property of William Marche, the Elder, 11 Feb. 1613/14, and also the inventory of Johane Marche, widow, 10 June 1616, his two associates in taking both inventories being Arthur Wakeman and William Randall. He had a daughter, Marie Marche, to whom Elizabeth March, in her will proved 14 May 1619, bequeathed 6s. This daughter may be identical with Mary Marche, whom Gregory Bickford, in his will dated 3 July 1630, called "my servant," to whom he bequeathed 10s. Whether this Thomas Marche of Sherford was identical with a Thomas Marche of Mattyscombe, whose name appears in an undated list of tenants (probably of 1608) of the manor of Stokenham, is uncertain; but presumably he was closely related to William Marche, the Elder, and perhaps was his brother or nephew.

## ADDENDUM

HENRY MARTYN, clerk, vicar of Rattery, co. Devon, called "my uncle, Mr. Henry Martyn," in the will of Elizabeth March, which was proved 14 May 1619, died between 13 Nov. 1619, when he made his will, and 31 Jan. 1619/20, when the inventory of his goods was taken by John Byckford and Thomas Head. His will was proved 25 Apr. 1620. In it he mentioned, among others, his brothers Thomas, Peter, and John Martyn, his cousins Robert Saverye, Esq., ———— [? Philip] Saverye, Johan Saverye, and Jane Saverye, Mrs. Philip Saverye, his cousin Thomas Beare (who had sons Thomas and Henry), his wife Lucy, his son Richard, and his daughter Christian, who was the wife of William Heale. The testator's cousin, Robert Saverye, Esq., and his son-in-law, William Heale, were named as overseers of the will, and they also witnessed it. The testator's wife, Lucy, and his son, Richard, were designated as residuary legatees and executors. The inventory showed property appraised at £534. 5s. 11d., including books valued at £20. (Cf. the will, *supra*, pp. 79-80.) The widow, Lucy Martin of Rattery, died intestate not

later than 15 Aug. 1639, when the inventory of her goods, valued at
£162. 18s. 10d., was taken; and administration was granted 20 Sept.
1639 to her son Richard, who, as "Richd. Martyn of Totnes, merchant," gave a bond for £300, signing it as "Richd. Martin thelder."
(*Vide supra*, p. 82.) He was called "my cousin" in the will of Gregory Bickford, dated 3 July 1630, of which he was an overseer, and,
as "Richd. Martyn, merchant," with three associates, took the inventory of Gregory Bickford's estate, 22 Sept. 1630.

## METCALF: ADDITIONAL RECORDS

Contributed by G. ANDREWS MORIARTY, A.M., LL.B., F.S.A.,
of Bristol, R. I.

THE following records throw additional light on the English connections and activities of Michael Metcalf, the dornick weaver, of
Norwich, co. Norfolk, England, and later of Dedham, Mass., concerning whom the Committee on English Research (now the Committee on English and Foreign Research) communicated to the
REGISTER (vol. 78, pp. 63-65) an article by the present writer and
also (vol. 80, pp. 312-313) an article by the late Charles Edward
Banks, M.D., Colonel, U.S.A., Retired.*

Considerable research shows the impossibility of establishing the
ancestry of Michael Metcalf beyond his father, Rev. Leonard Metcalf, rector of Tatterford in Norfolk, who, according to his deposition
(*infra*), was born in the hamlet of Apperside, in Wensleydale, Yorkshire. Examination of the records of this region shows that a large
proportion of the inhabitants bore the name of Metcalf. In the
extracts from the subsidy of 1542–1544 for Apperside (*infra*) a large
number of Metcalfs appear; and, when one remembers that this subsidy represents but a portion of the inhabitants, it is easy to see that
a large proportion of the inhabitants were named Metcalf. The
names *Michael* and *Leonard* were very common in the Metcalf family of this region, where the Metcalfs formed almost a clan. There
can be no doubt that the gentle family of the neighboring Nappa Hall
were related more or less remotely to the innumerable Metcalfs of the
vicinage, but just how it is impossible to say, owing to the lack of
wills. It may be suggested, however, that perhaps Rev. Leonard
Metcalf was the son of the Michael Metcalf who is found at Apperside in the subsidy of 1542–1544.

### FROM LAY SUBSIDIES FOR CO. YORK,
### 34–35 HENRY VIII [1542–1544]

#### APPERSIDE

| | |
|---|---|
| Henry Metcalf in goods 10d. | Jone Metcalf in goods 1d. |
| Michael Metcalf in goods 3s. 4d. | Edward Metcalf in goods 10d. |
| Denis Metcalf in goods 1d. | Reginald Metcalf in goods 2s. |
| Symon Metcalf in goods 18d. | John Metcalf, Sen., in goods 2s. |
| | Richard Metcalf in goods 1s. |

(Lay Subsidies, 22/166.)

*For pp. 63-65 see pp. 52-54, this volume; for pp. 312-313 see pp. 143-144,
this volume.

FROM THE RECORDS OF THE COURT OF REQUESTS

[Medcalf v. Browne, 1595]

Bill of Leonard Medcalf of Tatterfore, co. Norfolk, clerk, against Nicholas Browne of Walsingham, gentleman [endorsed 30 October, 37 Elizabeth, by warrant]:

Whereas complainant became bound with John Day of Walsingham, gentleman, about midsummer "last past was a Twelvemoneth," to Nicholas Browne, for the delivery, at the Feasts of the Nativity and the Purification of Our Lady next following,* of one hundred "combes" of barley sold by John Day to Nicholas Browne, so it is that John Daye has caused sixty "combes" of barley to be delivered, and has compounded with the said Browne for the residue; yet Nicholas Browne has given out that he will sue complainant upon the obligation of £40 or thereabouts, by reason that the form thereof was not kept, unless complainant will deliver to him, before the Purification of Our Lady next coming, eighty "combes" of barley, which at this time of dearth nearly amounts to the whole value of the said penalty. [Therefore your complainant] prays for a writ of privy seal against Nicholas Browne. (Court of Requests, Proceedings, 105/17.)

FROM PARISH REGISTERS

1579  James, son of Leonard Metcalf, baptized 14 March [1579/80].*†
1588  A daughter of Edmond Metcalf baptized.*
1590  Leonard Metcalf buried 10 August.*
1602  James Metcalf and Joan Cooke married 30 January [1602/3].*
              (St. Michael on the Hill, Lincoln.)
1603  Leonard Metcalfe and Margaret Smith married 17 July.
              (Kildwick, co. York.)
1607  Michael, son of Richard Metcalf, baptized 1 November.*
              (Tattershall, co. Lincoln.)
1607  John Mydcallf and Ellyn Benson married 19 July.
              (St. Andrew, Norwich, transcript.)
1613–1617  Children of Adam Metcalf baptized.*
              (St. Saviour, Norwich.)
1618  Mary, daughter of Michael Metcalfe, baptized 17 February [1618/19].*
              (St. Benedict, Norwich).
1627  Leonard, son of Edmund Metcalf, baptized.*
              (St. Augustine, Norwich.)
1630  Robt., son of Augustine Medcalfe, baptized 21 November.
              (St. Clement, Norwich, transcript.)

FROM DEPOSITIONS IN THE DIOCESAN REGISTRY, NORWICH

1614  Leonard Metcalf, clerk, rector of the parish of Tatterford, where he has been incumbent for forty years, born at Apperside, co. York, [deposed] aged 73 years. (Deposition Book, 1614.)*
1635  Michael Metcalfe of Norwich, dornick weaver, aged 45 years, born at Tatterford, co. Norfolk, testifies regarding the practices of the clergyman of St. Edmund's, Norwich. (Ib., 1635.)*

*That is, on 25 December and 2 February.
†For entries marked with an asterisk (*) the contributor is indebted to the late Col. Charles Edward Banks, M.D.

425

## FROM DEEDS ENROLLED

1617, 9 May. Wm. Doddesworth and wife to Adam Medcalfe of a tenement, etc., in St. Lawrence. (Roll 9.)

1617, 9 May. Adam Medcalfe and wife to Hen. Fawcett of a tenement in St. Lawrence. (Roll 10.)

1628, 23 June. Jno. Scottowe and others to Jeffry Medcalfe two messuages in St. James. (Roll 14.)

1630, 7 September. Francis Langley and wife to Jeffry Medcalfe and wife a messuage in St. Peter's, Mancroft. (Roll 31.)

1636 [? 1636/7], 18 February. Jno. Fayry and wife to Jeffry Medcalfe and wife of a tenement in St. Saviour's. (Roll 45.)

1638, 18 December. Pleasance Medcalfe and others to Thos. Watts three messuages in St. James. (Roll 67[?].)

1639, 29 April. Jeffry Medcalfe and wife to Jno. Askins of a tenement in St. James. (Roll 49.)

## FROM THE BOOKS OF THE MAYOR'S COURT

1624 Michael Metcalf and Xopher Church searchers of the dornix weavers.

1627 ⎫ Michael Metcalf and Thos. Tilney wardens of the dornix weav-
1628 ⎬ ers for one year.

1628/9, 3 January, 4 Charles I. Matthew Metcalf punished for disorder at the post.

1629 Michael Metcalf and Xopher Church sworn as wardens of the dornix weavers.

1632, 18 July, 8 Charles I. Dionis, wife of Silvester Medcalfe *alias* Parker, in a previous charge for disordered life, for entertaining of Edmond Allen, worsted weaver, dwelling in St. Peters Parmontergate, and one Farding of St. Michael of Coslany, weaver, and one Burton of St. Michael aforesaid, in her house between 12 and 1 o'clock last night, and for other misdemeanors, is committed to Bridewell. (Fo. 398.)

1632, Saturday, 21 July, 8 Charles I. Next Court. She [the said Dionis] is discharged out of Bridewell, upon her promise that she before this day sevenight will go over into Holland to her husband, or otherwise she consenteth to be whipped at the post.

1635, 25 November, 11 Charles I. Stephen Tye is put to St. Bennett's gates, and Susan Medcalfe agreeth to keep him till he be cured, and to receive 6s. 8d. when he is perfectly cured, whereof she hath received 3s. 4d. this Wednesday afternoon, 25 November 1635. (Fo. 84 b.)

1636, Saturday, 14 May. "Inquisicio artis de Dornix weavers." Michael Metcalfe, Simon Bowman, and others sworn. (Fo. 104 b.)

## FROM SESSIONS BOOKS AND SEARCH BOOKS

[Undated, probably about 1630.] Jeffery Medcalfe to pay 4d. to St. John Sepulchre [in list of persons paying to parishes other than those in which they are rated].

1630, 20 September, 6 Charles I. General Session of Peace at Guildhall. Geoffrey Medcalfe is fined 6s. 8d. and acknowledges the indictment.

1631. Order for payment to overseers of other parishes from 8 August 1631. Jeffery Medcalfe paid overseers of St. Michael at Thorn 3d.

1631, 12 December, 7 Charles I. Thomas Medcalf "ad respondendum" [probably for payment to other parishes].

1631, 12 December. In a list of those ordered to pay to overseers of other parishes appears the name of Jeffery Medcalfe, ordered to pay 1d. to St. Michael at Thorne, and Michael Medcalfe, ordered to pay ½d. to St. Paul's.

1633–34 (Easter to Easter). In Walter Rye's "The Norwich Rate Book" (p. 75), in St. Edmond's Parish, is listed Michael Medcalfe.

1634, 12 August. Presentments. Wards beyond the Water. Fibridge Ward. Augustin Metcalfe for not coming to church. (Norwich Sessions Rolls.)

1634, 16 December. Presentments for St. Peter's Mancroft Ward. The mark of Geoffrey Medcalfe. (Norwich Sessions Rolls.)

1634/5, Monday, 23 March, 10 Charles I. General Session of the Peace at the Guildhall, Norwich. In a list of recusants indicted and proclaimed according to the statute appears the name of Augustine Metcalfe of St. Clement's Parish, sadler, for absenting himself from his parish church for three months.

1634/5, 24 March. Presentments at Sessions. The Ward beyond the Water. "Wee present Augustine Medcalfe Sadler of St. Clement's parish for not coming to Church for the space of 3 months contrary to the statute." (Norwich Sessions Rolls.)

1635, 11 July. In the Court of the Mayor. Michaell Medcalfe, Simon Bowman, and diverse other dornix-weavers came into this Court and Informed that Augustine Thurton, who worketh with Thomas Mollett, and Tho: Evered, who worketh with John Brady, have an Intencion to gather a multitude of people together at the Unicorne this night, to doe (as they feare) some unlawfull Act, And have desired this Court to prevent the same. The said Augustine Thurton saith that hee and the said Tho: Evered did upon Tuesday last goe abroad to diverse dornix-weavers shopps in this City and did invite the severall Jorneymen to mete this afternoone at the Unicorne to elect 4 feast makers to make a feast for the Jorneymen dornix weavers.

Thomas Evered saith that the Jornymen dornix wevers have used to have yearely a feast amongest themselves, And upon Tuesday last hee and the said Augustine did speake to most of the Jornymen in the City to mete at the Unicorne this afternoone to consent howe they might drawe their severall masters to give greater wages, And he saith that the intent of this metinge was onely to knowe how the Journymen would holde all together concerning the mending of their wages and that they might have promised one annother that they would have no lesse then vj d. a weeke more then nowe they have, yf they could gett ytt.

Thurton and Evered bound in £40 each to answer at the Sessions. (Norwich Sessions, Minute Book 8.)

1640/1, 12 January. In "Alphabetical Lists of persons indicted at Sessions, both City and County," from 1624 onwards, is the entry: "Metcalfe Ric'us de Skyton pro non escur'. foveam ex' May 1641." (City of Norwich, Corporation Records, Search Books.)

EXTRACT FROM WREN'S "PARENTALIA"*

[Matthew Wren, D.D., 1585-1667, a prominent clergyman of the Church of England, elected Bishop of Hereford 5 Dec. 1634 and consecrated by

*"Parentalia, or Memoirs of the Family of the Wrens," was compiled by Christopher Wren, son of the famous architect, Sir Christopher Wren (who was a nephew of Bishop

Archbishop Laud 2 Mar. 1634/5, was elected Bishop of Norwich 10 Nov. 1635, and was translated to the See of Ely in April 1638. A follower of Archbishop Laud and a vigorous opponent of Puritanism, he was impeached by the Commons in 1641 and was imprisoned from time to time until the Restoration, when he recovered his episcopal rights and dignities. The following extract is from his answer to the Sixteenth Article of Impeachment against him.]

"He [Bishop Wren] further denieth, that *Daniel Sunning, Michael Metcalf,* and the rest in this Article named, or any other of his Majesty's Subjects, to the Number of 3000, did remove into the Parts beyond the Seas by reason of any thing done by this Defendant. And he humbly prayeth, that it may be consider'd, that the humour of separating themselves from the Church of *England* into foreign Parts is of a much higher Growth than since *Anno* 1636. And that out of these Dioceses where they could have no Pretence of vigorous Persecutions, they went so plentifully, as that the two chief Colonies in *New England,* long since took the Titles of *Plymouth* and *Boston.* And thither, into *New England,* of those which are named in this Article, went *Francis Lawes* a poor and mean Weaver, *John Dicks* a poor Joiner, *Nicholas Busby* a poor Weaver, *Michael Metcalf,* and *Nicholas* his Son, a Dornix Weaver (of some Estate, he only) but he was call'd in question for some Words against the King, and so slipt away. *John Durant* is supposed to be the same with *John Berant,* he a poor Weaver that went into the *Low-Countries,* and thither went *Richard Cook* a Draper newly set up, that kept but one Apprentice." (Wren's Parentalia, edition of 1750, p. 101.)

## FROM PROBATE RECORDS

The Will of NICHOLAS METCALFE of Blakeney [co. Norfolk], clerk, weak of body but of perfect memory, etc., dated 13 September 1661. I give my precious soul to God, [my] maker, hoping to be saved by the merits of Christ. My body I commit to the earth, not doubting but that it shall rise again a glorious body. As for my goods, I dispose of them as followeth:

To Leonard Metcalfe, the son of Leonard Metcalfe, my kinsman (dwelling in Norwich), when he shall attain fourteen years, the house wherein I now dwell, with yard and ground thereto, for him and his heirs for ever. My executors are to receive the rents of the same house and ground and to keep it in repair, until said Leonard Metcalfe is fourteen, and the surplus then in their hands is to be used to bind him out to some trade. To the said executors I give all household stuff and implements of household, to be sold by them to satisfy my debts, vizt., to Mary Cherch, my servant, 32s., and I give to Edmund Day, rector of this parish, 6s. 8d., to buy a pair of gloves. To each executor, for his pains, 10s. The rest of the money from the sale of my goods is to be used to discharge my funeral charges and for proving my will; and the remainder is to be divided equally between John Metcalfe and Elizabeth Metcalfe, the children of Leonard Metcalfe, now deceased. I appoint Thomas Youngman and Henry Basset executors. [Signed] Nicholas Metcalfe. Witnesses: Sam: Bacon, John Cressey[?], Tho: Abraham. Proved at Walsingham Parva [co. Norfolk], 16 September 1664, by the executors. (Archdeaconry of Norwich, 1664–65, fo. 113.)

Matthew Wren), and was published in London in 1750 by Stephen Wren, son of the compiler. A new edition was published in 1903. A life of Bishop Wren, from which the extract here given has been taken, is included in "Parentalia."

# MISCELLANEOUS RECORDS OF VARIOUS FAMILIES

Contributed by G. Andrews Moriarty, A.M., LL.B., F.S.A.,
of Bristol, R. I.

## COGGESHALL

1626   Ann Coxshall, daughter of John Coxshall, baptized 7 May.
1628   Marye Coghsall, daughter of John Cogeshall, baptized 22 June.
1629   Jeames Cogishall, son of John Cogeshall, baptized 14 March
       [1629/30].
1640   Catherine Coggeshall, daughter of John Coggeshall, buried 14 May.
       (Parish Registers of Castle Hedingham, co. Essex.)

[Cf. article on the English ancestry and connections of President John **
Coggeshall of the Colony of Rhode Island, in the REGISTER, vol. 73, pp. 19-32.]

## CUTLER

1636, 22 June.   This day Robt. Gallard of Sprowston [co. Norfolk],
Clerke, Saml. Gallard of the same Towne, Clerke, and John Cutler
of the same Towne, yeoman, came into this Court and brought into
this Court a writing conteyning the last will and testament of Susan
Haylett, widow, And offered to depose . . . that the writing
is . . . the last will of the said Susan, And was . . . so declared by her . . . in their presence, And the Subscription of
their severall names is the severall handwriting of the said severall
persons above-named.
(Mayor's Court Books, Norwich, co. Norfolk, 1634–1646, fo. 112.)

[This John Cutler was the early settler at Hingham, Mass., who, it is known,
came from Sprowston, co. Norfolk.]

## FOLGER

John Folger, the immigrant, who, according to Savage's "Genealogical
Dictionary," came from Norwich, co. Norfolk, in 1635, and had a
house lot of 6 acres at Watertown, Mass., was from Diss, co. Norfolk; and his wife, Meribeh Gibbs, was the daughter of John Gibbs
of Freudes Hall in that neighborhood, as is proved by the will of
John Gibbs, 1609, in which he mentioned his daughter, "Merraba
Folger."*

## HASKELL

William Haskell, whose wife's name was Elinor, was churchwarden in the
parish of Charlton-Musgrove, co. Somerset, in 1627. The registers
of that parish show that he had children baptized there, as follows:

| | |
|---|---|
| Roger, 6 March 1613/14. | Mark, 8 April 1621. |
| Cecilie, 5 June 1616. | Dorothy, 16 November 1623. |
| William (Hascoll), 8 Novem- | Elizabeth, 30 April 1626. |
| ber 1618. | Joan, 1 March 1628[1628/9]. |

William Haskell, the father of these children, was buried at
Charlton-Musgrove 11 May 1630, and his widow married John Stone,
who brought the Haskell children to Salem, Mass., in 1636. No
record, however, of the marriage of the Widow Haskell and John
Stone has been found, nor are there any Haskell records in the
registers of Charlton-Musgrove before or after the entries given
above; but other records show that a Mark Haskall was living in
that parish in 1623, aged 50 years. Perhaps he was father [or
brother] of William Haskell.*

*See p. 258, footnote. (Page 430, this volume.)

**See pp. 556-569, this volume.

## PERSE

1636, Saturday, 3 December. This day the wife of John Perse came, in the absence of her husband, who is now in New England, and desired to have a keeper chosen to succeed in that place at Christmas next, and this Court wth one consent did choose Nicholas Rix of St. Edmund's to perform that place, if he before Christmas next shall enter such surety as John Perse did formerly enter. [The "place" is not specified.]
(Mayor's Court Books, Norwich, co. Norfolk, 1634–1646, fo. 137.)

## ROSE

1632, 17 December, 8 Charles I. Henry Marsh, apprentice with Wm. Rose, late of Norwich, worsted weaver, complains that Wm. Rose has gone beyond the seas and left him destitute of maintenance, and that warrants have been made out, but he cannot be found. Marsh is, therefore, discharged of his apprenticeship, and shall serve the residue of his term with Robt. Brooke, worsted weaver.
(Sessions Minute Book, Norwich, co. Norfolk, 1630–35.)

## TARNE

Miles Tarne was living in Yorkshire in 1578. This is such an odd surname that it is possible that Yorkshire was the home county of the Miles Tarne, leather-dresser, who was in Boston, Mass., as early as 1638. (Cf. Savage's Genealogical Dictionary and Pope's Pioneers of Massachusetts.)*

*For entries marked with an asterisk (*) the contributor is indebted to the courtesy of Mrs. Charles Frederick White of Brookline, Mass., who obtained them in June 1929 from the late Col. Charles Edward Banks, M.D.

## GENEALOGICAL RESEARCH IN ENGLAND

Communicated by the Committee on English and Foreign Research

### THE FISKE FAMILY

Contributed by G. Andrews Moriarty, A.M., LL.B., F.S.A.,
of Bristol, R. I.

The ancient Suffolk family of Fiske and its connection with New England have long been known, and two books, one compiled by an American and the other by an Englishman, have been published about the family.* In spite of this the pedigree of the family has remained in great confusion and presents many difficulties that have not hitherto been cleared up. The American book is, in so far as the pages dealing with the family in England are concerned, of little value, as the very brief summaries of the wills there given contain numerous errors and omit many important details relating to the estates of the testators, their standing in their respective communities, their bequests, and their beneficiaries, while the conclusions of the compiler are often incorrect. The English book contains much valuable material, but it is not as carefully compiled as it should be, with the result that the pedigrees therein are often erroneous and misleading. From early times the family was very prolific, and the records of its various members about the beginning of the sixteenth century are, as is unusual in the case of a yeoman family of this sort, very voluminous and therefore confusing. In the American book the progenitor of the family in the fifteenth century, one branch of whose descendants became lords of the Manor of Stodleigh in Laxfield, co. Suffolk, is styled "Lord Symon Fiske," the compiler evidently being under the impression that the lord of a manor and his remote ancestors were peers of the realm and entitled to be called "Lords." In the sixteenth century the ancestors of the American family exercised the useful but hardly noble calling of wheelwrights,

*The two books are Fiske and Fisk Family, by Frederick Clifton Pierce, Chicago, 1896, and The Fiske Family Papers, by Henry Ffiske, Norwich [1902].

and they probably served the community in this capacity as well as they would have served it in the mythical capacity of barons of England which their American descendant has foisted upon them. There is a great difference between a peer and a wheelwright, and, although the latter may be and probably is the better man—well, he is not a peer.

In regard to the family arms, the branch which acquired the Manor of Stodleigh, whose pedigree appears in the heralds' visitations, undoubtedly used the checquy coat; but it is doubtful if their kinsmen from whom the American family descends ever claimed or used a coat of arms.

The pedigree of the branch which sent several members to America has been preserved in the Candler Manuscripts, the better copy of which is in the Bodleian Library at Oxford. Matthias and Philip Candler, who were descendants of this branch and lived in the middle of the seventeenth century, were excellent genealogists, and they were sufficiently near the persons of whom they wrote to know the facts. The pedigree of the Laxfield-New England Fiskes, as given by the Candlers, begins with a certain Richard Fiske, who was living in the Broadgates at Laxfield in the middle of the sixteenth century. After a careful study of the Laxfield Fiskes the present writer has come to the conclusion that this Richard Fiske was a son of Simon Fiske of Laxfield, the testator of 1536, for the following reasons: 1. The internal evidence of Simon's will shows that not all his children are named in the will. (It may be noted that this is also the case in the will of his nephew, William Fiske of Stodleigh, as well as in other early wills of the family.) 2. The name *Geoffrey* is found among the children of both Simon Fiske and Richard. 3. Simon Fiske had a daughter bearing the very unusual name of Gelion, and William Fiske, son of Richard, the testator of 1575, also had a daughter named Gelion. This name occurs in the Fiske family of Suffolk in only three instances, the third being in the family of George Fiske of Westhall, who was probably also of this branch. If Richard was not the son of Simon, the testator of 1536, he must have been the son of Geoffrey Fiske, son of Geoffrey of Laxfield, the testator of 1504, the elder Geoffrey being a brother of William Fiske of Laxfield, another testator of 1504, who was the father of Simon, the testator of 1536. In view, however, of the repetition of the name *Gelion* in the family of Simon Fiske and of William, son of Richard, there can be little doubt that Richard was a son of Simon, whose will, as has been stated, does not mention all his children. An examination of the records and of the pedigree that are given in this article will elucidate these points.

The ancestors of the New England Fiskes were notable for their adherence to the Reformed Religion and for their sufferings on its behalf in the dark days of Queen Mary; and this heritage is one on which their descendants may justly pride themselves far more than on any mythical peerage. At the time of the settlement of New England the Fiskes were a family of exceedingly prosperous artisans and yeomen, who sent several of their sons to the universities, whence they went forth to become Puritan ministers.

In this article abstracts of numerous records relating to the English ancestors and connections of the Fiskes of New England have been assembled and classified, and they will be followed by a pedigree based on them. It is not the purpose of the article to present a complete genealogy of the numerous Fiske families that resided in the various parishes of Suffolk. This research has been confined to the branch which may be called the Fiskes of Laxfield, and among them to the immediate families of the ancestors of the emigrants to America.

Attention is called to the inventory of the goods of William Fiske, the wheelwright of Laxfield, taken 7 January 1590/1, which should prove especially interesting to students of the social history of the period and of the Suffolk dialect. (See below, under Will No. 48.)

### From Probate Records

1. The Will of WILLIAM FISK of Laxfeld [Laxfield, co. Suffolk] the Elder, dated 6 March 1462 [1462/3]. To be buried in Laxfeld church. To the high altar there, for tithes forgotten, 3s. 4d. To a priest [to sing] for one year. Executors and residuary legatees: my wife Joan, Nicholas Noloth, and John Smyth, "Rafnam," of Laxfeld. Proved 21 April 1463 by Joan, the widow, and by John Smyth, "Raffman," Nicholas Noloth renouncing. (Archdeaconry of Suffolk [Ipswich Probate Registry], book 2, fo. 86.)

2. The Will of SIMON FYSK of Laxfeld [Laxfield, co. Suffolk], dated 22 December 1463. To be buried in Laxfeld church, whereof I am a parishioner. To the high altar 3s. 4d. To the stipend of the chaplain of the Gild of St. Mary in Laxfeld 6s. 8d. yearly, for sixteen years. For the health of my soul and my friends' souls I will that a chaplain shall celebrate in Laxfeld church for one year. For three trentals for my soul 30s. To the new bells in Laxfeld 20s. To my wife Katherine my utensils and moveables live and dead. To each of my three daughters £10 within a year of marriage; but, if any of them remain single, she shall enjoy her portion. To my son William 40s. To my son Geoffrey 40s. To my elder son John 40s. To my daughter Margaret Devsing 40s. To my son Edmund 40s. If any of my sons bring any action against my executors for lands in Laxfeld and Eston Bavent [Easton-Bavent, co. Suffolk], he shall lose his portion of 40s. Residuary legatees and executors: my wife Katherine, my younger son John, John Noloth, and Nicholas Noloth. To my wife Katherine lands in Laxfeld for life, with remainder to my younger son John, except 2 acres called Semams to my wife absolutely. If my younger son John be disturbed, he shall compensate himself from my lands in Eston Bavent. After his mother's decease he shall give my executors £30. For the health of my soul 10 marks. Proved at Laxfeld 26 February 1463/4 by the widow and John Fysk, the younger son. (Archdeaconry of Suffolk [Ipswich Probate Registry], book 2, fo. 117.)

3. The Will of WILLIAM FYSK of Rendham [co. Suffolk] the Elder, dated 16 July 1472. To be buried in the churchyard of St. Michaels, Rendham. To "frer" [i. e., Friar] John Lacy of the Friars Minors of Dunwich [co. Suffolk] and the other friars there, for a trental of St. Gregory, 30s.

To William, Robt., and Thomas, sons of John Fysk, my son, 40s., viz., to each 13s. 4d. To Richard, son of Walter Fysk of Pesenhale [Peasenhall, co. Suffolk], 13s. 4d. My wife Margaret is to have maintenance for life in my messuage in Rendham with John Fysk, my son, at his charge, or, if she prefers, 40s. a year from him. To my son John my tenement called Pysales and lands in Badyngham [Badingham, co. Suffolk] held at farm. Residue of my estate for pious works. Executor: my son John. [No witnesses.] Proved at Benhall [co. Suffolk] 22 October [1473]. (Archdeaconry of Suffolk [Ipswich Probate Registry], book 2, fo. 251.)

4. The Will of THOMAS FYSK of Badyngham [Badingham, co. Suffolk], yeoman, dated at Badyngham 14 September 1488. My wife "amnes" is to have her dwelling in my place "clepyd Dynnors," the parlour at the overend of my hall, with a little garden ground, and 6s. 8d. a year for life, and also one-half of my household stuff. To my son Wylliam my tenement called "pommanys." "I will that oldyr John my son" have Dynnors and one-half of my household stuff. To "yonger John hys brythyrne & systerin," to each of them 40s. If the "forsayd John my sun" be not able to pay it and 20s a year for my priest, the tenement and goods are to be sold, and the said John is to have 5 marks. Executors: "my true & faithful attornayse," my trusty "neve" [i. e., nephew], Wylliam Fyske, and Wylliam Grene. [No witnesses.] Proved 26 November 1488. (Archdeaconry of Suffolk [Ipswich Probate Registry], book 3, fo. 108.)

4a. The Will of JOHN FYSKE of Diss, co. Norfolk, dated in 1488, mentions the testator's wife Elizabeth and Mr. John Fiske, clerk. (The Fiske Family Papers, p. 380.)

5. The Will of MARGARET FYSKE of Laxfeld [Laxfield, co. Suffolk], wife of Jaffrey Fyske of the same town.* To be buried in Laxfeld churchyard. To the high altar of Denington [Dennington, co. Suffolk] 12d. To the high altar of Laxfeld 12d. To the Gild of Our Lady there 40d. To the Black Friars and Grey Friars of Dunwich [co. Suffolk] 40d. each. A reasonable stipend for a priest's service for the whole year. To Master John Fyske 10s. To Jaffrey, his brother, 6s. 8d. and a brass pan. To each godchild 4d. To Margaret Cryspe, the wife of Jaffrey Cryspe, wheelwright, a brass pot. To John Baas of Denington the Younger "a pot with a broke syde." To Ele Warner of Denyngton my best cap. To Odeny Baas a harnessed girdle with a "blew corse." To Johane Lefechyld of Norwich 12d. To Isabel West a coat, etc. To Draper's wife my cloak. Executor and residuary legatee: Master John Fyske, to dispose for me to God's honour and pleasure and for the soul's health. Proved 13 May 1504 by Master John Fiske. (Archdeaconry of Suffolk [Ipswich Probate Registry], book 4, fo. 135.)

6. The Will of JAFFREY FYSKE of Laxfeld [Laxfield, co. Suffolk], dated 3 May 1504. To be buried in Laxfeld parish. To the high altar there, for tithes forgotten, 3s. 4d. To the repair of the parish church 6s. 8d. To the repair of the bell 3s. 4d. To the repair of the Chapel of Our Lady in said parish and for arrear[s] of some rents pertaining to said chapel 6s. 8d. To Our Lady's Gild in Laxfeld 3s. 4d. Bequests to the

*In Pierce's Fiske and Fisk Family, p. 36 (No. 3), this testatrix is said to have made her will on 4 May 1504, the day after the date of her husband's will. But her husband, Jaffrey Fyske, in his will, dated 3 May 1504 (*vide infra*), makes no mention of his wife, and it is likely, therefore, that she was already dead or on the verge of death when he made his will. Both wills were proved 13 May 1504.

434

Friars of Dunwich and Orford [co. Suffolk]. To my son, Master John Fyske, to sing for me a year after my decease, a sufficient stipend. To the poor in Laxfeld 10s. To the mending of foul ways 20s. To each godchild 12d. To each "Bell chyld of myne" 12d. To my daughter Johane 5 marks. To my daughter Maryon* 6s. 8d. To Margaret Kempe a heifer. My house and land are to be sold, except a pightle bought of Nicholas Baas, [which is] to be sold him at a "meone" price. My son Jeffrey is to have the first purchase and within 40s of any other. "Nevertheless I am otherwyse counselled by my other children wherefore finally I put it to the discrescion of my executors & specially my son Master John Fyske to say how my son Jeffrey shall pay." He who purchases my place is to have the stock of "beys" [i. e., bees] there lying and to pay 2 lbs. wax to the light before the crucifix in Laxfeld church as long as the stock shall endure, if so much increase of wax come yearly off the said stock. Executors and residuary legatees: my sons Master John Fyske and Symond Fyske, to dispose to the health of my soul; and to each of them 6s. 8d. Proved 13 May 1504 by Master John Fyske, with power reserved to Simon Fyske. (Archdeaconry of Suffolk [Ipswich Probate Registry], book 4, fo. 134.)

7. The Will of JOHANE FYSKE, late the wife of William Fyske of Laxfeld [Laxfield, co. Suffolk], dated 15 July 1504. My soul "to our lady saynt Mary & all the saynts in heven." To be buried in the "Cherchyerd of all the Hallowen of Laxfeld." To Laxfeld church 10s. To the Gild of Our Lady there 3s. 4d. To "Agnes Arteyse servaunt" 3s. 4d. To a priest to sing for me in Laxfeld church for one-half a year. For a trental 10s. To the sepulchre light 40d. To the light before the rood 40d. To the repair of the chapel 40d. To every godchild 4d. To my daughters Margery and Margaret 13s. 4d. each. To Johan Davy 20d. To "Christian Margerye Elizabeth & Anne my sonys wyffes" 40d. each. To Sir John, my son [sic], 40d. To my son Austyn, to "pay down at my buryeng" to my executors, 6 marks for the lands called Gowches, and 4 marks which he shall allow himself twelve months after my decease for the purchase of said lands; and he is also to pay my executors, in the second year after my decease, for the priest's services, 5 marks, and, in the third year, 5 marks for my legacies. Executors: "Syr John Fyske the son of John Fyske [sic] and Simon Fyske my son," and they are to dispose of the residue [of my estate] to the most pleasure of God and the welfare of my soul. Proved at Horham [co. Suffolk] the last of February 1504/5 by the executors. (Archdeaconry of Suffolk [Ipswich Probate Registry] book 4, fo. 188.)

8. The Will of SYMON FISKE of Freston [co. Suffolk], being "of good and hole mynd," dated 25 June 1505. My soul to God, and my body to be buried in the churchyard of Freston. Legacies to the high altar, to the reparation of the church, to the high altar of Dersham, to the repair of the same church, to the Black Friars of Donwych [Donwich, co. Suffolk], to the Grey Friars there, and to the Friars of Orford [co. Suffolk]. To my brother, Master John Fyske, 10 marks, to sing for my soul and my friends' souls for a year. To each godchild 12d. To John Sparke, my servant, a "coombe" of rye. To Thos. Sewalle, my servant, 40d. To Alys Coke, servant, a sheep. To Mother Reynolde a half "comb" of malt. My wife Joan is to have my tenement in Dersham and lands in Dersham and Westylton [Westleton, co. Suffolk], and all household stuff, kine, ewes, etc., on condition that my children have meat, drink and

*Pierce, *op. cit.*, p. 36 (No. 3) gives this name as Margery.

clothing till they be able to go to service and that she make no claim for dower. On my wife's death the household goods [are to be divided] between my children. Each of my three daughters is to have five marks at marriage or [at the age of] twenty years. My house in Freston and lands are to be sold to carry out my will. The residue [is to be used] to pay my debts, etc., and any overplus [is to be used] for the good of my soul. Executors: Robert Knyts of Gt. [Great] Glemham and Richard Umfrey of Medylton [Middleton, co. Suffolk]. Supervisor: my brother, Master John Fyske. To each of them 10s. and their costs and labor "accordyng to Ryght." Proved 18 July 1505 by the executors. (Consistory Court of Norwich [Norwich, co. Norfolk], Register Garnon, fo. 58.)

9. The Will of WILLIAM FYSKE of Becyls [Beccles, co. Suffolk], being "of good mynd," dated in 1505. My soul to God, and my body to be buried in Beccles churchyard. To the high altar there, for tithes not paid, 12d. To the Gild of the Holy Ghost 12d., a pewter dish, and a saucer. To my wife Jone my tenement abutting on Newgate Street, to perform this will, and all household stuff "that perteynyth to the schoppe." My feoffees are to make estate to my wife when required. The residue of goods not bequeathed I give to Johanne, my wife, whom I make executrix. Witnesses: John Fiske and others. Proved 1 August 1505 by the executrix. (Consistory Court of Norwich [Norwich, co. Norfolk], Register Garnon, fo. 72.)

10. The Will of AUSTYN FYSKE of Laxfeld [Laxfield, co. Suffolk], dated 15 March 1507 [1507/8]. To be buried in Laxfeld churchyard. To the high altar of Laxfeld, for tithes, 20d. To the high altar at Cratfield [co. Suffolk] 20d. To my wife Johan my tenement, with lands free and bond, in Laxfeld, with remainder to my son William (under twenty-two). The "grovett" in Cratfield is to be sold to pay debts. My son William is to have lands in Cratfield and to pay to my son Thomas 20 marks from the year when he is twenty-four, in instalments. To my wife Johan my household stuff. Executors: Johan, my wife, and Symond Fyske and Thomas Fyske, my brethren. Witnesses: John Dowsyng and Robert Rows. Proved 11 April 1508 by the widow, Joan Fyske, Simon and Thomas renouncing. (Archdeaconry of Suffolk [Ipswich Probate Registry], book 6, fo. 16.)

11. The Will of JOHN FISKE of Laxfeld [Laxfield, co. Suffolk], being in good mind, dated 18 January 1512 [1512/13]. My soul to God, and my body to be buried in the churchyard there [i. e., at Laxfield]. To the high altar there, for tithes forgotten, 6s. 8d. To the "pathing of Mowbillston in sd. Church 20 marks." To Jone Fiske, daughter of Robert Fiske, 6s. 8d. To each of the four orders of friars "Gadryng in the town of Lawfield" [sic, Laxfield] 10s. To the repair of Brusierd [Bruisyard] Abbey 6s. 8d. To three friars in the same place 12d. To each of the nuns of Brusierd Abbey 4d. To the Abbot there 12d. John Fiske, chaplain, my son, is to sing for my soul for two years and is to have 20 marks, and to the said Sir John 10 marks. To Sir Robert, my son, 10 marks a year. To the canons in Leyston [Leiston] Abbey 6s. 8d. To the repair of the same place 6s. 8d. To Nicholas, my son, £4. and all the debts besides such as he oweth me. To the Gild of our Lady 6s. 8d. To the making of the gild house 10s. To the Church of St. Peter of Thorp [Thorpe, co. Norfolk] 3s. 4d. To Jone Downe 6s. 8d. To each godchild 4d. To Rose Payn 12d. To repairs of Laxfeld church and the chapel, to each 5 marks, "to be paid as yt growe of the sale of Falys house

according to such surrender & gift as I have made heretofore by my lyff." The residue of my goods are to be at the disposition of Sir John Fiske, priest, my son, Robt. Rowse of Laxfield, and Sir Robt. Fiske, canon of Leiston, whom I make my executors, for the benefit of my soul, "as yt may be payabill & grow of the sale of my place which I have sold to Robert, my son, of Suthwold [Southwold, co. Suffolk] for the sum of £110, to be paid £10 at Easter 1514 & so by £10 each Easter till paid. Proved 5 February 1512 [1512/13] by John, the son, with power reserved, etc. (Consistory Court of Norwich [Norwich, co. Norfolk], Register Coppinger, fo. 72.)

12. The Will of WILLIAM FYSKE of Hallysworth [Halesworth, co. Suffolk], dated 31 January 1512 [1512/13]. To be buried in the church or churchyard of Our Lady in Hallysworth. To the high altar of Rendham 2s., of Sot[t]erley 2s., and of Holton 6d. [all in co. Suffolk]. To the Gilds of St. John and St. Loye in Hallysworth, to each a comb of malt. To Brosyerd [Bruisyard] Abbey 20d., and to the sisters there 4d. each, and to the friars there 4d. To a priest, to sing for my "father mother my brothern" and others for whom I am bound to pray, in Hallysworth church. To my wife Johan my place which I dwell in, with a close called Schankys close and a meadow under the parson's hill called Paynys meadow, which place I lately bought of Mawte Sewall. To my wife Pycottys close and a meadow called Dame Meadow, for life, with remainder of the same and also of Schankys and Paynys to our son William; and he is to find a priest in Halesworth church, to sing for our souls and the soul of Johan Wryght otherwise called Pygott. To my son John my place in Rendham and my place in Sot[t]erley, with land in Sot[t]erley and Wyllyngham [Willingham, co. Suffolk], and he is to pay to Johan, my wife, his mother, 26s. 8d. a year, and to find a priest to sing for my soul and the souls of my father and mother and my "brothern" Robert and Thomas and for the souls of the "wyche the forseyd landys into our hands hath growen" in the parish of Rendham. To my wife Johan my household stuff for life, during her widowhood, and afterwards it is to be divided betwixt John and William, our sons. My brother Robert's place and lands in Rendham and Sweftlyng [Sweffling, co. Suffolk] are to remain in my executor's hands till such time as he assigned them to his children, the children "gydyd & fowndyn & sette to occupacion," and each to have 40s. on entering. To William Smyth and his wife Elizabeth, my daughter, a tenement called Hoggis. To Johan Smyth, my daughter's daughter, a calf. To Johan Smyth, my wife's goddaughter, the daughter of Symond Smyth, my two young kine, for such as were bequeathed her by her father and by her uncle, Robert Smyth. To Robert Stalworthey, my servant, a black cow in Sotyrley, and to his brother William a heifer. Executors: my son John Fyske, Johan Fyske, my wife, his mother, and William Fyske, my son. Proved at Halesworth 12 May 1513. (Archdeaconry of Suffolk [Ipswich Probate Registry], book 5, fo. 321.)

13. The Will of WILLIAM FYSKE of Hallysworth [Halesworth, co. Suffolk], yeoman, dated 25 January 1520 [1520/21]. To be buried in Hallysworth churchyard. To the high altar, for tithes forgotten, 12d. To the mother church of Norwich 4d. To my wife Johane the mese [messuage] where I now dwell, with closes called Westfeld and Chankys crosse and meadows called Wysett and Paynys meadows, for life, [she] finding my children and hers till they come to lawful age to be put forth to service and occupation as their mind shall serve them; and after her

death (a) to William, my son, the mese [messuage] and Westfeld close and Paynys meadow, with remainder to my son Roberd, and (b) to Roberd, my son, the meadow called Dame Meadow and the close called Chankys crosse, [he] paying 5 marks within three years to Anne, his sister, with remainder to my son William. My son William is to pay 5 marks to the child my wife is now with. After my wife's decease all such stuff as came to me by my father and mother is to be equally divided among my children. [Pious bequests, should none of his children survive his wife.] Executors and residuary legatees: my wife Johan and my brother John Fyske. Witnesses: John Fyske, priest, and Robt. Halle, priest. Proved at Halesworth 28 June 1522 by Johan, the widow, power being reserved to John Fyske, the other executor. (Archdeaconry of Suffolk [Ipswich Probate Registry], book 8, fo. 238.)

14. The Will of NICHOLAS FYSKE, late of Aldeburgh* [co. Suffolk], dated 10 April 1523. To be buried in Aldeburgh churchyard. To the high altar there, for tithes forgotten, 20d. Half my goods are to be sold for a priest. Residuary legatees and executors: my wife Johan and my daughter Johan. Witnesses: Mr. Doctor Grene and Sir Thomas Hollys. Proved at Snape [co. Suffolk] 6 June 1523 by the executors. Power to the vicar of Aldeburgh to take their oath. (Archdeaconry of Suffolk [Ipswich Probate Registry], book 8, fo. 315.)

15. The Will of THOMAS FYSKE the Elder of Laxfeld [Laxfield, co. Suffolk], being "in good and hole mynd," dated 27 October 1525. My soul to God, and my body to be buried in the churchyard of Laxfield. To the high altar there 6s. 8d. To the repair of the church 10s. To the "Black Fryers" 5s., to sing half a trental for me. To the Grey Friars 5s., for half a trental. To the Abbess of Brosyard [Bruisyard] 6d. To each friar and nun there 2d. To my son William the tenement [called] Stowes in Laxfield and all staff [sic] and "cattell" there except a cow; and he is to find a priest to sing for me at Laxfield. To my wife, at her choice, another cow. To Annes, my daughter, £6. 13s. 4d., and, if she be married, 40s., to be paid by my son William. My wife is to have from my son William 33s. 4d. a year, for her life, a chamber and dwelling in my parlour at the churchyard's side at Laxfield, the hall, buttery, and soler, and gardens and fruit, etc. To Thomas, my son, the rest of the tenement, and, on my wife's death, he is to have the whole tenement. My wife is to give to Agnes, my daughter, a part of my stuff in the house at the church that I occupy. To Harry, my son, land in Fressyngfeld [Fressingfield, co. Suffolk], and he is to deliver to Margaret Coslar, at her chamber, while she liveth, two loads of wood. My executors are to have all the cattle, except two heifers which I give to Agnes, my daughter, besides the two of her own that are there. Lands called Fales, Glemys, Herstofeld, and Conysfeld are to be used to pay my debts and perform my will; and then my son William is to have the same, if he pay 4 marks for the same, and so on until 24 marks is paid in all; and of these 24 marks my son Thomas is to have 16 marks and Herry, my son, 8 marks. To my wife and my son William all corn, etc. To my wife the cow that goeth with my brother Symon. Residue to my executors, my sons Harry and Thomas; and the latter is to have 2d. and Harry 1d. [Witnesses:] Thomas Gryggs, Sir John Fyske, Symond Fyske, Nycholas Ive. Proved 10 December 1525. (Consistory Court of Norwich [Norwich, co. Norfolk], Register Brigges, fo. 181.)

*The three words "late of Aldeburgh" are written on the margin.

16. The Will of NICOLAS FYSKE of Est Derham [East Dereham, co. Norfolk], "raffeman," dated 8 April 1529. To be buried in the church-yard there, before the image of St. Saviour. To the high altar there, for tithes forgotten, 20s. To the repairs of the said church, with the money that I owe for John Asoham, £4. To each gild there of which I be a brother 12d. [Legacies to various lights there.] To my wife Elizabeth my house I dwell in, for her life, some copyholds and other lands, tallow in the workhouse, candle to be weighed, etc., and my wife and John Fiske are to keep accounts of it. To the four orders of friars in Norwich, to sing for me, 10s. to each order. Patman's house is to be sold and the money used for the purposes of this will. To my wife all wares in the shop, to bring up the children; and, if not worth £20., then it is to be made up to that sum out of my goods. All household stuff, pewter, beds, etc., to my wife, except that I give to Wm. Fyske a good [*illegible*], a coverlet, etc., and certain pewter. My house and land at Kerbroke [Car-brooke, co. Norfolk] are to be sold (my wife may buy at less than others). To my son Thomas 100s. To Wm. Poynter and Elizh. Poynter, his wife, my daughter, £4. To John Fyske, my son, and to his wife, £20, in help to pay debts he oweth to Wm. Rogers, merchant, of Norwich, and to others, and also to him a close at the town's end. To Ambrose Fyske, my son, after his mother's death, the house I dwell in, and he is to pay to his sisters Cycely Fyske, Wyburgh Fyske, Anne Fyske, and Alice Fyske 5 marks each at marriage. If Ambrose die, his wife is to have the house. To John Tompson, "berebruer" [beer brewer] my best gowne. The feoffees of my lands in Norfolk or Suffolk are to make estate to my exec-utors when required. Residue to my executors, Elizh. Fyske, my wife, John Fyske, my son, and John Pavys of Norwich, to pay debts and to my soul's profit; and to each executor 40s. Witnesses: Roger Balkewell, Robert Dobbes, priests. Proved 8 November 1529 by Pavys, the wife renouncing, with power reserved to the son John, executor. (Consistory Court of Norwich [Norwich, co. Norfolk], Register Heywarde, fo. 139.)

17. The Will of JOHN FYSKE of Hallysworthe [Halesworth, co. Suf-folk], mercer, dated 5 October 1530. To be buried in Our Lady of Hal-lisworth churchyard by [the side of] my son Robert. To the high altar there, for tithes forgotten, 20d. To the mother church of Norwich 12d. To a priest to sing for me for one year in Hallysworth church, "whom I do name Sir Nicholas Bennett." To Felys, my wife, the tenement I bought of John Arnolde, in fee simple. The tenement I bought of Sharf-fordys' wife is to be sold, and of the money, 20s. given to the gilding of the high altar. To Felys, my wife, the tenement I dwell in, in fee simple, and she is to "bere out the purches thereof." To Halesworth church a corporas, price 6s. 8d. To Alys Harman, late my servant, 10s. To my brother Robert Fyske my best gown. To the Black Friars of Dunwich [co. Suffolk] 5s. To the Grey Friars of Dunwich 5s., for a trental. Residuary legatee: my wife Felyce, she bestowing 40s. on my burying. Executors: my wife Felys, John Fyske of Hotton, and Robert Baltoffe, and to each 16s. Supervisor: Robt. Amyllys, gent., of Braunfeld, [and to him] 6s. 8d. To Petyr Saunderson a hose cloth of my fine black karsey [i. e., kersey]. Witnesses: Sir Robt. Hall, Alexander Fylby, Thomas Pye, Peter Saunderson, John Rychardys. Proved 21 April 1531 by the widow Felicia, with power reserved to the other executors. (Arch-deaconry of Suffolk [Ipswich Probate Registry], book 10, fo. 177.)

18. The Will of SIR JOHN FYSKE of Laxfeld [Laxfield, co Suffolk], dated 2 October 1535. To be buried in the churchyard there by [the side

of] my mother. To Master Vycary of the same church, to pray for me, 3s. 4d. To the repairs of the same church 3s. 4d. To the four orders of friars 3s. 4d. To Brasyerd [Bruisyard] Abbey 6s. 8d. To John Fyske of Est Derham [East Dereham, co. Norfolk] 6s. 8d. To the repairs of Est Derham church three obligations of 33s. 4d. which I have delivered to Master Vycary of the same town, witness[es] Rychard Perry [or Percy] and John Fyske of Est Derham. To William Fyske of Est Derham 20s. of the £5 now remaining in the hands of Wm Peyntor of Est Derham, the residue, £4, to be paid to me or my executors. I forgive £6 that Thos. Fyske of Leystofte owes to me. A penny dole at my burial, and to every priest there 4d. A priest to sing for me in Laxfield church for one year, if it may be borne. Residue to Jaffrey Fyske the Elder [of] Laxfyld and to John Fiske, his son, executors, and to each 20s. John Fyske, son of Symond Fyske, is to make surrender to my executors of the house I dwell in. Witnesses: Master Roger Balkewell, clerk, Richard Perce of North Elmham [co. Norfolk], John Fyske of Est Derham. Proved in 1536 by the executors. (Consistory Court of Norwich [Norwich, co. Norfolk], Register Godsalve, fo. 105.)

19. The Will of SIMONDE FYSKE of Laxfeld [Laxfield, co. Suffolk], yeoman, dated 10 July 1536. My soul to "god allmyghtie to our ladye Saynt Marye & all the blyssed company of hevyn." To be buried in the churchyard of All Saints, Laxfeld, "at the Chauncells ende* ther next my father." To the high altar there, for tithes negligently forgotten and not paid, 20d. To the reparation of Laxfeld church 20d. To the three houses of friars in Dunwich and Orford [co. Suffolk], to each 3s. 4d., to have a trental of masses sung for my soul and my friends' souls as shortly as may be after my decease. To priests, clerks, and poor people, at my burial day, £6. 13s. 4d. To my son Robert Fyske my tenement in Laxfeld wherein now I dwell, with all my lands, meadows, feedings, rents, and services in Laxfeld, now "in the occupyeng and menuryng" of the same Robert, according to such bargain as I have made with him by indenture of 1 January, 25 Henry VIII [1 January 1533/4], he to pay £40, viz., (a) £6. 13s. 4d. to my executors, at the day of my burial; (b) to my son William Fyske 5 marks a year for three years, said William to discharge my executors of a bond of 20 marks wherein I am bound that he shall leave his wife Elizabeth, at his death, lands or moveables worth 20 marks; (c) to my son Symond Fyske, in the fourth year after my decease, £3. 6s. 8d.; (d) to my daughters Johan Jerelon and Olyve Warne £3. 6s. 8d., in the fifth year; (e) to my daughter Margerye £3. 6s. 8d., in the sixth year; (f) to my son Jafferye, £3. 6s. 8d., in the seventh year, and £3. 6s. 8d., in the eighth year; (g) to Johan, my younger daughter, £3. 6s. 8d., in the ninth year; (h) to Agnes, my younger daughter, £3. 6s. 8d., in the tenth year. If my younger children, viz., Jaffery, Margery, Johan the Younger, and Agnes the Younger die before being paid, their share is to be divided among the same my four younger children. My son Robert is to be bound to pay the above. My son Robert is to have the utensils, implements, and household stuff which I have not given or sold at the day of my decease. Residuary legatees and executors: John Goodynche, vicar of Laxfeld, Henry Smyth of Laxfeld, and John Noloth of Walpole [? co. Suffolk], to dispose to the pleasure of God and the health of my soul and my friends' souls. Supervisor: John Fyske of Holton [co. Suffolk]. Witnesses: James Lane, "balye" of Laxfeld, John Fyske of Holton the Younger, Nicholas Stannard of Lax-

*The chancel at Laxfield has been entirely rebuilt.

feld. Proved 15 July 1538 by the executors. (Archdeaconry of Suffolk [Ipswich Probate Registry], book 13, fo. 16.)

20. The Will of THOMAS FYSKE of Heddenham [Hedenham], co. Norfolk, dated 24 May 1541. My soul to God, Our Lady, etc. To be buried in the churchyard there. To the high altar there, for tithes forgotten, 3s. 4d. William, my son, is to have my tenement in Heddenham called Warners and lands thereto, for the term of thirty years "become ought [*sic*] fully ended and determined," which I had of Edward Cok, clerk, as by deeds appears, except such lands thereof with corn thereon at my decease, which I will to my executors, to sell said corn and occupy until reaped and carried, on condition that my son Wm. shall pay to my four daughters, Alyce, Margaret, Jhone, and Margery, 19 marks, and to Thomas Fyske, my son, 6 marks, and to John Fyske, my younger son, 10 marks, at stated intervals. If Wm. makes default, then my eldest son, John, is to enter on the same conditions, and, if he makes default, my executors are to enter the same. The said tenement at the end of thirty years is to belong to my son William and his heirs, and also all copyholds thereto. To John, my eldest son, the tenement called Kelyetts in Hedenham and lands thereto. To Raff, my son, the tenement called Clynke bells and lands thereto. To my son William three milch kine, my bald horse, and my young balled mare and cart, with trace and collars. To Margaret, my daughter, to my son Raff, to Thomas, my son, to John, my younger son, to Margery, my daughter, and to Jhone, my daughter, to each a cow. To Agnes Fyske, my "belchild," a "stirke" of a year old. To Anne Fyske, my "belchild," the like. To Robert Fyske, my "belchild," a "wene" calf of this year. To each godchild 4d. To my son William five combs of wheat and six of barley. All other household goods among all my other children. Residue to my executors, viz., Edward Cock, clerk, John Fyske of Holton [co. Suffolk], and John Fyske, my eldest son, and to each 6s. 8d. for his trouble. Witnesses: John Alboroughe, Roger Grenmere, Robt Gaye. Proved 15 July 1541 by the executors. (Archdeaconry Court of Norfolk [Norwich, co. Norfolk], Register for 1540–41, fo. 226.)

21. The Will of SYMON FISKE of Hekynham [Heckingham, co. Norfolk], being "hole of mynde," dated 8 November 1549. My soul to God, and my body to be buried in Heckingham church. To breaking the ground there 6s. 8d. To the high altar 12d. To Robt. Fiske, my son, a plow and cowlter [coulter] and share, with collars and trace and one "yren swyllwythe" and all other things necessary to a plow. Also four geldings or else £4 for them, four combs of wheat, twenty ewes with those that he hath of his own all ready to be delivered to him. To Anne, my daughter, 5 marks, two yearing [yearling] calves, and ten ewes. To Johan, my daughter, 5 marks, two cow calves, and ten ewes. To Elizabeth, my daughter, 5 marks, two cow calves, and ten ewes. If it happen Thos., my son, to depart this life seized of lands and tenements in Whenhaston [Wenhaston, co. Suffolk] and without heirs and on whose death shall descend to Robert Fiske, my son, then said Robert shall pay to Anna, his sister, £3, and to Joan, his sister, £2, and to Elizabeth, his sister, £3. All the rest of my goods to my wife Elizabeth, sole executrix, for God's pleasure and the performance of this will. Supervisor: Robert Fyske, my son, and to him 10s. for his pains. Witnesses: John Wrythocke, John Fyske, John Pratte, Wyllm Buxton, Phyllipe Haryson. Proved 8 December 1549. (Consistory Court of Norwich [Norwich, co. Norfolk], Register Wimer, fo. 386.)

441

22. The Will of ROBERT FISKE of Laxfield, co. Suffolk, being sick in body, dated 6 March 1549 [1549/50]. To be buried in the churchyard there "where all my frinds be buried aforetime." To my wife Alice the tenement I dwell in in Laxfield and lands thereto, for her life, and on condition that she keep it in repair and bring up my three children, viz., Nicholas, Anne, and Christian, until they be of age, and pay my daughter Anne £10 at [the age of] twenty. Also I give to Anne, my daughter, the house which I lately bought of John Storke of Laxfild as it is enclosed, to have it at fifteen years of age; and my wife also is to pay my daughter Christian £20, when twenty. If either die, the other is to be heir. If my wife.die before my son Nicholas is twenty, then the tenement I live in is to be let until the £30 is paid. To my son Nicholas the tenement I live in and lands subject to the said £30, and [he is] to have, when he enters the same, ten milch kine or £6. 13s. 4d. Also to Nicholas a gelding or 26s. 8d., a "cubbord" in the hall, and the tables, forms, and tressles there. To my wife Alice all kine and horses and all other goods, pewter, etc. To the poor of the towns adjoining 10s. Residue to my executors, John Jacobb of Fornecette [Forncett, co. Norfolk], Edmond Crispe of Laxfild, and Alice, my wife, and to each 10s. for their pains. Witnesses: John Nollothe, Robt Dalling, Robt Lane, Wm. Whiteman, Thos Plumpton, and others. Proved 5 April 1551 by the executrix, with power reserved to the other executors. (Consistory Court of Norwich [Norwich, co. Norfolk], Register for 1550–51, fo. 136.)

23. The Will of JOHN FYSKE of Hollton [Holton], co. Suffolk, being in health of body and "in love with all my neighbours," dated 23 November 1550. My soul to God, to Our Lady, etc. My body to be buried in Holton churchyard, nigh unto my children there. To the high altar there, for tithes not paid, 20d. Legacies to the poor box, to Halesworth high altar, to Blyforth [Blyford] high altar, and to the repairs of Holton [all in co. Suffolk]. My executors to take the rents of lands in Holton, Halesworth, and Blyforth, lately bought of Nichs. Smyth of Halesworth, now in farm of William Rossington, Robert Jermyn, and Richd Nepe, until my son William Fiske is eighteen, when I give the same to him, with remainder, in default of issue of William, to my son Francis and his heirs, and remainder, in default, to my right heirs. A close called Danyells Meares and a meadow called Broad meadow and a fen by the Mill Dam (copyhold of Mellis) [co. Suffolk], in default of issue [sic], [to] the said William, my son. Lands in Rendham [co. Suffolk], occupied by Edmd. Feveryere, to my son William. My "hartye" friend, Robt. Norton, gent., is to bring up said Wm Fiske, my son, until eighteen, and to have £5 a year from Feveryere and 33s. 4d., to find him in all things. Residue of lands in Holton, Halesworth, Blyforth, and Mellis to my son Francis and his heirs, with remainder to my son William, in default of issue. To my son Francis and William, my son, all my apparel between them. To my son Francis a silver salt, six silver spoons, and my signet of gold. To my son William a silver goblet (which his mother and I bought together), my silver pot with the cover, and six silver spoons. To Jane Kene, my daughter, four milch kine. To my son Francis my best horse, a draught bullock, two cart horses, a cart, a tambrell [tumbrel], a plow, a cart harness, etc., and six milch kine. To my wife Anne all her apparel, jewels, and money (£6. 13s.), in full satisfaction of £40, whereof I have delivered to her long before the date hereof, in bonds, money, plate, and household stuff, £37 and more, as appears by a bill indented between her and me and in my book of reckoning, which £40 is in satisfaction of dower. To my son William £4. To Anne Fiske,

442

my grandchild, 5 marks. To Margaret, her sister, 5 marks. To Anne Woulfe £3. 6s. 8d., at her marriage. To Katherine Wolfe £3. 6s. 8d., at her marriage. To Fraunces Wolfe 40s., when twenty. If my son William die under eighteen, then my son Francis is to have his bequests. To my son William four kine. Residue of my household stuff between my sons Francis and William. To each godchild 12d. To John Erne, my godson, 6s. 8d., when out of his "prenticehood." To the poor of Holton, Halesworth, Blyforth, and Wenhaston [co. Suffolk]. Residue to my executors, Francis Fyske and Wm. Fyske, and to each 20s. Witnesses: Thos. Erne, Gyles Farwhat, clerk, George Forest, William Rossington, Robert Norton, gent. Proved 2 July 1562 by Wm. Fiske, executor, the other executor having died beforehand. (Consistory Court of Norwich [Norwich, co. Norfolk], Register Cowlles, fo. 239.)

24. The Will of JOHN FYSKE thelder of Wenhaston [co. Suffolk], husbandman, dated 4 May 1558. To be buried in the parish churchyard of Wenhaston. To the poor men's box, Wenhaston, 20d. To my wife Marion the house that I dwell in and lands belonging in Wenhaston, Thuryngton, and Blythburgh [co. Suffolk], freehold and copyhold, for life, with remainder to my son John Fyske, on condition that he pay to my daughters Agnes Neve and Johan Barfote £6. 13s. 4d. each, payable by my son John, viz., 40s. evenly between them one year after my wife's decease and 40s. a year evenly for three years and 26s. 8d. after the said three years, the remainder (failing heirs of the body of my son John) to my said two daughters and the heirs of their bodies. Should the lands be sold, the next of my kindred and of my surname are to have preference. To my wife Maryon moveables. To my godchildren, 4d. each. Executors and residuary legatees: my wife Marion and my son John. Supervisor: Jaffrey Neve, my son-in-law. Witnesses: Hen. Thruston, Wm. Stinger, Nicholas Helwyse, John Thruston, Thos Thruston. Proved at Horham [co. Suffolk] 16 January 1558 [1558/9] by the executors, Sir Wm. Clarke, vicar of Wenhaston, to charge the executors in form of law. (Archdeaconry of Suffolk [Ipswich Probate Registry], book 18, fo. 626.)

25. The Will of THOMAS FYSKE of Northalls [North Hales, co. Suffolk], sick in body, dated 16 May 1558. My soul to Our Lady and all the Holy Company of Heaven. To be buried in the churchyard of Sowthcove [South Cove, co. Suffolk]. To my son John white hosen, russet hosen, a violet jacket, and a doublet with body of worsted and sleeves of canvas. To my daughter Margerye a pewter platter, etc. To my goddaughter Margaret Fyske, daughter of my son Wm. Fyske, a ewe and a lamb. To my godson Christopher Fyske a ewe and a lamb. Residuary legatee and executor: my wife Agnes. Witnesses: Wylliam Fyske of Southcove, William Allexaundre. Proved at Beccles [co. Suffolk] 27 May 1557 [sic, ? 1558] by the executrix. (Archdeaconry of Suffolk [Ipswich Probate Registry], book 18, fo. 38.)

26. The Will of HENRYE FYSKE of Cratfilde [Cratfield], co. Suffolk, being in good remembrance, dated 19 August 1558. To be buried in the churchyard there or elsewhere. To my son William all lands called Gooches in Fressingfelde [Fressingfield, co. Suffolk] and [other] lands there. To my son Jefferye £20, four milch kine, and a hefker [heifer]. To my son Thomas £10, four able milch kine, and a hefker [heifer]. Residue of my cattle, horse, and "neate" to my son William. To my son William such stuff as belongs to my "Dayer" [? dairy] house, with the

greatest milk pan, a trevett [trivet], a pair of querns, a stepinge [? steeping] tub, and "a hayer for a kill," and also all my husbandry things, carts, plow, tumbrel, corn, and hay. To my son Thomas my worst feather bed and things thereto and two sheets. To my son Thomas's eldest daughter, Mary Fiske, my godchild, 5 marks at her marriage. To my son Jefferye a one-fourth part of my household stuff, linen, and woollen. To my son William the rest of my household stuff, linen, and woollen. To my godson Francis Fiske 6s. 8d. If my son Thomas make any claim on lands, then his legacies are to be void. Executors: my son William and my brother Thomas Fiske of Stradbrooke [Stradbroke, co. Suffolk]. Witnesses: William Collman, Jafferye Hacnye of Stradbrooke, otherwise called Wiet. Proved 16 September 1558 by the executors. (Consistory Court of Norwich [Norwich, co. Norfolk], Register Jerves, fo. 238.)

27. The Will of WILLIAM FYSKE of Stodehaugh in Laxfeld [Laxfield], co. Suffolk, dated 15 October 1558. To be buried in Laxfild churchyard or where I shall die. To my wife Margaret, for life, my tenement called Stowes, with all lands and tenements in Laxfild or elsewhere, co. Suffolk, except my lands called Glemes Fales and Fales and Hersefeld Connisfeld [*sic*], with remainder to my son John Fyske and the heirs male of his body, provided he pay to my son Rauf £20, as appointed below. Should John die *s. p. m.*, the lands are to be sold and the money proceeding thence [shall be paid] to my daughters. To my wife the lands called Glemes Fales and the rest (as above), for six years, provided she pay £40, viz., £10 each at marriage to my daughters Alice, Marion, Jane, and Margarett, then to my son John and the heirs male of his body, or, if he die *s. p. m.*, the lands are to be sold (as above). William Fyske, son of my brother Henry Fyske, deceased, is to have preference in the purchase of said lands, if sold, and to have them within £20 of the price given by any other. To my son Rauff Fyske my tenement in Walberswyke [Walberswick, co. Suffolk], lately bought of [*blank*] Gybbon, and also £20 to be paid by my son John, at St. Michael after my wife's decease 40s., and thenceforward yearly 40s., provided Rauff do not vex my son. To my daughters Feithe and Katheryn £20, i. e., £10 each at marriage, and my wife is to bring them up and keep them at her own costs and charges till they be eighteen, [they] "doing for their said mother as yt becometh naturall children." To my son John twelve milch kine immediately after my wife's death, three horses or mares, my cart and plough, eight of my best milk "boilles," two of my best cheese "fatts" [vats], with the "bredes" [breds], and my cheese press and salting boards, immediately after my wife's death. Residuary legatee: my wife, [who is to be] executrix with my brother-in-law Robert Ball and Roger Wade of Bermondysh. Witnesses: William Dowsyng, William Fyske, Thomas Cower. [Signature of the testator not given.] Proved 4 May 1559 by Thomas Tower, procurator for the widow, Margaret, power being reserved to the other executors. (Prerogative Court of Canterbury [Somerset House, London], Chayney, 20.

Sentence 30 October 1560, in a cause between Ralph Fiske (impugning the above will) and Margaret Fiske, the widow and executrix, upholding the above will as made while the testator was of sound mind (with costs). (Prerogative Court of Canterbury [Somerset House, London], Mellershe, 52.)

28. The Will of THOMAS FISKE of Stradbroke [co. Suffolk], dated 20 January 1558/9. To be buried in Stradbroke churchyard. To my

daughter Christian, wife of Leonerde Sewell, and to my daughter Margaret, wife of Alan Borrett, copyholds in Hoxne [co. Suffolk]. To my daughter Margerie Fiske £20. To my daughter Alice Fiske the tenement I dwell in and ground called Irlondes held of Stradbroke Hall and a close, parcel of Eggescrofte in Stradbroke, [she] paying my daughter Margerie £10. To my daughter Alice my gelding, "Sorrell," a cupboard, and a brass pan. To my daughter Dorathe Fiske a tenement called Goldings and a close called Fydions in Stradbroke, a mare, and certain timber in my yard. To my daughter Johan Fiske lands, parcel of Shetyshyll by Buttleshawe Green in Stradbroke (she to pay my executors £5), my gelding, "Rudde," etc. To my daughter Margerie my sorrel bald gelding, my coral beads with paternoster, and "Gawdys" of silver and gilt. To Thomas and John Sewell and Johan Borrett and Elizabeth, my "belchildren," a calf each. Residuary legatees and executrices: my daughters Alice, Margerie, Dorathe, and Johan, with John Barker of Hoxne. Witnesses: Thos Richeman, John Godbolde, John Lone. Surrenders of copyholds of Stradbroke Hall and Stubcrofte. Proved 24 May 1559 by the executrices. (Archdeaconry of Suffolk [Ipswich Probate Registry], book 19, fo. 491.)

29. The Will of MARYON FYSKE of Wenhaston [co. Suffolk], widow, dated 30 January 1558 [1558/9]. To be buried in Wenhaston churchyard "by my husband aforeseide."* To the poor men's box in Wenhaston church 8d. To my daughter Agnes Neve 3s. 4d., to be paid by my son John Fyske at Michaelmas 1562. To my said daughter Agnes a red petticoat, etc. To Agnes Gybbon a kercher, etc. To Johan Barfott, my daughter, my best gown, etc. To Margaret Browne, widow, an old red petticoat. To Margaret Culh[a]m an old red kirtle. To Elizabeth Neve my hood. To Edmund Barfotte's four chilidren, Edmund, John, Thomas, and Elizabeth, a cow, to be delivered by my son John Fyske, when he shall receive the stock of cattle of John Snellynge that he had by lease for a term of years of John Fyske, late my husband. Residuary legatee and executor: my son John Fyske. Witnesses: John Bettes, Wm. Lambe, Thos Thurston. Proved 31 July 1559 by Jn. Fyske, at Horham [co. Suffolk]. (Archdeaconry of Suffolk [Ipswich Probate Registry], book 19, fo. 336.)

30. The Will of ANNE FYSKE of Beccles, co. Suffolk, widow, dated 9 January 1562 [1562/3]. To the church where [are] buried [names not given] 6s. To the poor of Beccles, to be distributed at their houses, 20s., if I die there. To my "nevye" Thomas Colvyle my ring "with the maiden face therein." To my "nevye" John Colvyle of Martham [co. Norfolk] the bed in the parlour, the cupboard and cypres[s] chest, and other household stuff [described; some of the cushions have roses, another a "splayed" eagle], all for the use of his son Copyldicke Colvyle, my godson. To my "nevye" and godson William Boyse two pairs of sheets and other household stuff [described], including two cushions with squirrels. To my niece, the wife of said William Boyse, a kirtle and other clothes [described]. To my godson John Buttolfe my little close truseing bed [trussing-bed] and other household stuff [described]. To Alice Bucknam, my niece, the mother of John Buttolfe aforesaid, two gowns and other clothes. To my daughter Kene of Thyrton [Thurton, co. Norfolk] my hoop of gold. To my "nevy" Robert Cudden a cushion with a rose thereon. To Anne Knightes a trundle-bed and other household stuff,

*The husband of the testatrix has not been mentioned previously in this will, but he is named below.

445

including the cushion with the red cross, clothes [described], one kettle that I bought of Brooke, and 20s. To my niece Grace Covyle my best gown and a little flat pan of brass. To the poor of Bestrete in Norwich 20d. To the poor of East Somarton and Wynterton [East Somerton and Winterton, co. Norfolk] 3s. 4d. Executors and residuary legatees: my "nevye" John Colvyle and Grace, his wife. Witnesses: Nicholas Chapleyn, Wm. Tebbolde, John Magnns [*sic*, ? Magnaus], "the writer." Proved at Beccles 16 February 1562 [1562/3] by John Colvyle, power being reserved to Grace Colvyle. Proved by Grace Colvyle 18 March 1562 [1562/3]. (Archdeaconry of Suffolk [Ipswich Probate Registry], book 20, fo. 228.)

30a. The Will of ROBERT DOWSYING of Laxfield [co. Suffolk], dated 12 April 1563. The testator names George Fyske, "my son in law and my belchildren Margaret and George his children." (Archdeaconry of Suffolk [Ipswich Probate Registry]. Cf. The Fiske Family Papers, p. 64.)

31. The Will of HARRY GOLDE of Ipswich [co. Suffolk], miller, dated 24 June 1563. To my Mr. Raffe Ingram £6. 6s. 8d. at present in his hands. To William Randbye the money due me from Geo. Wilkensone. To Thos. Taylor, who did marry my sister Elizabeth, £4. To John Estall the 10s. he oweth me. To my Mr. Ingram the horse which I bought out of Lincolnshire. To the poor men's box of St. Matthew 6s. 8d. To Robt. Goor my new hose. To Harry, the boy of the mill, my second hose and white fustian doublet. To Thos. Wyllowby a white petticoat. To Richard Tomson a petticoat. Executor and residuary legatee: Raffe I[n]grame. Witnesses: Thos. Willowbye, Richard Tomsone, John Dunckon, John Ramsy, minister. Proved 9 July 1563 by the executor. (Archdeaconry of Suffolk [Ipswich Probate Registry], book 20, fo. 477.)

32. The Will of ROBERTE FYSKE of Ipswich [co. Suffolk], clothmaker, "disquieted in body," dated 15 February 1563 [1563/4], 6 Elizabeth. To be buried in the churchyard of St. Mary Elms, Ipswich, near where my former wife was buried. To the repair of that church 10s. To the repair of the church of Randham [Rendham, co. Suffolk], where I was born, 10s. To the poor 40s. My wife Johanne is to have, for life, her free dwelling in the tenement wherein I now dwell, 20 nobles a year, £10 come two years after my decease, a silver and gilt salt, six silver spoons, household stuff including my cupboard in the hall, the countertable with the "state" in the hall, the flat hutch in the coller [soler], and all the hangings in the house where I now dwell; and she is to release all her right in my lands. To Thos. Stalworthye the Younger, Rachaell, Margery, and John Stalworthye, the children of Thos. Stalworthye the Elder and Margerye, my daughter, 5 marks each, at twenty-one. To my godson Robt. Cole, son of John Cole and Alice, his wife, £10., and to Magdelyn and John, their other children, 5 marks each at twenty-one. To Richard Marten, son of Robert Marten, 20s., and to every the residue of his children 6s. 8d., at twenty-one. To Robert Cottell, son of John Cottell, 20s., and to every other of the children of said John 6s. 8d., at twenty-one. To William Draper my gown faced with camlet, to his son Robt. Draper 20s., and to his daughter Elizh. Draper 6s. 8d., at twenty-one. To John Cole and my daughter Alice, his wife, the capital messuage where Robert Marten now inhabiteth in St. Mary Elms, Ipswich, with the grounds, free[hold] and copyhold, in and near Ipswich pertaining, and also the house wherein I dwell [*sic*, ? dwelt] after my wife's death,

subject to the payment of £100 to Edward Scarlet of Leostofte [? Lowestoft, co. Suffolk] and his wife Anne, Robert Marten to have the preference should they sell the house where he dwells. Executor and residuary legatee: the said John Cole of Ipswich. Supervisor: Wm. Draper, [to whom I give] 6s. 8d. Witnesses: Thos. Borage, John Gardyner, and Henry Hannam, "the writer hereof." Proved at Ipswich by the executor 4 March "1566" [apparently 1565/6, since the succeeding wills were proved in May 1566]. (Archdeaconry of Suffolk [Ipswich Probate Registry], book 21, fo. 353.)

33. The Will of JOHANNE FYSKE of Ipswich [co. Suffolk], widow, dated 22 May 1567. To be buried in the churchyard of St. Mary Elms. To my son John Cottell £5, to be paid of that I should have by force of my husband's will. If he die before Michaelmas 1569, the same is to be equally divided among his children, at twenty-one. To my son-in-law, Robert Marten of Ipswich, 50s. and six spoons. To Wm. Draper of Ipswich the Elder 50s. and a silver salt with cover, etc. All my other goods are to be divided between Robt. Marten and the said Wm. Draper, executors. Witnesses: John Gardiner, John Leman, John Hawis. Proved 12 July 1568 by the executors. (Archdeaconry of Suffolk [Ipswich Probate Registry], book 22, fo. 228.)

34. The Will of NICHOLAS FISKE of Dinnington [Dennington, co. Suffolk], dated 20 August 1569. To be buried in Dinnington churchyard. To my wife Johane, my father-in-law William Crispe of Laxfelde [Laxfield, co. Suffolk], my four children, Rachel, Ester, Mary, and Martha, my son William and my wife Johane, his mother, and my son Amos Fiske. Witnesses: John Fyske the Elder, John Fyske the Younger, and others. Proved 28 September 1569. (Archdeaconry of Suffolk [Ipswich Probate Registry], book 23, fo. 71.)

35. The Will of WILLIAM FISKE of Reidon [Reydon, co. Suffolk], dated 30 June 1572. To my wife Isabell all my goods, corn, "cattalls," and other implements of household, with plough and cart and all else that belongeth to husbandry. Executor: my wife Isabell. Witnesses: Simunde Nobbes, Thos. Aylmer. Proved 24 January 1576 [apparently 1575/6, for records of December 1576 follow] by the widow, Isabella, at Blithburgh [Blythburgh, co. Suffolk], by her proctor, Nichs Horneseye. (Archdeaconry of Suffolk [Ipswich Probate Registry], book 26, fo. 163.)

36. The Will of RICHARD FYSKE of Laxfelde [Laxfield, co. Suffolk], "sevemaker," dated 7 September 1572. "I do protest my self to die an humble and penitent synner." To be buried in Laxfelde churchyard, or wherever I die. To my wife Agnes the tenement wherein I dwell, with the lands, meadow, and pasture, for life, she to educate and bring up my children, with remainder to my daughters Marie and Margaret, or, in case they die s. p., to my daughters Anne and Elizabeth, who are to pay to my son Elye £10. To my daughter Anne my great meadow in Laxfield. To my son Elie my tenement lately purchased of my father-in-law, Edmunde Crispe, he paying to said Edmund £50, in accordance with agreement, and to my daughter Elizabeth £40, in instalments. To my son Elie my timber, tools, and all things belonging to my occupation. My wife is to have the residue and implements of husbandry, while sole, towards bringing up my children. If she marry, [she is to have] one-half only, and the other one-half to my children. Executor: my wife Agnes, with my son Elie, "in whom I repose a special trust & confi-

dence." Supervisor: my brother Robert Fiske, [to whom I give] 5s., praying him to be [of] assistance unto my wife and children. Witnesses: John Fiske, Jefferie Fiske, Nicholas Fiske, John Elwis, Nicholas Lane, John Petyver. Proved 5 November 1572 by the executors. (Archdeaconry of Suffolk [Ipswich Probate Registry], book 24, fo. 188.)

37. The Will of THOMAS FYSKE of Aldeburgh, co. Suffolk, cooper, dated 8 May 1573. To my wife Margaret one-half of the yearly farm of my house that John Catmere dwelleth in, for life. To my daughter Marie the other one-half, and after my wife's death the house is to remain to Marie. To my son John Fiske, after my wife's decease, my house, with ground, now dwelt in by Edward Ellis *alias* Martin, and also bedding [described in detail]. To my son George *alias* Fiske all my timber, "clappell borde," "hoopes," and "pompes" and "pompe" timber and tools belonging to a cooper's occupation, except the "shankes," on condition my "poompe wimbles" remain equally between George, my son, and William Fiske, my son, the said timber to be appraised and the said George to have the premises 40s. within the price, allowing to his brother John one-half the value of the premises. To my son George bedding [described in detail] and the house that was Tatswood's, with the lands, after my wife's decease. The house and lands beyond the Bulwarks, occupied by John Tailor and John Jaxon the Scott, and the part of my house and grounds belonging to it are to be sold, and of the said money £20 is to be paid to my daughter Anne Chaplin. To my daughters Margerie and Katherin 40 marks each, whereof Margerie is to have £6. 13s. 4d. at marriage and the residue is to be paid £5 yearly. My houses and grounds at Thorpe [co. Norfolk] are to be sold. My part of the wood bought of Mr. Rushe is to be sold, and my wife is to have £10. To my wife £20 which Robt. Holland, Senr., of Baddingham [Badingham, co. Suffolk] hath confessed he owed me. To Thomas Fiske and John Fiske, sons of William Fiske, my son, and to Thomas Chapleyn and Anne Chapleyn, children of my daughter Anne Chapleyn, 6s. 8d. each. My executors are to have my mare between them. George, my son, is to have one-fourth of my boat and one-half my "mackrell" nets. My executors are to have the little house that was Newton's to pay for John Allen's board and school, as is agreed between John Cressey and me, and to pay him £5 at the age of twenty. My executors are to have the house farm due from Jaxon the Scott, John Tailer, John Whiting, Edward Awsten, Edward Garnam, and Robt. Squier of Thorpe. To my son George my best gown, to my son John my best coat and frieze gown, and to both the rest of my apparel. To my son George five "flewes," as they be. My wife is to have one-half my rye and one-half my barley this year sown, and the other one-half to my sons George and John, and they are to "ynne" it with my wife. My executors are to have all my debts and my house "that is sett up" with the ground, so that my son William shall have one-third of the house. Residuary legatee: my wife Margaret. Executors: my sons George and John Fiske. Witnesses: Jeffrey Freman, John Bredley the Younger, Ric. Rooke, Senr. Memorandum that the testator surrendered his copyholds in the manor of Aldeburgh to the use of his will, and likewise his copyholds in Thorpe holden of Layson manor. Proved 15 February 1573/4 by Geo. Harrison, procurator of the executors. (Prerogative Court of Canterbury [Somerset House, London], Martyn, 7.)

38. The Will of WILLIAM FYSKE of the parish of St. Michael's of South Elmham [co. Suffolk], "whelewright," dated 10 October 1575.

My soul to "god my maker, Jhesus Christe my Savior and to the holye ghoste my sanctifier trusting to have full pardon and forgyvenes of all my synnes by the merightes of Jhesus Christe." To my daughter Gelyon Aldus a feather bed, etc. To my daughter Margaret Bancrofte 40s. To my daughter Agnes Borowghe a milch cow and 20s. Residuary legatee and executrix: my daughter Mary. Witnesses: William Rycord, minister, the writer hereof, Robarte Fyske, and William Fyske.

Codicil, dated 2 January 1578/9. To Elizabeth Wood, the lame wench in this parish, 20d. To Peter Wells 10d. To Robt. Kempe 10d. To "the afflicted for Christes his sake" 10s. To every grandchild of mine 20d. To "borowghes children" 40d. each. Witnesses: John Lauraunce, Robt. Fiske, Geofferye Fyske, William Rycorde.

Proved 30 January 1578/9 by Mary Fiske, the executrix. (Archdeaconry of Suffolk [Ipswich Probate Registry], book 27, fo. 129.)

39. The Will of WILLIAM FISKE of Sowthcove [South Cove], co. Suffolk, yeoman, dated 13 March 1576 [1576/7]. To be buried in the churchyard there. To the poor box there 3s. 4d. To my wife Elizabeth £5 a year for life, out of my lauds and tenements, on her releasing dower, also her dwelling in the parlour and a chamber on the same conditions, and also to her a silver goblet, a silver salt, six best silver spoons, two posted bedsteads in the parlour and bedding thereto, and a cupboard, hutches, etc., and she is to have use of the same for her life, and then to Judith Fiske and Dorothie Fiske, my grandchildren. To my said wife her apparel and body linen and all napery and other linen. To each child of Robert Pearse, as well as those to be born, 40s. at eighteen. To each child of Rychard Hause which he had by my daughter Alice, his late wife, deceased, 40s., at eighteen. To the poor of South Cove 20s. To Wm. Pearse, my grandchild, to his education, all the obligations in my custody at my death. To Judith and Dorothy Fiske, my grandchildren, all lands and tenements now occupied by Nycolas Hidis, my farmer, at their marriages or at eighteen, but my son-in-law Robert Pearse is to occupy the same and take rents for their use until they be married or eighteen. All residue to the said Robert Pearse, who, with my wife Elizabeth, is executor. Supervisor: John Duke, gent., [to whom I give] 40s. Witnesses: John Asshefeld, John Beare, and others. Proved 5 December 1581 by the executors. (Consistory Court of Norwich [Norwich, co. Norfolk], Register for 1581, fo. 341.)

40. The Nuncupative Will of EASTER FISKE of Framlingham ad Castrum, co. Suffolk, singlewoman, declared 20 March 1579 [1578/9], 21 Elizabeth, gave to her sister Marie Fiske two squares, "unto Mathewe her sister" two squares, and to her brother Amos Fyske all her money and raiment. Executor: her brother Amos Fyske. Witnesses: Anthonye Plomton, Johanne Blithe, Bridget Dowtie. Proved 21 March 1578 [1578/9] by the executor. (Archdeaconry of Suffolk [Ipswich Probate Registry], book 27, fo. 146.)

41. The Will of WILLIAM FYSKE of Denington [Dennington, co. Suffolk], yeoman, dated 13 August 1580. Testator mentions his wife Helen, his son Nicholas (under twenty-one), his late father Nicholas, his children under sixteen, his brother Amos, his sisters, and his daughters Anne Fyske, Rachaell, and Elizh. The witnesses include John Fiske and Amos Fiske. Proved 22 November 1580 by John Button, the testator's friend and executor. (Archdeaconry of Suffolk [Ipswich Probate Registry], book 28, fo. 163.)

42. The Will of KATHERINE FYSKE of Hensted [Henstead, co. Suffolk], widow, dated 5 May 1583. To be buried in Hensted churchyard. To the repairs of Hensted church 6s. To the poorest of the said parish 5s. To my godchildren Thos. Clement, Erasmus Watsonne, John Newman, Johane Feeke, daughter of John Feeke, Parnell Ringarborrowe and Margaret Harris, daughter of Wm. Harris the Younger of Benacre [co. Suffolk], 12d. each. To Mary Crosse, daughter of Thos. Crosse of Hensted, a bed, etc. To Alice Brigges, servant to Wm. Love of Hensted, a coffer. To Agnes Crosse, wife to the said Thos Crosse, my gown. To Janet Harris, wife of Wm. Harris the Younger of Benacre, a petticoat. To Elizh Bacon, wife of Richard Bacon of Gisleham [co. Suffolk], my French kirtle. To Michael Whiskine of Hensted 3s. 4d. To his wife my best "Axrene." To Johane Burter, wife of Owen Burter of Benacre, 2s. Alms at burial: five dozen of bread, as much cheese as can be bought for 3s., and a firkin of beer. To each of four persons who shall bear me to church 4d. Executor: Thos Crosse of Hensted, [and to him] 3s. 4d. Witnesses: Gabriel Thomlynson, Michael Whysken. Proved 2 May 1584 by the executor. (Archdeaconry of Suffolk [Ipswich Probate Registry], book 30, fo. 15.)

43. The Nuncupative Will of JONE FISKE of Ersham, co. Norfolk, widow, being of good and perfect remembrance, declared 7 December 1583. She gave to William Jaye, her son, a feather bed. To Agnes Jaye, her daughter-in-law, her next best gown. To Anne Jaye, daughter of the said William Jaye, her best gown and a silver pin. To Anne Jaye, wife of John Jaye, her son, her worsted kirtle. To Agnes Jaye, daughter of John Jaye the Younger, her taches. To Edward Jaye, son of John Jaye the Elder, a pewter platter. To William Jaye, son of William Jaye, her great colfer [sic, ? coffer]. To Henrie, son of William, a pewter porringer. All the rest of her goods not bequeathed she did give to William Jaye the Elder and John Jaye the Elder, her sons, to be equally divided between them, and she made them her sole executors. Witnesses: Robert Thacker, John Thorne, William Fiften of Ersham. Proved 15 February 1583 [1583/4] by Wm and John Jaye, executors. (Consistory Court of Norwich [Norwich, co. Norfolk], Register for 1583, fo. 268.)

44. The Will of WILLIAM FYSKE of Aldborough, co. Suffolk [sic, ? Norfolk], cooper, dated 3 September 1584. To be buried in the churchyard there. To Margaret Fyske, my wife, my houses in which Andrewe Blomefild [and] Frauncys Galley, the "Smyth," now dwelleth [sic], with the shop and yard, for her life, and then the same to Francis Fyske, my son, and his heirs. To Margerie Fyske, my daughter, the house and ground, fenced and enclosed, in which Robert Dey and Henrie Lambe now dwelleth [sic], when she is twenty-one, and my wife is to take the profits until that time. To Thomas, my son, and John, my son, houses and ground at the Watering. To William, my son, part of my land in Knodishall [Knoddishall, co. Suffolk] and the little house and ground wherein John Myles now dwelleth. The house and grounds in which Roger Busken lately dwelt are to be sold to pay debts. If my daughter Margerie die without lawful issue and under twenty-one, then the house and ground before given to her are to remain to the children of my brother John Fyske now living and their heirs. If my son Francis die before his mother and s. p., then his bequest is to remain, on my wife's death, to the children of my said brother John Fiske that be now living and to their heirs. If my brother George Fyske will take my son Thos as apprentice for five years and teach him his occupation, then George is

to have the profit of my said son Thomas's bequest till his time is up. If my brother John will take my son John as apprentice and bring him up to write and read and teach him his occupation, then my said brother is to have the profits of my said son John's bequest for his term of service. If my brother John shall take and bring up my son William and put him to a trade, my said brother is to have the profits of my son William's bequest, and my brother John is to be his guardian till he is twenty-one. To my wife Margaret my best posted bedstead and the bedding thereto. Residue of my goods between my said five children and my wife, equally. [Executors:] my son Thomas Fyske and John Fyske, my brother. [The proof is written out, but the words *Probatum fuit huius testamenti* are struck through and at the side are the words *non probavit sed renunciavit Iohes Fyske*, i. e., John Fyske, one of the executors, renounced, but nothing is said about Thomas, the other executor.] (Consistory Court of Norwich [Norwich, co. Norfolk], Register 84 [*sic*, ? for 1584], fo. 20.)

45.   The Will of GEORGE FISKE, "Cowper," of Aldeburgh [co. Suffolk], being sick in body, dated 25 January 1584 [1584/5], 27 Elizabeth. To be buried in Aldeburgh churchyard. To my wife Johane Fyske my house and ground, for life, with remainder to my brother John Fiske and his heirs, and he is to pay to my goddaughter Margerie Fiske, daughter to Wm. Fiske, £5. To Thos. Fiske, son of William Fiske, "2 shanks & all the pompe wimbles that belong to boring of pompes." Executrix: my wife Johane [to whom I give] my mare and all my other goods. Witnesses: Robt Bundiche, Dennis Browne, John Fiske, and Wm. Gildersleeve, the "wrighter hereof." I have surrendered my copyholds into the hands of Robt. Bundishe, copyholder, in the presence of Deonis Browne, John Fiske, and Robt. Bundiche, copyholders, to the use of my will. Proved 26 February 1584 [1584/5] by Johane, the widow. (Archdeaconry of Suffolk [Ipswich Probate Registry], book 30, fo. 259.)

46.   The Will of RICHARD FISKE of Shotley [co. Suffolk], husbandman, dated 6 April 1589. To my son Jonas Fiske the bed whereon I lie. To my wife Urselie my moveables, household stuff, and implements, she paying my debts. To my son Jonas a bay gelding, after my wife have [*sic*] had reasonable use of him until harvest be ended. Executrix: my wife. Witnesses: Richard Weston, George Redmaine, "writer." Proved 27 November 1589 by Ursula, the widow. (Archdeaconry of Suffolk [Ipswich Probate Registry], book 32, fo. 305.)

47.   The Will of ROBERT FISKE of the parish of St. James in Southelmam [South Elmham, co. Suffolk], "whelewright," "trusting and stedfastlie beleiving to be saved by the death and precious bloudshedding of our lord and saviour Jesus Christ," dated 10 April 1590. To my eldest son William Fiske my tenement called Hoves in the parish of St. James, according to the custom of the manor, he paying to my daughter Elizabeth, now the wife of Robert Barnard, or to the said Robert, in the dwelling house of my said tenement called Hoves, £18 (in instalments). To my son Eliezar and to Elizabeth, his wife, all my freehold lands in St. James, Elmham, [they] paying yearly to my son William 2½d., for their lives, and paying to my son Thomas Fiske, at the dwelling house of the said tenement called Hoves, £8, as follows: £4 within one month of my decease and £4 at the end of a year following that payment. The free lands are to pass to my son Thomas, if Eliezar and Elizabeth fail to be bound for the above payment. On the death of Eliezar and Elizabeth (and of Thomas, if tenant of the free lands) the free lands are to pass to my son

William, he paying to my son Thomas £3, in consideration thereof, one month after my decease. To the poor of St. James 10s., out of my moveables, after my decease, and 10s. more to such other godly poor people as shall be thought most needful and charitable by my executors, at such times as to them shall seem most convenient. To my "bedchildren" [*sic,* ? belchildren] 40s., to be equally divided among them and paid into the hands of their parents. To Nicholas Barbor of Chepenell Greene 30s., for him to divide equally among his children. My executors are to have those houses, parcel of the said tenement, which are now in my own hands and occupying, for one month after my decease. To my executors 6s. 8d. each. The residue of my estate is to be equally divided among my children then living, by agreement, or by the appointment of John Laurance the Elder, gent., and he is to have 6s. 8d. Executors: my sons Jefferie Fiske and Eliezar Fiske. Witnesses: Robert Lawter, Thomas Starke. Proved at Metfield [co. Suffolk], 28 July 1602, by the executors. (Archdeaconry of Suffolk [Ipswich Probate Registry], book for 1602–1603, fo. 144.)

48. The Will of WILLIAM FISKE of Laxfild [Laxfield, co. Suffolk], "whelewright," being "visited with sickness," dated 29 December, 33 Elizabeth [29 December 1590]. To be buried in Laxfild churchyard. To my wife Jane my messuage in Stradbroke [co. Suffolk], for life, with remainder to John Punchyard, my brother-in-law, till John Punchyard, his son, my nephew and godson, be twenty-one. To Anne Borret, my wife's daughter, a joined "chest of Abell [? abele]. To Susanna Borret, my wife's daughter, a joined chest. Residue, including a bond of £40 from my brother-in-law Jn. Punchyard, to my wife Jane. To my brother-in-law Jn. Punchyard £10 and three hundred oaken boards and the best trees of oak in my yard. To my wife Jane three handsaws, a "haggesawe" and other tools [named], oaken boards in the long shed, and other timber [described]. To my brother John Fiske oak and "poople" boards, etc. To my brother Jeremie Fiske my sorrel colt, the residue of my tools belonging to my science, and the residue of timber. To my brother-in-law Thomas Borret, my black mare, three hundred oaken boards, and five combs of wheat, with the straw. To the poor of Laxfield 20s. Executrix: my wife Jane. Proved 26 January 1590/1. (Archdeaconry of Suffolk [Ipswich Probate Registry], book 33, fo. 256.)

Inventory, taken 7 January 1590 [1590/1], £200. [A verbatim copy of the inventory follows here.]

An Inventory indented of all the Goodes Cattells & Cattell & Howssehold Stuff Implementes And utenssells of Howssehold And allso of all Sutche Tymber bords and other Thynges w of Late dyd appertayne and belonge unto Wyllm Ffyske Late of Laxfeld in the Countye of Suff. whellwryght deceassed Seane and p'sed the Seventhe daye of Januarij Anno 1590 By Robert Borret John Smithe of P'kefelde Roger Godbalde Edmonde Jesoppe and Crispen Dawlinge and others as ffolowethe

In the hawle.

|  | s d |
|---|---|
| In p'rnis One table wythe a frame Two Joyned fformes | 13—4 |
| It. one Square Table w<sup>t</sup> a Cubberd in it | 10—0 |
| Item One Joyned Cheste & one Coffer | 10—0 |
| It. on Calyver 'one ffowlyng piece fflaske & Tochebox | 20—0 |
| Item 2 greate Bake Chayers and 2 Lesse Chayers | 4—0 |
| It. one ffyre panne and Tonges | —12 |
| It. one payer of Bellowes & a gredyiron | —20 |
| It ffyve fflykkes of Bacons | 26—8 |

452

It ffyve Coffeyrs . . . . . . . 5—0
It. one pyke and one morion . . . . 5—0
It. Syxe Bookes greate and Small . . . 10—0
It. 2. Kandyll Styckes . . . . . 2—0
It 2 paynted Clothes . . . . . . 2—0
It one Woodknyfe one brushe & one Syckle . . —12
It one keepe or Glasse Casse . . . . 5—0
It one Brush-hooke . . . . . . . —8
It 6 panes of glasse in the wyndowe . . . 6—0

### In the Buttreye.

It one greate Brasse panne . . . . 20—0
It 12 peaces of pewter . . . . . 8—0
Item one greate Kettell and 4 Skylletts . . . 8—0
It. 4 Small Kettells . . . . . 5—0
It 9 Alle ffyrkyns . . . . . . 4—0
It. one Brasse poot & one Chaffyndyshe . . 5—0
Item 2 Spyttes and one Droppyng panne . . 3—0
It 2 payer of poothooks . . . . . —4
It one payer of Musterd Quecons . . . —10
It ffyve pewter porrengers . . . . —20
It 4 Steme pootts & one dosen Trenchers . . —12
It. 4 payles wᵗ Iron Bayles . . . . 2—0
It one Allestoole . . . . . . —4
It one Lether Botteli and one Skonse [sic] . . 2—0
It one Hatchet and one Hooke . . . . —8

### In the Lyttell Howsse by the Butterye

It one wollen whelle 3 Mandes a Bookeyenge Tubbe 2
  Temses a Bonchyng Blooke and the Byetells . . 3—0
It 2 payʳe of Bootes and two payer of Shooss . . 6—8
It 2 Bordynge Skeppes . . . . . —6
It one Passhyll and one Hagge Sawe . . . 2—4

### In the Chamber over the sayd Lyttell Howse.

Item one olde ffetherbed and Bollster . . . 6—8

### In the Chamber over the Butterye.

It in Wheate by Estimacion 10 busshell . . . 25—0

### In the Chamber behynde the Chymnys on the Northsyd

It one Joyned Bedsteade one olde fether bedde one
  Boullster one Blanket & one paynted Clothe . . 30—0
It 2 Old Coffers . . . . . . . —20
It one payer of Towe Combes a Rollyng pynne and a
  Battyldore . . . . . . . . 2—0
It Sartayne Towe Redys dressed . . . . 3—4

### In the upper Chamber behynde the Chemnye

Item one posted Bedsteade wᵗ a Joyned Testor Twoe
  ffetherbedds one boulster 2 blanketts . . . 3—6—8
Item 2 joyned Chestes . . . . . 20—0
Item 2 Downe pyllowes . . . . . 3—4
Item one paynted Clothe . . . . . 2—0
Item one Bowe of Ewe and sartayne arrowes and one
  Armyne Swoorde . . . . . . . 2—0
It. a sartayne old Iren and a Payer of Wolle Cardys . —16
It 2 old Coffers and Shellves to laye in Apparell . . 2—6
It all hys Apparell . . . . . . . 40—0

### In the other Chamber behynde the Chimnye

It. one joyned Bedsteade wᵗ a fetherbedd Boulster and a
  Coverynge . . . . . . . . 40—0
Itm one Trundell bedstead Joyned one ffetherbedde and
  one Boulster . . . . . . . 13—4

453

Itm one Joyned Cheste one Coffer  .    .    .    .
Item two Deskes  .    .    .    .    .    .    16—0
Item one Cappecase one Boxe  .    .    .    .    2—0

### The Lynnen and Naperye.

Itm 2 Soheales [*sic*] Table clothes table Napkins Towells
pyllowe Keepes and other Lynnen  .    .    .    .    5—0—0
It in Lynnen Yearnes  .    .    .    .    .    10—0

### On the Hawle Chamber

It. in Wheate by estimacion 6 busshells  .    .    .    15—0
Item in Malte 3 Barrells  .    .    .    .    9—0
Item in sartayne Apples and Peares  .    .    .    10—0
It. olde Bordes and Shellves to Laye apples upon and
other Sawen Tymber  .    .    .    .    .    6—8
Itm one Bownett one Batfoullyng nett and sartayne olde
Iron  .    .    .    .    .    .    .    2—0
Itm One Stylle & sartayne halfe Inche borde  .    .    6—8

### In the Bakehouse.

Itm One Salltyng Troughe w<sup>t</sup> a Cote [*sic*]  .    .    3—4
Itm one peele of Iron and one Spytte  .    .    .    —18
Itm one Longe Stoole and a Shelffe  .    .    .    —6
It one paryngs Iron and one Hall [*sic*]  .    .    —12

### In the Chesse Howsse

Item One Chessepresse and a Salltyng traye  .    .    6—8
It one Caudryon of Red Brasse  .    .    .    .    10—0
It. 2 Chayers 2 olde Tubbes  .    .    .    .    6—8
It 9 Mylk Bolles and one Traye  .    .    .    .    5—0
Itm 4 Chesse ffatts & 2 Breades  .    .    .    .    6—8
Itm 2 ffyrkyns of Whyght Heryngs  .    .    .    8—0
Itm 3 ffyrkyn of Swette Butter  .    .    .    .    40—0
It Chesse Bordes Shellves & one dressyng stoole  .    2—0
It one ffleshe Tubbe olde Erthen Poottes and 2 Bread
graates  .    .    .    .    .    .    .    2—0
It one Copper panne  .    .    .    .    .    2—6
It one Hallfe Barrell of Vergesse  .    .    .    2—6

### On the Chesse Chamber.

Item In Chesse by Estimacion 2 wayes  .    .    4—0—0
Itm. one Beame and Skooles & Leade wayghtes  .    8—0
It. sartayne Bee skeppes and Wheate Drosse  .    —20
Itm 4 Chesse Bordes and 3 Tressells  .    .    —20
It 1 Hallfe Barrell of Vergesse one Olde Tubbe and
sartayne Hoppes  .    .    .    .    .    3—4

### In the Shoppe behynde the Bakehowsse.

Ite one payer of malte Quearnes & one Boltynghutche  .  5—0
Item one olde Trewde and 8 postes for bedds  .    5—0
Item one Joyners Benche one planke a Lytell Troughe
and other Small Tryssells  .    .    .    .    2—0
Ite 3 Seaves and one olde Sakke  .    .    .    —12

### In the Chamber over the Bakehowsse

Itm poople bordes and other Tymber for Cartes Tum-
brells and other Thynges  .    .    .    .    13—4

### In the Bearne.

Item Wheate in the Shoffe by estimacion Twenty Combes  10—0—0
Itm 4 Chessepresse plankes  .    .    .    .    26—0
Itm Carte Strynges and sartayne tymber to make Ladders
a Saltyng Traye and Sartayn other Tymber of dyvers
soorts  .    .    .    .    .    .    4—0—0
Itm fyve pyckefforks  .    .    .    .    .    2—0

### In the Workehowsse or Shoppe

| | |
|---|---|
| Itm 2 longe Sawes Sartayn Wymbells and other Tooles belongyng to the Seyence . . . . | 4—3—4 |
| Itm. in sartayne Naves. ffellawes & other tymber . . | 30—0 |

### In the Stable

| | |
|---|---|
| Item. 2 Sadells 2 Brydells 2 Collers. 2 Dudffyns the Thyllers geare and 2 payer of traysse . . . | 17—0 |
| Itm 2 Shellves 1 matthooke 2 Sruppetts 2 Drafthookes & 2 mode skoppetts . . . . . . | 6—8 |

### In the Pasture

| | |
|---|---|
| Itm one Graye geldynge . . . . . . | 46—8 |
| Itm. one Baye Coulte . . . . . . | 40—0 |
| It. one Blacke Mare . . . . . . | 53—4 |
| Itm 2 Wenlyng Callves . . . . . . | 40—0 |
| Item 8 mylche Keyne and 3 heiffers . . . . | 20—0—0 |
| Item in Haye upon 2 Shoddes . . . . . | 5—0—0 |
| Itm in Haye Stakes at Stradbrook in yᵉ Lanne . . | 3—0—0 |

### In the Yeardes.

| | |
|---|---|
| Item in Naves ffellowes Spookes and other Tymber Redy Sawen . . . . . . . . | 17—0—0 |
| Itm in Oken Boordes and poople Bordes to the Valew of | 8—0—0 |
| Itm in Planks, Rayle, Beddsydes, bedds Whartes and Tymber for gates & other thynges . . . . | 20—0 |
| Itm in Rowghe Tymber and Same Redy hewen to the valew of . . . . . . . . | 4—0—0 |
| Itm sartayn plankes to goe upon and plankes and bordes at the Hogges Trowghes and the Hogges Troughes . | 5—0 |
| Itm sartayne ffyrewood Stendyng upp and other old Blookes for ffirewoode . . . . . . | 40—0 |
| Itm 10 Shooddes Coveryd with Chyppes & 2 Shoddes . | 40—0 |
| Itm one Carte at the Wedow Hellwys & Carte Roops . | 13—10 |
| Itm. One Grynstone as yᵗ hangeth . . . . | 6—0 |
| Redy money & One little Carte . . . . | 39—4 |
| Sum Total [*blank*] | |
|     Dothe [*sic*] owynge to Testate | [*blank*] |
|     Obligacions to the ffull Sume of | [*blank*] |
| Sum Total is £200 pounds.* | |

49. The Will of GEORGE FISKE of Westhall [co. Suffolk], dated 6 January 1591 [1591/2]. To be buried in Westhall churchyard. To my son George Fiske my tenement and lands in Westhall and Brampton [? co. Suffolk] bought of Nicholas Harvy, and he is to pay to my wife Anne £8 a year for two years and then £10 a year, the £10 to be paid by Geo. Fiske, "Thos Fiske & Margaret children of the said George,"† after the portion each shall have. My son Geo. is to pay to Thomas, my son, £100 and to Margaret, my daughter, £40. To my son Thomas my tenement and lands abovesaid, should conditions be unfulfilled. To my wife Anne the residue of my goods, the overplus on her death to be evenly departed among my children. If John Gille complete the purchase of the said lands and tenements, "as we have begun," my son George shall have £160, my son Thomas £100, and my said daughter £40, in occupation for life, and after her death the said £40 shall remain to John Wittingham, her

---

*The sum of the valuations given in the inventory is consiaerably less than £200, but it is to be noticed that the amounts for the debts due to the estate and for the obligations of the estate have not been entered in the inventory.

†Apparenty the words "the said George" refer to the testator, but the meaning is somewhat doubtful.

son. Executors: my wife Anne and my son George. Supervisor: Richard Aldus. Witnesses: Richard Aldows, John Baas, George Baas.

Codicil, dated 25 March 1593, annuls the bequest of the residue of goods to wife Anne; and said goods are to be appraised by four persons, two nominated by the widow and two by my two sons Geo. and Thos., my wife to have the use of the same for life and the residue to be parted on her death between my surviving children. Whereas a title is pretended by Thomas Harvey to my said lands and tenements my wife and Thomas, my son, shall bear part of the charges at law with my son George. Witnesses: John Baas and Geo. Baas.

Proved 7 April 1593 by the executors. (Archdeaconry of Suffolk [Ipswich Probate Registry], book 34, fo. 587.)

50. The Will of GREGORIE FISKE of Kirkton *alias* Kirton [co. Suffolk], husbandman, "sick in bodye," dated 7 June 1599. To be buried in the churchyard of Shotley [co. Suffolk]. To my wife Agnes my messuage and lands in Kirkton *alias* in Shotley for life, and she is to find two sureties, should she marry, to be bound to the churchwardens of Kirketon *alias* Shotley to perform the will, with remainder to my eldest son Richard Fiske, with remainder, failing issue of Richard, to my son William Fiske, with remainder, failing issue of William, to my daughter Elizabeth Fiske and her heirs for ever. My wife Agnes is to sell the ground called Diches (6 acres) and Allgoods meadow (1½ acres), to redeem my other lands which stand bound to [*blank*] Manhood of Ipswich, and to pay my debts, if she cannot otherwise redeem it. To my son William Fiske, out of said sale, £5 at twenty-one. To my daughter Elizh Fiske, out of said sale, £5 at twenty-one or marriage. Residuary legatee: my wife Agnes. Executors: my wife Agnes and John Sparke. Supervisor: Mr. Christopher Abbill [*sic*], minister of Shottley. Witnesses: Christopher Abbis [*sic*], minister, William Dennis. Proved at Ipswich, 12 December 1599, by Agnes, the widow. (Archdeaconry of Suffolk [Ipswich Probate Registry], book 37, fo. 534.)

51. The Will of ELIAS FISK of Laxfield [co. Suffolk], yeoman, dated 2 May 1601. To my wife Alice my lands and tenements in Laxfield and Stradbroke [co. Suffolk], free and copyhold, lately purchased of Edmund Jay, until my son Henrie be twenty-four, when he shall entere therein, on condition that he pay to my daughter Sara Fiske £5, £5, £5, £5, and £10 at stated times, to my daughter Marie Fiske £5, £5, £5, £5, and £10 at stated times, and to my daughter Margaret Fisk, £10, £10, and £10 at stated times, in the church porch of Laxfield. To my wife Alice my messuage in Laxfield wherein I inhabit and my lands in Laxfield and Stradbroke which late were of my father Richard Fiske, late deceased, with remainder to my son Henry. To my daughters Sara, Marie, and Margaret, and to Johane Cowper, my wife's daughter, to each £5 at twenty. To my son Henry household goods [described] and my horse mill, after the decease of my wife Alice. To my daughters Sara, Marie, and Margaret household goods [described], after the death of my wife Alice. Residuary legatee and executrix: my wife Alice, and she is to bind my son Henrie apprentice to such occupation or trade she thinks well. Witnesses: William Sandcrafte, John Buckenham, William Warner. [Signed] Elie Fiske. Proved 12 September 1601 by Alice, the widow. (Archdeaconry of Suffolk [Ipswich Probate Registry], book 38, fo. 394.)

52. The Nuncupative Will of ROBERT FISK of Great Lynstead [Great Linstead, co. Suffolk], single man, declared 8 March 1601 [1601/2]. He gave to his father, Thomas Fisk of Cratfield [co. Suffolk], 20s., to his mother, Alice, 20s., to his brother, William Fiske, 10s., to his sister, Alice Sparham, 10s., and to her four children 2s. 6d. each, to his sister, Ann Fiske, 10s., to his brother, John Fiske, whom he named executor, 20s., a cloak, etc., to his sister-in-law, Johane Fiske, wife to said John, 20s., to Marie Fiske, daughter to said John and Johane, 10s. and his best band, to Henry Fiske, son to said John and his godson, a heifer, to John Fiske, eldest son to said John, 5s. and his best girdle, to William Fiske, the other son to said John, 5s., and to John Backes wife 10s. due to her. Witnesses: Symon Barber, John Barber [or Barker, the one altered from the other], Thomas Wulnaughe, Thomas Welton. Proved 9 March 1601 [1601/2] by John Fisk, the brother. (Archdeaconry of Suffolk [Ipswich Probate Registry], book 38, fo. 485.)

53. The Will of JOHN FYSKE of Tyvetshall St. Marie [Tivetshall St. Mary], co. Norfolk, yeoman, sick in body, dated 1 October 1607. To be buried there or elsewhere. To Thomasyn, my wife, my messuage [and] lands in Tivetshall and Dicleburgh [Dickleburgh, co. Norfolk] (she to claim no dower), for her life or widowhood. If she remarry, then she is to have one-third only. If she makes claim for dower in my lands at Occolt [Occold], Thornden [Thorndon, co. Suffolk], or places near, then she is to forego the Tivetshall lands. To John Punchard the Younger, my sister's son, said property in Occolt and Thorndon, charged with £40 to his sister Margaret Punchard (by £10 a year). And to Jeremy Punchard, his brother, £30 (£10 a year). And to Mary Punchard, his other sister, £30 (£10 a year). To John Punchard aforesaid all my tools of a wheelwright and my joiner's tools. To John Bucknam [or Buckman, faded], my servant, 40s. To John Cobbrame [sic], my godson, 40s. To Richard Goothrame, my godson, 40s. To John Watlinge, my godson, 30s. at twenty-one. To John Dowson, my kinsman and godson, £3 when twenty. To Marie Cole, my goddaughter, 40s. at twenty-one. To Margerye Woodward, my goddaughter, 20s. when twenty. To Margaret Chapman, my goddaughter, 20s. To Fraunces Alpe, my nephew and godson, £30 at twenty-two. To Thomas Seaman 30s. To Edward Hickes, my godson, 20s., when twenty. To ———— Fisher, my kinsman and godson, 30s., when twenty-one. To Marie Alpe and Anne Alpe, my sister's daughters, my bond wherein Nicholas Haward of Darsham [co. Suffolk], William Haward of the same, and Jeffery Neve of Tivetshall St. Margaret [co. Norfolk] are bound to me in £20, [but] they are to take only the £10 debt and not the forfeiture. To Edward Alpe, my nephew, £5. To John Punchard the Elder of Beddingfield [Bedingfield, co. Suffolk], my brother[-in-]law, 40s. To Christopher Mercant of Tyvetshall St. Marie 40s. To the poor of Tivetshall St. Mary 30s. (10s. a year). If Thomasyn, my wife, enter bond in £80 [?, faded] to John Punchard the Elder of Bedingfield, to prove this will, pay legacies, etc., then she is to have all my goods, chattels, etc. Sole executrix: said Thomasyne, my wife. Witnesses: Paule Chapman, Edward Bateman. Proved the last of October 1609 by the executrix. (Consistory Court of Norwich [Norwich, co. Norfolk], Register for 1609, fo. 124.)

54. The Will of JOHN ALDUS of Fresingfield [Fressingfield, co. Suffolk], yeoman, dated 12 April 1610. Testator names his father, Robert Aldus, and bequeaths to Thomas Fiske, son of Thomas Fiske, 10s. within

a month of his decease, which 10s. is already in the hands of the said Thomas. The witnesses include Thomas Fiske. Proved 17 April 1610. (Archdeaconry of Suffolk [Ipswich Probate Registry], book 43, fo. 303.)

55. The Will of THOMAS FISKE of Fresingefield [Fressingfield, co. Suffolk], "whelewright," dated 20 February 1610 [1610/11]. Margerye, my wife, "shall have the occupation of the hole parcell of the tenement wherein I now dwell the holl Chamber and the Vaunce Rouffe over the same And the Twoe Butteries . . . & 2 coates wheareof the one is for Swine and the other for fowls," for life, with remainder to my son Thomas of all the term of years which I have therein. To my son Thomas my shop, the chamber over the same, and the chamber over the said two butteries, with the yards, gardens, and orchards, for the said term of years, on condition that he pay to my daughter Elizabeth £3. 6s. 8d., at Michaelmas 1619. To Phineas, my son, his executors, administrators, or assigns, £4, at Michaelmas 1621. To John, my son, £4, at Michaelmas 1624. To Mary, my daughter, £3. 6s. 8d., at Michaelmas 1627. To my wife Margery one-half of the fruit on the premises and the right to fetch water from the pond or ditch belonging to the tenement, to dry linen in the orchard, to lay wood in the yard, to plant herbs and seeds in the garden and take and use the same, and to keep her swine on the way adjoining the premises called Walslade Way and her fowls in the yards and orchards. My son John may remove to his own use, within four years, such young pear plants and apple plants which he has heretofore set or planted in the premises. My son Thomas shall keep the whole of the premises in repair. To my son Thomas all my timber and working tools. My wife Margery is to occupy all the residue of my goods, household stuff, and implements, for life, and then the same are to be divided equally among my children. Executor: my son Thomas. Witnesses: William Sancroft, Stephen Aldoes, Robert Aldoes, Thomas Fiske. Proved the last of February 1610 [1610/11] by Thos. Fiske, the son. (Archdeaconry of Suffolk [Ipswich Probate Registry], book 43, fo. 73.)

56. The Will of MARY FISKE of Ubston [Ubbeston, co. Suffolk], single woman, servant to Edmond Smyth of Ubston, being "visited by the hand of God," dated the last of February 1611/12. To my father and mother 20s. To my brothers and sisters 10s. each. To two of my sisters' children, "which I answered for," viz., Ann Mowling, my sister's daughter, and Jane Robertson, my other sister's daughter, 20s. each. To the residue of my brothers' and sisters' children 6s. 8d. each, at twenty-one. My apparel is to be at the disposition of "my master & dame." Residuary legatee and executor: Samuel Smyth, my master's son. Witnesses: Barthw. Aldred, Geo. Cole, John Smyth of Colshall. Proved 8 April 1612 by the executor. (Archdeaconry of Suffolk [Ipswich Probate Registry], book 45, fo. 13.)

57. The Will of THOMAS FISKE of Westhall, co. Suffolk, being in good and perfect remembrance, dated 15 April 1613. To the poor of Westhale 40s. To Mother Anne Fiske £30. To Anne Porter *alias* Fiske and Margery Fiske, daughters of my brother George Fiske, £10 between them. To my sister Margaret Wittingham £20. To the four children of 'my brother Jeffreye Fiske, namely, Elizabeth, Elizabeth [*sic*], Anne, and Millicent, £20 between them.* To Anthony Baldrye of Westhale the

*In The Fiske Family Papers, p. 64, the names of the four children of the testator's brother Jeffery are given, in a *very brief* abstract of this will, as Gelyon, Elizabeth, Anne, and Milicent.

profit of three milch neat, for life, and then the said neat or £10 to my nephew John Wittingham and also £5 which Anthony Baldry doth owe me, or the house of said Anthony Baldry for £4, parcel of the £5, and 20s., also two heifers in the hands of my cousin Lese of Sotherton [co. Suffolk], and also various [articles of] apparel, a musket, and other goods. To Elizabeth Clerke, my brother's maid, 10s. To Robert Hawle. his boy, 5s. To William Chapman 30s. in the hands of Thomas Bunting of Westhale. Executors: my brother George Fiske and Thomas Smyth of Westhale, [and I give them] £5. Witnesses: George Smythe, Nicholas Partriche. Proved 8 August 1613. (Archdeaconry of Suffolk [Ipswich Probate Registry], book 46, fo. 175.)

58. The Will of ELEAZER FISKE of Metfeild [Metfield, co Suffolk], "whelewright," dated 3 June 1613. My tenement and lands in the parishes of St. James and Sandcrofte in Southelmham [South Elmham, co. Suffolk] to my wife Elizabeth, for life, with remainder, as to the tenement in St. James, in the occupation of Robert Skepper, to my nephews Nathaniel Fiske and David Fiske, sons of my brethren William Fiske and Jefferye Fiske, and, as to the lands in Sandcroft, to Eleazer Lusher and Elizabeth Lusher, his sister (under twenty-one). To my wife Elizabeth my moveables. To the poor £3. To the children of my brother William £3 equally. To the children of my brother Jefferye £3 equally. To the children of my brother Thomas £3 equally. Executrix: my wife Elizabeth or, on her death, my nephews Nathaniel and David. Witnesses: Bartholomew Stiles, clerk, and Thos. Lancaster. Proved 4 July 1615 by Elizabeth, the widow. (Archdeaconry of Suffolk [Ipswich Probate Registry], book 48, fo. 72.)

59. The Will of WILLIAM WOLNOUGH of Metfield [co. Suffolk], yeoman, dated 17 July 1615, was witnessed by Jefferye Fiske and Eleazar Fiske. Proved 18 February 1615/16. (Archdeaconry of Suffolk [Ipswich Probate Registry], book 48, fo. 223.)

59a. The Will of WILLIAM FISKE of Ditchingham, co. Norfolk, dated 25 November 1616. The testator bequeaths to the poor of Ditchingham and of Bungay [co. Suffolk], mentions his now wife, Alice, and gives to his eldest son, John, lands in St. James, South Elmham, and in Metfield [both parishes being in co. Suffolk], the said John paying to his brothers Nathaniel and Eleazar and to his sister Esther sixscore pounds. The testator also mentions his grandchildren Matthias, John, and Mary Candler, his grandchildren John, Anne, Martha, Nathaniel, and Eleazar Fiske, all under twenty-one, and his daughter Anne Candler. Executor: testator's son John. Proved 17 May 1620. (Cf. The Fiske Family Papers, p. 71.)

60. The Will of ANN ALDRED of Laxfild [Laxfield, co. Suffolk], widow, dated 23 May, 19 James I [23 May 1621], was witnessed by Nicholas Fyske. Proved in 1621. (Archdeaconry of Suffolk [Ipswich Probate Registry], File for 1621, No. 35.)

61. The Will of JOHN SMYTH of Laxfield [co. Suffolk], tailor, dated 3 November, 19 James I [3 November 1621], was witnessed by Jerem. Fiske. Proved in 1625. (Archdeaconry of Suffolk [Ipswich Probate Registry], book for 1625, fo. 244.)

62. The Will of JAPHERIE FISKE of Metfielde [Metfield, co. Suffolk], yeoman, dated 10 October 1628. To my son Eliazer Fiske my messuage

in Metfield and Withersdale [co. Suffolk], with lands and freehold there, and he is to pay to my wife Sarah £15 a year, for life, at the south porch of Metfield church, quarterly. To my wife Sarah the parlour at the west end of said house, for life, and six loads of firewood from Eliazer's lands. To my wife Sarah all my moveables, for life, and after her death one-half [of the same] to my son-in-law John Sawer. To my son Eliazer a table in the parlour. To my "bedchild" [*sic*, ? belchild] John Sawer 20s. To my other "bedchild" [*sic*, ? belchild] Thomas Sawer 10s. To the poor of Metfield 20s. Executrix: my wife Sara. Witnesses: Stephen Lyllie, John Sawer, and Sarah [*altered from* Mary] Fiske, widow. Proved 25 November 1628 by Sarah, the widow. (Archdeaconry of Suffolk [Ipswich Probate Registry], book 58, fo. 369.)

63. The Will of JEFFERY FISKE "in the towne" of Great Bently [Great Bentley], co. Essex, yeoman, dated 11 May 1629. My soul to the Almighty God. To Samuel Fisk, my eldest son, living in Waybred [Weybread], co. Suffolk, my best suit of apparel. To Elizabeth Fisk, daughter of the said Samuel Fisk, 5s., to be paid at the end of her apprenticeship. I appoint David Fisk of Weley [Weeley, co. Essex] and Martine Underwood of Bentley executors, giving to them whatsoever remains at Bently, they paying all funeral expenses. [Signed] Jeffery Fysk. [Witnesses:] John Locke, the mark of Helen Hayes. Proved at Colchester 23 July 1629. (Archdeaconry of Colchester [Somerset House, London], original will, No. 8.)

64. The Will of JEROMIE FISKE of Laxfield [co. Suffolk], yeoman, sick in body, dated 22 August 1630. To be buried in Laxfield churchyard. To John Cocke, eldest son of Peter Cock, my son-in-law, a messuage and tenement in Tittleshall and Diskleborowe [Dickleburgh], co. Norfolk, freehold and copyhold, in the occupation of one Loter. To Anne Cock, daughter to the said Peter Cock, a messuage and tenement in the occupation of Wm. Smith, she paying her sister, Elizabeth Cocke, £10. To Peter Cock, son to the said Peter Cock, a messuage or tenement, free[hold] and copyhold, in Laxfield, now in my occupation, except the lands called Craiches. To Jeremie Cocke, son of the said Peter Cock, my son-in-law, a messuage or tenement, free[hold] and copyhold, called Craiches and [*illegible*] in Dennington [co. Suffolk] and Laxfield, in my occupation. To Margret Rackham, my servant, the house called Copphall, occupied by James Dallinger. To Alice Cocke and to Mary Cocke, daughters of the said Peter Cock, my son-in-law, to each £10. Executor: John Cocke, son of the said Peter Cock, my son-in-law. Supervisor: Peter Cock. Witnesses: John Cocke, Wm. Smith. Proved 15 September 1630 by John Cock. (Archdeaconry of Suffolk [Ipswich Probate Registry], book for 1629–30, fo. 227.)

# GENEALOGICAL RESEARCH IN ENGLAND

Communicated by the Committee on English and Foreign Research

## THE FISKE FAMILY

Contributed by G. Andrews Moriarty, A.M., LL.B., F.S.A.,
of Bristol, R. I.

From Parish Registers, co. Suffolk

CRATFIELD*

*Baptisms*

1555 Henry, son of Thomas Ffyske, 15 December.
1558 John Ffyske 7 September.
1561 Elizabeth, daughter of William Ffyske, 21 September.
1561 Bridget, daughter of George Ffyske, 2 October.
1562 Alice, daughter of Thomas Ffyske, 6 September.
1562 Eliazar, son of Jefria Ffyske and Christiana, 11 October.
1563 Maria, daughter of William and Alice Ffyske, May (middle day).
1564 Alice, daughter of William and Alice Ffyske, 13 February [1564/5].
1565 William, son of Jefria and Christiana Ffyske, 14 October.
1566 Gregory, son of Thomas and Alice Ffyske, 13 October.
1567 Henry, son of William and Alice Ffyske, 24 August.
1567 Alice, daughter of Gregory Ffyske, ———.
1568 John, son of Jefria and Christiana Ffyske, 29 September.
1569 William, son of William and Alice Ffyske, 4 January [1569/70].
1571 Alice, daughter of Jefria and Christiana Ffyske, 17 January [1571/2].
1572 John, son of William and Alice Ffyske, 1 May.
1572 Ann, daughter of Thomas and Alice Ffyske, 12 October.
1573 Gregory, son of William and Alice Ffyske, 4 February [1573/4].
1574 Ann, daughter of William and Alice Ffyske, 12 March [1574/5].
1575 Elizabeth, daughter of Jefria and Christiana Ffyske, 28 August.
1575 Robert, son of Thomas and Alice Ffyske, 27 December.
1578 Ann, daughter of William and Alice Ffyske, 6 March [1578/9].
1580 Margaret, daughter of William and Alice Ffyske, 24 August.
1591 Margaret, daughter of Henry and Margaret Ffyske, 12 December.
1593 William, son of Henry and Margaret Ffyske, 20 January [1593/4].
1596 Francis, son of Henry and Margaret Ffyske, 28 December.
1598 Elizabeth, daughter of Henry and Margaret Ffyske, 2 July.
1599 Henry, son of Henry and Margaret Ffyske, 17 November.
1602 Mary, daughter of Henry and Margaret Ffyske, 2 May.
1604 Elizabeth, daughter of Henry and Margaret Ffyske, 8 August.
1606 John, son of Henry and Margaret Ffyske, 22 February [1606/7].
1607 Alice, daughter of William and Elizabeth Ffyske, 21 March [1607/8].
1609 William, son of William and Elizabeth Ffyske, 22 August.
1610 Henry, son of Henry and Margaret Ffyske, 17 February [1610/11].

*Adapted from the copy of the Cratfield registers printed in The Fiske Family Papers, pp. 397–399.

461

1614 Ann, daughter of William and Elizabeth Ffiske, 18 August.
1629 Susana, daughter of Thomas ———— [*illegible*] by Mary Fyske, 11 June.
1632 Elizabeth, daughter of John and Elizabeth Fyske, 8 April.
1633 John, son of John and Elizabeth Fyske, 17 December.
1635 William, son of William and Mary Fyske, 22 December.
1637 Tobias, son of William and Mary Fyske, 22 August.
1638 Francis, son of William and Mary Fyske, 29 September.
1640 Frances, daughter of John and Frances Fyske, 20 April.
1641 Elizabeth, daughter of William and Mary Fyske, 14 April.
1642 Ann, daughter of William and Mary Fyske, 14 March [1642/3].
1643 Margaret, daughter of William and Mary Fyske, 12 March [1643/4].
1655 Henry Fyske, son of John and Mary, born 4 April and baptized soon after.
1657 William, son of John and Mary Fyske, born 11 May and baptized [? on same day].
1659 Francis, son of John and Mary Fyske, 14 November.
1662 Elizabeth, daughter of John and Mary Fyske of Linsted Magna, 29 April.

## Marriages

1554* Thomas Ffyske and Alice Bridge 11 November.
1555* Thomas Ffyske and Alice Bridges 11 November.
1558 William Ffyske and Alice Fulham 4 October.
1578 Thomas Keble and Joana Ffyske 24 April.
1581 Egilius Smith and Elizabeth Ffyske 5 January [1581/2].
1584 Thomas Butcher and Maria Ffyske September (nons die [*sic*]).
1600 Henry Robertson and Jane Ffyske 20 October.
1613 Isaac Stanard and Ann Fyske 28 October.
1617 William Fyske and Martha Chromer 3 June.
1622 Kobe Birton and Margaret Fyske 19 September.
1631 John Fyske and Elizabeth Day (last of) March.
1634 William Richard Ward [*sic*] and Ann Fyske 27 March.
1638 John Fyske and Frances Rouse 23 January [1638/9].
1657 William Warren of Nether Linsted and Elizabeth Fyske of Cratfield 4 February [1657/8].

## Burials

1553 Alice, wife of Henry Ffyske, 11 April.
1553 Peter Ffyske 4 February [1553/4].
1556 Henry Ffyske, son of Thomas, 17 May.
1558 Henry Ffyske 1 [*sic, vide supra,* Will No. 26] August.
1558 Joan, daughter of William Ffyske, 13 September.
1558 John and Joan Fyske 5 January [1558/9].
1561 Bridget, daughter of George Ffyske, 8 October.
1598 Elizabeth Ffyske 17 October.
1599 Elizabeth, daughter of Henry Ffyske, 17 November.
1602 Henry Ffyske, an infant, 28 May.
1603 Alice, wife of William Ffyske, 6 April.
1604 Infant son of Henry and Margaret Ffyske 13 August.
1608 William Ffyske 8 April.
1608 Alice Ffyske 4 October.
1609 Infant son of Henry Ffyske 9 November.
1612 Thomas Ffiske 21 October.

*Apparently one marriage recorded under two different years.

1613 Widow Fyske 26 June.
1616 The wife of William Fyske 26 February [1616/17].
1625 Elizabeth Ffiske 20 September.
1628 Henry Ffiske — July.
1637 Tobias Fyske 26 November.
1637 Elizabeth Fyske 5 March [1637/8].
1645 Widow Fyske, a Christian matron, ———.
1649 Bridget Fyske 3 December.
1660 Mary, wife of John Ffiske, 7 March [1660/1].
1661 Francis, son of William and Mary Ffiske, 15 January [1661/2].
1661 Henry, son of John and Frances Ffiske, 31 January [1661/2].
1663 Elizabeth, daughter of John and Mary Fyske, 31 May.

## DENNINGTON*

### Baptisms

1575 Joane Fyske, daughter of Amos and Mary, 23 July.
1578 Mary Fyske, daughter of Willon and Helen Fyske, 16 November.
1583 Mary, daughter of Amos and Mary Fyske, 12 May.
1587 Amos, son of Amos and Mary Fyske, 24 August.
1590 Witton, son of Amos and Mary Fyske, 10 January [1590/1].
1618 Francis, daughter of Amos and Margaret Ffiske, 15 April.
1620 Amos, son of Amos and Margaret Ffiske, 25 October.
1626 John, son of Amos and Margaret Ffiske, 10 October.
1628 Margaret, daughter of Amos and Margaret Ffiske, 13 February [1628/9].
1634 William and Margaret Ffiske 17 April.

### Marriages

1574 Willon Fyske and Hellyan ——— 27 September.
1574 Amos Fyske and Mary Gyrlynge 17 October.

### Burials

1584 Mary, daughter of Amos Fyske, 5 July.
1599 John, son of Amos and Mary Fyske, 7 November.
1609 Nicholas Ffiske, bachelor, about 28 years of age, 22 November.
1612 Amos and Mary Fyske, husband and wife, 31 May.
1612 Wyllyam, son of Amos and Mary Fyske, 31 May.
1632 Infant son of Amos Ffiske 7 June.
1632 Mary, daughter of Amos Ffiske, 10 June.
1633 Amos Ffiske 28 July.
1663 Margaret Ffiske, widow, 21 June.

## FRESSINGFIELD

### Baptisms

1554 Rychard fyscke, son of Robert fyscke, 16 July.
1556 Eleazar fyscke, son of Robert fyscke, 31 May.
1587 John fiske, son of John fiske, 28 January [1587/8].
1590 [Blank] fyske, the [blank], 1590/1 [between 22 January 1590/1 and the heading "1591," after which follows an entry of 18 June 1591].
1591 Phineas Cockram, son of Wyllyam cocrain, clercke, 22 August.
1592 Jonathan Cockrain, son of William Cockrain, "Schoolemaster," 8 September.

*Adapted from the copy of the Dennington registers printed in The Fiske Family Papers, pp. 403–405.

1594 Anne Fyske, daughter of John Fyske and Joan, 23 March [1594/5].
1595 William Fyske, son of William and Ann, 20 September.
1597 Elizabeth, daughter of William and Anne Fiske, 15 November.
1598 William Fiske, son of John and Johane, 21 September.
1600 Henry, son of John Fiske and Jene, his wife, 12 May.
1600 An, daughter of Wlm fisk and An, his wife, 29 August.
1612 Amie, daughter of John Fisk and An, his wife, 14 May.
1614 John, son of John and An Fisk, 11 October.
1616 Mary, daughter of John and An Fisk, 27 February [1616/17].
1618 Susan, daughter of John and An Fisk, 7 September.
1621 Antony, son of John Fisk and An, his wife, 17 June.
1624 Frances, son of John Fisk and An, his wife, 30 December.

### Marriages

1561 Thomas Alldowes and Gyllyan Fyske 14 October.
1594 Willm Fyske, son of Jeffrey [Fyske] of Fresyngfylde, and Anne
     Aldowes, daughter of William Aldowes of Fresyngfyld, 20 Sep-
     tember.
1596 John Wittam and Alys Fyske 1 June.
1613 James fisk and Alce Chetleborow 24 May.
1614 Philip Whisolcroft and Elisabeth fisk 25 April.
1618 Tho: greatrake and Mari Fisk 18 May.

### Burials

1586 Jefferye fyske his wife 23 September.
1603 Jeffery Fisk 22 February [1603/4].
1610 Thomas Fisk 26 February [1610/11].
1612 John Fisk 28 March.
1616 John fiske 4 May.
1616 Mary fisk 24 November.
1617 Mary Fisk 26 August.
1630 William Fiske 2 October.

## LAXFIELD*

### Baptisms, 1579–1651

1579 Ann, daughter of Nicholas Fiske, "the fiste [sic] of" July.†
1580 Elisabeth, daughter of Mathie Fiske, 12 February [1580/1].
1581 Mary, daughter of Nicholas Fyske, 12 November.
1584 Rebecca Fyske, daughter of Nycolas and Elizabeth, 26 July.
1588 Alice Fiske, daughter of Jerome and [blank], 22 December.
1589 Sara Fiske, daughter of Elye and Alice, 25 May.
1590 Henry Fyske, son of Elye and Alice, 24 May.
1591 Anne Fyske, daughter of Jerome, 12 March [1591/2].
1593 Mary Fyske, daughter of Elye, 16 April.
1596 Margaret Fiske, daughter of Elye, 16 November.
1601 Anne Fyske, daughter of John (son of Matthey), 17 May.
1602 John Fyske, son of John and Marye (son of Nycholas), 27 June.
1603 Margarett Fyske, daughter of Wylliam, late of Fresingfeld, 5
     April.

*Fiske entries in the parish registers of Laxfield are printed also in The Fiske Family
Papers, pp. 394–397. They extend from 1579, the year of the earliest entries in these registers, beyond the middle of the eighteenth century; and the dates and spellings do not always
agree with those given in the article. Words giving occupations are in many cases omitted.
Two entries have been inserted in the copy here printed on the authority of The Fiske Family Papers (see below).
†In The Fiske Family Papers, p. 394, this date is given as 5 July 1579.

464

1603 John Fyske, son of John (son of Matthey), 8 January [1603/4].
1604 Marye Fyske, daughter of John (the son of Nicholas), 27 January [1604/5].
1605 William Fyske, son of John Fyske, "wever," 23 February [1605/6].
1607 Elizabeth Fysk, daughter of John and Mary in Baynyards grene, 19 July.
1608 Elizabeth Fysk, daughter of John, the "wevour," 26 February [1608/9].
1613 Margrete Fyske, daughter of Jhon, 2 February [1613/14].
1614 Mathias Fiske, son of Jhon Fiske, weaver, 12 March [1614/15].
1640 John, son of John Fiske of Studhaw, 18 February [1640/1].
1642 John Fiske, son of John Fiske of Studhawe, 26 January [1642/3].
1644 Nicholas Fiske, son of John Fiske of Studhawe and Margaret, his wife, 17 October.
1645 Elizabeth, daughter of Matthias Fiske and Anne, his wife, 27 October.
1646 William, son of John Fiske of Studhawe and Margaret, his wife, 22 July.
1649 Deborah, daughter of Matthias Fiske and Anne, his wife, 26 March.
1651 Marie, daughter of Matthias Fiske and Anne, his wife, 29 October.

## Marriages, 1579–1654

1579 Thomas Borret and Anne fyske 26 July.
1579 Thomas Newson and Jane fyske 14 September.
1582 John Punchard and Margarett Fyske 20 May.
1590 Wollffran Balldreye and Elizabeth Fyske 18 August.
1590 Henry Fyske and Margarett Smithe 15 September.
1593 Mathey Fyske and Margaret Haywarde 24 October.
1599 Arthur Orffor and Rachell Fyske 21 June.
1600 John Fyske, son of Mathey, and Elizabeth Button, 5 May.
1600 Thomas Borrett and Anne Ffyske 8 July.*
1600 John Fyske, son of Nicholas, and Mary Eade, 23 September.
1604 Edmonde Stannarde and Elizabeth Fyske, daughter of Matthy, 25 July.
1611 Mathew Fyske and Ame Huggine 30 January [1611/12].
1629 John Fiske and Mary Haresone 30 June.

## Burials, 1579–1662

1579 William, son of Mathew Fiske, 23 June.
1590 William Fyske, "whellwryghte," 2 January [1590/1].
1591 Jeffrye Fyske, "Cowper," 29 April.
1592 Elizabeth, wife of Matthey Fyske, 6 January [1592/3].
1593 Alice Fiske, a "yonglynge," 7 April.
1595 Elizabeth fiske, "Singlewoman," 15 August.
1597 Marye Fyske, "Singlewoman," 18 November.
1597 Agnes Fyske, "wedowe," 16 January [1597/8].
1601 Elye Fyske, yeoman, 2 September.
1604 Jane Fyske, widow, 10 May.
1611 Margret Fyske, wife of Mathewe Fyske, 13 September.
1623 The "wyfe" of Nicholas Fiske 16 January [1623/4].
1624 The wife of Jerume Fiske 15 November.
1628 Mathias Fiske, "yeame," 5 November.
1628 Jhon Fiske of Studhaw, "yeman," at Vbbeston, "Fiske of Stow 6th November of Stow."

*This entry is inserted here on the authority of The Fiske Family Papers, p. 395.

1630 Jeremye Fyske, "yemane," 3 September.
1630 Nicholas Fiske, yeoman, 24 February [1630/1].
1639* "Vid." Fiske 8 June.
1641 John Fiske, infant, son of John Fiske, 12 November.
1648 Nicholas, son of Mr. John Fiske of Studhawe, 15 May.
1648 John Fiske, "ye elder," late of Broadgates, 21 March [1648/9].
1651 Marie, wife of John Ffiske, lately of Broadgates in Laxfield, 17 August.†
1659 Mathew Fiske, the "smyth" [blank].
1662 John Fiske, sen[i]or, a very aged man, 25 April.

## ST. JAMES, SOUTH ELMHAM.‡

### Baptisms, 1593-1657

1593 Clara, daughter of Jefferie and Marie Fiske, 10 March [1593/4].
1596 Anne, daughter of Jefferie and Marie Fiske, — October.
1599 Elizabeth, daughter of Geoffrey and Mary Fyske, 22 April.
1602 Martha, daughter of Jeffrie Fyske and [blank], 9 September.
1607 John, son of John and Anne Fyske, 20 March [1607/8].
1610 Ane, daughter of John and Anne Fyske, 1 April.
1618§ William, son of Thomas Fiske, 18 March [1618/19].
1623 Francis, son of Francis Fiske, 14 March [1623/4].

### Burials, 1558-1640

1587 Joan, wife of Robert Fiske, 3 August.
1600 Anne, wife of William Fiske, 13 February [1600/1].
1601 Nathaniel, son of Geoffrey and Mary Fiske, 13 September.
1614‖ Nathaniel, son of John and Anne Fyske, 27 March.
1614 Mary, wife of Jeffrey Fiske, 16 May.
1633 Goodman Fyske 14 May.

### Churchwardens

1601 Wm. Fiske.                    1628 John Fiske [?].

## WINGFIELD¶

### Baptisms

1622 Elizabeth, daughter of Phinehas Fiske, 22 April.
1627 John, son of Phinehas Fiske, 13 May.
1630 Thomas, son of Phineas Fyske, 25 March.

### Marriage

1594 Josua Brocke and Alice Fiske 17 June.

### Burials

1620 Martha Fiske 3 December.
1626 William Fiske 25 April.

[A continuation of this article on The Fiske Family will be published in the REGISTER of April 1933. — EDITORS.]

*There is a gap in the burial records from 1633 to 1638, inclusive.
†This entry is inserted here on the authority of The Fiske Family Papers, p. 396.
‡From a transcript by Rev. Lancelot Bird, 1924. Entries of marriages in these registers do not begin until 1668.
§There is a gap in the records of baptisms from 1610 to 1615.
‖There is a gap in the burial records from 1601 to 1605.
¶From Wingfield: Its Church, Castle and College, by S. W. H. Aldwell, Vicar of Wingfield.

466

# GENEALOGICAL RESEARCH IN ENGLAND

Communicated by the Committee on English and Foreign Research

## THE FISKE FAMILY

Contributed by G. Andrews Moriarty, A.M., LL.B., F.S.A.,
of Bristol, R. I.

### From Chancery Proceedings*

[Fyske *et al. v.* John, Abbot of St. Edmund's]

John Fyske and John Paryshe of Norwich, John Clubbe and Eliz., his wife, late the wife of Nicholas Fyske, *v.* John [Reeve], Abbot of St. Edmund's, *re* a debt of herrings bought by the cellarer of the abbey from Nicholas.

Complaint made to Sir Thomas Awdeley, Knight, Lord Chancellor of England, by John Fyske and John Parysshe of Norwich, executors of the will of Nicholas Fyske, deceased. and John Chiblee and Elizabeth, his wife, late the wife of Nicholas Fyske, coexecutrix, that Thomas Herset, late cellarer of the Monastery of St. Edmund's Bury, co. Suffolk, about

*Preserved in the Public Record Office, London.

1 February, 20 Henry VIII, at Norwich, bought of Nicholas Fyske aforesaid barrels of red and white herrings to the value of £28. 8s. and the said herrings were delivered to the monastery, but Fyske died before the money was paid. Thomas Ryngsted, now cellarer, has paid £12 of the sum, but John, the Abbot, although often requested, has refused to pay the residue of £16. 8s. They desire that John, the said Abbot, may be subpœnaed to appear to answer the premises.

(Early Chancery Proceedings, 1533–1538, File 795, No. 52.)

## [Garrad v. Fyske]

William Garrad v. Robert Fyske. Detention of deeds re land, etc., in Elmswell, late of John Hyll, grandfather of plaintiff and father-in-law of defendant.

[No. 20.] The Bill* of William Garrad [showeth] that, whereas John Hyll, late of Elmyswell, deceased, was seised, with others to his use, of land [specified] in Elmyswell, which he bequeathed to his son William Hyll, who entered into possession thereof, and after the death of William Hyll the premises descended to his daughters, Margaret, Elizabeth, Alys, and Anne, and Alice's share, on her death without heirs, came to the other three, and afterwards Margaret sold all her share to complainant, her heir apparent, now all the deeds touching complainant's share have come into the possession of Robert Fyske of Elmyswell, who had married Anne, and on the strength of the deeds lays claim to complainant's said share. Complainant asks for a writ subpena to be directed to Robert Fyske.

[No. 21.] The Answer† of Robert Fyske [states] that he does not know of the will. After Margaret had married Robert Garrad, Elizabeth . . . [mutilated] and Anne had married Robert Fyske, and Alice had come of full age, a lawful partition was made of the premises.

[No. 22.] The Replication of William Garrad denies that Alice, Robert Garrad and his wife Margaret, William Fyske and his wife Elizabeth, and defendant and Anne, his wife, ever made partition of the premises, or that Alice sold her share to defendant. The said Alice was "An Ideot borne."

[No. 23.] The Rejoinder of Robert Fyske denies that Alice's share should of right have descended to the other three daughters of William Hyll, or that Margaret could lawfully sell the third part of the said share to complainant. It denies also the other statements of the complainant.

(Early Chancery Proceedings, 1533–1538, Suffolk, File 805, Nos. 20–23.)

## [Fiske v. Fiske]

The Bill [filed 15 October 1566] of John Fiske of Laxfeld, co. Suffolk, complaining that, whereas William Fiske, late of Laxfeld, his father, was seised of lands called "glemes" and "harsfeld" in Laxfeld, which by his will, dated 15 October 1558, he bequeathed to his wife Margaret for six years, on condition she paid certain sums to his four daughters, with remainder, after the end of the six years, to complainant and his heirs male, and after the termination of the six years complainant possessed the premises until Mathye Fiske, one other son of the said devisor, older than complainant, has obtained the deeds of the premises

*An endorsement on this bill shows that a day, 20 April, 28 Henry VIII [20 April 1537], was set for hearing the replication of William Garrad.
†The answer of Robert Fyske is mutilated.

and entered into possession of the same, therefore complainant asks for a writ subpena directed to Mathye Fiske.

The Answer of Mathye Fyske [states] that the complainant's bill is the result of the sinister procurement of Thomas Tower and Margaret Armyger, late wife of John Armyger, sometime wife of the said William Fyske, and they are abettors in this suit, as they have been in divers other concerning the title to the premises.

William Fyske died at Laxfeld 30 October 1558, and the premises descended by right to Raffe Fyske, his eldest son, who, being seised thereof, made certain enfeoffments of parcel of the premises [to Thomas Browne, George Cowper, and Thomas Cryspe].

Rauffe Fyske died at Laxfelde 10 January, 7 Elizabeth [10 January 1564/5], without heirs; and therefore the rest of the premises [i.e., of the lands called "glemes"] descended to defendant.

Defendant denies the statements of complainant.

The Replication [torn] of John Fyske denies the statement as to Thomas Tower and Margaret Armiger and reiterates details as to the will of William Fyske. The said Rauf obtained possession of the will, and, finding that complainant's legacies amounted to more than his own, tried to conceal it.

The Rejoinder of Mathye Fiske denies the statements of complainant, or that Margaret caused a will to be made purporting to be that of William, or that he, the said defendant, was farmer of the premises for Margaret and unlawfully made the abovesaid enfeoffments.

(Chancery Proceedings, Series 2, File 67, No. 62.)

[Fastolfe v. Fyske]

The bill [filed 29 January 1568] of Elizabeth Fostalfe of Rednall, co. Norfolk, gentlewoman, complaining that, whereas she was lawfully possessed of £6 or £7 in old goods and of 57s. and odd money in silver and of an obligation in which Robert Jordayne and another stood bound for payment of £15 or £16 to her, and whereas John Fostalfe of Lytle Stonham, co. Suffolk, gentleman, executor of John Fastolfe, late of Petto, co. Suffolk, gentleman [stood bound] for £10 or thereabouts, part of a legacy given her by the testator, her late father, and whereas the said goods, silver, and the obligation with other writings and money about four years past came into the possession of Robert Fyske, also the £10 which was to be delivered to complainant, and he refuses to give them up, therefore complainant asks for a writ subpena to be directed to Robert Fyske.

The Answer of Robert Fyske to the bill of Elizabeth Fastolf [states that] there was a "comunycacion of Maryage" concluded about eight and one-half years past between complainant and defendant, and complainant received from defendant, to be kept to his use, money in French crowns, "pistoletes," and "Angelles," in part payment of which complainant delivered him about £7. Defendant has always been ready to deliver the obligation specified. At complainant's request he brought suit against John Fastolf in the Consistory Court at Norwich for the said £10, and has paid her £5, which was all that remained after defendant's costs in the suit had been deducted. He did not receive any other money or muniments of complainant.

The Replication of Elizabeth Fastolf denies the statements of defendant and that there was ever a communication of marriage between them, and prays that defendant may be ordered to make restitution.

469

The Rejoinder of Robert Fyske maintains the purport of his answer and denies all else contained in the bill and replication.
(Chancery Proceedings, Series 2, Bundle 67, No. 80.)

[Fiske v. Jollye]

The Bill [endorsed 3 October 1586] of Robert Fiske of Norton, co. Suffolk, yeoman, and Richard Cooke of Hunston, late of Walsham, co. Suffolk, yeoman, complaining that, whereas Robert Fiske about seven years past borrowed £20 of John Jollye of Langham, co. Suffolk, yeoman, and for repayment of £24. 2s. Robert and Richard Cooke became bound in an obligation of £40; and [whereas] John Jollye allowed the day of payment to pass and promised not to take advantage of the obligation, having received £12. 6s. 8d., or that value in money and corn, which, he said would satisfy him because of the friendship between himself and Robert, now John Jollye has begun a suit on the obligation, against complainants. Complainants beg for a writ subpena directed to John Jollye.

The Answer of John Jollye, dated 5 October, 28 Elizabeth [5 October 1586], [states that] he brought a suit against complainants for nonperformance of an obligation, and [that] verdict was given in his favour at the last assizes held at Bury St. Edmunds, by reason of which verdict he received some money and corn. He denies the said obligation of £40 or that he has begun a suit on the same.*
(Chancery Proceedings, Elizabeth, F 4/22.)

[Fiske v. Cutler]

The Bill [filed 27 January 1586/7] of John Fiske of Laxfeild, co. Suffolk, complaining that, whereas Henry Wase, being seised of 16 acres of land in Occolde, surrendered the same at a court of the Manor of Occolde held Thursday before the Feast of the Annunciation of Our Lady, 16 Henry VII [25 March 1501], that he might receive a regrant thereof to hold to himself and Margaret, his wife, and to his heirs, at the yearly rent of 11s., fealty, and suit of court for all manner of services and demands, and [whereas] afterwards Thomas Wells was seised of 15 acres, 1 rood, of the said lands, and a stranger was seised of the remaining parcel, and the share of Thomas Wells was surrendered 18 January, 27 Elizabeth [18 January 1584/5], to the use of the complainant and his heirs, now, the complainant being "a manne altogeath[e]r unlearned and desyrous of quiett, the rath[e]r for that he is of great yeres, beinge past fowerscore yeres old," and having paid a great fine for admittance to Nicholas Cutler, Lord of the Manor, said Cutler, knowing his simplicity, has inserted in complainant's copy that parcels of the premises are heriotable, whereas they were never subject to such charge, or, if so, the right is now extinct by reason of the grant to Henry Wase, and Cutler has also reserved a rent of 14s. 7d., which ought to be but 10s. 4d. Therefore complainant asks for a writ subpena to be directed to Nicholas Cutler.
(Chancery Proceedings, Elizabeth, F 8/6.)

[Fyske v. Springe]

The Bill [filed 2 November 1587] of Robert Fyske of Pakenham, co. Suffolk, yeoman, complaining that, whereas he is seised of lands [described] in Pakenham, which he, his ancestors, and any who had estate in the same have hitherto enjoyed peaceably, now Sir William

*A writ authorizing the examination of John Jollye is dated 8 June, 28 Elizabeth [8 June 1586] [sic].

470

Springe of Pakenham, desiring to enlarge his own lands, which adjoin those of complainant, has gained possession of complainant's title deeds and has made secret conveyances of his lands to divers persons, and persuades complainant's tenants to withhold their rents. Also, whereas complainant and Thomas Springe, about thirty years ago, by deed poll made an exchange of about 30 acres of land, the said Sir William, who has the inheritance of Thomas Springe, now claims the land which formerly belonged to Thomas, as well as the share allotted to him in exchange, of which the said Sir William possesses the title deeds, and complainant has no means of proving the agreement between himself and the said Thomas. Complainant begs for a writ subpena directed to Sir William Springe.

The Answer of Sir William Springe [sworn 24 January 1587/8] gives details as to the parcels in possession of complainant, with names of previous tenants, showing that complainant is as yet without title to certain of the premises and that he holds one parcel at will of the Lord of the Manor. Defendant does not know that he holds 20 acres of complainant's land, but, if complainant cannot show where the said 20 acres lie, defendant intends to enter upon the other 20 acres now held by complainant in virtue of the pretended exchange, of which defendant himself has no knowledge. Defendant denies that he has evidences belonging of right to complainant.

The Replication of Robert Fysk [states that] he can disprove defendant's title to the said lands, and is ready to prove by many witnesses and by ancient evidences that the lands both free and copyhold have been occupied by himself and his ancestors for the past sixty or eighty years. He denies the other statements of defendant.

The Rejoinder of Sir William Springe [declares that] he has sufficient proofs to maintain his title set forth in his answer.
(Chancery Proceedings, Elizabeth, F 4/58.)

[Fyske v. Botwright]

The Bill [filed 7 November 1589] of John Fyske of Ubston, co. Suffolk, yeoman, complaining that, whereas Symon Toppesfeld, late of Fresingfeld, co. Suffolk, about eight years past leased to Esdras Botwright lands called "Bancrofte hilles" and "lyttle Carters feld," in return for a loan of £80, [and whereas] seven years past complainant bought of Simon the said lands and other lands called "Stockes and Boultes" in Fresingfeld, agreeing to pay the debt to Botwright at the end of his term, and receiving from him a further loan of £30 in return for a lease of the lands called "Stockes and Boultes," both of which leases terminated at Michaelmas, 1587, [and whereas] the term was continued for another year, up to Michaelmas, 1588, and Botwright, being desirous of purchasing the lands and knowing that complainant was unwilling to sell, shortly before the end of the term gave notice that he would give up his occupation and desired payment of the money owing, and the complainant, not being able to meet the demand, was forced to agree to the sale of the premises for £440, on condition that his obligation to pay the above debts was annulled, as a first payment from Botwright, now Botwright, knowing that complainant has no written agreement and that, in expectation of the money, he has entered upon bargains with other men, not only refuses to fulfil their contract but also has begun an action against complainant upon the said obligation.

The Answer of Esdras Botwright [sworn 14 May 1590] restates the

471

details as to the loans of £80 and £30. About the Feast of the Birth of Our Lord, 1587, complainant, together with one Mathewe Fyske, became bound by an obligation for payment of £110 at Michaelmas, 1588. Defendant gives details as to transactions of defendant which were upset by nonpayment of the said sum and reasons why complainant's ability to make good assurance of the premises was doubted, so that defendant told complainant [that] he did not wish to make a purchase thereof. Defendant denies the other statements of complainant, but acknowledges that he is suing him upon his obligation.

(Chancery Proceedings, Elizabeth, F 7/38.)

[Murton *v.* Allington]

The Bill [undated, but the writ authorizing the examination of defendants is dated 27 June, 35 Elizabeth (27 June 1593)] of Robert Murton of Elmeswell, co. Suffolk, yeoman, complaining that, whereas Robert Fyske, late of Norton, co. Suffolk, yeoman, was seised of land in Elmeswell and Norton, and "the said Symonde Fyske and Roberte his sonne," in August, 20 Elizabeth [August 1578], granted a yearly rent charge of £16 to Thomas Andrewes, Esq., and Susan, his wife, for a term of sixty years, and afterwards Thomas died and Susan married Philip Allington of Burnt Pelham, co. Cambridge, now Philip Allington is suing complainant, for arrears of the said rent charge, upon complainant's bond which has already been fulfilled, and he also claims £16 awarded to him [i.e., Allington], in a suit brought against Robert Fyske in his lifetime, out of the "Landes and Tenementes nowe in the possession and ferme of yor said orator and subiecte to the distresse thereof [in the event of nonpayment of the rent charge] by reason whereof yor said orator standethe chargeable to John Fiske of Laxfeilde for the paymente of his yerely farme therefore." Complainant asks for a writ subpena to be directed to Philip and Susan Allington.

The Answer of Philip Allington and Susan, his wife, defendants. Defendant Philip Allington says that, if complainant Robert Moreton will satisfy him in certain demands amounting to £50. 13s. 4d. and will enter into bond to pay the rent charge hereafter as it shall fall due, at defendant's house in Burnt Pelham, co. Herts, then he will give up complainant's bond and discharge the judgment which he has secured against complainant.

(Chancery Proceedings, Elizabeth, M 8/22.)

# GENEALOGICAL RESEARCH IN ENGLAND

Communicated by the Committee on English and Foreign Research

## THE FISKE FAMILY

Contributed by G. ANDREWS MORIARTY, A.M., LL.B., F.S.A.,
of Bristol, R. I.

### FROM FEET OF FINES*

Final Concord made on the Feast of St. Michael in one month, 8 Elizabeth [October 1566], between John Fyske, Senior, and Christopher Hersante, querents, and John Cowper and Margaret, his wife, deforciants, concerning one messuage, four acres of land, five acres of meadow, forty acres of pasture, and one acre of wood in Laxfilde, which John and Margaret acknowledge to be the right of John Fyske. Warranty against all men from John and Margaret and the heirs of John to John Fyske and Christopher and the heirs of John Fyske for ever. John Fyske and Christopher have given £40. (Feet of Fines, Suffolk, Michaelmas Term, 8 and 9 Elizabeth, Part 1.)

Final Concord made on the Octave of St. Michael, 15 Elizabeth [6 October 1573], between William Dowsynge, querent, and John Fyske, deforciant, concerning six and one-half acres of pasture, with appurtenances, in Laxfylde, which John acknowledges to be the right of William. Warranty against all men from John and his heirs to William and his heirs for ever. William has given £40. (Feet of Fines, Suffolk, Michaelmas Term, 15 and 16 Elizabeth.)

Final Concord made on the Morrow of Holy Trinity, 20 Elizabeth [1578], between Robert Fyske, querent, and William Brooke, deforciant, concerning the Manor of Hardinges, with appurtenances, and concerning one messuage, twelve acres of meadow, twenty-five acres of pasture, twenty-four acres of wood, and 6s. yearly rent in Norton, which William acknowledges to be the right of Robert; and William has granted for himself and his heirs that the said manor and tenements, which on the day of this agreement are held of the heirs of William by Richard Cookie and Mary, his wife, for the term of the life of Mary, with remainder to William and his heirs, shall, on the death of Mary, remain to Robert and his heirs, to hold of the chief lords of that fee by the accustomed services. Warranty from William and his heirs, as aforesaid, to Robert and his heirs. Robert has given £220. (Feet of Fines, Suffolk, Trinity Term, 20 Elizabeth.)

Final Concord made on the Octave of St. Hilary, 22 Elizabeth [20 January 1579/80], between William Fyske and Henry Meane, querents, and Thomas Pulham and Margery, his wife, deforciants, concerning three acres of land and thirty-three acres of pasture in Stradbrooke, which the said Margery and Thomas acknowledge to be the right of William. Warranty against all men from Margery and Thomas and the heirs of

*Preserved in the Public Record Office, London. The text of the Feet of Fines in this article has been translated from the original Latin and abridged.

473

Thomas to William and Henry and the heirs of William for ever. William and Henry have given £100. (Feet of Fines, Suffolk, Hilary Term, 22 Elizabeth.)

Final Concord made on Easter in fifteen days, 25 Elizabeth [1583], between John Roo, querent, and William Fiske, deforciant, concerning three acres of land and forty acres of pasture in Stradbroke, which William acknowledges to be the right of John. Warranty against all men from William and his heirs to John and his heirs for ever. John has given 130 marks of silver. (Feet of Fines, Suffolk, Easter Term, 25 Elizabeth, Part 1.)

### From Additional Charters, in the British Museum

Grant [abstract only] dated at Laxfeld [co. Suffolk] on the Sunday after the Feast of St. Gregory the Pope, 19 Edward III [the Sunday after 12 March 1345/6], by Edmund le Glawyle of Laxfeld and Cristiana, his wife, to Peter Le Clerc of Westleton, of land in Laxfeld lying between the land of Roger Seman on one part and the land of Edmund Seman on the other, wherof one head abutts upon the land of Hugh Fisqs and the other upon the land of the said Edmund le Glawyle and Cristiana, in exchange for one half acre of land which the said Peter has acquired of Edmund and Cristiana. Witnesses: John Garneys, John Cloutyng, Geoffrey Crisp, Hugh Fisqs, John Banyard, and others. (British Museum Additional Charters, 32924.)

Grant [brief abstract only] dated at Laxfeld [co. Suffolk] 3 June, 6 Henry VI [3 June 1428], by Richard Gleme of Laxfeld to John Germyn, Knight, and others, of the site of a certain messuage, with lands, in Laxfeld, in the hamlet of Stodehagh [abuttals given]. Witnesses: Nicholas Stowe, William Donsyng, Simon Fysk, John Jurdon, Roger Smyth, and others. (British Museum Additional Charters, 32926.)

Translation of a charter dated at Laxfeld [co. Suffolk] 4 April, 23 Henry VI [4 April 1445].
"Know all present and to come that I, Robert Coupere of Laxfeld, have demised, enfeoffed, and by this present my charter have confirmed to Simon Fysk and William Crysp, 'whelewryghte,' of Laxfeld aforesaid, all my lands and tenements, meadows, feeding-grounds, pastures, ditches, rents, and services, with all their appurtenances in Laxfeld, which I have of the gift, grant, and confirmation of Geoffrey Covpere, my father, and which I have acquired of divers men, to have and to hold all those the aforesaid lands and tenements, meadows, feeding-grounds, pastures, ditches, rents, and services, with all their appurtenances, to the aforesaid Simon Fysk and William Crysp, their heirs and assigns, of the chief lords of that fee by the services therefrom due and by right accustomed for ever. In witness whereof, to this present charter I have put my seal. These being witnesses, William Chatyng, Henry Wylde, William Cone, Robert Pers, John Ede of Laxfeld aforesaid, and others." [Seal.] (British Museum Additional Charters, 32927.)

Grant [abstract only] dated at Laxfeld [co. Suffolk] 7 May, 2 Henry VIII [7 May 1510], from Thomas Blakeye, son and heir of Walter Blakeye, late of Huntyngfeld, deceased, to Robert Cowper, son of William Cowper, late of Laxfeld, Robert Noloth, John Cowper, tailor, and Nicholas Bradlawe, otherwise Jacob, of Laxfeld, of all lands and tenements and meadows [etc.], with all appurtenances, in the vil of Laxfeld, which the aforesaid Walter late held jointly with Robert Cowper of Laxfeld, William Cowper, son of the said Robert, and William Trusse of Stradbrook, now deceased, to them, their heirs and assigns, of the demise, grant, and charter of confirmation of Simon Fysk, late of Laxfeld, as by a certain charter of his dated at Laxfeld 24 December, 3 Edward IV [24 December 1463], manifestly appears. [No witnesses.]

[Endorsed:] Witnesses present at the time of the seisin, viz., John Cryspe *alias* Tur[*faded*] [? Turner], Geoffrey Fyske, John Heyward, William Fyske, and John Skarlett. (British Museum Additional Charters, 32928.)

Translation of a charter dated at Laxfeld [co. Suffolk] 12 January, 7 Elizabeth [12 January 1564/5].

"To all the faithful of Christ to whom this present charter shall have come, Ralph Fyske of Laxfelde in the county of Suffolk, son and heir of William Fyske, late of Laxfeld aforesaid, yeoman, deceased, eternal greeting in the Lord.

"Know that I, the aforesaid Ralph Fyske, for the sum of twenty-three pounds of good and lawful money of England, well and truly paid into the hands of me, the said Ralph, by a certain George Cowper of Laxfelde aforesaid, glover, whereof I acknowledge myself to be fully satisfied and content and the same George Cowper, his heirs, executors, and administrators, to be acquitted and exonerated therefrom by these presents, have sold, given, granted, enfeoffed, delivered, and by this present my charter have confirmed to the aforesaid George Cowper all that enclosure of pasture, parcel of a certain tenement called Glemes, containing by estimation three acres more or less, with appurtenances, in Laxfelde aforesaid, as it lies between the lands of the said Ralph, parcel of the said tenement on the south, and the lands now of the aforesaid George Cowper, parcel of the same tenement on the north, whereof one head abutts upon the common way there called 'Studhaugh Strete' towards the east, and the other head thereof abutts upon the lands of the said Ralph towards the west, which same aforesaid enclosure, with other lands and tenements, by right of inheritance descended, and of right ought to descend, to me, the aforesaid Ralph Fyske, my heirs and assigns, after the death of the aforesaid William Fyske, my father, because the aforesaid William Fyske, my father, died sole-seised therein and intestate, and which same enclosure aforesaid, with three other pieces of land, the aforesaid William Fyske, my father, first had and acquired to him and his heirs of John Jurdon, Robert Helwise, John Nolothe, Thomas Pype, and other persons, inhabitants of the township of Laxfeld aforesaid, as by their charter made thereof to the said William Fyske, dated 12 April, 6 Edward VI [12 April 1552], is more fully evident and appears, to have and to hold by these presents all the aforesaid enclosure of pasture, containing by estimation three acres, with all and singular its appurtenances and commodities whatsoever, to the aforesaid George Cowper, his heirs and assigns, to the sole use and profit of him, the aforesaid George Cowper, his heirs and assigns, for ever, of the chief lords of that fee by the services therefrom due and by right accustomed. And I, the aforesaid Ralph Fyske, my heirs and assigns, by these presents will warrant and for ever defend against all men all that the aforesaid enclosure of pasture, with all and singular its appurtenances and commodities, to the aforenamed George Cowper, his heirs and assigns, to the use abovesaid.

"In addition, know that I, the aforesaid Ralph Fyske, have constituted, deputed, and put in my place my beloved in Christ Charles Awstyne of

475

Laxfelde, aforesaid, my true and lawful attorney, to enter, for me and in my name, the aforesaid enclosure, with appurtenances, and to take possession and seisin thereof; and, after possession and seisin therein in this manner so taken and had, to deliver possession and seisin to the aforesaid George Cowper, his heirs and assigns, according to the force, form, tenor, and effect of this present my charter, taking and about to take as valid and acceptable all and whatever the said my attorney shall have done in the premises. In witness whereof, to this present my charter I have put my seal.

"Note that this present charter was read and sealed in the presence of John Cowper of Balstons, Thomas Cryspe, and Thomas ——— [faded]."

Endorsement that seisin was made the above day and year in the presence of Thos. Plumpton, clerk, vicar of Ubbeston, Jn. Cowper of Balstons, Thos. Cryspe, Thos. Browne, and others.

(British Museum Additional Charters, 32930.)

Copy [abstract only] by which George Cooper took up his lands in Laxfeld [co. Suffolk], endorsed: "Geo. Cooper 18 Apr. 1637."

Laxfeild. At a View of Frankpledge with Court Baron of Edward Coke, Knight, there holden 2 May, 12 James I [2 May 1614], was enrolled the surrender of all lands held by copy by William Cooper, bond-tenant, to the use of George Cooper, his son and heir, and also the admission of the said George Cooper to all the premises aforesaid, viz. [among others], "one piece of land, parcel of longsales,* lying between the way called Taylers lane on the east and the land partly of Thomas Crispe and partly of George Cooper on the west, one head thereof abutting partly onto the said land called longsales and partly onto Aldus Mcdowe towards the north, and the other head abutting onto the land of George Cooper towards the south, containing by estimation one acre, more or less, which the aforesaid William lately had to him and his heirs by the surrender of John Fiske, as appears at a View of Frankpledge with General Court here holden on the Tuesday next after Whitsunday, 28 Elizabeth" [1586].

(British Museum Additional Charters, 32932.)

FROM A CALENDAR OF DEEDS, LAXFIELD, CO. SUFFOLK†

12 Edward IV [4 March 1471/2–3 March 1472/3].
    Henry Rous, etc., [to] Geoffrey Fyske of Laxfield, William Fyske of the same, and Edward Fyske of Eye. (No. 33.)
17 Edward IV [4 March 1476/7–3 March 1477/8].
    William Fyske [to] Galfin [sic] Fyske. (No. 35.)
19 Edward IV [4 March 1478/9–3 March 1479/80].
    John Fyske of Laxfield [to] John Fyske of Disse [Diss, co. Norfolk], Simon Fyske of the same, etc., feoffees, etc. (No. 32.)
    William Fyske. (No. 36.)
11 Henry VII [22 August 1495–21 August 1496].
    William Smith, etc., [to] Geoffrey Fyske of Laxfeld, senior, Master John Fyske, and Geoffrey Fyske of Shadbrook. (No. 40.)
14 Henry VII [22 August 1498–21 August 1499].

*Also written "longfales."
†This calendar (or list of Laxfield deeds in which the name *Fyske* or variants is found) is printed in The Fiske Family Papers, p. 18, but the deeds themselves have not been discovered. The entries have been translated from the Latin, in which they are printed, *op. cit.*, except the last two entries (2 Edward VI and 17 Charles I), which were apparently written in English. Obvious typographical errors in the entries as printed, *op. cit.*, have been corrected.

Geoffrey Fyske, etc., [of] Laxfeld [to] Master John Fyske, etc.,
feoffees, etc. Simon Fyske *folio*, William Fyske of Laxfeld,
*et al.** (No. 42.)

19 Henry VII [22 August 1503–21 August 1504].
Simon Fiskith [*sic*]. (No. 44.)

22 Henry VII [22 August 1506–21 August 1507].
Know, etc., [that] Simon Fyske of Laxfeld, yeoman, etc. (No. 45.)

12 Henry VIII [22 April 1520–21 April 1521].
Simon Fyske of Laxfeld has granted, etc. (No. 58.)

2 Edward VI [28 January 1547/8–27 January 1548/9].
Jeffrey Fyske of Laxfeld, executor of Robert Rous of Laxfeld.
(Nos. 77–78.)

17 Charles I [27 March 1641–26 March 1642].
1641. Indenture between John Bradlaugh, etc., and William Ffiske
of Whenstead [*sic*], Gentleman. (No. 152.) Arms: *chequy on
a pale 3 mullets*.

FROM LAY SUBSIDIES FOR CO. SUFFOLK†

14 Edward III [1340–41].
Hundred of Hoxne. Inquisition taken 14 Edward III before the
Abbot of Leyston and others to inquire into the value of the
ninth part of sheaves, etc., of all churches, prebends, and bene-
fices, by the oath of . . . [several jurors including] Hugh Fiske.
(Lay Subsidies, 180/11.)

Particular of the account of the Abbot of Leysington and others,
assessors of the ninth part of sheaves, etc., in co. Suffolk, 14
Edward III. . . . Deanery of Hoxne. Laxfeld. King's writ.
And concerning the ninth part of the sheaves, etc., of the parish
church of Laxfeld which are taxed at £38 . . . [it is] committed
to Hugh Fiske and others for £21 and no more. (*Ib.*, 180/12.)

16 Henry VIII [1524–25].

| | |
|---|---|
| Eye. | John Whetyngham and James Seman in lands, late of John Fanner, John Fiske, and Robert Ystas, [valuation] £6. 13s. 4d., [tax] 6s. 8d. |
| Hacheston. | John Fyske, William Arnold, and John Harvy in goods, [valuation] £1. 6s. 8d., [tax] 2s. |
| Halesworth. | John Fiske the Elder in goods, [valuation] £13. 6s. 8d., [tax] 6s. 8d.<br>John Fiske, mercer, in goods, [valuation] £10, [tax] 5s.<br>Joan Fyske in goods, [valuation] £1, [tax] 4d. |
| Hunston. | Robert Feske, yeoman, in anticipation, [valuation] £40. |
| Ilketshall St. Andrew. | John Feek and William Fysk on wages, [valuation] £1, [tax] 8d. |
| Knettishall. | Robert Fiske in ———. |
| Laxfield. | William Jacob and Symon Fyske in goods, [valuation] £10, [tax] 10s. |

477

|  |  |
|---|---|
|  | Thomas Fyske in goods, [valuation] £12, [tax] 6s. |
|  | Jeffrey Fiske, Nicholas Heyward, and John Tayler ———. |
|  | John Vincent, William Fiske, and John Smyth in goods, [valuation] £2, [tax] 3s. |
| Long Melford. | John Fiske, [valuation] £5, [tax] 2s. 6d. |
| Mellis. | Thomas Fiske in goods, [valuation] £1, [tax] 4d. |
| Rendham. | Robert Fiske in goods, [valuation] £3, [tax] 1s. 6d. |
| South Cove. | Thomas Fiske in goods, [valuation] £10, [tax] 5s. |
| Southwold. | Robert Fysk in goods, [valuation] £4, [tax] 2s. |
| Wenhaston, with Mylles. | John Fyske in goods, [valuation] £5, [tax] 2s. 6d. |
|  | Simon Fiske in goods, [valuation] £1, [tax] 4d. |

(Lay Subsidies, published in Suffolk Green Books, No. X.)

34–35 Henry VIII [1542–1544].
Laxfield.*  Wylliam Fyske, [tax] —s. 4d.
John Fyske, [tax] 3s. 4d.
Jeffray Fyske the Yonger, [tax] 20d.
William Fyske, [tax] 8d.
Nycholas Fyske, [tax] 3d.
George Fyske, [tax] 12d.[?].
Jefferey Fyske, [tax] 2s. 4d.
Robert Fyske, [tax] 4s. 8d.[?]. (Lay Subsidies, 257/1.)

Indenture dated 17 April, 36 Henry VIII [17 April 1545].
Laxfield.  William Fyske in goods, [valuation] £20, [benevolence] 20s.
Robert Fyske in goods, [valuation] £13, [benevolence] 13s. (Ib., 181/253.)

Certificate dated 29 October, 37 Henry VIII [29 October 1545].
Wenhaston.  John Fyske in goods, [valuation] £6, [tax] 12d. (Ib., 181/250.)

Commission dated 28 February, 37 Henry VIII [28 February 1545/6].
Ilketshall St. Lawrence.  William Fyske in goods, [valuation] £6, [tax] 4s. (Ib., 181/267.)

4 March, 37 Henry VIII [4 March 1545/6].
Laxfield.  William Fyske in lands, [tax] 14s.
John Fyske in lands, [tax] 7s. 4d.
Jeffray Fyske in goods, [tax] 3s. 4d.
Robert Fyske in goods, [tax] 12s. (Ib., 181/273.)

10 Elizabeth [1567–68].
Aldeburgh.  Thomas Fiske in goods, [valuation] £11, [tax] 9s. 2d.
Botesdale.  William Fiske in lands, [valuation] £1, [tax] 1s. 4d.
Cratfield.  William Fiske in lands, [valuation] £8, [tax] 10s. 8d.

*Part of this return is illegible.

|  | Jeffrie Fiske in goods, [valuation] £3, [tax] 2s. 6d. |
| Dennington. | Nicholas Fyske in lands, [valuation] £2, [tax] 2s. 8d. |
| Elmswell. | Symon Fiske in lands, [valuation] £7, [tax] 9s. 4d. |
|  | Robert Fyske in goods, [valuation] £3, [tax] 2s. 6d. |
| Halesworth. | Amy Fiske, widow, in lands, [valuation] £10, [tax] 13s. 4d. |
| Hemley. | Richard Fiske in lands, [valuation] £1, [tax] 1s. 4d. |
| Laxfield. | John Fiske, Senior, in lands, [valuation] £6, [tax] 8s. |
|  | John Fiske of Studhaugue in lands, [valuation] £6, [tax] 8s. |
|  | Nicholas Fiske in lands, [valuation] £4, [tax] 9s. 4d. |
|  | Geoffry Fiske in lands, [valuation] £1, [tax] 5s. 4d. |
|  | Richard Fiske in lands, [valuation] £1, [tax] 2s. 8d. |
| Pakenham. | Robert Fiske in lands. [valuation] £4, in goods, [valuation] £8, [tax] 6s. 8d. |
| Reydon. | William Fiske in goods, [valuation] £3, [tax] 2s. 6d. |
| South Cove. | William Fiske in goods, [valuation] £15, [tax] 12s. 6d. |
| South Elmham St. James. St. Michael. | Robert Fiske and Robert Terrold in lands, each [valuation] £1, [tax] 2s. 8d. William Fyske and Stephen Elmye in goods, each [valuation] £3, [tax] 5s. |
| Wenhaston. | John Fiske in lands, [valuation] £5, [tax] 6s. 8d. |
| Westhall. | George Fiske in lands, [valuation] £1. 6s. 8d., [tax] 1s. 9½d. |
| Weybread. | William Fiske in lands, [valuation] £4, [tax] 5s. 4d. |
| Wortham. | Thomas Fiske in lands, [valuation] £1, [tax] 1s. 4d. |

(Lay Subsidies, published in Suffolk Green Books, No. XII.)

## From Rentals and Surveys

The town or parish* of Laxefeld, co. Suff[olk], is worth . . . the farm of one close lying between the land formerly of William Haughe on the east and the land of John Smythe on the west, with its southern head abutting on the close of the late Monastery [of Pleystow] called Milmount Close and its northern head abutting upon the land of St. John and the land of Geoffrey Cryspe, late of Geoffrey Fyske and before that of Marion Thrower, called Goddystroft—17s. 5d.

*Altered from "parcel of the manor."

[Endorsed:] Rental of parcel of the Manor of Laxfield, 37 Henry VIII [1545–46].

(Rentals and Surveys, Land Revenue, Miscellaneous Books, vol. 257, fo. 45 [Extract].)

## WILLIAM PYNCHON

Contributed by WINIFRED LOVERING HOLMAN, S.B.,
of Watertown, Mass.

THE two records of which abstracts are given below were found by E. Grogan, in a search made in England for the identity of the first wife of William Pynchon, the well-known settler at Springfield, Mass., and are published in the REGISTER through the courtesy of Chauncey Devereux Stillman, Esq., of New York City.

### FROM INQUISITIONS POST MORTEM*

Inquisition taken after the death of John Pynchon, late of Springfield, co. Essex, Gentleman, 7 October, 9 James I [7 October 1611]. The said John Pynchon held lands in Springfield and Writtle [co. Essex], and died at Springfield 4 September, 8 James I [4 September 1610]. William Pynchon is his son and heir, and at the time of his father's death was aged 19½ years and 10 weeks. (Chancery Inquisitions post Mortem, C. 142, 321/130.)

### FROM FEET OF FINES FOR CO. ESSEX*

Final Concord made in three weeks from Easter, 11 James I [1613], by which William Pynchon, Gentleman, and Frances Pynchon, widow, quitclaimed to Mathew Rudde, Gentleman, messuages and lands in Writtle [co. Essex], for which said Mathew gave them £100. (Feet of Fines, Essex, Easter Term, 11 James I, C.P. 25/2.)

*Preserved in the Public Record Office, London.

# GENEALOGICAL RESEARCH IN ENGLAND

Communicated by the Committee on English and Foreign Research

## THE FISKE FAMILY[*]

Contributed by G. Andrews Moriarty, A.M., LL.B., F.S.A.,
of Bristol, R. I.

From some of the records given in the four instalments of this article already published (see the REGISTER of October 1932 and of January, April, and July 1933), from the tabular pedigrees found in the "Candler Manuscripts," the better copy of which is in the Bodleian Library at Oxford (see the REGISTER, vol. 86, page 407, October 1932, for mention of these manuscripts and their compilers), and from other sources and authorities cited occasionally below, the following pedigree of the Fiskes of Laxfield, co. Suffolk, and some of their immediate connections, down to the members of this family who emigrated to New England in the seventeenth century, has been compiled.

The Fiske family has been settled in Suffolk from very early times, the first mention of the name that has been discovered being on 1 May 1208, when a grant of the park at Digneveton was made to the men of Laxfield and among the grantees appears the name of DANIEL FISC. (Rot. Chart., vol. 1, p. 177.) This Daniel Fisc was probably an ancestor of HUGH FISKE, who was one of the jurors in an inquisition taken in the hundred of Hoxne, co. Suffolk, 14 Edward III [1340–41], before the Abbot of Leiston and others, to inquire into the value of the ninth part of the sheaves, etc., of all churches, prebends, and benefices. The ninth part of the sheaves, etc., of the parish church of Laxfield, which were taxed at £38, was committed by the King's writ to Hugh Fiske and others for £21 and no more. (*Vide supra*, p. 221, Lay Subsidies, 180/11, 12.) As Hugh Fisqs this man appears as a landholder at Laxfield in a deed of 19 Edward III [1345–46], to which he was also a witness. (*Vide supra*, p. 218, British Museum Additional Charters, 32926.) He was probably the grandfather of SIMON FISKE of Laxfield, with whom the following pedigree begins.

1. SIMON FISKE, of Laxfield, co. Suffolk, 1428, 1445, wheelwright, the testator of 22 Dec. 1463 (Will No. 2), was born probably about 1400, and died between 22 Dec. 1463 and 26 Feb. 1463/4, when his will was proved at Laxfield by Katherine, his widow, and by his son John, the Younger. He married KATHERINE ———— [? CRISPE], who, perhaps, was not his first wife.

Simon Fiske was probably a grandson of Hugh Fiske or Fisqs, who appears as a landholder at Laxfield about the middle of the fourteenth century and in his turn was probably a descendant of Daniel

*The prior installments of "The Fiske Family" appear in this volume as follows: for Oct. 1932, pp. 406-435 see pp. 431-460, this volume; for Jan. 1933, pp. 40-45 see pp. 461-466, this volume; for Apr. 1933, pp. 141-146 see pp. 467-472, this volume; for July 1933, pp. 217-224 see pp. 473-480, this volume.

Fiske of Laxfield, 1208. (See the preceding paragraph.) The name of the wife of Hugh Fiske has not been discovered, nor the Christian name of his son, who is supposed to have been of Laxfield about 1390 and to have been the father of the Simon Fiske with whom this pedigree begins. William Fiske, the Elder, of Laxfield, the testator of 6 Mar. 1462/3 (Will No. 1), who died between that date and 21 Apr. 1463, when his will was proved by Joan, his widow, and by John Smyth, was probably a brother of Simon Fiske; and ———— Fiske, who married John Noleth of Laxfield and was probably the mother of Nicholas Noleth of Laxfield (one of the residuary legatees and executors of the will of William Fiske, who renounced his executorship), was probably a sister of Simon and William Fiske.

Children, the first four, perhaps, by an unknown earlier wife:

2. i. WILLIAM, a legatee (40s.) in his father's will in 1463, b. about 1425.
   ii. JOHN, THE ELDER, probably of Diss, co. Norfolk, the testator of 1488 (Will No. 4a), b. about 1428, a legatee (40s.) in his father's will in 1463, mentioned in 1478; m. ELIZABETH ————, living in 1488.
   iii. EDMUND, probably of Eye, co. Suffolk, in 1471, b. about 1430, a legatee (40s.) in his father's will in 1463.
   iv. MARGARET, b. about 1432, a legatee (40s.) in her father's will in 1463; m. before 22 Dec. 1463 ———— DEUSING.
   v. A DAUGHTER, ⎫ b. probably about 1434–1437; living unm. 22 Dec.
   vi. A DAUGHTER, ⎬ 1463. "To each of my three daughters £10 within a year of marriage; but if any of them remain single, she shall enjoy her portion." (Abstract
   vii. A DAUGHTER, ⎭ of Will of Simon Fiske.)
3. viii. JOHN, THE YOUNGER, a residuary legatee and an executor of his father's will, b. about 1440.
4. ix. GEOFFREY, a legatee (40s.) in his father's will in 1463, b. about 1442.
   x. SIMON (perhaps son of No. 1.), of Diss, co. Norfolk, 1478.

2. WILLIAM FISKE (*Simon*), of Laxfield, co. Suffolk, 1477, 1479, a legatee (40s.) in his father's will in 1463, born about 1425, died before 15 July 1504. He married JOAN ————, the testatrix of 15 July 1504 (Will No. 7), who died between 15 July 1504 and "the last of February" 1504/5, when her will was proved by her executors, "Syr John Fyske the son of John Fyske and Simon Fyske my son."

Children:

i. MARGERY, b. about 1450; living 15 July 1504, when she was named as a legatee (13s. 4d.) in her mother's will.
ii. MARGARET, b. about 1452; living 15 July 1504, when she was named as a legatee (13s. 4d.) in her mother's will; ? m. ———— COSLER.
iii. SIR JOHN, priest, b. about 1454; named 15 July 1504 as a legatee (40d.) in his mother's will; possibly the Sir John Fyske of Laxfield whose will, dated 2 Oct. 1535, was proved in 1536 (Will No. 18) by the executors, Jaffrey [Geoffrey] Fyske, the Elder, of Laxfield and John Fiske, his [Geoffrey's] son, who were the residuary legatees of the testator.*
iv. AUSTIN, of Laxfield, the testator of 15 Mar. 1507/8 (Will No. 10), b. about 1456; named in his mother's will, 15 July 1504;

*It is difficult to determine whether the testator of 2 Oct. 1535 (Will No. 18) was Sir John Fiske, priest (2, iii), son of William, Sir John Fiske, priest (3, i), son of John, or Master John Fiske, priest (4, i), son of Geoffrey.

482

d. between 15 Mar. 1507/8 and 11 Apr. 1508, when his will was proved by his widow, Joan Fyske, the testator's brothers, Simon and Thomas, Fyske, who had been named in the will as executors with the widow, renouncing; m. JOAN ———.

Children:

    1. *William*, of Laxfield, 1510, b. about 1490 (under twenty-two at the date of his father's will), to whom his father left lands in Cratfield, co. Suffolk.

    2. *Thomas*, perhaps of Lowestoft, co. Suffolk, 1535, b. about 1492 (under twenty-four at the date of his father's will).

v.    A SON, of Laxfield, 1504, b. about 1458; m. CHRISTIAN ———, who was a legatee (40d.) in the will of her mother-in-law, Joan Fyske, 15 July 1504.

5. vi.    SIMON, one of the executors of his mother's will, February 1504/5, b. about 1460.

vii.    A SON, of Laxfield, 1504, b. about 1462; m. ELIZABETH ———, who was a legatee (40d.) in the will of her mother-in-law, Joan Fyske, 15 July 1504.

6. viii.    THOMAS, named as one of the executors of his brother Austin's will, dated 15 Mar. 1507/8 (Will No. 10), b. about 1467.

3.  JOHN FISKE, THE YOUNGER (*Simon*), of Laxfield, co. Suffolk, 1478, one of the residuary legatees and executors of his father's will in 1463, the testator of 18 Jan. 1512/13 (Will No. 11), born about 1440, died between 18 Jan. 1512/13 and 5 Feb. 1512/13, when his will was proved by his son, Sir John Fiske, priest, one of the three executors named in the will. The name of his wife is unknown. She is not mentioned in his will, and probably died before her husband.

Children:

i.    SIR JOHN FISKE, of Laxfield, priest, a legatee and an executor of his father's will and perhaps the testator of 2 Oct. 1535 (Will No. 18),* b. about 1465; d., if he was the testator of 1535, not later than 1536, when his will was proved by his residuary legatees and executors, Jaffrey [Geoffrey] Fyske, the Elder, of Laxfield, and the latter's son, John Fiske.

ii.    SIR ROBERT FISKE, of Southwold, co. Suffolk, priest, canon of Leiston, co. Suffolk, b. about 1467; living 18 Jan. 1512/13, when he was a legatee (10 marks a year) and an executor of his father's will.

iii.    NICHOLAS, a legatee (£4 and all the debts "he oweth me") in his father's will, probably of East Dereham, co. Norfolk, "raffeman," and the testator of 8 Apr. 1529 (Will No. 16), b. about 1470; d. between 8 Apr. 1529 and 8 Nov. 1529, when his will was proved by John Pavys of Norwich, co. Norfolk, one of the three executors named in the will; m. ELIZABETH ———, who was named as an executor in his will, survived him, but renounced execution. He had lands in Norfolk and Suffolk, a dwelling, workhouse, and shop in East Dereham, and a house and land at Carbrooke, co. Norfolk. From his will he appears to have been a chandler.

Children (named as legatees in their father's will):

    1. *William* (probably son of Nicholas), of East Dereham, b. about 1500.

    2. *Ambrose*, b. about 1503; m. before 8 Apr. 1529 ———.

    3. *Thomas*, b. about 1505.

    4. *John*, an executor of his father's will, b. about 1507; m. before 8 Apr. 1529 ———.

    5. *Elizabeth*, m. before 8 Apr. 1529 William Poynter.

*See footnote, *supra*, p. 368.

6. *Cycely,*
7. *Wyburgh* (daughter), ⎫ all unm. and apparently all under
8. *Anne,* ⎬ age on 8 Apr. 1529.
9. *Alice,* ⎭

4. GEOFFREY FISKE (*Simon*), of Laxfield, co. Suffolk, 1472, 1477, 1496, 1499, a legatee in his father's will in 1463, the testator of 3 May 1504 (Will No. 6), born about 1442, died between 3 May 1504 and 13 May 1504, when his will was proved by Master John Fyske, his son. He married MARGARET ————, who was probably dead when her husband made his will, her own will (Will No. 5), undated, being proved by her son, Master John Fyske, on the same day as his father's will, 13 May 1504.

Children:

i. MASTER JOHN, priest, b. about 1465; living 25 June 1505, when he was named as supervisor of the will of his brother Simon (Will No. 8). On 13 May 1504, as residuary legatee and an executor of the wills of his father and his mother, he proved both wills. Possibly he was the testator of 2 Oct. 1535 (Will No. 18.)*

ii. JOHANE, b. about 1467; living 3 May 1504, when she was named as a legatee (5 marks) in her father's will.

iii. MARYON, b. about 1469; living 3 May 1504, when she was named as a legatee (6s. 8d.) in her father's will; probably m. THOMAS THROWER.

iv. MARGARET, b. about 1472; probably m. GEOFFREY (JAFFREY) CRYSPE (to Margaret Cryspe, the wife of Jaffrey Cryspe, wheelwright, a brass pot is bequeathed by the will of Margaret Fyske, wife of No. 4; cf. Will No. 5). She is not mentioned in the will of Geoffrey Fiske (No. 4), unless she is the Margaret Kempe to whom a heifer is bequeathed in that will.

v. GEOFFREY, probably of Shalbrook [?], 149–, of Laxfield, 1524, 1535, named as a legatee (6s. 8d. and a brass pan) in his mother's will and mentioned in his father's will, b. about 1474; living in 1536, when he and his son John Fiske, as residuary legatees and executors of the will of Sir John Fyske of Laxfield [priest], dated 2 Oct. 1535 (Will No. 18), proved that will; m. ————.

Children:
1. *John,* living in 1536 (see above, account of his father). Probably other children.

vi. SIMON, of Freston, co. Suffolk, a residuary legatee and an executor of his father's will, the testator of 25 June 1505 (Will No. 8), d. between 25 June 1505 and 18 July 1505, when his will was proved; m. JOAN ————, who was living when he made his will. His brother, Master John Fiske, was named as supervisor in his will. He had lands in Freston, in Dersham [? Dereham, co. Norfolk], and in Westleton, co. Suffolk.

Children:
1. *A daughter,* ⎫
2. *A daughter,* ⎬ unm. and under twenty on 25 June 1505.
3. *A daughter,* ⎭
Perhaps other children.

5. SIMON FISKE (*William, Simon*), of Laxfield, co. Suffolk, 1499, 1503, 1507/8, 1521, 1524, yeoman, one of the residuary legatees and executors of the will of his mother (Will No. 7,

*See footnote, *supra,* p. 368.

dated 15 July 1504) and named as one of the executors in the will of his brother, Austin Fiske (Will No. 10, dated 15 Mar. 1507/8—he renounced execution), the testator of 10 July 1536 (Will No. 19, which deserves careful study), born about 1462, died between 10 July 1536 and 15 July 1538, when his will was proved. He married first MARGERY ———; and secondly ———, who was not mentioned in his will and probably died before her husband.

Children by first wife:

7. i. RICHARD (probably son of No. 5), b. about 1493. For reasons for believing that this Richard was a son of Simon Fiske (No. 5) *vide supra*, vol. 86, p. 407 (October, 1932), the third introductory paragraph in this article.

ii. WILLIAM, a legatee (5 marks a year for three years) in his father's will, b. about 1495; m. before 10 July 1536 ELIZABETH ———, living at that date.

iii. SIMON, a legatee (£3. 6s. 8d.) in his father's will, b. about 1497; probably the Simon Fiske of Heckingham, co. Norfolk, whose will, dated 8 Nov. 1549, was proved 8 Dec. 1549; m. ELIZABETH ———, whom he appointed in his will residuary legatee and sole executrix.
Children, all named as living in their father's will in 1549:
1. *Robert*, named as supervisor of his father's will, to whom his father bequeathed farming implements, live stock, etc., b. about 1522.
2. *Anna,* b. about 1524,  ⎫ to each of whom their father be-
3. *Joan,* b. about 1525, ⎬ queathed 5 marks, 2 calves, and
4. *Elizabeth,* b. about 1527. ⎭ 10 ewes.
5. *Thomas,* seised of lands and tenements in Wenhaston, co. Suffolk, b. about 1528.

iv. JOAN, a legatee (£3. 6s. 8d.) in her father's will, b. about 1498.

v. JERELON [GELYON], a legatee (£3. 6s. 8d.) in her father's will, b. about 1500.

vi. OLIVE, a legatee (£3. 6s. 8d.) in her father's will, b. about 1502; m. before 10 July 1536 ——— WARNE.

vii. JOHN, of Laxfield, in 1568, and probably also in 1585, not mentioned in his father's will but mentioned in the will of Sir John Fiske, priest, dated 2 Oct. 1535, as son of Symond Fyske (Will No. 18), b. about 1504.

viii. ROBERT, of Laxfield, to whom his father bequeathed his dwelling house, with lands, etc., in Laxfield, the testator of 6 Mar. 1549/50 (Will No. 22), b. about 1506; d. between 6 Mar. 1549/50 and 5 Apr. 1551, when his will was proved; m. ALICE ———, who survived him and proved his will.
Children, named as legatees in their father's will:
1. *Nicholas,* of Laxfield, 1568, under twenty on 6 Mar. 1549/50.
2. *Anne,* under fifteen on 6 Mar. 1549/50.
3. *Christian,* under twenty on 6 Mar. 1549/50.

ix. AGNES, b. about 1508; probably d. before 10 July 1536, as she is not mentioned in her father's will of that date, but an "Agnes the Younger" is mentioned among his "younger" children.

Children by second wife, called in their father's will "my younger children:"

x. MARGERY, a legatee (£3. 6s. 8d.) in her father's will, b. about 1512.

xi. JAFFERY [GEOFFREY], a legatee (£3. 6s. 8d.+£3. 6s. 8d.) in his father's will, b. about 1514.

xii. JOAN, THE YOUNGER, a legatee (£3. 6s. 8d.) in her father's will, b. about 1516.

xiii.  AGNES, THE YOUNGER, a legatee (£3. 6s. 8d.) in her father's will, b. about 1518.

6.  THOMAS FISKE (*William, Simon*), of Stadhough in Laxfield, co. Suffolk, not named in his mother's will (Will No. 7), dated 15 July 1504, but named as one of the executors of his brother Austin's will (Will No. 10), dated 15 Mar. 1507/8, the testator of 27 Oct. 1525 (Will No. 15, in which he styled himself Thomas Fyske, the Elder, of Laxfield), born about 1467, died between 27 Oct. 1525 and 10 Dec. 1525, when his will was proved.  He married ANNES (AGNES or ANNE) ————, who was living 27 Oct. 1525 and was provided for in her husband's will, being mentioned there as "my wife," without any Christian name.  She was probably the Anne who was named in the will of her mother-in-law (Will No. 7) as one of the four sons' wives to whom the testatrix bequeathed 40d. each.
Children :

i.  WILLIAM, of Stadhough in Laxfield, a beneficiary in his father's will, the testator of 15 Oct. 1558 (Will No. 27), b. about 1500; d. at Laxfield 30 Oct. 1558 (Chancery suit, *supra*, p. 143) ; m. MARGARET BALL, who was named as executrix (with two executors) in her husband's will, which she proved by her procurator, Thomas Tower, 4 May 1559.  She m. (2) John Armyger, and was living, as John Armyger's widow, in 1566 (Chancery suit, *supra*, p. 143). *
    Children :
    1.  *Ralph*, a beneficiary in his father's will, b. about 1525; d. *s. p.* at Laxfield, 10 Jan. 1564/5 (Chancery suit, *supra*, p. 143). His attempt to contest his father's will on the ground that his father was not of sound mind when he made it was unsuccessful, a sentence of the Prerogative Court of Canterbury, 30 Oct. 1560, in a case between Ralph Fiske and Margaret Fiske, the widow and executrix, upholding the will as made while the testator was of sound mind. (See Will No. 27, additional paragraph.)
    2.  *Mathew*, b. about 1527; living in 1566.  He was not mentioned in his father's will, but was defendant in a Chancery suit brought by his younger brother John on 15 Oct. 1566 (*vide infra*, 6, i, 7).  From him descended the Fiskes of Stadhough.
    3.  *Alice*, b. about 1532.
    4.  *Marion*, b. about 1534.
    5.  *Jane*, b. about 1536; perhaps the Jane Fyske who m. at Laxfield, 14 Sept. 1579, Thomas Newson (parish register).
    6.  *Margaret*, b. about 1538.

    }  Each of these four daughters, according to their father's will, was to receive a conditional legacy of £10 at marriage.

    7.  *John*, of Laxfield, a beneficiary in his father's will, b. about 1540; living in 1593 (muster roll).  On 15 Oct. 1566 he brought a suit in Chancery against his elder brother, Mathew Fiske, for the possession of lands in Laxfield called Gleems and Harsfeld, of which his late father had been seized, and the records in this suit furnish much information about his father's family (*vide supra*, pp. 142– * 143).  The outcome of the suit is not known; but, as John Fiske is taxed on lands in Laxfield in the subsidy of
*See the footnote at the bottom of p. 481, this volume.

486

1567–68 and as the name of Mathew Fiske is not found there in this subsidy, it may perhaps be inferred that John Fiske won the case.

8. *Faith*, a legatee (£10 at marriage) in her father's will, b. about 1542; under eighteen on 15 Oct. 1558.

9. *Catherine*, a legatee (£10 at marriage) in her father's will, b. about 1544; under eighteen on 15 Oct. 1558.

ii. ANNES (or AGNES), a beneficiary (£6. 13s. 4d. and other bequests) in her father's will, b. about 1502; living unm. 27 Oct. 1525.

iii. THOMAS, of Stradbroke, co. Suffolk, a beneficiary and one of the two executors of his father's will (his brother Henry being the other executor), the testator of 20 Jan. 1558/9 (Will No. 28), b. about 1504; d. between 20 Jan. 1558/9 and 24 May 1559, when his will was proved by his four unmarried daughters, Alice, Margery, Dorothy, and Joan, who were named in the will as residuary legatees and executrices; m. ————, who probably d. before her husband, as she was not mentioned in his will. He held lands in Stradbroke and Hoxne, co. Suffolk.

Children, named as beneficiaries in their father's will:

1. *Christian*, living 20 Jan. 1558/9, when she was the wife of Leonard Sewell and had two sons, Thomas Sewell and John Sewell, who were named in her father's will.

2. *Margaret*, living 20 Jan. 1558/9, when she was the wife of Alan Borrett and had two daughters, Joan Borrett and Elizabeth, who were named in her father's will.

3. *Margery*, ⎫
4. *Alice*, ⎬ unm. 20 Jan. 1558/9; living 24 May 1559.
5. *Dorothy*, ⎪
6. *Joan*, ⎭

iv. HENRY, of Cratfield, co. Suffolk, a beneficiary and one of the two executors of his father's will (his brother Thomas being the other executor), the testator of 19 Aug. 1558 (Will No. 26), b. about 1506; bur. at Cratfield 1[*sic*] Aug. 1558 (parish register); m. ALICE ————, who was bur. at Cratfield 11 Apr. 1553 (*ib.*). His will was proved 16 Sept. 1558 by his son William and his (the testator's) brother Thomas Fiske of Stradbroke, co. Suffolk, the executors named in the will. He was the ancestor of the Fiskes of Cratfield.

Children:

1. *William*, a beneficiary (lands in Fressingfield, co. Suffolk, live stock, farming implements, household stuff, etc.) and one of the executors of his father's will, was bur. at Cratfield 8 Apr. 1608; m. at Cratfield, 4 Oct. 1558 (perhaps not his first marriage, for Joan, daughter of William Fiske, was bur. at Cratfield 13 Sept. 1558), Alice Fulham, who was bur. there 6 Apr. 1603. Children, bapt. at Cratfield: (1) Elizabeth, bapt. 21 Sept. 1561. (2) Mary, bapt. 16 May 1563. (3) Alice, bapt. 13 Feb. 1564/5. (4) Henry, bapt. 24 Aug. 1567. (5) William, bapt. 4 Jan. 1569/70. (6) John, bapt. 1 May 1572. (7) Gregory, bapt. 4 Feb. 1573/4. (8) Ann, bapt. 12 Mar. 1574/5. (9) Ann, bapt. 6 Mar. 1578/9. (10) Margaret, bapt. 24 Aug. 1580. (Cratfield register.)

2. *Geoffrey* (*Jeffery*), a legatee in his father's will, m. about 1562 Christiana ————. Children, bapt. at Cratfield: (1) Eliazar, bapt. 11 Oct. 1562. (2) William, bapt. 14 Oct. 1565. (3) John, bapt. 29 Sept. 1568. (4) Alice, bapt. 17 Jan. 1571/2. (5) Elizabeth, bapt. 28 Aug. 1575. (Cratfield register.)

3. *Thomas*, a legatee in his father's will, m. at Cratfield, 11 Nov. 1554 or 1555 (perhaps not his first marriage), Alice Bridge (or Bridges). To Mary Fiske, eldest daughter of

his (the testator's) son Thomas, her grandfather, Henry Fiske of Cratfield, bequeathed 5 marks at her marriage, calling her his godchild. (Will No. 26.) To his godson Francis Fiske (perhaps a son of Thomas) Henry Fiske bequeathed 6s. 8d. (*ib.*).* Children of Thomas and Alice Fiske, recorded at Cratfield: (1) Henry, bapt. 15 Dec. 1555; bur. 17 May 1556.† (2) Alice, bapt. 6 Sept. 1562.† (3) Gregory, bapt. 13 Oct. 1566.‡ (4) Ann, bapt. 12 Oct. 1572.‡ (5) Robert, bapt. 27 Dec. 1575.‡

*Mary and Francis (if he were a son of this Thomas Fiske) were probably children by an earlier marriage.
†Recorded as child of Thomas Fiske, the name of the mother being omitted.
‡Recorded as child of Thomas and Alice Fiske.

# GENEALOGICAL RESEARCH IN ENGLAND

Communicated by the Committee on English and Foreign Research

## THE FISKE FAMILY

Contributed by G. Andrews Moriarty, A.M., LL.B., F.S.A.,
of Bristol. R. I.

7. Richard Fiske (? *Simon, William, Simon*), of the Broadgates in Laxfield, co. Suffolk (Candler Manuscripts), appears in the pedigree by Candler without indication of his parentage, but he was probably a son of Simon Fiske (No. 5),* and was born about 1493. The name of his wife, the details of his life, and the date of his death are unknown.

Children :†

   i.   John, of Tittishall [Tittleshall] (Candler) or Tivetshall, co. Norfolk, b. about 1514; m. ———.

       Children:

       1.  *Jerome* (or *Jeromie*), of Laxfield, yeoman, the testator of 22 Aug. 1630 (Will No. 64), b. about 1545; bur. at Laxfield (as "Jeremye Fyske, yemane") 3 Sept. 1630; m. ———, who, as the wife of "Jerume" Fiske, was bur. at Laxfield 15 Nov. 1624.

          In his will, dated 22 Aug. 1630, Jeromie Fiske named various children of his son-in-law, Peter Cock, viz., John Cocke (eldest son of Peter Cock), to whom he left a messuage and tenement in Tittleshall and Diskleborowe, co. Norfolk, Anne Cock (a messuage and tenement), Elizabeth Cocke (to whom her sister Anne was to pay £10), Peter Cock (a messuage or tenement in Laxfield), Jeremie Cocke (lands, etc., in Dennington [co. Suffolk] and Laxfield), Alice Cocke (£10), and Mary Cocke (£10). To Margret Rackham, his servant, the testator gave a house. He named his son-in-law, Peter Cock, as supervisor, and appointed John Cocke, Peter's son, as executor; and the executor proved the will 15 Sept. 1630.

          Alice Fiske, daughter of Jerome, was bapt. at Laxfield 22 Dec. 1588, and was probably the Alice Fiske, a "yonglynge," who was bur. there 7 Apr. 1593; and Anne Fyske, daughter of Jerome, was bapt. there 12 Mar. 1591/2. Perhaps it was this Anne Fyske who m. Peter Cock and was evidently deceased by 22 Aug. 1630.

       2.  *John,* of Tivetshall, b. about 1548; living 29 Dec. 1590, when he was named as a legatee in his brother William's will.

       3.  *William,* of Laxfield, wheelwright, the testator of 29 Dec. 1590 (Will No. 48), b. about 1550; bur. at Laxfield 2 Jan. 1590/1; m. Jane (———) Borret, widow of ——— Borret. She was bur. at Laxfield 10 May 1604.

*See Register, vol. 86, p. 407. **(Page 432, this volume.)**

†The pedigree by Candler states that Richard Fiske of Laxfield (No. 7) had eleven sons in all, and gives the names of seven of them, omitting the son Richard, whose will, however, proves his parentage (*vide infra*). The dates given in this article for the births of these children are merely approximations. The names of the children are given in the order in which the seven occur in the pedigree by Candler, and the son Richard is added as the eighth child, although it is by no means certain that he should not be placed earlier in the list of children.

489

In his will, dated 29 Dec. 1590 and proved by Jane, his widow, the executrix, 25 Jan. 1590/1, William Fiske bequeathed to Anne Borret and Susanna Borret, his wife's daughters, left to his wife Jane, for life, his messuage in Stradbroke [co. Suffolk], with remainder to John Punchyard, the testator's brother-in-law, until the latter's son, John Punchyard, the testator's nephew and godson, should be twenty-one, gave the residue of his estate to his wife Jane, to whom also he left sundry tools and boards, and bequeathed to his brother-in-law John Punchyard £10 and boards and trees, to his brother John Fiske boards, etc., to his brother Jeremie Fiske a colt, tools, and timber, and to his brother-in-law Thomas Borret a mare, boards, wheat, etc. No children of the testator were mentioned in the will.*

4. *Anne,* probably b. about 1553; evidently deceased when her brother William made his will, 29 Dec. 1590; m. at Laxfield, 26 July 1579, Thomas Borret, who was living 29 Dec. 1590, when he was named as a legatee in the will of his brother-in-law, William Fiske.

5. *Margaret,* b. about 1555; evidently deceased when her brother William made his will, 29 Dec. 1590; m. at Laxfield, 20 May 1582, John Punchard (or Punchyard), who was living 29 Dec. 1590, when he was named as a legatee in the will of his brother-in-law, William Fiske. Child (surname *Punchyard*): John, under twenty-one on 29 Dec. 1590, when he was named in the will of his uncle, William Fiske.

8. ii. GEORGE, b. about 1516.

iii. NICHOLAS, of Laxfield and Dennington, co. Suffolk, the testator of 20 Aug. 1569 (Will No. 34), b. about 1517; d. between 20 Aug. and 28 Sept. 1569, when his will was proved; probably m. (1) ———; m. (probably a second wife) JOHANE CRISPE, who was living 20 Aug. 1569, daughter of William Crispe of Laxfield.

Nicholas Fiske appears on the Laxfield muster roll in 1543, and was taxed 3d. at Laxfield in 1542–1544. In the subsidy of 1567–68 he was taxed 2s. 8d. at Dennington, on lands valued at £2, and 9s. 4d. at Laxfield, on lands valued at £4.

In his will he named his wife Johane, his father-in-law, William Crispe of Laxfield, his four children, Rachel, Ester, Mary, and Martha, his son William and his (the testator's) wife Johane, William's mother, and his (the testator's) son Amos Fiske.

"Of him [Nicholas Fiske] Mr Foxe makes mention in his story of John Noyes burnt at Laxfield." (Candler Manuscripts.)

Children, probably by first wife (order of births uncertain):

1. *Amos,* of Dennington, perhaps b. as early as 1544;† bur. at Dennington 31 May 1612, on the same day on which his wife Mary and his son William were buried; m. at Dennington, 17 Oct. 1574, Mary Gyrlynge. Children, recorded at Dennington: (1) Joane, bapt. 23 July 1575. (2) Nicholas (probably son of Amos and Mary‡), bur. 22 Nov. 1609, a bachelor, about 28 years of age [and therefore b. about 1581]. (3) Mary, bapt. 12 May 1583; bur. 5 July 1584. (4) Amos, bapt. 24 Aug. 1587; bur.

*See the curious and interesting inventory of the goods and chattels of William Fiske, which is printed verbatim in the REGISTER, vol. 86, pp. 427–430. ✹✹

†Amos may have been younger than one or more of his sisters. He may even have been the youngest child of the supposed first marriage of his father. He was married some twenty days later than his supposed half brother, William (7, iii, 6).

‡Or possibly the son of William (7, iii, 6), if his age at death, about 28 years, be somewhat loosely interpreted.

✹✹See the footnote at the bottom of p. 481, this volume.

28 July 1633; m. Margaret ———, who was bur. 21 June 1663; at least six children, recorded at Dennington, 1618–1632. (5) Witton [sic, ? William], bapt. 10 Jan. 1590/1; bur. on the same day as his parents, 31 May 1612. (6) John, bur. 7 Nov. 1599.

2. *Rachel,* perhaps b. about 1546; probably d. before 20 Mar. 1578/9, as she was not mentioned in her sister Esther's will of that date.

3. *Esther,* the testatrix of 20 Mar. 1578/9 (Will No. 40), perhaps b. about 1548; d. unm., probably on 20 Mar. 1578/9, when, as "Easter Fiske of Framlingham ad Castrum," co. Suffolk, single woman, she declared her nuncupative will, which was proved the next day by Amos Fyske, her brother, the executor.

In her will she bequeathed to her sister Marie [Mary], to her sister Mathewe [sic, ? Martha], and to her brother, Amos Fyske.

4. *Mary,* a legatee in her sister Esther's will, 20 Mar. 1578/9, perhaps b. about 1550; m. ——— Fisher of Syleham, co. Suffolk (Candler). Children (surname *Fisher*): (1) Joshuah, b. about 1590, "who went with his family into New-England" (*ib.*). He was Dea. Joshua Fisher of Dedham, Mass., who d. in 1674. (Cf. Savage Genealogical Dictionary, vol. 2, p. 163.) (2) Anthony, b. about 1592, "who went with his family into New-England" (Candler). He was of Dedham, Mass., and d. in 1669/70. (Cf. Savage, *op. cit.,* vol. 2, p. 162.) (3) Amos, "farmer to Custrichhall in Weely in Essex" (Candler); m. Anne (Maurice) Locke, relict of Daniel Locke (*ib.*); the names of eight children, of whom four d. in infancy, are given by Candler. (4) Cornelius, M.A., who "taught the schoole at East Bergholt [co. Suffolk]," d. *s. p.*; m. ———, who, as his widow, m. "George Smyth one of the ministers of Dedham in Essex." (Candler.) (5) a daughter, m. Roger Bridges (or Briggs) of Dennington (*ib.*). (6) Martha, m. John Bokenham of Syleham; children: John Bokenham, "clark," and others. (*Ib.*).

5. *Martha,* a legatee in her sister Esther's will, 20 Mar. 1578/9, perhaps b. about 1552; d. *s. p.*; m. ——— Golding. (Marriage and death from Candler.)

Child by wife Johane (probably his second wife):

6. *William,* of Dennington, yeoman, the testator of 13 Aug. 1580 (Will No. 41), b. about 1553; d. between 13 Aug. and 22 Nov. 1580, when his will was proved; m. at Dennington, 27 Sept. 1574, Helen ———, who was living 13 Aug. 1580.

In his will he mentioned his wife Helen, his son Nicholas (under twenty-one), his late father, Nicholas, his children under sixteen, his brother Amos, his sisters, and his daughters Anne Fyske, Rachaell, and Eliz[abet]h. Mary Fyske, another daughter of Willon [i. e., William] and Helen Fyske, was bapt. at Dennington 16 Nov. 1578, and probably d. before 13 Aug. 1580.

iv. GEOFFREY (or JEFFERY), of Laxfield, "Cowper," b. about 1519; bur. at Laxfield 29 Apr. 1591; m. ———.

His name appears on the Laxfield muster roll in 1543; as "Jeffray Fyske the Yonger" he was taxed 20d. at Laxfield in 1542–1544; and in the subsidy of 1567–68 he was taxed 5s. 4d. at Laxfield, on lands valued at £1.

He left only two daughters, perhaps b. about 1550. (Cf. Candler.)

9. v. ROBERT, b. about 1521.

vi. JEREMIE, b. about 1523. The only authority for Jeremie as a son of Richard (No. 7) seems to be the pedigree by Candler, in which he is given as a son of Richard of the Broadgates in Laxfield, but no information is given about him except his name.

vii. WILLIAM, of the parish of St. Michael's of South Elmham [co. Suffolk], wheelwright, the testator of 10 Oct. 1575 (Will No. 38), b. about 1525; d. between 2 Jan. 1578/9, when he added a codicil to his will, and 30 Jan. 1578/9, when his will was proved; m. ———, who probably d. before 10 Oct. 1575, as she was not mentioned in his will.

According to the pedigree by Candler "he fled for religion in the dayes of Q[ueen] Mary."

In his will he bequeathed to his daughter Gelyon Aldus a feather bed, etc.; to his daughter Margaret Bancrofte 40s.; and to his daughter Agnes Borowghe a milch cow and 20s.; and he made his daughter Mary his residuary legatee and executrix. In the codicil he bequeathed 20d. "to every grand-child of mine," and to "borowghes children" 40d. each. Robert Fiske and William Fiske were two of the witnesses to the will, and Robert Fiske and Geoffrey Fiske were two of the witnesses to the codicil.

Children (in the order in which they were named in their father's will*) :

1. *Gelyon* (or *Gyllyan*), b. about 1546; living 10 Oct. 1575; m. at Fressingfield, co. Suffolk, 14 Oct. 1561, Thomas Aldowes [Aldus].

2. *Margaret,* living 10 Oct. 1575; m. before 10 Oct. 1575 ——— Bancrofte.

3. *Agnes,* living 10 Oct. 1575; m. before 10 Oct. 1575 ——— Borowghe [Burrough]. They had issue.

4. *Mary,* unm. 30 Jan. 1578/9, when, as Mary Fiske, she proved her father's will; m. after that date Robert Lawter. Children (surname *Lawter*) : (1) Joseph, "who killed his father and was executed at Bury" [Bury St. Edmunds, co. Suffolk]. He d. *s. p.* (2) Anne, m. John Fiske (No. 13), *q. v.* (3) Mary, m. Eleazar Fiske of Metfield, co. Suffolk (No. 8, i, 2), *q. v.* (4) Martha, d. *s. p.* (Information about the marriage of Mary Fiske to Robert Lawter and about her children is taken from the pedigree by Candler.)

viii. RICHARD, of Laxfield, "sevemaker," the testator of 7 Sept. 1572 (Will No. 36), b. about 1527;† d. between 7 Sept. and 5 Nov. 1572, when his will was proved; m. AGNES CRISPE, who survived him and was bur. at Laxfield 16 Jan. 1597/8, daughter of Edmund Crispe.

Richard Fiske was taxed 2s. 8d. at Laxfield, on lands valued at £1, in the subsidy of 1567–68.

In his will he named his wife Agnes, his daughters Marie [Mary], Margaret, Anne, and Elizabeth, his son Elie [Elias], and his father-in-law Edmunde Crispe. He appointed his wife Agnes "executor," with his son Elie, "in whom I repose a special trust & confidence." He made his brother Robert Fiske supervisor of his will; and among the witnesses were John Fiske, Jefferie Fiske, and Nicholas Fiske.

Children (in the order in which they are named in their father's will) :

1. *Mary,* living 7 Sept. 1572; perhaps the Marye Fyske, "Singlewoman," who was bur. at Laxfield 18 Nov. 1597.

---

*The pedigree of Candler gives the daughter who married a Bancroft as the eldest daughter and the daughter who married an Aldus as the second daughter.

†*Vide supra,* p. 142, second footnote. (Page 489, this volume.)

2. *Margaret,* } living 7 Sept. 1572.
3. *Anne,*
4. *Elizabeth,* m. at Laxfield, 18 Aug. 1590, Wollffran Balldreye [Wolfram Baldry].
5. *Elias (Elye, Elie),* of Laxfield, yeoman, the testator of 2 May 1601 (Will No. 51), bur. at Laxfield 2 Sept. 1601; m. about 1588 Alice (———) Cowper, widow of ——— Cowper. She survived him and, as executrix, proved his will 12 Sept. 1601.

In his will Elias Fisk left to his wife Alice his lands and tenements in Laxfield and Stradbroke [co. Suffolk], lately purchased of Edmund Jay, until his son Henry should be twenty-four, when Henry should enter therein, on condition that he pay to his [the testator's] daughters Sara Fiske, Marie [Mary] Fiske, and Margaret Fisk £30 apiece, at stated times and in stated instalments. To his wife Alice the testator left also his messuage in Laxfield "wherein I inhabit" and his lands in Laxfield and Stradbroke "which late were of my father Richard Fiske, late deceased, with remainder to my son Henry." To each of his daughters, Sara, Marie [Mary], and Margaret, and to Johane Cowper, his wife's daughter, the testator bequeathed £5, at twenty years of age. Household goods were to go, after the decease of his wife Alice, to the testator's son and the three daughters. The testator made his wife Alice his residuary legatee and executrix, and directed her "to bind my son Henrie apprentice to such occupation or trade [as] she thinks well." The will was signed "Elie Fiske." Children, recorded at Laxfield: (1) Sara, bapt. 25 May 1589. (2) Henry, bapt. 24 May 1590. (3) Mary, bapt. 16 Apr. 1593. (4) Margaret, bapt. 16 Nov. 1596.

Three other sons, whose names are unknown.*

*It is noteworthy that there is no mention of any daughters among the children of Richard Fiske (No. 7).

# GENEALOGICAL RESEARCH IN ENGLAND

Communicated by the Committee on English and Foreign Research

## THE FISKE FAMILY

Contributed by G. ANDREWS MORIARTY, A.M., LL.B., F.S.A.,
of Bristol, R. I.

8. GEORGE FISKE (*Richard, ? Simon, William, Simon*), of Laxfield, co. Suffolk (Candler Manuscripts), born about 1516,
was living in 1542–1544, when he was taxed at Laxfield in the
subsidy of 34–35 Henry VIII, and his name appears on the
Laxfield muster roll in 1543. The name of his wife, the details
of his life, and the date of his death are unknown.

Child:

i. GEOFFREY (or JEFFERY), of Metfield, co. Suffolk, yeoman, the
testator of 10 Oct. 1628 (Will No. 62), b. perhaps about 1540;
d. between 10 Oct. 1628 and 25 Nov. 1628, when his will was
proved; m. SARAH ———, who, as executrix, proved his will.
In his will he left to his son Eliazer Fiske his messuage in
Metfield and Withersdale, co. Suffolk, with lands and freehold
there, and Eliazer was to pay to the testator's wife Sarah £15
a year, for life, at the south porch of Metfield church, quarterly.
Sarah was also to have the parlour at the west end of the house,
for life, six loads of firewood from Eliazer's lands, all the testator's moveables, for life, and after her death one half of the
same were to go to the testator's son-in-law, John Sawer.
Eliazer, however, was to have also a table in the parlour. The
testator bequeathed 20s. to his belchild [grandchild], John
Sawer, 10s. to his other belchild [grandchild], Thomas Sawer,
and 20s. to the poor of Metfield.

Children:

1. *A daughter,* probably d. not later than 1628; m. John Sawer,
who was living 10 Oct. 1628, with two sons, John and
Thomas Sawer.
2. *Eleazar,* of Metfield, probably b. about 1580; m. his second
cousin, Mary Lawter, daughter of Robert and Mary
(Fiske) Lawter and grandson of William Fiske (No. 7,
vii), and had by her a son, Eleazar Fiske of Metfield.

9. ROBERT FISKE (*Richard, ? Simon, William, Simon*), of Fressingfield and St. James, South Elmham, co. Suffolk, wheel-

wright, the testator of 10 Apr. 1590 (Will No. 47), born about
1521, died not later than 28 July 1602, when his will was
proved at Metfield, co. Suffolk, by his sons Geoffrey (or Jeffery) and Eliezar Fiske, the executors named in the will. He
married first SIBILLA (GOLD) BARBOR, daughter of ———
Gold and widow of ——— Barbor;* and secondly JOAN
———, who was buried at St. James, South Elmham, 3 Aug.
1587.

Robert Fiske may have been the Robert Fyske who was
taxed at Laxfield in the subsidy of 34–35 Henry VIII [1542–
1544] and again on 17 Apr. 1545, in goods valued at £13, on
which a "benevolence" of 13s. was exacted, and again on
4 Mar. 1545/6, when he was taxed 12s. in goods at Laxfield.
He was of Fressingfield as early as 1554, the baptism of his
son Richard being recorded there on 16 July 1554 and that of
his son Eleazar on 31 May 1556. The records of the baptisms
of his eldest son, William, and of his other children have not
been found. It was probably soon after the baptism of his son
Eleazar that he moved to St. James, South Elmham, for he is
said (Candler Manuscripts) to have "fled for religion in Q.
Maries dayes," and he was then of St. James (ib.). In the
subsidy of 10 Elizabeth [1567–68] he was taxed at St. James
2s. 8d., in lands valued at £1.

In his will, dated 10 Apr. 1590 and proved at Metfield, co.
Suffolk, 28 July 1602, by his sons Jefferie and Eliezar Fiske,
the executors, he mentioned his eldest son William Fiske, to
whom he left his tenement called Hoves in the parish of St.
James, his daughter Elizabeth, "now" the wife of Robert Barnard, his son Eliezar and Elizabeth, his wife, his son Thomas
Fiske, and his son Jefferie Fiske. Various payments to be
made by his children to one another in connection with the
lands in the parish of St. James were prescribed in the will.
The testator bequeathed 40s. to his belchildren [grandchildren],
to be equally divided among them and paid into the hands of
their parents, 10s. to the poor of St. James, and 10s. more to
such other godly poor people as should be deemed by the executors most needful. The testator also bequeathed 30s. to Nicholas Barbor of Chepenell Greene [his stepson], for him to
divide equally among his children.† The residue of his estate

*Sibilla Gold, according to the Candler Manuscripts, had two brothers, one of whom,
whose wife's name is not given, was the father of Robert Gold, B.D., rector of Thorington,
co. Suffolk, who, although married, died s. p., of Paul Gold, "Doctor of Physicke," who
also married but died s. p., and of Peter Gold, a clergyman, "in high esteeme with the
Bishops, whom his two brothers did not much affect," who also married but died s. p.
Sibilla Gold "was in great danger in Q. Maries time," and her sister, Isabella Gold, who
was married to ——— Phillips, "was taken and imprisoned in the castle at Norwich for
her religion in Q. Maries time but by Gods providence [was] delivered through the great
power that her two brothers then had in the country." The Gold family was armigerous.
†According to the Candler Manuscripts Nicholas Barbor, son of ——— and Sibilla (Gold)
Barbor, had three sons, namely Nicolas Barbor of Waybred [Weybread, so. Suffolk], John
Barbor, and Samuel Barbor, and two daughters, one of whom married Martin Golding,
a cheesemonger in London, afterwards of Coddenham [co. Suffolk], and had two sons and
three daughters, while the other daughter married ——— Tallant, and had one daughter.

was eventually to be divided equally among the testator's children.

Children, all (according to the Candler Manuscripts) by first wife:

10. i. WILLIAM, b. probably about 1550.
11. ii. GEOFFREY (or JEFFERY), b. probably about 1552.
    iii. RICHARD, bapt. at Fressingfield 16 July 1554; d. young.
    iv. ELEAZAR, of Metfield, co. Suffolk, wheelwright, the testator of 3 June 1613 (Will No. 58), bapt. at Fressingfield 31 May 1556; d. *s. p.* between 3 June 1613 and 4 July 1615, when his will was proved by his widow, Elizabeth, the executrix; m. ELIZABETH ———.

> In his will he left his tenement and lands in the parishes of St. James and Sandcroft in South Elmham to his wife Elizabeth, for life, with remainder, as to the tenement in St. James, to his nephews Nathaniel Fiske and David Fiske, sons of his brothers William Fiske and Jefferye Fiske, and, as to the lands in Sandcroft, to Eleazer Lusher and Elizabeth Lusher, his sister (under twenty-one). He bequeathed to his wife Elizabeth his moveables, to the children of his brother William £3 equally, to the children of his brother Jefferye £3 equally, to the children of his brother Thomas £3 equally, and to the poor £3.

    v. ELIZABETH, b. perhaps about 1558; m. ROBERT BARNARD of Custrich Hall in Werley [Warley], co. Essex. Both were living on 10 Apr. 1590.
12. vi. THOMAS, b. probably about 1560.

10. WILLIAM FISKE (*Robert, Richard, ? Simon, William, Simon*), of St. James, South Elmham, co. Suffolk, and of Ditchingham, co. Norfolk, the testator of 25 Nov. 1616 (Will No. 59a), born probably about 1550, died between 25 Nov. 1616 and 17 May 1620, when his will was proved. He married first ANNA AUSTYE, who was buried at St. James 13 Feb. 1600/1, daughter of Walter Austye of Tibbenham, co. Norfolk (Candler Manuscripts); and secondly ALICE ———, described in her husband's will of 25 Nov. 1616 as his "now" wife.

According to the Candler Manuscripts William Fiske "fled with his father in Q. Maries dayes." He was a churchwarden in the parish of St. James in 1601.

In his will he styled himself of Ditchingham, co. Norfolk, bequeathed to the poor of Ditchingham and of Bungay [co. Suffolk], and left to his eldest son, John, lands in St. James, South Elmham, and in Metfield, co. Suffolk, the said John paying to his brothers Nathaniel and Eleazar and to his sister Esther sixscore pounds. The testator mentioned also his grandchildren Matthias, John, and Mary Candler, his grandchildren John, Anne, Martha, Nathaniel, and Eleazar Fiske— all under twenty-one, and his daughter Anne Candler. He appointed his son John executor.

Children, all (according to the Candler Manuscripts) by first wife:

13. i. JOHN, b. probably about 1580.
    ii. HANNAH (or ANNE), living 25 Nov. 1616; m. 4 May 1603 WILLIAM GILLETT *alias* CANDLER of Yoxford, co. Suffolk, b. in 1561, d. in 1612.

Children (surname *Candler*):

1. *Rev. Mathias,* B.A. (Trinity College, Cambridge, 1623/24), M.A. (Peterhouse College, Cambridge, 1628), b. about 1604; d. in 1663. He was ordained deacon and priest at Norwich, co. Norfolk, 18 Dec. 1625, became vicar of Coddenham, co. Suffolk, in 1629, and was ejected in 1662. He compiled the Candler Manuscripts. (Cf. Alumni Cantabrigienses, part 1, vol. 1, p. 287.)

    2. *John,* b. in 1607.     4. *Mary,* d. young.
    3. *Anne,* d. young.     5. *A daughter,* d. young.

iii. EUNICE, d. unm.

iv. NATHANIEL, of Weybread, co. Suffolk, m. ABRIA (HOVEL) LEMAN, widow of ———— Leman of Weybread.

    Children:

1. *Nathaniel,* of Weybread, m. Dorothy Simonds, daughter of John Simonds of Mendham, co. Suffolk and co. Norfolk. Children: (1) John. (2) Nathaniel, d. in infancy. (3) Esther.
2. *Sarah,* m. Robert Rogers. Children (surname *Rogers*): (1) Sarah. (2) Margaret.
3. *Abria,* m. Francis Wretts. Children (surname *Wretts*): (1) Sarah. (2) Benjamin. (3) Abria.

v. ESTHER, m., as his second wife, JOHN CHALKER of Rednall [? co. Norfolk].

    Children (surname *Chalker*):

1. *Esther,* m. Anthony Noblett.
2. *Matthias,* m. Susan Soame, daughter of Henry Soame of King's Lynn, co. Norfolk, gentleman, a rich tanner. Children: (1) Martha, d. in infancy. (2) Jonathan, b. in 1658.

vi. ELEAZER, of Norwich, co. Norfolk, m. MARY BRABOURNE.

    Children:

1. *A daughter.*     2. *A daughter,* d. young.

11. GEOFFREY (or JEFFERY) FISKE (*Robert, Richard, ? Simon, William, Simon*), of St. James, South Elmham, co. Suffolk, and of Great Bentley, co. Essex, yeoman, the testator of 11 May 1629 (Will No. 63), born probably about 1552, died between 11 May 1629 and 23 July 1629, when his will was proved at Colchester, co. Essex. He married MARY COOKE (whose maiden name is given in the Candler Manuscripts), who was buried at St. James 16 May 1614.

In his will he styled himself Jeffery Fiske of Great Bently [Great Bentley], co. Essex, yeoman, gave to Samuel Fisk, his eldest son, of Waybred [Weybread], co. Suffolk, his best suit of apparel, and to Elizabeth Fisk, daughter of the said Samuel Fisk, 5s., to be paid at the end of her apprenticeship, and appointed David Fisk of Weley [Weeley, co. Essex], undoubtedly another of his sons, and Martin Underwood of Bentley [his son-in-law] executors. That the testator did not make provision in his will for all his children then living and that he did not dispose therein of any substantial amount of property may be explained by assuming that his daughters had received their portions at marriage and that probably he had divided all his property in South Elmham and elsewhere among his children before he moved to Great Bentley, where in the last years of his life he may have made his home with his daughter, Martha Underwood, and her husband. His two executors were to have whatsoever remained at Bentley, and were to pay all the expenses of his funeral.

Children, probably all born at St. James, South Elmham (order of births somewhat uncertain) :

i.    SAMUEL, of Weybread, co. Suffolk, eldest son, b. probably about 1586; living 11 May 1629; m. ———.
        Child:
        1. *Elizabeth*, living 11 May 1629, when she was serving an apprenticeship.

ii.    NATHANIEL (not given in the Candler Manuscripts), b. probably about 1588; bur. at St. James 13 Sept. 1601.

iii.    MARY, b. probably about 1590; d. *s. p.*; m. (1) ——— BRAME; m. (2) JOHN MORE of Wissett, co. Suffolk.

iv.    NATHAN, b. probably about 1592; d. in New England (probably at Watertown, Mass.) 21 June 1676; m., probably in England, SUSANNA ———.

        In the Candler Manuscripts he is placed after his brother Samuel and before his brother David (the brother Nathaniel, who was bur. in 1601, not appearing in the Candler Manuscripts), and he is given there as "Nathan Fiske whose children went all into New England." It is clear, however, that he himself emigrated to New England and settled at Watertown, Mass., where his children were born, for his *sister*, Martha Underwood, who lived with him at Watertown after her husband's death, testified that he "was very crazy in his memory" before he died. He was in Watertown as early as 1642, the birth of his son Nathan being recorded there under date of 17 Oct. 1642, was admitted freeman 10 May 1643, bought land 10 Sept. 1643, and was a selectman in 1673.

        In his will, dated 19 June 1676 and proved 10 July 1676, he named his sons Nathan, John (executor), David, and Nathaniel, and his daughter Sarah Gale.

        Children, b. at Watertown :
        1. *Nathan*, b. 17 Oct. 1642.
        2. *John*, b. 25 Aug. 1647.   } For further history of these
        3. *David*, b. 29 Apr. 1650.   ⟩ sons and their descendants
        4. *Nathaniel*, b. 12 July 1653.  } see Bond's "Watertown."
        5. *Sarah*, d. 14 May 1728; m. at Watertown, 3 Sept. 1673, Abraham Gale of Watertown, who d. 15 Sept. 1718. Sixteen children. (Bond's Watertown.)

v.    CLARA (not given in the Candler Manuscripts), bapt. at St. James 10 Mar. 1593/4; probably d. young.

vi.    LYDIA, b. probably about 1595; d. *s. p.*; m. ———.

vii.    ANNE, bapt. at St. James in October 1596; m. WILLIAM BIRD of Kersey, co. Suffolk. In the Candler Manuscripts she is called "Anne Fiske (or rather Sarah)," and it is stated that of her ten children "the most died young."

        The four children (surname *Bird*) given in the Candler Manuscripts are:
        1. *Sarah*, m. John Twilter, and had a son named John Twilter.
        2. *William*.   3. *Bartholomew*, m. ———.   4. *Thomas*.

viii.    ELIZABETH, bapt. at St. James 22 Apr. 1599; d. *s. p.*; m. ——— PYGOTT.

ix.    DAVID, of Weeley, co. Essex, on 11 May 1629, when he was appointed one of the two executors of his father's will, and of of Watertown, Mass., as early as 1637, b. probably about 1601; d. in New England (probably at Watertown) between 10 Sept. 1660, when his will was dated, and 22 Jan. 1661/2, when it was proved; m. in England SARAH SMYTHE [SMITH], who d. probably before her husband migrated to New England, daughter of Edmund Smith of Wrentham, co. Suffolk. (Cf. the Candler

Manuscripts, which state that he "went with his family into New-England," Savage's Genealogical Dictionary, vol. 2, and Bond's Watertown.)

He was admitted a freeman in March 1637/8, and was a selectman of Watertown in 1640 and 1643 and a juror in 1652, 1654, 1655, and 1657. In 1644 he was proprietor of a homestall of 22 acres and of six other lots, amounting to 227 acres. (Bond's Watertown.)

In his will he mentioned no wife, but a daughter Fitch and a son David, whom he made his sole executor and residuary legatee, leaving to him his "houses, lands, cattle, and chattels." The will was signed with the mark of David Fiske, and a seal was attached. Inventory, 10 Jan. 1661/2, £78. 9s. 1d. On 6 Aug. 1673 the son David sold the homestead and two other lots of land in Watertown to John Coolidge. (Bond, *op. cit.*)

Children:

1. *Lieut. David,* of Cambridge Farms (now Lexington), Mass., planter, b. in England about 1623, for he deposed in Middlesex County, Mass., 1 Apr. 1672, aged about 49 years, and deposed again in 1686, aged 63. For him and some of his descendants see Bond, *op. cit.,* and Savage, *op. cit.*

2. *Martha,* b. undoubtedly in England; m. about 1656 Thomas Fitch of Boston, cordwainer, who d. in 1678, his wife Martha surviving him. For their children see Bond, *op. cit.,* and Savage, *op. cit.* (under name *Fitch*).

x.  MARTHA, bapt. at St. James 9 Sept. 1602; d. *s. p.* at Watertown, Mass., 6 May 1684; m. in England, probably before 11 May 1629, MARTIN UNDERWOOD, b. about 1596, d. at Watertown 7 Nov. 1672.

On 11 May 1629 Martin Underwood was of Great Bentley, co. Essex, England, and was named on that date as one of the two executors of the will of his father-in-law, Geoffrey (Jeffery) Fiske. In April 1634 Martin Underwood, aged 38, and his wife Martha, aged 31, embarked at Ipswich, co. Suffolk, in the *Elizabeth,* bound for New England. They settled at Watertown, and he was admitted freeman 3 Sept. 1634. He was a cloth manufacturer or weaver, and in his will, dated 23 Aug. 1663 and proved 10 Dec. 1672, left all of his property to his wife, for life, with remainder to his cousin [i. e., his wife's nephew] Nathan Fiske, Jr., and, after the death of the last-mentioned, to John Fiske, brother of Nathan Fiske, Jr. To his sister's children, if they should come over from England, he bequeathed 20s. each. After her husband's death the widow, Martha, lived with her brother, Nathan Fiske, at Watertown. (Cf. Watertown Records, vol. 1, Bond's Watertown, and Savage's Genealogical Dictionary, vol. 4.)

12. THOMAS FISKE (*Robert, Richard, ? Simon, William, Simon*), of Fressingfield, co. Suffolk, wheelwright, the testator of 20 Feb. 1610/11 (Will No. 55), born probably at St. James, South Elmham, co. Suffolk, about 1560, was buried at Fressingfield 26 Feb. 1610/11. He married probably about 1587, MARGERY ———, who was living 20 Feb. 1610/11, when he made his will.

How long before his death he had lived at Fressingfield, which about the middle of the sixteenth century had been the home of his father, has not been discovered, nor have the records of the baptisms of his children been obtained.

In his will he gave to his wife Margery the occupation for life of the whole of the tenement in which he then dwelt, with certain rights in regard to taking fruit, water, etc., and keeping swine and fowls, with remainder to his son Thomas of all the term of years which he (the testator) had therein. To his son Thomas he left his shop, with sundry chambers and with the yards, gardens, and orchards, for the said term of years, on condition that the said Thomas pay to the testator's daughter Elizabeth £3. 6s. 8d., at Michaelmas 1619 [probably the year in which she would come of age]. The son Thomas was to have all the testator's timber and working tools, and was to keep the whole of the premises in repair. To his son Phineas the testator bequeathed £4, to be paid at Michaelmas 1621; to his son John £4, at Michaelmas 1624; and to his daughter Mary £3. 6s. 8d., at Michaelmas 1627. The testator's wife Margery was to occupy all the residue of his goods, household stuff, and implements, for life, and then the same were to be divided equally among his children. The will was proved "the last of February" 1610 [1610/11] by the testator's son Thomas, the executor named therein. From this will the names of the testator's children who were living in 1610/11 (except a son James, who is not named in the will but is given in the Candler Manuscripts) and the approximate dates of their births (except the births of Thomas and James) may be learned.

Children:

i. THOMAS, of Fressingfield and later of Metfield, co. Suffolk, executor of his father's will in 1610/11, b. probably about 1588; m. at Metfield, 17 Oct. 1614, being then of Fressingfield, MARY WARD of Metfield.

ii. JAMES (given only in the Candler Manuscripts), of Weybread, co. Suffolk, b. probably about 1590; probably the James Fisk who m. at Fressingfield, 24 May 1613, ALCE [ALICE] CHETLE-BOROW.

iii. ELIZABETH, b. about 1598; perhaps the Elisabeth Fisk who m. at Fressingfield, 25 Apr. 1614, PHILIP WHISOLCROFT.

iv. PHINEAS, of Wingfield, co. Suffolk, and of Salem and Wenham, Mass., ancestor of one branch of the Fiskes of Massachusetts, b. about 1600; d., probably at Wenham, 7 Apr. 1673 (Wenham Vital Records); m. (1) at Metfield, co. Suffolk, 2 Oct. 1617 [sic], SARA FRANCIS (Suffolk Parish Registers, Marriages, vol. 3, p. 109), who d. in New England 10 Sept. 1659; m. (2) probably at Wenham, 4 Apr. 1660, ELIZABETH EASTWICK (Wenham Vital Records), who probably d. before her husband, as she was not mentioned in his will.

He emigrated to New England, with his wife and children, and was in Salem, Mass., as early as 1641, was admitted freeman 18 May 1642, and in 1644 moved to Wenham, a town set off from Salem in 1643. He was captain and, in 1653, a representative in the General Court.

In his will, dated 6, 1 mo. 1673 and proved in the court at Salem 26, 4 mo. 1673 by the witnesses, Samuel Fiske and Hannah Walden, Phineas Fiske gave to his son James Fiske one half of his house and lands and to his other two sons the other half, to be divided between them in equal portions. To his three sons also he bequeathed his chattels, to be divided

500

equally between them, except his great Bible, which the testator gave to Samuel Fiske, his nephew, and his "Best pillow & pillow beere," which he gave to Mara Fiske. He appointed his two sons, John and Thomas, his executors. The inventory of the estate of Phinehas Fiske of Wenham, deceased 7, 2 mo. 1673, amounted to £214. 10s. 6d., with debts amounting to £8. 9s. 3d. due from the estate. (Probate Records of Essex County, vol. 2, pp. 371–372.)

Children by first wife, b. in England:

1. *James,* b. about 1620; d. at Groton, Mass., 4 July 1689; m. at Haverhill, Mass., probably about 1648, Hannah Pike. He was admitted to the church in Salem 2 July 1641, was freeman 18 May 1642, moved to Newbury, Mass., and thence to Wenham, where he was received into the church from the church at Newbury in 1644, lived for several years at Haverhill, where he was proprietor in 1646, and moved finally to Groton. In his will, dated 14 June 1689 and proved at Cambridge, Mass., he bequeathed to his sons James, John, Samuel, and Thomas and to his daughter Hannah. His children by his wife Hannah, b. at Haverhill and all (except the first Ann) living 14 June 1689, were: (1) James, b. 8 Aug. 1649. (2) John, b. 10 Dec. 1651. (3) Ann, b. and d. 31 May 1654. (4) Thomas, b. 23 June 1655. (5) Ann (probably the Hannah of the will), b. 11 Feb. 1656/7. (6) Samuel, b. 1 Nov. 1658. (Cf. Haverhill Vital Records and Pope's Pioneers of Massachusetts.)

2. *Elizabeth,* bapt. at Wingfield 22 Apr. 1622.

3. *John,* bapt. at Wingfield 13 May 1627.

4. *Thomas,* bapt. at Wingfield 25 Mar. 1630.

   Perhaps others.

v. JOHN, b. about 1603; living 20 Feb. 1610/11.

vi. MARY, b. about 1606; living 20 Feb. 1610/11.

13. JOHN FISKE (*William, Robert, Richard, ? Simon, William, Simon*), of St. James, South Elmham, co. Suffolk, born probably about 1580, was buried at St. James, as "Goodman Fyske," 14 May 1633. He married his second cousin, ANNE LAWTER, who died on a voyage to New England, daughter of Robert and Mary (Fiske) Lawter and granddaughter of William Fiske (No. 7, vii).

Children:

i. REV. JOHN, B. A., of Salem, Wenham, and Chelmsford, Mass., planter, minister, physician, bapt. at St. James, South Elmham, 20 Mar. 1607/8; d. probably at Chelmsford, Mass., 14 Jan. 1676/7 (Chelmsford Vital Records); m. (1) in 1635 ANNE GIPPES of Frenze, co. Norfolk, who d. at Chelmsford 14 Feb. 1671/2; m. (2) at Chelmsford, 1 Aug. 1672, ELISABETH HINCHMAN (or HINCKSMAN), widow of Edmund Hinchman.

He was admitted sizar at Peterhouse College, Cambridge, 2 July 1625, and took the degree of Bachelor of Arts in 1628/9. In 1637, with his wife and one or two children, his two sisters, and his younger brother William, he emigrated to New England, and, after tarrying first at Cambridge, Mass., moved in the same year to Salem. He was admitted freeman 2 Nov. 1637, was preacher and schoolmaster at Salem for almost four years, moved to Wenham in 1641, gathered a church there, of which he was pastor, 1644–1656, and then went, with the greater part of his church, to Chelmsford, where he was the first pastor

501

and served both in that office and also as physician until his death.

In his will, dated 8 June 1676 and proved 22 Feb. 1676/7, he bequeathed to his wife Elizabeth, his son John and John's wife Lydia, his daughters Sarah, wife of John Farwell, and Anna, and his younger son Moses,* and also to William, eldest son of his (the testators) brother William, late of Wenham, and to his widow and their other children. (Cf. Alumni Cantabrigienses, part 1, vol. 2, p. 144, Savage's Genealogical Dictionary, vol. 2, Pope's Pioneers of Massachusetts, and Chelmsford Vital Records.)

ii.   ANNE, bapt. at St. James, South Elmham, 1 Apr. 1610; d. at Dedham, Mass., 5 Dec. 1649; m. FRANCIS CHICKERING. They went to Massachusetts in 1637 and settled at Dedham, where he was ensign, selectman, and deputy. They had issue.

iii.  NATHANIEL, d. in infancy; bur. at St. James, South Elmham, 27 Mar. 1614.

iv.   MARTHA, m. in England CAPT. EDMUND THOMPSON, master mariner, son of John Thompson of Holkham, co. Norfolk. They went to New England and settled at Salem, Mass., in 1637, where they had four children. After 4 July 1647, when their daughter *Hannah* was bapt., they returned to England and lived at Yarmouth, where they had three more children, who d. in infancy. (Cf. Savage, *op. cit.,* vol. 4.)

v.    WILLIAM, of Salem and Wenham, Mass., under twenty-four years of age in September 1638; d., probably at Wenham, about 1654, the inventory of his estate being taken 16 Sept. 1654; m. BRIDGET MATCHET, daughter of ——— Matchet of Pulham, co. Norfolk, England.

He went to Massachusetts in 1637 and settled at Salem. He was admitted freeman 18 May 1642, was a constable 26 Feb. 1643/4, and was licensed by the General Court to sell wine 13 Nov. 1644. He was a deputy to the General Court, and moved to Wenham.

Children, born in Massachusetts:
1. *William.*   2. *Samuel.*   3. *Joseph.*   4. *Benjamin.*
5. *Martha.*

*Moses Fiske, A.B. (Harvard, 1662), A.M. (*ib.,* 1665), died in 1708.

502

## GENEALOGICAL RESEARCH IN ENGLAND

Communicated by the Committee on English and Foreign Research

## ROBERT DANIEL, HUSBAND OF ELIZABETH MORSE

Contributed by Mrs. Mary Lovering Holman
of Watertown, Mass.

To the REGISTER of January and July 1929 (vol. 83, pages 70–84, 278–294) the Committee on English and Foreign Research communicated an able article by the chairman of the Committee, G. Andrews Moriarty, Jr., A.M., LL.B., now of Bristol, R. I., on the English ancestry of Samuel[1] Morse of Watertown, Dedham, and Medfield, Mass., and his wife, Elizabeth (Jasper) Morse. With his wife Elizabeth, aged 48, one of their sons, Joseph, aged 20, and Elizabeth Daniel, aged 2 years, Samuel[1] Morse, husbandman, aged 50, embarked on 15 Apr. 1635 on the ship *Increase,* bound from London for New England; and Mr. Moriarty stated that Elizabeth Daniel was probably a granddaughter of Samuel and Elizabeth Morse. (REGISTER, vol. 83, pages 70, 286.)

In the article in question, in the list of children of Samuel and Elizabeth (Jasper) Morse, appears the following account of their second child, Elizabeth (*ib.,* page 290) : *

> "ii.   ELIZABETH, bapt. at Redgrave, co. Suffolk, 6 Mar. 1605/6; probably m. ——— DANIEL, and d., leaving a daughter, *Elizabeth,*

*For pp. 70-84 & 278-294 see pp. 262-291, this volume.

b. about 1633, who was probably the Elizabeth Daniel, aged 2 years, who was taken to New England in 1635 by Samuel Morse and his wife."

Recent research confirms Mr. Moriarty's conjecture that Elizabeth Daniel was the granddaughter of Samuel Morse, but disproves the statement that her mother had died. It seems evident that Elizabeth Morse married Robert Daniel, and emigrated with him to New England before 1636/7, when Robert was admitted a proprietor of Watertown. As Elizabeth (Morse) Daniel had a second child about this time, she may have thought that the elder child would be better off on the voyage with her mother, or possibly she and her husband came to New England before her parents, and she, knowing that they would soon follow, left the little Elizabeth with them. On their arrival little Elizabeth Daniel, as might be expected, was united with her parents in Watertown, and, when the removal to Dedham of part of the Watertown settlers took place, the Daniel family remained in Watertown, and later moved to Cambridge, Mass. An account of Robert Daniel and his wives and children, with the names, birthplaces, and dates of birth of his grandchildren, is given here.

ROBERT[1] DANIEL, of Watertown and Cambridge, Mass., born in England about 1592 (he deposed in Middlesex County, Mass., 26 June 1652, aged 60 and upwards), died at Cambridge 6 July 1655. He married first, about 1630, ELIZABETH MORSE, baptized at Redgrave, co. Suffolk, England, 6 Mar. 1605/6, died at Cambridge 2 Oct. 1643, daughter of Samuel[1] and Elizabeth (Jasper) Morse; and secondly, at Cambridge, 2 May 1654, MRS. REANA (————) (JAMES) ANDREW, who died after 1672. He married, before 12 Apr. 1669, as her fourth husband, Elder Edmund Frost.

Robert Daniel was evidently a man of education. An abstract of his will follows:

The Will of ROBERT DANIELL of Cambridge [Mass.], dated 3 July 1655. To "my Loveing wife Reana over and besides that part of the estate wch by covenant was to returne unto her againe at my decease" I give 40s. a year during her life [with other provisions for her]. My household goods are to be equally divided amongst my five children. My eldest daughter, the now wife of Thomas Fanning, shall have her fifth part immediately after my decease, and the remainder shall remain with my son Samuell until the rest of his brothers and sisters shall come of age, of twenty-one years, or [until their] marriage. To my cousin Anna Newcomen a young cow, and to Elder Frost 40s. To my daughter Elizabeth, the wife of Thomas Fanning, £50. To my three youngest children £50 apiece, at twenty-one or marriage. "The remainder of my estate I do give & bequeath the whole & entire part" to my son Samuell, whom I nominate as my executor, together with my son-in-law Thomas Fanning. Supervisors: my loving friends Richard Jacson and Thomas Danforth, "to whom I do also . . . comitt the care & dispose of my Children both in their minority and in the change of their condicon by mariage . . . if it happen any of my children to Decease before their Marriage or ye Arivall to the aforesaid Age of twenty one years . . . then the portion of ym the deceased shalbe and remaine to such as shall survive." My executors shall pay yearly after my

504

decease to my son Joseph and my daughters Sarah and Mary £5 apiece, as part of their £50. My daughter Elizabeth shall have liberty to choose in the first place her part of the household stuff. [Signed] Robert Daniell. [Sealed with a seal bearing an anchor.] Witnesses: John Shepard, Thomas Danforth.* Proved 2 October 1655.

Inventory, including many books, a "Great Bible," and a sword, £359. 19s. 11d. (Middlesex Probate Files, 5939.)

Robert Daniel's widow, Reana Daniel of Cambridge, for a valuable sum of money paid by John Whitney, Jr., of Watertown, confirmed unto John Whitney, in 1656, 40 acres of land in Watertown; and the mark, R, of Mrs. Daniel was acknowledged by Reana Frost on 12 Apr. 1669. (Middlesex Deeds, vol. 3, page 364.)

Children by first wife:

i.   SAMUEL,[2] of Watertown and Medfield, b. about 1631; d., probably at Medfield, about or after 1683; m. at Watertown, 10 May 1671, MARY GRANT.
     He was admitted a freeman in 1652. On 26 Apr. 1656, being then of Watertown, he sold to Thomas Fanning of Watertown about 62 acres in Watertown, with a house thereon, and also cattle of all sorts and goods worth £50, household stuff, etc., in the custody of the said Samuel, "belonging to him the said Samuel by vertue of his Executorship upon the estate of his ffather Robert Daniel deceased." Thomas Fanning was to pay £74 in wheat and pease and the remainder in corn or cattle, the full amount being £89. 16s. 10d., and to satisfy debts, legacies, etc., due to any person by virtue of the will of Robert Daniel, excepting the debt then due to be paid to Reana Daniel, widow of the said Robert Daniel. (Middlesex Deeds, vol. 1, p. 212.)
     Children:
     1. *Robert,*[3] b. at Watertown 23 Apr. 1672.
     2. *Samuel,* b. at Watertown 1 Apr. 1674.
     3. *Joseph,* b. at Watertown 3 Feb. 1676/7.
     4. *Mary,* b. at Medfield 25 June 1679.
     5. *Elizabeth,* b. at Medfield 9 Apr. 1681.
     6. *Sarah,* b. at Medfield 23 Mar. 1683.

ii.  ELIZABETH, b. about 1633 (being recorded as 2 years old on 15 Apr. 1635, when she was taken on board the *Increase* by her Grandfather Morse for the voyage to New England); d. at Watertown 22 Jan. 1722/3, in her 92d year; m. at Watertown, 17 May 1655, THOMAS FANNING, who d. there in August 1685.
     Children (surname *Fanning*), b. at Watertown:
     1. *Elizabeth,* b. 5 Apr. 1656.
     2. *Mary,* b. 12 Nov. 1657; d. in infancy.
     3. *Mary,* b. 28 Oct. 1662; m. Benoni Learned.
     4. *Sarah,* b. 18 July 1665; d. 24 Aug. 1691.

iii. THOMAS, b. probably about 1635; bur. at Watertown 6 Nov. 1644.

iv.  SARAH, b. probably about 1638; living unm. in 1655.

v.   JOSEPH, of Medfield, b. about 1640 (he deposed 25 Apr. 1672, aged about 31); d. about or after 1689; m. (1) at Medfield, 16 Nov. 1665, MARY FAIRBANKS, bapt. at Dedham 29 Dec. 1650, d. at Medfield 9 June 1682, daughter of John and Sarah (————) Fairbanks; m. (2) about 1683 RACHEL ————, who d. at Medfield in 1697.
     Children by first wife, b. at Medfield:
     1. *Joseph,*[3] b. 23 Sept. 1666.
     2. *Mary,* b. in July 1669.

*The names of the witnesses are torn off from the original will, but are given in the recorded copy of the will.

3. *Samuel,* b. 20 Oct. 1671.
4. *Mehetabel,* b. 10 July 1674.
5. *Ebenezer,* b. 24 Apr. 1677.
6. *Elizabeth,* b. 9 Mar. 1678/9.
7. *Jeremiah,* b. 17 Mar. 1679/80.
8. *Eleazer,* b. 7 Mar. 1680/1.
    Children by second wife:
9. *Jeremiah,* b. 3 Nov. 1684.
10. *Rachel,* b. at Medway, Mass., 10 Oct. 1686.
11. *Zachariah,* b. 9 Apr. 1689.

vi.   MARY, b. at Cambridge 2 Sept. 1642; killed by the Indians on the
    road to Canada in 1704; m. at Medfield, 14 June 1660, SAMPSON
    FRARY, who was killed by the Indians at Deerfield, Mass., 29
    Feb. 1704, son of John and Prudence Frary. He moved from
    Medfield to Hadley, Mass., about 1666.
        Children (surname *Frary*), the first two b. at Medfield, the
    others at Hadley:
1. *Mary,* b. 24 July 1662.
2. *Mehetabel,* b. 29 Jan. 1664/5.
3. *Susanna,* b. 4 Mar. 1668 [1667/8].
4. *John,* b. 17 Sept. 1669.
5. *Nathaniel,* b. in 1675.

# GLEANINGS FROM ENGLISH RECORDS

Contributed by G. ANDREWS MORIARTY, A.M., LL.B., F.S.A.,
of Bristol, R. I.

## FROM ADMIRALTY EXAMINATIONS

Nicholas Shapleigh of Piscataqua in New England, merchant, deposed
22 May 1645, in the case of Alderman Berkeley, that he (the deponent)
was born at Dartmouth, co. Devon. The deposition concerned Stephen
Winthrop, his brother, and his father. (Admiralty Examinations, vol.
60.)

Thomas Hawkins of Boston in New England deposed 14 May 1646,
aged about 37 years.

Edward Bendall of Boston in New England deposed the same day,
aged about 38 years. He had been in Boston 17 years. (*Ib.*)

In the case of Joseph Grafton of Salem and Edmund Henfield of Boston in New England, 3 February 1650/1, Robert Henfield of Boston,
mariner, deposed on that date, aged about 28 years, that Joseph Grafton
of Salem in New England and William Andrews of Cambridge in New
England were owners of the ship *Diligence* of Boston, which was seized
between Cape Sable and Cape Cod in May last since four years by two
French men-of-war, and the crew were put ashore on an uninhabited
island off Cape Sable, in St. John's Bay, Newfoundland.

Roland Bever of Boston, mariner, aged 26 years, also deposed to the
above.

Nicholas Trewergy of Piscataqua, sailor, aged about 22 years, deposed that the ship was owned by Joseph Grafton, Robert Henfield, and
William Andrews.

Henry Parker of St. Matthew's, Friday Street, London, formerly of
Boston in New England, aged about 25 years, also deposed. (*Ib.,* vol.
64.)

[Edmund Henfield of Salem was a "kinsman" of Joseph Grafton, according
to the Salem records. Who was Robert Henfield of Boston?]

In the case of Maj. Edward Gibbons and ye French, 7 May 1651, John Richards of Boston in New England, merchant, deposed, aged about 26 years. He had lived in New England 19 years. (*Ib.*, vol. 64.)

In the case of David Sellick, Thomas Kimbold, Peter Butler, *et al.* of Boston, owners of the ship *Mayflower*, Peter Butler, master, taken at San Domingo by the Governour there, 17 August 1653, Peter Butler of Boston in New England, mariner, aged about 37 years, deposed that the *Mayflower* was built at Lynn in New England, that she went to Virginia for tobacco, and that she was driven, on her return voyage, into San Domingo, in the middle of November 1652, and was seized by the Governour, Don Andreas Perez Franto. (*Ib.*, vol. 67.)

[The gleanings given above were brought to the attention of the contributor by his friend, Richard Holworthy, Esq., of London. They have been taken from the recently discovered "Admiralty Examinations," which are a mine of information about early New England.]

## From the Records of the Court of Requests*

### Williams *v.* Gilman

[Undated.]    The complaint of SIDRACH WILLIAMS of London, merchant, shews that for many years he traded with Bartholomew Gilman of London, merchant, in sea horse [walrus] teeth, and that he had security for Gilman's account for money owed complainant. Gilman evaded making an accounting. In 1623 many ships were bound for Greenland. The complainant and Gilman sent the complainant's servant, John Duosley, to Hull, to buy sea horse teeth for both of them. Gilman has never paid for his share. They procured a letter of credit for £200 from Thomas Crathorne, Clerk of the Customs in London, to John Lister and Thomas Fen of Hull, merchants. They bought 228 sea horse teeth, weighing 470 pounds, 8 ounces, and valued at £156. 7s. 8d., as computed by Edward Dexter, servant of Gilman. The sea horse teeth were shipped overseas in Gilman's name and at his request, to enhance his credit. They were sent from London to Constantinople, to a merchant there, one Anthony Wilson, and complainant believed that he would receive satisfaction for his share and demanded the proceeds of his share. Shortly after there was war with Spain and the French King, and at that time the complainant, who was trafficking overseas, sustained great losses; and after the peace he travelled to Italy, seeking to recover some part of his estate in divers men's hands there. When he was returning to England out of Italy, he was seized and imprisoned by the Inquisition at Milan, and, if he had then died, the complainant's wife and children would have been defrauded by Gilman, who, when he heard of the complainant's imprisonment, denied his debt; but, on the complainant's return, he promised to account for the proceeds of the moiety of the sea horse teeth, but he has failed to do so. (Court of Requests, Charles I, B. 751.)

[This suit shews some of the vicissitudes experienced by Roger Williams's brother, Sidrach Williams, in carrying on his business as a merchant trading in Italy and Turkey. For abstracts of two Chancery cases, in 1626 and 1628, in which Sidrach Williams was complainant, which related to his business affairs, see REGISTER, vol. 75, pp. 234–235, and for a similar case in the Court of Requests, about 1636, in which also Williams was the complainant, see REGISTER, vol. 78, pp. 274–275.]

### Greenhill *v.* Collyns *et ux.*

18 November, 11 Charles I [18 November 1635].    The complaint of

*Preserved in the Public Record Office, London.

NICHOLAS GREENHILL of Shirley Hundred in Virginia against Walter Collyns and wife Elizabeth relates to the will of complainant's brother, Peter Greenhill of Cosham in Wymering, Hants, which was proved by his widow, Elizabeth, who married said Collins of Denmead in Hambledon, co. Somerset [*sic*], yeoman. (Court of Requests, Charles I, B. 23.)

### March *v.* Littlefield *et al.*

The complaint of STEPHEN MARCH of Newport, Isle of Wight [Hants], Esq., against Edmund Littlefield of Tichfield [Titchfield, Hants], clothier, Anne, his wife, and Nicholas Littlefield, his brother, sworn to on 12 February, 11 Charles I [12 February 1635/6], relates to eleven "Todds of Flees" of the value of 30s. per "Todd,"* and states that in February 1634 Edmund Littlefield came to complainant's house in Newport and agreed to buy the wool for £16. He carried the same away, and has since used it to his great profit. But, nevertheless, he has failed to make payment for the same, and has absented himself, conspiring with his wife Ann and his brother Nicholas to defraud your orator of his money, alleging that one Reinold Adams of Newport, deceased, owed him a large sum of money, whereby he is unable to settle accounts with your orator.

The answer of NICHOLAS LITTLEFIELD, one of the defendants, 17 January 1636 [? 1636/7], stated that his brother had been in trade many years as clothier, buying wool in various places, and that this defendant knew not whence the wool came, whether from complainant or others; that he bought wool of his brother and did not inquire as to the source; that he knows nothing beyond this, and prays for damages unjustly incurred in this suit. (Court of Requests, Charles I, Bundle 77, Part 4.)

[This suit was found by the late Col. Charles Edward Banks, and, while it adds nothing to our genealogical knowledge of the Littlefield family, it is interesting as supplementing the story of the life of Edmund[1] Littlefield prior to his emigration to New England. For Edmund[1] Littlefield of Exeter, N. H., and Wells, Maine, his parentage, his English home and relatives, and his children, see REGISTER, vol. 67, pp. 346–348 (October 1913).]

### Loder *v.* Way

20 May, 12 Charles I [20 May 1636]. The complaint of GILBERT LODER of Dorchester [co. Dorset], gentleman, shews that complainant two years since had cattle worth £40 then depasturing in New England, which were in the possession of Nicholas Upsall, who is living in New England and was a kinsman of George Way of Dorchester [co. Dorset], glover. Upshall proposed to buy the cattle from complainant, and, Way being on his way to New England, complainant authorized him to sell them. Four months later Way returned from New England, but Upshall was not able to buy the cattle, which were worth more than £40.

The answer of GEORGE WAY, defendant, states that complainant has only a one-twelfth share in the cattle. Upsall is still in New England, and defendant is willing to purchase the cattle, as he has servants shortly going thither. (Court of Requests, Charles I, B. 88.)

[Nicholas Upshall or Upsall, innkeeper, was of Dorchester, Mass., in 1630, and later of Boston, where he and his wife were admitted to the church in 1644. He was fined and imprisoned for opposing the harsh treatment of the Quakers by the Massachusetts authorities. Cf. Savage's "Genealogical Dictionary" and Pope's "Pioneers of Massachusetts."

George Way was a merchant of Dorchester, co. Dorset, and had grants of lands in New England, although he did not take up his residence there. In his will, 26 September 1641 (P.C.C., Evelyn, 155), he mentioned his dwelling house

---

*A tod was an old weight for wool, usually 28 pounds.

on the east side of North Street, Dorchester, houses in Bridport [co. Dorset], the moiety of a plantation in Pejepscot in New England, a lot in Dorchester in New England, and other lands in New England, which he left to his son Eleazer. He bequeathed also to his brother-in-law, Thomas Purchase, who was then apparently in New England. He appointed as trustees Mr. William Derbie, Mr. Richard Savage, and Mr. Thomas Church of Dorchester, and Mr. Walter Baily of Bridport. He mentioned his daughters Sarah, Mary, Elizabeth, and Martha, and moneys due from Thomas Forde in New England and from Henry Cogan.]

# GENEALOGICAL RESEARCH IN ENGLAND

Communicated by the Committee on English and Foreign Research

## ENGLISH CONNECTIONS OF DEA. EDWARD COLLINS OF CAMBRIDGE, MASS.

Contributed by WINIFRED LOVERING HOLMAN, S.B., of Watertown, Mass.

IT is the purpose of the contributor of this article to present briefly the facts that have already been published in regard to Dea. Edward[1] Collins of Cambridge, Mass., and his English connections, to add to them certain hitherto unpublished entries found in the registers of the parish of Bramford, co. Suffolk, England, the earliest home thus far discovered of this Collins family, and then to sum up, in the usual genealogical form, what has been brought to light about the English ancestry and connections of Deacon Collins and about his own family and one or two generations of his descendants.

In the first volume of his "Genealogical Dictionary," published in 1860, Savage placed Edward[1] Collins at Cambridge, Mass., in 1638, and stated that he was admitted a freeman 13 May 1640, that he was a deacon in the Cambridge church, that from 1654 to 1670, inclusive, except the year 1661, he was a representative in the General Court, and that he lived for many years on the plantation of Governor Cradock at Medford, Mass., finally buying it and selling 1600 acres of it to Richard Russell and other parts of it to other purchasers. He died, wrote Savage, at Charlestown, Mass., 9 Apr. 1689, aged about 86.

From the records of the First Church in Cambridge Savage found also that Edward[1] Collins brought over from England a wife, Martha ———, and four children, namely, Daniel (about 9 years old when his parents united with the Cambridge church), John, Samuel, and Sibyl; and the town records of Cambridge show that three other children were born in Cambridge, namely, Martha, in September 1639, Nathanael, 7 Mar. 1642 [1642/3], and Abigail, 20 Sept. 1644. Savage also added a son Edward, born in 1646, and stated that the children born in New England were all baptized in Cambridge. A brief history of the children of Dea. Edward[1] Collins will be given in the genealogical summary at the end of this article.

Savage also stated that John Collins of Boston, Mass., shoemaker, who was a member of the Ancient and Honorable Artillery Company in 1644, who had a wife Susanna and children John, Susanna, Thomas, and Elizabeth, and who died 29 Mar. 1670, was a brother of Dea. Edward Collins; but, in the opinion of the writer of this article, there is no proof that Dea. Edward of Cambridge and this John of Boston were brothers, there is no positive mention of *this* John in the will of Daniel Collins of London, dated 20 Nov. 1639, who is now known to have been a brother of Dea. Edward Collins (*vide infra*), and this John Collins of Boston, shoemaker, seems to have belonged to a very different social class from that of Edward Collins of Cambridge and his kin. It may be added here that Pope, in his "Pioneers of Massachusetts," published in 1900, in his account of John of Boston, makes no reference to this alleged relationship to Edward of Cambridge.

It appears, therefore, that in 1860, when the first volume of Savage's "Genealogical Dictionary" was published, nothing was known about the English ancestry, connections, and home of Dea. Edward Collins of Cambridge, although it was claimed, probably erroneously, that John Collins of Boston, shoemaker and member of the Ancient and Honorable Artillery Company, was his brother. The age of Edward Collins at death, about 86 years, indicated that he was born about 1603, and the knowledge of the approximate date of his birth might be helpful in searching English parish registers for the date of his baptism. But for twenty years more no further clue relating to his English origin and connections was found.

Then, to the *Essex Institute Historical Collections* for January 1880 (vol. 17, pages 1 and following), the late James A. Emmerton and the late Henry FitzGilbert Waters of Salem, Mass., communicated a lengthy article entitled "Gleanings from English Records about New England Families," included in which were very many brief abstracts of wills preserved chiefly in the Principal Probate Registry, in Somerset House, London, abstracts which had been made hastily by Messrs. Emmerton and Waters, while on a visit in London during the summer and fall of 1879. Among these abstracts was that of the will of one Daniel Collins (*op. cit.,* pages 20–21), the substance of which is as follows:*

The Will of Daniel Collins [of London], dated 20 November 1639 and signed 9 June 1643. To be buried in the parish of St. Peter the Poor, Broad Street [London], where my wife lies buried. The testator mentions the parish of Bramford [co. Suffolk]† where he was born and where his father lieth buried, Braintree, co. Essex, where his mother lieth buried, his sister Katherine Francknell, his nephew Samuel Collins, his brother Samuel Collins, vicar of Braintree, and his [the vicar's] five children, and his [the testator's] niece Sibill Linch. He bequeaths to Nathaniel Beadle the lease of the Dolphin, and mentions his [the testator's] nephew John Beadle and the latter's children, and his [the testator's] cousin Michael Powell, with the latter's wife and daughter Abigaell. He bequeaths to cousin Bowles, his wife [i. e., to the wife of cousin Bowles], and mentions Samuel Thompson, son of his [the testator's] sister Tomson. He bequeaths also *to Edward Collins, now in New England, to his daughter Sible, and to his other three sons [sic,? children], Daniel, John, and Samuel,*‡ and mentions the wife of John Russell and her children, the wife of cousin Markham, John Collins, Samuel Pordage, his [the testator's] partner John Cory, William Cory, John Bu[x]ton, Clement Palgrave, his [the testator's] five maidservants (namely, Katherine Scott, Benjaby Wilborne, Lidia, Mary, and Jane), sister Chiball, brother and sister Crabtree, sister Pordage, and brother Francknell, with the latter's

*The abstract here given is based on, but is not a verbatim copy of, the abstract published in the *Essex Institute Historical Collections.*

†The reading *Bramford* was questioned, as doubtful, in the abstract of the will published in the *Essex Institute Historical Collections*; but, as appears farther on in this article, it was the correct reading.

‡In the abstract published in the *Essex Institute Historical Collections* these words are not italicized. The italics have been substituted by the Editors of the REGISTER.

son Thomas and daughter Elizabeth. The testator appoints his sister Katherine Francknell and his nephew Samuel Collins executors, and makes ——— [unintelligible] and Samuel Pordage overseers. Proved 30 October 1643. (Commissary Court of London, at Somerset House, Twisse, 80.)

Appended to the abstract of the will of Daniel Collins, as published in the *Essex Institute Historical Collections,* are annotations by Messrs. Emmerton and Waters, identifying or suggesting possible identifications for several of the persons mentioned in the will. It is enough, however, to note here that the Edward Collins of New England, with daughter Sible and sons Daniel, John, and Samuel, was undoubtedly Dea. Edward Collins of Cambridge, but there is nothing in the abstract of the will to show why he and his children were beneficiaries in this will or what relationship, if any, existed between Dea. Edward Collins and the testator. The statements, however, that the testator was born in Bramford, co. Suffolk, that his father was buried there, and that the testator's brother, Samuel Collins, was vicar of Braintree, not to speak of the other persons named in the will, furnished clues which, if followed up, would probably throw light on the English connections of Edward Collins of Cambridge.

In January 1884 the statement was made in print that Daniel Collins of London, the testator whose will has been given in abstract above, was a brother of Edward[1] Collins of Cambridge. In July 1883 Mr. Waters, who, in association with Mr. Emmerton, had communicated to the *Essex Institute Historical Collections* in 1880 the abstract of the will of Daniel Collins of London, contributed to the REGISTER (vol. 37, pages 233–240) the first of his famous articles entitled "Genealogical Gleanings in England," in which for many years he made known the results of his researches in England on the possible origin of American families, chiefly in the form of abstracts of wills recorded in the Prerogative Court of Canterbury, the records of which are preserved in the Principal Registry of Probate, at Somerset House, London. In January 1884 his "Gleanings" included an abstract of the will of Thomas Bell, Sr., of London, merchant, dated 29 Jan. 1671 [1671/2] and proved 3 May 1672, in which the testator, sometime a member of Rev. John Eliot's church in Roxbury, Mass., who had returned to England in 1654, left £100 "to be distributed among poor necessitous men late ministers of the Gospel, of which number I will that Mʳ Knowles and Mʳ John Coling, both late of New England be accounted," and bequeathed also legacies to Mʳ John Colling and others. A note by the Editor of the REGISTER, the late John Ward Dean, attached to the abstract of Thomas Bell's will, stated that Mʳ John Colling was Rev. John Collins, "a son of Edward Collins, of Cambridge, N. E., who with sons Daniel, John and Samuel and daughter Sible, are [sic] mentioned in 1639, in the will of his brother Daniel Collins, of London." Thus in January 1884 Mr. Dean made the positive statement that Daniel Collins of London, the testator whose will had been published in abstract by Messrs, Emmerton and Waters in the *Essex Institute*

*Historical Collections* for January 1880, was a brother of Dea. Edward Collins of Cambridge.

That Mr. Dean's statement about the relationship of Daniel Collins of London to Dea. Edward Collins of Cambridge in New England was *substantially* correct has now been proved by the following entries, hitherto unpublished, which were found in the registers of the parish of Bramford, co. Suffolk, England, by the vicar of that parish, who, at the request of the writer of this article, examined these registers and sent to the writer in June 1933 a certified copy of the entries which seemed to him of importance in this quest.

FROM THE REGISTERS OF THE PARISH OF BRAMFORD, CO. SUFFOLK*

### Baptisms

1577  Madglen Trehone[?] 28 April.
1580  Samuell, sonne of Jo. Collinses, 19 December.
1583  Daniell, sonn of John Collins, 12 May.
1587  William, sonne of Samuell Bedle, 22 October.
1591  Abigail, daughter of John Collins, 17 October.
1595  John, sonne of Samuel Bedle, 28 September.
1596  Samuell, sonne of Samuel Bedell, 30 January [1596/7].
1600  Mandlene, da. of John Collins, 27 March.
1603  Edward, sonne of John & Mandelen Collins, 25 March.
1604  Phebe, da. of John & Mandlene Collins, 3 March [1604/5].

### Marriages

1586  Samuel Bedle and Abigail Collins 16 August.
1589  Abraham White and Elizabeth Collins — September.
1590  John Collins and ——— Dagger [or Wagger] 29 November.
1599  John Collins and Mandlene Trelhern[?] 29 May.
1614  William Cozzins and Mandelene Collins 6 August.

### Burials

1594  John Collins 14 September.
1605  Edward Collins, servant to Erasmous Nichols, 27 January [1605/6].

From entries found in the registers of the parish of Bramford, co. Suffolk, and given in substance above, from two short pedigrees (one of Bedle and the other of Collins) published in "The Visitation of London, 1633–4," vol. 1, pages 61, 181 (*Publications of the Harleian Society,* vol. 15, 1880), and communicated by Mr. Waters to the REGISTER of January 1884, from the abstract of the will of Daniel Collins of London, published in 1880 (*vide supra*), and from New England records and other statements relating to this Collins family, the following brief genealogy of the earliest known generations of the family has been compiled.

1.  JOHN COLLINS, who was buried at Bramford, co. Suffolk, 14 Sept. 1594, whose wife's name is unknown, was *probably* the father of the following
        Children:
    2. i.    JOHN.

*Adapted from a certified copy sent to the writer by the vicar of Bramford in June 1933.

513

ii.   ABIGAIL, m. at Bramford, 16 Aug. 1586, SAMUEL BEDLE (or BE-
      DELL).
         Children (surname *Bedle* or *Bedell*), bapt. at Bramford:*
         1.  *William,* bapt. 22 Oct. 1587.
         2.  *John,* bapt. 28 Sept. 1595.
         3.  *Samuel,* bapt. 30 Jan. 1596/7.
iii.  ELIZABETH, m. at Bramford, in September 1589, ABRAHAM WHITE

2.  JOHN COLLINS (? *John*), of Bramford, co. Suffolk, for a while
perhaps, of Braintree, co. Essex, and also of London, salter,
born probably about 1550, died before 20 Nov. 1639, the date
of the will of his son Daniel, and perhaps before 6 Aug. 1614,
and was buried at Bramford.  He married first ABIGAIL ROSE,
who died before 29 Nov. 1590 and was buried at Braintree,
co. Essex, daughter of Thomas Rose of Exmouth [? Ax-
mouth], co. Devon;† secondly, at Bramford, 29 Nov. 1590,
——— DAGGER [or WAGGER], who died before 29 May 1599;
and thirdly, at Bramford, 29 May 1599, MAGDALEN TREL-
HERN [?], who was baptized at Bramford 28 Apr. 1577, may
have survived her husband, and may have been the "Mandelene" Collins who married at Bramford, 6 Aug. 1614, William
Cozzins.‡
      Children by first wife:
i.    KATHERINE, probably a daughter of John Collins, salter, by his first
      wife,§ living 20 Nov. 1639, when, as his sister, Katherine Franck-
      nell, Daniel Collins named her in his will and appointed her and
      his nephew, Samuel Collins, executors; m., probably many years
      before 1639, ——— FRANCKNELL (called "brother Francknell"
      in the will of Daniel Collins).
         Children (surname *Francknell*), named as living in Daniel
      Collins's will:
         1.  *Thomas.*              2.  *Elizabeth.*
ii.   REV. SAMUEL, bapt. at Bramford 19 Dec. 1580; d. 2 May 1667;
      m. ———.
         He was matriculated sizar from Trinity College, University
      of Cambridge, about 1595, was admitted to the degree of Bach-
      elor of Arts in 1599/1600 and to that of Master of Arts in
      1603, and was ordained a deacon at Norwich, co. Norfolk, 29
      Sept. 1601 [*sic,* ? 1605 or 1606], aged 25.  He was curate of
      Ash–Bocking, co. Suffolk, vicar of Braintree, co. Essex, 1611–
      1661, and apparently surrendered his living in the last-named
      year.  (Cf. Alumni Cantabrigienses, part 1, vol. 1, p. 374.)
         Mark Mott of Braintree, Essex, gentleman, in his will dated

*It is evident that this Bedle or Bedell family, recorded at Bramford, in which William
was the eldest son, John the second son, and Samuel the third son, is not the family of
which two generations were entered by Nathaniel Bedle in the "Visitation of London" in
1633.
   †According to the brief Collins pedigree published in the "Visitation of London in 1633–4"
(vol. 1, p. 181) and signed by Daniel Collins, the testator of 1639, Abigall Rose, his mother,
was the third wife of John Collins of London, salter, the father of Daniel Collins; but a
study of the entries found in the parish registers of Bramford shows that she must have
been his first wife, or, at any rate, a wife who preceded the wife whom he married in 1590
and the wife whom he married in 1599.
   ‡One William Cozzins was of Boston, Mass., in 1649.  There are several different spellings of the name.  Cf. Savage, "Genealogical Dictionary."
   §Katherine, even if she was born as early as 1575, would not be too old to be named as
an executor of her brother's will in 1639.  If she was not an elder sister of Rev. Samuel
and Daniel Collins, there seems to be no place for her in the family, unless she were a
younger half sister of the two brothers.  It seems more likely that Daniel Collins would
appoint an own sister rather than a half sister as one of the executors of his will.

1 Mar. 1636 and proved 7 May 1638, mentioned Rev. Samuel
Collins as "My cousin Collyns, minister of Braintree," and Mark
Mott's son, Rev. Mark Mott, D.D., rector of Rayne Parva,
Essex, in his will dated 18 Dec. 1630 and proved 1 Apr. 1631,
called the vicar of Braintree his "cousin." (REGISTER, vol. 50,
p. 254, and vol. 46, p. 321, in wills communicated by Mr.
Waters.) Rev. Samuel Collins, vicar of Braintree, was named
by his brother, Daniel Collins, in his will of 20 Nov. 1639, and
Daniel Collins also mentioned in his will his (Daniel's) nephew,
Samuel Collins, and the vicar's five children.

    Children:
1. *Dr. Samuel,* eldest son, b. in 1619; d. in Paris, while on a
journey in France, 26 Oct. 1670, aged 50.

    He was admitted a pensioner at Corpus Christi College,
Cambridge, in 1635, and was matriculated at Michaelmas,
1637. He took no degree at Cambridge, but received the
degree of Doctor of Medicine from the University of
Padua in 1651. He served about nine years (1660–1669)
at Moscow as principal physician of the Czar Alexis of
Russia, father of Peter the Great. He was the author of
"The Present State of Russia," published in London in
1671, after the author's death, and issued in a French
translation in 1679. There is a mural inscription to him
at Braintree in Essex, outside the church, and his will is
in the Prerogative Court of Canterbury, Somerset House,
London. (Cf. Dictionary of National Biography and
Alumni Cantabrigienses, *loco citato.*)

    Other children, five children of the vicar of Braintree, prob-
ably in addition to Dr. Samuel Collins, being mentioned
in the will of their uncle, Daniel Collins.

iii.  DANIEL, of Broad Street, London, merchant, the testator of 20
Nov. 1639, bapt. at Bramford 12 May 1583; d *s. p.* between 9
June 1643, when he signed his will, and 30 Oct. 1643, when his
will was proved; m. SIBILL FRANKLYN, who d. before her husband, daughter of Thomas Franklyn of London, goldsmith. (Cf.
the pedigree which Daniel Collins entered in the "Visitation of
London" in 1633, vol. 1, p. 181, and also the abstract of his will,
*supra,* p. 74.) Some of the numerous relatives whom he men- *
tioned in his will can be identified; but it is difficult to determine
whether some of the "sisters" and "brothers" named were sis-
ters-in-law or brothers-in-law.

Child by second wife:

iv.  ABIGAIL, bapt. at Bramford 17 Oct. 1591; m. (1), being described
in the Visitation of London, 1633, as "da. of . . . . Collins of
Br. . . in Essex," SAMUEL BEDLE of Woluerston [Woolverstone],
co. Suffolk; probably m. (2) REV. WILLIAM THOMPSON, curate
of the church at Winwick in Lancashire, who emigrated with
his wife Abigail and family to New England about 1637 and
settled finally at Braintree, Mass. Daniel Collins in his will
mentioned Samuel Thompson, son of his [the testator's] sister
Tomson. Abigail, first wife of Rev. William Thompson of
Braintree, Mass., d. in New England 1 Jan. 1642/3, and he m.
(2) Ann, widow of Simon Crosby of Cambridge, Mass. (For
Rev. William Thompson and his family see Savage's Genealogical Dictionary, vol. 4, p. 289, Pope's Pioneers of Massachusetts, p. 457, and other New England works.)

    Children of Abigail Collins by her first husband (surname
*Bedle*):
1. *John ("eldest sonne").*          2. *Sam.*
3. *Nathaniel* ("3 sonne of London merch^t a° 1633"), m. at
    Wendover, co. Bucks, 1 Oct. 1629, Mary Rowell, daughter

*Page 511, this volume.

515

of Richard Rowell of Wendover. As "Nath'll Bedle" he
entered the brief Bedle pedigree, with coat or arms and
crest, in the "Visitation of London, 1633–4" (*Publications
of the Harleian Society*, vol. 15, p. 61), *q. v.*, and see also,
for date and place of marriage, Phillimore's "Buckinghamshire Parish Registers, Marriages," vol. 2, p. 5.

4. *Dorothy* [first wife of John Bowles of Roxbury, Mass.].
5. *Abigail* [wife of Michael Powell of Dedham and Boston,
Mass.].

Children by third wife:

   v.   MANDLENE [? MAGDALEN], bapt. at Bramford 27 Mar. 1600.
3. vi.  EDWARD, bapt. at Bramford 25 Mar. 1603.
  vii.  PHEBE, bapt. at Bramford 3 Mar. 1604/5; perhaps the Phoebe
      Collins who is recorded at Cambridge, Mass., as dying 5 Jan.
      1653 [1653/4].

---

# GENEALOGICAL RESEARCH IN ENGLAND

Communicated by the Committee on English and Foreign Research

## ENGLISH CONNECTIONS OF DEA. EDWARD COLLINS
## OF CAMBRIDGE, MASS.

Contributed by WINIFRED LOVERING HOLMAN, S.B., of Watertown, Mass.

3.  DEA. EDWARD[1] COLLINS (*John, ? John*), of Cambridge and
Charlestown, Mass., merchant, gentleman, baptized at Bramford, co. Suffolk, England, 25 Mar. 1603, died at Charlestown
9 Apr. 1689, aged 86 years. (He deposed in Middlesex
County, Mass., in 1659, aged 56, and again on 29 Apr. 1660,
aged about 57 years.) He married, probably in England about
1628, MARTHA ———, who was born about 1609 (she deposed
in 1693 in the Superior Court of Judicature in Massachusetts,
File 3925, aged 84), came with her husband and several children to New England, and died, probably at Charlestown,
either 22 Mar. 1699/1700 or a day or two earlier, "being very
aged."

The relations or narratives of persons joining the Cambridge
church give information about the life of Edward Collins in
England, stating that he was brought up by godly parents, that
after his father's death he was placed in a gentleman's house,
that afterwards he spent a year with old Mr. Rogers of
Wethersfield [co. Essex, England], that he was apprenticed in
a worthy family, and that later he went to Dedham [co. Essex],
England. (Cf. Pope, Pioneers of Massachusetts, p. 112, where
also may be found statements from the "relation" of his wife
and other statements about him.)

According to Pope, *op. cit.,* Edward Collins was a proprietor
of Cambridge, Mass., in 1636, but he probably did not arrive
in New England until a year or two later. He was a deacon

of the First Church in Cambridge in 1638, and was admitted a freeman 13 May 1640. He was a town officer, and, as already stated (*supra*, p. 73), he was a representative in the General Court of the Colony of the Massachusetts Bay from 1654 to 1670, inclusive, except the year 1661, and he lived for many years on the plantation of Governor Cradock at Medford, Mass. (where Pope, *op. cit.*, places him in 1656), finally buying this plantation and selling 1600 acres of it to Richard Russell and other parts of it to Dea. Thomas Willis of Medford and others. Although he lived many years on his estate in Medford, he retained his citizenship in Cambridge until his formal admission to Charlestown, 15 Jan. 1671 [? 1671/2]. (*Vide supra*, pp. 73–74, for reasons for doubting the statement of Savage that John Collins of Boston, Mass., shoemaker, was a brother of Dea. Edward Collins of Cambridge. An additional reason for doubting this relationship is found in the fact that no baptism of a John Collins is recorded among the entries in the Bramford registers given in the preceding instalment of this article, *supra*, p. 76.)**

Children :*

i.    DANIEL,[2] b. in England about 1629, as he was about 9 years old when his parents joined the Cambridge church; came with his parents to New England. He became a merchant, and was living at Königsberg in Prussia in 1658.

ii.   REV. JOHN, A.B. (Harvard, 1649), A.M. (*ib*)., b. in England about 1633; brought by his parents to New England; d. in London 3 Dec. 1687; m. ———.
He was a fellow and tutor at Harvard College, 1651–1653, went to England in the time of the Protectorate, and was a fellow of Pembroke College, Cambridge, and a minister in Edinburgh. He was chaplain to General Monk, before the latter marched out of Scotland into England and restored Charles II to the throne. He became pastor of a large Independent congregation at Pinner's Hall, London. No pastor, says Cotton Mather in the "Magnalia," ever called forth from the living church more veneration in life or deeper grief for his death.
His son, *Rev. John*,[3] b. in London about 1673, d. suddenly 19 Mar. 1714, when he was a little more than 40 years of age. He succeeded Rev. Nathaniel Mather as minister in Lime Street, London, and in 1702 took part in the ordination, in Mark Lane, of the celebrated Dr. Isaac Watts.

iii.   ENSIGN SAMUEL, of Cambridge and of Middletown, Conn., b. in

*Considerable information about Dea. Edward Collins and some of his descendants may be found in an article published in the REGISTER in July 1907 (vol. 61, pp. 281–288) and entitled "Edward and John Collins and Their Descendants," which was compiled by Hon. Ralph D. Smyth and communicated to the REGISTER by his grandson, Dr. Bernard Christian Steiner, librarian of the Pratt Free Library in Baltimore, Md. Hon. Ralph Dunning Smyth, B.A. (Yale, 1827), of Guilford, Conn., was born in 1804, was elected a corresponding member of the New England Historic Genealogical Society 4 Feb. 1846, and died 11 Sept. 1874. His article, therefore, was compiled not later than 1874, and, when he wrote it, his statement, "The place from which they [the Collinses] emigrated in England has not been ascertained," was correct. Mr. Smyth's article follows Savage in stating (erroneously, in the opinion of the present writer) that John Collins of Boston, shoemaker, a member of the Ancient and Honorable Artillery Company in 1644, was a brother of Dea. Edward Collins of Cambridge, and he gives several pages to an account of John Collins of Boston and his descendants. To the REGISTER of July 1908 (vol. 62, pp. 304–305) Frank Farnsworth Starr of Middletown, Conn., contributed several additions and corrections to Mr. Smyth's article, all of which, however, refer to descendants of Dea. Edward Collins only.

**Page 513, this volume.

517

England about 1635; brought by his parents to New England; d. at Middletown 10 Jan. 1695/6, aged 60; m. MARY MARVIN, bapt. at Great Bentley, co. Essex, Eng., 23 Oct. 1636, d. at Middletown 5 Mar. 1713/14, daughter of Reynold and Mary Marvin, later of Lyme (then a part of Saybrook), Conn. See REGISTER, vol. 62, p. 304 (July 1908). Mary, wife of Samuel Collins, was admitted to full communion with the church at Cambridge 31 May 1664.

Samuel Collins went to Scotland in 1658, when his brother John was at Edinburgh, but soon returned to New England. He probably resided in Cambridge until 1664, when he moved to Saybrook and soon afterwards to Middletown. He was a representative in 1672.

Children:

1. *Edward*,[3] b. at Cambridge 18 June 1664; bapt. there in same month.
2. *Martha*, b. at Middletown 3 Mar. 1666; m. 8 Jan. 1689/90 William Harris.
3. *Samuel*, b. 21 Oct. 1668; living unm. 25 Dec. 1690, when his father conveyed to him land in Middletown; deceased by 19 Jan. 1716/17, when Susannah, his only child, and her husband, conveyed land in Middletown; m. about 1694 ——— (perhaps the Susannah ——— who m. 18 Mar. 1702/3 John Harris of Middletown and d. 10 Feb. 1747/8, aged 80). Only child: Susannah, b. about 1694; m. 1 Dec. 1714 William Roberts of Middletown, who was living 19 Jan. 1716/17; bur., as the widow of William Roberts, 12 Nov. 1781, aged 87. William and Susannah (Collins) Roberts had children. (See REGISTER, vol. 62, p. 305.)
4. *Sibilla*, b. 24 Feb. and bapt. 27 Feb. 1669/70; m. (1) Isaac Rice of Sudbury, Mass.; m. (2) George Reed of Woburn, Mass.
5. *Mary*, b. 16 June 1672; m. Richard Moore of Needham and Oxford, Mass.
6. *Abigail*, b. 2 June 1673; m. 9 July 1702 William Ward of Middletown.
7. *Daniel*, b. 5 Oct. 1675; d. 6 June 1689.

iv.   SIBYL, b. in England about 1638; brought by her parents to New England; d. at Hartford, Conn., in June (4 June or earlier) 1672; m. at Cambridge, about 1654, REV. JOHN WHITING, A. B. (Harvard, 1653), A. M. (*ib.*, 1655), minister at Salem, Mass., and at Hartford, Conn., b. about 1635, d. at Hartford 8 Sept. 1689, son of Mr. William Whiting. Rev. John Whiting m. (2) Phebe ———, who survived him and m. Rev. John Russell of Hadley, Mass., A. B. (Harvard, 1645), A. M. (*ib.*), b. about 1627, d. 10 Dec. 1692, aged 65. (Cf. REGISTER, vol. 62, p. 304.)

v.    MARTHA, b. at Cambridge, Mass., in September 1639; d., probably at Portsmouth, N. H., by August 1674; m. about 1659 REV. JOSHUA MOODEY, A. B. (Harvard, 1653), A. M. (*ib.*, 1656), fellow and tutor at Harvard, 1656–1658, minister at Portsmouth, N. H., who d. in Boston, while on a visit there, 4 July 1697. He m. (2) Anna Jacobs, widow, who survived him.

Rev. Joshua Moodey was imprisoned by Cranfield, and later lived for a while in Boston, and during this period he declined the presidency of Harvard College. He returned to Portsmouth in 1692.

vi.   REV. NATHANIEL, A. B. (Harvard, 1660), A. M. (*ib.*, 1663), of Middletown, Conn., b. at Cambridge 7 Mar. 1642 [1642/3]; d. at Middletown 28 Dec. 1684; m. at Middletown, 3 Aug. 1664, MARY WHITING, b. about 1643, d. at Middletown 25 Oct. 1709, daughter of Mr. William Whiting.

He was invited to become minister at Middletown in 1663,

518

and was ordained and installed as pastor of the church there
on 4 Nov. 1668 [*sic*]. Lands were recorded to him at Middletown 24 Jan. 1664. Cotton Mather's "Magnalia" says of him:
"There were more wounds given [by his death] to the whole
colony in our New England, than the body of
Caesar did receive, when he fell wounded in the senate-house."
Children:

1. *Mary*,[3] b. 11 May 1666; d. 5 May 1722; m. in January 1684
   John Hamlin, b. 14 Dec. 1658, d. 2 Jan. 1732/3, son of
   Giles Hamlin of Middletown.
2. *John*, b. 31 Jan. 1667/8; m. 24 Dec. 1707 Mary Dixwell,
   daughter of Judge John Dixwell, the regicide. Seven
   children (see REGISTER, vol. 61, p. 283).
3. *Susannah*, b. 26 Nov. 1669; d. 24 Feb. 1721/2; m. 25 May
   1692 William Hamlin of Middletown, b. 3 Feb. 1667, d.
   22 May 1733.
4. *Sibbil*, b. 20 Aug. 1672; d. young.
5. *Martha*, b. 26 Dec. 1674; d. in June 1748; m. 15 Dec. 1705
   Thomas Hurlbut of Middletown, who d. in February 1752.
6. *Rev. Nathaniel*, A. B. (Harvard, 1697), minister of the
   church at Enfield, Conn., b. 13 June 1677; d. in 1756;
   m. in 1701 Alice Adams, who d. 19 Feb. 1755, daughter
   of Rev. William Adams of Dedham, Mass. Two children.
7. *Abigail*, b. 13 July 1681; d. 6 Feb. 1758; m. 27 Dec. 1706
   Samuel Wolcott of Wethersfield, Conn. (See REGISTER,
   vol. 62, p. 305.)
8. *Samuel*, b. 16 Apr. 1683; d. 23 Apr. 1683.

vii.   ABIGAIL, b. at Cambridge 20 Sept. 1644; d. at Charlestown 1 Feb.
1673/4, aged 29 years, 4 months, 14 days; m. (1) in 1663 JOHN
WILLETT, who d. at Charlestown 2 Feb. 1664, son of Capt.
Thomas Willett; m. (2) 12 May 1665, as his second wife, CAPT.
LAWRENCE HAMMOND, who d. 25 July 1699.

viii.  EDWARD, bapt. at Cambridge in June 1646; probably d. young.

## GLEANINGS FROM ENGLISH RECORDS

Contributed by G. ANDREWS MORIARTY, A.M., LL.B., F.S.A.,
of Bristol, R. I.

### MAKERNES : ADDITIONAL RECORDS*

#### FROM CHANCERY PROCEEDINGS†

Makernesse *v.* Mulsho

14 June 1613. The complaint of THOMAS MAKERNESSE of Thingdon
[Finedon‡], co. Northants, husbandman, shews that Thomas Makernesse,
late of Thingdon, yeoman, deceased, and Joahne, his wife, late father and
mother of your orator, were in their lifetime, that is, about October, 17
Elizabeth [1575], seised to themselves and to the heirs of Joahne, according to the custom of the manor of Thingdon, of and in a messuage,
4 crofts, 1 yardland called Lockeinges yardland, and ½ cottsettle of land
in Thingdon, being ancient customary and copyhold lands. They, Thomas
and Joahne, being so seised, Thomas Makernesse the father died, and the
estate passed to Joahne, as the survivor, and she possessed it as an estate
of inheritance, according to the custom of the manor. And being so

*The article on the Makernes family, to which the case in Chancery given in this article
supplies additional information, was published in the REGISTER, vol. 71, pp. 324–336 (October
1917).✱✱
   †Preserved in the Public Record Office, London.
   ‡Finedon, formerly also called Thingdon, is a parish situated about thirteen miles northeast from the town of Northampton.
✱✱See Volume I of this work, pp. 497-509.

seised, about fourteen years since, in her widowhood, the said Joahne, out of natural love for your orator, being her youngest son, out of full court, according to the custom of the manor, did surrender into the hands of the lord of the said manor, by the hand of George Makernesse and William Chapman, the said premises, to the use of Joahne for life and then to the use of your orator, her youngest son, and his heirs for ever; and, for better security, the said Joahne caused your orator to be bound in an obligation dated on or about 27 October, 40 Elizabeth [1598], in the sum of £200, that your orator would permit Joahne or her assigns to hold the said premises during her life. Afterwards, at the next court holden for the said manor, about one year after the making of the said surrender, George Makernesse and William Chapman did not, according to the custom of the manor, present the said surrender, albeit your orator in full court did will them to present the same, but entered as tenants, contrary to the custom of the manor, although the said Joahne and your orator did in open court entreat Thomas Mulshoe, Esq., the then lord of the manor, by his steward to admit them, the said Joahne and your orator, as tenants to the said estates, and offered such fine unto the said lord of the manor as should be due, but the lord of the manor refused to do that and George Makernesse and William Chapman refused to surrender the premises. About two years after the making of the said surrender Joahne died at Thingdon, in possession of the said copyhold. But now, although your orator, in the lifetime of the said Thomas Mulshoe, Esq., and after his decease in the lifetime of Robert Mulshoe, Esq., now deceased, brother and heir of the said Thomas, and lord also of the said manor, and now likewise also in the time of William Mulshoe, Esq., son and heir of the said Robert and now lord of the manor, hath often re- quested them to hold a court by his or their stewards and to cause the said George Makernesse and William Chapman to present the surrender of the said Joahne to her use for her life and then to the use of your orator and his heirs for ever, nevertheless William Mulshoe hath not only refused to do so but hath confederated with George Makernesse and William Chapman and one Richard Makernesse, son and heir of Richard Makernesse, deceased (who was the eldest son of the said Joahne), to suppress the said surrender by Joahne, and hath caused the said Richard Makernesse, grandchild of the said Joahne, to be found heir unto the said Joahne of and to the said premises; and at the last court holden for the said manor, about Michaelmas last past, William Mulshoe did admit the said Richard Makernesse to the said copyholds, contrary to equity. And now, by force thereof, the said Richard Makernesse doth go about to dispossess your orator of the said copyhold premises, who hath had pos- session of the same ever since the death of Joahne. And they have gotten into their hands the original copies which should prove that Joahne had full power and a sole and one absolute estate of inheritance in fee simple by copy of Court Roll, and they have gotten also the writings made by Joahne which should testify to the surrender made by her of the premises aforesaid, and they have gotten also the said bond for £200, intending to put the same into court against your orator. And your orator doth request a writ of subpoena, that George Makernesse and William Chap- man may be made to bring the said surrender into the court at Thingdon, whereby your orator may be admitted tenant thereunto (the said Richard being well advanced by your orator's father with a good estate of in- heritance within the same manor, and your orator having no other ad- vancement from his father and mother but only the said premises), and that William Mulshoe may be made to hold a court and to cause the grandchild of Joahne, Richard Makernesse, to deliver up copies of the writings.

Writ issued 22 June, 11 James I [1613].

The answers of WILLIAM MULSHO, ESQ., GEORGE MAKERNESSE, WILLIAM CHAPMAN and RICHARD MAKERNESSE, dated 2 October, 11 James I [1613].

WILLIAM MULSHO and RICHARD MAKERNESSE say that they are within the age of twenty-one years, to wit, William Mulsho under the age of twenty years and Richard Makernesse under the age of fifteen years, and therefore they ask whether they shall be compelled to answer unto the said bill; but they say that Thomas, deceased, and Joahne, his wife, were father and mother of the complainant, and that these defendants have seen a Court Roll, whereby Thomas Makernesse and Joahne did take of the lords of the manor the said copyhold lands about 17 Elizabeth [1574–75], to hold to themselves and to the heirs of Joahne, and Thomas the father shortly after died so seised, and Joahne did hold herself within by survivorship, and was sole seised of the premises of an estate of inheritance to her and her heirs, according to the custom of the manor.

And GEORGE MAKERNESSE and WILLIAM CHAPMAN say that Joahne did not surrender into the hands of the lords of the manor, by the hands of the said George Makernesse and William Chapman, the said premises to the use of Joahne for her life and then to the complainant for ever, but she did surrender the premises into the hands of the said lord of the manor, by the hand of William Chapman, to the use of the complainant and his heirs after the death of Joahne, and at the next court holden for the manor William Chapman did present the said surrender.* "Nevertheless the homage did not then find the same surrender," and before the next court Joahne died. After the decease of Joahne, who died about October, 43 Elizabeth [1601], at a court holden about that time, the homage of the same court, being then and there sworn, did find that since the last court before that court, holden for the said manor, Joahne died seised of such an estate, and that Richard Makernesse, her grandchild, son and heir of Richard Makernesse (son and heir of the said Joahne), was her next heir. Thomas Mulsho, Esq., now deceased, did not admit the complainant tenant to the premises, and, because he was not admitted tenant, complainant sued for the same admittance in the said court, but upon the oath of William Chapman and upon due examination of the right of the complainant and of this defendant, Richard Makernesse, he found homage against the complainant and his pretended title. At a court holden 15 October, 10 James I [1612], Richard Makernesse came and prayed to be admitted tenant to the premises, and they were granted to him by the then lord of the manor, and he then paid his fine for the same.

George Makernesse says that no surrender was made into his hands by the said Joahne.

William Chapman says that he hath presented the surrender made by Joahne unto him.

About 44 Elizabeth [1601–02] Richard Makernesse was found to be heir, as appears by copy of Court Roll, and about 15 October last past [15 October 1612] Robert Mulsho, lord of the manor, did at a court then holden for the said manor admit the said Richard.

*Apparently the surrender by Joahne had not been signed, and was therefore held to be invalid.

The replication of THOMAS MAKERNESSE.

He declares that all matters in the bill are true, and abides by his statements.

(Chancery Proceedings before 1714, Mitford 72/63, C. 8.)

[To the REGISTER of October 1917 (vol. 71, pp. 324–336) the present writer, *
under the heading "Genealogical Research in England," contributed abstracts
of a number of English wills and some entries from the parish registers of
Finedon, co. Northampton, with a pedigree based on them, relating to the
Makernes family of Finedon, to which belonged Ellen Makernes, wife of Roger
Sargent, mayor of Northampton, and mother of William Sargent, who emigrated to New England in 1638 and settled in that part of Charlestown, Mass.,
which was set off in 1649 as the town of Malden. The Chancery suit of which
records have been given in abstract above supplies additional information
about the Makernes family and makes it necessary to revise the pedigree
published in the REGISTER more than seventeen years ago.

Thomas Makernesse, the complainant in this suit, was a son of Thomas and
Joan Makernesse, the latter being the Joan Makernes of Thingdon, widow,
whose will, dated 17 Jan. 1600/1, was proved 12 May 1601. In it she named as
overseers her brother William Makernes and her cousin (i. e., nephew) George
Makernes. This William, the testator of 10 Mar. 1612/13, was the father of
George Makernes and of Ellen, wife of Roger Sargent, mayor of Northampton.
As Joan's husband, Thomas Makernes, is not named in the will of Thomas
Makernes, dated 28 May 1546, it is clear that Thomas (Joan's husband) and
his brother William must have been sons of William Makernes, brother of
Thomas (the testator of 28 May 1546), and that the William Makernesse who
married (1) 24 Apr. 1559 Agnes Sare (buried 29 Jan. 1564/5) and (2) 3 Feb.
1565/6 Marie Goodfellow was the son William whom Thomas Makernes (the
testator of 28 May 1546) mentioned in his will. Therefore the Makernes ancestral line of William Sargent of Malden, Mass., so far as it has been traced,
begins with John Makernes of Finedon, the testator of 14 Oct. 1515, and
descends through his son William (buried 8 May 1544), William (the testator
of 10 Mar. 1612/13), and Ellen (baptized 24 Nov. 1564), who married Roger
Sargent, to William Sargent of Malden.—G. ANDREWS MORIARTY.]

## ROBERT DANIEL, HUSBAND OF ELIZABETH MORSE
## CORRIGENDA

THE contributor of the article entitled "Robert Daniel, Husband of
Elizabeth Morse," which was published in the REGISTER of October 1934
(vol. 88, pages 383–386), as a part of the usual communication from the **
Committee on English and Foreign Research entitled "Genealogical Research in England," wishes to correct an error, to which her attention
has been called, in regard to the first wife of Joseph Daniel of Medfield
(No. v, page 385). His first wife, Mary Fairbanks, was *not* the daughter
of John and Sarah (———) Fairbanks, bapt. at Dedham 29 Dec. 1650,
as there stated, for their daughter Mary died in infancy; but she was
Mary Fairbanks, born at Dedham 10 Nov. 1647, daughter of Capt. George
and Mary (Adams) Fairbanks.

The Editors of the REGISTER also wish to express their regret for the
mistake by which the second wife of Robert Daniel (page 384) is referred to as "He," instead of "She," in the statement about her fourth
marriage.

*See the last footnote on p. 519.
**Pages 503-506, this volume.

# GENEALOGICAL RESEARCH IN ENGLAND

Communicated by the Committee on English and Foreign Research

## THE ENGLISH ANCESTRY OF JOSEPH PECK, OF HINGHAM, MASS., IN 1638

Compiled by S. Allyn Peck, B.A., of New York City, and contributed by Frederick Stanhope Peck, LL.D., of Barrington, R. I.

Among the passengers who arrived at Boston, in the Colony of the Massachusetts Bay in New England, on 10 Aug. 1638,* in the ship *Diligent,* from Ipswich, co. Suffolk, England, were Rev. Robert Peck, B.A., M.A., with his wife, two children, and two servants, and Joseph Peck, now known to have been a younger brother of Rev. Robert Peck, with his wife, three children, two men servants, and three maid servants. Both Rev. Robert Peck and his brother, Joseph Peck, took up their abode in Hingham, in the Bay Colony; and Daniel Cushing of that town, in "A list of the names of such persons as came out of the town of Hingham, and Towns adjacent in the County of Norfolk, in the Kingdom of England, into New England, and settled in Hingham in New England," a list extending from 1633 to 1639, inclusive,† begins his long list of arrivals in the year 1638 with the following entries:

"Mr. Robert Peck preacher of the Gospell in the Town of Hingham, in the County of Norfolk, in Old England, with his wife and 2 children and two servants came over the sea, and settled in this Town of Hingham, and he was teacher of the Church. 6 [persons]"

*The date of arrival is given in Savage's Genealogical Dictionary, vol. 3, p. 381.
†Printed in the Register, vol. 15, pp. 25–27 (January 1861).

523

"Mr. Joseph Peck and his wife with 3 sons and daughter, and 2 men servants and 3 maid servants came from Old Hingham and settled in New Hingham 10 [persons]"

Among additional entries by Daniel Cushing in regard to the settlers in Hingham of the year 1638 are the following:

"All the persons above named that came over in the year 1638, were 133 [they] came in one ship called the Diligent of Ipswich; the master was John Martin of said Ipswich. All before named that came before were 42 [sic, ? 49] persons."

"Mr. Robert Peck his wife his son Joseph and his maid went to England again in the year 1641."

Rev. Robert Peck, born at Beccles, co. Suffolk, England, about 1580, the third son of Robert and Helen Peck, was admitted at the University of Cambridge to his bachelor's degree in 1598–99, coming up from St. Catharine's College, and to his master's degree in 1603, coming up from Magdalene College. He was ordained a deacon and priest at Norwich, co. Norfolk, 24 Feb. 1604/5, aged 25, became curate of Oulton, co. Norfolk, and was rector of Hingham, co. Norfolk, 1605–1638, and again, after his return to England, from 1646 until his death, in 1656. He was a zealous Puritan, and through his influence a number of his parishioners became Nonconformists and emigrated to New England, where they took part in the founding of the town of Hingham, Mass., about 1635. During his many years of service as rector of Hingham in Norfolk his Puritan views brought down upon him the displeasure of the Bishops of Norwich, his ecclesiastical superiors, and at last, to escape from the jurisdiction of Bishop Wren, he was forced in 1638 to emigrate to New England and joined his former parishioners at Hingham, Mass. On 28 Nov. 1638 he was ordained a teacher in the church there, and was admitted a freeman 13 Mar. 1638/9; but on 27 Oct. 1641 he embarked with his wife and his son Joseph on his return voyage to England, where ultimately he was reinstated as rector of his former parish at Hingham, in Norfolk, Parliament having won in its long struggle with the King. More about him and his family will be given farther on in this article. His daughter Anne did not return with him to England, for she had been married at Hingham, Mass., in July 1639, as his second wife, to the famous Capt. John Mason, commander in the Pequot War and distinguished for his public services in Connecticut, to whom she bore several children.*

Rev. Robert Peck's younger brother, Joseph Peck, who also had lived at Hingham in England and had accompanied his brother to New England, was prominent in public affairs at Hingham, Mass., for about seven years, 1638–1645, and then moved to Rehoboth, which was incorporated as a town in 1645 and was in the jurisdiction of the Plymouth Colony until 1692, when that Colony was annexed to the Province of the Massachusetts Bay.

Joseph Peck was the immigrant ancestor of a numerous posterity,

*Cf. Venn's Alumni Cantabrigienses, part 1, vol. 3, p. 333, Savage's Genealogical Dictionary, vol. 3, pp. 167–168, 383, Pope's Pioneers of Massachusetts, pp. 304, 351, and History of Hingham (Mass.).

living for the most part in New England and especially in Massachusetts and Rhode Island; and the late Ira Ballou Peck of Woonsocket, R. I., who died in 1888,* a member and a benefactor of the New England Historic Genealogical Society, compiled a volume of 442 pages, which was printed in 1868 by Alfred Mudge & Son of Boston, and bears on its title page the ponderous legend, "A Genealogical History of the Descendants of Joseph Peck, who emigrated with his family to this country in 1638; and records of his father's and grandfather's families in England; with the pedigree extending back from son to father for twenty generations; with their coat of arms, and copies of wills." The book contains also an appendix, giving an account of various other Peck families in Massachusetts and Connecticut, and is embellished with portraits of distinguished persons.

The pedigree mentioned on the title page and given in tabular form in the "Genealogical History" may be found, according to the compiler of the volume, in the British Museum, "excepting the two last families, those of Robert and Joseph [the two brothers who came to New England in 1638], which are added to it." "The family of Robert," wrote Mr. Peck, "and the eldest children of Joseph, are from the parish records of Hingham, England. The three youngest children of Joseph are from the records at Hingham, Massachusetts, being born here."

This tabular pedigree, as printed in the "Genealogical History," begins with a John Peck of Belton in Yorkshire,† Esq., who married a daughter of one Melgrave and was the first of the twenty ancestors, in the direct paternal line, of Rev. Robert Peck and his brother Joseph. At what time this first John Peck of Belton lived is not stated, nor is any information given *in this pedigree* to show when any person of the first nineteen generations lived. Moreover, the pedigree for the first fourteen generations is little more than a skeleton pedigree. In the nine generations that follow the first generation only one son is named in each generation to carry on the line from the preceding generation (these Pecks are all of Belton, all are esquires, and each one is named either John, Thomas, or Robert), except that in the seventh generation, in which the line is continued through Thomas Peck of Belton, Esq., the name of his brother, John Peck, "2d son," who settled in Northamptonshire, is also given. In the eleventh generation the elder son, John Peck of Belton, Esq., appears to have inherited Belton, which descended to his daughter and

*See memoir (with portrait) of Ira Ballou Peck, by the late John Ward Dean, A.M., in the REGISTER, vol. 43, pp. 237–242 (July 1889).
†Although there are several parishes in England named Belton, among them a small parish near Beccles in Suffolk and a larger and more important parish in Lincolnshire, on the western border, near the place where Yorkshire and Nottinghamshire meet, no *parish* named Belton has been found in Yorkshire, and, since the elder son in the eleventh generation, John Peck of Belton, Esq., appears to have inherited Belton, it seems clear that Belton in Yorkshire, if it ever existed, was a family seat or a manor, and not a parish or a town. The earlier part of the pedigree, that purports to carry the ancestry of the Pecks of Wakefield back for many generations prior to their appearance at Wakefield, must be utterly unreliable, and was very likely forged by some one interested in connecting the Pecks of Beccles in Suffolk with the armigerous family of Pecks in Wakefield and in providing for the Suffolk Pecks an ancestral line going back at least to the beginning of the twelfth century, if not to the Conquest!

sole heir and came into the possession of her husband, John Ratcliffe of Todmorton, while Richard Peck, the second son in the eleventh generation and the ancestor of the Pecks of Wakefield, Yorkshire, was succeeded by his son, Richard Peck of Hesden,* Esq., who in turn was succeeded by his son, Thomas Peck of Hesden, Esq., and he was followed by his son, Richard Peck of Hesden, Esq., and of Wakefield in Yorkshire, of the fourteenth generation. Down to and including the fourteenth generation the Christian names of the wives of the Pecks are not given in the pedigree; only the surnames of the wives' fathers are there entered. With the establishment of the family at Wakefield, however, more information about each generation is given, more children of the head of a family are named, and the Christian names of the wives as well as of their fathers begin to appear. Many children of John Peck of Wakefield, Esq., of the eighteenth generation, are given, and included among his sons, *according to the pedigree,* is a Robert Peck of Beccles in Suffolk, to whom three sons and four daughters are assigned, the second of the three sons being Robert Peck, also of Beccles, of the twentieth generation, who was the father of Rev. Robert Peck and his brother, Joseph Peck of Hingham and Rehoboth in New England. According to the compiler of the "Genealogical History" a certificate from three officials of the Heralds' College accompanies the pedigree and the arms emblazoned on it, and reads as follows:

"20th Nov. 1620.

"Visum agnitum et in munimenta Collegii Heraldoru[m] relatum die et Anno suprascriptis.

"Testamur hoc.

"Henry St. George, Richmond.
"Henry Chitting, Chester.
"John Philpot, Rouge Dragon."†

The contents of Mr. Ira Ballou Peck's "Genealogical History" were analyzed and described in the REGISTER of January 1870 (vol. 24, pp. 96–97) by "W. H. W." (the initials of the late William Henry Whitmore, A.M.), who summed up his examination of the book by calling it "a very thorough and satisfactory genealogy, . . . evidently the result of extensive labor." The tabular pedigree, however, which purported to give twenty generations of ancestors, in the direct paternal line, of Rev. Robert Peck and his brother Joseph Peck, and represented their grandfather, Robert Peck of Beccles, co. Suffolk, as a son of John Peck of Wakefield, co. York, Esq., was regarded with some misgivings by Mr. Whitmore, who wrote:

"It is certainly to be regretted that the author did not give us more particulars about this pedigree. He should have specified where the original is, by whom compiled, and especially should have printed it as it is. We are inclined to believe in the authenticity of the descent, but Mr. Peck is evidently not familiar with such topics, and we should prefer to know more about the means of identifying this branch. Had this pedigree been

*This place also has not been found.
†These three officials of the Heralds' College, also known as the College of Arms, in London, are the Richmond and Chester Heralds and Rouge Dragon, one of the Pursuivants.

sanctioned by such experts as Mr. Somerby* or Col. Chester it would be sufficient, and if either of them did sanction it the author should have stated it. We hope Mr. Peck will favor the readers of this magazine with more particulars." '

To Mr. Whitmore's call for more particulars about the tabular pedigree Mr. Peck replied in the next issue of the REGISTER, that of April 1870 (vol. 24, pp. 187–188), and pointed out that the will of the second Robert Peck of Beccles, with its mention of the testator's son Robert at Cambridge and also of the testator's son Joseph (the later Rev. Robert Peck and his brother Joseph), proved that the pedigree was a pedigree of that branch of the Peck family to which these men belonged.† In regard to the correctness of the statements made in the pedigree Mr. Peck quoted the certificate of the officials of the Heralds' College which accompanied the pedigree (*vide supra*) and explained this certificate as meaning that they [the officials] "testify that they had seen or examined it [the pedigree] and knew it to be correct." "I considered this," added Mr. Peck, "sufficient authority for its correctness, and the best I could give, and supposed it would be satisfactory to others. No one who had examined the pedigree and certificate, with whom I had conversed or corresponded upon the subject, ever doubted its authenticity or correctness."

In reply to Mr. Whitmore's statement (*supra*), "Had this pedigree been sanctioned by such experts as Mr. Somerby or Col. Chester it would be sufficient," Mr. Peck wrote that his correspondence with Colonel Chester had been of recent date and related mainly to the "present" generations of Pecks in England, but that he had been in correspondence with Mr. Somerby for about twenty years, from 1850 or 1851 on. Mr. Somerby, he stated, had furnished him with much information upon such subjects as "heralds' visitations, pedigrees of the different branches of the name, coats of arms, crests, copies of wills, extracts from parish registers," etc., and in 1853, in sending to him (Mr. Peck) a copy of this pedigree, Mr. Somerby had written: "I assure you that few families in England, and none in America, have one [a pedigree] so complete and extensive." Mr. Somerby had also referred to the mention, in the will of the second Robert Peck of Beccles, of the testator's son Robert at Cambridge as proving positively "that the pedigree I sent you is correct." Mr. Somerby had also written: "I feel as well convinced that the document is correct as if I were living at the time and personally acquainted with the individuals mentioned therein." Satisfied with Mr. Somerby's sanction of the pedigree, Mr. Peck stated that it could be found among "Additional Manuscripts, No. 5524, fol. 152," in the library of the British Museum, and that it "was evidently prepared at much expense for Nicholas Peck, the elder brother of Robert and Joseph, who possessed, after

*At present few authorities on the English ancestry of the early settlers of New England would accept the statements of a pedigree merely because they had been "sanctioned" by the late Horatio Gates Somerby. Confirmation of such statements by thorough, independent research would be required.—EDITORS.

†This will is given in full by Mr. Peck in the Genealogical History, pp. 21–23, and an abstract of it will be printed in Section III (in the last instalment) of this article.

his mother's decease, the most of his father's and uncle's estates. Those who have examined this pedigree," continued Mr. Peck, "agree in its being very extensive and complete. It impales the arms of over thirty families, into which the Pecks married." Apparently Mr. Whitmore found the sanction of Mr. Somerby "sufficient," for, although he lived until 14 June 1900,* it does not appear that he challenged further the authenticity or correctness of the pedigree. Mr. Somerby died 14 Nov. 1872,† and the late John Ward Dean, A.M., Editor of the REGISTER and Librarian of the New England Historic Genealogical Society, referring, in his memoir of Mr. Peck published in the REGISTER of July 1889 (vol. 43, pp. 237–242), to Rev. Robert Peck and his brother, Joseph Peck of Hingham, wrote (p. 237): "Their ancestry has been traced back twenty generations, to John Peck of Belton, in Yorkshire."

In spite, however, of the apparent acceptance by Mr. Whitmore and Mr. Dean of the Peck pedigree "sanctioned" by Mr. Somerby and given by Mr. Peck in the "Genealogical History," in spite of the positive and extravagant assertions of Mr. Somerby as to its correctness, as revealed by his correspondence with Mr. Peck, and in view also of the well-known unreliability of visitation pedigrees and other such pedigrees unless their statements are supported by documentary evidence, and of the great distance—about 150 miles in a northwesterly direction—from Beccles in northeastern Suffolk to Wakefield in the West Riding of Yorkshire, it may well be asked whether proof should not be required for the statement in the pedigree that the first Robert Peck of Beccles, co. Suffolk, who was *undoubtedly* the grandfather of the New England settlers, was a son of John Peck of Wakefield in Yorkshire, Esq., of the eighteenth generation of the pedigree. If he were not a son of this John Peck of Wakefield, the wonderful chain of twenty generations of Peck ancestors for the New England settlers is broken. It is the purpose, therefore, of this article first to present abstracts of records that throw light on the probable date of birth and the Suffolk relatives of the first Robert Peck of Beccles, secondly to give abstracts of certain records of the Peck family of Wakefield in Yorkshire that will determine whether Robert Peck of Beccles could have been a son of John Peck of Wakefield, and thirdly to offer abstracts of wills and other records that relate to the connections by marriage of the first Robert Peck of Beccles and to his children and grandchildren, down to about the middle of the seventeenth century.

*A memoir of William Henry Whitmore, A.M., by the late George Augustus Gordon, A.M., may be found in the REGISTER of January 1902 (vol. 56, pp. 67–69).

†Horatio Gates Somerby of Boston, a native of Newburyport, Mass., was elected a resident member of the New England Historic Genealogical Society 7 Mar. 1845 and a corresponding member, as of London, England, 3 Aug. 1859. He established himself as a professional genealogist in England, and devoted himself to researches on the English ancestry of many of the early settlers of New England. The ancestry of some of these settlers he claimed that he had traced far back into the Middle Ages, but in several cases the pedigrees that he furnished to his clients have not been accepted by more recent investigators. There is no doubt, however, that *in his lifetime* he enjoyed a high reputation as an authority in his chosen field of genealogical research, and his memoir, by John Merrill Bradbury of Ipswich, Mass., which appeared in 1874 in the REGISTER (vol. 28, pp. 340–342), gives high praise to his genealogical work and casts no doubts on the correctness of his conclusions.—EDITORS.

# I

## ROBERT PECK OF BECCLES. CO. SUFFOLK,
### AND HIS RELATIVES

Beccles, the home of two Robert Pecks, the grandfather and the father of Rev. Robert Peck and of Joseph Peck of Hingham and Rehoboth in New England, is an important parish in the northeastern part of Suffolk, 41 miles northeast from Ipswich. It is situated on the River Waveney, which winds in a general northeasterly direction towards the North Sea and separates Suffolk from Norfolk. The parish church, dedicated to St. Michael the Archangel, stands on a point of land overlooking the meadows through which the Waveney flows. It was built probably about 1369, but the porch dates from about 1455 and the tower from about 1515. On 29 Nov. 1586 a fire at Beccles consumed eighty dwelling houses and damaged the roof and seats of the church, but probably did not damage the walls. A mile southward of the town there was formerly another parish church, called the Church of St. Mary Endgate, but it was taken down by order of Queen Elizabeth, and the two parishes were united into one.*

The earliest mention in the records here presented of a Robert Peck who can be *proved* to be the first Robert Peck of Beccles of the Peck pedigree is found in the will of John Leeke of Beccles, dated 6 Sept. 1529 (*vide infra*). The testator calls Robert Peck his "neve" [nephew], without naming his residence; but in the records in the Chancery suit of Drawer *v.* Pek (*vide infra*) his residence is given as Beccles, co. Suffolk. Below are given, in chronological order, abstracts of (1) the will of John Leeke of Beccles, dated, it seems likely, on the Thursday before Michaelmas, 1504, who was *probably* the father of the testator of 6 Sept. 1529, (2) the will of Thomas Leke, Parson, of Beccles, dated 12 Dec. 1504, who was brother of the testator of the Michaelmas season, 1504, (3) the will of Henry Peke of Carlton Colville, co. Suffolk, dated 16 Apr. 1525, who *may have been* the father of the Robert Peck named in the will of the testator of 6 Sept. 1529, and (4) the will of John Leeke of Beccles, dated 6 Sept. 1529. Then follow abstracts of (5) the proceedings in the Chancery suit of Drawer *v.* Pek, *circa* 1530, (6) the will of Alyce Leeke of Beccles, dated 14 June 1537, widow of the testator of 6 Sept. 1529, and (7) the will of Robert Pecke of Beccles, dated 31 Oct. 1556, nephew of the testator of 6 Sept. 1529 and grandfather of the emigrants to New England.

1. The Will of JOHN LEEKE of Beayles [Beccles], co. Suffolk, England, dated Thursday before All Saints' Day,† 1504. To be buried in the churchyard of St. Michael in Beccles. [Usual bequests for religious pur-

---

*This description of Beccles is based on that given in Moule's The English Counties Delineated, London, 1839, vol. 1, p. 278.

†This date is probably an error for the Thursday before Michaelmas, that is, the Thursday before 29 September, for a will dated on the Thursday before All Saints' Day, a festival which falls on 1 November, could not have been proved on 23 October of the same year. The date, as inserted near the end of the will, is given by the record searcher as the Thursday next before "ajyhelmasse" [probably a misreading of "Michaelmas"], . . . 1504. —EDITORS.

poses, etc.] To Alys, my wife, my two messuages to her proper use and to her assigns; also all my moveable goods. The residue of my goods not bequeathed are to be at the disposal of my executor, namely, Alys, my wife. Supervisor: my brother, parson of Beccles. Witnesses: William Cobbe, Rychard Robard, John Gylbert, and Robert Sele. Proved 23 October 1504 by the executrix named in the will. (Archdeaconry Court of Suffolk [Ipswich Probate Registry], Register 4 (1501–1506), fo. 161.)

[This testator was *probably* the father of John Leeke of Beccles, the testator of 6 September 1529. The testator of 1504 mentions no children in his will; but at that period it was not uncommon in Norfolk and Suffolk for a father to leave his estate to his wife and not to mention his children.]

2. The Will of THOMAS LEKE, Parson, of Beccles, co. Suffolk, England, dated 12 December 1504. [Many bequests for religious purposes, etc.] My garden at the "towns-end" to John Parker for the term of his life, and after his decease to Robert Sele for the term of his life, and, after both are deceased, I will that it be sold by my executors. To Robert Sele 10 marks. The residue of goods not bequeathed to my executors, namely, Robert Barker, Parson of Engate, and Sir William Payne, Chaplain there, and to either for his labour 40s. Supervisors: William Rede and John Parker, and to them 20s. apiece. [No witnesses given.] Proved 14 January 1504 [1504/5]. (Consistory Court of Norwich [Norwich Probate Registry], Register Rix (1504), fo. 64.)

[This testator, a priest, was a brother of John Leeke of Beccles, the testator of 1504, and was named as supervisor in John Leeke's will.]

3. The Will of HENRY PEKE of Carlton Colville, co. Suffolk, England, dated 16 April 1525. Testator styles himself Henry Peke of "Carletown." To be buried in the churchyard of St. Peter in "Carletown." To the High Altar for my tithes negligently forgotten 4d. To Margery, my wife, my house and the lands during her lifetime, and after her decease they are to remain to Robert, my son, and he is to pay 13s. 4d. to Kateryn, my daughter. If they die before their mother, then the said house is to be sold by my executors. All my moveable goods to my wife Margery. Executors: Margery, my wife, and Richard Sellyng of Loestoft [Lowestoft, co. Suffolk]. [No witnesses given.] Proved —— [day faded] November 1525. (Archdeaconry Court of Suffolk [Ipswich Probate Registry], Register 9 (1525–1527), fo. 120.)

[Carlton Colville is a little parish in northeastern Suffolk, 3½ miles southwest from Lowestoft (which is on the coast of the North Sea, on the most easterly point of land in England) and somewhat farther away, in an easterly direction, from Beccles. The church at Carlton Colville is dedicated to St. Peter. (Cf. Moule, *op. cit.*, vol. 1, p. 268.)

This will of Henry Peke (Peck), who had a wife Margery, a son Robert, and a daughter Kateryn (Katherine), is inserted here because some time the testator may be proved to have been the father of the first Robert Peck of Beccles. Thus far no proof of this relationship has been found.]

4. The Will of JOHN LEEKE of Beccles, co. Suffolk, England, Diocese of Norwich, dated 6 September 1529. To be buried in the Church of St. Michael the Archangel in Beccles. [Usual bequests to churches, etc.] To Kateryn, my daughter, and to her heirs for ever, all my lands and tenements in Gelingham, Wyndell, Wynston, Gelston, and Alby, or elsewhere within the county of Norfolk. I will that Alys, my wife, shall have her chamber and dwelling within the house of Robert Pecke, my "neve" [nephew], that is to say, in the "parlour" next the "mease" [messuage] of Richard Craske, with sufficient meat, etc., during her lifetime. Should she refuse to dwell there, then [she shall have] an annuity for

life of 20s., and the said Robert Pecke is to supply her with 10 combs of malt and 5 combs of wheat. [The testator bequeaths various items of household goods to his wife and daughter aforesaid.] To my said daughter £40, to be paid on the day of her marriage. To my said wife my land that I bought of Marsshe, for her life, and after her decease to the aforesaid Robert Pecke and his heirs. To my said wife and daughter and Robert Pecke all the residue of the household goods, equally. [Bequests to guilds.] To the said Robert Peck my "mease" [messuage] that I dwell in and all my other "measey" [sic, ? messuages], lands, and tenements in Beccles, co. Suffolk, as well bond as freehold, to him and his heirs, on condition that he pay unto Robert Leeke, John Leeke, and Richard Leeke 20 marks apiece and to Alys Leeke and Elyn Leeke 20 marks apiece. To Margaret Leke 40s., to be paid at the age of discretion. An obit is to be kept for me and my sons in Beccles church yearly by Robert Pecke, if he is able. To John Waters, my godson, 20s., and to each other of my godchildren 12d. To the said Robert Pecke all my pen cattle, moveables, and apparel. If my wife troubles, vexes, or sues my executors, her legacies are to be void. All the residue to my executors, namely, my well-beloved in Christ, the aforesaid Robert Peck, my nephew, and Kateryn, my daughter. Witnesses: John Waters, James Canne, Richard Robards, William Robards, Osbern Dering, John Pottes, William Hastings, Thomas Drurye, and others. Proved 17 November 1529. (Consistory Court of Norwich [Norwich Probate Registry], Register Attmer (1528–1537), fo. 65.)

[As has been already stated, it is in this will of John Leeke of Beccles, co. Suffolk, that the earliest *certain* reference to Robert Peck, grandfather of Rev. Robert Peck and his brother Joseph, has been found. Although John Leeke in his will does not mention the residence of this Robert Peck, the Chancery proceedings in the suit of Drawer *v.* Pek (Peck) (*infra,* No. 5) show that he was of Beccles, co. Suffolk.

The provisions of this will should be studied carefully, especially those referring to Alice, the testator's wife, and to Robert Peck, whom he calls his "neve," that is, nephew. That this nephew of John Leeke is identical with Robert Pecke of Beccles, co. Suffolk, the testator of 31 Oct. 1556 (*infra,* No. 7), is indicated by the provision in his will by which John Leeke leaves to his wife Alice, for her life, the land that he bought of "Marsshe," and directs that after her decease this land shall go to Robert Peck and his heirs, and by the provision in the will of the testator of 31 Oct. 1556 by which this later testator leaves to his son, John Peck, three acres of land, "late William Marshes." John Leeke leaves his lands in county Norfolk to his daughter Katherine and her heirs and his lands in Beccles to his nephew Robert Peck and his heirs, on condition that Robert Peck pay certain legacies, and, after stating what shall be done with his household goods and other moveables, he leaves all the residue of his estate to his executors, namely, the aforesaid Robert Peck, his nephew, and Katherine, his (the testator's) daughter.

From the provisions of this will, from the Chancery proceedings that follow it, and from the will of Alyce Leeke of Beccles, widow of John Leeke, dated 14 June 1537 (*infra,* No. 6), the following account of John Leeke and his family has been compiled.

John Leeke of Beccles, uncle of Robert Peck, died between 6 Sept. 1529, when his will was dated, and 17 Nov. 1529, when it was proved. He married twice, at least. His first wife, whose name has not been found, bore to him two or more sons, for in his will he directs Robert Peck, if he is able, to keep an obit annually in the church at Beccles for him (the testator) and his sons. In what way Robert, John, Richard, Alice, and Ellen Leeke, to whom Robert Peck was to pay 20 marks apiece, and Margaret Leke, to whom the testator bequeathed 40s., to be paid at the age of discretion, were related to the testator—whether they were grandchildren, nephews and nieces, or otherwise related, does not appear, although it is likely that those receiving the larger sum, 20 marks apiece, were grandchildren; but that neither they nor Robert

Peck, the testator's nephew, were blood relatives of the second wife, the testatrix of 14 June 1537, is probable, in view of the fact that not a single one of them was mentioned in her will. John Leeke's second wife, Alice Leeke, was, as is revealed by her will, the widow of Robert Bartram when she was married to John Leeke, and her maiden name is unknown. Two sons by her first husband, Thomas Bartram and William Bartram, and a daughter, Agnes (Bartram), wife of Robert Mikylburgh, were living in 1537, when their mother made her will, but they had not been mentioned in the will of John Leeke, their stepfather. John Leeke's daughter, Katherine, was his child by his second wife, and was a legatee in her father's will and also in her mother's will. To this daughter, Katherine, besides other bequests, her father left £40, to be paid on the day of her marriage. Not long afterwards, probably about 1530, Katherine appears in the records of a suit in Chancery as the wife of one Thomas Drawer (just when her marriage had been solemnized is not evident), and she and her husband brought in a bill of complaint against her cousin, Robert Peck, who was one of the two executors of her father's will, the other executor being Katherine herself. (*Vide infra*, No. 5, the case of Drawer *v.* Pek.) Katherine's mother seems to have been somewhat harshly treated by her second husband, John Leeke, in his will, and he directed that, if she should trouble, vex, or sue the executors of the will, her legacies should be void. Perhaps it is not unreasonable to suggest that Katherine's mother, debarred from bringing suit against the executors of the will under penalty of losing her legacies, instigated Katherine and her husband to appear as the complainants in a suit against Katherine's coexecutor, with whom, apparently, Katherine's mother and, perhaps, Katherine herself were not on friendly terms. The mistrust that John Leeke seemed to exhibit towards his wife Alice and the confidence that he placed in his nephew Robert Peck stand out unmistakably in the provisions of his will. It is clear that he intended that his nephew should be the leader of the two executors and that he relied on him to see that his wishes in regard to the distribution of his estate were duly carried out. The outcome of the Chancery suit is not known. Katherine (Leeke) Drawer, and her half sister, Agnes (Bartram) Mikylburgh, were legatees in their mother's will in 1537, and their mother named as residuary legatees and executors of that will her sons-in-law, her well-beloved Robert Mikylburgh and Thomas Drawer, desired of them that they would dispose of her goods to the most pleasure of Almighty God, and gave to each of them, for their labour, 40s.]

## 5. FROM EARLY CHANCERY PROCEEDINGS*

### Drawer *v.* Pek, *circa* 1530

No. 25. The Complaint of Thomas Drawer and Kathyn, his wife, against Robert Pek.

To the Right Honorable Thomas More, Knight, Lord Chancellor of England.

In full humble wise your poor orator, Thomas Drawer, and Kathyn, his wife, complaineth [*sic*] to Your Good Lordship that one John Leeke was seised in his demesne as of fee of and in a messuage and forty acres of land in Toft, in the County of Norfolk, and so seised died, after whose decease the said messuage and land descended and of right ought to descend to the said Katyn, as daughter and heir of the said John Leek, and that divers and sundry evidence, muniments, and writing concerning the premises have come to the hands and possession of Rbt Pek of Becles in the County of Suff[olk], of whom your said orator has often required to have delivery of the said evidences, muniments, and writings, which to do the same Robt Pek at all times has refused and does yet refuse, and, forsomuch as your said suppliants know not the number nor content of the same evidence, muniments, and writings, nor whether they be in

*Preserved in the Public Record Office, London. Bundles 601–694 cover the period 1529–1532, and the suit of Drawer v. Pek is in Bundle 627, Nos. 25–28.

bag, box, or chest sealed, therefore they have no remedy by the common law of this land to attain to the possession of the said evidence, muniments, and writings. It may, therefore, please Your Lordship the premises tenderly to consider and to grant a writ of subpoena to be directed to the said Robt Pek, demanding him to appear before the King in his Chancery at a certain day and upon a certain pain, by Your Good Lordship to be limited, then and there to answer unto the premises, and your said poor suppliants shall daily —— [? pray] for Your Good Lordship long to continue.

No. 26.  The Answer of Robert Pekk to the bill of Thomas Drawer and Katerin, his wife, whereby the defendant says that one William Davy had and yet hath good and just title to said lands and tenements mentioned in the bill, and that this defendant, long before the writ of subpoena, delivered to said William all evidences, charters, and muniments concerning said lands, except the "contrepain" of an indenture being cancelled, so that the defendant has no manner of evidences or writings in his possession, but only the said "contrepain," which he has now delivered to the Honourable Court, to be ordered as seems expedient to the said Court. The defendant further says that, if they will, the complainants may take their remedy against said William Davy for the evidences, by subpoena in this Honourable Court or else by such other means as by their learned counsel shall be thought most expedient, and not take their remedy against this defendant, for at the time of the delivery of said writings to Davy, he knew not nor yet knoweth of any manner of title of said complainants. And he prays to be dismissed with his costs.

No. 27.  The Replication of Thomas Drawer and Katherin, his wife, to the answer of Robert Pekke. [The replication is badly torn and practically illegible.]

No. 28.  The Rejoinder of Robert Pekke to the replication of Thomas Drawer and Katherin, his wife, whereby said defendant admits it to be true that William Davy bargained and sold said lands and tenements mentioned in the bill unto said John Leke for 20 marks, which bargain was made about July in the twenty-first year of our present sovereign lord the King [21 Henry VIII, July 1529], and it was agreed that if, at any time within seven years next ensuing, said Davy repaid to said Leke said 20 marks, the agreement made between them should be utterly void. But if said Davy were not disposed to buy back the premises within seven years, said Leke should pay to him a further 20 marks, for the lands and tenements are worth £40.  Now said Leke made his last will and ordained the defendant and others his executors.  And said Leke died within a year of making the aforesaid agreement, and the defendant took upon him the charge of said will.  Afterwards said Davy came to the defendant as executor of said Leke and offered the redemption sum of 20 marks for said lands and tenements, which sum the defendant received of him and delivered to him such evidences and writings as remained in his hands, as it was lawful for him to do.  And this defendant denies that John Leke paid any more money to said Davy.  Albeit one Richard Roberts, being put in trust to make an indenture by said Davy and Leke, craftily wrote in the indenture that said Leke paid 40 marks.  All which things said Robert Pekke is ready to aver in the Honourable Court.

[It is to be regretted that the decision of the Court in this case is not known. For comments on this suit see remarks that follow the abstract of the will of John Leeke (*supra*, No. 4).]

6.  The Will of ALYCE LEEKE of Beccles. co. Suffolk, England, Diocese of Norwich, widow, dated 14 June 1537.  To be buried in the Church of

St. Michael in Beccles, at my "stolys" [stool's] end, whereupon I will have a marble stone with inscription thereon remembering to pray for my soul, the souls of John Leeke and Robert Bartram, my husbands, and all my friends' souls. [Bequests to the church of Beccles and the church of Gislingham.] To each of my godchildren 4d. To Thomas Bartram, my son, my mazer and 5 marks in money, as soon as it may be born of my goods. To Kateryne Drawer, my daughter, my best gown, my "kyrtyll" next the best, and my best "gyrdyll" and a pair of white "Cambyr Beades gawdy with silver." To Agnes Mekylburgh, my daughter, my next best gown, my best "kyrtyll," my great white "Ambyr Beadys," my next best "gyrdyll," and 10s. To the aforesaid Kateryne, my daughter, 40s. Residuary legatees and executors: my sons-in-law, my well-beloved Robert Mikylburgh and Thomas Drawer, and I desire of them that they will dispose of my goods to the most pleasure of Almighty God, and to each of them for their labour 40s. Witnesses: William Roberdes, John Wakefelde, William Dobson, Isabell Coole. Item, to William Bartram, my son, my little feather bed, and to Margaret Kent my gown "purcled" with otter. Proved 25 September 1538. (Archdeaconry Court of Suffolk [Ipswich Probate Registry], Register 13 (1538–1540), fo. 30.)

[For information about John Leeke and his family supplied by this will see remarks that follow the abstract of the will of John Leeke (*supra*, No. 4).]

7. The Will of ROBERT PECKE of Beccles, co. Suffolk, England, dated 31 October 1556. My body to be buried in the churchyard of Beccles, near unto the grave of Johan, my wife. To every one of my household servants 12d. To John Pecke, my son, my messuage wherein I dwell and my tenement "late Mayster Rede" and the two meadows lying next the meadow in the "teno"" [tenure] of Mathew Prynte and my little garden "late Philippe Doddes," my close "sometyme Helyn Churches," my "fryttlell as the further Wynde Myll late Richard Tyde," and three acres of land "late William Marshes," upon condition that he shall pay —— [amount not given] to Thomas Pecke, my son, and to my three daughters Margret, Olyve, and Anne. To Robard Pecke, my son, my other two meadows in Barstun [*sic*, ? Barsham] "late Churchmans" and the meadows "date Doct$^{or}$ Rede sometyme Baldewyns," my close at Ingate church, one acre of land "late Tyde in Ingatefelds," and the "three roode acres called Bells acre." To Thomas Pecke, my son, my two tenements I purchased of John Walter [*sic*] and my tenter yard. To my daughters Margaret, Olyve, and Anne, to each £6. 13s. 4d. To every one of John Waters's and William Waters's children 4d. To every one of my godchildren 4d. Executors: Richard Crampton and Thomas Hagas. Supervisors: John Waters and Robert Bradley. My little "pyctell [pightel] called Caves pyctell" lying in Ingate shall be sold. To Johan Meriman, my daughter, a gown and a petticoat that were her mother's and the "worser paire of Corall beads." Witnesses: Sir John Gymbyn, Robert Tower, Robert Grene, Thomas Goodwyn, and John Waters. Proved 20 November 1556. (Archdeaconry Court of Suffolk [Ipswich Probate Registry], Register 17 (1554–1557), fo. 435.)

[Barsham was a small parish south of the Waveney, 2 miles west from Beccles.
John Waters and William Waters were brothers-in-law of the testator, their sister Johan having been the testator's second wife.
Robert Peck, from the nature of the services required of him and from the responsibility placed upon him under the terms of the will of John Leeke, his uncle (*supra*, No. 4), was probably at least twenty-one years old in 1529 and was therefore born in 1508 or earlier—very likely considerably earlier

than that year. From his will, dated 31 Oct. 1556 and proved 20 Nov. 1556, an abstract of which is given above, and from other records relating to his wives and children and to his connections by marriage, which will be given in Section III of this article, it appears that he had had two wives, that a married daughter (Johan Meriman) by his first wife was living when he made his will and that "all" the children of this daughter were referred to by her uncle, Robert Norton of Hallisworth (Halesworth), co. Suffolk, gentleman, in his will dated 4 Aug. 1561, that his second wife, Johan (Waters) Peck, daughter of John and Margaret Waters of Beccles, who was living 3 Aug. 1556, when she was named as a legatee in her mother's will, was dead and buried by 31 Oct. 1556, that six children by his second wife (three sons, John, Robert, and Thomas, and three daughters, Margaret, Olive, and Anne) were living on 31 Oct. 1556, and that his sons John and Robert and his daughter Margaret were born before 28 May 1547, when they were named as legatees in the will of their grandfather, John Waters, the two sons and their sister Margaret being under twenty-one on that date. In his will of 28 May 1547 John Waters also bequeathed to Jone Peck the younger "my boole," this legatee probably being the daughter of Robert Peck by his first wife. She was called Johan Meriman in Robert Peck's will, and, although not a grandchild of John Waters, she seems nevertheless to have been remembered by him, when he made bequests to her younger half brothers and half sister. These facts about Robert Peck's wives and children make it probable that his second marriage took place about 1540.

If Robert Peck of Beccles was a nephew by blood of John Leeke, the testator of 1529, his mother was probably a sister of John Leeke, and that relationship, if proved, would apparently make it impossible for him, whether born before, in, or after 1508, to have been a son of John Peck, Esq., of Wakefield, in the West Riding of Yorkshire, for the name of John Peck's wife and his family connections are known and will be given in the next following section of this article. But, disregarding for the present the probability that the maiden name of Robert Peck's mother was Leeke, it is the purpose of the compiler of this article to turn to the Pecks of Wakefield, and to present such records of that family as will determine whether the first Robert Peck of Beccles, co. Suffolk, could have been a son of John Peck of Wakefield, as he is represented to have been by the tabular pedigree in the British Museum.]

# GENEALOGICAL RESEARCH IN ENGLAND

Communicated by the Committee on English and Foreign Research

## THE ENGLISH ANCESTRY OF JOSEPH PECK
## OF HINGHAM, MASS., IN 1638

Compiled by S. Allyn Peck, B.A., of New York City, and contributed by Frederick Stanhope Peck, LL.D., of Barrington, R. I.

## II

### The Pecks of Wakefield, co. York

Wakefield, the home of the John Peck who, in the tabular pedigree in the British Museum described in the previous instalment of this article and accepted as authentic by the late Ira Ballou Peck in his "Genealogical History," is represented to have been the father of the first Robert Peck of Beccles, co. Suffolk, is a large and populous parish in the West Riding of Yorkshire, on the River Calder, a few miles south from Leeds and about 150 miles in a northwesterly direction from Beccles in northeastern Suffolk, where John Peck's alleged son Robert lived and died. Wakefield included five townships, and gave its name to the famous battle in 1460, in the Wars of the Roses, in which Richard, Duke of York, whose son became King Edward IV, was slain. The parish church, dedicated to All Saints, was built in the reign of Henry III, but part of it was rebuilt in 1724 and other parts have been rebuilt in later years. At the northern extremity of Wakefield was Heselden Hall, the timber roof and oaken panels of which bore the date 1583.*

Pedigrees entered in early heraldic visitations and confirmed in part by other records indicate that the Peck family had been settled in Wakefield for at least four generations prior to the generation to which the John Peck mentioned in the preceding paragraph belonged. Whatever may have been the origin and whoever may have been the author or forger of the tabular pedigree of the Pecks accepted by the late Ira Ballou Peck in his "Genealogical History," with its twenty generations of ancestors of Joseph Peck of Hingham and Rehoboth in New England—a line which, if proved, would go back at least to the beginning of the twelfth century, there can be little doubt that, as far as the family at Wakefield is concerned, this tabular pedigree is based to some extent on the Peck pedigrees given in "Tonge's Visitation of the Northern Counties," made in 1530, and in "The Visitation of Yorkshire," made in 1563 and 1564. As already stated (*supra*, REGISTER, vol. 89, p. 330), the tabular pedi-** gree represents Richard Peck of Hesden (a place which has not been identified), Esq., of the fourteenth (!!) generation from the beginning of the pedigree, as the first of the family to settle in Wakefield, and it also states that he married the daughter and heir of —— Heselden; and "The Visitation of Yorkshire," made by William Flower, Esq., Norroy King of Arms, in 1563 and 1564, begins its Peck pedigree with "Rychard Pecke of Wakefeld," who married "Margaret doughter & heyre of . . . . Heselden" (probably of Heselden Hall, mentioned in the preceding paragraph). (*The Publications of the Harleian Society,* vol. 16, p. 236, for the year 1881.) "The Visitation of Yorkshire" of 1563 and 1564 gives to Rychard and Margaret (Heselden) Pecke a son and heir, John Pecke, a lawyer, who married "Izabell doughter of John Lacy," a son Rychard, who died young, and a third son, Thomas Pecke, to whom the tabular pedigree of the British Museum gives four generations of descendants, said to be of Knoston, in Colchester [co. Essex], but no descendants of this Thomas Pecke are given in "The Visitation of Yorkshire." Of the greatest importance, however, in determining whether Robert Peck of Beccles, co. Suffolk, could have been a son or other near relative of the John Peck mentioned in the preceding paragraph, is the pedigree which John Peck himself entered in the earliest of these visitations, the heraldic visitation

*For a description of Wakefield cf. Moule's The English Counties Delineated, London, 1839, vol. 2, pp. 458–459.

**Page 526, this volume.

of the northern counties of England—Cumberland, Durham, Northumberland, Nottingham, Westmorland, and York, known as "Tonge's Visitation of the Northern Counties," which was made in 1530 by Thomas Tonge, Norroy King of Arms, most of the pedigrees and arms entered therein being, however, those of Yorkshire families and the arms of many monasteries, also, being given.

Two manuscripts of "Tonge's Visitation," both certainly drawn up in the reign of Henry VIII, have been preserved, one—perhaps the original draft of the author—in the College of Arms, and the other—probably a transcript of the former—in the Harleian Collections in the British Museum (Harleian MS. 1499). The Harleian manuscript, entitled "Heraldic Visitation of the Northern Counties, by Thomas Tonge, Norroy King of Armes," with an appendix containing other heraldic documents relating to the North of England, has been printed by the Surtees Society as volume 41 of its *Publications,* for the year 1862. Although collation of the Harleian manuscript with the manuscript in the College of Arms was not sought by the editor (W. Hylton Dyer Longstaffe, F. S. A.), the authorities of the College of Arms gave him the opportunity of becoming acquainted with the general character of their manuscript, and he stated in his preface that no material differences between the two manuscripts existed.

The pedigree entered in "Tonge's Visitation" in 1530 by John Peck of Wakefield begins with his great-grandfather, the John Peck who married Isabel, daughter of John Lacy, and ends with John Peck himself and his children; and it is evident that, whatever errors may be found in his statements about his more remote ancestors, such as his grandfather or great-grandfather, what he says about himself and his own children is the statement of a contemporary, who knew whereof he spoke, and, it is to be assumed, told the truth. This pedigree, as printed in *The Publications of the Surtees Society* for 1862 (vol. 41, p. 81), reads as follows:

THIS YS THE PETIGRE OF JOHN PEKE OF WAKEFELD.

ARMS. Argent, on a chevron engrailed gules three crosses patee of the field.

IMPALEMENT. Gules, three stags' heads caboshed argent.

JOHN PEKE maried Isabell, doughter of John Lacy : and by her had yssue, *Richard,* son and heyre ; Thomas ; and Robert ; Kateryn, maried to Skargill ; John,[1] maried to Richard Turton ; Margaret, maried to Norton.

RICHARD, son of John, maried Joan, doughter of John Haryngton, esquier : and by her had yssue, *Richard,* son and heyre ; Isabell ; Margaret ; Joan ; and Elisabeth.

RICHARD, son of Richard, maried Alice, doughter of Middelton of Stokell : and by her had yssue, *John,* son and heyre ; Margaret ; Anne ; Elisabeth ; and Isabell.

JOHN, son of Richard, maried Jane, doughter of John of Anne[2] [*sic,* John Anne] of Frekeley, esquier : and by her had yssue, RICHARD, son and heyre ; John, ij$^{de}$ sone ; Thomas, iij$^{de}$ son ; Willyam, iiij$^{th}$ son ; Nicholas, v$^{th}$ son ; Frances [*sic*], vj$^{te}$ son ; Kateryn, maried to John

Leyke ; Margaret, maried to John Talear ; Anne, married to John Hill ; Elisabeth ; Alice ; and Dorathe.

¹Joan.                                                    ²*Impalement.*

[In the list of his children entered by John Peck in "Tonge's Visitation" in 1530, as reproduced verbatim above, the names of six sons, beginning with Richard, son and heir, come first, and the names of three married daughters and three other daughters follow the name of the sixth son. The places of the daughters among the children, that is, the order of their births in relation to the births of the sons, cannot be ascertained from "Tonge's Visitation" alone, which shows only that in 1530 three daughters were old enough to be married and were already married, and that in the same year three other daughters were unmarried. "The Visitation of Yorkshire" of 1563 and 1564 gives later information about John Peck's children and adds the names of some of his grandchildren, but neither in the pedigree entered by John Peck in "Tonge's Visitation" in 1530 nor in "The Visitation of Yorkshire" of 1563 and 1564 is there any mention of a son of this John Peck named Robert. If a son named Robert had been born after 1530, his name would have appeared, probably, in "The Visitation of Yorkshire" of 1563 and 1564 and also, if he were living, in his father's will, dated 2 November 1558. There is a Robert Peck named in that will (*vide infra*), but the testator does not call him his son, and, if born after 1530, he would have been too young to have been identical with the Robert Pecke of Beccles, co. Suffolk, who made his will 31 October 1556 (*vide supra,* vol. 89, pp. 338–339). *On the other hand, if John Peck of Wakefield had a legitimate son named Robert, born before the eldest of the six sons named in "Tonge's Visitation," that son Robert must have died without leaving a male heir, for, even if the said Robert were dead when his father died, a male heir of Robert (and not Richard, the first son named in "Tonge's Visitation") would have been declared the next heir of the said John Peck.

Except for some differences in the spelling of proper names, the two Peck pedigrees, that of 1530 and that of 1563 and 1564, are in substantial agreement, in the parts that are common to them both. In order, therefore, to determine whether the first Robert Peck of Beccles, co. Suffolk, could have been a son of John Peck of Wakefield or could have been otherwise related to that armigerous Peck family of which the said John Peck was a member, it is necessary to present abstracts of other records, besides the visitation entries, concerning the Pecks of Wakefield; and included among such records will be found abstracts of documents relating to the grandfather and father of John Peck and to John Peck himself, his children, the Anne family, to which his wife belonged, and the Lake (not Leyke or Leake) family of Normanton, co. York, into which his daughter Katherine married.]

The other records (besides the visitation entries) mentioned above, relating to the Peck family of Wakefield, begin with certain items concerning the grandfather and the father of the John Peck (Peke) who entered his pedigree in "Tonge's Visitation" in 1530. These items are found in the first part of a calendar of Yorkshire Feet of Fines of the Tudor period, published in 1887 by the Yorkshire Archæological and Topographical Association as volume 2 of its Record Series, a volume which, after an introduction explaining what Feet of Fines are, gives a calendar of the Feet of Fines of Michaelmas Term, 2 Henry VII [1486], and the following terms, ending with the Feet of Fines of Hilary Term, 13 Elizabeth [1570/1].

In this calendar, in Michaelmas Term, 4 Henry VII [2–25 November 1488], Richard Pek, senr., and Johanna, his wife, and Richard Pek, junr., and Alice, his wife, appear as deforciants, admitting the manor of Shelf and a messuage with lands in Shelf [a township

*Pages 534–535, this volume.

538

in the large parish of Halifax, in the West Riding of Yorkshire] to belong to Richard Fournes and Richard Lyster, chaplain, the plaintiffs [or querents]. This Richard Pek, senr., with wife Johanna, was the grandfather of the John Peke of Wakefield who entered his pedigree in "Tonge's Visitation" in 1530, and Richard Pek, junr., with wife Alice, was the father of the said John Peke, the grandfather, according to "Tonge's Visitation," having married Joan, daughter of John Haryngton, Esq., and the father having married Alice, daughter of Middelton of Stokell. In Easter Term, 6 Henry VII [15 April–8 May 1491], Richard Pek (no longer called "junr.") and Alice, his wife, as deforciants, admitted the right of Nicholas Sayuyle [i. e., Savile], plaintiff [or querent], to three messuages, with lands, in Eland [another township in the parish of Halifax]. The grandfather, who was living in November 1488, was evidently dead in the spring of 1491, and in the parish church of Wakefield was a window, no longer to be found there, with a legend in Latin, reading: *Orate pro bono statu Ricardi Pek, armigeri, et Johanne, uxor* [*sic*] *ejus, et filuorum eorundem, qui istam fenestram fieri fecerunt,* that is, freely translated, "Pray for Richard Pek, Esq. and Johanne, his wife, and their children, who gave this window." (Dodsworth's Church Notes, in the Bodleian Library, Oxford.) In the parish church of Wakefield there was also formerly an inscription to the father of the John Peck (Peke) who entered his pedigree in "Tonge's Visitation," and this inscription read: "Here lyeth buried Richard Pek of Wakefield, esquire, and Alce, his wief, daughter of Peter Midleton of Stokeld, knight, and had yssue 2 sons and 4 daughters. He dyed anno Domini 1516, 24 Junii." (*Ib.*) One more inscription, formerly in the parish church of Wakefield, but now, like the two preceding inscriptions, no longer to be found there, may be given here, an inscription to John Peck himself and his wife Jane, which read as follows: "Here lyeth buried John Pek of Wakefeild and Jane, his wief, daughter of John Anne of Fricklay, who had yssue ix sons and ix daughters, and dyed att Wakefeild the 4 of January, anno Domini 1558." (*Ib.*)

The next entry in the calendar of Feet of Fines that relates to this Peck family of Wakefield occurs in the records of Michaelmas Term, 18 Henry VIII [2–25 November 1526], and shows John Peck (Peke) himself as plaintiff [or querent] and John Maunsell and Elizabeth, his wife, as deforciants, in a case concerning a messuage with lands in Sandall, near Wakefield, Walton, and Mylnthorp. [Sandall is a parish two miles south from Wakefield, and Walton a township in Sandall.] From this time on until his death in 1558/9 the name of John Peck (in various spellings) occurs frequently in the calendar of Feet of Fines, and, except in one case, he appears as plaintiff [or querent]. These entries will be mentioned, if necessary, in connection with the following records (chiefly abstracts of wills and inquisitions post mortem) of the Pecks of Wakefield and the families with which they were allied, records which will be helpful in passing judgment on the pedigree which the late Ira Ballou Peck, on the authority [!] of the late Horatio Gates Somerby, accepted

539

in his "Genealogical History," which differs considerably, as far as the children of the John Peck who entered his pedigree in "Tonge's Visitation" are concerned, not only from the pedigrees given in "Tonge's Visitation" and in "The Visitation of Yorkshire" of 1563 and 1564 but also, to some extent, from the actual forged [!] pedigree preserved in the British Museum. A facsimile of this forged pedigree will be given farther on in this article. The records that follow begin with an abstract of the will of the father of the John Peck who entered his pedigree in "Tonge's Visitation."

The Will of RICHARDE PEKE of Wakefield [co. York], Gentleman, dated 4 June 1516.* I commend my soul to God Almighty, to Our Lady Saint Marie, and to all the Saints in heaven, my body to be buried in the parish church of Allhallows in Wakefield, in the choir of Saint Nicholas. To the High Altar 4 marks, for a vestment flowered with my arms and my wife's arms. [Directions about the lights, and bequests to all priests and others employed in the church services, and to the four orders of friars for masses.] To the guild of Saint Christofer in York, for a mass, 20d. For prayers at Saint John's 3s. 4d. To Our Lady's guild at Boston all arrears due thereunto both for me and for my wife; our entry thereto was in the year of Our Lord God 1512, and I [am] to have a mass done at their Scala Cæli. For pilgrimages not done I bequeath to the "paviment in Northgatte" in Wakefield 6s. 8d., and 3s. 4d. where it is most needed, at the discretion of Sir William Joys, priest, "to ament a fowll holle abowt the brige." All these "parcelles" [i. e., items or bequests] above written I desire my wife to be performed and delivered [farther on in this will she is named as sole executrix] as soon after my burial as it can be conveniently done, by the oversight of John Anne, supervisor of this my last will. I will that a stone be laid upon my grave within a year; and, if they make an image of Saint Nicholas in the parish church, I assign thereto 3s. 4d., and require them to give the old [image] to Saint John's Church. I bequeath 6s. 8d. to the gilding of [the image of] Saint John, now new[ly] made, in the Church of Saint John in Wakefield.

All such "dewtyes" [i. e., payments] as I, the said Richard Peke, give with my hands or openly bid them to be given [are] to stand firm and stable. Elesabeth, my wife, [is] to pay to William Pallmer and Margaret, his wife, 4 marks, if any thereof be owing at the day of my burial, which "dewtie" I agreed to give them when I lay sick and at the mercy of God, at the instances of Master Thomas Knolles, subdean of the Cathedral Church of York, John Anne of Frikeley, Esq., my father-in-law ("fader in lawe"), and John Peke, my son, Thomas Grene, and Sir Robert Skelton, priest, which Sir Robert Skelton wrote the said agreement and will of me, the said Richard Peke, for my three daughters, for Margaret Palmer 53s. 4d., which her husband and she were fully agreed to for her full part—and they agreed to receive the said 53s. 3d. [sic] and to make general acquittance to me and my executors for her child's part for ever. And, in like manner, before the said subdean, with all these other gentlemen, I, the said Richard Peke, agreed to give to Anne Bolles, my daughter, for her part, 5 marks in full "contentacion" [i. e., satisfaction] thereof, and to Henry Brodeley [of Wakefield] and Isabell, his wife, my daughter,

*As abstracts only, not verbatim copies, of this and the following wills and inquisitions post mortem are given, no attempt has been made to reproduce the ancient spelling of the original records, except in names of persons and in a few other cases; and in these other cases the original spelling is placed within quotation marks.

£6. 13s. 4d. My priest, immediately after my decease and burial, [shall] say a trental of masses for me. The priest who shall happen to administer to me the sacrament with the suffrage [is] to have 12d. To John Peke, my son, and to his heirs [certain weapons, armor, bows and arrows, etc.] To the said John Peke my best doublet, my long riding knife, and my books, including two of law, the "Statutes with the booke of my fermys." To my uncle, Robert Peke, if he survive me, a doublet of buckskins [and other articles of apparel]. To every one of my servants their wages and 12d. in rewards. To every godchild that I have 4d. To Brian Brounhede one of the three jackets. As yet I, the said Richard Peke, cannot finish this [will] perfectly after my mind, because of such persons as are from home and of such "dewties" [i. e., payments] as are owing to me and also that I owe; but if aught should come to me, the said Richarde Peke, [I assign] Elesabeth, my wife, to be my "holl" [i. e., sole] executrix of this my last will, to pay all the "parcelles" [i. e., items or bequests] above written contained in this my last will. And to the said Elesabeth, my wife, I give all my goods [of every description, now in the testator's possession or that may come to him hereafter]. And I, the said Richard Peke, finish this my last will and [desire] to have this written and finished after the tenor of this written with my own hands. I make Elesabeth, my wife, my "holle" executrix of all my goods, as is above said, without any accounts. And I specially desire Master Thomas Knolles, our curate, subdean of the Cathedral Church of York, and John Anne, her father ("hir fader"), to give her their best mind and counsel and to see that she be not wronged.

[Here follow some instructions in regard to heirlooms, which *seem* to mean that certain items assigned as heirlooms in the presence of Master Thomas Knolles and John Anne and written down by Sir Robert Skelton as heirlooms (and no more of the testator's goods, unless the testator's wife of her own good will give them) are to go to John Peke, the testator's son, who is not to interfere further with nor "hurtt" the testator's wife; and the said John Peke is to "labour" for the goods of the testator's mother, "who hadd all the heyrloomes, and as yett I never hade none of theym." And, further, the testator charges his son not to interfere with any of his (the testator's) goods.]

In witness whereof I, the said Richard Peke, wrote and finished the tenor and effect of this my last will with my own hands, the day and year abovesaid. Witnesses: John Peke, gentleman, Sir Robert Skelton, priest, and Thomas Bayly, with many others. Proved 28 October 1516. (Exchequer and Prerogative Courts of York [at York], Register 9, fo. 38.)

Inquisition post Mortem on the death of Richard Peck (Pek) of Wakefield [co. York], Esq., held at Wentbridge [*sic*] 28 August, 10 Henry VIII [28 August 1518].*

The jurors say that before he died Richard Peck was seised of two messuages in Southowram and of messuages, etc., in Wakefield, Halifax, Thornes, and Stanley [co. York].

William Middelton, Knight, with Thomas Middelton, Thomas Lacy, and Richard Turton, now deceased, was enfeoffed of these properties to the use of Richard Peck and his heirs. Afterwards William Middelton, who outlived all the others, granted the two messuages in Southowram to John Peck, son and heir of Richard Peck, and Johan his wife, and the heirs male of John Peck. With the remainder of the properties William Middelton enfeoffed Thomas Middelton, his son ond heir, William Thwaites, Esq., of Marston, and others, their heirs and assigns, to the

*The inquisition post mortem, of which an abstract only is given here, is written in Latin.

use of an indenture made 23 July, 22 Henry VIII [*sic*, 23 July, 22 Henry VII, i. e., 23 July 1507],* between Richard Peck on the one part and John Anne on the other part, for the marriage of John Peck, son and heir of Richard Peck, and Johan Anne, one of the daughters of the said John Anne.

The said Richard Peck died on the last day of September, 8 Henry VIII [30 September 1516]. John Peck is his son and heir, and the said John Peck was twenty-six years and more of age at the death of his father. (Inquisitions post Mortem, Chancery Series, vol. 79, no. 283, preserved in the Public Record Office, London.)

[The date of Richard Peck's death, according to Dodsworth's "Church Notes," in the Bodleian Library at Oxford, was given as 24 June 1516, in an inscription that formerly could be read in the parish church of Wakefield but is no longer to be found there. The correct date is probably that in the inquisition post mortem, 30 September 1516, the earlier date being apparently an error either in the original inscription or in the copy made *by* Dodsworth or in a later copy made *from* Dodsworth.

Since John Peck, son and heir of Richard Peck, was over twenty-six years of age at the death of his father, he was born about 1489 or earlier, and the indenture for his marriage with Johan Anne, dated 23 July 1507, was made when he was about eighteen years of age or more.

Richard Peck ("Peke"), the testator of 4 June 1516, appears in the calendar of Yorkshire Feet of Fines in Michaelmas Term, 4 Henry VII [1488], and in Easter Term, 6 Henry VII [1491], with a wife named Alice, who in the pedigree entered by her son, John Peck ("Peke"), in "Tonge's Visitation" in 1530, is said to be a daughter of Middelton of Stokell. In the inscription that according to Dodsworth's "Church Notes" could formerly be read in the parish church of Wakefield she was called daughter of Peter Midleton of Stokeld, knight. "Peter," however, is apparently an error for "William," the "William Middelton, Knight," named in the inquisition post mortem above. The inscription in the parish church of Wakefield made Alice Midleton the mother of two sons and four daughters. One of the sons probably died young, for in "Tonge's Visitation" her son John gives only his own name, as son and heir of his father, and the names of his four sisters, Margaret, Anne, Elisabeth, and Isabell.

In the will of Richard Peck ("Peke"), however, the name of his wife is given as Elesabeth, and the testator calls John Anne of Frickeley [Frickley], Esq., his (the testator's) father-in-law and her (Elesabeth's) father. It appears, therefore, that the second wife of Richarde Peke, the testator of 1516, was Elisabeth Anne, daughter of John Anne of Frickley, co. York, Esq., and sister of Johan or Jane Anne, the wife of John Peck, son and heir of the testator. The will of Kateryn Anne, widow, dated 23 November 1523, and that of her son, John Anne, dated 24 April 1544, abstracts of both of which follow in this article, supply more information about the Anne family and further proof of the identity of the second wife of Richard Peck, the testator of 1516.

The marriage of John Peck and Johan or Jane Anne took place, according to the inquisition post mortem given above, about 1507. The marriage of Richard Peck and Elisabeth Anne took place not later than 1512, as Richard Peck in his will, given above, stated that he and his wife entered Our Lady's guild at Boston in that year. Richard Peck made John Anne supervisor of his will and designated his wife Elisabeth as sole executrix.

The will of Richard Peck shows that in 1516 he had three married daughters living, namely, Margaret, wife of William Pallmer [Palmer], Anne, wife of ——— Bolles, and Isabell, wife of Henry Brodeley [Bradley] of Wakefield. The testator's third daughter, Elisabeth, whose name was given by her brother John in his pedigree entered in "Tonge's Visitation" in 1530, is not mentioned

*As 23 July, 22 Henry VIII, was the same as 23 July 1530, and as Richard Peck died 30 September 1516, it is obvious that 22 Henry VIII ("henr octaui") was written by mistake where 22 Henry VII was intended. The indenture, therefore, was made 23 July, 22 Henry VII [23 July 1507].

in her father's will, and she probably died without issue before the will was made.]

The Will of . KATERYN ANNE [widow] of Hoton Pannall [Hooton-Pagnall, co. York], dated 23 November 1523. I bequeath my soul to God Almighty, to Our Blessed Lady Saint Mary, and to all the Saints of heaven, my body to be buried in the church of the aforesaid Hoton. I bequeath for my mortuary my best beast, after the custom of the country. To the High Altar for tithes forgotten 6s. 8d. To the church 6s. 8d. To my son, John Anne, my best salt and three pairs of my best sheets, to Kateryn, my daughter, his wife, my best kirtle and my best girdle; and to Cristofer Anne, my godson, 10s. To Jane Pek, my daughter, my best gown; to Alice Grene, my daughter, my other best gown; to Elizabeth Otes, my daughter, my other best gown; and to Anne More, my daughter, my best gown. To Nichales Peke 26s. 8d. To John Phaslay, my servant, a yoke of oxen. To Jenet, my servant, a cow. To Alicie, my servant, a cow. To John Ryley two sheep. To Robert, my servant, two sheep. To little Kateryn, my servant, an old gown or an old kirtle. To Kateryn More 6s. 8d. and a silver spoon. To Richard Ely's wife and to White['s] wife and to Rois, William Ely's wife, to each one of them a pair of sheets. To William Grene and to Kateryn Grene, to each a silver spoon. To a priest to sing for my soul a twelve-month 7 marks. The residue of my goods not bequeathed I give to John Anne, my son, to John Peke, my son-in-law, to Thomas Grene, my son-in-law, to Brian Otes, my son-in-law, and to George More, my son-in-law, whom I make my executors, [and they are] to dispose of all [my goods] for the health of my soul and profit to themselves. Witnesses: Sir William Sheperd, vicar, Robert Smythe, Thomas Wikham, and William England. Proved by the executors 3 March 1523 [1523/4]. (Exchequer and Prerogative Courts of York [at York], Register 9, fo. 277.)

The Will of JOHN ANNE of Frikley [Frickley, co. York], Esq., dated 24 April 1544. I commend my soul unto Christ Jesu [etc.], my body to be buried in the parish church of Frikley, in the choir between the pillars. To the church of Hoton Pannall [Hooton-Pagnall, co. York] 10s. To the High Altar of Hoton Pannall for tithes forgotten 5s. To the High Altar of Frikley for tithes forgotten 6s. 8d. To my sons Christofer Anne, Martyne Anne, Peter Anne, Gabriel Anne, and William Anne, and to my daughter, Dorithye Anlabie, various bequests [household furniture, livestock, corn, a house, etc.]. To John Anlabie, my godson, a yoke of oxen and two silver spoons. To Margaret Anlabie two cows and two silver spoons. To my brother William a horse and my brooch. To Marie More a cow and a quarter of barley. To Sir Richard Furnes a doublet and a jacket. To Christofer Uscrofte a jerkin and a velvet bonnet. I bequeath my ring, worth 26s. 8d., to my brother Peke, my brother Grene, and my three sisters, "for to make euery one of them a gymber rynge to have me in remembrance." To eight towns "next enioynynge me," that is, Clayton, Thurnscoughe, Hikilton, Marre, Brodesworth, Hoton Pannall, Elmsall, and Skelbrike, viij[th] quarters or corne," either wheat, barley, or pease, and to Hampall half a quarter of corn. To every one of my yeomen a quarter wage. To every one of my hinds 12d. To every one of my maids 12d. To John Marshall, my boy, 40s., "in penny or pennyworth." To every one of my god-children 12d. The residue to Katheryne Anne, my wife, and to my brother-in-law William Hothome, Esq., whom I make my full executors. Witnesses: Sir Richarde Fournes, curate, Christofer Uscrofte, Thomas Witt. Proved 21

## GENEALOGICAL RESEARCH IN ENGLAND

Communicated by the Committee on English and Foreign Research

### THE ENGLISH ANCESTRY OF JOSEPH PECK OF HINGHAM, MASS., IN 1638

Compiled by S. ALLYN PECK, B.A., of New York City, and contributed by FREDERICK STANHOPE PECK, LL.D., of Barrington, R. I.

## II

### THE PECKS OF WAKEFIELD, CO. YORK [CONTINUED]

The Will of JOHN PECKE of Wakefield, co. York, Esq., dated 2 November 1558. I commend my soul unto Christ Jesu, my maker and redeemer [etc.], my body to be buried within the parish church of Allhallows in Wakefield or else where it shall please Almighty God to call me to his mercy. To Mr. Vicar of Wakefield for tithes omitted and forgotten 12d. To the said Mr. Vicar for my mortuary according to the laws of this realm.

Mr. Thomas Robertson, Doctor of Divinity and Dean of the Cathedral Church of Durham, Mr. John Greene, and John Mylnes shall take and enjoy all the rents of one close in Wakefield lying near Wakefield bridge, now in the holding [i. e., tenure] of Richard Nayler, extending to the yearly rent of "viili" [8 pounds], to the use, profit, and commodity [i. e., advantage] of my three sons, John Peke, Thomas Peke, and Nicholas Peke, during their natural lives and the longest liver of those three; and after their deaths the said close thenceforth shall remain to the heirs male of my body, lawfully begotten, for ever.

Immediately after my decease the said Mr. Thomas Robertson, Mr. John Grene, and John Mylnes shall take and enjoy the rents and profits of all my lands, tenements. and hereditaments lying within the parish of Easbey Ardeslowe [sic, ? East Ardsley, co. York], to the use, profit, and commodity of John Peke, son and heir apparent of Richard Peke, my son, until the said John Peke shall come to the age of twenty-four years; and the said Mr. Thomas Robertson shall have the government and bringing-up (in virtue and learning) of the said John Peck until he come to the said age of twenty-four years, if it may please him at this my especial request to have his assistance therein, the said Mr. Thomas Robertson taking to himself at his discretion so much of the rents of the said lands, tenements, and hereditaments in Easte Ardeslowe [East Ardsley] aforesaid, for the education and bringing-up of the said John Peke, as [may seem necessary], the rest of the yearly rents to be reserved to the use of the said John Peke until he come to the said age of twenty-four years.

The aforesaid Richard Peke, my son, shall have all my purchased lands

[and] tenements, with their appurtenances, within the parish of Wakefield (except those parcels which I have already given to Lancelote Lake and Robert Peke), to have and to hold unto the said Richard and his heirs male for ever. Also [I give to the said Richard] all my lands and tenements in Halifax parish [co. York], with one house and a close thereto belonging in Criglestone, within the parish of Sandall [co. York], now or late in the tenure or occupation of John Norton, to have and to hold to the said Richard [and] his heirs male of his body, lawfully begotten, and for default of such issue to remain to me, the said John Peke, for ever.

I give and bequeath, immediately after my decease, all my lands, tenements, and hereditaments lying within the parish of East Ardeslow [East Ardsley] to John Peke aforesaid, son and heir apparent of the said Richard Peke, my son, and to the heirs male of his body, lawfully begotten, on condition that he or his heirs shall not alien the premises or any parcel thereof or do or procure to be done any act or acts, directly or indirectly, whereby to alter or transfer the possession of the premises or any parcel thereof contrary to the tenor of this my last will and testament, and "so that" [i. e., on condition that] he be ordered, as well in his education and bringing-up in learning as also in his marriage, by the Right Worshipful Mr. Thomas Robinson [sic] aforesaid, if it may please him at my special request to have his assistance therein, and [by] the said Richard Peke, his father, or the survivor of them. I give and bequeath unto the said John, son and heir of Richard Peck aforesaid, the use and occupation of my "chyne" of gold during his life, and after his decease I give and bequeath the said "chyne" of gold to the next heir male of me, the said John.

I give and assign to be heirlooms (which, I will, shall continue from time to time at my house in Wakefield wherein I now dwell) certain things expressed and mentioned in one schedule hereunto annexed.

To Agnes Peke, my daughter, 20 marks of current English money, in full satisfaction of her "filiall and childs portion" of my goods and chattels. To Alice Peke, my daughter, if she be now living, 20 marks of lawful money of England, in full satisfaction of her "filiall and childs portion" of my goods and chattels.

I make Mr. John Grene, Richard Peke and Nicholas, my sons, and John Mylnes mine executors, and I give unto every one of them for their pains herein 40s.

My said executors shall take and receive, to the use of Marie Poage, of one lease which I have of the demise and grant of Anne Poage in her widowhood, the sum of twenty pounds, to be received in the three half years next and immediately after my decease, to the use and marriage of the said Marie Poage, if she be then living. Moreover, I will and assign my said executors to take and receive the profits of all the lands in Nottingham and "within the Countie of the towne of Nottingham" and of all the lands within the "parishing" of Tyckell [? Tickhill, co. York] which I have at this present in lease, toward the education and bringing-up of John Poage in virtue and learning, until the said John shall come to the age of twenty-four years. My executors shall bestow of the finding of the said John Poage yearly of the rents and profits eight pounds, until he come to the full age of sixteen years; and from the end of the said sixteen years until she [sic] shall be of the full age of twenty-one years my executors shall bestow of his finding of the rents and profits aforesaid ten pounds in the year; and from the end of the said twenty-one years my executors shall bestow of his finding twenty marks yearly, until he shall be of the full age of twenty-four years.

Then, when the said John Poage shall be of the full age of twenty-four years, I give, bequeath, and assign unto him my whole lease which I have of the said lands, to have and to hold to his own use during all the term of years then to come and not finished in the said lease; and, if the said John Poage shall die before the said lease be finished, I give and assign the reversion of the said lease to my executors, during the term of years then unfinished in the said lease.

My executors shall take and receive all the rents and profits of one tenement in "northgate" in Wakefield called the Whyte Horse, with all the lands belonging to the same (which Thomas Killingbecke holdeth of me by one indenture of a lease), during all the term of years yet to come in the said lease, part thereof to be bestowed as hereafter followeth and the rest at the discretion of my executors, whereof I give and bequeath of the said rents of the Whyte Horse, yearly during the said lease thereof, 20s. in the year towards the repairing and amending of the most noisome highways about Wakefield, that is to say, 6s. 9d. [*sic*, 8d.] yearly to be bestowed from "northegate and to the wood syde at Sladely Lone gate" and 6s. 8d. yearly from "Northgate and to the brode foore and so to the Wood gate next allerthorp" and the other 6s. 8d. yearly at "Kirkgate end or Wrengate end" or other places at the discretion of a neighbor. I give and bequeath of the rents of the said tenement called the Whyte Horse, yearly during the said lease, unto Sir Edward Woode 6s. 8d., if the said Sir Edward live so long, and unto every one of the poorest of my god-children 4d., at the discretion of my executors, and the residue of the aforesaid yearly rents of the tenement called Whyte Horse, with the appurtenances, during the term of the lease, my executors shall give and bestow amongst my children's children, at the discretion of said executors. And after the said lease be finished and expired, the said tenement called the Whyte Horse and all other things mentioned in the said lease shall remain to Richard Peke aforesaid and to the heirs male of his body, lawfully begotten, and in default of such issue to the right heirs of me, the said John Peke, for ever, and in default of such issue to the heirs male of the body of me, the said John Peke.

To the said Richard Peke, my son, all my timber ready to build, with all my slate stone and "ashler" stone.

The residue of all my goods and chattels not bequeathed, my debts paid thereof and my legacies and funeral expenses discharged thereof, I give and bequeath unto all my children, to be divided amongst them at the discretion of my executors, and those of my children who have had the least benefit and help of my goods shall have the best part of the rest of my goods. I make the aforesaid Mr. Thomas Robertson the supervisor hereof, and I give unto him for his pains one ring of gold having a stone therein. In witness whereof I, the said John Peke, Esq., hereunto have subscribed my name with my own hand. Witnesses: Sir Edward Woode, Thomas Scrypynr, Peter Dighton, Willm Adamson, with others.

These parcels of goods following are given by John Peke, Esq., to my son and heir, Richard Peke, and to the heirs male of the said Richard, to remain from time to time for ever as heirlooms, according to my last will and testament; Inprimis, in two chambers, in either chamber one stand bed and in either of the said chambers two "chysts." Item, all such harness as is now remainng in the house of the said John Peke at Wakefield. Item, all the tables in the hall and the iron "chymnye" in the said hall. Item, the brewing leads.

Proved 17 February 1558 [1558/9] by John Grene, Richard Peke, John Mylnes, and Nicholas Peke, the executors. (Exchequer and Prerogative Courts of York [at York], Register 15, part 3, fo. 273.)

Inquisition post Mortem on the death of John Pecke (Peke) of Wakefield [co. York], Esq., held at Wakefield 30 April, 1 Elizabeth [30 April 1559].*

The said John Pecke died on 3 February last past [3 February 1558/9]. Richard Pecke, his son, is his next heir, and is forty-two years and more of age at the taking of this inquisition. (Inquisitions post Mortem, Chancery Series, vol. 122, no. 49, preserved in the Public Record Office, London.)

[In the explanatory notes given after the abstract of the will of Richard Peck,† the testator of 4 June 1516, and his inquisition post mortem, held on 28 August 1518 (*supra*, pp. 65–66), the two unusual marriage alliances that united the Peck family of Wakefield with the Anne family of Frickley, co. York, were made clear, and it was shown that Richard Peck, the testator of 1516, whose first wife, the mother of his children, was Alice Middelton, married secondly, not later than 1512, Elisabeth Anne, daughter of John Anne of Frickley and sister of the Johan or Jane Anne who about 1507 was married to John Peck, son and heir of the aforesaid Richard Peck. John Anne of Frickley, therefore, was the father-in-law of Richard Peck of Wakefield, Esq., the testator of 1516, and also of Richard Peck's son and heir, John Peck of Wakefield, Esq., the testator of 2 November 1558, who had entered his pedigree and given the names of his children in Tonge's Visitation of 1530.

Frickley, the seat of the Anne family, was a hamlet in the small parish of Clayton in the Field, a few miles northwest from Doncaster, in the West Riding of Yorkshire.

John Anne of Frickley died not later than 1520, when, according to data obtained by the compiler of this article, administration was granted on his estate; and from the will of his widow, Katherine Anne of Hooton-Pagnall, co. York, dated 23 November 1523 and proved 3 March 1523/4 (*supra*, p. 66), as well as from the will of his son, John Anne of Frickley, Esq., dated 24 April 1544 and proved 21 November 1545 (*ib.*), more information about the Peck and Anne families may be derived, which should be summarized before discussing the provisions of the will of John Peck, the testator of 2 November 1558.

Katherine Anne, widow of John Anne, in her will dated 23 November 1523, describes herself as of Hooton-Pagnall, co. York, and, after directing that she be buried in the church of Hooton-Pagnall and bequeathing to the high altar there, for tithes forgotten, 6s. 8d., and to the church there 6s. 8d., makes various bequests of personal property, such as wearing apparel, bedding, silver, and money, to John Anne, her only son mentioned in the will, to Katherine, "my daughter, his wife" [i.e., the daughter-in-law of the testatrix],‡ to Christopher Anne, "my godson" [shown by the will of the son, John Anne, to have been also the grandson of the testatrix], and to four married daughters, who, with their husbands and their children named in the will, may be grouped in the following order: daughter Jane Peck and son-in-law John Peck, known from other sources to have been the parents of Nicholas Peck, to whom a legacy of 26s. 8d. is left by the testatrix; daughter Alice Grene and son-in-law Thomas Grene, probably the parents of William Grene and Katherine Grene, to each of whom the testatrix bequeaths a silver spoon; daughter Elizabeth Otes and son-in-law Brian Otes;§ and daughter Anne More and son-in-law

---

*The Inquisition post Mortem, of which a brief abstract of the most important statements only is given here, is written in Latin.

†In the present explanatory notes the customary spelling, *Peck*, of the surname of the Wakefield family and the customary spellings of Christian names are used for convenience, without regard to the various spellings of such names in the original documents.

‡Information obtained by the compiler shows that John Anne, son of the testatrix, married first Margery Hercy and secondly Katherine Hotham, the daughter-in-law named in the will of the testatrix.

§Elizabeth Otes was the daughter who had married about 1512, as his second wife, Richard Peck, the testator of 1516 and the father of John Peck, the husband of her sister Jane. After Richard Peck's death Elizabeth married Brian Otes, who, according to information obtained by the compiler, was of Halifax, co. York. She married thirdly Richard Kepas, and fourthly Thomas Tatersal. She was probably living in 1544, when her brother, John Anne, in his will, mentions "my three sisters," the sister Jane, who had been the wife of John Peck, having probably died.

George More, probably the parents of Katherine More, to whom the testatrix bequeaths 6s. 8d. and a silver spoon. Other small bequests, in clothing, bedding, livestock, etc., are made to several servants and to some who are prehaps relatives, seven marks are left for a priest to sing a twelve-month for the soul of the testatrix, and the residue of her goods, not bequeathed, the testatrix gives to John Anne, her son, and to John Peck, Thomas Grene, Brian Otes, and George More, her sons-in-law, whom she makes her executors, directing them to dispose of all her goods for the health of her soul and profit to themselves.

The will of John Anne of Frickley, co. York, Esq. (son of the testatrix of 23 November 1523), dated 24 April 1544, directs that the testator be buried in the parish church of Frickley, and bequeaths 10s. to the church of Hooton-Pagnall, 5s. to the high altar of Hooton-Pagnall for tithes forgotten, and 6s. 8d. to the high altar of Frickley for tithes forgotten. Various bequests, consisting of household furniture, livestock, corn, a house, etc., are made to five sons of the testator, Christopher, Martin, Peter, Gabriel, and William Anne, and to a married daughter, Dorothy Anlabie, probably the mother of John Anlabie, the testator's godson, to whom the testator leaves a yoke of oxen and two silver spoons, and of Margaret Anlabie, to whom he leaves two cows and two silver spoons. To his brother [i.e., brother-in-law] William the testator leaves "a horse and my brooch," and to Marie More, perhaps a niece of the testator, a cow and a quarter of barley. There are bequests to various other persons, including the testator's yeomen, hinds, maids, and other servants, and 12d. to every one of his godchildren. His ring, worth 26s. 8d., the testator bequeaths to his brother Peck, his brother Grene, and his three sisters, to be made into "gymber" rings for every one of them, "to have me in remembrance." Brother Peck and brother Grene were actually brothers-in-law of the testator, and the fact that only three of the testator's sisters were living seems to indicate that the testator's sister Jane, wife of John Peck, was dead when her brother made his will, especially as no wife is mentioned in the will of the said John Peck, dated 2 November 1558. The residue of his estate the testator gives to Katherine Anne, his wife, and William Hothome, Esq., his brother-in-law, whom he makes his executors.

Almost fifteen years after John Anne of Frickley made his will, his brother-in-law, John Peck of Wakefield, Esq., signed with his own hand (2 November 1558) his last will and testament (of which an extended abstract is given above)—a document of the utmost importance in determining whether this testator was the ancestor, through a son Robert (as the tabular pedigree accepted as correct by the late Ira Ballou Peck states) or in any other way, of Joseph Peck of Hingham and Rehoboth in New England and his elder brother, Rev. Robert Peck.

As already related (*supra,* p. 62),[*]an inscription, formerly in the parish church of Wakefield but no longer to be found there, stated (according to Dodsworth's Church Notes) that John Peck of Wakefield and Jane, his wife, daughter of John Anne of Frickley, had nine sons and nine daughters, but the names of these children were not given.

It is possible that the inscription in the church at Wakefield that represented John Peck and his wife Jane as the parents of nine sons and nine daughters was copied incorrectly in Dodsworth's "Church Notes;" at any rate, the names of only six sons and seven daughters of John Peck—thirteen children in all—have been found by the compiler of this article.

*Page 539, this volume.

# GENEALOGICAL RESEARCH IN ENGLAND

Communicated by the Committee on English and Foreign Research

## THE ENGLISH ANCESTRY OF JOSEPH PECK OF HINGHAM, MASS., IN 1638

Compiled by S. ALLYN PECK, B.A., of New York City, and contributed by
FREDERICK STANHOPE PECK, LL.D., of Barrington, R. I.

## II

### THE PECKS OF WAKEFIELD, CO. YORK [CONTINUED]

[Continuation of Explanatory Notes]

The first son named by John Peck in "Tonge's Visitation" of 1530 was Richard, called there and also in John Peck's will in 1558 the son and heir of the said John Peck, and in the inquisition post mortem on the death of John Peck, held at Wakefield 30 April 1559, said to be the next heir of John Peck and to be forty-two years and more of age at the taking of the inquisition. Richard was born, therefore, about 1517 or perhaps somewhat earlier, and, as his parents were married about 1507, it is unlikely that he was their eldest child, although he was without doubt their eldest surviving son. As John Peck in 1530 names three married daughters and three unmarried daughters, presumably in the order of their births, it is probable that the three married daughters and perhaps one of the unmarried daughters were older than Richard, his father's son and heir. The first daughter named in 1530, Katherine, wife of John Leyke (i. e., Lake, as will be shown later), if born in 1508, would have been about twenty-two years old in 1530; the second daughter, Margaret, wife of John Talear (i. e., Taylor), may have been twenty in 1530; the third daughter, Anne, wife of John Hill, may have been eighteen in that year; and the fourth daughter, Elisabeth, although not married in 1530, may have been born about 1514. Four daughters, therefore, were probably older than their brother Richard, his father's eldest surviving son and his heir. Katherine, wife of John Lake, is not *named* in her father's will, but her husband was living in 1558 (see his will, *infra*) and Katherine herself was living, a widow, in 1578/9 (see her will, *infra*). She had probably received her portion of her father's estate on her marriage, and therefore was not *named* as a legatee in his will, although she would share, of course, with her brothers and sisters or their heirs, in the division, by the executors, of the final residue of her father's estate, which he bequeathed unto all his children. Margaret also, the second daughter named in "Tonge's Visitation" in 1530, who was then the wife of John Taylor, was not *named* in her father's will, and, like her sister Katherine, had probably received her portion at her marriage; but, as nothing has been found about her except that she was the wife of John Taylor in 1530, it is not possible to determine whether she was living or dead when her father made his will in 1558.

The third daughter, Anne, who in 1530 and also as late as Michaelmas Term, 25 Henry VIII [2—25 November 1533*] was the wife of John Hill [of Horbury, co. York], married secondly Robert [*sic*] Poge (or Poage) of Misterton, co. Nottingham [John Page of Nottinghamshire, according to "The Visitation

*In Michaelmas Term, 1533, John Peke, Esq., was plaintiff [or querent] in a suit against John Hyll, senr., and Isabel, his wife, deforciants, for a messuage, with lands, in Horbury, which after the decease of John Hyll, senr., and Isabel, his wife, was to remain to John Hyll, junr., and Anne, his wife, with remainder, in default of issue, to the right heirs of Isabel. (Calendar of Yorkshire Feet of Fines, 1486–1571, in vol. 2 of the Yorkshire Archæological and Topographical Association's Record Series.)

of Yorkshire" of 1563 and 1564], and thirdly, after 1542, Richard Burditt of Roystone, co. York. Her second marriage (and perhaps her third marriage also) took place in the lifetime of her father, who in his will directs his executors (Mr. John Grene, Richard Peke (Peck) and Nicholas [Peck], his (the testator's) sons, and John Mylnes) to take and receive to the use of Marie Poage, in the three half years immediately after his decease, of one lease which he (the testator) has of the demise and grant of Anne Poage in her widowhood [i. e., when she was the Widow Poage], the sum of 20 pounds, to the use and marriage of the said Marie Poage, if she be then living. The said executors are also to take and receive the profits of all the lands in Nottingham and "within the Countie of the towne of Nottingham" and of all the lands within the "parishing" of Tyckell [? Tickhill, co. York] which the testator has at this present in lease, towards the education and bringing-up of John Poage in virtue and learning, until the said John shall come to the age of twenty-four years, as follows: 8 pounds yearly until the said John Poage shall come to the full age of sixteen years, 10 pounds yearly from the end of the said sixteen years until he shall come to the full age of twenty-one years, and 20 marks yearly from the end of the said twenty-one years until he shall come to the full age of twenty-four years. Then, when the said John Poage has come to the full age of twenty-four years, the testator assigns to him his (the testator's) whole lease of the said lands, for the remainder of the term of the lease, and, if John Poage shall die before the lease expires, the testator assigns the reversion of the lease, for the unfinished term, to his (the testator's) executors. It seems clear that Marie Poage and John Poage, for whom provision was thus made in the will of John Peck of Wakefield, were grandchildren of the testator, the children of his daughter Anne by her second husband, Robert or John Poage, Poge, or Page of Nottinghamshire, and that the testator's grandson, John Poage, was under sixteen years of age on 2 November 1558, the date of John Peck's will. What became of the mother of Marie Poage and John Poage, who married a third husband after the death of the father of these two children, and whether she was living when her father made his will, does not appear. Born probably about 1512 and probably about eighteen in 1530, she was undoubtedly older than her brother Richard, her father's eldest surviving son and heir.

Of the three unmarried daughters, Elisabeth, Alice, and Dorathe (Dorothy), whose names were entered by their father in "Tonge's Visitation" in 1530, Elisabeth, who also may have been older than her brother Richard, was not mentioned in her father's will, dated 2 November 1558, and, according to "The Visitation of Yorkshire" of 1563 and 1564, she died without issue (whether married or single does not appear). The daughter Alice left home, and her father did not know, when he made his will on 2 November 1558, whether she was living or dead, but he provided for her in his will, bequeathing to "Alice Peke, my daughter, if she be now living," 20 marks of lawful money of England, in full satisfaction of her "filiall and childs portion" of his goods and chattels. The daughter Dorothy was not named in her father's will, but, according to "The Visitation of Yorkshire" of 1563 and 1564, she married William Rowke, and therefore she may have received her portion of her father's goods at the time of her marriage.

In his will John Peck mentioned another daughter, Agnes Peke, who was not named in "Tonge's Visitation" in 1530 and was probably born after 1530; and to this seventh daughter, unmarried, her father bequeathed 20 marks of current English money, in full satisfaction of her "filiall and childs portion" of his goods and chattels. Agnes was named in the will before Alice, probably because the father was uncertain whether Alice was living and would ever appear to claim her portion.

Of the six sons of John and Jane (Anne) Peck who were named in "Tonge's Visitation" in 1530, beginning with Richard, son and heir, and who were named also in "The Visitation of Yorkshire" of 1563 and 1564 (although it is not necessary to infer that all six were living when this later Visitation was compiled), four were living on 2 November 1558, and were named as legatees in their father's will of that date. William, the fourth son, and Francis, the sixth son, were not named in their father's will, and what had become of them

550

has not been ascertained, but it is probable that they had died between 1530 and 1558. No wife was mentioned in John Peck's will, and the mother of his children, as already stated, was probably dead by 24 April 1544, when the will of her brother, John Anne, was dated.

In making provision for the four sons mentioned in his will John Peck does not name them in the order of their births—that order is found in the entry of their names in "Tonge's Visitation" of 1530; but in this analysis of the will the order of births is followed.

To Richard Peke, his son and heir, the testator gives all his purchased lands [and] tenements, with their appurtenances, within the parish of Wakefield, except those parcels which he has already given to Lancelote Lake and Robert Peke (vide infra), to have and to hold unto the said Richard and his heirs male for ever; also all his (the testator's) lands and tenements in Halifax parish, with one house and a close thereto belonging in Criglestone, within the parish of Sandall, now or late in the tenure or occupation of John Norton, to have and to hold to the said Richard [and] the heirs male of his body, lawfully begotten, and for default of such issue to remain to him, the testator, for ever. To the said Richard Peke, his son, the testator leaves also a tenement in Wakefield called the "Whyte Horse," after the expiration of a lease from which the annual rents are to be used by his executors for certain designated purposes, such as repairing highways, sundry gifts, etc.; and to the said Richard, the testator's son and heir, is given all the testator's timber ready to build, together with his slate stone and "ashler" stone, and to Richard and his heirs male are given certain heirlooms that are to remain for ever as such in the testator's house at Wakefield.

To the use, profit, and advantage of the testator's three sons, John, Thomas, and Nicholas Peke, during their natural lives and the life of the longest liver of the three, the testator assigns all the rents of one close in Wakefield, in the tenure of Richard Nayler, extending to the yearly rent of 8 pounds,* and after the death of these three sons the said close is to remain to the heirs male of the testator's body, lawfully begotten, for ever.

The son John, according to "The Visitation of Yorkshire" in 1563 and 1564, lived in Rutlandshire, and no information is given in this Visitation about his marriage, children, or death. In Easter Term, 33 Henry VIII, 15 April— 8 May 1541, as John Pek, junr., he had been plaintiff [or querent], with his father, John Pek, senr., esq., in a suit for 5 messuages, with lands, in Wodhouse, in the township of Ardsley (Calendar of Yorkshire Feet of Fines, 1486–1571, in vol. 2 of the Yorkshire Archæological and Topographical Association's Record Series).

The son Thomas appears also in "The Visitation of Yorkshire" in 1563 and 1564, as the third son. No further information is given about him there; but in Hilary Term, 1 and 2 Philip and Mary, 11–31 January 1554/5, a Thomas Pek and Ann, his wife, were deforciants in a suit brought by John Sayvell [Savile], plaintiff [or querent], for 5 messuages in Wakefield (Calendar of Yorkshire Feet of Fines, as cited above).

To the son Nicholas, who appears also in "The Visitation of Yorkshire" in 1563 and 1564 as the fifth son, and is there said (in later additions) to have married Alice, daughter of Bryan Bradford and to have had six children (names given), of whom Jasper Peck, apparently the eldest son, was 17 years of age in 1585, Nicholas's grandmother, Katheryn Anne, widow, in her will, dated 23 November 1523, bequeathed 26s. 8d. Since Nicholas was the fifth son of his father, and his father's eldest son and heir, Richard, was born about 1516, Nicholas could hardly have been born before 1523, and was probably the latest born of her Peck grandsons when his Grandmother Anne bequeathed to him this legacy. With his eldest brother, Richard, and two others, he was named an executor of his father's will, and as such joined with the other three executors in proving the will, 17 February 1558/9. As Nicholas Pecke, gent., he was plaintiff [or querent] in a suit brought in Easter Term, 7 Elizabeth, 15 April–8 May 1565 (Calendar, etc., as cited above), and he was living 18 February 1578/9, when he was named as a supervisor in the will of his sister,

*Not 7 pounds, as might be understood from a typographical error in the abstract of this will, supra, p. 194.

Katherine Layke of Normanton, co. York, widow, and was also a witness to this will, being styled gentleman in both capacities.

As has been stated above, John Pecke of Wakefield, Esq., the testator of 2 November 1558, in his last will and testament, gives to his eldest surviving son, Richard Peke, and to all his (Richard's) heirs male for ever, all his (the testator's) purchased lands [and] tenements, with their appurtenances, within the parish of Wakefield, except those parcels which he has already given to Lancelote Lake and Robert Peke; and the question arises, "Who was this Robert Peke?" It is known (and will be proved later) that Lancelote Lake was a grandson of the testator, the son of his daughter Katherine, wife of John Lake; and therefore it has been suggested that perhaps Robert Peke (Peck) also was a grandson of the testator. In Easter Term, 20 Henry VIII (15 April–8 May 1528), a Robert Peke and Margaret, his wife, were deforciants in a suit brought by Thomas Fulwode, plaintiff [or querent], for land in Bentley near Doncaster (Calendar of Yorkshire Feet of Fines, 1486–1571, in vol. 2 of the Yorkshire Archæological and Topographical Association's Record Series), but the Robert Peke who had a wife in 1528 was, of course, too old to be a grandson of the testator of 2 November 1558. Perhaps he was "my uncle, Robert Peke," to whom Richard Peke of Wakefield, father of John Pecke, the testator of 1558, leaves sundry articles of apparel, in his will dated 4 June 1516, "if he survive me." It remains, therefore, to find out what information is given in the will of John Pecke or in other sources about his grandsons, and especially whether there was among them a grandson named Robert Peke (Peck).

In the first part of his will, after assigning the rents from a close in Wakefield for the use of his three sons, John, Thomas, and Nicholas Peke, during their lives and the life of the longest liver among them, John Pecke of Wakefield, Esq., directed Mr. Thomas Robertson (previously called Doctor of Divinity and Dean of the Cathedral Church of Durham), Mr. John Grene, and John Mylnes to take and enjoy, immediately after his (the testator's) decease, the rents and profits of all his lands, tenements, and hereditaments in the parish of East Ardsley, co. York, for the use of John Peke, son and heir apparent of Richard Peke, the testator's son, until the said John Peke shall come to the age of twenty-four years; and Mr. Thomas Robertson is to have the government and bringing-up (in virtue and learning) of the said John Peck until he come to the age of twenty-four years. These lands, etc., in East Ardsley are given to the said John Peke (son and heir apparent of the said Richard Peke, the testator's son) and to the heirs male of his body, lawfully begotten, on condition that he or his heirs shall not "alien" the premises or any parcel thereof, and on condition also that he be ordered, as well in his education and bringing-up in learning as also in his marriage, by the Right Worshipful Mr. Thomas Robinson [sic] aforesaid and by the said Richard Peke, his father, or the survivor of them. To the said John, son and heir of Richard Peck aforesaid, the testator bequeaths the use and occupation of his "chyne" of gold during his life, and after his decease the testator bequeaths the said "chyne" of gold to his (the testator's) next heir male. To sum up, the testator makes special provision for his grandson, John Peke (Peck), son and heir apparent of his (the testator's) son, Richard Peke, the said grandson being then, on 2 November 1558, apparently considerably under twenty-four years of age. According to "The Visitation of Yorkshire" of 1563 and 1564 both this grandson, John Pecke, and his next younger brother, Thomas Pecke, died without issue, and the third brother, Richard Pecke, became his father's heir. There was a fourth son in this family, Langton Pecke, and three daughters, but no mention in "The Visitation of Yorkshire" of a son in this family named Robert. If, therefore, the Robert Peke to whom John Pecke, Esq., had given lands in Wakefield prior to 2 November 1558 was a grandson of the testator, he was probably a son either of John or of Thomas Peck, the second and third sons of the testator of 1558. Nothing has been found about John's family. Thomas, it is probable, had a wife Ann in January 1554/5 (vide supra). No child named Robert is given in "The Visitation of Yorkshire" among the children of John Pecke's fifth son, Nicholas. In any event, the Robert Peke to whom John Pecke, Esq., had given lands in Wakefield prior to 2 November 1558, if he was a son of the testator's son John or his son Thomas, would be too young to be identical with the Robert Pecke of Beccles, co. Suffolk, who made his will 31 October 1556.

Only a few words more in regard to the will of John Pecke of Wakefield, Esq., are necessary.

Of the annual rents from the tenement in Wakefield called the "Whyte Horse," during the continuance of the lease thereof, in addition to what has been stated above, every one of the poorest of the testator's godchildren is to receive 4d., at the discretion of the executors of the will, and the residue of the yearly rents of the "Whyte Horse," during the term of the lease, the executors, at their discretion, "shall give and bestow amongst my children's children."

The residue of all his goods and chattels not bequeathed, after his debts and legacies and funeral expenses have been paid therefrom, the testator gives and bequeaths to all his children, to be divided amongst them at the discretion of the executors, "and those of my children who have had the least benefit and help of my goods shall have the best part of the rest of my goods."]

To complete the records that have been found about the Pecks of Wakefield, an abstract of the will of John Lake, son-in-law of John Peck of Wakefield, Esq., dated 24 December 1558, when his father-in-law was still living, and an abstract of the will of his widow, Katherine Layke (Lake), daughter of John Peck of Wakefield, Esq., dated 18 February 1578/9, with such brief comments as may be necessary, are here given.

The Will of JOHN LAKE of Normanton, co. York, Gentleman, dated 24 December 1558. I bequeath my soul unto Almighty God and my body to be buried within the parish church of Normanton, as nigh my mother as can be. I bequeath 3s. 4d. to the making of one case to the Blessed Sacrament, if it may be suffered; and, if not, my executors [are] to dispose [of] it to poor folks. To Thomas Lake, my son, 40s. in a year, yearly, for life, out of my lands and farms at "bottome house," in Stanley. To Launcelote Lake, Alexander Lake, and Robert Lake, every one of them, 20s. in a year, for life, out of two closes in the "graueship" of Thornes, called "Wilfeldes," now in the tenure of one Eamonson, widow, provided always that the said Launcelot Lake, Alexander Lake, and Robert Lake shall not receive any rents or profits of the said lands until my will be performed hereafter.

I constitute my trusty and well-beloved in Christ, Xpofer Twyseltone of Bartone [Barton, co. York], Esq., Richard Peke, Nicholas Peke, and John Buny feoffees and receivers of all my rents, lands, and tenements hereafter following, viz., in Wakefield and Wakefield parish, "Rodwell ryle mylne house," Credlinge, and Pounfret; and the rents and profits thereof yearly [are] to be divided betwixt my son John Lake and the rest of my children, namely, Thomas Lake, Launcelot Lake, Alexander Lake, Robert Lake, Katering Lake, Jane Lake, Brigett Lake, Marye Lake, and Elizabeth Lake, until every one of them has received toward their support and marriage 20 marks apiece, that is to say, to Thomas 20 marks, to Launcelot 20 marks, to Alexander 20 marks, as is above said, and to Elizabeth Lake, my youngest daughter, 25 marks.

My executors shall make one "sewere and straige stoke," well bound with iron, with three locks and three keys, to be delivered unto my said feoffees and receivers for the safe keeping of the said yearly rents to the use abovesaid. The said Xpofer Twiseltone shall have the keeping of one of the said three keys, to the said Richard Peke one other of the said keys [shall be given], and to the said Nicholas Peke the third of the said keys, and the said John Buny [is] to have the custody of the said "styke;" and my feoffees and receivers shall bestow the said yearly rents to my said children, to every of them as they shall be first ready to marry, from the first to the last, or when they come to the age of "xij$^{tie}$" [sic, "xij$^{tie}$," that is, "twelve," is undoubtedly a mistake for xxij$^{tie}$," that is "twenty-two"] years.

To Katherin, my wife, for life, various articles of bedding and household furniture, including "a leade with all suche ayre Lomes," and after her decease [they are] to remain to my son John Lake and to the right heirs of me, to be used and occupied in this house as continual "ayre Lomes" for ever. The rest of my moveable goods, my debts being paid, shall be divided into three parts, and my children [are] to have one part indifferently amongst them, and the other two parts I give to Katheryn, my wife, whom I make my executrix, and I make John Peke of Wakefield, Esq., supervisor of this my last will and testament. Witnesses: John Bunye of Wakefield, John Lake of Altoftes, Edward Allan of Wakefield, and John Lake the Younger, with others. Proved 18 May 1559. (Exchequer and Prerogative Courts of York [at York], Register 15, Part 3, fo. 414a.)

The Will of KATHERINE LAYKE of Normanton, co. York, widow, dated 18 February 1578 [1578/9]. To be buried in the Lady Choir in the parish church of Normanton, nigh unto my husband, John Laike, Gentleman, deceased. To Susan Lucas, daughter of Stephen Lucas and Jane, my daughter, £6. 13s. 4d. To the children of Mary, my daughter, £3. 6s. 8d. To Robert Laike, my son. To Alice Hardwicke. To Willm Hardwicke, son of Willm Hardwicke. Executors and residuary legatees: all my children, that is to say, John Laike, Thomas Lake, Lancelott Laike, Alexander Laike, Roberte Laike, Bettres Larley, Katherine Barghe, Jane Thorneton, Briggette Hardewicke, Mary Sleforthe, and Elizabeth Wilbore. Supervisors of this my last will and testament: my brother, Nicholas Pecke, and Richard Breaton, Gentlemen. Witnesses: Nicholas Pecke, Richard Breaton, [and] Roger Mallette, Gentlemen, [and] John Barghe [and] Willm Hardewicke, with others. Proved 9 February 1580 [1580/1]. (Exchequer and Prerogative Courts of York [at York], Register 22, fo. 1.)

[John Lake of Normanton, co. York, Gentleman, in his will, dated 24 December 1558, names his brothers-in-law Richard Peke and Nicholas Peke, as two of the feoffees constituted under the terms of the will, and makes his father-in-law, John Peke of Wakefield, Esq., supervisor of the will. His father-in-law died on 3 February 1558/9, and Richard Peke, the elder of the two brothers-in-law named, died about 1561. Nicholas Peke lived to be a supervisor of and a witness to the will of his sister Katherine Layke (Lake), widow of John Lake, which was dated 18 February 1578/9. John Lake died between 24 December 1558 and 18 May 1559, and his widow died between 18 February 1578/9 and 9 February 1580/1. John Lake, Jr., seems to have been their oldest son, and they named in their wills four other sons, Thomas, Lancelot, Alexander, and Robert Lake, and several daughters.]

# THE PECK PEDIGREE

PLATE I

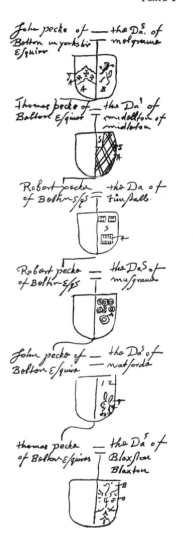

# THE PECK PEDIGREE

Plate II

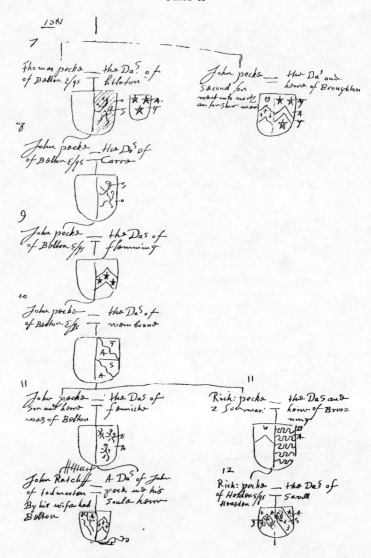

# THE PECK PEDIGREE

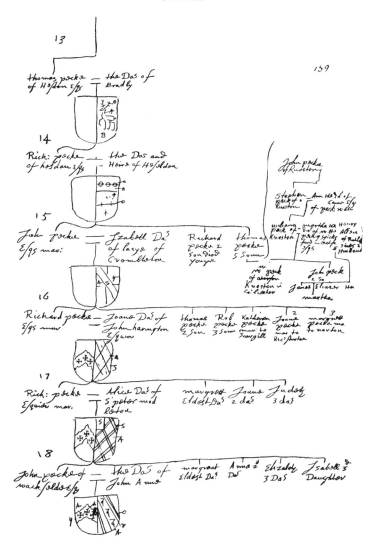

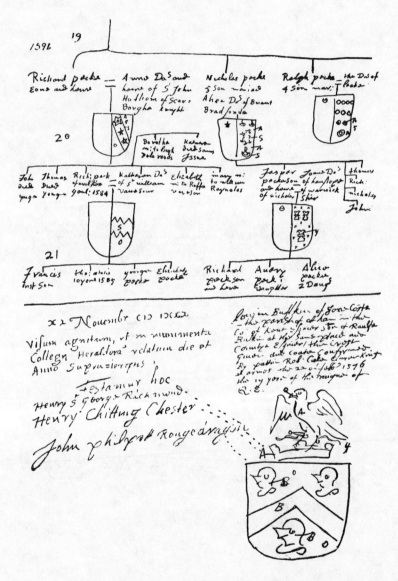

# THE PECK PEDIGREE

PLATE IVa

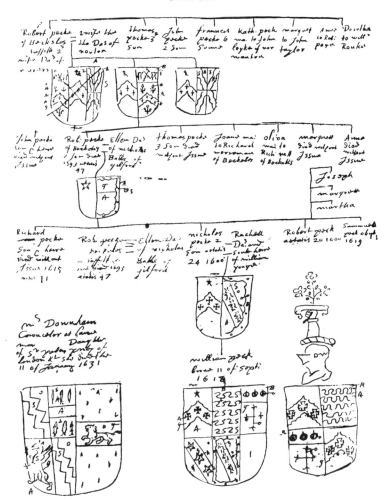

# GENEALOGICAL RESEARCH IN ENGLAND

Communicated by the Committee on English and Foreign Research

## THE ENGLISH ANCESTRY OF JOSEPH PECK
## OF HINGHAM, MASS., IN 1638

Compiled by S. ALLYN PECK, B.A., of New York City, and contributed by
FREDERICK STANHOPE PECK, LL.D., of Barrington, R. I.

## II

### THE PECKS OF WAKEFIELD, CO. YORK [CONCLUDED]

[Additional Note on the Lake Family]

[Katherine Layke (Lake) of Normanton, co. York, widow of John Lake,
in her will dated 18 February 1578/9 and proved 9 February 1580/1 (*supra*,
p. 268), names as living the same five sons that were named in their father's
will, dated 24 December 1558, viz., John (apparently the eldest son), Thomas,
Lancelott, Alexander, and Robert Lake, and, in addition to the five unmarried
daughters named in their father's will, she names another daughter (married)
and shows whom the five unmarried daughters of her husband's will married.
The daughter not named in the father's will is called by her mother "Bettres"
(i. e., Beatrice) Larley, and, as she comes first in the list of daughters, probably she was already married when her father made his will in 1558, had
already received her marriage portion, and therefore was not named in her
father's will.

The other five daughters, all unmarried when their father made his will, are
shown by their mother's will to be Katherine Barghe, whose husband was
probably John Barghe (a witness to the mother's will), Jane Thorneton, who
married first Stephen Lucas and had a daughter, Susan Lucas (to whom her
grandmother bequeathed £6. 13s. 4d.), and married secondly ——— Thorneton,
Briggette Hardewicke, who married William Hardwicke and had children
(Alice and William Hardwicke), Mary Sleforthe, who married ——— Sleforthe and had children (to whom their grandmother bequeathed £3. 6s. 8d.),
and Elizabeth Wilbore, who married ——— Wilbore.]

The records relating to the Pecks of Wakefield, co. York, and
the families connected with them by marriage, which have been given
—some verbatim and others in abstract—up to this point, have failed
to prove that John Peck of Wakefield, Esq., the testator of 2 November 1558 (who, it has been claimed, was the father of Robert
Peck of Beccles, co. Suffolk, the testator of 31 October 1556, ancestor of Joseph Peck of Hingham and Rehoboth in New England),
ever had a son named Robert Peck. It is true that in his will John
Peck of Wakefield, Esq., mentions a Robert Peck, to whom, together
with Lancelott Lake (known to be a grandson of the testator) he
states that he has given land in Wakefield, but he does not call this
Robert Peck his son, and this Robert Peck was probably, like Lancelott Lake, a grandson of the testator—not, however, a son of Richard
Peck, the testator's son and heir, for this Richard Peck had no son
named Robert (*supra*, p. 266), nor a son of the testator's fifth son,*

*Page 552, this volume.

Nicholas Peck, for he, too, had no son named Robert (*ib.*), but probably a son of John Peck or of Thomas Peck, the second and third sons of the testator of 2 November 1558 (*ib.*), or perhaps of William Peck or Francis Peck, the fourth and sixth sons of this testator, who are named by him in his pedigree entered in "Tonge's Visitation" in 1530 but probably died before their father, as they are not mentioned in his will.

It has been shown in the first instalment of this article that the Robert Peck who was named in the will of John Leeke of Beccles, co. Suffolk, dated 6 September 1529, as one of the testator's executors, was probably, from the nature of the services required of him and from the responsibility placed upon him under the terms of the will of John Leeke, at least twenty-one years old in 1529 and was therefore born in 1508 or earlier—very likely considerably earlier. It has been shown also that the Robert Peck named as an executor in the will of John Leeke was without doubt identical with the Robert Peck of Beccles whose will was dated 31 October 1556— a man who had had two wives (both then deceased), who by his first wife had a daughter who in 1556 was already grown up and married ("all" of whose children were mentioned in a will of 1561), and a man also who had six children by his second wife who were living on 31 October 1556, of whom three were born before 28 May 1547. Now the testator of 31 October 1556, from whom Rev. Robert Peck and his brother Joseph, who came to New England in 1638, are known to have been descended, could not have been a son or a grandson of John Peck, Esq., of Wakefield, the testator of 2 November 1558, for this Robert Peck of Beccles was probably born in 1508 or earlier, while the marriage of John Peck of Wakefield did not take place until 1507 and Richard Peck, his *eldest* son and heir, was not born until about 1516. Moreover, if the Robert Peck to whom, together with Lancelott Lake, land in Wakefield had been given by John Peck, Esq. (as stated in his will of 2 November 1558), was, as seems likely, a son of one of the younger sons of the said John Peck, he was too young to have been identical with Robert Peck of Beccles, the testator of 31 October 1556.*

Since the claim that Robert Peck of Beccles, the testator of 31 October 1556, was a son of John Peck of Wakefield, Esq., rests on the tabular pedigree in the British Museum which was accepted as authentic by the late Ira Ballou Peck in his "Genealogical History," on the guarantee of the late Horatio Gates Somerby, a facsimile of this tabular pedigree, in five pages, from its alleged beginning in the mists of the twelfth century, with all its armorial embellishments, is given in this issue of the REGISTER, immediately preceding page 371. ** The title, "The Peck Pedigree," and the plate numbers below it, that stand above each of the five line-cut plates, have been inserted by the Editors.

*See especially the abstracts of wills and of other records and the explanatory notes attached to them published in the REGISTER, vol. 89, pp. 334–339, as well as the records and explanatory notes relating to the Pecks of Wakefield given in the later instalments of this article. (For pp. 334-339 see pp. 530-535, this volume.)

**See pp. 555-559, this volume.

This pedigree, printed by the late Ira Ballou Peck in his "Genealogical History," has been described in the introduction to this article (*supra,* vol. 89, pp. 327–332). It may be found in the library of the ** British Museum, in Additional Manuscripts, No. 5524, folios 158–159b.* Plate IVA is an extension to the right of Plate IV, both plates purporting to give descendants of John Peck, Esq., of Wakefield, the testator of 2 November 1558. The sixth page of these three inserted sheets is necessarily a blank page.

The first part of this tabular pedigree, which gives an ancestral line for the Peck family of Wakefield that begins with a "John pecke of Belton in yorkshir Esquier," who, if he ever lived, probably lived as early as the twelfth century, needs no further comment here. (See Plates I, II, and the first two generations on Plate III.) The remainder of the pedigree, so far as it concerns the Pecks of Wakefield, seems to have been based, in general, on the pedigree entered in "Tonge's Visitation" of 1530 by John Peck of Wakefield, Esq., the testator of 2 November 1558, and on the Peck pedigree given in "The Visitation of Yorkshire" of 1563 and 1564. (See the last four generations on Plate III and also Plates IV and IVA.) But there are two important changes in the list of sons of John Peck of Wakefield, of the nineteenth generation, as given in this tabular pedigree. His children are given (Plates IV and IVA) as Richard Peck, son and heir, Nicholas Peck, 5th son, Ralph Peck, 4th son, who is substituted for William, the 4th son of "Tonge's Visitation" and "The Visitation of Yorkshire," who disappears entirely from the tabular pedigree, Robert Peck of Beccles, co. Suffolk, Thomas Peck, 3d son, John Peck, 2d son, Francis Peck, 6th son, and daughters about as given in "The Visitation of Yorkshire." Why a Ralph Peck should be substituted for William Peck, the 4th son in "Tonge's Visitation" and in "The Visitation of Yorkshire," does not appear, and the records given in the preceding instalments of this article furnish no justification, as already stated, for inserting the name of Robert Peck of Beccles, co. Suffolk, as an additional son (making seven sons in all) of John Peck, Esq., of Wakefield.

The last section of this article (Section III) will deal with the Pecks of Beccles, co. Suffolk, ancestors of Joseph Peck of Hingham and Rehoboth in New England.

---

*Mr. Ira Ballou Peck, in the REGISTER of April 1870 (vol. 24, p. 188), gave the folio number as 152; but the facsimile given in the present issue of the REGISTER begins with folio 158 and ends with folio 159b.

**Pages 523-528, this volume.

# GENEALOGICAL RESEARCH IN ENGLAND

Communicated by the Committee on English and Foreign Research

## THE ENGLISH ANCESTRY OF JOSEPH PECK
## OF HINGHAM, MASS., IN 1638

Compiled by S. Allyn Peck, B.A., of New York City, and contributed by
Frederick Stanhope Peck, LL.D., of Barrington, R. I.

## III

### Robert Peck of Beccles, co. Suffolk,
### and Some of His Descendants

[Editorial Note.—G. Andrews Moriarty, A.M., LL.B., F.S.A., of Bristol, R. I., Chairman of the Committee on English and Foreign Research, has called the attention of the Editors of the Register to the fact that the word "neve," which John Leeke of Beccles, co. Suffolk, in his will dated 6 September 1529 (*supra,* vol. 89, p. 334), applied to Robert Peck of Beccles, one of the executors of the will, and which the compiler of this article, Mr. S. Allyn Peck, B.A., interpreted as meaning "nephew," in the modern sense of the word, should have been interpreted as "grandson," its usual meaning at that period. (Cf. The Century Dictionary, under the word "neve.") A careful study of the will of John Leeke and of the records that follow it in the first instalment of this article shows that Robert Peck, whose identity with Robert Pecke of Beccles, the testator of 31 October 1556 (*supra,* vol. 89, p. 338), has been established, was far more likely to be a grandson of John Leeke than his nephew in the modern sense of the word. Assuming, therefore, that "neve" as used in the will of John Leeke means "grandson," the Editors propose to point out the changes that should be made in the account of John Leeke and his family that has been given in the first instalment of this article; and they can do this most clearly by presenting, in the usual genealogical form, a brief statement in regard to John Leeke, his wives, his children and grandchildren, and his stepchildren, as revealed by the wills and other records already published in the first instalment of this article (*supra,* vol. 89, pp. 333-339, * October, 1935).—Editors.]

John Leeke, of Beccles, co. Suffolk, died between 6 September 1529, when his will was dated, and 17 November 1529, when it was proved. It was suggested (*supra,* vol. 89, p. 334) that his father was probably the John Leeke of Beccles whose will, dated probably on the Thursday before Michaelmas (that is, on the Thursday before 29 September), 1504, was proved 23 October 1504 by his widow Alice, the executrix named in the will, of which the testator's brother, Thomas Leke (Leeke), parson of Beccles, was named as supervisor. John Leeke, however, the testator of 1504, mentioned no children in his will, but, after making the usual bequests for religious purposes and giving to his wife Alice his two messuages and all his moveable goods, he placed at the disposal of his wife Alice the residue of his goods not bequeathed. In the explanatory note attached to this will by the compiler of this article it is stated that

*For pp. 333-339 see pp. 529-535, this volume.

at that period it was not uncommon in Norfolk and Suffolk for a father to leave his estate to his wife and not to mention his children. Thomas Leke, also, the parson of Beccles, in his will, dated 12 December 1504 and proved 14 January 1504/5 (*ib.*), mentions no children or other descendants of his deceased brother John. He was rector of Beccles, 1467–1504, and, according to Venn's "Alumni Cantabrigienses" (part 1, vol. 3, p. 60), was perhaps identical with a Thomas Leeke who took his B.A. at Cambridge in 1456 and his M.A. there in 1460, and was probably a scholar at King's Hall. The Thomas Leeke who took his B.A. in 1456 was born probably about 1435, and, if he was the parson of Beccles and therefore brother of John Leeke, the testator of 1504, the latter was born probably *around* 1435, perhaps as early as 1430, and may have been the father of John Leeke, the testator of 1529, although proof of this relationship has not been found. (See the wills of the two brothers, *supra,* vol. 89, pp. 333–334.) If the testator of 1529 was born about 1460 or earlier, perhaps as early as 1453, he would have been well advanced in years at the time of his death, and might have been the grandfather of the Robert Peck whom he named in his will as one of his executors. **

John Leeke, the testator of 1529, married at least twice.* The name of his "first" wife, whom, if he were born about 1453, he may have married about 1475, has not been found. His last wife, ALICE, whose maiden name also is unknown, he married probably about 1510, and from her will, dated 14 June 1537 and proved 25 September 1538 (REGISTER, vol. 89, pp. 337–338), it is learned that, when John Leeke married her, she was the widow of Robert Bartram, to whom she had borne at least two sons, Thomas Bartram and William Bartram (both living in 1537 and both legatees in their mother's will), and at least one daughter, Agnes, who in 1537 was the wife of Robert Mekylburgh (or Mikylburgh) and was also a legatee in her mother's will. Alice (———) (Bartram) Leeke bore also to her second husband, as will appear below, a daughter, Katherine Leeke, who was unmarried when her father made his will, but about 1530 became the wife of Thomas Drawer and, together with her husband, was living in 1537, when her mother bequeathed to her 40s. and sundry articles of wearing apparel. Alice Leeke, of Beccles, widow of John Leeke, named in her will, as residuary legatees and executors, her sons-in-law, her well-beloved Robert Mikylburgh and Thomas Drawer. So far as known, she did not make bequests to any of John Leeke's relatives or descendants, except Katherine, her own daughter by John Leeke. Since she made bequests to the church of Gislingham, co. Suffolk, as well as to the church of Beccles, it may, perhaps, be inferred that she had at one time lived in Gislingham.

*He may have had more than one wife before he married Alice Bartram, widow, who survived him; but, as it is not possible to determine whether all the children who were born to him before his marriage with the Widow Bartram were children by *one* wife, it is convenient to refer to them as children by "first" wife.

**See the footnote on p. 563, this volume.

Children by "first" wife, in the probable order of their births:

i. A DAUGHTER, b. perhaps about 1480 or earlier; m. about 1498 ——— PECK.*

    Child (surname *Peck*):

    1. *Robert,* of Beccles, identified as the testator of 31 October 1556 (see will of John Leeke and comments thereon, *supra,* vol. 89, p. 335, and will of Robert Pecke of Beccles, *supra,* vol. 89, p. 338), b. perhaps as early as 1500, for he was evidently a man of mature years when his grandfather, John Leeke, made his will, in which he and Katherine Leeke, John Leeke's daughter by his last wife, were named as executors; d. between 31 October and 20 November 1556.

        Robert Peck was probably the eldest surviving *male* descendant of John Leeke, the testator of 1529, and his grandfather probably intended that he should be the leader of the two executors of his will and relied on him to see that his wishes in regard to the distribution of his estate were duly carried out. Details about Robert Peck's marriages and children will be given farther on in this section.

ii. <br> iii. Two SONS (at least), since John Leeke in his will stated that an obit was to be kept for himself and his sons in Beccles church yearly by Robert Peck, "if he is able."

    Children of one or more of these sons (surname *Leeke*):†

    1. *Robert,*   2. *John,*   3. *Richard,*   4. *Alice,*   5. *Ellen,* to whom Robert Peck, grandson of the testator of 6 September 1529, was to pay 20 marks apiece, and, on fulfilling this condition, was to receive, eventually, all the testator's messuages, lands, and tenements in Beccles, his cousins receiving their portions of their grandfather's estate in money.

    6. *Margaret,* to whom the testator bequeathed 40s., "to be paid at the age of discretion." Her exact relationship to the testator of 1529 is uncertain.

Child by last wife:

iv. KATHERINE, one of the executors of her father's will, to whom and to her heirs for ever her father bequeathed all his lands and tenements in Gelingham, Wyndell, Wynston, Gelston, and Alby, or elsewhere within the county of Norfolk, and also £40, to be paid on the day of her marriage, various items of household goods (to her and to her mother), the residue of the household goods (to be shared equally with her mother and with her co-executor, Robert Peck), and finally all the residue of her father's estate (except his pen cattle, moveables, and apparel, which he bequeathed to Robert Peck), to her and to Robert Peck, his two executors, b. probably about 1511; m. about 1530

*In the first instalment of this article (*supra,* vol. 89, p. 334) an abstract of the will of ** Henry Peke of Carlton Colville, co. Suffolk, dated 16 April 1525 and proved in November 1525, was printed. The testator named Margery, his wife, Robert, his son, and Kateryn, his daughter, and appointed his wife, Margery, and one Richard Sellyng executors. This will was printed because of the possibility that at some time the testator might be proved to have been the father of the first Robert Peck of Beccles, although no proof of such relationship had been found. On the assumption, however, that the first Robert Peck of Beccles, the testator of 31 October 1556, was a grandson (and not a nephew in the modern sense of the word) of John Leeke, the testator of 6 September 1529, and that the said Robert Peck may have been born as early as 1500, it is unlikely that Henry Peke of Carlton Colville, whose two children were apparently under age in 1525, was the father of the first Robert Peck of Beccles.

†In the usual English fashion these three grandsons of John Leeke, the testator of 6 September 1529, are named before the granddaughters.

**See the footnote on p. 563, this volume.

THOMAS DRAWER; and, as the wife of Thomas Drawer, was living in 1537, when she was a legatee in her mother's will. (*Vide supra.*) About 1530 she and her husband brought a bill of complaint in Chancery against her co-executor, Robert Peck, and abstracts of some of the records in this case have been given in the REGISTER, vol. 89, pp. 336–337. The comments ** and explanations already given in the REGISTER about the apparent ill-feeling between Katherine Drawer and her mother on the one hand and Robert Peck on the other hand should probably stand unchanged, if it is remembered that Robert Peck was undoubtedly the *grandson* of John Leeke, and not his nephew in the modern sense of the word. Nothing has been found to show whether Thomas and Katherine (Leeke) Drawer had issue.

From the following abstracts of wills, together with the abstract of the will of Robert Pecke of Beccles, co. Suffolk, the testator of 31 October 1556, given in the first instalment of this article (*supra,* vol. 89, p. 338), information is derived about the wives and children of the testator of 31 October 1556, who is now to be regarded as a *grandson* (and not a nephew in the present-day meaning of the word) of John Leeke of Beccles, the testator of 6 September 1529. This Robert Pecke of Beccles is known to have been an ancestor of Joseph Peck of Hingham, in the Colony of the Massachusetts Bay, and later of Rehoboth, who emigrated to New England in 1638.

The Will of WALTER NORTON of Hallesworth [Halesworth], co. Suffolk, England, dated 12 June 1542.*  To be buried in the Church of Our Lady of Hallesworth, near unto Jone Norton, my first wife. To the High Altar of said church for tithes forgotten 20d. To the reparation of said church 40s. To the mending of the highway between Halesworth and Chedston [Chediston, co. Suffolk] 40s. To the mending of the highway between Hallesworth and Beccles against my ground called Tympernells 13s. 4d.

To my wife Joone all such household stuff as she brought me and all her jewels, being here or at Bury St. Edmunds. I give to said Joone 100 marks and one cow, being at Richard Sapens, my farmer, and also all my swine. My said wife shall release all her rights of dower on my lands unto my executor within a quarter year after my decease, otherwise my bequests to her shall be void.

To Robert Norton, my son, my lands and tenements in Westhale [Westhall, co. Suffolk] purchased by me of Nicholas Bohin, Gentleman, and also my lands lying in the towns of Chedston and Cokeley [Chediston and Cookley, co. Suffolk]. After his death I will that said properties [shall go] to Water [*sic*, Walter] Norton, his son, and his heirs for ever. To William Norton, son of said Robert, the house where I dwell and the meadows belonging thereto, to him and his heirs for ever, but said Robert shall take the profits thereof until said William shall be twenty years old. To said William my household stuff, cloth in my shop, and plate, except two feather beds, and said Robert shall have custody thereof until said William shall reach twenty years. To Richard Norton, son of said Robert, my lands and tenements that were John Payne's, being in Halesworth and Wyssett [Wissett, co. Suffolk], now in the farm of Robert Yonges, to him and his heirs for ever, and said Robert shall take the profits thereof for bringing up said Richard till he reaches twenty

*The items in the two Norton wills have been rearranged by the Editors, in order to bring together the bequests to each legatee.

**See the footnote on p. 563, this volume.

years. To Thomas Norton, son of said Robert, £40 at twenty years. If said Walter, William, Richard, and Thomas die under age, the portion of one so dying shall go to the survivors. If said Water [*sic*, Walter] die before the age of twenty years, leaving no issue, the lands bequeathed to him shall go to his brother William and his heirs. If said William die before the age of twenty years, leaving no children, the properties bequeathed to him shall go to his brother Richard and his heirs. If said Richard die under the age of twenty, without children, the properties bequeathed to said Walter, William, and Richard shall remain to said Thomas and his heirs for ever. To Joone Norton and Elizabeth Norton, my belchildren [i. e., grandchildren], to each £20, to be paid to them by John Fyske of Holton [co. Suffolk], Gentleman, Alexander Fylby, and John Browne, on the bond of said Alexander and of John Browne, to pay said moneys to said Joone and Elizabeth at the age of eighteen years. To said Joone and Elizabeth, to each, one feather bed. If one of them dies, her portion is to go to the survivor. If they both die under age, their portions shall remain to the said Robert Norton. Said Johane and Elizabeth shall marry with the consent of said Robert, or the bequests to them shall be void. To said Joane and Elizabeth one cow. To said Robert my tenements and lands called Oranys, for him and his heirs for ever.

To John Winbyrche 20s. of the 40s. he owes me. To Raffe Bonett, my servant, 3s. 4d. To Mary Hopkyn, my servant, 5s. To Edward Fermage 5s. To Margaret Arnold, widow, 3s. 4d. To Richard Sipins and Robert Yongs, my farmers, to each 6s. 8d. My executors shall distribute among priests and clerks singing masses and to the poor of this town and other towns present at my burial £3. I desire an honest priest to sing for my soul in the church of Halleshame [*sic*] for a year after my death, and I devise to said priest £6.

The residue of my goods I leave to my executor, my said son Robert Norton. I make John Soone, Gentleman, my supervisor, and I give him 40s. Witnesses: John Sone, Gentleman, John Fyske, Gentleman, Thomas Baly, and Margaret Arnold, widow. [Signed] Walter Norton. Proved 8 November 1542 by Robert Norton. (P.C.C., Spert, 11.)

The Will of ROBERT NORTON of Hallisworth [Halesworth], co. Suffolk [England], Diocese of Norwich, Gentleman, dated 4 August 1561.

To my wife Mary, who is enfeoffed in the manor of Wright and lands in Shedstone [*sic*, ? Chedstone (Chediston), co. Suffolk] and Wisset [Wissett, co. Suffolk] to it belonging.

To my sons Walter, William, Richard, Francis (under twenty-one), and George (under eighteen), and to my daughter Jone.

To my son William my tenement late of Walter Norton, my father.

To all John Prynne's daughters had by my niece. To all the children of Johane Merryman, my niece, of Becclys [Beccles, co. Suffolk].

Proved 31 December 1561. (P.C.C., Loftes, 38.)

[Halesworth, the home of the Norton family, to which the first wife of Robert Peck of Beccles, the testator of 31 October 1556, apparently belonged, was a fairly populous parish in northeastern Suffolk, on the River Blyth, about 33 miles northeast from Ipswich and some 8 miles in a southerly direction from Beccles. The other places mentioned in these two Norton wills, except Beccles and except the important Bury St. Edmunds, far away in western Suffolk, were small parishes in the immediate neighborhood of and in various directions from Halesworth, no one of them being more than 5 miles distant from the last-named parish.

The first wife of Walter Norton, the testator of 12 June 1542, named Jone, was buried in the Church of Our Lady of Halesworth, and was evidently the mother of the testator's son Robert Norton, the only child of the testator named in the will, for the testator's second wife, also named Jone (Joone), although generously provided for in her husband's will, was required to release all her rights of dower in the testator's lands unto his executor (the son Robert) within a quarter year after the testator's decease, under penalty of forfeiting her bequests from the testator. A *very brief* abstract of the will of Walter Norton, the testator of 1542, is printed in the *Essex Institute Historical Collections* (published at Salem, Mass.) for 1880 (vol. 17, p. 95), among the "Gleanings from English Records about New England Families" communicated to that magazine by the late James A. Emmerton and the late Henry F. Waters; but the much more detailed abstract of the will of Walter Norton given above shows that Walter, William, Richard, and Thomas Norton, the four grandsons of the testator (sons of his son and executor Robert Norton) who were named in the will, were all under twenty years of age in 1542. Moreover, the abstract of the will of Robert Norton, son of the testator of 1542, dated 4 August 1561 and given above in this article, as well as in the *Essex Institute Historical Collections* for 1880 (vol. 17, pp. 95–96, among the "Gleanings" of the late Messrs. Emmerton and Waters), shows that Robert Norton's wife was named Mary, that his sons Walter, William, and Richard, named in their grandfather's will of 1542, were living on 4 August 1561, that the son Thomas, named in the grandfather's will of 1542, was not named in his father's will of 1561 and had presumably died in the interval, and that Robert Norton, in his will of 4 August 1561, names two other sons, who were evidently born after their grandfather made his will, namely Francis, under twenty-one, and George, under eighteen, as well as a daughter Jone, living in 1561, who may have been one of the two "belchildren" [i. e., grandchildren] of Walter Norton, the testator of 1542, Joone Norton and Elizabeth Norton, to each of whom their grandfather bequeathed £20, to be paid to them at the age of eighteen years. If one of them should die, her portion was to go to the survivor. If both should die under age, their portions were to remain to Robert Norton, the testator's son. They were apparently daughters of the said Robert Norton, for their grandfather prescribed that they should marry with the consent of the said Robert, or the bequests to them should be void. Perhaps the daughter Elizabeth was dead and Jone was the survivor of the two when Robert Norton made his will.

In the *Essex Institute Historical Collections* for 1880 the abstract of the will of Robert Norton is followed (vol. 17, p. 96, also among the "Gleanings" of Messrs. Emmerton and Waters) by an abstract of the Inquisition post Mortem taken at "Gipwic" [*sic*, ? Ipswich], co. Suffolk, 30 October, 3 Elizabeth [30 October 1561], after the death of Robert Norton, Gentleman, who had been seised of the manor of Wright and lands in Chedestan [Chediston], Wisset [Wissett], Walpoole [Walpole], Cokley [Cookley], and Hallisworthe [Halesworth], all in co. Suffolk. By a deed dated at Chedestan [Chediston] 5 April, 2 Edward VI [5 April 1548] the said Robert Norton granted to John Fiske, John Browne, and Alexander Filby the said manor of Wright, for the sole use of the said Robert Norton and Mary, his wife, for the life of the said Mary, and after her death to the said Robert Norton, his heirs and assigns. The said Robert Norton was also seised of lands in Wenhaston [co. Suffolk], Melles [Mellis, co. Suffolk], etc. He made his will 4 August, 3 Elizabeth [4 August 1561], and died 9 September last [9 September 1561]. Mary Norton, his wife, yet lives, and Walter Norton, eldest son of the said Robert, was twenty-five years of age and more at his father's death.

In his will, dated 4 August 1561, Robert Norton bequeathed to all John Prynne's daughters had by my "niece" and to all the children of Johane Merryman, my "niece," of Becclys [Beccles, co. Suffolk]. This Johane Merryman, who in 1561 appears as the mother of two or more children, is evidently the Johan Meriman whom Robert Pecke of Beccles, in his will dated 31 October 1556, calls "my daughter," the context showing that she was a married daughter of Robert Pecke by his first wife, and apparently had no children in 1556. She was born probably about 1540 or earlier. From what has been stated about the ages of the sons of Robert Norton, it seems as if the two nieces mentioned in his will must have been nieces in the present-day meaning of the word, and not granddaughters, and that their mothers were probably sisters of Robert Norton who had received their portions of their father's property on their marriages and therefore were not mentioned by their father, Walter Norton, in his will of 1542.]

The Will of JOHN WATERS, THE ELDER, of Beccles [co. Suffolk, England], Diocese of Norwich, dated 28 May 1547.* To be buried in the churchyard of Beccles, by my father and mother there, near to the window of St. Walston. To the High Altar of St. Michael the Archangel in Beccles 13s. 4d. To the building of the steeple in Beccles 6s. 8d. yearly, until [it is] completed. [Other religious bequests and bequests to the poor.]

To my wife Margarett all my lands, tenements, etc., for life, or so long as she keeps herself sole and not married. If my sons William and Robert die before my wife, then my son John is to have all messuages, etc., bequeathed to her for life. Cattle, etc., [and many other items] to my wife Margarett.

To my son John the messuage late Gedneys, cattle, corn, etc., [and many other items]. To William Waters, my son, and his heirs my tenement called Ballygate, etc. To Robert Waters, my son, and his heirs my meadow at Ringsfield [co. Suffolk], etc., and 6s. 8d. yearly during my wife's lifetime and until he is twenty-one.

To John Peck, my godson, 5 marks at the age of twenty-one years, but, if he dies before that age, then I bequeath it to Robert Peck and Margarett Peck, his brother and sister, equally, and, if either dies before the age of twenty-one, then [I bequeath it] to the survivor of them. To Robert Peck, my belchild [i. e., grandchild], a cow and a silver spoon. To Margaret Peck a cow and a silver spoon. To Jone Peck, the Younger, my "boole."

To Robert Peck, my son-in-law, one cow; to Joan, his wife, my daughter, another cow. [Many other bequests to the aforesaid legatees.]

To Annes Hapeled, my servant, two neats. To John Harman, my servant [sundry items].

Executors: my wife Margarett and my sons John and William. Supervisor: Robert Peck, my said son-in-law. Witnesses: William Robards, the Elder, John Storey, Wm. Payne, Thos. Deney, John Tylney, and others. Proved 28 July 1547 by the executors. (Archdeaconry Court of Suffolk, Register 15, 1544–1550, fo. 317.)

The Will of MARGARET WATERS of Beccles [co. Suffolk, England], late the wife of John Waters, the Elder, now deceased, dated 3 August 1556.* To be buried in the churchyard of Beccles, near to my said husband.

To my son John Waters, to him and his heirs, my tenement which I purchased of Adam Craske, provided he pays to Robert Waters, his brother, £6. 13s. 4d. To William Waters, my son, items of brass and pewter and three loads of wood in my yard. To William Waters's wife my cloth kirtle, etc. To Robert Waters, my son, the best bed, with blankets, etc., brass kettles, pewter dishes, etc. To Margarie Waters, my daughter-in-law, a gown.

To my goddaughter Margaret Waters, daughter of John Waters, my son, a feather bed, etc., and to William Waters and Margaret Waters, son and daughter of the said John, two neats, which are in the hands of my said son John. To William Waters, my godchild, son of my son, William Waters, the Elder, a milch cow, pillows, etc. To John Waters, son of William Waters, the Elder, two candlesticks, two pieces of pewter, etc. To Robert Waters, my belchild [i. e., grandchild], a cow.

Robert Pecke shall have the profits of my meadow, which I hold for

*The items in this will have been rearranged by the Editors, in order to bring together the bequests to each legatee.

years yet to come, until the Feast of St. Faith next,* and then they are to remain unto John Waters, my son. To Johane Peck, my daughter, my best petticoat and my best gown. To Robert Pecke, my godson, three silver spoons. To Margaret Pecke, daughter of Roberte Pecke, the Elder, a feather bed and the "traunsome" with the two blankets. To Thomas Pecke, son of the said Roberte Pecke, the Elder, one cow. To Olyve Pecke a bread pan of brass and another pan of "stele." To Anne Pecke two of my best platters.

To Johan Burney my mantle. To Elizabeth Bower a gown. To Alice Tyrrell my Holy Day petticoat. To Jane Mapledde [sundry items]. To Katheron Budde, my servant, two aprons, etc.

The residue of my goods not bequeathed to my executors [names not given]. Witnesses: Robert Pecke, William Roberds, David Goldspynke, Nicholas Tyrrell, William Waters, and others. Proved at Beccles 26 October 1556. (Archdeaconry Court of Suffolk, Register 17, 1554–1557, fo. 362.)

[John Leeke of Beccles (who, it has been assumed, was the grandfather, *not* the uncle, of Robert Peck of Beccles, the testator of 31 October 1556), in his will, dated 6 September 1529, bequeathed to John Waters, "my godson," 20s., and "to each other of my godchildren" 12d. The first of the numerous witnesses of John Leeke's will was John Waters, probably the father of John Leeke's godson of that name and identical with John Waters, the Elder, of Beccles, the testator of 28 May 1547. John Waters, the Elder, and his wife Margaret, the testatrix of 3 August 1556, were the parents of Johan (Joan), the second wife of Robert Peck of Beccles, who was already married to Robert Peck and had borne to him three children when her father made his will in 1547, was living 3 August 1556, the date of her mother's will, but was dead and buried when her husband made his will, on 31 October 1556.

Perhaps some relationship or early intermarriage between the Leeke family and the Waters family of Beccles may account for the bequest, in John Leeke's will, of 20s. to John Waters, his godson, and of 12d. to each other of his godchildren. John Waters may have been the eldest boy of these godchildren, and the other godchildren, who received 12d. each, may have been younger brothers or sisters (older or younger) of the godson John; but, be this as it may, the will of John Waters, the Elder, of Beccles, and that of Margaret Waters, his widow, together with the will of Robert Peck of Beccles, whose second wife was their daughter, contain much information about the Waters family and the Peck family of that parish.

The father and mother of John Waters, the Elder, were buried in the churchyard of Beccles, and there he, too, directed that he be buried. There, also, near to her husband, Margaret Waters, his widow, directed that she be buried.

Three sons, John Waters (probably John Leeke's godson of that name), apparently the eldest son, William Waters, and Robert Waters, were named in their father's will, in 1547, Robert being then under twenty-one, and the testator's wife Margaret and his sons John and William were named as executors. The testator of 1547 bequeathed to Robert Peck, his son-in-law, to Joan, Robert Peck's wife, the testator's daughter, to John Peck, the testator's godson [and grandson], under twenty-one, to Robert Peck and Margaret Peck, brother and sister of godson John Peck, both under twenty-one, and to Jone Peck, the Younger. This Jone Peck, the Younger, may have been the daughter of Robert Peck by his first wife, who appeared in her father's will, of 31 October 1556, as "Johan Meriman, my daughter," being a married daughter of the testator who apparently had no children in 1556 but who had two or more children in 1561, as the will of her uncle, Robert Norton, disclosed; or Jone Peck, the Younger, may have been a daughter of Robert and Johan (Waters) Peck, who died before her father made his will in 1556. Since Robert and Johan (Waters) Peck had at least three children, John, Robert, and Margaret Peck, all born before 28 May 1547, their marriage probably took

*The Feast of St. Faith, Virgin and Martyr, fell on 6 October.

place about 1540 or earlier, and Johan (Waters) Peck was perhaps older than her brother John Waters, the godson named in John Leeke's will.

When Margaret Waters, widow of John Waters, the Elder, made her will on 3 August 1556, a little more than nine years after her husband's will was dated, her sons John and William Waters were married and had children, and her son Robert Waters also was married and had at least one son, if the Robert Waters whom she called her belchild [i. e., grandchild] was the son of her son Robert. From the will of Margaret Waters, widow, and from the will of her son-in-law, Robert Peck, it appears that in the interval from 1547 to 1556 three more children of Robert and Johan (Waters) Peck had been born, namely, Thomas, Olive, and Anne Peck. Of the six children at least whom Johan Waters, second wife of Robert Peck of Beccles, bore to her husband, three sons and three daughters, all of whom were living when Robert Peck made his will, the eldest son, John, is said to have died without issue, the second son, Robert, of Beccles, is said to have been born about 1546, is known to have married Ellen or Helen Babbs, of Guildford, co. Surrey, and is said to have died in 1593, aged 47, his will being dated 22 March 1592/3 but not being proved until 10 November 1598, when it was proved at Beccles, and the third son, Thomas Peck, of Beccles, died without issue, leaving a will dated 16 February 1573/4. To each of his three daughters, Margaret, Olive, and Anne, their father bequeathed £6. 13s. 4d. Margaret is said to have died without issue, Olive married Richard Nott and was living in 1592/3, and Anne was living unmarried in 1573/4 and is said to have died without issue. The John Waters and the William Waters named in the will of Robert Peck, the testator of 1556, were the testator's brothers-in-law.

The remainder of this article will be devoted chiefly to an account of Robert Peck of Beccles (son of the testator of 31 October 1556) and his wife, Ellen Babbs, and some of their descendants, down to the later years of the seventeenth century. It will include the members of the family who migrated to New England in 1638 and remained there, as well as those who returned to England, and some of those who had never left the Mother Country. Some members of the Peck family won distinction in England by their personal merits and services; some became connected by marriage with families of high social standing and rank.]

---

# GENEALOGICAL RESEARCH IN ENGLAND

Communicated by the Committee on English and Foreign Research

## THE ENGLISH ANCESTRY OF JOSEPH PECK, OF HINGHAM, MASS., IN 1638

Compiled by S. ALLYN PECK, B.A., of New York City, and contributed by FREDERICK STANHOPE PECK, LL.D., of Barrington, R. I.

### III

### ROBERT PECK OF BECCLES, CO. SUFFOLK, AND SOME OF HIS DESCENDANTS [CONTINUED]

IN the last previous instalment of this article, printed in January[*] 1937 (*supra*, pages 7–15), it was shown, *inter alia*, that Robert Peck, the Elder, of Beccles, co. Suffolk, the testator of 31 October 1556 (an abstract of whose will was given in the REGISTER, vol. 89, page 338), should probably be regarded as a grandson (and not as a nephew in the present-day meaning of the word) of John Leeke of Beccles, the testator of 6 September 1529 (for abstract of whose will see the REGISTER, vol. 89, pages 334–335), and that by his second wife, Johan Waters (daughter of John Waters, the Elder, of Beccles, and his wife Margaret), this Robert Peck, the Elder, had six (or perhaps seven) children, namely, three sons, John, Robert, and Thomas, and at least three daughters, Margaret, Olive, and Anne, all of these six children being named as beneficiaries in their father's will. Their mother, who was living on 3 August 1556, when her mother, Margaret Waters, made her will, was dead on 31 October 1556, when their father made his will.

John Peck was evidently the oldest son of Robert Peck, the Elder, for he was the first son named in Robert Peck's will, and to him was left the messuage in which he (the testator) then dwelt and other lands, subject to payments to be made to the testator's third son Thomas and to the testator's three daughters. Other lands were left to the testator's second son Robert, two tenements which the testator had purchased of John Walter [*sic*, ? Waters] were left to the testator's son Thomas, and to each of the testator's three daughters, Margaret, Olive, and Anne, the sum of £6. 13s. 4d. was bequeathed.

The earliest mention that has been found of John Peck, of his brother, Robert Peck, and of their sister, Margaret Peck, occurs in the will of their maternal grandfather, John Waters, the Elder, dated 28 May 1547 (*supra*, page 13). This testator bequeaths to John Peck, his godson, 5 marks at the age of twenty-one years, but, if he dies before that age, then this money is to go to Robert Peck and Margaret Peck, his [John Peck's] brother and sister, equally, and,

[*]For pp. 7–15 see pp. 563–571, this volume; for Vol. 89, pp. 333–339 see pp. 529–535, this volume.

if either dies before the age of twenty-one, then the money is to go to the survivor of them. The testator bequeaths also to the said Robert Peck, his "belchild" [i. e., grandchild], a cow and a silver spoon, and makes a similar bequest to Margaret Peck. Thus, on 28 May 1547, John Waters, the Elder, had at least three Peck grandchildren, John, Robert, and Margaret, all three under twenty-one years of age. If Jone Peck, the Younger, to whom John Waters, the Elder, bequeathed his "boole," was also his grandchild, she probably died before her father, as she was not mentioned in her father's will.

Margaret Waters, widow of John Waters, the Elder, in her will of 3 August 1556 (*supra*, pages 13–14), bequeathed to all of her Peck\* grandchildren then living except John, her grandchildren Thomas, Olive, and Anne Peck having been born since their maternal grandfather made his will in 1547, and being, therefore, still of tender years.

That John Peck died without issue before 16 February 1573/4, and that John's sister Margaret also was no longer living on that date, is to be inferred from the will of that date of their brother Thomas, in which no mention is made of John or Margaret, but the testator leaves his two tenements, etc., to his nephew Richard Peck, son of his brother Robert Peck. This will is printed verbatim on pages 23–24 of the late Ira Ballou Peck's "Genealogical History," and is here given in abstract, in modern spelling. The date on which this will was proved and the court in which it was recorded are not stated in Mr. Peck's book; but the will of Robert Peck of Beccles, brother of Thomas, dated 22 March 1592/3, shows that Thomas died before that date (*vide infra*).

The Will of THOMAS PECKE of Beccles, co. Suffolk and diocese of Norwich, dated 16 February 1573 [1573/4], the testator being whole of mind and in perfect health of body, and intending to travel into foreign countries.

To be buried where it shall please God to call me. To Richard Pecke, my nephew (son of Robert Pecke, my brother), and his heirs for ever my two tenements, with appurtenances, situated together in Beccles, next unto a street called Balligate, on condition that the said Richard, his heirs, or assigns, pay to Olive, wife of Richard Note [Nott], and Anne Pecke, my sister [? sisters], to either of them, at such time as he doth enjoy the premises, the sum of five marks of lawful money of England. If the said Richard die before he comes of age, then I give all the premises, with appurtenances, to the above-named Robert Pecke, my brother, and his heirs for ever, on condition that the said Robert pay to the said Olive and Anne, my sister [? sisters], to either of them the sum of five marks, etc. I give to the said Richard and Robert or to that one of them who shall happen to enjoy my said tenements all my lease and term of years which I have of a certain ground adjoining the premises. All the residue of my goods I give to my said brother, Robert Pecke, whom, with the said Richard, my nephew, I make my executor. [Signed] Thomas Pecke. Witnesses: Richard Crompton, Simeon Smythe.

Thomas Peck, the testator of 16 February 1573/4, evidently died without issue; and his brother, the second Robert Peck of Beccles,
\*See the footnote on p. 572, this volume.

was the only one of the three sons of Robert Peck, the Elder, who left male descendants to hand down the family surname to later generations. He was the father of five sons and two daughters, and among his sons was Joseph Peck, who emigrated to New England in 1638. In the great events and religious movements of the seventeenth century in England the descendants of the second Robert Peck of Beccles played no small part, some of them, as has been already stated (*supra,* page 15), attaining distinction by their per-** sonal merits and services and some marrying into families of high social standing and rank.

The remainder of this article will consist of an account, in the usual genealogical form, of the second Robert Peck of Beccles and some of his descendants, the narrative extending into the second half of the seventeenth century and the statements made being supported by references to or extracts from the records.

1. ROBERT PECK (second son of Robert Peck, the Elder), of Beccles, co. Suffolk, was born prior to—perhaps three or four years before—28 May 1547, when he was named as a legatee in the will of his maternal grandfather, John Waters, the Elder, of Beccles, and died between 22 March 1592/3, when his will was dated, and 10 November 1598, when it was proved at Beccles. (*Vide infra.*) He married HELEN (or ELLEN) BABBS, who survived him, and, as "Ellenor Pecke widowe," was buried at Beccles 31 October 1614 (Beccles parish register), daughter of Nicholas Babbs of Guildford, co. Surrey (*vide infra,* Peck pedigree in The Visitation of Suffolk, 1664–1668, in *The Publications of the Harleian Society,* vol. 61).

The will of the second Robert Peck of Beccles was found at Ipswich, co. Suffolk, after a tedious search, and is printed verbatim in the late Ira Ballou Peck's "Genealogical History," pages 21–23. It was written by the testator himself, and a lengthy abstract of the will, in modern spelling, is given here, the reader being referred to the "Genealogical History" for the complete text of the will, in its original spelling.

The Will of ROBERT PECK of Beccles, co. Suffolk, dated 22 March 1592 [1592/3], 35 Elizabeth.

I, Robert Peck of Beccles, co. Suffolk, whole of mind and perfect of remembrance, although sick and weak of body at Chelmsford, co. Essex, at this present, of a pleurisy, dispose of my property [both real and personal], with appurtenances, as follows:

My body to be buried where it shall please God to call me.* To Helen, my well-loved wife (in consideration of the payment of my debts, the bringing up of my children, and the finishing of the houses which I am now building), I give all my houses, lands, tenements, etc., as well freehold as copyhold, and all my leases, plate, goods, and chattels within the towns of Beccles, Barsham, Ingate, or elsewhere, with the appurtenances—to the said Helen or her assigns during her natural life, in consideration of the things above-mentioned and also of paying such legacies to my chil-

*There seems to be no evidence that this testator died at Chelmsford in 1592/3. As his will was not proved until 10 November 1598, he may have lived until that year.

** See the footnote on p. 572, this volume.

dren as I shall appoint, or leave to her goodly consideration to provide for them according to her ability.

I give unto her [Helen] full authority to sell my woods in Barsham or my meadows in Barsham or both, if necessary. I desire my very good friends, Mr. Bartholomew Stiles and Mr. John Talbot, to aid my wife with their good counsel about the execution of this, my last will and testament.

To Richard Peck, my son, all my houses wherein I dwell in Blibergate [? Balligate] Street, my close at Ingate church, and my "pightill" in the same field—to him and his heirs for ever, and also all the lease lands adjoining the said close during the numbers of years yet to come, if his mother will vouchsafe him such favor, on condition that he pay such legacies as his mother shall appoint him to do.

Whereas Thomas Peck, my brother, deceased, by his last will gave unto the said Richard, my son, two tenements in Balligate Street, lately burnt, one of which has been built again on the same ground and the other on part of the said ground and on part of other free ground which I purchased of my uncle, William Waters, I will that the said Richard, my son, within one month after he shall become twenty-one years of age, shall make over an estate in fee simple to such of my sons and their heirs to whom I shall hereafter bequeath the said tenements, and also surrender my copyhold if it come to his hands. And if my son Richard shall not perform these things, he shall lose the benefit of such houses, lands, and leases as I have before assigned to him, and the same shall be [i. e., shall go] to those of my two sons to whom I shall give the forsaid new tenements and to their heirs and assigns for ever.

To Nicholas Peck, my son, my new tenement, partly builded on the tenement late of William Waters, and my meadows lying in Barsham (if his mother shall spare the said meadows)—to him, the said Nicholas, and his heirs for ever, he paying out of the same such sums of money as his mother shall assign him to do.

To Samuel Peck, my son, the other new tenement and little coyphold yard—to him and his heirs for ever, he paying out thereof to such of his brothers and sisters such money as his mother shall assign him to do.*

If, for paying my debts, bringing up my children, finding my son Robert† at Cambridge, and providing legacies for my two daughters and my son Joseph, my said wife shall make a lease of all or any part of my said lands and tenements, the same shall continue for so many years as she shall lease the same, her death or any legacies whatsoever before given or appointed to the contrary notwithstanding.

The residue of all my goods and chattels I give wholly to the said Helen, my wife, whom I make my sole executrix, desiring her to have care of those my children whose legacies I have left to her consideration, and also of Joane Babb and Elisabeth Babb and Robert Meriman and my sister Note [Nott] as she may.‡

Supervisors: Mr. Bartholomew Stiles, clerk, Mr. Roger Peirson, and Mr. John Talbot, whom I desire to aid my wife with their best counsel and advice.

*Since the testator left one of the two new tenements to his second son Nicholas and the other to his son Samuel, and since in the order of the testator's sons as given in the will Samuel is placed next to Nicholas, Samuel was probably older than the two other sons, Robert and Joseph.

†Afterwards Rev. Robert Peck.

‡Joane and Elisabeth Babb were perhaps sisters of the testator's wife, and Robert Meriman was probably the husband or son of the testator's half sister, Johan Meriman. The testator's sister Anne, who was living unmarried when her brother Thomas made his will in 1573/4, in which she was a legatee, is not named in this will of her brother Robert, dated 22 March 1592/3, and had probably died without issue.

Written with my own hand the day and year above said. By me [signed] Robert Peck.

Proved at Beccles 10 November 1598. (Archdeaconry Court of Suffolk [Ipswich Probate Registry].)

[To be continued]

# GENEALOGICAL RESEARCH IN ENGLAND

Communicated by the Committee on English and Foreign Research

## THE ENGLISH ANCESTRY OF JOSEPH PECK, OF HINGHAM, MASS., IN 1638

Compiled by S. ALLYN PECK, B.A., of New York City, and contributed by FREDERICK STANHOPE PECK, LL.D., of Barrington. R. I.

## III

### ROBERT PECK OF BECCLES, CO. SUFFOLK, AND SOME OF HIS DESCENDANTS [CONTINUED]

Children of Robert and Helen (Babbs) Peck:

i. RICHARD, born before 16 February 1573/4, when he was named as a beneficiary in the will of his uncle, Thomas Peck (*supra*, p. 283), and under twenty-one years of age at the date of his father's will, 22 March 1592/3. Nothing further is known about him, and he probably died without issue. There is no entry of his burial in the Beccles parish register, and no proof has been found of the statement made in the pedigree printed in the late Ira Ballou Peck's "Genealogical History," that he died in 1615, aged 41.

ii. NICHOLAS, not mentioned in the will of his uncle, Thomas Peck, dated 16 February 1573/4 (*supra*, p. 283), and probably not born until later,* perhaps not until about 1576, died about November 1648, according to the bill of complaint of Robert Hawes of Beccles, co. Suffolk, in a suit in Chancery brought against Bridget Peck, widow [of Nicholas Peck], William Peck [son of Nicholas Peck], and Henry Farrowe, dated 26 November 1649, in which it is stated that Nicholas Peck died "about a year ago." (*Vide infra.*)

Nicholas Peck married first, at Great Yarmouth, co. Norfolk, 19 February 1610/11, RACHEL YONGES, who, as "Mrs. Rachell Pecke wife of Nicholas Pecke gent," was buried at Beccles 4 October 1618 (Beccles parish register), only daughter and sole heir of William Yonges of Great Yarmouth. (*Vide infra.*) The date of this marriage of Nicholas Peck is given by the late Ira Ballou Peck, in the tabular pedigree in his "Genealogical History," as 19 February 1610 [i.e., 1610/11], and was probably taken from the parish registers of Great Yarmouth, which begin in 1558.

An abstract of the will of William Yonges of Great Yarmouth, dated 13 September 1611 and proved 11 November 1611 in the Prerogative Court of Canterbury (Register Wood, folio 93, at Somerset House, London), is printed in Waters's "Genealogical Gleanings in England," vol. 2, pp. 1411–1412, published by the New-England Historic Genealogical Society, Boston, 1901, the will of William Yonges being reprinted from the NEW-ENGLAND HISTORICAL AND GENEALOGICAL REGISTER, vol. 52, pp. 246–247, April 1898. The testator styles himself merchant, burgess, and alderman of the same town [Great Yarmouth], and mentions *his* daughter Rachael Peck and son-in-law Nicholas Pecke. The testator's wife Dorothy, apparently not the mother of his daughter Rachael Peck, had been previously married to —— Remington, for the testator mentions *her* [Dorothy's] daughter, Mary Remington, and *his* [the testator's] son-in-law [i.e., stepson] Nathaniel Remington, Agnes

*Page 573, this volume.

now his [Nathaniel Remington's] wife, and Mary, Nathaniel, and Samuel Remington, children of Nathaniel and Agnes Remington [and therefore grandchildren of the testator's wife Dorothy]. Among numerous Yonges kindred the testator names Augustine Yonges, the Elder, Henry Yonges, son of the testator's brother John, five daughters of the said Henry Yonges, and his [the testator's] brother Henry Yonges. Many other kindred or connections of the testator, whose exact relationship to him is difficult to determine in the brief abstract of his will given by Mr. Waters, are named. Not to be overlooked are three brothers-in-law of the testator, Benjamin Cooper and Hanna his wife and his children, Thomas Cooper and his wife, and Isaac Cooper. Other brothers-in-law mentioned are brother-in-law George Birche and children and Prisca his wife and brother-in-law Thomas Housegoe. A son-in-law [i.e., perhaps stepson] William Doughtie and Prisca his wife also are mentioned, and possibly the testator's wife Dorothy had at one time been the wife of ———— Doughtie.

Nicholas Peck married secondly, before 16 November 1619, BRIDGETT (————) SAYER, widow of Thomas Sayer of Fritton, co. Norfolk, gent., as appears from the following abstract of Chancery proceedings in the case of William Webbe *v.* Nicholas Pecke and his wife Bridgett, 1619–20:

To the Right Honourable Franncis, Lord Verulam, Lord Chancellor of England, 16 November 1619.*

The Bill of Complaint of WILLIAM WEBBE of Ewston [Euston], co. Suffolk, gent., declares that whereas your orator, together with Henry Branthwaite, late of Breckles [Breccles], co. Norfolk, gent., purchased of Henry Muskett, late of Fritton, co. Norfolk, gent., deceased, one messuage with fourscore acres of land thereunto belonging, lying in Fritton aforesaid, and whereas, since this purchase, said Henry Branthwaite has sold and conveyed his interest in the said property to Thomas Sayer, late of Fritton, gent., deceased, and his heirs, and whereas the said Henry, upon such sale, delivered the writings and evidences concerning said property to Thomas Sayer, after whose death they came, together with the interest in said premises, into the hands of Nicholas Pecke and Bridgett, his wife, late wife of said Thomas Sayer, and whereas by right of possession of such evidences said Nicholas and Bridget go about to defraud your orator of his right in said property and of the issues and profits thereof, now, seeing that your orator does not know any particulars concerning such evidences, he prays the Honourable Court to compel said Nicholas and Bridget Pecke to deliver them, or true copies of them, unto him, and asks that a writ of subpœna be directed to them, summoning them into the Court of Chancery.

The Answer of NICHOLAS PECKE, gent., and BRIDGET, his wife, to the Bill of Complaint of William Webbe, gent., dated Beccles, 19 January 1619 [1619/20], declares that the defendants believe that Edmond Read, late of Hempnall, co. Norfolk, yeoman, was seised of two messuages, one called Trotts and the other Kitts, with divers lands thereto belonging, whereof a great part are held by copy of Court Roll of the manor of Tasebourgh [Tasburgh] and Fritton [co. Norfolk], which they believe to be the property mentioned in the bill; and that said Edmond Read, in consideration of a marriage between Robert Read, son and heir of said Edmond, and Anne Morrys, one of the daughters of William Morris of Burgate, co. Suffolk, gent., for their maintenance and for their heirs, by deed dated 4 September, 34 Elizabeth [4 September 1592], granted to said Robert and Anne and their heirs an annuity of £20 out of said two messuages and his said lands in Fritton; and that this annuity was assured to the use of Thomas Sayer, named in the bill, and his heirs, during the lifetime of said Thomas; and that the complainant,

*Francis Bacon, the famous philosopher, first Baron Verulam, in 1621 made Viscount St. Albans and soon afterwards accused of taking bribes and disgraced.

together with Henry Branthwaite of the city of Norwich, gent., purchased of Henry Musket of Fritton, gent., one messuage and fourscore acres of land in Fritton. But if the said complainant refers in his bill to the two messuages called Trotts and Kitts and the land appurtaining thereto, then only about fifty acres of freehold land belong to them, the rest being copyhold, to which the complainant cannot pretend any title. It is truc [sic, ? not true] that Thomas Sayer purchased said two messuages of Henry Branthwaite, but on advice of his counsel he purchased said two messuages of Robert Read, next heir of Edmond Read. The complainant Webbe was named in the conveyance between Musket, the complainant, and Branthwaite, but he never paid any money nor took any profits of said lands. Further the defendants aver that the value of said lands does not amount to more than £20 yearly, such annual value being charged as aforesaid. Thomas Sayer, by his will, dated 25 October, 15 James I [25 October 1617], bequeathed said two messuages and lands to Bridget, one of the defendants, his then wife, with reversion to John, his son, and John's heirs, said John being now seven years old. Wherefore the defendants plead that the complainant shall not be allowed to prosecute any further during the nonage of said John Sayer, and they deny that they have any evidences in their custody, except such as concern the two messuages Trotts and Kitts. All which matters they will aver and prove in the Honourable Court. [Signed] Ncli Peck  Briget Peck.

The Replication of WILLIAM WEBBE, gent., complainant against Nicholas Pecke and Bridgett, his wife, defendants, declares that the Answer of the defendants is not sufficient and upholds the complainant's Bill of Complaint.

(Chancery Proceedings, James I, Bundle W 3, Number 76, in the Public Record Office, London.)

The outcome of the Chancery proceedings in the case of William Webbe v. Nicholas Peck and Bridget, second wife of Nicholas Peck, is unknown, for the final decree of the Court has not been found. But the abstracts of the proceedings given above show that before 16 November 1619 Nicholas Peck, gent., had married Bridget, widow of Thomas Sayer. More information about Thomas Sayer and his family is supplied by Thomas Sayer's will, an abstract of which is here given:

The Will of THOMAS SAYER of Fritton, co. Norfolk, gent., dated 25 October 1617. To be buried at the discretion of my executors. To Bridget, my wife, all my messuages, tenements, etc., until the seventh Feast Day of St. Michael the Archangel* following my decease. Certain fields are to remain to her during her lifetime, and after her decease the same are to go to John, my son, and his heirs. All my lands, messuages, etc., in Pulham, co. Norfolk, after the said seventh Feast Day, are to remain to Bridget, my wife, during her lifetime. To Elizabeth, my daughter, £300 at her age of twenty-one years, to be paid out of my said lands, etc., devised unto my said wife during the said term, as out of my moveable goods, etc. To Anne, my daughter, £200, to be paid unto her likewise. To Thomas Sayer, my son, all such household stuff, moveable goods, etc., as were the property of Thomas Sayer, my father, deceased. Residuary legatee: my said wife Bridget. Executors: Bridget, my said wife, and William Jacob, my brother-in-law. Supervisor: my uncle, Robert Sayer, Bachelor of Divinity. To Edward Bennett, my apprentice, £3. Per me Thomas Sayer. Witnesses: Thomas Gronshay, Robert Morse, Robert Dover. Proved 4 November 1617 by Bridget, the executrix. (Consistory Court of Norwich, at Norwich, Register Trotter, 1617.)

*The Feast of St. Michael the Archangel fell on 29 September.

579

The appointment by Thomas Sayer of Bridget, his wife, and William Jacob, his brother-in-law, as executors of his will may indicate that the maiden name of Bridget was Jacob. This Bridget, widow of Thomas Sayer and later widow of Nicholas Peck, was living as late as 16 November 1663, when John Sayer of Beccles [Beccles], co. Suffolk, gent., appears as plaintiff in a Chancery suit, the defendants being Thomas Sayer of Pulham, co. Norfolk, gent., eldest son of Thomas Sayer, deceased, and brother of the plaintiff, and Bridgett Pecke, widow, [formerly] wife of Thomas Sayer, and mother of the complainant [plaintiff]. (Chancery Proceedings before 1714, Reynardsons Division, Bundle S 232, No. 154.) The purpose of John Sayer in bringing this suit in Chancery against his elder brother and his mother is not given; but the relationship between the plaintiff and the defendants in this suit, together with the information supplied by the abstract of the will of Thomas Sayer, gent. (*vide supra*), shows that Thomas Sayer, gent., the first husband of Bridget (———) [? Jacob] Sayer, was son of a Thomas Sayer (whose brother, Robert Sayer, a Bachelor of Divinity, was supervisor of his nephew's will) and died between 25 October 1617, when his will was dated, and 4 November 1617, when it was proved by Bridget, the widow. Thomas Sayer, the testator of 1617, bequeathed to Thomas Sayer, his eldest son, all such household stuff, moveable goods, etc., as had belonged to Thomas Sayer, deceased, the testator's father. The testator bequeathed also to his son, John Sayer, and John's heirs certain lands after the decease of his [the testator's] widow. He bequeathed also to his [the testator's] daughter Elizabeth £300, at her age of twenty-one, and to his [the testator's] daughter Anne £200, to be paid unto her likewise. It appears, therefore, that Thomas Sayer and his wife Bridget had at least two sons, Thomas, the elder, and John, the younger, and two daughters, Elizabeth and Anne.

The Chancery suit of 1619–20 brought by William Webbe against Nicholas Peck and the latter's second wife, Bridget, the outcome of which is unknown, is the first of a number of Chancery suits found by the compiler of this article in which Nicholas Peck was a party, either as complainant or defendant. The only child of Nicholas Peck was a son by his first wife, Rachel Yonges, named William (undoubtedly for his maternal grandfather), who, as "William son of Nicholas Pecke, gent., and of his wife" was baptized at Beccles 23 September 1618 (Beccles parish register). The child's mother, as already stated, was buried at Beccles 4 October 1618, as "Mrs. Rachell Pecke wife of Nicholas Pecke, gent" (*ibid.*). It should not be overlooked that in both of these entries in the parish register of Beccles Nicholas Peck is styled "gent," and he is also so styled in the suit which he brought in November 1627 against Benjamin Cooper, one of the executors of the will of William Yonges (the grandfather of Nicholas Peck's son), an abstract of which follows:

To the Right Honourable Sir Thomas Coventrie, Knight, Lord Keeper of the Great Seal of England, 20 November 1627.

The Bill of Complaint of NICHOLAS PECKE of Beccles, co. Suffolk, gent., father and guardian of William Peck, an orphan of nine years or thereabouts declares that whereas William Yongs, late of Great Yarmouth, co. Norfolk, deceased, father-in-law of your orator and grandfather of said William Peck, son of your orator by Rachell, only daughter and sole heir of said Yongs, by his will dated 13 September, 9 James I [13 September 1611], directed that various properties of which said Yongs was seised, including the messuage where he dwelt and other messuages [described in said will] should be held in trust by certain trustees [named], who were to deliver said properties to the heirs of said Rachell after her death, the said Yongs appointing Beniamin Cooper and William Kendall as executors of his will, therefore, the said Rachell having died about 3 October 1618, leaving the said William Peck as her only child and heir, the said trustees, by their deed dated 28 October, 16 James I

[28 October 1618], conveyed all said properties to the said William. Notwithstanding, immediately after the decease of said Yongs, Beniamin Cooper entered into the closet of the deceased and took away the evidences, deeds, and other writings, and will not produce them, neither does your orator know whether they are in bag, box, or chest, all which writings properly belong to your orator during the minority of said infant. And as there is not any remedy for this cause in the common law, your orator prays for a writ of subpœna, to summon said Beniamin Cooper into the Court of Chancery to answer to the premises.

The Answer, not dated, of BENIAMIN COOPER, esq., alderman and burgess of Great Yarmouth, defendant, to the Bill of Nicholas Peck, complainant, declares that, as mentioned in said bill, the defendant was appointed executor [of the will] of said William Yongs, deceased, his brother-in-law, who left the property mentioned in said bill to the heirs of Rachell Pecke. Defendant says also that during the lifetime of Yongs, the said Yongs requested him to keep the deeds and other writings referring to said properties in his own custody, and never to deliver them to the complainant. This the said Yongs desired, knowing the complainant to be in debt to various persons and being unable to trust him in relation to the said property. Therefore, according to said request, the defendant has taken into his safe custody, but not concealed, such writings, and will not deliver them to the complainant, knowing said William Peck to be an infant unable to act, and thinking the complainant not to be within his right in bringing the matter to law. Defendant is prepared, on William Peck coming to full age, to deliver to him the said writings. Wherefore he prays the Court not to compel him to deliver said writings, and he is prepared to prove these premises in the Court of Chancery.

Order of the Court of Chancery at Westminster dated 30 November, Anno R. R. 3 [30 November, 3 Charles I, i.e., 30 November 1627].

(Chancery Proceedings, Charles I, Bundle P 62, Number 37, in the Public Record Office, London.)

Information as to the outcome of the Chancery suit brought in 1627 by Nicholas Peck against Benjamin Cooper is lacking, but that William Yongs distrusted his son-in-law, Nicholas Peck, who was heavily in debt, is clear from the abstracts of the proceedings in this Chancery suit that have been given above. A few days before Nicholas Peck brought in his bill of complaint against Benjamin Cooper, he became involved in litigation in Chancery with his [Peck's] brother-in-law, John Buckenham of Debenham, co. Suffolk, grocer, who brought suit against Peck in regard to the marriage portion of the latter's sister, Martha Peck, whom Buckenham had married several years earlier, and in the following year, 1628, Peck instituted a countersuit against Buckenham. The Chancery proceedings in these two suits furnish interesting information about the Peck family and their relations with Buckenham and also about the trust established by William Yongs for the benefit of his daughter Rachel Peck, Nicholas Peck's first wife, and her heirs. Abstracts of these proceedings in Chancery are here given:

To the Right Honourable Thomas, Lord Coventry, Lord Keeper of the Great Seal of England, 4 November 1627.

The Bill of Complaint of JOHN BUCKENHAM of Debenham, co. Suffolk, grocer, declares that whereas Nicholas Pecke of Beccles, co. Suffolk, later of Great Yarmouth, co. Norfolk, merchant, in consideration of a marriage between Martha Pecke, sister of said Nicholas, [and your orator,] became bound, about 3 May 1611, to your orator for £200, and whereas said Pecke has not dealt justly with your orator in the matter, your orator prays for a writ of subpœna, to summon him into the Court of Chancery to answer to the premises.

The Answer of NICHOLAS PECK, gent., defendant, to the Bill of John Buckenham, grocer, complainant, sworn 14 June, Anno R. R. 4 [14 June, 4 Charles I, i.e., 14 June 1628], states that it is true that, in consideration of a marriage to be solemnized between his sister, Martha Pecke, and the complainant, the defendant, for the marriage portion of the said Martha, was bound, together with Samuel Peck of Ipswich, co. Suffolk, his brother, in the sum of £200, the condition of the bond being the payment of £100 to the complainant. And this defendant was induced to enter into the bond by the persuasion of said Samuel Peck, who, in the lifetime of their mother, Ellen Peck of Beccles, co. Suffolk, widow, brought over the complainant to Beccles with the purpose of arranging a marriage between him and the said Martha. Now about 1611 said Samuel travelled beyond the seas and, having confidence in his brother-in-law, the complainant, left his goods in his charge and made an inventory of such goods. And the defendant says that he covenanted to pay to the complainant and said Martha, his sister, £100 more. But he denies that after the death in 1611 of his father-in-law, William Yonge, of Great Yarmouth, co. Norfolk, merchant, he ever enjoyed any houses or lands in his own right or in that of Rachell, his wife, daughter of said William Yonge. And he declares that under the will of said Yonge the residue of his property was left in the hands of [trustees] [six trustees (one gentleman and five merchants) named], in trust for said Rachell and her children. Moreover, the complainant has refused to come to any reckoning with the defendant regarding the goods of said Samuel Peck, who died about 1619, which goods were left in his charge. And the inventory made by said Samuel has been delivered to Joseph Peck, brother of this defendant. And the defendant allows it to be true that the complainant put in a suit in the King's Bench, and that he, the defendant, pleaded a former acquittance, as it was lawful for him to do. And the defendant is ready to aver and prove these matters in the Court of Chancery.

The Replication, not dated, of JOHN BUCKENHAM, complainant, to the Answer of Nicholas Pecke, gent, defendant, declares that the complainant maintains his bill, and he says further that he doubtless will prove that the defendant was present at the sealing of the acquittance. He says also that the defendant's wife, after the death of Yonges, her father, received for her own use £70 per annum, for some years duration, and that, after the sealing of the said covenant and the payment of £25 to Moyses Child, the repliant and the defendant accounted together for all matters between them and the defendant was indebted to the repliant for only £12. Nor was the defendant induced by Samuel Peck to seal the bond for £200, but did it freely. All which matters he will aver in the Honourable Court.

Decree of the Court in settlement of the suit given at Westminster 24 May [sic, ? June] Anno R. R. 4 [24 May [? June], 4 Charles I, i.e., 24 May [? June] 1628].

(Chancery Proceedings, Charles I, Bundle B 98, Number 11, for Bill of Complainant and Answer of Defendant, Bundle B 139, Number 3, for Replication of Complainant, in the Public Record Office, London.)

Whatever the decree of the Court of Chancery in settlement of the suit of John Buckenham v. Nicholas Pecke may have been, it was soon followed by a countersuit in Chancery brought by Nicholas Peck against John Buckingham, as the name is spelled in the Bill of Complaint, the only record of this suit which the compiler of this article has found. An abstract of this Bill of Complaint follows:

To the Right Honourable Thomas, Lord Coventry, Baron of Aldborooughe, Lord Keeper of the Great Seal of England, 19 November 1628.

The Bill of Complaint of NICHOLAS PECK of Beccles, co. Suffolk, gent, declares that whereas, about sixteen years past, John Buckingham of Debenham, co. Suffolk, grocer, became suitor to Martha Pecke, natural sister of your orator, who dwelt with her brother, Samuel Pecke of Ipswich, co. Suffolk, grocer, and whereas said John Buckingham, being of the same profession as said Samuel, persuaded him to journey with him to Beccles to make an offer of marriage for said Martha to her mother, Ellen Pecke, widow, to which said Ellen agreed, thereupon said Ellen Pecke, said Samuel Pecke, and your orator covenanted to give as a marriage portion £100, they being bound for £200, by a bond dated about 3 May 1611, to pay to said John Buckingham £50 on the day of marriage and £40 twelve months later, and, moreover, your orator covenanted about the same time to pay £100 more to said Buckingham and to his sister Martha and their issue, provided your orator survived his father-in-law, William Youngs of Great Yarmouth, and inherited the estate of said Youngs in common with Rachell, his then wife, daughter of said Youngs. This covenant was made in order that it might appear to the friends of Buckingham that he was receiving £200 as a marriage portion with his wife, and said Buckingham promised soon afterwards to cancel the covenant. Nevertheless, despite your orator, said Samuel, and said Ellen having sold a messuage in Beccles to expedite payment of their bond, and despite said Buckingham having in custody goods belonging to said Samuel while he was travelling beyond the seas and likewise goods belonging to your orator given into custody of his brother when he ceased to dwell in Ipswich, said Buckingham has brought a suit against your orator in the Court of King's Bench at Westminster, notwithstanding said Buckingham has used the goods of your orator for himself and knows that he is fully indemnified for the debt. However, as your orator had from said Buckingham a general acquittance, said Buckingham was unable to gain his suit, and made a bill of complaint in the Court of Chancery, whereby he made false allegations regarding your orator, endeavoring to prove that he had promised not to plead such acquittance in court. And whereas the inventory of the goods of said Samuel, now deceased, and all accounts relating to the aforesaid matters are in the hands of said Buckingham, including a book which he took from Joseph Pecke of Hingham, co. Norfolk, which had been delivered to said Joseph by his brother, said Samuel, and whereas your orator has not any witnesses to the deed of acquittance, having trusted to the good faith of John Buckingham, now your orator prays for a writ of subpœna, to summon John Buckingham into the Court of Chancery to answer to the premises.

(Chancery Proceedings, Charles I, Bundle P 79, Number 36, in the Public Record Office, London.)

The outcome of the countersuit in Chancery brought on 19 November 1628 by Nicholas Peck of Beccles, gent., against John Buckingham (or Buckenham), his brother-in-law, is unknown, and the next information available about Nicholas Peck is found in the bill of complaint in a Chancery suit brought on 26 November 1649, about a year after the death of said Nicholas, by one Robert Hawes of Beccles, woollen draper, who had been executor, together with Nicholas Peck, of the will of one Thomas Daynes, and claimed that Nicholas Peck had not reimbursed him [Hawes] for amounts due him from said Nicholas as a fellow executor of the above-mentioned will. In his later years Nicholas Peck apparently lived at North Cove, co. Suffolk, the home of his only son, William Peck, and Hawes sued Bridget Peck, the widow, and William Peck, the son, of said Nicholas, together with one Henry Farrowe, who also was indebted to the testator Daynes, for the amount due him as surviving executor of the will of Daynes. It is the bill of complaint of

Hawes that fixes the date of the death of Nicholas Peck at "about a year ago," i.e., about November 1648. An abstract of this bill of complaint follows:

To the Right Honourable the Lords Commissioners for the custody of the Great Seal of England, 26 November 1649.

The Bill of Complaint of ROBERT HAWES of Beccles, co. Suffolk, woollen draper, surviving executor of [the will of] Thomas Daynes, late of Beccles, clerk, deceased, declares that whereas said Daynes, being possessed of sundry personal estate, including a library of books, made his will on 19 February 1640, and appointed as executors Nicholas Pecke, gent., of North Cove, co. Suffolk, since deceased, and your orator, and whereas, after the death of said Daynes, your orator and said Pecke caused his goods to be valued, and afterwards exhibited the will at the registrar's office at Norwich, together with the inventory, and whereas, before the will was proved, the executors agreed to receive, each of them, part of the moneys to arise from the testator's personal estate, as it was sold, and to pay thereout the legacies left by the said will, and further they agreed that said Pecke should have the custody of the bonds, etc., connected with the estate, therefore, in pursuance of such agreement, said Pecke received and acknowledged the receipt of various moneys arising from the sale of the testator's estate, but when the legacies became due to be paid, said Pecke refused to pay his share, and your orator paid the whole, and when he required to be reimbursed, said Pecke affirmed that he had not the money then by him, but admitted, in the presence of Bridget, his wife, and William, his son, or one of them, that he had received the several sums of money out of the estate. And moreover your orator shows that Henry Farrowe, the Elder, of Beccles, was indebted to the testator for £5, which debt he never paid either to your orator or to said Pecke. And whereas said Pecke died about a year ago, before he had reimbursed your orator for the sum he had paid to the legatees as aforesaid, your orator has now required satisfaction from Bridget and William Pecke aforesaid, who not only refuse to accede to his request, pretending that said Nicholas Pecke has not left any personal estate, which your orator knows to be untrue, but also they refuse to render up the bonds and other writings connected with the estate of said Daynes, although they have not any rights in the administration thereof. And your orator likewise cannot get settlement of the debt from said Farrowe, who has combined with Bridget and William Pecke in order to deceive your orator, saying that he paid the money to said Nicholas in his lifetime. Therefore your orator prays for a writ of subpœna, to summon Bridget Pecke, widow, William Pecke, and Henry Farrowe to appear in the Court of Chancery to answer to these premises.

(Chancery Proceedings, Charles I, Bundle H 98, Number 21, in the Public Record Office, London.)

The result of the Chancery suit brought by Robert Hawes in 1649 against Bridget and William Peck and Henry Farrowe, the Elder, is unknown. The defendant Bridget Peck, widow of Thomas Sayer, gent., and later widow of Nicholas Peck (who is styled "gent." in Hawes's bill of complaint and in several other records already cited), was living as late as 16 November 1663, when John Sayer of Beccles, gent., her younger son by her earlier husband, brought a suit in Chancery against her and her elder son, Thomas Sayer of Pulham, co. Norfolk, gent. The defendant William Peck, stepson of Bridget Peck and only child of Nicholas Peck, had inherited from his mother, Rachel Yonges, first wife of Nicholas Peck, the estate left in trust for Rachel and her heirs by her [Rachel's] father, William Yonges of Great Yarmouth, who died in 1611. (*Vide supra, passim.*)

584

Baptized at Beccles 23 September 1618, as "son of Nicholas Pecke, gent., and of his wife" (who was buried at Beccles 4 October 1618, as "Mrs. Rachell Pecke wife of Nicholas Pecke gent"), William Peck lived at North Cove, co. Suffolk, and died not later than 25 April 1695, when administration of the goods, etc., of William Peck of North Cove, co. Suffolk, deceased, was granted to William Peck, his son. (Archdeaconry Court of Suffolk, Administrations, 1695, at Ipswich.) He married, about 1644, Dorothy Bacon, a daughter of Sir Butts Bacon of Herringfleet, co. Suffolk, baronet, and his wife, Lady Dorothy Bacon (who died before 18 March 1660/1, the date of her husband's will). Sir Butts Bacon was a relative of Francis Bacon, the famous scientist and philosopher, Lord Chancellor of England, and in his will, proved 30 January 1661/2, he bequeathed to his daughter, Dorothy Peck, and made his son-in-law, William Peck, and his [the testator's] son, Henry Bacon, executors. (Consistory Court of Norwich, at Norwich, Register 1661, folio 483.)*

In "The Visitation of Suffolk, 1664–1668" (*The Publications of the Harleian Society*, vol. 61, London, 1910, p. 81), there is published, under the title "Peck, of North Cove," a tabular pedigree, entered in 1664 by William Peck, son of Nicholas Peck, and giving the descent of this William Peck from the second Robert Peck of Beccles, his [William's] grandfather, with the names of William's six children. This pedigree not only describes the arms of Peck of North Cove, namely, *Argent, on a chevron engrailed Gules three crosses pattée of the field*, but is of special interest as the only known authority for the maiden name and parentage of Ellen [or Helen], wife of the second Robert Peck of Beccles. It shows that [the second] Robert Peck of Beccles, co. Suffolk, married Ellen, daughter of Nicholas Babbs of Guylford [Guildford, co. Surrey], that their son, Nicholas Peck of Beccles, married Rachell, daughter of "Will: Young" of Yarmouth, co. Norfolk, that the son of Nicholas and Rachell Peck, William Peck of North Cove, co. Suffolk g$^t$ [gent.]., 1664, married Dorothy, daughter of Sir Butts Bacon of Blundeston, co. Suffolk, bart., and that in 1664 the children of William Peck of North Cove and his wife Dorothy were four sons, William, son and heir, aged 19 in 1664, Thomas, John, and Samuel, and two daughters, Dorothy and Elizabeth. This pedigree is signed "Will$^m$ Peck." It is confirmed in part by the will of the second Robert Peck of Beccles, dated 22 March 1592/3 (*supra*, pp. 284–286).**

When William Peck's father-in-law, Sir Butts Bacon, baronet, made his will, dated 18 March 1660/1, he was of Herringfleet, co. Suffolk. In the tabular pedigree, entered by William Peck in 1664, Sir Butts Bacon, baronet, is described as of Blundeston, co. Suffolk. There his tombstone and that of his wife have been found recently (footnote), and there, probably, he lived in the last two or three years of his life. It should be noted that in the tabular pedigree William Peck styles neither his Grandfather Peck nor his father, Nicholas Peck, "gent.," but assumes that appellation for himself. No further information is at hand regarding the sons and daughters of William Peck of North Cove, co. Suffolk, gent.

[To be continued]

*Sir Butts Bacon, baronet, and his wife are buried in the church of Blundeston, co. Suffolk. The Latin inscriptions on their tombstones have recently been uncovered, and through the courtesy of the rector of Blundeston are given here. Each inscription consists of six lines, in capital letters, but they are printed here without regard to the capitalization and the division into lines of the original inscriptions:

"Hic iacet Butts Bacon baronettus Nicholai Bacon Anglie baronetti primi filius septimus qui obijt Maij 29 1661"

"Hic iacet Dorothea Bacon Butts Bacon baronetti marita Roberti Jermyn armigeri vidua Henrici Warner militis filia quae obijt Septembris [*illegible*]."

These inscriptions show that Sir Butts Bacon, baronet, was the seventh son of Sir Nicholas Bacon, the first baronet of England, and died 29 May 1661, and that his wife, Dorothea Bacon, was daughter of Henry Warner, knight, and widow of Robert Jermyn, esquire, and died in September, the day and year being illegible.

**Pages 574–576, this volume.

## GENEALOGICAL RESEARCH IN ENGLAND

Communicated by the Committee on English and Foreign Research

### THE STIBBS FAMILY

Contributed by G. Andrews Moriarty, A.M., LL.B., F.S.A.,
of Bristol, R. I.

In an article on the Haskett family, communicated by the
Committee on English Research, under the title "Genealogical
Research in England," and printed in the Register, vol. 77 (1923),
pp. 71–77, 110–133, it is shown that Stephen[1] Haskett, of Salem,*

*Pages 1-30, this volume.

Mass., was the son of Ellis (Elias) Haskett and his second wife, Eleanor Stibbs.

The following communication deals with the family of Eleanor Stibbs. The Stibbs were a yeoman family, tenants of the manor of Bowdon, in Henstridge, co. Somerset, England, in the latter part of the sixteenth century.

From the Bishop's Transcript of the Henstridge Parish Register *

*Baptisms*

1605 Elinor Stibbs daughter of William 18 October.
1622 Anna Stibbs daughter of William and Edith 15 December.
1639 William Stibbs son of William and Agnes 2 February [1639/40].

*Burials*

1605 Richard Stibbs 26 September.
1639 William Stibbs infant son of William and Agnes 16 February [1639/40].

From Lay Subsidies for co. Somerset †

39 Elizabeth [1596/7].
Henstridge.       William Stibbs in goods [valued at] £3. [tax] 8d.
7 James [1609/10].
Henstridge.       William Stibbs in lands [valued at] 20s. [tax] 4d.
3 Charles [1627/8].
Henstridge.       William Stibbs in lands [valued at] 20s. [tax] 4d.
4 Charles [1628/9].
Henstridge.       William Stibbs in lands [valued at] £1. [tax] 8d.
16 Charles [1640/41].
Henstridge.       William Stibbs in goods [valued at] £2. [tax] 2s.

From Star Chamber Proceedings

[Hayne *v.* Pope]

Bill endorsed 6 Feb. 38 Elizabeth [1596]

Complaint by William Hussey against William Pope of Milborne Port, co. Somerset, yeoman. Refers to a bill in Chancery brought against Thomas Hussey Esq. Robert Brooke yeoman and ——— Hayne by William Pope in 1594 to compel Hussey, Lord of Bowdon manor in Henstridge to cancel a lease made to Brooke and to grant a lease of the premises "late in the tenure of Hercules Stibbs" to the complainant, Pope, according to an agreement made on 24 Nov. 1592. In their answer in the chancery case Hussey, Hayne and Brooke stated that "one Stibbs pretended to have an estate for life in the copy hold" and that Pope learning that Stibbs was "suddenly dead" concealed the death and induced Hussey to grant him, Pope, a lease of the premises for a smaller sum than he would have demanded if he had known of the death of Stibbs. Thereafter, Hussey, at Haynes request, cancelled the agreement to lease to Pope and leased to Brooke for three lives. Hayne now complains in Star Chamber that Pope's three witnesses perjured themselves in the Chancery case. One of the witnesses, Richard Stibbs, perjured himself by swearing that one Robert Stibbs had at one time surrendered an estate in a copy hold of Bowdon manor for himself and another in remainder, when in fact there was no body in remainder, this testimony was given to prove the custom of the manor with respect to surrenders. Richard Stibbs on 13 Feb. 38 Elizabeth (1596) denied the perjury charges. (Star Chamber Proceedings, N. 27/22.)

* Preserved in the Diocesan Registry of Wells.
† Preserved in the Public Record Office, London.

[Pople *v.* Lambert (Collins 21/140)]

The bill [filed 12 Feb. 1660/1] of John Pople of Weeke in Milborne Port, co. Somerset, yeoman, against Samuel Lambert of Kingsbury Regis in Milborne Port.

About 28 years ago the said Samuel Lambert held a tenement called Lamberts' Hill in Milborne Port for 99 years determinable upon the death of the said Samuel Lambert and one John Lambert his son. By an indenture dated 10 March 1632/3 he assigned his interest in the premises to one Robert Stibbs, son of William Stibbs of Bowdon, co. Somerset, yeoman, upon an oral trust to the use of said William Stibbs. William Stibbs took the issues for 10 years until Robert died and thereafter for 12 years until 1654 when William died and bequeathed his interest to one of his daughters, Edith Stibbs, now the wife of Christopher French of Halstock, co. Dorset, charged with an annuity of 40/ for another of his daughters, Margaret Stibbs. Edith was executrix of William Stibbs's will and about 20 Dec. 1659 French sold the lease to the complainant Pople for 20 marks. Thereafter, the respondent Lambert persuaded someone to take out an administration on the estate of Robert Stibbs and about 6 months ago he got the administrator to convey the premises back to him, although he knew of the trust in favor of William Stibbs. Thereupon Lambert brought an action of trespass at the Common Law against Pople, who now prays for a subpoena against Lambert, Christopher and Edith French and Margaret Stibbs.

In his answer Lambert recites a lease to himself for 99 years dated 17 July 7 Charles I. He admits he assigned the said lease to Robert Stibbs, who took the issues up to his death. William Stibbs died intestate and did not devise to Edith and Margaret, "now since dead," even if he had the power to do so. Edith having got possession of the assignment, took the profits until her death, 2 years past, by permission of her sister Anne, now the wife of Thomas Galpen. On Edith's death Anne and Thomas Galpen took out administration on the estate of Robert Stibbs and on 13 Nov. 13 Charles II assigned the remainder of the lease back to Samuel Lambert. Answer dated 27 April 13 Charles II.

## FROM CHANCERY DEPOSITIONS

[Pople *v.* Lambert *et als.*]

(Chancery Depositions Before 1714, B 142/12, 7 July 15 Charles II [1663])

Deposition * of Elizabeth, late wife of William R—— of Bowdon, co. Somerset, yeoman, aged 50 years. She knows all the parties. William Stibbs died about 10 years since. Edith Stibbs died about 3 years since. Does not know how long since Robert Stibbs died. She was present at the treaty between the respondents French and Galpen for the marriage of said French with said Edith. Galpen on that occasion declared Edith had an estate for years in Lamberts Hill close, determinable on the death of Samuel Lambert or Margery his wife, since deceased, and of John Lambert his son and of the longest liver of them and also an estate for her own [Edith's] life in another close called Milborne Hill in Milborne Port and £100 in money, etc. The marriage took place and the father of Christopher French settled a considerable estate on Edith, to the satisfaction of Galpen.

Deposition * of —— of Milborne Port gent. aged about 55 years. He knows all the parties. William Stibbs died about 12 years since and Edith about 3 years since. Robert Stibbs died before William. He was present at the marriage treaty about 10 or 11 years ago between Galpen and French.

* This deposition is much injured by dampness.

Galpen promised that Edith should have the above property and William French settled certain closes for the use of Edith.

Deposition * of Richard H—— of Milborne Port weaver aged about 50 years. He knows the complainant and the respondents Samuel Lambert and —— [Thomas] Galpen and Anne his wife. He also knew William, Robert and Edith Stibbs. He was sometime suitor for Edith, late wife of the respondent French before she intermarried with the said Christopher. Galpen and his wife are reputed to be worth upwards of £100 . . . in two closes called Lambert's Hill . . . and one other close. . . .

FROM PROCESSES AND DECREES IN THE COURT OF DELEGATES

[Hasket *v.* Crumsey, vol. 269, no. 630 (cf. REGISTER, vol. 77 (1923), pp. 112–115)]

Giles Hallett aged about 80 years deposed 16 Sept. 1697 that he had lived since infancy in Henstridge. He well knew his near neighbor, William Stibbs, who lived in Bowdon. He was a farmer and kept sheep. The said William had five daughters, Eleanor, Susanna, Anne, Margaret and Edith Stibbs. He knew Ellis Hasket, who married Eleanor Stibbs. Anne, sister of Eleanor, married Thomas Galpen and had seven sons, the youngest of whom was Richard Galpen, a party defendant in the case of Hasket *v.* Crumsey *et als.*

From the above records we learn that at the close of the sixteenth century there were living in Bowdon manor, Henstridge, co. Somerset, several yeomen of the name of Stibbs, viz., Hercules, Robert, Richard, and William Stibbs. Hercules died very shortly before 24 Nov. 1592. In 1596/7 William Stibbs was taxed at Henstridge and Richard was alive on 12 Oct. 1596, when he answered to Hayne in the Star Chamber case and was buried in Henstridge on 26 Sept. 1605. Robert had died, apparently, some time before.

William Stibbs was married about 1604. He had issue: Eleanor bapt. 18 Oct. 1605 married about 1630–35 Ellis Hasket of Henstridge and had a son Stephen (afterwards of Salem, Mass.) bapt. 18 Dec. 1636; Robert born about 1608, died *s.p.* about 1642; Susanna born about 1612; Anne bapt. 15 Dec. 1622, married Thomas Galpen about 1640; Margaret born about 1623, died *s.p.* about 1662; Edith born about 1626 married about 1653 Christopher French of Halstock, co. Dorset, died about 1660; and William bapt. 2 Feb. 1639/40, buried 16 Feb. 1639/40. William Stibbs was apparently married thrice, first about 1604, secondly, prior to 15 Dec. 1622, Edith ——, and thirdly before 2 Feb. 1639/40 Agnes ——. William died in or about 1653–54.

It would appear that Robert (died some time prior to 1596), Hercules (died in 1592), Richard (died in 1605), and William (living in 1596/7) were brothers and that Robert was the father of William who died in 1654, in view of the fact that William named his son Robert.

   1. —— STIBBS of Somersetshire or Dorsetshire.
      Children (probably):
  2. i.  ROBERT, b. about 1540; d. about 1588.
    ii.  HERCULES, tenant of Bowdon manor, Henstridge, co. Somerset, b. about 1542; d. shortly before 24 Nov. 1592.
    iii.  RICHARD, of Henstridge, b. about 1545; bur. 26 Sept. 1605.
    iv.  WILLIAM, taxed at Henstridge in 1596/7, b. about 1547.

* This deposition is much injured by dampness.

2. ROBERT STIBBS (————), of Bowdon manor, Henstridge, co.
   Somerset, yeoman, born about 1540, died about 1588. He
   married ————.
   Child (probably):

   3. i.   WILLIAM, of Bowdon manor, Henstridge, co. Somerset, b. about 1580.

3. WILLIAM STIBBS (? *Robert*, ————), of Bowdon manor, Henstridge, co. Somerset, yeoman, grazier, born about 1580, died
   in 1653/54. He married first, about 1604, ————, secondly,
   prior to 15 Dec. 1622, EDITH ————, and thirdly, 2 Feb. 1639/
   40, AGNES ————.
   He was taxed at Hendridge in 1627, 1628, and 1640.
   Children by first wife:

   i.    ELEANOR, bapt. 18 Oct. 1605; bur. at Henstridge 17 June 1660; m.
         about 1630–1635 ELLIS HASKETT, of Henstridge, clothier, gentleman.
         They were the parents of Stephen Haskett, bapt. at Henstridge
         18 Dec. 1636. He emigrated about 1667 to Salem, Mass. For his
         family and descendants see REGISTER, vol. 77 (1923), pp. 128–131). *
   ii.   ROBERT, feoffee of Lambert's Hill in Milborne Port, co. Somerset,
         to the use of his father William in 1632, b. about 1608; d. *s.p.* in 1642.
   iii.  SUSANNA, b. about 1612; probably d. *s.p.*

   Children by second wife:

   iv.   ANNA, bapt. 15 Mar. 1622; living in 1663; m. about 1640 THOMAS
         GALPEN. Seven sons, the youngest of whom was *Richard.*
   v.    MARGARET, b. about 1625; d. unm. about 1662–3.
   vi.   EDITH, b. about 1628; d. in 1660; m. about 1653 CHRISTOPHER FRENCH
         of Halstock, co. Dorset, son of William French.

   Child by third wife:

   vii.  WILLIAM, bapt. 2 Feb. 1639/40; bur. 16 Feb. 1639/40.


THE ENGLISH ANCESTRY OF JOSEPH PECK,
OF HINGHAM, MASS., IN 1638

Compiled by S. ALLYN PECK, B.A., of New York City, and contributed by
FREDERICK STANHOPE PECK, LL.D., of Barrington, R. I.

[Continued from vol. 91, page 363]

III

ROBERT PECK OF BECCLES, CO. SUFFOLK,
AND SOME OF HIS DESCENDANTS [CONTINUED]

To the abstracts of records relating to Nicholas Peck, son of the second
Robert Peck of Beccles, co. Suffolk, England, which were published in the
REGISTER of October 1937 (vol. 91, pp. 355–363), there should be added the **
following abstract of a deposition by Nicholas Peck, gent., of North Cove,
co. Suffolk, recently obtained by the compiler of this article from Deposi-
tions by Commission in the Court of Exchequer, which are deposited in the
Public Record Office, London. These depositions were taken in 15 Charles I
1639–40), in connection with the suit of Robert Pearson, D.D., Archdeacon
of Suffolk, plaintiff, *v.* Sir William Hewett, knight, Thomas Hewett, esq.,
Dame Elizabeth Feltham, widow, Robert Lane, and John Lane, gent., de-
*See the footnote on p. 586, this volume.
**Pages 577-585, this volume.

fendants, in regard to the payment of procurations * to the Archdeaconry of Suffolk by the parsons, vicars, etc., of Wickham, Pettistry [Pettistree] *alias* Pistrie, Loudham, Brightwell, Foxall, Kesgrave, Rushmere, and Playford.

Depositions taken 4 October, 15 Charles I [4 October 1639], at Beccles, at the Sign of the King's Head there.

Nicholas Pecke of North Cove, co. Suffolk, gent., aged 63 years or thereabouts, being sworn and examined, saith as followeth:

To the first interrogatory he saith that he hath known the Complainant by the space of ten years and more last past, but for the Defendants [he] neither did nor doth know any of them.

To the ninth interrogatory he saith that he hath seen certain notes importing accounts which he, this deponent, knoweth well to be [in] the handwriting of Robte Pecke, deceased, this deponent's late father, of which one was an account of Margarett Crampton, executrix of the last will and testament of Richard Crampton, deceased, written in the handwriting of this deponent's said father for the year ending 1581, wherein she did charge herself with the receipt of all the procurations then due to John Maplerden, then Archdeacon of Suffolk, amounting to the entire sum of "fowerscore fowertene pounds five shilling & nyne pence" [£94. 5s. 9d.], and also one other account of the said Robte Pecke, this deponent's father, then register and collectoi, for the year 1582, in which accounts the said accountants have charged themselves with the afoi esaid sum of £94. 5s. 9d.; and this deponent verily believeth that the churches of Wickham, Pittistrie *alias* Pistrie, Lowdham, Brightwell, Foxall, Kesgrave, Rushmer, and Playford were then charged and did pay the said sums in the interrogatory mentioned for procurations unto the then Archdeacon of Suffolk. This deponent is induced so to believe for that [i.e., because] in the fore-mentioned accounts divers other churches are given [as] in arrearage, but the fore-mentioned churches are not mentioned in the said accounts to be in arrears; and this deponent further saith that he hath seen two small books, the one dated 1553, the other dated 1555, and these books this deponent verily believeth to be [in] the proper [i.e., own] handwriting of the afore-named Richard Crampton, then register and collector to the then Archdeacon of Suffolk. In these books are particularly set down all the parishes within said Archdeaconry, with the several sums charged upon them, viz., the church of Wickham 7s. 6d., the church of Pettistrie *alias* Pistrie 6s. 8d., the church of Lowdham 7s. 6d., the church of Brightwell 3s., the church of Foxall 5s., the church of Kesgrave 5s., the church of Rushmer 6s. 8d., and the church of Playford 6s. 8d., and these several sums this deponent conceiveth by the said accounts and books to have been paid and received at the several times mentioned in the said books, and further to this interrogatory he doth not depose.†

In several records relating to Nicholas Peck, of which abstracts were given in the instalment of this article which appeared in the REGISTER of October 1937, as well as in the deposition of Nicholas Peck given above, he is styled "gent." The earliest instance in which this rank is assigned to him seems

---

* Procurations, in ecclesiastical usage, were originally payments of the necessary expenses of bishops or archdeacons in making their visitations of parochial churches, monasteries, or other ecclesiastical foundations. They were paid by the churches, monasteries, etc., visited—in the case of a parochial church by the incumbent (rector, vicar, etc.) or by the patron who had the right of presentation to the living. In later usage procurations were customary sums of money paid to the visiting bishops or archdeacons by way of commutation for their necessary expenses. The defendants in the suit brought by Robert Pearson, D.D., Archdeacon of Suffolk, were probably the patrons of the several churches named.

† In this deposition of Nicholas Peck, taken at Beccles 4 October 1639, the deponent is described as of North Cove, co. Suffolk, "gent," and his age is given as 63 years or thereabouts. It is likely, therefore, that he was born in 1576, a date which harmonizes with the suggestion made in the REGISTER of October 1937 (vol. 91, p. 355). Although the deponent states that his late father [the second Robert Peck of Beccles] was register and collector [of the Archdeaconry of Suffolk] in the year 1582, nowhere in this deposition does the deponent style his father "gent." **

**Page 577, this volume.

591

to be in the entry, in the parish register of Beccles, co. Suffolk, of the baptism, on 23 September 1618, of his only son, William, who is there described as "son of Nicholas Pecke, gent., and of his wife," and the boy's mother, the first wife of Nicholas, was buried at Beccles on 4 October 1618 as "Mrs. Rachell Pecke wife of Nicholas Pecke gent." In the answer, dated Beccles, 19 January 1619/20, of Nicholas Peck and his second wife, Bridget, to the bill of complaint of William Webbe, gent., Nicholas is called "Nicholas Pecke, gent." (Register, vol. 91, p. 356), and a few years later, when Nicholas was much involved in litigation in Chancery, he brought in, as "Nicholas Pecke of Beccles, co. Suffolk, gent.," a bill of complaint, dated 20 November 1627, against Benjamin Cooper, one of the executors of the will of William Yongs, the father-in-law of Nicholas (*ibid.*, vol. 91, p. 358). A few days earlier, on * 4 November 1627, as Nicholas Pecke of Beccles, co. Suffolk, later of Great Yarmouth, co. Norfolk, "merchant," he had been sued by his brother-in-law, John Buckenham of Debenham, co. Suffolk, grocer (*ibid.*, vol. 91, p. 359), and in his answer (sworn to 14 June 1628) to John Buckenham's bill of complaint Nicholas Peck calls himself "gent." (*ibid.*, vol. 91, p. 360). The * replication, not dated, of John Buckenham mentions the answer of Nicholas Pecke, "gent" (*ibid.*). On 19 November 1628 Nicholas Peck of Beccles, co. Suffolk, "gent," brought a countersuit in Chancery against his brother-in-law, John Buckingham (as the name is spelled in this suit) of Debenham, co. Suffolk, grocer, the outcome of which is unknown (*ibid.*, vol. 91, pp. 360–361). In the deposition by Nicholas Peck taken 4 October 1639 and given above, the deponent, as already stated, is called Nicholas Peck of North Cove, co. Suffolk, "gent," and he is referred to in the same way, about a year after his death, in a suit in Chancery brought by Robert Hawes on 26 November 1649 (*ibid.*, vol. 91, pp. 361–362).

[To be continued]

*See the footnote on p. 586, this volume.

GENEALOGICAL RESEARCH IN ENGLAND

Communicated by the Committee on English and Foreign Research

THE FISKE FAMILY

Contributed by G. ANDREWS MORIARTY, A.M., LL.B., F.S.A.,
of Bristol, R. I.

IN the REGISTER, vol. 87, pp. 367–374, and vol. 88, pp. 142–146, 265–273, there is printed a pedigree of the Fiske Family of Laxfield, co. Suffolk, England, and New England. * Since this compilation appeared much new information concerning the earlier members of the family has come to light through the deposit in the public library of Ipswich, co. Suffolk, England, of many charters relating to the earlier members of the family.   These deeds not only disclose the name of the father of Simon Fiske of Laxfield, the testator of 22 Dec. 1463, but render it necessary to rearrange somewhat the chronology of the earlier members of the family.   Furthermore, an inexcusable error in the reading of the will of Simon Fiske, the testator of 10 July 1536 (cf. REGISTER, vol. 86, p. 415), renders it necessary to revise the account of the probable parentage of Richard Fiske of the Broadgates in Laxfield, with whom the Candler pedigree commenced.

In that will the testator bequeathed to his daughters Joan Jerelon (?Ireland) and Olive Warne.   The contributor read it as a bequest to his daughters Joan, Jerelon (Gillian), and Olive Warne and then argued that as William, son of Richard of the Broadgates, had a daughter Gillian, Richard was probably a son of this Simon, although not named in his will, as it was evident from the internal evidence of the will that all the children of Simon were not named therein. While this is true, the fact that Simon had no daughter Gillian destroys the argument of the former article.

Accordingly, after presenting the newly discovered evidence and a revised pedigree of the first three or four generations of the family, the contributor takes up the question of the parentage of Richard

*For pp. 367-374 see pp. 481-488, this volume; for pp. 142-146 see pp. 489-493, this volume; for pp. 265-273 see pp. 494-502, this volume.

Fiske and presents, he hopes, sufficient evidence to make out a strong case for his probable parentage.

18 Henry VI [1440]. At Laxfield. Charter of Thomas, son of Robert Cone, and Roger Smyth of Laxfield to William Cone, brother of said Thomas, William le Hawe and Thomas Bas all of Laxfield, cites a feoffment of land in Stodhaugh and parcels of land in Laxfield next the King's Highway and adjoining Sir Robert Wingfield, Knt., made by Nicholas Taylour and Simon Fiske then aged forty years. (*Ex penes* Randall Palmer Saunderson, Morpeth, England.)

## FROM CHARTERS OF THE FISKES OF LAXFIELD, CO. SUFFOLK

Friday before St. Luke the Evangelist, 14 Henry VI [14 Oct. 1435].
Charter whereby William Seman of Norwich grants to Simon Fiske of Laxfield two acres in said Laxfield bounded by the highway from Laxfield to Fressingfield on the East, West on John Edward, South on said Edward and on Joan Barwere, and North on the common way from Cratfield to Walterysditch in Laxfield. Witnessed by Hugh Fiske, William Dowsing, William Barwere, John Edward and Simon Jurdon of Laxfield et al. (Charter in the possession of G. Andrews Moriarty, F.S.A.)

8 Sept. 16 Henry VII [1500]. At Laxfield.
William Noyse of Laxfield grants to John Fiske, son of Simon Fiske, Nicholas Smyth, Thomas Fyske and William Blynde, all of Laxfield, a messuage called Hurleychys in Laxfield together with two adjacent closes and a piece of land belonging thereto lying in the close late of Robert Cone, seven acres more or less bounded East on Sir John Wingfield Knt. now in the tenure of John Cryspe, West on said Wingfield now in the tenure of John Barwere, North on Turrypestrete, South on John Cryspe, which premises I had with William Barwere, and Thomas Smyth of Laxfield, deceased, by feoffment of John Noloth, William Balston, Nicholas Noloth of Laxfield, John Fiske of Eye, the elder, and John Fiske aforesaid of Laxfield, the younger, as by a charter at Laxfield dated 16 June 15 Edward IV [1475]. Noyse appoints Robert Crispe *alias* Barker his attorney to give seisin to the grantees. (*Ex penes* New England Historic Genealogical Society.)

## FROM CHARTERS IN THE PUBLIC LIBRARY AT IPSWICH *

Tuesday, Purification of Blessed Virgin Mary, 41 Edward III [2 February 1368]. At Laxfelde, John de Stodhaghe of Laxfelde to William Gleme of Laxfelde the moiety of a tenement which John and William le Neve held of grantor in the hamlet of Laxfelde. Witnesses: William Cloutyng, John atte Brygge, Nicholas Talions, Seman le Hamuyle, Richard Rowe, John Gerard. (No. 1.)

10 May, 8 Henry V [1421]. At Laxfeld. John son of William Barwer late of Laxfeld to Edmund Seman of Laxfeld, William Crysp, "qwelwright," and Robert Barker of Laxfeld, their heirs and assigns, all my lands and tenements in Laxfeld Witnesses: Henry Seyly, John Edward, Alan Noyse, Edmund Hurlych, Simon Fysk. (No. 2.)

* These documents, brief abstracts of which follow, were deposited with the Ipswich Museum by William H. Fiske of Norwich, W. Sanders Fiske of London, and Edwin Burton Fiske of London, who acquired them in 1929 from Ruondell P. Sanderson of Morpeth, Northumberland, a retired official of the British Museum and a collector of old documents. He, in turn, received them from another collector some twenty-five years ago. These deeds, no doubt once in the parish church chest at Laxfield and later removed in an unknown manner, confirm the early pedigree of the Fiske family as recorded in the Fiske Family Papers by Henry Fiske.

1 December, 9 Henry V [1421]. At Laxfeld. William Dowsyng, son and heir of Stephen Dowsyng, deceased, late of Laxfeld, to Simon Fysk, son of Hugh Fysk of Laxfeld, two pieces of my land (2½ acres) there in the hamlet of Stoodh[a]wgh in the town of Laxfeld, between le Marketweye, W[est]; land of said William Dowsyng, E[ast]; land of said Simon Fysk, N[orth]; said Marketweye and land of John Sauage, S[outh]; to Simon Fysk, his heirs and assigns for ever. Witnesses: Nicholas Stowe, Edmund Hurlich, Richard Gleme, Robert Barker, John Edward. (Seal in good condition.) (No. 3.)

10 November, 29 Henry VI [1450]. At Laxfeld. Quitclaim by (1) Robert Broun of Laxfeld, son of John Broun late of the same, to (2) Geoffrey Fisk of Laxfeld, William Fisk of the same, the elder, Nicholas Noloth,' and William Fisk of the same, the younger, the messuage called Brounes, late of said John Broun, my father, and formerly of Roger Skynner in Laxfeld, and a piece of meadow called le mere, which (2) late had jointly of the demise and livery of Robert Thrower of Laxfeld and John Nicholl of the same, the younger, as the said messuage with gardens and croft(s) lies between (1) messuage and land of Prior of Eye in tenure of John Chirche, and land of the same Prior now in tenure of said Geoffrey Fisk, East; (2) land late of Margaret Balston, West; the way called le Cros Weye, N[orth]; land of said Prior in tenure of said Geoffrey Fiske, S[outh]; [and as] le Mere, which was formerly of John Nicholl, E[ast], W[est], and S[outh]; land of Robert Wyngefeld in tenure of said John Nicholl, N[orth]. Witnesses: John Ede of Laxfeld, Simon Fisk, John Noloth, John Smyth, Hugh Arteys, William Balston, John Hardyman. (No. 4.)

Thursday before SS. Philip and James, 30 Henry VI [1452]. Estreat of Court of the Rectory of Laxfeld. Surrender by John Clement of a messuage with the dyke opposite the said messuage lying next (iuxta) Crosweye, between messuage Clay, E[ast]; land of the Rector, W[est] and N[orth]; to the use of William Lynde and his heirs, upon condition that if William Lynde pay John Clement certain specified sums at certain dates the surrender shall be of effect forever. (No. 5.)

24 February, 15 Edward IV [1476]. At Laxfeld. Release, in accordance with Will of William Cone late of Laxfeld, by (1) William at Haugh of Laxfeld to (2) Robert Cone, son of said William Cone, John Smyth, otherwise called Dobbyng the younger, Nicholas Smyth, "le whilwrighte," and Simon Fiske, son of Geoffrey Fyske of Laxfeld, of three pieces of land of the tenement Newys (6 acres) in Laxfeld and in the hamlet of Stodhaugh, whereof (1) lies between the highway, S[outh]; land of John Wyngefeld, knt., late in the tenure of John Noyse, N[orth]; land of said John Wyngefeld now in tenure of William Fyske, E[ast]; land late of Edmund Noyse, W[est]; (2) between land of said John Wyngefeld now in tenure of said William Fyske, E[ast]; land of John Wyngefeld and Robert Cone and land late of Henry Wylde, W[est]; land of Wm. Coupere formerly Glemes, N[orth]; (3) between land of Robert Cone formerly Noyses, N[orth]; land late of said Henry Wylde, S[outh]; land late of said John Wyngefelde formerly Helwys, now in tenure of John Coupere, and lands late of Alan Noyse, W[est]; which William at Haugh late had jointly with William Coue, father of said Robert Coue, and Thomas Baas, deceased, of the demise and livery of Thomas Coue, late of Laxfeld, and Roger Smyth, late of the same, by deed at Laxfeld 24 October, 18 Henry VI [1439]; and which Thomas Cone and Roger Smyth late had jointly with Edmund Noyse, late of Laxfeld, of the feoffment of Nicholas Taylour, Robert Smyth, and Simon Fiske: to (2), their heirs and assigns forever. William at Haugh appoints William Noyes his attorney to deliver seisin. Witnesses: Nicholas Noloth of Laxfeld, Geoffrey Fyske, William Coupere, John Fyske, John Barwer of the same. (No. 6.)

12 October, 19 Edward IV [1479]. At Laxfeld. Enfeoffment by (1) Robert Cone of Laxfeld, John Smyth otherwise Dowsyng, Nicholas Smyth, "whelwright," and Simon Fiske, son of Geoffrey Fiske of the same, to (2) Thomas Crispe of Laxfeld, Thomas Heveningham, Esq., Robert Smyth of Cratfeld, and Robert Noloth of Laxfeld, (a) all rents and services in Laxfeld which (1) had of the demise and livery of William Barwer of Laxfeld by deed at Laxfeld, 24 February, 15 Edward IV [1476] and (b) three pieces of land of the tenement Neves (6 acres) in Laxfeld in the hamlet of Stodhaugh, abbutting [precisely as in Deed No. 6], which (1) late had of the demise of William at Haugh by deed of 24 February, 15 Edward IV [1476] (Deed No. 6); (c) a piece of land (1 acre) in Laxfeld and the hamlet of Stodhaugh between land of said John Wyngefeld late in tenure of John Noyse, S[outh]; land of said Robert Cone formerly Glemes, E[ast]; land now in tenure of William Barwer, W[est]; which (1) late had of the demise of Agnes Wylde, widow late wife of Henry Wylde, and William Blynde of Laxfeld by deed of 6 October, 17 Edward IV [1477] dated at Laxfeld; to (2), their heirs and assigns forever. Witnesses: Nicholas Noloth, William Coupere, Nicholas Basse, John Crisp, William Sancroft. (Four seals, none heraldic; the fourth, broken, appears to have an I in the dexter half.) (No. 7.)

10 March, 34 Elizabeth [1592]. Extracts of Court Rolls of the Manor of Forncett including (A) Extract of Court general there Friday, 4 March, 22 Elizabeth [1580]: whereas it was found at the last court that Nicholas Porter was dead and had surrendered all his bond messuages, lands, and tenements held of this manor to the use of his will, now come Augustine Dixe and Robert Stanton the younger, executors of the will, and are admitted to the said lands until John Porter, son of Nicholas, be 24. The lands include 1 acre of land near the market of Long Stratton called Denser's yard, which Nicholas Porter, the testator, and John Tyler took up (a) of the surrender of Robert Coggell, Agnes his wife, John Barker, Margaret his wife, Geoffrey Fiske and Christian his wife, and Edmund Browne and Alice his wife, and (b) by release of the said John Tyler, gent, Monday, 2 June, 14 Elizabeth [1572]; and (B) 2 June, 14 Elizabeth [1572]. Extract of Court General: A release by Nicholas Porter to John Tyler, gent. of his interest in two pieces of land in Stratton whereof (1) containing two acres lies between land of Stratton manor called Fortenacres W[est], and (2) containing half an acre in same field, etc., which the said Nicholas took up, together with the said John Tyler, of the surrender of Robert Coggell, Agnes his wife, John Barker, Margaret his wife, Geoffrey Fiske, Christian his wife, and Edmund Browne and Alice his wife. (No. 8.)

Monday, first week of Lent, 2 Elizabeth [1560]. Extract of Court of Laxfeld Rectory. Surrender by Thomas Browne and wife Margaret to the use of Thomas Cowper, tailor, his heirs and assigns, of (a) a messuage in Laxfeld (4 acres 1 rood 13 perches) of dyke opposite said house, lying next Crosse Weye, between a tenement late of Thomas Brown and land in tenure of Geoffrey Fyske, W[est]; Crosse Weye, S[outh]; meadow in tenure of John Cowper and the appurtenances upon (et ptin' sup) the meadow of Anthony Wingfeld, Knt., N[orth]; (b) a newly-built messuage, adjacent (lac.) between land of the lord of this manor on either side; Crosse Way, S[outh]; and meadow of Anthony Wingfeld, N[orth]; (c) the residue thereof, to wit the messuage aforesaid and the barn adjacent, in which Richard Aysheley dwells; (d) a moiety of the pond there; (e) egress and ingress; up to now in tenure of Thomas Browne, which he took up after the death of Simon Browne, his brother, Tuesday after Palm Sunday, 33 Henry VIII [1542]; and (f) a close, parcel of Parsonage Close (2 acres 1 rood) in Laxefyld between land of the lord of this manor in the tenure of Geoffrey Fyske, West; land in tenure of Thomas Brown, E[ast]; the highway, S[outh]; the meadow late of John Wyngfeld, Knt., and a meadow [*blank*], N[orth]; which Thomas took up from the lord's hands. (No. 9.)

Thursday, 6 December, 14 Elizabeth [1571]. Extracts of a Court Roll of the manor of Stratton Hall, at Court with leet there. Nicholas Porter, present, quitclaims to John Tyler, Gent., the bond lands in Stratton which John and Nicholas had jointly of the surrender of Francis Fyske and Elizabeth, his wife, and Robert Coggell and Agnes, his wife, in court of 30 October, 12 Elizabeth [1570]. (No. 10.)

Monday, 30 October, 12 Elizabeth [1570]. Extract of Court Roll of the manor of Welhams and Reesez Stratton. To this court came Francis Fyske and Elizabeth, his wife, and Robert Coggell and Agnes, his wife, Elizabeth and Agnes being examined apart by the steward and present here in court, surrendered their part and purparty of 5 roods bond land in Hallfeld Stratton St. Mary, and 4 acres bond land in two pieces, and 5 roods bond land in Stratton, all of which Elizabeth and Agnes together with Margaret, wife of John Barker, and Alice, wife of Edmund Browne, and Christian, wife of Geoffrey Fyske, had by inheritance after the death of John Armiger, their brother, as sisters and heirs of the said John, because John died seised thereof as appears in the court here holden. Tuesday, 19 May, 10 Elizabeth [1568], to the use of John Tyler, Gent., and wife Katherine, who are admitted. (No. 11.)

Thursday, 6 December, 14 Elizabeth [1571]. Extract of Court Roll of Welhams and Reesez Stratton. John Tyler, Gent., and wife Katherine, surrender five roods of bond land in Halfeld in Stratton St. Mary and 4 acres bond land in the same field in two pieces, which John and Katherine with others has in respect to three parts of the conditional surrender of John Armiger, second son of John Armiger, the elder, deceased, as appears in this court, 30 October, 12 Elizabeth [1570]; and in respect to two other parts of the surrender of Francis Fyske and wife Elizabeth, Robert Coggell and wife Agnes, to the use of Nicholas Porter, his heirs and assigns. (No. 12.)

Thursday after St. Mark, 16 Elizabeth [1574]. Extract of Court Roll of Laxfeld Rectory, manor. Thomas Browne and wife Margaret, and Thomas Cowper surrender one messuage now divided into two tenements, 4 acres 1 rood of land and 13 perches with a dyke, and another tenement, built, adjacent to the two tenements with 1 acre of land and a close called le Parsonage-close (2 acres 1 rood) between land of the manor in tenure of Geoffrey Fyske, E[ast] and W[est]; the highway called Crosse, S[outh]; the meadow late of Anthony Wyngfeld, Knt., and John Cowper, N[orth], which the lord regrants to Thomas Cowper and his heirs. (No. 13.)

Monday, 20 October, 20 Elizabeth [1578]. Extract of Court Roll of Studhaugh in Laxfeld. Presentment that John Barwar is dead since last court and John Barwar, his son, is heir, aged 2½ years. Elizabeth Mayes, now wife of James Mayes and late wife of John Barwar, is admitted to two pieces of land or pasture (2 acres ½ rood) whereof the first called Herstlond lies between land late of John Edwards now of John Noyse, W[est]; and free land of said John in the same close of the fee of this manor, E[ast]; the close late of Robert Cowper and now of Thomas Cryspe called le Herste, S[outh]; the close late of [*obliterated by scribe*] Simon Fiske, John Edwardes and late of John Borret, N[orth]; by 8d. per annum; the second (½ rood) formerly called Cookes between land formerly of Anthony Wyngfild Knt., late of Simon Fyske, E[ast]; and land formerly of Walter Barwar of the fee of this manor, W[est]; the Common Way, S[outh]; by service of 2d. and one hen, which John Barwar the father took up after the death of Nicholas Barwar his father, Monday before St. Edmund the King, 10 Elizabeth [1567], during the minority of John Barwar, the son. (No. 14.)

13 August, 43 Elizabeth [1601]. John Barwar of Kirby Bedon, co. Norfolk, yeoman, in consideration of £15 grants to John Borrett the elder, yeoman, for life, a piece of land (1 acre) in Laxfield and in the hamlet of Studhaugh, between lands of the manor of Studhaugh, W[est]; lands of the same John Borret in part, lands of Thomas Crispe in part and lands of John Fiske in part, E[ast]; le Markett waye in part and lands of John Borrett, N[orth]; meadow of Thomas Crispe called le Herst, S[outh], which descended to said John Barwer on death of his father Nicholas Barwer with remainder to Robert Borrett, son of said John. (No. 15.)

Tuesday in Whitweeke, 19 May, 6 Charles I [1630]. Extract of Court Roll of Cratfield manor. Presentment that John Borrett the elder, bond tenant of this manor, surrendered 12 Dec. 1627, out of court, by the hand of William Dowsing in presence of John Newson and William Aldus, to the use of his will, all his bond tenements of this manor. The will is brought in, proved, by Robert Borret, son of said John, and is dated 20 Oct. 1627. Testator bequeaths to "Robert Borret my son and his heirs one close conteyning by estimacion six acres lying in Laxfild commonly called . . . *Brodake.*" Robert Borret is thereupon admitted to two acres of land formerly of Simon Fiske between land of John Bowsing, N[orth]; and land of Robert Fiske, S[outh]; le Market Way, W[est]; and land of John Dowsing, E[ast]; in Laxfild, which John Borrett took up in the court holden 8 Elizabeth [1565–6]. (No. 16.)

7 August, 15 Charles I [1639]. Extract of Court Roll of Laxfield Rectory. First Court of Philip Earl of Pembroke, and Philip Lord Harbert and Penelope Viscountess Bayning of Sudbury, his wife, guardians of lands of Anne and Penelope Bayning, daughters and coheirs of Paul Viscountess [*sic*] Bayning of Sudbury. Jurors present that on 17 Oct. 1637, Robert Higate, Gent., bond tenant of this manor surrendered into the hands of the lords [by] the hands of Edmund Smythe bond tenant of this manor in the presence of John Fyske and John White likewise bond tenants a messuage or mansion house acquired from Isaac Stannard now in possession of Richard Chatinge of the demise of said Robert, being a piece of land and pond and newly built house to the use of John Ives and wife Margaret. (No. 17.)

The WILL OF SIMONDE FYSKE of Laxfeld, yeoman, dated 10 July 1536. To be buried in churchyard of All Saints, Laxfeld, at the Chancel's and next my father, high altar there for tithes forgotten 20d., repair of Laxfeld church 20d., 2 houses of Friars in Dunwich and Orford 3s. 4d. each for rental, etc.

To son Robert Fyske tent in Laxfeld where I now dwell with all lands in Laxfield in the occupation of said Robert, according to a bargain I made with him by indress 1 January, 25 Henry VIII [1534], he to pay £40, viz., to my exec[rs] at day of my burial £6 13s. 4d., my son Wm. Fyske in 3 years after my decease £10, viz., 5 marks a year upon this condition that the same William shall discharge my executors of an obligation of 20 marks, wherein I am bound, that he shall leave his wife Elizabeth lands or moveables worth 20 marks, to Symond Fyske my son in the 4th year next after my decease £3 63s. 8d., to Johan Jerelon and Olyue Warne my daughters in the fifth year after my decease other £3 6s. 8d., i.e., 33s. 4d. each, to Margery my daughter in the 6th year after my decease £3 6s. 8d., to Jaffery my son in the 7th year after my decease other £3 6s. 8d., to Jaffery my son in the 8th year after my decease other £3 6s. 8d., to Johan my younger daughter in the 9th year after my decease other £3 6s. 8d., to Agnes my younger daughter in the 10th year after my decease other £3 6s. 8d.

If it happen any of my said 4 youngest children, Margery, Johan the younger, and Agnes the younger*, to decease before time of payment, their shares to be parted among the rest of my 4 younger children.

Said Robert my son to be bound by obligation with 2 sufficient sureties with him to my executors and to the other my children being of Laxfeld for the payment of the said £40. To my son Robert all utensils, implements and stuff of household as I shall not have given or sold at the day of my decease. Residue to disposition of executors, viz., John Goodynche, vicar of Laxfeld, Henry Smyth of Laxfeld and John Noloth of Walpole. Supervisor, John Fyske of Holton. Witnesses: James Lane balye of Laxfeld, John Fyske of Holton the younger and Nicholas Stannard of Laxfeld. (Archdeaconry of Suffolk, book 13, f° 16.)

Friday next before the Feast of St. Luke the Evangelist, 14 Henry VI [1435]. At Laxfield. William Seman of Norwich to Simon Fyske of Laxfield a piece of land containing by estimation two acres of land, more or less, with its appurtenances, situated in Laxfield, next the King's Highway leading from Laxfield towards Fressingfield on the East side, and the land of John Edward of Laxfield aforesaid on the West side, and abutting upon the land of the said John Edward, and John Barwer towards the South, and upon the common road leading from Cratfield to Waltersfield in Laxfield towards the North. Witnesses: Hugh Fyske, William Dowsyng, William Barwer, John Edward, Simon Jurdon of Laxfield, and others.

5 June, 13 Charles II [1661]. At Cratfield. To the Court general with Leet came Robert Borrett, in full court, and surrendered into the hand of the lord of the manor all that close of land, called Brodoake, containing by estimation two acres more or less, formerly of Simon Fyske, situate in Laxfield between the land, now or lately, of John Dowsing on the North, and the land, now or lately, of Robert Fyske on the South, and abutting on the common road, called Le Marketwaye, towards the West, and the land, now or lately, of the said John Dowsing towards the East, and the aforesaid Robert Borrett for himself and his heirs surrenders this his inheritance under the last will of John Borrett at the Court general held here 19 May, 6 Charles I [1630] to the use of Christopher Barry of Sileham (Sylam) in co. Suffolk, Gentleman.

[To be continued]

---

* It is evident that one child is omitted here, probably Jeffray.

# GENEALOGICAL RESEARCH IN ENGLAND

Communicated by the Committee on English and Foreign Research

## THE FISKE FAMILY

Contributed by G. ANDREWS MORIARTY, A.M., LL.B., F.S.A.,
of Bristol, R. I.

The Will of NICHOLAS FISKE of Dinnington [co. York], dated 20 August 1569. I betake my soul to the great and infinite mercy of Almighty God my creator redeemer and saviour. To be buried in Dinnington churchyard. To Wife Johane, my messuages, lands, tenements, meadows, feedings, and pastures in Dinnington, which I lately purchased of my father-in-law William Crispe of Laxfield, for life. Wife Johane shall well and honestly educate and bring up my four children, namely, Rachel, Ester, Mary, and Martha, my daughters, until they shall be of lawful age. To "the sayde William my sonne" and his heirs for ever all my said messuages and lands both free and bond after the death of my wife Johane, on condition he pay to "his brother and sisters" £80, as follows: to Amos Fyske my son £30; to Rachell Fyske, Ester Fiske, Marye Fiske, and to Martha Fiske, my daughters £10 each; payment to be made at the rate of £5 a year after the entry on the premises, to my daughter Rachel her £10 by even portions the 7th and 8th years after the entry, to my daughter Ester £10 equally the 9th and 10th years after the entry, to my daughter Mary £10 equally the 11th and 12th years, and to my daughter Martha £10 equally the 13th and 14th years. If "the sayde William Fyske the elder my son" die without heirs of his body or refuse to pay the £80, the lands and tenements shall remain to my son Amos Fyske, his heirs and assigns on the same condition. The other £10 [of the £80] to the poor, to be paid the 15th and 16th years after the entry on the premises, to be distributed by the churchwardens within one month after receipt. "If William dye afore his mother" having a child or children, Amos shall have the land paying to William's child or children £10 and to my daughters five marks apiece "beginning again at the eldest." To my wife, all my moveables and implements.

Wife appointed executrix. Witnesses: John Marshall, John Fiske the elder, John Fiske the younger, Christopher Harsaunte, Robert Capon.

Proved at Hoxne [co. Suffolk] 28 September 1569 by the executrix. (Archdeaconry of Suffolk (Ipswich Probate Registry), Book 23, fo 71.)

These charters compel us to place the birth of Simon Fiske who died in 1463/4 and the births of his sons William and Geoffrey somewhat earlier than they appear in the pedigree set forth in the REGISTER, vol. 87, p. 368. * These two latter men must both have been born prior to 1429 and about 1420–1425, while their father must have been born about 1400. His father Hugh was, therefore, born about 1370 and is probably the son or grandson of the Hugh who appears in Laxfield in 1340 and 1345.

We now turn to the problem of the parentage of Richard Fiske "of the Broadgates" in Laxfield, who heads the Candler pedigree. The early evidence for his existence is the Candler pedigree, but as Matthias Candler, the compiler (born in 1604). was the great-grand-

*See the footnote on p. 593, this volume.

son of Robert Fiske, the testator of 1602, and as in other respects the contributor has found his pedigree of the family accurate, he thinks we may accept Richard as his great-great-grandfather. Now this Richard must have been born as early as 1500 as his sons were mature men in the middle of the 16th century and he was undoubtedly born somewhat earlier, about 1480–1485. This Richard does not appear in the great Subsidy of 1524 and it is reasonable to suppose that at this date he was dead, leaving a family of 11 children, according to Candler, who must have all been born prior to that date. Now we find no Fiskes in Laxfield in the 16th century who were not descendants of Simon Fiske who died in 1463/4. It is, therefore, reasonable to suppose that Richard was also a descendant of Simon, in which case he must have been a great-grandson in order to square with the known chronology of the family. On examination, the families of the grandsons of Simon show that all their children are known with the exception of the family of Geoffrey Fiske (son of Geoffrey, the testator of 1504, son of the first Simon). Of the latter's family we know only of his son John (named as such in the will of "Sir" John Fiske, the testator of 1535). It is reasonable to suppose that this Geoffrey had other children and that Richard was one of them. This idea is greatly strengthened by the fact that Richard named his fourth son, according to Candler, Geoffrey— a name which again appears in the family of Richard's son Robert. It would seem, accordingly, both by elimination and the repetition of the name Geoffrey in the family of Richard, that the latter must have been a son of Geoffrey (son of Geoffrey the 1504 testator) and the great-grandson of the first Simon.

## GENEALOGICAL RESEARCH IN ENGLAND

Communicated by the Committee on English and Foreign Research

### THE GURDON FAMILY

Contributed by G. ANDREWS MORIARTY, A.M., LL.B., F.S.A.,
of Bristol, R. I.

THE family of Gurdon has now occupied a prominent position among the county families of East Anglia for nigh four hundred years. At the end of the reign of Henry VIII they purchased Assington from the spoils of the monastery of Bury St. Edmunds. More recently the branch at Letton, co. Norfolk, has enjoyed the honors of the peerage under the title of the Lords Cranworth. In New England, although none of the name ever settled, their blood is widely diffused in the female lines. It has always been known that the second Richard Saltonstall of New England married Muriel, daughter of Brampton Gurdon of Assington, Esq., by his second wife, Muriel, daughter of Martin Sedley, Esq., of Morley, co. Norfolk, and the name of Gurdon has been faithfully handed down in the Saltonstall family, especially the branch which settled in Connecticut. What will be shown here, however, for the first time, is that John Coggeshall, the early settler and chief magistrate of Rhode Island, was the great-grandson of Anne, daughter of John Gurdon of Dedham, who, with his son Robert, purchased Assington in the county of Suffolk.

In the Tudor or Stuart days the family, as was so common at that period, was duly provided with a long pedigree, which may be found in Muskett's "Suffolk Memorial Families," tracing their descent from one John de Gurdon, living in 1220, who is called the father of Sir Adam de Gurdon of Shropshire. Now Adam de Gurdon, a very real character, living in the reigns of Edward I and II, founded a family in that county, but the descent of the East Anglian Gurdons from the Shropshire family rests upon nothing better than their Tudor or Stuart compilation, which makes their descent run through one Robert Gurdon, sheriff of London (called son of Sir Adam), John of London, merchant, who died in 1385, Thomas of London and Kent, who died in 1436, and John of Kent, who died in 1465 and is styled the father of John Gurdon of Dedham, co. Essex, who died in 1487. This last John of Dedham was a very tangible person. His will, proved 14 January 1487/8, shows that he was a substantial clothier in that town and that his father was named John. Beyond this we have no proof of the descent of the Dedham Gurdons from the Shropshire family except the fact that it is stated in the old pedigrees that "Sir Adam Gurdon of Shropshire, the latter end of Queen Eliz. told Brampton Gurdon that the Essex and Suff. Gurdons were descended from his family thro' the city." Any competent genealogist can judge the probative value of this statement. As against this we have a long series of entries from the Dedham Manor Court Rolls showing that the family were small tenants in Dedham as early as the reign of Henry IV.

The contributor of this article has also been accorded by Lady Cranworth the privilege of having the Gurdon muniments examined. From them much valuable material was extracted, especially the document proving the marriage of William Butter and Anne Gurdon, the great-grandparents of John Coggeshall of New England. Acknowledgment of this courtesy is herewith gratefully made.

The real early history of the Gurdons of Assington and Letton will now be presented, based upon the Dedham Court Rolls, the wills of the family, and other documents from the Gurdon muniments. These records show the Gurdons at the beginning of the fifteenth century as small clothiers and land holders in Dedham, who rose gradually, as the century wore on, into considerable wealth so that at its close they appear as substantial Dedham cloth workers. In the succeeding century they continued to prosper and their wealth was augmented by several fortunate marriages. Robert Gurdon of Little Waldingfield, son of John Gurdon of Dedham, by his wife Anne, daughter of John Coleman of Little Waldingfield, bought Assington Hall of Sir Miles Corbet and founded the county family of Gurdon of Assington. His marriage to Rose, widow of William Appleton of Little Waldingfield and sister and coheiress of Thomas Sexton of Lavenham, co. Suffolk, greatly augmented the family fortunes.

The subsequent history of the family is too well known to require full treatment, consequently this article will confine itself to establishing the early generations of the Gurdons of Dedham prior to the time of this Robert and will then give briefly the descent of Muriel, the wife of Richard Saltonstall, and of John Coggeshall of Halsted, co. Essex, and Portsmouth, R. I., from the Gurdons.

In closing the contributor would say that while there is no evidence of the descent by the Suffolk and Essex family from the one in Shropshire, such a descent, in view of the rarity of the name, may well be true, but proof thereof will probably never be forthcoming.

## FROM COURT ROLLS OF DEDHAM, CO. ESSEX.

### RECORDS OF THE DUCHY OF LANCASTER

#### [Series 30, Bundle 58, Roll 729]

Dedham. Court held there Thursday before the feast of St. George, 7 Henry IV [22 April 1406]. John Stor, by licence of the court, hath let to Simon Gurdon one acre and a half of the tenement Longes in Dedham for the term of three years beginning at the feast of the Purification of the Blessed Mary last past [2 February 1405/6]. And he gives for fine 3d. for having a term [of years]. (m. 13.)

Same court. From Simon Gurdon for trespass done against John Brown to damages assessed at 3d. which [he is ordered to pay]. 1d. amercement. (m. 13ᵈ.)

Dedham. Court of the Prioress of Campsea held there Tuesday before St. Michael the Archangel, 9 Henry IV [25 September 1408].* 1 d. amercement from Robert Gurden for an unjust complaint against William Fybrygge in a plea of detention of chattels. (m. 15.)

Dedham. Court held there Tuesday before St. Martin the Bishop, 9 Henry IV [8 November 1407]. 6d. amercement from William Pycard because he made rescue from the lady and from Robert Gurdon, farmer † of the lady, of one horse, taken and arrested for trespass upon the herbage of the lady without leave. (m. 16.)

Dedham. Court held there Tuesday before St. Michael the Archangel, 10 Henry IV.‡ Jurors present that William Fybregge surrendered into the hands of the lady one close (½ acre) of meadow to the use of John Curdon [sic], to whom seisin is delivered to hold to the same John and his heirs by the rod at lady's will, doing service, saving the right of anyone. He fines 2s. and hath done fealty. (m. 18.)

Same court. The lady hath granted and let to farm to John Curdon 3 roods of meadow in Cheldewalle to hold to him or his attorneys from the feast of St. Michael next to come until the end and term of ten years following, paying to the lady yearly 2s. 7d. at said two terms equally (Easter and Michaelmas). He gives the lady 4d. for having the term [of years].

The lady hath granted and let to farm to Roger Eye and John Curdon 3 acres of meadow in Lorbregge to hold to them or their attorneys from Michaelmas after the date of these presents for the term of 10 years, paying 10s. a year. They fine 8d.

* Unless the Courts are out of order this seems to be an error of the scribe who should have put 8 Henry IV, since Henry IV's regnal years date from 30 September (morrow of St. Michael).

† In the previous court (dated Tuesday before St. Michael the Archangel, 9 Henry IV, *vide* above footnote) the lady's farmers (*firmarii*) unnamed were ordered to have sufficient straw and stubble for the thatching of the lady's houses.

‡ Probably intended for 1408; the preceding court is for Friday before Palm Sunday, 9 Henry IV [6 April 1408].

The lady hath granted and let to Simon Curdon [Webbe written above the word Curdon] and Christian, his wife, the end of the hall on the north part with easement in the hall and the garden below the hall on the North and West, to hold to them and their attorneys from the feast of St. Michael next for the term of ten years, paying 5s. a year at said two terms equally. They shall maintain the said hall and the end thereof with thatching and daubing. They give to the lady, as fine, 4d. (m. 18.)

Same court. The lady hath granted and let to farm to Robert Curdon one acre of meadow in Westfen next the meadow of Henry Webbe to hold to him and his attorneys from Michaelmas next for ten years paying 4s. 3d. yearly at said terms. He fines 4d. [Walter Reyland and Hugh Stefne have lease of the acre next the above.] (m. 18d.)

Dedham. Court held there Thursday before the Purification, 10 Henry IV [31 January 1408/9]. Isabella Terry, present in court, surrenders into the lord's hands one cottage with 5 acres of bond land, enclosed, of tenement Gores in Dedham to the use of Robert Gurdon and Alice, his wife, and their heirs. Seisin is delivered to them. They give fine 40d. and have done fealty. (m. 19.)

Same court. Presentment that John Gurdon and John Pygewell broke the door of the granary and the door of the barn and carried off the lady's barley and wheat. They are amerced 40s. (m. 19d.)

Dedham. Court held there St. Faith's day, 12 Henry IV [6 October 1410]. Agnes Warde amerced 1d. because she did not prosecute a suit of debt against Simon Gurdon. (m. 21.)

Dedham. Court held there Tuesday after St. John before Latin Gate, 12 Henry IV [May 1411]. John Gurdon falls by an inquest against Christian Canceler in a plea of trespass because he grazed the pasture with her beasts to her damage 3d., which is to be levied, and he is in mercy 3d.

The same John falls by an inquest against Christian Canceler for not cleaning his ditch next the meadow of the said Christian, whereby her meadow was drowned to her damage in 4d., and he is in mercy 3d.

The same John falls by an inquest against Roger Eyr in a plea of trespass to his damage in 6d. In mercy 3d. (m. 22.)

Dedham. Court held there Friday before St. Barnabas, 13 Henry IV [June 1412]. Inquest of office taken by oaths of Roger Eyr and thirteen others, including Robert Gurdon. (m. 24.)

Same court. Held the Friday after St. Luke the Evangelist, 14 Henry IV [21 October 1412]. Inquest of office by oath of Roger Eyr and others, including Robert Gordon [sic].

John atte Ry gives the lady for fine to have licence to let to farm to Robert Gurdon one messuage with two acres of land of the tenement Peryes for the life of John from St. Michael last past, 2s. (m. 25.)

Same court. Held the Tuesday after St. Matthew the Apostle, 14 Henry IV.* Inquest by oath of Roger Eyr and others, including Robert Gurdon. (m. 26.)

### [Series 30, Bundle 59, Roll 730]

Dedham Campsea. Court General held there Thursday after St. Luke the Evangelist, 2 Henry VI [October 1423]. Essoins: Robert Gurdon of the common suit, by Robert Brook. Elections: They choose tenement Gores in the hands of Robert Gurdon to perform the office of harvest-reeve (messor) this year. (m. 2.)

* The preceding court (m. 25) is Friday after St. Luke, 14 Henry IV [21 October 1412]. Perhaps Matthew (plainly here written Sancti Matthei) is a slip here for Matthias; in which case the date would be 28 February 1412/13.

Dedham Campsea. Court held there Tuesday before St. Katherine the Virgin, 3 Henry VI. Robert Gurdon among the jurors. (m. 3.)

Dedham Campsea. Court held there Thursday after St. Martin, 5 Henry VI [November 1426]. The inquest presents that John Gourdon, without the court, surrendered into the hands of Robert Pertre bond tenant, in the presence of Robert Gourdon and others, of the homage half an acre of meadow of the bond tenement Fybregges in Dedham to the use of John Sculton, who is admitted. Fine 20d. (m. 5.)

Dedham Campsea. Court held there Thursday in Easter Week, 7 Henry VI [1429]. Essoins: Robert Gurdon by John Brown, of the common suit.

Dedham [Campsea]. Court held there Tuesday before Epiphany, 8 Henry VI [January 1429/30]. [A very large number of tenants surrender their tenements which are regranted in accordance with a new rental made this year, including], and Robert Gurdon surrendered into the lady's hands one messuage with a curtilage, two crofts of land [of] tenement Peryes, one croft [? at the head of] tenement Terryes and tenement Gores, with one croft, one messuage, and two acres of land of the same tenement Gores, that the lady might do her will thercin; and she regranted to the same Robert the said messuage with the curtilage and the crofts and land belonging, to hold to him and his heirs, by the rod, paying by the year 6s. 11¾ d. as in the new Rental. The fine discharged [as in other cases]. (m. 8ᵈ.)

Dedham Campsea. Court General held there Thursday after St. Edmund the King, 8 Henry VI [November 1429]. Robert Gurdon is amerced 3d. for not having warranted his essoin in the preceding court. (m. 9.)

Dedham [Campsea]. Court General held there Thursday in First Week of Lent, 11 Henry VI [1433]. Essoins: John Gurdon by John Calk, of common suit. At this court Robert Gurdon gives the lady as fine for licence to let to farm to John Skulton four crofts containing 1 acre 1 rood for two years begining Easter next, 4d.

Robert Gurdon and others are amerced 3d. each for defaulting at the preceding court.

Presentment that John Skulton out of court surrendered a piece of meadow of the bond tenement Fibrigg, late of John Gurdon (3 roods), and a piece of meadow, late of William Stansour in Dedham, to the use of Nicholas Louekyn, who has seisin to hold at the will of the lady to sell and dispose for the soul of the said John Skulton and [the souls] of his friends. He fines 2s.

William Wodegate and John Gurdon amerced 3d. each for keeping the watercourse stopped up by the lady's meadow called Lorbregge to the annoyance of the tenants. Pain set, 12d. (m. 11.)

Dedham. Court General held there Saturday after All Saints, 15 Henry VI [November 1436]. Robert Gurdon, present in court, surrenders into the lady's hand one piece of bond land, enclosed, formerly built upon, containing by estimation five acres of the tenement Gores in Dedham to the use of William Thedam, who is admitted; fine 3s. 4d. (m. 14.)

Undated rental, sewn between the court of the Saturday after All Saints, 15 Henry VI [November 1436] and the Monday after St. Margaret the Virgin, 15 Henry VI [July 1437]. Headed: Roll of the names of the Suitors at the Court of the Prioress of Campsea in Dedham. These are common suitors, viz., Robert Gourdon for a messuage formerly of John Terry and Gorys. (m. 14.)

Dedham. Court General held there Tuesday after St. Faith, 16 Henry VI [October 1437]. Robert Gurdon amerced 3d. for default of suit of court. (m. 15ᵈ.)

Dedham. Court General held there Monday after St. Martin, 18 Henry VI [November 1439]. The jurors say that Alice, late wife of Robert Gurdon, who [*que*, i.e., Alice] died 19 years past, before her death surrendered into the lady's hands by the hands of William Brook bond tenant in the presence of John Bakere, John Alyn, and others, the reversion, after the death of her said husband Robert, of 2½ acres bond land . . . of tenement Peryes and one croft of bond land called Custynescroft, containing 3 acres in Dedham, to the use of John Broun, to whom seisin is delivered, to sell and dispose for the fulfilment of the will of said Alice.

The said John Brown, present, surrendered the said lands and tenements, late of Alice Gurdon, to the use of John Mayston, who is admitted and fines 10d.

The jurors say that Robert Gurdon, out of court, surrendered by the hands of William Brook, the lord's bailiff, in the presence of John Bakere and John Broun, all right which he ever had in the said lands and tenements to the use of said John Mayston, who is admitted and fines 10d. (m. 16.)

Dedham Campsea. Court General held there Monday after All Saints, 36 Henry VI [November 1457]. Presentment that William Wodegate lately deceased surrendered out of court various bond tenements including a piece of meadow (3 roods) of tenement Fibrigge formerly of John Gurdon and late of Nicholas Lovekyn in Dedham to the use of John Wodehous and wife Agnes, who are admitted. (m. 23.)

### [Series 30, Bundle 59, Roll 732]

Dedham Campsea. Court General held there Friday Morrow of St. George, 7 Edward IV [24 April 1467]. Presentment that John Mayston, who died of late, surrendered by the hands of Thomas Cranefen in presence of William Webbe, the elder, and William Webbe, the younger, 2½ acres bond land, enclosed, of tenement Peryes, and one croft called Custynescroft (3 acres), late of Alice, wife of Robert Gurdon, in Dedham, to the use of William Warner, Henry Warner, and John Warner, who are admitted. (m. 3.)

Dedham Campsea. Court General held there Wednesday, 16 May, 10 Edward IV. Presentment that William Webbe, junior, out of court surrendered by the hands of William Brook, bond tenant, in presence of John Smyth, senior, his purparty, viz., ½ of one acre and one rood of bond meadow, late of John Hood in Lordbregge, held of the lady wholly by the service of 12d. in Dedham, to the use of John Gurdon, senior, and Stephen Wodegate, their heirs, and assigns; they fine 12d., and are admitted.

And that Richard Peverel surrendered, out of court, by the hands of John Wilye, bond tenant, in the presence of Walter Brook, his purparty of said meadow to the use of John Gurdon and Stephen Wodegate [as above]; they fine 12d. and are admitted. (m. 4ᵈ.)

Dedham Campsea. Court held there Friday after St. James the Apostle, 12 Edward IV [July 1472]. Iurors include John Gurdon the elder. They say that William Lovekyn who died of late, out of court, surrendered by the hands of John Gurdon, bond tenant, in presence of John Bakeler, one acre of bond land of tenement Holtlond, late of Christian Lovekyn in Dedham, to the use of Alice, his wife, and Stephen Lovekyn, executors of his will. They are admitted and fine 20d.

Afterwards at this court Robert Merveyn and the said Alice, now his wife, and the said Stephen surrender the said acre to the use of John Gurdon, aforesaid, and Margaret, his wife, and the heirs and assigns of John Gurdon; they are admitted and fine 2s.

The jurors say that John Moyse and William Whelere, out of court, surrendered by the hands of the bailiff in the presence of John Hall and Thomas Wodehous 3 roods of meadow, late of John Hunt, in the meadow called Esthousmedewe in Dedham, to the use of John Gurdon the elder; he is admitted and fines 20d.  (m. 4ᵈ.)

Dedham Campsea.  Court General held there Monday after St. Faith, 12 Edward IV (October 1472].  Jurors include John Gurdon the elder.

William Webbe the elder, present in court, surrenders one messuage with a garden containing ½ acre and one croft of bondland containing 6 acres 3 roods of tenement Hertstretelond and a wood (3 acres) late of Isabella Felbrygge in Dedham to the use of John Gurdon, the elder, and John, his son, to whom [cui] seisin is delivered to hold to them, their heirs and assigns; upon condition that if they pay William Webbe £10 at Michaelmas next, and £10 at Michaelmas following, and £10 at the Michaelmas after that, as well for the said lands and tenements as for lands and tenements of the fee of the manor formerly Waldens in Dedham, the surrender shall be of full effect.  John and John fine 20s.  (m. 5.)

Dedham Campsea.  Court General held there Monday the Morrow of St. Edmund, 14 Edward IV [21 November 1474].  John Snow, present, surrenders 1 acre 1 rood of meadow of bond tenement Seman, late of John Mayston and William Martyn, and before that of Thomas Wellok in Dedham, to the use of John Gurdon the elder who is admitted and fines 3s. 4d.  (m. 6.)

Dedham Campsea.  Court General held there Wednesday in the fourth week of Lent, 16 Edward IV [1476].  Jurors include John Gurdon.  (m. 6ᵈ.)

Dedham Campsea.  Court General held there Tuesday within the Octave of St. Hilary, 17 Edward IV [January 1477/78].  Jurors include John Gurdon. (m. 6ᵈ.)

Same court.  Agnes Clerk widow and Robert Clerk, out of court, surrendered by the hands of John Halk in presence of John Brook, senior, and John Ry, a toft late built upon (4 acres), late of William Snow, and a croft called Caledon (4 acres) in Dedham, to the use of John Gurdon, junior, and John Gurdon, senior, to whom seisin is delivered; they fine 4s.  (m. 6ᵈ.)

Same court.  Court General held there Tuesday after St. Hilary, 20 Edward IV [January 1480/81].  Jurors include John Gurdon, senior, John Gurdon, junior.  (m. 8.)

Same court.  Jurors say that Henry Vyne, out of court, surrendered by the hands of Walter Brook in presence of "*Johannis Gurdon junioris et Johannis Gurdon medij*" a parcel of tenement Mechilboys to the use of John Gurdon, the elder (*senioris*), and John Gurdon, his son, and the heirs and assigns of John Gurdon, the elder; they are admitted and fine 3d.

And that Henry Vyne surrendered a meadow (7 acres) enclosed, called Brookmedewe, of the demesnes of the manor, formerly of Robert Dedham, in Dedham, which he late took up by fee farm of 40s., to the use of John Gurdon, junior, and Robert Gurdon, his brother.  (m. 8ᵈ.)

Dedham Campsea.  Court held there Monday after the Assumption of the Blessed Virgin, 21 Edward IV [20 August 1481].  Jurors include John Gurdon, senior, and John Gurdon, junior.

Same court.  Whereas John Gurdon, junior, and John Gurdon, senior, have and hold for the life of Rose, late wife of Hugh Leme, one messuage with a close adjacent (3½ acres) called Brownesdowne in Dedham, with reversion to right heirs of Hugh; now the jurors say that John Leme, brother of Hugh, is heir to the reversion; he is admitted to the reversion and fines 20d.

Afterwards at this court John Gurdon and John Gurdon, aforesaid (*predicti*), surrendered all their estate for the life of Rose to the use of John Leme on condition that if John Leme pay John Gurdon, junior, and his attorneys or executors 60s., viz., at Michaelmas 1481, 10s., and yearly 10s., then the surrender shall be of effect. (m. 9.)

Dedham Campsea. Court held there Monday after the Assumption of the Blessed Virgin, 21 Edward IV [20 August 1481]. Thomas Wodehous, present, surrenders the reversion after the death of his mother, Agnes, of a piece of meadow (1 acre) of tenement Hertstretelond, a piece of meadow (3 roods) of tenement Fibrygg formerly Michael Lovekyn and 4 acres of land, with a little grove, in a close called Leygh, formerly of William Fibrygge, late of John Wodehouse, to use of John Gurdon, senior, and Walter Brook. (m. 9.)

Dedham Campsea. Court held there Tuesday after St. Hilary, 22 Edward IV [January 1482/83]. Jurors: John Gurdon, senior, and John Gurdon, junior.

Dedham Campsea. Court held there Wednesday in the fourth Week of Lent, 1 Richard III [1484]. Jurors: John Gurdon, senior.

[To be continued]

---

608

# GENEALOGICAL RESEARCH IN ENGLAND

Communicated by the Committee on English and Foreign Research

## THE GURDON FAMILY

Contributed by G. Andrews Moriarty, A.M., LL.B., F.S.A.,
of Bristol, R. I.


From Court Rolls of Dedham, co. Essex.

Records of the Duchy of Lancaster

[Series 30, Bundle 59, Roll 734]

Dedham Campsea. Court General held there Monday after the Exaltation of the Holy Cross,* 2 Henry VII [September 1486]. Jurors include John Gurdon.

They say that William Marlere, out of court, surrendered into the lady's hand by the hands of Walter Brook in presence of William Pekeryng, bailiff, and William Rand (Isabell, wife of William, being examined severally), one cottage and one acre of land, late of Margaret Mashcal, widow, formerly daughter of Robert Bertlot in Dedham, to the use of John Gurdon, senior, and Robert, his son, who are admitted and fine 18d. (m. 11.)

Dedham Campsea. Court held there Tuesday after Saints Philip and James,† 3 Henry VII [May 1488]. Jurors include John Gurdon the middle (*medius*).

They say that John Gurdon the elder, who lately died, surrendered by the hands of Robert Herre in presence of Walter Brook, and John Erlyng and Stephen Wodegate likewise surrendered by hands of John Warnere in presence of John Thorn, one piece of meadow (1 acre 1 rood) late of William Webbe and Ric'. Peverel held by service of 12d. per annum in Dedham to use of John Gurdon, his son, and of John, son of the same John Gurdon, the younger (*Johannis Gurdon filij sui et Johannis filij eiusdem Johannis Gurdon jun*'). They are admitted and fine 20d.

And that the said John Gurdon the elder surrendered in the same manner 1 acre of meadow of tenement Holtlond, late of Alice Lovekyn and Stephen Lovekyn, 1 acre 1 rood of tenement Seman, late of William Snow, before of John Maysten and William Martyn, in Dedham to the use of John Gurdon, his son, and John, son of the same John Gurdon, the younger, they are admitted and fine 3d.

And that the said John Gurdon, after the same form, and Robert Gurdon, his son, who is present in court, surrendered a cottage and 1 acre of land late of William Marlere and wife Isabel, before of Margaret Mashcal in Dedham, to the use of the said John Gurdon, junior, and of John, his son (*predictorum Johannis Gurdon junr et Johannis filij sui*). They are admitted and fine 18d.

And that the said John Gurdon, the elder, after the said form, and Walter Brook, who is present in court, surrendered a piece of meadow of tenement Herlstreetelond (1 acre) and a piece of meadow of tenement Fibrygge, and 4 peces of land with a little grove and pightel enclosed, called Leye (7 acres) late of Thomas Wodehous and [before] of John Wodehous in Dedham to the

---

* The Feast of the Exaltation of the Holy Cross falls on 14 September.
† The Feast of Saints Philip and James falls on 1 May.

use of John Gurdon, junior, and of John, his (*sui*) son. They are admitted and fine 3s. 4d.

And that the said John Gurdon, senior, after the said form, and John, his (*eius*) son, who is present in court, surrendered one parcel of land of tenement Mekilboyes (1 rood), late of Henry Vyne, before of Robert Copyn in Dedham, to the use of Robert Gurdon and Thomas Webbe, who are admitted and fine 3d.

And that the said John Gurdon, senior, surrendered 3 roods of meadow, late of John Moyse and William Whelere, before of John Hunte in Esthousmedowe in Dedham, to the use of Robert Gurdon and of Robert Gurdon, his son (*filij sui*), who are admitted and fine 18d. (m. 11ᵈ.)

Same Court. William Warnere surrenders a cottage (½ acre) and 2 crofts of land (5 acres 1½ roods) called Helhoustenement, late of John Pertre, before of John Hood, in Dedham to the use of Richard Rycheman, who is admitted and fines 6s.

And afterwards at this court the said Richard, present, surrenders the said lands and tenements to the use of Stephen Dunton and John Gurdon, senior, who are admitted and fine 7s.

And the said William Warnere and John Warnere, his brother, present, surrender a croft called Sotilfeld, with an aldergrove, in all 7½ acres, late of William Thedam, in Dedham to the use of Thomas Webbe and of John Gurdon, son of John Gurdon, the elder (*senʳ*), who are admitted and fine 6s. 8d. (m. 11ᵈ.)

Dedham Campsea. Court General held there Monday before St. Luke the Evangelist,* 7 Henry VII [October 1491]. Jurors include John Gurdon.

Presentment of a surrender by John Tranas and wife Marion, late wife of John Ry, in the presence of Robert Gurdon and Walter Brook and others of the homage.

Jacob Liens surrenders a parcel of bond land built upon (3 roods), late of John Pertre, to the use of Robert Gurdon and John Gurdon, his brother (*fratris sui*), who are admitted and fine 8d.

The lady granted to Robert Gurdon and Thomas Ry the fields (*campos*) called R          of the demesnes, lying in the meadow called Prioreshalle-medwe, late in the farm of divers tenants in Dedham, to hold to them, their heirs and assigns by the rod, at the will of the lady, paying 32s. yearly and doing suit of court. They shall have sufficient underwood for repairs. They fine 3s. 4d. (m. 12.)

Dedham Campsea. Court General held there Thursday, St. Luke the Evangelist,* 8 Henry VII [18 October 1492]. Jurors include John Gurdon.

Whereas at a former court John Gurdon, senior, and John Gurdon, junior, present in court, surrendered their title for the life of Rose, late wife of Hugh Leme, in a close in Dedham, to John Leme, on certain conditions and it has been ordered that the bailiff should summon the said John Leme to show cause why John Gurdon, junior, should not have reentry in the same. There come Richard Mounk and Agnes, his wife, late wife of John Leme, and cannot gain-say that the said John Gurdon, junior, should have reentry. Thereupon John Gurdon aforesaid comes and craves to be admitted. He has seisin and fines 3s. 4d.

Afterwards the said John Gurdon, junior, present, surrenders the said title to the use of the said Richard Mounke and Robert Gurdon and of John Brooke "lez Sexteyn," who are admitted. (m. 12ᵈ.)

Court held there Monday before the Ascension of Our Lord,† 8 Henry VII [1493]. Jurors include John Gurdon, junior.

* The Feast of St. Luke the Evangelist falls on 18 October.
† The Feast of the Ascension of Our Lord falls on Holy Thursday.

At this court come Thomas Gurdon and Robert [blank] and do fealty for a piece of meadow enclosed (1 acre), late of William Webbe, before of John Michell, between the meadow of Richard Cranefen and Stephen Sturioun and Alice Smert, south; the river running to Manningtree, north; the way to Cranefen and the meadow of said Richard, east; and the meadow called le lound, west.

John Brook, son of Robert Broke, out of court, surrendered 2 closes and a croft (5 acres), with a way out of the heath to the said tenement and croft in Dedham, late of Thomas Brooke, to the use of Robert Halk and Thomas Gurdon, who are admitted and fine 13s. 4d.    (m. 13.)

Same court.    Jurors say that John Hadleygh, present, surrendered, and John Broke, son of Robert Broke, out of court, surrendered by the hands of John Lofekyn, in the presence of William Gurdon and Stephen Lofkeyn and others, of the homage to the use of the heirs and assigns of John Hadleygh, 2 crofts, etc.    (m. 13.)

[Dedham Campsea.]    Court held there Monday after St. Mark the Evangelist,* 9 Henry VII [1494].

Robert Gurdon of Dedham brings a plea against Henry Nevard for trespass in le Brichet with his beasts; and against Robert Veysy for pound breach. Jurors include John Gurdon.

They say that Robert Gurdon sold to John Gurdon, his brother, a tenement built upon (3 roods), late parcel of the tenement late of James (*Jacobi*) Liem without licence, and that the same John sold it to Stephen Dunton and Robert Lerlyng.    Therefore the bailiff is ordered to seize it into the lady's hands. (13ᵈ.)

Dedham Campsea.    Court held there Thursday after St. Peter,† 11 Henry VII [1495–1496].    Jurors include John Gurdon.

Robert Gurdon, the lady's bailiff, sues Robert Bakeler for trespass in lez Byrchet with his beasts and William Pacche for the like.    (m. 14.)

[Dedham Campsea.]    Court held there Monday before the Purification [of the Holy Virgin],‡ 12 Henry VII [1496/7].    Jurors include John Gurdon.

They say that Robert Gurdon, out of court, alienated to John Barker a field called Langefeld and 2 acres of meadow [without licence].    Therefore the bailiff is ordered to seize them into the lady's hand.

The said Robert Gurdon, present in court, surrenders a field called Longefeld (12 acres) and 2 acres of meadow next the meadow of Simon Crane, newly divided at the costs of Robert and Simon to the use of the said (Robert and) ‖ Simon and Anne and their heirs, who are admitted and fine 4d.    (m. 14ᵈ.)

[Dedham Campsea.]    Court held there Saturday, 20 January, 13 Henry VII [1497/8].    Jurors include John Gurdon.

They say that John Gurdon, junior, sold to John Thorne, junior, a parcel of meadow called Brokemedewe (½ acre 8 feet) as enclosed at the charge of the said Thomas [*sic*], to which John seisin is delivered and he fines 4d.    (m. 15.)

[Dedham Campsea.]    Court held there Wednesday before St. Andrew,§ 14 Henry VII [1498].    Jurors include John Gurdon.    (m. 15ᵈ.)

Same court.    The lady granted to John Herre, John Gurdon, son of John Gurdon, junior (*junʳ*), Robert Gurdon, son of Robert Gurdon, John Webbe, son of Thos. Webbe, and four others (named), two sandpits (described). (m. 15ᵈ.)

* The Feast of St. Mark the Evangelist falls on 25 April.
† The Feast of St. Peter falls on 29 June.
‡ The Feast of the Purification of the Holy Virgin falls on 2 February.
‖ Underlined for erasure.
§ The Feast of St. Andrew falls on 30 November.

611

Dedham Campsea. Court General held there Wednesday before St. Andrew, 14 Henry VII [November 1499]. Jurors include John Gurdon, junior. (m. 16.)

[Dedham Campsea.] Court held there Monday after St. Hilary,* 15 Henry VII [January 1499/1500]. Jurors include John Gurdon.†

Presentment that Walter Broke, who died of late, surrendered by the hands of Robert Gurdon,‡ bond tenant, a messuage with a croft called Mekylboys and other tenements (described) to the use of Thomas Webbe, who is admitted.

Other surrenders, out of court, by hands of Robert Gurdon, are here presented.

John Warner, out of court, surrendered by hands of Robert Gurdon in presence of Thomas Webbe and John Hadleygh a bond tenement called Crowchehouse (5 acres) and 1 piece of meadow (3 roods) called Peryesmedwe, late of Idonia Warner; and thereupon Thomas Webbe and Robert Gurdon, present in court, surrender all right in said lands as appears 3 Henry VII to the use of William Clerk and his heirs and of John Gurdion, the elder, son of John Gurdon, the younger (*Johannis Gurdon sen' filij Johannis Gurdon jun'*), and of John Warner and the heirs William Clerk.

The said John Warner, out of court, surrendered by the hands of Robert Gurdon in presence of Thomas Webbe and John Hadleygh, two closes called Cherchehousefeld [*sic*] (20 acres) and one close called Losnefeld (6 acres) of the demesnes of Overhall in Dedham held by fee farm of 20s. and suit of court to the use of William Clerk and his heirs, John Gurdon the elder, son of John Gurdon the younger, and John Warner, who are admitted.

William Pertre and Robert Gurdon, present in court, surrender the East end of a granary in Dedham to the use of Hugh Turnour.

Stephen Dunton and John Hadleigh, executors of the will of Robert Lerlyng, surrender a pice of demesne land called Cheldewellewent to the use of Robert Gurdon. (m. 17ᵈ.)

Dedham Campsea. Court held there Monday before the Ascension of Our Lord,‖ 16 Henry VII [1501]. Jurors include John Gurdon. Surrenders out of court made by hands of Robert Gurdon the lady's bailiff. (m. 19.)

Dedham Campsea. Court held there Monday after Epiphany,§ 17 Henry VII [1501/2]. Jurors include John Gurdon. (m. 20.)

Dedham Campsea. Court General held there Monday after Epiphany,§ 17 Henry VII [1501/2].

William Gurdon, present in court, surrenders a cottage called Crabhalle, late of Marion Reade and John her son (which Marion and John took up at the Court holden Monday the Eve of St. Peter the Apostle, 5 Henry VII [1490], in Dedham to the use of John Wright of Holton and Henry Grene, who are admitted. (m. 20.)

Same Court. Thursday before St. Edmund,¶ 18 Henry VII [1502]. Jurors include John Gurdon. Jurors present that Robert Gurdon who lately died surrendered into the lady's hands by the hands of John Gurdon, bond tenant, in presence of William Thorne and Ralph Bredman one piece of demesne land (10 acres) in Hallefeld called Cheldewallewent and one-half acre of meadow held by service of 5s. 4d. (of which 2s. for the meadow) to the use of Robert Denham and Joan, his wife, who are admitted to them, their heirs and assigns,

* The Feast of St. Hilary falls on 13 January.
† A duplicate of same court (m. 18) has John Gurdon, Junior.
‡ A duplicate of same court (m. 18) has "the lady's bailiff."
‖ The Feast of the Ascension of Our Lord falls on Holy Thursday.
§ The Feast of Epiphany falls on 6 January.
¶ The Feast of St. Edmund falls on 20 November.

and fine 4d. And that he surrendered by the hands of Stephen Dunton in the presence of William Clerk the rest of his bond tenements to the use of John Gurdon, his brother, who is admitted. John Gurdon brings a plea of land against Robert Hewet and wife Alice, late wife of John Barker, being Barker's land. (m. 21.)

The jurors say that Robert Gurdon late son of John Gurdon the elder (*senʳ*) who lately died surrendered into the lady's hand by the hands of Stephen Dunton in the presence of William Clerk a parcel of bond land of tenement Mekylboyes (1 rood) late of the said John Gurdon the elder and before of Henry Vyne, 3 roods meadow late of said John Gurdon the elder before of Henry Vyne and before that of John Moyse and William Wheler in Esthousemedewe as in the year 3 Henry VII, two fields (*campos*) called Westefeldes containing respectively 9 acres and 10 acres and 7 acres meadow in the lady's meadow called Prioreshallemedewe held by fee farm of 32s. and suit of court as in 7 Henry VII to the use of John Gurdon, brother of said Robert, who is admitted.

Afterwards at this court Robert Gurdon son of the said Robert Gurdon surrendered all right in the said lands to the said John Gurdon.

Dedham Campsea. Court held there Thursday after St. Edmund,* 19 Henry VII.

Jurors say that Richard Monke sold to John Gurdon a tenement close and garden in Dedham. And that Richard Monke, out of court, surrendered a cottage with a croft (3 acres) late of Agnes Leem to the use of John Gurdon and John his son, who are admitted.

Dedham Campsea. Court held there Monday after St. Matthias,† 20 Henry VII [1504/5].

Jurors say that John Gurdon under the style of (*nomine*) John Gurdon, junior, who lately died, held of the lady at his death one bond croft lately built (4 acres), formerly of William Snowe and one croft called Caledon (4 acres) late of Agnes Clarke, widow, and Robert Clarke as in 18 Edward IV in Dedham, and that John, his son, is his next heir thereof.

John Gurdon, son of John Gurdon, present in court, surrenders a parcel of land late of Robert Copyn (½ acre) at Mychelboyes, between the brook running from "le Wodehowse" of the said John Gurdon towards the tenement of John Pynkyrnell, north; the land of the said John Gurdon, south; the stable of John Pynkyrnell, east; land of the said John Gurdon, west; in Dedham to the use of Stephen Dunton and William Clarke, who are admitted. (m. 23.)

[Dedham Campsea.] Court held there Thursday after St. Mary Magdalene,‡ 21 Henry VII [1506]. Jurors include John Gurdon. (m. 24.)

[Dedham Campsea.] Court held there Monday, feast of St. Luke,‖ 23 Henry VII [1507]. Jurors include John Gurdon. (m. 25.)

[Dedham Campsea.] Court held there Tuesday after St. Luke,‖ 24 Henry VII [1508]. Jurors include John Curdon.

William Clarke and John Gurdon, present in court, surrender 2 closes called Chesehowsfeldes [*sic*] (20 acres) and one close called Losnefeld (6 acres) of the demesnes of the manor of Overehall held at fee farms by 20s. *v* suit of court late of John Warner, as in 15 Henry VII,§ which the said William and John received jointly with John Warnere, junior, now deceased, of the surrender of

* The Feast of St. Edmund falls on 20 November.
† The Feast of St. Matthias falls on 24 February.
‡ The Feast of St. Mary Magdalene falls on 22 July.
‖ The Feast of St. Luke falls on 18 October.
§ The same tenements surrendered Monday after St. Hilary, 15 Henry VII [1499/1500] (*vide* m. 17ᵈ. *supra*) the duplicate of that court on m. 18 seems imperfect.

John Warner, the elder, in Dedham to the use of Robert Warnere, who is admitted. (m. 25ᵈ.)

Dedham. Court * held there Thursday after the Octave of Easter, 8 Henry VII [1493]. Jurors include John Gurdon, senior.

Ordered that John Gurdon, junior, make clean the stream in his meadow, under pain of 20d. Affeerers, John Gurdon, senior, and John Hadleych. (m. 1.)

Dedham. Leet held there Tuesday after the Octave of Easter, 8 Henry VII [1493].

Capital pledges include John Gurdon, senior, and John Gurdon, junior. John Gurdon, senior, is one of the affeerers. (m. 2.)

Dedham. Court held there Monday after St. Faith,† 9 Henry VII [1493]. Jurors include John Gurdon, senior.

Twenty acres of land and meadow, parcel of tenement Greylonds, are granted by the lady to Robert Hall, Thomas Gurdon, John Rye and John Herre [feoffees to uses]. John Gurdon, senior, an affeerer. (m. 3.)

Dedham. Leet held there Monday after the Octave of Easter, 9 Henry VII [1494]. Capital Pledges include John Gurdon, senior, John Gurdon, junior, and Robert Gurdon.

Dedham. Leet held there Tuesday after Octave of Easter, 12 Henry VII [1497].

Capital pledges include John Gurdon, senior, and John Gurdon, junior. John Gurdon, senior, an affeerer. (m. 5.)

Dedham. Court held there Monday after All Saints,‡ 13 Henry VII [1497]. Jurors include John Gurdon, senior.

They present that John Clerke and his wife Agnes surrendered 7 acres parcel of 15 acres called Caldweyland in Dedham, later of Peter Perpound, to the use of William Veyse and John Gurdon, junior, their heirs and assigns, admitted. (m. 6.)

"Mᵈ that it is covenantyd and agreed betweene John Gurdon thelder and William Veyse paynter in fourme foloyng that is to say that the sayd William Veyse shall haue a tenement of the sayd John Gurdon thelder callyd Knyghtes immediatly after the decesse of the sayd John Gurdon payng therfor as much as a noder man wyll wuthout frawde or gyle the wych payment shall be in fourme foloyng that is to say the fyrst yere after the decease of the sayd John xl s. and euery yere after xx s. onto the tyme such summe as they shall be agreyd vpon be fully content and payd. In wytness wherof the sayd John Gurdon hath resceyuyd 1d. of the sayd William Veyse in Ernest in the presens of Richard Sutton Esquier." (m. 6ᵈ.)

Dedham. Court held there Thursday in Whitweek, 14 Henry VII [1499]. Jurors include John Gurdon.

At this court come John Gurdon, late called (*nup voc'*) John Gurdon, junior, and Thomas Wodehous, and surrender into the lady's hand a tenement called Knightes and 3 acres 3 roods of land to the use of Stephen Dunton and Dionysia, his wife, during the life of John Gurdon aforesaid and Olive, his wife, with remainder after the death of said John Gurdon and Olive, his wife, to the heirs and assigns of the same John Gurdon. (m. 7.)

Same court. Presentment that William Mynot, who lately died on his deathbed, surrendered into the lady's hand by the hands of Ric. Mannyng in the presence of Robert Gurdon and William Myldenale a messuage, 5 acres of land and ½ acre of meadow, in Dedham to the use of John Webbe and his

* The Courts here are out of order.
† The Feast of St. Faith falls on 6 October.
‡ The Feast of All Saints falls on 1 November.

heirs, to whom seisin is delivered, to hold to the same John Webbe and to Robert Gurdon, their heirs and assigns, in accordance with the will of the said William Mynot, on condition that if John Webbe pay William Myldenale and William Dawes, executors of William Mynot, £20, in certain portions [described], the surrender should be of effect, with clause of re-entry in case of John Webbe's default.

Same court. At this court come Joan Wulfard, wife of William Wulfard and late wife of Thomas Cranefen, John Gurdon, junior, and James Cranefen, and surrender half an acre enclosed to the use of John Gurdon, senior, Stephen Dunton and their heirs; they are admitted. (m. 7.)

Dedham. Leet held Tuesday after Octave of Easter, 14 Henry VII [1499]. Capital pledges include John Gurdon, junior, sworn; John Gurdon, senior, sworn. William Gurdon amerced 3d. for default of suit. (m. 8.)

Dedham. Leet held Tuesday after Octave of Easter, 15 Henry VII [1500]. Capital pledges include John Gurdon, junior.

[Dedham.] Court held there Monday in Whitweek, 15 Henry VII [1500]. John Gurdon, junior, brings a plea of debt upon demand against William Wodegate, 39s. 11½d.; Wodegate acknowledges the debt. William Wodegate brings a plea of debt upon demand against said John Gurdon, who puts himself fivehanded, 39s. 11½d. Jurors include John Gurdon.

[Dedham.] Leet held there Tuesday after the Octave of Easter, 16 Henry VII [1501]. Capital pledges include John Gurdon.
Order to Robert Gurdon to scour ditches towards Bolles Hyll. (m. 10.)

Dedham. Leet held there Tuesday after the Octave of Easter, 17 Henry VII [1502]. Capital pledges include John Gurdon.
Order to John Webbe "wever" to scour his ditch opposite the way leading from his house to the house of John Gurdon. (m. 11.)

Dedham. First Court of Queen Elizabeth held there Wednesday in Whitweek, 17 Henry VII [1502].
All bond tenants were summoned [to attorn tenant], of whom there appeared John Gurdon and others, who did fealty.
John Gurdon brings a plea of trespass against Thomas Northen of Ardleigh. Inquest includes John Gurdon.
They say that Walter Broke, junior, on his deathbed surrendered by the hands of Robert Gurdon, bond tenant, a piece of land (3 roods) called Dokkecroft to the use of Thomas Webbe.
And that William Gurdon, junior, died since the last court seised of a cottage called Reymes with 3 acres of land in Dedham, and that Robert Gurdon, his younger brother (*Robertus G. frater eius jun*[r]) is heir thereof and of full age. He is admitted.
At this court come William Gurdon and John Gurdon, late called John Gurdon, junior, and surrender a croft in Dedham (1 acre) formerly of Stephen Sturgeon to the use of Henry Grene and John Wright of Holton.

Same court. At this court come John Webbe and Robert Gurdon and surrender ½ acre of customary meadow in Dedham, which they late had jointly of the surrender of William Mynoot, as appears in court on Thursday in Whitweek, 14 Henry VII [1499] to the use of Stephen Dunton and Thomas Webbe, who are admitted. (m. 12.)

Dedham. Court held there Monday after Corpus Christi,* 20 Henry VII [1505].
John Mynott, executor of the will of Thomas Gurdon, brings a plea of debt upon demand (5 marks) against John Gurdon. Mynott [as executor of said

* The Feast of Corpus Christi falls on the Thursday after Trinity Sunday.

will] also brings pleas of debt (4 marks) against John Greneleff and of detention of 5 yards of woollen cloth price 10s. against Agnes Edward.

The inquest includes John Gurdon.

Robert Cranefen surrenders a croft (2½ acres) to the use of John Gordon and his heirs, who is admitted to hold to himself and Stephen Dunton and their heirs and assigns.

John Cardon* surrenders a cottage called Peperis and land in Brodweyfeld in Dedham. (m. 13.)

[Dedham.] Leet held there Tuesday after Whitsunday, 20 Henry VII [1505]. Capital Pledges include John Gurdon. (m. 14.)

[To be continued]

---

## GENEALOGICAL RESEARCH IN ENGLAND

Communicated by the Committee on English and Foreign Research

### THE GURDON FAMILY

Contributed by G. ANDREWS MORIARTY, A.M., LL.B., F.S.A.,<br>of Bristol, R. I.

#### FROM COURT ROLLS OF DEDHAM, CO. ESSEX.

RECORDS OF THE DUCHY OF LANCASTER<br>[Series 30, Bundle 59, Roll 734]<br>(Concluded)

Dedham. Leet held there Tuesday after Whitsunday,* 21 Henry VII [1506]. Capital pledges include John Gurdon.

Orders that John Gurdon scour the ditch between his house and Dorkys, and the ditch by Westfeld. (m. 15.)

Dedham. Leet held there Tuesday after Whitsunday, 22 Henry VII [1507]. Capital pledges include John Gurdon.

John Gurdon to scour a ditch towards Copynyslane.

[Dedham.] Court held there Friday after Pentecost, 23 Henry VII [1508]. Inquest includes John Gurdon. (m. 17.)

[Dedham.] Leet held there Tuesday after Whitsunday, 24 Henry VII 1509]. Capital pledges include John Gurdon. (m. 18.)

[Dedham.] Leet held there Tuesday after Whitsunday, 23 Henry VII [1508]. As at m. 17, a draft. (m. 18ᵈ.)

[Dedham.] Draft [in bad condition]. [On the face, the last court is Monday after Holy Trinity, 22 Henry VII.] [1507.]

The date has almost gone; it reads: "Dedham Court there holden Wednesday before [St. Martin] in winter [torn] Henry [illegible]." A Sixteenth Century scribe writes "H vij xxiiij vt opinor."

The inquest includes John Gurdon.

Same court. They present that Robert Denham with his cofeoffees held a

---

* The name Cardon occurs quite distinctly a number of times.

* The person who copied and translated these records writes that she translated *Dominica in Albis* as Whitsunday and *Pentecostis* as Whitsuntide.

She finds that she was in error and that *Dominica in Albis* is the Octave of Easter.

Therefore all the Whitsuntide dates in Roll 734, are incorrect, but the Anno Domine in the reign of Henry VII is not affected.

The earliest possible date for Hock Tuesday is 31 March, the latest 4 May.

Courts were held Tuesday "*post dominicam in Albis*" (Hock Tuesday), and Wednesday in the week of Pentecost (Whit Wednesday).

messuage [close] and a pightel (3½ acres), which they had late of John Gurdon under certain conditions; and afterwards the said John Gurdon died, and before his death made Stephen Dunton executor of his will, and the conditional payments were in arrear at the Feast of St. Michael 1506, and therefore Stephen Dunton, as assignee of the said John Gurdon, has re-entered into the said messuage close and pightel and surrenders the same to the use of Henry Palmer and John Webbe.

Stephen Dunton, present in court, surrenders a messuage called Knytes with 5 acres of land in Dedham to the use of W[illiam] Veysy, who is admitted to hold to himself and to John Gurdon and their heirs and assigns to the use of the said William Veysy, conditionally upon certain payments by Veysy to Dunton. Affeerees: James Judy and John Gurdon. (m. 19ᵈ.)

[Series 30, Bundle 59, Roll 735]

Dedham Campsea. Court held there Monday after St. Swithin,* 1 Henry VIII [July 1509]. Inquest includes John Gurdon. (m. 26.)

Dedham Campsea. Monday after St. Luke the Evangelist,† 1 Henry VIII [October 1509]. John Gurdon, present in court, surrenders one parcel of meadow in Brookmedow (1 rood) in Dedham to the use of John Pynkernell. (m. 26.)

Dedham Campsea. Court held Friday after the Annunciation,‡ 2 Henry VIII [March 1511]. Inquest includes John Gurdon. (m. 27.)

Dedham Campsea. Court held Tuesday after All Saints,§ 5 Henry VIII [November 1513]. Inquest includes John Gurdon.

They say Henry Grene, who late died, held a cottage called Crabbishalle, which he received jointly with John Wright of the surrender of William Gurdon, as in the court of Monday after Epiphany, 17 Henry VII [1502]. (m. 28.)

Same Court. John Gurdon, present in court, surrenders 2 crofts called Wadisfeld (10 acres), late of Robert Halk, before of John Halke, in Dedham to the use of Adam Nycolle and Joan, his wife, their heirs and assigns. (m. 28ᵈ.)

Dedham Campsea. Court held Tuesday before SS. Simon and Jude,‖ 6 Henry VIII [October 1514]. Inquest includes John Gurdon. (m. 29.)

Same Court. Tuesday, the feast of St. Martin the Bishop, 8 Henry VIII. Inquest includes John Gurdon.

They say that John Ry who is lately dead, surrendered into the lady's hands a cottage and other premises (described) late of John Ry senior, as in 7 Edward IV, and a cottage and croft called Bollys (described), late of said John Ry, senior, formerly of John Smert, in which lands and tenements John Traves and his wife, Marion, surrendered into the lady's hands by the hands of John Gurdon, in the presence of Robert Gurdon, all their interest for the life of Marion—as in 7 Henry VII [1491–92]—in Dedham, to the use of Walter Ry son of said John. (m. 30.)

Same court. They say that John Curde, who is lately dead, surrendered into the lord's hands in the presence of Thomas Upsher, a messuage with a curtilage adjacent (½ rood) and 2 crofts lying together (2½ acres and ½ rood) of tenement Peries, late of Isabel Kebill and formerly of Maud Canceler, in

* The Feast of St. Swithin falls on 15 July.
† The Feast of St. Luke the Evangelist falls on 18 October.
‡ The Feast of the Annunciation of the Blessed Virgin falls on 25 March.
§ The Feast of All Saints falls on 1 November.
‖ The Feast of SS. Simon and Jude falls on 28 October.

617

Dedham, to the use of John Gurdon, who is admitted to himself, his heirs and assigns, and surrenders to the use of Robert Cradok upon condition that if the said Robert pay John Gurdon, his heirs and executors 100s. at certain dates (specified), the surrender to Cradok shall be of effect. (m. 30<sup>d</sup>.)

Dedham Campsea. Court held there Monday before SS. Simon and Jude,* 9 Henry VIII [October 1517]. Inquest includes John Gurdon.

They present a surrender out of court by the hands of John Gurdon and Thomas Webbe, of land late of William Webbe, junr., and wife, Margaret, to the use of John Webbe, son of said Thomas Webbe.

The jurors present that John Gurdon, who died many years past, held of the lady at his death a parcel of land of tenement Mekylboys (1 rood), 3 roods of meadow in Esthonsmedow, which Robert Gurdon late received of the surrender of John Gurdon, senior, as in 3 Henry VII [1487–88], 2 fields of the demesnes of the manor called Westfeld, whereof one contains 9 acres, the other 10 acres, and 7 acres of meadow in Prioreshallemedow, held at fee farm [by] 32s. per annum, which the said Robert Gurdon late received jointly with Thomas Ry of the grant of the lady, the lady to find underwood for their repair, as in 7 Henry VII, and which were late of the said Robert Gurdon in Dedham.

And that John Gurdon, son of said John, is heir thereto of full age and comes into court craving to be admitted; and is admitted to hold to himself his heirs and assigns. Fine of 5s. 1d. paid to the lady. (m. 31.)

Court held there Tuesday before St. Michael,† 10 Henry VII [September 1518]. The homage present the death of Stephen Dunton, who surrendered out of court, by hands of John Gurdon, bond tenant, a messuage and 36 acres of land and the reversion thereof, after the death of Olive,‡ late wife of William Dunton, and before wife of Thomas Kyng, [which] Stephen received jointly with the said William Dunton, John Clapton, Esq., and John Hubberd, now deceased, of the surrender of William Stevene and John Stevene, as appears Tuesday after St. Hilary, 22 Edward IV [January 1483], in Dedham, to the use of John Warnere, on condition that if John Warnere pay William Clerk, John Gurdon, and William Budde, executors of the will of said Stephen, 100 marks at dates (specified), the surrender shall take effect; otherwise the said executors (including Gurdon) shall enter. John Warnere is admitted. (m. 31.)

Dedham Campsea. Court held there Tuesday 12 April, 10 Henry VIII [1519]. Inquest includes John Gurdon.

Jurors present that John Halke and Robert Halke, out of court, sold to John Gurdon, junior, father of John Gurdon, now living, 8 acres, parcel of 3 crofts, of tenement Gerolds which John and Robert Halke had taken up in the court held Friday morrow of St. George,§ 5 Edward IV [April 1465], and also William Bounde, gent., of Colchester, and Thomas Glender, about the same time, out of court, sold to the same John Gurdon, the father, one pasture called Swetmanesey (6 acres) and one pasture called Mellefen (8 acres) which the said Bownde and Glender had taken up. Monday the feast of St. Mark,‖ 9 Henry VII [April 1494], which land, crofts, and pasture, the said John Gurdon, the father, had and occupied without licence of the lady and her predecessors. And the said John Gurdon, the son, likewise occupied them after his father's death.

The bailiff is therefore ordered to seize the said land, etc. (m. 28<sup>d</sup>.)

* The Feast of SS. Simon and Jude falls on 28 October.
† The Feast of St. Michael falls on 29 September.
‡ This name may be Alina.
§ The Feast of St. George falls on 23 April.
‖ The Feast of St. Mark falls on 25 April.

Court held there Monday before St. Edward the King and Confessor,* 12 Henry VIII [January 1521]. Inquest includes John Gurdon.

Robert [obliterated, but not Gurdon] surrendered into the lady's hand, out of court, parcel of a close and pasture (1 acre) to the use of John Gurdon and Robert Cradock, who are admitted to the sole use of the said John, his heirs and assigns.

The lady of her grace grants to John Gurdon the land seized from him at last Court.

Same Court. The lady granted to John Gurdon and Robert Cradock all her fishery in the river of Dedham from "le Planker' mill" of Dedham and from "le Flote Gates" there to the corner called Swetmonesey corner and throughout the whole liberty. She delivers to them the custody within the river and two white swans. They have seisin thereof to the use of John Gurdon, his heirs and assigns, for service of 4s. 6d. and suit of court. They fine 3s. 4d. (m. 32d.)

Dedham Campsea. First Court of Dame Agnes Valentyne, Prioress of Campsea. Monday after Conception of the Blessed Virgin Mary,† 13 Henry VIII [December 1521]. John Gurdon [one only] attorns tenant. Inquest includes John Gurdon. (m. 33.)

Court held there Tuesday, Feast of St. Edward the King and Confessor,* 15 Henry VIII [January 1524]. Inquest includes John Gurdon.

They present that John Webbe on his deathbed surrendered by the hands of John Gurdon all his bondlands to the use of his will. And that Dionesia Felix, widow, sold to Thomas Botour, a tenement late of Thomas Ry. (m. 34.)

Robert Petwell comes and surrenders 1 acre parcel of Overwent *alias* Gravelpetwent (abbutals given), which the same Robert with others took up Tuesday after All Saints,‡ 5 Henry VIII [November 1513], to the use of John Pynkernell, churchwarden of Dedham for the time being, Thomas Clerk, son of William Clerk, Robert Gurdon, son of John Gurdon, Bartholomew Lufkyn, son of Bartholomew Lufkyn the elder, James Petwell and Thomas Cradock, their heirs and assigns who are admitted to the use of the parishioners and inhabitants of the town of Dedham. (m. 34d.)

Dedham Campsea. Court held there Thursday after St. Martin, Bishop,§ 16 Henry VIII [November 1524]. Inquest includes John Gurdon. (m. 35.)

They present that James Thomson surrendered, out of court, by the hands of William Derbye, in presence of Robert Cradock, John Gurdon, and others of the homage, a piece of land newly built (1 rood) parcel of 7 crofts of tenement Blunts, which he took up in the last Court, to the use of Robert Gurdon and Robert Gurdon, his son. They are admitted and fine 2s. (m. 35d.)

Dedham Campsea. Court held there Thursday after St. Leonard,‖ 17 Henry VIII [November 1525].

William Clerk, executor of the will of Stephen Dunton, surrenders a cottage, etc., etc., and one parcel of land, late of Robert Copyn, at Mechelboys between the brook running from le Woodehows of John Gurdon to the tenement of John Pynkernell, north; the land of John Gurdon, south; the east head abutting on land of John Pynkernell; and the west head upon land of the said John Gurdon, in Dedham, which William Clerk took up jointly with said Stephen Dunton, now deceased, of the surrender of John Gurdon, son of

* The Feast of St. Edward the King and Confessor falls on 18 March.
† The Feast of the Conception of the Blessed Virgin falls on 8 December.
‡ The Feast of All Saints falls on 1 November.
§ The Feast of St. Martin, Bishop, falls on 11 November.
‖ The Feast of St. Leonard falls on 6 November.

619

John Gurdon, Monday after St. Matthias,* 20 Henry VII [February 1505,] to the use of Thomas, son of said Stephen, who is admitted. (m. 35ᵈ.)

Same court. Affeerers include John Gurdon. (m. 36.)

Dedham Campsea. Monday after St. Edward the King and Confessor,† 18 Henry VIII. Attornment of tenants, including John Gurdon. Inquest includes John Gurdon. (m. 36.)

Same court. Monday after St. Edward the King and Confessor,† 18 Henry VIII [October 1526]. Jurors say whereas in court Thursday after St. Edmund,‡ 19 Henry VIII [November 1503] William Thorn surrendered a parcel of a barn, with a garner, tiled, in Dedham, to the use of Margaret, his wife, for life, remainder to John Thorn, son of said William, and now it is testified that Margaret is dead and John Thorn craves to be admitted; there are admitted John Thorn, John Gurdon, and John Milis, son of Robert Mylys, their heirs and assigns, to the use of John Thorn. (m. 36ᵈ.)

Dedham Campsea. Tuesday after St. Edward,† 19 Henry VIII [October 1527]. Inquest includes John Gurdon.

Same court. At this court comes John Gurdon present in court and surrenders one rood of land late of John Gurdon, his father, before of Robert Gurdon, and before that of Henry Vyne in Dedham, which he took up in the court, Monday before SS. Simon and Jude,§ 9 Henry VIII [October 1517], to the use of John Cole and Joan, his wife, who are admitted by their attorney, John Pynkernell. They fine 4d.

The jurors say that John Gurdon, brother of Robert Gurdon, died 22 years ago and was seised of 3 roods of land, parcel of 2 closes of Mekilboys tenement, late in tenure of Robert Copyn, held by service of 12d. rent in Dedham, which same John took them up jointly with the same Robert in the court here, Monday before Ascension, 8 Henry VII [1493]; and that the said John survived the said John [sic]. Further they say that John Gurdon, son of the said John Gurdon, is his heir and of full age, who comes and craves to be admitted as to his inheritance. He is admitted and fines 6d.

Afterwards the said John, the son, surrenders the same to the use of John Cole and Joan, his wife, by the hands of John Pynkernell, their attorney. Fine 6d. (m. 37.)

Dedham Campsea. Court held there Monday after All Souls,‖ 20 Henry VIII [November 1528]. Inquest includes John Gurdon. (m. 38.)

Same court. At this court comes John Gurdon, one of the executors of Stephen Dunton, and acknowledges that he and the other executors, William Clerk and William Budde, have been paid 100 marks by John Warner, as appears in court of Monday before SS. Simon and Jude,§ 9 Henry VIII [October 1517].

Dedham Campsea. Court held there Thursday before Palm Sunday, 20 Henry VIII [1529]. Inquest includes John Gurdon.

Dedham Campsea. Court held there Monday after St. Martin, Bishop,¶ 21 Henry VIII [July 1529]. Inquest includes John Gurdon. (m. 38.)

They say that Kakys Dernell surrendered, out of court, a messuage in tenure of John Bonde, and late of John Wylye, new built (except a parcel of land in the lady's hand on which the lady's pinfold is built) in Dedham, which the

* The Feast of St. Matthias falls on 24 February.
† The Feast of St. Edward the King and Confessor falls on 18 March.
‡ The Feast of St. Edmund falls on 20 November.
§ The Feast of SS. Simon and Jude falls on 28 October.
‖ The Feast of All Souls falls on 2 November.
¶ The Feast of St. Martin, Bishop, falls on 11 November.

said Jakys took up in the court here 15 December, 14 Henry VIII [1522] to the use of John Mynott, John Gurdon, and Robert Pettewell, junior, who are admitted to them and the heirs of John Mynott. (m. 39ᵈ.)

[Dedham Campsea.] Court held there Monday after St. Lucy,* 22 Henry VIII [December 1530]. Inquest includes John Gurdon.

They say that William Webbe surrendered a messuage in presence of William Clerk and 8 others including John Gurdon. (m. 39ᵈ.)

[Dedham Campsea.] Court held there Monday after All Saints,† 22 Henry VIII [November 1530]. Inquest includes John Gurdon. (m. 39ᵈ.)

Same court. At this court come Ralph Warner and Isabella, his wife, and surrender one acre in Brodemedow, late of James Judge, before of Lawrence Wodehous, which Ralph and Isabella took up Wednesday after All Saints,† 5 Henry VIII [1513] to the use of John Cole and Robert Gurdon, son of John Gurdon, who are admitted. (m. 39.)

[To be continued]

## ADDITIONAL RECORDS
### LEACHLAND

An account of the Leachland family, of whom Alice Leachland (daughter of Roger Leachland of Chard, co. Somerset, and his wife, Margaret (Jones) Leachland), who married about 1642 Richard Derby, father of Roger Derby of Salem, Mass., was a member, was printed in the REGISTER, vol. 81, pp. 320–323, 486–487, and vol. 82, pp. 63–65. **

The following abstracts from chancery proceedings relate to this family.

### FROM CHANCERY PROCEEDINGS ‡
#### [Lechland v. Hill]

Writ to commissioners to examine defendant, 24 November, 30 Elizabeth [1587].

Bill of Thomas Lecheland of Taunton, Somerset, now prisoner in the Fleet.

Whereas William Leonard late of Taunton, deceased, his master, about 20 years ago bequeathed £50 each to his daughters Elizabeth and Emma Leonard, payable on marriage, and appointed Margery his wife, their mother, executrix, and Robert Hill, Esq., William Chaplyn late deceased, and the plaintiff, his overseers, the plaintiff had nothing to do with the legacies except to borrow sums from Hill at interest; and 3 years ago the said Elizabeth and Emma exhibited bills in this court against Eleanor, widow and executrix of Robert Hill, and against this plaintiff, for payment of their portions, and judgment was awarded against him because he had confessed to money received from reckonings with Hill. He has been in prison for twelve months through inability to pay, to the undoing of his wife and children.

He asks for a writ of subpena against Eleanor Hill, who has sufficient money and ought to pay the legacies.

Answer of the defendant.

The bill of Elizabeth and Emma Leonard was exhibited 5 years ago, whereupon the court ordered each defendant to pay £58. 6s. 8d., which she has done. There is no new cause why this defendant should be further chargeable.

---

\* The Feast of St. Lucy falls on 13 December.
† The Feast of All Saints falls on 1 November.
‡ Elizabeth, L, 3/22. Preserved in the Public Record Office, London.
\*\*For Vol. 81, pp. 320-323 & 486-487 see pp. 205-210, this volume; for Vol. 82, pp. 63-65 see pp. 224-225, this volume.

# MOHUN

## (OR MOONE)

An account of the Mohun (or Moone) and Hyde families was printed in the REGISTER, vol. 81, pp. 91–94, 178–186, and 314–320. **
The following abstract from Chancery Proceedings relates to this Mohun (or Moone) family.

### FROM CHANCERY PROCEEDINGS *

#### [Moone *v.* Sidwaye and Pitt]

Bill of Margaret Moone widow, late the wife of Robert Moone late of Baunton, Dorset, gent., deceased, his executrix,

Whereas about 10 years ago her husband mortgaged to Thomas Hardye gent. the rectory and parsonage of Chalden, co. Dorset, for a sum not repayed within the limited term because her husband became senseless from sickness, and afterwards the mortgage was assigned to Henry Pytt of "Weymouth Melcombe Regis," co. Dorset, merchant, who married a daughter of Robert Moone and the plaintiff; about 8 years ago, being desirous to settle matters for her husband, the plaintiff found that he was endebted to Henry Pytt for £340 for the said mortgage, his daughter's marriage-portion and other matters. Whereupon she paid £70 and had assurances made for the rest, including a bond by Richard Sydwaye gent., who had married another daughter, together with Gilbert Holman. Sydwaye received the lease, and, after her husband's death, an additional bond from the plaintiff. Pytt has now been fully satisfied by the plaintiff, yet by confederacy with Sydwaye, he is bringing suits against him to recover more money from plaintiff upon both the bonds.

## THE ENGLISH ANCESTRY OF JOSEPH PECK, OF HINGHAM, MASS., IN 1638

Compiled by S. ALLYN PECK, B.A., of New York City, and contributed by FREDERICK STANHOPE PECK, LL.D., of Barrington, R. I.

[EDITORIAL NOTE.—Since the publication, in the REGISTER of January 1938 (vol. 92, pp. 71–73), of the last preceding instalment of this article, much new material relating to the Pecks of Wakefield, co. York, and the Pecks of Beccles, co. Suffolk, has been collected by Mr. S. Allyn Peck and placed in the hands of the editor of the REGISTER by Frederick Stanhope Peck, LL.D., the contributor of this article. Therefore it seems best to the editor, before going on with the history of Nicholas Peck, son of the second Robert Peck of Beccles, from the point where it was left in the REGISTER of January 1938, to edit, arrange, and present in their proper order the various items of new material relating to the part of the article already published.—EDITOR.] ***

ADDITIONS AND CORRECTIONS FOR THE HISTORY OF THE PECKS OF WAKEFIELD, CO. YORK, AS PUBLISHED IN THE REGISTER: ****

Vol. 90, p. 59, lines 42–43 (January 1936), "Knoston, in Colchester (co. Essex)." Knoston is an abbreviated form for Knossington, which lies in co. Leicester. "Colchester" is a typographical error for "co. Leicester," occurring in Mr. Ira B. Peck's "Genealogical History." The facsimile of the Peck pedigree shows that this passage should read "Knoston in co.

---

* Elizabeth, M, 3/9.  No date is shown.  Preserved in the Public Record Office, London.
**See pp. 186-205, this volume.
***Pages 590-592, this volume.
****For Vol. 90, pp. 59, 62, 65, 263-264 & 265 see pp. 536, 539, 542, 549-550, & 551 this volume.

Leicester." A pedigree of the Peck family of Knoston or Knossington, co. Leicester, may be found in "The Visitation of Leicestershire, 1619," vol. 2, pp. 146–148 (*The Publications of the Harleian Society*), but the compiler has material on hand that disproves conclusively any connection between this Leicestershire family of Pecks and the Pecks of Wakefield.

Vol. 90, p. 62, lines 14 and following: Among the heriots appearing in the court rolls of the Wakefield Manor for 1490 is that paid by Richard Peck on the death of his father, Richard Peck. Therefore the grandfather of John Peck, Esq., of Wakefield was dead by 1490.

Vol. 90, p. 65, lines 28 and following: It is here argued that Sir Peter Middleton, Knight, was not the father of Alice Middleton, the first wife of Richard Peck of Wakefield (who was the father of John Peck, Esq., of Wakefield), but that a Sir William Middleton, Knight, was her father. Sir William was a son of Sir Peter, and Sir William's will, dated 2 August 1549, was proved 11 March 1552 [1551/2]. (Prerogative Court of York, vol. 13, folio 958.) Richard Peck of Wakefield died in 1516, and was then of an age to have grandchildren. It is highly improbable that this Richard who died in 1516 had a wife as early as 1491 (Yorkshire Feet of Fines) who was the daughter of a man who was living as late as 1549. No mention of the Pecks is found in Sir William's will. The administration of Sir Peter Middleton, Knight, is dated 21 April 1499 (Prerogative Court of York, vol. 3, folio 335), but gives no information as to Sir Peter's children. The father of Sir Peter was named John, and his grandfather, although his name was William, was never knighted, and died in 1474.

Vol. 90, pp. 263–264 (July 1936): In regard to the Poge or Poage family mentioned on these pages, the name of the Poge who married Anne Peck, daughter of John Peck, Esq., of Wakefield, was definitely Robert Poge, and not John Poge. At the Inquisition post Mortem of his father, Thomas Poge, Gentleman, Robert Poge was aged twenty-two years and upwards, on 19 November, 35 Henry VIII [1543]. It is stated in the Inquisition post Mortem of Robert Poge, 3 Edward VI [1549–50], that his widow Anne was living at Wakefield.

Vol. 90, p. 265, lines 9 and following, and p. 266, lines 3 and following: The question arose as to the identity of the Robert Peke [Peck] to whom, with Lancelot Lake, John Peck of Wakefield, Esq., the testator of 2 November 1558, had already, prior to the date of his will, given certain parcels of land in Wakefield, and it was suggested (p. 266) that, since Lancelot Lake was a grandson of the testator, perhaps Robert Peke [Peck] was also a grandson of this testator. The recent discovery of the will of Robert Cockson of Wakefield, clothier, dated 24 September 1561 and proved 1 February 1563/4 (Prerogative Court of York, vol. 17, folio 313), probably explains the parentage of this Robert Peck and his relationship to John Peck of Wakefield, Esq. In his will Robert Cockson mentions his daughter, Mrs. Anne Peck, and a Thomas Peck and his wife Anne are known to have sold five messuages in Wakefield in 1554–5 (Yorkshire Feet of Fines). Therefore Thomas Peck, son of John Peck of Wakefield, Esq., probably married Anne Cockson, daughter of Robert Cockson, clothier, and their son was named Robert for his Grandfather Cockson. This Robert Peck was therefore probably a grandson of John Peck of Wakefield, Esq., as previously suggested. Proof has been obtained that John Peck, son of John Peck of Wakefield, Esq., left no sons at his death. Nicholas Peck, another of the surviving sons of John Peck, Esq., married Alice Bradford, and of this marriage there is ample proof, as there is also of the marriage of Richard Peck, the eldest son, to Anne Hotham.

FROM THE RECORDS OF THE COURT OF REQUESTS

[Robert Young *v.* Robert Peck and Katherine Drawer,
Wife of Thomas Drawer]

[Not dated] To the King, our Sovereign Lord:

The Bill of Complaint of Robert Yong of Pakefylde [Pakefield], co. Suffolk, "Bocher," complaining as follows: Whereas on 11 March in the 20 [th] year of this present reign [20 Henry VIII, 1528/9], at Beccles in said county, the complainant sold to John Leke of Beccles, tanner, all slaughtered hides that said complainant should chance to slay by space of one year next following, for which hides said Leke agreed to pay for every "satyn" hide 2s. 4d. and for every ox hide 3s. 4d. and for every "bolks" [? bullock's] or steer's hide 20d., after which bargain the complainant delivered to John Leke 75 hides, each 20d., 4 hides, each 4d., etc., amounting in all to £7. 4s. worth, which was due to him for the same, now afterwards said Leke made his last will and testament and appointed Robert Pekke [Peck] and Katherine Drawer, wife of Thomas Drawer, his executors, and afterwards died, after whose death said Pekke [Peck] and Katherine Drawer, by her husband, took upon them[selves] administration of his goods. And said Pekke [Peck] paid to the complainant 26s. 8d., part of said sum owing to him, but the residue of 17s. 8d. has never been paid, and the executors of said Leke refuse to disburse it, contrary to all right. Wherefore your orator asks for a commission to be directed to some worshipful gentlemen within said shire of Suffolk, commanding them to examine the premises.

The Answer of Robert Pekk [Peck], denying the Bill [not dated].

The Replication of Robert Young [not dated].

The Rejoinder of Robert Pekk [Peck] [not dated].

By the King. Commission [appointed] to examine the case of Robert Young against Robert Pekke [Peck] and Katherine Drawer, wife of Thomas Drawer, [and] to report by Saint Michael next. Given under the Privy Seal at York Place, the 8th day of July. Commissioners: William Prior of Saint Olaves of Pryngfield, Robert Bruster, amd Hamfride Yarmouth [*sic*]. Richard Sampson, Dean. (Court of Requests, Bundle 12, No. 77, preserved in the Public Record Office, London.)

[This case should be compared with the statements about the will, family, executors, etc., of John Leeke of Beccles given in the REGISTER, vol. 89, pp. 334–339 (October 1935), the reader keeping in mind the fact that Robert Peck, one of the executors of the will of John Leeke, should probably be regarded as a grandson, rather than a nephew, of John Leeke. See Editorial Note in REGISTER, vol. 91, p. 7 (January 1937).* The records of this case have been given here chiefly because they show that John Leeke was a tanner.—EDITOR.]

[To be continued]

*Page 563, this volume.

# GENEALOGICAL RESEARCH IN ENGLAND

Communicated by the Committee on English and Foreign Research

## THE GURDON FAMILY

Contributed by G. Andrews Moriarty, A.M., LL.B., F.S.A.,
of Bristol, R. I.

### From Court Rolls of Dedham, co. Essex

Records of the Duchy of Lancaster
[Series 30, Bundle 59, Roll 735]
(Concluded)

Dedham Campsea. Monday Feast of St. Edmund,* King and Martyr, 23 Henry VIII [1531].

Robert Went, junior, in a plea of trespass against John Weye, junior. They submit to the arbitration of Thomas Botour and John Warner on behalf of Robert Went, John Gurdon and Robert Cradock on behalf of John Weye.

John Gurdon is of the inquest.

Jurors say that John Gurdon present in court surrendered a parcel of a barn with a garner, tiled (½ rood), late of William Snowe in Dedham (which the same John Gurdon took up jointly with John Milis, son of Robert Milis, surviving, and John Thorn, deceased, to

_____
* The Feast of St. Edmund falls on 20 November.

625

the use of John Thorn and his heirs as appears Monday after St. Edward,* 18 Henry VIII [1527], to the use of William Thorn, his son, in accordance with John Thorn's will.   (m. 40.)

Court held there, Monday before St. Martin the Bishop,† 25 Henry VIII [1533].   Inquest included John Gurdon.   (m. 40ᵈ.)

Manors of Overhall and Netherhall in Dedham.   First Court of Sir Humphrey Wyngfield.   Tuesday, 16 July, 29 Henry VIII [1537]. Attornment of tenants, bond and free.   No Gurdon; but Thomas Butter.   (m. 42.)

Overhall and Netherhall in Dedham.   Court held Monday, 6 May, 30 Henry VIII [1537].
Inquest includes John Gurdon.
At this court comes Robert Gurdon and shows a charter dated Thursday after St. Martin the Bishop,† 16 Henry VIII [1524], being his copy for a piece of bondland built upon, containing 1 rood, parcel of seven crofts of tenement Bluntes.   (m. 42ᵈ.)

Overhall and Netherhall in Dedham.   Court held 16 April, 30 Henry VIII [1539].   Jurors present that Robert Petywell died and had surrendered (*inter alia*) a parcel of land of the demesnes (10 acres) held by fee farm of 3s. 4d. and ½ acre of meadow by fee farm of 2s., formerly of Robert Gurdon, to the use of his wife.   (m. 43ᵈ.)

Overhall and Netherhall in Dedham.   Court general held 27 April, 34 Henry VIII [1542].   The jurors present that John Gurdon ought to pay 8d. a year for a parcel of land next his 'le beverpytts.' (m. 47.)

Court held Tuesday Eve of St. Luke,‡ 34 Henry VIII [1542]. Recites entry above as to lands of Robert Petywell and that his wife Rose is dead; now Thomas Petwell, younger son of said Robert, comes in person, and John Petwell, the elder son, comes by John Gordon his attorney, and they are admitted.   (m. 47ᵈ.)

Overhall and Netherhall in Dedham.   Court held Tuesday after St. Faith,§ 31 Henry VIII [1539].

Essoins: John Gordon by Richard Lawrons [*sic*].   At this court comes John Gordon in person [*sic*] and surrenders the greater part of a meadow called Broke medowe (6 acres) to the use of Richard Lawrence; who is admitted and fines 5s.   (m. 50ᵈ.)

Same Court.   Homage present that it was found at the last court‖ that John Sander had sold to John Gourdon 1 acre meadow in le Lady Meadow, formerly of William Chandeler and before that of John Crane; and that John Gourdon, being present in court, the lord of his special grace granted the said meadow to the same John Gordon his heirs and assigns to held by the rod.   Note that it is of the demesnes.   (m. 51.)

* The Feast of St. Edward the King and Confessor falls on 18 March.
† The Feast of St. Martin the Bishop falls on 11 November.
‡ The Feast of St. Luke the Evangelist falls on 18 October.
§ The Feast of St. Faith falls on 6 October.
‖ No entry appears in that court.

Overhall and Netherhall. Court held Tuesday after St. Mark,* 37 Henry VIII. Essoins: John Gurdon by Richard Lawrence. (m. 51ᵈ.)

Overhall and Netherhall. Attornment of tenants and first court of Robert Wingfield, Esq., son of Sir Humphrey, 30 March, 37 Henry VIII [1546].
Attornment of tenants. No Gurdon here or among essoins. (m. 52ᵈ.)

Same Court. The jurors say that Robert Gurdon [sic], bond tenant, died since the last court [i.e., since Tuesday before St. Luke,† 37 Henry VIII [1546]] and before his death had surrendered by the hands of John Rande in the presence of John Gurdon and Richard Clarke a cottage, with one rood of land, late called Tomsons in Dedham, to the use of Olive, his wife, for her life and after her death to Richard Gordon [sic], his son, and his heirs and assigns. Livery to said Olive. She fines 3s. 4d. Marginal reference to 16 Henry VIII [1524–25]. (m. 53.)

Overhall and Netherhall. Thursday after the Annunciation,‡ 1 Edward VI [1547].
Jurors say that John Gurdon, bond tenant, out of court surrendered by the hands of John Sopham in presence of Richard Lawrence and John Mynott a pasture called Swetemanesye (3 acres) held by 7s. a year, a pasture called Mellefen (8 acres), by 13s. 4d. a year, which he took up of the lady, Monday before St. Edward,§ 12 Henry VIII [1521], to the use of William Litlebury who is admitted and fines 6s. 8d. (m. 54ᵈ.)

Dedham Hall. Court with View of frankpledge of Anne of Cleves, Friday after All Saints,‖ 36 Henry VIII [1544].
Now concerning the court [Baron]. At this court John Gurdon and others (named), who are suitors in default, are pardoned because they did not have notice. (m. 2.)

Dedham. View of frankpledge of Anne of Cleves, Thursday after All Saints,‖ 36 Henry VIII [1544].
John Gurdon pardoned as above, as he had not notice.
Thomas Butter lies sick (infirmus), therefore pardoned his absence.
Ordered that John Gurdon scour his ditch at Cancellors as far as the land of Margaret Clerk and Grace Smyth, on pain of 3s. 4d., and his ditch towards the highway next his field called le Teyntourfeld opposite the house of Richard Lawrence, on pain of 4s.; and that Thomas Butter should set at large (ponend ad largu) the highway in le Hawle Feld as freely and in as good condition as it was, on pain of £4. (m. 3.)

* The Feast of St. Mark falls on 25 April.
† The Feast of St. Luke the Evangelist falls on 18 October.
‡ The Feast of the Annunciation of the Blessed Virgin falls on 25 March.
§ The Feast of St. Edward the King and Confessor falls on 18 March.
‖ The Feast of All Saints falls on 1 November.

Dedham. View of frankpledge with Court, 13 April, 37 Henry VIII [1546]. [Under the court baron.]

This court is informed as well by Edward Reynold gent., the lady's bailiff, as by William Cardon, deputy bailiff, and by testimony of divers credible persons, that William Budd and John Gurdon, who hold jointly to them and their heirs, among other things, 3 roods of meadow next the tenement of John Soffham for the fulfilment of the will of Stephen Dunton, deceased, have withholden the rent from the lady these two years and still refuse to pay it; therefore the bailiff is ordered to seize the meadow; and the steward at the special instance of John Soffham, and by advice of Thomas Carewe, Esq., who pays the lady a sum of money, delivers the same to Soffham his heirs and assigns, at 1d. a year, to perform the will of Stephen Dunton. (m. 4.)

Dedham. View of frankpledge of Anne of Cleves, Tuesday after St. Barnabas,* 37 Henry VIII [1545]. Essoins: John Gurdon by John Vygerous. (m. 5.)

Dedham. Court held there Tuesday after Whitsunday, 1 Henry VIII [1509]. Inquest includes John Gurdon. (m. 1.)

Dedham. Leet held there Tuesday after Whitsunday, 1 Henry VIII [1509]. Capital pledges include John Gurdon. (m. 2.)

Dedham. Leet held there Wednesday in Whitweek, 3 Henry VIII [1511]. The capital pledges choose John Smart "barbour" and John Gurdun to be constables for two years to come; they are sworn. (m. 4.)

Dedham. Leet held there Tuesday after Whitsunday,† 4 [sic] Henry VIII [1512]. Capital pledges include John Gurdon. (m. 5.) [On the dorse is leet for Tuesday after dominicam in Albis 6 Henry VIII [1514]. No Gurdon.]

Dedham. Court with leet held there, Wednesday in the week of Pentecost, 4 [sic] Henry VIII [1512]. Capital pledges include John Gurdon; he is also of the inquest, and one of the affeerees. Ordered that John Gurdon scour his beuerdycke and his ditch towards le Hooyate. (m. 6.)

Dedham. Court held there Wednesday in the week of Pentecost, 6 Henry VIII [1514]. John Gurdon essoined of the common suit by Robert Cradok. (m. 8.)

Dedham. Leet held there Tuesday after dominicam in Albis, 6 Henry VIII [1514]. John Gurdon one of the capital pledges. (m. 9.)

Dedham. Leet held there Tuesday after dominicam in Albis, 8 Henry VIII [1516]. John Gurdon one of the capital pledges. (m. 9.)

* The Feast of St. Barnabas falls on 11 June.
† Dominicam in Albis. The copyist mistook this phrase for Whitsunday throughout these records. The date is the Octave of Easter.

Dedham.   Court held there Wednesday in the week of Pentecost, 7 Henry VIII [1515].   John Gurdon essoined.   (m. 10.)

Dedham.   Court held there Wednesday in the week of Pentecost, 8 Henry VIII [1516].   John Gurdon is of the inquest.   (m. 10.)

Dedham.   Court held there Wednesday in the week of Pentecost, 10 Henry VIII [1518].   John Gurdon is of the inquest.   (m. 11.)

Same Court.   They present that Stephen Dunton on his deathbed surrendered by the hands of Robert Pettewell, by testimony of James Revet, bailiff, and Robert Cradok, nine cottages and one rood of land, formerly of James Aleyn and late of William Smart, and a piece of meadow, enclosed, in Dedham (1½ acres), late of Isabel Woodgate, and ½ acre of customary meadow in Dedham which he took up in the court Wednesday in the week of Pentecost, 17 Henry VII to the use of William Clerke, William Budde and John Gurdon, his executors, to fulfil his will. They are delivered seisin and fine 12d. (m. 11ᵈ.)

Dedham.   Court held there Wednesday in the week of Pentecost, 11 Henry VIII [1519].

At this court came John Coppyn, warden of the Guild of St. Nicholas in Dedham, William Clerke,——— Lufkyn, John Gurdon, Robert Cradok, John Pynkemell, John Smarte, and William Woodehows, brethren (*confratres*) of the same Guild, and sold and surrendered into the lady's hand one acre of land, parcel of Chesehowsfeld, late in the tenure of Robert Fynche, to the use of Robert Petewell who is admitted and fines 8d.   (m. 12.)

Dedham.   Leet held there Tuesday after Dominicam in Albis, 11 Henry VIII.   John Gurdon amerced 3d. for default of suit at the leet.   (m. 12ᵈ.)

Dedham.   View of frankpledge, Tuesday after Dominicam in Albis, 14 Henry VIII.

Order to John Gurdon to scour 10 perches of ditch lying towards the highway from Dedham to Colchester before the Invention of Holy Cross on pain of 6s. 8d.   (m. 15.)

Dedham.   Court held there Wednesday in Pentecost Week, 14 Henry VIII [1522].   Inquest includes John Gurdon.

The homage find that Isabella Harre and Margaret Harre, who held of the Queen* to them and their heirs in copartnership (in copcen ia) after the custom of the manor together with Katherine Gurdon, now wife of Robert Gurdon, 2 crofts of bond land and one little grove called le Haye, by the death of Robert Harre as cousins (*consanguinee*) and heirs of the said Robert Harre have died since the last court† seized of such estate.   And that Katherine Gurdon is their sister and next heir and of full age.   Now come Robert Gurdon and Katherine, his wife, as in her right, and crave to be admitted

* Katherine, Queen of England, lady of the manor (see m. 17).

† A leet (only) was held Tuesday after Dominicam in Albis, 14 Henry VIII (m. 15); m. 14, a court of which the heading has gone; m. 13, a court held Wednesday in Pentecost week, 12 Henry VIII.

629

to the said ⅔ of the crofts and hay, and are admitted to them and the heirs and assigns of Katherine. They fine 6d. Afterwards they come into court in person and surrender to the Queen, who regrants to them and their heirs and assigns; they fine 8d. and Robert hath done fealty. (m. 16.)

View of frankpledge of Queen Katherine, Tuesday after Sunday in Albis, viz. 29 April, 14 Henry VIII [1522]. [Tuesday after Sunday the Octave of Easter or Hock Tuesday.] (m. 17.)

Dedham. Court held there Wednesday in the week of Pentecost, 16 Henry VIII [1524]. Inquest includes John Gurdon. (m. 19.)

Dedham. View of frankpledge, Tuesday after dominicam in Albis, 16 Henry VIII. Capital pledges include John Gurdon. (m. 20.)

Dedham. Court held there Wednesday in the week of Pentecost, 17 Henry VIII [1525].
At this court the Queen [lady of manor] granted to John Gurdon a piece of meadow, 3 perches by 2 perches, within le lordys medowe at the south end thereof and abutting upon Westfeld; to hold to him his heirs and assigns, by the rod. He hath done fealty and fined 4d.

Dedham. View of frankpledge, Tuesday, the feast of St. Mark,* 17 Henry VIII [1525]. Capital pledges include John Gurdon. (m. 21.)

Dedham. Court General, Wednesday in the week of Pentecost, 18 Henry VIII [1526]. Homage include John Gurdon. (m. 22.)

Dedham. View of frankpledge, Tuesday after dominicam in Albis, 18 Henry VIII. Capital pledges include John Gurdon. (m. 23.)

Dedham. View of frankpledge, Tuesday, 30 April, 19 Henry VIII [1527]. Capital pledges with homage include John Gurdon. (m. 24.)

Dedham. Court held there Wednesday in Pentecost Week, 19 Henry VIII [1527]. Homage includes John Gurdon.
At this court comes John Gurdon and alienates, sells, and surrenders 2 acres bondland enclosed with a cottage built thereon, formerly of Henry Vyne, 2 crofts of land called Stansworth (3 acres), one piece of bondland, parcel of Bowere tenement (1 acre enclosed) in Dedham to the use of John Coole and wife, Joan, their heirs and assigns. (m. 25.)

Dedham. Court held there Wednesday in Pentecost Week, 20 Henry VIII [1528].
Homage. 45 names of whom 16 are sworn. John Gurdon sworn.
Robert Cradok surrenders a croft (2 acres) and 1 piece of land, late grove now arable, called Bowyere and the greater part of a lane,

* The Feast of St. Mark falls on 25 April.

parcel of 13 acres, late of Robert Cranefen to the use of John Gurdon, paying 10d. yearly to said Cradok.

John Gurdon comes and surrenderes a barn (?) (*grangiam*)* with all the land between the running water and the said "*grangiam*" (½ rood) called Bowyere in Dedham, with an entry way at le Hogate and so going to the said "*grangiam*" [barn] to the use of Robert Cradok. (m. 26.)

Same court. Robert Cradok comes and shows a copy of the court Tuesday after Pentecost, 21 Henry VIII [1529], whereby Robert Cranefen surrendered a barn (*grangiam*), etc., called Bowyere (as above) to the use of John Gurdon† and his heirs. (m. 27.)

Dedham. View of frankpledge Tuesday, 6 April, 20 Henry VIII [1528]. Order to Widow More to scour her ditch between her house towards [*sic*] Robert Gurdon. (m. 28.)

Dedham. View of frankpledge Tuesday, 26 April, 22 Henry VIII [1530].

"It is commaunded to the bailly to warne John Warner, Robert Cradok, John Gurdon" and seven others (named) "to make and every of them to make a sufficient beverpitt and them alweise to kepe sufficiently clene and scoured so that they kepe the past and the thik bevere oute and from the broke there before the feast of Whitsontide next" on pain of 40s. each. (m. 29.)

Dedham. Court held there Wednesday in Pentecost Week, 22 Henry VIII [1530]. Homage:—John Gurdon, named but not sworn. (m. 29.)

John Thorne comes and surrenders a messuage called Holtys and 10 acres of customary land in Dedham to the use of Thomas Levows *alias* Lewes, Robert Gurdon, the son of John Gurdon, Thomas Clerk, the son of William Clerk, and Bartholomew Luffekyn, junior, their heirs and assigns, on condition that if Thomas Lewis pay £20 at Pentecost next and £3. 6s. 8d. at Pentecost following, the surrender shall be of effect. (m. 29ᵈ.)

Dedham. View of frankpledge Tuesday, 22 April, 24 Henry VIII [1532]. Capital pledges include John Gurdon. (m. 33.)

Dedham. Court held there Wednesday in Pentecost Week, 26 Henry VIII [1534]. Homage includes John Gurdon.

Thomas Knappe and wife, Agnes, surrender a messuage and 15 acres of land to the use of John Gurdon, reserving to Agnes a parlour with a chamber and half the fruit in the orchard, with the occupation of 2 crofts, and on condition John Gurdon pays her 10s. a year for life. Gurdon thereupon surrenders to the use of Thomas Birchett, John Cole and Thomas Levous. (m. 25ᵈ.)

Dedham. View of frankpledge Tuesday, 6 April, 26 Henry VIII [1534]. Capital pledges include John Gurdon. (m. 36.)

---

* Possibly a marsh, or a groin.
† Does not say the "said John Gurdon."

Dedham.   Court held there Wednesday in Pentecost Week, 27 Henry VIII [1535].   Inquest includes John Gurdon.   (m. 36.)

View of frankpledge held there Monday after Dominicam in Albis, 28 Henry VIII.

Capital pledges include John Gurdon.   (m. 37.)

Dedham.   Court held there Monday after Ascension, 29 Henry VIII [1537].   John Gurdon amerced 6d. for not warranting his essoin at the last court.   (m. 38.)

Dedham.   Court held there Tuesday after Exaltation of the Holy Cross,* 29 Henry VIII [1537].   Homage includes John Gurdon. (m. 38ᵈ.)

Dedham.   Court General held Wednesday after Epiphany,† 29 Henry VIII [1538].   Homage includes John Jurdon.

John Jurdon, present, surrenders a piece of meadow, 3 perches by 2 perches, between (*inter*) the meadow called Lords Meadow, to the intent that the lord should regrant to the same John Jurdon and Alice, his wife, and the heirs of John.   (m. 39.)

Thomas Botor, present, surrenders 4 acres of meadow, parcel of le lords meadow, which is regranted to him his heirs and assigns.   (m. 39ᵈ.)

Dedham.   First Court of King Henry VIII, Wednesday after St. John the Baptist,‡ 31 Henry VIII [1539].

All free, bond and leasehold tenants attorn, including John Gurdon, who appears and is also sworn of the homage.   Thomas Boter is destrained to appear.   (m. 40.)

[To be continued]

---

* The Feast of the Exaltation of the Holy Cross falls on 14 September.
† The Feast of the Epiphany falls on 6 January.
‡ The feast of St. John the Baptist falls on 24 June.

# GENEALOGICAL RESEARCH IN ENGLAND

Communicated by the Committee on English and Foreign Research

## THE ENGLISH ANCESTRY OF JOSEPH PECK, OF HINGHAM, MASS., IN 1638

Compiled by S. ALLYN PECK, B.A., of New York City, and contributed by
FREDERICK STANHOPE PECK, LL.D., of Barrington, R. I.

DEPOSITION OF JOHN WATERS OF BECCLES, CO. SUFFOLK,
DESCRIBING THE MARRIAGE OF THOMAS DRAWER
AND KATHERINE LEEK

IN the last preceding instalment of this article, which appeared
in the REGISTER of April 1939, records of the Court of Requests were
given (*supra*, page 178) pertaining to the case of Robert Young *v.*\*\*
Robert Peck and Katherine Drawer, wife of Thomas Drawer.
Robert Young sought to recover from Robert Peck and Katherine
Drawer, who were executors of the will of John Leek of Beccles, co.
Suffolk, tanner, an unpaid balance due for the sale of hides to said
John Leek. Below is given a deposition of John Waters of Beccles,
who was the father of the second wife of the said Robert Peck, the
first Robert Peck of Beccles, and according to this deposition was
born about 1490.

John Waters, of Beccles, resident there since birth; aged 40 years; [deposed
that he] had known Thomas Drawer for one year and more, and Katherine
Leek since her birth. Dated: 26 July 1530.

[Deponent] Saith that in the Feast of St. Mar^te last past in the house of
John Leek at Beccles in the present [*sic*] of John Leek, Kateryne Leek, and
Thomas Drawer and others, this Deponent heard the said Thomas say:
"Masters this is the cause that ye be called for hither at this time for to witness of a contract betwixt Kat: Leek and me," and then the said Thomas said
to the said Kateryne Leek: "I trust ye be the same woman that ye have been
in times past;" the said Kateryn saying: "Yeh!" then he took her by the hand
and said; "I Thomas take you Kat. to my wife, and I plight ye my troth"; the
said Kateryn saying in like wise to him; "I Kateryn take you Thomas to my
husband, and that I plight you my troth"; there being also present, Osbert
Dering, and Richard James. There was no blood relationship between the
said Thomas and Kateryn. . . . (Norwich Diocesan Records, Evidence
Book 1518–1530, folio 323 a.) *

* It is difficult to fix the exact date of the marriage of Thomas Drawer and Katherine Leek described above, because of the uncertainty as to who the saint ("St. Mar^te") was on whose Feast,
"last past," the marriage took place, for the saint's name may have been copied incorrectly by the
person who copied this deposition of John Waters. The will of John Leeke of Beccles, co. Suffolk,
England, Diocese of Norwich, an abstract of which was given in the first instalment of this article \*\*\*
(REGISTER, vol. 89, pp. 334–335, October 1935), was dated 6 September 1529, and that his daughter
Katherine was then unmarried is evident by his bequest to her of £40, "to be paid on the day of her
marriage." The deposition of John Waters, dated 26 July 1530, shows that the marriage took place
in the house of John Leek at Beccles and in the present [*sic*, ? presence] of John Leek and others.
The Feast of Martinianus, Bishop, fell on 12 September, that of Matthæus, Apostle and Evangelist,
on 21 September, that of Marcus, Pope, on 7 October, that of Martinus Turonensis, Bishop and
Confessor (St. Martin of Tours) on 11 November, and that of Martinus, Pope and Confessor, on 12
November; but no one of these Feasts can be identified with certainty as the Feast on which the
\*\*See p. 624, this volume.
\*\*\*See pp. 530-531, this volume.

## INVESTIGATIONS REGARDING THE EARLY HOME
## OF THE FIRST ROBERT PECK OF BECCLES

That the first Robert Peck of Beccles, one of the two executors of the will of John Leek of Beccles, was not a native of Beccles, but had taken up his residence there about 1525, is proved by his deposition, dated 23 May 1537, in a case concerning the testament of John Coke, late of Beccles, deceased.

In this case " Robert Were, of Beccles, where he had lived since birth, of the age of 60 years, of free condition, sworn and examined, saith:
"That John Coke desired Sir John Burton one of his executors to write his Will which the said John did and which testament was read openly in the presence of this Deponent, Roberte Peke, Thomas Murdocke, John Cane, and Robert Coke, who were present the same time. The testament now exhibited agrees in every thing with the Testament then read to this Deponent. And more he cannot Depose."
"Robert Pecke, of Beccles, where he had resided for 12 years, of free condition, saith he has known testator and executor for seven years. Duly sworn and examined he saith that the Testament then exhibited agrees in everything with the Testament read to him." (Causes Ecclesiastical, Diocese of Norwich, year 1537, folio 150.)

This first Robert Peck of Beccles, who in 1537 deposed that he had resided in Beccles for twelve years, probably was related to the Peck families of Halesworth and Southelmham, co. Suffolk. He married twice. His first wife was a daughter of Walter Norton of Halesworth, and Walter Norton was a native of one of the Southelmhams, namely, Southelmham St. Margaret, and was therefore connected with the only two places, Halesworth and the Southelmhams, in Suffolk, in the environs of Beccles, in which Peck families resided at that time and had resided for generations past. Before Robert Peck went to Beccles, it is likely that he was known to Walter Norton, who in the lay subsidy in Suffolk in 1524 was taxed at Halesworth in goods [valued at] £20. The names "Richard Pek" and "Maryon Pek" also are found at Halesworth in this subsidy. In the same subsidy, at Southelmham St. Margaret, Walter Norton was taxed in lands [valued at] £1. 13s. 4d., while at Southelmham St. James William Pek was taxed in goods [valued] at £9. 3s. 4d. and Robert Pek in goods [valued at] £2. (Suffolk Green Books, vol. 10.) Whether the last-mentioned Robert Pek was identical with the first Robert Peck of Beccles is unknown; but in 3 Edward VI, 14 March 1549/50, mention is made of three acres of land and pasture, in Southelmham St. James, in the tenure of Robert Pecke and Anne Carre, widow. (Calendar of Patent Rolls, Edward VI, vol. 2, p. 278.) The first Robert Peck of Beccles may have held lands in Southelmham St. James or elsewhere long after he settled at Beccles about 1525; but, if he held such lands as late as March

marriage of Thomas Drawer and Katherine Leek took place, and the last two Feasts came so late as hardly to allow time enough to elapse between the death of John Leek and the proving of his will on 17 November. Perhaps John Leek, foreseeing his approaching death, desired that the marriage should take place while he was still living.

1549/50, he probably disposed of them before his death seven years later.*

The name of the first Robert Peck of Beccles does not, of course, appear under Beccles in the subsidy of 1524, for he was not then a resident of Beccles. Since, however, he was living in Beccles as early as 1525 and in 1529 was one of the executors of the will of John Leek, it is evident that he was then a man of mature years, and, considering the tender years at that time of the children of John Peck of Wakefield, co. York, Esq., who died in 1559, that he was not a son of John Peck of Wakefield by his wife Joan Anne.

Probably this first Robert Peck of Beccles was born in the vicinity of Beccles. The surname is common both to Norfolk and to Suffolk from a very early date. The lay subsidy tax for Suffolk for 1524, as already stated, is in print (in volume 10 of the Suffolk Green Books), and with this as a guide it is possible to enumerate all the Peck families living at this time in Suffolk, in the neighborhood of Beccles. Beccles, however, lies on the Waveney River, which separates Norfolk from Suffolk, and the list of the Peck families residing in the neighborhood of Beccles but across the Waveney in Norfolk must remain incomplete until a lay subsidy for Norfolk of the same period has been examined. It is evident, nevertheless, that the Pecks in that section of Norfolk, near Beccles, were not very prolific, as no testators of the name have been found there in the records of the Norfolk probate courts.

[To be continued]

## JOAN (SAVAGE) EARL, OF NEWPORT, R. I.

Contributed by G. Andrews Moriarty, A.M., LL.B., F.S.A.,
of Bristol, R. I.

Hon. Samuel Sewall (1652–1730) of Boston, Mass., jurist and diarist, writes in his diary under the date of 15 Sept. 1699: "Mr. Newton and I ride to Newport [R.I.], see aged Joan Savage, (now Earl), by the way. Her husband, Ralph Earl, was born 1606. and his wife was 10. or 11 years older than he. So she is esteemed to be hundred and five years old."

The following records, taken from the Registers of Widford Parish, co. Herts, England, deal with Joan (Savage) Earl† and members of

---

* Halesworth is a market town in Suffolk, about eight miles south from Beccles and slightly west of a line drawn due south from that place. Southelmham St. James lies about five miles to the northwest from Halesworth and about nine miles in a southwesterly direction from Beccles. The lands of Walter Norton were in the parish of Southelmham St. Margaret, which adjoins the parish of Southelmham St. James. In an editorial statement about Halesworth and some of the neighboring parishes, published in an earlier instalment of this article (REGISTER, vol. 91, p. 11, January 1937), ** the parish of Halesworth is described as the home of the Norton family, to which the first wife of the first Robert Peck of Beccles belonged, and as situated in northeastern Suffolk, on the River Blyth.

† Ralph Earl married Joan Savage 29 June 1631 at Bishop's Stortford, co. Herts, England. (See "Earl Family of Bishop's Stortford, co. Herts, England," in *The New York Genealogical and Biographical Record*, vol. 67 (1936). pp. 390-393.)

**Page 567, this volume.

her family, and show that her reputed age was not correct.　Records of baptisms (1562–1626), marriages (1558–1625), and burials (1558–1650) were examined.

## Baptisms

1585　　Mary, daughter of Thomas and Mary Isacke, 11 July.
1586/7　Thomas and William, Twins of Thomas and Mary Isacke, 29 January.
1592　　John, son of Thomas and Mary Isake, 3 December.
1598/9　Daniel, son of Thomas and Mary Isake, 21 January.
1600　　Ric., son of Ric. Savage, 19 October.
1602　　Elizabeth, daughter of Ric. Savage, 19 December.
1607　　Ric., son of Ric. Savage, 12 April.
1609/10　Joan, daughter of Ric. Savage, 18 February.

## Burials

1598　　William, son of Thomas and Mary Isacke, 10 October.
1598　　Thomas Isacke, 22 October.
1602　　Ric., son of Ric. Savage, 25 September.
1625/6　Ric., son of Ric. Savage, 18 March.
1636　　Mary, wife of Ric. Savage, 5 May.
1637　　Ric. Savage, 17 December.

## Marriages

1599/1600　Ric. Savidg and Mary Isake widow, 14 January.
1608/9　William Crofte and Ellenor Savage, 30 January.

# GENEALOGICAL RESEARCH IN ENGLAND

Communicated by the Committee on English and Foreign Research

## THE ENGLISH ANCESTRY OF JOSEPH PECK, OF HINGHAM, MASS., IN 1638

Compiled by S. ALLYN PECK, B.A., of New York City, and contributed by
FREDERICK STANHOPE PECK, LL.D., of Barrington, R. I.

IN the first installment of this article (vol. 89, pp. 327–339, October 1935) abstracts of records were given (on pp. 336–337) relating to the suit in Chancery brought about 1530 by Katherine Drawer *

*For pp. 336-337 see pp. 532-533, this volume.

(daughter of John Leek of Beccles, co. Suffolk, deceased) and her husband, Thomas Drawer, against the first Robert Peck of Beccles, who was one of the two executors of the will of the said John Leek, the other executor being the above-named Katherine Drawer. In his will, dated 6 September 1529, John Leek called Robert Peck his "neve," a word which the compiler of this article interpreted as meaning "nephew" in the modern sense of the word, but which, according to G. Andrews Moriarty, A.M., LL.B., F.S.A., Chairman of the Committee on English and Foreign Research of the New England Historic Genealogical Society, should have been interpreted as "grandson," its usual meaning at that period. (See REGISTER, vol. 91, p. 7, January 1937.) * A few years before his death the first Robert Peck of Beccles was one of the defendants in another suit in Chancery, brought by one William Rede of Beccles against John Waters, father of Robert Peck's second wife, and Robert Peck himself. Below is given the Bill of Complaint in this suit, in so far as possible in its original form and spelling. Although this Bill of Complaint is undated, it is addressed to the Right Honorable Sir Thomas Wryothesley, who was appointed Lord Chancellor of England on 3 May 1544, in the reign of Henry VIII, and ceased to be Lord Chancellor on 5 March 1546/7, when the great seal was taken from him. He never was Lord Chancellor again, although he was readmitted for a while to the Privy Council; and therefore the following Bill of Complaint must have been addressed to the Lord Chancellor not earlier than 3 May 1544 and not later than about 5 March 1546/7. It is, of course, conceivable that a complainant, not knowing that Lord Chancellor Wryothesley had been deprived of the Chancellorship, might have addressed a Bill of Complaint to him after 5 March 1546/7. Lord Chancellor Wryothesley (or Wriothesley) was born 21 December 1505 and died 30 July 1550, in the reign of King Edward VI. A full account of the career of this notorious and unscrupulous man may be found in the great English "Dictionary of National Biography," under "Wriothesley, Sir Thomas."

The Bill of Complaint in the case of Rede v. Waters and Peck is an interesting old document, which, unfortunately, in many places has crumbled to pieces or is illegible, and is very difficult to read. One William Robard [sic, ? Roberts] of Beccles and Robert Peck were churchwardens of Beccles at the time of this dispute about the custody of the property of St. Michael's Gild in Beccles, and John Waters, father-in-law of Robert Peck, was one of the aldermen of the Gild.

[Rede v. Waters and Peck, not dated]

To the Right honorable Syr Thomas Wryothe[crumbled] Knygh[t] lord Wryothesley and lord Chauncello$^r$ of England.

In his most humble wyse sheweth & compleynythe vnto yo$^r$ good lordshyp your dayly supplyant & orato$^r$ Wyllm Rede of Becclys in the County of Suffolke That where ys [crumbled, ? whereas yo$^r$] sayd supplyant & other Inhabitants of the sayd Town of Becclys beyng aldermen of a s'teyn [i.e., certain] Gylde in Becclys aforesayde called Seynt Mychellys Gyld ware seasyd to the

*Page 563, this volume.

vse [*sic*] Gyld of [*crumbled*] beyng the hole stocke of the sayd Gylde and also of
[*illegible*] belongying to [*crumbled*] of the sayd Goodys to the vse aforesayd
delyuyd the sayd Goodys sayfe vnto one John Waters of Becclys aforesayd
shomaker yett beyng in [*illegible*] lyf & to one Robard ffrancys of [*crumbled*]
aldermen to the sayd Gylde then newe electyd & Chosyn and for [*crumbled*] of
the sayd mony & Goods the sayd John Waters & Rbd ffrancys wer bound vnto
yor sayd [*crumbled*] aldermen of the sayd Gylde whoos Namys yor sayd supplyant dothe not Remember in a s'teyn [i.e., certain] booke of Rekenyng
[*illegible*] to the sayd Gylde wherein the sayd [*illegible*] is contaynyd [*crumbled*]
sayd boke was delyuyd vnto one Willm Robard of Becclys aforsayd one of the
aldermen of the sayd Gyld he beyng one of the Chyrchewardyngᵉ of Becclys
aforesayd wythe one Robard Pecke [*illegible*] kepe to the vse of yor sayd suppliant Thomas [*sic*] Rede & other aldermen In[ha]bitants of the sayd Towne to
the entent the sayd mony goods should be wele & [*crumbled*] Rede & other att a
s'teyn [i.e., certain] daye by them appoyntyd wyche daye w'out syght of the
sayd booke yor sayd Orator dothe nor can not Remember and for the suer
kepyng of the sayd booke [*crumbled*] or hows called the vestry in the sayd
Chyrche the sayd Robd Pecke hauyng a kye to the dore of the sayd vestry So
it is good lord that the same Robd Peck of his [*crumbled*] [*illegible*] the sayd
John Waters for that he maryed his doughter wythout the assent or knowlege
of the sayd Wyllm Robard the same Wyllm beyng [*crumbled*] att [*crumbled*]
awaye the sayd boke ffrom the possession of the same Wyllm Robard to
thentent to defraude yor sayd supplyant & other aldermen Inh[ab]itants of the
sayd [*crumbled*] from [*crumbled*] the same boke vnto the sayd John Waters who
hathe delyued the same booke out of his possession & custody to whom yor
sayd suppliant knowyth not (By Reason whereof [*crumbled*] allso the sayd
stuffe vtenstyles & goods of the sayd Gylde to his owne vse contr[ar]y to the
confydens & truste that was put vnto hym & contr[ar]y to all Ryght & good
confydns and for asmoche as ys sayd [*crumbled*] was chefly put in truste for to
receyve the sayd mony & vtensalys of the same John Waters & Robd ffranceys
to the vse of the sayd aldermen & other Inh[ab]itants of the sayd town of
Becclys [*illegible*] not [*illegible*] have any p[ar]te or p'cell of the sayd mony
vtensyles & stuffe before declaryd to his owne vse but onely to the vse of the
Inh[ab]ytants of sayd town of Becclys and for asmoche as yor sayd Supplyant
dothe not know the sume s'teyn [i.e., certain] of the sayd mony nor yett the
s'tayn [i.e., certain] nomber of the sayd Pewter brasse Pottys pannys ketylls
speats & other soundry vtensyles & stuffe nor also to whom he shuld resorte
for the [*illegible*] of the sayd boke wyche [*illegible*] the s'teynty [i.e., certainty] of
the vtensyles & mony before [*illegible*] yor sayd orator is w'out Remady by the
order of the Commyn Lawe onlesse yor Good lordeshyppe save [*sic*] to hym be
shewyd in this behalf & Consyderacon where it maye please yor sayd good
lordeshyp the p'missez tenderly consyderyd to g'nnte [i.e., grant] the Kyngs
most gracyous Wrytte of Suppena to be dyrectyd aswell vnto the sayd Rbd
Peck to shawe why he convayd awaye the say[d]e booke and who hathe nowe
the kepyng of the sayd boke as to the sayd John Waters for what cause he
deteynyth the sayd mony vtensyles stuffe & goodes comandyng them &
either of them p[er]sonally to apeare before the Kyng in his moste hon'able
court of Chansery at a s'teyn [i.e., certain] daye be yt [by] yor Good lordshyp
assynd & appoyntyd Then & theare to answer to the p'missz and ffurther be
orderyd therin as your Good lordshyp shall thyncke to seend wythe Ryght &
Good consyence and you[r] sayd supplyant shall dayly praye to God for the
psp'erous astate of you[r] sayd Good lordshyp longe to [*illegible*]. (Early
Chancery Proceedings, 1544–1553, file 1155, no. 17, in the Public Record
Office, London.)*

[To be continued]

* Further information about this suit in Chancery is lacking.

# THE GURDON FAMILY

Contributed by G. Andrews Moriarty, A.M., LL.B., F.S.A.,
of Bristol, R. I.

## From Court Rolls of Dedham, co. Essex.

### Records of the Duchy of Lancaster

#### [Series 30, Bundle 59, Roll 731]

Dedham. [Another tenement] surrendered 3 Henry VII [1487–1488] by John Gurdon to use of his son John and of John, son of said son.

Dedham. 2 & 3 Philip and Mary [1555–1556]. John Gurdon died seised; admission of son John, who surrendered to use of Robert Sterlinge. (f° 6ᵇ.)

Dedham. 2 & 3 Philip and Mary [1555–1556]. John Went, to use of Thomas Butter* and heirs. Thomas died and surrendered to use of John Butter his son and his heirs male, tenement named Brownes. (f° 8.)

Dedham. 5 Elizabeth [1562–1563]. John Butter, to use of Arthur Gylgate. (f° 8.)

#### [Series 30, Bundle 59, Roll 735]

Dedham Campesse. Monday after St. Lucy,† 22 Henry VIII [1530]. John Wente surrendered a messuage, etc., to use of Thomas Botour, admitted. (m. 38ᵈ.)

Dedham Campesse. Monday after All Saints,‡ 22 Henry VIII [1530]. Rph Warner and wife Isabella surrender 1 acre meadow, which they took up jointly with John Cole and Robt. Gurdon son of John Gurdon Tuesday after All Saints, 5 Henry VIII [1513], to use of John Cole. (m. 39.)

#### [Series 30, Bundle 59, Roll 746]

Overhall and Netherhall in Dedham. 12 October, 21 Elizabeth [1579]. John Butter proffered a libel as to claim to lands called Brownes and Cranfens.

#### [Series 30, Bundle 59, Roll 730]

Dedham Campsea.§ List of suitors, viz. common suitors and those who only owe suit at Michaelmas. No Butter included. Robert Gourdon, common suitor, for a messuage formerly of John Perry and Gorys. (m. 14.)

#### [Series 30, Bundle 59, Roll 734]

Dedham. Thursday in Whitweek, 14 Henry VII [1499]. John Gurdon late called John Gurdon junior and Thos. Wodhous come and surrender tenement Knightes to use of Stephen Dunton and wife during the life of the said John Gurdon and of Olive his wife. (?m. 7.)

Dedham. Wednesday in Whitweek, 17 Henry VII [1502]. First Court of the Queen [Elizabeth]. Attornments of tenants include John Gurdon, John Butter. Presentment of death of William Gurdon, junior; his heir is Robert Gurdon his younger brother. (m. 12.)

#### [Series 30, Bundle 60, Roll 736]‖

Dedham. View of frankpledge with Court, Wednesday in Easter Week, 2 Edward VI [1548].

* An account of the Butter family of Dedham, co. Essex, England, compiled by Mr. Moriarty, was printed in the Register, vol. 76 (1922), pp. 278–295. **
† The Feast of St. Lucy falls on 13 December.
‡ The Feast of All Saints falls on 1 November.
§ Undated, probably Henry VI.
‖ Dedham View of frankpledge with Courts Baron, 1 April, 1 Edward VI [1547] onwards. This is a made-up roll and included Stratford, Langham, and Hingham Courts. The whole roll has been remade from scattered membranes.
**See Volume I of this work, pp. 732–749.

Now concerning the Court:

Essoins    Richard Lawrence essoined of the common suit by John Gurdon

The inquest present that John Gurdon out of court and since the last court*
surrendered by the hands of John Soffham, deputy of the bailiff, in the presence of Richard Lawrence and John Mynott, tenants of this manor, one acre
of meadow formerly pasture parcel of Thornett lying in Stratford, having its
west part lying upon the river running between Dedham and Stratford to the
use of William Lyttylbury, who is admitted.    (m. 8.)

Langham.    View of frankpledge with Court, Thursday in Easter Week,
2 Edward VI [1548].    Order to John Gurdon to scour his ditch, 10 perches
long, towards Alens Grove, on pain of 20d.    (m. 8ᵈ.)

Dedham.    View of frankpledge with court, Monday before Easter, 3
Edward VI [1549].    Now concerning the Court:    Inquest of Office includes
Thomas Buttor, sworn.    (m. 10.)

Overhall and Netherhall in Dedham.    Court ‡ held there, Tuesday after
SS. Simon and Jude,† 2 Edward VI [1548].    Inquest of Office: Thomas Buttour, sworn.    (m. 56.)

Dedham    Overhall and Netherhall    Court held there Thursday after St.
Faith,§ 4 Edward VI [1550].

Inquest present that Richard Gurdon, bond-tenant of this manor, hath died
since the last court seised of a cottage and one rood of land late called Thomp-
sons in Dedham.    Bridget and Anne are his daughters and heirs, Bridget
aged 5, Anne aged 2.    They are admitted by Margaret, their mother, who has
seisin during their minority (Marginal reference to 16 Henry VIII [1524–
1525]).

Whereas at the court held here Tuesday after St. Faith,§ 35 Henry VIII
[1543] it was found that John Sawnder had sold to John Gourdon one acre in
le Lady Medowe, formerly of William Chaundeler; now to this court comes
John Sawnder and surrenders the same to the use of John Gourdon, his heirs
and assigns.    John Gourdon comes by John Chandeler his attorney and is
admitted.    Fealty respited to the next court.    (m. 58.)

[Series 30, Bundle 60, Roll 737]

Dedham    Overhall and Netherhall.    Court of Thomas Nevill, knt., farmer
of the said manor, 27 April, 2 & 3 Philip and Mary [1556].

[A]

Order to John Butter or the tenants of the land late of Thomas Rutter
(*sic* Butter) called Brownes to scour 20 perches of ditch towards Walter Ryes
on pain of 6s. 8d.

[A]

The homage present upon their oath that John Gurden, the elder, of Great
Wallyngfeld in the county of Suffolk, gentleman, a bond-tenant of this manor,
before this court and out of court surrendered into the lord's hand by the
hands of John Browne and Richard Wake two customary tenants and of
William Litelberye in the stead of the bailiff a tenement called "his hede-
house" with a parcel of land called Garroldes and one acre lying within the
"said" pasture called Garroldes late of Robert Warners to the use of John
Web of Langham and his heirs for ever.    Web is admitted and fines 13s. 4d.

---

* A court for Overhall and Netherhall in Dedham, later in roll, is dated Tuesday after SS. Simon
and Jude.†
† The Feast of SS. Simon and Jude falls on 28 October.
‡ The "C" has a finely-executed drawing of a man's head, plainly a portrait.
§ The Feast of St. Faith falls on 6 October.

641

## [A]

The homage present that John Gurden the elder of Great Wallyngfeld gentleman surrendered [as above] a field called the West fylde next the church with a meadow called 'the Lady Meddowe' containing 8½ acres to the use of John Web of Langham and his heirs for ever.    Web is admitted and fines 40s.

## [A]

The homage present that Thomas Butter is dead since the last court and held for life a bond tenement called Brownes which he surrendered before his death in the presence of John Rye the elder and John Whitlock, and of John Rande in the stead of the bailiff, to the use of John Butter his son and his heirs male and further to the use of the will of the said Thomas Butter.    John Butter comes and is admitted.    He fines 15s.    (m. 1.)

## [B]

[Under same court] [the last entry]    Whereas at the court of Thomas Neville knt., farmer of the said manor there holden (by reason of an indenture between the same Thomas Neville knt. and Robert Wyngfeld of Brampton, co. Suffolk, Esq., dated 30 June, 1 Mary [1554], granting to Neville the said manors for the term of 21 years) it was found by the homage that John Gurden late [*nuper*] * of Wallyngfyld in the co. of Suffolk, gentleman, after the last court and out of court by the hands of William Littelbery in the stead of the bailiff and in the presence of Richard Woode, John Web the elder † and John Browne, customary tenants of the said manors, surrendered into the lord's hand one messuage called his head house (*capit' mesuagium*) with a field called le Taynterfeld containing 7 acres and 2 acres 3 rods of wood, and a bond-tenement called "the hedehousse" otherwise "the olde housse" and one piece of pasture or meadow containing 2 acres called the leye and diverse closes of land called Garroldes and one parcel of enclosed land and pasture, containing one acre lying at the south end thereof and one field called "the Westfeld" containing 9 acres in the occupation of Richard Bredgewater and all that meadow called "Lady Meddowe" containing 9 acres to the use of John Web the younger and his heirs for ever on condition that the said John Web or his heirs pay Robert Gurden his heirs or assigns at the feast of St. Michael next at Ossyngton [*sic*] Hall, co. Suffolk £80. which John Web was admitted at this court upon this condition.    (m. 1ᵈ.)

Manors of Overhall and Netherhall in Dedham.   Court held Monday, 27 April, 2 & 3 Philip and Mary [1556].

The homage find that John Gurden late of Wallyngfeld, co. Suffolk, gentleman, after the last court by the hands of William Litelbery [etc., as on m. 1ᵈ.] surrendered into the lord's hands a messuage [etc., as on m. 1ᵈ.] to the use of John Web the younger and his heirs for ever on condition [as on m. 1ᵈ.] (m. 2.)

## [C]

At the court here holden Monday before St. Edward the Confessor,‡ 12 Henry VIII [1521], the lady granted to John Gurdon § and Robert Cradock all her fishery in the river of Dedham from the "plankez" of the mill of Dedham and from the "Floote Gates" there to the corner called Swetmensey Corner and thence for (*pro*) the whole liberty of the lady there, and delivered to the said custodians within the river and liberty two white swans; which John Gurden and Robert Cradock had seisin thereof to them, their heirs and assigns, at the will of the lady, to hold to them their heirs and assigns to the

---

* This word does not occur in the previous entries.
† Does not occur in previous entries.
‡ The Feast of St. Edward the King and Confessor falls on 18 March.
§ Spelt "Gurden."

sole use of the same John his heirs and assigns by rent of 4s. 6d. yearly and suit of courts. (m. 2.)*

[There is nothing further here, but "Willm butter" is written below in another Sixteenth Century hand.]

Manors of Overhall and Netherhall in Dedham. Court of Thomas Neville, knight, farmer, of the said manors there held 27 April, 2 & 3 Philip and Mary [1556]. (m. 3.)

[The first part follows the same order as m. 1. and has the entries which are under [A] above.]

Same court, continued [In place of [B] above, on m. 1ᵈ.]:

The jurors present upon their oath that John Gurdon late of Waldyngfyld was a bond-tenant of these manors [and] has died since the last court, and that he was seised in his lifetime and died seised of a tenement with the appurtenances called Cauncelers and another tenement with the appurtenances called monkes and another tenement called bartlettes and was likewise seised of a field called the West fyld and 5 roods of meadow in Hawkes medow and that all the said premises ought to descend, according to the custom of the manors, to a certain Robert Gurden his son and next heir, to all the premises by the custom † of the said manors. (m. 3ᵈ.)

[Marginal note]: Fine for Caunclers, etc., 8s. Fine for Bartlettes and others, 10s.

Another copy of the same court in the same form as m. 1. (m. 4.)

[Another copy of m. 2. It includes entry which are under [C] above, with the addition in another hand "Willelmo butter." (m. 5.)]

Overhall and Netherhall in Dedham. First Court General of Humphrey Wyngfeld, gent., son and heir of Robert Wingfeld, Esq. Tuesday, 15 October, 2 & 3 Philip and Mary [1555].

At this court it was found by the homage that John Gurdon the elder died diverse years now past seised of one acre one rood of bond meadow late of John Hood and Richard Peuerell in Lezebredge Medowe held by 12d rent yearly, which the said John took up in the Court holden 16 May in the [omitted] year of the reign of Edward IV, and of one acre of bond meadow of tenement Ha'tlond byling in le Brodmeadow late of Cristine larckyn in Dedham which the said John Gurdon late took up in the court holden Friday after St. James,‡ 12 Edward IV [1472]; and that John Gurdon the younger is his son and next heir, who for many years hath holden the said meadow without any surrender or just title of inheritance to the lord and his heirs.

Therefor the bailiff is commanded to seize them into the lord's hands until, etc. And whilst the court is sitting the said John Gurdon comes by John Chaundeler, his attorney on this behalf, craves by the lord's grace to be admitted to all and singular the premises as to his right and inheritance. To whom the lord, for divers considerations and of his special grace by his steward delivered seisin, to hold to him his heirs and assigns at the lord's will. He fines 6s. 8d. and hath done fealty, saving the rights of anyone, etc.

And whilst the Court is sitting, it is likewise found by the homage that the said John Gurdon out of court surrendered, by the hands of Hugh Breton bond tenant in the presence of Ralph Starlyng and John Woodhouse all the above mentioned premises to the use of Robert Sterlyng and his heirs, who is admitted. (m. 6.)

* A duplicate of some entries from this and other courts. The whole membrane contains four entries from this court, two from earlier courts, not all relating to Gurdon.

† Throughout the rolls the customary descent of bond-tenements is to the youngest son; but nothing here shows whether Robert is eldest, youngest, or only son. [Robert was an only son. G. A. M.]

‡ The Feast of St. James falls on 25 July.

643

Same Court. At this court it was found by the homage that Thomas Buttour on his deathbed surrendered in the presence of John Rande the elder, William Baynynez and John Whystok his capital tenement in which William Buttour his son now dwells with all the lands, meadows, feedings, and pastures belonging in Dedham, containing 4 acres, to the use of William his son to such intents as in the will of the said Thomas are more fully contained. William Buttour is admitted.

They say that John Gurdon alienated to John Webbe the younger certain bond lands and tenements of this manor, the particulars whereof they do not know; they are to inquire better by the next court. (m. 6ᵈ.)

Another copy of the court of 27 April, 2 & 3 Philip & Mary (as on mm. 1 and 1ᵈ) is found as m. 7.

Another copy of m. 2 is found as m. 8.

Overhall and Netherhall in Dedham. First Court of Thomas Nevell, knt., farmer, held there, Wednesday, 3 October, 1 & 2 Philip and Mary [1554].

Jurors say that Christiana Thorne, widow, late wife of John Thorne, died since the last court and held for life a parcel of the meadow called Brodmedow containing ½ acres 8 feet, enclosed, for 2s. 9d yearly and suit of court in Dedham, formerly of John Gurdon the younger, with reversion to John Thorne son of said John Thorne, who is admitted. (m. 9.)

Court there, Monday after dominica in albis, 3 & 4 Philip and Mary [1557].

The jurors say that Thomas Buttour, bond tenant, died before this court having surrendered 3 roods meadow in Chaldwall to the East of the river there, which he took up 23 Henry 8 [1531–1535] to the use of his will, namely to the use of Alice wife of Christopher Percyvall for life and afterwards as is contained in the said will. She is admitted. (m. 9.)

Dedham. View of frankpledge with First Court of Robert Bogas, gent.. Monday, 7 October, 2 & 3 Philip and Mary [1555]. Order to [blank] Warner to scour the ditch against the highway through (per) Gordons Grove

Order to John Gordon to scour his ditch from the grove to the cart gate towards the land of John Lawrence. (m. 12.)

Same Court. They present that John Gurdon without the court and after the last court surrendered by the hands of Hugh Borage in stead of the bailiff and in the presence of Ralph Sterlyng and John Wodehowse customary tenants a messuage and 7½ acres of land called Coles and 2 acres of pasture called le Holye, which the said John Gurdon took up jointly with John Gurdon his father deceased to them and their heirs, as is contained in the court roll of Monday, the feast of St. Giles,* 4 Henry VIII [1512], to the use of Robert Sklyng his heirs and assigns, on condition that Robert pay the same John Gurdon £40 at the Annunciation next; otherwise Gurdon to reenter. Fine 13s. 4d. (m. 13.)

[To be continued]

* The Feast of St. Giles falls on 1 September.

## GENEALOGICAL RESEARCH IN ENGLAND
Communicated by the Committee on English and Foreign Research

### THE GURDON FAMILY

Contributed by G. Andrews Moriarty, A.M., LL.B., F.S.A.,
of Wells, Maine.

From Ministers' Accounts
For Dedham Campsea, co. Essex.
Records of the Duchy of Lancaster
[Bundle 40, Number 742]

Account of the Reeve of Dedham, Michaelmas 2–Michaelmas 3, Henry V
[1414–1415].

Under farm of land, meadows and pasture.

He answers for:

| | | |
|---|---|---|
| 11s. | | from Wm. Webbe and Matthew Sturioun for 14 acres called Cheldewellswente with 2 acres 1 rood called Fenselowe late demised to Thomas Songers at 13s. 4d. |
| 5s. | 3d. | from Wm. Webbe for 6½ acres in Leuynglond, demised to him for 10 years, this being the 6th. |
| 10s. | | from Roger Eyr and John Gurdon for 3 acres of meadow in Lorbregge, demised for 10 years, this being the 6th. |
| 12s. | 6d. | from John Skulton and Henry Webbe for 28 acres in Westfeld with one long house in the manor called le Shepene, demised for 10 years, this being the 6th, they to maintain the said house at their own costs in roofing, covering and daubing. |
| 10s. | | from John Webbe for the northern end of the hall with easement into the hall and garden beneath the said hall on the north and west, demised for 9 years, this being the 5th.; the said John to maintain the said hall and end of the same in covering and daubing at his own costs. |

* Rev. Comfort Starr, Jr., perhaps had a personal acquaintance with John Sadler, M.A., a graduate of Emanuel College, Cambridge, England, who was born at Patchen, County Sussex near Lewes, 6 Apr., 1617, the son of Rev. John Sadler, and the brother of Ann Sadler, who was born there 24 Aug. 1614, and married at South Malling, co. Sussex, near Lewes, 19 Apr. 1636, John Harvard, who gave his name to Harvard College in 1638. In 1662 on the restoration of King Charles II, John Sadler was, like Comfort Starr, deprived of his living.

A Thomas Starr was for some years auditor for the Dean and Chapter of Canterbury Cathedral, as noted on a tablet there in the center aisle. Perhaps he was one of the descendants of Rev. Comfort Starr (1624–1711) and was connected with Jehoshaphat Starr of the precincts of Christ Church, Canterbury. In the church yard of St. Martin's at Canterbury is also a recent stone to commemorate a Mr. John Starr who died in 1883, perhaps also a descendant of Rev. Comfort Starr. As the contributor recalls, it was this John Starr who was a guest at a hotel in Belgium some sixty years ago, when Mr. John Starr (1827–1909) of Halifax, Nova Scotia, was also a guest at the same hotel; and as he once told the contributor, he received mail clearly intended for his namesake from England. Mr. John Starr of Halifax met his namesake in Belgium, and while unable to determine their exact relationship, he said they resembled each other in appearance.

| | | |
|---|---|---|
| 4s. | 3d. | from Henry Webbe for 1 acre of meadow by the meadow which John Skulton holds in Westfen, demised for 10 years, this being the 6th. |
| 4s. | 3d. | from Robert Gurdon for one acre of meadow in Westfen lying (*iuxta*) the meadow of Henry Webbe, demised for 10 years, this being the 6th. |
| | | [Thomas Ry holds a similar tenement next to that of Robert Gurdon.] |
| | 20d. | from Wm. Webbe for land called Levoteslynton demised for 3 years, this being the 2nd. |
| 36s. | 8d. | from Wm. Webbe for cow pasture called le Roye, demised for 10 years, this being the 6th. |
| | 12d. | from John Gurdon for the herbage of a piece of meadow in Porbregge after the first crop this year. |

Under livery of moneys.

To the steward of the Lady's household:

By the hand of Henry Webbe in full payment of his arrears, without tally, 18d.

By the hand of the same Henry for part of £7.6s. 8d. for farm of the mill without tally, 100s.

By the hand of John Webbe for part of 10s. 10d., whereof 10d. is arrears, and for farm of the end of the hall as above, 7s. 7d.

By the hand of Robert Gurdon for part of 5s. 7d. whereof 19d. is arrears, and for his farm as above 4s. 12d.

By the hand of William Webbe for part of 20s., whereof 8s. 9d. is arrears, and for divers farms 11s. 3d., 12s. 6d.

Under respites.

[Sums owing for rent by all the above named people as arrears from divers years back to 11 Henry IV, also from Baldwin Webbe, 2s. for rent of a house from 2nd year last past.]

Under farm of the mill.

He answers for:

£7 6. 8.     for the moeity of £4. 13. 4. being part of £16. 13. 4. the yearly farm of the watermill belonging in common to the manor of the prioress of Campsea and the manor called Waldonesmaner in Dedham, the tenants of the latter manor having £2 above their moeity of £14. 13. 4d. by agreement [cited].

[i.e., Henry Webbe presumably paid the whole farm of £16. 13. 4.]

### Bundle 40, Number 743

Account of the bailiff of Dedham Campsea, Michaelmas, 9 Henry V, Michaelmas, 1 Henry VI [1421–1422].

Beginning of this roll is mutilated but the items are apparently all as on the succeeding roll, number 744. The leases are for 10 years, this being the 3rd year.

### Bundle 40, Number 744

Account of the bailiff of Dedham Campsea, Michaelmas 1–Michaelmas 2, Henry VI [1422–1423].

Under farms.

He answers for:

| | | |
|---|---|---|
| 4s. | 4d. | from Wm. Webbe for 14 acres called Cheldewellewente. |
| 5s. | 3d. | from Wm. Webbe for 6½ acres in Levynglond. |

| | |
|---|---|
| 24s. | from Wm. Webbe for 3 acres, 3 roods meadow and 12 acres in Twlefacres. |
| 6s. 8d. | from Henry Webbe for 14 acres in Westfeld. |
| 20d. | from Wm. Webbe for a piece of land called Levoteslynton. |
| 12s. | from Wm. Webbe for meadow called Redene containing 3½ acres and 3 roods meadow called Poyntlesacre, demised for 10 years, this being the 4th. year. |

Under farm of the mills.

He answers for:

113s. 4d.  from Henry Webbe for farm of the corn and fulling mills, for the Lady's share this year.

Bundle 40, Number 745

Account of the bailiff of Dedham, Michaelmas 14–Michaelmas 15, Henry VI [1435–1436].

Under farms.

He answers for:

7s.  for William Webbe for 6½ acres of land in Levynglond, and one piece of land and aldergrove called Levottislynton containing by estimation 15 acres late demised for 8s. 6d. by the year.

Account of the bailiff of Dedham, Michaelmas 28–Michaelmas 29, Henry VI [1449–1450].

Under allowances.

Arrears of fines and amercements of divers tenants, . . . whereof, of William Webbe, 3s. 4d.—pardoned by the Lady upon the account.

Account of the bailiff of Dedham, Michaelmas 30–Michaelmas 31, Henry VI [1451–1452].

Under farm of land, meadows and pasture.

He answers for:

13s. 4d.  from Gilbert Lovekyn and John Gurdon jun. for 3 acres 3 roods of meadow called 'le londe.'

[To be continued]

647

# GENEALOGICAL RESEARCH IN ENGLAND

Communicated by the Committee on English and Foreign Research

## THE GURDON FAMILY

Contributed by G. Andrews Moriarty, A.M., L.L.B., F.S.A.,
of Wells, Maine.

### From Court Rolls of Dedham, co. Essex *

#### Records of the Duchy of Lancaster

[Series 30, Bundle 59, Roll 731]

*Re* Robert Gurdon, 8 Henry VI [1429–1430].

Surrender by John Gurdon to use of Robert Cradock of premises to which Gurdon was admitted same year by surrender of John Curde.   8 Henry VIII [1516–1517].

John Snowe to use of John Gurdon, senior.   14 Edward IV [1474–1475].

John Gurdon senior to use of son John and of his son John.   3 Henry VII [1487–1488].

William Webbe to use of John Gurdon the elder and William Woodgate (one moiety).

Ric. Peverell, the like, the other moiety.   10 Edward IV [1470–1471].

Said John Gurdon to use of his son John and his son John.   3 Henry VII [1487–1488].

John Gurdon died seized; son John admitted (*sic* Robert).   2 & 3 Philip & Mary [1555–1556].

Ric. Richeman to use of John Gurdon & Stephen Dunton.   3 Henry VII [1487–1488].

Thomas Woodhouse to use of John Gurdon the elder and Walter Broke and their heirs.   21 Edward IV [1481–1482].

The same party to the use of John Gurdon, his son and John son of John. 3 Henry VII [1487–1488].

#### From Lay Subsidies
#### For Lexden, co. Essex

Lexden Hundred.

Assessment dated 12 December 15 Henry VIII [1523].

> Dedham.                                        Lay Subsidies 108/154
>
> William Clark in goods £100 whereof Anticipation £4   Subsidy 20s.
>
> John Gourdon in goodes £80 whereof paid by Anticipation 65s. Subsidy 15s.
>
> Thomas "Button" in goodes £6.   Anticipation [*blank*]   Subsidy 3s.
>
> William Clarke and John Gourdon of £100 in money remaynyng in ther handes to "Thuse" (the use) of Thomas Dunton and Margarete Dunton within age.   Anticipation 100s.   Subsidy [*blank*].
>
> Robert Gourdon in Earnings 20s.   Anticipation [*blank*]   Subsidy 4d. Sum £40. 2s. 5d. whereof Anticipation £28. 5s.   Subsidy £11. 16s. 5d. (m.1.)

* A late memorandum book drawn up from the rolls.   Abstracts of the Gurdon entries have been taken.

Lexden Hundred.
Dated 35 Henry VIII [1543–1544]. Lay Subsidies (E 179) 108/253.
Dedham.
[begins] John Gurdon in goods £4. 13s. 4d.
[4th name] Thomas Butter in Goods 53s. 4d.
William Butter in goods 13s. 4d.
Robert Gurdon in goods 4d.
William Cardynall for John Coolle orphan in goods 32s. 4d.
The same William for Alice Coole orphan in goods 53s. 4d.   (m. 2.)

FROM PROBATE RECORDS

The Will of THOMAS GURDON, dated 12 December 1495.   To be buried in the church of Dedham; to the high altar for "my forgetfull tithes" 10s.; to the steeple £5.   Unto Grace my wife 40 marks.   Unto Kateryn my daughter 10 marks   Unto Johane my daughter 10 marks   Unto Anne my daughter 10 marks   if my goods extend so far.   If wife Grace be with child with a son it shall have the meadow which I bought of James Gransen; if it be a daughter 10 marks, and the meadow to be sold "to one of the name if it so be that he will geue as mykill as a nother man will."   "If it please God to take all my children out of this present life be fore as they be married," the money bequeathed to said children to be disposed for my soul.   Executors, wife Grace and Master John Barforde Vicar of Dedham to be supervisor.   My house to be sold to pay me debts.   Proved 10 July 1495 by oath of Master John Barforde, Vicar of Dedham and admon. committed to Grace the widow in the person of said Master John her proctor.   (P. C. C., Vox. 23.)

The Will of JONE GURDON of Dedham, late wife of John Gurdon of the same town, dated 28 December 1512.   To be buried in churchyard of Our Blessed Lady of Dedham.   To Dedham church 13s. 4d.   The Grey Friars in Colchester to sing a trental for my soul and all my good friends' souls 10s. The nuns of Campsea Abbey to pray for my soul 6s. 8d.   To the hermit of Dedham, if he be a priest, 10s. to sing a trental for my soul and all my good friends' souls, otherwise another honest priest to have it.   To Johan Cradok daughter of Christiane my daughter 3s. 4d. at marriage.   To Alis the sister of said Johan 3s. 4d. at marriage.   Son John Gurdon executor to dispose of residue for the health of my soul.   Witnesses: John Bradshay, clerk, Robert Cradokk, Robert Ayleward.   (Archdeaconry of Colchester, Reg. Clerke fo 208b.)
[No Acts to any of these wills, the one preceding is dated 12 July 1499, the one following 10 Jan. 1512/13.]

FROM PROBATE RECORDS

The Will of JOHN GURDON senr of Dedham in London Dioces dated 13 Aug: Año 1487, first bequeathed his soule to ye Allmighty God St Mary ye Virgin & all ye Saints, & his Body to be Buryed in ye North Portch of ye Church of St Mary ye Virgin of Dedham.   Also gave to ye High Altar of ye same Church for his Tiths forgotten 20s.   And gives for ye building of ye Tabernacle of St John ye Evangelist in ye foresd Church 20 Marks.   And willeth that his Executors shall buy one marble stone for his Grave, and procure one fit Presbiter to celebrate masses for his Soule, & for ye Souls of John Gurdon & Joane his wife parents of him ye sd testator, & for ye Soules of Margaret his owne wife & of Joane & Alice his daughters, in ye sd church of Dedham by ye space of 3 yeares, they giving to him a competent stipend.   And gives to Matilda his own wife 20l sterling & 4 woollen clothes containing each of them in length 24 yards, & all her own utensills wh she had before he (ye testator) maried her.

649

And willeth that John Gurdon his son shall have his tenement in wh ye same John (ye Son) now liveth, & one acre lying in a large meadow called Lufkyns meadow, on ye condition that ye foresd John shall pay therefore 20l in mañer following, vizt:—to Agnes daughter of ye testators son Robert Gurdon 40s, also to Robert son of ye sd Robert 40s, and to Margaret daughter of ye sd Robert 40s. And if any of ye sd 3 children shall die before it be 16 years old, then ye part of ye deceased child shall be equally divided between ye other two surviving. And if all ye sd 3 children shall die before they be 16 years old, then ye sd 6l given to them, shall be distributed in pious uses & in works of charity for ye health or welfare of his own soule & of their souls & for all ye souls to whom he is obliged (teneor). And in like mañer that his sd son John shall pay to Joane daughter of his same sonne John 40s, & to John ye eldest son of his foresd son John 40s and to John younger son of his foresd son John 40s. And if all ye foresd 3 children shall die before ye sd age then ye foresd 6l shall be distributed by his executors in ye mañer abovesd. And likewise 8l ye residue of ye sd mony, to be expended by his executors in ye same mañer. Also willeth that ye foresd John his son shall have his tenemt in wh ye sd testator now inhabiteth paying therefore 30l sterling in mañer following viz: to Will Gurdon son of ye sd testator 20l, And 10 marks for making of ye abovesd tabernacle in a better forme. And ye residue thereof viz: 5 marks to be distributed and expended for his Soule & for ye Soules to whom he is obliged. Also he gives to ye foresd William his son all his tenemt called Ramys in Dedham and all mañer of things pertaining to ye arts both of a Weaver & ffuller, and all his own utensills, except one little chest wh he gives to Agnes daughter of his aforesd son Robert. Also except 12 pieces of plate wh he orders to be equally devided between ye foresd 3 children of his sd son Robert & ye foresd 3 children of his sd son John. Also except One Table called ye Dowble Cownter wh he orders to be sold & that ye money be disposed for his soule. Also gives to his sd son Robert all his Tenemt late of Hen: Vyne, & one ffield late of John Taston lying in Dedham, & all his Tenemt called Bodys in Langham. And willeth that his sd son John shall have 5 roods of meadow called Snowes meadow lying in West meadow, And that his sd son Robt shall have 3 roods of meadow lying in Easthows meadow to hold to them & their heirs in maner underwritten, viz:— that his sd sons John & Robert shall keep his Anniversary for 20 yeares next after his death; in ye first yeare of his aforesd term to be disbursed in his funerall exequies & other works of Charity 20s, & in every year next during ye sd terme 10s. And gives to his sd son Robert to pay his ye said Robts debts 13l sterling. Also willeth that his sd son Robt may have for his life all ye easements of him ye sd Robt in ye Dying house called ye Whodhows scituate betw: ye foresd Tenemt in wh his sd son John now dwelleth & ye Gate called Howegate for working ye art of Dying in ye same house of his proper goods with liberty of ingress & egress as he shall please except at such times in wh his sd son John hath any Dying work in ye same house. Provided that his sd son Robt shall bear a third part of ye charge of ye repaires of ye sd house & apurt during his life & receiving ye third part of ye profits thereof if any other in ye meane time shall have any Dying. And willeth that Thomas Martyn junr son of Tho: Martyn senr of Wrabnase & Isabella his wife daughter of ye testator may have all his tenemt & apurtenañs called Bowyers lying in the town of Sutton on condition that if ye sd Tho: Martin senr shall infeoff ye sd Isabell in so many lands & tenemts as shall be of ye yearly value of his sd tenemt called Bowyers. And if ye sd Tho: Martin senr shall not do so then ye sd tenemt called Bowyers to remaine to ye sd Isabell her heirs & Assigns for ever. Also he gives to William Gurdon his Brother yearly 6s 8d for 6 years towards ye ffarme of his mansion house. Also to Stephen Lufkyn his servant 40s. The rest of his Goods he giveth to ye foresd John & Robert his sons to dispose for ye health of his soule as they shall see best. W^h John & Robert he maketh executors of this his will. And M^r John Barfoot vicar of y^e fores^d Church Supervisor of y^e same Testament. In witness whereof he hereto set his Seale, witness Will Mynot, Steph: Lufkin, John Hunt, &c. This will was Proved before John Aleyn *als* Kerver Bachellor of Lawes Comissary of Thomas Bishop of London, & y^e Administration of y^e goods comitted to y^e executors within named, Dat 14 Janu: Año Dñi within written 1487.

From the Gurdon Papers.

In his will, Lambeth Registers, Morton II, fo. 13, dated 20th March 1498, William Mynot of Ipswich, the above-named witness, desires "to be buried bifore the chapel dore of oure Lady of grace, the grave to be coulyd w^t a stone aftre John Gordonys in the porche of the churche of Dedham."

The Will of JOHN GURDON of Dedham in y^e Diocess of London, dated 3 Apr: 1594 first bequeaths his soule to Almighty God our blessed Lady S^t Mary y^e Virgin & to all y^e holy company in Heaven. His Body to be Buryed in y^e Church or Church yard of our Lady in Dedham. And gives to y^e High Altar of y^e s^d Church for Tithes & offerings negligently forgotten & witholden 26^s 8^d. And to y^e Grey ffrerys of Yepyswych for a trentall to be said for his Soule 10^s. And to y^e White ffrerys of Yeypswich for a trentall 10^s. And to y^e Black ffrerys of y^e same town 10^s for a trentall. And to ye Grey ffrerys of Colchester for a trentall 10^s. And willeth that there be given & disposed at his Burying day 11^l. And that there be disposed in Almes deedes to y^e poore for me at my Seven day 5^l & also at his thirty day 4^l. And ordreth a secular Priest to sing for y^e soules of himself friend & all Christian soulis in y^e s^d church of Dedham by y^e space of 2 years, the s^d Priest to have for his stipend 20 marks. And gives to y^e making of a new Isle of y^e North side of y^e s^d Church of our Lady in Dedham 40^l on condition that y^e Parishioners will beare y^e charges to finish y^e s^d Isle or else y^e s^d 40^l to be disposed for y^e pleasure of God & profit of his soule & all his friends souls. And gives to y^e building of y^e Steeple in Dedham 10^l to be paid out of y^e next setting. And orders that his executors buy a Vestment for Priest Decon & Subdecon with a Cope of White cloth of Tissew. And gives to y^e Prioress & Convent of Campsey for a Dirigi & masse to be sunge for his soule & all his friends souls 26^s 8^d. And orders that his executors shall observe his Year day by y^e space of 12 years, disposing in costs & charges y^e first yeare 26^s 8^d & every yeare after 13^s 4^d for y^e s^d 12 years. And bequeths to Joane his wife 30^l. And willeth that Joane his wife & John his son part equally his houshold as in Brass Pewter Latton Coper Spitts Andirons & Trevets. And ordreth that all clothes belonging to his Body & Bedding be parted equally between Joane his wife & John his son. And his Jewells to be equally divided between Joane his wife & John his son, except y^t John his son shall have 4 of y^e best siluer spoones & 2 of y^e lightest. And gives to John his son 100^l starling at y^e age of 20 years, & if y^e s^d John die within y^e age of 20 years than y^e s^d mony to be disposed by y^e discretion of his executors for his soul and his friends soules. And gives to his son John his house w^h Will Clerk dwelleth in with y^e tenem^t called Bernards & y^e lands meadows and Grove called Woodgate lands with Lovebrigg meadow, on condition that Joane his wife shall have y^e nether part of y^e fores^d house that Will Clerke dwelleth in, with Parlour Chamber & Soler for terme of her life. And gives to John his son his place w^h he y^e testator dwelleth in with y^e wood-house & y^e Leygh thereto belonging, And his tenem^t called Cancelerys (Chancellors) & his meadow that was Thomas Gurdons, Also an acre of meadow lying in Broad meadow, Also 5 roods of meadow lying in Halkys meadow late called Snowes. And gives to John his son his tenem^t lying in Ardelegh called Beres tenem^t with y^e lands called Schetheth, Also a field called Pett field with a lane called Perkyn's lane, And his lands & Grove in Langham called Aldo-

651

wennys, on condition that if yᵉ sᵈ John die within yᵉ age of 20 years then all yᵉ foresᵈ tenemᵗˢ lands meadows & Groves be sold by his executors, except his wifes part above rehersed for terme of her life, & yᵉ mony of yᵉ sᵈ premisses to be disposed by yᵉ discression of his executors to yᵉ most pleasure to God & profit of his soule & all his friends souls.   And gives to John his son his Sprewse table in yᵉ Hall.   And to Cristion his daughter 20ˡ sterling at yᵉ age of 20 years.   And if yᵉ sᵈ Cristian die within yᵉ age of 20 years then yᵉ sᵈ mony to remaine to Joane his wife & John his son.   And willeth that Joane his wife shall have after his (yᵉ testators) death yᵉ keeping & rule of Christion his daughter & of yᵉ 20ˡ beuqeathed to yᵉ sᵈ Cristion till yᵉ sᵈ Cristion be 20 years old.   And ordereth & requireth all his ffeoffees & cofeoffees in all his lands tenemᵗˢ meadows pastures woods & Groves rents or services that they shall deliver a sufficient estate & seasin of & in such lands tenemᵗˢ & premisses when they shall be required by his executors.   The residue of all his Goods he comitts to yᵉ disposall & discretion of my executors to be disposed to yᵉ most pleasure of God & weale of his soule his friends souls & all christian soules. And makes for his executors John Gurdon his son, Stephen Dunton & Will Clerke of Dedham, & yᵉ sᵈ Steph: Dunton & Will Clerke each of them to have for their labour 4ˡ starling.   And supervisors Master John Barfoott Vicar of Dedham, & Thomas Woodhowse of yᵉ same.   Witnesses Tho: Grenlyng, Will Aleyn &c.   In witness whereof he set his seale.   This will was proved 21 May Año 1504 at Lambeth before Will Archbishop of Canterbury, yᵉ sᵈ John Gurdon yᵉ testator deceased having Goods in divers Dioceses of yᵉ Province of Canterbury.   I suppose it was Arch Bp. Warham, his Armes at yᵉ bottom of yᵉ seale of yᵉ office, is first yᵉ Arms of yᵉ A: Bishoprick of Canterbury impaled with his own, viz. a fess, in chief a Goat's head erased & in base 3 escallops shells 2. 1.

Abstract from the Gurdon Papers.   P. C. C. 5 Holgrave.

The Will of ROBERT WINCOLL the elder of Little Waldingfeld, dated 31 July 1559 'as a man·... by [God's] grace . . . indued with some temporall substance.'   A godly preacher to make a sermon in said parish church at my burial, 6s. 8d.   To the finding of an able minister in said parish church 40s. yearly for 5 years if John Hopkins do be minister there, otherwise at executors' discretion.   To the poor there 20s. a year for 3 years.   To a teacher for children to be chosen by advice of executors and the parish 40s. a year, for 5 years.   £4 to church repairs.   Wife Thomasin instead of her ⅓ to have £20 yearly paid by John Wyncoll my son.   Wife Thomasin, my capital messuage I dwell in with the croft and wood adjoining and other lands belonging to Mr. Spring and now in my occupation in Waldingfeld for life.   Money due from Thomas Algar of Little Waldingfield blacksmith and Wᵐ Harris of same clothier for land sold them to my son John Wincoll.   Julian Lufkin and [blank] his wife; Thos. Rise and wife Anne; all children of Edwarde Collman of Much Waldingfield and [blank] his wife my daughter, at 21; Alice Bogarys one of daughters of Wᵐ Bogais and [blank] his wife deceased now dwelling with me, monetary bequests.   Wife and son John Wyncoll residuary legatees and executors   Witnesses: John Hopkins Roger Wincoll the younger Raffe Garth.   Proved 31 October 1560 by John Wincoll the younger in person and as proctor for the relict.   (P. C. C. Mellershe 52.)

The Will of ROBERT GURDON of Assington, Esq., dated 3 April 1578, 20 Elizabeth.   Soul to God.   To wife Rose £100 per annuum, to be paid by his son John Gurdon.   To daughter Elizabeth Waldegrave lease and term of years in parsonage of Much Coggeshall and Little Coggeshall in Essex.   To her 3 children Thomas, John and Elizabeth Waldgrove £20 each to be paid to his son Thomas Waldegrave their father to hold until they be fit to have

652

same. To son John Gurdon lands and tenements purchased of John Wyncoll of Waldingfield for life remainder to Brampton. Gwelon son of said son John in fee tail remainder to heirs of testator Robert Gurdon. To sister Wyncoll £10. To Mary wife of John Glamefeld. To Francis wife of John Duke. To Robert Lawrence. Bequests to minister of Little Waldingfield and Mr. Knewstub, Mr Crokes and Mr. Bind. To daughter Appleton for use of her son Isaac Appleton 20 marks. Bequests to servants. Residue to son John Gurdon his sole executor. Witnesses: Thomas Crooke John Knewstub and John Hanna. Proved 12 May 1579. (P. C. C. Bakon 19.)

The Will of JOHN WINCOLL of Little Waldingfield, gent., dated 14 Oct. 1576, proved 25 Feb. 1576/7. Mentions daughter-in-law Elizabeth Wintroppe. Mentions children Isaac W., John W., Thomazin W., Jane W., Anne W., Bridget W., and Amye. M: Walshe, curate of Little Waldingfield. M: Cooke parson of Great Waldingfield. Mr. Newstubbes, 40s. Mentions sisters Coo, Rice, Mrs. Apleton jun., Margaret wife of cousin John Wincoll. To Robert Wincoll senior 20s. To Agnes Wincoll widow 10s. To Servants (named). Daughter-in-law Margaret Betts. Lands in Great Cornard, Alphamton and Twynsted, Essex, bought of Thomas Wyllet. Manors of Twynsted and Harberds, etc. (Archdeaconry of Sudbury Book 33, f⁰ 222.)

The Will of RICHARD COLEMAN of Waldyingfield Parva [undated], proved 3 February 1457/8. To the High Altar 13s. 4d. To wife Agnes his tenement, household good and 1 acre of pasture also 2 crofts of land at her will. A priest to say masses at Waldyngfield Church for one year. To each son and daughter 5 marks. Residue to his executors, i.e., wife Agnes and his son Stephen Coleman. (Archdeaconry of Sudbury Book II, f⁰ 206.)

The Will of AGNES COLEMAN of Waldingfield Parva, dated 10 December 1476, proved 18 May 1477. To be buried in Waldingfield Parva Churchyard next her husband. To daughter Joan £10. in recompense of the will of Richard Coleman "my husband." To son Richard Coleman 10 marks for same. To each of the daughters and sons now living of son Stephen Coleman 6s. 8d. at 14 years of age, if any die their portion to be disposed of for the good of "my soul" and that of "my husband Richard Coleman." To each son and daughter of "my son" Richard Coleman on the same condition. To the servants of "my son John Coleman." Residue to son John Colman the executor. To son John Coleman a messuage and garden and adjacent land called "Calowe" and 6 crofts of land and 2 pightels belonging to the said messuage and the reversion of 3 tenements in Great Street, he paying my executors 25 marks etc. Executors sons Stephen, John and Richard Coleman. (Archdeaconry of Sudbury Book III, f⁰ 83.)

The Will of RICHARD COLEMAN of Waldingfield Parva [no date], proved 30 Jan. 1493/4. To son John Coleman tenement in Great Waldingfield. Residue to John and Stephen Coleman. (Archdeaconry of Sudbury Book III, f⁰ 444.)

The Will of JOHN COLEMAN the elder of Little Waldingfield, dated 19 Dec. 1505, proved 5 Mar. 1505/6. To be buried in Little Waldingfield church before the choir door. To the High Altar. To every good clerke 2d. and every poor man, woman and child 1d. A Placebo dirge and mass to be said every day for 30 days. Bequests for souls of his father and mother and three of his children. To a priest at Rome £10 and to the friars of Sudbury, Clare Babwell and the White Friars of Norwich. To wife Katherine the tenement where I dwell with the dye house, 2 tenements adjoining and other lands in Little Waldingfield for life, but if any of my male children become cloth workers they to use the dye house. Bequests of wool, cloths and plate etc. to wife for life and then to my 2 sons. To son Edward the tenement where I dwell etc after wife's death together with other lands specified. Executors to use profits to educate Edward at school until he is 21 years old, and to pay him 100 marks at 21 years. To son William the tenement in Little Waldingfield which was my brother Richard's in tail male remainder to son Edward. If both sons die without issue male the lands are to be sold and ½ the price to heirs male and ½ to wife and children. To son William 100 marks at 21 and to be educated at school until he is 21 years. If both sons die under 21 one half their bequests to wife and daughters. Residue of lands to wife for life and then to the one of my sons "which is best disposed and towardest." To daughter Agnes 50 marks at marriage and the like to daughter Alice. If they die the money to go to my 2 sons, and if they die under 21 "amongst my other daughters then alive." To each married daughter £5. To Robert and Richard the sons of my brother Richard Coleman 20s. and to their sister Katherine 13s. 4d. to each apprentice 10s. Executors wife Katherine, Thomas Manser and "John Gurdon my sone in lawe," they to have 40s each. Proved by executors. (P. C. C. Adeane 4.)

## FROM CHANCERY PROCEEDINGS

Bill of John Gurdon, vicar of the church of Fyngryngho, co. Essex, complaining that the bailiff of Colchester arrested him at Romynbrigge, outside their bailiwick, as he was riding to Coggeshall to appear before the Vicar General of the Bishop of London for a visitation of his church of Fyngryngho. (Early Chancery Proceedings, Bundle 12, No. 273, 11 Henry VI [1433–1434].)

Bill [French] [without any direction] of John Gordon. Whereas he was bound in a simple bond to Robert Steerte in £20, because petitioner had slandered Steerte, and because Steerte had afterwards forgiven him in the court Christian of the Archdeacon of Essex; but now Steerte has arrested him upon pretext of the said bond in the City of Colchester and causes him to be detained.

Prays for a writ of *corpus cum causa* to the bailiff of Colchester and for a subpoena for appearance of Steert with the bond. (Early Chancery Proceedings, Bundle 69, No. 336.)

[Undated; on the dorse is a commission for gaol delivery in Warwickshire 12 February, 6 Henry [blank] of John Cokayn [d. 1438], James Strangways and Richard Knyght. [d. *circa* 21 Henry V [1442–1443]].

## FROM INQUISITIONS POST MORTEM *

Inquisition on Robert Gurdon at Sudbury, Suffolk. He [the said Robert named in writ] died seised of manors of Assington, Stratton, Shiplingforde, and Serles in Assington, Bures St Mary, Stoke by Nayland, Boxford, Little Nayland, Great Cornard, Newton, Edwardeston, Groton and Wiston, which manors the said Robert and a certain John Gurdon the elder his father (whom Robert survived) had of the feoffment of Nicholas Spring and Henry Stapleton gents with the assent of Ric. Corbett knt. and Mary his wife. He died seised of Ronshall in Clopton by inheritance after the death of his said father John Gurdon. The said Robert Gurdon died seised of 4 messuages, 200 acres land, 40 acres meadow, 100 acres pasture and 10 acres wood in Assington, Bures St Mary, Cornard Magna and Parva, Newton, Edwardeston, Groton, Boxford and Wiston late parcel of said manor of Asington which messuages etc. Robert [sic] Gurdon aforesaid the father [sic] acquired to him and his

* Series 2 (C. 142), Bundle 187, No. 600. 7 April, 21 Elizabeth [1579].

heirs of John Wyncoll clothier and the said Robert [*sic*] Gurdon, the father [*sic*], made his will 3 April, 20 Elizabeth, at Assington bequeathing the 4 messuages etc. to John Gurdon esq. his son, then his heirs apparent for life, and after his death to John Bramptom Gurdon son and heir apparent of the said John.

Rose Gurdon widow late wife of Robert Gurdon the father survives at Assington.

Rous hall in Clopton is held of [*blank*] Rouse Esq. as of his manor of Bournehall.

Robert Gurdon the father died at Assington 5 April, 20 Elizabeth [1578] Said John Gurdon his son and heir is aged 34.

[No Essex inquisition remains extant.]

[To be continued]

---

## GENEALOGICAL RESEARCH IN ENGLAND

Communicated by the Committee on English and Foreign Research

### THE GURDON FAMILY

Contributed by G. ANDREW MORIARTY, A.M., L.L.A., F.S.A.,
of Wells, Maine.

ENTRIES FROM THE PARISH REGISTERS OF LITTLE WALDINGFIELD,
CO. SUFFOLK.*

*Mixed Entries*

1573   An Winckooll the wiff of Jhon Winckoull was beried the xxiij of May.
1573   Jhon Winckovll and margret garner was mareid the vij of November.
1574   Mystries Winckovll was bereid the xij of Jenuary [1574/5].†
1581   An tolman daughter to tomas tolman was baptized the vj of October.
1583   An tolman the wiff of tomas tolman was bereid the xxvij of september.
1583   John Winckovll ‡ the ssonne of Roger Winckull was baptised the vj of
        October.
1584   Susan Winckovll daughter to tomas Winckovll was baptised the xix
        of Juley; buried xxj August.
1585   "Sara Winckovll the daughter of Roger Winckoll was baptissed the x
        of November."
1586   Abegaill Winckoull the daughter of tomas Winckoull was baptissed
        the xvj of October.
1588   Ellyzabeth Wincoll the daughter of George Wincoll was baptyzed the
        17th of November 1588.§
1588   Marey Winckoull the daughter of Roger Winckovll was baptised the
        iiij Februarey [1587/8].‖
1589   Roger Winckoll was bereid the xxix of Aprell.
1589   Jon Winckoll the daughter of Isack Winckovll Jentelman was baptised
        the 20 of Febrewarey [1589/90].
1590   George Wincoll the sonne of George Wincoll was babtyzed the 27th of
        January 1590   [This entry had been inserted and struck out after
        December 1590, but was later added in another current hand be-
        tween April and May of that year.]

[*No entries for* 1591.]

1592   An Winckovll the daughter to tomas was baptysed the 10 of Juley.
1593   Alis Wincoll daughter of George Wincoll was babtysed the 26 of Maye
        1593.¶
1593   Juda Winckovll daughter to master Isack Windcovll was baptissed the
        27 of September.
1593   An Winckovll daughter to tomas Winckovll was baptissed the 20 of
        August.

---

* These Registers begin in 1568.
† New style is plainly being used throughout.
‡ The 'c' resembles very closely the 't' of "tomas" and "tolman."
§ Inserted in another more current hand.
‖ The recorder is using new style throughout and this entry occurs under 1588; but the dates are
not in proper order in this year.
¶ Interlineated.   It had been interlineated in 1594 and struck through.

1596   Robart Winckoll ssone to gorge * Winckoll was baptised the 14 of November.

1598   Jhon Winckoll the sonne of Apolo Winckoull was baptissed the 17 of Dessember.

1599   Frances Winckoull sonne to gorg Winckill was baptissed the 15 of Aprell 1599 † ye 41 of quen [Elizabeth].

1600   Sara Corten the daughter of William Corten was baptissed the 14 of November.

      William Winckoull the sonne of appollo Winckill was baptised the 16 of Dessember.

1601   Marey Winckovll the wiffe of apolo Winckovll was bereid in Dessember the —— xvj.‡

1612   Anna Winckoll daughter to John Winkoll was baptyzed the 7 of Martch [1612/13].

1615   John Winckkoll sonne to M<sup>r</sup>. Johne Winckoll was Baptysed the 5th of Octobar.

1617   Susan Wincoll daughter to M<sup>r</sup>. John Wincoll was baptized 19th March [1617/18].

1619   Martha Wincoll daughter of M<sup>r</sup>. John Wincoll was baptized 13th July.

1624   Elizabeth Wincoll daughter of John Wincoll was baptized 6th March [1624/5].

1627   Roger Wincoll sonne to John Wincoll was baptized 13th July.

1628   Elizabeth Wincoll daughter to Francis Wincoll baptized [? 15] February [1628/9].

1629   Joane Wincoll daughter of John Wincoll baptized 4 January [1629/30].

1630   Anna daughter of Francis Wincoll baptized 23 January [1630/1].

1631   Mary daughter of William Wincoll baptized 21 August.

1632   Thomas son of Mr. John Wincoll baptized 19 August.

1632   George son of Francis Wincoll baptized 20 January [1632/3].

      1633   Mr. John Wincoll churchwarden 25 Mar.

1634   Elizabeth daughter of Francis Wincoll baptized 15 March [1634/5].

*Burials* §

1610   Martha Wincoll daughter John Wincoll buried 16th March [1610/11].

*Marriages* ‖

1630   marryed William Wincoll and Dorothy Clopton both of this parish 23 September.

1632   marryed John Bowsser of Stanstead and Anne Wincoll of this parish 3 May.

*Burials*

1617   Susan Wincoll daughter to Mr. John Wincoll buried 22 March [1617/18].

1622   M<sup>rs.</sup> Wincoll wife to M<sup>r.</sup> John Wincoll [after July].

1630   Elizabeth y<sup>e</sup> daughter of Francis Wincoll buried 11 April.

1630   Elizabeth y<sup>e</sup> daughter of M<sup>r</sup>. John Wincoll buried 16 August.

* Altered from Jorge. This entry is not interlineated. In 1597 there is an entry "Sam Gosse sonne of Thomas Gosse was babtised Aug. 2." [The copyist thinks this is in the hand which inserted the earlier baptisms of children of George Wincoll.]

† This is not an insertion; but "ye 41 of quen [Elizabeth]" is added.

‡ The copyist thinks that the earlier interlineations are in the hand which begins to make regular entries 10 Sept, 1602 onwards.

§ These entries were kept separate from 1605 to 1616.

‖ These entries were kept separate from 1605 to 1635.

1633 Thomas son of Mr. John Wincoll buried 11 April.
1635 Alice wife of George Wincoll buried 23 April.
1635 William Wincoll 30 April.

## Transcript from the Parish Registers of Great Waldingfield, co. Suffolk *

### Baptisms, 1539–October 1595 †

1554 Ann Colman daughter of Edward 23 December.
1555 Daniel Colman son of Edward 17 June.
1558 Frances Colman daughter of Edward 27 September.
1572 Samuel Colman son of Edward 31 August.
1572 Ann Colman daughter of William 14 December.
1574 Jane Colman daughter of William ———‡.
1574 Abigail Colman daughter of Edward 27 June.
1575 Edward Colman son of William 15 May.
1576 Judith Colman daughter of William 22 July.
1577 Judith Colman daughter of William 3 November.
1579 Isaack Colman son of William 6 September.
1582 John and Robert Colman sons of William, twins, 9 December
1586 Edward Colman son of William 9 October.

### Marriages, 1539–1609 §

1549 William Colman and Joan Firmin 17 June.
1564 Edward Colman and Ann Rophe 13 November.
1569 William Colman and Margaret Rophe 4 July.
1569 Robert Gale [or Gate] and Rachel Colman 4 July.
1595 Christopher Robins and Jane Colman 16 November.
1609 Robert Colman and Mary [blank] 4 May.

### Burials, 1539–1604 ||

1562 Alice Colman 2 January [1562/3].
1572 Joseph Colman 23 May.
1573 Ann Colman 9 April.
1576 Edward Colman 9 January [1576/7].
1577 Abigail Colman 31 December.
1580 Isaac Colman 4 August.
1590 Ann wife of Edward Colman 10 January [1590/1].
1598 Edward Colman 26 August.

### Register Bills of Waldingfield Magna, From the Archdeaconry of Sudbury, co. Suffolk ¶

1565 Anne Collman daughter of Edward baptized 11 November.
1567 Alice Colman daughter of Edward baptized 1 August.
1575 Edm. [? Edward] Collman son of William and Margaret baptized 15 May.
1577 Judeth Colman daughter of William and Anne baptized 3 November.
1577 Abigail Collman buried 31 December.

* These transcripts were made by Charles Partridge, Esq., and recently deposited in the Ipswich Public Library.
† There are gaps in these transcripts of baptisms from October 1542 to May 1549, August 1560 to March 1571/2, March 1582/3 to June 1590, and October 1595 to April 1604. Some of the gaps between 1584 and 1598 have been filled from Archdeacon's Bills.
‡ This date is between 10 January 1573/4 and 2 May 1574.
§ There is gap in these transcripts between February 1569/70 and September 1584.
|| There are gaps in these transcripts from 1543 to 1548, 1554 to 1558, 1582 to 1584, in 1596/7, and later brief ones.
¶ All the existing Register Bills before 1600 were examined.

1580 Isaac Colman son of William buried 4 August.
1581 William Colman a child buried 14 October.
1581 John Colman son of William and Margaret buried 30 November.
1582 Robert and John Colman sons of William and Margaret baptized 9 December.
1586 Edward Colman son of William baptized 9 October.
1598 Edward Colman buried 26 August.

REGISTER BILLS OF WALDINGFIELD PARVA,
FROM THE ARCHDEACONRY OF SUDBURY, CO. SUFFOLK *

1580 John Wincoll buried 30 May.
1584 Susan Wincoll daughter of Thomas baptized 19 July; buried 21 August.
1585 Susan Wincoll daughter of Roger baptized 10 November.
1586 Abigaill Wynckoll baptized 16 October.
1588 Elizabeth Wynkolls baptized 7 October.
1592 [blank] Wincoll daughter of Isaac and Judith baptized 24 September.
1592 Nan Wincoll daughter of Thomas Wincoll baptized 20 August.
1593 Alice Wyncoll daughter of George Wyncoll baptized 1 June.
1595 Robert Wincoll son of George Wincoll baptized 17 November.
       George Wincoll, Churchwarden.
1615 John Wyncolne son of Mr. John Wyncolne baptized 5 October.
1618        John Wincoll, churchwarden.
1619 Martha Wincoll daughter of Mr. John baptized 13 July.
       John Wincoll, churchwarden.
1634 Elizabeth Wincoll daughter of Francis baptized 15 March [1634/5].
       John Wincoll, churchwarden.
1637 Isaac Wincoll son of Francis and Alice baptized 13 April.
1637 Thomas Cooke widower married Dorothy Wincoll, widow, 19 January [1637/8].
       John Wincoll, churchwarden.
1639 Francis Wincoll son of Francis and Alice baptized 25 August.
1639 George Wincoll buried 11 October.
1639 Thomas Ryely servant of Francis Wincoll buried 6 February [1639/40].

NOTES FROM "GURDON PAPERS" *penes* BARON CRANWORTH (OF LETTON AND GRUNDISBURGH)

John Gurdon the fourth bearing that name in immediate succession married first Mary, daughter of John Butter, Esq., of Dedham, by whom he had no issue, and secondly Anne, daughter of John Coleman, Esq., of Lynes Hall in Suffolk. He died in 1536 [sic].† (From a volume called "History," p. 29, by Sir William Brampton Gurdon, undated.)

A volume entitled "Deeds" begins with the early deeds (starting in 1317) relating to Brampton properties at Cranworth and elsewhere in co. Norfolk, with the marriage settlement of John Gurdon and Amy Brampton, in 1561, and are abstracts from originals.

Gurdon and Brampton Wills and Settlements of Letton and Stow. In Box 13, pp. 143 ff.

The Will of JOHN GURDON of Dedham, 3 April 1504. Bequests to son John under 20. (p. 144.)

The Will‡ of JOHN GURDON (part only, no date), bequeathing to his daughter Alice 52 pistolets his sons-in-law William Butter and Richard Lawrens,

---

* The following years were examined: 1564, 1566, 1571, 1572, 1575, 1577, 1580, 1584, 1585, 1586, 1588, 1591/2, 1593, 1595, 1603, 1606, 1609, 1615, 1618, 1619, 1620, 1634, 1636, 1637, 1638, 1639, 1641.

† Refers to the fragment of his will.

‡ Obviously made about and before 27 April 1556.

each 40 marks  sons-in-law Roger Wyncoll and Robert Thorpe £40 each
John Cole and his sister Alice £10 each   Executors: son Robert Gurdon and
son-in-law Robert Thorpe.

"I suppose it was after yᵉ Reformation from Popery because no praiers for
yᵉ dead.  he might be the son of yᵉ former John & father of Robt."   (p. 144.)

Examination was made of volume IX (Supplementary) of a series entitled
"Letters and Papers of the Gurdon Family, 1524–1691.  During the Lifetime
of John Gurdon (died in 1536) and Others."  These papers were discovered
after the other volumes were compiled.  The earlier papers are Letton and
Brampton records.

### From Muskett's Collections

William Butter of Dedham, co. Essex, clothier, 27 Elizabeth [1584–85], became bound to pay Robert Burman of Ipswich, merchant.   35 Elizabeth
[1592–93] residue of a debt assigned to Samuel Johnson of Ipswich—money
matters.  (Requests, Uncalendared.  Elizabeth B. 4.  Add. 38099 fᵒ 176.)

Suffolk Feet of Fines   Michaelmas, 14 Charles I [1638].   John Butter *v.*
Thomas Bacon &c.  Wiston.  (fᵒ 157.)

The following genealogical table is based on an outline recon-
structed by Muskett from contemporary evidences in the Suffolk
Visitation of 1664.   (Add. 33864, Muskett Collections, fᵒ 102.)

JOHN GORDON of Assington, Esq., and Dedham, married ANNE
COLMAN, daughter of John Colman of Lynnes Hall in Edwardstone,
co. Suffolk, etc.

Children:

- i.  A DAUGHTER, m. before 1664 HENRY BUTTER of Dedham.
- ii.  ALLICE, m. (1) ———— BUNNE of Mannitree; m. (2) ROBERT THORPE.
- iii.  ROBERT of Assington, Esq., testator of 3 Apr. 1578.
   Other children.

The following pedigree is based on a copy of the Gurdon pedigree
in the handwriting of Thornhagh Gurdon *penes* Sir W. Brampton
Gurdon, 18 March 1884.   (Add. 33869, Muskett's Collections, fᵒˢ
204 ff.)

1.  JOHN GURDON of Dedham, co. Essex, died in 1487.   He married first ————, and secondly MATHILDA ————, widow of a
clothier in Dedham, who, being well stocked for the clothing trade,
she and her husband carried that trade until his death.

In his will John Gurdon gave several gifts to the church, viz., to
building in a better form or repairing the tabernacle of St. John the
Evangelist in Dedham Church, and to prayers for John Gurdon and
Joan his wife.

   Child by first wife:
   2. i.   JOHN.

2.  JOHN GURDON (*John*), died about 1504.   He married JOAN
————.

   Children:
   i.   JOAN.
   3. ii.   JOHN.
   iii.   CHRISTIAN.

660

**3.** JOHN GURDON (*John, John*), of Dedham, died in 1586. He married first MARY BUTTER, third daughter of John Butter of Dedham, and secondly ANN COLMAN, daughter of John Colman of Lynnes hall, in Edwardstone, co. Suffolk. Children:

    i.  A DAUGHTER, m. WILLIAM BUTTER of Dedham Hall.
    ii.  ALICE, m. ROBERT THORPE of Brent Ely Hall.
           Children (surname *Thorpe*):
              1.  *John.*
                 Others.
   iii.  A DAUGHTER, m. ———— FOX.
   iv.  A DAUGHTER, m. ROGER WINCOLL of Waldingfield.
    v.  A DAUGHTER, m. ———— NOTTINGHAM.
   vi.  A DAUGHTER, m. ———— COLMAN.
  vii.  A DAUGHTER, m. RICHARD LAWRENCE.
 viii.  JONE, m. WILLIAM CARDINALL of North Bromly.
   ix.  ROBERT of Waldingfield parva, and later of Assington, d. in 1577.

The Will of JOHN COLMAN thelder of Little Waldingfield, dated 19 December [1505], proved 5 March 1505 [1505/6] [P.C.C. 4 Adeane] Wife Kateryn sons William and Edward daughters Agnes and Alice my two daughters John Gurdone my son-in-law to my other daughters which be married John Gurdon one of executors. (Add. 33870, p. 268.)

The following abstracts are taken from "The Manors of Suffolk", by Copinger, vol. 1, pp. 237–249, and vol. 3, p. 33.

Waldingfield<br>Great Waldingfield

Manors

Carbonels or Butler's.

Badley *alias* Peyton Hall. At the time of Henry VIII it was vested in Sir William Drury, but at the time of Elizabeth it had passed to the Coleman family, for Edward Coleman died seised of it in 1599.
    The Rental at the time of Henry VIII may be found in Bodl. Suff. Rolls. 35.

Brandeston Hall. The Appletons had a lease about 1500, and it was bequeathed in 1504 by Thomas Appleton to son Robert Appleton, whose son William Appleton bequeathed it to his wife Rose in 1538. It belonged "on the Dissolution" to Sir Edmund Bacon of Redgrave, Bart.[*sic*] (Copinger, however, states that former owners (Nunnery of Dartford in Kent) had surrendered to the King in 1371.)

Moreves *alias* Morefes *alias* Sarres with Storkenest. In 1474 this manor was granted by the Crown to Henry Lord Bourchier, Earl of Essex, and it passed in 1484 to his grandson and heir, Henry Earl of Essex. In 1528 it was in possession of Henry Bures.

Sandesfords *alias* Stanford. This belonged to the Knyvet family (1420–1500), then to John Rainsford, and in 1507 to the Clopton family.

Dowres or Dowayres. In possession of the de Peytons from 1294 on.

Little Waldingfield

Woodhall *alias* Waldingfield Parva. This belonged to the Lutterell family of Dunster (1370–1521); possibly in 1540 to John Purpett of Newborne; at

661

the time of Elizabeth it "passed to Roger Wincoll of Hitcham. He was son of Roger Wyncoll by Anne his wife daughter of John Gurdon of Dedham, which Roger was the son of John son of John Wyncoll of Little Waldingfield."

Netherhall. In possession of the Wincolls (descent given 1542–1710).

Holbrook Hall. Owned by the Appleton family.

Luns Hall

Rousehall in Clopton. This was held by John Audeley who died in June 1534, when it devolved upon Edward Audeley. It passed to Robert Gurdon who died in 1579.

## From Feet of Fines, co. Suffolk

The following records are taken from Copinger's "Index to Suffolk Feet of Fines, 1 Henry VIII to Elizabeth," now at the Ipswich Public Library.

All reference to Gurdon during the reign of Henry VIII are given.

There are no references to the name Butter earlier than that of Peter Butter deforciant in Kersey. (Easter, 22 Elizabeth [1580].)

*Gurdon* John Gurdon and Anthony Stapelton of the manor of Alverston Hall and Chamberlayns and tenements in Clopton, Burgh and Grundisburgh. (Hilary 34 Henry VIII [1543], Easter, 38 Henry VIII [1546].)

Robert Gurdon and Edward Weldon of the manor of Stratton, Asington *alias* Lovenes and tenements in Assington, Boxford, Newton, Cornard and Stoke by Nayland. (Easter, 38 Henry VIII [1546].)

The following pedigree is based on Davy's "Suffolk Pedigrees," Add. 19133 f° 259.

JOHN GURDON of Dedham, Esq., died in 1536. He married first MARY BUTTER, who died *s.p.*, daughter of John Butter of Dedham, Esq.; and secondly, ANNE COLMAN, daughter of John Colman, Esq. of Lynnes Hall, co. Suffolk.

Children * by second wife:

    i.  ROBERT, Esq., son and heir, high sheriff of Suffolk, who bought Assington, died 5 Apr. 1577 † dictus aged 63, and was buried at Assington.
    ii. JOAN, m. WILLIAN CARDINALL of Great Bromley, Essex, Esq.

Add. 19133 f° 272 [part of a MS. communicated by G. B. Jermyn [? from] Mr. Almack]:

John Gurdon Esq. of Dedham obᵗ 1536[*sic*].
John Gurdon Esq. of Dedham and Waldingfield married Mary daughter of John Butter Esq. of Dedham[*sic*].
Robert Gurdon Esq. bought the manor of Assington.

f° 273. Cites charters belonging to Brampton Gurdon from Harl. 639 art. 13 f° 77.

[To be continued]

* Davy gives no other children of this John Gurdon, and no other Butter connections.
† Or 1579, altered over from the other.

## GENEALOGICAL RESEARCH IN ENGLAND
Communicated by the Committee on English and Foreign Research
### THE GURDON FAMILY

Contributed by G. ANDREWS MORIARTY, A.M., LL.B., F.S.A.,
of Wells, Maine.

At the commencement of the fifteenth century Simon Gurdon, Robert Gurdon, and John Gurdon were living at Dedham, co. Essex, England.

SIMON GURDON, of Dedham, perhaps a brother of Robert Gurdon, living 6 Oct. 1410, when, with his wife CHRISTIAN, he took up the north end of Dedham Hall with easement in the hall and garden below the hall on the north and west (REGISTER,† vol. 92, p. 383).* As the name of Simon Gurdon disappears from the court rolls at this time, it is supposed that he died soon after 1410.

ROBERT GURDON, of Dedham, perhaps a brother of Simon Gurdon, died probably between 1440 and 1450. He married ALICE ———, who died in 1420–1 (ibid., p. 385).
The name of Robert Gurdon appears in the court rolls as early as 1408 (ibid., p. 382) and as late as November 1439 (ibid., p. 385), but following the gap in these records from 1440 to 1457, it disappears.

1. JOHN GURDON (? Robert), of Dedham, whose name appears in the court roll as early as 8 Nov. 1407 (ibid., p. 382), and by inference as late as 1451/2, when John Gurdon, Jr.,‡ is mentioned (vol.

---

† All references hereafter indicate the REGISTER.
‡ This John Gurdon, Jr., cannot refer to John Gurdon who died in 1487, because that son was probably a young lad in 1451/2, as his children were not born until after 1471. It seems likely, therefore, that the first John Gurdon was a son of Robert Gurdon (the name Robert is perpetuated in the family, but that of Simon is not).
*All references to Vol. 92, pp. 380-387 refer to pp. 601-608, this volume.

94, p. 182), died perhaps soon after 1451–2. He married JOAN ———.

He may well be the John Gurdon called father by John Gurdon, the testator of 1487, in his will.

Children:

2.    i.    JOHN.
       ii.    WILLIAM, probably of Dedham.
      iii.    JOHN, probably "the middler," of Dedham, called "senior," 1492–1498; d. about 1498; m. OLIVE ———.

The Court Roll of Octave Easter, 14 Henry VII [1498–9] mentions John Gurdon, Sr., and John Gurdon, Jr., as pledges. It may well be that John the middler, after the death of his elder brother John (who died in 1487), became John Gurdon, Sr., and died soon after as in a Court held in 1502 there is mention of "John Gurdon, late called John Gurdon, junior" (vol. 73, p. 81). But here the John, Jr., is probably he who died in 1504; and at a Court held in February 1504/5 there is reference to "John Gurdon under the style of John Gurdon, junior, who lately died." (Vol. 93, p. 79.)

Thomas Gurdon of Dedham, probably a son, d. in 1495; m. Grace ———, who, with three unmarried daughters, Katherine, Joan, and Ann, survived him.

For the will of Thomas Gurdon see vol. 94, p. 232.

2. JOHN GURDON (*John, ? Robert*), called John the elder in 1480,[*] died, an old man, between 13 Aug. 1487, the date of his will, and 14 Jan. 1487/8, the date it was proved. He married first MARGARET ———, who died after 1472 (vol. 92, p. 385), and secondly MATILDA ———, who died 13 Aug. 1487.

For the will of John Gurdon see vol. 94, pp. 232–234.

Children:

       i.    JONE, d. before 13 Aug. 1487.
      ii.    ALICE, d. before 13 Aug. 1487.
3.    iii.    JOHN.
      iv.    WILLIAM, d. *s.p.* in 1502. The Court Roll, dated at Dedham on Wednesday in Whitweek, 17 Henry VII [1502], states that "William Gurdon, Junior, died since the last court."
      v.    ROBERT, clothier and dyer, b. about 1455; d. in 1503; m. ———. Robert and his three children are named in the will of John Gurdon, his father.

Children:

     1.  *Agnes*, living in 1487.
     2.  *Robert*, b. after 1470 and before 1487; d. in 1546; m. (1) in 1522 Katherine Hane; m. (2) Olive ———, who was living in 1546. Child by second wife: (1) Richard.
     3.  *Margaret*, living in 1487.
      vi.    ISOBEL, m. THOMAS MARTIN of Wrabness.

Child (surname *Martin*):
     1.  *Thomas*, living in 1487.

3. JOHN GURDON (*John, John, ? Robert*), of Dedham, clothier, testator of 1504, died between 3 Apr. 1504, the date of his will, and 21 May 1504, the date it was proved. He married JOAN ———, whose will was dated 28 Dec. 1512.

After the death of his father, John Gurdon was sometimes called John Gurdon, and sometimes John Gurdon, Jr.

---

✻ In 1480 there were also living John Gurdon, "the middler," and John Gurdon, Jr., the testator of 1504. (See vol. 92, p. 386.) ✳✳

✳✳See the last footnote on p. 663.

In the Court Roll of Whitweek 1499 the names of John Gurdon, Jr., and his wife Olive appear (vol. 93, p. 80).* This must be an error for John Gurdon in his will, dated 3 Apr. 1504, calls his wife Joan, and her will shows her to be the mother of his children.

For the will of John Gurdon see vol. 94, pp. 234–235; and of Joan Gurdon see *ibid.*, p. 232. **

Children:

    i.    JOHN, the elder, under 16 years of age in 1487; d. *s.p.* He is called "John Gurdon the elder, son of John Gurdon the younger," i.e., the elder John of John Gurdon, Jr.'s two sons John.

    ii.   JOAN, under 16 years of age in 1487.

4.  iii.  JOHN, the younger, under 20 years of age 3 Apr. 1504.

    iv.  CHRISTINA, b. about 1480; m. ROBERT CRADDOCK of Dedham, b. after 1474.

        Children (surname *Craddock*):

        1.  *Johan*, b. before 28 Dec. 1512.

        2.  *Alice*, b. before 28 Dec. 1512.

4. JOHN GURDON (*John, John, John, ? Robert*), of Dedham, Little Waldingfield, and Great Waldingfield, co. Suffolk, England, gentleman, born about 1485, died in 1556. He married first, before 19 Dec. 1505 (vol. 94, p. 237) ANNE COLEMAN, daughter of John Coleman of Little Waldingfield, and secondly, before 1537/8, ALICE ——— (vol. 93, p. 229).**

In the pedigrees it is stated that he previously married Mary Butter, daughter of John Butter, but there is no evidence of this and it is clearly wrong. He is also said to have died in 1536, but the court rolls show that he died shortly before 27 Apr. 1556 (vol. 94, p. 76).**

Although his heir was his son Robert Gurdon, yet on 27 Apr. 1556 he is called John Gurdon the elder of Great Waldingfield, hence it appears that he had a son John who died shortly before him.

The will is not recorded, but there is a fragment of it among Lord Cranworth's muniments.

A portion (undated) of the will of John Gurdon bequeaths to his daughter Alice 52 pistolets; to his sons-in-law William Butter and Richard Lawrence, 40 marks each; to his sons-in-law Roger Wyncoll and Robert Thorpe, £40 each; and to John Cole and his sister Alice, £10 each. The executors were his son Robert Gurdon and his son-in-law Robert Thorpe.

"I suppose that it was after yᵉ Reformation from Popery because no praiers for yᵉ dead. He might be the son of yᵉ former John and father of Robert." (Letters and Papers of the Gurdon Family, vol. ix, supplementary, 1524–1691.)

The pedigrees state that his daughter Anne Gurdon married Robert Wyncoll. In this event he must also have had another daughter named Anne, a not uncommon thing in the sixteenth century, because William Butter's first wife Anne,

*Page 614, this volume.
**For Vol. 93, p. 229 see p. 632, this volume; for Vol. 94, pp. 76, 232 & 234-235 see pp. 643, 649 & 651-652, this volume.

the mother of all his children except his youngest daughter, was buried at Dedham 22 Aug. 1563.

John Gurdon, with his son Robert, purchased the Manor of Assington in Suffolk.

Children:

i. JOHN, d. *s.p.* in 1555/6.
ii. ROBERT, of Assington, m. ROSE (SEXTON) APPLETON, daughter of Robert Sexton and widow of William Appleton.

> John Gurdon of Assington, co. Suffolk, a son, m. Amy Brampton, daughter of William Brampton of Letton, co. Norfolk, and had a son, Brampton Gurdon of Assington, who m. Muriel Sedley (daughter of Martin Sedley of Morley, co. Norfolk), and their daughter, Muriel Gurdon, m. in June 1633 Richard Saltonstall, Esq. (eldest son of Sir Richard Saltonstall of Essex, who began the settlement of Watertown, Mass., in 1630). Richard Saltonstall, b. in 1610, came with his father to New England in 1630, but returned to England in 1631. In 1635, with his wife Muriel and young daughter, he left England and settled at Ipswich, Mass. (For a complete account of the Saltonstall family see "Ancestry and Descendants of Sir Richard Saltonstall of New England," by Richard A. Saltonstall, 1897.)

iii. ANNE, buried at Dedham 22 Aug. 1563; m. as his first wife WILLIAM BUTTER of Dedham, clothier, b. perhaps about 1521; was buried at Dedham 8 Nov. 1594.

> Children (surname *Butter*): *
> 1. *Pierce.* A daughter Anne Butter m. John Coggeshall the Younger of Halstead, co. Essex, gentleman, and was the mother of John Coggeshall of Rhode Island.
> 2. *Thomas.*
> 3. *Richard.*
> 4. *Edward.*
> 5. *Alice.*

iv. ANNE, m. ROGER WINCOLL of Little Waldingfield.
v. MARY, m. ANTHONY ROWS of Badinghouse, who, in his will dated 22 Nov. 1559, calls Robert Gurdon his brother-in-law.
vi. ALICE, m. (1) ——— BUNNE; m. (2) ROBERT THORPE of Brent Ely.
vii. KATHERINE, d. before 1561; m. RICHARD LAWRENCE of Spexhall, co. Suffolk, the testator of 1560.
viii. JANE, m. (1) ——— COLE; m. (2) WILLIAM CARDINAL of North Bromley, co. Essex.

> Children by first husband (surname *Cole*):
> 1. *John.*
> 2. *Alice.*

[GENEALOGICAL RESEARCH IN ENGLAND to be continued]

———

* See REGISTER, vol. 76, pp. 293–295. (See Vol. I of this work, pp. 747-749.)

# GENEALOGICAL RESEARCH IN ENGLAND

Communicated by the Committee on English and Foreign Research

## THE ORIGIN OF THE PUTENHAMS
## OF PUTENHAM, CO. HERTS., AND PENN, CO. BUCKS., ENGLAND

By A. VERE WOODMAN, ESQUIRE, of Wing, Bucks., England

WHILE the great antiquity of the Putenham family has always been manifest, their early history has hitherto remained altogether obscure. Recently, however, it has been found possible to trace the descent of the lords of Putenham to an ancestor so unusually early as to have died even before the date of the great survey of Doomsday Book. Few, indeed, are they who possess so ancient a pedigree, and some account of the origin of a family able to make such a claim can hardly fail to be of interest to their many descendants, both in England and America.

For four generations the story of the Putenhams is linked with that of the prominent Norman family who left a lasting memorial of their consequence in the second name of their principal manor and castle site of Weston Turville in the county of Buckingham.

One of the greatest lords that accompanied Duke William upon his memorable invasion of England in 1066 was his half-brother Odo, Bishop of Bayeux. Among the Bishop's followers was a certain Anschitil, who may have been actually present at Hastings—possibly one of the young men whom the Bayeux tapestry shows the warlike prelate exhorting to renewed offensive against the Saxon host.* Be this as it may, all that is beyond doubt is that Anschitil was dead before 1086, when his son Roger is found holding extensive estates of the Bishop in the counties of Buckingham, Kent, and Hertford. By far the greater part of his possessions lay in Buckinghamshire where he held, besides several lesser lordships, Weston, Taplow, Chalfont, and Saunderton; in Kent, where he is called "son of Anschitil," he held Hastingleight† and Eastling; in Hertford he held the manor of Putenham‡. These holdings, assessed at upwards of fifty hides, constituted a very large estate for a Doomsday under-tenant.

On Roger's death his inheritance passed to Geoffrey de Turville whose grandsons, William and Richard de Turville, were sued, in 1212, by Herbert de Bolebec, great-grandson and heir of Isabel, the daughter of Roger, son of Anschitil, for seven and a quarter knights' fees in Weston, Penn, and Taplow, and two knights' fees in Chalfont.§ The suit was obviously unsuccessful and it may therefore be fairly presumed that Geoffrey was Roger's son and heir, for it is quite

---

* "Hic Odo Episcopus, baculum tenens, confortat pueros."
† In 1242–3, Michael de Hastingel' held three quarters of a fee there of the heir of William de Turville (Testa de Nevill).
‡ Doomsday Book.
§ Curia Regis Rolls, 14 John.

667

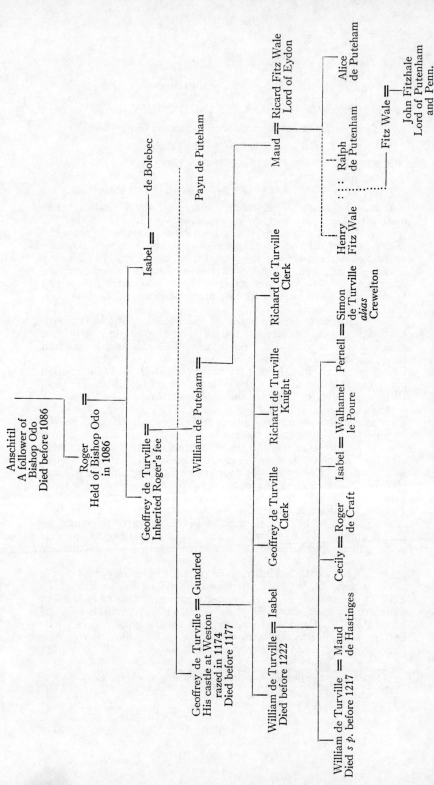

THE PUTEHAM PEDIGREE

unlikely that the Turvilles could otherwise have resisted so strong a claim.

There can be no doubt but that this Geoffrey is identical with the Geoffrey de Turville whose cruel mutilation by Henry I is recorded by Ordericus Vitalis. After Bishop Odo's forfeiture many of his lordships passed to Robert de Beaumont, Earl of Leicester and Count of Meulan. His son Waleran, Count of Meulan, whose fortunes Geoffrey would naturally follow, rebelled against the King in 1123, and was utterly defeated at the battle of Rougemontier, where he and some eighty of his men-at-arms were taken prisoners. At Rouen, the following year, the King pronounced judgment on the captives and caused the eyes of Geoffrey de Turville and another knight named Odard du Pin to be put out. The Count of Flanders, who was then at the court, commiserated the lot of the condemned and said to the King, "my lord King, you are doing what is quite abhorrent to our usages when you mutilate captives taken in the service of their lords;" to which the King replied, "Sir Count, I do what is right, and I will prove it by good reasons. Geoffrey and Odard became my liege men with the consent of their lords and, breaking their oaths of fealty, proved false to me and therefore incurred the penalty of death or mutilation." It is not known for certain if Geoffrey survived this terrible punishment. It is, however, evident that a Geoffrey de Turville, either this man or his son of the same name, was, to some extent, in the King's favour in 1130, when he was pardoned £4-8-6 of geld—an amount corresponding very closely to the sum that would have been due on the Doomsday assessment—on his land in Bucks.* At the same time smaller sums, representing the geld on some twenty-five hides, were remitted on his lands in the counties of Warwick, Northants, and Cambridge.† These considerable estates were probably of the Earl of Leicester's grant.

Geoffrey de Turville was succeeded by his son another Geoffrey. In 1146 he acknowledged that, with the consent of Gundred, his wife, he had given to the church of St. Mary of Missenden, for the souls of his father Geoffrey, his brother William, himself, his wife and his sons, all the land of "la Lega" that Ralf de Haltuna held.‡

By another charter of about the same date Geoffrey gave to John de "Leia" and to his heirs a hide of land of his demesne in Weston and the mill that William held, free from all service save that John and his heirs should do castle-guard in the castle of Weston for forty days in time of war, with a destrier and a rouncey, and for three weeks in time of peace. And this he did because John had surrendered to him his own inheritance, to wit, the land of "Leia" which he had given to the canons of Missenden in alms. This deed was witnessed by the abbot of Missenden, Hugh de Noers, William de Puteham, Payn de Puteham, Osbert de Saunderton and many others, including the whole halvimote of Weston.§

* Pipe Rolls, 31 Henry I.
† *Ibid.*
‡ Cartulary of Missenden Abbey, No. 201. This charter, missing from Harl. MS. 3688, is preserved in the Browne Willis Transcript at the Bodleian.
§ *Ibid.* No. 248. Payn may have been a brother of William de Puteham.

Before proceeding to the identification of these earliest known Putenhams, the history of the Turvilles will be briefly traced until the failure in the male line of the main branch of the family.

Weston Castle, toward the garrisoning of which such careful provisions had been made, had no long duration. In 1174 the Pipe Rolls record the payment of 59s. 6d. "for the custody of the castle of Weston which was of Geoffrey de Turville before it was razed." The entry suggests that it had been forfeited and it may, perhaps, be inferred that once again a Turville had followed his overlord into rebellion for the Earl of Leicester was, in 1173, among the chief supporters of the Princes in their revolt against their father King Henry. As, however, the Princes' adherents were reinstated in their possessions on the conclusion of peace, this forfeiture could only have been temporary.

Geoffrey died before 1177. His heir was the William de Turville, who at the beginning of the xiiith century held nineteen knights' fees of the honour of Leicester,* and he had at least three other sons: Geoffrey de Turville the clerk, to whom his father gave the church of Chalfont; Richard de Turville the knight, to whom his brother William gave the manor of Chalfont;† and Richard de Turville the clerk, who was his brother Geoffrey's attorney in a fine, levied in 1196, concerning the advowson of the church of St. Peter of Chalfont.

William de Turville, by his wife Isabel, had a son William who died without issue before 1217.‡ His father survived him but was dead before 1222 when his three daughters, Cecily, the wife of Roger de Craft, Isabel, the wife of Walhamet le Poure, and Pernell, the wife of Simon de "Creullona" or, as he is usually called, de Turville,§ are named as his heirs.‖

That the earliest Putenhams were descended from Roger, who was lord of the place in 1086, is, in itself, probable. Moreover, as has been seen, instances are known in which the Turvilles bestowed churches and manors on younger sons and brothers. These facts suggest the possibility that Geoffrey's brother William and the William de Puteham who attested Geoffrey's grant to John de Leia may have been one and the same man.

The first reference to Putenham, after its mention in Doomsday Book, occurs in the charter by which Ricard Fitz Wale, lord of Eydon, and Maud his wife gave to the priory of Canons' Ashby, in which they intended to be buried, the church of Putenham with its appurtenances, to wit, sixteen acres of land in one field, sixteen acres of land in the other field, four acres of meadow and all the moor under their garden.¶

By another charter Maud, the daughter of William de Putenham,

* Red Book of the Exchequer.
† Curia Regis Rolls, 1194–5. (Pipe Roll Soc., vol. xiv.)
‡ Bracton's Note Book, no. 1355.
§ Crewellon or Croughton, co. Northants, was a Turville fee and Simon—the son of Simon and grandson of Robert de Turville [Ancient Deeds B 309]—was apparently a cadet of the family.
‖ Bracton's Note Book no. 203.
¶ The cartulary of this convent [Egerton M. S. 3033], owing to the War, is at present inaccessible, and I am indebted to Baker's "History of Northants" for the abstracts of the three Putenham charters which I have used.

670

confirmed the above grant for the soul of her husband Ricard Fitz Wale.

These deeds show that Ricard Fitz Wale, who occurs in a XII[th] century Survey of Northants * as holding two hides in "Cydona" of the fee of Leicester, had married Maud the daughter, and obviously the heir, of William de Putenham.

Now in 1177 the Pipe Roll for Bucks. records that "Ricard Fitz Wale owes 40 s for the right of half a knight's fee that he has not yet had." Similar entries recur every year up to and including the 33rd year of Henry II when more precise information is afforded. "Ricard Fitz Wale owes four marks that Maud his wife may have recognition of the death of her uncle for his fee of half a knight in Penna de Tapeslawe." The following year he pays the four marks and is quit, and there is no further reference to the matter.

The Turvilles alone at this date had any interest in Penn, which was anciently accounted a member of Taplow and is so described in a fine levied in 1197, by which William de Turville granted Taplow to the prior of Merton reserving, however, to himself and his heirs "totam villam de Lapenne que dicebatur membrum de Tappelow."

It follows, from these facts, that Maud's uncle was Geoffrey de Turville and that her father was his brother William mentioned in the deed of 1146.

The exact descent of the Putenhams from Ricard Fitz Wale and Maud de Putenham, which must remain, for the present, doubtful, will probably be revealed when the muniments of the monastic houses to which they were benefactors become once more available. Additional information may well be provided by the Canon's Ashby cartulary and Ricard Fitz Wale's grant of Eydon church to the abbey of St. Mary of Leicester, which was subsequently confirmed by charters and final concords † preserved in the cartulary of that convent.‡ Together these sources should supply the evidence necessary to complete the pedigree of the family.

While it is apparent that Maude de Putenham had a daughter Alice, who by a recorded charter gave her marriage of Stoke to the monks of Wardon,§ nothing has so far been discovered concerning her sons. There are, however, slight indications that Ricard Fitz Wale was succeeded by a son Henry‖ and perhaps the Ralf who held Putenham during the first third of the XIII[th] century was Ricard's younger son. But that Ralf was not the heir of the Fitz Wales is

* Cott. MS. Vesp. E XXII.

† A XV[th] century Rental of the abbey [Bodleian Lib. Land M. S. H 72] states "we have three confirmation charters of this church and three final concords."

‡ Cott. MS. Vitell. F. XVII.

§ *Sciant tam futuri quam presentes quod ego Aliz filia Matildis de Putheam dedi et concessi et hae carta confirmavi deo et sancte Marie et monachis de Wardona ibidem deo servientibus maritagium meum de Stoche in liberam et perpetuam elemosinam Ita quod predictam terram a predictis monachis quam diu vixero tenebo Reddendo annuatim duos solidos scilicet infra octavas sancte Andree apostoli Hiis testibus Philippo persona de Enidona Willelmo de Cantebruge Matheo filio eius.* [Cartulary of Wardon Abbey. Beds. Hist. Rec. Soc. XIII. no. 149.]

‖ A Henry Fitz Wale gave to the monks of Wardon twenty acres in Eydon [*ibid.*, no. 121] and a grant [*ibid.*, no. 123] by Walkelin, son of Ricard of Eydon, mentions the land "Ricardi filii Henrici domini mei."

evident, for in 1219, while he was still living, a Ricard Fitz Wale was at law with the abbot of Leicester concerning the advowson of Eydon church which his grandfather Ricard had given to the convent.* Presumably Ralf died without issue, for the manor seems to have reverted to the Fitz Wales, and when it is next mentioned—in 1265—was held by Hugh de Herdebergh, knight—one of the heirs of the Turvilles—as guardian of John Fitz Wale of Putenham.†

It was this John who abandoned the patronymic and took as his surname the de Putenham by which his descendants were henceforth known. In 1278, as John Fitz Wale, he confirmed the grant of the church to Canon's Ashby, "as in the charter of his uncle Richard de Puteham."‡ In 1288 he attests as John, lord of Putenham.§ In 1305 Sir Thomas Wale, lord of Eydon, granted—or rather confirmed as mesne overlord—to Roger, son of John de Putenham, the manors of Putenham and Penn to be held for the service of one knight's fee and a pair of gilt spurs.||

In conclusion it must be stressed that this attempt to elucidate the origin of the family is based almost entirely upon records already in print, and no claim is made that it has involved research in original documents. Even before the contributor had appreciated the significance of the Turvilles association with the manor, the cartularies indispensable to the completion of the pedigree had all been removed for safety and will be wholly inaccessible until the War is over. But, defective as his account is, he submits that there can be no doubt of essential accuracy, and he looks forward to the time when it may be possible not only to trace the descent of the Fitz Wales more perfectly but also, perhaps, to add details of interest to what is known of the later history of the Putenhams.

Since writing the above, I have become aware that Baker, under Woodford, mentions the confirmation, to St. Andrew's priory, Northampton, by Ralf, son of Osmund Basset, of a virgate of land in Woodford which Osmund his father gave to Alice, his sister in marriage with Richard Fitz Wale of Eydon and which Henry their son gave to the priory. Obviously this charter, which implies that the Putenhams were descended from Richard Fitz Wale and Alice Basset, is a most important piece of evidence. It is, however, incompatible with Baker's pedigree of the Fitz Wales, which states that Alice Basset married Ralf Fitz Wale, Richard's brother, and this assertion is to a certain extent supported by the fact that a Ralf Fitz Wale is known to have had some interest in Woodford, where Walkelin, son of Richard of Eydon, gave six acres, "quas Radulfus filius Walonis dedit miehi pro servitio et homagio meo," to the monks of Wardon [Wardon Cartulary. no. 125]. It is, of course, possible that Alice Basset may have been Richard's first

* Curia Regis Rolls. 3–4 Henry III.
† Misc. Inqns. no. 709. His description as "John son of Wale de Puteham," due to misunderstanding on the part of the translator, is altogether misleading.
‡ This Richard was, I suspect, Richard Fitz Wale, lord of Eydon and Putenham.
§ Ancient Deeds C 5691.
|| De Banco Roll 155. m. 23. d.

wife and that the Putenham inheritance reverted to his children by her on the failure of his issue by his second wife Maud de Putenham. Judgment on this matter must, however, be suspended until the cartulary of St. Andrew's priory [Cott: M. S. Vesp. E XVII] has been examined. [A. V. W.]

[GENEALOGICAL RESEARCH IN ENGLAND to be continued]

## GENEALOGICAL RESEARCH IN ENGLAND

Communicated by the Committee on English and Foreign Research

### GIFFARD OF DRY DRAYTON, CO. CAMBRIDGE, ENGLAND

By Anthony R. Wagner, F.S.A.

Portcullis Pursuivant of the College of Arms, London

Reviewing General Wrottesley's work on the Giffards[1] Oswald Barron wrote,[2] "With such a name as Giffard, a mere epithet name after the fashion of so many Norman patronymics, and with houses whose very shields of arms show bearings as widely unlike as the three passant lions of Giffard of Brimpsfield, the three stirrups of Giffard of Chillington, and the indented fesse of the west country branches, we should at the outset look with suspicion upon any attempt to range all bearers of the name of Giffard as kinsmen one to another. Yet it may be said that General Wrottesley, without unduly straining probabilities, has done much to show that for the most part Giffard was Giffard's cousin all England over, and in Scotland and Ireland to boot."

Walter Giffard came with the Conqueror in 1066, a great leader with thirty ships and a hundred men at arms, and his son received the Earldom of Buckingham. Osbern, ancestor of the Brimpsfield Giffards and a tenant in chief in four counties at Domesday, was stated in 1221 to have come to the conquest of England. That he was of kin to Walter is shown by his grandson Elis witnessing a charter of the Earl of Buckingham.[3] The senior line of Brimpsfield expired in 1322, but two younger branches continued and survive to this day. The relationship of both to the main stem has been established by Mr. G. A. Moriarty.[4] Giffard of Twyford is represented by a family of generals and admirals descending from the younger line of Middle Claydon and Rushall;[5] while Giffard of Weston under Edge and Itchull survives in an Irish branch.[6] One of the Giffards of Fonthill Giffard held of a Giffard of Brimpsfield and General Wrottesley makes out a good case for deriving the Chillington line, which still continues there, from Fonthill, and a less good one for tracing the Devon Giffards to the same source.

There is, however, one family of Giffard still extant, barely noticed by Wrottesley, which can be shown, as the contributor believes, with certainty to have no connection whatever with this stock; a family remarkable especially on this, that though never of great wealth or consequence its continuity can be established from the time of

[1] William Salt Society, N.S. vol. V, 1902.
[2] *The Ancestor*, no. 3, p. 222.
[3] J. H. Round, "Calendar of Documents in France," p. 76.    *
[4] The REGISTER, vol. 74, pp. 231–237, 267–283; vol. 75, pp. 57–63, 129–142; *The Genealogist*, vol. 38, pp. 91–98, 128–134; *Genealogists' Magazine*, vol. 7, pp. 110, 250.
[5] Burkes' "Landed Gentry," 1937, pp. 881–883. The writer recorded this pedigree at the College of Arms in 1937.
[6] Burkes' "Landed Gentry of Ireland," 1912, p. 265.
*See Vol. I of this work, pp. 595–638.

Domesday to the present day, and that for more than six out of those eight and a half centuries it continued to live and hold land in the same Cambridgeshire parish of Dry Drayton. The pedigree cannot be proved without a break. There are weak or doubtful links in the thirteenth, fourteenth and fifteenth centuries and a slight uncertainty at the end of the sixteenth. But there are Giffard names in Dry Drayton for every generation and though the actual line of descent is in places doubtful, it cannot be doubted that it exists.

In 1086, at the Domesday survey, Giffard of Drayton was a juror for Chesterton hundred,[7] and Robert the Usher, Rodbertus Ostiarius, held one hide in the adjoining manor of Westwick.[8] There is nothing so far to connect these two together, but in the Pipe Roll of 1130 the Cambridgeshire return records the payment by Robert the Usher, son of Giffard, of one gold mark and seven ounces for his father's office. There can be little doubt that this Robert son of Giffard was identical with the Robert Giffard who held a sixth of a knight's fee in Cambridgeshire (and almost certainly in Dry Drayton [9]) of Stephen de Scalers from 1135 or earlier to 1166 or later,[10] and was party with Edward, abbot of Crowland from 1143 to 1173, and other lords of manors there to a division of lands in Dry Drayton.[11]

If this identification be accepted, it follows that Giffard father of Robert, that is Giffard of Drayton, the Domesday juror, was his predecessor in the office of Usher; and it can hardly be doubted that he in turn had succeeded his neighbour and his son's namesake, Robert the Usher, Domesday tenant in Westwick. The office being evidently a hereditary one Giffard will have been Robert's son or brother, and chronology suggests the latter. But we can go back further. Robert the Usher's appearance in Domesday is not confined to Cambridgeshire. We find him in Leicestershire also, holding two carucates in Howes and six in Claxton.[12] The section which includes these entries is given twice, a fact of interest to students of Domesday for reasons discussed by Round [13] and to us because of a small variation between them, for Robert is entered in one place as Robert the Usher but in another as Robert son of William the Usher. The pedigree and the office of Usher are thus carried back yet one more generation, and to a man independently known. William the Usher makes a more considerable figure in Domesday than his son. He held in chief in Nottinghamshire in Bromcote and Trowell [14] and in Devon is returned among the Servientes Regis as holding in no fewer than ten places.[15]

From Robert Giffard the Usher, who was probably as we have shown grandson of William the Usher, the descent is clear for three,

[7] Inquisitic Eliensis, ed. N.E.S.A., Hamilton, 1876, p. 99.
[8] *Ibid.:* pp. 115, 177.
[9] Farrer. Feudal Cambridgeshire, p. 39.
[10] Red Book of the Exchequer, ed. Hall, vol. I, p. 368.
[11] Gentlemen's Society, Spalding, Wrest. Park Cartulary of Crowland, f° 242.
[12] Domesday Book, 1783, vol. I, p. 237.
[13] Feudal England, pp. 26–27.
[14] Domesday, vol. I, p. 292.
[15] Domesday, vol. I, p. 117b; Exon Domesday, pp. 61, 63, 439; Devon Association Transactions, 1896, vol. XXVIII, pp. 401, 450; Whale and Ruchel, Analysis of Exon Domesday.

perhaps four, generations.    His son Reginald was a party with him
to the division of lands in Drayton before 1173, already mentioned,
gave land there to Crowland for his father's soul made a later gift
with his son Roger,[16] and is mentioned in several other records.[17]
He was dead in 1209 when his widow Matilda made over her dower
land there to Crowland.[18]    The son Roger, who held both in Drayton
and adjoining Oakington,[19] was dead by 1225, leaving a son and
namesake.[20]    The Memoranda Book of Barnwell Priory preserves a
return of the tenants of this Roger Giffard and their holdings.[21]
Among a number of others are some of his name; Robert Giffard
enfeoffed of 10 acres in the reign of King John; Reginald Giffard
with 15 acres; William Giffard enfeoffed of 25½ acres in King John's
reign; Cecilia Wambe, Roger's stepmother; Ralph Giffard with 13½
acres; and Joan Giffard with 8.    Several of these occur also in Curia
Regis Rolls, Hundred Rolls, and Feet of Fines, but their relationship
to Roger Giffard and one another has not been established.    The
same is true of a number of other Cambridgeshire Giffards of the
thirteenth and early fourteenth centuries.    Another Roger was
taxed on the Oakington fee in 1284–1286.[22]    In 1286 a Ralph Giffard
had licence to alienate 2½ acres in Dry Drayton to Barnwell Priory.[23]
In 1303 he had given them 2 more acres there.[24]    In 1318 he was in
trouble for breaking into the prior of Barnwell's house at Madingley,
assaulting his men and driving away 160 of his sheep worth £30.[25]
In 1323 he was pardoned for adherence to the rebels,[26] and is last
mentioned as receiving a pardon in 1330.[27]    It is possible of course
that these entries do not all relate to one man, but at least all relate
to men of one place and family.    What is harder to decide but also
more interesting is whether this man or any of these men can be
identified, either with Ralph Giffard, sheriff of Cambridgeshire and
Huntingdonshire, and Constable of Cambridge Castle in 1315, 1318
and 1319, and sheriff of Essex and Hertfordshire and Constable of
Colchester Castle in 1319 and 1320, or with Ralph Giffard of Great
Sampford, Essex, and Giffard's Gilston in Sawbridgeworth, Hertfordshire.    This last Ralph was son of a William Giffard of Great
Sampford who has been identified with Sir William Giffard of Bowers Giffard, Essex.    The latter married Gundreda, daughter of
William Bigod and grand-daughter of Roger Earl of Norfolk.    He
was succeeded at Bowers Giffard by a son Robert and grandson
John who, dying in 1348, was commemorated by a brass which still
survives though mutilated.    The Sampford and Gilston line ended

[16] Wrest. Park Cartulary of Crowland, fo 241.
[17] Pipe Rolls 1191–1195; Curia Regis Rolls 1198–1203; Oxford Historical Society, Cartulary
of Eynsham, vol. I, p. 116.
[18] Feet of Fines; ed. Hunter, 1835, vol. I, p. 330; Wrest. Park Cartulary, fo 241.
[19] Curia Regis Rolls, vol. I, p. 141.
[20] Feet of Fines, Cambs. 9 Henry III, 2 C.P. 25 (1). 23/10.
[21] Liber Memorandum Ecclesia de Bernewelle, ed. J. W. Clark, Cambridge, 1907, p. 136.
[22] Feudal Aids, 1284–1431, vol. I, p. 138.
[23] Calendar of Patent Rolls, Edward I, vol. II, p. 235.
[24] 16, vol. IV, p. 117.
[25] Cal. Pat. Rolls, Edward II, vol. III, p. 174.
[26] 16, vol. IV, p. 236.
[27] Cal. Pat. Rolls, Edward III, vol. I, p. 493.

with John whose heir at his death in 1414 was his sister Margaret, wife of John Chauncy, ancestress of Sir Henry Chauncy, the historian of Hertfordshire,[28] and Charles Chauncy, the New England settler. Neither of these lines has been definitely connected with the Dry Drayton family. On the other hand no other origin for them has been put forward and what is known of Ralph of Dry Drayton fits in, so far as it goes, with Ralph of Great Sampford.

Meanwhile the senior Dry Drayton line appears either to have expired or to have lost its former holding. With one or two doubtful exceptions[29] we hear no more of the Giffard fee there after the thirteenth century. But younger lines continue the name there and gradually gain wealth and local standing. Our information for the fourteenth and fifteenth centuries comes mainly from the splendid series of court rolls of the Abbot of Crowland's manor in Oakington (which included Dry Drayton), now belonging to Queen's College, Cambridge. Much interesting material, including the early history of the Pepys family, was gathered from these rolls by Miss F. M. Page for her "Estates of Crowland Abbey" (Cambridge, 1934). The contributor has to thank the President of Queen's, Dr. J. A. Venn, for his courtesy in putting them at his disposal. They run without a break from 1290 to 1528 and throughout this period Giffards appear frequently. The record, like most of its sort, is a chronicle of small beer, nor do successive generations retain the same holdings with sufficient constancy to give us the full and unbroken genealogical record that might have been hoped for. Isolated pieces of pedigree are proved however and a probable line of descent can be made out from 1328 downward. In 1291 William Giffard came into court and said that he held nothing of the Abbot of Crowland, but only payed him twopence from old time for a tenement which was of the fee of Giffard. In 1297 we meet with a Reginald Giffard, in 1307 with a Roger, and in 1308 with Ralph. Between 1328 and 1344 John Giffard is often mentioned in connection with small fines and offences. In 1345 John son of John Giffard is named and is probably the same John Giffard who appears as a juror from 1350 to 1362 and in the latter year surrenders 30 acres in Drayton to his son Robert. This Robert attained some local prominence, for the Patent Roll records the appointment in 1375 of a commission to enquire into the truth of an allegation that Robert Giffard of Dry Drayton, bailiff of the hundred of Leighton Ston, co. Huntingdon, had committed many damages, extortions and excesses by colour of his office.[30] The Court Rolls mention his wife Agnes and son John in 1380 and record his death in 1393. John died in 1416 and was probably father of another John, who continues up to 1460 and was probably father of Henry Giffard from whom the descent is clear.

Henry Giffard's will, made in 1496, was proved in the Cambridge Consistory Court. He left a son William who in his will proved in 1537 names seven sons and two daughters. From this the pedigree

28 Chauncy, "Historical Antiquities of Hertfordshire," 1700, pp. 60, 188.
29 Calendarium Inquisitionum post mortem, vol. III, 1821, p. 241; vol. IV, 1828, p. 87.
30 Cal. Pat. Rolls, 1374–1377, p. 150.

spreads out and evidence for several lines grows plentiful in wills, and the Dry Drayton parish register. Between 1564 and 1664 the latter has no fewer than 193 Giffard baptisms. A large proportion of these can be fitted into their place in the pedigree.

Boniface Giffard was one of William's younger sons and was living as late as 1569. His name heads a pedigree entered in 1634 [31] at the Herald's Visitation of London by his grandson "John Giffard of Hockston in Com. Midd. Doctor in Deuinitie." In 1626 this John had obtained a grant of arms and crest from Richard St. George, Clarenaux, so far as is known the only one this family has ever owned. The design is amusing for it combines elements from the coats of both the Brimpsfield and the Chillington Giffards, who were connected only remotely if at all with each other and not at all with the Giffards of Dry Drayton. The coat is Argent a leopard gules, on a chief azure three stirrups or, and the crest A demi lion rampant azure holding a stirrup or.

The Rector of Hoxton was son of a divine of some distinction, George Giffard, Vicar of All Saints Maldon. He was a son, as stated above, of Boniface of Dry Drayton; entered Christ's College, Cambridge, in 1569/70, was ordained priest in 1578, then aged 30, went to Maldon in 1582 but was ejected before 1585. He was preacher and lecturer at Paul's Cross in 1591, engaged in controversy with the Brownists and is described as a leader of the Puritan party in Essex.[32] He died in 1600 and was buried at Maldon, his will dated in that year describing him as "Preacher of Gods Worde in Maulden."

He had a brother Henry who remained in Dry Drayton where he died in 1612 and almost certainly another brother William buried at Dry Drayton in 1604. The evidence that William was brother to George is that George had a son Daniel and Daniel Giffard witnessed William's will in 1602, that William named his eldest son George and that in his will he names a daughter Sibell, wife of Nicholas Mathew of Maldon.

From this William the descent is at length clear to the present day. His great-great-grandson James was baptized at Dry Drayton in 1686. Whether he himself moved into Cambridge is uncertain, but at all events his son and namesake, born in 1714, was apprenticed there in 1729, and prospering as a wine and spirit merchant became an alderman and several times mayor of that town, dying in 1774. His elder son James served in the American war as a captain in the 14th Regiment of foot, and married an American lady, but returning to England settled at Potton in Bedfordshire where he died in 1813, aged 77. He left four sons and three daughters. His younger brother William (1745–1786) was "designed to succeed to his father's business," but "disliking trade" retired from it and lived on his fortune, settling first at Greenwich, "passing his summers at a house in the Isle of Thanet, or in France," and then at Quy Hall near Cambridge, where he died leaving a widow and two young sons. The elder of these, James Giffard (1775–1849), wrote about 1815

[31] C24. 572.
[32] Alumni Cantabrigienses, vol. II, p. 213.

a full and entertaining narrative of his own life, addressed to his son with the idea that "according to usual calculations, the chances are much against my living until you shall come to Man's estate." It is now in the possession of his great-grandson, Major W. L. Giffard of Epsom. He writes with much interesting detail of his early education in the house of Jeffery Bentham, minor canon of Ely, in the close there: of a short, unhappy time as a King's Scholar at Eton; then some years with a private tutor at Quy Hall, to which he succeeded on his father's death, preparatory to entrance at Trinity College, Cambridge. There unhappily he failed to secure a fellowship, and to make matters worse he found his affairs much embarrassed. He had to sell Quy Hall and taking orders became first curate at Whaplode, Lincolnshire, then at East Meon, Hampshire, and then at the neighbouring parish of West Meon. After this he was for a time a Chaplain in the Navy, after which he returned to Lincolnshire as curate of Wrawby. During his time there he married in 1808 Anne daughter of John Goodwin of Brigg (an ancestor of the present writer) and widow of Thomas Swan of Gainsborough. By 1814 his fortunes had so far improved that he was able to purchase the advowson of the neighbouring parish of Wootton. This remains with his family to the present day and the living was held successively by his son and grandson, the latter dying in 1923.

To recapitulate—the living members of this family can trace a clear descent from William Giffard, living at Dry Drayton in 1566. William was almost certainly a son of Boniface, grandson of Henry who made his will in 1496. A highly probable ancestry for Henry can be gathered from the Oakington Court Rolls back to John, who appears in 1328. Here we run into a tangle of disconnected Giffards occurring sporadically in Dry Drayton over a period of about a century. So far we have found no evidence to show their relationship to each other or to the main line which can be traced from Giffard of Drayton, the Domesday juror (or from William the Usher, his probable father) down to Roger Giffard in 1236, or the later Roger in 1284. It is a descent not easily paralleled.

---

## GENEALOGICAL RESEARCH IN ENGLAND

Communicated by the Committee on English and Foreign Research

### THE CHAMBER AND HATHORNE FAMILIES.

Contributed by G. ANDREWS MORIARTY, A.M., LL.B., F.S.A.
of Ogunquit, Maine.

In the REGISTER, vol. 67 (1913), pp. 248–260,[*] there was published an account of the ancestry of Major William Hawthorne of Salem. The following records prove that Thomas Hathorne of Bray, co. Berks, England, with whom the pedigree commences married Joan Chamber, daughter of Robert Chamber and granddaughter of William Chamber. It further seems quite probable that the said Thomas Hathorne was a younger son of John Hathorne of Bray who died in 1520, leaving a son and heir Henry Hathorne, and that Rob-
*See Vol. I of this work, pp. 267-279.

ert Hathorne who appears in the Subsidy of 1524 as of Bray was another brother.

## FROM KERRY'S "HISTORY OF THE PARISH OF BRAY"

1475 Thomas Chambour chaplain of Bray.
1520 John Hothorne died, leaving Henry his son and heir.
1531 Henry Hothorne died, leaving Roger his son and heir.
1533 Thomas Hathorn appointed Collector for Chaunters.
1535 John Bysshop held 4 closes at Crychefeld adjoining Thomas Hothorne.
1538 William Hathorn died, leaving William his son and heir.
1602 William Hathorne copy tenant and church warden.

## FROM RENTAL ROLL OF BRAY, 1650

East and Water Ockley
William Hathorne    £1.
Thomas Hathorne    3s.
Heirs of Robert Hathorne    5s.
William Hawthorne, Jr.    5d.

## FROM ASSART RENT, 1658

Ockley
Robert Hawthorn for house and lands 0/6/4
Thomas Hawthorn 0/3/3½
John Chamber house and close 0/1/4

On Lady Day [25 March] 1586 William Hathorne, grandfather of Major William Hathorne of Salem, held "Chambers" in Water Ocley; but at Michaelmas [29 Sept.] 1586 "Chambers" was held by Robert Golding. (Cf. REGISTER, vol. 67, p. 255.) **

From Kerry's "History of the Parish of Bray" (p. 10) we learn that on 1 May, 8 James I [1610], the King by letters patent granted to Richard Winch, Sr., William Hawthorne, George Bishop *et als.*, the improvement of the Queen's Lease in Old Field at Bray.

## FROM RENTALS AND SURVEYS PORT. 20/44 G. S.

22 Henry VIII [1530–31]
Brey
Thomas Chambers 15d.

## FROM LAY SUBSIDIES 14 AND 15 HENRY VIII [1523–24]

Binfield
Robert Hatheern goods 20/4.

It seems highly probable that "Chambers" in Water Ockley which William Hathorne held in 1586 descended to him from his grandmother Joan Chamber. The absence of the name of Hathorne in the early Bray and Cookham Court Rolls shows that the Hathornes came into Bray from the neighboring parish of Warfield, where the family was very numerous and where they gave their name to the well known Hawthorne Hill.

## FROM EARLY CHANCERY PROCEEDINGS *

### [Hathorn v. Chamber]

[Undated; between 1533 and 1538.]
[No Answer.]
Bill of Thomas Hotorne and his wife Johanne, one of the cousins and heirs

* Early Chancery Proceedings, 814, No. 8.

**See the footnote on p. 679, this volume.

of Johan Chamber, widow, deceased, sometime wife of William Chamber, deceased, John Garmon and "Alice his wiff the second & an other of the Cosyns and heires of the said Johan Chamber," Thomas Martin and "Agnes his wiff the third & an other of the Cosyns and heires of the said Johan Chamber" and Thomas Kyng and Isabell "his wiffe the fourthe and an other of the Cosyns [i.e., grandchildren] & heires of the said Johan Chamber."

Whereas the said Johan Chamber was seised of a messuage and garden and 60 acres of land, meadow and pasture in the parishes of Cokham and Braye, co. Berks, in fee by copy of court-roll and custom of the manor of Ivisplate in Maydenhed, co. Berks, at whose death the premises should descend to complts in right of the same Johan, Alice, Agnes, and Isabell, as daughters of Robert Chamber, son of the said Johanne Chamber; the evidences have come into the hands of William Chamber the younger and Thomas Davy and Jeffrey Holland and Johan his wife, and William Chambers the younger has wrongfully deforced complts of their possession and taken the profits by a long time.

FROM COURT ROLLS *

[Examined for Chamber, Ha(w)thorne, Martin, and Garmon.]

Braye   Court holden there 14 October, 5 Henry VI [1426]. Fines for release from suit of court—John Martyn 4d. Affeerers of this court: Richard Chambour, with John Westwode.

Braye   Court holden there 4 November, 5 Henry VI [1426]. Enrolment of charter of quitclaim. Robert Felton clerk comes into court and shows a charter of quitclaim to him from Agnes Newby of Windsor, widow, concerning her lands in Braye   Dated at Braye 31 May, 4 Henry VI [1426] and witnessed by John Palmere, John Est, Richard Chambour, John Westwood, and Richard Bedyll.

Braye   Court held there 16 December, 5 Henry VI [1426]. Twelve freemen on inquest as to payment for pannage [avisamentis] of pigs include Richard Chambour   they present "all well." Affeerers: John Est and Richard Chambour.

Braye   Court to be held there 6 January, 5 Henry VI [1427], adjourned to 27 January because it fell within the Feast of the Nativity. William Watford puts himself in mercy (2d) for licence to agree with Richard Chambour in a plea of debt.

Braye   Court held there 17 February, 5 Henry VI [1427]. Ordered that Richard Chambour, Thomas Euhurst and four others (named), set the bounds between the land of William Stauerton and the land of the College of Windsor in Slofur; and between the highway from Maidenhead to Windsor and the land of Thomas Boyer at Perystobbe.

Braye   Court held there 6 October, 6 Henry VI [1427]. John Adam comes to this court and fines to be released from suit 4d. . . . John Martyn the like   4d.

Braye   Court held there 8 December, 6 Henry VI [1427]. Richard Chambour amerced 2d. for breaking the assize of ale once.

Braye   Court held there 19 January, 6 Henry VI [1428]. John Martyn the elder appointed with others to make oath in a plea of trespass between Lucas and March.   in default.

Braye    Court held there 19 January, 6 Henry VI [1428].    Richard Chambour and John Westwood, affeerers.

Braye    View of frankpledge held there 2 May, 6 Henry VI [1428].    Braytowne [tithing]    John Martyn amerced 3d. as a butcher selling meat at too high a price.    John Martyn, junior, one of the 12 freemen, jurors for the King.

Braye    View of frankpledge held there 14 June, following 24 May, 6 Henry VI [1428], from which day the court had been adjourned.    Petty Court    Hugh Ryng brings a plea of debt against John Martyn the elder; ordered that he be summoned.    John Westwood and Richard Chambour, affeerers.

Braye    Court held there 5 July, 6 Henry VI [1428].    John Martyn in mercy (2d) for licence to agree with Hugh Ryng.

Braye    Court held there 27 September, 7 Henry VI [1428].    Richard Chambour amerced 2d. for breaking the assize of ale once.

Braye    Court held there 10 October, 8 Henry VI [1429].    John Martyn the younger comes and fines to be released from suit of court    4d.

Braye    Court held there 31 October, 8 Henry VI [1429].    Essoins from the common suit:    Richard Chambour, by John Herewood.

Braye    Court held there 2 January, 8 Henry VI [1430] adjourned (as to all business) to 23 January.    Richard Chambour among the suitors of the court before whom is heard a plea of land, by little writ of right, between William and Isabel Tilehurst and Thomas Euhurst.

Braye    Court held there 27 March, 8 Henry VI [1430].    William Aylward *v.* John Martyn and John Coeterell in a plea of debt.    Ordered that they be summoned.

Braye    Court to be held there 7 April, 8 Henry VI [1430], adjourned till 8 May.    Braytowne tithing.    John Martyn the elder amerced 4d. for being a butcher and selling meat at excessive rates.    Martyn *v.* Coterell default in the Aylward *v.* Martyn plea (above).

Bray    Second view of frankpledge held 29 May, 8 Henry VI [1430] John Martyn *v.* John Coterell put themselves in mercy (2d) in a plea of debt, for licence to agree with Aylward.

Braye    Court held there 10 July, 8 Henry VI [1430].    John Martyn in mercy because he did not prosecute against Thomas Purchas in a plea of debt.

FROM THE COURT ROLLS OF COOKHAM, CO. BERKS.*

[Examined for Chamber, Hathorne, Garmond, Kyng, and Martin.]

Cokham    Court held there 5 December, 9 Henry VI [1430].    John Garmond essoined in a plea of debt against John Elys    by John Pynkeny.

Cokham    Court held there 26 December, 9 Henry VI [1430], and adjourned to 16 January following.    John Garmond puts himself in mercy (2d) for licence to agree with John Elys in a plea of debt.    William Bangour *v.* John Garmond in a plea of debt; order to summon him.    Robert Kyng *v.* Richard Chambour summoned among other jurors to make their oath (touching a plea) between John Colyngbourne and John Millward in a plea of detention; Robert Kyng defaults with several others of the jury.

* Preserved in the Public Record Office, Court Rolls 154/14.

| | |
|---|---|
| Cokham | Court held there 6 February, 9 Henry VI [1431]. John Garmond pledge for John Tod "webbe." John Garmond puts himself in mercy (2d) for licence to agree with William Bangour; and with Philip Cook in a plea of debt. Plea between John Smyth and John Garmond in a plea of debt, adjourned. The beadle returns that Robert Kyng and Richard Chambour were summoned upon the same jury as in the previous court and Kyng defaulted. Philip Cook in mercy (2d) for an unjust complaint against John Garmond in a plea of trespass. Philip Cook complains against John Garmond and Christian his wife in a plea of trespass; therefore order is given to attach them. |
| Cokham | Court held there 27 February, 9 Henry VI [1431]. John Garmond puts himself in mercy (2d) for licence to agree with John Smyth in a plea of debt. Philip Cook in mercy (2d) for not prosecuting a plea against John Garmond and his wife Christian. |
| Cokham | Court held there 20 March, 9 Henry VI [1431]. John Garmond and Nicholas Tod in mercy (4d) for not having John Tod to answer John Horne. |
| Cokham | Court held there 10 April, 9 Henry VI [1431]. John Garmond in mercy for licence to agree with John Pynkeny in a plea of debt. John Milward aletaster of Northtowne presents John Garmond for brewing once; amerced 2d. |
| Cokham | View of frankpledge with court held there 1 May, 9 Henry VI [1431]. Maydenhithe [tithing] William Brown, tithing-man there with his tithing, presents that Richard Chambour is a taverner and takes excess [money for his sales]; he is amerced 4d. |
| Braye | Second view of frankpledge with court to be held there 22 May, 9 Henry VI [1431]. None of the view nor jury was attached because the day fell in Pentecost, therefore the court was adjourned till 12 June following, when John Passingiam tithingman for "Who" tithing presented that John Garmond dug a ditch upon the common opposite his garden; he is amerced 4d. |
| Cokham | Court held there 3 July, 9 Henry VI [1431]. John Garmond puts himself in mercy (2d) for licence to agree with Richard Chambour in a plea of debt. |
| Cokham | Court there 24 July, 9 Henry VI [1431]. John Garmond and Nicholas Tod pledges for John Milward in a plea of debt. |
| Cokeham | Court held there Tuesday, 10 October, 15 Edward IV [1475]. Thomas Garten, Esq., did suit of court and again, Tuesday, 10 October, 20 Edward IV [1480]. |
| Cokeham | Court held there Tuesday, Feast of St. Clement the Pope [23 November], 20 Edward IV [1480]. Thomas Lane brings a plea of debt against William Chamber who is to be summoned. |
| Cokeham | Court held there Tuesday, 12 December, 20 Edward IV [1480]. William Chamber is summoned to answer Thomas Lane. |
| Cokeham | Court held there 23 January, 20 Edward IV [1481]. Thomas Lane in mercy because he did not prosecute his plea against William Chambour, 2d. |
| Cokeham | Court (First Court, 5 Henry VII) held there 24 November, 5 Henry VII [1489]. Richard Chamber brings a plea of debt against William Smyth. (Court Rolls, P.R.O., 154/15.) |

Cokeham   Court held there 26 January, 5 Henry VII [1490].   William
        Smythe in mercy for licence to agree with Richard Chambre in
        a plea of debt.   (Court Rolls, P.R.O., 154/15.)

In 1586 William Hathorne, grandson of Thomas and Joan, held
"Chambres" in Water Ockley in Bray, which probably descended
to him from his grandmother; and his own mother, Joan, lived close
by at East Ockley in Bray.

William Chambre (the grandfather of Joan, wife of Thomas
Hathorne) is evidently identical with the man in the Cookham Court
Rolls of 1480–1481, and he is undoubtedly the son of Richard Chambre of Bray, the innkeeper, whose name occurs in the same Rolls
from 1426 to 1431.   The William Chambre, the younger, of the
chancery, is undoubtedly identical with William Chambre, citizen
and goldsmith, of London, whose will, dated 9 March 1558/9, was
proved 7 Nov. 1559.   This William, who lived in the parish of St.
Ethelborough, left a bequest to the parish of Bray and to his sisters
there.   He left to his sister, Joan Wigmore, wife of John; to sister
Katherine Wylcocks "now of Fulham;" and to sister-in-law Maud
Porter.   He mentions his lands in Essex, Bucks, and Berks, his
house and land in Raynham, co. Essex, and his land called "Hol-
ands" in Maydenhithe in the parish of Bray, "now in the occupation of Henry Roberts" (P. C. C., 61 Chayney).

From the foregoing records the following pedigree has been compiled.

1. RICHARD CHAMBER, of Bray, co. Berks, England, taverner, was
    born about 1398.   His name occurs in the Bray Court Rolls
    from 14 October, 5 Henry VI [1426], to 3 July, 9 Henry VI
    [1431].   He married ———.
        Child:
    2. i.   WILLIAM, b. about 1430.

2. WILLIAM CHAMBER (*Richard*), of Bray, co. Berks, England,
    yeoman, born about 1430, died about 1460.   He married
    JOAN ———, possessor of lands in Corkham, co. Berks, and
    Bray, born in 1440, died before 1533.
        The name of William Chambers occurs in the Cookham
    Court Roll, 20 Edward IV [1480–81].
        Children:
    3. i.   ROBERT, b. in 1461.
            Perhaps also,
        ii.  WILLIAM, the younger, alive 1533.
        iii. RICHARD, of Bray, 5 Henry VII [1489–90].

3. ROBERT CHAMBER (*William, Richard*), of Bray, co. Berks, Eng-
    land, was born in 1461.   He married ———.
        Children:
        i.   JOAN, b. about 1490; m. before 1533 THOMAS HATHORNE * of Bray,
                b. about 1490, died before 1557, when administration was granted
                on his estate.

* For a more detailed account of Thomas Hathorne and his descendants, among whom were the
founders of the Hathorne family of Salem, Mass., see the REGISTER, vol. 67 (1913), pp. 255–260. **

**See the footnote on p. 679, this volume.

Child (surname *Hathorne*):

1. *Thomas*, b. about 1520; d. before 16 Jan. 1565/6, when administration was granted on his estate; m. Jone Powney, widow, whose will was dated in 1575.   Children: (1) William, holder of "Chambers" in Water Ockley in the parish of Bray, 25 Mar. 1586; m. Agnes Perkins. (2) Christopher. (3) Thomas. (4) John. (5) Jone, m. William Winch.

ii.   ALICE, m. JOHN GARMON of Bray.
iii.   AGNES, m. THOMAS MARTIN.
iv.   ISOBEL, m. THOMAS KYNG.

[GENEALOGICAL RESEARCH IN ENGLAND to be continued]

685

## GENEALOGICAL RESEARCH IN ENGLAND

Communicated by the Committee on English and Foreign Research

### The Origin of the Hastings

Contributed by G. Andrews Moriarty, A.M., LL.B., F.S.A.,
of Ogunquit, Maine

Among the families which figure in that strange conglomeration, the British Peerage, that of Hastings has an exceedingly rare distinction, for the present Earl of Huntingdon descends in the male line from a man who occupied a reasonably important position in the England of the first Henry. Two branches of the family held two earldoms, that of Pembroke in the later middle ages and that of Huntingdon since the days of Henry VIII, and the present Earl descends from William Lord Hastings, the great minister of Edward IV, who has been immortalized in the pages of Shakespeare. Notwithstanding their great and distinguished descent, the early generations of this house are shrouded in uncertainty and it is somewhat remarkable that more study has not been bestowed upon them. The most exhaustive account of the family, "The Rise and Race of Hastings" by Dr. G. F. Clark, F.S.A., appeared in the *Archaeological Journal* (1869), vol. xxvi, pp. 12–19, 121–'36, 236–'56), which has, with some justice, been criticized by Dr. Round (*The Ancestor*, vol. II, pp. 91–92). It must be observed, however, that while the pedigree compiled by Dr. Clark contains serious errors, all students of the family owe him a lasting debt for the great amount of original source material collected by him, which is of vital importance to the study of this house. It is to be regretted that Dr. Round himself never undertook to compile the Hastings pedigree. The editors of the Hastings Manuscripts in the Historical Manuscripts Commission Series cautiously refrain from giving any detailed account of the early generations and the best account extant is that of Dr.

Eyton in his great History of Shropshire (vol. V, p. 135), but this account is only incidental to that of the Shropshire Banasters.

The following account, which is by no means exhaustive, is an attempt to elucidate the confusion of the earlier generations and has, at least, the virtue of fitting with the extant records. At the outset it should be observed that in the twelfth century there were two distinct families bearing the name of Hastings; that from which the historic house descends and another family which held Wix in Essex and the Barony of Little Eston in that county. No connection can be proved between these two families, but the contributor will suggest a possible connection which will, at least, fit with the records.

## PART I

In Domesday Robert the Seneschal of Hastings was a tenant in Sussex of the Abbey of Fécamp, but his holdings do not appear to have passed to the later Hastings and he cannot be definitely connected with the later bearers of the name (Victoria County History, Sussex, vol. i, pp. 375, 391), and the same is true of Ralf de Hastings, an undertenant in Essex. However, the contributor of this article is inclined to believe that William de Hastings in the next generation, with whom our pedigree commences, was a son of Robert of the Domesday. In the Pipe Roll of 31 Henry I (1130), William de Hastings owed 70/ in Essex for a debt of Goislin of London, and William owed also in Sussex, and in that county "William son of Robert de Hastings" rendered an account for Lestgo, Hastings and Rye (Pipe Roll, 31 Henry I, P. R. Soc., pp. 58, 68). It seems likely that this entry refers to the first proved ancestor of the family.

There appears to be some reasonable ground to suppose that the historic house of Hastings descended from the sieurs of Vernoix, who held Vernoix near Caen and were the hereditary Marshals of the Stable to the Norman Dukes, an office corresponding to the Staller of the English Kings. It is further likely that the great house of Marshal, Earls of Pembroke, derive from the same stock. (*Cf.* Mem. de Soc. des Antiq. de Norman., vol. xii, p. 15.) About 1050 the Duchess Maud purchased from Miles de Venoix and Lesceline, his wife, the lands at Vaucelles to endow her foundation of the St. Trinité at Caen (*ibid.*). Miles and Lesceline are said to have been the parents of Ralf de Venoix, the Marshal, and he is said to have had issue: Robert Fitz Ralf or de Hastings, also styled the "Marshal", Seneschal of Hastings and the Domesday tenant in Sussex (Domesday, 17, 73, 74b, 160b) and of Goisfred, the Domesday tenant in Hants. and Wilts., and who may have been the father of Gilbert the Marshal, ancestor of the House of Marshal. Robert Fitz Ralph may have been the father of Robert de Venoix and of William de Hastings, who impleaded Gilbert the Marshal and John his son, for the Marshalship prior to 1130, about which year Gilbert died (P. R., 31 Henry I; Dugdale's Baronage, vol. I, p. 599; Round's Geoffrey de Mandeville, p. 171, *n.;* Charter R., 1 John). It is reasonable to suppose that Robert de Venoix and William de Hastings were brothers, and that Robert succeeded to the Norman fief, while William, who remained in England, retained the name of

Hastings. In this event, however, it is difficult to understand why he did not succeed to the English fee.

With William de Hastings we emerge upon surer ground. William married the sister of Maurice de Windsor,* dapifer of the Abbey of St. Edmund's and the daughter of Walter Fitz Other, the ancestor of the Irish Fitz Geralds and of the Windsors. Maurice flourished about 1115–1148. Between 1115–1119 Abbot Albold granted to Maurice de "Windleshore" the dapifership of the Abbey, together with the knights' fees, which Ralf the former dapifer had held (Jocelyn de Braklond, Chron., Camden Soc.; Dr. Round in *The Ancestor*, vol. II, pp. 92–94). It is not unlikely that Ralf the former dapifer may have been a brother of William de Hastings. King Stephen confirmed Maurice in the dapifership (*ibid.*, p. 93). William de Hastings died about and shortly before 1130 (Eyton's Shropshire, vol. V, p. 135). In or about 1155, by a writ addressed to William Bishop of Norwich and the King's servants in Norfolk, Suffolk, Essex, Beds., and Northants, Henry II confirmed to Ralf de Hastings the dapifership of St. Edmund's and the lands which his maternal uncle Maurice de Windsor, the dapifer, and Ralf the previous dapifer had held. Ralf is described as "the Queen's dapifer" (Brakelond, *op. cit.*, p. 119; Round, *op. cit.*; Page's Suffolk Traveller; Dr. Clark, *op. cit.*). In the return of 12 Henry II (1166), Ralf de Hastings held 5 kts. fees of St. Edmund's (Red Book, ed. Hall; Round, *op. cit.*). This was the fee of Maurice de Windsor in Norfolk, Suffolk, Essex, Beds., and Northants. About 1152 Ralf gave the Templars his lands at Templehurst in the West Riding of Yorks (Mon. Ang., 1st ed., vol. II, p. 551; Tanner's Not. Yorks., LVIII). This gift he made in conjunction with William de Hastings. He occurs as "the Queen's Dapifer" in the Pipe Roll of 2 Henry II (1155/6) and in that of 5 Henry II (1158/9) as Sheriff of Kent. He was given 20 librates of land in Fordham, co. Camb., and in Witham by the King (N. Foedra, vol. I, p. 41, Clark; *op. cit.*). He was in frequent attendance on the King and frequently witnessed the royal charters (*ibid.*). Ralf died about 1166 and was succeeded by his nephew William.

Ralf had a younger brother, Hugh, who was the direct ancestor of the family. In the Pipe Roll of 31 Henry I (1130), Hugh de Hastings was excused from danegeld in Leics., Bucks., Warws., and Middlesex, on the lands of Robert de Flamville his uncle (P. R., 31 Henry I). Robert de Flamville was his wife's uncle. This Hugh died, apparently, prior to 1152, when Ralf and William made their gift to the Templars.

About 1166 William de Hastings succeeded to the dapifership of St. Edmund's. Henry II confirmed to William de Hastings, "my despenser", the dapifership of St. Edmund's as it had been held by his paternal uncle, Ralf, and by the latter's maternal uncle (*i.e.*, William's grandmother's brother), Maurice de Windsor (Clark, *op.*

---

* It is significant to note that Gerald de Windsor, the brother of Maurice, held the dapifership of the Bishopric of St. David's and was Seneschal of Pembroke. He was the ancestor of the Irish house of Fitz Gerald.

*cit.;* Brekelond, *op. cit.,* p. 120; Page's Suffolk Traveller; *cf.* Round, *op. cit.*), and the same King confirmed to William de Hastings his inheritance which came from his grandfather, William de Hastings, and from Hugh de Hastings, his father, in the time of Henry I, and also the lands given to Robert de Flamville by Robert de Limesi, Bishop of Coventry (Bishop, 1100–1117), which came from his mother, Erneberga de Flamville (Eyton's Shropshire, vol. V, pp. 137, 151). Dugdale, in his Baronage (vol. I, p. 574), cites from the collections of Robert Glover, Somerset Herald, the confirmation by Henry II to his dapifer, William de Hastings, of the fees of Burbache, Barewell, and Birdingbury, with their appurtenances, *i.e.* Scerescleve (Sketchley) and Eston (Aston-Flamville), and Stapleton, together with his houses in Coventry, with a burges there and a croft in Wilie to hold by service of 2 kts. fees as freely as Henry I gave them to his grandfather, Hugh de Hastings, with Erneberga, daughter of Hugh de Flamville; and he also confirmed to him the lands of William de Hastings, his grandfather, and of Hugh, his father, which they held in the time of Henry I. The lands, which came from Erneberga, were those given by Robert de Limesi, Bishop of Coventry, to Robert de Flamville. This is evidently the same charter as that cited by Eyton. These lands descended in the eldest line of Hastings, and were held in 1375/6, at his death, by John de Hastings, Earl of Pembroke (Dugdale, *op. cit.,* p. 577b). William de Hastings * attested a royal charter in 1163 (Clark, *op. cit.*). William married Maud, daughter of Thurstan le Banaster of Shropshire (Eyton, *op. cit.,* vol. V, p. 135), and died prior to 1 Apr. 1182, leaving at least two sons, Henry and William. On 1 Apr. 1182 Thomas de Hastings appeared before the Abbot of St. Edmund's, leading "his nephew Henry de Hastings", who was not yet a knight, and demanded for him his hereditary office of dapifer of the Abbey (Brakelond, *op. cit.,* pp. 116, 117, 118; Eyton's Shropshire, vol. V, p. 138; Clark, *op. cit.*). In 1188 he was still a minor when Robert de Flamville, evidently a kinsman, was exercising his office of dapifer (Brekelond, *op. cit,*. 6, 117). Henry went with King Richard on the Third Crusade and died in the East before 1194, when William paid 100 marks relief and had livery of his brother's lands (Pipe R., 6 Richard I, in Norfolk and Suffolk). This William was the ancestor of the Earls of Pembroke and the Lords Hastings, now extinct, and from him the descent is quite clear. The entry of 1182 from Brakelond shows, moreover, that Hugh and Erneberga also had a younger son, who appears as uncle of Henry, and it is from him that the present Earl of Huntingdon descends. Before we deal with him, however, it will be well to notice some of the cadets of the family who were flourishing in the twelfth century, but who cannot be placed in the pedigree with certainty. Roger, Bishop of Litchfield (1129–1148), and Hugh, son of Richard, the overlord, confirmed to Poleworth Convent (co. Warw.) the lands in Aldbury given by Walter de Hastings and

---

* William as dapifer of Henry II was granted by that King the manor of Ashele, co. Norfolk, held by the sargeantry of taking charge of the table linen at the Coronation (Testa de Neville, Cl. R., 15 Richard II, m. 23).

# CHART 1, PART 1.

Miles de Venoix, = Lesceline . . . . .
Lord of Venoix near Caen.
Marshal of the Stable to
the Norman Dukes. Occ.
1050.

Ralf de Venoix, =
Lord of Venoix.

Roger the Marshal,
Tenant in Essex 1086.

Gerard,
Tenant in
Sussex 1086.

Goisfred, = . .
Tenant in
Hants and
Wilts.
1086.

Gilbert the Marshal = . . .
Tenant in Wilts, d.
before 1130, but
about this date.

John the Marshal
Held in 1165/6.
d. in 1165/6.
Marshal Earls of
Pembroke.

Robert Fitz Ralf =
"The Marshal."
Domesday tenant
in Sussex (1086).
Bailiff of Hastings.

William de Hastings = . . . sister of Maurice
Party to the suit
against the Marshals
before 1130. d. after
1130.

de Windsor, dapifer of
St. Edmund's Abbey
(occ. 1115—ca. 1148),
dau. of Walter de
Windsor.

Ralf dapifer
of St. Edmunds',
ca. 1115—20.

( . . . de Hastings = Robert de Hastings
(daughter)

of Wix, co. Essex,
ca. 1120.
See Chart 2.

William de Etton,
Tenant in Bucks.
d. in 1189.

Walter de Hastings = Hawis . . . . .
of Oldbury 1129—
1135.

Robert de Vernoix
Occ. before 1130 in
suit for Marshalship
vs. Gilbert the Mar-
shal and John his son

Hugh de Hastings =
of Barawell, co.
Leics., etc., jure
uxoris. (Pipe R.
1130). d. before
1166.

Erneburga, dau. of
Hugh de Flamville
and niece and suc-
cessor of her uncle,
Robert de Flam-
ville.

John de Hastings = . . .
Held Gissing, co.
Norfolk, and gave
it to Thomas.
Occ. 1189.

Henry de Hastings
Confirmed Gissing
to Hugh ca. 1195—
1203.

Richard de Hastings,
Master of the Temple
in England, temp.
Henry II.

Philip
(Mon. Aug.; old ed.,
II, 1021).

Ralf de Hastings,
Dapifer of Queen Eleanor.
Confirmed as dapifer of
St. Edmunds ca. 1155. d.
s.p. in 1166. Occ. 1130.

William de Hastings = Maud, dau. of Thurstan
Dapifer of St. Ed-
mund's. Dispenser
of Henry II. d. be-
fore 1 Apr. 1182.

le Bannastre, tenant in
Shropshire.

Thomas de Hastings =
Enfeoffed of Gissing
by John. Occ. as
uncle of Henry, 1
Apr. 1182. d. before
1194/5.

→ A    → B

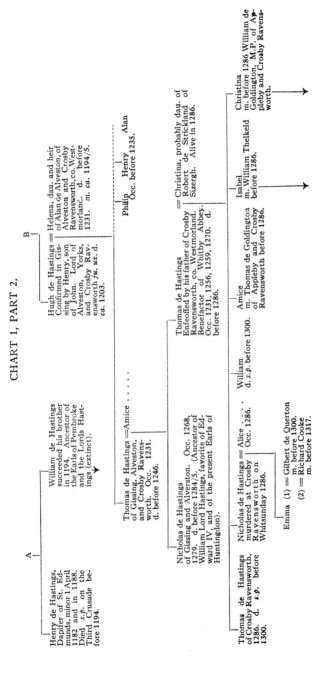

CHART 1, PART 2.

# CHART 2.

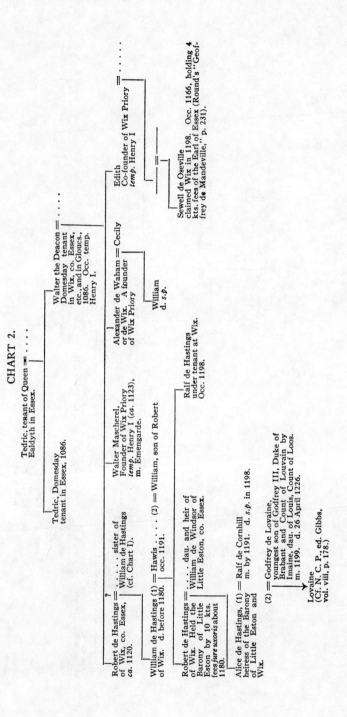

Tedric, tenant of Queen Ealdyth in Essex.

Tedric, Domesday tenant in Essex, 1086.

Walter the Deacon = ..... Domesday tenant in Wix, co. Essex, etc., and in Gloucs., 1086. Occ. temp. Henry I.

Edith = ..... Co-founder of Wix Priory temp. Henry I

Sewell de Oseville claimed Wix in 1198. Occ. 1166, holding 4 kts. fees of the Earl of Essex (Round's "Geoffrey de Mandeville," p. 231).

Robert de Hastings = .....sister of of Wix, co. Essex, William de Hastings ca. 1120. (cf. Chart I).

Walter Mascherel, = Founder of Wix Priory temp. Henry I (ca. 1123). m. Emengarde.

William, son of Robert

Alexander de Waham = Cecily or de Wix. A founder of Wix Priory

William d. s.p.

Ralf de Hastings under tenant at Wix. Occ. 1198.

William de Hastings (1) = Hawis..... (2) = William, son of Robert of Wix. d. before 1180. | occ. 1191.

Robert de Hastings = .....dau. and heir of of Wix. Held the William de Windsor of Barony of Little Little Eston, co. Essex. Eston by 10 kts. fees jure uxoris about 1180.

Alice de Hastings, (1) = Ralf de Cornhill heiress of the Barony m. by 1191. d. s.p. in 1198. of Little Eston and Wix. (2) = Godfrey de Lovaine, youngest son of Godfrey III, Duke of Brabant and Count of Louvain by Imaine, dau. of Louis, Count of Loos. m. 1199. d. 26 April 1226.

Lovaine (Cf. N. C. P., ed. Gibbs, vol. viii, p. 178.)

Hawise, his wife (Mon. Ang., 1st ed., vol. I, p. 199). It may be suggested that he was a son of the first William de Hastings and that he was named for his maternal grandfather, Walter Fitz Other (de Windsor). In 12 Henry II (1166), William de Etton held a knight's fee at "Budefuset", Bucks., as the maritagium of Annia, his father's wife, of the fee of William de Windsor (Lib. Nig., vol. I, p. 193), and in the Pipe Roll of 1 Richard I (1188/9), John de Hastings rendered an account for having the lands and inheritance of William de Etton, his brother (P. R., 1 Richard I). It may be suggested that they were the sons of the first William de Hastings by the sister of Maurice de Windsor. William de Windsor, his overlord, was the head of the house in 1166 (*cf.* Round in *The Ancestor*, vol. I, p. 124). John de Hastings is probably the man we shall meet again in connection with Thomas de Hastings. In the reign of Henry II, Richard de Hastings,* probably a brother of William II and Thomas, was Master of the Templers in England (Mon. Ang., 1st ed., vol. I, p. 436). Miles de Hastings, who witnessed the charter of Henry, son of John de Hastings, confirming Gissing to Hugh, son of Thomas de Hastings, may have been a son of John and brother of Henry (Hastings Manuscripts, Hist. Mss. Comm., vol. I, p. 206).

We now return to Thomas, brother of William II. In the reign of Henry II, John de Hastings gave Gissing, co. Norfolk, to Thomas de Hastings, and this gift was confirmed by Henry, son of John de Hastings, to Hugh, son of the said Thomas, at the end of the twelfth century (Hastings Manuscripts, *op. cit.*, 1925, vol. I, p. 206). Among the witnesses were Robert, Hugh, and William de Flamville. The date of Thomas's death is uncertain, but he was, as we have seen, alive on 1 April 1182, and he was certainly dead by 1195 and evidently before the accession of Richard I (1189). His son and successor in Gissing was Hugh de Hastings, to whom Henry, son of John, confirmed the gift of Gissing made by his father to Thomas, the father of Hugh.

Hugh de Hastings, who succeeded to Gissing, made a great marriage with Helen, daughter and heiress of Alan de Alveston of Alveston, co. Yorks., and Crosby Ravensworth, co. Westmorland. Alan de Alveston, who was the member of a great native house in the North, descended in the male line from Arkill Egfridson, the great Yorkshire thegn in the Conqueror's time. It was in this way that Thomas and his descendants became seised of Alveston and Crosby Ravensworth. Hugh de Hastings, for his soul and that of Helen, his wife, confirmed to St. Peter's, York, all the lands in Alveston which Torfin de Alveston and Alan, his son, gave them (Reg. St. Leonard's Hosp. York, Cott. Mss., f° 138; cited in Dugdale *op. cit.*, vol. I, p. 579). Helen de Hastings gave to Eggleston Abbey her rights in the pasturage of the church at Startforth; this was witnessed by Honorius Archdeacon of Richmond, William Abbot of Jervaulx, Roald the Constable (of Richmond), and Henry Fitz Henry. Dated early in the thirteenth century (Inspeximus Edward II, Cal. Pat. R.,

---

* An inspeximus of Edward III confirmed to Wroxhall Priory a gift made by Master Richard de Hastings, Master of the Temple in England (Col. Pat. R., Edw. III).

1307–1313, p. 574). This gift was confirmed by Thomas, son of Helena (*ibid.*). Hugh died prior to 1203, when the King granted the wardship of his lands and the marriage of his widow (*Cart. Antiq.*, X, p. 27). Helena was dead by 1231 (Ft. Fines Yorks., 15 Henry III, no. 104). They had as issue a son Thomas. There may also have been another son Philip, who witnessed the charter of Thomas de Hastings about 1220–1225 to Whitby (*vide post*). This Philip may have been named for an earlier one, who witnessed a charter of John de Coucy late in the twelfth century (Mon. Ang., 1st ed., vol. II, p. 1021).

We have to consider next Thomas, son of Hugh of Gissing. This Thomas inherited his father's manor of Gissing, co. Norfolk, and his mother's manors of Alveston and Crosby Ravensworth. About 1220–1235 he confirmed to Whitby Abbey the gifts of Torfin de Alveston and Alan his son, "my grandfather", in Crosby Ravensworth, and this charter was witnessed by Philip de Hastings (*cf.* above), Gilbert de Aton (*ca.* 1202–35) and by Henry and Alan de Hastings (Whitby Chart., Surt. Soc., vol. I, p. 37, no. 31). Henry and Alan were probably his brothers. Thomas died prior to 1247, as in that year his son Nicholas settled dower upon his mother, Amice, widow of Thomas de Hastings (Harl. MSS., 3881, f° 2). Thomas and Amice had issue at least two sons, Nicholas, the elder, who succeeded to Gissing, Alveston and the overlordship of Crosby Ravensworth, while Thomas, the younger son, succeeded to Crosby Ravensworth. In 1279 Nicholas was lord of Alveston (Plac. Quo Warr.). Nicholas died prior to 1284/5 and was succeeded by his son, Hugh (omitted in Dugdale's Baronage) (Kirkby's Inquest, Yorks., Surt. Soc., p. 147); and Hugh in turn was succeeded by his son Nicholas, from whom the present Earl of Huntingdon descends. The descent of Alveston will be found in the Victoria County History, Yorkshire, North Riding, Vol. II, p. 421.

Thomas the younger, son of Thomas de Hastings and Amice, was granted by his father, prior to his death, in fee tail, his lands in Westmorland and Cumberland (*i.e.* Crosby Ravensworth, etc.). This grant was witnessed by Thomas, son of John, Sheriff of Westmorland, and Richard le Brun, Sheriff of Cumberland (sheriff, 1233–1235) (Hastings Manuscripts, *op. cit.*, vol. I, p. 201). On 16 Oct. 1256, Thomas de Hastings was granted exemption from knighthood (Pat. R., 40 Henry III, m.1). In 1255/6 he held Crosby Ravensworth of Nicholas de Hastings, who held of the Viponts (Westmdld. Assize R., 979; *cf. Cumb. & Westmdld. Ant. & Archaeol. Soc. Trans.*, n.s., vol. VIII, p. 263; *ibid.*, n.s., vol. XIV, 11n.).

In 1256 Thomas, son of Thomas de Hastings, quitclaimed to Whitby Abbey his rights in the advowson of Crosby Ravensworth given by Torfin de Alveston. Witnessed by William de Goldington (Whitby Chart, *op. cit.*, no. 321, p. 272). In 1263 he witnessed a charter of Sir Matthew de Rosgill to Sap Abbey (Levens MSS., Hist. Manuscripts Comm.). This Thomas gave his peat and heather, together with his commons at Crosby Ravensworth, to St. Peter's,

York, for the keeping of their grange at Gartham. Among the witnesses were Gilbert de Kirketer, Sheriff of Appleby, Philip de Hastings, and William de Morville (mid-thirteenth century) (C. & W. Trans., *op. cit.*, vol. XI, n.s., 318–9). Thomas de Hastings of Crosby Ranvensworth, brother of Nicholas de Alveston (Nicholas de Hastings of Alveston), quitclaimed to Whitby the pasturage at Crosby Ravensworth Church given to Whitby by Torfin de Alveston. Witnessed among others by Master William de Goldington (Whitby Chart., *op. cit.*, p. 269, no. 318). He was alive about 1270, when he witnessed a charter of Eda de Pinckney (C. & W. Trans., n.s., XII, 357–8), but he died before 1286 (*vide post*). His wife was named Christina and, in view of the fact that their granddaughter, Elena de Goldington's marriage to Walter de Strickland of Sizergh was dissolved, undoubtedly for consanguinity, it may be suggested that she was probably a daughter of Robert de Strickland, and a granddaughter of Walter de Strickland and Christina de Letham. Thomas and Christina had issue: Thomas, Nicholas, William, Amice, Isabel, and Christina.

Thomas, the eldest son, died shortly before 1300, in which year Henry de Threlkeld, Emma (daughter of Nicholas de Hastings), and Gilbert de Querton, her husband, together with William de Goldington and Christina, his wife, were heirs to a messuage and 50 acres in Crosby Ravensworth, which they had obtained from the heirs of William de Hastings (Assize R. 990, year 1300). In 1317 Emma, now the wife of Richard Cooke, quitclaimed her rights in Crosby Ravensworth to Henry de Threlkeld (*cf.* Canon Ragg's account of de Threlkeld in C. & W. Trans., *op. cit.*, n.s., vol. XXIII, p. 154). In his article upon the Threlkelds, Canon Ragg goes fully into the division of Crosby Ravensworth between the three sisters of Thomas de Hastings, who died without issue about 1300; William, his brother, died without issue, apparently, prior to Thomas, and Nicholas was murdered in 1286. Emma, daughter of Nicholas, does not appear to have had issue by either of her husbands. Of the sisters of Thomas, Amice married Thomas de Goldington of Appleby and Crosby Ravensworth; Isabel married William de Threlkeld; and Christina married William de Goldington of Appleby and Crosby Ravensworth, the brother of Thomas. The Goldingtons belonged to a burgess family of Appleby, who had probably come north from Beds. or Essex in the service of the Viponts in the middle of the century. William de Goldington was burgess for Appleby in 1302 and knight of the shire for Westmorland in 1306/7. Previously he had been Mayor of Appleby. The Goldingtons are an interesting example of a mediaeval burgess family, who became knightly feudal tenants. William's daughter, Elena, who was the first wife of Walter de Strickland of Sizergh, was the ancestress of that ancient house.

Nicholas de Hastings, the younger son of Thomas and Christina, met a violent end. In the Westmorland Assize Roll of 20 Edward I (1291/2), Amice, Isabel, and Christina accused Richard le Francys of Mauld's Meaburn, William de Harcla *et als.* of having murdered their brother, Nicholas de Hastings, on Whitsunday in 1286, while he was standing outside his mother Christina's house at Crosby Ravensworth. From this case it appears that Nicholas had a wife Alice and a brother Thomas, as well as a brother William. The jury found that Thomas de Hastings, brother of Nicholas, Thomas, son of William de Goldington (*i.e.* the elder), and Amice, his wife, and William de Goldington and Christina, his wife, and John de Goldington had made complaint against the accused at the town's head in Crosby Ravensworth (Assize R., no. 987). The murder was a brutal one and is a typical example of the manner in which the gentlemen of England, at this period, were accustomed to settle their little differences with their neighbors.

This completes the story of the earlier generations of the historic house of Hastings. The later generations can be connected quite certainly with the above described persons and it now remains to consider the other family of Hastings, the Barons of Little Eston, co. Essex.

## PART II

### The Barons of Little Eston
#### of the Family of Hastings

In Domesday Walter the Deacon and his brother Tedric held lands which descended to them from their ancestor Tedric, who held them by the gift of Queen Ealdgyth (wife of Harold). Walter the Deacon held in Essex and Gloucs. In Essex he held 2 hides in Bury of his brother Tedric, and he also held Purley, Little Eston, Ferne, Coln, Wix, and Estreford in that county. Wix was the gift of Queen Ealdgyth. It is somewhat doubtful whether these men were Normans or natives. Walter is clearly a Norman name, but Tedric is doubtful; in any event Tedric, their father, was domiciled in England prior to the Conquest. It may be suggested that they were of mixed blood. Walter and his children were founders of Wix Priory. Little Eston appears to have passed in some way out of the family and was the caput of a small barony of 10 kts. fees given by Henry I to Robert de Windsor, another brother of Maurice and Gerald de Windsor. Henry I, and Henry II, also, confirmed to Wix Priory the church there and 2 carucates of land, together with 7 villeins and the houses around the church, which had belonged to Walter Mascherel and Alexander, his brother, and Edith, their sister, and to Walter the Deacon, their father; and the same King confirmed ⅓ of Wixvill with which Cecily, wife of Alexander, was dowered, as per a charter of Alexander and one of William, son of Robert, his lord. (Cart. Ant. L., 2, 31, 14; *ibid.*, Rot. C m. 20d; Mon. Ang., vol. IV, p. 513; old ed., vol. II, pp. 282–83); and he also confirmed the gift of 10/ rent in Fratings vill which Alwin Wereward and Godheigh held of the said Walter Mascherel and which Alexander his brother gave at the request of Edith, their sister. This was witnessed by Robert, Bishop of London (1108–1128) (Cart. Ant. L., 2, 31, 14; Mon. Ang., vol. IV, p. 513). About 1130 Henry I confirmed the foundation charter of Wix made by Walter and Alexander Mascherel at the request of their sister Edith. Witnessed by Bernard, Bishop of St. David's, Geoffrey the Chancellor, and Richard the Keeper (Facsimile of National MSS. cited by Dr. Clark, *op. cit.*). They also settled on Wix Priory their lands in Wix Fen or Fen in Purley and 2 carucates in Wix held in demesne, and Alexander added thereunto his demesnes in Purley (Cart. Ant. L., 2, 3, 16, 19). There was still another brother, the eldest apparently, named Robert, whose son William confirmed to Wix the gifts of Walter Mascherel and Alexander his brother, "my uncles" (Cart. Ant. L., 2, 31, 10).

Alexander de Waham confirmed to Ralf son of William his own acquisitions and purchases in the vill of Wix, together with his lands in Hansell and Cokesete, etc. This charter was witnessed by William de Hastings and Robert de Windsor at Little Eston, after the death of William the lord (*ibid.*, L., 231, 7). Alexander de Waham, having no issue (surviving) by his wife Cecily (or Aelia), granted his lands at Wix, Wenberg, etc., to Ralf, son of William, son of Robert, for which his lord, William, son of Robert, and father of Ralf gave him 30 marks of silver, and Ralf confirmed to Wix the gift of Alexander de Waham, his father's uncle, which gift his own father William and his own brother Robert had previously confirmed (Charter in St. George MSS. cited in Morant's Essex, vol. II, p. 466). Henry I confirmed to Wix the grant of the "Isle of Siricheshire" and the tithes and demesnes of Alexander de Waham in Purley, etc. (Cart. Ant. L., 2, 31, 19), and Henry II confirmed the above gift of "Alexander de Wix", together with the gift of a virgate of land in Wendelby which was given by Sewel de Oseville, and also a gift of land in Oteley made by Ralf de Hastings (Cart. Ant. L., 2, 31, 16). This last charter was witnessed by Gilbert Foliot, Bishop of London (1163–1187), Ranulf de Glanville (the Justiciar), Herbert Walter (before he became Archbishop), Bartholomes and Roger de Glanville and Richard de Hastings (Facsimiles of Charters, cited by Dr. Clark).

It now appears that Walter the Deacon had issue: Robert, his eldest son; Walter Mascherel; Alexander, styled de Waham and Mascherel; and a daughter, Edith. They flourished in the reign of Henry I. Robert, who was overlord of Wix, was succeeded by his son, William de Hastings. This William had a wife named Hawis, who married, after his death, William son of Robert (Ft. Fin. P.R.S., Henry II-Richard I, p. 37). William and Hawis had two sons, Robert the heir, and Ralf, who acquired the demesnes of his great uncle (Alexander de Waham) in Wix, and those which he held of his brother.

Robert de Hastings, the eldest son of William, married the daughter and heiress of William de Windsor, the Baron of Little Eston and the son and heir of that Robert de Windsor, noted above, who received Little Eston from Henry I (Dr. Round in *The Ancestor*, vol. II, p. 92). Robert de Hastings made a return of his fees, but it was of a later date than the great return of 1166 (*ibid.*). This Carta of Robert de Hastings is as follows:

Walter de Windsor held 1 kts. fee in Swineland.

697

Ralf de Hastings held 1 kts. fee in Wix.

William son of Robert held 4 kts. fees in Godemanston, co. Dorset, and Bromley, co. Essex.

Robert himself held in demesne Little Eston in Essex by service of 1 kts. fee and a kts. fee in Bildeston in Suffolk.

Reynold le Bret held 2 kts. fees in Costreford, co. Essex.

The total number of fees in the Carta of Robert de Hastings was 10.

In 1199 Sewel de Oseville impleaded Ralf de Hastings for ½ kts. fee in Wix, which descended to him from his ancestors. He stated that Robert de Hastings gave it to Alexander, his brother, and on the decease of Robert, Alexander held it of William, son of the said Robert, and, after the decease of Alexander, his son (named William) * held it of William, son of Robert, and he declared that Ralf de Hastings is the overlord and so cannot hold it in demesne; moreover on the death of William, son of Alexander, it should have descended to the sister of Alexander, who was the grandmother of Sewel the plaintiff, as of right, because he (Sewel) and the aforesaid Ralf are of one stock and Ralf cannot be the overlord and the tenant in possession at the same time. In his answer Ralf declared that he was not the overlord because he had an elder brother, Robert, who had the right (of overlordship) and was the heir of his father's barony and this brother had a daughter, who is now the wife of Ralf de Cornhill (Curia Regis R., Rec. Com., vol. I, p. 318).

Robert de Hastings was assessed for the Norman scutage as late as 1206 (P. R., 7 John, cited by Dr. Clark). His first wife was, as we have seen, the daughter and heiress of William de Windsor of Little Eston, but he had, apparently, a second wife, Maud, daughter of Roger de Flamville (died 1164), and a sister and co-heiress of Hugh de Flamville (Farrer's Early Yorkshire Charters, vol. I, p. 420; vol. II, pp. 89–95). By his first wife, Robert de Hastings had as issue an only daughter and heiress, Alice, who carried Little Eston and Wix to her two husbands successively. She married first, prior to May 1191, Ralf de Cornhill, a member of the great City family of that name (Ft. Fines, P.R.S., Henry II-Richard I, p. 7). He was alive in October 1198 (Rot. Cur. Reg., Rec. Com., vol. I, p. 184), but died soon after as she remarried by 1199 Godfrey de Louvain, youngest son of Godfrey III, Duke of Brabant and Count of Louvain by his second wife Imaine, daughter of Louis Count of Loos (Rot. de Obl. et Fin., pp. 24, 37; N.C.P. ed. Gibbs, vol. VIII, p. 178). They were the ancestors of the baronial house of Lovaine in England.

The question which naturally arises is—what connection, if any, existed between the family of Hastings and that discussed in the first part of this article? The contributor would suggest that Robert, son of Walter the Deacon, also called Robert de Hastings, married a sister of the first William de Hastings and of Robert de Vernoix, and that her husband and their descendants thereupon assumed the name of Hastings.

[GENEALOGICAL RESEARCH IN ENGLAND to be continued]

* This statement disagrees with the charter noted above which stated that Alexander died without issue.

THE HASTINGS-WHARTON CONNECTION.—Mr. G. Andrews Moriarty has supplied us with the most valuable contribution yet made to the early history of the Hastings Family. His article, published in the January 1942 issue of the REGISTER, correctly supercedes all previous pedigrees of the early Hastings and, I believe, for the first time portrays the proper junction of the junior or Gissing branch with the senior branch. All pedigrees and biographies of the early Hastings personnel, including Burke's Peerage *re* the Earls of Huntingdon, should be made to conform with Mr. Moriarty's outline in order to offset some of the many errors now in print.

Mr. Moriarty has kindly given me permission to correct an assumption contained in his article. He had assumed that the Emma de Hastings who married Gilbert de Querton died without issue. As a matter of well-established fact Emma de Hastings and Gilbert de Querton were the founders of the Wharton Family of Westmorland county.

For the children and descendants of Emma de Hastings and Gilbert de Querton we are indebted to Edward Ross Wharton, M.A., a professor of Oxford University, who spent the last five years of his life making an intensive study of the origins of the Wharton family. In his "The Whartons of Wharton Hall", printed by the University Press at Oxford in 1898, on page 20 we find the following:

"In 1292 Gilbert de Querton (as the name was then written: the form WHARTON appears first in 1310) proved before the justices at Appleby his right to the manor of Querton. . . . Gilbert had improved his fortunes by marrying Emma Hastings, coheiress of the manor of Croglin, in Cumberland: and his descendants have ever since borne the 'maunch' or lady's sleeve, the ensign of the great family of Hastings. In 1304 Gilbert and Emma settled the manor of Croglin on their son Henry and his wife Margaret 'by service of a rose', i.e. on condition of his presenting them yearly with a rose."

Additional data may be found in six manuscript volumes, along with nine other volumes of Whartoniana, which Edward Ross Wharton deposited with the Bodleian Library where I was privileged to examine them. In Volume I of these Bodleian manuscripts ERW names three surviving sons of Gilbert and Emma; Henry, Thomas and William. Henry was named for his father's brother and Thomas and William were named for their mother's uncles. Henry was the ancestor of the main line of the family; Thomas had an only daughter who, by the way, was named Emma; and William left descendants in Beverly, Co. York and in Cockney, co Notts.

N. EARL WHARTON.

The above interesting note of Mr. Wharton is undoubtedly correct, and it seems clear that Gilbert de Querton and Emma de Hastings were the progenitors of the historic house of Wharton, later so prominent in English history. In this connection the well-known Wharton arms, "sable a maunch silver, on a border gold 8 pairs of lions' gambs saltaireways erased gules", is evidently derived from the maunch coat of Hastings, in accordance with the well-known mediaeval custom of assuming a wife's coat, when her family was of more importance than that of the husband. In his article on "De Threlkeld" (Cumb. & Westmd. Ant. & Arch. Soc. Trans., n.s., vol. 23, p. 15409) the late Canon Frederick W. Ragg, M.A., cites a deed, dated Wednesday in Epiphany 12 Edward III (1339), by which William de Goldington enfeoffed William de Threlkeld and Alice, his wife, and the heirs of their bodies, remainder to the heirs of William de Threlkeld of certain lands in Odelingal, Moseburgywanes and his part in the mill of Crosby Ravensworth. Among the witnesses we find *Henry de Querton*, who is undoubtedly the son of Gilbert and Emma. This deed helps to confirm the proposition that Emma left issue a son Henry.

I should like to point out that my article dealt with the family of Hastings exclusively and did not attempt to cover the issue and descendants of the daughters of the house, hence I made no detailed study of them and made the assumption that, as the bulk of the Hasting estates passed to the Threlkelds and Goldingtons, Emma died without issue; this was undoubtedly wrong and Emma was in all probability the progenetrix of the Whartons. In any event her descendants were beyond the scope of my article.

*Ogunquit, Maine.*　　　　　　　　　　　　　G. ANDREWS MORIARTY, F.S.A.

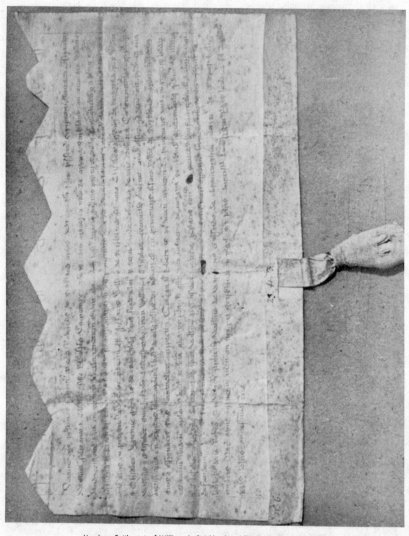

Marriage Settlement of William de Strickland and Elizabeth d'Eyncourt, 1239.

*From the original at Sizergh Castle.*

## GENEALOGICAL RESEARCH IN ENGLAND

Communicated by the Committee on English and Foreign Research

### The Early History of the Stricklands of Sizergh, Ancestors of the Carletons of Massachusetts and the Washingtons of Virginia

By S. H. Lee Washington, M.A., of Cambridge, Mass.

The following article by a very able Anglo-American antiquary upon the early generations of the ancient Westmorland house of Strickland of Sizergh is of more than passing interest to both American and English readers.   The Stricklands are one of the comparatively few English families still flourishing in their ancestral home which possess a proved pedigree reaching back into the 12th century.   Their present seat, Sizergh Castle, came into their possession in the 13th century by the marriage of the heiress of d'Eyncourt of Sizergh with a Strickland, and their muniment room contains charters and other family documents dating from the early 13th century.   Such families are rare in the England of the 20th century.   To Americans the story of their origin has an absorbing interest.   Not only were the Virginia Washingtons, the ancestors of the great George, directly descended from the earlier members of the house, but Edward Carleton, the early settler of Rowley, Mass., as has been shown by Professor Hazen, was a great-grandson of Walter Strickland of Sizergh (died in 1569), the head of the house in the middle of the 16th century (Register, January 1939).

No less than four accounts of the family are in print, the latest and best being that of Mr. Hornyold-Strickland, who married a daughter of the late Lord Strickland and resides at Sizergh.   Mr. Hornyold-Strickland's excellent account of the family is based largely upon the rich collections of charters in the muniment room at Sizergh, and he has cleared up several obscure points in the long descent in his critical history of the family.   However, his book does not show sufficient research, especially as regards the earlier generations, in the public records, with the result that the descent in the early 13th century is a bit uncertain and not as fully proven as one could wish.   This is especially true of the parentage of the William Strickland who in 1239 married Elizabeth d'Eyncourt, the heiress of Sizergh, and brought Sizergh to the Stricklands. This point has now happily been cleared up by Mr. Washington, who also shows the probability of the Stricklands being sprung from a cadet of the great Norman house of Vaux, so prominent in the North in the 12th century. It may be of interest to readers of the REGISTER to know that these points were also considered by the writer of this foreword and that, quite independently of Mr. Washington, he arrived at identical conclusions with him both as to the parentage of William of Sizergh and also as to the descent of the family from that of Vaux. In addition to these discoveries in which Mr. Washington and I are agreed the former has, thanks to his opportunity to examine the documents contained in the local muniment rooms of Cumberland and Westmorland, discovered for the first time the maiden name of Christian, the wife of Sir Walter de Strickland, first of the name (died 1236–1239), the son of Adam de Castle Carrock, the first *proved* ancestor of the family, and who was undoubtedly a cadet of the Vaux family. This discovery of Mr. Washington has disproved the conjectures of previous writers that Christian was the daughter of the Westmorland magnate, Gilbert fitz Renfrid, ancestor of the baronial house of de Lancaster. In addition to this, Mr. Washington has discovered much new material regarding the other wives of early members of the Strickland family, has also corrected the question of the eldest son of the house at the end of the 13th century, and has added much new information regarding the early cadets of the house and the descent of the Washingtons from the Stricklands. He has also made some new and startling discoveries regarding the descent of the d'Eyncourts, correcting the erroneous descent of that family printed by the late Rev. F. W. Ragg in the Cumberland and Westmorland A. & A. Society Transactions (*Cumberland and Westmorland Ant. & Arch. Soc. Trans.*, n.s., vol. xvi, p. 168). Among other things he has shown that Elizabeth d'Eyncourt descended maternally from the great house of Dunbar, cadets of the Scottish kings, and from the Uchtred Earldorman of Northumberland and his third wife Aelfgifu, daughter of King Aethelred the Unready. [G. Andrews Moriarty, F. S. A.]

THE history of the time-honoured English house of Strickland of Sizergh is one of very special interest: for, through intermarriage with the Washingtons and the Carletons, the Stricklands were ancestors both of the Washingtons of Virginia and the Carletons of Rowley, Mass. (cf. Burke's "Landed Gentry," 1940 edition, and the REGISTER, vol. 93, no. 1, January 1939). Not only do the Stricklands themselves still boast a male representative, but Sizergh, co. Westmorland, which they acquired by marriage with a d'Eyncourt heiress in the thirteenth century, continues to this day to be the seat of the family of the late Lord Strickland, a former Governor of New South Wales. Nevertheless it is only with the greatest diffidence that the contributor is venturing to present another paper on the Strickland pedigree; and his sole excuse is that the various genealogists who have dealt with this subject in the past [1] have perforce neglected the resources of the London Public Record Office, on ac-

---

[1] Curiously enough, the Stricklands were omitted from all the Visitations: and the first coherent account of them is that contained in Nicolson and Burn's "History of Westmorland and Cumberland" (1777), vol. I, pp. 87 *et seq.*, which is based almost entirely on the MS. pedigree and abstracts of Sizergh documents prepared *circa* 1770, at the request of Mrs. Cecilia Strickland, by the Rev. Thomas West, S.J. In 1887 an elaborate article, entitled "Genealogy of the Stricklands of Sizergh," was contributed by Edward Bellasis, of the College of Arms, to the *Transactions of the Cumberland and Westmorland Antiquarian Society*, Old Series, vol. X, pp. 75 *et seq.* More recently, two separate publications dealing in detail with the family descent have appeared in England, viz., Daniel Scott's "The Stricklands of Sizergh Castle" (1908), and H. Hornyold-Strickland's "Strickland of Sizergh" (1928). Plantagenet-Harrison's "History of Yorkshire" (1878) includes a partial genealogy (*ibid.*, p. 375), which, like the other products of its learned but misguided author, is a curious blend of fact and fiction: and shorter references will also be found in Archdeacon Prescott's "Register of the Priory of Wetherhal" (1897) and in Canon Wilson's "Register of the Priory of St. Bees" (Surtees Society, 1915).

count of the extraordinarily rich collection of family archives which is preserved at Sizergh Castle. He thus hopes that his own researches amongst the Plea Rolls and other unpublished material at the Record Office and elsewhere may help to supplement the existing information;[2] since, despite the attention of scholars, there is much in the early generations that has remained obscure, whilst the descent of the original lords of Sizergh—the d'Eyncourts —has never been properly investigated. In the first half of this paper an attempt will therefore be made to contribute some *addenda et corrigenda* to the Strickland pedigree prior to the reign of Edward III: and the second section will be devoted to the ancestry of Elizabeth d'Eyncourt, the heiress who brought Sizergh in marriage to Sir William de Strickland in the thirteenth century, and who was descended (as will presently appear) not only from such distinguished feudal houses as Stuteville and Greystoke, but even from the great Gospatric, Earl of Northumberland, and hence from the ancient Scottish and English kings.

## PART I

### THE STRICKLANDS

It has long been established that the founder of the Strickland family was a certain Walter de Strickland, *alias* Walter fitz Adam, living in the first quarter of the thirteenth century, who has been rightly placed by Mr. Hornyold-Strickland (in his admirable work, *Strickland of Sizergh* [1928], p. 10) as a younger son of Adam, lord of Castlecarrock in Cumberland.[3] This identification of Walter's parentage leads to a still more interesting possibility; for, although Mr. Hornyold-Strickland carries his pedigree no further, there seems a reasonable presumption that Adam's father was none other than Eustace de Vaux, who had been enfeoffed of Castlecarrock *circa* 1160 by Hubert de Vaux,[4] baron of Gilsland,—in which

---

[2] The contributor has likewise at various times enjoyed access to the Sizergh muniments (not all of which have been previously made use of), as well as to the great mass of private charters and evidences at Levens Hall, Rydal Hall, and Lowther Castle: and his best thanks are hereby tendered to the late Lord Strickland, Henry Hornyold-Strickland, Esq., F.S.A., and the late John F. Curwen, Esq., F.S.A.. also to Col. Anthony Lowther and the Trustees of the Lowther Estates, to the late Col. John Parker, C.B., and to the late M. G. Hughes Le Fleming, Esq., of Rydal Hall, for their courteous assistance in facilitating his enquiries during the past few years.

[3] Adam's eldest son and successor, Robert of Castlecarrock, is called "brother" of Walter de Strickland in the latter's charter to the monks of Wetheral (Prescott, "Wetherhal," p. 327). This disposes of the absurd legend, fostered by Agnes Strickland, the historian, that the Stricklands descended from an imaginary Sir Adam "Stryke-land," so-called from being the first Norman to reach the English shore at the time of William the Conqueror's invasion of 1066!

[4] The family of Vaux derived their surname from the *terram et feodum de Vallibus* in Normandy, which King John, on 14 July 1199, confirmed to the abbey of St. Jean de Falaise (Rot. Chart. [Record Com.], p. 5). Robert de Vaux (of Pentney) and Aitard de Vaux (of Surlingham), who were apparently brothers, appear in the Doomsday Survey as holding of the fee of Bigod extensive lands in Norfolk, Suffolk, and Essex. In 1246 Maud, daughter and heiress of the last Hubert de Vaux of Gilsland, claimed Aitard de Vaux as her "ancestor" (Assize Roll, Norfolk and Suffolk, no. 818, m. 19d.); but he was presumably only a collateral progenitor, since the direct descent was unquestionably from his brother, Robert de Vaux of Pentney (see R. S. Ferguson, "The Barony of Gilsland and its Owners," in *Transactions of the Cumb. and Westd. Antiq. Soc.*, Old Series, vol. IV, pp. 446 *et seq.*). This Robert, who in 1086 gave part of his tithes of Bernières in Normandy to St. Évroult, left issue four sons (cp. R. S. Ferguson, *ibid.*): (1) Robert, the founder of Pentney priory and a benefactor of the monks of Castleacre, Norfolk (Dugdale, *Monasticon* [1st edit.], vol. I, p. 628b; *ibid.*, vol. II, p. 19). He rendered the sum of £4 6s. 8d. in 1131 for having the inheritance of his wife (Agnes) at "Hocton" [Houghton], co. Norfolk (*Pipe Roll*, 31 Henry I. [Rec. Com.], p. 92); (2) Robert, surnamed *pinguis* ("the fat"); (3) Gilbert; (4) Hubert, afterwards the 1st. Norman lord of Gilsland. A fifth son, called Ranulf de Vaux, is traditionally stated to have been enfeoffed by Ranulf "le Meschin" (lord of Carlisle and subsequently Earl of Chester) of the three Cumberland townships of Castle Sowerby, Upperby, and Carlatton (Wilson, "St. Bees" [Surtees Soc.], p. 492). But the second Rob-

case the Stricklands themselves can claim direct male descent from Robert de Vaux, the Domesday tenant of Pentney under Roger Bigod. Eustace de "Vallibus" is duly mentioned by Mr. Hornyold-Strickland (*op. cit.*, p. 6), who does not, however, definitely affiliate him to Adam of Castlecarrock; but that the Christian name "Adam" was in use amongst the Vauxes at this period is evidenced by the occurrence of an Adam de Vaux as mesne-lord of Torcrossoc in Gilsland *circa* 1200.[5] It should also be observed that the Strickland arms, *Sable three escallops argent*, as well as their ancient crest of a holly tree, closely resemble the crest and arms borne by the Dacres of Gilsland, the Vauxes' heirs-general. Moreover, if this view of Adam of Castlecarrock's parentage be accepted (and there can be no question that, at least territorially speaking, he was Eustace de Vaux's successor), an equally noteworthy descent would be involved on the maternal side: since, according to the antiquary Denton ("Accompt of Cumberland," ed. Ferguson, pp. 195–6), Eustace had married one of the two sisters and co-heiresses of Robert son of Bueth, who was the last direct male descendant of a native chieftain, Gilles son of Bueth, the original owner of Gilsland (Gilles-land) in the days of Henry I.[6]

---

ert de Vaux (the founder of Pentney), in his charter to Castleacre, gives the names of his brothers as Robert *pinguis*, Gilbert, and Hubert, without any mention of Ranulf (Dugdale, *Monasticon*, vol. I, p. 628b): and not improbably there is simply a confusion here with Hubert de Vaux's younger **son**, Ranulf (afterwards 3rd lord of Gilsland)—especially as Hubert's eldest son, Robert (2nd lord of Gilsland), was undoubtedly in possession of Castle Sowerby in 1186. Hubert de Vaux himself was at the Court of the Empress Maud before the accession of Henry II (Round, *Cal. Docs. preserved in France*, pp. 72, 208), and received the barony of Gilsland, co. Cumb., from the latter monarch in November 1158 ("Victoria County History of Cumberland," vol. I, p. 306). The story that he and his brother Robert [Robert *pinguis?*] had been in possession respectively of Gilsland and Dalston some thirty years earlier, as feoffees of Ranulf "le Meschin" (Wilson, "St. Bees," p. 492), is probably apocryphal. Hubert died in 1165, leaving by Grace, his wife, at least two sons:—Robert, who d., *s.p.* in 1195, and Ranulf, who became his brother's successor and from whom the later lords of Gilsland derived (see G. E. C.'s "Complete Peerage" [ed. Gibbs], vol. IX, p. 397). Very likely Eustace de Vaux, who held Castlecarrock and Hayton of the fee of Gilsland (Denton, "Accompt," pp. 103, 139), was a third son of Hubert: he, at all events, must have been a near relative. Incidentally, it is interesting to observe that the Vauxes of Gilsland continued to maintain their East Anglian associations, despite their acquisition of a Cumbrian barony; since Hubert II de Vaux (died 1234) was in possession of Surlingham, co. Norfolk, and Denham, co. Suffolk, both of which had belonged to Aitard de Vaux in 1086 (Assize Roll, no. 818, m. 19d.). The christian name "Hubert" perhaps points to some ancestral connection of the Vauxes in Norfolk and Suffolk with the neighbouring families of Walter and Munchensy. Archbishop Hubert Walter was the guardian of Robert son of Ranulf de Vaux (grandson of the first Hubert of Gilsland) in 1199 (Pipe Roll, I John [1199–1200]); and *circa* 1150 Hubert III de Munchensy confirmed to William de Vaux land in Stratford [co. Essex?] which the latter's father, William de Vaux, Senior, had formerly held (*Cal. Ancient Deeds*, C. 2421). The original Hubert de Munchensy was a tenant-in-chief in East Anglia at the time of Doomsday Book.

[5] It seems not altogether impossible that this Adam de Vaux and Adam of Castlecarrock were identical. Nothing is known of Adam de Vaux's connection with Torcrossoc, beyond the statement of Denton (Accompt, p. 163) that he alienated the property to Robert son of William [de Corby], by a charter issued in the presence of Archbishop Hubert Walter and Robert de "Vallibus" (evidently Robert, son of Ranulf de Vaux of Gilsland). The names of these two witnesses date the charter itself as having been granted between 1199 and 1205.

[6] Eustace de Vaux's posterity could thus boast the blood of both the native and the Norman lords of Gilsland—a circumstance made more romantic by the fact that a fierce rivalry long existed between them (cf. "Victoria County History of Cumberland," vol. I, pp. 306, 310). Gilles son of Bueth only actually occurs twice in contemporary records—first, amongst the *judices Cumbrenses* who officiated at David of Scotland's inquest concerning the lands of the See of Glasgow *circa* 1124 (Lawrie, "Early Scottish Charters," p. 46), and, secondly, as a witness to the perambulation of the bounds of Stobo, co. Galloway, *circa* 1150 (*Scottish Antiquary*, vol. XVII, pp. 105–11). There are other indications, however, that he and his family long remained a thorn in the side of the Norman invaders ("Victoria County History of Cumberland," *loc. cit.*; *Transactions of the Cumberland and*

The outstanding problem in the early Strickland genealogy, however, is not so much the descent of Walter de Strickland as that of his wife Christian, about whose origin nothing definite has ever been ascertained, beyond the fact that a Fine of 1208 (quoted in a succeeding paragraph) proves that she was actually the heiress of the manor of Great Strickland, co. Westmorland, from which the family surname was derived (Scott, "Stricklands of Sizergh Castle," p. 10). Two rival theories as to her identity have, it is true, long held the field: but neither of them appears to rest on a sufficiently substantial foundation.

Thus, theory number one is based on the circumstance that Great Strickland itself, although situated in the parish of Morland a few miles from Appleby, was a "member" not of the barony of Appleby but of the barony of Kendal:[7] and hence it has been argued that Christian was a sister of the contemporary baron of Kendal, Gilbert fitz Renfrid, and that she received the manor of Great Strickland as her *maritagium* (Hornyold-Strickland, *op. cit.*, pp. 10–12). This hypothesis, however, appears entirely inadmissible. For, quite apart from there being no vestige of proof of any such relationship between Christian and Gilbert, we must remember that Gilbert's own title to the barony of Kendal was merely derived through his marriage to Helewise de Lancaster, so that he would be unlikely to enfeoff his sister and her descendants of land which he himself could only claim to hold *jure uxoris*.[8]

---

*Westmorland Antiquarian Society*, Old Series, vol. IV, p. 450). By one means or another, he himself seems to have retained possession of Gilsland right up till the date of Henry II's recovery of the northern counties from Scottish domination in 1156: and, though his death is expressly referred to in Henry's transfer of Gilsland to Hubert de Vaux two years later, his son, Bueth *barn* (i.e. "the younger"), and grandson, Robert son of Bueth, evidently made desperate attempts to recover their lost inheritance (cf. *Transactions of the Cumberland and Westmorland Antiquarian Society*, New Series, vol. XXVI, pp. 285 *et seq.*). This last mentioned Robert son of Bueth was an adherent of King William the Lion of Scotland in his invasion of England in 1174, but in 1177 procured a pardon from the English Crown on payment of a fine (Pipe Roll). He appears to have died without issue, and to have left two sisters as his co-heirs (cf. Denton, "Accompt," pp. 103, 195–6), married respectively to Eustace de Vaux of Castlecarrock and to Robert son of Asketill of Over Denton. (The latter's son, John de Denton, confirmed in 1214 to the monks of Wetheral a gift previously made to them by "Robert son of Bueth, my uncle.")

[7] (*Cal. Inqs.*, vol. VIII, p. 202; *ibid.*, vol. X, pp. 467–8; and *vide postea*, footnotes nos. 18 and 68). It seems worthwhile to point out that Mr. Hornyold-Strickland, in his remarks upon the early history of Great Strickland (*op. cit.*, p. 15), has been misled into confusing it with the manor of Strickland in south Westmorland, which was afterwards represented by the two townships of Strickland Roger and Strickland Ketel. Worse still, he has identified a native thegn called Gillemichael, who is mentioned in Doomsday as having held this same manor of Strickland under Edward the Confessor, with the Gilles son of Bueth who was lord of Gilsland *circa* 1150 (*ibid*, p. 4)! The latter statement has since found its way into Burke's *Peerage* and other publications, although Gilles and Gillemichael not only lived in different centuries but were wholly unconnected with each other. Moreover, Great Strickland near Appleby (i.e. in north Westmorland)—with which we are concerned in the present article—is not even so much as mentioned in the Doomsday Survey, being at that period part of a district that had not yet been effectually brought under Norman control.

[8] Helewise was the daughter and heiress of the second William de Lancaster, lord of Kendal (died 1184), and granddaughter of the first William de Lancaster (who died 1170). Mr. Hornyold-Strickland devotes considerable space to the ancestry of Helewise's husband, Gilbert fitz Renfrid, whom he represents (*op. cit.*, pp. 2–3) as son of Roger fitz Renfrid by Rohese, widow of Gilbert de Gant, Earl of Lincoln, and daughter and heiress of William de "Romare," Earl of Lincoln, son of Roger fitz Gerald (de "Romare") by Lucy, daughter and heiress of Ivo de [*sic*] Taillebois by Lucy, sister of Earls Edwin and Morcar and granddaughter of no less a personage than the celebrated Lady Godiva. The real object of this pedigree—apart from the splendour of the actual descent involved—is apparently to affiliate Gilbert fitz Renfrid, the alleged brother of Christian wife of Walter de Strickland, with Ivo Taillebois [his surname of "Taillebois" was not territorial, but simply a

The second, and rival, theory,—which was originally propounded by the late Dr. William Farrer,[9]—seeks to identify Christian as the daughter and co-heiress of a certain Uctred:[10] but here, too, the arguments fall to the ground for lack of proof, nor, indeed, did Dr. Farrer ever intend this supposition as anything save an interesting possibility. He founded his conjecture solely and simply on the Westmorland Fine of 1208 (previously mentioned), which records that Walter de "Stircland" and Christian his wife made an agreement with "Sigrid daughter of Uctred" regarding a carucate of land in "Stircland" [Great Strickland], whereby Walter and Christian acknowledged the said property to be the right of Sigrid to hold of them and of the heirs of Christian by the free service of a two shilling render yearly.[11] Thereupon, Sigrid granted to them all her land "from Aspelgile to Groshousic and from Groshousic to Bounwath," with remainder to Christian and her issue; and it was specified that Sigrid and her heirs were not to be amerced in the Court of the said Walter and Christian above an amercement of two shillings (Feet of Fines, Westmorland, 10 John [1208–1209], no. 28).[12] On the basis of the above document, Dr. Farrer proceeded to infer that Christian

---

nickname], who is known to have received a grant of the manor of Strickland *circa* 1090. Unfortunately, however, it can be demonstrated that Ivo's estate was not Great Strickland near Appleby, but the south Westmorland Strickland previously owned by Gillemichael (see footnote no. 7); and, moreover, Gilbert fitz Renfrid was not even descended from Ivo Taillebois at all. Indeed, the actual marriage of his father, Roger fitz Renfrid, with Earl Gilbert de Gant's widow, Rohese, has still to be established: and, apart from that, it has long ago been proved that Rohese, so far from being the daughter of William de Roumare, Earl of Lincoln, was in reality the daughter of the latter's maternal cousin, Richard de Clare. True, in either case she would have derived from Lucy, the wife of Ivo Taillebois and the grandchild (as Mr. Hornyold-Strickland has it) of the immortal Maid of Coventry (*vide infra*). But it can be shown that Lucy and Ivo's marriage was childless and, furthermore, that there were not two Lucys (mother and daughter) but only one (cf. G. E. C.'s "Complete Peerage" [ed. Gibbs], vol. IX). In other words, Lucy herself was married thrice: first to Ivo Taillebois (by whom she had no issue), secondly to Roger fitz Gerald (by whom she became the mother of William de Roumare, Earl of Lincoln), and thirdly to Ranulf "le Meschin," Earl of Chester (by whom she left *inter alia* a daughter, Alice, wife of Richard de Clare and mother of the Rohese who espoused Earl Gilbert de Gant). Not the least astounding feature of Mr. Hornyold-Strickland's pedigree is the resurrection of the long-exploded theory which places Lucy as the sister of Earls Edwin and Morcar. On the contrary, nothing whatever can be proved about Lucy's parentage except that she was, maternally, the niece of Robert Malet of Eye. After a prolonged study of the question, however, the present contributor has become convinced of the soundness of the hypothesis which identifies her father with Turold the Sheriff (of Lincoln). But Turold's own origin and ancestry remain wrapped in mystery; and certainly neither he nor Robert Malet could boast the faintest relationship to Lady Godiva!

In all this the writer does not mean to cavil unduly at Mr. Hornyold-Strickland's statements, his principal aim being merely to demonstrate once and for all that Gilbert fitz Renfrid was not a descendant of Ivo Taillebois and that Ivo himself was totally unconnected with the manor of Great Strickland.

[9] Quoted in Scott, "The Stricklands of Sizergh Castle," pp. 12–13.

[10] "This Ughtred had two daughters—the contributor supposes—Christiana, married to Walter de Stirkland, and Siegrid, a widow or unmarried in 1208" (cf. Scott, *op. cit.*, p. 12). Dr. Farrer also placed Robert of Castlecarrock as brother of Sigrid and son of Uctred, which is unquestionably at variance with the facts (see footnote no. 3).

[11] As a matter of interest, the contributor might mention that a Final Concord of 1200 shows that Sigrid had married a certain Maldred, who is described as *quondam viri sui* in a claim which she then brought against Walter son of Durand [of Great Asby] for dower in her deceased husband's property at "Werfton," co. Westmorland (Feet of Fines, Westmorland, 2 John [1200-1201]). Another Fine of the year 1208 refers to an agreement touching two bovates of land in "Stirkeland," made between "Sigrith" daughter of Uctred and Gilbert de Lancaster (*ibid.*, 10 John [1208-1209]). Incidentally, the names "Maldred" and "Uctred" are curiously reminiscent of those borne by the early paternal ancestors of the historic house of Neville.

[12] A further example may be cited in the case of the "Thomas Long of Stirkland" who was evidently a landowner in Great Strickland at about the same period (see p. 122).

wife of Walter de Strickland and Sigrid daughter of Uctred were sisters, and that Uctred must have been mesne-lord of Great Strickland under the barons of Kendal. But such a supposition is scarcely warranted by the language of the Fine. In the first place Christian is nowhere described, either in the Fine or in any other record, as Uctred's daughter; and in the second place there is nothing to show that this Uctred had ever possessed the *manor* of Great Strickland at all. That his daughter Sigrid (who was probably his sole heiress) did succeed him in the tenure of a carcucate or ploughland there, is apparent from the Fine itself; but this assuredly does not imply that Uctred's own status had been anything more than that of a freeholder or an under-tenant of Christian's actual father. Indeed, a somewhat analogous position would seem to have been occupied by another native landowner named Dolfin, whose daughter Eve occurs in 1246 as claiming various lands in "Stirkland" against Adam, son of the said Christian and Walter,—the lands in question having previously been held by the plaintiff's father (Dolfin) "*in dominico ut de feodo et jure tempore domini Johannis regis, patris domini regis qui nunc est*" (Assize Roll, Westmorland, 31 Henry III [1246–1247], no. 454).

Meanwhile, although far from being able himself to provide a complete solution to Christian's origin, the contributor can at least, he believes, offer a partial key to the mystery. For in the following hitherto undiscovered extract from the Westmorland Assize Rolls, Sir William de Strickland—who is known to have been Walter and Christian's great-grandson—explicitly refers to the latter as his "great-grandmother, Christian *de Leteham:*"

Michaelmas Term, 1291: "Alan son of Thomas son of Bernard de Midelton seeks against William de Burgh of Lonesdale one messuage and eight acres of land and three acres of meadow in Midelton in Lonesdale [in the parish of Kirkby Lonsdale, co. Westmorland], which he claims by a grant from Ralph de Berburne. And William de Striklaund [Strickland] seeks against the said William de Burgh one messuage and sixteen acres of land, which his great-grandmother Christian de Leteham (*Cristiana de Leteham proauia predicti Willelmi de Stirklaund*), whose heir he is, held on the day of her death. And William de Burgh comes and calls to warrant Matthew de Burgh and Avice his wife, who come and say that they hold the said land in right of the said Avice—along with Gregory de Thorneton and Agnes his wife, John de Bolton and Eve his wife, and Gilbert de Burnolfsheved [Burneside] and Christian his wife—of the inheritance of Ralph de Berburne, father of the aforesaid Avice, Agnes, Eve, and Christian. But all the above-named lands and tenements are now in the King's hands for felony owing to the imprisonment of the said Gilbert (de Burnolfsheved); wherefore the said Alan (de Midelton) and William (de Stirklaund) are without a day," etc. (Assize Roll, Westmorland, no. 985, m. 23).[13]

This record is incidentally of value as establishing for the first

[13] In February 1292/3 Sir William confirmed to the monks of Wetheral the charter previously granted them by Walter de Strickland, *proaui sui* (Prescott, "Wetherhal," pp. 326–327; Hornyold-Strickland, *op. cit.*, p. 18). There is also recorded a release from John de Reygate, curate of Morland, to Sir William de Stirkelande of an annual rent of four pounds of wax for having a chantry in his chapel of Stirkelande, etc., the said chantry having been originally founded by Walter de Stirkelande, "great-grandfather of the said Sir William" (Hist. MSS. Com., Various Collections [1903], vol. II, p. 339).

time the identity of the wife of Gilbert de Burneside, or Burneshead (a prominent figure in Westmorland *temp*. Edward I), as one of the four daughters and co-heiresses of Ralph de Berburne;[14] and we further'learn that another daughter had married Sir Gregory de Thornton, who served as Knight of the Shire for Yorkshire on no less than eleven different occasions between 1313 and 1333. The Berburnes had had possessions at Middleton-in-Lonsdale from a very early period. In 1280 Ralph de Berburne, above named, was defendant in an assize of novel disseisin regarding a tenement in "Midelton" brought by Adam del Eskes (Dep. Keeper's Report, XLIX, appendix, p. 119); and about the same date, as "Ralph son of Gilbert de Berebrun," he acquired property there from William son of Gilbert de Layfite (Farrer MSS.). Moreover, nearly a century beforehand, Richard de Berburne, lord of Berburne (*alias* Barbon in Kendal), granted land at Middleton in frank-almoign to the canons of Cockersand (*Cockersand Chartulary* [Chetham Society], p. 927).

But our interest naturally centres chiefly in Christian "de Leteham," wife of Walter de Strickland and great-grandmother of Sir William de Strickland, the claimant in the above suit against William de Burgh: and it thus becomes apparent that her own inheritance—in addition to the manor of Great Strickland near Appleby—had likewise included considerable holdings in South Westmorland at Middleton-in-Lonsdale, where her great-grandson still retained interests in 1291. Nevertheless, in spite of this fresh information and of the vital new fact regarding Christian's previous surname, we are not even yet in a position to identify with certainty the family to which she belonged.

The very name "de Leteham," for instance, presents difficulty; for there are no place-names in Westmorland which furnish any corresponding equivalents, though there is a Leatham in northern Northumberland and a Kirkleatham in the Northeast Riding of Yorkshire,—not to mention Lytham in the Hundred of Amoundness, co. Lancaster, which was not infrequently written "Liteham" or "Letham" in records of the twelfth and thirteenth centuries (cf. Baines, "History of Lancashire," ed. Harland [1870], vol. II, p. 503). It seems impossible, however, to connect Christian herself with any of the families associated with those three localities:[15] and at

[14] Ralph de Berburne, father of the four co-heiresses, held Whitwell and Godwinscales (in Kendal), co. Westmorland, of William de Lindsay in 1283 (*Cal. Inqs.*, vol. II, p. 269), and seems to have left a widow named Christian, who in 1298 was the relict of Adam de Layrwatholm (De Banco Roll, no. 122, m. 70; *ibid*, no. 118, ms. 59d. and 74d.). He was the son and heir of Gilbert de Berburne by his wife Joan, the eldest of the three daughters and co-heiresses of Roland de Reagill (Levens Hall MSS.; *Excerp. e Rot. Fin.*, vol. II, p. 278). This Gilbert was apparently the son of Gilbert, younger brother of Richard, lord of Berburne (already mentioned), whose daughter and heiress, Sybil, married Robert Fossard and became the ancestress of the family of Lascelles of Escrick (*Cockersand Chartulary* [Chetham Soc.], pp. 927–928; *Plac. de quo Waranto* [Record Com.], p. 787).

[15] Cf. Hodgson-Hinde, "History of Northumberland," pt. II; *Victoria County History of Yorks.* [North Riding], vol. II, pp. 103–105; and *Victoria County History of Lancashire*, vol. VII, pp. 214, 285–287. The early Lancashire lords of Lytham—the descendants of Roger son of Ravenkil, thegn of Woodplumpton—had lands (at Whittington, etc.) near Middleton-in-Lonsdale, where part of Christian's own inheritance was situated: and no less than three of the daughters and co-heiresses of the last thegn of Woodplumpton, Richard fitz Roger (who died in 1200 without male issue), married into families possessing Westmorland or Cumberland affiliations (*e.g.* one daughter, Margaret, became the wife of Hugh de Multon of co. Westmorland; another, Avice, married William

present the most that one dare say is that it would appear probable that she was the daughter and heiress of ——— de Leteham [first name unknown], who held the manor of Great Strickland and property at Middleton-in-Lonsdale of the barony of Kendal.[16] In the meantime, besides younger sons Robert and William and a daughter Amabel, wife of Sir Richard de Preston,[17] Walter and Christian de Strickland also left an elder son, Adam (who was presumably called after his paternal grandfather, Adam of Castlecarrock). There seems no doubt that this Adam son of Walter was indeed his father's heir, since—along with Robert of Castlecarrock, the grantor's brother—he was witness as a consenting party to Walter de Strickland's well-known charter to the priory of Wetheral (Prescott, "Wetherhal," pp. 326–327; Scott, *op. cit.*, p. 9; Hornyold-Strickland, *op. cit.*, pp. 10–11). But, apart from that, practically nothing has been learned about him; and the available evidence is both scanty and conflicting. In the first place, it is generally assumed that Adam died *vita patris* "about 1230" (cf. Hornyold-Strickland, *op. cit.*, p. 12), on the grounds that Walter de Strickland (Adam's father) was still living in September, 1238, when he officiated as a Justice at Appleby, and that Sir Robert de Strickland—who is known to have been Walter's grandson—made a settlement of the manor of Great Strickland in the year 1239. We shall return to the difficulties raised by the last-mentioned settlement in a moment; but in the meantime it also should be noticed that four separate documents demonstrate that Adam himself—far from dying "about 1230," as alleged—was still alive at least twenty years afterwards. The earliest of these records consists of an entry on the Westmorland Pipe Roll of 26 Henry III [1242–1243], showing

---

de Millum of Millum, co. Cumberland; and a third, Amice, married Thomas de Beetham of Beetham in Kendal, great-great-grandfather of the Sir Thomas de Beetham who was M.P. for Westmorland in 1302). But, unluckily, none of Richard fitz Roger's daughters was called "Christian" (cf. George Ormerod, "Parentalia," p. 7); and, moreover, they did not even inherit the manor of Lytham, which their father had granted to the Benedictine priory of Durham by charter issued between 1189 and 1194 (Farrer, "Lancs. Pipe Rolls and Early Charters," p. 346; *Reginald of Durham* [Surtees Society, vol. I], pp. 280-4).

[16] Conceivably some ancestral relationship with the Berburnes (for whom see footnote no. 14) lay behind the Middleton-in-Lonsdale lawsuit of 1291; and, moreover, in the twelfth century the Berburnes held considerable property at Lowther, which adjoins Great Strickland (*Transactions of the Cumberland and Westmorland Society*, New Series, vol. XVI, p. 114). But, in the absence of more concrete evidence, it is profitless to indulge in further speculations.

[17] For the son Robert (who was living in 1220 and from whom the later generations of the family descended), see page 111. The son William occurs in a Westmorland Fine of 1246, when William son of Walter [de Strickland] and Amabel his wife were the defendants in a claim for property at "Stirkeland" brought by Roger son of Jordan [de Lancaster] (Feet of Fines, Westmorland, 31 Henry III [1246–1247], no. 4). The daughter Amabel (who must not be confused with her sister-in-law Amabel, wife of William son of Walter) can be identified from a charter granted by Walter de Strickland to the priory of St. Bees, in which he confirms a gift made by Richard de Preston and the said Richard's wife Amabel, *filia mea* (Wilson, "St. Bees" [Surtees Soc.], p. 414). The early Preston pedigree has not hitherto been worked out; but the above Richard de Preston, who was of Preston Richard in Kendal, co. Westmorland, appears to have died before 1256, leaving by Amabel de Strickland (who survived him [cf. Wilson, "St. Bees," pp. 414–415]), a son and heir, Sir Richard, whose wife was named Alice (Feet of Fines, Westmorland, 40 Henry III [1255–1256], no. 30). The latter was father of a third Sir Richard, who married Amabel [?de Burton] and was M. P. for Westmorland in 1290, dying shortly before the year 1315 (see S. H. Lee Washington, "The Early Parliamentary Representation of Westmorland"). Thanks to this Strickland alliance the Prestons acquired property at Great Strickland (cf. Wilson, "St. Bees," pp. 412–415), which was considerably increased by later generations. It is interesting to note that the first Richard, husband of Amabel de Strickland, was a cousin-german of Sir Ralph d'Eyncourt of Sizergh (see Part II).

# THE CONNECTION OF THE FAMILIES OF STRICKLAND, WASHINGTON, AND CARLETON

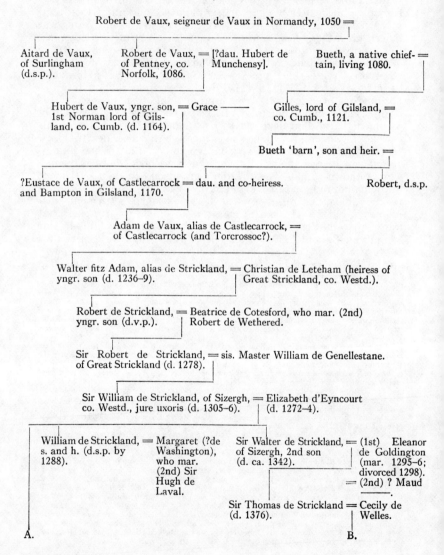

Robert de Vaux, seigneur de Vaux in Normandy, 1050 =

Aitard de Vaux, of Surlingham (d.s.p.).

Robert de Vaux, = [?dau. Hubert de of Pentney, co. | Munchensy]. Norfolk, 1086.

Bueth, a native chief- = tain, living 1080.

Hubert de Vaux, yngr. son, = Grace ——— 1st Norman lord of Gils- | land, co. Cumb. (d. 1164).

Gilles, lord of Gilsland, = co. Cumb., 1121.

Bueth 'barn', son and heir. =

?Eustace de Vaux, of Castlecarrock = dau. and co-heiress. and Bampton in Gilsland, 1170. |

Robert, d.s.p.

Adam de Vaux, alias de Castlecarrock, = of Castlecarrock (and Torcrossoc?). |

Walter fitz Adam, alias de Strickland, = Christian de Leteham (heiress of yngr. son (d. 1236–9). | Great Strickland, co. Westd.).

Robert de Strickland, = Beatrice de Cotesford, who mar. (2nd) yngr. son (d.v.p.). | Robert de Wethered.

Sir Robert de Strickland, = sis. Master William de Genellestane. of Great Strickland (d. 1278). |

Sir William de Strickland, of Sizergh, = Elizabeth d'Eyncourt co. Westd., jure uxoris (d. 1305–6). | (d. 1272–4).

William de Strickland, = Margaret (?de s. and h. (d.s.p. by | Washington), 1288). | who mar. | (2nd) Sir | Hugh de | Laval.

Sir Walter de Strickland, = (1st) Eleanor of Sizergh, 2nd son | de Goldington (d. ca. 1342). | (mar. 1295–6; | divorced 1298). = (2nd) ? Maud ———.

Sir Thomas de Strickland = Cecily de (d. 1376). | Welles.

A.

B.

A.                                                                B.

```
                    ┌──────────────────────────────────────────┐
                    Sir Walter de Strickland (d. 1407–8). = (1st) Margaret de Lathom.

                            ┌────────────────────────── = (2nd) Alice, who mar. (2nd)
                            │                                      Thomas Warcop.
                    Sir Thomas de Strickland (d. 1455). = Mabel de Beetham.

                    ┌───────────────────────────────┘
                    Walter Strickland (d. 1467). = Douce Croft.

                        ┌──────────────────┐
                    Sir Thomas Strickland (d. 1497). ⌐ (1st) Agnes Parr.

                            ┌────────────────────── = (2nd) Margaret Fowlehurst,
                            │                             widow Sir John Byron.
                    Sir Walter Strickland, K. B. = Elizabeth Pennington, widow of
                    (d. 1506).                  ───── Salkeld.  She mar. (3rd)
                                                  Sir Richard Cholmeley, and (4th),
                                                  Sir William Gascoigne.

                        ┌───────┘
                    Sir Walter Strickland = Elizabeth Neville, who mar. (2nd)
                    (d. 1528).              Henry Burgh; mar. (3rd) ───── Darcy;
                                            and mar. (4th) William Knyvett.

                    ┌──────┘
                    Walter Strickland, of Sizergh, = (1st) Margaret Hamerton.
                    co. Westd. (d. 1569).

                            │                  = (2nd) Agnes ──────.

                            │                  = (3rd) Alice Tempest, widow of
                            │                    Christopher Place.  She mar.
                            │                    (3rd) Sir Thomas Boynton.
                        ┌───┘
                    Sir Thomas Strickland, K. B. = (1st) ────── Seymour.
                    (1563–1612).                 = (2nd) Margaret Curwen.
                                         ↓
                                   LORD STRICKLAND.

            Ellen Strickland (half-sister of Sir Thomas), = John Carleton, of Beeford,
            mar. by 1582.                                   co. Yorks.  (d. 1623).


Joan de Strickland, = Robert de Washington
mar. 1292; living  │ of Carnforth in Warton,
1324.              │ co. Lancs. (d. 1324).
        ↓                                        ↓
WASHINGTONS OF VIRGINIA.          CARLETONS OF MASSACHUSETTS.
```

that Adam son of Walter paid 40s. "quia retraxit se," and that Roger [? *recte*, Robert] de Stirkland and Hugh le Despenser paid the sum of one mark by pledge of the same Adam (Parker, *Pipe Rolls of Cumberland and Westmorland*, p. 206). Next, in 1246 we have the claim (*ante*, p. 105) brought by Eve daughter of Dolfin against Adam son of Walter for a bovate and two acres of land in "Stirkland," and against Robert son of Robert de Stirkland for another bovate and thirteen acres there "with the appurtenances" (Assize Roll, Westmorland, no. 454). Moreover, yet a third document vouchsafes us details of a Final Concord levied at Appleby on the morrow of St. Martin, 31 Henry III [12 November 1246], by which Adam son of Walter agreed that a moiety of the manor of "Stirkeland" was the right of Robert son of Robert de Stirkland, in return for which the latter gave Adam eight bovates thereof for life and undertook to provide him with seven and a half quarters of oatmeal *per annum*. The aforesaid lands were to revert to Robert son of Robert de Stirkland at Adam's decease; and we also meet with the names (as interim feoffees) of Ralph d'Eyncourt (of Sizergh) and Rowland de Reagill (Feet of Fines, Westmorland, 31 Henry III [1246–1247], no. 14).[18] Finally, in 1250 Robert son of Robert de Stirkeland was impleaded by Adam son of Walter for dower at "Stirkeland,"—a claim which was clearly an echo of the Final Concord of four years before (Assize Roll, Westmorland, 35 Henry III [1250–1251]).[19]

There can thus be no question, in the light of the above records, that Adam son of Walter died, not "about 1230," but some time after the year 1250: and the problem which next confronts us is how to reconcile such a fact with Sir Robert de Strickland's settlement of the manor of Great Strickland as early as 1239. The contributor should explain that the settlement itself had been made by Sir Robert upon the occasion of the marriage of his young son William (the Sir William de Strickland of 1291, etc.) with Elizabeth d'Eyncourt of Sizergh,—a marriage which, owing to the broad acres that the bride afterwards inherited, was to have a far-reaching effect upon the future destinies of the race. But, although every writer on the Strickland pedigree from Nicolson and Burn onwards has duly mentioned this famous document, not one of them has quoted it *verbatim;* and that eminent authority, the late Archdeacon Prescott, even doubted whether 1239 were really the correct date of the settlement at all ("Register of Wetherhal," p. 326, note 3). However, the clarity of the original charter effectually excludes the possibility of errors. Moreover, apart from its value in confirming the charter's date as 1239, the context reveals other illuminating details:

[18] The document adds that, in the case of the vill of "Stirkeland," sixteen carucates comprised a single knight's fee. Therefore, as the vill itself owed the service of a quarter of a knight's fee (*ante*, footnote no. 7), it must accordingly have been rated at four carucates. Now one carucate equals eight bovates; from which it is evident that Robert son of Robert de Stirkland was allowing Adam one-fourth of the manor (*i.e.* half of the moiety).

[19] The last-mentioned entry was known to Plantagenet-Harrison (see his "History of Yorkshire," p. 373): but, unluckily, he translated the *Adae* of the original record not as "Adam" but as "Ada" and promptly identified this mythical lady as Adam's widow—a piece of carelessness that has served, not unnaturally, still further to mislead those dealing with the family genealogy (cf. Hornyold-Strickland, *op. cit.*, p. 12).

and consequently the contributor ventures to append a full transcription:

*Sciant omnes presentes et futuri quod ego Robertus de Stirkland, miles, dedi, concessi, et hoc presenti scripto indentato confirmaui Willelmo filio meo et Elisabete filie Radulpho* [*sic*] *Daincourt militis totum manerium meum de Magna Stirkland in comitatu Westmerland existente una cum seruicio liberorum tenencium ibidem molendo, boscis, pratis, pascuis, pasturis, et omnibus pasturis et omnibus aliis qualitercumquibus et ubiquibus eidem manerio spectantibus, tenendum et habendum predictum manerium cum pertinenciis una cum seruiciis liberorum tenencium ibidem, molendo, boscis, et omnibus aliis cum pertinenciis predictis ut predictum est prefatis Willelmo de Stirkland filio meo* [*et*] *Elisabete et heredibus de corporibus ipsorum Willelmi et Elisabete legitime procreatis, de capitalibus dominis feodis illius per servicium inde debita et de inde consueta. Et si contingat quod predicti Willelmus et Elisabeta sine heredibus de corporibus ipsorum Willelmi et Elisabete exeuntibus obierint, quod absit quod tunc omnia predicta manerium una cum seruiciis liberorum* [*tenencium*] *molendo, boscis, et omnibus aliis ut predictum est cum pertinenciis prefato Roberto de Stirkland, militi, heredibus suis et assignatis suis remaneant imperpetuum. Et ego vero Robertus predictum manerium cum pertinenciis una cum seruiciis liberorum tenencium ibidem molendo, boscis, ac omnia alia ut predictum est dicto manerio de Magna Stirkland spectantibus predictis Willelmo et Elisabete et heredibus de corporibus ipsorum Willelmo et Elisabete et heredibus de corporibus ipsorum Willelmi et Elisabete legitime procreatis contra omnes gentes warrantizabim et imperpetuum defendem. In cuius rei testimonium huic presenti scripto* [*inden-*] *tato sigillum meum apposui. Hiis testibus domino Thoma de Helbek, domino Roberto de Enewyth, militibus, Willelmo de Warthcopp, Galfrido de Brantingham, Henrico de Tyrer, et aliis multis. Datum apud manerium meum in Magna Stirkland in vigilia Sancti Johannis Baptisti* [*23 June*], *anno regni regis Henrici filii domini regis Johannis vicessimo tercio.* [Seal missing.]

Of the witnesses, Sir Thomas de "Helbek" (of Hillbeck in Brough) was the predecessor of a second Sir Thomas, deputy-sheriff of Westmorland 1292–1295; Henry de "Tyrer" held the township of Tirergh (now Tirrell) in the parish of Barton; and William de "Warcopp"[20] became the grandfather of Henry de Warcop, M.P. for Westmorland 1315 and 1316, from whom descended the Warcops of Warcop and Smardale. But the really significant clauses to observe are those dealing with the manor of Great Strickland: for here we see Sir Robert de Strickland already a knight,[21] and in possession of the entire Great Strickland estate (*totum manerium meum de Magna Stirkland*) less than three years after Walter de Strickland's death and over eleven years prior to the death of Walter's son, Adam.[22] What, then, is the explanation?

[20] The mention of this William de Warcop in 1239 supplies us with a missing generation in the early Warcop pedigree, of which a very inaccurate account was given by the late Canon Ragg in *Transactions of the Cumberland and Westmorland Antiquarian Society*, New Series, vol. XVI, p. 168. William himself seems to have been still living on 13 September 1265, when he occurs in company with Henry de Tirergh (*Cal. Close Rolls*, 1265, p. 131). Sir Thomas de Helbeck, Sir Robert de Yanwath, and Henry de Tirergh all attested a grant to Thomas Black made by Gilbert Engaine of Clifton, near Appleby, which, from its reference to Ralph de Nottingham as "then sheriff of Westmorland," must have been issued *circa* 1247–1248 (*vide* Nicolson and Burn, "History of Westmorland and Cumberland," vol. I, p. 416). For additional particulars about Sir Robert de Yanwath, who was related in some way to the d'Eyncourts, see Part II.

[21] He is again given the designation of *miles* when attesting (*circa* 1250–1260) a charter of John son of William de Thrimby to the priory of Wetheral (Prescott, "Wetherhal," p. 332).

[22] As has previously been shown, Adam, son of Walter, was alive at least as late as the year 1250 (*ante*, p. 108).

Clearly, the contributor thinks, there is only one,—and that is, that Adam, in spite of being Walter's eldest son, never actually succeeded to the Great Strickland heritage. (That Adam—like his younger brother, William, and his sister, Amabel—had certain holdings at Great Strickland, is of course beside the point.)[23] Moreover, we must remember that the manor of Great Strickland was actually the inheritance of Adam's mother, Christian; and such maternal possessions were frequently entailed on the second son, whilst the eldest son fell heir to the paternal property.[24] It should also be noted that Adam himself, unlike his father Walter, is never once styled "de Stirkland" in contemporary records, but invariably appears simply as *Adam' filius Walteri*. But in that case, who was Sir Robert de Strickland, the lord of Great Strickland in 1239 and the father of the (Sir) William who married Elizabeth d'Eyncourt? From this last-named Sir William's specific references to Walter and Christian de Strickland as his great-grandparents (*ante*, page 105), we at any rate learn that Sir Robert de Strickland was Walter and Christian's *grandson:* and Mr. Hornyold-Strickland (following Bellasis and Nicolson and Burn) concludes that he must have been Adam's son and heir (*op. cit.*, p. 12),—an argument based (*a*) on the fallacious premise that Adam died *vita patris* and (*b*) on a charter amongst the muniments at Sizergh which has "Robert son of Adam de Stirkeland" as one of its witnesses. But internal evidence would date the charter in question as *circa* 1280–1290;[25] and nothing indicates that the "Robert son of Adam de Stirkeland," there mentioned, was identical with Sir Robert de Strickland of 1239 or that he was more than a stray cadet of the main family.[26] On

[23] Cf. footnote no. 17.

[24] Some hint that Walter de Strickland did have lands of his own (apart from what he had obtained *jure uxoris*) is contained in one of his charters to St. Bees, in which he bestows upon that house two acres of arable land *de dominico meo in Crosrig* (Wilson, "St. Bees" [Surtees Soc.], pp. 413–4).

[25] The deed itself, which no one (including Mr. Hornyold-Strickland) has thus far quoted, records a release by "Alice del Hawes, late the wife of Thomas, son of Thomas de Levenes," of the two moieties of "Le Howes" [*i.e.* The Howes in Helsington, co. Westmorland],—one moiety of which she settled upon her son, Thomas, and the second moiety of which she divided between her two younger sons, Benedict and John. The witnesses, in addition to Robert son of Adam de Strickland, included Sir Roger de Burton and Sir Richard de Preston (Sizergh MSS.). As has been said, this release is *sans date;* but it should be compared with three other documents at Sizergh, which obviously form part of a single series and of which the substance is as follows:—(I) General release [undated] from Alice del Howes to "William son of Robert de Stirkeland, knight," of both moieties of Le Howes (previously settled upon her sons Thomas, Benedict, and John). Attested by Sir Roger de Burton, Sir Richard de Preston, etc. (II) Quitclaim [undated] to the aforesaid Sir William son of Sir Robert de Strickland by John son of Thomas de Levenes, confirming "all my [*i.e.* the grantor's] land in Le Houwes which the said [Sir] William has by gift of Alice, my mother." Attested by Sir Roger de Burton, Sir Richard de Preston, etc. (III) Grant from Sir William son of Sir Robert de Strickland to John "de Camera" and Sybil, his wife, of all the land of Le Howys, etc., "which Alice del Howys holds for life." Dated "at Great Stirkeland in Westmorland" on the Sunday after Michaelmas, 1288; and witnessed, *inter alia*, by Sir Roger de Burton, Sir Richard de Preston, William de Windsor, and Gilbert de Burneside (Sizergh MSS., *ibid.*). Now although in only one of the above documents is the actual date given, yet all of them are clearly of the same period, since not only do they relate to the same set of transactions, but they even have virtually the same group of witnesses. Moreover, Sir Roger de Burton did not succeed his elder brother (Sir John) until shortly before 1278 (cf. *Cal. Patent Rolls*, 1270, p. 500; De Banco Roll, no. 27, m. 119): he was M.P. for Westmorland in 1298, and died in 1302 or 1303 (*Cal. Fine Rolls*, I, p. 480; *Cal. Inqs.*, IV, p. 86).

[26] Very possibly he was the son of an "Adam son of Robert de Stirkland" who attested, *circa* 1245–1255, a grant by William de "Schelmergh" to Roger son of Simon of land at "Schelmergh" [Skelsmergh], co. Westmorland (*Cal. Ancient Deeds*, A. 9342). For the probable place of this Adam son of Robert in the Strickland pedigree, see the illustrative chart on page 111. Robert son of Alan [*recte*, Adam] de Stirkeland obtained a pardon from the Crown at the instance of Sir Roger de Clifford (of Appleby) for the death of Alan son of William Mustel, 25 October 1269 (*Cal. Patent Rolls*, 1269, p. 372).

714

the contrary, all the accumulated evidence tends to identify Sir Robert himself with the "Robert son of Robert de Stirkeland" who made an allowance of land and oatmeal [27] to Adam son of Walter in 1246,[28] and from whom the said Adam claimed his endowment at Great Strickland in 1250 (*vide supra*, page 108). Such an identification, moreover, is the only one which provides a solution that is both reasonable and in harmony with all the known facts. A Robert de Strickland served as a juror at Appleby in 1220 (Assize Roll, Westmorland, no. 312, m. 27): and doubtless the latter was Sir Robert de Strickland's father, and in consequence a younger son of Walter de Strickland and Christian de Leteham. We may further assume that this Robert de Strickland (Senior) died during Walter and Christian's lifetime; for judging by the dates, his son, Sir Robert, succeeded to Great Strickland immediately following the said Walter and Christian's decease.[29]

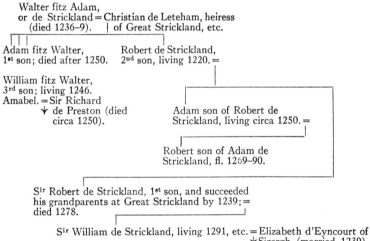

Walter fitz Adam,
or de Strickland = Christian de Leteham, heiress
(died 1236–9). | of Great Strickland, etc.

Adam fitz Walter,
1st son; died after 1250.

Robert de Strickland,
2nd son, living 1220. =

William fitz Walter,
3rd son; living 1246.
Amabel. = Sir Richard
de Preston (died
circa 1250).

Adam son of Robert de
Strickland, living circa 1250. =

Robert son of Adam de
Strickland, fl. 1269–90.

Sir Robert de Strickland, 1st son, and succeeded
his grandparents at Great Strickland by 1239; =
died 1278.

Sir William de Strickland, living 1291, etc. = Elizabeth d'Eyncourt of
Sizergh (married 1239).

[27] It is also significant that one of the interim feoffees named in this transaction was Sir Ralph d'Eyncourt of Sizergh, whose daughter had already married Sir Robert de Strickland's son, William.

[28] See also footnote no. 18. Perhaps the agreement had been designed to compromise some claim brought by Adam son of Walter as heir male. Incidentally, this Final Concord of 1246 did not escape the vigilant eye of Dr. Farrer, who wrote that "Robert son of Robert de Stirkland, dealing with the manor in 1246, makes it highly improbable, even impossible . . . that Adam [son of Walter] had a son Robert in the line of the lords of Strickland" (cited in Scott, *op. cit.*, p. 13). Dr. Farrer, however, was not aware of the full circumstances of the case, and interpreted the Final Concord as meaning that Adam son of Walter was actually lord of Great Strickland at the time. In addition, he avoided the *chimera* of Sir Robert de Strickland's settlement of some seven years earlier by assuming, like Archdeacon Prescott, that the date "1239" was erroneous (*vide supra*, p. 108).

[29] Or rather, to speak more accurately, following the decease of Christian; since it was she, and not Walter, who possessed the Great Strickland estate. Indeed, the contributor has come across a charter amongst the muniments at Lowther which records a grant from Thomas de Hastings to the Hospital of St. Peter's at York of certain privileges at Crosby Ravensworth, co. Westmorland, for the use of their grange at Garthorne; the witnesses to which included Walter de Strickland and Gilbert de Kirketon, "then sheriff of Appleby" [*i.e.* of Westmorland]. Gilbert de Kirketon was certainly sheriff of the county in 26 Henry III (cf. Parker, "Pipe Rolls of Cumberland and Westmorland," p. 201), which would date the charter itself as *circa* 1242–1243: but of course it is always possible that he had been (deputy) sheriff under the Vieuxponts (the hereditary sheriffs) at some earlier period.

From the period of Sir Robert de Strickland onwards we are, happily, upon firmer ground: but there are, none the less, still problems connected with Sir Robert's own career that merit attention. For example, the name of his wife is usually given as "Alice del Howes", while Adam son of Walter is credited with having espoused a certain "Alice de Levens" (Scott, *op. cit.*, pp. 10, 13).[30] In point of fact, however, both these ladies are imaginary—or rather, each of them has been evolved out of a single Alice del Howes (or Hawes), *alias* de Levens, who was the heiress of property called The Hawes in Helsington (in the parish of Kendal) and occurs with her husband, Thomas son of Thomas de Levens, in several deeds between 1270 and 1285.[31] Needless to say, however, this real Alice never became the wife of a Strickland at all;[32] and probably Adam son of Walter died unmarried. In the case of Sir Robert de Strickland, an entry on the Westmorland Assize Roll of 1256 suggests that his mother may have been a co-heiress of the manor of Melcanthorpe: for in that year Robert de "Styrkeland" was defendant in a claim for dower in a moiety of the manor of "Melkinthorp" at the suit of Beatrice, widow of Robert de "Wytheheved" (Assize Roll, 41 Henry III [1256–1257], No. 979),[33] and the same moiety reappears as in the possession of William de "Stirkeland" (Robert's son and heir) in the Assize Roll of 1291–1292 (*ibid.*, 20 Edward I [1291–1292], no. 987). Who Beatrice herself was, is not clear; but this moiety of the manor of Melcanthorpe had shortly beforehand been in the hands of Geoffrey de "Cotesford" [Coatsforth] of Asby Coatsforth, co. Westmorland, who died *circa* 1230 without male issue. His Asby lands were afterwards held by William l'Engleys and Christian his wife, who was Geoffrey's daughter; and it seems to the contributor not unlikely that there was another daughter [? Beatrice, later married to Robert de Wethered] who brought the Melcanthorpe property in marriage to Sir Robert de Strickland's father.[34]

[30] Adam son of Walter has, in addition, been supplied (by Plantagenet-Harrison) with an equally fictitious wife named Ada. *Vide* footnote no. 19.

[31] See footnote no. 25, where abstracts of the deeds are given. In view of Canon Ragg's wild suggestion that Alice was identical with the daughter of an "Adam son of Howe", named in a Westmorland document of *circa* 1220 (*Transactions of the Cumberland and Westmorland Antiquarian Society* New Series, vol. XVI), it should perhaps be added that the Sizergh muniments make it clear that Alice's father was Thomas del Howes, who (along with Thomas de Levens and Ralph de Nottingham, "then sheriff") witnessed a charter from Robert de Kendal to Sir Ralph d'Eyncourt *circa* 1247 (Sizergh MSS.) and is further mentioned in a division of the lands of Peter de Brus and Walter de Lindsay in 1256 (*Transactions of the Cumberland and Westmorland Antiquarian Society*, New Series, vol. XIII, p. 69).

[32] The deeds cited in footnote no. 25 will show how easy it was for previous writers to be misled regarding Alice's matrimonial career. For example, the third deed records a quitclaim from John son of Thomas de Levens to Sir William son of Sir Robert de Strickland of lands at Le Howes in possession of Alice, his mother (*ibid.*). A careless reading of this passage (as given in the Rev. Thomas West's transcripts), without reference to the original, might well lead one to infer that Alice was the mother of the grantee and not of the grantor.

[33] *i.e.* Wethered. Before 1226 a William de "Wytheheved" witnessed a grant made by Ivo de Vieuxpont of the manor of Garthorne, co. Westmorland, to St. Peter's, York (Lowther MSS.).

[34] A somewhat confused account of the Cotesfords of Asby Coatsforth and Melcanthorpe was printed by Canon Ragg in *Transactions of the Cumberland and Westmorland Antiquarian Society*, New Series, vol. XX, p. 66–94. Evidently Geoffrey de Cotesford was the nephew of Hugh de Cotesford (*fl.* 1180–1210), and grandnephew of Richard de Cotesford who was among those fined in 1176 for the treacherous surrender of Appleby Castle to the King of Scots. Perhaps Geoffrey's father was an elder Geoffrey (of Melcanthorpe), who is called "brother" of Hugh de Cotesford in

The identity of Sir Robert de Strickland's wife can be virtually established by a deed in the muniment room at Balliol College, Oxford, dated at "Burgh" [Brough, near Appleby] on the Feast of the Assumption of our Lady [25 August], 1271. This document, which is in Norman-French, records an agreement then made between "Sire Johan de Balyels" [*i.e.* Sir John de Balliol, of Barnard Castle, co. Durham] and "Sire Thomas de Musgrave" [of Great Musgrave, co. Westmorland] concerning the imprisonment at Appleby by the said Sir Thomas of Master William de Genellestane and of "la Dame de Stirkeland, sa sore." Sir Thomas agreed to reimburse Master William and his sister, the Lady of Strickland, for the losses which their imprisonment had cost them in money and goods, as well as to present five hundred shillings and two tuns of good wine to Sir John de "Balyels:" and he further secured as pledges Sir John de Morville, Sir Thomas de Helbeck, Sir Henry de Staveley, and Sir Thomas de Hastings, and as mainpernors Sir Peter de Brus and Sir Roger de Lancaster. No reasons for the imprisonment are given; but it should be noted that in 1270–1271 Sir Thomas de Musgrave was under-sheriff of Westmorland and constable of Appleby Castle, so that he had doubtless been acting in his official capacity.[35] Moreover, the chronology leaves little room for doubt that "la Dame de Stirkelaund" was wife of the contemporary head of the family, Sir Robert de Strickland, who survived till 1278; and the latter's son, Sir William de Strickland, was not improbably named for Master William de Genellestane, who would thus have been his maternal uncle.

Entries in the early Close and Patent Rolls shows that in August 1257 Robert de "Stirkeland" was removed from the position of coroner in co. Westmorland since the King by letters patent had specially exempted the said Robert from acting as sheriff, coroner, or in any other office unless he so desired (*Cal. Close Rolls*, 1257, pp. 85–6; *Cal. Patent Rolls*, 1257, p. 574). The interesting fact is added that the above exemption had been granted at the instance of Alexander, King of Scotland (*ibid.*). Evidently, however, Sir Robert subsequently consented to be reappointed; for he was again serving as coroner in 1278 at the time of his decease (Hornyold-Strickland, *op. cit.*, p. 13). But the most memorable event in Sir

---

a Lowther charter of *circa* 1200. At all events, the younger Geoffrey de Cotesford was granted "half my manor of Melkinthorpe" *circa* 1190 by his uncle, Hugh, who seems to have divided both the Asby and Melcanthorpe estates between this same Geoffrey and the latter's brother, Robert. One moiety of Melcanthorpe (together with property in Asby) was inherited by Robert's son, Peter, and grandson, Richard (Ragg, *ut supra*): and lands at Asby and Melcanthorpe were possessed by another Richard de Cotesford as late as 1362 (*Cal. Inqs.*, vol. XI, no. 312). The second moiety of Melcanthorpe passed to Geoffrey; but Canon Ragg observed (*ibid.*, p. 73) that "It does not appear that the Lengleys family succeeded" to it—although William l'Engleys certainly succeeded *jure uxoris* to Geoffrey's Asby possessions. All of this lends support to the hypothesis that Geoffrey himself must have left two daughters and co-heirs: (1) Christian (of Asby), wife of William l'Engleys, and (2) Beatrice (of Melcanthorpe), the mother of Sir Robert de Strickland. Sir Robert l'Engleys (grandson and heir of William l'Engleys and Christian) was M.P. for Westmorland in 1295, etc., and was a contemporary and companion in arms of Sir William de Strickland (the grandson, if this theory be correct, of Christian's sister Beatrice).

[35] Another of the Balliol College deeds records the acknowledgment of a debt of 123 marks owed by Sir Thomas de Musgrave to Sir John de Balliol, and payable at Barnard Castle in specified instalments during the years 1265 and 1266.

Robert's career was undoubtedly his election as one of the four knights to represent Westmorland in the Michaelmas Parliament of 1258; his other colleagues being Sir John de Morville (of Helton Flecket), Sir Robert de Asby (of Great Asby), and Sir Patrick fitz Thomas (of Preston Patrick), ancestor of the Curwens of Workington (See S. H. Lee Washington, "The Early Parliamentary Representation of Westmorland"). Curiously enough, this important episode has been ignored without exception by all authorities, although it was to prove the precursor of a notable series of Parliamentary services performed by virtually every generation of Stricklands up until the close of the seventeenth century.

Meanwhile, of Sir William de Strickland—who succeeded his father, Sir Robert, in 1278 [36]—there is little further that need be said. We have already sufficiently enlarged upon the arrangements for his marriage to Elizabeth d'Eyncourt in 1239; and it only remains to add that at the last-named date Sir William himself must have been scarcely more than nine or ten years old—very possibly less. [37] For a Coram Rege Roll of 4 Edward I proves that his eldest son by Elizabeth was still under age as late as 1276:—"The King *versus* William de Stirkeland concerning the manor of Strosdermod [Tristermont, co. Westmorland], which is alleged to belong to the Crown as having been an escheat *de terris Normannorum*. But the said William de Stirkeland declares that he holds it by the courtesy of England of the inheritance of Elizabeth, formerly his wife, by whom he has begotten William, his son, without whom he cannot answer. And he [*i.e.* William the son] appears in Court, and is a minor (*de qua suscitauit Willelmum filium suum, sinequo non potest respondere, qui visus* [*est*] *in Curia et est infra etate*). Therefore, the King," etc. (Coram Rege Roll, Westmorland, Michaelmas, 4 Edward I [1276], m. 1). Moreover, Sir William de Strickland's only daughter, Joan—the sister of the young William de Strickland of 1276—did not marry till 1292, while another son, Sir John, survived until 1352 (*vide postea*). Consequently, Sir William's children by Elizabeth d'Eyncourt can not have been born before 1256 at the earliest; whilst several of them—including the daughter Joan —doubtless made their appearance at an even later period.

Elizabeth d'Eyncourt herself died between 1272 and 1274 (see Part II); but her husband outlived her for over thirty years, and was still alive on 1 May 1305, when he entered into a covenant regarding waste and destruction in the lands of his late wife's inheritance at Barton, Hackthorpe, and Heversham (Hornyold-Strickland, *op. cit.*, p. 19). Along with his cousin Sir Richard de Preston, Sir William de Strickland represented Westmorland in the Easter Parliament of July 1290; and amongst some miscellaneous

[36] Sir Robert's life is dealt with at length in the present writer's "Early Parliamentary Representation of Westmoreland" (*passim*).

[37] Aside from the settlement of 1239, Sir William's initial appearance is in 1265, when he received letters of protection (dated September 17th) as being one of the followers of Roger de Clifford (*Cal. Patent Rolls*, 1265, p. 452). So far as the contributor can discover, Sir William first occurs as a knight in a charter of 1281, which recites a mortgage from Sir Roger de Burton to "Willelmus de Stirkeland, miles", of £10 worth of land at Hincaster (Sizergh MSS.).

**PORTRAIT OF SIR THOMAS STRICKLAND, K.B. (1563–1612), HALF-BROTHER OF ELLEN (STRICKLAND) CARLETON**

*From the original at Sizergh Castle*

Sheriffs' Accounts at the Public Record Office is preserved a highly interesting return of the revenues of the Strickland estates made in 1295 by the deputy-sheriff of Westmorland, Sir Thomas de Helbeck, who was then apparently at Sizergh for the purpose of levying the King's Fifteenth (Exchequer Q. R., Miscellanea, Sheriffs' Accounts, bdle. 46, m. 2). Like his father Sir Robert, Sir William de Strickland obtained in 1267 a life exemption from serving as sheriff, coroner, etc. (*Cal. Patent Rolls*, 1267, p. 64): but he, too, subsequently relented, since he acted as deputy-sheriff of Westmorland in 1275 and as coroner until 25 November 1303, at which date he was removed from office as incapacitated by age and infirmity (*Cal. Close Rolls*, 1303, p. 113).

By his marriage with the heiress of Sizergh, Sir William left several children. It has hitherto been supposed that his eldest son was the Sir Walter de Strickland who succeeded him shortly after 1305: but the entry from the Assize Roll of 1276 concerning the manor of Tristermont (*passim*) implies that the young William de "Stirkeland", there mentioned, was then his father's actual heir-presumptive. Fortunately, satisfactory confirmation on this point is supplied by a De Banco Roll of 5 Edward II [1311–1312], which specifically states that Elizabeth d'Eyncourt, wife of Sir William de Strickland, had an elder son, William (Junior), who deceased without issue, when his next brother, (Sir) Walter, became his successor (*vide infra*). Therefore, it may be confidently asserted that William de Strickland, Junior, was the first-born son of the family, and her heir to his mother (although still a minor) in 1276. He is again mentioned in a grant made by Margaret de Ros in November 1281, which speaks of various lands of his mother's inheritance at Stainton-in-Kendal, co. Westmorland, that his father, Sir William de Strickland, had recently given him (Nichols, "Topographer", vol. II, p. 187; and cf. *Cal. Close Rolls*, 1281, pp. 90, 106). Presumably, however, he died *vita patris* prior to 1292, in which year Sir William de Strickland made fresh settlements of the d'Eyncourt properties upon (Sir) Walter de Strickland, William's younger brother (Hornyold-Strickland, *ibid.*, p. 18).[38] But, despite the fact that he thus deceased at an early age and left no descendants,[39] young William de Strickland had evidently found time to marry. For one of the Sizergh deeds quoted by Nicolson and Burn ("History of Westmorland and Cumberland", vol. I, p. 89) shows that in 1303 Margaret,

[38] Walter de Strickland seems actually to have been in possession of the d'Eyncourt holdings at Natland as early as October 1290, when he brought suit against Sir Roger de Burton, Sir Richard de Preston, and others for having lately entered his land of "Natelond", carried away his goods and those of Nicholas de Crakehall, his bondman, abducted the latter, and assaulted his men (*Cal. Patent Rolls*, 1290, p. 408): and in 1294 Walter impleaded Nicholas de Crakehall to render account of the time when he (Nicholas) was the said Walter's bailiff at Natland, co. Westmorland (De Banco Roll, no. 103, m. 72). See *supra*, where evidence is produced to show that William de Strickland, Junior, was already dead by 1288.

[39] John, son of William de Stirkeland, "an idiot", died in 1310 leaving property in Strickland Ketel, and was succeeded by a brother and heir, Thomas son of William de Stirkeland, then aged thirty-five (Roberts, *Cal. Geneal.*, no. 5; *Abbrev. Rot. Original.* [Record Com.], vol. I, p. 175b). But it is plain that he derived his surname from Strickland Ketel itself, and not from Great Strickland, and that he was totally unconnected with the Sizergh family. Indeed, his brother Thomas is specifically described as "son of William de Stirkeland Ketle" in a charter of *circa* 1311 (Add. MS. 32106, fo 141b; and cf. *ibid.*, 32109, fo 14b).

"late the wife of Hugh de la Vale," quitclaimed in her widowhood to (Sir) Walter de Strickland (young William's brother and heir) her rights in the property at Stainton-in-Kendal "which William de Stirkeland (Senior) formerly gave to her in free marriage with William de Stirkeland (Junior), her first husband." Margaret's own origin is elusive, though certain evidences in the contributor's possession indicate that she may have been born a Washington.[40] But her second husband, Sir Hugh "de la Vale," *i.e.* de Laval (died 1302), was a well known man in Northumberland, who had acquired large territorial interests through his previous wife, Maud (died 1281), one of the three co-heiresses to the barony of Bolbec.[41] By his second marriage to young William de Strickland's widow Margaret, Sir Hugh left three children:—Sir Robert,[42] Walter, and Katherine, wife of the notorious rebel, Sir Walter de Selby. We also learn from an Inquisition that Margaret's eldest son, Sir Robert de Laval, was born 5 August 1289—a fact which demonstrates that young William de Strickland must have been dead at least by the year 1288 (*Cal. Inqs.*, vol. V, p. 202).

Sir Walter de Strickland—who thereupon succeeded the latter as heir-presumptive to the family estates—was hence the second son of Sir William de Strickland and Elizabeth d'Eyncourt. He is alleged to have been already knighted by 1276–1277, on the strength of one of Father West's abstracts at Sizergh, which professes to be dated "5 Edward I [1276–1277]" and records a release to "Sir. Walter de Stirkland, knight," from Adam Warde of Kendal. The witnesses were "Sir Nicholas de Leyburn, Roger de Kernetby [Carnaby], vicar of Kyrkeby in Kendale, John de Wessington [Washington], Thomas d'Aunay, Roland de Patton, Richard de Derley, Thomas de Stirkland, and Alan de Elmed, clerk" (cf. Hornyold-Strickland, *op. cit.*, p. 26): but these names alone prove that the date "5 Edward I" is impossible. For, to take only two instances, Sir Nicholas de Leybourne (who was M.P. for Westmorland in 1305, 1307, 1313, and 1314) was not knighted till after 1303, while Roger de Carnaby (M.P. for Westmorland in 1318) did not even become vicar of Kendal until 1307 (see Washington, "The Early Parliamentary Representation of Westmorland," *ibid*): and the most likely explanation seems to be that "5 Edward I" is simply a textual misreading for "5 Edward II"—so that the release would in reality have been issued not in 1276–1277 but in 1311. Indeed, Sir Walter de Strickland himself only actually took up knighthood in 1306 (when he occurs amongst the numerous company knighted on May 22nd with Edward, Prince of Wales)[43]: and, remembering that

[40] See S. H. Lee Washington, "The English Washingtons" (now in press).
[41] *Northumberland County History*, vol. VIII. The name of Sir Hugh de Laval's second wife has not hitherto been known.
[42] This Sir Robert—the ancestor of the Delavals of Seaton Delaval (now represented by Lord Hastings)—was father *inter alia* of a son, Sir William de Laval, who in 1322 espoused Eleanor, daughter of Sir Robert de Leybourne (M.P. for Westmorland in 1315) by Sarah, sister of Andrew de "Harcla," Earl of Carlisle (*Cal. Close Rolls*, 1322, pp. 552–553; *ibid.*, 1328, pp. 364, 404).
[43] The story, which apparently originated with Shaw ("Knights of England," p. 115) that Sir Walter was made a Knight of the Bath on this occasion—or, as one writer puts it, "was created K.C.B." (!)—is, of course, a palpable anachronism.

his elder brother William was still a minor in 1276, we shall probably not go far wrong in placing his own birth at *circa* 1260.

Sir Walter is supposed to have married Eleanor de Goldington (Scott, *op. cit.*, p. 30; Hornyold-Strickland, *op. cit.*, p. 33); but up to the present the sole basis for this belief has been the unsupported assertion of that eccentric antiquary, General Plantagenet-Harrison ("History of Yorkshire," p. 375). The contributor has, however, found full proof of the Goldington alliance in the Westmorland Assize Rolls; and the following unpublished record hence becomes of unusual importance:

The Friday within Whitsun week, 1301: "The Assize came to enquire if Walter son of William de Stirklaund, Robert de Wessington [Washington] and Joan, his wife,[44] and John Gretason unjustly disseised Eleanor, daughter of William de Goldington, of her free tenement in Nateland and Stanton [Stainton-in-Kendal, co. Westmorland], and whereof she complains that they disseised her of twenty-two messuages, fourteen oxgangs, and fifty acres of land, ten acres of meadow, forty acres of wood, and one water-mill. . . . The Jurors say that there was talk of a marriage to take place between the said Walter, son of William de Stirklaund, and the said Eleanor, daughter of William de Goldington, and that William de Stirklaund (father of Walter) should enfeoff them with the above-named property. The marriage was duly solemnized, whereupon William de Stirklaund enfeoffed them and the heirs of their bodies for ever. And they were accordingly seised thereof during the space of two and a half years, until the said Walter withdrew himself from the society of the said Eleanor, and brought a plea into an Ecclesiastical Court for a divorce between them on the grounds of consanguinity. The divorce was granted in the Archbishop's Court at York three years before [1298]. Therefore, the said Eleanor has no right in the aforesaid lands" (Assize Roll, Westmorland, no. 989, m. 2).

It is thus evident that Eleanor de Goldington married Sir Walter de Strickland in 1295–1296, and that he obtained a divorce from her in 1298 on the grounds that the marriage was within the prohibited degrees. This plea of consanguinity is extremely interesting, although it is not clear just in what way the relationship arose. However, Eleanor de Goldington's mother was Christian, daughter and eventually co-heiress of Sir Thomas de Hastings (of Crosby Ravensworth, co. Westmorland) by Christian his wife;[45] and the latter (whose surname is unknown) may well have been a daughter—or, more probably, a grand-daughter—of the original Walter de Strickland and Christian de Leteham.[46]

[44] Sister of Walter de "Stirklaund" and daughter of Sir William (see pp. 125–6).

[45] In 1292 Thomas, son of Sir Thomas de Hastings, and his sisters, Amice wife of Thomas de Goldington and Christian wife of William de Goldington, petitioned at Appleby against the murderers of Nicholas de Hastings, their brother, who had been slain in a ditch at Crosby Ravensworth six years before (Assize Roll, Westmorland, no. 987, m. 34 d., etc.). The above suit was printed by Canon Ragg in *Transactions of the Cumberland and Westmorland Antiquarian Society*, New Series, vol. XI, p. 237, where a certain passage is misquoted as referring to "William de Goldington, and Christian [de Hastings] wife of *John* de Goldington" (*ibid.*). However, an examination of the original Assize Roll shows that this phrase actually translates "William de Goldington and Christian [de Hastings] his wife, and John de Goldington,"—a correction which obviates the difficulty that would otherwise arise as regards the name of Christian's husband.

[46] She was most likely a sister of Sir Robert de Strickland who died in 1278 (see illustrative chart, p. 111). Sir Thomas de Hastings was a younger brother of Nicholas de Hastings, lord of Alverston, co. Yorks., ancestor of the Earls of Huntingdon. By his marriage with Christian [? de Strickland],

As for Eleanor herself, we are expressly told that she and her husband, Sir Walter, lived together for less than three years, from which it follows that she cannot by any means have been the mother of all of Sir Walter's issue. An entail of 1323 (cf. Scott, *op. cit.*, p. 30) proves that Sir Walter left at least three children,—Thomas (his heir), John, and Ralph; and of these it seems probable that Thomas alone was a son of the Goldington marriage—if, indeed, the whole of Sir Walter's issue were not by a later wife.[47]   For in truth it is difficult to resist the conclusion that the divorce itself had been instigated by something more than purely religious scruples, and that sterility— rather than the artificial excuse of consanguinity—was the real cause that lay behind Sir Walter's premature desire to get rid of the unhappy Eleanor.

Be that as it may, the immediate results of such a drastic step were, not unnaturally, to provoke a feud between the Strickland and Goldington families.   Not only did the Goldingtons (as we have seen) sue the Stricklands to recover Eleanor's dower, but in 1296 Sir William de Strickland (Sir Walter's father) brought a writ of *scire facias* against Eleanor's father, William de Goldington (Coram Rege Roll, Westmorland, no. 149, in 24d.), while in 1297 he claimed damages against the said William in the sum of twenty marks and was still continuing to prosecute in 1304 (Coram Rege Roll, Westmoreland, no. 150, *m.* 10d.; *ibid.*, no. 178, *m.* 41d.).   Incidentally, during these proceedings William de Goldington is referred to as "late Mayor of Appleby", a borough which he represented in Parliament both in 1302 and in 1305.[48]   In 1307, moreover, he was twice returned as Knight of the Shire for Westmorland, his colleague on the second occasion being none other than Sir Walter de Strickland, his erstwhile son-in-law.

It might be added that Sir Walter de Strickland's own career was a long and active one.[49]   He served as M.P. for his native county in 1307, 1312, 1313,[50] 1322 (May and November), 1324, and 1332: and

Sir Thomas de Hastings had three sons—Thomas, Nicholas (murdered at Crosby Ravensworth in 1286), and William, all of whom died *sine prole*.   He also appears to have left four daughters, who ultimately became his co-heiresses, viz., Isabel, wife of William de Threlkeld (and mother of Sir Henry de Threlkeld of Yanwath); Amice, wife of Thomas de Goldington; Christian, wife of William de Goldington (and mother *inter alia* of Christian, wife of Sir Walter de Strickland); and ? Emma, wife of Gilbert de Wharton.   In 1300 Henry de Threlkeld, William de Goldington and Christian his wife, and Gilbert de Querton [Wharton] and Emma, his wife, succeeded to property in Crosby Ravensworth, co. Westmorland, as the next heirs of William de Hastings, deceased (Assize Roll, Westmorland, 29 Edward I [1300–1301], no. 990).

[47] Plantagenet-Harrison states, although without quoting his authority, that Sir Walter married secondly a lady named "Matilda" or Maud ("History of Yorkshire", p. 373).

[48] The Goldingtons (who possibly were a junior branch of the knightly family of Goldington in Bedfordshire) were prominent merchants at Appleby, having become established there towards the middle of the twelfth century as officials and clerics under the baronial house of Vieuxpont (Washington, "Early Parliamentary Representation of Westmorland", *ibid.*).   William de Goldington, Junior—son of William, above-mentioned, and brother of Eleanor de Strickland—was M.P. for Appleby in 1322 along with his kinsman, William son of John de Goldington: and a Cuthbert de Goldington served as M.P. for the same borough in 1313, as did Robert de Goldington in 1295 and 1315 (cf. Washington, *op. cit.*).

[49] For details, cf. Washington, "Early Parliamentary Representation of Westmorland" (*ibid.*).

[50] Sir Walter de Strickland and Sir Thomas de Beetham were actually elected to the Parliament of July, 1313; but the enrolment of the writ *de expensis* gives the names of Sir Mathew de Redman and Sir Nicholas de Leybourne.   Doubtless the two former became unable to serve at the last moment owing to absence in the Scottish wars.

on 10 February, 1321/2 he succeeded Sir Hugh de Lowther (the younger) as sheriff of Westmorland, being further entrusted nine months later (October 31st) with the custody of Appleby Castle (*Cal. Fine Rolls*, 1322, pp. 95, 193; cf. also Ministers' Accounts, file 1044, m. 1).[51] However, on December 30th of the same year Sir Hugh de Lowther again replaced him as sheriff, whilst the castle of Appleby was at the same time transferred to Sir Anthony de Lucy (*Cal. Fine Rolls*, 1322, pp. 192–193).[52] Local historians have invariably been misled as to the nature of these appointments, and have inferred that Sir Walter himself was simply serving in 1322 as deputy-sheriff under the Cliffords (cf. Sir George Duckett, "The Sheriffs of Westmorland, with the Early Sheriffs of Cumberland," in *Cumberland and Westmorland Antiquarian Society*, Old Series, vol. IV, pp. 285 *et seq.*; Hornyold-Strickland, *op. cit.*, p. 30, etc.). It is true that the Cliffords were the hereditary sheriffs, and normally nominated deputies to act for them.[53] But at the period of Sir Walter de Strickland's tenure of the shrievalty, the county was temporarily in the king's hands, following the attainter of Roger de Clifford (one of the leaders in the Earl of Lancaster's rebellion during the previous autumn);[54] and Sir Walter, and his immediate successors and predecessors in office, were thus ministers interposed by the Crown, who occupied positions closely analogous to that of *custos*.

The third son of Sir William de Strickland and Elizabeth d'Eyncourt was Sir John de Strickland, about whom very little appears to be known.[55] Sir William Betham ("Baronetage," vol. I, p. 412) cited a record that purported to mention an Alice de Strickland as Sir John's widow in 1318; and later writers have accordingly assumed that Sir John's death must have occurred prior to that year (see Hornyold-Strickland, *op. cit.*, p. 24). In reality, however, it can be

---

[51] These rewards make it clear that Sir Walter, unlike most of his family and friends, had escaped being implicated in the Earl of Lancaster's rebellion in the summer of 1321 and the spring of 1322. He had, however, been actively engaged in the Earl's previous rising (Palgrave, "Parliamentary Writs," vol. II, pt. ii, p. 243); and, although he had already obtained a pardon from the Crown in 1318, his former adherence to the Earl was again raked up against him in 1323 (see the next footnote).

[52] It is conceivable that Sir Walter was the victim of some intrigue—or possibly the fact that his brother, Sir John de Strickland, and another kinsman, Hugh de Strickland, both fought with Roger de Clifford under the Earl of Lancaster's banner at Boroughbridge in March 1322 (*postea*, pp. 120, 124), may have made him an object of suspicion. At all events, at the beginning of 1323 he was suddenly charged with his old adherence to the Earl five years before, and his previous pardon of 1318 was rescinded (Palgrave, "Parliamentary Writs," vol. II, pt. ii, p. 243). Presumably, however, he succeeded in clearing himself; for later in 1323 we find him acting as Commissioner of Array in Westmorland and Cumberland, and on 5 Feb. 1323/4 he was empowered to receive into the king's peace the rebel followers of the ill-fated Andrew de "Harcla," Earl of Carlisle (Palgrave, *ibid.*, p. 244). He was still living 1341 (*Cal. Inqs.*, VIII, p. 202), and probably died about 1342. From his eldest son, Sir Thomas de Strickland, who married Cecily, daughter of Sir Robert de Welles, the late Lord Strickland of Sizergh was directly descended.

[53] The Cliffords were the heirs of the Vieuxponts (de Veteriponts), barons of Appleby, who held the hereditary shrievalty by grant of King John.

[54] Roger de Clifford (Lord Clifford of Appleby) was subsequently captured at the battle of Boroughbridge (16 March 1321/2), and executed a week afterwards. (His half-sister, Cecily de Welles, was married in 1322–1323 to Thomas, son and heir of Sir Walter de Strickland, which may have been another factor that contributed to the latter's temporary fall from favour. Cf. footnote no. 51.)

[55] For some reason it is claimed that Robert de Strickland (for whom see p. 123) was the third son, and Sir John de Strickland the fourth son (Hornyold-Strickland, *op. cit.*, pp. 23–24); but the fact that Sir John received the paternal estate of Great Strickland (*vide infra*) is evidence that he was older than Robert, and next brother to Sir Walter.

*Page 728, this volume.

shown that the Alice in question did not even marry Sir John until 1319, and that the latter, so far from having died "before 1318," actually lived until 1352! Indeed, Sir John's career was quite as long and distinguished as that of Sir Walter, his elder brother: and, although there is not space to consider it fully here, yet, in view of the general dearth of information, some details may perhaps prove of interest. At the Assize at Appleby in 1301, Sir William de "Stirkeland" and John de "Stirkeland," his son, were impleaded by John de la Chamber (de Camera) for four marks' rent from land which the latter occupied as tenant of the defendants. In the course of his reply, Sir William de "Stirkeland" declared that he then held the whole manor of "Stirkeland" [Great Strickland] of Margaret de Ros (one of the co-heirs to the barony of Kendal),[56] and that another of his sons, Walter, held the townships of Natland and Sizergh, as well as possessions in Stainton worth £20 per annum. He added that he himself also held £20 worth of land in Whinfell, Winder, and Tristermont as tenant of his son Walter, to whom the said land belonged—but that the manor of "Stirkeland" was his (Sir William's) own paternal inheritance (Assize Roll, Westmorland, 29 Edward I [1300–1301], no. 990). In 1302 Sir William formally settled the Great Strickland estate on his son, John de Strickland, and his heirs (Feet of Fines, Westmorland, case 249, file 5, no. 41): and the above records give us a valuable insight into the arrangements that had been effected regarding the distribution of the various ancestral properties. Like the rest of his family at this period, Sir John de Strickland took an active part in the Scottish wars: and in March 1312 he was granted remission of a debt to the crown of £100 (originally incurred by Sir William de Strickland many years before) "in consideration of his good service in Scotland both to the King [Edward II] and to the King's late father" (Cal. Close Rolls, 1312, p. 408). Sir John was amongst those pardoned, on the testimony of Roger de Clifford, for having been implicated in the Earl of Lancaster's rising in 1321 (Cal. Patent Rolls, 1321, p. 20): and he no doubt fought with Clifford at the disastrous battle of Boroughbridge on 16 March 1321/2,—since on 3 August 1322 he received restoration of his lands and goods which had been forfeited for his adherence to Roger de Clifford, a rebel (Palgrave, "Parliamentary Writs").[57] He acted as Commissioner of Array in Westmorland in 1326, represented the county in Parliament in 1326 and 1327, and is described as (deputy) sheriff of Westmorland on 9 July 1337,[58] when attesting a settlement made by John le Franceys of the manor of Cliburn (cf.

[56] She was widow of Robert de Ros of Wark (died 1274), and granddaughter and co-heiress of Gilbert fitz Renfrid, baron of Kendal, and his wife Helewise de Lancaster (vide footnote no. 8). She died in 1307 (Cal. Inqs., vol. IV, p. 284), having transferred a considerable portion of her share of the barony to her nephew, Sir Marmaduke de Thweng (1st Lord Thweng, of Thwing and Kilton), between 1297 and 1301 (Cal. Patent Rolls, 1297, p. 304; Feet of Fines, Westmorland, 29 Edward 1 [1300–1301], no. 62). Included in the transfer of 1301 was the manor of Great Strickland (Levens MSS., vol. II, f° 12), of which the Thwengs henceforth became the overlords.

[57] This act of clemency was doubtless facilitated by Sir John's elder brother, Sir Walter de Strickland, who (as we know) had been placed in Roger de Clifford's shoes as sheriff of Westmorland and constable of Appleby Castle (ante, p. 119).✱

[58] He was appointed 12 Oct. 1335 (MS. List of Sheriffs in the Public Record Office).

✱Page 726, this volume.

Assize Roll, Westmorland, 14 Edward III [1340–1341], no. 1426b). His wife Alice seems to have been previously married to Sir John de Byron of Clayton in Droylsden, Lancs. (ancester of Lord Byron, the poet), who died shortly before Easter 1318, leaving Alice as his widow (De Banco Roll, no. 222, m. 229). The latter[59] first appears as the wife of Sir John de Strickland in 1319 (Assize Roll, Lancashire, no. 424, m. 9);[60] and in 1321 and later Sir John and Alice were prosecuting claims for dower out of the Byron estates against Sir Richard de Byron, Alice's step-son (De Banco Roll, no. 240, m. 192; *ibid.*, no. 276, m. 159). In 1329 Sir John de Strickland settled the manor of Great Strickland on his wife, Alice, and their issue (Feet of Fines, Westmorland, 3 Edward III); but evidently the marriage was childless—for in 1340 Sir John made a fresh entail with remainder to his nephew John son of Robert de Strickland, Joan his wife, and their heirs (*ibid.*, 14 Edward III).[61] In 1341 Sir John is recorded as holding Great Strickland of the heir of William de Thweng (*Cal. Inqs.*, vol. VIII, p. 202): and in 1342 Richard Warde of Walesby, Lincs., obtained pardon of his outlawry "in the county [court] of Westmorland for failing to answer the plea of Sir John de Stirkeland, knight, that he [Richard] render an account of the time when he acted as the said Sir John's receiver of monies" (*Cal. Patent Rolls*, 1342, p. 468). In 1348, we find mention of Sir John and his wife, Alice, as defendants in a claim for property in Lancashire at the suit of Robert de Fallowfield (De Banco Roll, no. 356, m. 140); and four years after this (1352) Sir John was gathered to his fathers, being probably at least eighty at the date of his death.

The *inquisitio post mortem* (which has hitherto been ignored by all authorities) was taken at Appleby on Monday after the Feast of the Decollation of St. John the Baptist, 34 Edward III [1361] pursuant to a writ addressed to the escheator of Westmorland on the 16th of May. The document itself recites that Sir John de Stirkeland had died on the Thursday following the Feast of the Invention of the Holy Cross, 25 Edward III [1352], holding Great Stirkeland manor of Sir John de Thweng by the service of 16s. "cornage" yearly, and that his heir was his kinsman (*consanguineus*), Robert de Stirkeland, "now [*i.e.* in 1361] aged sixteen years and upwards." During his own lifetime, the said Sir John de Stirkeland had settled the aforesaid manor, etc., upon his heirs by his wife, Alice, with remainder to John son of Robert de Stirkeland, Joan his wife, and their issue [cf. the Final Concords already quoted in the text]. John, son of Robert de Stirkeland died, leaving Robert de Stirkeland (above-named) and other sons and daughters; and his wife, Joan, survived him and married, secondly, Thomas de Berewys. And since Sir John de Stirkeland and his wife Alice died childless, the said Thomas de Berewys and Joan entered into possession of the manor

[59] She is alleged to have been one of the heirs of Robert Banaster of Hindley, Lancs. (Betham, "Baronetage," vol. I, p. 412). Plantagenet-Harrison ("History of Yorkshire," p. 373) calls her "daughter and co-heir of William de Stopham, lord of Baildon in Ayrdale."

[60] When Henry de Trafford impleaded John la Warre and his wife, Joan (Grelley), and Sir John de Stirkeland and his wife, Alice, concerning lands in Chorlton, co. Lancs. (Assize Roll, *ut supra*).

[61] Sir Edmund de Neville and John de Lowther, clerk, were named as the two interim feoffees

and enjoyed the profits thereof from the time of the decease of Sir John and Alice until the manor was taken by the escheator into the King's hands (Chanc. Inq. P.M.'s, Edward III, file 150, no. 6; *Cal. Inqs.*, vol. X, pp. 467–468).

Along with this same inquisition are included the following writ and inquest, which disclose further interesting particulars:—(I) Writ of *plenius certiorari* to the escheator in Westmorland, dated 3 December, 33 Edward III [1359]: The said escheator had previously answered to a writ of *certiorari super causa capcionis* regarding the title of Thomas de Berewys and Joan his wife to the manor of (Great) Stirkeland that he had found by an inquisition taken *ex officio* that Margaret de Ros, tenant-in-chief, alienated an annual rent of 50s. from divers tenements in Stirkeland and two quarters and two bushels of oatmeal from the mill there to Richard de Preston and Amabel, his wife,[62] who thereupon enfeoffed (Sir) John de Stirkeland, who included the same in his settlement upon his wife, Alice; after whose death without heirs the said rent—along with the manor of Stirkeland which (Sir) John de Stirkeland held of Thomas de Thweng by knight's service—was seized into the king's hands by the customary royal prerogative. "But now Thomas de Berewys and Joan his wife petition that the king's hand be removed, since they assert that they hold a messuage, sixty acres of land, and six acres of meadow in [Great] Stirkeland from which the aforesaid rent used to come, and have informed the king that the above premises are held of Thomas de Thweng and not of the king *in capite*." (II) Inquest taken at Appleby on the Monday after Palm Sunday, 33 Edward III [1359/60]: One Richard de Laton was seised in demesne as of fee of a messuage, sixty acres, and six acres of meadow in Stirkeland, from which the rent, etc., mentioned in the above writ used to come, and held them of one Thomas Long of Stirkeland, as of a third part of the manor of Stirkeland, by the service of 2s. yearly for "cornage;"[63] and he alienated the said tenements to Robert de Stirkeland [*i.e.* Sir Robert de Strickland, d. in 1278], to hold of the chief lords of the fee by the rent aforesaid. Robert de Stirkeland died in possession; and upon his death his son, William de Stirkeland [Sir William de Strickland, husband of Elizabeth d'Eyncourt], entered as his heir, and afterwards gave the lands to Sir John de Stirkeland and the heirs of his body. But the above-named Richard de Laton, having retained the actual rent by a special reservation, granted it to Margaret

[62] In 1315 Amabel, widow of Sir Richard de Preston, obtained a pardon for having, in conjunction with her late husband, acquired 50s. rent in "Stirkeland" from Margaret de Ros without licence of the Crown (*Abbrev. Rot. Original*, vol. I, p. 214; *Cal. Patent Rolls*, 1315, p. 302). Sir Richard de Preston (he was the M.P. of 1290, for whom see footnote no. 17) was still living in 1310, when he witnessed a release to Sir Walter de Strickland from John son of Sir Roger de Burton (Sizergh MSS.). But Margaret de Ros had died in 1307 (cf. footnote no. 56), so that her grant of the rent to Sir Richard and Amabel must have actually occurred prior to that year.

[63] Thomas Long seems to have a freeholder at Great Strickland *temp.* Henry III (cf. *ante*, p. 104, * and footnote no. 12); while Richard de Laton was possibly some cadet of the Yorkshire Laytons, who from early times held land at East and West Layton of the honour of Richmond. A deed of *circa* 1290 mentions the sale from John Gudeberd to (Sir) Richard de Preston and Amabel his wife of a messuage "lying between 'Latuneland and Richards land' in Great Stirkeland" (Sizergh MSS.): and "Latuneland in Great Stirkeland" is again referred to in a record of the year 1335 (*Cal. Close Rolls*, 1335, p. 378).

*Page 706, this volume.

de Ros, who gave it to Richard de Preston and his wife Amabel, who in turn enfeoffed Sir John de Stirkeland (who was already in possession of the tenements on which the rent was charged). Amabel de Preston, after the death of her husband, released to Sir John de Stirkeland all claims, etc., by virtue of which deeds the rent itself became totally extinguished. Consequently, neither Margaret de Ros nor Sir John de Stirkeland nor any other ever held the said rent of the king *in capite;* nor are the tenements from which the rent came held in chief, but of Thomas de Thweng by the service of 2s. yearly for "cornage" and by homage (Chanc. Inq. P.M.'s, *ibid.*).

From the records just quoted it is apparent that Sir John de Strickland's eventual successor in the Great Strickland property was Robert de Strickland, a minor, who was aged sixteen in 1361 and was hence born about 1345; and we are further informed that the latter was the eldest son[64] of the "John, son of Robert de Stirkeland" upon whom Sir John de Strickland had entailed his possessions in 1340. This John son of Robert was himself born *circa* 1293; for he is described as "aged forty" in 1337, when he volunteered the curious piece of information that a bastard son of his had been killed by mischance "at the schools at Oxford" eighteen years before (*Cal. Inqs.*, vol. IX, pp. 34–5).[65] Between 1348 and 1350 he served as a Collector of the Subsidy in Westmorland and Cumberland (*Cal. Fine Rolls*, 1348–1350), and was a Juror on an inquisition at Kendal in 1354 (Dodsworth MSS., vol. 70, f° 148b). But he was evidently dead before the year 1361, by which date his widow, Joan, had become the wife of Thomas de "Berewys"—probably the Thomas de Barwise (of Barwise in Appleby) who was M.P. for Westmorland in 1360. From 1320 onwards, John son of Robert de Strickland's name is frequently associated with that of Sir John de Strickland in attesting charters, etc.;[66] and it is reasonable to suppose that his father, Robert, was yet another of Sir John de Strickland's brothers —a supposition which is supported by the mention of "Robert de Stirkland" as "brother" of (Sir) John de Stirkland and "son" of (Sir) William de Stirkland in a Westmorland Coram Rege Roll of 1302 (*ibid.*, no. 168, m. 45).[67]

It only remains to add that by the beginning of the fifteenth century Great Strickland manor had passed to Nicholas de Fallowfield, against whom Sir Thomas de Strickland—the then head of the Sizergh branch—appears to have claimed the estate as heir male

[64] The inquisition itself speaks of "other sons and daughters" (*ibid.*), without, however, referring to them by name.

[65] This bastard son was likewise named Robert (*Cal. Inqs., loc. cit.*); but as he died in youth there is no risk of confusing him with the legitimate heir.

[66] *e.g.* in 1330 Sir John de Stirkeland and John son of Robert de Stirkeland witnessed a settlement of the manor of Sockbridge (*Transactions of the Cumberland and Westmorland Antiquarian Society*, New Series, vol. X, pp. 456–460); and in 1339 they both witnessed two grants of land in Crosby Ravensworth made to William son of Sir Henry de Threlkeld (Lowther MSS.). A deed enrolled on the Westmorland Assize Roll of 14 Edward III [1340], and dated at "Clibrun" (Cliburn) 9 July, 1337, was attested by Sir John de Stirkeland, (deputy) sheriff of Westmorland, John son of Robert de Stirkeland, and Sir Thomas de Stirkeland (eldest son of Sir Walter de Strickland of Sizergh).

[67] Mr. Hornyold-Strickland follows Bellasis and others in making this Robert the third son of Sir William de Strickland, but gives no proof of his parentage (*op. cit.*, p. 23). There seems little doubt that Robert was really the *fourth* son, and that Sir John de Strickland was his older brother (cf. footnote no. 55).

(Sizergh MSS.).[68] Nicholas, however, continued to retain possession, as did his descendants up to the close of the seventeenth century (cf. Nicolson and Burn, "History of Westmorland and Cumberland," vol. I, p. 360): and since the later Fallowfield arms, *Sable three escallops or*, are similar to those of Strickland save for a change of tincture, it would seem highly probable that the Fallowfields themselves succeeded to Great Strickland by marriage with the heiress of the young Robert de Strickland who was born in 1345.[69]

Meanwhile, besides the children whom we have already enumerated (William, Sir Walter, Sir John, and Robert), Sir William de Strickland and Elizabeth d'Eyncourt are also alleged to have left two additional sons, named Hugh and Roger (Bellasis, "Genealogy of the Stricklands of Sizergh," *Transactions of the Cumberland and Westmorland Antiquarian Society*, Old Series, vol. X, p. 75; Hornyold-Strickland, *op. cit.*, p. 24). The name of a Hugh de Stirkland does indeed appear in a list of the northern knights (who included Sir John de Strickland) captured at the battle of Boroughbridge in 1322 (Palgrave, "Parliamentary Writs," vol. II, p. 201); but the writer has been unable to find any further reference to him and his exact relationship remains unproven, although there is little doubt that he belonged to the same stock.[70] On the other hand, Roger de Strickland, so far from having been a son or relative of Sir William de Strickland, in all probability possessed no connection with the Sizergh family whatever. The only mention of him which Mr. Hornyold-Strickland adduces (*ibid.*, p. 24) is Plantagenet-Harrison's assertion (unsupported as usual) that in 1311–12 Roger de Stirkeland "was defendant in a suit by Sir Richard de Bermingham . . . for hunting without license on his lands at Berborne," *i.e.* Barbon in Kendal. But this Roger de Stirkeland of Barbon was almost certainly the same man who occurs in Kendal records of the period as Roger "de Stirkeland Ketell," *alias* Roger "de Kendale" (cf. *Cal. Close Rolls*, 1296, pp. 509–510; De Banco Roll, no. 108, m. 23; *ibid.*, no. 109, m. 21d.): and he would thus have derived his

---

[68] This claim is dated by the Rev. Thomas West (in his MS. abstracts of Sizergh deeds) as *temp.* Edward III; but it quite obviously belongs to a later period. For Sir Thomas de Strickland is expressly described as "son of Walter, son of Thomas, son of Walter, son and heir of William de Stirkeland, to whom his father Sir Robert de Stirkeland gave the said manor (of Great Stirkeland) with remainder to his heirs by his wife Elizabeth, daughter of Sir Ralph Daincurt" (Sizergh MSS.). The claimant was therefore the second Sir Thomas de Strickland, who succeeded to Sizergh in 1407/8, was knighted in 1425, and died in 1455: and the claim itself may thus be assigned to *circa* 1430.

[69] The latter was plaintiff in a plea concerning property in Great Strickland against Sir Thomas de Strickland (the husband of Cecily de Welles) in 1375 (Assize Roll, Westmorland, 49 Edward III); and on 14 Mar. 1378/9 he was pardoned for having acquired without licence a tenement called Ravewyk in Applethwaite (near Great Strickland), co. Westmorland, which Ingram de Coucy, Earl of Bedford, had granted him for life (*Cal. Patent Rolls*, 1379, p. 334). No doubt he was the same Robert de Stirkeland who served as escheator of Northumberland in 1391 (Bain, *Cal. Docs. Scots.*, IV).

[70] Presumably another kinsman was the Thomas de "Sterkland" who occurs with Sir William de Strickland in 1299 as witness to a grant of lands in Newby, co. Westmorland, and who attested a release from Adam Warde to Sir Walter de Strickland in 1311 (Sizergh MSS.). A Duchy of Lancaster Assize Roll of the year 1292 mentions that during the sittings of the Justices at Lancaster "Richard Tothay, serjeant, chattered in the hall and made a great tumult which impeded the court, and Thomas de Stirkland was also in mercy for the same" (Assize Roll, Lancs., no. 416, m. 28).

surname from Strickland Ketel in Kendal, and not (like the Sizergh Stricklands) from Great Strickland near Appleby.[71]

One genuine member of the Sizergh line does, however, yet require to be noticed, viz., Joan de Strickland, who was Sir William de Strickland's only known daughter by his marriage with the Sizergh heiress. She espoused Robert de Washington, who, thanks to the powerful Strickland influence, was returned as M.P. for Westmorland to the Parliament of May 1300.[72] This Strickland-Washington alliance took place (as the Sizergh muniments show) in 1292, when (Sir) Walter de Strickland, by a grant dated "on the Wednesday next after the Feast of St. Matthew the Apostle 24 September, 20 Edward I [1292]", settled upon his sister, Joan, and Robert de "Wessington," her husband, nine messuages, five bovates, a hundred and fifteen and a half acres, and one rod of land in Natland, also a meadow called Le Quaghe and the land of John Gretason, and a moiety of the land of "Lowkerig" [Loughrigg in Kendal], all in co. Westmorland (Sizergh MSS.). Sir Walter further endowed Joan and her heirs with the manor of Routhworth in Helsington, co. Westmorland (Washington, "Early Parliamentary Representation of Westmorland")—as well as with a moiety of the manor of Carnforth in the parish of Warton, co. Lancs., which Robert de Washington was holding *jure uxoris* at the time of his decease in 1324 (*Cal. Close Rolls*, 1324, p. 249; *Cal. Inqs.*, vol. VI, p. 357). Nothing has heretofore been ascertained regarding the manorial history of Carnforth prior to the fourteenth century, beyond the fact that the estate was from early times comprised in the Lancashire fee of the barons of Kendal (see "Victoria County History of Lancashire," vol. VIII, pp. 168–169). It can be shown, however, that all of the Westmorland properties which Sir Walter de Strickland gave to his sister as her *maritagium* had formerly belonged to his mother, Elizabeth d'Eyncourt; and the contributor concludes that Carnforth must also have been part of the d'Eyncourt inheritance. Such a view is strengthened by the circumstance that Sir William de Strickland—father of Sir Walter and Joan—was still flourishing in 1292 (the year of Joan's marriage): and it seems extremely unlikely that at that date Sir Walter himself possessed any lands in his own right, other than those to which he had already succeeded *jure matris*. Indeed, a Curia Regis Roll of 1261 (to be quoted presently) suggests the possibility that Sir Walter's moiety of Carnforth may have been originally acquired by his maternal grandfather, Sir Ralph d'Eyncourt of Sizergh, through espousing a certain Alice de Boyville; but the writer will have to reserve the last-named point for discussion in Section Two (*vide infra*). A curious feature about the tenure of the Carnforth moiety—and one which, incidentally, entirely escaped the attention of the learned editors of the "Victoria County History"—is that, although Robert de Washington was plainly holding

---

[71] He was most probably identical with Roger de Carnaby (or de Kendal), M. P. for Westmorland in 1318 (*vide supra*, page 116). Cf. also the case of John, son of William de Strickland (Ketel), cited in footnote no. 39. *

[72] Washington, "Early Parliamentary Representation of Westmorland."

*Page 721, this volume.

it in 1301 under Sir Marmaduke de Thweng, one of the co-heirs to the barony of Kendal (*Lancs. Final Concords* [Rec. Soc. Lancs. and Cheshire,] vol. I, p. 214), yet before Robert's death this Thweng overlordship had been eliminated: for in 1324 it is recorded that the property had then lately been held by "Robert de Wessington, tenant-in-chief, deceased," directly of the King *in capite* as of the earldom of Lancaster (*Cal. Inqs.*, vol. VI, p. 357). Possibly the explanation lies in the fact that Robert (as the writer's own researches prove) was closely associated throughout his life with Sir Marmaduke de Thweng, whom he attended with great gallantry as personal Esquire in the Scottish campaigns:[73] and Sir Marmaduke may well have released Robert and his descendants from the feudal obligations due from the manor of Carnforth, as a partial reward for these long and faithful services.

[*To be concluded*]

---

[73] Cf. Washington, *op. cit.*, and the new "History of Parliament," vol. III (to which the present writer has contributed).

# GENEALOGICAL RESEARCH IN ENGLAND

Communicated by the Committee on English and Foreign Research

## THE BAYFORD FAMILY

By G. ANDREWS MORIARTY, A.M., LL.B., F.S.A.

In the REGISTER, volume 85, pages 133–145, is found an account of the [*] English ancestry of William Chandler, the early settler of Roxbury, Mass. The following article relates to the ancestry of his wife Annis or Agnes Bayford of Fornham, co. Essex, England. It may be here noted that the parish register of Fornham has not been searched and such items as appear therefrom were copied by the late J. Gardner Bartlett in connection with his search for the family of William Chandler.

The Bayfords were a yeoman family which was flourishing in eastern Hertfordshire and western Essex at the end of the sixteenth and the beginning of the seventeenth century. The distinguished K.C. of our own times was descended from this family.

1. RICHARD BAYFORD, of Fornham, co. Essex, England, born about 1535, died between 17 Apr. 1599, the date of his will, and 15 May 1599, the date of its probate. He married at Fornham, 10 Apr. 1564, JOAN SEARLE.

Richard Bayford was a ploughwright and held copyhold lands and tenements in Fornham and in Bishop's Stortford (co. Herts.), within the royal manor of Earlsbury. On 17 Apr. 1599 he surrendered his tenement in Fornham, "where William Sturge dwelt", together with a lease of twelve acres, to his son Thomas Bayford.

In his will he left his lands to his son William, who was to pay his brother, Francis Bayford, £7:3:0 and bequeathed goods to his wife Joan and his daughters Mary and Elizabeth. (Original Will, Comm. Court of London, Essex and Herts.)

Children (order of last three uncertain):

   i.   WILLIAM, b. about 1565.
2. ii.  FRANCIS, bapt. at Fornham 13 Apr. 1567.
  iii.  THOMAS, b. about 1569.
  iv.  MARY, b. about 1572.
   v.  ELIZABETH, b. about 1575.

2. FRANCIS BAYFORD (*Richard*), of Fornham, co. Essex, England, baptized 13 Apr. 1567, died shortly before 3 Dec. 1622. He married JOAN ———

Francis Bayford was a husbandman, and held customary lands at Fornham within the manor of Earlsbury.

In his will, dated 9 June 1614, and proved at Bishop's

*Pages 354-366, this volume.

Stortford, co. Herts., England, 3 Dec. 1622, he left the tenement where he lived, after his wife's decease, to his son, Richard, except "Running House", and including "Long Croft", "Little Croft", and "Lancote Croft", but Richard was to pay £6 to his sister Agnes, when he was 21 years of age. To his younger son, John, he left "Running House", "Rosemary Close", and "New Close"; he also was to pay £6 to his sister Agnes, when he reached 21 years of age. The residue of the estate he left to his widow Joan. (Original Will, Comm. Court of London, Essex and Herts.)

Children:

i. RICHARD, b. about 1600; living, underage, 9 June 1614.
ii. AGNES or ANNIS, bapt. at Fornham 12 June 1603; d. at Roxbury, Mass., 15 Mar. 1682/3; m. (1) at Fornham, 6 Nov. 1625, WILLIAM CHANDLER of Bishop's Stortford, an emigrant in 1635–6 to New England, where he settled at Roxbury, d. 26: 11: 1641/2; m. (2) at Roxbury, 2 July 1643, as his second wife, JOHN DANE of Ipswich and Roxbury, Mass., who was buried at Roxbury 14 Sept. 1658; m. (3) at Roxbury, 9 Aug. 1660, as his second wife, DEA. JOHN PARMENTER of Sudbury and Roxbury, Mass., who d. at Roxbury 15 Mar. 1682/3.

Children by first husband (surname *Chandler*), all but last baptized at Bishop's Stortford:

1. *William*, bapt. 26 Mar. 1627; was buried at Bishop's Stortford 27 Nov. 1633.
2. *Capt. Thomas*, of Andover, Mass., bapt. 9 Aug. 1628; d. early in 1702/3.
3. *Hannah*, bapt. 22 May 1630; d. 2 June 1711; m. (1) at Roxbury, 12 Dec. 1646, George Abbott of Roxbury and Andover; m. (2) about 1690 her stepbrother, Rev. Francis Dane of Andover.
4. *Henry*, bapt. 13 Aug. 1632; d. young.
5. *Dea. John*, of Roxbury, and Woodstock, Conn., bapt. 27 July 1834; d. at Woodstock 15 Apr. 1703.
6. *William*, of Andover, bapt. 20 Mar. 1635/6; d. in 1698.
7. *Sarah*,* of Sandwich on Cape Cod in 1689, b. at Roxbury about 1638; m. (1) at Roxbury, 4 Nov. 1659, William Cleves of Roxbury, who was killed in the Sudbury Fight in Phillip's War on 29 Apr. 1676; m. (2) before 4: 7 mo: 1681 ——— Stevens; m. (3) before 13: 11 mo: 1683 ——— Parker (Roxbury Church Records, pp. 95–96).

iii. JOHN, b. about 1605; living, underage, 9 June 1614.

---

* In the account of the family of William Chandler, printed in the REGISTER, volume 85, p. 145, ** it is stated that Sarah Chandler married thirdly, 11 Oct. 1688, Ephraim Stevens of Andover. This is an error as on 11 Oct. 1680 Ephraim Stevens married her niece, Sarah Abbott, born 14 Nov. 1659, daughter of George and Hannah (Chandler) Abbott of Andover, and was having children by his wife Sarah as late as 10 Sept. 1700.

**Page 366, this volume.

THE OLD TOWER, SIZERGH CASTLE

## GENEALOGICAL RESEARCH IN ENGLAND

Communicated by the Committee on English and Foreign Research

### THE EARLY HISTORY OF THE STRICKLANDS OF SIZERGH, ANCESTORS OF THE CARLETONS OF MASSACHUSETTS AND THE WASHINGTONS OF VIRGINIA

By S. H. LEE WASHINGTON, M.A., of Cambridge, Mass.

### Part II

#### THE D'EYNCOURTS AND LE FLEMINGS

So much for the Stricklands; and it now becomes necessary to turn to the pedigree of Elizabeth d'Eyncourt and to the illustrious descent which she was the means of introducing into the Strickland family. Elizabeth's earliest ancestor in Westmorland is known to have been a certain Gervase d'Eyncourt, who was granted Sizergh towards the end of the twelfth century by William de Lancaster II, lord of Kendal; but the intervening generations have never been correctly worked out, and the printed information on the subject is too fragmentary to be of much assistance. A tentative chart of the Westmorland d'Eyncourts (though without any supporting proofs) was, indeed, published some years ago by the late Canon Ragg (*Trans. Cumb. and Westd. Antiq. Soc.*, New Series, vol. XVI, pp. 167-8), which made Elizabeth the sister and heiress of Ralph d'Eyncourt and daughter of another Ralph by Helen (or Eleanor) de Furness—the last-named Ralph (Elizabeth's father) being given as son of Peter d'Eyncourt by Avice de "Apelthwayt", and grandson of Gervase d'Eyncourt, the Sizergh grantee. This genealogy, however, is contradicted by the Sizergh evidences (*vide infra*),[*] which show clearly that Elizabeth's brother was named not Ralph but Richard, and that she herself was the granddaughter (instead of being the daughter) of the Ralph d'Eyncourt who married Eleanor de Furness; and, moreover, there is ample evidence that Peter d'Eyncourt, the husband of Avice de Applethwaite, was not in the direct line at all, but, on the contrary, was the progenitor of a younger branch seated at Applethwaite, co. Westmoreland, which preserved

*For Vol. 96, pp. 99-126 see pp. 701-731, this volume.

a male succession until the fourteenth century. What clinches the matter is an entry on a Westmoreland De Banco Roll of 1312, where the entire d'Eyncourt descent is appended during the course of some proceedings between Sir Walter de Strickland and John, son of Sir Roger de Lancaster of Sockbridge. This valuable entry states that in the Easter Term of the year 1312 "John, son of Roger de Lancaster was summoned to answer Walter de Stirkeland regarding common of pasture in the vill of Barton. And the said Walter, by Adam de Burton, his attorney,[74] claimed common of pasture in two thousand acres of moor and pasture and three hundred acres of wood in Barton for all manner of cattle throughout the year, of which his ancester Gervase [d'Eyncourt] was seised in the time of King Henry, grandfather of the King [Edward II] that now is. And from Gervase the right descended to a certain Ralph as son and heir, and from Ralph to Ralph [the second] as son and heir, and from Ralph [the second] to Gervase as son and heir; and from Gervase, because he died without any heirs of his body, the right went to Richard as brother and heir. And Richard similarly dying childless, the right went to Elizabeth, as sister and heir of Richard and Gervase; and from Elizabeth the right descended to William (de Stirkeland) as her son and heir. And because William died without issue, the right descended to his brother and heir, Walter (de Stirkeland), the present claimant" (De Banco Roll, Westmorland, Easter, 5 Edward II [1312], no. 192, *m.* 158 *d.* There is a further reference to the case on the same Roll, *m.* 171 *d.*, where Sir Walter de Strickland's mother is specifically called "Elizabeth, daughter of Ralph de Ayncourt"). Bearing the foregoing pedigree in mind, we can accordingly turn to consider such illustrative and corroborative material as is afforded by the Sizergh muniments and other contemporary sources.

Gervase d'Eyncourt, the Sizergh grantee, was undoubtedly some cadet of the great baronial house of d'Eyncourt of Thurgarton, co. Nottingham, and Blankney, co. Lincs.; for the arms of the two families differed only in tincture, the Sizergh branch bearing *Silver a fesse dancetté between six billets sable*, while the d'Eyncourts of Blankney bore *Azure a fesse dancetté between six billets or*.[75] It is not impossible that Gervase's father was Ralph, third and youngest son of the first Ralph d'Eyncourt, lord of Blankney and Thurgarton.

---

[74] According to the Westmorland Assize Rolls, Adam de Burton had married Sigrid, widow of Ralph de Berburne (for whom see REGISTER, vol. 96, pp. 105–6), and mother of Christian, wife of Gilbert de Burneside, whose daughter Elizabeth de Burneside married *circa* 1310 (as his second wife) John de Washington, brother of Robert de Washington, the husband of Walter de Strickland's sister Joan (cf. Assize Rolls, Westmorland, no. 985, *m.* 23).

[75] The quarterly arms of d'Eyncourt and Strickland (those of d'Eyncourt being given precedence and placed in the left quarter) are still to be seen on the fourteenth century tower of Sizergh Castle, which is believed to have been built by Elizabeth d'Eyncourt's son, Sir Walter de Strickland. It is an interesting fact, however, that the seal of Sir Ralph d'Eyncourt (Elizabeth's father), appended to one of his charters to John Gernet, bears the coat: *Two bars, in chief a canton* (Dodsworth MSS., vol. 149, f° 136). These arms are a variant of those of Sir Ralph's overlord, William III de Lancaster, lord of Kendal: (*Silver*) *two bars* (*gules*), *on a quarter* (*gules*) *a leopard* (*or*); and another variation of the de Lancaster coat had evidently occasionally been used by the Stricklands, who like the d'Eyncourts, held of the Kendal barony. In the Parliamentary Roll of Arms, *circa* 1310–1315, it is recorded that "Sire Wauter de Striklande" bore "de argent a ij barres e un quarter de goules"; although the ordinary Strickland coat was *Sable three escollops argent* (cf. REGISTER, *ibid.*, p. 102). ✵

*See the footnote on p. 735, this volume.

The latter in turn was the eldest surviving son of the Domesday tenant, Walter d'Eyncourt or d'Aincourt, one of the leading Norman magnates in the North Midlands *temp.* William the Conqueror.[76]

Gervase himself makes his initial appearance in Westmorland as a knight of the household of the second William de Lancaster, who was lord of Kendal between 1170 and 1184; and it is interesting to observe that Gervase witnessed the aforesaid William's confirmation of the manor of Docker to the hospital of St. Peter's, York, simply as *Geruasio milite* (cf. Charter Roll, 22 Edward I [1293–94], no. 80, *m.* 9). Gervase's name does not occur as attesting any of the grants of the earlier William de Lancaster (died 1170)—with the solitary exception of this William's conveyance of the manors of Heversham, Morland, and Grayrigg to Alexander de Windsor, his son-in-law. The last-named charter was printed by Sir George Duckett (*Duchetiana*, p. 15), and purports to have been given in the presence of Geoffrey, Earl of Richmond, Hubert de Vaux, William de Lancaster, Junior (eldest son of the grantor), Gervase "de Aencurt", Gilbert son of William (de Lancaster), and Jordan his brother. But clearly the text must be corrupt, since, although Hubert de Vaux (of Gilsland) died in 1165, Geoffrey (Plantagenet) did not become Earl of Richmond until 1181, while both Gilbert and Jordan were illegitimate sons of the *second* William de Lancaster who died in 1184. The most likely explanation is that the document in its existing form represents a combination of two separate charters issued by successive lords of Kendal, and that the witnesses to both charters have been accidentally combined by the mediaeval transcriber.

In the meantime, further documents illustrate Gervase d'Eyncourt's position as one of the second William de Lancaster's *familia.* Thus, along with William's second wife, Helewise (de Stuteville), Gervase attested a grant of half the land of Crook (in Strickland Ketel, co. Westmorland) made by William to his cook, Walter, and another grant of the remaining portion of Crook to William fitz Geoffrey (Levens Hall MSS.). He also attested William de Lancaster's conveyance bestowing half of Sockbridge in Kendal upon his natural son, Gilbert—among the other witnesses on that occasion being Walter, Abbot of Furness, Norman (de Redman) the Sewer, "Michael le Fleming of Furness and Anselm his son" (Lowther MSS.). Moreover, *circa* 1175–1180 Gervase was formally enfeoffed of fifteen "librates" in Westmorland, including the lands of Sizergh, to hold by the service of three-fourths of a knight's fee: and the charter of feoffment, which is the first in the long series of family muniments preserved at Sizergh Castle, would seem to be of sufficient importance to warrant its being quoted *in toto:*

[76] Walter derived his surname from Aincourt in the French Vexin, between Mantes and Magny. He appears as a tenent-in-chief in Domesday, holding over sixty manors, Blankney being the *caput* of his barony. In 1670 an inscription was discovered in Lincoln Cathedral commemorating Walter's son William who died in his father's lifetime. William is described as "*filius Walteri Aiencuriensis, consanguinei Remigii episcopi Lincoliensis* [Remigius of Fécamp, Bishop of Lincoln] *qui hanc ecclesiam fecit*", and also as "*regia stirpe progenitus*". William's royal blood probably came through his mother (the wife of Walter d'Aincourt), who was no doubt some relative of the Dukes of Normandy.

*Notum sit tam futuris quam presentibus quod ego Willelmus de Lancastre dedi et concessi Geruasio de Aiencurt pro homagio suo et seruicio suo XV libratas terre [scilicet tres partes feodi] unius militis [in Natalaund et Bothelford. . . . us] que ad riuulum de furcis et sic totum campum in sursum usque ad viam de Hotun. . . emus et de . . . illa usque ad diuisam de Hotun et de Stainton, et Sigaritherge *[77]* cum pertinentiis suis et Winderge cum pertinentiis suis et alteram Windergam cum pertinentiis suis et meam partem de Louder, et illam partem de Socabret que fuit Walteui. Has predictas terras dedi ei pro XII libratis terre et dimidia librata terre, et de L. solidatis terre que retro sunt tradidi ei seruicium de Hacatorp in vagium pro L. solidatis donec sibi perficiam XV libratas terre, in feodo et hereditate sibi et heredibus suis de me et de meis heredibus tenere libere et quiete et honorifice, in bosco, in plano, in aquis, in pratis, in pascuis, et in omnibus libertatibus. Testibus: Normanno dapifero, Jordano filio domini, Gilberto filio domini, Grumbaldo, Roberto de Heriez, Anselmo,*[78]* Ormo filio Tore, Rogero de Croft, Rogero filio Ade, Ormo filio Bernulfi, Roberto Mustel, Willelmo persona de Warton, Johanne clerico, Ricardo camerario, Willelmo [de Pultyngton]. Vale.* [mutilated; seals missing].*

About the same date, for the witnesses are similar, William de Lancaster granted Gervase an additional twelve and a half "librates" in Whelpside and Whinfell (which lies adjacent to Sizergh), for which he was to render the service of one-fourth of a fee (Sizergh MSS.); and another Sizergh charter (in Norman-French) records that the said William de Lancaster afterwards released him from all services due from his lands in Westmorland, in exchange for a rent of 50s:

*Sachent presens et advenir q je Gillam de Lancastre garaunte et quite ay clayme a Gervase de Haencurt et ses heiers de moy et mes heiers et a cest ma present chartre ay conferme au dit Gervase tous maniers de rentes et services a il et ces heiers dount fair a moy et mes heiers pour aucun de ces maniers, terres, ou tenemens dedans la Counte de Westmerland, en la exchainge pour la vente de sinc quant souvs en Westmerland les que anoc le dit Gervase et ces heiers avaunt dellesse a moy et mes heiers a toue jours. Tesmoignes: Norman dapifer, Robert de Heriic, Anselme, Orme fitz Rober le Chamurleyn, Gillem de Croft, Gillem le Person de Warton, Johan le Clerk, Ricardyn le Chamburleyn, Gillem de Pultyngton, et autres.*

Gervase thus became the holder of a considerable fief in the Kendal district, including Sizergh, Natland, Hutton, Stainton, High Windergh and Low Windergh, Whinfell, and Whelpside, besides other holdings in North Westmorland at Sockbridge, Hackthorpe, and Lowther.[79]    After the death of William de Lancaster in 1184, William Marshall (afterwards Earl of Pembroke), the guardian of de Lancaster's young daughter and heiress Helewise, confirmed Gervase in these possessions (Sizergh MSS.): and a few years later the latter received a fresh confirmation from Gilbert fitz Renfrid, who had become lord of Kendal through his marriage to Helewise in 1189 (Levens Hall MSS.).    Gilbert fitz Renfrid likewise gave Ger-

---

[77] Sizergh.

[78] Anselm le Fleming, whose daughter Eleanor became the wife of Gervase's son Ralph (*vide infra*).

[79] It is apparent from the Assize Rolls that the d'Eyncourts also possessed rights in the presentation to Lowther church, which passed from them to the Stricklands (cf. Assize Roll, Westmorland, no. 980, *m.* 6 *d.*).    In 1278 the three patrons of the church were stated to be the Prior of Watton, (Sir) William de Strickland, and Alice, wife of Robert de Morville (*ibid.*, no. 982, *m.* 11 *d.*).

vase quittance from the ancient tribute of "noutgeld",[80] for which release Gervase paid twenty marks in silver (Sizergh MSS.); and in the Dodsworth MSS. are two charters of property in Levens, co. Westmorland, granted to Gervase de "Aencurt" by Ketel de Levens and Orm de Ninezergh (*ibid.*, vol. 149, f[os] 134 *d.*, 135 *d.*). Gervase himself was still living as late as 1210, when he served on two inquisitions at Carlisle (Prescott, *Wetherhal*, p. 339); but he probably died before May 1211, when the name of his son and successor, Ralph d'Eyncourt, replaces his own as witness to a grant made by Robert de Vieuxpont to the Abbey of Shap (Dugdale, *Monasticon*, 1st edit., II, p. 595).[81]

Ralph d'Eyncourt was one of the two knights in attendance on Gilbert fitz Renfrid who were taken prisoner, along with their suzerain, at the capture of Rochester Castle, 30 Nov. 1215. On 22 Jan. 1215/16, Gilbert fitz Renfrid became obliged to pay King John the enormous sum of twelve thousand marks to purchase a pardon for his "confederacy with the King's enemies and that his son William de Lancastre [82] and his knights, Ralph de Aencurt and Lambert de Bussay,[83] might be delivered from the King's prison, having been taken at the castle of Rochester in arms against the King", etc. (*Rotuli de Oblatis et Finibus* [Rec. Com.], p. 570). The unfortunate Gilbert was further required to furnish hostages from amongst the sons or daughters of his principal mesne-tenants in the barony of Kendal; and we learn that among those selected were "the heir (son or daughter) of Ralph de Aencurt" and "the heir of Walter de Stirkeland", the husband of Christian de Leteham and the founder of the Stricklands of Sizergh (*Rot. Chart.* [Rec. Com.], p. 221 b).[84] Nor was it until 1217, after King John's death, that Ralph d'Eyncourt received a pardon from the young Henry III, and was allowed to leave his place of confinement at Corfe castle and return to his allegiance (*Rot. Litt. Claus.* [Rec. Com.], I, p. 376). The fact that the new King was then under the regency of William Marshal, the quondam guardian of Gilbert fitz Renfrid's wife Helewise, had doubtless helped to expedite Ralph's release. About the year 1220, the latter demised five acres of land in Levens, which he "had from Roger de Lancastre of the fee of Orm de Niandsherg" [Ninezergh], to Gilbert de Osmotherley, the witnesses including Matthew de Sizergh and Robert d'Eyncourt (probably the grantor's younger brother); [85] and by another charter, of *circa* 1224-6, he transferred the holding to a certain Roger Abbot (Dodsworth MSS., vol. 149, f[o] 135). Ralph was dead by 1228-1233, when Eleanor his

[80] "Noutgeld", or "geld of cows", was a survival of pre-Conquest days, being a rent incumbent on the land and paid in kind, *i.e.* in cattle. The assessment was reckoned "by head" or "by horn" on the animals kept by the tenant.

[81] The names of Gervase and Ralph occur together in several earlier charters. Together they witnessed Gilbert fitz Renfrid's grant of Lambrigg, co. Westmorland, to Lambert de Bussy (*Northamptonshire Charters* [Northants. Rec.], and his confirmation to Henry de Redman of the manors of Levens and Selside (Levens Hall MSS., f[o] 95).

[82] He was the heir of his mother Helewise, the daughter and heiress of William II de Lancaster, and assumed the de Lancaster arms and surname (*vide* REGISTER, *supra*, p. 103, footnote 8).

[83] The grantee of Lambrigg.

[84] *vide* REGISTER, *supra*, pp. 106-7. *

[85] He attested the grant to Ralph made by Anselm le Fleming *circa* 1210-1215 (*vide infra*).

*See the footnote on p. 735, this volume.

widow, for the soul of her "lord, Ralph de Haynecurth, and of Helewise de Lancastre", confirmed a rent of 2s. 6d. for one moiety of the vill of "Siggeswich" [Sedgwick in Kendal], formerly held by Herbert de Ellel, to the canons of Cockersand (*Cockersand Chartulary* [Chetham Soc.], p. 1044). The Sizergh muniments make it clear that Eleanor herself was one of the daughters and co-heiresses of Anselm le Fleming, *alias* de Furness. For by a charter of *circa* 1210–1215 Anselm de "Furnesia" gave to Ralph de "Aien-curt", in further increase of the property which the said Ralph held in free marriage with Eleanor, the grantor's daughter, "the hall of Stayneton [Stainton in Kendal, co. Westmorland], with its pre-cincts, garden, and vivary"—the witnesses comprising William, Prior of Cartmel, Robert d'Eyncourt, Richard fitz Alard, Thomas de Esseby, and Thomas de Linacre (Sizergh MSS.). As will pres-ently appear, Anselm was the younger son of Michael le Fleming, lord of Aldingham, co. Lancs.; while his wife Alice was a niece, maternally, of Walter de Greystoke and a daughter of the great Scottish house of Dunbar.

Ralph d'Eyncourt and his wife Eleanor (le Fleming) seem to have left at least two sons, viz., Sir Ralph of Sizergh—who is called "son of Ralph (Senior) and grandson of Gervase" in a charter of *circa* 1245 (*vide infra*)—and Peter, who married Avice, daughter and co-heiress of William de Applethwaite,[86] by whom he was father of another Sir Ralph d'Eyncourt (of Applethwaite and Arcleby, co. Cumb.), who served as Coroner of Cumberland in 1300 and a Com-missioner to assess the Subsidy there in 1301.[87] An Adam d'Eyn-court, chaplain, occurs in a Final Concord with John de "Hoton-rofe" and Eleanor his wife concerning the manor of Hutton Roof, co. Westmorland, as late as 1327 (De Banco Roll, Easter, 12 Ed-ward II [1319], *m.* 121 *d.*; *ibid.*, Trinity, 12 Edward II [1319], *m.* 35).

But it is Sir Ralph d'Eyncourt of Sizergh—the eldest grandson of Gervase, the knight of William de Lancaster—who chiefly concerns us here: and Sir Ralph's name appears as witness to numerous Westmorland charters during the second quarter of the thirteenth century. His parentage is proven by a quitclaim of *circa* 1245–1250, by which Roger Abbot released to Ralph "son of Ralph de Aynecurt" property at Levens, co. Westmorland, the witnesses in-cluding Walter de Strickland, Gervase d'Eyncourt,[88] and Richard de Preston (Dodsworth MSS., vol. 149, fº 135 *d.*); while Thomas de Levens granted him further holdings there, as well as the land which Ketel de Levens gave to "Gervase de Aynecurt, the said Ralph's grandfather" (Sizergh MSS.). In 1235 Ralph d'Eyncourt and Pat-rick fitz Thomas (de Curwen)[89] are mentioned as holding one knight's fee of the barony of Kendal (*Rot. Chart.* [Rec. Com.], I, p. 412); and

[86] In 1246 Thomas de Lowther and Beatrice, his wife, had a Final Concord with Peter d'Eyncourt and Avice, his wife, regarding the manor of Crosthwaite, co. Cumb. (Feet of Fines, Cumberland, 30 Henry III [1245–1246]). The manors of Crosthwaite and Applethwaite descended to Beatrice and Avice from William de Applethwaite, their father.
[87] He held Applethwaite of Thomas de Lucy in 1305 (*Cal. Inqs.*).
[88] This was, of course, a second Gervase, for whom see below.
[89] Ancestor of the Curwens of Workington.

in 1240 the former, having not yet become a knight, was granted a respite until the next Feast of Pentecost (*Cal. Close Rolls*, 1240, p. 343). But, although holding a whole knight's fee, Ralph had still not taken up knighthood by the following year—since on 24 Apr. 1241 the King ordered the sheriff of Westmorland to distrain Roger de Burton, Ralph d'Eyncourt, and Guy de Boyville for their failure in this respect (*Cal. Patent Rolls*, 1241, p. 352). On 7 Dec. 1237 Ralph d'Eyncourt and Richard de Denton, clerk, were appointed to collect the subsidy in co. Westmorland, in place of Thomas fitz John, deceased (*Cal. Patent Rolls*, 1237, p. 206); and the King issued a writ on 13 Feb. 1239/40 commanding that Ralph be reimbursed with the sum of 100s. for his expenses as Collector (*Cal. Liberate Rolls*, 1240, p. 450). In 1242 the latter was again in official employment, when we find that Sir Ralph d'Eyncourt (now evidently a knight) and Sir Robert de Asby received appointments in Westmorland as Conservators of the Peace (*Cal. Patent Rolls*, 1242, p. 484): and in 1243, during a suit in the Court of King's Bench between Matthew de Redman and William de Lancaster (the son of Gilbert fitz Renfrid), William was attached by Ralph de "Ayncurt" and Richard de Heyham (Curia Regis Rolls, no. 128, *m.* 2 *d.*). In 1246 Sir Ralph impleaded William de Lancaster at Appleby for the right of having "estovers" (*i.e.*, taking wood from an estate for reasonable purposes) in the manor of Barton (Assize Roll, Westmorland, no. 1045, *m.* 55 *d.*): and in the same year he officiated as a juror at Lancaster (*Lancs. Inqs.* [Lancs. and Cheshire Rec. Soc.], pt. I, p. 166), while in 1247 he was amerced half a mark for a default (*Pipe Rolls of Cumb. and Westd.*, ed. Parker, p. 204). In addition to his paternal lands of Sizergh, etc., and the property which he inherited from his mother Eleanor le Fleming at Natland and Heversham, Sir Ralph purchased the manor of Tristermont, on Ullswater, from Hugh de la Chamber (cf. Coram Rege Rolls, Westmorland, Michaelmas, 4 Edward I [1276], *m.* 1), and also acquired *jure uxoris* lands at Blencarn and Carnforth (*vide infra*). Moreover, Roger Pepin, Rector of the mediety of the church of Kendal (subsequently sub-Dean of York),[90] granted to him and his heirs the privilege of having a private chapel in their "court at Natelond for the celebration of divine service" (Feet of Fines, Westmorland, 31 Henry III [1246–47], file 4, no. 15), which suggests that Sir Ralph made his chief seat at Natland, rather than at Sizergh; and, indeed, the oldest existing portion of Sizergh Castle only dates from the time of Sir Walter de Strickland, his grandson. Sir Ralph likewise served as Steward of the barony of Kendal under William de Lancaster, third and last of the name; and he was amongst those present at William's death-bed on 29 Nov., 1246 (*Cal. Inqs.*, *Henry III*, p. 28; cf. *Trans. Cumb. and Westd. Antiq. Soc.*, New Series, vol. X, pp. 440–442). Shortly afterwards, William son of Henry [de Wrayton] was summoned to answer the Abbot of Cockersand in a plea to acquit him of the service that Ralph de "Aynecurt" demanded of the Abbot for the free tenement which he held of William (the

90 Cf. *Cal. Papal Registers*, I, p. 338.

defendant) in "Quinnefell" [Whinfell], co. Westmorland, viz., "thirty acres of land in that vill held in free alms by the Abbot by the gift of Adam fitz Orm, uncle of the said William, and for which, by reason of William's default, Ralph de Ayencurt distrained him (the Abbot) to do suit at his court [? at Natland] in Strickland Ketel" (Assize Roll, Westmorland, no. 454, *m.* 12). Sir Ralph was still living in 1251, when he was sued for entering the Abbot of Byland's demesne at Bannisdale, co. Westmorland, with force and arms (*ibid.*, no. 1046, *m.* 1; no. 1048, *m.* 4 *d.*). But he must have died soon afterwards, leaving a widow, Dame Alice de "Aynecurt", who *circa* 1260 was demised property at Sizergh by Robert son of Matthew de "Syzittsergh" which Sir Ralph de "Aynecurt", her late husband, had granted to the said Robert in exchange for land called "Ewode" (Dodsworth MSS., vol. 149, f⁰ 137 *d.*). It appears probable that it was this Dame Alice who brought to the d'Eyn-courts as her *maritagium* half the manor of Blencarn, co. Cumber-land, as well as half the manor of Carnforth in Warton, co. Lancs.,— both of which holdings were later in possession of her grandson, Sir Walter de Strickland, as part of his maternal inheritance (cf. *supra,* pp. 125–6; also *Cal. Inqs.*, 5 Edward II [1311–1312], p. 183). For in a claim regarding a moiety of Blencarn, initiated by Juliana widow of Adam de Ireby against William de Thursby, it is stated that the said moiety was then held by Alice de "Eincurt" (*Abbrev. Placit.* [Rec. Com.], p. 78). The other moiety belonged to William de Thursby, whose daughter and heiress married Guy de Boyville (Denton, *Accompt of Cumberland*, p. 57); and in 1261 their son will-iam de Boyville, together with his wife Alice, sued Walter de Lind-say (one of the co-heirs of William de Lancaster, the last lord of Kendal) that he keep the agreement which he had with them con-cerning a messuage, two bovates, and fifty acres of land in Carn-forth (Curia Regis Rolls, Michaelmas, 45 Henry III [1260–61], no. 171, *m.* 44 *d.*). The paternity of Alice, wife of Sir Ralph d'Eyn-court, is difficult to determine; but it seems possible that she, too, was an heiress of the de Thursby family.[91]

According to the entry on the De Banco Roll quoted at the com-mencement of this section, Sir Ralph d'Eyncourt was the father of three children: Gervase, his heir (who died *sine prole*), Richard, (who also died without issue), and Elizabeth (the mother of Walter de Strickland). Of Gervase, named for his great-grandfather, we know nothing beyond the fact that he witnessed Roger Abbot's quitclaim to his father of property at ˎLevens (*vide supra*). Richard, the second son, occurs in two Sizergh charters, both of which are *sans date* but must have been issued at some period between 1251 and 1271.[92] By the first of these, William son of Patrick de Sedgwick

[91] The Thursbys, lords of Blencarn, Ainstable, and Thursby, co. Cumb., descended from a certain Herbert who had been granted "Thoresby" towards the middle of the twelfth century by Alan, son of Waldeve, lord of Allerdale (*Reg. St. Bees* [Surtees Soc.], p. 493). A Robert de Thursby wit-nessed a deed of *circa* 1163 relating to Culgaith, near Ainstable (Prescott, *Wetherhal*, p. 308), and occurs in the Cumberland Pipe Roll of 1182.

[92] Sir Ralph d'Eyncourt was a defendant in 1251, and his daughter Elizabeth, wife of Sir William de Strickland, had succeeded as sole heiress of the family before 30 Oct. 1271 (*vide infra*).

Michael I. le Fleming, of Aldingham, fl. 1127–50. = dau. Robert de Stuteville.

Gospatric II., Earl of Dunbar, = Christian ——.
d. 1138.

Michael II. le Fleming, fl. 1160–80. = Christian de Stainton.

Edgar "Unniting". = Alice de Greystoke.

Anselm le Fleming, yngr. son; d. 1210–17. = Agnes of Dunbar.

Gervase d'Eyncourt, grantee of Sizergh, 1175–80. =

Erneburga. = Richard de Preston.

Isabel. = Thomas fitz John.

daughter. = Patrick de Borwick.

Eleanor le Fleming. = Ralph d'Eyncourt, of Sizergh; d. 1228–33.

Robert d'Eyncourt, fl. 1210–15.

Avice de Applethwaite. = Peter d'Eyncourt, jure ux. of Applethwaite.

Sir Ralph d'Eyncourt, = Alice, ? dau. and coh.
of Sizergh; d. ca. 1251. William de Thursby.

Sir Ralph d'Eyncourt, of Applethwaite; fl. 1300.

? Adam d'Eyncourt, chaplain.

Gervase d'Eyncourt, d.s.p. before 1271.

Richard d'Eyncourt, d.s.p. before October 1271.

Sir William de Strickland, = Elizabeth d'Eyncourt,
jure ux. of Sizergh; heiress of Sizergh;
d. 1305–6. m. 1239, d. 1272–4.

released to Richard de "Ayncurt" the land at Sedgwick in Kendal which Sir Ralph de "Ayncurt" held at his death of the said William's fee; whilst by a further charter Hugh de "Sockebrede" quitclaimed to him all the holdings in Stainton which he had from "Sir Ralph de Eyncurt, father of the said Richard", in exchange for his own property at "Sockebrede" [Sockbridge, near Penrith]. As to Elizabeth, the sister of Richard and Gervase, we have already seen that she was married at a tender age (June 1239) to William, the young son and heir of Sir Robert de Strickland of Great Strickland, co. Westmorland; and she must have succeeded as heiress of the d'Eyncourt family in or before 1271. For Peter de Brus (nephew and one of the co-heirs of William de Lancaster III), who was dead by October 30th of that year (*Cal. Inqs.*, II, pp. 189–90), confirmed to William de Strickland and Elizabeth his wife their lands of Natland, Sizergh, Hackthorpe, etc., free from "pulture" of his master-forester and from service in the baronial court (Sizergh MSS.). Elizabeth is named as wife of William de "Stirkeland" in a Westmorland Final Concord of 1272 (*Excerp. e Rot. Fin.* [Rec. Com.], II, p. 567): but she died between that date and 1276, when she is referred to as "deceased" in the course of a plea concerning the manor of Tristermont (Coram Rege Roll, Westmorland, Michaelmas, 4 Edward I [1276], m. I).

In conclusion, et us consider briefly the ancestry of Eleanor le Fleming, Elizabeth d'Eyncourt's grandmother; since not only are there problems in the Fleming pedigree that still await solution, but it was Eleanor herself who brought to the d'Eyncourts, and ultimately to the Stricklands and the Washingtons, that strain of royal blood derived from Earl Uctred and his wife Edith (Aelfgifu), daughter of King Ethelred the Unready. The early Fleming descent has never been worked out; but Michael le Fleming and Rainer le Fleming were both landowners in Cumberland during the first quarter of the twelfth century. Rainer, who was the father of sons named William, Walter, and Hugh, was the original feoffee of Beckermet in Coupland, co. Cumberland, under William "le Meschin", lord of Coupland and Skipton, to whom he acted as *dapifer*, and whose foundation charter of the priory of St. Bees he witnessed in 1120–25 (*Reg. St. Bees* [Surtees Soc.], pp. 28–40, 107).[93] Michael, who was the immediate progenitor of Anselm (the father of Eleanor le Fleming, wife of Ralph d'Eyncourt), acquired the Cumberland manor of Drigg in Coupland, and was also lord of Aldingham in Furness, co. Lancs., in the year 1127, having evidently been enfeoffed of his Lancashire estates by Henry I.[94] The parentage of

[93] He also appears to have been enfeoffed of the manor of Wath upon Dearne in Yorkshire, since his grandson, Rainer II, held two knights' fees of the Honour of Skipton in that county in 1166.

[94] In 1127 Stephen of Blois (afterwards King Stephen), lord of the Honour of Lancaster, specially excepted the lands of Michael le Fleming from his charter of endowment of the Abbey of Furness. Michael held a moiety of the original lordship of Furness, comprising twenty and a half carucates situated in the vills of Aldingham, Leece, Hart, Gleaston, Dendron, Sunton, Bolton, Stainton in Urswick (which must be distinguished from Stainton in Kendal), and Fordbottle (*Lancs. Pipe Rolls*, ed. Farrer, pp. 302–317; *V.C.H. Lancs.*, II, pp. 114–120; *ibid.*, VIII, pp. 286–301). Michael's moiety, formerly called Aldingham from its principal seat, became later known as Muchland, *i.e.* "Michael's land". For his acquisitions of Drigg, see below.

neither Michael nor Rainer is known, but they were probably brothers: and the writer would suggest that they very likely belonged to the family of le Fleming, barons of Wahull (now Odell) in Bedfordshire, amongst whom the names Michael, Rainer, Hugh, and Walter were common at this period. At the date of the compilation of Domesday Book in 1086, Walter "Flandrensis" (*i.e.* le Fleming) was one of the principal tenants-in-chief in co. Bedford, where he held Wahull, Thurleigh, and other broad estates. His eldest son, Walter II, was father of Simon le Fleming, or de Wahull, who had sons named Michael and Rainer,[95] and whose heir-general, Sir Richard Chetwode, claimed to be "Lord Wahull" (by virtue of his possession of the "barony" of Wahull) in 1613.[96] The first Walter of Wahull may well have been the father of Rainer le Fleming of Beckermet and Michael le Fleming of Aldingham.

The origin of the lords of Wahull has never been ascertained; but Domesday shows that Walter "Flandrensis" (of 1086) had succeeded a certain Saier in the manor of Southill, co. Bedford, prior to the date of the General Survey; and as this unusual Christian name was afterwards borne by Walter's great-grandson, Saier de Wahull, there seems good reason for regarding the original Saier of Southill as Walter's father.[97] Now it is a remarkable circumstance that the arms as well as the Christian names of the early lords of Wahull were identical with those of the powerful Flemish family of d'Oisy, castellans of Cambrai, who claimed descent from the ancient Counts of Lens. Not only do the three crescents of Wahull closely resemble the one crescent coat borne by d'Oisy, but Walter, castellan of Cambrai, who was assassinated in 1041, had a brother named Saier, who aspired unsuccessfully to the bishopric of Cambrai in 1054. Still more curious, Hugh I. d'Oisy, castellan of Cambrai—who was the grandson and heir of the Walter of 1041, and whose grandson, Simon d'Oisy, succeeded to the *chatéllenie* of Cambrai in 1131—was in his youth under the guardianship of his kinsman (*propinquus*) Anselm de Ribemont, Count of Ostrevant, whose Christian name recalls that of Anselm le Fleming, the father of Eleanor d'Eyncourt! We may therefore conclude that Walter, the Domesday lord of Wahull, was a cadet of this distinguished house; and most probably his (presumed) father, Saier of Southill, was a younger brother of Hugh I. d'Oisy, castellan of Cambrai, and of Walter de Cambrai, castellan of Douai.[98]

[95] Cf. Assize Roll, Bedfordshire, 46 Henry III [1261–1262], *m.* 4. In the twelfth century the lords of Wahull owed the service of no less than thirty knights' fees.

[96] Sir Richard's claim was rejected on the grounds that none of his ancestors were ever summoned as barons by writ. For the later lords of Wahull see *V. C. H. Beds.*, III, pp. 69–73.

[97] "Walter brother of Saier" and Walter le Fleming (of Wahull) each had the same English predecessor in their Domesday estates, the English thegn Leofnoth; and Saier gave his name to Segenhoe (Beds.), which was afterwards held as part of the Wahull barony. Rainer le Fleming of Thurleigh was most likely another son of Saier, and this Walter of Wahull's younger brother.

[98] An excellent account of the castellans of Cambrai, from the Continental point of view, is given by M. Leon Vanderkindere in "La Formation Territoriale des Principautés Belges au Moyen Age," II, pp. 56–59. Walter, castellan of Lens, was made castellan of Cambrai between 972 and 979, and left two sons, Walter II and Saier, the latter of whom has already been mentioned as an unsuccessful candidate for the bishopric of Cambrai. The elder son, Walter II, was assassinated in 1041; and upon his death his next heir was an infant grandson, Hugh d'Oisy, son of his only daugh-

Meanwhile, we must return to Michael le Fleming, the feoffee of Aldingham *temp.* Henry I, and to his brother (?) Rainer le Fleming, lord of Beckermet. Rainer's grandson and namesake founded Kirklees Priory, Yorks., in the reign of Henry II, and became the ancestor of the Flemings, baronets, of Rydal Hall, who erroneously trace descent from the Flemings of Aldingham.[99] As for Michael, the founder of the Aldingham branch, he appears to have married a daughter of Robert de Stuteville by his wife Erneburga, and thus to have obtained the Cumberland manor of Drigg, which was held under the Stutevilles by the Flemings during the twelfth and thirteenth centuries;[100] and, moreover, one of the daughters and co-heiresses of his grandson Anselm le Fleming bore the rare Christian name of "Erneburga", which affords additional indication of a Stuteville connection.[101] A later Michael le Fleming, who died about 1186,

ter, Adela, by her marriage to Hugh, castellan of Douai. During the latter's minority the *chatéllenie* of Cambrai was usurped by John, hereditary advocate of Arras, the second husband of Walter II's widow, Ermentrude. But *circa* 1057 Bishop Liebert of Cambrai restored the heir to his rights and placed him under the guardianship of his relative, Anselm I de Ribemont, Count of Ostrevant, who, besides the *comté* of Ostrevant in Flanders, possessed the fief of Ribemont in the Vermandois (Vanderkindere, *op. cit.*, I, pp. 135–137). Hugh d'Oisy, who eventually succeeded as castellan of Cambrai, had a brother Walter who inherited the *chatéllenie* of Douai, as well, probably, as another brother, Saier, the original feoffee of Southill and Segenhoe. Hence the writer would further suggest that "Walter brother of Saier" of the Bedfordshire Domesday, was identical with Walter d'Oisy, castellan of Douai, and that Hugh le Fleming, the Domesday tenant of Poddington (who also held lands in 1086 of the Wahull barony) was identical with Hugh d'Oisy, castellan of Cambrai. Both Hugh and Walter d'Oisy were alive in 1086.

[99] According to Burke and other authorities the Flemings of Rydal descend from "Sir Michael Fleming, lord of Beckermet", although Michael le Fleming never possessed the manor of Beckermet, the earliest recorded holder being his contemporary (and brother?) Rainer. The error appears to have originated with Sir Daniel Fleming, the seventeenth century historian of the house, who placed Richard le Fleming (husband of Elizabeth de Urswick, the heiress of Coniston), living in 1275 and the undoubted ancestor of the Rydal family, as a son of a Sir John le Fleming, stated to be the grandson of Michael, living apparently in the reign of the Conqueror! On the contrary, the descent of the manor of Beckermet shows that Richard le Fleming, who held Beckermet as well as Coniston (cf. Kuerden MSS., vol. II, fᵒ 221 *d.*), was identical with Richard, brother of Rainer le Fleming, lord of Beckermet and Wath upon Dearne, mentioned in a charter of 1342 (Dodsworth MSS., vol. 8, fᵒˢ 21, 71; and cf. De Banco Roll, no. 9, *m.* 27 *d.*). This Rainer appears to have been the son of another Rainer le Fleming, who gave Lindale to the Knights of St. John of Jerusalem in 1191 (*V. C. H. Lancs.*, VIII, p. 269), and grandson of a third Rainer, the founder of Kirklees priory.) It should be added that the Richard le Fleming of 1275 was father of a son called Rainer, whose son John le Fleming (no doubt identical with the "Sir John le Fleming" whom Sir Daniel Fleming transformed into the father of Richard!) died in 1352, when his son and heir, Richard (second of the name), was aged thirty (Inq. P. M., 28 Edward III, no. 37). The latter settled Beckermet in 1373 on the marriage of his son Thomas with Margaret, daughter of William de Bardsey (Kuerden MSS., vol. II, fᵒ 211 *d.*). In 1418 Thomas, son of Sir Thomas Fleming, made a feoffment of the manor of Coniston, as well as the reversion of the manor of Beckermet (then held as dower by Dame Isabel, his mother). Thomas, Junior, acquired Rydal, co. Westmorland, in marriage with one of the daughters and co-heiresses of Sir John de Lancaster; and both Rydal and Coniston were in possession of his descendant, the late M. J. Hughes Le Fleming, Esq., of Rydal Hall.

[100] Canon Wilson suggested the possibility of a connection between the Flemings and Turgis Brundas, who had preceded the Stutevilles in the ownership of the Cumbrian barony of Lydal (cf. *Reg. St. Bees*, pp. 456–7). But there is no evidence that Turgis Brundas, who was lord of Rosedale in Yorkshire, was ever connected with Drigg, which was a member not of the barony of Lydal (as Canon Wilson asserts) but of the barony of Coupland.

[101] For the early descent of the Stutevilles see article by G. Andrews Moriarty in the REGISTER for October, 1925, pp. 373–378. Robert de Stuteville, the *caput* of whose barony was at Cottingham, Yorks., had been one of the northern lords at the battle of the Standard in 1138, and was son of Robert "Fronte-boeuf", governor in 1085 of the castle of Ambrières in Normandy, who was taken prisoner after the battle of Tinchebrai in 1107 and died in captivity. This elder Robert, who apparently took his surname from Estouteville-sur-mer in the Pays de Caux, is said to have married Joan, daughter of Hugh Talbot, lord of Cleuville by his wife Mary, sister of Waleran, Count of Meulan (*Dict. de la Noblesse*, VII, p. 558). Erneburga, the wife of his son Robert, was probably the daughter and heiress of Hugh fitz Baldric, the Domesday lord of Cottingham. They were the

granted the manor of Fordbottle (a "member" of the lordship of Aldingham) to Furness Abbey in 1153, which was confirmed *circa* 1216 by Michael (son of William) le Fleming, who is described in the charter of confirmation as the grantor's "grandson" (*Dep. Keeper's Rep.*, XXVI, Appendix, p. 162; *Coucher Book of Furness* [Chetham Soc.], pt. II, p. 455). This Michael of 1153, etc., was presumably the son of the first Michael of 1127, who probably died about the year 1150. Michael II in 1157-8 obtained Little Urswick and Foss in Coupland from the Abbot of Furness, besides Bardsea, co. Lancs., in exchange for the vills of Roose and Crivelton (P. R. O., Duchy of Lancs. Anc. Deeds, L. 342; Farrer, *Lancs. Pipe Rolls*, pp. 307-8). He was a Juror on the division of the Furness Fells *circa* 1160 (Farrer, *op. cit.*, p. 311); and his name occurs in the Lancashire Pipe Rolls between 1168 and 1176 (*ibid.*, pp. 13, 23, 29, 34),—while *circa* 1180, along with his son Anselm, he attested a grant made by William II de Lancaster of the manor of Sockbridge (*ante*, p. 10).[102] He married a lady called Christian (cf. *Cockersand Chartulary* [Chetham Soc.], pt. I, p. 765); and from a later charter, in which his son Anselm refers to "my uncle (*avunculus*) Bernard de Staynton" (*vide infra*), it is evident that she was the sister and heiress of Bernard fitz Gilbert and daughter of Gilbert, lord of Stainton in Kendal. The latter may possibly have been identical with Gilbert, younger brother of William I de Lancaster, lord of Kendal, and son of Ketel (son of Eldred) of Workington and Christian, his wife.[103]

Michael II and Christian (de Stainton) had several children. William, the eldest son, attested several of his father's charters as "William son of Michael de Furness", and in 1186 paid twenty marks to the Crown *pro fine terrae*, doubtless upon succeeding to the paternal estates (*Lancs. Pipe Rolls*, ed. Farrer, p. 60). *Circa* 1190 he obtained a grant of various liberties in his lordship of Aldingham, including the right of gallows and judgment by iron, water, and duel (*Rot. Chart.* [Rec. Com.], p. xl); and in 1193 he was amongst those fined for having taken part in the rebellion of King John, then Count of Mortain, against Richard I (Farrer, *Lancs. Pipe Rolls*, p. 78). He apparently died about 1203, leaving a widow, Eleanor or Ada (who married, secondly, William le Butler, lord of Warrington),[104] besides two sons, Michael III and Daniel, the former of whom was six years old at his father's death (P. R. O., Ancient Deeds, A. 13453; Farrer, *Lancs. Pipe Rolls*, pp. 180, 191; *Lancs. Inqs. and Extents* [Lancs. and

parents of a third Robert, who married Helewise, daughter and co-heiress of Geoffrey Murdac, and left issue (Farrer, *Early Yorkshire Charters*).

[102] See *Trans. Cumb. and Westd. Antiq. Soc.*, New Series, vol. x.

[103] It has been assumed that the Michael of 1127 survived until 1176-7, after which is no further mention of his name in the Lancashire Pipe Rolls, and that the William "de Furness" who paid his relief in 1186 did so upon attaining his majority, being accordingly born in 1164-5 (cf. *Trans. Cumb. and Westd. Antiq. Society*, New Series, vol. XXXI, pp. 30-32). But, on chronological grounds, we must conclude that there were at least two Michaels during this long interval; while the assumption that William became his father's heir in 1176-7, but did not pay his relief until 1186 on account of being under age, is scarcely warranted by the other facts in the case. From a consideration of all the evidence, it seems probable that William's father died in 1185-6 and that he himself was born *circa* 1150.

[104] She was daughter of Thomas son of Gospatric, lord of Workington, co. Cumberland, son of Orm (younger brother of Gilbert son of Ketel, ancestor of the de Lancasters) and his wife Gunhilda, daughter of Gospatric I, Earl of Dunbar.

Cheshire Rec. Soc.], pt. I, p. 82).[105]   Other sons of Michael II by his wife Christian were Anselm (of whom hereafter), Marsilius, Jordan, and Daniel, Rector of Aldingham and Little Urswick, where his son, Daniel, Junior, was a benefactor of the Priory of St. Bees (*Coucher Book of Furness* [Chetham Soc.], pt. II, pp. 452–7; *Reg. St. Bees* [Surtees Soc.], pp. 98–9, 382, 541).   There was also a daughter Godith, who became the second wife *circa* 1163 of William de Esseby, or Esseville (the latter's first wife, Uctreda, was widow of Ranulf de Lindsay, and daughter of Waldeve son of Earl Gospatric), and subsequently seems to have married Ulf son of Efward, lord of Hyton, co. Cumb. (*Reg. St. Bees*, pp. 57, 381–2; *Trans. Cumb. and Westd. Antiq. Soc.*, New Series, vol. XXVI, pp. 39–40).[106]

   This brings us to Anselm le Fleming, apparently the second son of Michael II and Christian de Stainton, from whom he inherited the manor of Stainton in Kendal (most of which afterwards passed to the d'Eyncourts), as well as the paternal lands at Drigg.   Like his father and elder brother, Anselm is usually styled "de Furness" in charters of the period, though he attests a grant made by William II de Lancaster to Walter "Cocus" shortly before 1184 as Anselm "de Staynton" (Levens Hall MSS., fº 247).   It appears from a later charter that Anselm built and endowed a chapel on his Stainton property: for *circa* 1280 William de Strickland (the husband of his great-granddaughter, Elizabeth d'Eyncourt) confirmed to the Priory of Cartmel the perpetual cure and custody of the chapel of Croscrake, formerly founded by Anselm son of Michael de Furness in the grantor's territory of Stainton in Kendal, with a proviso that "when the Prior and Convent appoint a priest in the said chapel to celebrate divine service for the grantor's ancestors and successors, none of his heirs shall distrain the Prior or his chaplain to give refuge to any lepers or infirm in the said chapel nor to render hospitality to such against their will" (Sizergh MSS.; cf. Hornyold-Strickland, *Strickland of Sizergh*, p. 18).   In 1198 a day was given to Anselm de Furness and Uctred son of Osulf (of Preston Richard, co. Westmorland) to hear their record and judgment of a plea of perambulation and division of lands on the Octaves of St. John the Baptist (*Cal. Curia Regis Rolls*, I, p. 51).   Anselm was still living in 1210, when he was amerced sixty marks for trespass (*Pipe Rolls, Cumb. and Westd.*, ed. Parker, p. 194).   However, he had died prior to 1217, in which year Richard de Preston and Adam son of Patrick de Borwick undertook to render yearly to the Abbey and monks of Furness one stone's weight of wax which Anselm son of Michael de Furness had given to the monks there during his lifetime (*Coucher Book of Furness* [Chetham Soc.], II, p. 92).

[105] Michael III married Agatha, daughter of Henry fitz Hervey, lord of Ravensworth (ancestor of the Lords Fitzhugh), and by her, who married secondly Marmaduke Darell of Sesay, Yorks. (De Banco Roll, no. 54, *m.* 67), had issue a son William, who left two sons and two daughters: (a) Michael IV, who died without issue in March 1169, having been drowned whilst returning to Aldingham after dining with the Prior of Cartmel (*Chronicles of Stephen, etc.* [Rolls Ser.], II, p. 555). (b) William, Rector of Aldingham.   (a) Eleanor, who eventually succeeded as lady of Aldingham, married Sir Richard de Cantsfield, through whom she became ancestress of the Lords Harrington of Aldingham. (b) Margery, wife of Henry de Clifton (*V. C. H. Lancs.*, VIII, pp. 300–301).

[106] There is no proof that Godith was ever the wife of de Coupland, as stated in *Trans. Cumb. and Westd. Antiq. Soc.*, New Series, vol. XXVI.

Amongst the unpublished documents at Rydal Hall is a charter of *circa* 1180, by which Edgar [of Dunbar] and his wife Alice, daughter of Ivo [de Greystoke], settled upon Agnes their daughter, in free marriage with Anselm son of Michael de Furness, half their land of "Euenwit" [Yanwath], co. Westmorland (Rydal MSS.). By an earlier charter, of *circa* 1150–60, Walter son of Ivo confirmed to Alice his sister, on her marriage to Edgar son of Earl Gospatric, "Euenwit" and "Chonoc Salchild" [Knock Salcock], co. Westmorland, as well as other property in Cumberland, Northumberland, and Yorkshire (*Newminster Chartulary* [Surtees Soc.], p. 117). Alice was thus the sister of Walter de Greystoke (died 1162), ancestor of the Lords Greystoke, and daughter of Ivo (son of Forne, son of Sigulf), lord of Greystoke, whose sister Edith became celebrated as the mistress of King Henry I (Farrer, *Early Yorkshire Charters*, II, pp. 505–12). Alice's husband Edgar, called *Unnitting* ("the Dauntless") by contemporary chroniclers owing to his fiery spirit, was the second son of Gospatric II, Earl of Dunbar in Scotland, who was slain at the battle of the Standard in 1138. He, in turn, was son of Gospatric I, Earl of Dunbar and Northumberland, whose mother Edith was the daughter of King Ethelred and whose father Maldred, lord of Cumbria, was a younger brother of the "gracious" King Duncan of Shakespeare's *Macbeth* (*Northumberland County History*, pp. 103–4; *Scots Peerage*, VII, pp. 30–50). The records make it clear that Anselm and his wife Agnes of Dunbar left four daughters and co-heiresses: (a) Eleanor, wife of Ralph d'Eyncourt, and great-grandmother of Sir Walter de Strickland of Sizergh and of Joan de Strickland, wife of Robert de Washington. (b) Erneburga, wife of Richard de Preston (Feet of Fines, Westmorland, 10 John, no. 30; *Coucher Book of Furness* [Chetham Soc.], pt. II, p. 94). Their son Richard married Amabel de Strickland, and was ancestor of the Prestons of Preston Richard, co. Westmorland. (c) Isabel, wife of Thomas fitz John (*Reg. St. Bees* [Surtees Soc.], pp. 538–9). (d) daughter (Christian name unknown), wife of Patrick de Borwick, of Borwick in Warton, co. Lancs., and mother of Adam de Borwick, from whom descended the Borwicks and the Whittingtons of Borwick Hall (*Cal. Inqs.*, V, p. 118; *Lancs. Pipe Rolls*, ed. Farrer, p. 420; *V. C. H. Lancs.*, VIII, pp. 170–1).[107]

In conclusion, it seems worthwhile to point out that the Stricklands, the d'Eyncourts, and the Flemings all three derived (probably) from ancestors mentioned in Domesday Book—two of the ancestors in question (Walter d'Eyncourt and Walter le Fleming) being tenants-in-chief. Moreover, it is a remarkable fact that both the Stricklands and the Flemings still possess representatives in the male line. Nor must it be forgotten that the present owner of Sizergh Castle is the lineal descendant of Gervase d'Eyncourt, the grantee of the estate in the twelfth century, and that the Stricklands themselves have lived at Sizergh for seven hundred years.

[107] Jane, daughter of Miles Whittington of Borwick Hall (the heir-general of the de Borwicks), married *circa* 1475-1480, as his second wife, Robert Washington of Warton, Lancs., grandfather of the first Lawrence Washington of Sulgrave.

## GENEALOGICAL RESEARCH IN ENGLAND

Communicated by the Committee on English and Foreign Research

### SOME NOTES UPON THE FAMILY OF ROGER WILLIAMS

By G. ANDREWS MORIARTY, A.M., LL.B., F.S.A., of Ogunquit, Maine

Fifty-three years ago my old friend, the late Henry Fitz Gilbert Waters, A.M., of Salem, Mass., printed in the REGISTER (vol. 43, pp. 290–303, 427) his important discovery of the parentage of Roger Williams. In this article he established the fact that Roger was the son of James Williams (a citizen of London and a member of the Great Livery Company of the Merchant Taylors) by Alice Pemberton, his wife. Since that date much additional information has come to light regarding the family of Roger Williams. Walter Angell of Providence, R. I., following up a suggestion of Mr. Waters, secured the Chancery Suits mentioned by Roger, and they were printed by the late Sydney Rider in his "Book Notes". The present writer also secured much information regarding the maternal relations of Roger (the Pembertons of St. Albans, co. Herts.), which he deposited in the Library of the Rhode Island Historical Society; and in 1917 he secured for that Society from Elizabeth (French) Bartlett (Mrs. J. Gardner), a professional genealogist, the marriage of Roger Williams and Mary Barnard at Hatfield Broadoak, co. Essex; and this record was printed in due course in the Society's *Collections*. The Herts. Genealogist and Antiquary (vol. III, p. 241 *seq.*) contains many original documents regarding the Pemberton family of St. Albans. In 1923 the Rev. R. Pemberton, Rector of Ingatestone, co. Essex, published his "Pemberton Pedigrees", which, while not entirely accurate as regards the earlier generations contains much useful information concerning the family.

Alice Pemberton, mother of Roger Williams, was the daughter of Robert and Catherine (Stokes) Pemberton of St. Albans and the sister of Roger Pemberton, Esq., of that Borough, who was godfather to Roger Williams, sometime High Sheriff of Hertfordshire and the donor to St. Albans of the "Pemberton Alms Houses", which are still in existence. He was the father of Ralph Pemberton (Mayor of St. Albans) and the grandfather of the famous Sir Francis Pemberton, Lord Chief Justice of England, and the senior counsel for the Seven Bishops in their trial in the reign of James II.

The following records throw additional light upon the Pembertons:

The WILL of JOAN STOKES of Redbourne, co. Herts., dated 30 June and proved 12 Oct. 1560 leaves to Joan Wetherhedde; to Robert and Roger Stokes; to Walter and John Beche; and mentions "my brother Roger Stokes" (Archdeaconry of St. Albans, Register Fankelcaster, f° 230).

The WILL of ROGER STOKES, mercer, of St. Albans (parish of St. Peter's), dated 18 Feb. 1572/3. To his sons Robert and Roger, who are to be educated at the Universities. To nephew Roger Pemberton. "My brother-in-law Robert Pemberton" (Archdec. of St. Albans, Reg. Fankelcaster 66).

These wills show that Catherine Pemberton, the maternal grandmother of Roger Williams, was born Catherine Stokes. (For Robert and Roger, sons of the testator of 1573, see REGISTER, *op. cit.*, p. 294.)

The Inquisition Post Mortem of Roger Pemberton, Esq., of St. Albans, was taken on 17 May, 4 Charles I [1628]. In it we have the following:

Roger Pemberton and James Williams were seised in fee of a messuage called Hedges in St. Peter's parish in St. Albans and of 80 acres belonging thereto and also of Bockett's *alias* Bockas Fields; of Spencer's Field (late in the tenure of William Spencer); of 30 acres late in the tenure of Matthew Davis; of Faunton Wood and Munck Wood (in the tenure of Thomas Studman); of Cadmale *alias* Cadmer Heath and of Park Moore, all of which premises were bought by Roger Pemberton and James Williams of Raphael Pemberton and Anne, his wife. By an indenture dated 10 January, 7 James I [1609/10] between Roger Pemberton of St. Albans gent. and John his son and heir and James Williams, citizen and merchant taylor of London, of the one part, and Robert Angell, citizen and merchant of London, of the other part, the said premises were granted to William Angell and Robert Angell to the uses of John Pemberton * and Katherine Angell for life &c. (*Herts. Gen. and Ant.*, vol. III, p. 241).

The arms of the St. Albans Pembertons, as given in the Visitation of Herts. for 1634 (Harl. Soc. Pub.) were: "Quarterly 1st. and 4th. Silver, a chevron between 3 buckets sable hooped and handled gold. 2nd. and 3rd. Silver 3 dragons' heads sable couped and langued gules". These are the arms of the Pembertons of Northamptonshire, whose connection with the St. Albans family has not been established. The 1st. and 4th. quarterings are the arms of the ancient Lancashire house of Pemberton of Pemberton, whose pedigree can be traced to the thirteenth century. The funeral certificate of Roger Pemberton of St. Albans at the College of Arms states that he claimed that his ancestors came out of Cheshire (the county adjoining Lancashire).

It will thus be seen that a good deal is known about the maternal ancestry of Roger Williams, but up to date nothing has been learned concerning the parentage of his father James Williams. The latter was admitted free of the Merchant Taylors Company by servitude on 7 Apr. 1587, a date at which he must have been about 21 years old. He lived in Cow Lane within the parish of St. Sepulchres without Newgate in London. It is reasonable to suppose, however, that he had a connection with St. Albans, where he found his wife. The Rector of St. Albans at the close of the sixteenth century was the Rev. Roger Williams, B.D. He was ordained a deacon and priest by Richard, Bishop of Gloucester, on 18 Sept. 1575 in the chantry superior of "Le Lodge" in Paynswick parish, diocese of Gloucester, and was inducted into the rectory of St. Albans on 7 Mar. 1681/2 by John, Bishop of London ("Records of the Old Archdeaconry of St. Albans, 1575–1637", by H. R. Wilton Hall) and into the vicarage of St. Peter's in the same borough on 1 Mar. 1591/2 (REGISTER, *op. cit.*, p. 295). His will shows that he died without issue (*ibid.*). There was also a Mr. Lewis Williams of St. Albans, who had a son Roger baptized there in August 1607 (*ibid.*, p. 300). These items suggest that the Rev. Roger Williams, the parson at St. Albans, was a close kinsman to James Williams. He *may* also have come from the west in Gloucestershire near the Welsh border. James Williams *may* have gone to London from St. Albans as some of the Pembertons did.

* John Pemberton, citizen and Grocer of London, eldest son and heir of Roger Pemberton and ancestor of the Pembertons, lords of the manor of Wootton, co. Beds., married Katherine Angell, daughter of William Angell, citizen of London and Sergeant of the Catery (Vis. of London, Harl. Soc. Pub., vol. I, p. 18). This William Angell had a son James Angell, whose will mentions a son Thomas (REGISTER, *op. cit.*, p. 299). There can be but little doubt but that this Thomas is identical with the Thomas Angell who came to New England, as a lad, with Roger Williams and became the ancestor of the well-known Providence family.

The following items, taken from the Hertfordshire records, were printed in the *Herts. Genealogist and Antiquary*. They seem suggestive, although they do not prove anything regarding the parentage of James Williams. They are, however, useful as a basis for further research in the paternal ancestry of Roger Williams of Rhode Island.

Subsidy for Herts. 37 Henry VIII [1545] Tring Magna.
James Williams gent., taxed 4s.
(*Herts. Gen. and Ant.*, vol. II, p. 27).

The WILL of JOAN AUDLEY of Hitchin, co. Herts., widow, dated 14 Mar. 1580/1 and proved 6 Feb. 1583/4. To be buried in Hitchin. To daughter, Joan Audley. To sons William and John Audley. To daughter Agnes Williams and her children James and Joan. To daughter Elizabeth Coop and her children. To son Robert Papworth and his children and his son William. Mentions "William Audley my last husband". James Tydye of Dunstable. Executor, son William Audley. Overseers, son Robert Papworth and friend Mr. Thomas Parrys (*ibid.*, vol. II, p. 229).

Subsidy for Herts. 37 Henry VIII [1545] Hitchin vill.
William Audley taxed 40s.
(*Ibid.*, vol. I, p. 329).

Herts. Feet of Fines. Hilary Term 25 Elizabeth [1582/3].
John Bowyer, Esq., querant, and William Audley and Mark Williams and Agnes, his wife, deforciants. A messuage in Hitchin *alias* Hutchyn.
(*Ibid.*, vol. II, p. 307).

It may be suggested that the James Williams, of Tring Magna in 1545, was the father of Mark Williams, who married Agnes Audley, daughter of William and Joan Audley of Hitchin, and had issue James Williams and Joan Williams, who were evidently young in 1581. This James Williams *may* be identical with James Williams who was admitted to the Merchant Taylors Company in 1587, and is the known father of the founder of Providence. The Rev. Roger Williams, parson of St. Albans, may be another son of James Williams, of Tring Magna, and a brother of Mark Williams. In any event this combination is worthy of further investigation.

---

## AN ENGLISH BILL IN CHANCERY, 1644
## CONCERNING ROGER WILLIAMS AND HIS BROTHERS *

By HARLEY HARRIS BARTLETT, A.B., of Ann Arbor, Mich.

Evidence regarding the immediate English ancestry of Roger Williams of Rhode Island was first brought to light by Henry F. Waters, who published with critical comments (REGISTER, vol. 43 (1889), pp. 291–303) the wills of James Williams, merchant tailor of London, whom he correctly surmised to be Roger's father; Alice

* The late Sidney S. Rider of Providence, R. I., published in his *Book Notes*, under the date of 8 June 1912 (vol. 29, pp. 89–93), an announcement of the discovery of this Chancery case by Walter F. Angell of Providence in London in 1910; and a copy of the bill was also printed in the article.

(Pemberton) Williams, his mother; Ralph Wightman, his brother-in-law; and Roger Pemberton, his uncle and godfather. These wills mention three brothers, Robert, Sidrach (variously spelled), and Roger, the latter indicated in his mother's will of 1 Aug. 1634, as "beyond the seas". This latter circumstance agreed with the fact regarding Roger Williams of Rhode Island, and there was also Roger's own testimony that he had a brother Robert, who, in 1672, was residing at Newport. Nevertheless the identification of Roger's family could hardly be considered satisfactorily established until the third brother, the one with the unusual name Sidrach, could be accounted for.

On one occasion (in his "George Fox digg'd out of his Burrowes") Roger Williams mentioned a brother who had been "a Turkey merchant in London", a member of the Levant or Turkey Company of Merchants. In 1921 the Committee for Genealogical Research in England of the New England Historic Genealogical Society published (REGISTER, vol. 75, pp. 234–235) two cases from Chancery ** Proceedings preserved in the Public Record Office, London, one of which showed that there was a Sydrack Williams who was actually a "Turkey merchant". The bill in question, dated 28 May 1628, was brought by Sydrack Williams of London, against one John Freeman, complaining of the non-delivery of "Suffolk cloths" which the said Freeman was to have delivered before a certain time. In his answer the defendant referred to the "usual time that the Turkey merchants ship their cloths for to be transported", thus proving certainly that Sydrack Williams was a "Turkey merchant" as Roger had described that brother whom his extant published writings did not refer to by name.

Since 1921, therefore, the evidence has been convincing, even if not quite complete, that Roger Williams was the son of James Williams, citizen and merchant tailor of London, and his wife, Alice (Pemberton) Williams "of St. Sepulchre's, without Newgate, London". The proof has rested (1) upon the testimony of Roger that Robert Williams of Newport, Rhode Island, was his brother; (2) upon Roger's reference to a brother who was a "Turkey merchant"; and (3) the proof that at the right time there was a certain Sydrach Williams who was actually a "Turkey merchant".

Nevertheless, in spite of the practical certainty already attained, it is a satisfaction to find the absolutely confirmatory evidence that all the records of Sydrack pertain to one and the same individual.

Such confirmation is provided by a chancery case brought jointly on 15 Aug. 1644 by Sidrach (i.e., Sydrack) and Roger Williams against their brother, Robert Williams, sole executor of the estate of their mother, Alice Williams, and John Davies,* Robert King, and Robert Bartopp, "overseers of her will".

The case coincides in time with Roger Williams' visit to England

---

* Katherine Williams, sister of Roger, "married first Ralph Wightman, citizen and merchant tailor, and later John Davies, clerk (minister)". (Easton, Emily, "Roger Williams, Prophet and Pioneer". Boston and New York, 1930. See p. 15.) If this John Davies was the same one against whom Sidrach and Roger Williams made complaint to the Court in Chancery, he was not only their brother-in-law, but also a clergyman.

**See Vol. I of this work, pp. 646-647.

in 1643 and 1644 to procure a charter for the Colonies of Rhode Island and Providence Plantations.

A typewritten transcript of the bill in question, copied from the Chancery Proceedings of the reign of Charles I (endorsed W 5/22, dated 15 Aug. 1644), was presented in 1920 to the Library of the University of Michigan by the late Professor Claude H. Van Tyne. He seems to have made no published use of it. Certain passages of the original are omitted in the typed copy, all presumably on account of illegibility, since one indicated omission is accounted for by the annotation "illegible". The complaint and the answer thereto extend to more than nine foolscap pages. Since the text of this verbose document is incomplete anyway, there seems to be no reason for quoting more than is needed to present the facts that throw light upon the family to which Roger Williams belonged.

Addressed "To the right honorable the Lords and others the Commissioners for the great Seal of England", it recites the complaint of "Sidrach Williams, citizen and Merchant tailor of London, and Roger Williams of London, clerke," that whereas Alice Williams, widow, their deceased Mother, "was in her life time possessed of a personall estate of great value in leases moneyes debts upon specialties and divers other goods and chattels (her own debts being discharged) And amongst the said severall leases the said Alice Williams was possessed and interested for the term of thirty and fyfty yeares or thereabouts, yet to come and unexpired, of Two Messuages or Tenements in Cow Lane in the parish of St. Sepulcher without Newgate, London"; and whereas she bequeathed legacies of one hundred pounds and two hundred pounds, respectively, to her sons Sydrack and Roger, to be paid in yearly installments of ten pounds to each; and whereas "the said Alice Williams therein Constituted and appointed one Robert Williams her Sonne sole Executor and thereby willed that her Executor should give . . . security to John Davies, Robert King and Robert Bartopp, overseers of her will for the due payment of the said legacyes by assignemt. Of the said lease or leases of her dwelling house and other Tenemtes."; and whereas "the said Robert Williams proved the said Will and tooke uppon him the execucion thereof"; and whereas "yor. orator. Sidrach Williams (your other orator. Roger being then alsoe beyond the Seas) relying upon the integrity and in [the] sufficiency of the said Robert, and also upon the fidelity and honesty of the said overseers touching the execution of the said trust did forbeare to presse the speedy and Sudden performance thereof," but "Conceyved that the said Messuages and houses were sufficiently tyed and bound for the said legacyes by the said Will, so that yor. orators. as was conceived could not receyve any prejudice therein And thereupon yor. orator. Sidrach Williams having then very urgent occassions to goe into the parts beyond the Seas to manage his grade and affairs of a merchant was by reason thereof inforced to goe into Italy and other parts beyond the Seas and there continued for the Space of Seven yeares to geather or thereabouts without returning into England, yor. other orator. Roger remaynng then alsoe beyond the Seas—

"But now so it is, may it please yor. Honors. that the said Robert shortly after yor. orators. being beyond the Seas failed in Creditt and became unexpectedly much impoverished by reason of some accidentall misfortunes, and the said Robert Williams and the said Overseers combined and confederated together with Walter Chauncey Citizen and goldsmith of London and John Wright of the Strand in the County of Middx. coachman to defeat and defraud yor. orators. of their said legacyes and also neglected the trust originally reposed in them for Securing yor. orators. legacyes by assignemt. as aforesaid and do yet share and divide the said houses amongst them; And now the said Walter Chauncey and John Wright, (the said Robert having Conveyed himself beyond the Seas as your orator. is informed) give out in Speeches that they have severally lent unto the said Robert Williams the Executor the Severall and respective Somes of twoe hundred poundes by way of mortgage upon the said houses and pretend that they have severall deeds of mortgages thereof, Whereas yor. orators. by the originall intention of the said Will ought to have had their legacyes secured by the said houses as aforesaid and the said Robert Williams the Executor ought not to have destroyed the said trust by mortgaging the said houses. . . .

"May it therefore please [your Honors, in] the premises Considered to grant unto yor. orators. his Mates. [Majesty's] most gracious writt of Suppena to be directed to the said Walter Chauncey, John Wright, John Davies, Robert King and Robert Bartopp commanding them and every [one] of them . . . and under a certaine paine therein to be lymitted personally to be and appeare before yor. honors in his Mates. hight Court of Chancery then and there to answer the premises and further to stand by and abide such [judgment] as may stand with equity and good conscience."

The aforesaid complaint places Robert Williams in a very unfavorable light. There seems to be no exact record of when Robert arrived in Rhode Island, but the chancery case just cited shows that it could hardly have been before 1643 when Roger Williams returned to London, and, finding that his brother Robert had gone abroad after having been guilty of fraud and dishonesty as executor of the will, joined Sydrack in an effort to recover damages by recourse to the courts.*

The answer of two of the defendants, Chauncey and Wright, dated 28 Aug. 1644, is filed with the complaint. It denies the charges "to be just and true in such manner as they are herein sett forth." So far as complainant Roger Williams is concerned they refer to earlier litigation which Sydrack had entered into in behalf of himself and Roger. "Roger Williams together with the sayd Complt. [complainant] Sydrack Williams did heretofore exhibit a petition to the right Honble. the Committee for obstructions in Courts of Justice against these defts. [defendants] concerning the same matters now complayned of, upon which petition by an order of the 12th of Oct. last [1643] it was ordered by the said committee . . . that the now defts. should exhibit their Bill in Chancery and that the now Complts. should forthwith appeare gratis and answere the said Bill. . . . In pursuance of which order . . . the sayd Sydracke Williams answered but the said Roger Williams would not answere but stands in contempt for not answearing the same. Whereupon by an order of this Honble. Cort. made the one and twentith daye of June last it amongst other things ordered that the said Roger Williams should have no benefitt of the sayd proceedings in regard hee doth not answeare the sayd

---

* The writer does not know the original authority for the statement that "Robert Williams had followed Roger to the New World in 1635". (See "Roger Williams, Prophet and Pioneer", Emily Easton, p. 234.) All that Roger himself seems to have said about his brother's coming (see "Early Records of the Town of Providence", vol. V, p. 307) is a statement of 1661 to the effect that "besides the first that were admitted [1635] our Town Recordes declare that afterwardes we received . . . Robert Williams, Gregorey Dexter, and others. . . ." Since the name of Gregory Dexter, Roger Williams's "dear and faithful friend", who printed his "Key to the Indian Language" in London in 1643 and then followed Roger to Providence about 1644 directly follows the name of Robert Williams, it is a fair inference that the latter arrived in 1643 or 1644 while Roger was in England. Robert Williams bought land on 27 Nov. 1644 from Robert Morris and William Reynolds ("Early Records of the Town of Providence", vol. II, p. 4). This seems to be the first record of his presence in the colony.

bill. . . ." The defendants "demand the judgement of this Honble. Court whether they shall be put to any further or other answer unto soe much of the sayd bill of Complaynt as anywayes concerneth the sayd Roger Williams untill he the sayd Roger Williams shall in obedience submitt and conforme himselfe to the orders of this Honble. Court and clear his contempt and putt in an Answeare to the sayd bill exhibited against him, and for soe much of the sayd bill of complaynt these defts. pray to be dismist with their reasonable costs on that behalfe wrongfully sustayned."

So much from the defendants by way of disposing of Roger's case. In acknowledging that Sydrack's claim might possibly have to be paid they said: "But these deftes. doe denye that they or either of them at or before the sayd severall morgages thus made unto them were privie to the sayd trust in the sayd will mentioned concerning the payment of the one hundred poundes unto the sayd Complt. Sydrach Williams and in that respect not subject or liable to any such Trust as they are advised by theire Counsayle and these defts. do likewise deny that they or either of them untill long after the sayd morgages thus made did knowe or weare made acquaynted to the best of their remembrance that the lease of the sayd messuages was appointed by the sayd will to bee assigned over for the satisfying of the sayd one hundred poundes unto the complt. Sydrach Williams as by the bill of complt. [complaint] is pretended."

The question at once arises: Was Roger Williams in England when adjudged guilty of contempt of court for failing to appear as summoned 12 Oct. 1643? The mission to procure a charter for the civil government of Rhode Island and Providence colonies had been intrusted to him, following the decision of an assembly, held at Newport 19 Sept. 1642, that such a charter must be obtained if the claims of the confederated colonies were to be withstood. Since Williams was an exile from Massachusetts, he had determined to sail for England from Manhattoes (New Amsterdam). He was detained there, but only until late June or early July 1643, in order to make peace with the Indians in behalf of the Long Island settlers. He must, therefore, have been in England in time to join Sydrach in the prosecution of their joint case.* The probability is that his conscientious objection to placing himself under oath except as an act of religious worship prevented him from appearing before the court, since he would have had to submit to being sworn if he had done so.†

The decision of the court does not appear from the available record, but on the face of the evidence, before his emigration to America Robert Williams would seem to have been the black sheep of the family. It accords with all that is known of Roger's charity that his delinquent brother should have ventured to settle within the jurisdiction of Rhode Island, apparently confident that his mis-

* "Williams remained in England a little over a year, from about the middle of July 1643 to about the middle of August 1644" ("Roger Williams the Pioneer of Religious Liberty", Oscar S. Straus, New York, 1894. See p. 124).

† There is much evidence on this matter of Williams' objection to giving testimony under oath, one of his cardinal tenets. For instance, he affirmed in a controversy with John Cotton regarding the cause of his banishment from Massachusetts that he was correctly quoted as having said: "That it is not lawful to call a wicked person to Sweare, to Pray, as being actions of God's worship." ("Roger Williams: A Study of the Life, Times and Character of a Political Pioneer", Edmund J. Carpenter, New York, 1909. See quotation on p. 170, from *Publications of Narragansett Club*, vol. 1, p. 40.)

deeds in London would be forgiven and forgotten, as they must have been on Roger's part, even though relations between the brothers may never have become intimate. Certainly Roger interposed no obstacle to Robert's becoming prominent in public affairs, as he was during the period 1651–54, while Roger was a second time in England.

In this connection it is interesting to note that in August 1647 the brothers Roger and Robert were among the group of eight (including the first Town Council of Providence, chosen after the first General Assembly in August 1647) who made a covenant that brotherly love was to guide the administration of affairs in Providence. Among other matters they pledged themselves never to mention in their assembly any previous differences they may have had, public or private, but to let "love cover the multitude of them in the grave of oblivion". In 1651 Roger wrote a letter regarding public business to Robert Williams and Thomas Harris, but this cannot be considered a special indication of confidence and friendship, for these two were elected deputies in June 1650 and Robert Williams was generally moderator of the Town Council from 1651 to 1654 ("Early Records of the Town of Providence", vol. II, pp. 47–57), until Roger Williams returned from England.

---

# GENEALOGICAL RESEARCH IN ENGLAND

Communicated by the Committee on English and Foreign Research

## THE WOODMAN FAMILY

By G. ANDREWS MORIARTY, A.M., LL.B., F.S.A., of Ogunquit, Maine

More than sixty years ago the late Cyrus Woodman, Esq., A.M., of Cambridge, Mass., commissioned Mrs. Harriet de Salis, an English genealogist of those days, to search for the ancestry of his emigrant ancestor, Edward Woodman of Newbury, Mass. The choice of his searcher was unfortunate. This lady was more noted for the exuberance of her imagination than for the accuracy of her deductions and her productions, and while her errors were not so numerous as those of the late Horatio Somerby, still they occasionally arise to plague the present-day genealogist. The pedigree furnished to Mr. Woodman was no exception to the rule and would have done credit to a Dethick or a Cooke as a flowery figment of the imagination.

A clue to the English home of the family had long been known and was in print as far back as 1860 (REGISTER, vol. 14, p. 333); and in the list of passengers who embarked at Southampton for New England in the *James* about 5 Apr. 1635, we find the name of Hercules (Archelaus) Woodman, mercer, of Malford (Christian Malford, co. Wilts.). Archelaus was an early settler of Newbury, where he was admitted a freeman on 17 May 1637.

Edward Woodman, ancestor of those of the name in New England, was admitted a freeman at Newbury on 25 May 1636. He had a wife Joan and children, Edward (born 1628), John, Joshua (born 1636/7, said to have been the first English child born in Newbury), Mary, Sarah (born 12 Jan. 1640/1), Jonathan (born 5 Nov. 1643), and Ruth (born 28 Mar. 1646). Of these children Edward was of Newbury, where he had a son Archelaus, born 9 June 1672; and John moved to Dover, N. H., where the name Archelaus was perpetuated in that branch of the family.

The close association at Newbury of the first Archelaus Woodman and the first Edward Woodman and the repetition of the name Archelaus among the descendants of Edward lend weight to the family tradition that they were brothers, a statement which the contributor expects to show was undoubtedly the case.

Starting at this point, Harriet de Salis furnished the will of Nicholas Woodman of Corsham, co. Wilts. (a parish hard by Christian Malford), dated 1564, and the wills of "Edward" Woodman of Corsham, 1573, and of "Valentine" Woodman of Christian Malford, 1630. She gave no references for these wills beyond calling them "Salisbury" wills. Examination of the Salisbury probate records, preserved at Somerset House, reveals the will of Nicholas Woodman of Corsham, dated 11 Mar. 1563/4 and proved 5 May 1564, but it is entirely different from the version furnished to Cyrus Woodman.

759

The wills of "Edward" and "Valentine" appear to have been the offspring of Harriet de Salis' vivid imagination—at least no such wills can now be found. After this auspicious beginning she proceeded to construct a wondrous pedigree making Nicholas the ancestor of the two New England progenitors and deducing his descent from the ancient and gentle family of Woodman of Surrey. Concerning all this one can only say that the pedigree is utterly worthless and the production of the, to say the least, peculiar methods of the lady who compiled it.

A good many years ago the writer of this article examined the Corsham parish register and the Salisbury wills for the purpose of compiling a true account of the family of Edward Woodman and Archelaus Woodman. At the end of the sixteenth and the beginning of the seventeenth centuries the parish of Corsham was filled with Woodmans, whose number was so great as almost to constitute a tribe. The wills also are very numerous. Several members of the family appear in the great subsidy of 1524, and it is quite evident that the Woodmans must, at this date, have been residing for several centuries in and about Corsham and during that period have raised large families. This fact, together with lack of wills at vital points, has rendered it impossible to construct a satisfactory pedigree of the family back of the grandfather of Archelaus. In the present article not all the numerous entries from the Corsham parish register will be given, but only such as appear to have a bearing on the immediate family of the emigrants. In like manner only such wills as appear to belong to these people will be given from among the numerous Woodman wills taken from the various probate courts of the Bishopric of Salisbury.

Unfortunately it will not be possible to give the references for these wills for the following reason. A number of years ago a Woodman living in the Middle West announced that he was compiling a genealogy of the family, and this contributor, more trustingly than wisely, loaned him the entire collection of wills. All efforts to secure its return from this gentleman or his widow have proved fruitless. Fortunately copies of the wills were made before they were sent away, but the copyist failed to note the references. These wills were taken from the various probate courts of the Bishopric of Salisbury and will be found in the calendars of those courts now on file, together with the wills themselves, at Somerset House.

The Corsham Woodmans were a numerous group of middle class yeomen and artisans who had long been settled in and about Corsham, so that at the beginning of the seventeenth century they formed a large part of the inhabitants of the parish.

FROM LAY SUBSIDIES *

Parish of Corsham, co. Wilts.

16 Henry VIII [1524–25]   John Woodman, [valuation] £8, [tax] 4s. (197/155.)
Richard Woodman, in goods [valuation] £7, [tax] 3s. 6d. (197/155.)

41 Elizabeth [1598–1599]   Richard Woodman, [valuation] 20s., [tax] 4s. (198/331.)

William Woodman, [valuation] 20s., [tax] 4s.
(198/331, returned 20 September, 41 Elizabeth
[1599].)

FROM MISCELLANEOUS BOOK T.R. 46.

Wiltshire Musters,     1539, f° 35b Liberty of Corsham.
Nicholas Woodman an archer.
William and John Woodman billmen.

WILLS FROM THE PROBATE COURTS OF THE BISHOP OF SALISBURY.

The WILL of NICHOLAS WOODMAN of Corsham, dated 11 March 1563/4 and proved 5 May 1564. To sons Nicholas, Richard, Robert, Thomas and William the younger. To daughters Joan Woodman and Margaret Pinchin. To nephew John Hulbert. To Elizabeth, daughter of young Nicholas Woodman. To son John. Residuary legatee and executrix, wife Elizabeth. Richard Pinchin overseer. Witnessed by Richard Pinchin, William and Robert Woodman *et als.*

The WILL of RICHARD WOODMAN of Corsham, dated 27 March 1567. No probate act. To be buried in Corsham Church [this indicates a superior social position]. To son Robert, son John the elder, sons Richard and Thomas, son John the younger. To my sons' children. To son Robert's children. Residuary legatee and executor son Richard. To daughters Agnes and Alice. Witnessed by Thomas Woodman *et als.*

The WILL of ELIZABETH WOODMAN, dated 30 March 1575. No probate act. To be buried in Corsham churchyard. To sons John, Nicholas, Richard, Thomas and Robert Woodman. To daughters Margaret and Joan, wife of Thomas Becfer. Residuary legatee and executor, son William Woodman, who is to keep the child of John Watts until he is 21 years old.

The WILL of THOMAS WOODMAN of Pickwick in Corsham, husbandman, dated 16 Sept. 1600 and proved 25 Sept. 1601. To daughter Jane and sons Anthony, Thomas the younger, and wife Elizabeth.

The WILL of THOMAS WOODMAN of Corsham, roughmason, dated March 1612/13 and proved April 1613. To sons Robert and Thomas, daughter Jane Hayward and wife Agnes. Witnessed by Nicholas and William Woodman *et al.*

The WILL of PETER SMITH *alias* WOODMAN of Christian Malford, dated 15 Feb. 1566/7 and proved 23 May 1567. To daughters Joan and Alice Woodman, brother-in-law Nicholas Rimell and his daughter Joan. To sister Maud Rimell and brother-in-law William Wellstede. To wife Agnes and son Hugh Woodman.

The WILL of EDWARD WOODMAN "late of Corsham" (nuncupative will). To all his children "now living" 2s. each. To wife Edith, who is residuary legatee and executrix. Witnessed by Edward Dyer, John and David Woodman. Proved 16 July 1654.

FROM THE CORSHAM PARISH REGISTERS (1563–1634)

*Baptisms* *

1565  Thomas, son of Thomas, 8 April.
1566  Elizabeth, of Thomas, 3 November.
1567  Prudence, of Thomas, 25 January [1567/8].
1568  Maulde, of Thomas, 4 April.
1574  Joan, of Thomas, 25 July.
1574  Edward, of Thomas, 9 October.

* Preserved in the Public Record Office, London.

761

1576    Anthony, of Thomas, 13 May.
1577    John, of Thomas, 11 August.
1578    Jane, of Thomas, 25 October.
1578    Robert, of Thomas, 1 November.
1581    Jane, of Thomas, 18 March.
1583    Jane, of Thomas, 8 March [1583/4].
1585    Agnes, of Thomas, 1 August.
1588    Anne, of Thomas, 27 May.
1591    Thomas, of Thomas, 26 September.
1601    Mary, of Edward, 24 January [1601/2].
1604    Elizabeth, of Edward, 1 July.
1606    Edward, of Edward, 27 December.
1612    Edward, of John, 28 October.
1613    Archelaus, of Edward, 23 January [1613/14].
1616    Rebecca, of Edward, 15 December.
1617    Thomas, of Thomas, 2 July.
1620    Walter, of Edward, 25 March.
1621    Jonathan, of Edward, 12 August.
1623    Anna, of Edward, 23 November.
1625    Ruth, of Edward, 27 December.
1628    David, of Edward, 17 August.

## Marriages

1566    Thomas Woodman and Jane Champion 12 September.
1574    Thomas Woodman and Elizabeth Pryor 24 April.
1600    Edward Woodman and Collet Mallet 30 June.
1615    Thomas Woodman and Sarah Bolwell 7 January [1615/16].

## Burials *

1563    Nicholas Woodman 27 March [1563/4].
1567    Richard Woodman 9 April.
1568    Jane Woodman wife of Thomas 20 April.
1568    Alice Woodman wife of Thomas 18 May.
1575    Elizabeth Woodman 1 April.
1577    John Woodman son of Thomas 6 December.
1581    John Woodman son of Thomas 27 December.
1586    Mary Woodman daughter of Thomas 9 March [1586/7].
1611    Collice Woodman wife of Edward 5 July.
1612    Thomas Woodman 17 March [1612/13].
1614    Edward Woodman 21 April.
1633    Jane Woodman daughter of Edward 4 July.

From the above records it will appear that early in the seventeenth century there were two Edward Woodmans in Corsham.
One of these was buried there on 21 Apr. 1614, the other was the
father of Archelaus (baptized 23 Jan. 1613/14), and this latter Edward evidently had children down to 1628 when David, son of
Edward Woodman, was baptized on 17 Aug. 1628. It may be suggested that this latter Edward is identical with the Edward Woodman who married Collet Mallet on 30 June 1600 and had Edward,
baptized 27 Dec. 1606 (who is undoubtedly the Edward Woodman
who settled in Newbury, Mass.). Collet Woodman was buried at
Corsham on 5 July 1611. Edward remarried and had Archelaus,
baptized 23 Jan. 1613/14 (Archelaus deposed on 9 Nov. 1695, aged
80 years, Suffolk County, Mass. Old Supreme Jud. Ct. Files, no.

* These are all of the name of Woodman.

3217). It would seem that the elder Edward is the testator of Corsham of 1654, who was evidently, from the wording of his will, which left to each of his children "now living", an old man. He was, then, the father of the two settlers of Newbury, who were evidently half-brothers. He, in turn, was probably the Edward Woodman, baptized at Corsham on 9 Oct. 1574, the son of Thomas Woodman. It is impossible to say whether this Thomas Woodman was the Thomas, son of Nicholas, the testator of 1563, or the Thomas, who was the son of Richard, the testator of 1567. Nicholas and Richard may have been brothers and the sons of either John or Richard Woodman, who appear in the Subsidy of 1524. Nicholas occurs in the Muster Roll of 1539. As there were two Thomas Woodmans living in Corsham around 1575, each with families, we are not able to give with certainty the brothers and sisters of Edward, the father of the emigrants, but it seems probable that Edward was the son of the Thomas Woodman who married Elizabeth Pryor on 24 April 1574.

1. THOMAS WOODMAN, of Corsham, co. Wilts., England, was born about 1545. He is probably the Thomas Woodman who married at Corsham, 24 Apr. 1574, Elizabeth Pryor.
   Child:
   2. i. EDWARD, bapt. at Corsham 9 Oct. 1574.

2. EDWARD WOODMAN (*Thomas*), was baptized 9 Oct. 1574, and is probably the Edward Woodman whose nuncupative will was proved 16 July 1654. He married first, at Corsham, 30 June 1600, COLLET MALLET, who was buried there 5 July 1611; and secondly EDITH ——.
   Children by first wife, baptized at Corsham:
   i. MARY, bapt. 24 Jan. 1601/2.
   ii. ELIZABETH, bapt. 1 July 1604.
   3. iii. EDWARD, bapt. 27 Dec. 1606.

   Children by second wife, baptized at Corsham:
   4. iv. ARCHELAUS, bapt. 23 Jan. 1613/14.
   v. REBECCA, bapt. 15 Dec. 1616.
   vi. WALTER, bapt. 25 Mar. 1620.
   vii. JONATHAN, bapt. 12 Aug. 1621.
   viii. ANNE, bapt. 23 Nov. 1623.
   ix. DAVID, bapt. 17 Aug. 1628.

3. EDWARD[1] WOODMAN (*Edward, Thomas*), of Corsham, was baptized there 27 Dec. 1606. He married JOAN ——, living 9 Nov. 1653.
   Edward Woodman moved to New England and settled at Newbury about 1635, where he was admitted a freeman on 25 May 1636. He was conspicuous and active in the affairs of the Newbury Church, and was usually styled "Mr.", thereby indicating his good position in the community. On 8 Sept. 1636 he was chosen the deputy from Newbury to the General Court, and was thereafter frequently the deputy from that town. On 17:3:1637 he was a lieutenant of the Newbury

company; on 6 Sept. 1638 he was a commissioner to end small causes; and thereafter he frequently held these offices. On 12:1 mo.: 1637/8 he was licenced to sell strong drink. As his name last appears in the Colonial records on 11 May 1670 as the deputy from Newbury, he evidently died not long afterwards.

Children:

i.   EDWARD, of Newbury, b. about 1628.  A son, Archelaus, b. at Newbury 9 June 1672.
ii.  JANE, b. probably about 1630; buried at Corsham 4 July 1633.
iii. JOHN, b. about 1634; moved to Dover, N. H., where he was an inhabitant 17 June 1657.  The name Archelaus appears among his immediate descendants.
iv.  JOSHUA, of Newbury, b. about 1636; d. 30 May 1703.
v.   MARY, b. about 1638; m. JOHN BROWN.
vi.  SARAH, b. at Newbury 12 Jan. 1640/1; m. JOHN KENT, JR.
vii. JONATHAN, of Newbury, b. 5 Nov. 1643.
viii. RUTH, b. 28 Mar. 1646; m. BENJAMIN LOWELL of Newbury.

4. ARCHELAUS (HERCULES)[1] WOODMAN (*Edward, Thomas*), of Christian Malford, co. Wilts., England, baptized at Corsham 23 Jan. 1613/14, died 7 Oct. 1702.  He married first ELIZABETH ———, who died 17 Dec. 1677; and secondly, 13 Nov. 1678, DOROTHY CHAPMAN.

Archelaus Woodman moved to the neighboring parish of Christian Malford, where he was a mercer.  On or about 5 Apr. 1635 he embarked on the *James* at Southampton for New England and settled at Newbury, where he was admitted a freeman 17 May 1637.  He was a freeholder in that town in 1642, and in 1645 was granted a house lot there.  He does not appear much in the Colonial records until after the decease of his brother Edward Woodman.  He is mentioned in the will of John Pemberton of Lawford, co. Essex, England, on 9 Sept. 1653 as "Hercules Woodman of Newbury" (REGISTER, vol. 39, pp. 61–62).  He was constable at Newbury on 27 Apr. 1648 and selectman in 1661.  In 1670–1 he was a commissioner at Newbury to try small causes and on 31 May 1670 lieutenant of the Newbury company, an office from which he was discharged on 4 June 1685.  He was deputy to the General Court from Newbury on 7:8 mo.:1674, 12 May 1675, and 9 July 1675.  He was "Prudential Man" at Newbury on 6 Mar. 1674/5 and also a tythingman in 1679.  In 1677 he took the oath of allegiance.  He was taxed at Newbury in August 1688 (REGISTER, vol. 32, p. 160).  He deposed on 9 Nov. 1695 "aged 80 years" (Suffolk Supreme Jud. Ct. Files, old, no. 3217).

Child:

i.   SARAH, b. about 1638; m. (1) 26 Sept. 1657 JOHN BROCKLEBANK of Rowley, who was buried 5 Apr. 1666; m. (2) in 1667 JOHN ADAMS of Newbury.
     A daughter by her first husband, Sarah Brocklebank, m. Lieut. James Putnam of Salem prior to 6 Jan. 1686.  A son by her second husband was Archelaus Adams.

# GENEALOGICAL RESEARCH IN ENGLAND

Communicated by the Committee on English and Foreign Research

## THE EAST ANGLIAN BLENNERHASSETS

By G. ANDREWS MORIARTY, A.M., LL.B., F.A.S.G., F.S.A.

This is an account of a family of East Anglian gentry, which flourished in the counties of Norfolk and Suffolk in the fifteenth and sixteenth centuries. Elizabeth Blennerhasset, grandmother of John Throckmorton, the early settler of Providence, was a member of this family, whose principal seat was at Frense in Norfolk, where their memorials are very numerous in the church.

The affiliation of the East Anglian family with the parent stock in distant Cumberland will, the writer believes, be shown for the first time and it is interesting to note that the evidence enabling us to make the connection between the two families is largely heraldic and is a striking example of the value of heraldry to the genealogist, before it became a debased science in the social and economic upheaval of the sixteenth century.

The family of Blennerhasset derives its name from a village in Cumberland but there is today no extant evidence of the connection between the family and the hamlet in which they clearly originated, as the earliest members of the race appear in the middle of the fourteenth century, as burgesses of the ancient Roman city of Carlisle, which was for centuries the bulwark of the Western Marches against the Scots. Being a burgess family, without landed estates, their earliest history is difficult to ascertain and must of necessity remain somewhat conjectural. It was not until their marriage with Joan Skelton, the heiress of the families of Skelton and Orton, two families of considerable landed importance, that their story becomes more certain.

The will of Robert de Broamfeld, rector of Melmerby, near Carlisle, dated 17 Nov. 1353, left a legacy to Alan de Blennerhasset (Testamenta Karleolensia, Cumb. & Westmdld. Ant. & Arch. Soc., p. 5). The will of Sir Adam de Wygeton, vicar of Adynham, dated Monday before 20 July 1362, proved 30 June 1382, made Alan de Blennerhasset his residuary legatee (*ibid.*, p. 49). The will of Ellen, daughter of William de Blennerhasset, was not recorded, but it was proved 12 Sept. 1362 and administration was granted to Thomas del Gill (*ibid.*, p. 72). The will of William Arthuret, mayor of Carlisle, dated Sunday after 15 Aug. 1369, made Alan de Blennerhasset his residuary legatee (*ibid.*, p. 89).

In 5 Richard II (1381) John Blennerhasset was M.P. for Carlisle and again in 1384 (Parl. of Eng. 1213-1702, pp. 208, 222).

In 1382 Alan de Blennerhasset was mayor of Carlisle (Hist. & Ant. of Carlisle by Samuel Jefferson, p. 447, where by error the name is written "Adam").

Mary, daughter of this Alan Blennerhasset, married William Aglionby, M.P. for Carlisle in 1385 and 1387-88 (V.C.H. Cumberland, vol. II, p. 325; Parl. of England 1213-1702, pp. 225, 231). Hutchinson in his "History of Cumberland" says that this marriage took place in 1391 (Cumb. & West. A. & A. Soc. Trans. n.s., vol. 13, p. 107).

In the reign of Richard II, John de Mulcaster entailed lands near Carlisle, with remainder in fee to the heirs of Alan de Blennerhasset (*ibid.*, n.s., vol. 18, p. 120).

At Easter 1400 William and Joan Osmunderlaw released to Alan Blennerhasset et als. lands in Carlisle, Cummersdale, Anthorne and Sollom for 100 silver marks (Cumb. Ft. Fines 1 Henry IV, Cumb. & West. A. & A. Soc. Trans. n.s., vol. 16, p. 174).

In 1413 Ralfe Blennerhasset was M.P. for Carlisle (Parl. of Eng. *op. cit.*, p. 278) and in 1441/2 John Blennerhasset was M.P. for that city (*ibid.*, p. 332). There is an excellent account of this John by the late Lord Wedgwood in his "History of the Parliament". He was born about 1405-08 and died shortly before 2 Oct. 1471. He was "perhaps the son of Ralfe (M.P. Carlisle 1413) by Jane, who remarried Sir John Middleton". This statement is undoubtedly correct. John was mayor of Carlisle 8 Nov. 1440 (Cal. Pat. R. 1440, p. 502). Soon after the mayor and citizens of Carlisle sued John Blennerhasset gent., late mayor, for detaining money belonging to the citizens, which should be "dispensed" for the defense of the city (Early Chanc. Proc. 27/194). On 24 Oct. 1452 the manor of Orton was librated to John Blennerhasset, as son and heir of Jane, late wife of John Middleton knt. (Fine R. 31 Henry VI, m. 4). He was an elector for Cumberland in 1442, 1447, 1453, 1455 (when he was also mayor of Carlisle) and 1467. On 11 Sept. 1457 John Denton of Carlisle gent. and John Blennerhasset of the same were mainprizes for Thomas Stanlaw (Fine R. 36 Henry VI, m. 7). He died shortly before 2 Oct. 1471 when his writ of *diem clausit extremum* issued to

SIR THOMAS BLENNERHASSETT

IN FRENSE CHURCH, NORFOLK, 1531

*After Cotman*

the Cumberland excheator (Fine R. 11 Edward IV, m. 23).   His son John was an elector for Cumberland in 1478 and in 1484 a pardon for outlawry was granted to "John Blennerhasset of Carlisle gent. alias son and heir of John Blennerhasset of Carlisle gent." (Cal. Pat. R. 1484, p. 357) (cf. Hist. of the Parl., 1439–1509, Wedgwood, p. 82).   From this John descended the gentle family of Blennerhasset of Cumberland, a branch of which emigrated to the County of Kerry, Ireland, where it still flourishes among the gentry of that region.   The Blennerhasset, who was such a tragic figure in the career of Aaron Burr belonged to the Kerry family.

It may be suggested that William, father of Ellen Blennerhasset, whose will was proved in 1362, was either the father or brother of Alan de Blennerhasset, who occurs in 1353, 1362 and 1369 and that the latter was the father of Alan, mayor of Carlisle in 1382 and of John, the M.P. for Carlisle in 1381 and 1384.   This John was undoubtedly the father of Ralfe, the M.P. for Carlisle in 1413, and he was the father of John, the mayor and M.P., who died in 1471.   Ralfe the M.P. of 1413 married, as her first husband, Jane or Joan,[1] daughter and co-heiress of Sir Clement Skelton by Joan (born in 1345), daughter and co-heiress of Giles de Orton, of Orton and Stainton, co. Cumberland, whose writ of *d. cl. ex.* issued 15 Aug. 1369.   She carried Orton and Stainton to Clement Skelton and they descended to their daughter Jane, wife of Ralfe Blennerhasset, who remarried Sir John Middleton, and from her it descended to her son, John Blennerhasset, the mayor and M.P., who died in 1471.   The Inquisition Post Mortem of Joan, late wife of Sir John Middleton, was taken on 30 Oct., 27 Henry VI (1450).   She held ⅓ of the manor of Great Stainton.   She died on 17 March 1449/50 and her son, John Blennerhasset, aged 40 years and more was her heir.

We now turn to the East Anglian branch of the family founded by Ralfe Blennerhasset.   The pedigree of the family in the Visitation of Suffolk for 1561 is near enough in time to the persons treated therein to be reliable and it is further confirmed by record evidence. Ralfe married about 1423 Jane,[2] widow of Thomas de Heveringham and daughter and heiress of John Lowdham of Lowdham and Boy-

[1] Joan Skelton was the daughter of Sir Clement de Skelton of Orton, *jure uxoris*, who was M.P. for Cumberland in 1382 by Joan (born in 1345), daughter and co-heiress of Gyles de Orton of Orton, M.P. for Carlisle in 1337/8.   Sir Clement was grandson of Hugh Skelton, who flourished about 1325.   Joan de Orton descended from Robert de Orton of Orton who occurs about 1252.   Alice Skelton, sister of Joan, married first Nicholas Ridley and was the ancestress of Bishop Ridley, the Marian martyr.

The arms of the Cumberland Skeltons were: "Azure a fess gules between 3 fleur de lys."   They appear as a quartering in the shield on the tomb of Margaret, wife of Sir Thomas Blennerhasset, in Frense church.   The arms of Orton were: "Azure a lion rampant silver" (cf. Foster's "Some Feudal Coats of Arms", p. 152).

(For Skelton see Cumb. & Westmdld. A. & A. Soc. Trans. n. s., vol. 12, p. 1 sq. and for Orton see Nicolson and Burne's Hist. of Cumb. and Westmdld., vol. II, p. 207, where there is a pedigree of Orton, which contains some errors.)

[2] The Lowdhams of Lowdham and Frense were an ancient East Anglian family which occurs at Frense as early as 1280 (Blomfield's Norfolk, vol. I, p. 141; Coppinger's Manors of Suffolk, vol. III, p. 108).

# BLENNERHASSET OF FRENSE

Arms of Blennerhasset of Frense:
1st. & 6th. Gules, a chevron ermine between 3 dolphins embowed silver (Blennerhasset)
2nd. Azure, a fesse gules between 3 fleur de lys gold (Skelton)
3rd. Azure, a lion rampant silver (Orton)
4th. Silver 3 scutchons sable (Lowdham)
5th. Gules, a pale ermine (Kelvedon).

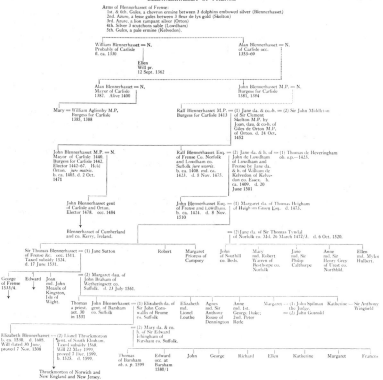

William Blennerhasset = N.
Probably of Carlisle
fl. ca. 1330

Ellen
Will pr.
12 Sept. 1362

Alan Blennerhasset = N.
of Carlisle occ.
1353–69

Alan Blennerhasset = N.
Mayor of Carlisle
1382. Alive 1400

John Blennerhasset M.P. = N.
Burgess for Carlisle
1381, 1384

Mary = William Aglionby M.P.
Burgess for Carlisle
1385, 1388

Ralf Blennerhasset M.P. = (1) Jane da. & co.-h. = (2) Sir John Middleton
Burgess for Carlisle 1413     of Sir Clement
Skelton M.P. by
Joan, dau. & co-h. of
Giles de Orton M.P.
of Orton. d. 24 Oct.
1452

John Blennerhasset M.P. = N.
Mayor of Carlisle 1440.
Burgess for Carlisle 1442.
Elector 1442–67. Held
Orton. *jure matris.*
b. ca. 1405. d. 2 Oct.
1471

Ralf Blennerhasset Esq. = (2) Jane da. & h. of = (1) Thomas de Heveringham
of Frense Co. Norfolk     John de Lowdham     ob. s.p.–1423.
and Lowdham co.     of Lowdham and
Suffolk *jure uxoris.*     Frense by Jane da.
b. ca. 1408. md. ca.     & h. of William de
1423. d. 8 Nov. 1475.     Kelvedon of Kelvedon co. Essex. b.
ca. 1409. d. 20
June 1501

John Blennerhasset gent
of Carlisle and Orton.
Elector 1478. occ. 1484

Blennerhasset of Cumberland
and co. Kerry, Ireland.

John Blennerhasset Esq. = (1) Margaret da. of Thomas Heigham
of Frense and Lowdham.     of Heigham Green Esq. d. 1473.
b. ca. 1424. d. 8 Nov.
1510

= (2) Jane da. of Sir Thomas Tyndal
of Norfolk co. Md. 26 March 1472/3. d. 6 Oct. 1520.

Sir Thomas Blennerhasset = (1) Jane Sutton
of Frense &c. occ. 1511.
Taxed subsidy 1524.
d. 17 June 1531.

Robert

Margaret
Prioress of
Campsey

John
of Southill
co. Beds.

Mary
md. Robert
Warren of
Besthorpe co.
Norfolk

Jane
md. Sir
Philip
Calthorpe

Anne
md. Sir
Henry Grey
of Urest co.
Northbld.

Ellen
md. Myles
Hulbert.

George
of Frense
1533/4.

Edward

Joan
md. John
Meaulx of
Kingston,
Isle of
Wight.

= (2) Margaret dau. of
John Braham of
Wetheringsett co.
Suffolk. d. 23 July 1561.

Thomas John Blennerhasset = (1) Elizabeth da. of
a priest.     gent. of Barsham     Sir John Corn-
aet. 30     co. Suffolk     wallis of Brome
in 1531     co. Suffolk.

Elizabeth
md.
Lionel
Louthe

Agnes
md. Sir
Anthony
Rouse of
Dennington

Anne
md. 1st,
George Duke;
2nd. Peter
Rede

Margaret = (1: John Spilman
the Judge.
= (2) John Gosnold.

Katherine = Sir Anthony
Wingfield

= (2) Mary da. & co.
h. of Sir Edward
Ichingham of
Barsham co. Suffolk.

Elizabeth Blennerhasset = (2) Lionel Throckmorton
b. ca. 1530. d. 1608.     gent. of South Elmham.
Will dated 30 June,     Taxed subsidy 1568.
proved 7 Nov. 1508     Will 22 May 1599,
proved 7 Dec. 1599.
b. 1525. d. 1599.

Throckmorton of Norwich and
New England and New Jersey.

Thomas
of Barsham
ob. s. p. 1599

Edward
occ. at
Barsham
1580/1

John

George

Richard

Ellen

Katherine

Margaret

Frances

lands, co. Suffolk, and Frense, co. Norfolk, by his wife Jane, daughter and heiress of William Kelvedon of Kelvedon in Great Braxsted, co. Essex, whereby he acquired the manors of Frense, Lowdham, Boylands and Kelvedon (Coppinger's Manors of Suffolk, vol. III, p. 108; Blomfield's Norfolk, vol. I, p. 141). The monumental inscription of Jane Blennerhasset in Frense church makes her born in 1404 but her age as given in her father's Inq. P.M. in 1423 is as 14 years and this is undoubtedly correct (Inq. P.M. 2 Henry VI, Norf. Inq. ed. Rye).

Ralfe Blennerhasset is mentioned in a letter of Sir John Paston to his brother, John Paston Esq. 2 April 1473: "Raff Blaundrehasset wer a name to styrte an hare. I warrant ther shall come no suche name in our bokys, ner in our house; it myght per case styrt xxti harys at onys; ware that jd perse" (beware of that stingy fellow) (Paston Letters, ed. Gardner, vol. III, p. 83). He is buried in Frense church with this inscription in Latin: "Here lies that honnoured man Ralfe Blennerhasset Esq., who died 8 Nov. 1475, on whose soul God have mercy". Upon his tomb are his arms, which conclusively show his connection with the Cumberland family. They are "quarterly 1st. and 4th. Blennerhasset of Cumberland, 2nd. and 3rd. Orton of Cumberland impaling Lowdham" (Blomfield's Norfolk vol. I, p. 142). The Orton quartering shows his descent from Ralfe of Carlisle and his wife Jane Skelton, whose mother was the Orton heiress. He must, therefore, have been a younger son of Ralfe the M.P. of 1413 and a younger brother of John, who died in 1471.

Jane (Lowdham) Blennerhasset, who is also buried in Frense church, died on 20 June 1501 "aged 97 years" (*ibid.*). Her Inq. P.M. in Essex was taken on 12 Oct. 1501 (Blomfield's Norfolk, *op. cit.*, pp. 141–42; Morant's Essex, vol. II, p. 153). Her son and heir John Blennerhasset was aged 77 years.

John, son and heir of Ralfe and Jane (Lowdham) Blennerhasset, succeeded to his mother's manors and died 8 Nov. 1510 in his 87th. year. He was buried in Frense church with this inscription: "Here lies that honnoured man John Blennerhasset Esq. who died 8 Nov. 1510 in his 87th. year". On his tomb are four armorial shields. Two of these are the arms of Blennerhasset. The third shield is quarterly 1st. and 4th. Blennerhasset, 2nd. Lowdham and 3rd. Orton. The fourth shield shows Orton impaling Heigham, which is obviously an error for Blennerhasset impaling Heigham (Blomfield, *op. cit.;* Coppinger's Manors of Suffolk vol. III, p. 108; Harvey's Vis. of Suffolk 1561, vol. II, p. 229). He married first, Margaret,[3] daughter of Thomas Heigham Esq. of Heigham Green in Gaseley parish, co. Suffolk, by Isabel, daughter and co-heiress of Sir Hugh Francis of Giffard's in Wickhambrook in that county (Harvey's Vis. of Suffolk, *op. cit.*). She was buried in Gaseley church. The inscription is gone but two shields of arms remain. The first shows quarterly 1st.

[3] The Heighams of Heigham Green arose in the 15th century through the law. Thomas Heigham, father of Margaret, was a Justice of Assize in Suffolk in 1457 and was apparently a Lancastrian in politics. Sir Clement Heigham, Chief Baron of the Exchequer in the time of Queen Mary, belonged to this family.

and 4th. Blennerhasset, 2nd. Orton, 4rd. Lowdham. The second
shield is quarterly 1st. Blennerhasset, 2nd. and 3rd. Lowdham, 4th.
Orton impaling Heigham (Harvey's Vis., *op. cit.*, vol. II, p. 228;
"Pedigree of the Heigham Family" by Charles William Heigham).
He married secondly, before 26 March 1473, Jane, daughter of Sir
Thomas Tindal of co. Norfolk. She is buried at Frense with this
inscription: "Pray for the soul of Jane late wife of John Blennerhasset
Esq., who died 6 October 1520" (Blomfield, *op. cit.*). Margaret
Tyndal wife of Gov. John Winthrop belonged to this family.

John Blennerhasset is mentioned in a letter of John Paston to
his brother Sir John Paston, dated 26 March 1473: "As I was wryght-
yng this bylle, Mastresse Jane Harsset comandyd me streyghtly that
I shold recomand hyr to yow in hyr best wyse, and she sendyth
yow word she wold be as fayne to here fro yow as another poore
body. Syr, it is so that my cosyn John Blenerhasset is enformyd
that for verry serteyn he is chosyn to be on the colectours of the
taske in Norfolk, wher in verry trowthe he hathe not a foot of lond
with in the shyer; wherefor I beseche yow that, as hastyly as ye may
aftyr the syght of thys bylle, that it may please yow to take the
labore to comon with Sir Rychard Harrecorte, and to let hym have
knowlage that thys gentyllman hathe nowght with in the shyer, and
that ye tweyne may find the meane to get hym owght of that thank-
lesse offyce for I promyse yow it encomberthe hym evyll, and my
mastresse hys wyffe, and alle us hys frendys here; and if so be that ye
and Sir R. Harcort may not fynd the meane betwyx yow, that then
it may please yow to meve my Lord Chamberleyn with thys mater,
and so Master Harsset prayithe yow, and Mastresse Jane, hys wyff
also, for she lyekyth no thyng by the ofyce" (Paston Letters *op. cit.*,
vol. III, p. 81). In his reply dated 2 April 1473 Sir John writes: "a
son trescher & bon ame Freer, John de Paston Esquier. Weel
belovyd brother, I recomand me to yow, letyng yow wete that at the
request of Mestresse Jane Hasset and yow, I have laboryd the
knyghtys off the sheer of Norfolk, and the knyghtys off the sheer of
Suffolk. I understand ther had ben made labor that suche thing
shulde have ben as ye wrotte to me off, but now it is saff." Sir John
then goes on with his uncomplimentary remarks about John's father
Raffe quoted above (*ibid.*, vol. III, pp. 81, 83).

In 9 Henry VII (1493/4) John Blennerhasset was holding Bore-
lands (Boylands), one of the Lowdham fees lying partly in Norfolk
and partly in Suffolk, *in capite* (Suckling's Suffolk, vol. I, p. 37).
His Inq. P.M. was taken in 1510/11 (Inq. P.M. 2 Henry VIII, no.
33).

By his first wife Margaret Heigham he had issue, Sir Thomas his
heir, Robert of Warwickshire, and Margaret, prioress of Campsey.

By his second wife Jane Tindal he had John of Southill, co. Beds.,
who died *s.p.*, Mary, married Robert Warren of Besthorpe, co.
Norfolk, Jane, married Sir Philip Calthorpe, Anne, married Sir
Henry Grey of Urest, co. Northumberland and Ellen, married Myles
Hulbert.

Sir Thomas Blennerhasset of Frense &c. succeeded his father in

1510 and died on 17 June 1531. On 12 May 1511 John Heigham et als., feoffees, had license to enfeoff Thomas Blennerhasset in fee tail, remainder to the heirs of John Blennerhasset, with the manor of Boylands and messuages in Osmondeston and Scole, co. Norfolk and Stuston, Thrandeston, Okley, Brome and Palgrave, co. Suffolk (Papers For. & Dom. Henry VIII; Heigham Pedigree *op. cit.*). He was taxed at Framlingham, co. Suffolk, in the Subsidy of 1524 for £13 on £200 (Suff. Sub. 1524, Suff. Green Bks., p. 417). He was buried in Frense church under an elaborate tomb with his effigy in full armor and several shields of arms. The first shield is quarterly 1st. and 4th. Blennerhasset, 2nd. and 3rd. Orton impaling quarterly 1st. and 4th. Lowdham, 2nd. and 3rd. Kelvedon. The second shield is quarterly 1st. and 4th. Blennerhasset, 2nd. and 3rd. Lowdham impaling Heigham (Harvey's Vis. of Suffolk vol. II, p. 229). The third shield is quarterly 1st. Blennerhasset, 2nd. Lowdham, 3rd. Orton, 4th. Kelvedon impaling Braham. The fourth shield is quarterly 1st. Blennerhasset, 2nd. Lowdham, 3rd. Orton, 4th. Kelvedon impaling 2 lions rampant (probably Sutton) (Blomfield *op. cit.*). His Inq. P.M. was taken in 1531 (Inq. P.M. Henry VIII; Coppinger, *op. cit.*, vol. III, p. 108).

He married first Jane Sutton and had issue George his heir, who inherited Frense, Boylands &c. and continued the line (Suckling's Suffolk, vol. I, p. 37), Edward, who left issue, and Joan, wife of John Meaulx of Kingston, Isle of Wight.

He married secondly Margaret,[4] daughter of John Braham of Wetheringsett, co. Suffolk, Esq. She is buried in Frense church with the following inscription: "Here lyeth Dame Margaret, widow of Sir Thomas Blennerhasset of Frense knt. and daughter of John Braham of Wetheringsett Esq. and had issue two sons, Thomas a priest and John of Barsham by Beccles co. Suffolk and five daughters, Elizabeth, wife of Lionel Louthe and next of Francis Clopton, Anne, wife of Sir Anthony Rouse knt., Anne, wife 1st. of George Duke and and then of Peter Rede, Margaret, wife of John Gosnold (she had previously been the wife of John Spilman the Judge) and Katherine, wife of Anthony Wingfield. The said Dame Margaret died on 23 July 1561" (Blomfield's Norfolk, *op. cit.*). On her monument are two shields. The first is Braham impaling Rydon and the second is quarterly 1st. and 6th. Blennerhasset, 2nd. Lowdham, 3rd. Kelvedon, 4th. Orton, 5th. Skelton impaling Braham (Blomfield *op. cit.*).

John Blennerhasset gent., the fourth son of Sir Thomas, and his second son by his second wife, held Barsham, in right of his second wife and it descended to her son Thomas Blennerhasset, who held it at his death in 1599 (Blennerhasset Pedigree in Vis. of Suffolk 1561, ed. Metcalf; Suckling's Suffolk, vol. I, p. 37).

John Blennerhasset married first Elizabeth,[5] daughter of Sir

---

[4] The Suffolk Brahams early divided into several branches. In 49 Edward III (1375/6) John de Braham held Brome Hall (Coppinger, *op. cit.*, vol. III, p. 239; Gipp's "Ancient Families of Suffolk", pp. 18, 21).
[5] The Cornwallis family descended from Thomas Cornwallis, citizen and goldsmith of London. He was alderman in 1376 and sheriff of London in 1378. He

John Cornwallis of Brome by Mary,[6] daughter of Edward Sulyard of Otes in High Lever, co. Essex. By her he had issue one daughter Elizabeth, born about 1522, who married Lionel Throckmorton gent. of South Elmham, co. Suffolk. She was the grandmother of John Throckmorton, the early settler of Providence, R. I., and the ancestor of the New Jersey Throckmortons.

He married secondly Mary, daughter and co-heiress of Sir Edward Ichingham of Barsham, co. Suffolk, and had issue, Thomas of Barsham his heir, d. *s.p.* 1599, Edward, occurs at Barsham 1580/1, John, George, Richard (wrongly called Ralph in the Vis. of 1561), Ellen, Katherine, Margaret and Frances.

---

was M.P. for London in 1380. He died on 4 Jan. 1385/6 and was buried in the church of St. Martin's Vintry. His son John acquired Brome by his marriage with Philippa, daughter and co-heiress of Robert de Buckton of Brome, by the daughter and heiress of Sir John Braham of Capell, co. Suffolk.

Sir John Cornwallis, father of Elizabeth Blennerhasset, was knighted at the taking of Morlaix in Brittany in 1522. He was Steward of the Household to Prince Edward (Edward VI) and died in 1554. His son, Sir Thomas of Brome, was Privy Counsellor and Comptroller of the Household to Queen Mary and Treasurer of Calais. He was sheriff of Suffolk and Norfolk in 1553 and M.P. for Suffolk in 1557. He was the direct ancestor of the Marquis of Cornwallis, the British general in the Revolution.

[6] The Sulyards descended from John Sulyard gent. of Eye, co. Suffolk, in 1425. His son, Sir John, grandfather of Mary Cornwallis, was of Wetherden, co. Suffolk. He was tutor to Edward Prince of Wales and Governor of Lincoln's Inn in 1459. In 1484 he was raised to King's Bench as a puisne Judge·and died on 18 March 1487/8. In politics he was a faithful adherent of the House of York (cf. Vis. of Suffolk 1561; Foss's "Lives of the Judges", vol. V, p. 74; Wedgwood's Hist. of the Parl., 1439–1509, pp. 827–8).

776

Beltofte (cont.)
John 367, 368, 369,
370, 371, 372, 373,
376, 377, 378, 379,
380
Laurence 377
Marg'ett --- 380
Margarett --- 372
Richard 368, 376, 377,
378
Richarde 375
Ricu 380
Rychard 370
Thomas 376, 377
Benchall, Geo: 236
Bendall, Edward 506
Benett, Mary 254, 259
Ralph 220
Benfeild, Allan 420
Allan (or Belfeild)
420, 421
Allan (sic) 411
Joane 411
Joane (or Belfeild)
420, 421
Margaret (or Belfeild)
420, 421
Margarett 410, 411
Bennett, Edward 579
Mary 330
Nicholas (Sir) 439
Benolte, Thomas 203
Benslye, Elizabeth 144
Benson, Ellyn 425
Margaret --- (widow)
301
Bentham, Jeffery 679
Bentley, John 220
Berant, John 428
Berburne, --- 708
--- (lord of) 708
--- (lord of) (alias
Barbon) 708
Berburnes, --- 709
Berd, Allen 412
Henry 412
John 412
Berkeley, --- (Alderman)
506
Berkenhead, Wm. (Mr.) 50
Berkinshaw, William 237
Berry, Agnes 392
Margery 60
Thomas 392
Bertlot, Margaret
(Mashcal) 609
Robert 609
Bertune, John 301
Best, John 298
Beswyck, Roger 235
Thomas 235
Betham, William (Sir)
724
Betscombe, Christopher
194
Betson, William 239, 248
Bettes, John 445
Bettey, John 196
Betts, Margaret --- 653
Bever, Roland 506
Bewlde, Thomas 298
Bexwicke, Alexander 233
Edward 234
John 233, 234
Bickeford, Anne 409
Gregorye 409
Jaune 409
Marye 409
Bickeforde, Gregory 409

Gregorye 409
Jane --- 409
Richard 409
Richd. 409
Symon 409
Bickford, Anne 409
Gregorie 410
Gregory 407, 410, 420,
421, 422, 423, 424
Jane --- 411, 420
John 407, 410, 421
Thomas 409, 410, 411
Bickforde, --- 421
Gregory 420
John 409, 420
Bickham, Aldred 74, 75,
76
Aldred, Jr. 76
Anne 76
Charitie (Slocombe)
76
Charity 74, 77
Charity (Slocombe) 73
Charity (Slocum) 76
Ellen 76
Ellen (Escott) 76
Ellen --- 76
Ellen --- (widow) 76
Hugh 76
Isott 76
Joan (Studdier) 76
Joane (Studdier) (?)
75
Johan 76
Mary 76
Richard 76
Thomasine --- 76
William 76
Biggs, Ambrose 156
Anne 156
Jo: 253
Bigod, --- 703
Gundreda 676
Roger 704
Williamm 676
Billingsby, Margaret 402
Bind, --- (Mr.) 653
Bindon, --- (Lord
Vicount) 109
--- (Viscount) 116
Bingham, --- 14
--- (Mr.) 49
George 14
John 47
Nicholas 328
Binson, John 403
Birch, Alice 359
Ambrose 242
Thomas 233
Birche, --- 578
Alexander 250
George 578
Birchett, Thomas 631
Bird, --- 498
--- (Dr.) 68
--- --- 498
Alice 151
Bartholomew 498
Lancelot (Rev.) 466
Sarah 498
Thomas 498
William 498
Birder, Robert (Mr.) 36,
40
Biron, --- 242
John (Sir) 242
Birtenshall, --- ---
(widow) 234

Robert 234
Birtinshaw, Miles 242
Birton, Kobe 462
Bishop, --- 87
George 680
Henry, Esq. 107
Humphrey, Esq. 107
James 87
John 87
Margaret 218
Richard 257
Robert 87
Thomas 651
William 688
Bishopp, Elizabeth 218
Jane 218, 224, 226
Julian 218
Thomas 218
Bishoppe, Joan 219
Robert 216
Bisse, --- 325
Bitfield, Elizabeth (?)
405
Black, Thomas 713
Blackborne, William 60
Blackeledge, John 234
Blackledge, John 234
Blackmoore, Robert 330
Blackstone, William 334
Blackwell, Isbell 61
Blake, Humphry 222
Richard 212, 214
Blakeye, Thomas 474
Walter 474, 475
Blakkaller, Elles 342
Blanchard, John 44
Joseph 632
Blaundrehasset, Raff 770
Blaxston, --- 555
Blaxton, --- 555
Blenerhasset, John 771
Blennerhasset, --- 765,
768, 769, 770, 771,
772
--- --- 769
Agnes 769
Alan 766, 769
Anne 769, 771, 772
Edward 769, 772, 773
Elizabeth 765, 769,
772, 773
Ellen 768, 769, 771,
773
Frances 769, 773
George 769, 772, 773
Jane 769, 770, 771
Jane --- (Middleton)
766
Joan 769, 772
John 766, 768, 769,
770, 771, 772, 773
John (Sir) 771
John, Esq. 769, 770,
771
Katherine 769, 772,
773
Margaret 769, 771, 772,
773
Margaret --- 768
Mary 766, 769, 771
Raffe 771
Ralf 769
Ralf, Esq. 769
Ralfe 766, 768, 770
Ralfe, Esq. 770
Ralph 773
Richard 769, 773
Robert 769, 771

Blennerhasset (cont.)
  Thomas 769, 772, 773
  Thomas (Sir) 767, 768,
    769, 771, 772
  William 768, 769
Blish, --- 121
  Abraham (or Blush)
    121
  Ann --- (or Blush)
    121
  Joseph (or Blush) 121
  Sarah (or Blush) 121
  Sarah (or Blush)
    (Orchyard) 121
Bliss, --- 417
  John 417
Blithe, Johanne 449
Blomefild, Andrewe 450
Blomfeild, Steven 266
Blomfield, --- 770, 771,
    772
Bloyse, --- (Sister) 263
Blush, --- 121
  --- (Widow) 124
  Abraham 121, 124
  Abraham (or Blish)
    121
  Ann --- (or Blish)
    121
  Joseph (or Blish) 121
  Sarah (or Blish) 121
  Sarah (or Blish)
    (Orchyard) 121
Blynde, William 594, 596
Boadman, Andrew 35, 36
  Elizabeth --- 35
  Giles 35, 36
Boandman, Andrew (sic)
    38
  Ann 38
Boardma-, Andrew 38
  Ann 38
Boardman, --- (Bordman)
    35
  --- (Boreman) 35
  --- (or Bordman) 39
  Andrew 36, 40
  Andrew (or Bordman)
    39
  Giles 39
  Giles (or Bordman) 39
  Grace --- 36, 38, 40
  Rebecca 36, 38
  Rebecca (Linsey) 38
  Rebecca (Lynsey) 38
  Thomas 123, 239, 250
  William 36
  William (Maj.) (or
    Boardman) 35
  William (Maj.) (or
    Bordman) 35
  Andrew 38
Bodd, --- 299
  --- --- 299
  Agnes (Borden) 299
  Parnell (Semarke) 299
Bogais, --- --- 652
  Wm. 652
Bogarys, Alice 652
Bogas, John 270
  Margret 270
  Robert 270, 644
  Wm. 270
Boggas, Ann 270
  Edward 270
  John 270
  Margery 281
  Margerye 270
Bogwell, Heracles 54

Bohin, Nicholas 566
Bokenham, --- 183, 491
  Henry (Sir) 183
  John 491
  Wiseman, Esq. 183
Bold, --- 242
  John 242
Bolde, Henry 242
Boldero, Francis 151
  John 156
  Mary 150, 156
Boler, Mary --- 107
  William 107, 121
Bolles, --- 542
  --- (Capt.) 12, 27
Bolwell, Sarah 762
Bond, --- (Cousin) 264
  --- --- 264
  Agnes --- 221
  George 213
  Thomas 221
Bonde, John 620
Bondon, --- (Lord
    Vicount) 109
Bonett, Raffe 567
Boodes, Nicholas 299
Boods, Nycholas 299
Boolle, Richard 187
Boone, Margarie 298
  William 298
Boorden, Agnes (Borden)
    302
  Edward (Borden) 302
  Elizabeth (Borden)
    302
Booreman, Agnes 302, 310
  Anne 301
  Edward 301, 302
  Elizabeth 301
  Stephen 302
Boorman, Edward 302
  Xtopher 302
Booth, John 136
  Rychard 135
Boothe, William 239, 240
  William (Mr.) 239
Borage, Hugh 644
  Thos. 447
Bordeman, Andrewe 36
Borden, --- 293, 294,
    295, 298, 302, 307,
    308, 311, 312, 328
  --- (Joan) 302
  --- (John) 302
  --- --- 299, 301, 302,
    310, 328
  --- --- (Widow) 302
  Agnes 296, 299, 301,
    302, 310
  Agnes (Boorden) 302
  Agnes (Gorham) 300
  Agnes (or Ann) 310
  Agnes --- (widow) 299,
    302
  Alexander 301
  Alice 298, 301, 309
  Alice --- 297, 307
  Amey 312
  Amy (Anne) 310
  Amye 300
  Amye (Anne?) 302
  Ann 297, 298
  Ann (or Agnes) 310
  Anna 298
  Anne (Amy) 310
  Anne (Amye?) 302
  Benedicta --- 294
  Benet --- 297

Benjamin 312
Bennett 296
Bennett --- 293
Bennett --- (widow)
    293, 297
Dionisia --- 297
Edmond 308
Edmund 293, 294, 298,
    302, 309, 310, 311
Edmund (Edward) 312
Edmunde 299
Edward 297, 298, 299,
    300, 301, 302, 303,
    304, 309, 310, 312
Edward (Boorden) 302
Edward (Edmund) 312
Eleanor 301
Elizabeth 296, 297,
    298, 299, 300, 310,
    311, 312
Elizabeth (Barden)
    302
Elizabeth (Boorden)
    302
Francis 311
Henry 293, 294, 296,
    297
Hope --- 312
Isabel 296, 297
Isabel --- 294
Isabella 296
Joan 297, 298, 300,
    302, 309, 310
Joan (---) 302
Joan --- 297, 300, 304,
    309, 310
Joane 302
Johane (Jone) 302
John 293, 294, 296,
    297, 298, 299, 300,
    302, 309, 310, 312,
    328
John (---) 302
John (Bourden) 328
Jone (Johane) 302
Joseph 312
Julian 309
Julyan 298
Katherin 302
Katherine 297, 298
Leticia --- (widow)
    296
Margaret 298, 309
Margaret --- 298, 299,
    302, 309
Margaret --- (Burden)
    (widow) 302
Marion 309
Mary 302, 310, 311
Mary (Rowe) 300
Maryon 298
Mathew 301, 302, 306,
    308
Matthew 293, 300, 301,
    302, 307, 310, 311,
    312
Matthewe 302
Richard 293, 294, 296,
    300, 301, 302, 305,
    306, 307, 309, 310,
    311, 328
Roberga --- 294
Roberge 297
Robergie 296
Robert 296, 297
Robert, Jr. 295
Roger 296, 297
Rose --- 298

Burden (cont.)
Emma --- 296
George 299
Godleve--- 295
Godlove --- 295
Henry 308
Herry 309
James 295, 299
Jane 299
Joan 296
Joan --- 295
John 295, 298, 299,
304, 309
John, Jr. 308
Lettys 299
Margaret --- (Borden)
(widow) 302
Petronilla --- 304,
305
Richard 295, 304, 305,
309
Roberge --- 309
Robert 298, 308
Stephen 298, 299
Thomas 299, 308, 309
Thos. 309
Ursula --- 299
William 295, 296, 298,
309
Burditt, Richard 550
Burdn, --- (sic) 309
Burdon, Alice ---
(widow) 299
Ann 299, 301
Christian (?) 301
Christopher 298
Edmonde 299
Edward 299
Elizabeth 299
Gilbert 301
Grace 301
Joan --- 299
John 299, 301
Judeth 301
Petronilla --- 304,
305
Richard 301, 304, 305
Robert 298, 299
Rose 301
Stephen 298, 299
Thomas 299, 301
Thomesy 299
William 299, 301, 305
Burdune, Joan 301
Bures, Henry 661
Burg, John (Burgess) 125
Burge, Richard 5
Burgeant, --- 153
Thomas 152, 153
Burgent, --- 151
Thomas 151
Burgess, Anthony 234
John 125
John (Burg) 125
Burgesse, Josias 47
Burgh, --- (Mr.) 266
Henry 711
Buriman, Andrew (sic) 37
Burk, Richard 417
Sarah --- (widow) 417
Burke, --- 699, 705, 746
Burman, Robert 660
Burn, --- 712, 713, 714,
720, 729
Burnap, Dorothy 282
Thomas 282
Burne, --- 768
John 333
Burneside, Gilbert (de

Burnolfsheved) 707
Burnet, Mary 10
Burney, Johan 570
Burns, --- 702
Burr, Aaron 768
Burrough, --- 492
--- (Borowghe) 492
Bursley, Elizabeth 260
John (Mr.) 260
Burt, --- 406, 413, 415,
417, 418, 419, 422,
423
--- (Wm.?) 413
--- --- 412, 417
Abigail 417
Ann --- 413
Christian 412
David 412, 417
Dorcas 418
Elizabeth 412, 417
Eulalia --- 412
Eulaliah --- 412
Hannah 418
Henrie 412
Henry 406, 410, 411,
412, 414, 415, 416,
417, 418, 419, 422
Isack 412
John 410, 412, 414,
416
Jonathan 412
Jonathan (Dea.) 417
Luke 411
Mary 412, 417
Mercy 417
Nathaniel 412, 416,
417
Patience 417
Samuel 412, 416, 417
Samuell 412
Sarah 412, 417
Ulaiah --- 412
William 413
Wilmote --- 412, 416
Wm. 413
Burte, Agnes 410, 415
Elizabeth 410, 415
Henry 410
Isott --- 410
Isott --- (widow) 415
John 408, 410, 414
Richard 414
Will. 412
William 412
Burter, Johane --- 450
Owen 450
Burton, --- 426
Hanah (Osborne) 132
Hannah (Osborn) 26
John (Sir) 634
Susanna 249
William 251
Burtt, --- 408, 415
Agnes 408, 415, 416
Alice (Allies) 415,
416
Allies 408
Allies (Alice) 415,
416
Elizabeth 408, 415,
416
Henry 407, 415, 416
Isett 415
Isett (or Isott) ---
415
Isett --- 407
Isott (or Isett) ---
415

Johan 408, 416
Johan (Saunders) 415
John 410, 415, 416
Raddegan 407, 415, 416
Burtun, Thomas 301
Bury, Henry 142
Busby, Anne (Nickerson)
124
Nicholas 428
Bush, --- 362
Phillologus 362
Philologus 360
Busken, Roger 450
Butcher, Rebecca 268
Thomas 462
Butler, John 186
Margaret 204
Peter 507
William 204
Butte, William 659
Butter, --- 640, 662
Alice 666
Anne 666
Anne --- 665
Edward 666
Henry 660
John 640, 641, 642,
660, 661, 665
John, Esq. 659, 662
Mary 659, 661, 662,
665
Peter 662
Pierce 666
Richard 666
Thomas 626, 627, 640,
642, 649, 666
Thomas (Rutter?) 641
Willelmo 643
William 602, 649, 660,
661, 665, 666
Willm 643
Buttolfe, John 445
Button, Elizabeth 465
John 449
Thomas 648
Buttor, Thomas 641
Buttour, Thomas 641, 644
William 644
Butts, Anne, --- (widow)
281
Buxton, John (Bu[x]ton)
511
Wyllm 441
Byccombe, Aldred 76
Ann (Lanham) 76
Charitie 76
Helen 76
Hellen --- 76
Joane 76
Mary 76
William 76
Byckford, John 423
Byland, --- (Abbot of)
742
Byles, Elizabeth ---
(widow) 18
William 18
Bynkys, William 333
Byrch, Richard 61
Byrche, John 210
Byrd, John (Sr.) 233
Byrde, --- (?) 95, 175,
265
--- (Mr.) 145
Beatrice 152
John 209
Byron, --- 247, 726
--- (Lord) 726

Chandler (cont.)
  Edward 359, 361, 362
  Edward (Old) 361
  Elizabeth 358, 359, 362, 363, 365
  Elizabeth --- 361, 362
  Frances 357, 358, 359
  Francis 361, 362
  George 358, 359
  George (Dr.) 366
  Grace 358, 359, 360
  Hana 365
  Hannah 351, 354, 365, 733
  Hannah (Abbott) 405
  Henry 358, 359, 360, 361, 362, 363, 365, 733
  Jane 359
  Jeremy 359
  Jhone 358
  Joane 359, 360
  Joane --- 357, 358, 360
  Job 362
  Johane 358
  John 357, 358, 359, 362
  John (Capt.) 352
  John (Dea.) 365, 733
  Jone 359
  Margaret 358, 359, 362
  Martha 360, 362
  Mary 357, 359, 360, 363
  Mary (Holley) 362
  Noah 362
  Rebecca 362
  Richard 358, 361, 363
  Robert 357, 358, 359
  Samuel 363
  Sarah 359, 361, 362, 363, 365, 366, 733
  Sarah --- 359
  Susan 361, 362
  Susanna 360
  Thomas 352, 354, 355, 356, 357, 358, 359, 360, 361, 362, 363
  Thomas (Capt.) 365, 733
  Thomas, Jr. 356
  Tobias 358, 359
  Willia' 363, 365
  William 351, 352, 354, 359, 360, 362, 363, 364, 365, 366, 732, 733
  Winifred 362
  Wm 365
Chandoll, William 3
Chanler, Thomas 356
Channler, Tobias 363
Chant, Richard 324
Chapleyn, Anne 448
  Nicholas 446
  Thomas 448
Chaplin, William 207
Chaplyn, --- 172, 173, 175, 178
  John 172, 173, 174, 175, 177, 178
  William 621
Chapman, Dorothy 764
  Margaret 457
  Paule 457
  Thomas 108
  William 459, 520, 521
Chappell, John 220

Charington, Epa 27
Charles, Diego 338
Chase, Aquila 405
  Mary 405
  William 122, 123
Chatinge, Richard 598
Chatyng, William 474
Chauncey, --- 374
  --- (Mr.) 383, 385
  --- 756
  Henri 371
  Henry 381, 386
  Henry, Esq. 374
  Henry, Sr. 385
  Walter, 755
Chauncy, --- 677
  Charles 677
  Henric. 374
  Henry 372, 373, 376
  Henry (Sir) 677
  John 677
  Robert 379
Chaundeler, --- (old) 355
  --- --- 355
  Agneis --- 356, 357
  Agnes --- 356
  Henry 362
  Joan --- 357
  Joane --- 358, 360
  John 358, 643
  Robert 357
  Thomas 355, 356, 358, 360, 361
  Thomas, Sr. 355, 356
  Tobias, Sr. 358, 361
  William 641
Chaundler, --- 356, 357
  Agnes --- 357
  Anne 357
  Barbara 357
  John 356
  Robert 357
  Thomas 355, 357, 361
  Thomas, Jr. 360
Chawcott, Elizabeth (or Chaldecot) 201
  Francis (or Chaldecot) 201
Chawcy, --- 381
  Henry 381
Chayney, --- (?) 444
Cheeke, Thomas 206
Cherch, Mary 428
Chersley, Jane 254, 258
Chester, --- (?) 526
  --- (Col.) 527
  --- (Earl of) 703, 706
  Robert 268
Chetleborow, Alce 464
  Alce (Alice) 500
  Alice (Alice) 500
Chetwode, Richard (Sir) 745
Cheverell, --- 102, 103, 114
  Anne --- 103
  Hugh 102, 103
  Hugh, Esq. 102, 105, 107, 114
  Hughe 102
  Hughe (Mr) 102
Cheverrye, John 147
Chiball, --- (sister) 511
Chiblee, Elizabeth --- (Fyske) 467
  John 467

Chick, --- --- (widow) 214
  Alexander 172
  John 211
  Robert 214
Chicke, Robert 212
Chickering, --- 502
  Annas 288
  Francis 288, 502
  Susanna --- (Mrs. Chickerin[g]) 405
Chilcott, Joyce 214
  Symon 214
  Thomas 212, 214
  William 100, 101, 116, 119, 130
Child, Edith 318
  Moyses 582
Chiles, --- 319, 320
  Edith --- 320
  Thomas 319, 320, 321
Chipman, --- 110, 118, 127
  --- --- 110
  Hannah (Hanner) 117
  Hanner 112
  Hanner (Hannah) 117
  John 117, 110, 111, 112, 118, 121, 122, 126, 127
  John (Elder) 111
  Richard Manning (Rev.) 111
  Tamson 112
  Tamson (Thomasine) 117
  Thomas 117, 111
  Thomas (Mr) 111
  Thomas (Mr.) 117, 118
  Thomasine 118
  Thomasine ("Tamson") 117
  William Churchill 111
Chippingdale, George 82
Chippman, Richard 5
Chirche, John 595
Chitting, Henry 526, 559
Cholmeley, Richard (Sir) 711
Chorlton, Margaret 239, 248
Chromer, Martha 462
Chubb, Matthew 108
Chubbe, John 166
Church, Thomas (Mr.) 509
  Xopher 426
Churche, Helyn 534
Churchill, --- 201
  Ann 201
  Johannis 201
  John 189, 201
  William 189
Churchman, --- 534
Chute, Anne --- 222
  Robert 211, 221, 222
City, --- (?) 698
Clagget, Elizabeth 302, 310
Clap, Increase 260
Clapton, John, Esq. 618
Clare, John 194
Clarendon, --- (Lord) 17
Clark, --- 688
  --- (Dr.) 686, 688, 697
  Alice 263
  Eleanor (Dane) 366
  G. F. (Dr.) 686

Clark (cont.)
  John 33
  Richard 128
  William 648
Clarke, --- 70
  --- (?) 148, 265, 267
  Agnes 150, 151, 154
  Agnes --- 151
  Agnes --- (widow) 613
  Ann --- (Darby) 96
  Anne --- 104
  Catherine (Gould) 34
  Henry 69, 70
  John 96, 104, 111, 119
  Jonas 55
  Loader (?) 96
  Richard 627
  Robert 613
  Roger 330
  Thomas 10
  Walter (Gov.) 34
  William 70, 151, 613,
    648
  Wm. (Sir) 443
Clavell, --- 192
  --- --- 192
  Henry 192
  Roger 191
  Walter 192
Clayton, Sarah 312
Cleaton, Hughe 235
Clegg, John 104
Clement, Edmund 70
  Edward 73
  John 595
  Thos. 450
Clerico, Johanne (?) 738
Clerk, Agnes ---
    (widow) 607
  Margaret 627
  Robert 607
  Thomas 619, 631
  Will 651
  William 612, 613, 618,
    619, 620, 621, 631
Clerke, Agnes --- 614
  Elizabeth 459
  John 614
  Will 651, 652
  William 629
Cleuville, --- (lord
    of) 746
Clevehanger, --- 176
  William 173, 176
  Wm. 176
Cleves, William 366, 733
Clifford, --- 724, 725
  --- (Lord) 724
Clopton, --- 661
  Anne 165, 182
  Dorothy 657
  Francis 772
  William (Sir) 165, 182
Clough, Raph 242
  Richard 128, 242
Cloutyng, John 474
  William 594
Clover, Thomas 149, 157
Clowler, --- (Mr.) 213
Clowther, Edmond 221
Clubbe, Eliz. ---
    (Fyske) 467
  John 467
Cluett, James 323
Clutterbucke, Samuel 251
Clyffe, --- 191, 192
  Richard 191
Clyfton, Andrew 355
  Joan --- 356

  Thomas 356
Coas, Joanna 393
  Mary 393
  William 393
Cobbe, William 530
Cobbrame, John 457
Cobham, --- (?) 264
Cock, --- (Mrs.
    William) 61
  Agnes 57, 59, 62
  Agnes --- 59, 60, 62
  Agnes --- (widow) 61
  Anne 58, 60, 460, 489
  Anne --- 58, 59, 62
  Bennet 61 62
  Christian 61
  Daniel 59
  Edward 441
  Elenor 61
  Elizabeth --- 60
  Ellen --- 62
  Ellen --- (widow) 62
  Ellenor --- 59
  Elyzabeth 58, 59, 60,
    61, 62
  Elyzabeth --- 58, 59,
    61, 62
  Emme --- 59
  George 59, 60
  Henry 58, 60, 61
  Hester 62
  Hugh 58
  Isabel (Gold) 57
  Isbell 61
  Isbell --- 59, 62
  Jaane 59
  James 60
  Jane 57
  Joan 57, 58
  Joan --- 57, 59, 60,
    61
  Joan --- (widow) 60,
    63
  Joane --- 60
  John 58, 61
  John (Old) 62
  John, Jr. 59, 62
  John, Jr. (?) 62
  Jone --- (widow) 63
  Josias 59
  Margaret --- 60
  Margarite 60
  Margarite --- 59
  Martha 59, 60
  Mary 58, 59, 62
  Nathanael 59, 62
  Nicholas 58, 59, 60,
    61
  Nicholas, Jr. 62
  Nicholas, Jr. (?) 59,
    62
  Nicholas, Sr. 61
  Peter 460, 489
  Phillip 59
  Phillip (or Cocke) 57
  Priscilla 59
  Rebecca --- 60
  Richard 57, 58, 59, 60,
    61, 62
  Ro. 57
  Robert 59, 62
  Rychard 58, 60, 61
  S Isbell --- 62
  Samuel 59
  Sara 59, 62
  Sara --- 62
  Sarah 60
  Susan 62

  Susanna 59, 62
  Thomas 57, 58, 59, 60,
    61, 62
  Timothie 59, 60
  William 57, 58, 59, 60,
    61
  William (Mrs.) 61
  William (Old) 62
Cocke, --- 57
  --- (Mother) 61
  --- (Mr) 378
  --- (Mr.) 384
  --- (widow) 61
  --- --- 62
  Abraham 59
  Agnes 58, 60, 62
  Agnes (or Ann) 63
  Agnes --- 59, 61, 62
  Alice 58, 60, 63, 460,
    489
  Alice --- 58, 60
  Alice --- (widow) 62
  Ann 58
  Ann (or Agnes) 63
  Ann --- 58
  Anne 60, 61, 63
  Bennet 59, 60, 61
  Christian 60
  Daniel 59
  Dorcas 59
  Dorothie --- 60
  Elenor 63
  Elizabeth 63, 460, 489
  Elyzabeth 60, 61
  Elyzabeth --- 58, 59,
    60
  Elyzabeth --- (widow)
    60, 61
  Emme --- 59
  George 59, 60, 61
  Helenor 58
  Henry 58, 60, 61, 63
  Hester 59
  Isabel 62
  Isbel --- 59, 61
  Jaane 58
  Jane 63
  Jeremie 460, 489
  Jeremy 60
  Joan 58, 60, 60, 61,
    63
  Joan (Jone?) 63
  Joan --- 57, 59, 60,
    61, 62, 63
  Joan --- (widow) 62
  Joane --- 60
  John 58, 59, 60, 61,
    62, 237, 460, 489
  Jone 58
  Jone (Joan?) 63
  Lidia 59
  Margarite 61
  Margarite --- 59, 60
  Martha 60, 63
  Martha --- 60
  Mary 63, 460, 489
  Mathew 62
  Nicholas 58, 59, 60,
    61, 62, 63
  Nicholas, Jr. (?) 59
  Phillip 62, 63
  Phillip (or Cock) 57
  Raufe 58
  Richard 60, 61, 63
  Robert 58, 63
  Rychard 58, 59, 61, 62
  Samuell 59
  Susan 59

794

Cocke (cont.)
  Symon 58
  Thomas 58, 59, 60, 61,
    62, 63
  Timothie 59
  William 57, 58, 59, 60,
    61, 62, 63
Cocker, John 247
Cockersand, --- (Abbot
  of) 741
Cockrain, Jonathan 463
  William 463
Cocks, Sibly 218
Cockson, ---
    (Grandfather) 623
  Anne 623
  Anne (Peck) 623
  Robert 623
Cocky, Thomas 78
Cocrain, Wyllyam 463
Cocus, Walter 748
Coe, Samuel 361
Coels, --- (?) 185
Coeterell, John 682
Cogan, Henry 509
  Robert 165
Cogeshall, John 429
Coggan, Edmond 206
  William (Mr.) 96, 207
Coggell, Agnes --- 596,
    597
  Robert 596, 597
Coggeshall, --- 80, 429
  Abbe --- (widow) 80
  Catherine 429
  John 80, 429, 601, 602,
    603, 666
  John (Pres.) 429
Coghsall, Marye 429
Cogishall, Jeames 429
Cok, Edward 441
Cokayn, John 654
Coke, Alys 435
  Edward 476
  John 634
  Robert 634
Coker, --- 103
  Matthew 103
  R. 269
  Thomas 186
Cokke, Joan --- 57
  John 57
  William 57, 62
Colaton, Dorothy 391
Colborn, William 322
Cole, --- 666
  Alice 660, 665, 666
  Alice --- 446
  Daniel 250
  Geo. 458
  Joan --- 620
  John 45, 121, 446, 447,
    620, 621, 631, 640,
    660, 665, 666
  Magdelyn 446
  Marie 457
  Robt. 446
Coleman, --- 653, 654,
    661
  Agnes 654
  Agnes --- 653
  Alice 654
  Anne 602, 659, 665
  Edward 654, 661
  Joan 653
  John 602, 653, 665
  John, Esq. 659
  Katherine 654
  Katherine --- 653, 654

Richard 653, 654
Robert 654
Stephen 653
William 654
Coles, Barnard 319
Colford, John 220, 221
  Margaret --- 220
Colingham, John 300
  Thomas 300
Collens, --- 251, 257
  Thomas 251, 257
Collerd, William 179
Colles, --- (Mr.) 177
  --- (widow) 76
  Humphrey, Esq. 176
  John 76
  Nicholas 76
  Roger 76
Colley, William 346
Collier, Wm 92
Colling, John (Mr) 512
Collins, --- 106, 508,
    510, 511, 512, 513,
    514, 515, 516, 517,
    519
  --- (?) 18, 107, 588
  --- (Dea.) 510
  --- (Tomson) 511
  --- --- 511, 514, 517,
    518
  Abigail 510, 513, 514,
    515, 518, 519
  Daniel 510, 511, 512,
    513, 514, 515, 517,
    518
  Daniell 513
  Edward 510, 511, 512,
    513, 516, 518, 519
  Edward (Dea.) 510, 511,
    512, 513, 516, 517
  Elizabeth 510, 513,
    514
  John 510, 511, 512,
    513, 514, 516, 517,
    518, 519
  John (?) 514, 516
  John (Rev.) 512, 517
  Katherine 514
  Katherine (Francknell)
    511, 512, 514
  Magdalen (Mandlene)
    (?) 516
  Mandelen --- 513
  Mandelene 513
  Mandelene (Cozzins)
    (?) 514
  Mandlene 513
  Mandlene (Magdalen?)
    516
  Mandlene --- 513
  Martha 510, 518, 519
  Martha --- 510, 516
  Mary 518, 519
  Nathanael 510
  Nathaniel (Rev.) 518,
    519
  Phebe 513, 516
  Phoebe 516
  Samuel 510, 511, 512,
    514, 515, 518, 519
  Samuel (Dr.) 515
  Samuel (Ensign) 517
  Samuel (Rev.) 514, 515
  Sibbil 519
  Sibilla 518
  Sible 511, 512
  Sibyl 510, 518
  Susanna 510

Susanna --- 510
Susannah 518, 519
Susannah (Roberts)
  518
Susannah --- (?) 518
Thomas 510
Collinses, Jo. 513
  Samuell 513
Collis, John 5
  Rose --- 5
  William 5
Collman, --- 652
  Abigail 658
  Anne 658
  Edm. (Edward?) 658
  Edward 658
  Edward (Edm.) 658
  Edwarde 652
  Margaret --- 658
  William 444, 658
Collyer, Thomas 298
Collyn, Agnes 150
Collyns, --- 507
  --- (cousin) 515
  Elizabeth --- 508
  Walter 508
Colman, --- 661
  --- (Gurdon) 661
  Abigail 658
  Agnes 661
  Alice 658, 661
  Ann 658, 661
  Ann --- 658
  Anne 660, 662
  Anne --- 658
  Daniel 658
  Edward 658, 659, 661
  Frances 658
  Isaac 658, 659
  Isaack 658
  Jane 658
  John 653, 658, 659,
    660, 661
  John, Esq. 662
  Joseph 658
  Judeth 658
  Judith 658
  Kateryn --- 661
  Margaret --- 659
  Mary --- 658
  Rachel 658
  Robert 658, 659
  Samuel 658
  William 659, 661
Colridge, --- (Widow)
  213
Colstone, Margery 266
Colthurst, Mathew 192,
    194
  Matthew 202
  Thomas 408
Colvord, John 220
  Nicholas 168
  Nicholas (or Calvarte)
    179, 184
Colvyle, Copyldicke 445
  Grace 446
  Grace --- 446
  John 445, 446
  Thomas 445
Colyngbourne, John 682
Combe, --- 170, 172, 174,
    175, 176
  --- (good wyfe) 178
  --- (Mistress) 177,
    178
  Andrew 44, 45
  Elizabeth 44, 172, 173,

d'Eyncourt (cont.)
  743, 744
  Robert 739, 740,
    743
  Walter 749
  Walter (or d'Aincourt)
    737
d'Oisy, --- 745
  Hugh 746
  Hugh I. 745
  Saier 746
  Simon 745
  Walter 746
Daccomb, --- 323
Dacres, --- 704
Dagger, --- (or Wagger)
    513, 514
Daincourt, Elisabeta 713
  Elisabete 713
  Elizabeth 729
  Radulpho 713
  Ralph (Sir) 729
Dajne, John 365
Dakcomb, ---, (or
    Jackson), 201
Dale, --- (?) 95, 206
  Danell 266
  Humfrey 234
Dalling, Robt 442
Dallinger, James 460
Dame, Tabitha 300
Dan, --- (Mr.) 12
Dane, Frances --- 365
  Francis (Rev.) 351,
    365, 733
  John 363, 364, 365,
    733
  John (Dr.) 366
  Mary 366
Danford, John 129
Danforth, Thomas 504,
    505
Daniel, --- 288, 503,
    504
  --- (Fanning) 504
  --- (Mrs.) 505
  Ebenezer 506
  Eleazer 506
  Elizabeth 262, 288,
    503, 504, 505, 506
  Elizabeth (Fanning)
    504
  Jeremiah 506
  Joseph 505, 522
  Mary 505, 506
  Mehetabel 506
  Rachel 506
  Rachel --- 505
  Reana --- (James,
    Andrew) 504
  Reana --- (widow) 505
  Robert 503, 504, 505,
    522
  Samuel 505, 506
  Samuell 504
  Sarah 505
  Thomas 505
  Zachariah 506
Daniell, --- (?) 55
  Elizabeth 284
  Robert 505
Dann, Robert 50
Dannett, --- (Mr) 196
  --- (Mr.) 196
  John 196
Dany, Mary 231
Darbey, --- (Mr) 127
  --- (Mr.) 110
  --- (widow) 123

Abraham 123, 124
Joane --- 98
John 110, 118, 122,
    123
Mary 124
Mathew 125
Richard 110, 127
Richard (Mr.) 110, 127
Tristrum 98
Darbeye, --- 126
--- (Mr.) 110
Darbie, Elizabeth 97
Nicholas 115
Darby, --- 99, 103, 109,
    112
Agnes 216
Agnes --- 97
Alice --- 104
Ann 96, 131
Anne 97, 104, 121, 123
Bartilmew 94
Christopher 97, 98, 99,
    102, 103, 108, 109,
    113, 115, 116
Christr 113
Cristofer 100, 101,
    109
Dorothy 97
Edith --- (widow) 97
Elizabeth 97
Henry 117, 94, 100,
    113, 114
Joan 97
Joane 113
Joane (Fowkes) 113
Joane (Peasinge) 113
Joane --- 94, 113
John 98, 99, 122, 123,
    124, 218, 219
John (A. B.) 99
John (Mr.) 122
John, Jr. 99
Laurence 99, 115
Nichas 103
Nicholas 94, 97, 99,
    103, 108, 109, 113,
    115
Oswald 98
Richard 103, 104, 105,
    106, 130
Richard (Mr.) 97, 130
Robert 97, 101, 108
Robert (Sir) 94
Robt. 276
Roger 97, 99, 115, 130,
    131
Samuel 97, 131
Samuell 97
Thomas 96, 100
Will'm 120
William 103, 110
William (Mr.) 97, 121
Darbye, --- 108
--- (Mr.) 126
Christopher 94, 100,
    102
Henry 99
Joane 97
John 218
Jone (Fowkes) 94
Jone (Peason) 94
Lawrence 94
Nicholas 94, 98, 102,
    108
Oswald 99
Richard 102, 126
Robert 98, 101
Robert (Sir) 94

Roger 94
William 110
Darcy, --- 711
--- (?) 187
Darell, Henry 186
Marmaduke 748
Dassell, Richard 210
Dasset, William 20
Davage, Richard 199
Thomas 177
Davedge, John (Mr.) 207
Davenish, Francis 328
Davesse, --- --- 230
John 230
Davey, --- 107
Andrew 107
Davidge, Anthony 3
Christopher 187, 203
John 330
John (alias Moone)
    187
Martha (alias Moone)
    187
Mary 330
Richard 186, 194, 196
Robert 330
Davie, John 212
Davies, Agnes 217
John 754, 755, 756
Davis, Aaron 34
John 260
John, Jr. 260
Mary 260
Mary --- 34
Matthew 751
Sarah 34, 405
Davy, --- 533
Jn 220
Johan 435
Mary 106
Thomas 681
William 106, 533
Davydge, --- 175
Dawes, Edmond 213
William 615
Dawley, William 179
Dawlie, --- 174
Dawlinge, Crispen 452
Dawlye, --- 175
Dawson, James 239, 250
Day, --- 41
--- --- 40
Ann 37
Edmund 428
Elizabeth 462
Grace 37, 40
Jane 37
John 425
Matthew 40, 41
Stephen 35, 37, 40, 40,
    41
Daye, John 96, 207, 425
Dayne, --- 364
John 364
Daynes, --- 583, 584
Thomas 583, 584
de Aencurt, Gervase 737,
    739
Ralph 739
de Aiencurt, Geruasio
    738
Ralph 740
de Alveston, Alan 691,
    693, 694
Helen 693
Helena 691
Nicholas 695
Torfin 693, 694, 695

799

803

Fiske (cont.)
Anne (Candler)   459,
  496
Anne (or Hannah)   496
Anne (or rather Sarah)
  498
Anne ---   455, 456, 464,
  465, 466, 486
Anne --- (Agnes or
  Annes)   486
Anne --- (Mother)   458
Annes (or Agnes)   487
Annes --- (Agnes or
  Anne)   486
Austin   482, 483, 485,
  486
Benjamin   502
Catherine   487
Christian   442, 445,
  485, 487
Christian ---   483, 596
Christiana ---   487
Clara   466, 498
Cycely   484
Daniel   481, 482
David   459, 496, 498,
  499
David (Lt.)   499
Deborah   465
Dorathe   445
Dorothie   449
Dorothy   449, 487
Easter   449, 491
Edmund   482
Edwin Burton   594
Eleazar   459, 492, 494,
  495, 496
Eleazer   459, 497
Elias (Elie)   492
Elias (Elye, Elie)
  493
Eliazar   487
Eliazer   459, 460, 494
Elie   456, 492, 493
Elie (Elias)   492
Elie (Elias, Elye)
  493
Eliezar   451, 452, 495
Elisabeth   464
Elisabeth --- (widow
  Hinchman or
  Hincksman)   501
Elizabeth   441, 456,
  458, 464, 465, 466,
  483, 485, 487, 492,
  493, 495, 496, 498,
  500, 501
Elizabeth (?)   445
Elizabeth (Barnard)
  451
Elizabeth ---   441, 449,
  451, 459, 482, 483,
  485, 495, 496, 502
Elizabeth --- (widow)
  459, 496
Elizh   456
Elye   464
Elye (Elias, Elie)
  493
Ester   447, 490, 600
Esther   459, 491, 496,
  497
Eunice   497
Faith   487
Francis   444, 466, 488
Gelion   432
Gelyon   458
Gelyon (Aldus)   492
Gelyon (Jerelon)   485

Gelyon (or Gyllyan)
  ˙92
Geo.   455, 456
Geoffrey   432, 466, 482,
  484, 492, 595, 596,
  600, 601
Geoffrey (Jeffery)
  487, 499
Geoffrey (or Jeffery)
  491, 494, 495, 496,
  497
Geoffry   479
George   432, 448, 451,
  455, 456, 458, 459,
  479, 490, 494
Gillian   593
Gillian (Jerelon)   593
Gregorie   456
Gregory   487, 488
Gyllyan (or Gelyon)
  492
Hannah   501
Hannah (Ann)   501
Hannah (or Anne)   496
Helen ---   491
Henrie   493
Henry   457, 464, 487,
  488, 493, 594
Hugh   477, 481, 482,
  594, 600
Hugh (or Fisqs)   481
Isabell ---   447
Isabella --- (widow)
  447
Jaffery (Geoffrey)
  485
James   500, 501
Jane   486
Jane ---   452
Jane --- (Borret)   489,
  490
Jane --- (widow)   490
Japherie   459
Jefferie   448, 452, 466,
  492, 495
Jeffery   458, 460, 497
Jeffery (Geoffrey)
  487, 499
Jeffery (or Geoffrey)
  491, 494, 495, 497
Jeffery or (Geoffrey)
  496
Jefferye   459, 496
Jeffrey   466, 478
Jeffreye   458
Jeffrie   479
Jene ---   464
Jerelon (Gelyon)   485
Jerelon (Gillian)   593
Jerem.   459
Jeremie   452, 490, 492
Jerome   464, 489
Jerome (or Jeromie)
  489
Jeromie   460
Jeromie (or Jerome)
  489
Jerume   465, 489
Jhon   465
Joan   441, 485, 487
Joan (Jerelon
  [Irelan?])   593
Joan ---   466, 482, 484,
  495
Joan --- (widow)   482
Joane   490
Johan   441, 445
Johane   484

Johane ---   457, 464,
  491, 600
Johane --- (widow)
  451
John   436, 437, 439,
  440, 448, 449, 450,
  451, 452, 457, 458,
  459, 463, 464, 465,
  466, 468, 470, 472,
  476, 477, 478, 479,
  482, 483, 484, 485,
  486, 487, 489, 490,
  491, 492, 496, 497,
  498, 499, 500, 501,
  502, 568, 594, 598,
  600, 601
John (Master)   482, 484
John (Mr.)   434, 466
John (Rev.)   501
John (Sir)   436, 437,
  482, 483, 485, 601
John, Sr.   466, 479
Jonas   451
Jone   436
Jone --- (widow)   450
Joseph   502
Judith   449
Katherine --- (widow)
  481
Lydia   498
Lydia ---   502
Mara   501
Margaret   443, 445, 455,
  464, 482, 484, 486,
  487, 490, 492, 493
Margaret (Bancrofte)
  492
Margaret (Wittingham)
  458
Margaret ---   465, 468,
  484, 491
Margaret --- (?)   470
Margaret --- (widow)
  444, 486
Margerie   445, 451
Margery   458, 482, 485,
  487
Margery ---   458, 485,
  499, 500
Margerye ---   458
Marie   449, 456, 457,
  465
Marie (Mary)   491, 492,
  493
Marie ---   466
Marion   486
Martha   447, 459, 466,
  490, 491, 496, 499,
  502, 600
Martha (Mathewe?)   491
Martha (Underwood)
  497, 498
Mary   444, 447, 449,
  458, 487, 488, 490,
  491, 492, 493, 498,
  500, 501, 600
Mary (Lawter)   494, 501
Mary (Marie)   491, 492,
  493
Mary (Sarah) ---
  (widow)   460
Mary ---   466
Marye   600
Maryon   484
Mathew   465, 466, 486,
  487
Mathewe   449
Mathewe (sic, Martha?)

807

Fiske (cont.)
491
Mathias 465
Mathie 464
Mathye 468, 469
Matthias 465
Milicent 458
Millicent 458
Moses 502
Nathan 498, 499
Nathan, Jr. 499
Nathaniel 459, 466,
  496, 497, 498, 502
Nicholas 436, 442, 447,
  448, 464, 465, 466,
  479, 483, 485, 490,
  491, 492, 600
Olive 485
Olive (Warne) 593
Phineas 458, 500
Phinehas 466, 501
Rachel 447, 490, 491,
  600
Ralph 444, 486
Richard 432, 451, 456,
  479, 485, 489, 492,
  493, 494, 495, 496,
  497, 499, 501, 593,
  594, 600, 601
Robert 436, 437,
  441, 442, 448,
  466, 470, 478,
  479, 485, 488,
  491, 492, 494, 495,
  496, 497, 499, 501,
  598, 601
Robert (Sir) 436, 483
Robt. 441, 449
Robt. (Sir) 437
Samuel 498, 500, 501,
  502
Sara 456, 464, 493
Sara --- 460
Sarah 497, 498, 502
Sarah (Anne?) 498
Sarah (Gale) 498
Sarah (Mary) ---
  (widow) 460
Sarah --- 460, 494
Sarah --- (widow) 460
Simon 432, 478, 481,
  482, 483, 484, 485,
  486, 489, 494, 496,
  497, 499, 501, 503,
  594, 595, 596, 597,
  598, 600, 601
Simon (?) 489, 494,
  496, 497, 499, 501
Susanna --- 498
Symon 435, 441, 479
Symon (Lord) 431
Thomas 444, 448, 451,
  452, 455, 456, 457,
  458, 459, 466, 478,
  479, 483, 485, 486,
  487, 488, 495, 496,
  499, 500, 501
Thos 455
Thos. 441, 451, 456,
  458
Urselie --- 451
Ursula --- (widow)
  451
Vid. ("Vid.") 466
W. Sanders 594
William 432, 433, 447,
  448, 449, 451, 452,
  456, 457, 459, 464,
  465, 466, 468, 474,

478, 479, 482, 483,
484, 485, 486, 487,
489, 490, 491, 492,
494, 495, 496, 497,
499, 501, 502, 593,
600
William H. 594
Witton (sic, William?)
  491
Wm. 443, 451, 466
Wyburgh 484
Fiskith, Simon (sic) 477
Fisqs, Hugh 474, 481
  Hugh (or Fiske) 481
Fitch, --- 499
  Thomas 499
Fitton, Susan 139
fitz Adam, Walter (alias
  de Strickland) 703,
  710
  Walter (or de
  Strickland) 715
fitz Alard, Richard 740
fitz Baldric, Erneburga
  (?) 746
  Hugh 746
fitz Geoffrey, William
  737
Fitz Gerald, --- 688
fitz Gerald, Roger 706
  Roger (de Romare) 705
fitz Gilbert, Bernard
  747
Fitz Henry, Henry 693
fitz Hervey, Agatha 748
  Henry 748
Fitz James, --- 90
  --- (?) 89
  James 89
  John 90
  John, Esq. 89
fitz John, Thomas 741,
  743, 749
fitz Orm, Adam 742
Fitz Other, --- 688
  Walter 688
  Walter (de Windsor)
  693
Fitz Ralf, --- --- 691
  Robert (or de
  Hastings) 687
  Robert (the Marshal)
  691
Fitz Ralph, Gilbert (?)
  687
  John (?) 687
  Robert 687
fitz Renfrid, Gilbert
  702, 705, 706, 725,
  738, 739, 741
  Helewise --- 739
  Roger 705, 706
fitz Rober le Chamurleyn,
  Orme, 738
fitz Roger, Richard 708,
  709
fitz Thomas, Patrick (de
  Curwen) 740
  Patrick (Sir) 718
Fitz Wale, --- 668, 672
  --- --- 668
  Alice 671
  Henrici (?) 671
  Henry 668, 671, 672
  John 672
  Maud --- 670
  Ralf 671, 672
  Ricard 668, 670, 671,

672
  Ricardi (?) 671
  Richard 672
  Walkelin (?) 671
fitz Walter, Adam 715
  Amabel (?) 715
  Walter 715
Fitzhale, John 668
FitzHerbert, Anthony 313
Fitzhugh, --- (Lords)
  748
Fitzpaine, Walton 103
Fitzpayne, Wotton (?)
  188
Flamell, Henry (Mr.) 72
Flanders, --- (Count
  of) 669
Flandrensis, Walter 745
  Walter (i.e., le
  Fleming) 745
Flecher, Ellis 137
Fleetwood, --- (Mr.) 136
Fleming, --- 744, 746,
  749
  Daniel (Sir) 746
  Isabel --- (Dame) 746
  Michael (Sir) 746
  Thomas 746
  Thomas (Sir) 746
  Thomas, Jr. 746
Flemming, --- 556
Fletcher, Alice 139, 141
  Alice (Dunster) 139
  Anne (Gorton) 239
  Elizabeth 137, 139
  Isabel 139
  James 135
  Jane 139
  John 136
  Richard 135
  Robert 135
  Ryc. 134
  Thomas 135
  William 137, 139, 141
Flint, Joseph 132
Flitcroft, George 236
Flouerd, Nathaniel 268
Flower, William, Esq.
  536
Foackes, Henry (alias
  Gorton) 234
Folger, --- 429
  John 429
Foliot, Gilbert 697
Foote, --- 36
  Alice --- 36
  Thomas 88
Ford, --- 88
  Agnes --- 303
  John 390, 391
  Thomas 303
Forde, Thomas 509
Fordham, --- 351
  Daniel 351
Forest, George 443
Forster, Thomas 244
Forth, Julyan (Morse)
  264, 285
Foss, --- 773
Fossard, Robert 708
Fostalfe, Elizabeth 469
  John 469
Foster, --- 242, 243,
  244
  Agnes 332
  Margaret --- (als.
  French) 236
  Thomas 243

Gollop, John 202
Golloppe, Thomas 166
Golupp, Thomas 166
Gooday, Robert 349
Goodaye, --- 373, 375
  Robarte 374
  Robt. 375
Goodday, Robert, Sr. 385
Gooddaye, Robt. 373
Gooddynge, John 78
Goodfellow, Marie 522
Goodland, Nicholas (Mr.)
  166
Goodspead, Nicholas 255
Goodspeade, Nicholas 254,
  255
Goodspede, ---na 254
  Nicholas 254, 257
  Robert 255, 257
Goodspeed, --- 251, 255,
  257, 259, 260, 261
  --- (Gurney) 258
  --- --- 252, 257, 259
  Agnes 253, 254, 259
  Agnes (Ann) 259
  Alice 253, 254, 257,
    258, 259
  Alice (Lucas) 252
  Alice --- 254, 257
  Ann 253, 254
  Ann (Agnes) 259
  Anna --- 257
  Anne 252, 258
  Anne --- 252
  Bartholomew 251
  Benett 254
  Benjamin 260
  Bennett 252, 253, 257,
    259, 260
  Dorothy 253, 258
  Ebenezer 261
  Edw. 254
  Edward 253, 257, 258
  Eliz. 253
  Elizabeth 253, 257,
    258, 259, 261
  Elizabeth (Brookes)
    252
  Elizabeth --- 253, 257
  Henry 252, 253, 259,
    260
  Hugh 251, 254
  Isabel --- 253, 254
  Jane 251, 254, 260
  Jane --- 254
  Jane --- (widow) 254
  Jo. 253, 254
  Jo: 253, 259
  Joan 253, 257, 258,
    259
  Joan (Gaffield) 252
  Joan --- 253, 258
  John 252, 253, 254,
    255, 257, 258, 259,
    260, 261
  Katheine 253
  Katherine 252, 258
  Margaret 251, 253, 254,
    257, 258, 259, 260,
    261
  Margaret --- 257
  Margaret --- (widow)
    254
  Margt. --- 253
  Mary 253, 254, 258,
    260
  Mary (Peaseley) 252
  Mary (Peeasley) 252

  Mathew 260
  Matthew 253, 258
  Nathaniel 260
  Nicholas 252, 253, 254,
    257, 258, 259, 260
  Richard 253, 259
  Robert 251, 252, 253,
    254, 255, 257, 258,
    259, 260
  Roger 251, 252, 253,
    254, 257, 259, 260,
    261
  Ruth 260
  Susan 253, 258
  Thomas 251, 252, 253,
    254, 257, 258, 259,
    260
  Thos. 253
  Weston A. 261
  Willaim 251
  William 251, 252, 253,
    254, 255, 257, 258
  Wm. 253
Goodspeede, --- 251, 252
  --- --- 252
  Alice --- 252
  Alicia 254
  Bennett 252
  Edward 251
  Henry 252
  Hugh 255
  Jane (Lucas) 252
  Jane --- 251
  John 252, 255, 257
  Margaret (Bate) 252
  Mary (Seabrooke) 252
  Mathew (Moores) 252
  Nathaniel 261
  Nicholas 254, 255
  Robert 252
  Roger 261
  Thomas 251, 252
  William 251, 254, 255
Goodwin, Anne 679
  John 679
Goodwyn, Thomas 534
Goodynche, John 440, 599
Gooinche, William 146
Goolde, Wm. 220
Goor, Robt. 446
Goorde, Isacke 231
  John 231
Goothrame, Rihard 457
Gord, Christian 231
  John 231
Gordon, --- 660
  Allice 660
  John 616, 626, 644
  John (Gordonys) 651
  John, Esq. 660
  Richard 627
  Robert (sic) 604
  Robert, Esq. 660
Gordonys, John (?) 651
Gore, William (Sir) 269
Gorges, Ferdinando (Sir)
  230, 232
  Thomas 232
Gorham, John 124
  Jonas 300, 310
  Jonas (Gorram) 302
Gorram, Jonas (Gorham)
  302
Gortō, Edmund 239
Gorton, --- 232, 233,
  238, 240, 241, 242,
  244, 247, 249
  --- --- 238, 240, 247,

    249
  --- --- (widow) 233
  Adam 235, 236, 237,
    238, 239, 240, 247
  Adame 235
  Agnes 233
  Agnes --- 249
  Ales (Hudson) 236
  Alice 233, 238, 239,
    248
  Alice (alias Carter)
    234
  Alice --- (widow) 236
  Ann 239, 240, 250
  Ann --- (widow) 247
  Anna 239
  Anne 239, 250
  Anne --- 235, 248
  Anne --- (widow) 240
  Benjamin 249
  Catherine 235
  Catterin --- 237
  Cicely 240
  Cicely --- 248
  Dorothie --- 236
  Edmunde 239
  Edward 235, 239, 240,
    247, 250
  Edwarde 239
  Elizabeth 234, 235,
    238, 239, 246, 247,
    248, 250
  Elizabeth (alias
    Carter) 234
  Elizabeth --- 240
  Elizabeth --- (?) 248
  Elizabeth --- (widow)
    240, 248
  Elizabethe 238
  Ellen 248, 250
  Ellen --- (widow) 246
  Ellin 239, 240
  Elline 238, 239
  Ellys 246
  Elys 246
  Frances 240
  Francis 234, 240, 241,
    247, 248, 249, 250
  Francys 240
  Frannces 233, 238, 239
  Franncis 238, 239, 240
  Franncys 238, 240
  Georg 238
  George 238, 239, 240,
    248, 250
  Grace 239
  Grace --- (widow) 242
  Henrie 234
  Henry 242
  Henry (alias Foackes)
    234
  Isabel 250
  Isabell 239
  Isabell --- 234, 240
  Issabell 235, 238, 239,
    240
  Issabell --- 235
  James 233, 236, 238,
    239, 240, 241, 248
  Jane 240
  Jane --- 240
  Joan --- 233, 248
  Joane --- (widow) 240
  Johane (Smethurste)
    (?) 235
  John 234, 237, 238,
    239, 240, 246, 249
  Jone --- 238

Gorton (cont.)
Katharine --- 240
Katherin 233, 239
Katherine 238, 240, 248
Katherine --- (widow) 240
Mahershalalhashbaz 250
Margaret 234, 235, 250
Margaret --- 234, 240
Margerye 240
Margrett 239
Marie 239
Marie (Knott) 236
Martha 238, 239, 240, 248
Mary 235, 237, 238, 239, 250
Marye 239, 240
Marye (Boothe) 239
Nicholas 235, 238, 240, 246, 247, 248
Nichols 239
Nicolas 242
Rauffe 240
Ric. 233
Ric: 238
Richard 233, 236, 240, 242, 246, 247, 248, 250
Robarte 239
Robert 233, 236, 240, 241, 242
Roger 246
Samuel 232, 233, 235, 238, 239, 242, 244, 247, 248, 249, 250
Samuell 239, 240, 244
Sarah 250
Susanna 250
Tho: 240
Thomas 232, 233, 234, 235, 236, 237, 238, 239, 240, 241, 246, 247, 248, 249, 250
Thomas (Bridge?) 248
William 233, 235, 238, 239, 240, 241, 242, 247, 248, 249, 250
Wm. 240
Gortonn, Franncis 238
George 238
Margaret 238
Thomas 238, 240
William 238
Gortonne, Adam 238
Adame 238
Elizabeth --- (widow) 240
Otywell 238
Samuell 238
Thomas 238, 240
William 238
Williame 238
Gortoun, William 234
Gorum, John, Sr. 124
Gory, --- (?) 640
Gosling, Anthony 395
Gosnold, John 769, 772
Gosse, Sam 657
Thomas 657
Gostwyk, John (Sir) 257
Gostwyke, John 255
Gould, James 34
William 102, 114, 116
Gourdon, John 605, 626, 641, 648
Robert 605, 640, 648

Grace, Alice 254, 259
Richard 61
Grafton, Elizabeth (Sanders, Kitchen) 42
Joseph 506
Gransen, James 649
Grant, Mary 505
Grante, John 60
Grauer, Thomas 237
Graver, Thomas 235
Graves, Dorcas 352
Hannah 353
Mark 352, 353
Gray, George 213, 214
Hannah 353
Margaret 363
Sara --- 214
Graye, George 213
Greade, Richard 231
Greatrake, Tho: 464
Gredy, Jasper 323
Green, Anne 239
Francis 397
Prensall (?) 268
Greene, --- 250
Anne 248
John 108
John (Mr.) 544
Maryan --- 268
Peter 250
Robert 157
Roberte 149
Thomas 268, 353
Thomas (Cousin) 268
Greenehalghe, Richard 136
Greeneham, Oliver (Mr.) (?) 37
Greenestrete, George 6
Greenhalgh, John 138
John, Jr. 138
Richard 135
Greenhalghe, William 136
Greenhill, --- 507
Elizabeth --- (widow) 508
Nicholas 508
Peter 508
Gregorie, John (alias Whetcombe) 94, 114
Thomas 206
Gregory, Agnes 61, 63
John 63
Judah 417
Grelley, Joan 726
Grene, --- 543, 548
--- (Mr. Doctor) 438
Chepenell 495
Henry 612, 615, 617
John 191, 546
John (Mr.) 544, 545, 550, 552
Kateryn 543
Katherine 547
Richard 146, 147
Robert 534
Thomas 540, 543, 547, 548
William 543, 547
Wylliam 434
Grenealgh, Thomas 138
Grenehaulghe, Richard 138
Greneleff, John 616
Grenlyng, Tho: 652
Grenmere, Roger 441
Grennaugh, John 136

Grenough, Oliver 36
Oliver (Mr.) 36, 39
Oliver (Mr.) (?) 37
Grenwud, Oliver (Mr.) (?) 37
Gresham, --- 174
Gressham, John 174
Gretason, John 722, 730
Grey, --- (?) 362, 395
--- (Master) 100
Geo. 221
Henry (Sir) 769, 771
John (Sir) 99, 112
Robert (Sir) 89
Thomas 101
Walter 100
Walter, Esq. 100, 101
Greystoke, --- 703
--- (Lords) 749
Ivo 749
Gribham, Thomas (?) 20
Gridley, Richard 41
Griffith, James 27
Grimshaw, Agnes 232, 239, 249
Agnes (Gorton) 232
Raphe 236
Grinhalgh, Richard 135
Grinnell, Matthew 63
Grome, Robert 65
Gromishaw, James 236
John 236
Gronshay, Thomas 579
Groome, Robert 65
Grove, John 15
Grover, Abigail 312
James 312
Rychard 58
Gryce, John 358
Gryffin, William 60
Gryggs, Thomas 438
Grynehaulgh, John, Esq. (Mr.) 135
Guddicker, Elizabeth 234
Gudeberd, John 727
Gudspede, Richard 255
Gulliler, Catherine 330
Gunnison, Hugh 345, 346
Guppie, John 103
William 103
Guppy, Ezekiel 55
Gurden, John 642
Gurden, Robert 603, 642, 643
Gurdon, --- 601, 602, 603, 609, 616, 625, 626, 627, 628, 640, 643, 644, 645, 648, 649, 651, 652, 656, 659, 660, 661, 662, 663, 665
--- (Appleton) 653
--- (Butter) 661
--- (Colman) 661
--- (Fox) 661
--- (Lawrence) 661
--- (Wincoll) 661
--- --- 660, 664
Agnes 650, 664
Alice 649, 659, 661, 664, 665, 666
Alice --- 604, 606, 663, 665
Alis 649
Ann 664
Anne 602, 641, 649, 665
Anne (Butter) 666

813

Haskett (cont.)
  47, 48, 49, 49, 50,
  51, 52, 326
Elias (Capt.) 27
Elias (Col.) 27
Elias (Ellis) 25, 28,
  29, 29, 587
Elias (Gov.) 28
Elias (Mr.) 50
Elias (or Ellis) 44,
  326, 331
Elias, Esq. (Hon.
  Col.) 28
Elizabeth 4, 25, 26,
  29, 47, 325
Elizabeth (Dynn) 131,
  132
Elizabeth (Young) 8
Elizabeth --- 1, 4, 8,
  25, 26, 29
Elizabeth --- (widow)
  48
Elize 14
Elizeno 4
Elizer, Sr. 3
Elizeus 313, 330
Elizeus (Ellis) 330
Ellioc 8
Ellis 2, 5, 5, 8, 15,
  16, 17, 23, 28, 44,
  323, 324, 325, 326,
  327, 329, 330, 332,
  590
Ellis (?) 25, 28, 29,
  324
Ellis (Elias) 25, 28,
  29, 29, 587
Ellis (Elizeus) 330
Ellis (or Elias) 44,
  326, 331
Ellis, Jr. 16, 331
Ellis, Sr. 16, 330,
  331
Elnor 3
Frances 29
Hanna 28
James 316
Jane 29
Joan 3, 29
Joan --- 3, 29, 317
Joane 6
John 3, 4, 4, 6, 8, 25,
  29, 45, 313, 316, 317,
  319, 320, 321, 322,
  323, 330
Jonathan 29
Judith --- 317, 318
Margaret 25, 316, 330
Margaret --- 12, 315
Margaret --- (widow)
  316, 317
Margarett 4
Marie 5
Martha 28, 132
Martha --- 3, 331
Martha --- (widow)
  325
Mary 3, 8, 9, 10, 28,
  29, 29, 46, 326, 331
Mary (Hoddinot) 9
Mary --- 4, 9, 11, 18,
  19, 29, 49, 49, 52,
  326, 331
Michael 6
Rebecca --- 45, 318,
  331
Robert 4, 317, 318,
  330
Roger 330

Samuel 29
Sara 28, 29
Sarah 9, 46
Sarah --- 28
Stephen 1, 2, 4, 6, 8,
  8, 9, 9, 19, 22, 23,
  24, 25, 26, 27, 28,
  29, 29, 43, 44, 45,
  47, 48, 51, 52, 131,
  132, 312, 317, 323,
  325, 329, 330, 332,
  586
Stephen 590
Susanna 29
Susanna (Hobbs) 9
Susannah (widow Hobbs)
  46
Thomas 4, 29, 29, 44,
  45, 327, 330
William 3, 4, 5, 6, 6,
  8, 10, 11, 12, 15, 17,
  18, 22, 23, 24, 25,
  29, 45, 313, 314, 315,
  316, 317, 318, 319,
  320, 321, 322, 323,
  324, 325, 327, 328,
  329, 330, 331
Willm 4
Wm. 319, 322
Haskette, Ellis 5
Haskine, --- --- 236
  Edward 236
Haskit, --- 2
Haskitt, Elias 2
  Elizabeth 2, 26
  Elizabeth (Mrs.) 2
  Ellis 5
  Hannah 2
  Martha 2
  Mary 2
  Sarah 2
  Stephen 2
Haskot, Elizabeth --- 3
  Elizog (?) 3
  Ellis 3
  Joan 3
  Joan --- 3
  Mary 3, 29
  Robert 3
  Samuel 3
  William 3
  Wm. 3
Haskott, Elizabeth --- 3
  Ellis 3
  Jane 3
  Joan 3
  Joan --- 3
  Johanna 3
  John 318, 319
  Mary 3
  Mary --- 3
  Rebecca --- 3
  Samuel 3
  Sara 3
  William 3, 318
  Wm. 3
Hassem, Joan 330
Hasset, Jane (Mestresse)
  771
Hasting, Edward (Sir) 71
Hastings, --- 686, 687,
  688, 693, 694, 696,
  698, 699
  --- (Lord) 721
  --- (Lords) 689, 691
  Emma 699
  William 531
  William (Lord) 686

Hatheern, Robert 680
Hathorn, --- 680
  Thomas 680
  William 680
Hathorne, --- 87, 89,
  679, 680, 682, 684
  Christopher 685
  Elizabeth 88
  Elizabeth --- (Bishop)
    87
  Henry 679
  Jane 87
  Joan (Winch) 92
  Joan (Winch) (or
    Joane) 91
  Joan --- 684
  Joane 92
  Joane (Winch) 92
  Joane (Winch) (or
    Joan) 91
  John 2, 87, 87, 679,
    685
  John (or Horthorne)
    88
  Jone 88, 685
  Jone --- 89
  Marie 88
  Nathaniel 88, 89, 90,
    91, 92
  Richard 88
  Robert 87, 88, 89, 679,
    680
  Thomas 87, 88, 89, 679,
    680, 684, 685
  William 87, 88, 91, 92,
    680, 684, 685
  William (Maj.) 87, 92,
    680
Hatton, --- (Mr.) 236
Hauersham, Thomas 295
Haughe, William 479
Haunce, Richard 251
Haurmersham, Nicholas
  299
Hause, --- 449
  Rychard 449
Hauthorne, Nathaniel 89
Haward, Nicholas 457
  William 457
Hawers, --- (?) 356
Hawes, --- 583, 584
  Edmund 123
  Robert 577, 583, 584,
    592
  Rychard 61
Hawis, John 447
Hawkins, Thomas 506
Hawkyns, George 357
Hawle, Robert 459
  Thomas 239, 248
Hawly, --- (Mr.) 269
  --- --- 269
Hawthorn, Robert 680
  Thomas 680
Hawthorne, --- 680, 681
  Nathaniel 87, 91
  William 90, 91, 680
  William (Maj.) 679
  William, Jr. 680
Hawton, George 397
Haydocke, Lawrence 234
Haydon, Alan 209
Haye, John 82
Hayes, --- (?) 36
  Helen 460
Haylett, Susan ---
  (widow) 429
Hayne, --- 331, 332, 587

March (cont.)
Nicholas 412
Peter 414
Richard 417
Stephen, Esq. 508
Thomas 407, 408
Ulalia 406, 407, 412,
415, 418, 419, 421
Ulalia (Burt) 419
Ulalia (or Eulalia)
416
William 407, 408, 415,
420, 421, 422
William, Sr. 414
Margaret 212, 214
Marche, --- 407, 420,
421, 422
--- --- 419
Alce (Alice) 422
Alce --- 420
Alice 422
Alice (Alce) 422
Ames 409, 423
Amias (or Amyas) 423
Amyas 422
Amyas (or Amias) 423
Elizabeth 412, 422,
423
Geo. 415
George 420
Grace 414, 420
Grace (Neale) 407, 420
Jane 420, 423
Jane (Bickforde) 407,
420
Joane 420
Joane (Hinde?) 407,
420
Joane --- 407, 421
Joane --- (Martyn?)
421
Joane --- (widow) 420
Johane 423
Johane --- (widow)
407, 420, 421, 423
John 412, 414, 419
Marie 408, 422, 423
Mary 411, 420, 422,
423
Nichola 414
Nicholas 412
Peter 414, 419
Prudence 421
Prudence (Jackson?)
407, 420
Richard 407, 414, 419,
420, 421
Robert 414, 419
Sarah 421
Sarah (Pounde) 407,
420
Thomas 407, 422, 423
Thos. 414
Ulalia 422
Will 414, 419
Will. 415
William 406, 414, 419,
420, 421, 422, 423
William, Sr. 419
Marden, John 302, 310
Nicholas 356
Maris, Mary (?) 150, 153
Marketman, Richard 295
Roger 295
Markham, --- (cousin)
511
--- --- 511
Marler, Raffe 235
Robarte 235

Marlere, Isabel --- 609
William 609
Marrance, Robert 300
Marrante, Robert 300
Marsh, --- 351, 430
Henry 430
Thomas 32
Marshal, ---, (Earls of
Pembroke) 687, 691
--- (House of) 687
William 739
Marshall, John 543, 600
William 738
Marshe, --- 350
--- (Abbott) 350
William 531, 534
Marsshe, --- 531
Marten, Henry 408, 422
Richard 411, 446
Robert 446, 447
Robt. 447
Martin, --- 681, 682
Agnes --- 681
Edward (alias Ellis)
448
John 524
Lucy --- (widow) 411,
423
Richard 411
Richd. 411, 424
Tho:, Sr. 650
Thomas 664, 681, 685
Tom 154
Martine, --- (Uncle) 408,
422
Martyn, --- 146, 421,
682
--- (?) 448
Christian 423
Christian (Heale or
Hele) 422
Chrystijan 408
Chrystyan 409
Hannah 391
Heale 408
Henry 100, 408, 421,
422, 423
Henry (Mr.) 408, 421,
422, 423
Henry (Rev.) 421, 423
Joan (?) (March) 417
Joane (?) (Marche)
421
John 409, 423, 681,
682
John, Jr. 682
Late (?) 411
Luce 408, 414
Luce --- 409, 422
Lucee --- 409
Lucy --- 421, 423
Peter 409, 423
Richard 408, 409, 423,
424
Richd. 411, 424
Robert 82
Thomas 87, 187, 408,
423
Thomas, Jr. 650
Thomas, Sr. 650
William 607, 609
Martyne, Henrie (Mr.)
408, 422
Marvin, Mary 518
Mary --- 518
Reynold 518
Mascherel, --- (Robert?)
697

Alexander 696, 697
Cecily --- 696
Edith 696, 697
Emengarde --- 692
Robert (?) 697
Walter 692, 696, 697
William (?) 692, 697
Mashcal, Margaret 609
Margaret --- (widow)
609
Mason, --- (?) 145
--- (Mr.) 154
John (Capt.) 524
Robert 108, 114, 235
Thomas 193
Masshantampaine, --- 122,
123
Masters, Ralphe 211
Matchet, --- 502
Bridget 502
Mather, Cotton 517, 519
Nathaniel (Rev.) 517
Mathew, George 380
Nicholas 678
Mathewe, --- 381
Francis (als. Saunton)
349
George 380, 381, 386
John (alias Philip)
147
Mathie, Eleanor 402
Matlat, Anna (or
Motley) 365
Matthew, Richard 178
Matthews, Robert 90
Maunsell, Elizabeth ---
539
John 539
Maurice, --- (Prince)
110
Anne (Locke) 491
Maverick, Nath. 337
Nathaniel 337, 340
Samuel 337
Samuel (Mr) 340
Mavericke, Nathaniel 337
Maxwell-Lyte, Henry
Churchill, (Sir) 228
Maycock, John 6
Mayes, Elizabeth ---
(Barwar) 597
James 597
Mayne, John 95, 167, 299
Maysten, John 609
Mayston, John 606, 607
Mcdowe, Aldus 476
Meadowcroft, Ann 136
Margaret --- (widow)
138
Meane, Henry 473, 474
Mears, William 332
Meaulx, John 769, 772
Medcalf, --- 425
Leonard 425
Michael 53
Sara --- 53
Thomas 53, 427
Medcalfe, --- --- 426
Adam 426
Augustine 425, 427
Dionis --- (alias
Parker) 426
Elizabeth 53
Geoffrey 426, 427
Jeffery 426, 427
Jeffry 426
Martha 53
Mary (Saray) 53

Moone (cont.)
202
Gilbert 188, 196
Joan 186, 187, 203
Joan (alias Mohun)
200, 202
Joan --- (Howman)
(alias Mohun) 227
John 186, 187, 188,
189, 191, 203
John (alias Davidge)
187
John (alias Mohun)
202
Margaret 187, 189
Margaret (alias Mohun)
200, 201, 202
Margaret --- 171, 187,
189, 194
Margaret --- (widow)
187, 195, 196, 622
Martha 186, 203
Martha (alias Davidge)
187
Mary 187
Mary (alias Mohun)
200, 201, 202
Max (Mr) 201
Maximilian 187, 188,
191, 194, 195, 197
Maximilian (alias
Mohun) 201, 202
Maximilian, Esq. 189
Maximilian, Esq.
(alias Mohun) 201
Meliora 189
Meliora (alias Mohun)
201
Meliora --- 188
Morgaine 171
Morgan 171, 181, 186,
187, 188, 192, 194,
197, 198, 202, 203
Richard 170, 171, 186,
187, 192, 194, 195,
196, 197, 202, 203
Richard (alias Mohun)
199, 200, 227
Robert 116, 170, 171,
180, 186, 187, 188,
189, 190, 191, 192,
193, 194, 195, 196,
197, 198, 205, 622
Robert (alias Mohun)
180, 186, 200, 201,
202, 203, 204, 228
Robert, Esq. (alias
Mohun) 202
Robert, Jr. 189
Thomasine (alias
Mohun) 202
Walter 171, 186, 188,
192, 193, 194, 195,
196, 197, 198, 202
Walter (alias Mohun)
200
Water 191
Moore, Aphrodoza ---
(Mrs.) 68
Elizabeth 290
Elizabeth (Morse) 290
Jeffery 184
Jeffery, Esq. 179
Ralph 65
Richard 518
William 68
Moores, --- 260
John 5
Mary 252, 260

Mathew 252
Morant, --- 770
More, --- (Mr.) 176
--- --- (Widow) 631
George 543, 548
Helen 217
John 498
Kateryn 543
Katherine 548
Marie 543, 548
Thomas (Rt. Hon.) 532
Moreton, Robert 472
Morgan, Anne --- 100
Cristofer, Esq. 100
Luodovic 10
Mary --- 10
Morise, Philip 275
Morriff, --- (Mistris,
widow) 275
Morris, Abraham 319
Judith --- (widow)
267, 290
Richard 249
Robert 756
Thomas 6
William 578
Morrison, Richard (?)
559
Morriss, --- (Mistris,
widow) 275
Morrys, Anne 578
Mors, Anne 271
Daniel 268
Daniell 268, 269, 270
Jane 271
John 268, 269, 272
Joseph 268, 269
Josephe 272
Nathaniel 268, 271
Nathaniell 269
Philip 271
Richard 269
Robert 268
Samuel 268
Samuell 269
Sarae 269
Thomas 268, 269, 270,
271
Thomas (Mr.) 270
Morse, --- 262, 263, 264,
266, 267, 268, 270,
275, 276, 277, 278,
279, 281, 282, 283,
284, 285, 286, 287,
288, 289, 290, 291,
292
--- (Grandfather) 505
--- (Mr.) 285, 292
--- (Wellam?) 263
--- --- 279, 283, 504
--- --- (Widow) 264,
290
Abigail 288, 290
Abigail --- 283
Abner (Rev.) 278, 285,
290
Agnes --- 263, 278
Agnes --- (Mosse) 280
Agnes --- (widow) 281
Ales --- (sic) 271
Alice 263, 279, 284
Alice --- 267
Ann 274
Ann --- 265
Ann --- (widow) 288
Anne 276, 279, 280
Anne --- 271, 275, 284
Annes 264, 282

Anthonie 277
Anthony 263, 264, 277,
285
Asabell (?Asahell)
275
Asahel (or Azaell)
285
Asahell (?Asabell)
275
Azaell 264
Azaell (or Asahel)
285
Azell 264
Barbara --- (widow)
269
Bathiah (Perry) 289
Bathsheba (Bathshua)
289
Bathsheba (Fiske) 289
Bathshua (Bathsheba)
289
Benjamin 268, 283
Bethia 288, 289, 290
Brian 271
Bridget 276, 279
Daniel 262, 281, 282,
283, 285, 286, 287,
288, 289, 291
Daniell 263, 266, 269
Dinah --- 291
Dorcas 289
Dorothe 267
Dorothe --- 267
Dorothy 282
Dorothy --- 262, 290,
291
Dorothy --- (widow)
267
Edward 263, 264, 266,
276, 277, 284, 285
Elizabeth 262, 264,
267, 271, 273, 280,
281, 282, 283, 288,
289, 290, 291, 503,
504, 522
Elizabeth (Daniel)
504
Elizabeth --- 262, 263,
264, 265, 267, 277,
282, 284, 285, 286,
287, 288, 291
Ephraim 288
Esther 291
Ezra 288
Francis 265, 274, 276,
280
Hanna 271, 283
Hannah 289, 291
Henry 276
Henry (alias Femall)
168
Isaac 291
J. Howard 278, 288
James 263, 267, 269,
271, 282, 283, 284,
286, 289
Jeames 266
Jeremiah 271, 283, 286,
289, 290, 291
Jeremie 265, 271, 279
Jeremy 276, 283
Jeremye 263
Jerimiah 265
Joan 271, 279
John 262, 263, 264,
265, 267, 269, 270,
271, 273, 274, 275,
276, 279, 280, 282,

828

Morse (cont.)
283, 284, 285, 287,
288, 291
John (Mr.) 266, 283,
286
John (Rev.) 278, 282
Jonathan 289, 291
Jone 263
Joseph 262, 263, 264,
265, 266, 267, 272,
273, 276, 278, 280,
282, 283, 284, 285,
286, 287, 288, 289,
290, 291, 292, 503
Joseph, Jr. 276, 282
Joseph, Sr. 265, 290
Josephe 272
Judith 271
Judith --- 266
Katherine 263, 279
Katherine --- 263, 279
Lancelot 280, 283
Lawrence (alias
Femall) 168
Lawrence (alias
Femell) 168
Lydia 265, 274, 280,
282, 289
Lydia (Wight) 289
Margaret 263, 264, 271,
276, 279, 280, 281
Margaret --- 264, 266,
272, 276, 282
Margereth 266
Margerie 281
Margery --- 271
Marie 272
Martha 269
Mary 262, 270, 271,
272, 275, 276, 280,
283, 286, 289, 291
Mary (Bullen) 287
Mary (Sister) 264
Mary (West) 289
Mary --- 268, 285
Michaell 270
Nath'l 271
Nathaniel 263, 264,
268, 270, 271, 281,
283, 285, 286, 288,
289
Nathaniell 266
Nicholas 276
Obadiah 289
Obediah 289
Philip 263, 281, 283,
286
Phillip 266
Rachel 288
Rachel --- 284
Recherd 266
Richard 263, 265, 266,
270, 271, 275, 276,
277, 278, 279, 280,
281, 283, 285, 290
Robert 263, 265, 268,
269, 271, 272, 274,
275, 276, 278, 279,
280, 281, 283, 284,
285, 290, 579
Robt. 266
Ruth 288
Samuel 262, 263, 264,
265, 270, 273, 278,
282, 283, 284, 285,
286, 287, 288, 289,
291, 292, 503, 504
Samuel, Jr. 270
Samuell 266, 273

Sara 263, 270, 271,
276, 281, 282, 283,
285, 286, 289, 290
Sarah 289, 291
Sarah (Hornigold) 268
Sidney (Mrs.) 263
Spachett 269
Susan 268
Susan --- (Morse) 268
Thomas 262, 263, 271,
272, 274, 276, 279,
280, 281, 282, 283,
286, 288, 290
Thomas (?) 283, 290
Thomas (Rev.) 278, 280,
281, 282, 283, 284,
285, 286, 287, 290,
292
Thos. 276
Wellam 263
William 263, 264, 269,
270, 275, 276, 279,
284, 285
Wm. 271, 275
Morss, Edw. 275
John 275
Margarett 273
Marye 275
Rachell 275
Sara 275
Wm. 275
Morsse, --- (Mother) 275
--- --- 274, 280
Agnes --- (widow) 274,
275
Alice 275
Ann 274
Anne 274, 275
Anne --- 275
Briget 274
Charles 272
Edward 277
Elizabeth 274, 280
Elizh. 274
Francis 274
George 274
Jeremie 274
John 274, 275
John, Jr. 274
John, Sr. 275
Katherine 274, 279
Katherine --- (widow)
275, 279
Leedye 275
Margarite 274
Margerie 274
Nath'l 275
Richard 274, 275, 280
Robert 274, 275, 276
Robt. 274, 275
Susan 272
Thomas 274, 275
William 274
Wm. 275
Morton, Nathaniel 232
Morys, John 209
Mose, Alce --- 267
Anne --- 271
Henry 277
John 274
Margett (Bechshop)
267
Richard 275
Robard 274
Samuell 267
Wm. 275
Moseley, --- 242
Rowland, Esq. 242

Moss, --- --- (Widow)
271
Ann 270, 271
Goodman Jeremy 271
Henry 270
Jeremy (Goodman) 271,
283
John 270, 273
Martha --- 270
Mosse, --- 265, 267
--- (Mr.) 276, 282
--- --- 263
Abigael --- 267
Abigail 268
Abigail --- (widow)
268
Abigall --- 267
Agnes --- 263, 279,
280, 283
Agnes --- (Morse) 280
Alice 279
Amye --- 273
Anne 272, 275, 280
Anne --- 272, 275
Benjamin 272
Charles 269
Chas. 269
Daniel, Jr. 268
Daniel, Sr. 268
Elizabeth 275, 280
Elizabeth --- 273
Elizh. 274
Elizh. (Mary) 274
Francis 269, 275
Geo. 275
George 274
Gervase 269
Grace 274, 275
James 271
Jeames 272
Jeremy 265, 267
John 263, 272, 273,
274, 275, 276, 280,
281
John --- 273
Joseph 269, 274
Josephe 272
Judith --- (widow)
272
Katherin --- 275
Katherine 279
Lancelot 263
Margaret 263, 272
Margaret --- 272
Margery 275
Margt. 265
Marie 274
Mary 265, 269, 272,
273
Mary (Elizh.) 274
Mary --- 269
Rich. 275
Richard 263, 264, 270,
271, 272, 273, 274,
275, 280, 281
Robert 263, 264, 269,
271, 272, 275, 280
Robert (Mr.) 269
Robertt (sic) 275
Robt. 269, 271, 274
Robte 271, 272
Robte. 271, 272
Ruth --- 273
Samuel 269
Susa --- 272
Susan 272
Susan --- 272
Thomas 263, 271, 273,

829

Mosse (cont.)
  280, 281
  William 271, 272, 274,
    275
  Wm. 269
Mosy, Edward 267
  James 267
  Robart 267
Mote, Thomas 218
Motley, Anna, (or
    Matlat), 365
Mott, Mark 515
  Mark 514
  Mark (Rev.) 515
Moun, Roberti (alias
    Mohun) 200, 201
Moundyn, Thomas 108
Moundyne, --- 108
Mounk, Agnes --- (Leme)
    610
  Richard 610
Mounke, Richard 610
Mountjoy, George 231
Mountjoye, George 230
Mouse, Grisle 271
  Wm. 271
Mower, Margaret --- 303
  William 303
Mowling, Ann 458
Mowne, Joan ---
    (Howman) 229
  Richard 228, 229
  Robert 229
  Walter 229
Moyne, Richard 228
Moyon, --- 199
Moyse, Henry 277
  John 606, 610, 613
Mugford, --- 28
  George (Capt.) 28
Mullyns, Robert 220
Mulsho, --- 519
  Robert 521
  Thomas, Esq. 521
  William 521
  William, Esq. 521
Mulshoe, Robert, Esq.
    520
  Thomas, Esq. 520
  William 520
  William, Esq. 520
Mun, --- 185
  John (Muns) 179
  Thomas 185
Munchensy, --- 704
Munck, Henry (or Monck)
    359
Munn, --- 417
  Benjamin 417
Munnings, John 51
Munns, John 395
Muns, Elizabeth 179
  John (Mun) 179
Murdac, Geoffrey 747
  Helewise 747
Murdocke, Thomas 634
Murton, --- 472
  Robert 472
Musgrame, --- 555
Musket, Henry 579
Muskett, --- 660
  Henry 578
Mustel, Alan 714
  Roberto 738
  William 714
Mychell, Agnes 217, 223
  Henry 187
Mydcallf, John 425
Myldenale, William 614,
    615
Myles, John 450
Myller, Thomas 350
Mylnes, John 544, 545,
    546, 550, 552
Mylys, Robert 620
Mynoot, William 615
Mynot, Will 651
  William 614, 615, 651
Mynott, --- 615
  John 615, 621, 627,
    641

N

Narracot, David 413
Nash, Christian 402
Natsorda, --- (?) 555
Nayle, John 324
Nayler, Richard 544, 551
Neale, --- 420
  Alexr. 213
  George 219
  Joan 216, 218, 223
  John 84, 216, 218
  Thomas 217, 218
  William 216, 219
Nell, Rich 559
Nelson, Willm 129
Nepe, Richd 442
Nesmith, Robert 27
Nethersole, John, Esq.
    164, 181
Nettar, John 296
Nevard, Henry 611
Neve, Elizabeth 445
  Jaffrey 443
  Jeffery 457
Nevell, Thomas 644
Neves, --- 596
  Agnes 80
  Agnes (Payne) 78
  Ann (or Agnes) (Payne)
    79
Nevill, Thomas 641
Neville, --- 642, 706
  Elizabeth 711
  Thomas 642, 643
Newby, Agnes ---
    (widow) 681
Newcomen, Anna 504
Newe, --- 108
Newell, Richard 251
Newenden, Joan --- 304
  William 304
Newman, --- (Mr.) 394,
    397
  Barnaby (Mr.) 394, 397
  John 148, 251, 450
  Richard 212
  Thomas 291
Newport, Emanuel 207
  Florence 207
  Frances 207
Newporte, Florence 207
Newson, John 598
  Thomas 465, 486
Newstubbes, --- (Mr.)
    653
Newton, --- 448
  --- (Mr.) 635
Neylsonn, Agnes 82
Nicarson, --- (Goodman)
    123
  --- (Widow) 124
  Goodman 123

Nicholas 125
Nicolas 122
Willam 122
Nicholl, John 595
Nicholls, John 172
Nichols, --- 720
  Erasmous 513
  Richard (alias
    Smethurst) 135
Nicholson, Mary --- 247
  Marye 239
  Paul 247
Nickerson, --- 125
  --- --- 124
  Elizabeth 124, 125
  Hester 125
  John 124, 125
  Mary 125
  Nicholas 124, 125
  Patience 124, 125
  Sarah 125
  William 124, 125
Nicolson, --- 702, 712,
    713, 714, 720, 729,
    768
Nicson, --- (Mr.) 251
Ninezergh, Orm (de
    Niandsherg) 739
Nobbes, Simunde 447
Nobill, Joane --- 356
  John 356
Noble, Christopher 679
Noblett, Anthony 497
Nodds, Robert 376
Nokes, Joan --- 306
  Thomas 306
Noleth, John 482
  Nicholas 482
Nollothe, John 442
Noloth, John 433, 440,
    594, 595, 599
  Nicholas 433, 594, 595,
    596
  Robert 474, 596
Nolothe, John 475
Nombonne, --- 556
Nomys, John 175
Norfold, --- (Earl of)
    676
Normandy, --- (Dukes
    of) 737
Nurres, John 88
Norrice, Henry 234
  James 234
Northen, Thomas 615
Northumberland, ---
    (Earl of) 703, 749
Norton, --- 537, 539,
    557, 566, 567, 568,
    635
  --- (Peck) 634, 635
  --- (Peck) (?) 567
  --- (Pecke) 539
  Bonus 393
  Elizabeth 567, 568
  Francis 567, 568
  George 567, 568
  Joane 567
  Johane 567
  John 545, 551
  Jone 567, 568
  Jone (Joone) --- 568
  Jone --- 566, 567
  Joone 567, 568
  Joone --- 566
  Mary --- 567, 568
  Richard 566, 567, 568
  Robert 443, 535, 566,

830

Payne (cont.)
Phebe 78
Richard 78, 80
Robert 78, 79
Roger 78
Rose 78
Susan 79
Thomas 78, 80, 167
Walter 79
William 78, 79, 80
William (Sir) 530
Wm. 569
Paynne, John (sic) 78
Peacock, Robert 153
Pearce, --- 340
Ancilla 206
Anne 34
John 34, 214, 340
William 206
Pearse, --- 449
--- (goodman) 123
Andrew 407
Elizabeth --- 122
Johan 407
Robert 449
Willam (sic) 122
William 123
Wm. 449
Pearson, Robert 590, 591
Peaseley, --- 258
Hugh 252, 258
William 252, 258
Peasinge, --- 113
Joh: 113
Peason, --- 94, 113
John 94, 113
Peat, Joan 185
Mary 185
Pechell, John (Sir) 82
Peck, --- 523, 524, 525,
526, 527, 528, 529,
535, 536, 537, 538,
544, 547, 548, 549,
551, 553, 554, 555,
556, 557, 560, 561,
562, 570, 571, 573,
574, 575, 581, 585,
622, 623, 634, 635,
638
--- (Grandfather) 585
--- (Mr.) 525, 526,
527, 528, 573
--- (Pek) 531
--- (Pekke) 624
--- --- 523, 524, 526,
570
Alice 550
Alice --- (Peke) 542
Amie 559
Ann --- 552
Ann --- (Sawer?) 557
Anne 524, 535, 542,
571, 572, 573, 575,
623
Anne (Bolles) 542
Anne (Hill) 549
Anne (Hill, Poge or
Poage or Page) 549
Anne (Hill, Poge or
Poage or Page,
Burditt) 550
Anne (Poge) 623
Anne --- 623
Anne --- (Mrs.) 623
Audry 559
Bridget --- 579, 580,
592
Bridget --- (Sayer)
584

Bridget --- (Sayer)
(widow) 580
Bridget --- (widow)
577, 583
Briget 579
Dorathe (Dorothy) 550
Dorothe 559
Dorothy 550, 585
Dorothy (Dorathe) 550
Elianor 557
Elisabeth 542, 549,
550
Elizabeth 585
Ellen --- 582
Ellen --- (widow) 582
Francis 550, 561, 562
Frederick Stanhope
523, 535, 544, 549,
560, 563, 572, 577,
590, 622, 633, 637
Helen --- 524, 574,
575
Henry (Peke) 530
Ira B. (Mr.) 622
Ira Ballou 525, 535,
539, 548, 561, 562,
574, 577
Ira Ballou (Mr.) 526
Ira Balou 536, 573
Isabell 542
Isabell (Brodeley or
Bradley) 542
James 557
Jane --- 539
Jasper 551
Joan --- 569
Johan (Meriman) 535,
570, 575
Johan --- 541
John 525, 528, 535,
536, 537, 538, 540,
541, 542, 544, 545,
547, 548, 549, 551,
552, 557, 561, 562,
569, 570, 572, 573,
585, 623
John (Peke) 539, 552
John, Esq. 525, 526,
528, 535, 548, 549,
553, 560, 561, 5623
Jone 569, 570, 573
Joseph 523, 524, 525,
526, 527, 528, 529,
531, 535, 536, 544,
548, 549, 559, 560,
561, 562, 563, 566,
572, 574, 575, 577,
582, 622, 633, 637
Joseph 590
Joseph (Mr.) 524
Kateryn (Katherine)
(Peke) 530
Kath. 559
Katherin (?) 559
Katherine (Kateryn)
(Peke) 530
Katherine (Lake) 549,
552, 554
Katherine (Lake, Leyke
or, Leake) 538
Katherine (Layke or
Lake) 553, 560
Katherine (Layke) 552
Katherine (Leyke, i.
e., Lake) 549
Katheryn (Lake) 554
Margaret 535, 542, 569,
570, 572, 573

Margaret (Pallmer or
Palmer) 542
Margaret (Talear, i.
e., Taylor) 549
Margaret --- (Peke)
552
Margarett 569
Margery --- (Peke)
530
Margret 559
Martha 557, 559, 581
Martha --- (Noth?)
557
Ncli 579
Nicholas 527, 547, 550,
561, 562, 575, 577,
578, 579, 580, 581,
582, 583, 584, 585,
590, 591, 592, 623
Noni (?) 557
Olive 535, 571, 572,
573
Rachell --- 585
Ralph 562
Rbd 639
Richard 526, 538, 541,
542, 545, 547, 549,
552, 559, 560, 561,
562, 573, 575, 577,
623
Richard (Peke) 542,
550
Richard, Esq. 526, 536,
547
Richard, Esq. (Pek)
541
Richi 559
Robd 639
Robert 524, 525, 526,
527, 528, 529, 531,
532, 534, 535, 536,
538, 548, 559, 560,
561, 562, 563, 564,
565, 566, 567, 569,
570, 571, 572, 573,
574, 575, 576, 577,
585, 590, 591, 622,
623, 624, 633, 634,
635, 638
Robert (Mr.) 523, 524
Robert (Peke) 530, 552,
623
Robert (Pekk) 624
Robert (Pekke) 624
Robert (Rev.) 523, 524,
525, 526, 527, 528,
529, 531, 548, 561,
575
S. Allyn 523, 535, 544,
549, 560, 563, 572,
577, 590, 622, 633,
637
S. Allyn (Mr.) 622
Samuel 575, 582, 585
Samuell 559
Stephen 557
Thomas 525, 535, 552,
561, 562, 571, 572,
573, 575, 577, 585,
623
Thomas, Esq. 525, 526
Wilano (?) 557
William 550, 559, 561,
562, 577, 580, 581,
583, 584, 585
Willm 585
Pecke, --- 552, 581, 584
--- --- 568, 592

832

844

846